Heart of Europe

PETER H. WILSON

Heart of Europe

A History of the Holy Roman Empire

THE BELKNAP PRESS *of*
HARVARD UNIVERSITY PRESS
Cambridge, Massachusetts   2016

First published in the United Kingdom as *The Holy Roman Empire: A
Thousand Years of Europe's History* by Penguin Books Ltd. 2016
First Harvard University Press edition, 2016
First Printing

Library of Congress Cataloging-in-Publication Data

Names: Wilson, Peter H. (Peter Hamish), author.
Title: Heart of Europe : a history of the Holy Roman Empire / Peter H. Wilson.
Description: First Harvard University Press edition, 2016. | Cambridge, MA :
The Belknap Press of Harvard University Press, 2016. | "First published in
the United Kingdom as The Holy Roman Empire: A Thousand Years of Europe's
History by Penguin Books Ltd. 2016."—Title page verso. | Includes
bibliographical references and index.
Identifiers: LCCN 2015037932 | ISBN 9780674058095 (cloth : alk. paper)
Subjects: LCSH: Holy Roman Empire—History. | Holy Roman Empire—Politics and
government.
Classification: LCC DD125 .W55 2016 | DDC 943/.02—dc23
LC record available at http://lccn.loc.gov/2015037932

For Janine Marret

Contents

CONTENTS

PART IV
Society

List of Illustrations

List of Tables

Maps

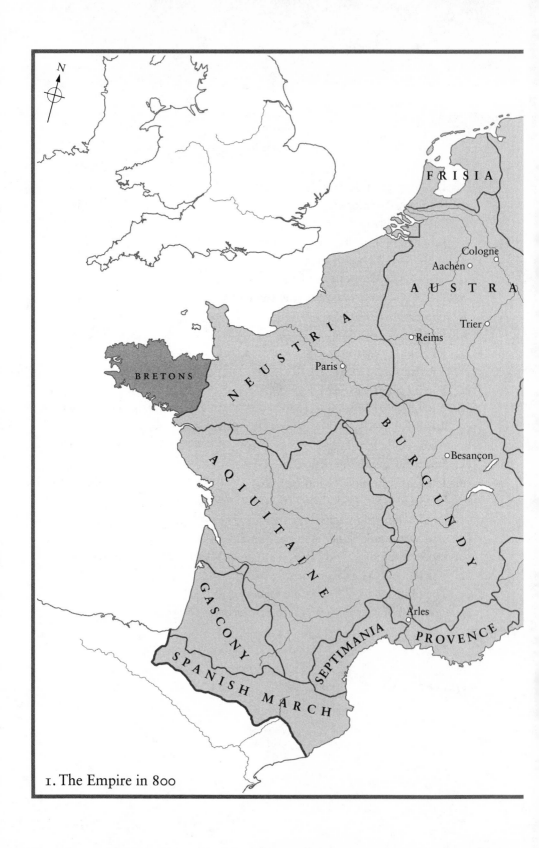

FRISIA

Cologne
Aachen ○

AUSTRA

Trier ○
Reims ○

Paris ○

N E U S T R I A

B U R G U N D Y

○ Besançon

BRETONS

A Q U I T A I N E

GASCONY

Arles
○

SEPTIMANIA

PROVENCE

SPANISH MARCH

1. The Empire in 800

Rügen Island

ABODRITES

LIUTIANS

SORBS

BOHEMIANS

MORAVIANS

SAXONY

Bremen

Paderborn

THURINGIA

SIA

Mainz

ALEMANNIA

BAVARIA

Regensburg

CARINTHIANS

ne]

CROATIANS

Aquileia

ISTRIA

Pavia

FORMER
EXARCHATE
OF RAVENNA

PAPAL PATRIMONIUM

DUCHY OF
SPOLETO

Rome

DUCHY OF
BENEVENTO

Imperial Empire

Tributaries of the Empire

SORBS Peoples

0   100   200 km

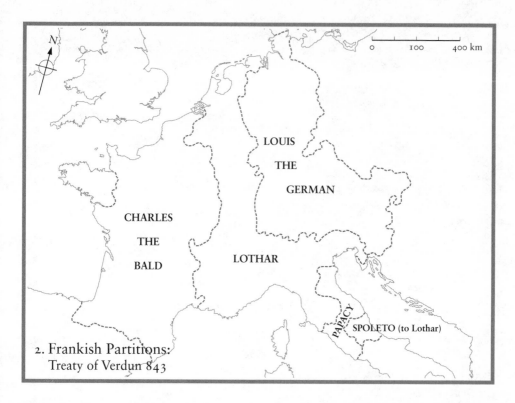

2. Frankish Partitions:
Treaty of Verdun 843

2. Frankish Partitions:
Divisions in 855

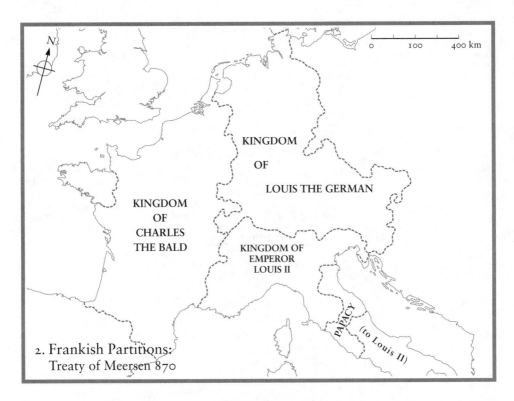

2. Frankish Partitions:
Treaty of Meersen 870

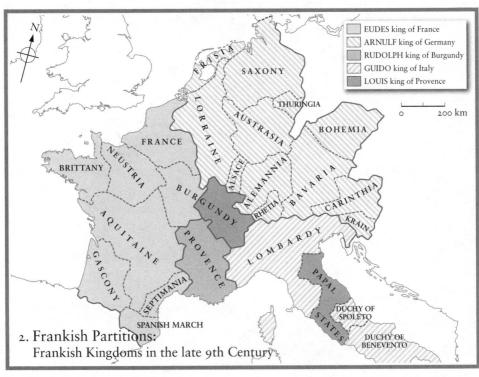

EUDES king of France
ARNULF king of Germany
RUDOLPH king of Burgundy
GUIDO king of Italy
LOUIS king of Provence

2. Frankish Partitions:
Frankish Kingdoms in the late 9th Century

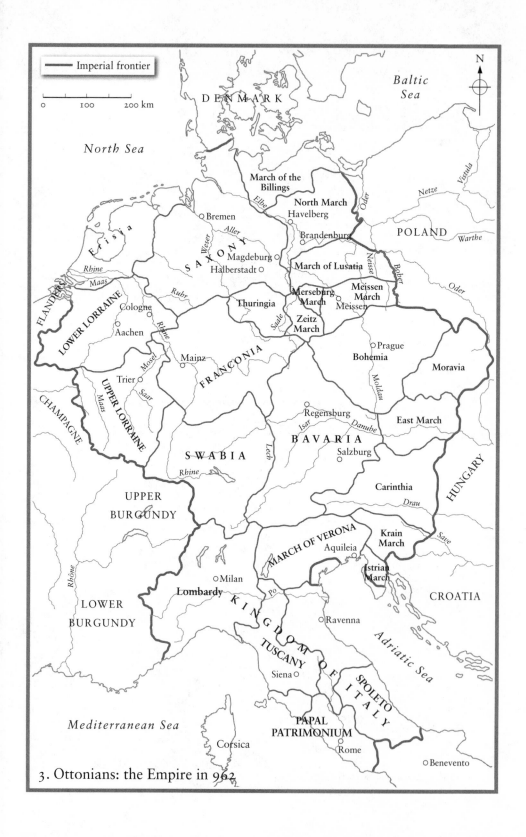

Imperial frontier

0   100   200 km

DENMARK

Baltic
Sea

North Sea

March of the
Billings

Bremen

North March
Havelberg

Brandenburg

POLAND

Netze

Vistula

Warthe

Elbe

Oder

Frisia

Weser

Aller

SAXONY

Magdeburg

Halberstadt

March of Lusatia

Neisse

Bober

Rhine

Maas

FLANDERS

Ruhr

Cologne

LOWER LORRAINE

Aachen

Thuringia

Saale

Merseburg
March

Zeitz
March

Meissen
March

Meissen

Oder

Rhine

Mainz

FRANCONIA

Prague

Bohemia

Moravia

CHAMPAGNE

Trier

Mosel

Saar

UPPER LORRAINE

Maas

Regensburg

Isar

Danube

East March

SWABIA

Lech

BAVARIA

Salzburg

HUNGARY

Rhine

UPPER
BURGUNDY

Carinthia

Drau

Save

MARCH OF VERONA

Aquileia

Krain
March

Istrian
March

Rhône

Milan

Lombardy

Po

KINGDOM OF ITALY

CROATIA

LOWER
BURGUNDY

Ravenna

Adriatic Sea

TUSCANY

Siena

SPOLETO

Mediterranean Sea

PAPAL
PATRIMONIUM

Corsica

Rome

Benevento

3. Ottonians: the Empire in 962

Legend:
— Imperial frontier
▨ Ecclesiastical territory
▨ Imperial lands in Italy
POLES People

0   100   200 km

Baltic Sea

North Sea

DENMARK

March of Schleswig

Hamburg

ABODRITES

POMERANIANS

Bremen

Elbe

LIUTIANS

Oder

Frisia

Weser

SAXONY

Saxon Marches

POLES

Rhine

Oder

LOWER LORRAINE

Cologne

Maas

Frankfurt

BOHEMIA

UPPER LORRAINE

Trier

Rhine

Mainz

FRANCONIA

Moravia

Verdun

Maas

Alsace

Strasbourg

Augsburg

Regensburg

Danube

March of Austria

Vienna

SWABIA

BAVARIA

Salzburg

CARINTHIA

Drau

Upper Burgundy

Rhine

Save

KINGDOM OF BURGUNDY

March of Krain

Lombardy

Verona

Venice

Po

KINGDOM OF ITALY

Turin

Rhône

Lower Burgundy

Ravenna

Romagna

Adriatic Sea

Artes

Tuscan March

SPOLETO

Mediterranean Sea

Papal Patrimonium

Corsica

Rome

4. Salians: the Empire around 1050

N

North Sea

DENMARK

Baltic Sea

County of
Holstein

Principality of
Mecklenburg

DUCHY OF
POMERANIA

POLAND

Elbe

Ascanian
possessions

Weser

Welf

Oder

Duchy of Silesia

DUCHY OF
SAXONY

Cologne

possessions

Wettin
possessions

Duchy of
Brabant

Rhine

T h u r i n g i a

KINGDOM
OF
BOHEMIA

Maas

Mainz

County of
Moravia

Trier

Duchy of
Franconia

Duchy of
Lorraine

DUCHY OF
SWABIA

DUCHY OF
BAVARIA

DUCHY OF
AUSTRIA

Danube

County of
Burgundy

KINGDOM OF BURGUNDY

County of
Tirol

Duchy of
Carinthia

DUCHY OF STYRIA

KINGDOM
OF
HUNGARY

Drau

County of
Savoy

K
I
N
G
D
O
M

March of
Friaul

March of
Krain

Save

March of
Verona

Po

Lombardy

County of
Provence

O
F

I
T
A
L
Y

Tuscany

PAPACY

Adriatic Sea

KINGDOM
OF
SERBIA

Rhône

Corsica

Mediterranean Sea

Duchy of
Benevento

Sardinia

Imperial frontier

Imperial Crown
lands and Staufer
allodial possessions

KINGDOM
OF SICILY
(Staufer possession 1194–1266)

0   100   200 km

5. Staufers: the Empire in 1195

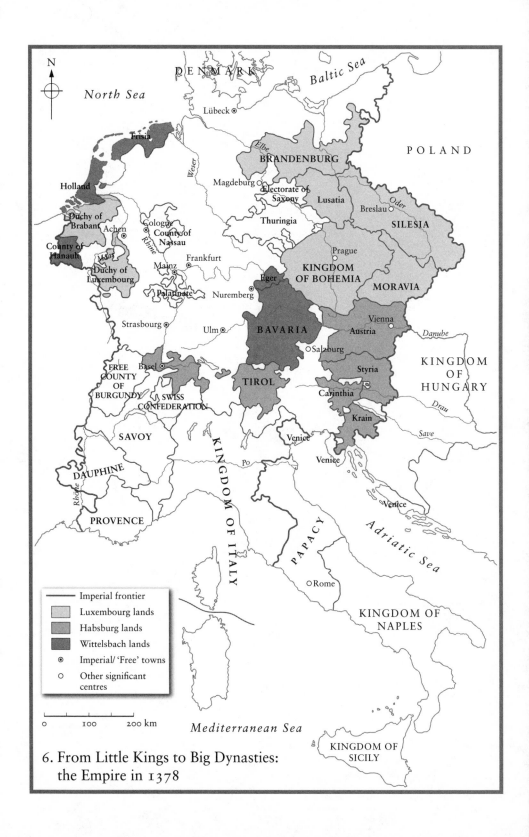

North Sea

DENMARK

Baltic Sea

Lübeck

POLAND

Frisia

Elbe

BRANDENBURG

Holland

Weser

Magdeburg

Electorate of
Saxony

Lusatia

Oder

Breslau

SILESIA

Duchy of
Brabant

Achen

Cologne

County of
Nassau

Rhine

County of
Hanault

Maas

Duchy of
Luxembourg

Mainz

Frankfurt

Prague

KINGDOM
OF BOHEMIA

MORAVIA

Thuringia

Palatinate

Eger

Nuremberg

Strasbourg

Ulm

BAVARIA

Salzburg

Vienna

Austria

Danube

KINGDOM
OF
HUNGARY

FREE
COUNTY
OF
BURGUNDY

Basel

SWISS
CONFEDERATION

TIROL

Styria

Carinthia

Krain

Drau

SAVOY

Venice

Save

DAUPHINE

Rhone

Po

KINGDOM OF ITALY

Venice

Venice

Adriatic Sea

PROVENCE

PAPACY

Rome

KINGDOM OF
NAPLES

Imperial frontier

Luxembourg lands

Habsburg lands

Wittelsbach lands

⊙ Imperial/ 'Free' towns

○ Other significant
centres

0   100   200 km

Mediterranean Sea

KINGDOM OF
SICILY

6. From Little Kings to Big Dynasties:
the Empire in 1378

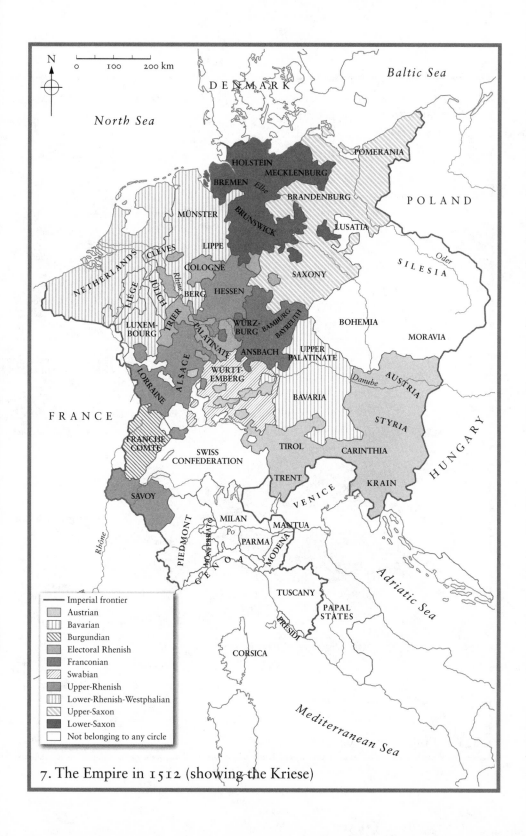

N

0   100   200 km

Baltic Sea

North Sea

D E N M A R K

P O L A N D

POMERANIA

HOLSTEIN
MECKLENBURG
BREMEN
Elbe
BRANDENBURG
MÜNSTER
BRUNSWICK
LUSATIA

CLEVES
LIPPE
COLOGNE
SAXONY

NETHERLANDS
Rhine
LIÈGE
JÜLICH
BERG
HESSEN
Oder
S I L E S I A

TRIER
WÜRZ-
BURG
BAMBURG
BAYREUTH
BOHEMIA

LUXEM-
BOURG
PALATINATE
ANSBACH
MORAVIA

ALSACE
UPPER
PALATINATE

LORRAINE
WURTT-
EMBERG
Danube
AUSTRIA

BAVARIA
STYRIA

F R A N C E

FRANCHE
COMTÉ
SWISS
CONFEDERATION
TIROL
CARINTHIA

H U N G A R Y

TRENT
KRAIN

SAVOY
Rhône

V E N I C E
Adriatic Sea

PIEDMONT
MILAN
MANTUA
Po
PARMA
MODENA

MONTFERRATO
G E N O A

TUSCANY
PAPAL
STATES

CORSICA
PRESIDI

Mediterranean Sea

—— Imperial frontier
    Austrian
    Bavarian
    Burgundian
    Electoral Rhenish
    Franconian
    Swabian
    Upper-Rhenish
    Lower-Rhenish-Westphalian
    Upper-Saxon
    Lower-Saxon
    Not belonging to any circle

7. The Empire in 1512 (showing the Kriese)

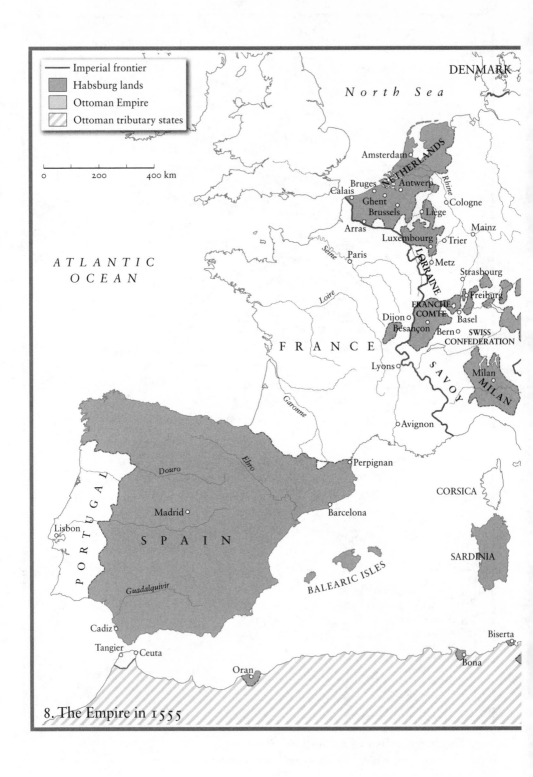

8. The Empire in 1555

N

Baltic Sea

DUCAL
PRUSSIA

RUSSIA

POMERANIA

BRANDENBURG
Berlin

Magdeburg

Vistula

P O L A N D

Leipzig

Oder

SILESIA

SAXONY
Dresden

Breslau

BOHEMIA

GALICIA

Dniester

Prague

Olmütz

BUKOVINA

Nuremberg

MORAVIA

Danube

T R A N S Y L V A N I A

AUSTRIA

Pressburg

Augsburg

Linz
Enns

Vienna

Munich

Salzburg

Budapest

Innsbruck

STYRIA

Graz

H U N G A R Y

TIROL

CARINTHIA

Temesvar

Trent

CROATIA

Drau

SLAVONIA

BANAT

Mantua

V E N E T I A N   T E R R I T O R Y

Karlowitz

Venice

Mirandola

PAPAL

FLORENCE

Florence

Adriatic Sea

STATES

Danube

O T T O M A N   E M P I R E

Black Sea

Rome

Benevento

Naples

Palermo

SICILY

Goletta

Tunis

CRETE
(to Venice)

M e d i t e r r a n e a n   S e a

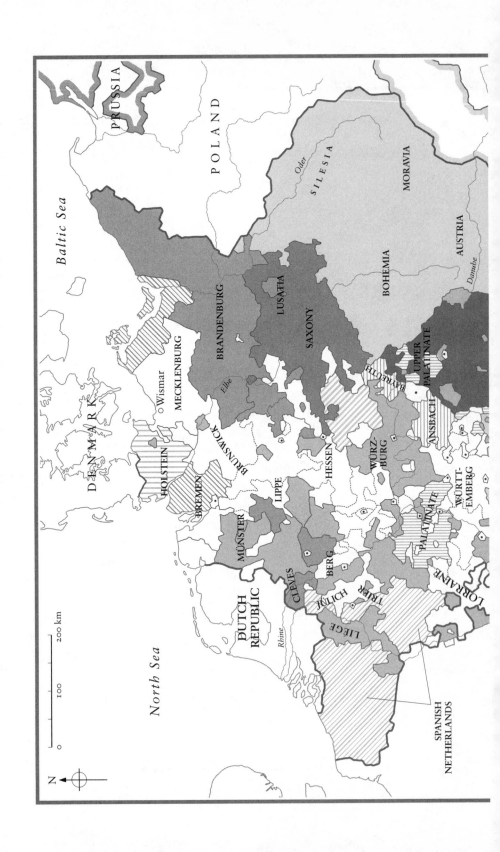

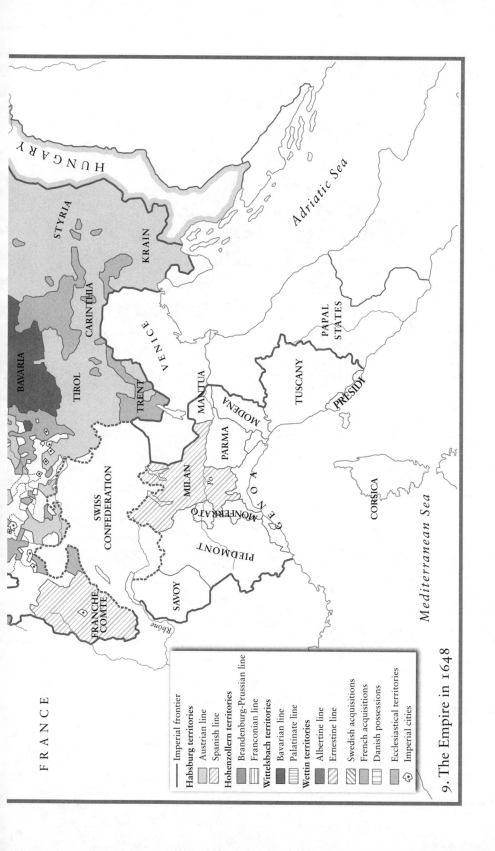

FRANCE

HUNGARY

STYRIA

KRAIN

CARINTHIA

BAVARIA

TIROL

TRENT

VENICE

SWISS
CONFEDERATION

FRANCHE
COMTÉ

SAVOY

PIEDMONT

MONFERRATO

MILAN

MANTUA

PARMA

MODENA

GENOA

TUSCANY

PRESIDI

PAPAL
STATES

Po

Rhône

CORSICA

Adriatic Sea

Mediterranean Sea

Imperial frontier
Habsburg territories
  Austrian line
  Spanish line
Hohenzollern territories
  Brandenburg-Prussian line
  Franconian line
Wittelsbach territories
  Bavarian line
  Palatinate line
Wettin territories
  Albertine line
  Ernestine line
  Swedish acquisitions
  French acquisitions
  Danish possessions
  Ecclesiastical territories
  Imperial cities

9. The Empire in 1648

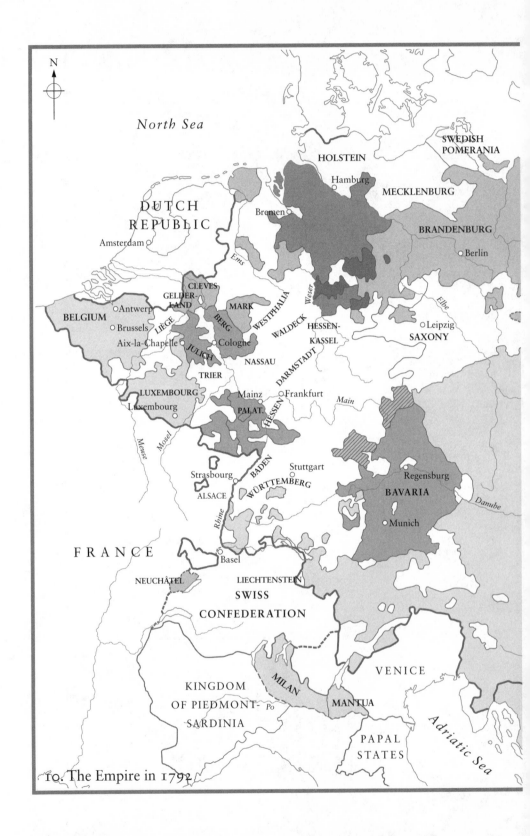

N

North Sea

SWEDISH
POMERANIA

HOLSTEIN

Hamburg

MECKLENBURG

Bremen

BRANDENBURG

DUTCH
REPUBLIC

Berlin

Amsterdam

CLEVES

GELDER-
LAND

MARK

WESTPHALIA

Weser

Ems

Antwerp

BERG

WALDECK

HESSEN-
KASSEL

Elbe

BELGIUM

LIÈGE

Leipzig

Brussels

SAXONY

Aix-la-Chapelle

JÜLICH

Cologne

NASSAU

DARMSTADT

TRIER

LUXEMBOURG

Mainz

Frankfurt

Main

Luxembourg

PALAT.

HESSEN

Meuse

Mosel

BADEN

Stuttgart

Regensburg

Strasbourg

WÜRTTEMBERG

BAVARIA

ALSACE

Rhine

Danube

Munich

FRANCE

Basel

NEUCHÂTEL

LIECHTENSTEIN

SWISS

CONFEDERATION

VENICE

KINGDOM

MILAN

OF PIEDMONT-

Po

MANTUA

SARDINIA

PAPAL

STATES

Adriatic Sea

10. The Empire in 1792

Baltic Sea

PRUSSIA

POLISH-LITHUANIAN
COMMONWEALTH

Vistula

Oder

SILESIA

BOHEMIA

AUSTRIA

Vienna

HUNGARY

Save

	Habsburg
	Hohenzollern Franconian branch
	Wittelsbach Zweibrücken branch
	Hanover (Electoral branch)
	Brunswick (Ducal branch)
———	Boundary of the Empire
– – –	Fief of the Empire
------	Boundary of extra-imperial possessions

0   100   200 km

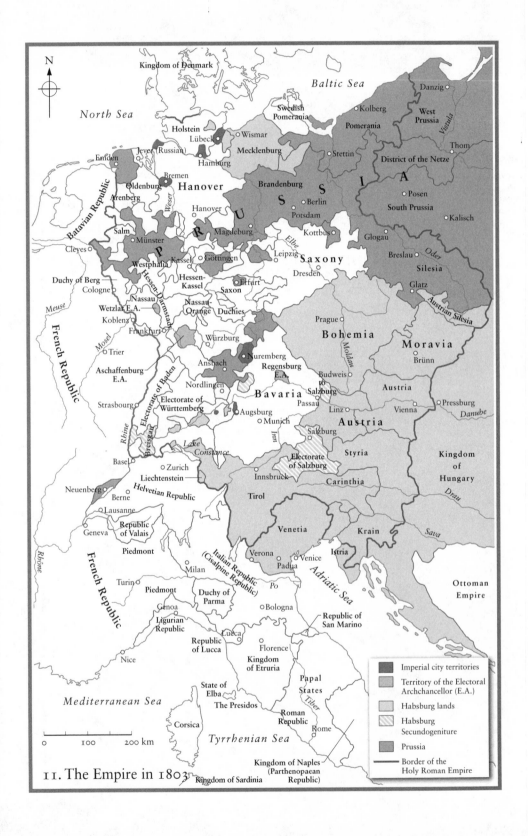

N

Kingdom of Denmark

Baltic Sea

North Sea

Holstein
Lübeck
Jever (Russian)
Wismar
Emden
Hamburg
Bremen
Oldenburg
Arenberg
Hanover
Salm
Cleves
Münster
Westphalia
Duchy of Berg
Cologne
Nassau
Wetzlar E.A.
Koblenz
Frankfurt
Trier
Aschaffenburg E.A.
Strasbourg
Nordlingen
Basel
Zurich
Liechtenstein
Neuenberg
Berne
Lausanne
Geneva
Piedmont
Turin
Milan
Genoa
Nice

Batavian Republic

Kassel
Göttingen
Hessen-Kassel
Saxon
Nassau-Orange Duchies
Würzburg
Ansbach
Nuremberg
Regensburg E.A.

Swedish Pomerania
Mecklenburg
Brandenburg
Berlin
Potsdam
Magdeburg
Elbe
Leipzig
Erfurt
Dresden
Saxony

Kolberg
Pomerania
Stettin

Danzig
West Prussia
Thorn

District of the Netze

Posen
South Prussia
Kalisch

Glogau
Kottbus
Breslau
Silesia
Glatz
Austrian Silesia

Prague
Bohemia
Moldau

Moravia
Brünn

Electorate of Baden
Electorate of Württemberg
Augsburg
Munich
Bavaria

Budweis
to
Salzburg
Passau
Linz

Austria

Vienna
Pressburg
Danube

Salzburg
Electorate of Salzburg
Innsbruck
Tirol

Austria

Styria
Carinthia

Kingdom of Hungary

Drau

Lake Constance

Helvetian Republic

Republic of Valais

Krain
Sava

Italian Republic (Cisalpine Republic)

Venetia
Verona
Padua
Venice
Po
Istria
Adriatic Sea

Ottoman Empire

Piedmont
Duchy of Parma
Bologna

Ligurian Republic
Lucca
Republic of Lucca
Florence

Republic of San Marino

Kingdom of Etruria

State of Elba

Papal States
Tiber

Mediterranean Sea

Corsica

The Presidos

Roman Republic
Rome

Tyrrhenian Sea

Kingdom of Sardinia

Kingdom of Naples (Parthenopaean Republic)

French Republic

Rhine
Mosel
Meuse
Breisgau

French Republic

Rhône

0   100   200 km

Imperial city territories

Territory of the Electoral Archchancellor (E.A.)

Habsburg lands

Habsburg Secundogeniture

Prussia

Border of the Holy Roman Empire

11. The Empire in 1803

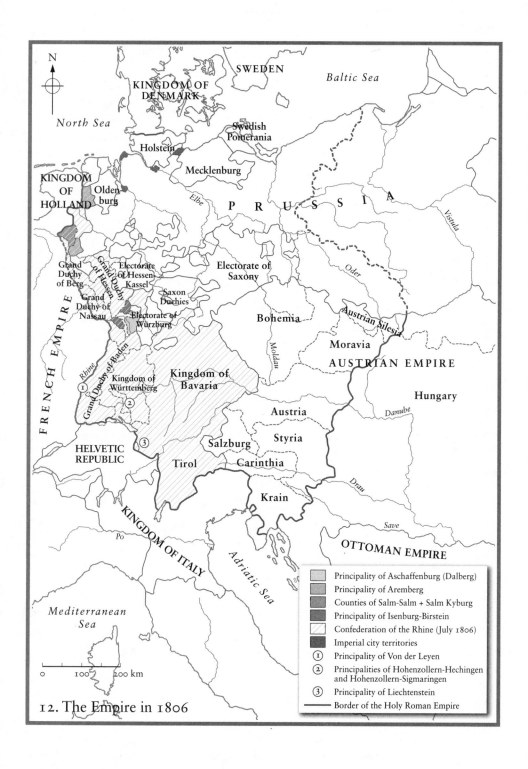

N

SWEDEN
Baltic Sea

KINGDOM OF
DENMARK

North Sea

Swedish
Pomerania

Holstein

Mecklenburg

KINGDOM
OF
HOLLAND

Olden-
burg

P R U S S I A

Elbe

Vistula

Grand
Duchy
of Berg

Grand
Duchy
of Hessen

Electorate
of Hessen-
Kassel

Electorate of
Saxony

Oder

Grand
Duchy of
Nassau

Saxon
Duchies

Austrian Silesia

Electorate of
Würzburg

Bohemia

Moravia

Rhine

Moldau

AUSTRIAN EMPIRE

FRENCH EMPIRE

Grand Duchy of Baden

① Kingdom of
Württemberg

Kingdom of
Bavaria

Hungary

②

Austria

Danube

③

Styria

HELVETIC
REPUBLIC

Salzburg

Carinthia

Tirol

Krain

Drau

KINGDOM OF ITALY

Po

Adriatic Sea

Save

OTTOMAN EMPIRE

Mediterranean
Sea

0   100   200 km

12. The Empire in 1806

Principality of Aschaffenburg (Dalberg)
Principality of Aremberg
Counties of Salm-Salm + Salm Kyburg
Principality of Isenburg-Birstein
Confederation of the Rhine (July 1806)
Imperial city territories
① Principality of Von der Leyen
② Principalities of Hohenzollern-Hechingen
   and Hohenzollern-Sigmaringen
③ Principality of Liechtenstein
—— Border of the Holy Roman Empire

N

North Sea

† Schleswig

† Ratzeburg

† Bremen ○

† Verden ● Lüneburg
† Havelberg

† Osnabrück ● Minden ● St Michael
Herford ● Hildesheim ● Magdeburg ○
Münster ● Paderborn ● Gandersheim ● Halberstadt
Corvey ● Quedlinburg
Essen ● Pöhlde ● Gernrode
Werden ● Memleben ● Merseburg
Brauweiler ‡ Cologne ○ Naumburg
St Trond ● St Pantaleon Hersfeld
St Gembloux ● † Liège Fulda ●
Cambrai ● Laubach ● Brogne
Stavelot ● Prüm ○ Mainz
Trier ‡ ○ Lorsch ● Bamberg †
Worms † Würzburg †
Verdun † Gorze Metz ● Speyer †
St Vanne ● Lorsch
St Mihiel ● St Symphorian Weissenburg ● Eichstätt
St Toul ● Strasbourg † Freising
St Evre Augsburg †
Moyenmoutier Kempten Tegernsee †
Murbach Reichenau ● Konstanz Benediktbeuern
Basle † St Gallen Brixen †
Besançon ‡ ○ Chur †
Cluny ● Chur
Vienne ‡ ○ Tarentaise ‡ ○ Milan ○
Fruttuaria ● Pavia †

13. The Imperial Church, c. 1020

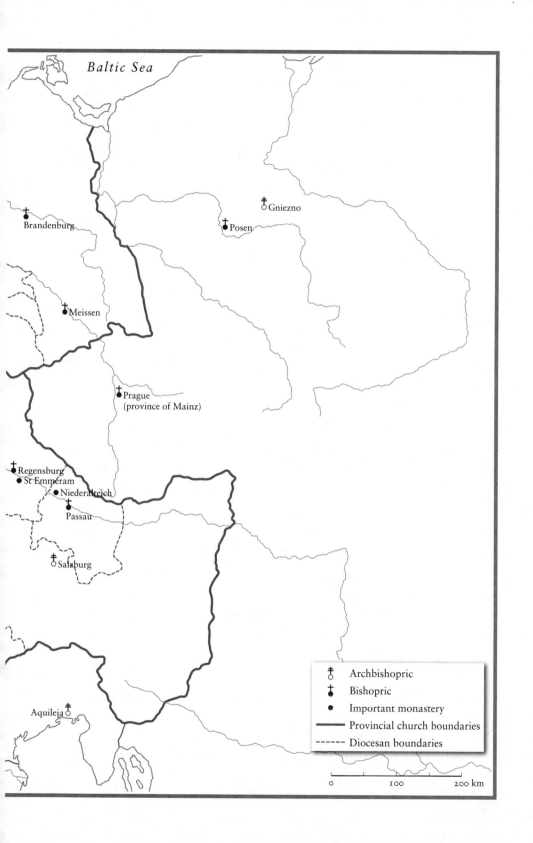

Baltic Sea

Brandenburg

Gniezno
Posen

Meissen

Prague
(province of Mainz)

Regensburg
St Emmeram
Niederaltreich
Passau

Salzburg

Aquileia

	Archbishopric
	Bishopric
•	Important monastery
——	Provincial church boundaries
- - -	Diocesan boundaries

0   100   200 km

N
0   50   100 km

North Sea

Conrad II
Elected in Kamba 6 Sept. 1024,
crowned in Aachen 23 Sept. 1024,
final assembly in Tribur
26 July 1025

Weser

Elbe

S A X O N Y

Aller

Rhine

Vreden

Minden
Corvey

Hildesheim

Magdeburg

Goslar   Werla   Halberstadt

Nijmegen

Paderborn
Dortmund

Gandisheim
Grone

Pöhlde

Quedlinburg

SAXON

LOWER

Fritzlar

Allstedt

Merseburg

MARCHES

LORRAINE

Cologne

Aachen

Sinzig

HESSEN

Werra
Fulda

THURINGIA
Erfurt

Liège

Fulda

Frankfurt

Salz

Moselle
Ingelheim

Mainz   Tribur

Bamberg

BOHEMIA

Trier

Kamba

Würzburg

Forchheim

Worms

Diedenhofen

Speyer

FRANCONIA

Metz

UPPER

Regensburg

LORRAINE

Strasbourg

SWABIA

Danube

Erstein

Neckar

Ulm

Augsburg

Altötting

Selestat

FRANCE

ALSACE

Bodman
Konstanz

Inn

BAVARIA

Basel   Zürich

Rhine

Chur

Imperial frontier

● Carolingian Palace

■ Ottonian Palace

▲ Palace of Henry II and Salian Prince

⚲ Episcopal City

Episcopal City with Carolingian/
Ottonian/Salian Palace

BURGUNDY

14.Royal Palaces (showing Conrad II's
Royal Progress, 1024–5)

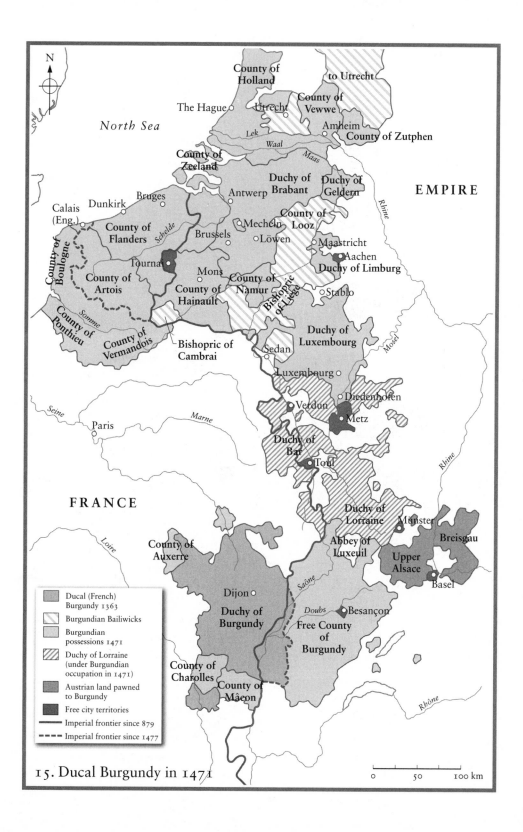

N

North Sea

County of
Holland

to Utrecht

The Hague ○   Utrecht ○   County of
                                Vewwe

                        Amheim
                        ○   County of Zutphen

                                    Lek
                                    Waal
County of   Maas
Zeeland

                Antwerp ○   Duchy of   Duchy of
Bruges ○   Brabant   Geldern

Calais   Mecheln ○   County of
(Eng.) ○ Dunkirk   County of   Löwen ○ Looz
County of   Flanders   Brussels ○   Maastricht
Boulogne   Schelde   ○
                    Tournay ●   Aachen
                                    Mons ○   ○
County of   County of   Duchy of Limburg
Artois   County of   Namur
                Hainault   Stablo ○
County of   Somme   Bishopric
Ponthieu   of Liège   Duchy of
        County of   Bishopric of   Luxembourg
        Vermandois   Cambrai
                        Sedan ○

                                    Luxembourg ○

Seine   Diedenhofen ○
        Marne   Verdun ○   Metz ●

Paris ○   Duchy of
                                    Bar   Toul ●

                                                    Rhine
FRANCE
                                    Duchy of
                                    Lorraine   Münster ○
        Loire   Breisgau
                County of   Abbey of
                Auxerre   Luxeuil   Upper
                                                Alsace
                                                    Basel ○

                        Dijon ○   Besançon ○
Ducal (French)   Duchy of   Doubs
Burgundy 1363   Burgundy   Free County
                                    of
Burgundian Bailiwicks   Burgundy

Burgundian
possessions 1471

Duchy of Lorraine
(under Burgundian   County of
occupation in 1471)   Charolles
                        County of
Austrian land pawned   Mâcon   Rhône
to Burgundy

Free city territories

Imperial frontier since 879

Imperial frontier since 1477

EMPIRE

15. Ducal Burgundy in 1471

0   50   100 km

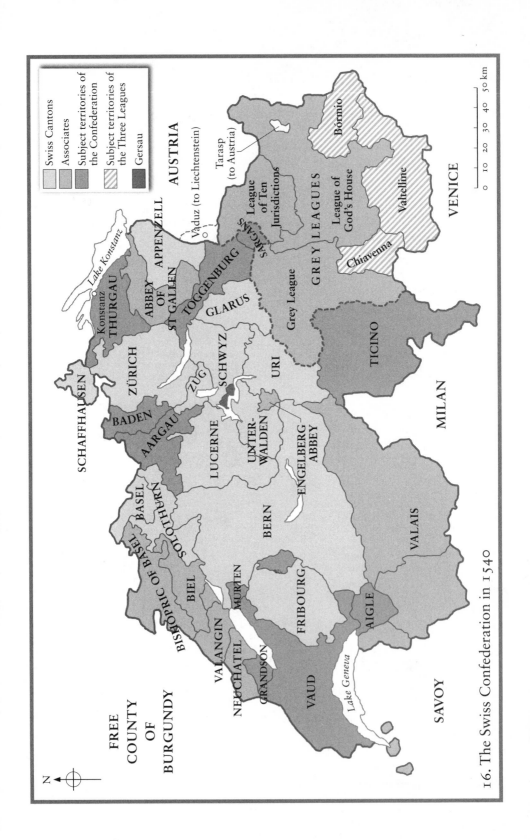

16. The Swiss Confederation in 1540

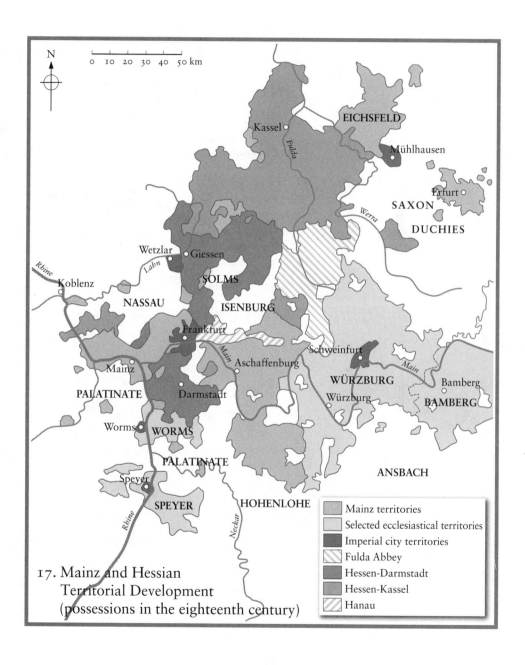

N

0 10 20 30 40 50 km

EICHSFELD

Kassel

Mühlhausen

Fulda

Werra

SAXON

Erfurt

DUCHIES

Rhine

Wetzlar   Giessen

Lahn

Koblenz

SOLMS

NASSAU

ISENBURG

Frankfurt

Schweinfurt

Main

Mainz

Aschaffenburg

WÜRZBURG

Bamberg

PALATINATE

Darmstadt

Würzburg

BAMBERG

Worms

WORMS

PALATINATE

ANSBACH

Speyer

SPEYER   HOHENLOHE

Neckar

Mainz territories

Selected ecclesiastical territories

Imperial city territories

Fulda Abbey

Hessen-Darmstadt

Hessen-Kassel

Hanau

17. Mainz and Hessian
Territorial Development
(possessions in the eighteenth century)

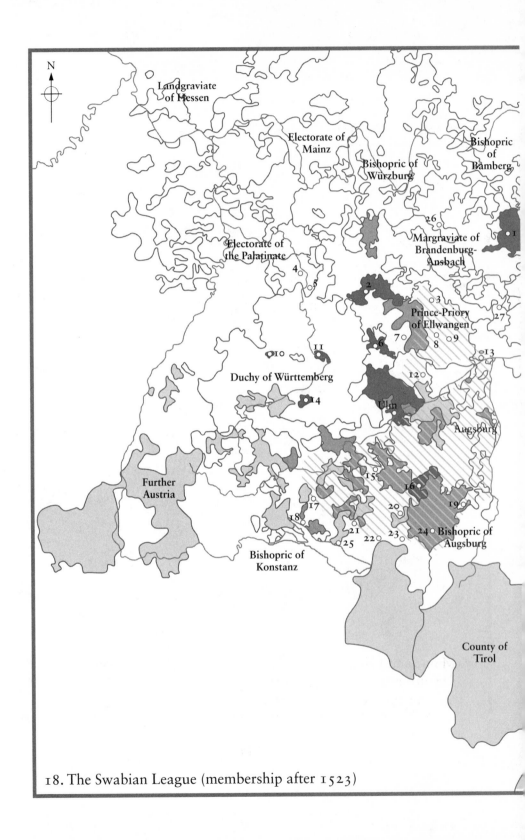

N

Landgraviate
of Hessen

Electorate of
Mainz

Bishopric of
Würzburg

Bishopric
of
Bamberg

26

Margraviate of
Brandenburg-
Ansbach

•1

Electorate of
the Palatinate

4

5

2

3

Prince-Priory
of Ellwangen

27

7

6

8

9

10

11

13

Duchy of Württemberg

12

14

Ulm

Augsburg

Further
Austria

15

16

17

19

18

20

21

22

23

24 Bishopric of
Augsburg

25

Bishopric of
Konstanz

County of
Tirol

18. The Swabian League (membership after 1523)

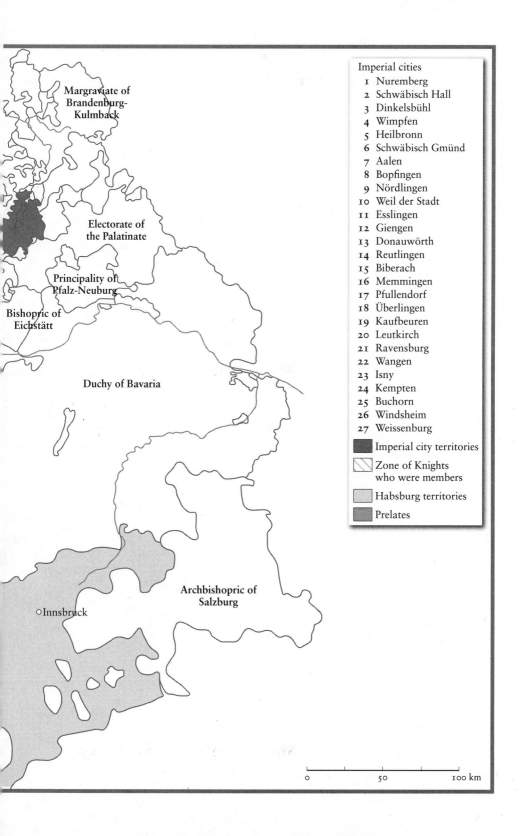

Imperial cities
1 Nuremberg
2 Schwäbisch Hall
3 Dinkelsbühl
4 Wimpfen
5 Heilbronn
6 Schwäbisch Gmünd
7 Aalen
8 Bopfingen
9 Nördlingen
10 Weil der Stadt
11 Esslingen
12 Giengen
13 Donauwörth
14 Reutlingen
15 Biberach
16 Memmingen
17 Pfullendorf
18 Überlingen
19 Kaufbeuren
20 Leutkirch
21 Ravensburg
22 Wangen
23 Isny
24 Kempten
25 Buchorn
26 Windsheim
27 Weissenburg

Imperial city territories

Zone of Knights
who were members

Habsburg territories

Prelates

Margraviate of
Brandenburg-
Kulmback

Electorate of
the Palatinate

Principality of
Pfalz-Neuburg

Bishopric of
Eichstätt

Duchy of Bavaria

Archbishopric of
Salzburg

○Innsbruck

0   50   100 km

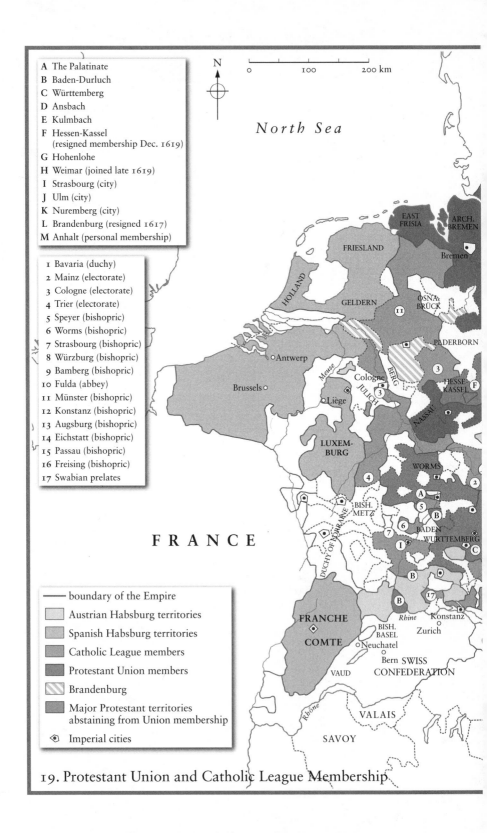

A The Palatinate
B Baden-Durluch
C Württemberg
D Ansbach
E Kulmbach
F Hessen-Kassel
  (resigned membership Dec. 1619)
G Hohenlohe
H Weimar (joined late 1619)
I Strasbourg (city)
J Ulm (city)
K Nuremberg (city)
L Brandenburg (resigned 1617)
M Anhalt (personal membership)

1 Bavaria (duchy)
2 Mainz (electorate)
3 Cologne (electorate)
4 Trier (electorate)
5 Speyer (bishopric)
6 Worms (bishopric)
7 Strasbourg (bishopric)
8 Würzburg (bishopric)
9 Bamberg (bishopric)
10 Fulda (abbey)
11 Münster (bishopric)
12 Konstanz (bishopric)
13 Augsburg (bishopric)
14 Eichstatt (bishopric)
15 Passau (bishopric)
16 Freising (bishopric)
17 Swabian prelates

N

0   100   200 km

North Sea

FRANCE

EAST FRISIA
ARCH. BREMEN
FRIESLAND
Bremen
HOLLAND
GELDERN
OSNA-BRÜCK
PADERBORN
Antwerp
Meuse
Cologne
BERG
HESSE-KASSEL
Brussels
Liège
JÜLICH
NASSAU
LUXEM-BURG
WORMS
BISH. METZ
DUCHY OF LORRAINE
FRANCHE COMTE
BISH. BASEL
Neuchatel
Bern
Rhine
Konstanz
Zurich
SWISS CONFEDERATION
VAUD
Rhône
VALAIS
SAVOY

——— boundary of the Empire
Austrian Habsburg territories
Spanish Habsburg territories
Catholic League members
Protestant Union members
Brandenburg
Major Protestant territories
  abstaining from Union membership
Imperial cities

19. Protestant Union and Catholic League Membership

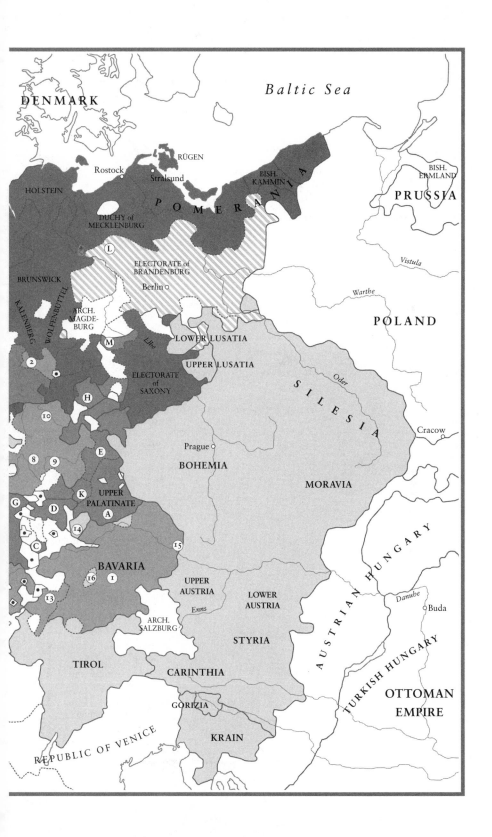

Baltic Sea

DENMARK

HOLSTEIN

RÜGEN
Rostock
Stralsund

BISH.
KAMMIN

P O M E R A N I A

BISH.
ERMLAND

PRUSSIA

DUCHY of
MECKLENBURG

BRUNSWICK

KALENBERG

WOLFENBÜTTEL

L

ARCH.
MAGDE-
BURG

M

2

ELECTORATE of
BRANDENBURG

Berlin

LOWER LUSATIA

UPPER LUSATIA

ELECTORATE
of
SAXONY

H

10

8   9

E

K   UPPER
      PALATINATE

G   A

D

14

C

BAVARIA

16   1

13

Vistula

POLAND

Warthe

S I L E S I A

Oder

Cracow

Prague

BOHEMIA

MORAVIA

UPPER
AUSTRIA

LOWER
AUSTRIA

Enns

ARCH.
SALZBURG

STYRIA

TIROL

CARINTHIA

GORIZIA

KRAIN

REPUBLIC OF VENICE

A U S T R I A N   H U N G A R Y

Danube

Buda

T U R K I S H   H U N G A R Y

OTTOMAN

EMPIRE

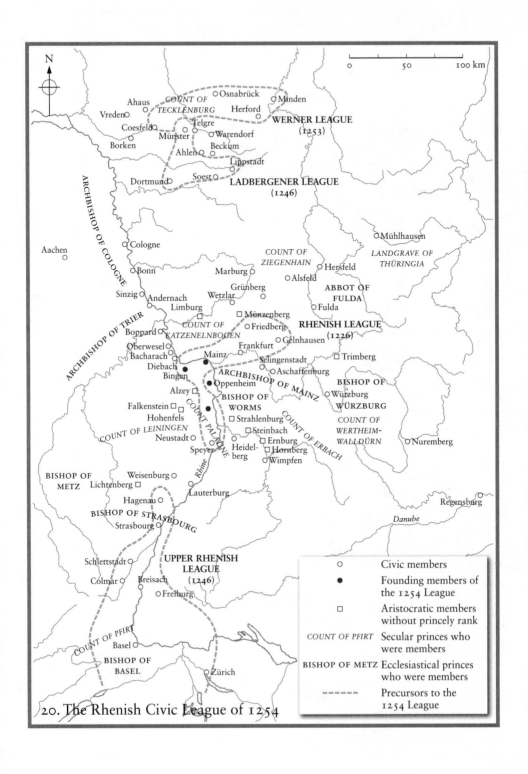

N

50   100 km

Osnabrück
Ahaus   *COUNT OF*   Minden
Vreden   *TECKLENBURG* Herford
Coesfeld   Telgre   **WERNER LEAGUE**
Münster   Warendorf   (1253)
Borken   Ahlen   Beckum
Lippstadt
Dortmund   Soest   **LADBERGENER LEAGUE**
(1246)

ARCHBISHOP OF COLOGNE

Aachen
Cologne
Mühlhausen
Bonn   *COUNT OF*   *LANDGRAVE OF*
Marburg   *ZIEGENHAIN* Hersfeld   *THÜRINGIA*
Sinzig   Andernach   Alsfeld
Grünberg   **ABBOT OF**
Wetzlar   **FULDA**
Limburg   Münzenberg   Fulda
COUNT OF   Friedberg   **RHENISH LEAGUE**
ARCHBISHOP OF TRIER   Boppard   *KATZENELNBOGEN*   (1226)
Oberwesel   Frankfurt   Gelnhausen
Bacharach   Trimberg
Diebach   Mainz   Selingenstadt
Bingen   *ARCHBISHOP OF MAINZ* Aschaffenburg
Oppenheim   **BISHOP OF**
Alzey   **BISHOP OF**   Würzburg   **WÜRZBURG**
Falkenstein   **WORMS**
Hohenfels   Strahlenburg   *COUNT OF*
COUNT OF LEININGEN   Steinbach   *WERTHEIM-*   Nuremberg
Neustadt   Ernburg   *WALLDÜRN*
Speyer   Heidel- Hornbach
berg   Wimpfen
BISHOP OF
METZ   Weisenburg
Lichtenberg
Lauterburg   Regensburg
Hagenau
BISHOP OF STRASBOURG   *Danube*
Strasbourg

UPPER RHENISH
LEAGUE
(1246)
Schlettstadt
Colmar   Breisach
Freiburg

COUNT OF PFIRT
Basel
BISHOP OF
BASEL   Zürich

○	Civic members
●	Founding members of the 1254 League
□	Aristocratic members without princely rank
COUNT OF PFIRT	Secular princes who were members
BISHOP OF METZ	Ecclesiastical princes who were members
- - - - -	Precursors to the 1254 League

20. The Rhenish Civic League of 1254

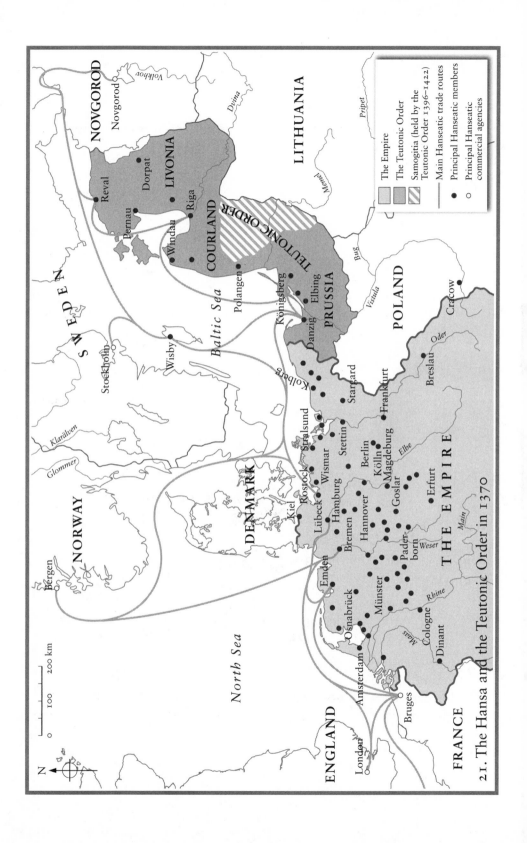

200 km

100

0

North Sea

NORWAY

Bergen

SWEDEN

Klarälven

Glommer

Stockholm

Baltic Sea

Wisby

DENMARK

Kiel

Rostock

Wismar

Stralsund

Lübeck

Hamburg

Bremen

Hannover

Berlin

Kölln

Magdeburg

Elbe

Goslar

Erfurt

Stettin

Stargard

Frankfurt

THE EMPIRE

Main

Paderborn

Weser

Münster

Rhine

Cologne

Dinant

Maas

Osnabrück

Emden

Amsterdam

Bruges

London

ENGLAND

FRANCE

Kolberg

Danzig

Elbing

Königsberg

Polangen

PRUSSIA

POLAND

Breslau

Oder

Cracow

Vistula

Bug

TEUTONIC ORDER

COURLAND

Windau

Riga

Pernau

Reval

Dorpat

LIVONIA

Dvina

Novgorod

NOVGOROD

Volkov

LITHUANIA

Memel

Pripet

2.1. The Hansa and the Teutonic Order in 1370

The Empire

The Teutonic Order

Samogitia (held by the
Teutonic Order 1396–1422)

Main Hanseatic trade routes

● Principal Hanseatic members

○ Principal Hanseatic
commercial agencies

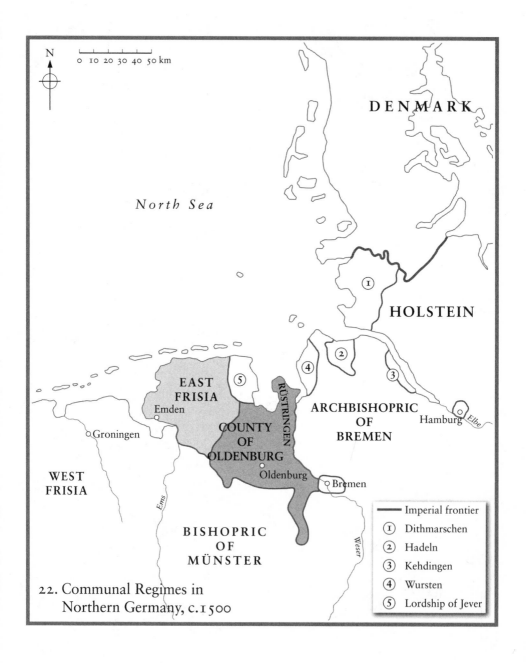

N

0 10 20 30 40 50 km

North Sea

DENMARK

HOLSTEIN

①

②

③

④ ⑤

EAST
FRISIA
Emden

RÜSTRINGEN

ARCHBISHOPRIC
OF
BREMEN

Hamburg

Elbe

○Groningen

COUNTY
OF
OLDENBURG

Oldenburg

○Bremen

WEST
FRISIA

Ems

BISHOPRIC
OF
MÜNSTER

Weser

22. Communal Regimes in
Northern Germany, c.1500

—— Imperial frontier
① Dithmarschen
② Hadeln
③ Kehdingen
④ Wursten
⑤ Lordship of Jever

Family Trees

TREE 1: CAROLINGIANS

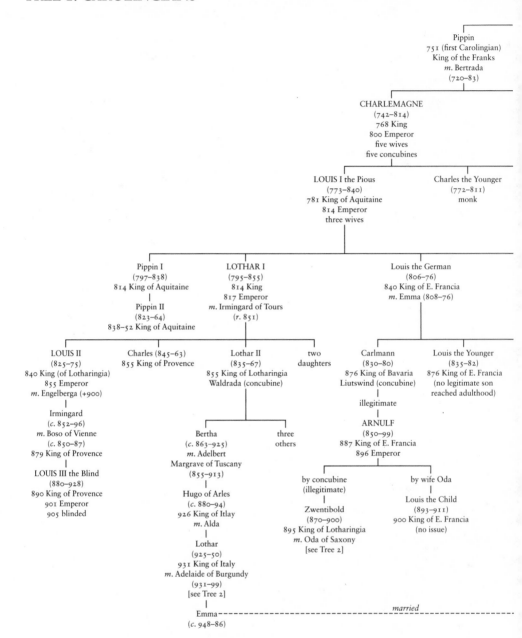

Pippin
751 (first Carolingian)
King of the Franks
m. Bertrada
(720–83)

CHARLEMAGNE
(742–814)
768 King
800 Emperor
five wives
five concubines

LOUIS I the Pious
(773–840)
781 King of Aquitaine
814 Emperor
three wives

Charles the Younger
(772–811)
monk

Pippin I
(797–838)
814 King of Aquitaine

Pippin II
(823–64)
838–52 King of Aquitaine

LOTHAR I
(795–855)
814 King
817 Emperor
m. Irmingard of Tours
(*r.* 851)

Louis the German
(806–76)
840 King of E. Francia
m. Emma (808–76)

LOUIS II
(825–75)
840 King (of Lotharingia)
855 Emperor
m. Engelberga (+900)

Charles (845–63)
855 King of Provence

Lothar II
(835–67)
855 King of Lotharingia
Waldrada (concubine)

two
daughters

Carlmann
(830–80)
876 King of Bavaria
Liutswind (concubine)

illegitimate

Louis the Younger
(835–82)
876 King of E. Francia
(no legitimate son
reached adulthood)

Irmingard
(c. 852–96)
m. Boso of Vienne
(c. 850–87)
879 King of Provence

LOUIS III the Blind
(880–928)
890 King of Provence
901 Emperor
905 blinded

Bertha
(c. 863–925)
m. Adelbert
Margrave of Tuscany
(855–913)

Hugo of Arles
(c. 880–94)
926 King of Itlay
m. Alda

Lothar
(925–50)
931 King of Italy
m. Adelaide of Burgundy
(931–99)
[see Tree 2]

Emma
(c. 948–86)

three
others

ARNULF
(850–99)
887 King of E. Francia
896 Emperor

by concubine
(illegitimate)

Zwentibold
(870–900)
895 King of Lotharingia
m. Oda of Saxony
[see Tree 2]

by wife Oda

Louis the Child
(893–911)
900 King of E. Francia
(no issue)

married

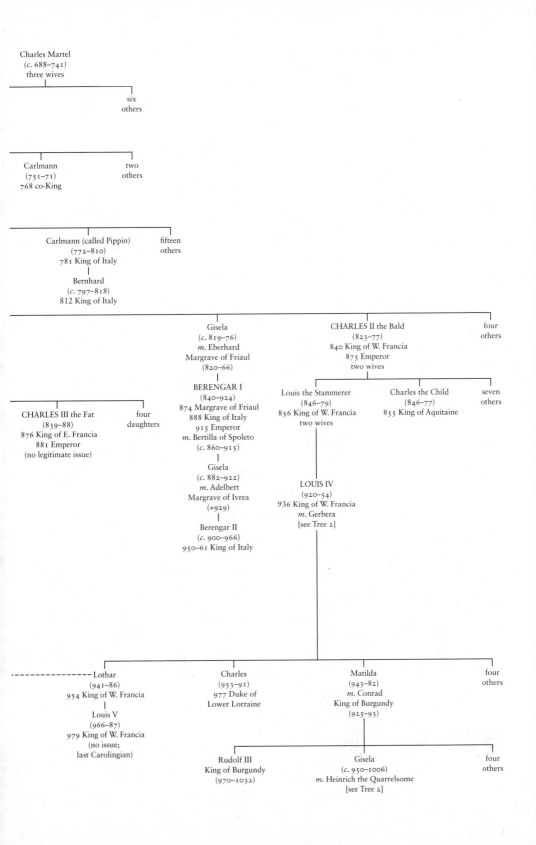

Charles Martel
(c. 688–741)
three wives

six
others

Carlmann
(751–71)
768 co-King

two
others

Carlmann (called Pippin)
(772–810)
781 King of Italy

fifteen
others

Bernhard
(c. 797–818)
812 King of Italy

Gisela
(c. 819–76)
m. Eberhard
Margrave of Friaul
(820–66)

CHARLES II the Bald
(823–77)
840 King of W. Francia
875 Emperor
two wives

four
others

BERENGAR I
(840–924)
874 Margrave of Friaul
888 King of Italy
915 Emperor
m. Bertilla of Spoleto
(c. 860–915)

Louis the Stammerer
(846–79)
856 King of W. Francia
two wives

Charles the Child
(846–77)
855 King of Aquitaine

seven
others

CHARLES III the Fat
(839–88)
876 King of E. Francia
881 Emperor
(no legitimate issue)

four
daughters

Gisela
(c. 882–922)
m. Adelbert
Margrave of Ivrea
(+929)

LOUIS IV
(920–54)
936 King of W. Francia
m. Gerbera
[see Tree 2]

Berengar II
(c. 900–966)
950–61 King of Italy

- - - - - - - - - - - - - - Lothar
(941–86)
954 King of W. Francia

Charles
(953–91)
977 Duke of
Lower Lorraine

Matilda
(943–82)
m. Conrad
King of Burgundy
(925–93)

four
others

Louis V
(966–87)
979 King of W. Francia
(no issue;
last Carolingian)

Rudolf III
King of Burgundy
(970–1032)

Gisela
(c. 950–1006)
m. Heinrich the Quarrelsome
[see Tree 2]

four
others

TREE 2: OTTONIANS

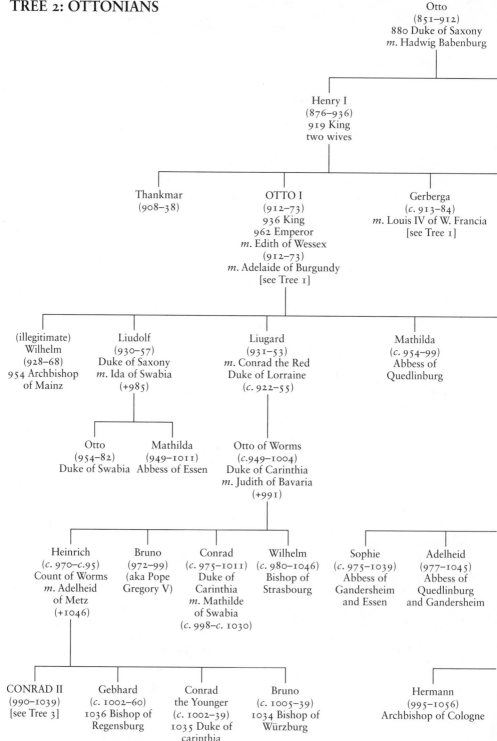

Otto
(851–912)
880 Duke of Saxony
m. Hadwig Babenburg

Henry I
(876–936)
919 King
two wives

Thankmar
(908–38)

OTTO I
(912–73)
936 King
962 Emperor
m. Edith of Wessex
(912–73)
m. Adelaide of Burgundy
[see Tree 1]

Gerberga
(c. 913–84)
m. Louis IV of W. Francia
[see Tree 1]

(illegitimate)
Wilhelm
(928–68)
954 Archbishop
of Mainz

Liudolf
(930–57)
Duke of Saxony
m. Ida of Swabia
(+985)

Liugard
(931–53)
m. Conrad the Red
Duke of Lorraine
(c. 922–55)

Mathilda
(c. 954–99)
Abbess of
Quedlinburg

Otto
(954–82)
Duke of Swabia

Mathilda
(949–1011)
Abbess of Essen

Otto of Worms
(c.949–1004)
Duke of Carinthia
m. Judith of Bavaria
(+991)

Heinrich
(c. 970–c.95)
Count of Worms
m. Adelheid
of Metz
(+1046)

Bruno
(972–99)
(aka Pope
Gregory V)

Conrad
(c. 975–1011)
Duke of
Carinthia
m. Mathilde
of Swabia
(c. 998–c. 1030)

Wilhelm
(c. 980–1046)
Bishop of
Strasbourg

Sophie
(c. 975–1039)
Abbess of
Gandersheim
and Essen

Adelheid
(977–1045)
Abbess of
Quedlinburg
and Gandersheim

CONRAD II
(990–1039)
[see Tree 3]

Gebhard
(c. 1002–60)
1036 Bishop of
Regensburg

Conrad
the Younger
(c. 1002–39)
1035 Duke of
carinthia

Bruno
(c. 1005–39)
1034 Bishop of
Würzburg

Hermann
(995–1056)
Archbishop of Cologne

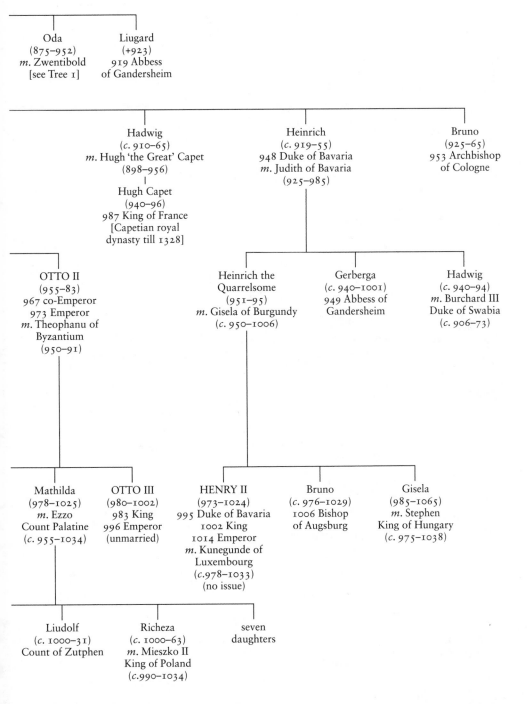

Oda
(875–952)
m. Zwentibold
[see Tree 1]

Liugard
(+923)
919 Abbess
of Gandersheim

Hadwig
(c. 910–65)
m. Hugh 'the Great' Capet
(898–956)

Hugh Capet
(940–96)
987 King of France
[Capetian royal
dynasty till 1328]

Heinrich
(c. 919–55)
948 Duke of Bavaria
m. Judith of Bavaria
(925–985)

Bruno
(925–65)
953 Archbishop
of Cologne

OTTO II
(955–83)
967 co-Emperor
973 Emperor
m. Theophanu of
Byzantium
(950–91)

Heinrich the
Quarrelsome
(951–95)
m. Gisela of Burgundy
(c. 950–1006)

Gerberga
(c. 940–1001)
949 Abbess of
Gandersheim

Hadwig
(c. 940–94)
m. Burchard III
Duke of Swabia
(c. 906–73)

Mathilda
(978–1025)
m. Ezzo
Count Palatine
(c. 955–1034)

OTTO III
(980–1002)
983 King
996 Emperor
(unmarried)

HENRY II
(973–1024)
995 Duke of Bavaria
1002 King
1014 Emperor
m. Kunegunde of
Luxembourg
(c.978–1033)
(no issue)

Bruno
(c. 976–1029)
1006 Bishop
of Augsburg

Gisela
(985–1065)
m. Stephen
King of Hungary
(c. 975–1038)

Liudolf
(c. 1000–31)
Count of Zutphen

Richeza
(c. 1000–63)
m. Mieszko II
King of Poland
(c.990–1034)

seven
daughters

TREE 3: SALIANS

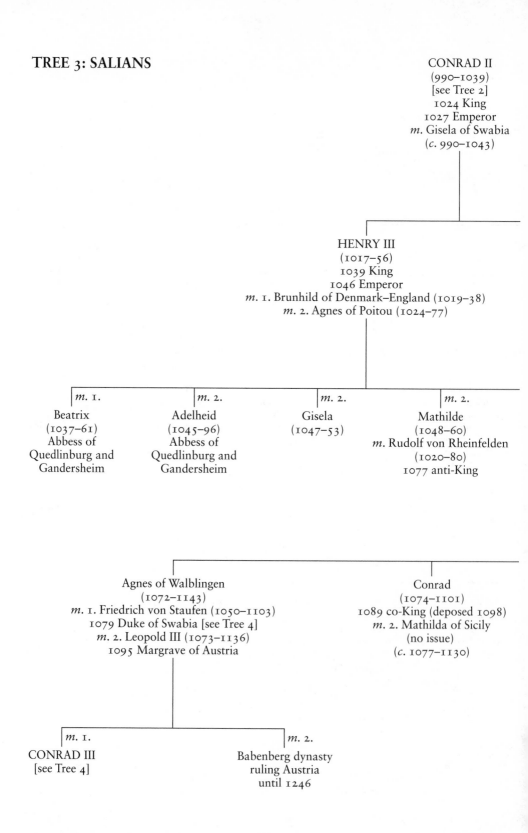

CONRAD II
(990–1039)
[see Tree 2]
1024 King
1027 Emperor
m. Gisela of Swabia
(*c.* 990–1043)

HENRY III
(1017–56)
1039 King
1046 Emperor
m. 1. Brunhild of Denmark–England (1019–38)
m. 2. Agnes of Poitou (1024–77)

m. 1.
Beatrix
(1037–61)
Abbess of
Quedlinburg and
Gandersheim

m. 2.
Adelheid
(1045–96)
Abbess of
Quedlinburg and
Gandersheim

m. 2.
Gisela
(1047–53)

m. 2.
Mathilde
(1048–60)
m. Rudolf von Rheinfelden
(1020–80)
1077 anti-King

Agnes of Walblingen
(1072–1143)
m. 1. Friedrich von Staufen (1050–1103)
1079 Duke of Swabia [see Tree 4]
m. 2. Leopold III (1073–1136)
1095 Margrave of Austria

Conrad
(1074–1101)
1089 co-King (deposed 1098)
m. 2. Mathilda of Sicily
(no issue)
(*c.* 1077–1130)

m. 1.
CONRAD III
[see Tree 4]

m. 2.
Babenberg dynasty
ruling Austria
until 1246

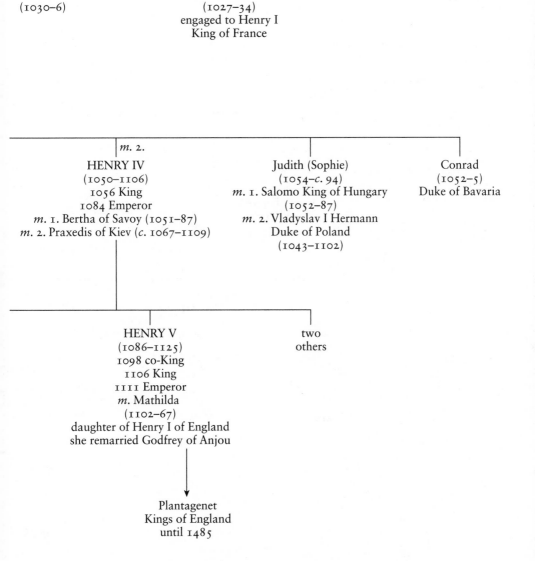

Beatrix
(1030–6)

Mathilde
(1027–34)
engaged to Henry I
King of France

m. 2.

HENRY IV
(1050–1106)
1056 King
1084 Emperor
m. 1. Bertha of Savoy (1051–87)
m. 2. Praxedis of Kiev (*c.* 1067–1109)

Judith (Sophie)
(1054–*c.* 94)
m. 1. Salomo King of Hungary
(1052–87)
m. 2. Vladyslav I Hermann
Duke of Poland
(1043–1102)

Conrad
(1052–5)
Duke of Bavaria

HENRY V
(1086–1125)
1098 co-King
1106 King
1111 Emperor
m. Mathilda
(1102–67)
daughter of Henry I of England
she remarried Godfrey of Anjou

two
others

Plantagenet
Kings of England
until 1485

TREE 4: STAUFERS AND WELFS

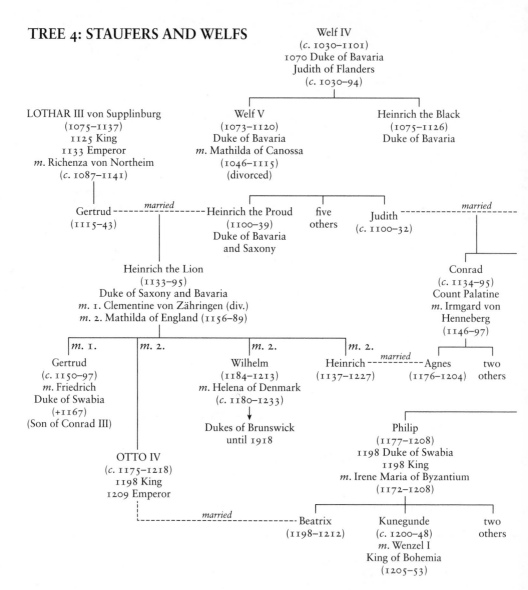

Welf IV
(c. 1030–1101)
1070 Duke of Bavaria
Judith of Flanders
(c. 1030–94)

LOTHAR III von Supplinburg
(1075–1137)
1125 King
1133 Emperor
m. Richenza von Northeim
(c. 1087–1141)

Welf V
(1073–1120)
Duke of Bavaria
m. Mathilda of Canossa
(1046–1115)
(divorced)

Heinrich the Black
(1075–1126)
Duke of Bavaria

Gertrud - - - - - - - - - - - - - - - - married - - - - - - - - - - - - Heinrich the Proud
(1115–43)   (1100–39)
                                                   Duke of Bavaria
                                                   and Saxony

five
others

Judith - - - - - - - - - - - married - - - - - - - - - -
(c. 1100–32)

Conrad
(c. 1134–95)
Count Palatine
m. Irmgard von
Henneberg
(1146–97)

Heinrich the Lion
(1133–95)
Duke of Saxony and Bavaria
m. 1. Clementine von Zähringen (div.)
m. 2. Mathilda of England (1156–89)

m. 1.	*m.* 2.	*m.* 2.	*m.* 2.	
Gertrud		Wilhelm	Heinrich - - - - married - - - - Agnes	two
(c. 1150–97)		(1184–1213)	(1137–1227) (1176–1204)	others
m. Friedrich		*m.* Helena of Denmark		
Duke of Swabia		(c. 1180–1233)		
(+1167)		↓		
(Son of Conrad III)		Dukes of Brunswick		
		until 1918		

Philip
(1177–1208)
1198 Duke of Swabia
1198 King
m. Irene Maria of Byzantium
(1172–1208)

OTTO IV
(c. 1175–1218)
1198 King
1209 Emperor

- - - - - - - - - - married - - - - - - - - - - - Beatrix
(1198–1212)

Kunegunde
(c. 1200–48)
m. Wenzel I
King of Bohemia
(1205–53)

two
others

m. 1.
Henry VII
(1211–42)
1220 King (deposed)

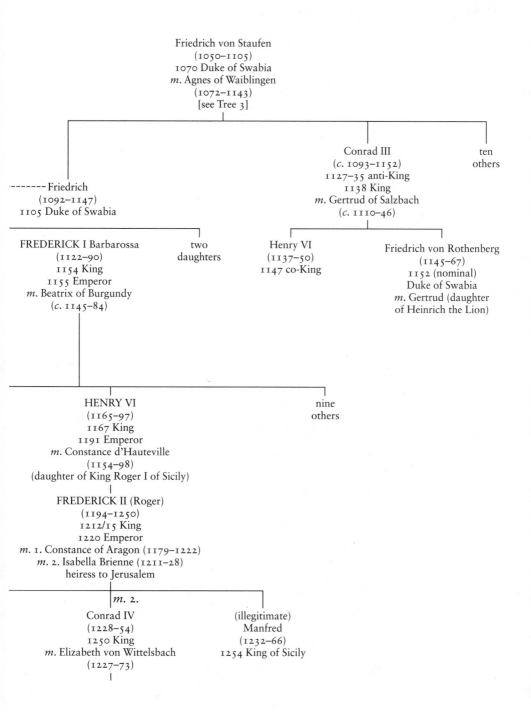

Friedrich von Staufen
(1050–1105)
1070 Duke of Swabia
m. Agnes of Waiblingen
(1072–1143)
[see Tree 3]

Conrad III
(c. 1093–1152)
1127–35 anti-King
1138 King
m. Gertrud of Salzbach
(c. 1110–46)

ten
others

⸱⸱⸱⸱⸱⸱⸱ Friedrich
(1092–1147)
1105 Duke of Swabia

FREDERICK I Barbarossa
(1122–90)
1154 King
1155 Emperor
m. Beatrix of Burgundy
(c. 1145–84)

two
daughters

Henry VI
(1137–50)
1147 co-King

Friedrich von Rothenberg
(1145–67)
1152 (nominal)
Duke of Swabia
m. Gertrud (daughter
of Heinrich the Lion)

HENRY VI
(1165–97)
1167 King
1191 Emperor
m. Constance d'Hauteville
(1154–98)
(daughter of King Roger I of Sicily)

nine
others

FREDERICK II (Roger)
(1194–1250)
1212/15 King
1220 Emperor
m. 1. Constance of Aragon (1179–1222)
m. 2. Isabella Brienne (1211–28)
heiress to Jerusalem

m. 2.

Conrad IV
(1228–54)
1250 King
m. Elizabeth von Wittelsbach
(1227–73)

(illegitimate)
Manfred
(1232–66)
1254 King of Sicily

TREE 5: LUXEMBOURGS

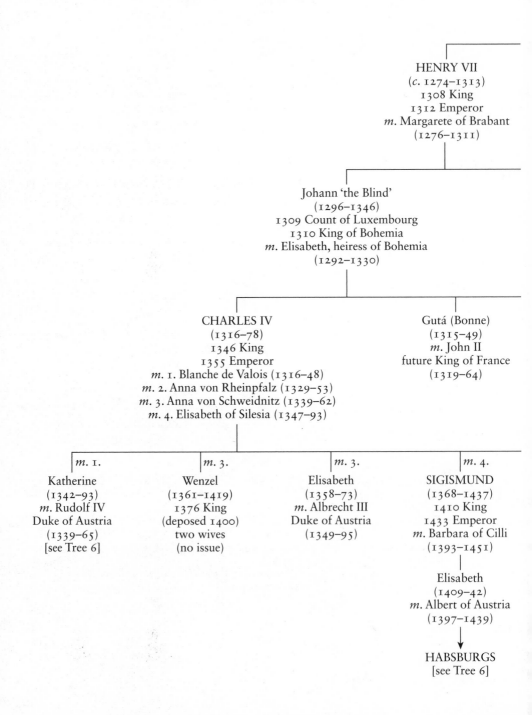

HENRY VII
(*c.* 1274–1313)
1308 King
1312 Emperor
m. Margarete of Brabant
(1276–1311)

Johann 'the Blind'
(1296–1346)
1309 Count of Luxembourg
1310 King of Bohemia
m. Elisabeth, heiress of Bohemia
(1292–1330)

CHARLES IV
(1316–78)
1346 King
1355 Emperor
m. 1. Blanche de Valois (1316–48)
m. 2. Anna von Rheinpfalz (1329–53)
m. 3. Anna von Schweidnitz (1339–62)
m. 4. Elisabeth of Silesia (1347–93)

Gutá (Bonne)
(1315–49)
m. John II
future King of France
(1319–64)

m. 1.
Katherine
(1342–93)
m. Rudolf IV
Duke of Austria
(1339–65)
[see Tree 6]

m. 3.
Wenzel
(1361–1419)
1376 King
(deposed 1400)
two wives
(no issue)

m. 3.
Elisabeth
(1358–73)
m. Albrecht III
Duke of Austria
(1349–95)

m. 4.
SIGISMUND
(1368–1437)
1410 King
1433 Emperor
m. Barbara of Cilli
(1393–1451)

Elisabeth
(1409–42)
m. Albert of Austria
(1397–1439)

HABSBURGS
[see Tree 6]

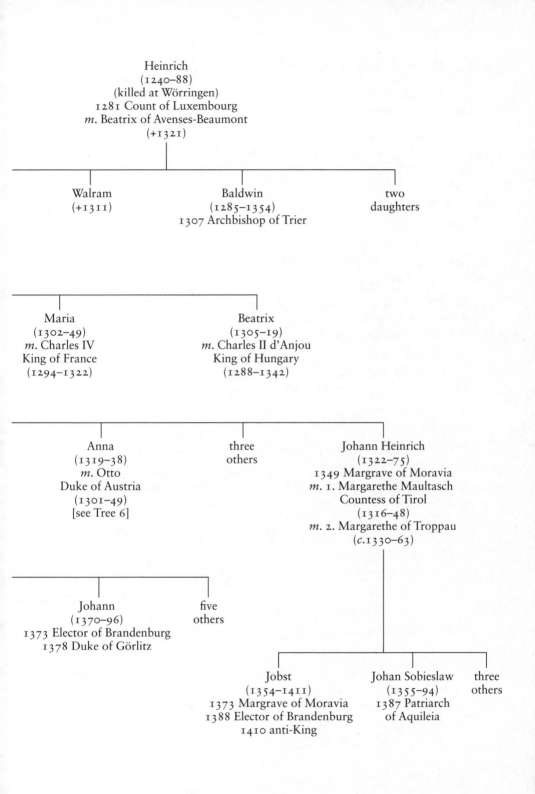

Heinrich
(1240–88)
(killed at Wörringen)
1281 Count of Luxembourg
m. Beatrix of Avenses-Beaumont
(+1321)

Walram
(+1311)

Baldwin
(1285–1354)
1307 Archbishop of Trier

two
daughters

Maria
(1302–49)
m. Charles IV
King of France
(1294–1322)

Beatrix
(1305–19)
m. Charles II d'Anjou
King of Hungary
(1288–1342)

Anna
(1319–38)
m. Otto
Duke of Austria
(1301–49)
[see Tree 6]

three
others

Johann Heinrich
(1322–75)
1349 Margrave of Moravia
m. 1. Margarethe Maultasch
Countess of Tirol
(1316–48)
m. 2. Margarethe of Troppau
(*c.*1330–63)

Johann
(1370–96)
1373 Elector of Brandenburg
1378 Duke of Görlitz

five
others

Jobst
(1354–1411)
1373 Margrave of Moravia
1388 Elector of Brandenburg
1410 anti-King

Johan Sobieslaw
(1355–94)
1387 Patriarch
of Aquileia

three
others

TREE 6: HABSBURGS (Part 1)

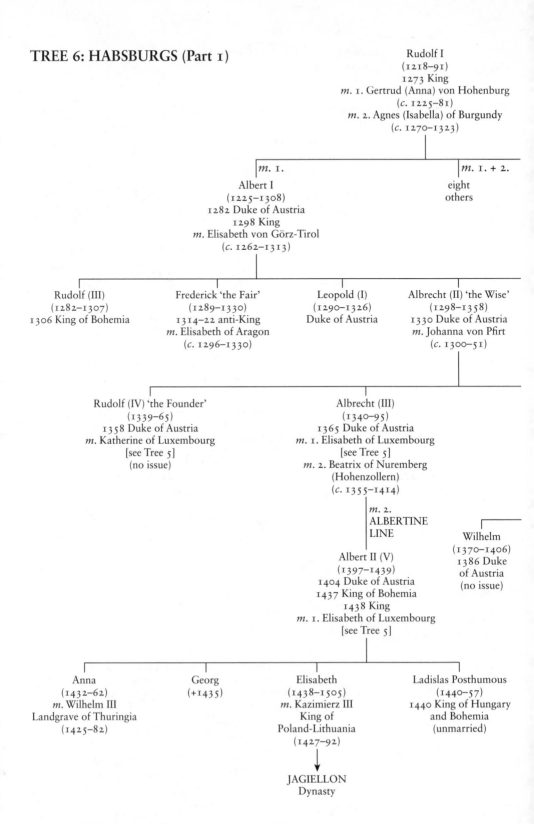

Rudolf I
(1218–91)
1273 King
m. 1. Gertrud (Anna) von Hohenburg
(c. 1225–81)
m. 2. Agnes (Isabella) of Burgundy
(c. 1270–1323)

m. 1.

Albert I
(1225–1308)
1282 Duke of Austria
1298 King
m. Elisabeth von Görz-Tirol
(c. 1262–1313)

m. 1. + 2.

eight
others

Rudolf (III)
(1282–1307)
1306 King of Bohemia

Frederick 'the Fair'
(1289–1330)
1314–22 anti-King
m. Elisabeth of Aragon
(c. 1296–1330)

Leopold (I)
(1290–1326)
Duke of Austria

Albrecht (II) 'the Wise'
(1298–1358)
1330 Duke of Austria
m. Johanna von Pfirt
(c. 1300–51)

Rudolf (IV) 'the Founder'
(1339–65)
1358 Duke of Austria
m. Katherine of Luxembourg
[see Tree 5]
(no issue)

Albrecht (III)
(1340–95)
1365 Duke of Austria
m. 1. Elisabeth of Luxembourg
[see Tree 5]
m. 2. Beatrix of Nuremberg
(Hohenzollern)
(c. 1355–1414)

m. 2.
ALBERTINE
LINE

Wilhelm
(1370–1406)
1386 Duke
of Austria
(no issue)

Albert II (V)
(1397–1439)
1404 Duke of Austria
1437 King of Bohemia
1438 King
m. 1. Elisabeth of Luxembourg
[see Tree 5]

Anna
(1432–62)
m. Wilhelm III
Landgrave of Thuringia
(1425–82)

Georg
(+1435)

Elisabeth
(1438–1505)
m. Kazimierz III
King of
Poland-Lithuania
(1427–92)

Ladislas Posthumous
(1440–57)
1440 King of Hungary
and Bohemia
(unmarried)

JAGIELLON
Dynasty

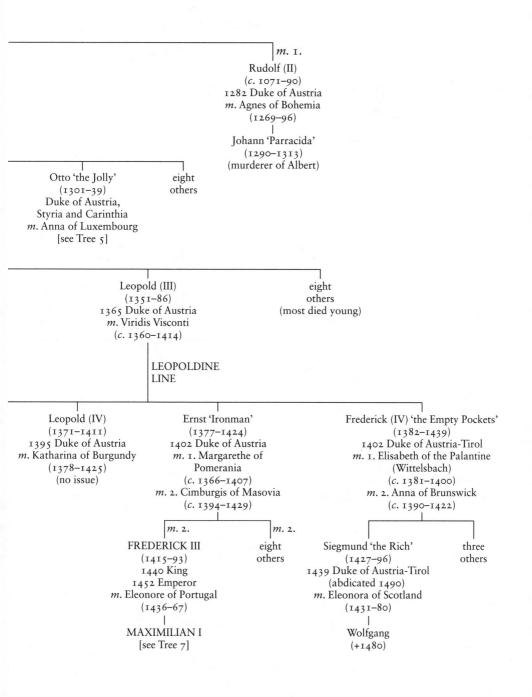

m. 1.
Rudolf (II)
(*c.* 1071–90)
1282 Duke of Austria
m. Agnes of Bohemia
(1269–96)

Johann 'Parracida'
(1290–1313)
(murderer of Albert)

Otto 'the Jolly'
(1301–39)
Duke of Austria,
Styria and Carinthia
m. Anna of Luxembourg
[see Tree 5]

eight
others

Leopold (III)
(1351–86)
1365 Duke of Austria
m. Viridis Visconti
(*c.* 1360–1414)

eight
others
(most died young)

LEOPOLDINE
LINE

Leopold (IV)
(1371–1411)
1395 Duke of Austria
m. Katharina of Burgundy
(1378–1425)
(no issue)

Ernst 'Ironman'
(1377–1424)
1402 Duke of Austria
m. 1. Margarethe of
Pomerania
(*c.* 1366–1407)
m. 2. Cimburgis of Masovia
(*c.* 1394–1429)

Frederick (IV) 'the Empty Pockets'
(1382–1439)
1402 Duke of Austria-Tirol
m. 1. Elisabeth of the Palantine
(Wittelsbach)
(*c.* 1381–1400)
m. 2. Anna of Brunswick
(*c.* 1390–1422)

m. 2.
FREDERICK III
(1415–93)
1440 King
1452 Emperor
m. Eleonore of Portugal
(1436–67)

m. 2.
eight
others

Siegmund 'the Rich'
(1427–96)
1439 Duke of Austria-Tirol
(abdicated 1490)
m. Eleonora of Scotland
(1431–80)

three
others

MAXIMILIAN I
[see Tree 7]

Wolfgang
(+1480)

TREE 7: HABSBURGS (Part 2)

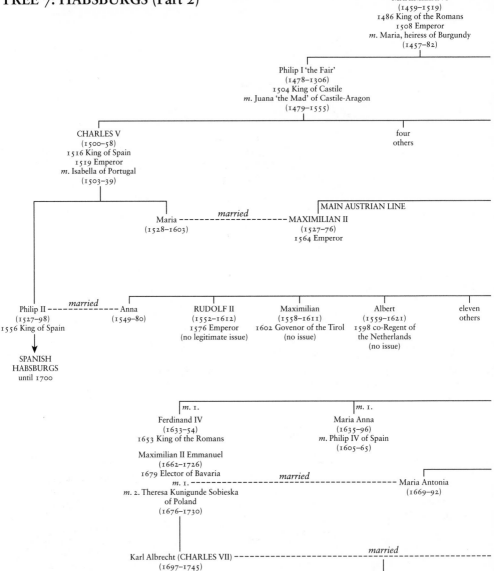

MAXIMILIAN I
(1459–1519)
1486 King of the Romans
1508 Emperor
m. Maria, heiress of Burgundy
(1457–82)

Philip I 'the Fair'
(1478–1306)
1504 King of Castile
m. Juana 'the Mad' of Castile-Aragon
(1479–1555)

CHARLES V
(1500–58)
1516 King of Spain
1519 Emperor
m. Isabella of Portugal
(1503–39)

four
others

MAIN AUSTRIAN LINE

Maria -------- *married* -------- MAXIMILIAN II
(1528–1603)   (1527–76)
                                   1564 Emperor

Philip II -- *married* -- Anna
(1527–98)   (1549–80)
1556 King of Spain

RUDOLF II
(1552–1612)
1576 Emperor
(no legitimate issue)

Maximilian
(1558–1611)
1602 Govenor of the Tirol
(no issue)

Albert
(1559–1621)
1598 co-Regent of
the Netherlands
(no issue)

eleven
others

SPANISH
HABSBURGS
until 1700

m. 1.
Ferdinand IV
(1633–54)
1653 King of the Romans

m. 1.
Maria Anna
(1635–96)
m. Philip IV of Spain
(1605–65)

Maximilian II Emmanuel
(1662–1726)
1679 Elector of Bavaria
m. 1. -------- *married* -------- Maria Antonia
m. 2. Theresa Kunigunde Sobieska   (1669–92)
of Poland
(1676–1730)

Karl Albrecht (CHARLES VII) -------- *married* --------
(1697–1745)
1726 Elector of Bavaria
1742 Emperor

Maimilian III Joseph
(1727–77)
Last Bavarian Wittelsbach

Margarete
(1480–1530)
1506 Regent of
The Netherlands

FERDINAND I
(1503–64)
1525 King of Bohemia and Hungary
1530 King of the Romans
1558 Emperor
m. Anna Jagiellon of Bohemia and Hungary
(1503–47)

TIROLEAN LINE   STYRIAN LINE

Anna
(1528–90)
m. Albrecht V
Duke of Bavaria
(1528–79)

Ferdinand
(1529–95)
m. Anna Catherina of Mantua
(1566–1621)

Karl II
(1540–90)
m. Anna of Bavaria
(1551–1608)

FERDINAND II
(1578–1637)
1617 King of Bohemia
1618 King of Hungary
1619 Emperor
m. Maria Anna of Bavaria
(1574–1616)

BAVARIAN WITTELSBACHS until 1777

MATTHIAS ----------- *married* ----------- Anna
(1557–1619)   (1585–1618)
1608 King of Hungary
1612 Emperor
(no issue)

FERDINAND III
(1608–37)
1637 Emperor
m. 1. Maria Anna of Spain (1608–46)
m. 2. Maria Leopoldine of Tirol (1632–49)
m. 3. Eleonore Gonzaga (1630–86)

m. 1.

LEOPOLD I
(1640–1705)
1658 Emperor
m. Eleonor Magdalena von Pfatz-Neuburg
(1653–1720)

seven
others

m. 3.

Eleonore Maria
(1633–97)
m. Charles IV Leopold
Duke of Lorraine
(1643–90)

JOSEPH I
(1678–1711)
1690 King of the Romans
1705 Emperor
m. Amalia Wilhelmine of
Brunswick-Lüneburg (Hanover)
(1673–1742)

CHARLES VI
(1685–1740)
1706–14 King of Spain
1711 Emperor
m. Elisabeth Charlotte of
Brunswick-Wolfenbüttel
(1691–1750)

Leopold Joseph
(1679–1729)
Duke of Lorraine
m. Elisabeth Charlotte d'Orleans
(1676–1744)

-------- Amalia Maria
(1701–56)

Maria Theresa ---------------------- *married* ---------------------- FRANCIS I Stephen
(1717–80)   (1708–65)
1729–36 Duke of Lorraine
1745 Emperor

JOSEPH II
(1741–90)
1765 Emperor
two wives
(no adult issue)

LEOPOLD II
(1747–92)
1790 Emperor
m. Maria Ludovika of Spain
(1745–92)

Marie Antoinette
(1755–93)
m. Louis XVI
King of France
(1754–93)

thirteen
others

FRANCIS II
(1768–1835)
1792 Emperor (abdicated 1806)
1804 Emperor of Austria

fifteen
others

HABSBURGS until 1918

Note on Form

Place names and those of emperors, kings and other well-known historical figures are given in the form most commonly used in English-language writing. For east central European locations, this tends to be the German version. Lesser-known individuals are generally identified using the modern version of their names. This at least helps distinguish royalty (e.g. Henry) from aristocracy (e.g. Heinrich) for periods where only a few names predominated amongst the elite. The term 'Empire' is used throughout for the Holy Roman Empire, distinguishing this from references to other empires, such as those of the Byzantines and Ottomans. Likewise, 'Estates' refers to corporate social groups, like the nobility and clergy, and to the assemblies of such groups, whereas 'estates' identifies land and property. The Empire endured throughout the periods when it was ruled by a king who had not been crowned emperor. Use of the terms 'king' and 'emperor' reflects the status of the Empire's monarch at any given period. Foreign terms are italicized and explained at first mention, generally with additional information provided in the glossary. Terms and their definitions can also be accessed using the index.

Acknowledgements

This book would have been impossible without the kind assistance of numerous good people. I am particularly grateful to Barbara Stollberg-Rilinger and Gerd Althoff for their kind hospitality and lively critique of my ideas during my time as visiting fellow at the Excellence Cluster at Münster University. My colleagues Julian Haseldine and Colin Veach, as well as Simon Winder at Penguin, read and commented on the entire book, offering innumerable insightful comments and suggestions. Additionally, I have benefited from long discussions on all or parts of what eventually became this book with Thomas Biskup, Tim Blanning, Karin Friedrich, Georg Schmidt, Hamish Scott, Siegfried Westphal and Jo Whaley. Virginia Aksan, Leopold Auer, Henry Cohn, Suzanne Friedrich, Karl Härter, Beat Kümin, Graham Loud and Theo Riches all kindly sent useful material or pointed me in the direction of books I had overlooked. Rudi Wurzel and Liz Monaghan of the Centre of European Union Studies at the University of Hull provided me with an opportunity to test out ideas before an interdisciplinary audience, which help give shape to the concluding chapter. Some elements of the introduction and conclusion were presented at a conference on the Reichstag at the University of Regensburg, for which I am especially grateful to Harriet Rudolph.

The University of Hull provided a semester's research leave during which the book assumed its general shape, while the staff of the Brynmor Jones Library performed miracles in locating obscure literature that I needed to use. Cecilia Mackay tracked down my picture requests with her customary efficiency, while Jeff Edwards transformed my sketches into beautiful maps. Richard Duguid expertly oversaw the book's production. Richard Mason's eagle-eyed copy-editing saved me from innumerable potential errors, and the proofreading of Stephen Ryan and Michael Page was invaluable. I am also grateful to Kathleen McDermott and the staff at Harvard University Press for putting the book into production in the US. As always, Eliane, Alec, Tom and Nina have contributed to my work in more ways than they know, for which I am eternally thankful.

Introduction

The Holy Roman Empire's history lies at the heart of the European experience. Understanding that history explains how much of the continent developed between the early Middle Ages and the nineteenth century. It reveals important aspects which have become obscured by the more familiar story of European history as that of separate nation states. The Empire lasted for more than a millennium, well over twice as long as imperial Rome itself, and encompassed much of the continent. In addition to present-day Germany, it included all or part of ten other modern countries: Austria, Belgium, the Czech Republic, Denmark, France, Italy, Luxembourg, the Netherlands, Poland and Switzerland. Others were also linked to it, like Hungary, Spain and Sweden, or involved in its history in often forgotten ways, such as England, which provided one German king (Richard of Cornwall, 1257–72). More fundamentally, the east–west and north–south tensions in Europe both intersect in the old core lands of the Empire between the Rhine, Elbe and Oder rivers and the Alps. These tensions were reflected in the fluidity of the Empire's borders and the patchwork character of its internal subdivisions. In short, the Empire's history is not merely part of numerous distinct national histories, but lies at the heart of the continent's general development.

This, however, is not how the Empire's history is usually presented. Preparing for the Continental Congress that would give his country its constitution in 1787, the future US president James Madison looked to Europe's past and present states to build his case for a strong federal union. Reviewing the Holy Roman Empire, then still one of the largest European states, he concluded it was 'a nerveless body; incapable of regulating its own members; insecure against external dangers; and agitated with unceasing fermentation in its own bowels.' Its history was simply a catalogue 'of the licentiousness of the strong, and the oppression of the weak ... of general imbecility, confusion and misery.'[1]

Madison was far from alone in this opinion. The seventeenth-century philosopher Samuel Pufendorf famously described the Empire as a 'monstrosity' because he felt it had degenerated from a 'regular' monarchy into an 'irregular body'. A century later, Voltaire quipped it was neither holy, Roman nor an empire.[2] This negative interpretation was entrenched by the Empire's inglorious demise, dissolved by Emperor Francis II on 6 August 1806 to prevent Napoleon Bonaparte from usurping it. Yet this final act itself already tells us that the Empire retained some value in its last hours, especially as the Austrians had already gone to considerable lengths to prevent the French from seizing the imperial regalia. The Empire would be plundered when later generations wrote the stories of their own nations, in which it appears positively or negatively according to the author's circumstance and purpose. This trend has grown more pronounced since the later twentieth century, with some writers proclaiming the Empire as the first German nation state or even a model for greater European integration.

The Empire's demise coincided with the emergence of modern nationalism as a popular phenomenon, as well as the establishment of western historical method, institutionalized by professionals like Leopold von Ranke who held publicly funded university posts. Their task was to record their national story, and to shape it they constructed linear narratives based around the centralization of political power or their people's emancipation from foreign domination. The Empire had no place in a world where every nation was supposed to have its own state. Its history was reduced to that of medieval Germany, and in many ways the Empire's greatest posthumous influence lay in how criticism of its structures created the discipline of modern history.

Ranke established the basic framework in the 1850s which others, notably Heinrich von Treitschke, popularized over the course of the next century. The Frankish king Charles the Great, who was crowned first Holy Roman emperor on Christmas Day 800, appears in this story as the German *Karl der Grosse*, not the Francophone *Charlemagne*. The partition of his realm in 843 is interpreted as the birth of France, Italy and Germany, with the Empire thereafter discussed in terms of repeated, thwarted attempts to construct a viable German national monarchy. Individual monarchs were praised or condemned according to an anachronistic scale of 'German interests'. Rather than entrench the imperial title in Germany itself as the basis of a strong, centralized monarchy, too many monarchs, it seemed, pursued the pointless dream of re-creating the Roman empire. To rally support, they allegedly dissipated central power in debilitating concessions to their senior lords, who emerged as virtually independent princes. After several centuries of heroic efforts and glorious failures, this project finally succumbed in a titanic clash around 1250 between German *Kultur* and the treacherous Italianate civilization represented by the papacy. 'Germany' was now condemned to weakness, divided by the dualism between an impotent emperor and selfish princes. For many, especially Protestant writers, the Austrian Habsburgs wasted their chance once they obtained an almost permanent monopoly of the imperial title after 1438, by again pursuing the dream of a transnational empire rather than a strong German state. Only the Prussian Hohenzollerns, emerging on the Empire's north-eastern margins, carefully husbanded their resources, preparing for their 'German mission' to reunite the country as a strong, centralized nation state. Although shorn of its nationalist excesses, this story still continues as the 'basso continuo' of German historical writing and perception, not least because it appears to make sense of an otherwise thoroughly confusing past.[3]

The Empire took the blame for Germany being a 'delayed nation', receiving only the 'consolation prize' of becoming a cultural nation during the eighteenth century, before Prussian-led unification finally made it a political one in 1871.[4] For many observers this had fatal consequences, pushing German development along a deviant 'special path' (*Sonderweg*) away from western civilization and liberal democracy and towards authoritarianism and the Holocaust.[5] Only after two world wars had discredited the earlier celebration of militarized nation states did a more positive historical reception of the Empire emerge. The concluding chapter of this book will return to this in the context of how the Empire's history is being used to comment on and inform discussions of Europe's immediate future.

The term 'empire' requires some clarification before proceeding further. The Empire lacked a fixed title but was always referred to as imperial, even during the long periods when it was governed by a king rather than an emperor. The Latin term *imperium* was gradually displaced by the German *Reich* from the thirteenth century. As an adjective, the word *reich* means 'rich', while as a noun it means both 'empire' and 'realm', appearing in the terms *Kaiserreich* (empire) and *Königreich* (kingdom).[6] There is no universally accepted definition of an empire, though three elements are common to most interpretations.[7] The least useful is a stress on size. Canada covers nearly 10 million square kilometres, over 4 million square kilometres larger than either the ancient Persian empire or that of Alexander the Great, yet few would contend that it is an imperial state. Emperors and their subjects have generally lacked the obsession of social scientists with quantification; on the contrary, a more meaningful defining characteristic of empire would be its absolute refusal to define limits to either its physical extent or its power pretentions.[8]

Longevity is a second factor, with empires being judged of 'world historical importance' if they pass the 'Augustan threshold' – a term derived from Emperor Augustus's transformation of the Roman republic into a stable imperium.[9] This approach has the merit of drawing attention to identifying why some empires outlived their founders, but it should be recognized that many which did not nonetheless left important legacies, such as those of Alexander and Napoleon.

Hegemony is the third element and perhaps the most ideologically charged. Some influential discussions of empire reduce it to the dominance of a single people over others.[10] Depending on perspective, the history of empire becomes a story of conquest or resistance. Empires bring oppression and exploitation, while resistance is usually equated with national self-determination and democracy. This approach certainly makes sense in some contexts.[11] However, it often fails to explain how empires expand and endure, especially when these processes are at least partly peaceful. It also tends to conceive of empires as composed of a fairly stable 'core' people or territory, dominating a number of peripheral regions. Here – to use another common metaphor – imperial rule becomes a 'rimless wheel', with the peripheries connected to the hub but not to each other. This allows the imperial core to govern through 'divide and rule', keeping each peripheral population separate, and preventing them combining against the numerically inferior core. Such a system relies heavily on brokerage provided by local elites acting as the spokes between the hub and each periphery. Rule does not have to be overtly oppressive, since the brokers can be coopted and can transmit some benefits of imperial rule to the peripheral population. However, imperial rule is tied to numerous local bargains which can make it difficult to mobilize substantial resources for common purposes, because the core has to negotiate separately with each set of brokers.[12] The core–periphery model is helpful in explaining how relatively small groups of people can govern large areas, but brokerage has been a part of most states as they have expanded and consolidated and is, in itself, not necessarily 'imperial'.

A major reason for the Empire's relative scholarly neglect is that its history is so difficult to tell. The Empire lacked the things giving shape to conventional national history: a stable heartland, a capital city, centralized political institutions and, perhaps most fundamentally, a single 'nation'. It was also very large and lasted a long time. A conventional chronological approach would become unfeasibly long, or risk conveying a false sense of linear development and reduce the Empire's history to a high political narrative. I would like to stress instead the multiple paths, detours and dead ends of the Empire's development, and to give the reader a clear sense of what it was, how it worked, why it mattered, and its legacy for today. An extended chronology is included after the appendices for general orientation. The rest of the book is divided into 12 chapters, grouped equally in four parts that examine the Empire through the themes of ideal, belonging, governance and society. The themes have been grouped for natural progression so the reader approaches the material like an eagle flying over the Empire. The basic outline will be visible in Part I, with the other details becoming clearer as the reader nears ground level by the time he or she reaches Part IV.

It makes sense to examine how the Empire legitimated its existence and how it defined itself relative to outsiders. This is the task of Part I, which opens with a discussion of the Holy Roman Empire's basis as the secular arm of western Christianity. Historically, European development has been characterized by three levels of organization: the universal level of transcendental ideals that provide a sense of unity and common bonds (e.g. Christianity, Roman law); the particular and local level of everyday action (resource extraction, law enforcement, etc.); and the intermediary level of the sovereign state.[13] The Empire was characterized for most of its existence only by the first two of these. The emergence of the third from the thirteenth century was a major contributory factor in its eventual demise. However, the evolutionary progression once imagined by historians, culminating in a Europe of competing nation states, no longer appears the terminus of political development, contributing to the recent renewed interest in the Empire and to comparisons between it and the European Union.

Chapter 1 opens with the circumstances of the Empire's foundation through an agreement between Charlemagne and the papacy, which expressed the belief that Christendom constituted a singular order under the twin management of emperor and pope. This imparted a lasting imperial mission, anchored on the premise that the emperor was the pre-eminent Christian monarch within a common order containing lesser rulers. Moral leadership and guardianship of the church were the emperor's tasks, not hegemonic, direct rule over the continent. As with other empires, this imperial mission imparted a 'quasi-religious sense of purpose' transcending immediate self-interest.[14] The belief that the Empire was far bigger than its ruler and transcended whoever was currently emperor took root very early on, and explains why so many emperors struggled to fulfil that mission rather than settle for what, with hindsight, seems the more realistic option of a national monarchy. The rest of the chapter examines the holy, Roman and imperial elements of this mission, and explains the often difficult relationship between Empire and papacy into early modernity.[15]

The specifically religious dimension is explored in Chapter 2, which shows how the Empire embraced the typically 'imperial' distinction between itself as a single civilization in contrast to all outsiders, who were 'barbarians'.[16] Civilization was defined as Christianity and the ancient imperial Roman legacy as embodied by the Empire after 800. However, the Empire's dealings with outsiders were not always violent, while its continued expansion into northern and eastern Europe in the high Middle Ages was partly through assimilation. Chapter 3 shows how the concept of a singular civilization prevented the Empire dealing with other states on equal terms. This became increasingly problematic as Latin Christian Europe divided into more clearly distinct sovereign states, each with monarchs claiming to be 'emperors in their own kingdoms'.

Part II aims to transcend the traditional dismemberment of the Empire by nationalist and regionalist historians in discussing how its many different lands and peoples related to it. The Empire lacked a stable core, unlike those provided by the Thames valley and the Île de

France for the English and French national states respectively. It never had a permanent capital or a single patron saint, common language or culture. Identity was always multiple and multilayered, reflecting its imperial extent over many peoples and places. The number of layers grew over time as part of the evolution of a more complex and nuanced political hierarchy sustaining imperial governance. The general core came to rest in the German kingdom in the mid-tenth century, though imperial monarchy remained itinerant into the fourteenth century. A stable hierarchy emerged by the 1030s, establishing that whoever was German king also ruled the Empire's other two primary kingdoms of Italy and Burgundy and was the only candidate worthy of the imperial title. Chapter 4 explores the actual shape of these kingdoms and their component lands, as well as how the Empire related to other European peoples. The relative significance of ethnicity, social organization and place to identities is discussed in Chapter 5. Chapter 6 examines how concepts of the nation, emerging from the thirteenth century, reinforced rather than undermined the identification of many inhabitants with the Empire. Germans already saw themselves as a political nation well before unification in 1871, identifying the Empire as their natural home. The Empire never demanded the absolute, exclusive loyalty expected by later nationalists. This reduced its capacity to mobilize resources and command active support, but it also allowed heterogeneous communities to coexist, each identifying its own distinctiveness as safeguarded by belonging to a common home.

Part III explains how the Empire was governed without creating a large, centralized infrastructure. Historians long expected and wanted kings to be 'state builders', or at least to have consistent, long-term plans. States are judged by a singular model, expressed most succinctly by the sociologist Max Weber as 'the monopoly of the legitimate use of physical force within a given territory'.[17] National history thus becomes the story of creating an infrastructure to centralize and exercise exclusive sovereign authority, and the articulation of arguments to legitimate these processes. Equally, the arguments delegitimate rival claims both from insiders, like would-be autonomous nobles or regions, and from outsiders seeking hegemony over the 'national' territory. Measured against this yardstick, it is scarcely surprising that the Empire's history is reduced to a repetitive and chaotic cycle lasting at least into the fifteenth century. Each ruler assumed the throne as king recognized by his peers amongst the senior nobles. He then toured the German kingdom seeking homage, thereby providing opportunities for his rivals to deny this and rebel. Most kings at least asserted their authority, though there were lengthy periods involving rival kings and even civil war, notably 1077–1106, 1198–1214 and 1314–25. Many kings faced external raids and invasions by the Vikings, Slavs or Magyars until the tenth century. Once secure, these kings generally made a Roman expedition (*Romzug*) to seek coronation as emperor by the pope. Those that dallied too long were apt to face renewed rebellion north of the Alps, often precipitating an early return. Others found repeated expeditions necessary to assert even a modicum of authority in Italy. They either died prematurely of malaria whilst on campaign, or, worn out, hastened to some appropriate spot in Germany for a 'good death'. Then the whole wearisome cycle seems to begin again, continuing until the Habsburgs finally established their own dynastic territorial dominions in the early sixteenth century that partially overlapped those of the Empire.

This narrative rests on Ranke's influential conception of the Empire's history as the story of failed nation building. Most observers have followed his lead in arguing that the 'decline' of central authority was inversely proportionate to the growth of the princes as semi-independent rulers. This argument has been underpinned by a century and a half of national and regional histories, charting the separate stories of modern countries like Belgium or the Czech Republic, as well as those of the regions of modern Germany and Italy, such as Bavaria or Tuscany. Each of these stories is so persuasive, because it is constructed around the development of centralized political authority and associated identity focused exclusively on its given territory. The overall conclusion is often that the Empire was some kind of federal system, which it became either immediately after Charlemagne's death in 814 or by the Peace of Westphalia in 1648 at the latest.[18] The enormous difference between these dates is an indicator of the problems with confidently pinning down these structures. Nonetheless, this is an attractive idea not only because, as we shall see, some of the Empire's inhabitants claimed it was a confederation, but also because this definition at least allows it to be fitted into the accepted taxonomy of political systems. It was this aspect that drew Madison's attention and his conclusion that it was 'a feeble and precarious union', a conclusion intended to encourage his fellow Americans to agree to a stronger federal government.[19]

8

Federal systems are not unitary, in that they have two or more levels of government rather than a single, central authority. Additionally, they combine elements of shared rule through common institutions with regional self-rule in constituent territorial segments.[20] These elements were certainly present in the Empire after the 'imperial reform' of the late fifteenth and early sixteenth centuries gave the imperial constitution its definitive, early modern form. However, the concept of federalism requires careful handling, because it easily confuses more than it clarifies. Defining the Empire as federal perpetuates the narrow, dualist view of its development as solely defined by emperor-princely tensions, with the latter winning out by establishing fully sovereign kingdoms and principalities in 1806. Worse, it is very difficult to disassociate the term from its modern political usage, particularly in the German and Austrian federal republics, as well as Switzerland and other contemporary states, including the USA. In all these cases the component elements interact as equals, sharing a common status as parts of a political union. The differences are genuinely dualist: their dynamics provided by how far key powers are shared through common central institutions, and how far they are devolved as 'states rights' to the component units. Finally, modern federal states act directly on all their citizens equally. Each citizen is meant to have an equal participation in his or her own state, and in the union as a whole. All are bound directly by the same federal laws, even if some aspects of life are covered by arrangements specific to each component state. These forms of equality were completely and fundamentally alien to the Empire, which always had a dominant, if shifting, political core, and always ruled its population through a complex hierarchy defined by socio-legal status.

Part III charts the evolution of this hierarchy, with each of the three chapters 7–9 covering one of the fundamental shifts in the basis of imperial governance. Carolingian rule established a basic political and legal framework for the Empire, but this did not develop further and even partially disappeared around 900. The absence of formal institutions should not, however, be taken as the lack of effective governance. This book follows the lead of those who have drawn attention to the informal aspects of a political culture based on personal presence rather than written, formalized rules.[21] Symbols and rituals were as much a part of politics as formal institutions; indeed formal institutions cannot function without the former, even though their role is often no longer acknowledged openly in the modern era. Any organization is partly 'fictive' in that it depends on the conviction amongst those who engage with it that it really exists. The organization is sustained because each individual acts in the expectation that others will behave similarly. Symbols and rituals provide markers for participants, helping to sustain the belief in the organization's continued existence. The organization is threatened if its symbols lose their meaning, or are challenged, such as during the iconoclasm of the Protestant Reformation. Likewise, an organization risks being exposed as fictive if it no longer meets common expectations, for example if the anticipated repression fails to materialize or is exposed as feeble when a government is confronted with open defiance.

Imperial governance entailed fostering a consensus amongst the Empire's political elite to ensure at least minimum compliance with agreed policy, enabling the emperor to dispense with the burden of both forcing cooperation and of ruling the bulk of the population directly.[22] Consensus did not necessarily mean harmony or stability, but it did achieve the 'crude simplicity' of imperial rule, allowing the emperor and elites to pursue policies without requiring a radical transformation of the societies they governed.[23] This imposed limits on what emperors could do. They needed to uphold the legitimacy of imperial rule through demonstrative acts, such as punishing obvious wrongdoers; yet emperors also had to avoid personal failures that would undermine their aura of power and could be interpreted as the loss of divine favour.

A key characteristic of imperial governance was that institutional development was primarily driven by the need to foster and sustain consensus, rather than by attempts by the centre to reach directly into the peripheries and localities. The Ottonian line of kings during the tenth century ruled through a relatively flat hierarchy of senior lay and spiritual lords. The Salians, their successors after 1024, shifted to more of a command style without breaching the established pattern. Broader socio-economic changes meanwhile supported a longer and more complex lordly hierarchy, both reducing the average size of each jurisdiction while multiplying their numbers. The Staufer family ruling after 1138 responded by formalizing the lordly hierarchy, creating a more distinct princely elite internally stratified by ranks denoted by different titles, but united through a common immediacy under the emperor. Lesser lords and subjects were now more clearly 'mediate', meaning that their relationship to the emperor and Empire ran through at least one intervening level of authority. This hierarchy crystallized around 1200, consolidating the complementary division of responsibilities within the Empire. The emperor got on with the business of the imperial mission, assisted by the immediate princely elite who meanwhile assumed more functions within their own jurisdictions, including peace-keeping, conflict resolution and resource mobilization. These jurisdictions became 'territorialized' through the need to demarcate areas of responsibility. The Staufers' demise around 1250 was a personal, not structural failure, since the basic pattern of imperial governance continued to evolve along the same lines into the fourteenth century.

The next shift came during the line of Luxembourg kings (1347–1437), who changed the emphasis from imperial prerogatives to hereditary dynastic possessions to provide the material basis sustaining imperial governance. The new methods were perfected after 1438 by the Habsburgs, who amassed not only the largest hereditary lands in the Empire, but acquired a separate dynastic empire outside it, initially including Spain and the New World. The transition to Habsburg rule occurred amidst new internal and external challenges, prompting the period of imperial reform that intensified around 1480–1520. The reforms channelled established patterns of consensus-seeking through new, formalized institutions, and entrenched the complementary distribution of responsibilities between imperial structures and princely and civic territories.

The development of imperial governance through a long lordly hierarchy appears to detach the Empire from its subjects. Certainly this is how most general accounts have treated its history: as high politics, far removed from daily life. This has had the unfortunate consequence of contributing to the widespread sense of the Empire's irrelevance, especially as social and economic historians have largely followed their political counterparts and traced developments like population size or economic output using anachronistic national frontiers. Part IV addresses this, arguing that both the governance and patterns of identity within the Empire were closely entwined with socio-economic developments, notably the emergence of a corporate social structure combining both hierarchical-authoritarian and horizontal-associative elements. This structure was replicated – with variations – at all levels of the Empire's socio-political order.

A full social history of the Empire is beyond the scope of this book. Rather, Chapter 10 traces the emergence of the corporate social order, showing how it embraced both lords and commons, and how it became anchored in rural and urban communities with varying but generally wide degrees of self-governance. These associative aspects are explored further in Chapter 11, which demonstrates the importance of corporate status in all forms of leagues and communual organizations from the high Middle Ages onwards, from the smallest guild to groupings that resulted in major challenges to imperial rule, such as the Lombard League or the Swiss Confederation. Like jurisdictions, corporate identities and rights were local, specific and related to status. They reflected the belief in an idealized socio-political order, which placed a premium on preserving peace through consensus rather than through any absolute, abstract concept of justice. The consequences of this are explored in Chapter 12, which shows how conflict resolution remained open-ended, like the Empire's political processes generally. Imperial institutions could judge, punish and coerce, but they mainly brokered settlements intended as workable compromises rather than as definitive judgements based on absolute concepts of right and wrong.

The Empire thus fostered a deep-rooted, conservative ideal of freedom as local and particular, shared by members of corporate groups and incorporated communities. These were local and particular *liberties*, not abstract *Liberty* shared equally by all inhabitants. Here, this book offers an alternative explanation for the hotly contested 'genesis of German conservatism', without, however, claiming any continuity beyond the mid-nineteenth century. Usually, the authoritarianism of nineteenth- and early twentieth-century Germany is attributed to the supposedly dualist political development prior to the Empire's demise in 1806.[24] Attempts at genuine egalitarian liberty are ascribed solely to 'the people' who are crushed by 'the princes', notably during the bloody Peasants War of 1524–6. Meanwhile, the princes usurped the ideal of freedom for themselves to legitimate their privileged position as autonomous rulers. 'German liberty' thus supposedly narrowed to the defence of princely autonomy against potential imperial 'tyranny'. Simultaneously, as the 'real' governments in the Empire, the princes allegedly introduced the rule of law, protecting their subjects' right to property, whilst denying any meaningful political representation. Liberty thus became associated with the bureaucratic state and transposed to national government when this was created in the later nineteenth century.

This argument has never explained why central Europeans remained so unreceptive to nineteenth-century liberalism. Either they were too cowed by a repressive police state to embrace it, or they were duped by a naive faith in princely benevolence and their own ingrained sense of subordination.[25] Yet liberals discovered that ordinary people often did not want their version of liberty, because uniform equality conflicted with treasured corporate rights which appeared to offer superior safeguards against capitalist market exploitation.[26] Later problems stem at least partly from how those corporate rights were stripped away amidst rapid industrialization and urbanization after the 1840s. These matters lie beyond the scope of this book.

The attachment to corporate identities and rights helps explain why the Empire endured despite internal tensions and stark inequalities in life chances. However, it was neither a bucolic, harmonious old-worldly utopia, nor a direct blueprint for the European Union.[27] The question of the Empire's long-term viability by the late eighteenth century is tackled at the end of Chapter 12. For now we need to note, as an important factor in changing the Empire across time, the long-term shift from a culture of personal presence and oral communication to one based on written communication. This transition was common throughout Europe and is one of the general markers of the shift to modernity. However, it had particular consequences in the Empire since this relied so heavily on consensus-seeking and on delineating power, rights and responsibilities along a status hierarchy.

Oral communication and written culture co-existed throughout the Empire's lifespan, so the transition is one of degrees, not absolutes. Christianity is a religion of the book, while both ecclesiastical and secular authorities used written rules and communication (see Chapter 7, pp. 320–25, and Chapter 12, pp. 603–10). Yet messages generally only acquired full meaning when delivered in person by someone of appropriate rank. Early medieval theology believed God's intentions to be transparent, with individual actions merely demonstrating divine will. Face-to-face contact was generally necessary for binding decisions to be reached. However, writing was a good way to fix such decisions and to avoid potential ambiguities and misunderstandings. Like the more recent and certainly more rapid media revolution, participants found the new forms of written communication unsettling, but appreciated their benefits. Ancillary techniques, like the use of seals and particular forms of address and styles of writing, were developed in the eleventh and twelfth centuries to convince recipients of letters that such techniques represented the authentic voice of the writer by imparting a permanent authority to the text.[28] The use of paper rather than parchment facilitated a significant growth of written culture from the mid-fourteenth century, while the invention of printing a century later changed both its volume and its use.

Unfortunately, writing also makes discrepancies more obvious, as the papacy already discovered during the twelfth century when it began to be criticized for issuing patently contradictory pronouncements. A paper trail could also demonstrate how knowledge was conveyed, making it harder for authorities to claim ignorance of wrongdoing. Theologians and political theorists responded by elaborating a hierarchy of communication. The idea that divine intentions were directly manifest in human action already threatened to make God the servant of His own creation. From this it was logical to develop the idea of a mysterious God whose actions were beyond the comprehension of ordinary mortals. To elevate themselves above their subjects, secular authorities were credited with an exclusive ability to understand the 'mysteries of state' that would otherwise only baffle common folk. Those in power tailored their choice of words and images to suit specific target audiences. Communication became as much – if not more – about signalling the authorities' superiority over their subjects as about conveying messages.[29]

The elevated language of the mysteries of state used to promote centralization elsewhere in Europe was ill-suited to an imperial governance based more on consensus than command and where high politics continued to rely primarily on face-to-face communication. Although the princes did adopt a more exalted style of rule during the sixteenth century, they remained bound within a common framework, which exposed their actions and pronouncements to audiences they could not control. The imperial chancellery was usually at the forefront of employing written culture, but used this to record and fix the status and privileges of those entitled to participate in the political process. Broadly similar developments took place within the Empire's constituent territories, where communal and corporate rights were enshrined in charters and other legal documents. Increasingly, imperial institutions were called upon to broker disputes arising from the interpretation of these rights. While the system retained some flexibility, contemporaries were increasingly aware of the discrepancies as settlements relied on compromise and fudge, almost inevitably contravening some formal rules. In the late eighteenth century, the gap between formal status and material power became glaring at the highest political level with the growth of Austria and Prussia as European powers in their own right. While the refusal to abandon hallowed practices gave the Empire some coherence, this also made it impossible for its inhabitants to conceive of any alternative structure. Reform narrowed down to mere tinkering with existing arrangements and ultimately proved unable to cope with the overwhelming impact of the French Revolutionary Wars, forcing Francis II's decision in 1806 to dissolve the Empire.

PART I

Ideal

I

Two Swords

HOLY

The problems of defining the Empire are already apparent in the confusion over its title. For most of its existence it was simply 'the Empire'. The words Holy, Roman and Empire were only combined as *Sacrum Romanum Imperium* in June 1180, and though used more frequently from 1254, they never appeared consistently in official documents.[1] Nonetheless, all three terms formed core elements of the imperial ideal present from the Empire's foundation. This chapter will consider each in turn, before investigating the Empire's troubled relationship with the papacy.

The holy element was integral to the Empire's primary purpose in providing a stable political order for all Christians and defending them against heretics and infidels. To this end, the emperor should act as chief advocate, or guardian, of the pope, who was the head of a single, universal Christian church. Since this was considered a divine mission, entrusted by God, it opened the possibility that the emperor and Empire were themselves sacred. Like the Roman and imperial elements, the holy character of the Empire was rooted in the later, Christian phase of the ancient Roman empire, rather than the pagan past of the first Caesars or the earlier Roman republic.

Christian Rome

After more than three centuries of persecuting Christians, Rome adopted Christianity as its sole, official religion in AD 391. This step partially desacralized the imperial office, since the singular Christian

God would not tolerate a rival. The emperor no longer considered himself divine and had to accept the church's development as a separate institution throughout his empire. These changes were eased by the church's adoption of a clerical hierarchy modelled on Roman imperial infrastructure. Christian bishops resided in the chief towns, exercising spiritual jurisdictions (dioceses) that generally matched the political boundaries of the empire's provinces. Moreover, though no longer considered a god, the emperor retained a sacral role as mediator between heaven and earth. The *Pax Romanum* remained an imperial mission, but changed from providing an earthly paradise to advancing Christianity as the sole path to salvation.

The later Roman empire faced internal tensions and external pressures. Parts of the empire were already devolved to co-emperors after 284, and this resumed after a brief reunification under Constantine I, who revived the ancient Greek town of Byzantium as a new capital, immodestly dubbed Constantinople in the 330s. The split into eastern and western empires became permanent after 395. Both halves survived through accommodating invading warriors, especially the western empire, which absorbed successive waves of Germanic invaders, notably the Goths and, later, the Vandals. These poachers were turned into gamekeepers through the attractions of Roman culture and settled life. They abandoned raiding to serve as the empire's border guards and became partly Romanized, including adopting forms of Christianity.

Their embrace of Rome was always conditional on the benefits of subordination outweighing the lure of independence. This balance tipped against the western empire during the fourth and fifth centuries. The western Gothic tribes, known as the Visigoths, established their own kingdom in former Roman Spain and southern Gaul in 395, and sacked the imperial capital only fifteen years later. The Franks – another tribe about which we will hear more shortly – assumed control of northern Gaul around 420 after 170 years of alternately attacking and serving the local Roman defenders.[2] Having seen off the Huns, a fresh set of armed migrants arriving in the mid-fifth century, the victorious Goths under Odovacar toppled the last western emperor, fittingly called Augustulus, or 'Little Augustus', in 476.

Only later was this regarded as the 'fall of the Rome empire'. For contemporaries, Rome simply contracted to its eastern half based in Constantinople, which still regarded itself as a direct continuation of ancient Rome, despite its much later distinctive label as the Byzantine empire. Nonetheless, the events of 476 were significant. The city of Rome was no longer capital of the known world, but a precarious outpost on the western periphery of an empire whose primary interests now lay in the Balkans, Holy Land and north Africa, and whose culture was predominantly Greek rather than Latin by the seventh century. Byzantium underwent periodic revivals, but was short of manpower, especially after costly wars against the Islamic Arabs, generally known as Saracens or Moors, who emerged as a new enemy as they overran Palestine and north Africa by 640.

Byzantium was obliged to secure Rome by relying on the Ostrogoths, another tribe displaced by the Huns' eruption into central Europe in the fifth century. Following established practice, Byzantium offered status and legitimacy in return for political subordination and military service. The Ostrogoth leader, Theodoric, had been raised in Constantinople and combined Romanized culture with the Gothic warrior ethos. Having defeated Odovacar, he was recognized as ruler of Italy by Byzantium in 497. Cooperation broke down during the reign of Emperor Justinian, who capitalized on his temporary reconquest of north Africa to try to assert more direct control over Italy. The resulting Gothic War (535–62) saw the eventual defeat of the Ostrogoths and the establishment of a permanent Byzantine presence in Italy. Known as the Exarchate, this had its political and military base at Ravenna in the north, with the rest of the peninsula divided into provinces, each under a military commander called a *dux* – the origins of both the word 'duke' and the title *duce* taken by Benito Mussolini.

Success proved temporary as the Lombards, another Gothic tribe that had served as Byzantine auxiliaries in the recent war, launched their own invasion of Italy in 568. Unlike Odovacar's Goths, they failed to take Rome, or the new Byzantine outpost at Ravenna, but nonetheless established their own kingdom based initially in Milan, and then Pavia from 616.[3] Italy was now split in three. The invaders' new kingdom of Langobardia extended along the Po valley, giving that region its modern name of Lombardy. Lombard kings exercised only loose control over southern Italy, which was largely organized as the separate Lombard duchy of Benevento. The remainder was known as the Romagna, or 'Roman' territory belonging to Byzantium, and surviving today as the name of the region around Ravenna.

The Emergence of the Papacy

A fourth political factor emerged with the growing influence of the papacy, based in Rome. The popes traced their origins as the church's 'father' (*papa*) through 'Apostolic Succession' from St Peter, though they were only really free to function once ancient Rome tolerated Christianity. Rome was only one of five primary Christian centres, but the loss of Jerusalem, Antioch and Alexandria to the Arabs (638–42) increased its importance alongside Constantinople. Additional prestige derived from Rome's own continued importance as an imperial city, and its emotional and spiritual significance in the development of early Christianity. Beginning with the execution of St Peter and St Paul in the year 64, all 30 Roman bishops prior to Constantine's toleration Edict of Milan (313) were subsequently recognized as saints and claimed as martyrs by the church.[4]

It was important for the later Holy Roman Empire that the Roman papacy developed differently to the eastern patriarchate in Constantinople. Byzantium retained the centralized imperial structure, with its culture of hierarchical subordination and written administration deriving directly from ancient Rome. This imparted two characteristics largely absent in the early western church. The patriarch remained subordinate to the emperor, while the desire to fix theology in written statements made doctrinal differences much more pronounced than those in the western church, which was both more decentralized and less concerned with communication in writing. The eastern church distanced itself from the version of Christianity known as Arianism, which retained a strong following amongst the Lombards, while a dispute over the human and divine aspects of Christ's nature had forced the emergence of a separate Coptic church in Syria and Egypt when these were still Byzantine provinces.

The absence of durable imperial structures in the west deprived the Roman popes of the strong political backing afforded the eastern patriarch. Papal authority relied on asserting moral rather than direct administrative leadership of the western church, which remained a loose agglomeration of dioceses and churches. Since the fifth century, popes used the argument of Apostolic Succession to claim the right to pronounce on doctrine without reference to any political authority. This was extended to the right to judge whether the candidates chosen by the various Christian Gothic kings and nobles were suitable to become bishops or archbishops. Authority was symbolized through the practice of investiture developed in the seventh century: no archbishop could take office without receiving a special vestment known as the *pallium* from the pope. In turn, popes made archbishops responsible for checking the credentials of bishops within their archdiocese, thus extending papal influence indirectly deeper into the localities. Wynfrith, an Anglo-Saxon monk later known as St Boniface, who was the first archbishop of Mainz and a key figure in the Empire's church history, was given cloth that had lain across St Peter's tomb as his *pallium* in 752. The message was clear: opposing the pope was equated with disobeying St Peter.

The early medieval popes would have preferred a strong emperor who could protect them and allow them to pursue their spiritual mission. Rome was one of the military duchies established in Italy after the Gothic War, but Byzantine power was flickering, while Byzantium had to deal with its own practical problems. As bishops of Rome, popes were further bound to local society through canon law, the as yet largely uncodified customs governing the management of the church and its personnel. Bishops were to be elected by the clergy and inhabitants of their diocese. Local young men tended to be preferred: 13 of the 15 popes in the century before 654 were Romans who often had an uncomfortable relationship with their city's clans, or leading families, who held much of local wealth and power. Gregory I, the most important of these popes, hailed from a family of Roman senators and pushed the papacy into the void left by contracting Byzantine power. Within a century, his successors had assumed ducal authority across the city and its hinterland, known as St Peter's Patrimonium (*Patrimonium Petri*), a coastal strip either side of the Tiber.[5] Over time, this territory became the material basis for papal claims to supremacy over the western church. Popes steadily appropriated the symbols and political claims of Byzantine emperors, whilst simultaneously deliberately obscuring or minimizing their continued ties to Constantinople. For example, by the late eighth century, popes issued their own coins and dated their pontificates like the reigns of kings.[6] Meanwhile, their spiritual influence grew while Byzantine political authority contracted. Gregory I and his successors sent missionaries to Christianize Britain and Germany, areas long since outside any Roman imperial orbit.

However, the popes did not follow seventh-century Islamic leaders in establishing their own imperial state. Latin Christianity alone proved insufficient to reunite the kingdoms and principalities emerging from the former western Roman empire. The papacy still needed a protector, but Byzantium proved increasingly unhelpful. Constans II made the last serious attempt to eject the Lombards from southern Italy in 662–8, and was the last Byzantine emperor to visit Rome, but he spent his time transferring ancient treasures to Constantinople. Friction increased after 717 through Byzantine tax demands and interference in western Christian practices. The Lombards seized the opportunity to capture Ravenna in 751, essentially extinguishing Byzantine influence. The pope was left alone facing the Lombards, who now claimed former Byzantine rights, including secular jurisdiction over Rome and thus the papacy.

The Franks

The pope looked north-west to the Franks as alternative protectors. Like many of the peoples of post-Roman western Europe, the Franks had emerged as a tribal confederacy; in their case in the Weser-Rhine area of north-western Germany known then as Austrasia and later, loosely, as Franconia. Unlike their southern neighbours, the Alamanni of Swabia, the Franks assimilated much from Rome as they spread westwards into Gaul after 250.[7] By 500 they controlled all Gaul under their great warrior, Clovis, who united all the Frankish tribes and was proclaimed king. Clovis accepted baptism directly into the Roman church, rather than the usual Germanic choice of Arianism, while his successors cooperated with papal missionaries, notably St Boniface's activities on the eastern and northern fringes of their realm.

These factors probably influenced the pope's choice, as did the extent and proximity of the Frankish realm. By 750 it extended beyond Gaul and north-western Germany to include Swabia, and – crucially – Burgundy, which then encompassed western Switzerland and south-east France, and so controlled access over the Alps into Lombardy. These huge territories, known as Francia, were ruled by the Merovingian family descended from Clovis. Unfairly criticized by later French historians as *les rois fainéants* ('the do-nothing kings'), the Merovingians had achieved much, but they were suffering from inbreeding and the

Frankish custom of partitioning property amongst sons, which led to repeated civil wars during the seventh and early eighth centuries. Power slipped to what became known as the Carolingian family, which held the office of 'mayor of the palace' controlling the royal household.[8]

Accordingly, the first papal appeal was addressed not to the Meroving-ian king, but to his mayor Charles, known as *Martel* ('the Hammer') after his victory over the invading Moors at Poitiers in 732. Cooper-ation was frustrated by Charles's death within a year, followed by renewed Frankish civil war. As the pope's situation deteriorated after the fall of Ravenna, he took the bold step of assuming the Romano-Byzantine strategy of offering status to a 'barbarian' leader in return for submission and support. Acting through Boniface, Pope Zachary crowned Martel's son Pippin the Short as Frankish king in 751, thereby sanctioning Pippin's coup overthrowing the Merovingians. Pippin sig-nalled his subordination to the pope at two meetings in 753 and 754 by prostrating himself, kissing the papal stirrup and helping the pontiff dismount. Unsurprisingly, Frankish accounts contain no record of this 'Strator service', which was to assume considerable significance in later papal-imperial relations as a highly visible means of demarcating super-iority.[9] More practically, Pippin invaded Lombardy (754–6), capturing Ravenna and relieving the pressure on Rome without removing it entirely.

The papal-Frankish alliance was renewed in 773 by Charlemagne, Pippin's eldest son, who answered renewed calls for assistance as the Lombards again tried to assert secular jurisdiction over Rome. The future emperor looked the part at 1.8 metres, towering over his con-temporaries, even if he was developing a pot belly from over-eating. Detesting drunkenness and dressing modestly, Charlemagne nonethe-less clearly enjoyed being the centre of attention.[10] Recent attempts to debunk him as a military leader are unconvincing.[11] The Franks were simply the best organized for war of all the major post-Roman king-doms, as Charlemagne amply demonstrated in his campaign to rescue the pope in 773–4 (see Plate 4). Charlemagne besieged Pavia for a year, and its capture in June 774 ended two hundred years of Lombard royal rule. In keeping with Frankish custom, Lombardy was not annexed dir-ectly, but preserved as a distinct kingdom under Charlemagne. Following the suppression of a rebellion in 776, Charlemagne replaced most of the Lombard elite with loyal Franks and spent the next three decades ruthlessly consolidating his authority throughout Francia and extending his influence with new conquests in Bavaria and Saxony.

Foundation of the Empire

The Holy Roman Empire owed its foundation to the pope's decision to dignify this expansion by conferring an imperial title on Charlemagne. The reasons for this step remain obscure, but can be reconstructed with reasonable certainty. It seems likely that the pope initially regarded Charlemagne as a second Theodoric, the fifth-century Ostrogothic chieftain who acted as Byzantine governor of Italy: a useful, domesticated barbarian king, rather than a substitute for the Byzantine emperor. However, the failure of a Byzantine expedition in 788 to eject the Franks from Benevento, which they had just conquered, seemed to confirm the new balance of power. In December 795 Leo III notified Charlemagne of his election as pope, a favour normally reserved for the Byzantine emperor. Nonetheless, contingency rather than systematic planning characterized the next five years leading to Charlemagne's coronation.[12]

Three aspects stand out. First, the Empire was a joint creation of Charlemagne and Leo III, 'one of the shiftiest occupants of the throne of St Peter'.[13] Accused of perjury and adultery, Leo was unable to assert authority over the Roman clans, who orchestrated a mob which attacked him in April 799, nearly cutting out his eyes and tongue – acts of mutilation that were considered to render their victim unfit for office. Already at his accession, Leo had sent Charlemagne a banner and the keys to St Peter's tomb, symbolically placing the papacy under Frankish protection. Charlemagne was reluctant to assume this responsibility, which could require him to judge and possibly remove a wayward pontiff.[14]

Writing a generation later, the Frankish chronicler Einhard claimed Leo sprang the idea of an imperial coronation when Charlemagne finally visited Rome in November 800. We should not be misled by this typical hagiographic device stressing Charlemagne's supposed modesty in not seeking worldly ambition.[15] The details were agreed in advance and carefully choreographed, with the participants fully aware they were taking a significant step. Leo rode 12 miles from Rome to meet Charlemagne, double the usual distance accorded a mere king. The ambassador from the patriarch of Jerusalem was on hand to present the keys to the Holy Sepulchre. Although the actual site was in Arab possession since 636, this act symbolized Charlemagne's assumption of the ancient Roman mission of protecting Christianity. Finally, the choice of Christmas Day 800 for the coronation was deliberate. This was not only a central Christian holy day, but that year fell on a Sunday and was believed to be exactly 7,000 years since the Creation.[16]

Just what Charlemagne thought he was getting into is not clear, because – like virtually all medieval emperors – he left no written insight into his motives. His concern was unlikely to have been the purely immediate one of convincing the recalcitrant Saxons to accept his rule.[17] The Franks had long regarded themselves as rightful rulers over the Saxons and the other Germanic tribes that were not formally constituted as monarchies. Rather, it is more likely Charlemagne saw his accession as a way to consolidate his hold over all Italy, since the former Lombard kingdom only covered the north, whereas the idea of the Roman empire had great resonance throughout the entire peninsula.[18] Additionally, in accepting the various religious symbols, Charlemagne signalled his partnership with the pope as joint leaders of Christendom.[19]

Alongside the joint effort and careful choreography, the third factor is that it is highly likely Charlemagne believed he was being made *Roman* emperor. The Byzantine throne was technically vacant, since Emperor Constantine VI had been deposed and blinded in 796 by his mother Irene, who assumed power herself. As the first woman to rule openly in Byzantium, her authority remained hotly contested, with her immediate opponents claiming the throne as vacant to legitimize their own counter-coup, which toppled her in 802.[20] This had lasting significance. To its supporters, the Empire was not an inferior, new creation, but a direct continuation of the ancient Roman one with the title simply being 'translated' (transferred) by Leo from Byzantium to Charlemagne and his successors.

Spiritual and Secular Authority

Nonetheless, a whiff of illegitimacy still surrounded the Empire's birth. It was questionable whether the disreputable Leo had the authority to transfer the imperial title to the Frankish strongman, not least since the pope had already symbolically submitted to Charlemagne by greeting him outside Rome. These specific problems betray the deeper difficulties that contemporaries faced over the relationship between spiritual and secular authority.[21] Two biblical passages exemplify this. Jesus's response to Pontius Pilate's question 'Are you the king of the Jews?' was the potentially revolutionary: 'My kingdom does not belong to this world . . . My kingly authority comes from elsewhere' (John 18:33, 36). This opposition to secular authority made sense during Christianity's time of persecution by the Romans, and was underpinned by the doctrine of Christ's second coming, which suggested the secular world was of little significance. However, the delay in the Messiah's return made accommodation with secular authority unavoidable, as exemplified by St Paul's response to the Romans: 'Every person must submit to the supreme authorities. There is no authority but by act of God, and the existing authorities are instituted by him; consequently anyone who rebels against authority is resisting a divine institution' (Romans 13:1–2).

Christians owed obedience to all authority, but their duty to God trumped that to secular power. It proved impossible to agree whether they should suffer tyrants as a test of faith or were entitled to oppose them as 'ungodly' rulers. Attempts to resolve these tensions also drew on Scripture, notably Christ to the Pharisees: 'Render unto Caesar the things that are Caesars; and unto God the things that are God's' (Mark 12:17). In short, Christian thought tried to distinguish separate spheres of *regnum*, denoting the political realm, and *sacerdotium* for the spiritual world of the church.

Delineation of separate spheres merely raised the new problem of their mutual relationship. St Augustine was in no doubt of the superiority of *sacerdotium* over *regnum*.[22] Responding to Roman intellectuals' attribution of the Gothic sack of their city in 410 as the wrath of their former pagan gods, Augustine argued this merely demonstrated the transience of temporal existence compared to the enduring Christian 'city of God' in heaven. This distinction was later elaborated by Latin theologians to reject Byzantium's continuation of a semi-divine imperial office. Pope Gelesius I used the influential metaphor of two swords, both provided by God (see Plate 1). The church received the sword of spiritual authority (*auctoritas*), symbolizing responsibility for guiding humanity through divine grace to salvation. The state received the secular sword of power (*potestas*) to maintain order and provide the physical conditions to enable the church to perform its role. Christendom had two leaders. Both pope and emperor were considered essential to proper order. Neither could ignore the other without negating his own position.[23] Both remained locked in a dance that each struggled to lead, yet neither was prepared to release his partner and go solo.

Disagreements were expressed in texts that circulated in only a few handwritten copies and that are much more widely known now than they were at the time. They were position statements prepared to provide arguments to wield in oral debate, rather than to be used as mass propaganda.[24] Their impact on daily life was limited. Clergy and laity generally worked together, while spiritual and secular authority generally proved mutually reinforcing rather than conflictual. Nonetheless, the issues remained clear enough. Secular power was inconceivable without reference to divine authority. Likewise, the clergy could not dispense with the material world, despite waves of enthusiasm for those seeking 'freedom' from earthly constraints as hermits or monks. The Franks gave Ravenna to the pope through the *Donation of Pippin* in 754, presenting this as restoring it to the *Patrimonium*, yet they retained secular jurisdiction over the entire area, asserting claims not dissimilar to those of the Lombards they had just displaced.

The difficulties with ultimate authority were obvious at the Empire's birth. Pope Leo's public obsequiousness extended – if we believe the Frankish accounts – to prostrating himself before the newly crowned emperor. Yet, moments before, he had placed the crown on Charlemagne's head in a ceremony invented for the occasion; Byzantine emperors did not use crowns before the tenth century. The coronation thus enabled both parties to claim superiority. It was not in Charlemagne's interest to contest papal claims directly, since the process of translating his imperial title from east to west required a pope with wide-ranging authority. Thus, the Franks did not seriously question the inventions of previous popes; notably Symmachus, who claimed in 502 on dubious precedents that no secular power could judge a pontiff. Nor did they challenge the *Donation of Constantine*, purportedly dating from 317, but probably written around 760, which presented the pope as temporal lord of the western empire as well as head of the church.[25]

From Sacral Kingship to Holy Empire

Other arguments favoured imperial supremacy. The idea of the secular sword elevated the emperor above other kings as 'defender of the church' (*defensor ecclesiae*), extending the Franks' existing Christianizing mission to include repelling external threats from the Arabs, Magyars and Vikings. Defence could also entail combating internal enemies, including corrupt or heretical clergy, thus suggesting a spiritual as well as a military and political mission. Petrus Damiani, shortly to become one of the Empire's most vocal critics, called the Empire a *sanctum imperium* in 1055. By that stage, many had gone further to assert that the emperor was not merely sanctified, but intrinsically sacred (*sacrum*).[26]

Ancient Roman emperors had been regarded as demigods, with Caesar posthumously pronounced divine by the senate. The idea continued under his successors, but the need to respect Rome's still powerful republican traditions prevented this developing into full, theocratic kingship – something that was further curbed by the conversion to Christianity early in the fourth century. While ancient practice continued in Byzantium, the western Empire emerged amidst post-Roman ideas of piety as a guide to public behaviour.

Charlemagne's son and successor, Louis I, is known in Germany as 'the Pious', but in France as *le Débonnaire*; both soubriquets capture aspects of his behaviour. He was sufficiently sinful to require three rites of penance during his reign, yet devout enough to perform them. His more grievous sins included cloistering his relations to remove them as rivals to his succession in 814, mortally blinding his nephew for revolt, breaking a sworn treaty with his sons, and allowing his marriage to deteriorate to the point of his wife having an affair with a courtier. Interpretations differ whether the Carolingian bishops regarded him as an errant member of their flock or used the rites of penance as show trials to discredit him politically.[27] Either way, Louis certainly emerged stronger, even though he never silenced his opponents.

The obvious benefit of penitential acts was that they allowed you to do bad things and get away with them. For example, the tenth-century Emperor Otto III walked barefoot from Rome to Benevento to spend two weeks as a hermit after violently crushing a rebellion in 996.[28] Piety peaked under Henry III, who banished musicians seeking work at his wedding in 1043, and who often wore penitential clothes and even asked for forgiveness *after* his victory over the Hungarians at Menfö in 1044, in contrast to the usual prayers before battle.[29] Nonetheless, as the controversy over Louis I's behaviour shows, penitence could easily appear humiliating, as will be seen later with Henry IV's experience at Canossa (see pp. 57–8).

Piety remained important, particularly with the start of the First Crusade in 1095, but otherwise it became less obviously politicized until the emergence of baroque Catholicism in the seventeenth century when emperors regularly led religious processions and dedicated elaborate monuments as thanksgiving for victories or deliveries from danger. Throughout the Empire's existence, the routine of the imperial court remained regulated by the Christian calendar, with the highly visible presence of the imperial family at important religious services.[30]

The notion that emperors were sacred rather than merely pious took hold during the tenth century. Its most visible expression was the practice of appearing at public events accompanied by 12 bishops, such as the consecration of new cathedrals – something that contemporaries clearly understood as *imitatio Christi* with the Apostles. Otto I's deliberate *Renovatio*, or renewal of the Empire in the 960s, included emphasis on his role as Christ's vicar (*vicarius Christi*) wielding a divine mandate to rule.[31] Some caution is required in interpreting such acts, not least because the primary evidence is liturgical texts. Early medieval emperors remained warriors, including Henry II, who was subsequently canonized in 1146 and who consciously presented the Empire as God's House. Nonetheless, the period 960–1050 clearly saw a more sacral style of kingship (*regale sacerdotium*) intended to manifest the divine imperial mission through public acts. The most prominent of these was Otto III's grand tour in the millennial year 1000, which assumed the character of a pilgrimage via Rome and Gniezno, culminating in Aachen, where the young emperor personally opened Charlemagne's tomb. Finding his predecessor sitting upright 'as if he were living', Otto 'robed him on the spot with white garments, cut his nails, and [replaced his decayed nose] with gold, took a tooth from Charles's mouth, walled up the entrance to the chamber, and withdrew again'.[32] Treating the imperial corpse like a holy relic was an obvious first step towards canonization; this project was interrupted by Otto's death shortly after, but completed by Frederick I 'Barbarossa' in 1165.

Like their Roman predecessors, the Empire's rulers stopped short of claiming to be priests, but their coronation ritual resembled a bishop's ordination by the mid-tenth century, including anointing, assuming vestments and receiving objects that symbolized spiritual as well as secular authority.[33] In the two centuries following Charlemagne, emperors regularly followed Constantine's example from 325 and convened church synods to discuss ecclesiastical management and doctrine. Otto II introduced new images on coins, seals and illuminated liturgical texts showing him elevated on a high throne, receiving his crown directly from God, while the royal insignia were increasingly treated like holy relics.[34] Otto and his next three successors assumed positions as cathedral and abbey canons, thereby combining secular and ecclesiastical roles, though not in top clerical positions.[35]

This trend was interrupted by the seismic clash with the papacy known as the Investiture Dispute (see pp. 56–60 below), in which Henry IV suffered the humiliation of being excommunicated by the pope in 1076. After this blow, it was harder to believe the emperor was holy, let alone pious, and the stress on the divinity of the imperial mission sounded increasingly shrill. It proved impossible for kings to live up to the ideal of Christ in their personal lives and public actions. More fundamentally, as Henry IV's notary Gottschalk pointed out, claims for the emperor's sacrality derived from anointing by the pope and so risked acknowledging papal supremacy.[36] Thus, the Empire did not pursue sacral monarchy to the extent found in England and France, where kings claimed the miraculous powers of the Royal Touch.[37] This probably explains why the cult of St Charlemagne took firmer roots in France, where it was celebrated as a public holiday from 1475 to the Revolution of 1789.[38] Neither Charlemagne, nor Henry II and his wife Kunigunde – both of whom were canonized (in 1146 and 1200, respectively) – emerged as royal national saints of the Empire, unlike Wenceslas in Bohemia (from 985), Stephen in Hungary (1083), Knut in Denmark (1100), Edward the Confessor in England (1165), or Louis IX in France (1297).

A renewed bout of papal-imperial tension in the mid-twelfth century (see pp. 63–7) confirmed the impracticality of sacral kingship to legitimate power in the Empire. The Staufer family, ruling from 1138, changed the emphasis from the monarch to a transpersonal holy Empire, first using the title *Sacrum Imperium* in March 1157.[39] Already sanctified by its divine mission, the Empire did not need the pope's approbation. This powerful idea survived the Staufers' political demise in 1250, persisting thereafter even in the long periods when no German king was crowned emperor.

ROMAN

The Legacy of Rome

The Roman legacy was powerfully attractive, but hard to assimilate within the new Empire. Knowledge of ancient Rome was imperfect, though it improved during the ninth century with the intellectual and literary movement known as the Carolingian Renaissance.[40] The Bible and classical sources presented Rome as the last and greatest in a succession of world empires. Both the German *Kaiser* and Russian *tsar* derive from *Caesar*, while the name *Augustus* was also synonymous with 'emperor'. Charlemagne was depicted on coins in profile dressed as a Roman emperor crowned with oak leaves.[41] However, he quickly dropped the title *Imperator Romanorum* conferred by Leo III, perhaps to avoid provoking Byzantium, which still regarded itself as the Roman empire (see pp. 138–43). Another reason was that the adjective 'Roman' was not considered necessary since there was no need of such a qualification at a time when no other power was recognized as 'imperial'.

There were also domestic pressures against embracing Rome. Charlemagne already ruled his own realm, which itself stimulated imitation: the Polish *król*, Czech *král* and Russian *korol*, all meaning 'king', derive from 'Charles'. The Franks were not prepared to renounce their own identity and merge themselves with the peoples they had recently conquered to become a common body of Roman citizens. While the Franks were Romanized, the centre of their power lay on or beyond the *Limes* – the frontiers of the ancient Roman empire. Memories lingered, such as the widespread stories that Caesar himself had laid the foundations of various important buildings, but most Roman settlements had contracted or been abandoned completely. Likewise, Roman institutions influenced Merovingian governance, but had also been heavily modified or replaced by entirely new methods.[42] The situation was different in Italy, where three-quarters of ancient towns were still economic and population centres in the tenth century, often retaining their original street pattern.[43] Frankish control of Italy only dated from 774 and was disrupted by the partition of the Carolingian empire in 843. Italy and the imperial title were reunited with the former eastern Frankish lands in 962, but by this point these were ruled by the Ottonians from Saxony – a region that had never been part of the Roman empire.

The Ottonians curried favour north of the Alps by ostentatiously incorporating Frankish traditions. Otto I dressed as a Frankish noble and presented himself at Aachen as the direct continuation of Carolingian, rather than Roman, rule. His court chronicler, Widukind of Corvey, ignored the lavish imperial coronation in Rome (962) in his history, and instead presented Otto as already 'Father of the Fatherland, Master of the World and Emperor' after his victory over the Magyars at Lechfeld in 955.[44] Nonetheless, Roman traditions were important to Otto I and his successors. It is unlikely that Otto III's adoption of the motto *Renovatio imperii Romanorum* in 998 was part of a coherent plan, but the subsequent historical controversy is useful in pointing to Rome's dual significance both as a secular imperial centre and as the city of the Apostles and mother of the Christian church.[45]

The title *imperator* originally meant 'military commander'. It acquired political meaning through Caesar and, especially, his adoptive son and successor, Octavian, who assumed the name Augustus and ruled as the first full emperor from 27 BC. The title avoided offending Roman identity, which rested on the expulsion of the original kings at the end of the sixth century BC, and disguised the transition from republican to monarchical rule. A victorious general's acclamation as emperor by his troops suggested choice by merit and ability, rather than hereditary succession, and could be reconciled with the continuation of the Roman senate, which formally endorsed the soldiers' action.[46] This method could be easily accommodated within Frankish and Christian traditions. Germanic kingship also rested on the idea that rulers were acclaimed by their warriors, allowing the Frankish elite to buy into Charlemagne's coronation in 800. Victory was regarded as a sign of divine favour, while the fiction that all present voiced their consent unanimously was interpreted as a direct expression of God's will.[47]

While Roman traditions could be accommodated, the actual city of Rome was another matter. In 754 the pope had already granted Pippin the title of Roman patrician, suggesting some kind of stewardship for the city. However, Frankish nobles were warrior-landlords with no desire to reside in Rome as senators. Some later emperors also accepted the title of patrician, probably because they hoped it would bring influence in papal elections, but they were not prepared to receive their imperial dignity from the Romans directly. The best opportunity to forge closer ties to Rome's inhabitants came as the senate re-emerged to challenge papal control of the city in the 1140s. Despite their own troubled relationship with the pope, the Staufer kings rebuffed Roman delegations offering them the imperial title in 1149 and 1154. At least the pope was head of the universal church, whereas the senators merely governed a large Italian city. The Romans felt betrayed and the knights of Frederick 'Barbarossa' had to prevent an angry mob from disrupting his coronation by Pope Hadrian IV in 1155. Only Louis IV accepted a Roman invitation, in January 1328, but under the special circumstances of a papal schism and when he had been excommunicated by Pope John XXII. Once his position improved four months later he had himself crowned by his own pliant pope, Nicholas V. The last offer came from Cola di Rienzo, who had seized control of Rome in 1347, later during the same schism. His arrival in Prague proved an embarrassment for King Charles IV, who arrested him and sent him home, where he was murdered by local opponents.[48]

A Rome-free Empire?

There were only about 50,000 people in Rome in 800, and despite some Carolingian rebuilding, the numerous ancient ruins indicated just how much time had passed since it had been capital of the known world. Although still large by contemporary standards, it was not big enough to accommodate pope and emperor simultaneously. Following the Carolingian partition of the Empire in 843 into three kingdoms (West Francia, East Francia and Lotharingia), the imperial title was generally held by the Frankish kings of Italy until 924, but they were relatively weak, especially after 870, and they usually resided in the old Lombard capital at Pavia, or in the former Byzantine base at Ravenna. While imperial coronations were often years in the planning, subsequent emperors rarely stayed in Rome for long. Otto III did build a new imperial palace, but even he returned to Aachen after his coronation and began fresh construction there too.

Although they sometimes wanted to displace the pope as emperor-maker, the Romans shared the pontiff's hostility towards a prolonged presence. Emperors might be feted with sumptuous banquets and even applauded for deposing unpopular popes, but they should not outstay their welcome. Rome was in any case too far from Germany, which became the main seat of imperial power after 962. The Frankish expeditions to Italy in 754–6 and 773–4 by Pippin and Charlemagne respectively attracted strong support from Carolingian nobles, who welcomed an excuse to plunder the Lombards, but such opportunities declined once Italy was incorporated into Charlemagne's realm. Plunder remained possible if the emperor was engaged on a punitive expedition to punish Italian rebels, depose a pope, or assert control over the still largely independent southern part of the peninsula. However, a prolonged presence required more peaceful methods, removing the incentive for most northerners to cooperate. Usually, support swiftly transformed into accusations that the emperor was neglecting his subjects north of the Alps.

The possibility of dispensing with Rome altogether was strongest during the early Carolingian era. Charlemagne never returned to Italy after the spring of 801, and it was 22 years before another emperor visited Rome; whereas popes crossed the Alps three times, including for the coronation of Charlemagne's son and successor, Louis I, in Reims (816). Louis had already been crowned co-emperor without papal involvement in 813 (before his father's death next year), as was his eldest son Lothar I four years later. Aachen was the site of an important palace from 765 and was already known as *nova Roma* and *Roma secunda* before Charlemagne's coronation in 800. The Aachen chapel was modelled on the Byzantine palace chapel at San Vitale in Ravenna and incorporated ancient columns and statues thought to represent Theodoric, thus symbolizing a link as much to the glorious Gothic past as to a Roman one.[49] However, the turbulence of Carolingian politics from the 820s both made it imperative to involve the pope in legitimizing possession of the imperial title and decreased the incentive for the pope to travel over the Alps to please the Franks. Lothar's decision to have his son Louis II crowned co-emperor in 850 is usually accepted as definitively fixing imperial coronations in Rome. Thereafter, it proved hard to break what appeared to be tradition.

While it became impossible to become emperor without being crowned by the pope, papal involvement was not necessary to rule the Empire. The so-called 'interregna' are misleading. The Empire had an almost unbroken succession of *kings*; it was just that not all of them were crowned *emperors* by the pope (see Table 1 and Appendices 1 and 2). Otto I established the convention that the German king was automatically *imperator futurus*, or, as Conrad II asserted in 1026 before his coronation, 'designated for the imperial crown of the Romans'.[50] However, it proved fundamental to the Empire's subsequent history that Otto did not merge the imperial with the German royal title. Despite being proclaimed emperor by his victorious army at Lechfeld, he waited until his coronation in 962 before presenting himself as such. Unlike later nationalist historians, Otto and his successors never regarded the Empire as a German nation state. In their eyes, what made them worthy to be emperor was that they already ruled such extensive lands. By the early eleventh century it had become accepted that whoever was German king was also king of Italy and Burgundy, even without separate coronations. The title King of the Romans (*Romanorum rex*) was added from 1110 in a bid to assert authority over Rome and reinforce claims that only the German king could be emperor.[51]

Table 1. Imperial Reigns and German Kings

Timeframe	Dynastic Era	Number of Kings	Total Years	Years with an Emperor
800–918	Carolingians	8	119	52
919–1024	Ottonians	5	105	50
1024–1125	Salians	4	101	58
1125–37	Lothar III	1	12	4.5
1138–1254	Staufers	7*	116	80
1254–1347	'Little Kings'	8	93	20
1347–1437	Luxembourgs	4	90	27
1438–1806	Habsburgs	18**	368	365

*including Otto IV (Welf family), 1198–1218

**including Charles VII (Wittelsbach), 1742–5

Translatio imperii

German claims evolved in response to the difficulties in dealing with the papacy, rather than rejection of the Roman imperial tradition. Indeed, the idea of unbroken continuity grew stronger with the spread of new ideas about the 'imperial translation' enacted in 800 by Leo III and Charlemagne. Like all powerful medieval ideas, this was rooted in the Bible. The Book of Daniel (2:31ff.) recounts how the Old Testament prophet responded to a request to interpret Nebuchadnezzar's dream about the future of his empire. Thanks to an influential reading by St Jerome in the fourth century, this was understood as a succession of four 'world monarchies': Babylon, Persia, Macedonia and Rome. The notion of 'empire' was singular and exclusive. Empires could not co-exist, but followed each other in a strict sequence that was epochal, involving the transfer of divinely ordained power and responsibility for humanity, rather than merely changes of ruler or dynasty. The Roman empire had to continue, since the appearance of a fifth monarchy would invalidate Daniel's prophecy and contradict God's plan.[52]

These beliefs hindered any Byzantine-imperial mutual recognition (see pp. 138–43), and are a reason why the Carolingians and Ottonians were often unclear how far they were directly continuing the Roman empire or merely reviving power which Byzantium had allowed to lapse. The mood changed around 1100 in response to the Investiture Dispute and scholastic interest in classical history. Frutolf of Michelsberg compiled a list of 87 emperors since Augustus, suggesting that Charlemagne had succeeded to the original Roman empire in 800, rather than merely reviving it.[53] Translation ideology became increasingly flexible as other authors presented the shifts from Rome to Constantinople (fourth century), to Charlemagne (800), to his Carolingian successors in Italy (843), and finally to the German king (962), as merely a succession of glorious dynasties ruling the same empire. The papacy was obliged to endorse these arguments, since it wanted to preserve its role as agent in each 'translation' of the imperial title.

The belief that the Roman empire was the last monarchy included the idea of it as *Katechon*, or restrainer, keeping the divine schedule on track and preventing the premature destruction of the world by the Anti-Christ. Byzantine readings of the Book of Revelation produced the idea of the 'last world emperor', who would unite all Christians, defeat Christ's enemies, travel to Jerusalem and submit earthly power to God. Having already spread to western Europe, this idea readily lent itself to eulogizing Charlemagne, who, by the 970s, many believed was merely resting in Jerusalem, where he had allegedly gone as a pilgrim at the end of his reign.[54] Abbot Adso articulated similar ideas in his *Book of the Anti-Christ*, written around 950 at the request of Gerberga, Otto I's sister. Otto III and Henry II both had ceremonial cloaks embroidered with cosmic symbols and may have considered themselves emperors at the end of time. Frederick 'Barbarossa' is known to have attended a play about the Anti-Christ in 1160, and certainly apocalyptic arguments helped emperors justify deposing 'false' popes as potential Anti-Christs.[55]

As with all futurology, these ideas encouraged people to relate real events to the predictions. A central concern was to distinguish the good last world emperor from the evil Anti-Christ, since both were associated with Jerusalem and an expanding empire. It was thought that the Empire would reach its highest perfection as an earthly paradise under the former, suggesting that any signs of decline portended the latter. Already in the eleventh century, the monk Rodulfus Glaber identified the emergence of distinct Christian kingdoms as such a portent.[56] The most influential writer was Joachim of Fiore (1135–1202), a Cistercian abbot who claimed the world would end 42 generations after Christ, predicting Judgement Day would fall sometime between 1200 and 1260 – precisely in the period of renewed papal–imperial conflict. Many people longed for the end, which was expected to herald a golden age of social justice and open all human hearts to God. Such ideas took hold amongst the radical Franciscans, Waldensians and other groups flourishing after 1200, who were swiftly condemned as heretics by the church establishment, which in 1215 also dropped its initial acceptance of Joachim's arguments.[57]

Emperor Frederick II's recovery of Jerusalem in 1229 intensified debate, since he had acted outside the official crusading movement and whilst excommunicated by the pope. His death in 1250 reinforced his place in Joachimist chronology and swiftly led to rumours that he was still alive. Initially, this took the form of various imposters, one of whom briefly issued his own decrees in the Rhineland using a forged imperial seal. By 1290 this rumour had transformed along the lines of the myths surrounding Charlemagne; the emperor was merely resting and would return as part of the end of days. While it was initially claimed Frederick had disappeared into Mount Etna, by 1421 it was believed he was slumbering under the steep Kyffhäuser mountain near Nordhausen in the Harz region. The unrealistic expectations accompanying the accession of Charles V in 1519 prompted the last flowering of the Joachimist fantasy, by which time Frederick II had become confused with his grandfather, Frederick 'Barbarossa'. This was probably because Barbarossa's frequent visits to the Harz had embedded him in local memory, while his death on crusade and absence of a grave fitted the story better.[58]

EMPIRE

Singular and Universal

The belief in imperial translation might strike modern readers as far detached from the Empire's reality, especially after the demise of the Staufers around 1250. Yet, of all the Latin European states, only the Empire developed a consistent, fully imperial (as opposed to simply monarchical-sovereign) ideal prior to the new age of global maritime empires in the sixteenth century.[59] There were only 25 years with a crowned emperor between 1245 and 1415, but the Empire's monarch continued to be considered more than an ordinary king.

Imperial apologists fully recognized that the Empire's territory was much smaller than the extent of the known world (Map 1). Like the ancient Romans, they distinguished between the Empire's actual territory and its divine imperial mission, which they considered limitless. French, Spanish and other western monarchs increasingly emphasized their own sovereign royal authority, but this did little to diminish arguments that the emperor was still superior. Even if they acknowledged practical limits to imperial authority, most writers still believed in the desirability of a single, secular Christian leader.[60]

The Empire was considered indivisible, since the theory of imperial translation ruled that there could only be one empire at a time. The clergy pressured the Franks to abandon their practice of partible inheritance. It is not clear how far Charlemagne accepted this, since two of his sons predeceased him, leaving only Louis I as heir in 814.[61] Louis declared the Empire indivisible in 817 on the grounds that it was a gift from God. However, it was the Franks' own conception of Empire that proved more significant since this envisaged imperial leadership of subordinate kingdoms, rather than a centralized, unitary state. Thus, Louis assigned Aquitaine (southern France) and Bavaria to his younger sons, with the bulk of the land going to the eldest, Lothar I, as emperor, while his nephew Bernard continued as king of Italy.[62] Family jealousies wrecked these arrangements, leading to civil wars from 829 and a series of partitions after the Treaty of Verdun in 843 (Map 2), but the Carolingians continued to regard their lands as part of a wider unit and held at least 70 summit meetings between 843 and 877 alone.[63] It is only subsequent historical convention that sees these partitions as creating distinct nation states. The same convention also stresses discontinuity, especially by ignoring the emperors based in Italy between 843 and 924, and instead interpreting Otto I's acquisition of the title in 962 as the foundation of a new, 'German' empire.[64] Although the last reunion of eastern and western Francia broke up in 887, none of the Paris-based Carolingian kings ever claimed their own imperial title. The singularity of empire was too deeply rooted in Christian political thought; there could only be one emperor, because there was only one God in heaven.

Practical politics reinforced this. For most of the Middle Ages, the Empire remained its own political world. Indeed, for the first four centuries of its existence, Byzantium and France were the only significant outsiders, and the latter remained ruled by kings from the Carolingian family until 987 when the western Frankish Carolingian line died out. There were no major external threats to the Empire between the defeat of the Magyars at Lechfeld in 955 and the approach of the Mongols around 1240 – and these later fortunately turned back before they did serious harm. All other rulers could be considered peripheral to both the Empire and Christendom generally. Even as the Empire's actual territory contracted, it remained far larger than that of any other Latin monarch (see Chapter 4).

The Frankish ideas imparted important characteristics to the Empire, giving it a strong ideological continuity, but ultimately contributing to its inability to match new political ideas emerging in Europe by the eighteenth century. Although different in many ways, one aspect of ancient Rome is strikingly modern. Romans believed their empire was a unitary state inhabited by a common people who had submerged any previous identities through the acceptance of common citizenship. By contrast, the Franks and their imperial successors were more like other pre-modern emperors in Persia, India, China and Ethiopia who saw themselves as 'kings of kings', ruling empires composed of discrete kingdoms inhabited by different peoples.

This was a source of great strength to the Franks and their successors. It meant that the imperial title retained prestige, remaining a much more realistic goal than trying to establish direct hegemony over the subjects of other rulers. Peoples and lands were mostly only indirectly subject to the emperor, whose authority was mediated by a variety of other, lesser lords. This hierarchy would lengthen, especially under the Staufers, eventually becoming more elaborate and rigid as it began to be fixed in copious written and printed documents from the fifteenth century. Although ultimately hindering adaptation to change, this aspect provided coherence since status and rights depended on each lord or community's continued membership of the Empire. It also rendered the creation of a national monarchy undesirable, because the Empire was defined as many kingdoms, rather than just one kingdom.

Peace

As in other empires, the emperor was expected to preserve peace. Charlemagne blended Merovingian and late Roman ideals by presenting peace as the fruit of justice. The Salians and Staufers asserted a more active style of kingship, reversing the church's argument that good governance was a precondition of faith and justice.[65] This shift should not be misunderstood as deliberate state-building. It was not until the eighteenth century that Europeans embraced the modern idea of progress, which envisaged the future as an improved version of the present, encouraging both the elaboration of new utopias and the expectation that politics should deliver these.[66] Previously, people generally viewed the future in terms of salvation and secular ideals of fame and posthumous reputation. They might bemoan current problems like disorder, disease and misrule, but saw these as deviations from an essentially static, idealized order. The discrepancy between ideal and reality was not too troubling, since it was considered an expression of the imperfection of human, earthly existence. The ruler was expected to

42

embody idealized harmony (*Concordia*) and to manifest it through symbolic-laden actions.

The emphasis on consensus remained fundamental to imperial politics until 1806, but it would be wrong to replace the earlier narrative of emperors as failed state-builders with a new one of them as honest peace-brokers.[67] Virtually all the men ruling the Empire before the sixteenth century were successful warriors, with many of them owing their position to victory over domestic rivals.

Freedom

Likewise, we should not confuse the Empire's much cherished freedoms with the modern, democratic ideal of Liberty. The latter derives inspiration from republican Rome and the ancient Greek city states, neither of which feature significantly in the classical legacy embraced by the Empire. Instead, Frankish warrior culture imparted a distinctly pre-modern idea of local and particular liberties, which started to shape the Empire as a status hierarchy, distributing political and social capital unevenly across society. The emperor's coronation and mission elevated him above other lords, but these lords still played a role in his accession as king. The Franks' success as conquerors bred a culture of entitlement amongst the aristocracy that Carolingian rulers never escaped. No king could afford to ignore his leading lords for long. However, these rarely sought to displace the king, or to establish fully independent kingdoms of their own. As we shall see in Chapter 7, the Carolingian and Ottonian aristocracy repeatedly declined opportunities to break up the Empire during periods of weak royal rule. Rebellions were about individual influence, not alternative forms of governance.

The most important liberty was the right of lords to participate in the greater affairs of the Empire by having a voice in forming the political consensus. Rather than a constant battle between centralism and princely independence, the Empire's political history is better understood as a long process of delineating these rights and fixing them with greater precision. As will become clearer in Chapter 8, the graduations became sharper with the fundamental distinction from the later twelfth century between those with 'imperial immediacy' and those whose relationship to the emperor was mediated by one or more intervening levels of lordship. Over the next five centuries, immediacy became more firmly associated with the rule of increasingly distinct territories and their mediate subjects. Meanwhile, those possessing immediacy shared common political rights that came to be exercised through more formal institutions from the later fifteenth century.

Freedoms and status were corporate in the sense of being shared communally by members of a legally recognized social group, such as the clergy. They were also local and specific, varying across different parts of the Empire, and even between those of nominally the same social rank. Fundamentally, however, their freedoms and status related all inhabitants in some way to the Empire as the ultimate source of individual or communal liberties. The Empire's hierarchy was not a chain of command, but a multilayered structure allowing individuals and groups to disobey one authority whilst still professing loyalty to another. This was exemplified by the refusal of Counts Frederick and Anselm to join their immediate lord, Duke Ernst II of Swabia, in rebelling against Conrad II in 1026: 'If we were slaves of our king and emperor, subjected by him to your jurisdiction, it would not be permissible for us to separate ourselves from you. But now, since we are free, and hold our king and emperor the supreme defender of our liberty on earth, as soon as we desert him, we lose our liberty, which no good man, as someone says, loses save with his life.'[68]

Power

Imperial rule was not hegemonic, despite periodic moves towards a more command-style monarchy, notably under the Salians, but was characterized more by brokerage and negotiation. It worked because the main participants usually had more to gain from preserving the imperial order than by overturning or fragmenting it. The Carolingians extended a broadly standard system of general governance across their entire realm, entrenching it by adapting the specifics of rule to local circumstances (see pp. 334–52). The Empire was divided into duchies as military districts, subdivided into counties for the maintenance of public order. The duchies largely mapped onto the diocesan structure west of the Rhine, and onto the fewer, but larger tribal areas east of that river. Land was endowed as fiefs or benefices to enable the dukes and counts to sustain themselves and carry out their functions, as well as to support bishops and abbots in developing a more extensive and dense church infrastructure (see pp. 79–89 and 326–30).

Later chapters will explore how far these institutions provided political continuity, but for now it is important to note that the Carolingians already distinguished between the kingdom (*regnum*) and the king (*rex*), with the former persisting even if it was ruled by several kings.[69] The transition from the Carolingians to the Ottonians as German kings in 919 was regarded by contemporaries as a significant event. Like Otto I's assumption of the imperial title in 962, they disagreed how far this represented a break with the past, but by the twelfth century most emphasized continuity even if they did not all fully accept the wider claims of imperial translation.[70]

Continuity persisted despite subsequent changes of ruling family and the long periods without a crowned emperor. History records the Empire's kings as members of different dynasties, and this is certainly a useful shorthand. However, true dynasticism only emerged in the fourteenth century, and in fact simply reinforced existing ideas that each ruler could claim descent from his illustrious predecessors. Wipo of Burgundy expressed this as 'Charlemagne's stirrups hang from Conrad [II]'s saddle'.[71] Most medieval kings tried at least once in their reign to sit on Charlemagne's stone throne, which was carefully preserved in Aachen. Frederick I renovated the Carolingian palaces at Ingelheim and Nimwegen. As time progressed, Charlemagne became an idealized role model. Even the Ottonians, who, as Saxons, came from a people once defeated by Charlemagne, could still celebrate him as the bringer of Christianity.[72]

Continuity suggested that power was transpersonal, transcending the lives of individual monarchs. This idea developed in France, England and Bohemia around 1150 where it was expressed through the idea of the crown symbolizing the kingdom as a combination of inalienable royal rights and property. The loyalty that all subjects owed to the crown transferred automatically from one king to the next. This idea did not take firm hold in the Empire, despite its having Europe's oldest crown in continuous use.[73] While royal rule remained continuous in the Empire, imperial coronations depended on papal cooperation before 1530. Consequently, it was the Empire itself that was abstracted as transpersonal. This was most famously demonstrated in 1024 by Conrad II's furious response to a delegation from Pavia that defended their demolition of the imperial palace there on the grounds that his predecessor Henry II had died: 'Even if the king had died, the kingdom remained, just as the ship whose steersman falls remains. They were state, not private buildings; they were under another law, not yours.'[74]

Abstracting the Empire helped divorce political continuity from specific territory, unlike western European monarchies, where power was increasingly associated with ruling a distinct people and place.[75] The sacrality of the imperial mission reinforced this. Continuity was only seriously challenged with changes in historical perception emerging from Renaissance Humanism, which was more likely to contest claims that lacked foundation in verifiable written sources. The Protestant Reformation proved a second challenge, since continuity with ancient Rome was automatically suspect to those busy renouncing papal supremacy over their church. Finally, political changes became more obvious as imperial governance shifted under the Habsburgs to possession of lands controlled directly by the emperor, including parts of the New World during the reign of Charles V in the sixteenth century. However, it was not until 1641 that anyone published a serious critique of the ideology of imperial translation, while imperial political culture continued to celebrate aspects of the Holy Roman imperial past right up to 1806, such as the belief in unbroken imperial rule since Charlemagne.[76]

POPE AND EMPEROR TO 1250

The Papacy and the Carolingians

The relationship between spiritual and secular authority broadly followed the common European trend for power to become less personal and more institutional. As institutionalized politics has long been associated with progress, individual popes and emperors have been criticized for putting what are perceived as private interests before their public roles. Medieval emperors, in particular, have been accused of pursuing the 'chimera' of imperial power in Italy, rather than building a strong German national monarchy.[77] Individuals were certainly important in shaping events, notably through the deaths of key figures at critical moments. Yet, Italy was an integral part of the Empire, and defence of the church was central to the imperial mission.

Popes and emperors were not necessarily predestined to clash. Indeed, their relationship in the ninth century was more about assistance than assertiveness. The church remained underdeveloped and decentralized. Clergy were relatively few and scattered, especially north of the Alps, where they faced many challenges (see pp. 77–83). While the pope enjoyed prestige and a measure of spiritual authority, he was not yet the commanding international figure he would become by 1200 and was often at the mercy of the feuding Roman clans. Over two-thirds of the 61 popes between 752 and 1054 were Romans and another 11 came from other parts of Italy.[78] Lothar I confirmed the free election of popes by the clergy and congregation of Rome in 824, but required successful candidates to seek confirmation from the emperor. This assertion of imperial authority did not unduly trouble most popes at this point, since they wanted an emperor who was strong enough to protect them, yet not so close by as to be an oppressor. The Carolingian civil wars after 829 exposed Rome to the Arabs, who sailed up the Tiber and sacked St Peter's in 846.

The Empire's partition in 843 following the Treaty of Verdun widened papal autonomy, since the pope could choose between three, still relatively powerful Carolingian kings – of West Francia, East Francia (Germany) and Lotharingia – who each saw the imperial title as a way of asserting leadership over the others. This gave the pope a vested interest in perpetuating the idea of a singular, enduring Empire to sustain his role as emperor-maker. Lothar I already held the title co-emperor alongside his father Louis I since 817. Lothar retained this title in the partition of 843 and, as the eldest Carolingian, was allowed to choose his share of empire, selecting Aachen and the middle strip of territory running up the Rhine and over the Alps to Italy, which became known as Lotharingia. This arrangement suited the pope, since it kept the emperor interested in defending Rome. The incidence of papal-imperial meetings indicates the generally good cooperation. Lothar's successor as emperor, Louis II, met the pope nine times during his reign (855–75), thrice more than any of his immediate successors.[79] However, the balance clearly shifted in the pope's favour, as symbolized by Louis' performance of Strator service for Pope Nicholas I in 858 – the first time for over a century, and possibly the first ever occasion if we believe Frankish accounts that Pippin had not acted as papal groom in 752. Some contemporary observers criticized Louis as only 'emperor of

Italy', a charge levelled against his successors, whose lands shrank still further after the 880s.[80]

The extinction of the central Lotharingian branch in 875 intensified the civil wars amongst the Carolingian elite. The deposition of Charles III 'the Fat' as German king in 887 unravelled the last reunification of East and West Francia and ended Carolingian rule in Italy, where control passed to the leading Carolingian-Lombard aristocrats, notably the dukes of Spoleto. These events underscored the importance of a viable Empire for the papacy, which was again caught between the Roman clans and regional strongmen like Guido of Spoleto, whom Pope Stephen V was obliged to crown emperor in 891. Stephen's successor, Pope Formosus, tried to escape subordination by transferring the title in 896 to the East Frankish king Arnulf of Carinthia, only to be paralysed by a stroke and, afrer the 15-day reign of Boniface VI, replaced by Stephen VI. The new pope was obliged to recognize Guido's son Lambert II as emperor, disinter Formosus's recently buried corpse and put it on show trial. The corpse was duly condemned and thrown into the Tiber, but subsequent reports of miracles discredited Stephen VI, who in turn was himself strangled in August 897. His successor, Pope Romanus, ruled for only four months and was followed by Theodore II, whose pontificate of just 20 days nonetheless proved long enough to overturn the verdict and rebury the somewhat fragmenting Formosus.[81]

Some stability within the papacy returned once the Theophylact clan seized power in 901 and established a more durable relationship with the dukes of Spoleto, and then with the powerful lord of the southern Alps, Hugo of Arles, who did not receive the imperial title but nonetheless ruled as king of Italy from 926 to 947.[82] Some of the Theophylact popes were no more sinful than other medieval pontiffs, but the state of the papacy was still shocking, especially to senior clergy north of the Alps, who were growing more confident with their own efforts to promote Christianity. A sentiment emerged that would later be labelled as 'reform'. This lacked clear ideological coherence prior to the mid-eleventh century, but nonetheless it already argued that the church had to be freed from the ungodly and entrusted to better men. Prior to the later eleventh century, all reformers looked to the emperor to achieve this.

Ottonian Imperial Rule

The lack of a crowned emperor from 925 to 961 was largely due to the reluctance of the Theophylact popes to play their last card in their game against increasingly powerful kings of Italy. Hugo of Arles had been succeeded by Berengar II, margrave of Ivrea, who, by 959, had conquered Spoleto and was threatening Rome as the Lombards had done two centuries before. The best chance of relief appeared to be the Ottonians, who followed the Carolingians in eastern Francia from 919. Otto I had already made two botched attempts to assert authority in northern Italy between 951 and 952. He spent the next decade consolidating his hold over Germany, whilst carefully cultivating contact with bishops fleeing the troubles in Italy. Otto was determined to present himself as liberator, not conqueror, and thus worthy to be crowned emperor.[83] His great victory over the heathen Magyars at Lechfeld in 955 convinced many contemporaries, including Pope John XII, that Otto was divinely favoured. Despite being unable to capture Berengar, Otto's invasion of northern Italy succeeded in 961 and he was crowned emperor on 2 February 962.[84]

Otto's coronation did not 'refound' the Empire, nor create a new empire, since a sense of the original Carolingian realm had persisted and there had been plenty of individual emperors after Charlemagne. Nonetheless, his coronation was a significant event and clearly intended to put papal-imperial relations on a new, improved footing. To this end, Otto issued his own charter (the *Ottonianum*), confirming the 'donations' of Pippin and Charlemagne of extensive lands in central Italy to sustain the pope. As with his predecessors, Otto envisaged these lands remaining under his suzerainty. He likewise bound himself to protect the pope, to whom he transferred large amounts of gold and silver, receiving numerous holy relics in return for his programme of Christianization north of the Alps.[85]

Otto's 'Roman expedition' (*Romzug*) lasted three years and already displayed all the features shaping subsequent imperial interventions in medieval Italy. The convergence of interests facilitating Otto's coronation was insufficiently stable for prolonged papal-imperial collaboration. Emperors wanted popes to possess sufficient personal integrity not to demean the imperial honour they conferred, but otherwise to be pliant executors of the emperor's will. In Otto's case, this included the controversial elevation of Magdeburg to an archbishopric (see p. 85). Like his successors, Pope John XII wanted a protector, not a master, and he rebelled against the 'Frankenstein's monster' of Ottonian emperorship by conspiring with Berengar and the Magyars in 963.[86] The next moves established the template for subsequent emperors towards disobedient pontiffs. Otto returned to Rome, while John fled to Tivoli. After a brief exchange of letters failed to restore harmony, Otto convened a synod in St Peter's, which deposed John on the grounds of murder, incest and apostasy – a charge sheet sufficiently grievous to justify the first ever deposition of a pope, and one that became standard for such actions in the future. Otto confirmed Lothar I's papal constitution of 824, allowing the Roman clergy a fairly free choice in electing Leo VIII as replacement in December 963.

Deposition was the easy part. As Otto and his successors soon discovered, it was extremely hard to maintain their own pope without firm local support, which, for the next century or so, meant the backing of the Roman clans, Italian lords and bishops. John was still at large, creating a papal schism that threatened the integrity and legitimacy of the church. The Romans rebelled as soon as Otto left their city in January 964, allowing John to return and hold his own synod to depose his rival. Leo was restored by force later that month, expelling John, who died in May – allegedly in the arms of a married woman, another story typical of the mudslinging during later papal schisms. What followed merely underscored the intractability of the problem. The Romans elected Benedict V as their own anti-pope. Enforcement of Leo VIII was now a matter of imperial prestige. Otto besieged Rome until the starving inhabitants handed over the unfortunate Benedict, who was demoted and packed off as a missionary to Hamburg. Otto sent two bishops to oversee a new election following Leo's death in March 965, but the successful candidate was in turn expelled by another Roman revolt nine months later. The emperor was obliged to return personally, crushing Roman opposition in December 966. The socially inferior were executed, while the rich were exiled. Those who had died in the meantime were disinterred and their bones scattered in what was clearly intended as exemplary punishment.[87]

Subsequent opposition drew an equally harsh response. The leader of the Crescenti clan was beheaded and hung by his feet along with 12 supporters in 998. Simultaneously, anti-pope John XVI was blinded, mutilated and forced to ride through Rome seated backwards on a don-key. A riot after Henry II's coronation in Pavia as king of Italy in 1002 ended in a massacre by imperial troops in which the city burned down. Further rioting after the imperial coronation of 1027 prompted Conrad II to force the Romans to walk barefoot, though this time they were spared execution. This 'German fury' (*furor teutonicus*) reflected general attitudes to justice in the Empire, which permitted harsh pun-ishment of those who ignored opportunities to negotiate, or who rebelled having been previously pardoned.[88] It also betrayed the basic strategic weakness of the imperial presence in Italy throughout the Middle Ages. Rome was not a pleasant billet for an imperial army. The nearby pestilent marshes made their presence felt each summer through malaria epidemics. That of 964 killed the archbishop of Trier, the duke of Lorraine and a sizeable part of Otto's army. Campaigns in southern Italy often encountered the same problem: malaria killed both Otto II (983) and Otto III (1002), while Conrad II lost his wife and most of his troops to disease in 1038. Losses were hard to take, because Ottonian and Salian armies were quite small (see pp. 321–2). While they did have some capacity for laying sieges, Italy was a land of numerous, well-fortified cities. Violent shock and awe appeared a quick fix to these problems, but as later regimes have discovered, it generally alien-ated local support and discredited those who used it.

The Empire and Church Reform

Conflict within Rome produced another schism with three rival popes after 1044, including the pious but naive Gregory VI, who had bought his title. Concerned this would tarnish his imperial office, Henry III deposed all three at the Synod of Sutri in December 1046 and appointed Suitger, bishop of Bamberg, as Pope Clement II. This initiated a succes-sion of four popes selected from loyal incumbents of German bishoprics lasting until 1057, and was most likely intended simply to restore the papacy as a reliable partner rather than subordinate it directly as part of the imperial church.[89]

Imperial intervention came precisely when the papacy faced new challenges emerging from the anxieties produced by rapid population growth and economic change.[90] Many believed the church was losing its way amidst the new materialism, fuelling a broader reform agenda encapsulated by the slogan 'freedom of the church' (*libertas ecclesiae*). Better standards were demanded of the clergy, with key papal advisors becoming more critical of long-standing issues around the mid-eleventh century. Gregory VI's deposition focused attention on the problem of simony, the purchasing of ecclesiastical office, named after Simon Magus, who had tried to buy salvation from the Apostles. This was broadened into a generalized condemnation of the sale of spiritual office as well as favours. A second bugbear was nikolaitism, or clerical concubinage, associated with Nikolaos, a member of the early church who had defended elements of pagan practice. Both issues were part of a general renunciation of earthly life, which expected all clergy to live like monks and renounce worldly activities. By 1100, reformers also expected them to look different from laity by cutting their hair as a tonsure. Such demands were in fact part of a general reconceptualization of the social order along functional lines, with each group allotted a task to perform for the benefit of all.

A parallel and partially contradictory element emerged with the demand for greater spirituality among the laity too. This had a common root in the yearning of individuals for a simpler life free of worldly burdens. The most obvious manifestation was a new wave of monasticism particularly associated with Gorze in Lorraine and Cluny in the French part of Burgundy. The number of Cluniac houses increased fivefold across the eleventh century. A key element in the new monasticism was the renunciation of local control in favour of placing each religious house under the direct – but largely nominal – control of the pope. The movement spread to Italy where it was known as the Fruttuaria, and to Germany through the influential abbey of Hirsau where it was adopted by over two hundred monasteries.[91] Reformed monasticism largely catered to elite interests, and its connections to wider lay piety were complex and not always amicable, but its coincidence with a broader yearning for a simpler, more Christian life added to the general sense of change.[92]

It was no coincidence that reform emerged in Lorraine and Burgundy where royal rule was relatively weak. Both Gorze and Cluny benefited from strong local lordly patronage, a factor exposing one of the main contradictions of reform. The new asceticism improved the clergy's social prestige, enhancing the attractions of monasteries as convenient accommodation for the unmarried children of lords. Founding and promoting churches was a good way to extend local influence and earn spiritual credit. Lords were happy for the monks to escape the jurisdiction of local bishops by placing their house under papal authority, because the pope generally entrusted them, as the primary donors, with supervisory and protectorate rights.[93] Asceticism appealed also to the growing urban population, most of which was still under the jurisdiction of bishops as lords of cathedral towns. Attacks on simony and concubinage lent moral force to political demands for civic autonomy. Popular movements called *Patarenes* developed in Milan and Cremona during the 1030s, calling for sworn associations of the godly to provide a more moral and autonomous government.

The reformers' demands were not immediately anti-imperial. Henry II had already held a synod at Pavia in 1024 that wrote most of the moral agenda into imperial law, including bans on clerical marriage, concubinage and some forms of simony. He personally forced Fulda abbey to observe Gorze rules, while other members of the imperial family promoted the new monasticism into the 1070s. Imperial support no doubt owed much to personal conviction and to the general mission to promote Christianity. The reform agenda served concrete, political goals too, since improved clerical discipline also promoted better management of the huge properties that emperors had given the church, which in turn enabled abbots and bishops to support the imperial household and military campaigns.[94] Likewise, *libertas ecclesiae* could improve the emperor's access to these resources by liberating them from local lordly influence.

Two developments conspired to pit pope against emperor over the reform agenda. First, the Salians were victims of their own success, since their rehabilitation of the papacy between 1046 and 1056 made it an agent rather than object of reform. Leo IX held at least 12 synods on his own initiative across Italy, France and Germany between 1049 and 1053, demonstrating active and credible leadership with decrees against simony and nikolaitism. Papal action was supported by the parallel development of canon law, which saw more systematic efforts to elaborate rules governing church management based on Scripture, the writings of the church fathers and the papal registers. Partial codification of the canons (i.e. decisions) and other papal decrees helped remove some of the ambiguities and gave greater credibility to papal claims to direct the church.[95] The pope asserted himself as the ultimate judge on doctrine and ritual, demanding that all true Christians share his opinions. The desire for clarity and uniformity opened a rift with Byzantium, which widened into the separation of the Latin and Orthodox churches after 1054. Latin definitively displaced vernacular languages in communicating Christianity in the west, while the role of priests was enhanced as they became the sole official intercessors between the laity and God. By the early twelfth century, the papacy wrested control over canonization from bishops and local synods, and within another century it was taking the initiative in selecting and approving candidates for sainthood.[96]

These measures had effect thanks to a more sophisticated papal bureaucracy that emerged in the second half of the eleventh century, together with a treasury whose resources grew exponentially with the new taxes levied on Christians to support the crusades declared after 1095. The papal library and archive ensured the pope was less forgetful than other monarchs, and could usually produce documentary evidence to support his claims. Simultaneously, the advisory group around Leo IX assumed greater coherence as the *curia Romana*. Staffed initially mostly by Lorrainers closely involved in monastic reform, the curia expanded the pope's capacity for sustained action and curbed the pernicious influence of the Roman clans. The reformers' moment came in December 1058 when they got one of their number elected as Pope Nicholas II. Four months later, a reform synod revised papal election rules restricting participation to the (then) seven cardinals, or auxiliary bishops of Rome. Although the rules still contained a vague reference to notifying the emperor, the chances of external manipulation had been severely curtailed.[97] Having captured the papacy, the reformers had less need to respect imperial interests.

The wider political context proved a second factor in deteriorating papal-imperial relations. The Salians were at loggerheads with the duke of Lorraine in the 1040s. The duke married into the family ruling Tuscany, a province which had demonstrated great loyalty to the emperor and which occupied a strategic location between Rome and the main imperial centres at Pavia and Ravenna. Although the problem of Lorraine was neutralized, the Tuscan heiress, Matilda of Canossa, remained firmly anti-imperial.[98] Tuscany's subsequent defection assumed importance because it coincided with a still more momentous change to the south. Nicholas II abandoned two centuries of papal support for

ineffectual imperial control over southern Italy by allying with the
Normans in 1059. Arriving around 1000, these ruthless freebooters
rapidly expunged the last Byzantine outposts and remnants of Lombard principalities to take control of the entire south. By the time the
alliance was renewed by Gregory VII in 1080, the Normans were well
on their way to conquering Sicily as well. For the first time, the pope
had a credible alternative to imperial protection, because the Normans
were not only nearby and militarily effective, but as newcomers, they
craved recognition and accepted papal suzerainty over their possessions in return for acceptance as legitimate rulers.[99]

Henry III's death in 1056 had frustrated an effective imperial
response. His son Henry IV, though accepted in Germany as king, was
only six and could not be crowned emperor until an adult. Government
of the Empire devolved to a regency council until 1065. This remained
preoccupied with more immediate affairs and failed to see the dangers
ahead. Intervention in the 1061 papal election in favour of Alexander
II was particularly ill-judged, leading to the imperial court being condemned for dividing rather than defending the church. Imperial prestige
suffered while the pope's identification with reform was reinforced.[100]

The next pope, Gregory VII, still saw the emperor as a valuable
partner, but a decidedly junior one. Originally from Tuscany and usually presented as of humble origins, Gregory came from a family well
connected within the papacy and rose rapidly in the expanding administration. Having embraced reform, he became a prime mover in papal
elections from the 1050s before being accepted as pope himself in 1073.
Controversial in his own lifetime, he survived an assassination attempt
in 1075 to give the reform agenda its later name 'Gregorianism'.[101]
While Gregory did not initiate reform, he certainly radicalized it with
his uncompromising assumption that his opponents must be agents of
the Anti-Christ. His political views were encapsulated in his *Dictatus
Papae* of 1075, a set of 27 maxims that were only published later. The
church as immortal soul was superior to the mortal body of the state.
The pope was supreme over both, entitled to reject bishops and kings
if they were unfit for office. However, Gregory's thinking remained
moral, rather than constitutional, and he and his supporters never
systematized these ideas or resolved their implications.

Initially well disposed towards Henry IV, Gregory underestimated
the young king's need to appear strong in the face of constant

challenges to his authority in Germany. Scarcely less obstinate, Henry contributed to a series of misunderstandings and lost opportunities between 1073 and 1076 that left both men viewing the other as rival not partner. The clash widened as each buttressed his position with ideological arguments, drawing in others who often had their own, local agendas. The complexity and multiplicity of the issues broke previous bounds, producing an explosive situation that could not be resolved through conventional means.[102]

The Problem of Investiture

The dispute crystallized over the problem of investiture, which eventually came to name the entire papal–imperial struggle lasting until 1122.[103] The trigger was Henry's investiture of Archbishop Godfrey of Milan, whom the reformers charged with simony in 1073. Investiture proved so controversial because it touched the basis of both material and ideological power in the Empire. The vast endowments to the church were still considered integral parts of the crown lands, particularly north of the Alps. In an age largely without written rules, obligations were affirmed through rituals. The process of appointing an abbot or a bishop involved his investiture. Royal patronage already gave the king a role, while clergy regarded it as a special honour to be invested by the monarch, since this reinforced their place in the social order. Local congregations and clergy did play a role in electing abbots and bishops, but this often rested on royal charters and not yet clearly on canon law. Thus, it was established practice for the king to hand the new cleric a staff, while the archbishop would give him a ring. Under Henry III, both items were presented by the king. Given the heightened sacrality of kingship in the Empire around 1020, this was not immediately contentious. Moreover, it was not entirely clear which item symbolized the cleric's acceptance of his military and political obligations in return for his lands, especially as these same lands also supported his spiritual activities.[104] The problem was that Gregorian criticism extended beyond the conventional (whether Godfrey was a suitable archbishop for Milan) to challenge royal involvement altogether and, in doing so, broke several centuries of unarticulated theocratic consensus. Worse, this occurred precisely at a time when the monarchy was involving bishops and abbots more heavily in the Empire's governance.

Since the twelfth century, chroniclers have simplified events into a clash between Guelphs and Ghibellines. The former derived from the German aristocratic Welf family, which briefly backed the reform papacy, while the latter was a corruption of Waiblingen in Swabia, which was erroneously believed to be the Salian family home.[105] These names did assume importance in the factionalism of later medieval Italian politics, but the Investiture Dispute was waged by loose coalitions rather than disciplined parties. Many clerics opposed Gregorian reform as excessive. For example, the monks of Hersfeld abbey were convinced Gregory divided the church further each time he opened his mouth. Those clergy with female partners considered themselves legally married. The eventual triumph of reform by the 1120s reduced the wife of a priest to the legal status of a concubine, while their children became serfs of the church. Bishops often opposed the cause of church liberty, because this could be used to undermine their authority and withhold tithes at local level.[106] Likewise, the attractions of reform asceticism drew many laity to support the papacy.

The Investiture Dispute

The dispute in Milan was the culmination of a decade of bitter, local conflict between the reforming Patarene movement, supported by the pope, and the wealthy, pro-imperial archbishop and clergy.[107] Unable to resolve the matter, Henry IV convened a synod at Worms in January 1076, which renounced obedience to Gregory VII and demanded he abdicate. The fact that the assembled bishops stopped short of full deposition implicitly acknowledged they were not entitled to do so, while the whole event lacked credibility as it was too late to complain at irregularities in Gregory's election three years into his pontificate. The new balance was revealed a month later when Gregory went further than any previous pope by not merely excommunicating Henry, but deposing him, releasing all his subjects from their oath of loyalty.

Henry's situation worsened across the year with growing opposition in parts of Germany, but he seized the initiative in late December by dodging his opponents in the Alps and crossing the Mont Cenis pass. Allegedly, the snow forced him to crawl up the mountain, while his wife and the other royal women had to slide down the other side on a cow hide. Nonetheless, Henry intercepted Gregory, who was on his way to meet the anti-royalist German lords and bishops at Augsburg. This was not a royal commando mission to kidnap the pope, but instead an attempt by Henry to force Gregory to rescind his excommunication and deposition by appearing as a penitent. Having 'waited, clad in wool, barefoot, freezing, in the open air outside the castle', the king was finally allowed into Canossa, a fortress belonging to Matilda of Tuscany and where Gregory was staying (see Plate 5).[108]

Henry's action divided contemporary and subsequent opinion. He won considerable sympathy and appeared to achieve his immediate objectives. Gregory was prevented from joining the German opposition and obliged to lift the royal excommunication. Despite the positive spin of some recent interpretations, it is hard not to agree with the earlier perception of royal humiliation, regardless whether Henry performed an act of penance or political submission.[109] By going to Canossa, Henry implicitly acknowledged that Gregory had the power to excommunicate and depose him, whereas the king's own supporters regarded these actions as illegal. The contrast with his father could not have been stronger. Henry III had deposed two popes and appointed his own in 1046, whereas Henry IV had failed even to reverse his own deposition, since Gregory subsequently claimed he had merely absolved a penitent, not reinstated a king.

The political opposition in Germany carried on regardless, electing Rudolf of Rheinfelden as the first ever anti-king at an assembly in Forchheim on 15 March 1077. Although two papal legates were present, the rebel dukes acted independently of Gregory and advanced their own contractual theory of monarchy, arguing that they, not the pope, were responsible for the Empire's collective welfare. Their actions reveal the complexity of the issues that were emerging as well as an important trend in imperial politics, which ultimately ensured the Empire survived its monarchs' successive defeats by the papacy.[110]

Henry's repeated demands that Gregory condemn Rudolf eventually forced the pope to pick sides and excommunicate him again in March 1080, this time permanently. Henry retaliated by summoning another synod, which not only formally deposed Gregory but elected an anti-pope, creating another schism, lasting until 1100. These actions finally led to open warfare from October 1080. Henry was obliged to operate either side of the Alps, backing his own anti-pope Clement III in Italy, whilst confronting his political opponents in Germany. Initial successes in Italy enabled Henry to be crowned emperor by Clement in March 1084. Having seen off Rudolf and two further anti-kings by 1090, Henry found himself opposed three years later by his own eldest son, Conrad, whom he had made co-king in 1087. Unlike the previous anti-kings, Conrad was widely shunned as a papal stooge after he made extensive concessions at the expense of imperial prerogatives.[111]

Meanwhile, Pope Gregory and his reformist successors received strong backing from Matilda until her death in 1115, as well as intermittent assistance from the self-seeking Normans, who burned much of Rome when they rescued Gregory from an imperial siege in 1084. German support was limited, but could prove strategically significant, especially in 1089 with the temporary defection of the duke of Bavaria, who facilitated Conrad's rebellion by closing the Alpine passes and trapping Henry in northern Italy. Henry only broke out after making concessions to Bavaria in 1096.

Despite his considerable military skill and dogged determination, Henry was defeated and never returned to Italy. His numerous mistakes and chaotic personal life made him an easy target for Gregorian propaganda, especially once his second wife, Praxedis, fled alleging brutality.[112] Combined with his prolonged excommunication, these accusations demolished the sacral kingship developed since the later Ottonians and which Henry still claimed to exercise. He remained within established patterns of kingship rather than finding new ways of working with Italian lords, bishops and urban communes, many of which had their own reasons to oppose the pope and Matilda. Henry might have rallied wider European support once Gregory widened his claims to supremacy beyond the Empire to cover all kings after 1078. Instead the French king Philip I outflanked him, forging closer ties to the papacy by backing the First Crusade in 1095, thus assuming the position of Christendom's defender that many had expected Henry as the emperor to fulfil.

The perception of royal failure was a factor behind another rebellion in Germany, this time led by Henry's second son, Henry V, whom he had recognized as king and legitimate successor in 1098. Henry IV's death in 1106 after a year of inconclusive skirmishing opened the possibility for a new direction, but Henry V essentially continued his father's line towards the papacy and failed to exploit mistakes of the new pope, Paschalis II.[113] This contrasted sharply with the success of the French and English kings in reaching agreements over similar issues with the papacy in 1104 and 1107 respectively. As neither had challenged papal authority directly, compromise was easier, while the agreements also reinforced the pope's claim that the dispute was entirely the German king's fault.

These settlements rested on ideas advanced since the 1080s by Ivo, bishop of Chartres, and others, who distinguished between spiritual office (*spiritualia*) and temporal powers and properties (*bona exterior*). The latter, now increasingly understood collectively as 'regalia', were associated with the material world and duties to the monarch.[114] This distinction was welcomed by German and Italian bishops who needed their temporal jurisdictions to secure resources and the labour required for cathedral-building and other projects. The French and English agreements showed that conceding spiritual investiture did not impair royal authority over regalia. Pope Paschalis's death in 1118 meant that Henry V could compromise without losing face, though further misunderstandings delayed the actual agreement until 23 September 1122.

The Concordat of Worms

The agreement consisted of two documents known collectively as the Concordat of Worms, though this name actually dates from seventeenth-century accounts. The emperor conceded spiritual investiture with vestments, ring and staff to the pope. German bishops were to be chosen according to canon law and free from simony, but the emperor was allowed to be present at elections and could adjudicate any disputes. The emperor invested each bishop with a sceptre symbolizing the temporal authority associated with regalia. This was to take place before ordination in Germany, but after it in Italy and Burgundy. The clause was revised in 1133 to emphasize that the new bishop had to swear loyalty to the emperor before receiving his temporal powers. The papacy's own possessions were exempt from these arrangements, suggesting they were entirely outside imperial jurisdiction.

The Concordat has widely been interpreted as marking an epochal shift from the early to the high Middle Ages, and the start of secularization.[115] In fact, religion remained closely entwined with politics, but the agreement nonetheless regulated papal-imperial relations until 1803. Later generations have joined contemporaries in debating who

benefited most. Pope Callistus II certainly thought he had won, celebrating with commemorative frescos in the Lateran palace and sending
copies of the Concordat around Europe. The corporate distinctions of
the clergy had been preserved, while the new investiture ceremonies
made it clear that the German king lacked spiritual powers – in this
sense, politics were indeed desacralized. Henry V's disavowal of the
last imperial-backed anti-pope in 1119 underscored the emperor's
inability to make and break popes. However, the Empire had not been
weakened. Rather, the outcome reinforced underlining trends, accelerating the transformation of church property from parts of the crown
lands to possessions held by spiritual princes bound in more formalized
feudal relations to the monarch. Meanwhile, the sense of collective
responsibility for the Empire expressed through the rebellions against
Henry IV continued with the Concordat, which had been negotiated
with the assistance of lay and spiritual lords. These swore collectively
to ensure that Henry V adhered to the terms. The Salians' command
monarchy was being replaced by a mixed system where the emperor
shared more responsibility with his leading lords.[116]

The papacy changed too. The original Gregorian goal of church
liberty had been defeated. The more radical reformers were forced to
accept that the papacy had political as well as spiritual responsibilities.
The repeated papal schisms since 1080 had spawned multiple local
ones as rival pontiffs consecrated their own bishops in the same sees.
Reform was compromised as the papacy sold church property to finance
its war against the emperor. The papacy was increasingly monarchical,
imitating the Empire from the mid-eleventh century in the use of imperial purple and elaborate coronations. A century later, the popes assumed
the title Christ's Vicar, which had been used by the Salian kings but
was now employed to assert papal authority over all monarchs. Papal
territory expanded as the pope claimed Tuscany after Matilda of
Canossa's death. The Latin church was subject to greater central
control, underpinned by the expanding papal administration and the
establishment of the Inquisition in 1231 to police belief. The free election of abbots and bishops had largely ceased by 1380 as successive
popes claimed the right to vet candidates and approve appointments.

Far from freeing the church, reform embedded it deeper into politics.
The church alienated many of the people it claimed to serve and who
now saw it as corrupt and detached from their spiritual needs. The

result was further waves of monasticism and new forms of lay piety. The latter were further stimulated by the heightened concern for personal salvation emerging in the twelfth century. The Waldensians and other grassroots fundamentalists embraced extreme poverty and rites increasingly at odds with the official church's growing insistence on uniformity of belief and practice. Crusader indulgences were extended from the Holy Land to include combating heresy in a series of brutal campaigns in southern Europe after 1208. The requirement to confess at least once a year from 1215 opened the door to greater policing of inner thoughts. From 1231 heresy was punishable by death, and by 1252 the Inquisition was authorized to use torture to root out heresy.[117]

The Empire's rulers largely refrained from direct involvement in these issues after Henry V's death in 1125 ended the Salian line. Pope Honorius II reversed the earlier papal-imperial relationship by claiming the right to confirm the next German king, and intervened in imperial politics by excommunicating the anti-king Conrad Staufer in 1127. The successful candidate, Lothar III, performed Strator service when he met the next pope in 1131. The Lateran palace was quickly redecorated with new frescos depicting this, which were then showed at the next imperial visit as evidence for what was now claimed as traditional practice. The emperor's inferior status was further emphasized by the pope's insistence on riding a white horse, symbolizing his purity and proximity to God.[118]

The Staufers and the Papacy

As with so much in the Empire's history, this apparent decline was soon reversed by new trends beginning in 1138 with the reign of Conrad III, who initiated the line of kings from the Staufer family lasting until the mid-thirteenth century. The Staufers capitalized on the fact that the pope still regarded the German king as the only monarch worthy of being crowned emperor. Conrad referred to himself as emperor even without being crowned.[119] This practice was continued by his nephew and successor, Frederick I 'Barbarossa', who assumed imperial status immediately at his royal coronation in 1152, and named his own son 'Caesar' without papal involvement in 1186 (see Plate 25). The later Staufers followed suit, with Frederick II taking the title 'elected Roman emperor' in 1211, and it is likely that this practice would have become firmly established had he emerged victorious in his struggle with the papacy after his imperial election in 1220. This assertion of imperial identity rested on the further development of the Empire as a collective political structure, since it tied imperial powers to the German royal election involving the major lords, and not to the coronation by the pope. Henry IV had already proclaimed 'the honour of the Empire' (*honor imperii*), and the Staufers developed this as something in which all lords shared, giving them a stake in defending it against the papacy.[120]

The stress on honour unfortunately hindered imperial policy in Italy by discouraging concessions that might have secured compromises, or won allies like the cities that combined in the powerful Lombard League in 1167 to demand self-government. Frederick Barbarossa's expedition to Italy in 1154 was the first for 17 years and ended a 57-year period in which German monarchs had spent only two years south of the Alps. The prolonged absence weakened the personal networks that might have assisted peaceful negotiations. The emperor did not seek conflict, but was determined to reassert imperial authority. The 1,800 knights accompanying his first expedition were already considered a large army, and he returned with 15,000 on his second campaign in 1158.[121] However, the armies were never sufficient to master such an extensive and populous country. The need for local bases added urgency to Barbarossa's insistence on reviving imperial regalia, including the right to garrison towns, levy taxes and demand military assistance. Inevitably, he was sucked into local politics. Northern Italy was a dense mosaic of bishoprics, lordships and cities, often enmeshed in their own conflicts. Support from one for the emperor usually prompted its rivals to back the papacy. Already on the first expedition Tortona was sacked and destroyed after it had surrendered, because Barbarossa was unable to restrain his Pavian allies.[122] The return of the notorious 'German fury' damaged imperial prestige, further hindering the desired pacification. The pattern was repeated in four subsequent campaigns between 1158 and 1178. Barbarossa achieved local successes, but he could never control all of Lombardy.

The pope was not averse to cooperating with the emperor to escape the now oppressive influence of the Normans, whom he had been forced to raise to royalty as kings of Sicily in 1130. The Normans and the French had through their interference in Roman politics already created a schism (1130–39). However, they now combined to back a majority candidate as pope against an imperial-backed anti-pope in a renewed schism (1159–80). Like Henry IV, Barbarossa was excommunicated, but unlike the Salian emperor he accepted a compromise in the Treaty of Venice 1177. The presence of Sicilian and English representatives at the negotiations revealed the internationalization of Italian affairs, which were clearly no longer an internal matter for the Empire. Although he made significant concessions to the Lombard League, Barbarossa was acknowledged as suzerain of northern Italy.

He was able to return to Italy from 1184 to 1186, this time without an army, and consolidate peace through an additional agreement with the Normans involving the marriage of Barbarossa's son Henry to Constanza d'Hauteville, daughter of the king of Sicily. The unexpected death of the Norman king in 1189 opened the prospect of the Staufers acquiring both Sicily and its dependent territories, later known as Naples, in southern Italy. Timing favoured the Staufers, because the Saracen victory at Hattin in 1187 and subsequent capture of Jerusalem distracted the papacy, which now also needed imperial assistance for the planned Third Crusade. Despite opposition from many Norman lords, by 1194 Barbarossa's son, now Henry VI, had secured Sicily. This success encouraged an escalation of his ambition. Already in 1191, Henry had rejected papal claims to suzerainty over Naples and argued this was under imperial jurisdiction. Within five years he was planning to integrate the former Norman kingdom within the Empire and convert the German monarchy into an hereditary possession (see pp. 192 and 303–4). Papal-imperial relations had shifted dramatically in the emperor's favour. The extinction of the Normans deprived the pope of a counterweight to imperial influence, reduced his temporal jurisdiction to the Patrimonium, and left him facing an emperor more powerful than any since Otto I (Map 5).

Contingency again intervened, this time with Henry's unexpectedly early death at 31 in September 1197, followed by that of his wife Constanza 14 months later, which left their four-year-old son, Frederick II, as a ward of the pope. The Staufers' German supporters picked Frederick's uncle, Philip of Swabia, as a more viable candidate in the royal election of 1198, but the situation was exploited by their local rivals, who elected Otto IV from the Welf (Guelph) family, leading to civil war until 1214.[123]

The response from Pope Innocent III reflected the political high stakes. After some initial hesitation, in 1202 Innocent issued a decretal, or judgement of the papal court, called *Venerabilem*. This restated the Gregorian interpretation of the Two Swords doctrine that all authority, including temporal, flowed from God through the pope to kings. Innocent did not challenge the division of spiritual and secular authority enshrined in the Worms Concordat, and agreed that the Germans were free to elect their king, but claimed that popes had the right of approbation. This suggested he could veto candidates, for example on the grounds they had sinned. He also rebutted the Staufer practice of assuming imperial prerogatives immediately on their accession as kings, arguing that only popes crowned emperors. By distinguishing the wider Empire from the German kingdom, Innocent sought to usurp imperial authority in Italy and southern Burgundy. He claimed the status of imperial vicar, or governor if either there was no emperor or he was absent from Italy. Within 50 years, canon lawyers were claiming the pope was really the true emperor, since he had translated authority from Byzantium.[124]

Venerabilem entirely reversed the position under the Ottonians, who had claimed broadly similar powers over the papacy. However, it also revealed how the papacy remained bound to the Empire. No pope could reduce the Empire to the status of any other kingdom without devaluing his own pretentions as sole emperor-maker. This explains why, despite extensive periodic tensions, popes crowned every German king from Otto I to Frederick II, except Conrad III and Philip of Swabia.

In practice, Innocent was unable to steer events. Both sides in the German civil war shared a desire to restrict papal influence. Hoping to prevent a union of the Empire and Sicily, Innocent eventually endorsed Otto IV, but this merely alienated some of that king's supporters who now viewed him with suspicion. By 1207 Otto was obliged to ask for a truce, only for Philip of Swabia to be murdered in an unrelated dispute the following year.[125] Otto skilfully rallied most of Philip's supporters by assuming the same imperial goals in Italy, including attempting to control the south. Having just crowned Otto emperor, Innocent was compelled to excommunicate him a year later in 1210 and join France in supporting the young Frederick II of Sicily as the new Staufer candidate. Otto overreached himself by joining his uncle, King John of England, in an invasion of France that ended in a rout of the imperial army at Bouvines, east of Lille, on 27 July 1214. Having already been crowned German king in 1212, Frederick was able to assume power unchallenged.

Frederick II is probably the most controversial of all emperors (crowned in 1220). The English chronicler Matthew Paris called him *Stupor Mundi*, or the 'amazement of the world'. He was certainly astonishing. Intelligent, charming, ruthless and unpredictable, he often appeared to act on a whim. His supporters saw him as fulfilling a messianic mission, especially after his recovery of Jerusalem in 1229 (see pp. 146–7). His papal opponents called him the Beast of the Apocalypse and compared him to Nero in destroying the Empire. Later generations have shared this mix of awe and revulsion: hated by Luther, Frederick was celebrated by Nietzsche as a 'free spirit'. The emperor had 19 children by 12 different women and deposed his son and designated heir. Frederick regarded himself as a true Christian, yet spoke some Arabic, tolerated Muslims, and had his own Saracen bodyguard. However, he was not a modern multiculturalist, nor as innovative as some biographers have claimed.[126]

Frederick reneged on his agreement with Pope Innocent as soon as he felt sufficiently secure in Germany. By 1220 it was obvious he had resumed his father's programme of uniting Sicily and the Empire. The papacy reluctantly played along, hoping the emperor would lead a new crusade. Relations broke down, leading to Frederick's excommunication in 1227, which had to be lifted after he recovered Jerusalem through bloodless negotiation. Problems resumed after 1236, leading to his renewed excommunication for alleged heresy three years later – this time permanently. The issues remained the same as those under the previous three emperors, but now the pope employed the new weapon of crusader indulgences to rally military assistance in addition to backing a series of German anti-kings from 1246. The situation returned to that under Barbarossa where neither side could gain a decisive preponderance, yet this time no one was in the mood to negotiate. Imperial defeats in Italy between 1246 and 1248 were reversed in later counter-attacks, and the situation remained open at Frederick II's death in 1250. The Staufer failure was contingent, not structural (see pp. 377–8).

Frederick's son Conrad IV and other relations rapidly lost control of Germany after 1250, in turn hastening their demise in Italy in the face of local revolts in Naples and papal support for Charles of Anjou, the

French king's younger brother, whose conquest of Sicily was sanctioned as a crusade.[127] The death of the last Staufer claimant in 1268 secured the papacy's primary goal of preserving its suzerainty over Sicily and Naples whilst keeping these separate from the Empire. However, the failure of either pope or emperor to gain the upper hand in the prolonged war since 1236 increasingly encouraged contemporaries to regard both as merely ordinary monarchs.[128]

PAPACY AND EMPIRE FROM 1250

Empire and Papacy in the Age of the 'Little Kings'

The period from Frederick II's death in 1250 to Henry VII's imperial coronation in 1312 was the longest without a crowned emperor in the Empire's history. Without coronation journeys, there was also no royal presence in Italy. However, the imperial ideal remained potent, attracting the first 'foreign' candidates in what proved a second 'double election' in 1257 when both Alfonso X of Castile and Richard, earl of Cornwall, were elected German king. Between 1273 and 1313 the German kingdom was ruled by a succession of men who had only been counts prior to their election. All saw the imperial title as a means of asserting themselves over the more powerful dukes (see pp. 377–96). Imperial traditions remained strong. Rudolf I, Adolf of Nassau and Albert I were all buried in the imperial crypt in Speyer Cathedral next to the illustrious Salian emperors. Henry even had Adolf and Albert expressly moved there to convey a sense of legitimate continuity after a brief renewed civil war in 1298.

The papacy also remained interested in the Empire. Like their previous choices of protectors, the popes found that the Angevins (the Anjou family) quickly escaped their control as they added Sicily and Naples to their existing possessions in Provence. The revolt known as the Sicilian Vespers led to the loss of the island to the king of Aragon in 1282. This severed the link between Sicily and mainland Naples that had existed since the Norman conquest around 1070, and so released the papacy from the threat of encirclement.[129] However, the Angevins remained powerful, even exercising a protectorate over the papacy for about twenty years after 1313. Additionally, the popes had to deal with increasingly assertive western monarchs like the kings of France. Embarking on a prolonged series of wars with England, the French kings redirected annual fees paid by their clergy from the papacy to their own war chest. Faced with these problems, a strong but largely absent emperor again appeared an attractive option to the papacy.

Pope Gregory X urged the German electors not to repeat their double election of 1257 when Richard of Cornwall died in 1272. Three years later the pope also persuaded Alfonso of Castile to renounce the German royal title he had never actually exercised. The new king, Rudolf I, thrice planned to go to Rome for a prearranged coronation, only for other events to intervene.[130] Meanwhile, French pressure on the papacy mounted, encouraging Clement V to welcome the arrival of Henry VII, who had been elected German king in November 1308.[131] Henry's arrival late in 1310 encouraged unrealistic expectations amongst those, like Dante, who identified themselves as Ghibellines and hoped Henry would restore order and end the violent factionalism raging in many Italian cities. All initially went well as Henry was crowned king of Italy in Milan in January 1311. However, the Italian cities were no longer accustomed to accommodating imperial expeditions, while the Angevins marched north from Naples to block any attempt to reassert imperial jurisdiction over southern Italy. Some cities paid Henry to go away, but others resisted, providing excuses for his largely mercenary army to repeat the 'German fury' of old. Henry's brother Walrum was killed, while his wife died (of natural causes) and most of his troops went home. Delays meant that Henry missed the planned date of 2 February 1312 for his imperial coronation, which had been scheduled to coincide with the 350th anniversary of Otto I's coronation. Roman resistance had to be overcome by a violent assault in which Archbishop Baldwin of Trier, the only senior German lord accompanying Henry, split the skull of a defender with his own sword (see Plate 6).

Clement had meanwhile decamped to Avignon, where the papacy was obliged by French pressure to remain until 1377. With St Peter's still held by his opponents, Henry was forced to stage his imperial coronation (the first since 1220) in the Lateran palace on 29 June 1312. Only three cardinals officiated on Clement's behalf, while Guelph crossbowmen fired at the imperial party in the banqueting hall afterwards.[132] It was hardly an auspicious beginning. The end came soon.

Having failed to capture Florence, Henry caught malaria and died at Buonconvento, near Siena, on 24 August 1313.

Another double election to the German throne in 1314 saw Louis IV 'the Bavarian' pitted against Frederick 'the Fair' until the latter renounced his claim in 1325. Learning from Innocent III's failure in 1198, Pope John XXII refrained from posing as arbiter and instead declared the throne vacant, establishing the new idea of *vacante imperio* to strengthen papal claims to exercise imperial prerogatives in the absence of an emperor.[133] Louis' determination to dispute this opened what proved to be the final round of old-style papal-imperial conflict. Louis appointed Count Berthold of Neuffen as his own imperial vicar in 1323 to exercise prerogatives in Italy, thereby directly challenging papal claims. Pope John responded with the full range of measures developed since 1073, but now underpinned by a much more substantial administration. Proceedings were opened at the papal court in Avignon, which predictably condemned Louis as a usurper, hence John's reference to him as merely 'the Bavarian' to deny him legitimacy in Germany. Louis' excommunication (1324) and a crusade (1327) followed as the dispute escalated.[134]

Unlike his predecessors, Louis enjoyed support from leading intellectuals who were alienated both by the papacy's move to Avignon and by its condemnation of popular movements such as the Franciscan Spirituals, who took the vow of poverty literally. Those arguing for imperial supremacy as a way to a new order included Dante, William of Ockham, Marsilius of Padua and Johannes of Jandun, but their writings were not widely disseminated for another century.[135] In practice, Louis relied on traditional methods, forcing his way into Italy in 1327–8 aided by local supporters. His imperial coronation by two Italian bishops on 17 January 1328 was the first since 817 without either a pope or at least a papal legate officiating. Advised by his supporters, Louis cited Otto I's example in order to depose John XXII on the grounds he had abandoned Rome and to install his own pope, creating the first schism since 1180. This had little effect given that John was safe under French protection in Avignon.

French involvement continued the trend present since at least the 1170s that papal-imperial disputes were open to external influence. France repeatedly hindered negotiations, because the dispute allowed it to prolong what Petrarch called the papacy's 'Babylonian Captivity' in

Avignon. John's imposition of the interdict suspending church services in Germany was widely resented and ignored, and cost him the moral high ground by appearing to punish ordinary Germans. Already in 1300, the leading German lords had rejected papal attempts to fan their dispute with King Albert I. Now in 1338 they backed Louis' decree *Licet iuris* explicitly endorsing the Staufer's earlier idea that the German king was already emperor-designate entitled automatically to exercise imperial prerogatives immediately after his election. For once, an intellectual directly influenced events, as Lupold of Bebenburg supplied the legal and historical arguments for Louis' decree. This programme was continued by Charles IV, who emerged as Louis' challenger and, soon, successor, culminating in the Golden Bull of 1356, which excluded the pope entirely from German royal elections (see pp. 301 and 307).

The Luxembourgs and the Papacy

Like Pope Innocent's *Venerabilem*, the imperial statements implicitly acknowledged limits. It was difficult to nationalize the imperial title without accepting it no longer represented superiority over other kings. In short, Louis and Charles still sought the idealized cooperation with the papacy that their predecessors had failed to secure. Charles used a brief coincidence of Guelph and Ghibelline sentiment in Italy to travel with only 300 troops for his imperial coronation, which was conducted by a papal legate in Rome in April 1355. This was the first coronation since 1046 not to be marred by serious violence.[136] The papacy still insisted on the prerogatives claimed in *Venerabilem*, while the German lords continued the line resumed in 1338. Pope Gregory XI was ignored in 1376 when Charles's son Wenzel was chosen as king of the Romans, the title henceforth used for the successor designate in the Empire.

Gregory's death in March 1378 changed the direction of papal-imperial relations. Gregory had only moved the papacy back to Rome from Avignon 22 months earlier. The Romans had grown accustomed to self-government, while the cardinals regarded themselves like the electors in the Empire and were not prepared to be treated as papal functionaries. France's reluctance to lose its influence added a third factor. The result was the Great Schism lasting until 1417 and coinciding with a period of dramatic intellectual and religious development. The founding of universities during the twelfth century ended the church's monopoly over education. The Great Schism accelerated this, since central Europeans were no longer as keen to attend Paris or the Italian universities due to the disruption in public life. Charles IV had already provided an alternative by founding Prague University in 1348. This had been followed by Vienna (1365) and fifteen more universities by 1500, while student numbers in the Empire more than doubled across the fifteenth century to reach over 4,200.[137] New, critical approaches associated with Renaissance Humanism increasingly challenged established claims, including the *Donation of Constantine*, which was proved by Lorenzo Valla to be a forgery in 1440.[138] Such criticism appeared most suspicious amidst the surge in popular religious practices, which threatened to escape official supervision. These included new shrines attracting thousands of pilgrims, such as Wilsnack in Brandenburg between 1383 and 1552, as well as Marian cults, fresh waves of monasticism and relic collecting.[139]

Debates surrounding faith and practice gave urgency to those about church governance, since one could not be resolved without the other. They also merged with reform discussions in the Empire, where the idea of the electors and lords exercising collective responsibility meshed with the new concept known as conciliarism emanating from the University of Paris, which argued that papal monarchy should be balanced by a general council of bishops and cardinals. Practical politics added further impetus. Both Wenzel and Richard II of England were deposed by aristocratic conspiracies within a year of each other, while France descended into civil war from 1407, which widened with England's involvement eight years later. The instability prevented imperial coronations for either Wenzel or his rival after 1400, Ruprecht (Rupert) of the Palatinate. Wenzel's refusal to stand down, even after the election of his younger brother Sigismund in 1410, extended the political uncertainty in the Empire until his death in 1419. By that point, the Empire faced its own heretical movement, the Hussites in Bohemia, as well as the menacing advance of the Ottomans through Sigismund's own kingdom of Hungary to the east.

Sigismund's decisive intervention demonstrated the continued potency of the imperial ideal, whilst also showing how much had changed since Henry III ended the earlier schism in 1046. Whereas Henry had acted unilaterally, Sigismund had to consider other kings and the multiple influences within the church. First, he allied himself with the conciliarists who had convened a general council in Pisa and elected their own pope in 1409 in defiance of both Avignon and Rome. Having won support to convene his own council in Constance in November 1414, Sigismund outmanoeuvred all three popes, who either abdicated or were deposed by 1417, allowing the church to be reunited under the reform-minded Pope Martin V.[140]

The Great Schism greatly weakened the papacy, which now confronted the more radical conciliarists who chose Duke Amadeus VIII of Savoy in 1439 as what proved to be the last anti-pope. Although conciliarism fizzled out with his abdication ten years later, the renewed schism extended the time for European monarchs to bargain concessions from the Roman papacy. This proved particularly important for the Empire, where monarchical authority was shifting from reliance on imperial prerogatives to the direct control of extensive dynastic possessions – a method perfected by the Habsburgs, who ruled the Empire from 1438 with only a single break until its demise in 1806. The Vienna Concordat secured by Frederick III on 17 February 1448 joined that of Worms from 1122 as the fundamental document regulating the imperial church until 1803. It did not go as far as its French equivalent in halting all papal taxes within the realm, but nonetheless curtailed papal influence over appointments at all levels of the Empire's church hierarchy. Unlike the nationalized Gallican church in France, there was no single *ecclesia Germania*. Instead, other leading princes negotiated their own concordats on the Viennese model between the 1450s and 1470s to cover the lesser clergy within their jurisdictions.

Nonetheless, conciliarism had fostered greater cohesion amongst what were increasingly regarded as national episcopates, including that in Germany. A synod of German bishops at Mainz in 1455 drew up the first *Gravamina nationis Germanicae*, or complaints of the German church, to be presented to the pope. The issues were taken up at the Empire's assembly in 1458, and subsequent Gravamina became integral elements of imperial politics, especially because they often served imperial interests in the continuing disputes with the papacy over jurisdictions in northern Italy.[141]

Habsburg-Papal Relations

Sigismund's success in ending the Great Schism in 1417 appeared to reset papal-imperial relations to the era of Charles IV. Sigismund was the first German monarch to go to Italy after the fiasco of Ruprecht's abortive Roman expedition in 1401–2. His imperial coronation on 31 May 1433 was the first since 1220 by a universally accepted pope and represented the culmination of two-year's peaceful presence in Italy. The Vienna Concordat smoothed the way for Frederick III's imperial coronation on 19 March 1452, which proved to be the last in Rome.[142] It was also the last occasion on which an emperor performed Strator service for a pope. The ceremony was already at odds with the new political balance, as the Habsburgs were amassing what would soon become the largest personal possessions held by any imperial family and which provided an entirely new basis for imperial authority.

The new reality was obvious with Habsburg involvement in the Italian Wars, which opened in 1494 with a French attempt to supplant imperial influence over northern Italy whilst asserting direct control of the south. French ambitions were first checked by Frederick III's son and successor, Maximilian I, and then completely reversed by his great-grandson, Charles V, who was both Spanish king and emperor by 1519. Charles's power far exceeded even that of Henry VI, enabling the Habsburgs to complete the process under way intermittently since the 1130s and remove papal involvement from the imperial title. Already in 1508 the pope agreed that Maximilian I could simply assume the title Elected Emperor when the way over the Alps to his coronation was blocked by his Franco-Venetian enemies. That year, Lupold von Bebenburg's most important treatise on the imperial title appeared in book form, using the newly invented print media that now disseminated the arguments behind the fourteenth-century constitutional changes. Meanwhile, the Empire was undergoing a fundamental transformation through rapid institutional growth, consolidating its definitive, early modern form as a mixed monarchy in which the emperor shared power with an increasingly finely graduated hierarchy of princes, lords and cities collectively known as the imperial Estates (see pp. 402–21). The formalization of new forms of representation in the imperial diet (Reichstag) around 1490 distinguished the members of the Empire more clearly. Popes continued to send legates to participate in the

Reichstag into the 1540s, but already before the Protestant Reformation made them unwelcome it was becoming obvious they were merely representatives of a foreign potentate.[143]

Nonetheless, the Habsburgs were not ready to sever all ties to the papacy. Arriving in the Empire from Spain in 1521, Charles V rejected the calls of evangelical reformers to purge Rome of what they considered the Anti-Christ. There was no return to the earlier imperial intervention to reform the church. Instead, Charles responded in line with the division between secular and spiritual responsibility that had slowly emerged since the Worms Concordat. The Reformation was dealt with as an issue of public order, with doctrinal questions left to the papacy (see pp. 108–17). The pope's reluctance to compromise on doctrine made Charles's position extremely difficult in the Empire, while both clashed in Italy over conflicting territorial ambitions. The low point was the infamous sack of Rome by imperial troops on 6 May 1527, an event still commemorated annually at the memorial to the 147 Swiss Guards killed defending the Vatican.[144]

Chastised, Pope Clement VII crowned Charles as emperor in Bologna on 24 February 1530 in the last such ceremony where a pontiff officiated (see Plate 7). The venue was chosen to fit with Charles's campaign, but was still staged with great pomp and was intended to assist efforts to conclude the Italian Wars with a successful peace. Charles's triumphal entry into the city presented him as a victorious Roman emperor.[145] Charles obtained papal recognition in 1531 that his younger brother, Ferdinand, would succeed him directly without a coronation. By the time this occurred in 1558, Ferdinand had already concluded the Peace of Augsburg (1555) accepting Lutheranism alongside Catholicism as an official religion in the Empire. Ferdinand I's accession provided the first opportunity since the Reformation to alter the emperor's place in the imperial constitution. Protestants wanted to strike the clause committing the emperor to act as *advocatus ecclesiae,* and substitute an obligation to uphold the Peace of Augsburg. The Catholic imperial Estates eventually persuaded them to retain the original language. At Maximilian II's election as king of the Romans in 1562 this was reworded as general protection of the Christian church, omitting any reference to the papacy; a formula retained thereafter, though clearly interpreted along more traditional lines by the still Catholic Habsburgs.[146]

The imperial and German royal titles had been merged, consolidating the change of 1508 and ensuring the undisputed assumption of imperial prerogatives immediately upon election. There was now a single coronation, conducted by the archbishop of Cologne, who had generally presided over German royal coronations since the Carolingian kings and whose role was accepted even by the Protestant imperial Estates. Ferdinand IV's coronation as king of the Romans in 1653 made liturgical concessions to Protestantism, and merely required the monarch to respect rather than obey the pope.[147] The ceremonial alterations freed the emperor from the need to go to Rome, removing a major reason for cooperation with the papacy at a time when both were struggling to redefine their roles in a rapidly changing international order.

It was politically impossible for the emperor to cooperate unconditionally with the Counter-Reformation agenda embraced by the papacy at the Council of Trent (1545–63). The constitutional rights secured by Lutherans in the Peace of Augsburg were part of the Empire's increasingly elaborate web of collective liberties that could only be altered through mutual agreement. The Habsburgs managed the Empire by presenting themselves as impartial guardians of all liberties, whilst remaining personally Catholic and imposing their faith on their own direct subjects. While the pope applauded Habsburg efforts in their own lands, even zealous emperors like Ferdinand II were heavily criticized for not capitalizing on moments of military strength to rescind all Protestant rights in the Empire (see pp. 125–7). France and especially Spain (which became independent of Habsburg Austria in 1558) displaced the emperor as the pope's primary international champions.[148]

The pope's influence in the Empire declined sharply, and efforts to influence a more zealous Catholic line by delaying recognition of Ferdinand III's accession in 1637 failed to inconvenience the emperor. From 1641 publication of papal decrees in the Habsburgs' own lands required the emperor's permission, and a year later demands for papal book censorship were rejected on the grounds that this was a sovereign right of all monarchs. The papal reform of holy days was ignored, because this interfered with events important to the political calendar. More momentously, the pope's protest when the Peace of Westphalia ended the Thirty Years War in 1648 was already pre-empted by a clause asserting the treaty's validity regardless of what the pontiff thought.[149]

The last papal–imperial clash – and the first since 1527 – occurred in 1708–9 when Austrian troops invaded the Papal States to assert

Habsburg and imperial feudal jurisdictions in Italy over the pontiff's counter-claims. There were also tense moments in the late eighteenth century when Emperor Joseph II championed the dissolution of the Jesuit order and secularized hundreds of Austrian monasteries. However, Joseph and Pope Pius VI also exchanged official visits in 1782–3.[150] Relations were never quite those of equal sovereign states. Vestiges of the shared past lingered beyond the Empire's demise in 1806, especially as the papacy generally now saw Austria as a more reliable protector than France, which was tainted with revolution after 1789. Concern for his traditional place as head of universal Catholicism prevented Pius IX from assuming the leadership of a liberal united Italy in 1848 as this would have entailed declaring war on Austria, which still controlled most of the north. Austria allowed thousands of its troops to serve as volunteers in the papal army until 1870, and did the same in the ill-fated Catholic-imperial project of Archduke Maximilian in Mexico between 1864 and 1867. Pius IX performed a symbolic translation of the old Empire in 1860 by reworking the still-official prayers for the *Imperator Romanorum* to one explicitly for the Habsburg emperor. Finally, Austria retained a formal veto in papal elections until 1904.[151] As we shall see, these lingering connections were typical of the Empire's legacy in later European history.

2

Christendom

THE CHRISTIAN MISSION

Christendom and Christianization

The early Middle Ages recognized Christianity (faith) and Christians (believers), but had no geographic concept of Christendom. Faith began with baptism (christening). The role of kings, lords and bishops was to oversee this, and to enforce observance of holy days and other outward markers of inner belief. The slogan 'defence of Christendom' (*defensio Christianitatis*) emerged during the ninth century in response to the Muslim Arab threat, especially in southern Europe, and it identified the wider lay community beyond the church (*ecclesia*) which the emperor should defend. Christendom only assumed closer associations with Europe through Gregory VII's promotion of the papacy as sole and exclusive leader of all Christians, reducing the emperor to being mere ruler of the largest Christian kingdom. The geographic demarcation was consolidated by the First Crusade of 1095 and those that followed, which involved military expeditions against what was regarded as an eastern 'other'.[1]

The Empire's southern reaches encompassed Italy, including Rome into the eleventh century. The absence of a religious boundary in the west contributed to the lack of clear demarcation between the Empire and what became France. Differences were sharper with the pagan Scandinavians, Slavs and Magyars to the north and east. An extensive belt of pagan peoples across south-east Europe separated the Empire from its Christian counterpart in Byzantium – a major factor in the ability of both empires to ignore each other. Thus, though geographically located in the heart of what is now considered Europe, the Empire lay on the northern and eastern edges of Latin Christianity, and provided the principal means by which that faith penetrated these regions.

A sense of east–west distinctions was already present in the inhabitants' myths of origins. The Franks considered themselves descendants of Noah's son Japheth, and thought the Slavs stemmed from another of Noah's sons, Ham.[2] The Slavs worshipped forest and sky gods, practised bigamy, cremation and other customs totally alien to Christians, such as digging their houses into the ground in contrast to the wooden-post construction used by the Franks. Slavs had little affinity for Christian practices and regarded tithes as tribute to an alien, unwanted god. Even those willing to embrace Christianity encountered significant cultural barriers. The boundaries between past and present in Slavic culture were more fluid than among Christians accustomed to the Bible's linear chronology. The refusal of Christian priests to baptize ancestors made no sense to Slavs.[3]

Christianization aided the consolidation of imperial authority and promoted its extension north and eastwards across the river Elbe. However, unlike the Muslim Ottomans, who would form a majority in their own empire only late in the nineteenth century, the Empire's population was always overwhelmingly Christian with only a small Jewish minority; the population included relatively few pagan Slavs in the ambiguous border zones of the north-east, who were largely Christianized by the thirteenth century.[4]

Christianization was not a 'clash of civilizations'.[5] This popular yet controversial approach defines civilization largely through religion and regards cultures as mutually exclusive, homogeneous entities that either clash or engage in dialogue. The Empire's expansion was certainly legitimated in language which later generations would consider that of civilization overcoming barbarianism. Religious texts and laws certainly distinguished Christians from Slavs, Jews and Muslims. However, culture offers a repertoire of behaviour, experience and attitudes allowing individuals to select what is meaningful or useful in their own context. Interactions depend on circumstances. Boundaries are blurred by negotiation, exchange and integration, and contact is rarely exclusively either benign or violent. Christianity underwent considerable changes in practice and belief throughout this period. What was considered acceptable at one point could be condemned later. The sense of a fully defined Christendom only assumed its true shape as a singular, exclusive civilization in the period of Romantic nostalgia following the French and Industrial Revolutions.[6]

Motives

It is unlikely that Charlemagne and the Franks had a conscious policy to create a single *populus Christianus*.[7] The principal sources for this view are clerics who put their own gloss on Carolingian actions. Carolingian society was primarily organized for war, not prayer. Its goal was to acquire wealth through plunder and extorting tribute, and to translate claims to authority into reality by gaining prestige, reputation and dominion.[8] Christianity channelled these ambitions by identifying non-Christians as 'legitimate' targets. Crucially, the Empire's foundation coincided with the revival of the western European slave trade, which had declined with the demise of ancient Rome and the development of a servile rural population working the land. Demand for slaves returned with the rise of the Arabs, their growing wealth and their switch from tribal to slave armies.[9] The Vikings emerged to service this economy by seizing captives in northern and western Europe for sale in the Mediterranean. The Carolingians and Ottonians provided a second supply through their campaigns across the Elbe. The word 'slave' is cognate with Slav and began to displace the earlier Latin term *servus* during this period.[10] Meanwhile, both the Saxons and Slavs engaged in more localized raiding for women. These practices only ceased with a general growth in population and the assimilation of east Elbian areas into the Empire around 1200.

There were other reasons for laity to answer the clergy's call to spread the Gospel. The Empire's elite was uniformly Christian and shared a concern for salvation and the belief that God influenced earthly events. The idea of penance was powerfully attractive to a warrior elite engaged in killing, fitted with Germanic legal customs that demanded reparations for victims, and encouraged lavish endowments of material resources to the church. The development of indulgences at the end of the eleventh century allowed warriors to gain remission from sin by serving in the crusades. Endowments were additionally encouraged by the belief in vicarious merit in which prayers and intercessions by the living benefited the donor's soul long after their death. These beliefs in turn encouraged the laity's concern for monastic discipline and good ecclesiastical management, since 'a community of lax and negligent monks was a poor investment'.[11]

Endowments removed wealth from the grasp of rivals and entrusted it to a transpersonal institution headed by Christ. The clergy enjoyed considerable social prestige through their proximity to God and their role as transmitters of written culture. The church offered a secure and attractive career for those of the elite who did not fit into the secular world, either because they were surplus to requirements as younger sons or unmarried daughters, or through personal misfortune. Hermann 'the Lame' probably had cerebral palsy and, unable to train as a warrior like his brothers, was placed instead in Reichenau abbey, where he could develop his prodigious literary and musical talents.[12] Religious houses were also secure places to confine wayward relatives and rivals.

Spiritual Goals

Thus, Christianization was driven by a powerful mix of conviction and self-interest. The objective was outward conformity and submission. In contrast to Byzantium, before the twelfth century the western church did not enquire too deeply into what people believed. Conversion and winning souls entailed persuading powerful local figures to join the clergy or enter a monastery. The captured sons of Slav nobles were often educated by monks in the ninth and tenth centuries. Later, as Christians, these Slavs used their personal connections to advance conversion among their own people by acting as baptismal sponsors. The Carolingians and Ottonians were likewise quite successful in persuading Viking warlords to convert, thereby assimilating 'barbarians' in the same way as did the ancient Roman empire.[13]

Carolingian kings were already coordinating these activities before 800. A series of church synods between 780 and 820 increased the incentives for lay patronage through written guidelines (*capitulares*) to improve monastic discipline. Monks and nuns were distinguished by their vows and strictly circumscribed lives, setting them apart from secular canons and canonesses who lived a communal life and acted as political and economic managers of church assets. While the first group prayed for benefactors, the second provided suitable roles for noble sons and daughters.[14]

The synods ensured clergy had the tools of their trade. Eighth- and ninth-century inventories show that most of the Empire's churches contained at least one religious book – a remarkable achievement in an age without printing.[15] The Christian message was also conveyed through non-written methods like wall paintings, sculptures, sermons and mystery plays. Objectives remained realistic. Bishops were to ensure liturgical uniformity and check that lesser clergy preached on Sundays and holy days, visited the sick, and performed baptisms and burials. Burial rites were an important marker of Christianity, displacing earlier customs of interring horses and weapons in warrior graves. However, saints' days only became regular calendar fixtures in the twelfth century, while it was not until 1215 that confession became at least an annual obligation. Considerable scope remained for local toleration of pagan practices and heterodoxy, all of which eased assimilation.

Missionaries

Christianization varied across the Empire. The church had enjoyed support from local elites in Burgundy and Italy since late antiquity, in contrast to Britain, where Christianity had largely expired by the late sixth century and had to be reintroduced by missionaries. Meanwhile, much of Germany had escaped both Romanization and Christianization. Frankish influence remained limited to the Rhine–Main nexus prior to the rapid conquest of Alamania, Bavaria and Saxony completed by Charlemagne around 800. For most of what became the kingdom of Germany, conquest and Christianization proceeded together and the entire church structure had to be created from scratch. The new German church was both a 'national' (i.e. general) and local institution, owing its overall shape to royal initiative, but its specific character to lords and missionaries on the ground.

Frankish kings sent missionaries to Frisia on the North Sea coast from the 690s, and others into central and northern Germany to work among the heathen Saxons from 718.[16] St Boniface, the most famous of these missionaries, felled the sacred oak at Geismar in Thuringia to prove the impotence of pagan gods. A major push followed between 775 and 777 when around 70 priests and deacons travelled to north-west Germany, including Willehard, who became the first north German bishop in 787.[17] Liudger was a prominent, yet fairly typical missionary.

A third-generation Christian Anglo-Saxon, he had been educated in Utrecht and York, imbibing the literate, cosmopolitan culture characteristic of a period without clear political or national boundaries. He worked among the Frisians from 787, moving his base in 793 to Mimigernaford, an important ford and crossroads, where he established a *monasterium*, giving the later name of Münster to the settlement that slowly developed around it.[18]

Like Boniface's felling of the sacred oak, military victories were intended to prove that God favoured only Christians. Acceptance of the conqueror's religion was a powerful sign of submission, hence the significance attached to the baptism of the Saxon leader Widukind in 785. Germanic warrior culture provided common ground, easing assimilation. The Saxon elite embraced Christianity within two generations. Already in 845, the Saxon Count Liudolf and his wife Oda travelled to Rome to fetch relics and papal approval for a convent at Gandersheim. Five years later, Widukind's grandson Walbert collected Roman relics for his own monastery at Wildeshausen.[19]

Christianization and imperial expansion both slowed as the Carolingian civil wars coincided with intensified external raids by Vikings, Arabs and Magyars during the middle and later ninth century. The stabilization of the northern and eastern frontiers allowed renewed activity from the early 930s. The king and his cleric advisors selected suitable monks who were sent to Rome to secure papal backing and holy relics, before being despatched to establish new churches and persuade local pagans to convert.[20] In time, these churches were placed on a firmer footing through incorporation within new or existing dioceses. A notable example was the mission of Abbot Hadomir of Fulda in 947, which revived Willehard's archbishopric of Hamburg-Bremen as the primary centre for the Christianization of Scandinavia and the Baltic.

The emperor was rarely able to help missionaries once they set off into the wild north and east. Those sent to Denmark were expelled in the 820s and Christianization made no headway there until the conversion of Harald Bluetooth in the mid-tenth century. The cooperation of local elites proved indispensable, especially as conversion entailed simultaneous acceptance of imperial suzerainty and payment of tithes. The Bohemian leader (and later saint) Wenceslas had been educated as a Christian and accepted imperial overlordship, only to be murdered on his brother's orders in 929. Bohemia was forced to acknowledge imperial suzerainty in 950, though resistance to Christianity persisted into the eleventh century. Nonetheless, conversion of much of its elite proved significant in spreading Christianity and imperial influence to the East Elbian Slavs and to the Poles and Magyars. Vojtech (Adalbert), a missionary martyred by the Prussians in 997, came from the Bohemian ruling family.

Despite the impressive scope of its activity, Ottonian Christianization rested on insecure foundations, with few churches and only a tenuous hold on most of the East Elbian and Baltic populations. Its vulnerability was exposed during the massive Slav rising of July 983, which, in turn, was probably encouraged by Otto II's catastrophic defeat by the Arabs at Cotrone the previous year. Churches and castles were swept away, leaving the partially Christianized Sorbs around Meissen as a last outpost. The other East Elbian bishoprics remained only nominally in existence, and it was not until the twelfth century that the bishops of Brandenburg and Havelberg could visit their dioceses.[21]

Nonetheless, many Slavs found Christianity attractive, especially the elite, who saw it as a way to enhance their own status through association with Latin culture and power. Bohemian and Polish nobles had already converted before 983 and refused to join the revolt. The Polish Duke Boleslav I Chrobry ('the Brave') ransomed Vojtech's body from the Prussians and placed it in his capital at Gniezno just prior to Otto III's pilgrimage during Lent 1000. The emperor's visit resulted in Gniezno's elevation to an archbishopric with jurisdiction over missionary bishops in Cracow, Kolberg and Breslau (Wroclaw). This entailed the transfer of jurisdictions that were previously part of the Magdeburg and Hamburg-Bremen archdioceses, as well as recognition of Boleslav Chrobry as an allied if still subordinate prince sharing in the imperial Christianizing mission. Cooperation was symbolized by Otto's gift of a copy of the Holy Lance in exchange for the prized relic of Vojtech's arm. Boleslav was clearly elevated above his local rivals, while the establishment of a separate Polish ecclesiastical structure provided the basis for that country as an independent monarchy. Polish Christianity was swept away by a pagan rising between 1037 and 1039 during which the rest of Vojtech's corpse was retrieved and installed in Prague, where it became the focus of a cult extending across Germany, Bohemia, Poland and Hungary. Polish Christianity was rebuilt through new monastic foundations in the later eleventh century.[22]

Building the German Church

Burgundy and Italy already had established ecclesiastical structures dating from late antiquity when dioceses had been established on the framework provided by the Roman imperial provinces. The emperor's primary contribution to the development of the Italian church was to encourage the pope to create new institutions in southern Italy to curb Byzantine influence during the late tenth century. These factors ensured there were 26 archdioceses in Italy in 1000, compared to six in Burgundy, seven in France, two in Britain, and one each in Poland and Hungary.

The general framework for the German church was laid out in just twenty years by Charlemagne in collaboration with the pope. Already an important base during St Boniface's mission, Mainz was elevated to an archdiocese in 780 to oversee all missionary work east of the Rhine. The rapidity of subsequent conquests necessitated more subdivisions to allow closer supervision of the population being incorporated into the Frankish realm (Map 13). Cologne was raised to an archbishopric in 794 with responsibility for north-west Germany and the Frisian missions. Hamburg-Bremen was initially one of its subordinate bishoprics, but was itself raised to archiepiscopal status during the 860s with responsibility for lands beyond the Elbe. Bavaria's submission to Carolingian rule led to Salzburg's elevation as an archbishopric in 798. The Empire's foundation in 800 was preceded the year before by an assembly held by Charlemagne and Leo III in Paderborn, which had served as the main military and missionary base in the campaigns against the Saxons since 770. It was agreed to leave Saxony as part of the archdiocese of Mainz, which was simultaneously confirmed as Germany's premier archbishopric.[23] Trier was raised to an archdiocese around 800 with jurisdiction over what became Lorraine, a factor in this province's eventual attachment to Germany rather than France. Besançon was meanwhile made the senior archdiocese for Burgundy.

Complete by 800, this basic framework survived a millennium. The only major modification was made by Otto I, and the difficulties he encountered amply illustrate the role of local elites in developing the imperial church. Otto wanted to commemorate his victory at Lechfeld over the Magyars in 955 and improve coordination of missionary activity beyond the Elbe. At his imperial coronation in 962 he announced the establishment of a new archbishopric based at Magdeburg equal in status to Mainz, which was expected to relinquish its jurisdiction over the Saxons. The bishoprics of Brandenburg and Havelberg were transferred from Mainz. The bishop of Halberstadt (also under Mainz) was required to surrender part of his diocese to create a new bishopric of Merseburg, while additional bishops were to be installed at Meissen and Zeitz in the missionary areas.

Implementation was delayed until 968 by opposition from Otto's son, Archbishop Wilhelm of Mainz. Otto I's death in 973 opened the way to reverse his pet project. The pope adjusted the German hierarchy in 975–6, reasserting Mainz's premiership and extending it to include Bohemia's bishopric, created in Prague in 973.[24] Otto II used the death of the first archbishop of Magdeburg in 981 as an opportunity to suppress the bishopric of Merseburg and redistribute its resources and jurisdictions to Halberstadt, Zeitz and Meissen, which were all considered under-endowed. Giselher, the former Merseburg bishop, was compensated by promotion to the vacant see of Magdeburg. However, this still left lesser clergy deeply disgruntled, including Thietmar, a Merseburg Cathedral canon who interpreted the 983 Slav rising as divine punishment for the suppression of his beloved diocese.[25] Even the imperial family were divided over the issue. Otto II's wife Theophanu supported Thietmar, while the emperor's mother Adelheid backed Archbishop Giselher in opposing Merseburg's restoration. The imperial women intervened, because Merseburg's dissolution affected the jurisdiction over convents under their patronage. Otto III ordered Merseburg's restoration in 998, but this was only achieved when Giselher died six years later and the new king Henry II made a large donation to compensate Magdeburg and Halberstadt.[26]

No further archdioceses were added after Magdeburg, but the number of bishoprics grew through a subdivision of existing dioceses, and the creation of new ones as the Empire expanded eastwards again from the twelfth century. Charlemagne's realm had contained 180 bishoprics, of which 45 were under direct papal control. A significant number were detached in the Empire's partition in 843 following the Treaty of Verdun, but the development of the German church created 32 bishoprics and 6 archbishoprics there by 973. This total grew to over 50 by 1500, or around a tenth of all those in Latin Christendom. There were another nine that remained unincorporated within an archdiocese, as well as five more outside all archiepiscopal control because they had been placed under direct papal supervision, like Bamberg, founded by Henry II in 1024.[27]

Abbeys

The eighth century already saw the foundation of abbeys as a third ecclesiastical tier junior to bishoprics and archbishoprics. Abbeys had smaller jurisdictions and were initially closer than diocesan centres to the monastic ideal of prayer. Frankish conquests both created the need for a local ecclesiastical infrastructure and secured the slave labour necessary to build it. Charlemagne is credited with founding 27 cathedrals, and 232 monasteries and abbeys, compared to 65 palaces.[28] This activity created a new sacral landscape in Germany where only Mainz, Cologne and Trier had relatively old churches. Some important monasteries traced their origins to early missionary churches like St Gallen, established in Switzerland by an Irish monk in 612, though the actual church dated from the 830s. Association with a martyred missionary often influenced the choice of location, but royal or lordly initiative was important too.

Patronage of churches and abbeys helped preserve lordly family identity. The Ottonians traced their origins to Liudolf and Oda, the pious founders of Gandersheim convent. In praying for them, the Gandersheim nuns helped perpetuate the Ottonians' *memoria*, including Abbess Hrotsvith, who wrote an early family history. Moreover, the Ottonians broke even more sharply than the Carolingians with the old Frankish practice of partible inheritance, thereby increasing the need for suitable accommodation for younger or unmarried children excluded from inheritance. All Gandersheim's early abbesses, including Hrotsvith, were Liudolf and Oda's direct descendants.[29]

Patronage extended to multiple sites, especially amongst the royal family, which remained without a fixed capital into the later Middle Ages and needed staging posts for their journeys around the Empire. Extended kinship continued to outweigh patrilinear descent in family structure, also encouraging the use of different places. In addition to Gandersheim, for instance, the Ottonians developed the former Carolingian castle of Quedlinburg into another important family convent, promoted by Henry I's widow, Matilda. Matilda held the status of canoness regular created by the earlier Carolingian legislation, allowing her to become Quedlinburg's first rector without taking vows as a nun.[30]

The Imperial Church

This ecclesiastical infrastructure emerged as the Empire developed, creating what became known as the imperial church and serving as a primary pillar of the political order into the early nineteenth century. As a new foundation, the imperial church rested on recently endowed land, most of which came directly from the emperor. The Franks had donated about a third of their land to the church between the fifth and eighth centuries, but Charles Martel had secularized much of this to fund his campaigns. Donations resumed under his grandson Charlemagne, but were most extensive in the newly conquered areas east of the Rhine where property could be redistributed from defeated peoples.[31]

Prüm abbey north of Trier was especially favoured, acquiring 1,700 individual properties scattered across Lotharingia, inhabited by 16,000 to 20,000 people in 893. The 12 manors belonging to St Bertin abbey in ninth-century Flanders encompassed 11,000 hectares, while Nyvel abbey near Ghent had 14,000 dependent farms when it was given by Otto II to Theophanu after their marriage in 972.[32] These properties were gifted as benefices, remaining ultimately royal possessions whilst used by the beneficiaries. The Carolingians also finally achieved the long-standing Merovingian goal of enforcing the tithe as a one-tenth tax on all Christians. Bishops were charged with coordinating collection, but the role of assigning tithes to specific churches often lay with the king.[33]

The emperor expected a significant return on his investment. Senior clergy represented a readily identifiable group of vassals who could be summoned, in contrast to the much larger and fluctuating numbers of secular lords. The advice of clerics was valued, especially as they were usually literate, well travelled and widely connected. They could draw on their substantial endowments to supply troops for royal campaigns and coronation journeys. These burdens increased at the end of the tenth century when German kings largely stopped living in palaces and instead stayed with bishops and abbots as they toured the Empire.

Clerics critical of such displays compared royal visits with biblical plagues of locusts.[34]

However, the imperial church was never an exclusive instrument of royal dominion, since lesser lords were also partners in these arrangements. This point is important, since it explains why the imperial church became so deeply embedded in the Empire's socio-political hierarchy. Secular lords were already important local donors before the ninth-century civil wars disrupted royal supervision of abbeys. Lorsch, Fulda and other important imperial abbeys acquired additional, local patrons.[35] Some houses slipped entirely under local control. Others were founded by lords on their own land. These trends created a second, mediate ecclesiastical layer under lordly jurisdiction and only indirectly subject to imperial authority. Carolingian lords passed monasteries directly to their sons, and lordly control remained pronounced until revised as protectorate powers during the Investiture Dispute that began in the 1070s (see pp. 56–60).

Prior to Gregory VII, lordly influence was generally welcomed. The early missionaries faced a monumental task and needed lordly protection and assistance. The term parish (*parochium*) and priest (*sacerdos*) still meant diocese and bishop respectively until well into the eleventh century. Clergy remained based in the primary religious sites like cathedral towns, travelling to outlying oratories and churches to perform services. Missionary activity further promoted the incipient hierarchy through founding mother–daughter networks with satellite churches surrounding their abbeys. Further church-building allowed the initially large parishes to be subdivided. By the eleventh century, most dioceses contained sufficient numbers of parishes to require an intermediary level of deaconries to supervise them. Demarcation was often driven by the desire to define control over tithes and other resources.[36] Clergy also responded to growing demands for their services from the tenth century, as well as new ideas emerging from Gregorian reform and the requirement after 1215 to confess annually. The parish structures envisaged in Carolingian legislation around 800 finally became reality in the later Middle Ages when there were 50,000 parishes in the Empire, compared to 9,000 in England and a total of 160,000 across Latin Europe.[37] The impact was profound. Christianity extended beyond the elite to become a more genuinely popular religion, changing many of its practices in the process.

The 'incorporation' or assignment of a parish to an abbey, a dea-conry, or other higher jurisdiction entailed control over its resources, including tithes and any endowments associated with its church. With this often came the power to appoint the parish priest. By 1500, half of German parishes had been incorporated in this way, often with the priests' functions entrusted to poorly paid vicars as substitutes. This formed a major grievance fuelling what would become the Reforma-tion, but it also illustrates the growing complexity of overlapping jurisdictions, and interconnected spiritual, economic and political interests in the Empire.

These local networks remained mediate, subject to one or more intervening levels of secular supervision below the emperor's overall authority, as well as subordination to at least one layer of spiritual authority, such as that of an abbot or a bishop. The extensive lordly influence remained acceptable to the emperor, because he retained overall supervision of the imperial church, including the appointment of archbishops, bishops and many abbots who remained his immediate vassals on account of their benefices. There was no significant breach in this control until 1198 when the secular supervision of the bishopric of Prague was transferred to the Bohemian king. The Bohemian church acquired full autonomy in 1344 when Prague was raised to an arch-bishopric, freeing it from Mainz's spiritual jurisdiction. A separate Habsburg territorial church followed Frederick III's concordat with the pope in 1448, which was consolidated with the establishment of new bishoprics in Vienna and Wiener Neustadt in 1469, subject to Frederick's jurisdiction as Austrian archduke rather than as emperor. However, both bishoprics would remain under the spiritual jurisdic-tion of the archbishop of Salzburg, despite some reduction of that cleric's powers by Joseph II in the 1780s.

The 'Imperial Church System'

Before exploring the impact of the Reformation, we need to turn from the imperial church's structure to its place in medieval imperial politics. The monarch's influence over senior clerical appointments was a key royal prerogative that assumed even greater significance with the Otto-nian kings after 919. Despite widespread clerical concubinage, the senior clergy were still celibate and lived under rules distinguishing them from the laity. As such, they could not pass their benefices directly to sons or relations, and so did not exhibit the trend to hereditary possession that was a constant feature of secular jurisdictions in the Empire. Consequently, the Ottonians saw the senior clergy as potentially more reliable partners than the great secular lords. Growing reliance on the imperial clergy changed the episcopate from the cosmopolitan, learned monks of the Carolingian era to a more aristocratic, politically engaged group, and created what has been termed the 'imperial church system' (*Reichskirchensystem*).[38]

This label remains useful provided we remember that the political use of the imperial church was never a coherent policy.[39] Much depended on circumstances and personalities. Kings had to respect local interests, not simply through the formal requirements of canon law, but because ignoring these usually caused trouble. Two-thirds of eleventh-century bishops were either born in their see or had served there prior to appointment. Bishops 'married' their church, displaying a sense of transpersonal office by the eleventh century and seeking to raise their see's prestige through cathedral-building, relic-collecting and territorial acquisitions. Simultaneously, the old ideal of the monk-like bishop was displaced around 1050 by a new model of the energetic shepherd actively promoting his flock's welfare.[40]

The itinerant royal chapel was central to the king's influence. Established under the Carolingians to provide religious services at court, it was developed by Otto I from the 950s to test the loyalty of his secular vassals by encouraging them to send their sons there to be educated. Soon, those who showed promise were rewarded with the next vacant bishopric or abbey. Turnover was relatively high, offering numerous opportunities: Henry II installed at least 42 bishops across his 22-year reign.[41] The practice peaked under Henry III when half of all bishops emerged from the chapel. Capacity expanded with the foundation in 1050 as an additional training school of the St Simon and St Jude monastery at the royal palace in Goslar, Lower Saxony. Connections to royalty did not automatically make bishops more reliable partners. Kinship was at least as important, with families directly related to the king providing a quarter of both senior secular lords and bishops in the eleventh century. In the longer term, the monarchy was a victim of its own success. Royal patronage of the church increased the attractions of clerical appointments for lords, who began expecting appointments.

The later Salians were unable – or possibly unwilling – to open the epis-copate to the new class of unfree vassals called *ministeriales* who emerged in the eleventh century and might have provided a counter-weight to aristocratic influence.[42]

The demographic and economic expansion from 950 was another factor behind royal patronage, because kings saw senior clergy as ideal agents to tap the growing resources. This explains why the later Otto-nian and Salian kings accelerated the transfer of crown lands to the imperial church and entrusted senior clergy with new secular powers like mint and market rights, and jurisdiction for crime and public order. Far from representing a dissipation of central authority, this entailed the replacement of relatively inefficient direct management by a more productive partnership with the imperial church. Henry II began donating imperial abbeys to bishops whose sees overlay duchies where royal control was weak. For example, Bishop Meinward of Paderborn received several abbeys, strengthening him relative to the powerful duke of Saxony. The bishops of Metz, Toul and Verdun were likewise patronized as counterweights to the duke of Upper Lorraine. Italian bishops had already acquired county jurisdictions by the early tenth century, and this was extended by Henry II to Germany, where 54 coun-ties had transferred into episcopal hands by 1056.[43]

This explains why the early Salians saw no danger in the cause of 'church liberty' emerging from eleventh-century reform, since it appeared to free valuable assets from the influence of potentially diffi-cult secular lords. Bishops also welcomed the greater powers that assisted their conscription of peasant labour and the resources needed for cathedral construction. The invention of new techniques like frame construction increased the scale of both buildings and clerical ambi-tions. Within four days of arriving in Paderborn in 1009, Meinward ordered the half-finished cathedral to be demolished and resumed on a grander scale. Meanwhile, his colleague in Mainz embarked on a lavish construction programme to underpin his claim as Germany's senior churchman. Bishops also adopted the new royal symbolism that had been introduced by Otto II by representing themselves in sculpture and pictures as seated on thrones.[44] Episcopal and royal splendour were still mutually reinforcing at this point, and kings participated fully in the building boom. Henry III dramatically expanded Speyer Cathedral, making it the largest religious building north of the Alps in the mid-eleventh century and setting aside 189 square metres of the nave for the royal tomb. The symmetry of royal and ecclesiastical power was symbolized by the addition of two towers of equal height and a throne room above the western portico from where the emperor could see the mass; these modifications were replicated in many other cathedrals.[45]

Relations were not always so harmonious, even before the Investiture Dispute beginning in the 1070s. The most notorious case involved the rivalry of archbishop Anno II of Cologne, archbishop Adelbert of Hamburg-Bremen and Bishop Heinrich II of Augsburg during the regency for Henry IV (1056–65), and underscores the importance of personalities in imperial politics. Anno wanted to assert his own, exclusive control and persuaded the young king to inspect a boat moored outside the royal palace at Kaiserswerth on an island in the Rhine on 31 March 1062. No sooner was the king aboard than Anno's co-conspirators cast off. Henry tried to escape by jumping overboard, but was fished out by Count Ekbert of Brunswick, and the boat sailed to Cologne, allegedly for the king's safety.[46]

Secular lords did not always cooperate with imperial bishops, as illustrated in the defeat of Adelbert's plans to revive Hamburg-Bremen's earlier role as sole archbishopric for the Baltic and Scandinavia. He used his influence in the regency to acquire additional benefices and planned to incorporate 12 north German bishoprics within his jurisdiction. The Saxon lords compelled Henry IV to oblige Adelbert to relinquish two-thirds of his assets to their two leaders in 1066. The significance of Adelbert's alienation of secular support was revealed later that year by the largest Slav rising since 983. Antagonized by Adelbert's missionary zeal, the pagan Wends burned Hamburg and Schleswig, stoned Christians in Ratzeburg, and murdered one of their own princes who had cooperated.[47]

The Imperial Church after the Investiture Dispute

The Investiture Dispute changed how the church related to the emperor, but it did not diminish the church's political role. The re-emergence of the monk-bishop ideal challenged political appointments, but it made little difference, as the aristocracy retained the best access to education and continued to dominate senior church positions. The Worms Concordat of 1122 confirmed that local clergy and laity were to participate in selecting their bishop. In practice, the wider population was excluded by the twelfth century through the emergence of cathedral and abbey chapters composed of lay canons, or senior clergy who had not taken full vows and who managed their church's secular affairs. The royal chapel lost much of its political significance, since the way to become a bishop now lay through winning influence in the relevant chapter. This contrasted with the situation in France, where the king had displaced the chapters' role in selection by the later Middle Ages.[48]

Although the Worms Concordat allowed the king to be present at elections, it was scarcely possible to coordinate royal movements with the death and succession of individual bishops. Conrad III's presence is documented for only eight of the 36 episcopal elections during his reign, while Frederick I 'Barbarossa' was present at just 18 of the 94 elections under his kingship. Nonetheless, monarchs retained considerable influence, sending envoys to express their views and, less directly, through their ability to favour clients with appointments as canons. They were aided by the generational shift around 1140 as the imperial church passed into the hands of men who had not participated in the Investiture Dispute and who viewed royal influence more pragmatically.

This explains why the transfer of secular jurisdictions to the imperial church resumed with even greater force under the Staufers, who enfeoffed favoured bishops with not merely counties but also ducal powers after 1168. The new relationship was codified in a general charter favouring what were now explicitly called 'ecclesiastical princes', which was issued in April 1220.[49] This consolidated church lands as a distinct category of imperial fief held by senior clerics elected by their abbey or cathedral chapter. Like their hereditary secular counterparts, ecclesiastical lords only exercised their privileges once the emperor confirmed them in office. Their secular authority rested on the clutch of jurisdictions and material assets acquired over time and now permanently associated with their abbey or diocese. These jurisdictions were extensive, collectively covering a third of the German kingdom, but they remained fiefs held immediately under the emperor's authority and entailed obligations to support him with advice, troops and other assistance. Simultaneously, the ecclesiastical lords exercised spiritual jurisdictions that generally extended far beyond their own lands and across neighbouring fiefs held by hereditary secular lords. These spiritual jurisdictions were bolstered by the ongoing incorporation of parishes within diocesan control and included powers to supervise local clergy and religious practice.

Abbots and bishops participated in the general trend to territorialize rights through clearer, more exclusive demarcation of jurisdictions under way from the thirteenth century. However, unlike their secular counterparts, they suffered from the Staufer's demise around 1250, because the persistence of weaker monarchs into the fourteenth century reduced the flow of patronage and benefices. Abbeys with nuns were especially hard hit, with many disappearing during the twelfth and thirteenth centuries through incorporation within the domains of their secular protectors.[50] Many abbeys and bishoprics now appeared under-resourced compared to the larger secular fiefs. Secular lords tried to curtail spiritual jurisdiction where this conflicted with their own powers to adjudicate criminal behaviour, especially as the growing significance on personal piety and morality from the thirteenth century changed how many misdemeanours were perceived. Ecclesiastical lords frequently lost lands that they had previously pawned to secular neighbours to avoid insolvency. Some ecclesiastical lords agreed treaties of protection, whereby secular lords assumed various functions on their behalf, including honouring their obligations as imperial vassals. Over time, such agreements eroded the ecclesiastical lords' immediacy and by the later fifteenth century 15 bishoprics, including Brandenburg and Meissen, were well on their way to being fully incorporated within secular principalities.

Colonization

Efforts to rebuild ecclesiastical structures in north-eastern Germany after 983 were wrecked by the renewed Slav rising of 1066. Expansion of the Empire and imperial church only resumed around 1140, but this time it continued until virtually the entire southern Baltic shore had been Christianized and incorporated within the Empire. The extensive forests and underpopulated regions east of the Elbe had attracted western settlers since at least the eighth century, but the movement only became general and coordinated after 1100. Acutely aware that Germany had lost out in the European scramble to steal other peoples' lands, nineteenth-century historians adopted the language of high imperialism to present this migration as a legitimate 'drive to the east' (*Drang nach Osten*) to colonize 'virgin land' and spread a supposedly superior culture.[51] In fact, eastwards migration was part of a much wider movement of peoples throughout the Empire, which included forest clearance, marsh drainage, land reclamation and urbanization, all frequently in areas already viewed as 'settled'. People were moving elsewhere in Europe at the same time, such as Spaniards crossing into Arab lands south of the river Ebro, or southern Italians settling in Sicily after its conquest by the Normans.[52]

The initial impetus came from the more densely populated areas of Holland, Flanders and the Lower Rhine, from where people were already moving around 1100 into the western Saxon lands around Bremen. Flemings and Dutch also continued east across the Elbe into the eastern Saxon areas of Altmark and Brandenburg during the twelfth century, and were later joined by further waves of Saxon and West-phalian migrants. Hessians and Thuringians from central Germany moved east into the area between the Elbe and the middle Saale, set-tling the region that would later become electoral Saxony. Altogether, 400,000 people crossed the Elbe during the twelfth and thirteenth cen-turies, causing an eightfold increase in the population of the region immediately beyond, compared to a 39 per cent increase over the next 250 years.[53] Meanwhile, south Germans joined migrants from Luxem-bourg and the Moselle region in crossing Hungary to settle in Transylvania in the late twelfth century. Saxons, Rhinelanders and Thuringians also headed north to the Baltic coast, while Italians crossed the Alps to live in Germany. New Polish towns attracted Ger-mans, Italians, Jews, Armenians and Tartars, while Polish settlers headed into Lithuania, Prussia and later Russia.

Each group brought its own legal system, though most lived under what was called 'German law'. This was always an amalgam of differ-ent elements, some originating in Flanders. Each successive wave of migrants transformed this law as they moved further east, creating entirely new elements unknown in the west. Certain broad patterns existed through the influence of Lübeck, Magdeburg and other import-ant cities, providing models for the laws of new eastern settlements.[54]

The legal arrangements help explain why people moved. Although the impetus came from areas with high population density, migration was not primarily a product of overpopulation. As Flemish migrants put it: 'We want to go east together . . . there'll be a better life there.'[55] The new laws included better property rights, lower inheritance dues and reduced feudal obligations. Migrants faced considerable hardship, as expressed by the thirteenth-century German proverb *Tod-Not-Brot*: the first generation found death, the second experienced want, but the third finally got bread. The greater personal freedoms were guaranteed by eastern lords who used them to attract settlers to their sparsely inhabited domains. Slav lords participated in this, like the Polish Prince Henryk the Bearded of Silesia, who called on 10,000 Germans to settle 400 new villages he established in 1205.[56]

Newcomers almost always faced mistrust, not least because they enjoyed privileges denied indigenous inhabitants, who remained tied to manorial farms. Assimilation was also slowed by the successive arrival of fresh migrants. Areas experiencing significant initial settlement were transformed, such as Brandenburg, where already by 1220 Slavic-speaking Wends were only a third of the population. Migrants had generally merged with the indigenous population by the fifteenth century, though some Slavic areas retained their distinct identity, most notably the Sorbs, who remain a distinct group today around Bautzen and Cottbus in eastern Germany. Germans comprised only 40 per cent of Prussia's population, while Slovenes predominated in Krain and Lower Styria. Assimilation could work in the other direction. Germans arriving in rural parts of Prussia and Poland became Polonized, and though they predominated in the towns, this was not invariably the case and by the sixteenth century, German was no longer understood in Cracow. Descendants of medieval settlers often reacted with hostility when a new wave of German eastwards migration began in the eighteenth century.[57]

The initial phase of colonization was accompanied by considerable violence, reinforcing a sense of a frontier and contributing to the lasting contradistinction between German and Slavic identities. The arrival of additional labour reduced the dependency of frontier communities on slave raiding, whereas those Slav communities still further east continued attacks for captives. Coupled with factors like material and technological differences, this fostered the self-perception among German communities of their inherent cultural superiority.[58]

The Northern Crusades

Animosities were inflamed by the new language of holy war accompanying the Empire's eastwards expansion. Popes already blessed warriors and their weapons in the tenth century and from 1053 offered remission from sin to men fighting their enemies. Initially, these indulgences were granted to those fighting the Normans, but from 1064 they were extended to campaigns against Muslims. Gregory VII prepared the ground for what became the crusades by stigmatizing his enemies as heretics. The ideologically charged Investiture Dispute nurtured new ideas about violence, involving sharper distinctions between Christendom as a realm of peace where killing was condemned as murder, and an external world where exterminating infidels glorified God and Christians dying in combat became martyrs directly entering heaven.

The most concrete expression of these beliefs were the new military orders whose members combined monastic vows with the duty to protect pilgrims travelling to the Holy Land. The Templars are perhaps the best remembered today, but never had a significant presence in the Empire, in contrast to the Hospitallers, who were founded in 1099 and known in the Empire as the *Johanniter*, or Knights of St John. They established their first German house at Duisburg in 1150, and were followed by the Teutonic Order formed in the Holy Land in 1190, which had seven houses in the Lower Rhine by 1261.[59]

The crushing defeat by the Turks at Manzikert in 1071 forced the Byzantine emperor to call on the despised Latins for assistance. The first full crusade was eventually proclaimed by Pope Urban II at the Council of Clermont in November 1095. The initial part of the ambitious programme was achieved with surprising ease when Jerusalem was recovered after 463 years of Muslim rule in 1099, leading to the establishment of a new crusader state in the Holy Land. The second goal of reunifying the eastern and western churches quickly foundered on the pope's insistence on supremacy over Constantinople's patriarch. By 1105, the papacy was actively encouraging the Normans to conquer Byzantium, a redirection of resources that ultimately contributed to the failure of the entire crusading enterprise over the following three centuries.[60]

Crusader ideology was employed against western Christian opponents already in 1102 when Pope Paschalis II backed one of Henry IV's opponents in a struggle over the bishopric of Cambrai; this was one of the many local conflicts characterizing the confused final phase of the Investiture Dispute. The ideology was employed more extensively by Gregory IX and Innocent IV, who redirected armies bound for the Holy Land to fight Frederick II in the final stage of the papacy's conflict with the Staufers.

Outside Italy, crusader ideology assisted the Empire's expansion. What became known as the Northern Crusades opened as a second front declared by the pope in 1147 to attack the Wends and other Slavs north of the Elbe. The initiative lay with Count Adolf II of Holstein, who began by evicting Slavs from Wagria and replacing them with Flemish and German settlers, many of whom helped found the new town of Lübeck in 1143. Official sanction as a crusade attracted Germans, Danes, Poles and some Bohemians to Adolf's army, allowing him to greatly expand operations. 'Indulgences on this front could be won at a lower cost and in a fraction of the time necessary to complete a pilgrimage to Jerusalem.'[61] The cooperation of the Polish and Pomeranian dukes proved crucial to success. These Slavic princes were engaged in Christianizing their own lands as a means to enhance their authority and possessions. Their involvement expanded the scope of the Northern Crusades from the area immediately north of the Elbe eastwards along the Baltic shore through Prussia and into modern Estonia, Latvia and Lithuania. Much of this region had been conquered by 1224, assisted by the pope's sanction of the Knights of the Sword, a new military order who soon became rulers of the area north of Riga, known as Livonia.

The heathen Prussians were driven from the Vistula estuary in the later eleventh century, only to spread across the Polish duchy of Masovia, prompting Duke Conrad to appeal for aid in 1226. The call was answered by the Teutonic Order, which had transferred to fight in Hungary only to be expelled in 1225 for being out of control. Operations were temporarily dislocated by the devastating Mongol invasion of Poland in 1240–41, which eliminated much of the Polish elite. Although the Mongols soon retreated, Pope Innocent IV had been persuaded to proclaim a permanent Baltic crusade in 1245, legitimizing regular recruitment for the Teutonic Order. Four hard-fought campaigns secured Prussia by 1280.[62]

The emperor was hardly involved in either colonization or the

Northern Crusades, which, together, achieved the largest expansion of the Empire since Charlemagne. Although Frederick II issued his own authorization to the Teutonic Knights, the Order acted independently in carving out its own state, which eventually succumbed to a resurgent Poland around 1500 (see pp. 209–11). Secularization of the Order's territory in Prussia by the (then) relatively insignificant Hohenzollern dynasty in 1525 did not affect its other possessions, which were grouped into 12 bailiwicks across the Rhineland, south and central Germany, and Austria. The Order retained its crusader privileges, making membership highly attractive for German nobles. Any land donated to it was immediately freed from previous debts. The senior Grand Master remained based in Germany and had been raised to the status of imperial prince in 1494, followed by his counterpart in the Knights of St John in 1548. These elevations integrated both Orders and their leaders into the imperial church, with their lands becoming immediate imperial fiefs, though the Knights of St John remained part of an international organization based in Malta. The Teutonic Grand Master remained Catholic, but the Order accepted Protestant nobles after the Reformation.[63]

The Hussites

A century after the Northern Crusades, the Empire engaged in a final, internal crusade, against Bohemian Hussitism, the most important heretical movement prior to the Reformation, as well as the largest popular rising prior to the Peasants War of 1524–6. The late medieval concern for individual belief intersected with the growth of written culture to make heresy easier to identify as deviance from approved texts and practices. The Hussites took inspiration from Jan Hus, the rector of Prague University who was treacherously burned at the stake in 1415 after the Luxembourg monarch Sigismund reneged on a promised safe conduct to present Hus's case at the Council of Constance (1414–18). Although the Hussites established their own national church in 1417, their movement soon split into millennialist Taborites, operating from the town of Tabor, and moderate Utraquists, named after their practice of communion 'in both kinds' (*sub utraque specie*), bread and wine. Opposition to Sigismund's accession as Bohemian king in 1419 briefly reunited the factions and led to their conquest of most of the kingdom.

Sigismund received papal indulgences for five major expeditions between 1420 and 1431. Most crusaders came from Germany, Holland and Hungary (where Sigismund was also king), despite the appeal being directed throughout Christendom. A 3,000-strong English detachment arrived on the continent in 1427, but they were redirected to fight Jeanne d'Arc in the Hundred Years War – a further indication of the manipulation of indulgences to advance secular goals. The imperial counter-attacks were repulsed by the Hussites' determination and superior tactics, but also because the emperor was simultaneously engaged in defending Hungary against renewed Turkish invasion.

Eventually, the situation was defused through the *Compacta* of 1436 between the Bohemian Catholic elite and the Utraquists, who formed the majority of the population. Utraquist practices were tolerated in return for their formal submission to Rome. The defeat was greater for the papacy than for the Empire. For the first time, the pope had allowed heretics to present their case and made significant concessions. Sigismund's rule was secure in Bohemia, while the episode provided a significant boost to constitutional reform, eventually giving the Empire its definitive shape around 1500. Bohemia remained within the Empire despite its distinctive religious arrangements and even the accession of an openly Utraquist king, George Podibrad, in 1458.[64]

THE EMPEROR AS JEWISH ADVOCATE

The Jews and the Empire

The story of the Jews in the Empire is much like imperial history generally: far from perfect, occasionally tragic, but generally more benign than that of other places or times. Although marginalized in most accounts, their history reveals much about the Empire's social and political order. Charlemagne revived late Roman imperial patronage of the Jews, who had retained legal recognition in most of the Germanic successor kingdoms since the fall of western Rome in the late fifth century. Jews made significant contributions to Carolingian artistic and commercial development, particularly through their roles as intermediaries in selling captive Slavs as slave soldiers to Iberian Muslim armies. There were around 20,000 Ashkenazi Jews in the Empire north of the

Alps in 1000, mainly in Mainz, Worms and other Rhenish episcopal towns.[65]

The Carolingian and Ottonian elite remained ambivalent, conscious that Jews and Christians shared the Old Testament, yet only Jews could read the original Hebrew text.[66] Imperial protection was inconsistent. Otto II often assigned powers over Jews to bishops as part of broader privileges intended to boost the development of cathedral towns. Adverse circumstances could prompt punitive measures against Jews, notably under Henry II, who was decidedly less tolerant. Two thousand Jews were expelled from Mainz in 1012, though the decree was revoked the following year.[67]

The most significant step came in 1090 when Henry IV issued a general privilege to Jews modelled on those granted to individuals by Louis II over two centuries earlier. Probably prompted by the significant growth in the Jewish population in Worms and Speyer, Henry assumed the position of *Advocatis Imperatoris Judaica*, or general protector of all Jews in the Empire. This established arrangements that persisted until the Empire's demise in 1806. The safeguarding of Jewish economic, legal and religious rights was reserved as an imperial prerogative, linking imperial prestige to effective protection. Like other arrangements in the Empire, implementation varied according to circumstances, while protection rights were often devolved along with other privileges to more local figures. Enforcement became less consistent, but over time Jewish privileges were woven into the general web of imperial law, affording Jews by early modernity a surprising degree of autonomous protection.

Pre-modern toleration should not be confused with modern multiculturalism, equality, and the celebration of diversity as intrinsically good. Jews remained protected provided they accepted their second-class status. Diversity was feared, but also recognized as beneficial. Jews had a specific socio-economic role, assuming tasks that Christians were unwilling or unable to perform. Jews also played a cultural part as 'the other' reinforcing Christian group identity – often at considerable cost to themselves.

Pogroms and Extortion

Imperial protection of the Jews foundered almost immediately when Henry IV was trapped by his enemies in northern Italy and unable to prevent the first serious pogrom in German history in 1096. Proclamation of the First Crusade in November 1095 coincided with widespread suffering from flooding and famine. French preachers spread the standard accusations of Jews as usurers and 'Christ killers', calling on the crusaders to eradicate them as they marched to the Holy Land. Already licensed to kill by papal indulgences, the crusading army wreaked havoc as it moved east from Rouen into the Empire, where it was joined by impoverished German knights who saw a chance for plunder. Jews were told to convert or die, with many choosing suicide as the crusaders marched up the Rhine. Only the pro-imperial bishop Johannes of Speyer used force to uphold imperial protection. Once he managed to escape to Germany in 1097, Henry blamed Archbishop Ruthard of Mainz for the pogrom. Jews who had been forcibly converted were allowed to return to Judaism, despite Ruthard's protests. Imperial protection was renewed and incorporated in the general public peace declared for the Empire in 1103.[68]

Frederick Barbarossa acted swiftly to prevent a repeat of the pogrom when 10,000 gathered in Mainz to take the cross for the Third Crusade in March 1188. He publicly praised loyal Jews, and when a mob threatened violence against them, the imperial marshal, 'taking his servants with him and his staff in his hand . . . smote and wounded them, until they all dispersed'.[69]

Frederick II made an important adjustment when he renewed Henry IV's legislation in 1234. As with many of Frederick's actions, this was not as progressive as it first appears. The emperor vigorously rejected the myth of Jews committing ritual child murder, which so often provided an excuse for pogroms. Christians killed 30 Jews in Fulda after five Christian children died in a house fire at Christmas 1235. The case was considered sufficiently serious to be transferred to Frederick's own royal tribunal, which publicly rejected the excuse of ritual murder and renewed imperial protection for all Jews early the next year. Frederick's legislation inspired similar measures in Hungary (1251), Bohemia (1254) and Poland (1264). Unfortunately, it also incorporated Pope Innocent III's transfer of religious animosity to secular law promulgated a few decades earlier. Arguing that Jews inherited the guilt of Christ's death, Innocent had imposed permanent servitude as a punishment. This aspect was expressed in Frederick's verdict in 1236, which subordinated the Empire's Jews as 'servants of the chamber' (*Kammerknechte*).[70] Protection was now dependent on payment of an annual tax, known since 1324 as the 'Sacrificial Penny', levied on all Jews older than 12. An additional 'crown tax' was payable on the accession of each new king.

Imperial protection for Jews remained patchy. Three-quarters of Frankfurt's 200-strong Jewish community died in a pogrom in 1241, while Jews joined other migrants heading east in search of a better life. Nonetheless, the situation was probably similar to that in Spain and compared favourably to England or France.[71] More significantly, this persisted despite weaker royal power after 1250, providing a further indication that 'decentralization' should not be misconstrued as 'decline' in the Empire's history. Later thirteenth-century kings sold or devolved to lords those rights to protect Jews as part of a wider strategy to buy support. Consequently, both the number of Jewish communities and their lordly protectors multiplied so that there were 350 communities across Germany by the mid-fourteenth century.

This did not immediately strengthen protection for the Jews, since overall responsibility remained with the monarch, who could switch track, as Charles IV demonstrated with fatal results. Charles assumed power in the middle of a civil war in 1346. The papal interdict against his predecessor, Louis IV, had left large parts of the Empire without Christian services by 1338, stoking anxiety that deepened dramatically with the Black Death a decade later. Charles crudely exploited his prerogatives to win support by encouraging pogroms, even offering immunity in return for a share in the spoils. Six hundred Jews died in Nuremberg, where the Marienkirche was built on the ruins of their synagogue, while only around 50 communities across the Empire survived, largely by paying huge ransoms.[72] The privilege of protecting Jews (*Judenregal*) was included in the wider bundle of rights granted to the electors in the Golden Bull cementing the new alliance between Charles and the Empire's political elite in 1356. His son and successor Wenzel repeated this shameful extortion, receiving 40,000 florins from the Swabian cities in return for allowing them to plunder their Jewish populations in June 1385, and he did this again five years later in alliance with several princes. Meanwhile, Jews faced growing discrimination, including exclusion from long-distance trade. Again, much of this was fuelled by the Empire's elite, who were imposing heavier taxes on Jews, who were then obliged to pass increased costs on to their Christian customers by charging higher interest on loans.[73]

Early Modern Protection

Nonetheless, in the longer term the devolution of protection for Jews blunted this abuse of power by widening the circle of those with a vested interest in better relations. Throughout the bad times of the fourteenth century, individual lords and imperial cities preferred peaceful coexistence. Regensburg and Ulm refused to cooperate with Charles's measures, and while Frankfurt expelled its Jews in 1349, it allowed them to return in 1360. The community thrived, doubling across the late fifteenth century to total 250 by 1522, and then rising rapidly, reaching 3,000 or 11 per cent of all inhabitants by 1610.[74] The Habsburg Albert II was the last monarch to attempt extortion and, significantly, this failed to raise much money, despite the richer and larger Jewish population.[75]

His successor, Frederick III, reactivated imperial protection by claiming all Jews were his immediate subjects. Frederick too hoped to raise money, but this time through the regular Sacrificial Penny, and he vigorously resisted calls from Christians to reinstitute extortion. He was criticized as too soft, and mocked as 'king of the Jews'.[76] More positive attitudes were emerging around the time of Frederick's death in 1493. Humanists and early Protestant reformers were interested in Hebrew as a means to understand Christianity's origins. Sebastian Münster's book *Hebraica* sold 100,000 copies, making it one of the world's first best-sellers. The personally anti-Semitic Maximilian I, Frederick's successor, was dissuaded from renewing persecution by the Humanist Johannes Reuchlin, who argued in 1511 that Jews had been Roman citizens since late antiquity.

Rapid socio-economic change, passions stirred by the Reformation, and the reformers' disappointment at failing to convert Jews to Protestantism all contributed to a more threatening atmosphere around 1530. Jews were expelled from at least 13 Protestant and Catholic territories and cities between 1519 and 1614, reducing their main communities to

Frankfurt, Friedberg, Worms, Speyer, Vienna, Prague and Fulda abbey. Anti-Semitism remained a depressing feature of rural as well as urban protest throughout early modernity. However, the continued grant of Jewish protection rights to princes created new communities in Fürth, Minden, Hildesheim, Essen, Altona, Crailsheim and the duchy of Westphalia from the 1570s. Others, like Ansbach, readmitted communities they had previously expelled. The new pattern of protection again changed the character of Jewish settlement, which now spread into the countryside from imperial cities and princely residence towns. Meanwhile, refugees from the Dutch Revolt founded the Empire's first Sephardic community in Hamburg during the 1580s.

Jews and Imperial Law

Emperor Rudolf II (r. 1576–1612) was genuinely interested in Jewish culture and banned Luther's anti-Semitic books.[77] However, the Empire's development as a mixed monarchy proved a far more significant factor in the improving conditions. Unlike in centralized monarchies, toleration no longer depended on the whim of individual monarchs. Devolution of protection for Jews embedded responsibility within the general web of privileges and rights enshrined in imperial law. Imperial protection was renewed five times between 1530 and 1551, and became part of the general legislation passed by all imperial Estates through the Reichstag, linking the integrity and prestige of all political authorities to ensuring observance. The 1530 law did oblige all Jews to wear a yellow star. This was widely ignored and then formally overturned by the Reichstag in 1544. All forms of harassment were now prohibited. Jews were guaranteed free mobility, protection for their property and synagogues and against forced conversion, and were permitted to charge higher interest rates than Christians. Jewish self-government also secured legal recognition.[78]

Local authorities had to obtain permission from higher sources before expelling a Jewish community. Individual Jews remained subject to numerous restrictions, such as denial of full citizenship in cities, but could own property, including weapons, and could participate in wider aspects of the Empire, including using the imperial postal service. Imperial criminal justice remained neutral towards religion. Prejudice certainly affected judgements, but the new imperial supreme courts created in the 1490s were concerned with adhering to formal procedures. For instance, Jewish prisoners could observe religious rituals, even where they had not requested this.[79]

Like peasants and other socially disadvantaged groups, Jews were able to make effective use of imperial laws to defend their rights after 1530. For example, Emperor Ferdinand I's own supreme tribunal (the *Reichshofrat*) disregarded his anti-Semitism and upheld an appeal from the Jewish community in Worms against the city council's decision to expel them.[80] Such cases have wider significance, because the Empire's judicial system is widely perceived as deficient thanks to a systematic late sixteenth-century campaign by Protestant zealots to discredit their Catholic opponents, much of which was accepted as fact by later historians. Precisely when some Protestant princes were complaining loudly at religious bias, Jewish communities were quietly and effectively obtaining legal protection against princely and civic persecution.[81]

This is best demonstrated by the notorious Fettmilch incident, the worst anti-Semitic outburst between the mid-fourteenth century and the 1930s.[82] Frankfurt's Jewish community became the scapegoats for wider problems in the city around 1600, including rising taxation, falling wages, and an increasingly oligarchical government perceived as out of touch with ordinary inhabitants. The artisan leader Vincenz Fettmilch accused Jews and patricians of exploiting the poor, inciting a mob that attacked both the city hall and the ghetto where the city's Jews had lived since 1462, murdering 262 and plundering property worth 176,000 florins in 1612. Violence spread to Worms, where Jews were expelled. Although the outbreak had not been prevented, punishment was swift and effective. Fettmilch and six associates were executed, while legal injunctions prevented other cities from expelling their communities. Worms was forced to readmit its Jews in 1617. Overall, Jews brought 1,021 cases to the Empire's supreme court (the *Reichskammergericht*), representing 1.3 per cent of its entire case load between 1495 and 1806, though they only numbered 0.5 per cent of the Empire's population. Meanwhile, they were also involved in 1,200 cases before the Reichshofrat between 1559 and 1670, or 3 per cent of that court's business.[83]

The Persistence of Established Structures

Protection for the Jews continued despite the upheavals of the Thirty Years War (1618–48), while the surge in violent anti-Semitism accompanying the hyper-inflation of 1621–3 did not see a repeat of the earlier pogroms. The immediate post-war decades after 1648 saw a renewed wave of expulsions, with Jews driven from ten territories and cities, including Vienna, but these were more limited than those of the sixteenth century, while many authorities now actively encouraged Jewish immigration to help repopulate their lands. Already in 1675, 250 families were allowed to return to Vienna, while that year Duisburg University admitted its first Jewish students, far ahead of institutions elsewhere in Europe.[84] Territorial governments observed their legal obligations, even though they no longer derived significant financial benefit. Only Frankfurt's Jews still paid the Sacrificial Penny in the eighteenth century, which brought the emperor a mere 3,000 florins annually, while Jewish taxes in Münster accounted for just 0.1 per cent of the bishopric's revenue.[85]

The Jewish population grew faster than that of the Empire overall, rising from under 40,000 in 1600 to 60,000 by the later seventeenth century, with an additional 50,000 in Bohemia and Moravia. Although main centres were still urban, notably Frankfurt and Prague, nine out of ten Jews now lived in the countryside, either in the 30 principalities with communities or amongst the 20,000 living on the lands of the imperial knights by the late eighteenth century. The knights saw Jewish protection as a way of asserting their otherwise vulnerable autonomy. The Jewish population continued to grow faster than that of Christians, totalling 250,000 by 1800, with a further 150,000 in the lands recently annexed by Austria and Prussia from Poland.[86]

Economic arguments and liberal ideas associated with the Enlightenment are usually used to explain the improving conditions leading to nineteenth-century emancipation. This links the standard narrative of progress to the centralized state, exemplified in central Europe by Prussia and Austria. Both these lands were largely outside the web of imperial laws by the late eighteenth century, so we would expect the position of Jews there to be better than in the more politically fragmented areas of the Empire. This was not the case. The situation in the Habsburg monarchy was not always favourable prior to the 1781

toleration edict, and in 1745 the Ottoman sultan lodged a formal protest at Empress Maria Theresa's treatment of the Bohemian Jews.[87]
Frederick William I forced Prussia's Jews to pay a new tax in 1714 in
return for dropping requirements to make them wear a distinctive red
hat. The Berlin court printer circumvented the imperial censor to pub-
lish Johannes Andreas Eisenmenger's *Jewishness Revealed*, the first
modern anti-Semitic book that was banned in the Empire, but it now
appeared from a press supposedly based in the Prussian town of
Königsberg beyond the imperial frontier. The brilliant Jewish intellectual, Moses Mendelssohn, visiting Berlin in 1776, was made to pay a
head tax fixed at the rate levied on cattle passing the main city gate in
a deliberate effort to ridicule him. His treatment reveals the hollowness
of Frederick II of Prussia's much-celebrated toleration.[88]

Legal protection for Jews could still fail elsewhere in the Empire, as
exemplified by the notorious show trial and execution of the financier
Joseph Süss Oppenheimer, who was made the scapegoat for discredited
government policies in Württemberg in 1738.[89] However, the authorities had a vested interest in upholding protection, since their own
privileges and status were at risk if they failed to do so.[90] The contrast
with other parts of Europe is perhaps best illustrated by one final case.
Prince de Rohan fled revolution in his homeland of France by moving
to his German properties at Ettenheim in 1790, where he evicted
several Jewish families to make room for his courtiers. The families
promptly obtained redress from the Reichskammergericht.[91]

REFORMATIONS

The Reformation in the Context of Imperial History

The Jews formed the Empire's only religious minority between the
decline of paganism amongst the Slavic populations around 1200 and
the emergence of Hussitism over two centuries later. The most significant challenge to conformity came with the Reformation after 1517.[92]
The Reformation's uneven outcome reinforced the political and cultural distinctions between the Empire's primary territorial components,
including the drift of Switzerland and the Netherlands towards
independence.

The causes of this cultural earthquake lie beyond this book's scope, but we need to note the context in which it emerged, since this explains why the new religious controversy differed from those of the medieval Empire. Papal concordats with individual monarchs since the early twelfth century fostered the growth of more distinct national churches across much of Europe. This process accelerated rapidly around 1450 and contributed to Charles V's inability during the 1520s to repeat Sigismund's success at the Council of Constance by addressing the Reformation through a single church council under his leadership. Meanwhile, the Empire was also changing rapidly through the institutional changes collectively labelled 'imperial reform' around 1500 (see pp. 398–406). Crucially, these changes were incomplete by 1517, ensuring that resolution of the crisis became enmeshed with constitutional developments.

The context also contributed to Luther's failure to restore what he regarded as the original 'pure' Christianity by elevating Scripture to the sole basis of truth. The relative decline in papal and imperial authority meant there was now no single authority to judge his beliefs, which were as a result accepted, rejected or adapted by a host of national and local communities. Religious issues affected broad aspects of daily life, as well as personal salvation, adding to the urgency of their resolution. Attempts to defuse controversy by clarifying doctrine proved counterproductive, since fixing arguments in writing simply made the disagreements more obvious. Moreover, the new print media ensured rapid dissemination of the diverging views, igniting arguments across Europe.[93] Once the initial splits had occurred, it became harder for those involved to repair them.

The Problem of Authority

The failure of clerical leadership prompted theologians and laity to call on the secular authorities for protection and support. Religious issues became impossible to disentangle from political questions as political backing for Luther expanded the evangelical movement from simply protesting within the Roman church to creating a rival structure. The real question by 1530 was one of authority. It was not clear who among the emperor, princes, magistrates or people was entitled to decide which version of Christianity was correct. Nor was it clear how to resolve who owned church property or how to deal with dissent.

Some reformers like Caspar Schwenckfeld and Melchior Hoffmann rejected virtually all established authority, while a few like Thomas Müntzer envisaged a communistic godly society. Such radicalism was discredited by the violence accompanying the Knights Revolt (1522–3) and Peasants War (1524–6) (see pp. 557–8 and 591–3). Regardless of belief, the Empire's authorities had closed ranks to exclude common folk from these decisions by 1526. However, evangelicals continued to elaborate theological arguments to resist those who opposed their goals, by claiming that duty to God trumped political obedience.[94] Unfortunately, even they disagreed about who possessed such rights of resistance. While most restricted such resistance to 'godly magistrates', it was far from clear who these were given the Empire's multiple layers of authority.

Luther's protest came at entirely the wrong time for the ageing emperor Maximilian I, who was in the middle of brokering the election of his grandson, Charles, king of Spain, as his successor. The pressure of other events ensured that nearly two years elapsed between Charles's election as emperor in 1519 and his arrival in the Empire to open his first Reichstag at Worms in April 1521. The delay fuelled not only mounting (and unrealistic) expectations, but also frustration at the pace of constitutional reform. The decisions over the next three years proved decisive in determining how religion affected later imperial politics.[95] Luther's refusal to recant at Worms prompted Charles to impose the imperial ban, effectively criminalizing the evangelicals as outlaws who threatened the Empire's internal 'public peace'. Under the judicial system developed since 1495, all imperial Estates were supposed to enforce this decision, but Charles acted more honourably than Sigismund had behaved towards Jan Hus. Having allowed Luther to enter Worms under safe conduct, Charles permitted him to leave unmolested. The elector of Saxony, who sympathized with Luther, then arranged to have him hidden in Wartburg castle, where he stayed for ten months while others spread his message largely unchecked.

Having sought to detach theological issues from public order, Charles issued the Edict of Burgos on 15 July 1524, expressly rejecting calls to hold a national council to debate church reform. This completed his attempt to separate religion and politics along the traditional lines expressed by the Two Swords doctrine: the pope was to decide what constituted the correct version of Christianity, while Charles as emperor would enforce this using the Empire's legal machinery to crush dissent as a public-order issue.

A Lost Opportunity?

The controversy surrounding the decisions of 1521–4 persisted into the nineteenth century. Protestant German nationalists condemned what they regarded as a lost opportunity to embrace their faith as a truly 'German' religion, thereby forging the Empire as a nation state.[96] This 'failure' was often woven into explanations of later German woes: the country was supposedly left divided, hindering unification under Bismarck, who regarded Catholics as disloyal after 1871, because of their continued religious allegiance to Rome. These charges rest on a partisan, Protestant reading of history and the self-identification of that faith as inherently 'German', as well as a gross oversimplification of the situation facing people in the sixteenth-century Empire – that is, a supposedly simple choice between Catholicism and Protestantism. The vast majority hoped the controversy could be resolved without shattering Christian unity. Wholehearted support for Luther made little political sense for Charles V, regardless of his own fairly conservative views on faith. Ruling the birthplace of the Reformation, Charles confronted evangelism when it appeared indelibly associated with political subversion and challenges to the socio-economic order, and before it had acquired the theological and institutional footing making it acceptable later in other countries such as England. Charles's imperial title was tied to a universal, not a national, church, and it remained inconceivable, both to himself and to many of his subjects, that he should not follow the same faith as the pope.[97]

These considerations help explain why the Empire did not adopt what became the general western European solution to the religious controversy of imposing a monarchical civil peace. This entailed the ruler deciding on a single official faith enshrined in a written statement prepared by his theologians (as, for example, in England), or through publicly defending Catholicism. Regardless of the precise theology, this produced a 'confessional state' with a single, established church allied institutionally and politically to the crown.[98] Toleration of dissenters was a matter of political expediency, granted when the monarchy was weak, as in the case of late sixteenth-century France, or where the official church remained opposed by a significant minority, as in England. Either way, dissenters depended on special royal dispensations which could be curtailed, or revoked, unilaterally, as the French Huguenots discovered in 1685. Toleration might be widened incrementally through further dispensations, like the Catholic Emancipation Act (1829) in Britain, but a privileged, established church remained. Few countries have ever gone as far as the French Republic, which separated church and state in 1905, establishing a modern, secular peace treating all faiths equally provided their followers do not transgress state laws.

Secularization

Rather than imposing a solution by fiat from above, the Empire negotiated its solution collectively through the new constitutional structures emerging from imperial reform. Unity rested on consensus, not central power, and the result was religious and legal pluralism, not orthodoxy and a disadvantaged or persecuted minority. This outcome emerged from fierce and sometimes violent disputes over constitutional rights rather than through ecumenical compromise.

Once all parties had agreed by 1526 that matters should be settled by the 'proper authorities' rather than the 'common man', two core issues remained. One involved the question of spiritual jurisdiction, since this determined the authority to direct the religious belief and practices of ordinary folk in specific areas. The other concerned the management of clergy and church assets like buildings, property and revenue streams. These had always been important issues in imperial history. The Ottonians had already revoked donations and transferred land to secular lords. This process accelerated after 1100 as the emperor needed more resources to compensate nobles for their military expenses. Meanwhile, secular lords curtailed or usurped the secular jurisdictions of their ecclesiastical neighbours, removing them as imperial Estates, but not as functioning Catholic institutions. This continued beyond the Reformation as the archbishop of Salzburg incorporated the possessions of the bishops of Gurk, Seckau and Lavant. Charles V himself bought the secular jurisdiction of the bishop of Utrecht in 1528, and in 1533 would have accepted a similar offer from the archbishop of Bremen if the pope had not objected. However, secularization in these cases mostly involved smaller properties, and rarely threatened spiritual jurisdiction.[99]

The evangelical movement posed an entirely new challenge through its objection to papal jurisdiction and its rejection of good works and prayer for the dead as justifying monasticism. Georg the Pious of Ansbach-Kulmbach did sequestrate religious houses in 1529 and then sell them to fund road and fortress construction in a move prefiguring Henry VIII's Dissolution of the Monasteries (1536–40). However, this was exceptional in the Empire, where 'secularization' generally meant a change of public use. Church assets were placed in public trusts by reform-minded princes and used to fund a more numerous and better-educated clergy, evangelize by teaching the population to read the Bible, and improve welfare through hospitals and poor relief. For example, the duke of Württemberg converted 13 monasteries into schools to train pastors in 1556.[100] Conflict was not always inevitable. The complexity of legal and property rights in the Empire prevented a clear demarcation of jurisdiction and ownership, necessitating fairly frequent discussion between the different authorities. These discussions often continued despite religious animosities.[101] However, many Catholics regarded the evangelicals' re-designation of church property and use of spiritual jurisdictions as robbery breaching the public peace, and opened the so-called 'religious cases' in the imperial courts.[102]

Becoming Protestants

The problem fell to Charles's younger brother Ferdinand I, who was left to oversee the Empire during the emperor's prolonged absences after 1522. Ferdinand had inherited Hungary in 1526 amidst an Ottoman invasion. This existential threat to the Empire encouraged the imperial Estates to avoid matters that might escalate to civil war. The 1526 Reichstag at Speyer tried to uphold the Burgos edict by allowing imperial Estates to act according to their consciences until the papal-chaired church council ruled on doctrine. The decision essentially settled the question of authority by identifying the imperial Estates as responsible for religious affairs in their own territories. Electoral Saxony, Hessen, Lüneburg, Ansbach and Anhalt now followed the example of some imperial cities two years earlier and began converting church assets and jurisdictions to serve evangelical objectives. These decisions were influenced by the personal convictions of princes, the location of their lands, regional influence, and their relations to the Empire and papacy. For instance, thanks to its earlier concordats, Bavaria already enjoyed considerable control over the church on its territory and had little incentive to break with Rome.[103]

Given the long history of secular supervision of church affairs in the Empire, these changes did not automatically identify a territory as evangelical. Several important princes kept arrangements deliberately ambiguous, like the elector of Brandenburg, while religious practices amongst the bulk of the population remained heterodox. The new Lutheran territorial churches issued several revisions to its initial statement of faith, while other reformers like Huldrych Zwingli and Jean Calvin produced their own competing confessions. Similarly, Catholic thought and practice were hardly monolithic, and contained their own reforming impulses, so that we should speak of multiple Reformations.[104]

The growing divergence was nonetheless clear by the next Reichstag in Speyer in 1529. Catholics disputed the evangelicals' interpretation of the 1526 meeting as a licence to forge ahead with religious reform. Since the majority of imperial Estates were still Catholic, they reversed the earlier decision and insisted on full enforcement of Charles V's Edict of Worms banning Luther and his adherents. The ruling prompted the famous *Protestatio*, giving rise to the word 'Protestant' as the elector of Saxony led five princes and magistrates from 14 imperial cities in dissenting from the majority. This was the first open breach in the political unity of the Empire.

Failure of the Military Solution

The Protestants formed the Schmalkaldic League in 1531 for mutual defence (see pp. 564–5). The Ottoman threat encouraged Ferdinand to suspend the Worms edict in 1532 and then extend this truce three times by 1544. Meanwhile, the League was weakened by internal divisions and scandals amongst its princely leadership. Having temporarily gained ascendancy over France and the Ottomans in 1544–5, Charles V returned to the Empire with a large army. The elector of Saxony and the landgrave of Hessen were declared outlaws after they attacked their regional rival, the duke of Brunswick. This allowed Charles to present his intervention as restoring the Empire's public peace. The resulting Schmalkaldic War of 1546–7 saw the League's comprehensive defeat, culminating in Charles's victory at Mühlberg, which was celebrated in Titian's famous portrait of the emperor as triumphant general (see Plate 8).

Charles held the 'Armoured Reichstag' (*Geharnischte Reichstag*) at Augsburg between September 1547 and June 1548 under a strong imperial military presence. Intended to consolidate his victory, this Reichstag represented the only time the emperor attempted to define doctrine by issuing a statement of faith that he hoped would last until the pope's council, meeting in Trent, passed judgement. Known as the Interim, Charles's statement offered 'a new hybrid imperial religion' incorporating some Protestant elements. Although the Interim was endorsed by the archbishop of Mainz, most Catholics already disavowed it ahead of its promulgation, while Protestants rejected it as an imposition.[105]

The unsatisfactory settlement was widely resented as a breach of consensus, and Charles was accused of exceeding his authority. Magdeburg's armed defiance of the Interim galvanized more general opposition across 1551, leading to the Princes Revolt the following year that was backed by France, which had renewed its own war with the Habsburgs. Three months of manoeuvring convinced Ferdinand – who had again been left by Charles to manage the Empire – to agree the Peace of Passau on 31 July 1552. This provided the basis for a general settlement through the mutual renunciation of violence to settle religious disagreements.[106]

The Peace of Augsburg

The initiative had slipped from Charles to Ferdinand, who won support through his more consistent dealings with princes and adherence to constitutional norms. This allowed Ferdinand to convert the temporary arrangements evolving since 1521 into a more stable peace, securing broad acceptance of this as necessary to preserve the cherished imperial unity.[107] The result was the agreement concluded at the 1555 Reichstag, which has entered history as the 'Religious Peace' but was known to contemporaries as the 'Religious and Profane Peace'. The differences are important. The treaty annulled the Interim and deliberately avoided any religious statement.[108] Rather than grant toleration, as was soon to be attempted in France, the peace extended political and legal rights to both Catholics and Lutherans. These privileges were part of a much longer document adjusting the Empire's police, defence and financial arrangements as parts of a comprehensive constitutional package. The key questions of authority, property and jurisdiction were encompassed by the right of Reformation (*ius Reformandi*) granted to imperial Estates to manage the church and religious affairs in their territories. Possession of church property was fixed at the date of the Peace of Passau as the Empire's 'normative year' (*Normaljahr*). Protestants accepted that the Reichskammergericht should resolve specific disputes. No imperial Estate was to transgress the property or jurisdiction of another, meaning that Catholic spiritual jurisdiction was now suspended over those territories embracing Lutheranism. Limited freedom of conscience and rights of emigration were extended to inhabitants who dissented from their territory's official faith.

These arrangements have entered history as 'he who rules decides the religion' (*cuius regio, eius religio*), though the phrase is absent from the Peace and was only coined by Joachim Stephan, a Greifswald University law professor, in 1586. They are usually credited with strengthening the Empire's supposed dualism between a weak emperor and more distinct principalities. Yet although rights were granted equally to both confessions, Catholic and Lutheran, they were distributed unevenly along the status hierarchy among imperial Estates. Regardless of faith, imperial cities lacked the full right of Reformation, as they were obliged to stick to whichever faith they had adopted by 1555. The imperial knights were excluded, while it was uncertain how far counts enjoyed the same powers as princes to change their subjects' faith. In short, the Reformation's political outcome reinforced the Empire's existing development towards a mixed monarchy where the emperor shared power to differing degrees with a complex hierarchy of imperial Estates.

The imperial church was covered by a special clause known as the Ecclesiastical Reservation, because it obliged all incumbent bishops who converted from Catholicism to stand down, whilst also ruling that Protestants were ineligible for election as church princes. These restrictions were modified by Ferdinand's Declaration, issued on his own authority separate from the Peace, which extended toleration to Protestant minorities in the imperial church lands.

Apart from Ferdinand's Declaration, the Peace was collectively 'owned' by all imperial Estates, setting it apart from other western European settlements. Whereas other monarchies became confessionalized through identification with a single, official faith, the Empire remained simply Christian, while the legal position of Jews remained unaffected. This was potentially a source of great strength, since the autonomy and identity of both major religions rested on shared rights guaranteed by the confessionally neutral constitutional order. There was, however, a price: a modern separation of church and state was impossible, and religion remained integral to imperial politics. Formal political action remained open-ended: the Catholic majority ruling of the 1529 Reichstag had remained unenforceable, and it now appeared that future majority decisions would remain provisional until those in favour won acceptance from dissenters. The real decision of 1552–5 was the mutual renunciation of violence by the imperial Estates as part of this process.[109]

The Outcome beyond Germany

Most accounts of the Reformation in the Empire stop at this point, interpreting developments as simply 'German' history. Yet all the major reformers thought in terms of a single, universal church, while the Empire was still much bigger than just Germany. The Peace of Augsburg settled matters between the emperor and those parts of the Empire that had acquired the status of imperial Estates during the late fifteenth-century constitutional reforms. The largest Estates were those areas under direct Habsburg rule in Austria and Burgundy, meaning that the imperial family shared the same rights granted to other princes. The treaties of Passau (1552) and Augsburg (1555) did not alter the Burgundian Treaty, which was part of the package of measures that Charles secured at the Armoured Reichstag in 1548. This assigned the Burgundian lands to his son, the future Philip II of Spain, who retained them when Charles partitioned his entire inheritance into Spanish and Austrian branches across 1551–8. As an imperial prince, Philip exercised his right of Reformation to instruct his Burgundian subjects to remain Catholic, but his violent methods contributed to what became the Dutch Revolt after 1566, leading to the eventual independence of the northern provinces (see pp. 228–9 and 594–8).

Bohemian religious affairs continued along their own route, reflecting that kingdom's special place within the imperial constitution. The 1436 *Compacta* had been revised as the Treaty of Kuttenberg in 1485, guaranteeing the Utraquists autonomy at parish level through the appointment of their own priests, while forbidding lords to dictate their peasants' faith. This arrangement prefigured that at Augsburg seventy years later in that it accepted only two confessions (in this case, Catholicism and Utraquism), whilst denying rights to dissenting minorities like the Bohemian Brethren. The Treaty of Kuttenberg was confirmed in 1512 and accepted by Ferdinand I when he became Bohemian king in 1526. For outsiders, Utraquists remained tainted by Hussite subversion and no one saw Kuttenberg as a desirable model for domestic religious peace.[110] Yet the agreement remained legally binding despite the Peace of Augsburg, thanks to Bohemia's political autonomy and the Habsburgs' need to retain support amongst the Bohemian nobility. The spread of Lutheranism among German-speakers during the 1570s added to the kingdom's religious pluralism. In his capacity as Bohemian king, Maximilian II gave oral sanction to the *confessio Bohemica* agreed between Utraquists, Lutherans and the Bohemian Brethren in 1575. Written confirmation was later extorted from his successor Rudolf II in 1609 in the form of the Letter of Majesty allowing dissenters to establish parallel administrative and ecclesiastical institutions. Although this was overturned during the Thirty Years War, the distinct course of Bohemian religious developments reinforced that kingdom's autonomous place within the Empire.

The Reformation also strengthened similar political trends amongst the Swiss, who were still redefining their relationship to the Empire when the religious crisis broke. Theological differences reinforced this, because Swiss evangelicals followed their own reformer, Huldrych Zwingli, rather than Luther.[111] The Swiss agreed their own version of *cuius regio, eius religio* in 1529, resolving the question of authority in favour of the cantonal governments. This collapsed in 1531, but the Catholic victory in the ensuing civil war ended Protestant expansion in the Confederation's core regions. Protestants conceded legal guarantees for Catholic minorities in the condominia, the lands jointly administered by two or more cantons. Protestant minorities belatedly secured equivalent rights after another brief war in 1712. Like Bohemia, Switzerland was able to pursue its own path, because it already enjoyed considerable political autonomy, and remained outside the institutions created by imperial reform. The common heritage of the Empire is nonetheless apparent in the broad similarity of political and legal solutions to the problem of religious division.

Imperial Italy also lay largely outside the new common institutions, but was bound more closely to the Empire through the Habsburgs' possession of Milan, as well as their acquisition through Spain of Naples and Sicily to the south. Itinerant evangelical preachers drew huge crowds, while senior clerics like Cardinal Contarini conceded the need for reform. The Italian Wars since 1494 were widely interpreted as a sign of divine displeasure and added to the sense of urgency. Charles V pressured a succession of popes to respond positively to the Protestant criticism of the Italian church. However, he remained within his interpretation of the Two Swords doctrine. After theologians failed to resolve their difference during talks at the 1541 Regensburg Reichstag, Charles allowed Pope Paul III to enforce Catholicism in Italy through the Inquisition and the new Jesuit Order.[112]

The Italian principalities were excluded from the Peace of Augsburg, because they were not imperial Estates, except the duchy of Savoy, which had been incorporated within the German kingdom during the fourteenth century. However, Savoy refrained from direct engagement in the events leading to Augsburg, pursuing instead its own, more western European-style settlement towards the Waldensian communities that had persisted in its Alpine and Piedmontese territories since the late twelfth century and had been reinvigorated through contact with Swiss reformers after 1532. The duke of Savoy granted special dispensation to designated villages in the Peace of Cavour on 5 June 1561, and allowed exiles to return provided the Waldensians refrained from proselytizing.[113] This agreement was close to those adopted in France after 1562 and proved equally unstable, especially because the duke remained susceptible to pressure from other Catholic monarchs to renew persecution. The persistence of at least some form of toleration nonetheless contributed to the generally positive impression among German Protestant princes, who continued to regard the duke as a potential ally into the seventeenth century.

RELIGION AND IMPERIAL POLITICS AFTER 1555

Preserving the Augsburg Settlement

The Peace of Augsburg suffered from the same divergence of interpretation undermining the earlier agreement at Speyer in 1526, though it survived far longer without serious trouble. Catholics regarded it as limiting further encroachments on their church, while Protestants believed the legal protection licensed the continued expansion of their own religion. Many now openly embraced Lutheranism by reforming clergy and churches in their territories along evangelical lines. The basic religious balance within Germany was complete by the late 1550s, at which point Lutheranism had been officially adopted in around 50 principalities and counties and three dozen imperial cities. These included some very substantial territories, notably the electorates of Saxony, Brandenburg and the Palatinate, as well as most of the old, established princely houses: the Ernestine Saxons, all branches of Hessen, the Franconian Hohenzollerns in Ansbach and what became known as Bayreuth, as well as Württemberg, Holstein, Mecklenburg, Pomerania, Anhalt, and the majority of Westphalian and Lower Saxon counties.

Catholicism was reduced in Germany to only three large principalities: Lorraine, which was already semi-autonomous, Bavaria and Austria, which was by far the largest principality in the Empire. Elsewhere, Catholicism held out in the small counties of the south-west and in two-fifths of the imperial cities. However, since the numerous (but individually fairly small) church lands were reserved for them, Catholics still ruled around 200 imperial Estates, giving them a decisive majority in the Empire's common institutions.

Lutherans did not establish any national organizations. Instead, each prince or city council assumed the powers formerly exercised by a Catholic bishop in their territory. In practice, these powers were entrusted to church councils, considerably expanding the scope of territorial administration and increasing its presence at parish level. Catholic authorities implemented similar reforms in their own lands, though they still accepted the spiritual jurisdiction of their bishops.

Regardless of belief, all secular and ecclesiastical authorities pursued similar policies of 'confessionalization' intended to impose the official faith of their territory through education, improved clerical supervision and more intensive 'visitations' to probe individual belief and monitor religious practices.[114] Such measures were far from universally effective. Heterodoxy and dissent persisted, while there were often considerable discrepancies between outward conformity and inner belief. Many people simply adopted a pragmatic approach, embracing those beliefs and practices that made most sense to their own circumstances.[115] Nonetheless, confessionalization initially helped preserve the Augsburg settlement by directing official energies inwards and away from activities likely to cause friction with neighbouring territories.

Ferdinand I and his successor Maximilian II worked hard to maintain the peace through good personal relations with influential princes, not least since consensus was in their own interests in the face of the constant Ottoman threat to their own possessions. Moreover, the benefits of peace were soon clear to all, as first France and then the Netherlands descended into violent religious civil war after the 1560s. Most German observers were horrified by such atrocities as the St Bartholomew's Day massacre in France in August 1572, and urged a culture of self-restraint.[116] Moreover, unlike France, where the monarchy was a participant in the struggles, the Empire remained a neutral, cross-confessional legal framework. Lutherans and Catholics might disagree, but they largely refrained from criticizing the Empire since their own rights and status derived from imperial law. The later sixteenth century saw a strong 'irenic' current, providing additional arguments to bridge religious divisions in favour of preserving political harmony.[117]

Confessional and Political Tension

Three developments challenged harmony after 1555. One was the emergence of Calvinism during the 1560s. Calvinists distinguished themselves from Lutherans theologically, yet considered they were simply continuing Luther's 'Reformation of the Word' with their own moral 'Reformation of Life'.[118] Calvinism made most of its converts in the Empire among the aristocracy, unlike the French Huguenots and English Puritans, who evolved into more genuinely popular movements. Apart from Emden in East Frisia, which adopted a Presbyterian structure, Calvinism spread through its acceptance by Lutheran princes who then used their right of Reformation and the territorial church to impose the new faith on their subjects. The first and most significant conversion was the elector Palatine, who abandoned Lutheranism in 1559. Calvinism slowly gained ground from the 1580s, including the conversion of the landgrave of Hessen-Kassel (1604) and the elector of Brandenburg (1613), but had been adopted by only 28 territories, including a single city (Bremen) by 1618.[119]

Lutherans increasingly resented these inroads into their own faith, but minimized the differences to preserve the Peace of Augsburg. The elector Palatine, as self-appointed Calvinist leader, promoted his own, narrow form of irenicism to remain within the Peace by finding common ground with Lutherans. Internally, the Palatine government remained dominated by Calvinists who bullied the largely Lutheran population, persecuted Jews and refused dialogue with Catholics.[120] Calvinism threatened the peace by seemingly adding substance to Catholic zealots' arguments that no Protestant could be trusted. More seriously, the elector Palatine deliberately fanned fears of Catholic plots to persuade Lutherans to accept his leadership and his demands for constitutional change. The Palatinate had lost influence to Bavaria, ruled by a rival branch of the same Wittelsbach family who had conquered much of its territory in 1504 and who had remained Catholic.[121] The elector Palatine's demand for religious parity in imperial institutions promised not merely to remove the inbuilt Catholic majority, but also to level some of the status distinctions that currently disadvantaged the minor princes and aristocrats who formed the bulk of his political clientele. A hierarchy dominated by the electors and a few senior princes would be replaced by a political structure of two confessional blocs, with that of the Protestants firmly under Palatine leadership.

Developments in the imperial church represented a second challenge to peace.[122] Protestant princes and nobles were not prepared to forgo the benefits of engagement in the imperial church, which still offered around 1,000 lucrative benefices for cathedral canons, as well as the considerable political influence through the 50 bishoprics and 80-odd abbeys recognized as imperial Estates. Although these were reserved for Catholics in 1555, Ferdinand's Declaration extended toleration to individual

Protestants living in church territories. Under this protection, Protestant nobles gained majorities in several important chapters, enabling them to elect their own candidates on the death of each Catholic bishop. Maximilian II and Rudolf II refused to accept these men as imperial princes, but tolerated them as 'administrators' to preserve peace. Ten sees passed this way into Protestant hands, including the substantial archbishoprics of Magdeburg and Bremen. The duke of Bavaria meanwhile promoted his relations in the church lands as a means of pushing his own family as Catholic champions in the Empire. Thanks to Spanish support, Bavaria blocked a Calvinist takeover of Cologne in 1583, establishing a Bavarian monopoly of this important archbishopric lasting until 1761. To advance these objectives, Bavaria pushed the emperor to deny the Protestant administrators rights of imperial Estates.

The dispute over the ecclesiastical imperial Estates was complicated by problems surrounding mediate church property, such as monasteries under secular jurisdiction. Enforcement of the 1552 normative year was hindered by the often confused legal arrangements, involving rights and assets which had been pawned or were shared by several lords. The Peace of Augsburg charged the Reichskammergericht with resolving any disputes by entrusting cases to bipartisan panels composed equally of Lutheran and Catholic judges. The court made sincere efforts to judge according to law, encountering few complaints until cases became increasingly politicized through Palatine and Bavarian propaganda during the later sixteenth century.

It is likely that the Peace would have survived the challenge of both Calvinism and disputes over the imperial church had the Habsburg monarchy not encountered serious difficulties of its own around 1600. Charles's partition of his inheritance left Austria with the imperial title, but cut off from Spain's vast resources. Problems were compounded by a further internal partition creating three separate Austrian lines in 1564: the Tirolean branch (based in Innsbruck), that of Inner Austria, or Styria (in Graz), and the main line based in Vienna. Each branch traded limited toleration for cash grants from the largely Lutheran nobility who dominated their provincial assemblies. Lutheran nobles in turn used their powers over parish churches to install Protestant pastors and encourage their tenants to adopt their faith. Around three-quarters of Habsburg subjects followed some kind of Protestantism by the time the dynasty began to reverse this by restricting court and military appointments to loyal Catholics during the 1590s.[123] Coordination of this roll-back broke down amidst bankruptcy following the protracted and unsuccessful Long Turkish War (1593–1606) and subsequent quarrelling amongst Rudolf II's relations over his succession, leading to renewed concessions to Protestant nobles in Bohemia and parts of Austria.

The distraction created a political vacuum in Germany, adding to anxiety fanned by extremists. The Palatinate was finally able to rally sufficient support to form the Protestant Union in 1608, answered the following year by the Bavarian-led Catholic League. Despite these ominous developments, support for the Augsburg settlement remained strong among moderate Catholics and most Lutherans, and there was no inevitable slide towards war.[124]

The Thirty Years War

The famous Defenestration of Prague on 23 May 1618 was the work of a small group of disaffected Bohemian aristocrats who felt their gains from the Letter of Majesty were being eroded by the Habsburgs' practice of restricting government appointments to Catholics. The aristocrats acted independently of the Protestant Union, which was in a state of near collapse. By throwing three Habsburg officials from a window in Prague castle, the Defenestrators hoped to force the moderate majority to take sides in their dispute with the dynasty.[125]

The Defenestrators presented their cause as common for all Protestants. Confessionalization had forged new connections across Europe, especially among radicals of the same faith. Militants tended to interpret events in providential terms, feeling personally summoned by God and believing their religious goals were almost within reach. Setbacks were interpreted as tests of faith. Such zealots were a minority within all confessional groups, confined mainly to exiles, clergy and external observers frustrated with their own government's policies. Militants dominated public discussions, but rarely influenced decision-making directly. Most people were more moderate, wanting to advance their faith by pragmatic and peaceful means.[126]

These insights explain the fragility of confessionally based alliances during the ensuing conflict. Contrary to popular memory, military operations did not escape political control, but remained tied to negotiations that continued almost unbroken throughout the war. All belligerents fought as members of complex, often delicate coalitions and knew that peace would entail compromise. Generals were asked to achieve a position of strength so that concessions would appear magnanimous gestures rather than signs of weakness, which could endanger the established authorities and cause further problems.[127]

The war escalated through the failure to contain successive crises. The initial revolt widened through the decision of Elector Palatine Frederick V, one of the few genuinely militant leaders, to accept the rebels' offer of the Bohemian crown in 1619. This set him against the Austrian Habsburgs, who now received substantial Bavarian support. Outsiders were drawn in. Spain aided Austria in the hope that assistance against its own Dutch rebels would follow a swift victory in the Empire. The Dutch, English and French sent men and money to help Bohemia and the Palatinate, largely because they saw war in the Empire as a useful way of distracting Spain.

Habsburg policy became more determined with Ferdinand II's accession in 1619, because he regarded his opponents as rebels who forfeited their constitutional rights. The comprehensive victory at White Mountain, outside Prague, in November 1620, allowed him to start the largest transfer of private property in central Europe prior to the Communist land seizures after 1945. Assets were redistributed from defeated rebels to Habsburg loyalists. Following further victories in western Germany, this policy was extended across the Empire, culminating in the transfer of Frederick V's lands and titles to Duke Maximilian of Bavaria in 1623. The war was essentially over, though Danish intervention reignited it in May 1625, shifting the focus to northern Germany. Danish defeats by 1629 merely extended the area covered by Ferdinand's policy of redistribution and reward.[128]

Ferdinand sought a comprehensive settlement, securing Danish acceptance through generous terms, but overreaching himself by issuing the Edict of Restitution in March 1629. This sought to resolve the ambiguities in the Peace of Augsburg by asserting a narrowly Catholic interpretation of the disputed terms, which included excluding Calvinists from legal protection and ordering Protestants to return all church lands usurped since 1552. The Edict was widely condemned, even by many Catholics who felt Ferdinand had exceeded his prerogatives by issuing it as a definitive verdict for immediate enforcement, rather than as guidelines to assist the imperial courts in resolving disputes case by case. Coming after the substantial redistribution of land to Habsburg supporters, Restitution appeared a further step towards converting the Empire into a more centralized monarchy. Despite their confessional differences, the electors closed ranks at their congress in Regensburg in 1630 to block the emperor's bid to have his son Ferdinand III made king of the Romans, and to force him to dismiss his controversial general, Albrecht von Wallenstein, and reduce the expensive imperial army.[129]

Any hope that negotiations might ease tensions over Restitution were wrecked by the Swedish invasion in June 1630. Sweden had its own security and economic reasons for intervention, which it only subsequently officially masked as saving German Protestants from Ferdinand's Counter-Reformation. The religious dimension grew pronounced following the death of Sweden's king Gustavus Adolphus at the battle of Lützen in November 1632. The site later became a virtual shrine after locals celebrated the battle's bicentenary, and the subsequent hagiography profoundly influenced later interpretations of the Thirty Years War as a religious conflict.[130] At the time, though, Sweden legitimated its involvement principally as defending the Palatinate's more aristocratic interpretation of the imperial constitution, since this would weaken Habsburg management of the Empire. Sweden's operations were facilitated by the exiled rebels and those imperial Estates most threatened by Ferdinand's edict. This ensured that the new round of conflict was a continuation of that which began in 1618 and not an entirely separate war as Ferdinand claimed.

German support grew after Sweden's victory at Breitenfeld in September 1631 made it a credible ally. Subsequent successes enabled Sweden to copy Ferdinand II's methods and redistribute captured imperial church lands to its allies. Gustavus Adolphus clearly intended usurping constitutional structures to tie these allies within a new Swedish imperial system, though it is not entirely clear how far he intended to displace the emperor. His death in 1632 and subsequent Swedish defeats forced these ambitions to be scaled back. The imperial victory at Nördlingen in September 1634 gave Ferdinand another chance to make 'peace with honour' through concessions to moderate Lutheran states like Saxony. He agreed the Peace of Prague in May 1635, suspending the Edict and revising the normative year to 1627, allowing

Lutherans to keep many of the church lands acquired since 1552, though not all those they had held in 1618. The need to retain Bavarian support meant the Palatinate's exclusion from the amnesty, along with several other important principalities. These exclusions allowed Sweden to claim it was still fighting to restore 'German freedom'.

Opportunities slipped from Ferdinand's grasp as he delegated negotiations with Sweden to Saxony, while he embarked on ill-advised support for Spain in its new war with France.[131] France had sponsored Austria's opponents since 1625 and now moved over to direct involvement. The full impact was delayed until France and Sweden agreed a more coordinated strategy in 1642, now concentrating on forcing a succession of pro-imperial principalities into neutrality. The war was channelled into fewer areas, but fought with desperate intensity, contributing to the lasting impression of all-destructive fury.

The Peace of Westphalia

The Westphalian towns of Münster and Osnabrück were declared neutral in 1643 as venues for a peace congress intended to resolve the Thirty Years War in the Empire, Spain's struggle with the Dutch rebels, which had resumed in 1621, and the Franco-Spanish war waged since 1635. Military operations continued as the belligerents fought to improve their bargaining positions. Spain eventually accepted Dutch independence in a treaty concluded in Münster in May 1648, but the Franco-Spanish war continued for another 11 years, because both powers overestimated their chances of future military successes.

However, the diplomats successfully concluded an end to the Empire's war in two treaties negotiated in Münster and Osnabrück and signed simultaneously on 24 October 1648, known respectively from the abbreviations of their Latin titles as IPM and IPO.[132] Together with the first peace of Münster, the two treaties formed the Peace of Westphalia, which was both an international agreement and a revision to the Empire's constitution. France and Sweden received territorial compensation, but the Peace neither made the princes independent sovereigns nor reduced the Empire to a weak confederation. Instead, the existing trend towards a mixed monarchy continued. This can be seen by examining the adjustments to the place of religion in imperial politics.

The Peace of Augsburg was renewed but also revised by adjusting the normative year to 1624, agreed as a compromise. This allowed Catholics to recover some church lands, but not as many as they would have done had either the Edict of Restitution or the Peace of Prague been fully implemented.[133] Calvinism was included alongside Lutheranism and Catholicism, but other faiths remained excluded, except for the Jews' existing privileges that remained unaffected. Contrary to the later perception that Westphalia widened princely powers, Article V of the IPO in fact significantly curtailed the right of Reformation granted at Augsburg by removing the power of imperial Estates to change their subjects' faith. Henceforth, the official faith of each territory was permanently fixed as it had existed in the new normative year of 1624. Individual freedoms were extended to ease implementation of this rule by protecting dissenters from discrimination over emigration, education, marriage, burial and worship. Violence was again renounced in favour of arbitration through the Empire's judicial system. The Palatine programme of constitutional change was definitively rejected. Fixing each territory's official religious identity cemented the permanent Catholic majority in imperial institutions. However, new voting arrangements (known as *itio in partes*) were introduced in the Reichstag to allow that body to debate as two confessional bodies (*corpora*) if religious matters had to be discussed.[134]

Tension and Toleration after 1648

From this review of the key terms, it is obvious that the Westphalian settlement did not remove religion from imperial politics, still less inaugurate a fully secular international order, but it did signal the defeat of militant confessionalism. Imperial Estates lodged 750 official complaints at breaches of the religious terms between 1648 and 1803, but virtually all these concerned jurisdictions and possessions. Many were relatively trivial: a fifth involved individual farms or houses, and only 5 per cent were about entire districts.[135] Church and state had not been separated, but doctrinal issues had been quarantined to allow the Empire's courts to settle 'religious' disputes like other disagreements over demarcating legal rights and privileges. None of the 74 allegations of religious bias in Reichshofrat judgements were upheld by reviews conducted by the Reichstag between 1663 and 1788.[136]

Only three issues proved significantly difficult. One concerned

Protestant anxiety at the Catholic revival after 1648. Calvinism's political defeat during the Thirty Years War compounded its inability to attract further influential adherents after the conversion of the elector of Brandenburg in 1613. Likewise, Lutheranism lost ground, apart from new grass-roots activism known as Pietism, which was generally viewed with suspicion by the authorities, except in Prussia.[137] By contrast, even minor Catholic abbeys embarked on massive building and cultural projects associated with the baroque, while the emperor's wealth and prestige (all signs he had *not* lost the war) attracted nobles from across the Empire into his service. Competition for imperial favour encouraged 31 leading princes to convert to Catholicism between 1651 and 1769, including Elector Friedrich August I 'the Strong' of Saxony in 1697, followed by his son in 1712. Saxony, birthplace of Protestantism, was now under Catholic rule.[138] Each major conversion caused momentary tension, but the constitutional problems were resolved fairly easily, indicating the Empire's continued flexibility into the eighteenth century. The revised normative-year rules prevented princes from requiring their subjects to follow their new faith. Instead, the ruling family was allowed to worship in their palace chapel, but had to sign documents known as *Reversalien* guaranteeing the unimpeded management of their Lutheran territorial church by officials sworn to uphold these arrangements regardless of their prince's own beliefs. The agreements were usually guaranteed by the territorial assembly and often other Protestant princes, extending the basis upon which appeals could be lodged with the imperial courts in the event of disputes.[139]

Despite the Reversalien, many Protestants suspected princes of secretly promoting Catholicism through the priests attached to the court chapel. This helps explain the furore surrounding developments in the Palatinate, which formed a second major difficulty. On the extinction of the Calvinist ruling line, the Palatinate passed to a junior, Catholic branch of the Wittelsbachs in 1685. The new elector collaborated with the French occupying his lands during the Nine Years War (1688–97) to reintroduce Catholicism. France then secured international recognition for the changes as part of the Peace of Rijswijk in 1697, despite this breaching the 1624 normative year (which France, as a guarantor of the Westphalian settlement, was supposed to uphold). The impact was magnified by its coincidence with the conversion of the Saxon elector to Catholicism and Louis XIV's expulsion of the

Huguenots from France, where their religious rights had been revoked in 1685. The depth of concern is apparent from the fact that 258 of the 750 official complaints were about this one issue.

The response opened the third major difficulty, because Protestants invoked their right to 'debate in parts' by splitting the Reichstag into two confessional groups. While legal under the post-1648 constitution, this threatened to deadlock debate at a time when the Empire needed to respond to the outbreak of the Great Northern War (1700–1721) and the looming dispute over the Spanish inheritance, which embroiled it directly in renewed war with France (1701–14). Despite the intensity of public discussion, there was little political appetite to abandon established ways of working in the Reichstag and other institutions. The Protestants did meet separately as a *Corpus Evangelicorum* from 1712 to 1725, 1750 to 1769, and 1774 to 1778, but continued to participate throughout in the other imperial institutions. The Catholics regarded existing structures as satisfactory and never convened a separate body. The Protestant Corpus was hamstrung by a struggle over its leadership between Prussia, Hanover and Saxony (whose elector, despite becoming a Catholic, refused to relinquish his leadership). The practice of formally debating in parts was used only four times (1727, 1758, 1761 and 1764), largely as a tactical device for Prussia to hinder Habsburg management of the Empire. In the longer term, Prussian manipulation of religious issues eroded their potential to cause trouble and by the late eighteenth century the established constitution was regarded as sufficient protection for religious freedoms.[140]

The Westphalian settlement also proved successful in resolving more local, everyday disputes, again indicating how the Empire remained meaningful to its inhabitants into early modernity. The new normative year left Brandenburg, the Palatinate, several Lower Rhenish principalities, and the bishoprics of Osnabrück, Lübeck and Hildesheim as confessionally mixed. Four imperial cities had been officially bi-confessional since 1548. The IPO imposed parity in civic office and there are signs that confessional identities hardened into an 'invisible frontier' dividing each community.[141] The number of cross-confessional marriages declined in Augsburg and it was said that even Protestant and Catholic pigs had separate sties. The adoption by Catholics of the Gregorian calendar in 1584 had placed them ten days ahead of their Protestant neighbours, who only caught up in 1700. However, the riots accompanying the calendar's adoption were not repeated. Inhabitants might be acutely aware of subtle differences, but they now preferred court cases to violent protest.

Clergy, especially in border areas, placed innumerable petty obstacles in the way of ordinary folk exercising their religious freedoms. Mixed marriages were regarded as divided houses, and individuals were often pressured to convert. Nonetheless, pragmatism generally prevailed. A fifth of marriages in Osnabrück were cross-confessional, while Protestants joined Catholic religious processions and in a few communities different congregations even shared the same church. Official policy remained toleration not tolerance, suffering minorities as a political and legal necessity. Attitudes did change during the later eighteenth century, notably following Joseph II's patent in 1781, which allowed greater equality and was adopted by most other German governments between 1785 and the 1840s.

THE IMPERIAL CHURCH DURING EARLY MODERNITY

Size

The register prepared for the 1521 Reichstag in Worms recorded 3 ecclesiastical electors, 4 archbishops, 46 bishops and 83 lesser prelates, compared to 180 secular lords. By 1792 only 3 electors, 1 archbishop, 29 bishops and prince abbots, and 40 prelates remained, alongside 165 secular Estates. This decline is only partly attributable to the Reformation, which merely accelerated the existing trend for secular rulers to incorporate the material assets of church fiefs within their own territories. Many of the ecclesiastical Estates listed in the 1521 register were already disappearing this way, including 15 bishoprics. While the Reformation added new theological arguments for this, political changes associated with imperial reform were equally important, because they tied the status of imperial Estates more clearly to imperial fiscal and military obligations. Many prelates voluntarily accepted incorporation within secular jurisdiction in the hope of escaping these obligations.[142] Thus, all 'secularization' up to 1552 involved a reduction from immediate to mediate status by removing a fief's political rights. By contrast, the

Peace of Westphalia sanctioned the secularization of two archbishoprics and six bishoprics by converting them into secular duchies with full political rights and obligations.

Movement was not only in one direction. Some ecclesiastical territories emancipated themselves from secular influence, notably the bishopric of Speyer that had been under the Palatinate's protection from 1396 to 1552, though it did lose all its mediate monasteries and two-thirds of its churches and benefices in the process. Twelve prelates were promoted to princely rank, while a few mediate monasteries bought out their secular protectors to become full immediate Estates.[143]

As Speyer's experience indicates, losses amongst mediate church property were far greater. Protestant rulers in the Palatinate, Württemberg, Hessen, Ansbach and elsewhere suppressed religious houses that lacked full immediacy yet had been vibrant parts of Catholic cultural and political life – often for centuries. Nonetheless, many Catholic institutions survived in Protestant territories. Magdeburg retained half its convents and a fifth of its monasteries after its conversion to a secular duchy by the Peace of Westphalia. The bishopric of Lübeck even remained part of the imperial church, despite its official designation as a Lutheran territory permanently assigned to Holstein-Gottorp. Three imperial convents likewise remained within the imperial church as Lutheran institutions, because Protestant princely families valued them for their unmarried daughters. Altogether, there were still 78 mediate foundations and 209 abbeys worth 2.87 million florins in annual revenue east of the Rhine in 1802, in addition to hundreds of monasteries, mainly in Catholic territories. The 73 immediate ecclesiastical Estates controlled 95,000 square kilometres, with nearly 3.2 million subjects generating 18.16 million florins of annual revenue.[144]

Social Composition

This vast wealth extended the political influence of the Empire's aristocracy, which held virtually all the roughly one thousand cathedral and abbey benefices and dominated the imperial church. The geographical distribution of church lands reflected their origins in the areas of densest population, which had supported higher concentrations of lordships since the Middle Ages. The majority of the counts and knights were in the same regions as the surviving church lands:

Westphalia, the Rhineland, and the Upper Rhine–Main nexus across Swabia and Franconia. Election as bishop automatically elevated the successful candidate to full princely rank, and so was especially attractive for the knights who otherwise remained disadvantaged by the Empire's hierarchical distribution of political rights. The knights provided a third of all early modern prince-bishops, with the Schönborn family being the most successful, twice securing election in the premier see of Mainz.[145] Aristocratic domination was already well advanced in the Middle Ages and was strengthened during early modernity by additional barriers, such as requiring canons to prove they had 16 noble ancestors. Of the 166 archbishops in the Empire between 900 and 1500, only 4 are known to have been commoners, while there were only 120 known commoners among the 2,074 German bishops from the seventh to fifteenth centuries. This proportion remained broadly the same with 332 nobles, 10 commoners and 5 foreigners serving as archbishops or bishops between 1500 and 1803.[146]

Unfortunately for the knights and counts, the princes also had long pedigrees. The Wittelsbachs emerged as strong contenders to be archbishops or bishops, especially once Protestants officially disqualified themselves by their faith after 1555. The papacy relaxed the rules prohibiting the accumulation of bishoprics to prevent these falling into Protestant hands. The Bavarian Duke Ernst secured Cologne and four bishoprics in the late sixteenth century, while his relation Clemens August was known as 'Mr Five Churches' for securing a similar number around 150 years later.[147] The accumulation of bishoprics was often welcomed by cathedral canons, because it could link a weaker bishopric to a more powerful one, such as Münster to Cologne, or allow neighbours to cooperate, like Bamberg and Würzburg.

Such unions remained temporary with each bishopric retaining its own administration. This apparent failure to participate in wider institutional development attracted criticism after 1648, especially from Protestants and Enlightened thinkers who complained about the 'dead hand' of the church tying up valuable resources that might be put to better uses. These arguments for renewed secularization grew stronger after 1740, because they appeared to offer a way to defuse Austro-Prussian tension, or to improve the viability of the middling principalities, all at the expense of their ecclesiastical neighbours. Some later historians accepted this discussion at face value and presented the imperial church as a fossilized medieval relic.[148] In practice, the internal development of the church lands was broadly similar to that of the secular territories and included many of the measures advocated by Enlightened thinkers. Unfortunately, this meant the church lands were also not the benevolent backwaters claimed by some Catholics, as all of them established their own armies and many participated in the same European wars as the secular princes.[149]

Political reform was supplemented by a grass-roots movement for spiritual renewal across Catholic Germany from the 1760s. This faltered in the 1770s, but recovered renewed vigour in response to Joseph II's suppression of 700 mediate monasteries in the Habsburg lands and curtailment of the spiritual jurisdiction of several south German prince-bishops after 1782.[150] Renewal and reform became known as Febronism after the pseudonym adopted by the Trier suffragan bishop Nikolaus von Hontheim in a manifesto published in 1763. Hontheim asked the pope to settle the remaining Protestant Gravamina, or formal complaints, to permit the reunification of all German Christians within a national church. The anti-papal element deepened as several bishops called for an end to all-papal jurisdiction and the recall of the papal nuncios in Vienna, Cologne and Luzern. This contributed to the alienation of all those whom Febronism hoped to enlist as supporters, including the largely conservative Catholic peasantry who opposed many of the bishops' social reforms. The association of Febronist bishops with Prussia's League of Princes in 1785 angered Joseph II and left the imperial church politically vulnerable by the outbreak of the French Revolutionary Wars in 1792.[151]

Carl Theodor von Dalberg was prominent in these efforts to defend the imperial church. He came from a family of imperial knights that had owned estates between Speyer and Oppenheim since the fourteenth century and was related to the influential Metternich, Stadion and von der Leyen families. Having been a cathedral canon for ten years, Dalberg rose in the service of the elector of Mainz to become his successor as imperial arch-chancellor and head of the Empire's church in 1802. His promotion came precisely at a time when the world he loved was coming to an end through the demise of the three interrelated institutions of the imperial church, imperial knights and imperial constitution. Dalberg struggled amidst rapidly changing circumstances to preserve the old order, remaining optimistic (his critics say naive) despite what

appear with hindsight to have been impossible odds. Napoleon Bonaparte used him to legitimate his reorganization of Germany between
1802 and 1806. Dalberg's lavish flattery of Napoleon did nothing to
deflect accusations of treachery and led to his being made a scapegoat
for the end of the Empire.[152]

In fact, the imperial church's fate was sealed by arrangements under
the Peace of Campo Formio accompanying Austria's surrender of the
left bank of the Rhine to France in 1797. Secular princes who lost possessions were to be compensated at the expense of church lands east of
the Rhine. The Habsburgs hoped to limit the damage, but the process
gathered its own momentum in the wake of further French victories
culminating in a final, extensive wave of secularization between
1802 and 1803. This went far beyond all previous changes, irrevocably
changing the Empire by effectively destroying the imperial church.
Only Dalberg's electorate was relocated, to the former bishopric of
Regensburg, while Mergentheim and Heitersheim remained in the
hands of the Teutonic Order and Knights of St John as preserves of the
German aristocracy. The rest of the imperial church passed into secular
hands, including its mediate properties. Austria alone seized property
worth 15 million florins, while Württemberg suppressed 95 abbeys,
converting them into barracks, schools, mental hospitals, government
offices and palaces to accommodate the secular lords of the lands it had
also annexed by 1806. The former Augustinian monastery at Obern-
dorf became an arms factory, later famous for producing the Mauser
rifle.[153] Property, artworks and records were scattered or destroyed,
and 18 Catholic universities closed, though most of the wealth was
used initially to provide pensions for the former imperial clergy.[154]

Dalberg saved his principality by acting as a figurehead of the
16 princes who left the Empire through a pact with Napoleon in July
1806, precipitating Emperor Francis II's abdication three weeks later
(see Plate 31). Dalberg was rewarded with additional territory and the
title of Grand Duke of Frankfurt, but was obliged to accept Napoleon's
stepson Eugène de Beauharnais as his designated successor. Austria
assumed the Teutonic Grand Master title, but the Knights of St John were
eliminated as a political element entirely in 1805. Dalberg became the
Empire's executor, working hard to reorganize the Catholic church and
redefine its relations to the now sovereign principalities. He was hindered by laws passed by the Reichstag in 1803 exempting Austria and

Prussia from future imperial concordats with the papacy. Prussia annexed most of the Westphalian bishoprics in 1802, reorganizing them without reference to the pope. Meanwhile, the papacy rebuffed Dalberg's overtures on behalf of the rest of the Empire after 1803, because it saw him as continuing Febronism. Bavaria fanned papal suspicions, hoping as it did to obtain the autonomy enjoyed by Austria and Prussia. Other princes made their own arrangements, reducing Dalberg's supporters to those whose lands were too small or poor to support their own bishops. The project failed. Dalberg's death in 1817 cleared the way for the papacy to agree concordats with the surviving sovereign states, thereby participating in the Empire's demise by adjusting to the federalization of Germany, which was left without a national church.[155] However, this story was not simply one of loss, since the imperial church's destruction freed energies and resources that fuelled the dynamism of German Catholicism in the nineteenth century.

3

Sovereignty

THE PILLARS OF HERCULES

Not Beyond Metz

For three miserable months in the autumn of 1552, Charles V besieged Metz with the largest army he ever commanded. The French had taken the city five months earlier in agreement with the Protestant princes opposing Charles's unpopular solution to the Empire's religious tension. The princes had already forced his younger brother Ferdinand to agree the Peace of Passau on 31 July. Charles needed a major victory to restore prestige. Instead, he suffered his worst defeat. With his forces reduced by disease and desertion, he finally abandoned the siege of Metz on 1 January 1553. The outcome demonstrated clear limits to imperial authority and hastened the political process culminating in the Peace of Augsburg two years later.[1]

These limits had already been marked symbolically during the siege by the French defenders, who taunted Charles by displaying an image of the imperial eagle chained between two pillars and the motto *Non ultra Metas* – a clever double pun, literally meaning 'not beyond Metz', but also 'not exceeding proper limits', since *Metas* could mean both 'Metz' and 'boundary'. The design mocked the motif invented at Charles's accession in Spain in 1516, but which drew on ideas already expressed by Dante. According to ancient legend, Hercules had marked the limits to the known world by placing pillars either side of the Straits of Gibraltar. As part of their pseudo-genealogy, Habsburg apologists claimed Hercules along with other suitable heroes as Charles's direct ancestors. In 1519 the motto *plus ultra* ('still further') was added to the device showing the two pillars to symbolize both the traditional view of the Empire as encompassing Christian civilization and the new vision associated with Spain, which was then conquering its New World imperium in Mexico and Peru (see Plate 10).

Even as this device was being prepared, it was obvious that the known world was divided into many different states. What was not yet clear was how far each was independent and whether they should interact as equals. These problems were present at the Empire's foundation, but they never developed sufficiently to render imperial pretensions entirely meaningless, or to undermine the emperor's authority within his own territories.

Byzantium

Charlemagne and Pope Leo III had established an empire in 800 that was neither singular nor the only one claiming to be Roman. Byzantium's survival for another 653 years proved fundamental in dividing Christian Europe into eastern and western political and religious spheres, leaving a legacy persisting today. In contrast to the Empire, Byzantium could legitimately claim direct continuity from ancient Rome through an unbroken line of emperors. Unlike the western emperor, who was always also a king, his Byzantine counterpart was only ever imperial. There were regencies in the east, but never interregna as in the west where there were long periods without a crowned emperor. Byzantium never evolved clear rules governing succession like those that eventually emerged in the late medieval Empire. The army, senate and people participated in varying combinations in electing eastern emperors between the fourth and ninth centuries. Successful candidates were raised upon a shield amidst acclamation of their soldiers, rather than being crowned at a church service. No more than four generations of the same family ruled prior to the Makedonian dynasty, which held power between 867 and 1056. The practice of naming a successor emerged during the tenth century, establishing hereditary rule under the Comnenians (1081–1185) and again under the Palaiologians (1259–1453).

Byzantine emperors assumed office directly. A coronation had been used since 474, but without any sacral element until this gradually appeared through western influence in the thirteenth century. The emperor was expected to rule like an Old Testament king, and, while not considered a god, he was nonetheless believed to be *like* one, ruling *Dei gratia* – by God's grace in direct pious submission to the divine will. Following Constantine's example in the fourth century, Byzantine emperors exercised overall management of their church through their appointment of the patriarch of Constantinople. Patriarchs retained moral authority and could impose penance on wayward emperors. The failure of the imperial family to remove images from worship between 717 and 843 also demonstrated limits to their direction of religious affairs. Nonetheless, they could depose obstructive patriarchs and asserted greater control of doctrine from the eleventh century, ultimately forcing their clergy into an unwilling and short-lived reunification with Rome in 1439. This combination of imperial and papal powers was condemned by westerners as *Caesaropapism*.[2]

Unlike Rome, Constantinople remained a world-class capital until the later Middle Ages. Although its population declined from a peak of about half a million in the sixth century, it still totalled 300,000 five centuries later when the Byzantine empire had 12 million inhabitants. The Great Palace, begun by Constantine and now the Topkapi, was full of marvels like mechanical lions, a self-elevating throne and a golden organ, offering a dazzling vision of imperial splendour to awestruck western visitors. Elaborate court etiquette perpetuated a sense of solid traditions despite the collapse of much of the ancient infrastructure, like the education system. Although changed substantially, the empire maintained a large standing army, bureaucracy and regular tax system – all features missing in the west. Continuity and coherence enabled Byzantium to develop what has been termed a 'grand strategy' by the seventh century. Combining diplomacy, avoidance of unnecessary risk and careful application of scarce military assets, this enabled it to survive against often formidable odds, as well as stage several impressive recoveries after serious defeats.[3]

East–west theological differences were apparent since disagreements over religious images in 794 and became more pronounced with the Gregorian drive for doctrinal uniformity. This hardened disagreements into permanent schism after 1054, with the final separation of the eastern and western Christian churches.[4] However, even zealous clerics regarded a divided Christendom and the existence of two empires with unease. Outside polemic, east–west religious tensions were largely confined to competition for the hearts and minds of east-central and northern Europeans between the ninth and twelfth centuries. Acceptance of either Latin or Greek Christianity was a crucial marker of imperial influence, and the outcome reflected the balance between the Empire and Byzantium. Pagan leaders swiftly appreciated this, manipulating imperial rivalry to enhance their own prestige and influence.

The clash was most obvious in the area of the 'Great Moravian empire', which emerged on the Empire's eastern frontier in the early ninth century, only to collapse around 907. A Byzantine missionary expedition led by Cyril and Methodius had some success there by translating the Scriptures into Slavonic in the 860s. Pope Hadrian II was obliged to accept this in order to retain the region's recognition of the Latin church. Although the Slavonic liturgy was largely expunged by Gregorianism in the eleventh century, the Croats retained it whilst still acknowledging Rome. The Ottonians succeeded in drawing Poland and Hungary into the Latin church through recognition of their rules as kings. Bulgaria, however, gravitated towards the eastern church, especially thanks to Cyril, who devised a new script (Cyrillic) enabling its population to retain their vernacular when embracing Christianity in the 890s. Kiev likewise chose Christian Orthodoxy in 988, thus spreading it to what became Russia, and was followed by Serbia in 1219, despite Byzantium's growing political problems.[5]

The Armenians were regarded in Byzantium as schismatics and used the First Crusade in 1095–6 to contact Rome and the Empire. Like his counterparts in Poland and Hungary, Prince Leo of Armenia hoped for recognition as king in return for accepting incorporation within the western political and Christian orbit. Eventually, Henry VI sent Bishop Conrad of Hildesheim to crown both Leo and Prince Amalric of Cyprus as kings under nominal imperial suzerainty in 1195. The Empire maintained intermittent contact as Armenia became a battleground between Persia and the rising Turkish empire after 1375. Seventeenth-century emperors wrote on behalf of Jesuit missionaries to persuade the Persian shah to rescind repressive laws against Christians. Although irredeemably lost, a sense of connection remained sufficiently strong for Elector Palatine Johann Wilhelm in 1698 to toy with the idea of making himself Armenian king in order to secure the region for Catholicism and elevate his family to European royalty.[6]

Religious rivalry was matched politically by the 'two emperors problem' caused by Byzantium and the Empire rejecting the ancient solution of two parallel Roman empires.[7] Each claimed exclusive pre-eminence, but neither had much appetite to assert this through war. Charlemagne conquered Istria, the last Byzantine outpost in northern Italy, between 806 and 809. Louis II tried to subordinate the remaining Byzantine and Lombard possessions in the south during the 860s, and Otto II made another serious effort a century later. Otherwise, the two empires refrained from fighting, choosing largely to ignore each other. At best, Byzantium was prepared to accept the rival western emperor as a new Theodoric, governing lands it still officially claimed as its own. Byzantine documents used the term *basileus*, translating as 'emperor', but falling short of the full 'Caesar'. Western claims to be *Imperator Romanorum* angered the Byzantine court and contributed to the repeated failure of Carolingian and Ottonian diplomatic missions. Westerners responded in kind, calling the Byzantine emperor *Rex Graecorum* and presenting Charlemagne as conqueror of the effeminate Greeks.[8]

The Byzantine empress Irene proposed a marriage alliance and even allegedly offered herself to Charlemagne after his coronation. The scheme came to nought, but the prospect of a Byzantine bride remained attractive to western emperors into the high Middle Ages as a way to assert supremacy over truculent lords by marrying way above their circle. The lure of Byzantine riches as a dowry and hopes of securing precedence ahead of the eastern empire were added inducements. Otto I followed his own imperial coronation by obtaining the Byzantine princess Theophanu for his son in 972, perhaps believing this would also consolidate his hold over southern Italy. Otto ignored pressure from his lords to send Theophanu home when it transpired she was only the niece, and not the daughter, of the Byzantine emperor. Otto III – himself half-Byzantine – sent two embassies to the east to woo a wife. Princess Zoe set out as his expectant bride, only to turn back on news of the emperor's death in 1002. Conrad II made a similar attempt on behalf of his own son Henry III, while Conrad III became the first emperor to visit Constantinople when he passed through during the Second Crusade in the late 1140s. His sister-in-law Bertha married the Byzantine emperor Manuel I in 1146, taking the Greek name Irene. Henry VI's brother, Philip of Swabia, married another Irene, daughter of the Byzantine emperor Isaac II Angelus, a year before he became German king in 1198.[9]

Western influence peaked between 1195 and 1197 when Byzantium

paid tribute to Emperor Henry VI, who simultaneously obtained formal submission from the rulers of England, Cyprus, Armenia, Syria,
Tunis and Tripoli. The tribute remained symbolic. Byzantine emperors
often paid their enemies, regarding this as a temporary expedient similar to Danegeld payments from western kings to the Vikings. The
Ottonians did the same with the Magyars in the early tenth century.
The deliberate ambiguity of these arrangements allowed each party to
present them more favourably to their followers.

Changing Byzantine attitudes reflected that empire's own fortunes.
Emperor Michael I's tacit acknowledgement of Charlemagne's imperial
status in 812 followed the defeat of his predecessor Nicephorus by the
Bulgar khan, who used his victim's skull as a drinking cup. Byzantium
became less receptive to western overtures as it managed to Christianize the Bulgars in the 860s. Bulgaria claimed its own imperial status in
direct imitation of Byzantium after 914, leading to a long war of attri-
tion, culminating in a major Byzantine victory in 1014. Emperor Basil
II blinded 14,000 Bulgarian prisoners, earning the title of the 'Bulgar
Slayer'. By the time of his death in 1025, Byzantium was twice as large
as it had been in the eighth century. This expansion proved unsustain-
able and was reversed by the serious defeat by the Seljuk Turks at
Manzikert in 1071. The Crusades, launched nominally to aid Byzantium, inflicted more damage.[10] The Normans established kingdoms in
the Holy Land and participated in the sack of Constantinople in 1204,
establishing their own rival Latin emperor there until 1261. The Palaio-
logian family recovered Constantinople, but Byzantium was now
reduced to a narrow area along the Bosphorus, plus an outpost at Trebizond in north-east Anatolia. The Byzantines relied heavily on the
Turks, who defeated a resurgent Bulgarian empire in 1393 and crushed
a Serbian one (established 1346) at Kosovo Polje in 1389. But by
1391 the Turks had completely surrounded Byzantium, which had
shrunk to a tenth of its former size.[11]

Byzantine emperors twice offered reunification with the Latin church
(in 1274 and 1439), and thrice travelled west personally to seek aid
between 1400 and 1423. These moves stirred internal opposition and
failed to bring about the desired results. The last western Crusade
ended in disaster at Varna (eastern Bulgaria) in 1444. Nine years later
Constantinople faced its thirteenth siege by a Muslim-led army since
650. The city's population had shrunk to 50,000, but Constantinople's

eventual loss in 1453 was nonetheless perceived as a huge disaster for all Christians. In 1461 the fall of the Trebizond empire (north-eastern Anatolia and southern Crimea) removed the last outpost.[12]

Byzantine decline occurred during a period of western imperial weakness. None of the German kings between 1251 and 1311 were crowned emperor, while those that followed were embroiled in renewed problems with the papacy into the 1340s. The subsequent Great Schism further hindered any coordinated response until it was too late. Thus, the two-emperor problem was largely resolved by default. Its longer-term significance lay in the slow secularization of imperial titles as superior monarchical ranks, rather than singular and uniquely tied to a universal Christian mission.[13]

The prolonged existence of two Christian emperors also helped embed east–west distinctions. Ancient and medieval geographers identified Europe, Asia and Africa as continents, but these meant little in political or ideological terms, especially as ancient Rome had straddled all three. The ancient view persisted in Byzantium where the Bosphorus flowed through the heart of its empire. 'Europe' was simply the ecclesiastical and administrative district of Thrace immediately to the west. This was politically unacceptable in the west, where the foundation of the Empire necessitated sharper demarcation with the east. Anything else would have entailed either acknowledging that there were two emperors, or that one was not fully imperial. 'Europe' came to denote western civilization, bounded to the east by the limits of the Empire and Latin Christianity. The Empire's place in these ideas was expressed most clearly by Charlemagne's early medieval hagiographers, who hailed him as Father of Europe.[14]

The Sultan

Their capture of Constantinople in 1453 fixed the Ottoman Turks in western minds as the Muslim 'other', despite continued trade and other points of contact between east and west.[15] With the eventual establishment of the Ottomans in Hungary and on the Adriatic coast, the Empire would come to define itself as Christendom's bulwark against Islam. The rapid spread of prejudice was facilitated by the coincidence of the Ottoman advance with the invention of printing. Hostility in the west to the Ottomans overlaid and reinforced earlier resentment of the

Byzantines, extending far deeper than antagonism towards any western people and creating a sense of existential threat persisting into the
later eighteenth century. Yet the Ottomans were only one of several Muslim imperial powers succeeding the Caliphates that framed the Muslim
world between seventh-century expansion and the shock of the thirteenth-
century Mongol invasions. The Shiite Safavid family forged a new Persian
empire by 1501. The Mamalukes were originally Turkic slave soldiers
who seized power in Egypt around 1250, and were the only power to
inflict a serious military defeat on the Mongols, routing them in Syria in
1260. The Mamaluke empire survived until conquered by the Ottomans
in 1517. The Mongols toppled the last Caliphate, based in Baghdad, in
1268, but converted to Islam soon after. Although the vast Mongol
empire soon fragmented, one group re-emerged as the Mughuls in India
by 1526. Thus, Spain's rise to global imperial power under Charles V
coincided with the consolidation of the Ottoman, Safavid and Mughul
Islamic empires, which together controlled 130 to 160 million people
across the Mediterranean, Anatolia, Iran and South Asia.[16]

The Ottomans traced their origins to Osman, their first sultan and a
tribal leader in Bithynia, a landlocked province south of the Sea of
Marmara. Osman completed the transition of his people from a
nomadic to a settled existence around 1320. Like the Safavids, Mughuls
and Habsburgs, the Ottomans cultivated what became a dynastic monarchy, emerging to dominate all other Turkic groups after the decline of
the Seljuks and Byzantines, both of whom they ultimately replaced.[17]
Westerners viewed the Ottomans as Muslims, not least because of their
culture of holy war. Yet their rise depended on accommodation with
Christians. Osman's great-grandson, Bayezid I, named his own sons
Jesus, Moses, Solomon, Muhammed and Joseph. Mehmet II signalled
his desire to make Islam the unifying force for his empire by expelling
30,000 Christians from Constantinople after he took it in 1453. However, Sunni Muslims only became the largest population group following
further conquests in Anatolia, Arabia and north Africa around seventy
years later. They thus controlled the holy sites of Medina, Jerusalem and
Mecca, but self-identification with Sunni Islam was primarily a response
to the rise of Shiite Persia immediately to the east, rather than through
conflict with the west. Additional gains in the Balkans between the
1460s and 1540s ensured that Christians still formed a substantial proportion of Ottoman subjects.[18]

The emergence of three empires in the Muslim world offers instruct-ive comparisons for the Empire's position amongst Christians. Unlike Christianity, which converted the Roman empire and used Roman structures to build its church, Islam developed in the seventh century as a community largely outside a formal imperial framework.[19] The Caliphate was created subsequently to advance the faith, deriving its authority through descent from Muhammed by marriage, in contrast to the direct links to the divine claimed by western kings. The Caliph-ate became dynastic, splitting into Spanish, north African and Middle Eastern branches. Meanwhile, religious structures remained decentral-ized without a single priestly hierarchy equivalent to Christendom's bishops. Spiritual authority was diffused amongst a multitude of holy men, teachers and interpreters of Koranic law, whose influence depended on their personal reputations for learning and morality.

Lying outside the Christian political order, Muslim rulers did not challenge the Empire's singular imperial pretensions. Charlemagne's reign coincided with a surge of fresh Arab conquests, including Sar-dinia (809) and Sicily (827). From the Carolingian perspective, this was simply the kind of behaviour to be expected from 'barbarians'. Charle-magne sent an embassy to tell the Baghdad caliph Harun al-Rashid of his coronation. After many adventures, the survivors returned with rich gifts, including an elephant called Abolabas – a traditional sign of authority in the Near East since Alexander the Great. The caliph simply regarded Charlemagne as a potentially useful ally against his Muslim rival in Spain. As with imperial-Byzantine relations, both par-ties were free to interpret signs as they wished. Political and geographic distance lessened the incentive to formalize relations. Otto I tried to contact the al-Andalus Caliphate in Córdoba in 953, but failed to pro-vide suitable credentials for his envoys. The caliph was already well informed about the Empire and remained decidedly unimpressed.[20]

The Norman conquest of southern Italy and Sicily in the eleventh century drove a wedge between the Empire and Islamic north Africa. Together with papal hostility during the Investiture Dispute, this ensured that the emperor did not emerge as Crusader leader after the First Crusade of 1095. Conrad III joined the Second Crusade in the late 1140s under incompetent French leadership, personally contributing to the disastrous, unprovoked attack on Damascus in 1148. The young Frederick I 'Barbarossa' fought in this crusade, as well as leading the

Third Crusade in 1190, becoming the only major ruler to participate in two crusading expeditions. Barbarossa's prestige as emperor assisted his negotiations with Byzantium, Hungary, Serbia, Armenia, the Seljuk sultan and even Saladin. Although diplomacy failed to bring a peaceful solution, it at least secured the long route chosen through Anatolia. Barbarossa's huge army included his son Freidrich VI of Swabia, 12 bishops 2 margraves and 26 counts.[21] Barbarossa himself died en route, but though the expedition failed to recover Jerusalem, it relieved the pressure on the Crusader kingdoms and forged closer connections between crusading and the imperial office.

The illness of Barbarossa's successor, Henry VI, prevented his personal participation, but he sent a major expeditionary force in 1197. Large numbers of Germans, Frisians and Austrians joined the next three crusading campaigns between 1199 and 1229. Frederick II led 3,000 men in June 1228, though his excommunication by the pope prevented this from being classed a full crusade. The emperor succeeded by peaceful means where others had failed with more violent methods, though he was fortunate in arriving at the Holy Land as Saladin's realm split into three rival sultanates amidst Mongol attacks. Sultan Al-Malik al-Kamil was also impressed by Frederick's relative openness to Islam and patronage of Muslim refugees in Lucera, near Foggia in southern Italy. Most of the latter were in fact deportees, who had been forced from Sicily by Henry VI to curry favour with Christian inhabitants after his conquest of that island in 1194. Frederick stepped up these deportations after 1223 until Lucera's population reached 60,000. The Byzantines and Normans had already used expulsion as a method of control, but Frederick's action was unique in that he resettled the population, creating a community on his mainland possessions who depended on his patronage. Lucera provided around 3,000 elite troops who, as Muslims, had the added value of being impervious to papal excommunication and served Frederick faithfully, including on his Jerusalem expedition.[22] Favoured by these circumstances, Frederick and al-Kamil concluded the Treaty of Jaffa in February 1229, giving the emperor control of Jerusalem for 10 years, 5 months and 40 days – the maximum permitted under Islamic law for the alienation of property to non-Muslims. Although he retained control of the Dome of the Rock, al-Kamil also conceded access corridors to Bethlehem and Nazareth and gave Frederick an elephant. Frederick was crowned king of Jerusalem in the Holy Sepulchre on 17 March 1229, the only Holy Roman emperor actually to visit the city.

Frederick's supporters hailed it as the dawn of a new age, fanning unrealistic expectations and inevitable disappointment. The Templars and Knights of St John condemned the treaty for failing to restore their lost lands. Frederick remained nominal king of Jerusalem, but left actual government to Alice of Champagne (aunt of his second wife) as regent. The city was surrendered to the Saracens when the lease expired in 1239, and within five years the Latin kingdom was restricted to five Lebanese coastal towns. It passed to the Angevins, who had assumed the Staufers' Mediterranean interests in 1269, but the last crusader outpost (Acre) fell to the Muslims in 1291.

Meanwhile, papal propaganda capitalized on the imperial patronage of Lucera to present Frederick as an oriental despot, complete with harem. The Lucera 'Saracens' served loyally, but the Staufers' final defeat in 1268 left them no choice but to transfer allegiance to the Angevins, serving them in turn against Byzantines, Tunisians, Turks and Sicilian rebels. However, the presence of a large Muslim community proved increasingly embarrassing to the Angevins, who were seeking to displace the Empire as the papacy's protectors. Lucera's inhabitants were forced to convert to Christianity in August 1300 when the town was renamed Città Santa Maria.

Rudolf I took the crusader vow in 1275, but was prevented by domestic events from honouring it. His successors also faced more immediate problems, while crusading increasingly appeared a risky and hopeless enterprise. Nonetheless, direct participation in the Second and Third Crusades had left a lasting impression on the Empire's inhabitants during the later thirteenth and fourteenth centuries.[23] Prior to becoming emperor, Sigismund led an unsuccessful crusade to save his own kingdom of Hungary from Turkish invasion in 1396. His successor Albert II also regarded Hungary's defence as a crusade, preferring to fight and die there than consolidate his authority in the Empire.[24]

The Ottoman advance through the Balkans after 1453 transformed what had been crusades with distant geographical goals organized by individual emperors into a collective defence of the Empire. This reinforced the wider process of imperial reform, encouraging a more collective form of power-sharing and responsibility in the Empire's governance (see pp. 396–408). The Ottomans took Belgrade in 1521, invading Hungary again the following year. Within four years they had conquered around half of that kingdom. Within another three they were at the gates of Vienna, threatening the Habsburgs and the Empire directly. The pace of events fused with traditions brought by the Habsburgs to reinvigorate the ideal of the emperor as Christendom's defender. The Habsburgs had become kings of Spain as Iberia was freed from Muslim Moorish rule. Begun in the eleventh century, this *Reconquista* had stalled around 1270, but revived in 1455 in response to papal crusading appeals, gathering pace after 1482 to culminate in the defeat of the last Muslim kingdom, Granada, in 1492. Charles V carried this success story with him, as well as Spain's Mediterranean interests, when he became emperor in 1519. Seven years later, his brother Ferdinand assumed Hungary's own traditions when he inherited that kingdom from King Louis II, who died in battle against the victorious Turks at Mohács in August 1526.[25] Spain continued to oppose the Ottomans in the Mediterranean, scoring the notable naval victory at Lepanto in 1571, but the Empire carried the main burden of defending central Europe.

The ideological clash was sharpened by the Ottomans' assumption of Byzantine imperial traditions, setting them apart from previous Muslim empires and reviving the two-emperor problem in new form. The Ottomans already combined Romano-Byzantine traditions with Turkic and Islamic ones before 1453, but became self-consciously imperial after taking Constantinople that year.[26] They moved their capital from Adrianople (Edirne) to Constantinople, taking up residence in the former Byzantine imperial palace. Shari'a civil law and Ottoman secular fiscal and administrative practice were all combined with Byzantine Caesaropapism, entrenching the ruler as legislator and inhibiting the transition to the rule of law ultimately made in the Empire.[27] Byzantine infrastructure was retained in modified form. Mehmet II adopted the title *Kaysar* and presented himself as the successor to ancient Rome and Alexander the Great, claiming he would unite east and west under Islam. Latin and Greek scholars were commissioned to write official histories incorporating mythic Byzantine emperors from Solomon onwards in tales of Muhammed.[28]

The adoption of imperial imagery and rhetoric was complex. In part, it was about presenting the sultan to his new Christian subjects in ways already familiar to them. It was also encouraged by the Venetian and Genoese merchants, long-standing intermediaries between the Latin and Greek worlds, who continued trading after the latter passed under Ottoman rule. It also stemmed from westerners who tended to apply their own political language when dealing with the Ottomans.

Following the rapid conquest of Mamaluke Egypt (1514–17) and victory over Persia, the new sultan Süleyman I turned west again in 1521. Having plucked the Red Apple of Constantinople, Ottoman aspirations increasingly focused on the Golden Apple of Vienna, heightened by the coincidence of the growth of their imperial power with that of the Habsburgs. Charles V refused to be diverted by the Ottoman siege of Vienna in 1529, going ahead with his own imperial coronation by Pope Clement VII in Bologna in 1530.[29] Süleyman was forced to retire, having waited in vain for Charles to meet him in battle. The sultan masked the anticlimax by staging a triumphal homeward journey, hoping to outshine Charles's recent coronation. A huge crown was commissioned from Venetian craftsmen, costing 115,000 ducats, equivalent to a tenth of Castile's annual revenue. The design mixed Charles's crown with a papal tiara, but added a fourth diadem deliberately to upstage the sultan's western rivals. The success of this PR stunt is demonstrated by Süleyman's lasting fame in the west as 'the Magnificent'.

After 1536 Süleyman progressively abandoned western trappings in favour of a more Islamic Ottoman style distinct from both the Christian imperial tradition and that of Safavid Persia. The Ottoman conquests of Egypt and Arabia had redressed the religious balance, while the majority of Anatolian and Balkan elites had converted to Islam. Sultans had already presented themselves as new caliphs since 1453 in a bid for leadership of the entire Muslim world. Byzantine distinctions between civilization and barbarism were sublimated within the Islamic division of the world into antagonistic 'Houses' of Islam and War, making permanent peace with Christians politically impossible.

The fault line ran through Hungary, where Habsburg efforts at reconquest stalled by 1541, compounded by the failures of Charles V's expensive expeditions to Tunis and Algiers.[30] The Habsburgs were obliged to accept a tripartite division between imperial (Habsburg) Hungary in the west (including Croatia), Ottoman Hungary in the centre and south-east, and Transylvania in the north-east. Possession of Transylvania and the right to use the Hungarian royal title remained contested until 1699, further hindering permanent peace. Ferdinand I bought a truce by paying 30,000 florins in tribute to the Ottomans in 1541. Further defeats forced him to pay this annually after 1547. The sultan refused to recognize the Habsburgs as emperors, claiming they were merely his tributaries. The truce forbade major military operations, but allowed raiding by militia across the frontier. The constant friction provided a ready excuse for war, but Habsburg efforts to end tribute to the Ottomans through renewed campaigns from 1565 to 1567 and 1593 to 1606 failed.[31]

Although not full crusades, Habsburg operations were backed by the papacy and drew strong support from across Europe, attracting foreign volunteers such as John Smith, the future founder of Virginia.[32] Days of prayer and penance were decreed from the 1530s to tackle the perceived causes of the Turkish menace in the sin of the Christian population. So-called Turkish Bells were rung throughout the Empire daily at midday during campaigns to remind people to pray for the success of imperial armies. The ideological impossibility of peace encouraged acceptance of the Empire's structural reforms, requiring all imperial Estates to contribute to collective defence (see pp. 398–406 and 445–62).

Relations between east and west nonetheless fell short of a 'clash of civilizations'. Not only did Hungarians and the Empire's subjects continue to trade with the Ottomans, but the emperor regarded Shiite Persia as a potential ally. The Persian shah first proposed an alliance to Charles V in 1523. Intermittent contacts intensified around 1600 as a large Persian embassy arrived in Prague. Talks ultimately collapsed in 1610 due to differing expectations. Shah Abbas mistook vague Habsburg expressions of friendship for firm commitment and attacked Ottoman Kurdistan in 1603. He regarded the Habsburgs' separate peace with the Ottomans at Zsitva Torok in 1606 as a betrayal, leaving long-standing resentment and wrecking all attempts to renew contact between the Habsburgs and the Persians.[33]

Zsitva Torok extended the pre-war truce between Habsburgs and Ottomans, but required that both parties 'should address each other as emperor, not just as King'.[34] It was renewed five times by 1642, improving relations by granting Habsburg subjects favourable trading status within the Ottoman empire. The annual tribute paid to the Ottomans ended in 1606, but each renewal of the truce cost the Habsburgs 200,000 florins. Good relations proved vital for the Habsburgs' survival, since the sultan, preoccupied with his own problems, rejected opportunities to exploit the Thirty Years War, having toyed with the idea of backing the Bohemian rebels. The truce was renewed again for 20 years in July 1649 when the Habsburgs' 'free gift' was reduced to 40,000 florins. Friction persisted, because Habsburg efforts to crush malcontents in their part of Hungary opened the door to Ottoman intervention, which escalated into full war by 1662. The need to coordinate aid from the Empire consolidated the constitutional changes enacted through the Westphalian settlement and led to the Reichstag remaining permanently in session after 1663.[35] The Habsburgs bought another 20 years' truce by paying 200,000 florins in 1664, but this time the sultan also sent gifts, suggesting a more equal relationship.

The pattern appeared to repeat itself in 1683 when the Ottoman leadership attacked Vienna again in the hope of reasserting authority after prolonged internal unrest in their empire. Instead, the city resisted until it was relieved by Polish and imperial troops in a truly international victory, hailed in the west as another Lepanto. The huge amount of booty included tents, carpets and at least 500 Turkish prisoners who were forcibly settled in Germany. Orientalism swept central Europe well before the better-known wave following Napoleon's invasion of Egypt in 1798.[36] It was hoped that even Jerusalem might be recovered, but the initial euphoria instead soon gave way to a long, successful but grinding war of reconquest in Hungary between 1684 and 1699.

Internally, this continued the trend towards mixed monarchy in the Empire. Internationally, it represented a significant shift in the Habsburgs relative to the Ottomans, who finally accepted a permanent peace at Karlowitz in 1699. The Habsburgs secured all Hungary and Transylvania, swiftly eradicating all trace of 150 years of Muslim presence. The sultan also promised better treatment of Catholics in his territories. However, the religious element was waning. The emperor continued to receive German and Italian aid in further Turkish wars into the 1730s, but these conflicts were increasingly regarded as purely Austrian concerns. The Turkish Bells rang for the last time during the 1736–9 war, and suggestions of repeating this in the next conflict (1787–91) were rejected as unenlightened.[37] Meanwhile, further gains from the Turks in 1716–18 cemented the Habsburgs as a great power independent of the imperial title, transforming their relationship to the Empire and other European powers.

The Tsar

The prolonged warfare against the Ottomans between 1683 and 1718 drew in Russia, hastening that country's integration within the nascent European states system. Although initially regarded as a useful ally against the Ottomans, it soon became clear that the tsar was replacing the sultan as chief challenger to the Habsburgs' claim to be Europe's pre-eminent monarchs.

Russia originated in the Varangians (Vikings) who conquered Kiev and were called Rus by the Slavs. The ruling Rurik family were wooed by Byzantine and Latin missionaries and they ultimately adopted eastern Christianity, which allowed them to use a Slavonic liturgy. The conversion of Prince Vladimir in 988 established the basis of a highly personalized sacral monarchy. Rurik princes contributed one third of the 180 Russian saints from the tenth to thirteenth centuries.[38] Internal disputes produced rival Rurik principalities after 1054, all of which were conquered by the Mongols, who overcame the fearsome Russian winter by using the frozen rivers as roads for their cavalry. The Mongols established themselves by 1240 as the Golden Horde on the Lower Volga, extorting tribute from the Rurik princes. The principality of Moscovy emerged from the wreckage after 1325, facilitated subsequent to 1438 by the fragmentation of the Golden Horde. Tribute was stopped in 1480. Five years later, Moscovy took Novgorod, eliminating a major rival and signalling a desire to extend towards the Baltic.

As with the Ottomans, rapid expansion encouraged ambitions to formalize prestige through more overt imperial imagery. Ivan III 'the Great' married Zoe Palaiologina, niece of the last Byzantine emperor, in 1472 and proclaimed himself ruler of all the Russias. He took the title *tsar*, again a word derived from *Caesar*, which had been used before but was now employed more consciously to mean emperor in contrast to the old Kievan title *knyaz*, meaning prince or king.[39] The link to ancient Rome was reinforced by the Russian Orthodox church's rejection of the brief reunification of the Greek and Latin churches imposed by the Byzantine emperor in 1439. Philotheus, abbot of Pskov, developed his own version of imperial translation, arguing that the first Rome fell through heresy, the second (Constantinople) was conquered by the infidel, but the third (Moscow) would endure until Judgement Day. Like their western equivalents, such ideas derived their importance not as practical programmes, but through fostering an intellectual climate conducive to imperialism. Russian rulers aimed to 'liberate' Constantinople and claimed to protect Christian holy places – both as late as 1853 contributory factors in the outbreak of the Crimean War.[40]

Byzantine traditions were readily adaptable to Russian circumstances, as they did not challenge the idea of a sacred ruler. The tsar already exercised greater control over his metropolitan than the Byzantine emperor over his patriarch – one metropolitan was strangled in 1568 for daring to criticize the tsar. The Russian church secured full autonomy in 1685 when the tsar declared the metropolitan independent from the Greek patriarch, who still lived under Ottoman rule in Constantinople. The move deliberately undercut the sultan's authority over his Christian subjects whilst bolstering his Russian rival's pretensions as champion of the true church.

The imperial double eagle first appeared as a tsarist symbol in 1480, though it only became the primary one under Peter I 'the Great', displaying icons and other religious symbols on military flags around 1700.[41] Ivan IV 'the Terrible' staged a coronation 14 years into his rule, in 1561, that deliberately asserted Russia as a continuation of ancient Rome. The ceremony used a Slavonic translation of the Byzantine coronation service, while the regalia were presented as those of the former Byzantine emperor. Ivan regarded himself as a direct descendant of Emperor Augustus, and even the tsar's notorious terror was influenced by ancient examples.[42]

Assumption of the Byzantine legacy reinforced western perceptions of Russia as an alien civilization, but it also raised the tsar's profile as a potential ally. The first imperial embassy to Russia was despatched in 1488 by Frederick III. This revealed how the two-emperor problem had also translated to Moscow. Frederick approached negotiations from the perspective of his pre-eminence, while Tsar Ivan III (rightly) stressed that neither he nor his ancestors had ever been imperial vassals. Ivan and his successors wanted international recognition that their title of tsar meant emperor, while westerners continued to ignore it and to refer to Russian rulers as merely 'dukes'. Civil wars eventually saw the Ruriks replaced by the Romanovs in 1613, but these events simply reinforced westerners' prejudices of Russia as barbaric and discouraged acceptance that its new rulers directly continued Romano-Byzantine imperialism. Russians for their part remained baffled by the Empire, despite increasing efforts to understand it – for example, the tsar's government obtained copies of the Peace of Westphalia just three months after its conclusion in 1648. The Empire's constitution contained many elements for which there was no Russian equivalent, and the tsar and his advisors found it hard to understand that feudal relations did not mean the princes' servitude under the emperor.[43]

The desire to learn more grew as Russia's frontiers advanced westwards after 1653, bringing greater influence in Poland and direct contact with the eastern edge of the Ottoman empire by 1667. German traders and immigrants were an important source of information, but the main shift came with Peter the Great, who personally travelled across the Empire on his famous European tour in 1697–8. Russia's involvement in the Great Northern War (1700–1721) not only secured access to the Baltic but brought direct contact with imperial politics as Peter's army pursued the Swedes across northern Germany. On 19 April 1716, Peter the Great's niece Ekaterina Ivanovna married Duke Carl Leopold of Mecklenburg-Schwerin, initiating two centuries of close dynastic relations between the Romanovs and German princely families.[44]

Russian imperial imagery became increasingly western, though without entirely jettisoning Byzantine elements. Peter issued a two-rouble coin depicting himself as an ancient Roman emperor to celebrate his victory over Swedish forces at Poltava in 1709. His officials then discovered a letter from Maximilian I sent in 1514 seeking an alliance. Whether by accident or design, the Habsburg chancellery had addressed Vasily III as *Kayser*, implicitly recognizing the Russians' insistence on translating tsar as emperor. Peter had the letter published in 1718 as part of the careful preparations culminating in his self-proclamation as *imperator* in October 1721.[45] The coincidence of this act with the successful outcome of the Great Northern War underscored Russia as an imperial power.

The Habsburgs persisted in refusing to recognize the Russian emperor as their equal, rebuffing a proposal that the two emperors alternate as Europe's foremost monarch. Backed diplomatically by France, Emperor Charles VI recycled old arguments that Europe could not have two emperors.[46] Deteriorating relations with western European powers forced Charles to compromise, recognizing the tsar's imperial title as part of a wider alliance in 1726, though Charles still claimed formal pre-eminence. Russia remained content until 1762, because it saw Austria as a useful ally against the still-powerful Ottomans. The alliance drew it deeper into imperial politics. Russian troops thrice entered the Empire to assist Austria in wars between 1733 and 1762. The Romanovs were now closely related to the princely families of Mecklenburg, Holstein, Württemberg, Hessen-Darmstadt and Anhalt-Zerbst, with the last providing the princess who ruled Russia as Catherine II 'the Great' between 1762 and 1796. The purpose of involvement shifted from payback for Austrian assistance in the Balkans to a growing concern for the Empire's internal political balance as a factor in Russia's own wider strategic interests. Russia brokered the Peace of Teschen ending the Austro-Prussian War of the Bavarian Succession (1778–9), and thereafter claimed this made it a guarantor of the Peace of Westphalia. Although he was never fully recognized, a permanent envoy at the Reichstag was maintained by Russia after 1782 to safeguard its interests.[47]

The Most Christian King

A factor in Austria's accommodation with Russia was the growth of France as a western European great power. France shared common roots with the Empire in the Carolingian realm. The Treaty of Verdun (843), which divided the Empire into three kingdoms (West Francia, East Francia and Lotharingia), was celebrated later as the foundation of France and Germany, but at the time there was no sense that this had created separate countries. Reunification efforts continued into the 880s, while ties amongst the elite persisted across the Rhine long after that. Distinctions became clearer as the Ottonians succeeded the defunct eastern Carolingian royal line in 919. The meeting between the Ottonian Henry I and the 'French' King Rudolf I near Sedan in 935 was carefully choreographed to stress parity – something that was repeated during further royal summits in 1006–7. However, none of the monarchs involved held the imperial title at the time of the meetings.[48]

Common origins allowed French kings to claim the imperial tradition themselves. King Lothar reacted angrily to Otto I's imperial coronation in 962, while the Capetian family ruling France after 987 were prepared to recognize Byzantium's imperial title if this would secure an anti-Ottonian alliance. From the tenth century onwards, French writers Frenchified Charlemagne and the Franks, stressing an unbroken line of Christian kings since Clovis. They disputed the concept of imperial translation, instead presenting the empire as a

Carolingian creation always centred on Paris, not Aachen. A central feature was the myth that Charlemagne had gone to Jerusalem and brought back the relics of St Denis to found a Parisian monastery – a story vigorously propagated by the monks to assert their house as home to French royal and national identity. Unable to ignore Ottonian possession of the actual imperial title, they sought to reduce the emperor's role to protecting the pope, judging the emperor's actions according to the current state of Franco-papal relations.[49]

The initial goal was to maintain parity with the former East Frankish realm, but after 1100 French writers increasingly distinguished between the German kingdom as a foreign country and the imperial title that they claimed for their own king. However, some went further, arguing that, as direct heir to the Franks, the French king should rule all former Frankish territory, including Germany. The victory of King Philip II Augustus over Otto IV at Bouvines in 1214 decided the Welf–Staufer civil war and appeared to make France the arbiter of imperial affairs. Philip's troops carried the *Oriflamme*, the blood-red banner of St Denis abbey that was traditionally considered Charlemagne's own flag, while their superiority appeared confirmed by their capture of Otto's imperial standard in the battle.[50]

Heavy French involvement in the Crusades after 1095 added interest, because the emperor was widely regarded as the Crusaders' 'natural' leader. French observers interpreted the prolonged absence of a crowned emperor between 1251 and 1311 as a factor in the failure of later crusading ventures.[51] Opposition to individual emperors remained contingent on specific circumstances, not principled objections to the idea of the Empire. For instance, action against Henry VII stemmed from a desire to protect French interests in Italy and the belief that the pope had crowned the wrong king as emperor. Prayers for the emperor continued in France and Spain into the fourteenth century. French kings made serious efforts to secure the imperial title in 1273–4, 1308, 1313 and 1324–8. Charles Valois, brother of Philip IV, even married the granddaughter of Baldwin II, the last Latin emperor of Byzantium, in the hope of reuniting the eastern and western empires. These attempts failed, but thanks to their growing power, French kings did assert themselves as the papacy's protectors by the late thirteenth century. The propagandists of Philip Augustus already presented him as Charlemagne's true heir. 'Augustus' was in fact a nickname given the king by Rigord, a senior monk of St Denis, to celebrate Philip's appropriately 'imperial' expansion of monarchical authority across France. Rigord also repeatedly referred to him as 'Most Christian King' (*rex Christianissimus*), a rank chosen to outflank the imperial title by emphasizing the French monarch's special mission. This title was later confirmed by the pope, while further papal concessions since the twelfth century cemented the separate identity of the French church.[52]

Failure to obtain the imperial title encouraged the assertion that the French monarchy already possessed imperial, in the sense of sovereign, powers. Charlemagne had been a great king before his imperial coronation. This became the standard argument into the mid-seventeenth century, serving to justify continued bids to obtain the title, and to deflect any criticism when these attempts failed. The belief in both the independence of the French monarchy and its continued membership of a single, universal Christian order did not strike contemporaries as contradictory. While later nationalist writers played up the former whilst ignoring the latter, late medieval and early modern opinion was in fact strikingly modern: twenty-first-century France is clearly still a sovereign country despite being part of the European Union.[53]

The myth of Charlemagne helped inspire Charles VIII's invasion of Italy in 1494, especially as his immediate target, Naples, claimed the defunct title of king of Jerusalem since 1477. François I had more concrete imperial ambitions, securing papal backing and canvassing German support from 1516. In his attempt to cover all the ideological bases he claimed Trojan descent, presented himself as embodying Roman virtues, and argued that French and Germans shared common Frankish ancestry. He pushed universalism to its logical conclusion: the title was not a purely German possession, but open to all worthy candidates. However, the process of becoming emperor was by now firmly associated with election as German king. The German electors regarded Charlemagne and the Franks as their own, exclusive ancestors and rejected François' overtures in favour of Charles V.[54]

Louis XIV and his advisor, Cardinal Mazarin, made the last attempt at securing the imperial title, following Ferdinand III's death in 1657. Mazarin backed the candidacy of the duke of Pfalz-Neuburg as a stalking horse to test German support for Louis. But the primary motive was to prevent another Austrian Habsburg emperor who might involve the Empire in France's ongoing war (since 1635) with Spain. The ploy contributed to what became the longest imperial interregnum since 1494–1507, but failed to prevent the election of Leopold I in 1658. Speculation about another French candidacy persisted into the 1670s, but was rendered irrelevant by Leopold's longevity (he died in 1705). French diplomats swiftly fell back on arguments advanced since the 1640s that their king was the German princes' natural ally in defending their constitutional liberties against the threat of 'imperial absolutism'.[55]

The abandonment of direct imperial ambitions inevitably led to assertions that France was already superior. The experience of civil war between 1562 and 1598 had produced new arguments for strong royal rule as the foundation of a stable social and political order. French writers increasingly drew disparaging contrasts with the Empire, which they presented as declining from an (allegedly) hereditary monarchy under Charlemagne's 'French' rule into a degenerately elective one under the Germans. It was no longer an empire, but merely a sorry shadow of one, whereas the continuous line of Christian French kings had existed beyond the combined span of republican and imperial Rome. France was a divine monarchy, with its king chosen by God through hereditary succession. As the Sun King, Louis outshone any other ruler. Thanks to his Christian credentials and practical power, he, not the emperor, was the natural arbiter of Europe.[56]

French pretensions to be Europe's arbiter foundered in a series of wars between 1667 and 1714. Louis achieved the long-standing French goal of keeping Spain and Austria apart by defeating Habsburg claims to the entire Spanish succession after 1700. Yet by the Sun King's death in 1715 it was clear that most diplomats favoured ideas of a power balance rather than a single peacekeeper (see pp. 170–76). France also struggled to assert itself as arbiter of the Empire's internal balance, because it proved hard to find a reliable German partner to facilitate intervention. Bavaria was preferred since the 1620s as suitably Catholic and large enough that, with help, it could serve as a counterweight to the Austrian Habsburgs. Franco-Bavarian cooperation intensified when Charles VI's death without a male heir in October 1740 broke the line of Habsburg rulers since 1438 and opened the War of the Austrian Succession, lasting until 1748. Carl Albrecht of Bavaria was eventually elected as Charles VII with French backing in 1742. His brief reign of just under three years proved a disastrous failure for both Bavaria and the Empire.[57] The setback encouraged the French foreign minister, the Marquis d'Argenson, to propose federalizing Germany and Italy by reorganizing them into fewer, larger territories in 1745. The plan was opposed by Prussia and Savoy, who saw greater opportunities for themselves through preserving the old order. Austria's recovery of the imperial title through Francis I's election later in 1745 ended d'Argenson's scheme.[58]

A Fool's Hat?

Habsburg statesmen realized long before this point that the imperial title no longer meant what it had done in the Middle Ages. Following successful wars against the Ottomans, by 1699 the Habsburgs had more land outside the Empire than within it, inevitably changing how they regarded the imperial title. Plans to raise Austria to a kingdom had been abandoned in 1623. Nonetheless, the term 'Austrian monarchy' was employed from 1703 as a vague yet suitably regal designation for the Habsburg lands, which in fact included several genuine kingdoms: Bohemia, Hungary, Croatia, Naples (between 1714 and 1735), plus Galicia, annexed from Poland in 1772, and nominal claims to Jerusalem.[59] These developments raised questions about the continued utility of the imperial title, especially as the Habsburgs survived without it between 1740 and 1745 during the international War of the Austrian Succession. They felt betrayed by the failure of the imperial Estates to back them against France, Bavaria and their allies. Francis I's wife, Maria Theresa, took an especially dim view, calling the imperial crown a 'fool's hat', refusing to be crowned empress and referring to her husband's coronation in 1745 as a 'Punch and Judy Show' (*Kaspar Theater*). These misgivings persisted even when their son Joseph II succeeded his father in 1765. Joseph described the position of emperor as 'a ghost of an honorific power' and was quickly frustrated by the imperial constitution, which was indeed functioning to constrain Habsburg management of the Empire as French diplomats hoped.[60]

Historians have often cited these comments as evidence for the Empire's supposed irrelevance after the Peace of Westphalia in 1648. However, Francis I's advisors replied to his questions on 7 March 1749 by stressing that the imperial title was a 'brilliant symbol of the highest political honour in the West ... bringing precedence ahead of all other powers' (see Plate 7).[61] The entire Habsburg government – including the imperial couple – were convinced that the loss of the imperial title in 1740 had been disastrous, and resolved to defend the Empire's internal political hierarchy since this gave Austria a privileged position and helped maintain its international influence. Austria was obliged to concede ceremonial parity with France in 1757 as part of an anti-Prussian alliance. Even the French Revolutionaries remained sufficiently status conscious to get this confirmed in 1797 and 1801. The imperial title was now the sole marker of this pre-eminence and the Habsburgs clung to earlier arguments that all others calling themselves 'emperors' were really only 'kings'.[62] For the Habsburgs, both the Empire and Europe as a whole were hierarchical political systems. These arguments were useful in putting upstarts like Prussia in their place, and were backed by many of the smaller imperial Estates, which felt any levelling of the established order would lead to the kind of federalism proposed by d'Argenson, thereby threatening their autonomy.

Having found Prussia an unreliable German partner after 1740, France switched to an Austrian alliance in 1756, lasting until the Revolutionary Wars after 1792. The resulting Seven Years War (1756–63) failed to eliminate Prussia as challenger to Austria. The French envoy to the Reichstag after 1763 identified the other imperial Estates as 'inert resources' (*forces mortes*), which France should preserve from both Austria and Prussia to prevent either German great power from dominating central Europe.[63] The French public failed to appreciate the subtleties of this policy, seeing only surface aspects like the arrival of the unpopular Austrian princess, Marie-Antoinette, as symbolizing their country's humiliating association with its long-standing enemy. Few were interested in the complexities of imperial politics, and those that were believed the Empire could not be reformed without destroying it.[64]

French hostility grew after 1789 when some German princes sheltered the émigrés fleeing the Revolution. The Girondin and Jacobin factions were both disappointed by their failure to replace their country's established ties to German princes with a new alliance with the 'German nation'. Revolutionary policy became ever more extreme as it departed from accepted diplomatic norms. French policy-makers now considered the Westphalian settlement as 'absurd', while still using it in negotiations to further their goals. Even this lost its relevance once advocates among the French revolutionaries of 'natural frontiers' seized power in Paris by 1795, intending to annex the entire left bank of the Rhine to France.[65]

A New Charlemagne

French military successes by 1797 raised urgent questions about the Empire's reorganization, renewal or dissolution. Many answers focused on Napoleon, the rising figure within the French Republic. Beethoven was not the only central European disappointed by Napoleon. The smaller imperial Estates hoped Napoleon would renew the Empire, especially Arch-chancellor Dalberg, who sent him numerous proposals.[66] Napoleon initially continued earlier French policy, writing in May 1797 that if the Empire did not already exist, France would have to invent it to keep Germany weak.[67] Differing interpretations of Charlemagne's legacy reflect how Napoleon's attitudes soon diverged radically. Central Europeans, like Dalberg, who hoped to preserve the Empire, regarded Charlemagne as the progenitor of a thousand years of power tempered by law and propriety through the Empire's constitution. Napoleon's interpretation was rather closer to the historical reality, seeing Charlemagne as a heroic warrior and conqueror.

Napoleon's use of Charlemagne's memory was primarily directed at consolidating his authority within France, where he used his position as First Consul to foster a personality cult, replacing the Revolution's classical republican iconography with royalist-imperial images. The words *Karolus Magnus* are carved into the rock at Napoleon's feet in Jacques-Louis David's famous portrait of him crossing the Alps, painted in 1801–2. The idea of a heroic strongman asserting order had considerable popular appeal after the revolutionary disorders. The appropriation of Charlemagne was part of a wider strategy to legitimate the regime without tying it to any single tradition. More specifically, the Frankish king's role as papal protector proved useful when Napoleon urgently needed a compromise with the papacy to end the Revolution's war with French Catholics, which had killed 317,000 people since 1793. These moves culminated in Napoleon's proclamation of himself as 'emperor of the French' on 18 May 1804, followed by his coronation on 2 December where Pope Pius VII read the same text used by Leo III when investing Charlemagne over a millennium before. Replicas of Charlemagne's sword and crown had to be used, because the Austrians still had the originals. Napoleon hoped to reconcile republicans by issuing a new constitution, but he did not regard the French as new Roman citizens. He declared Rome a free city when he annexed the Papal States to France in 1809, rather than making it his imperial capital.[68]

The Napoleonic empire promised to guarantee order by sweeping away defective socio-political arrangements and defeating all possible external enemies. Napoleon's universalism rested on the hegemony of decisive victory and rational uniformity exemplified by his civil code and the metric system.[69] His deployment of Charlemagne's legacy directly challenged the Empire by suggesting his territorial ambitions extended to the entire former Frankish realm. Initially, he still formally deferred, promising in May 1804 that he would only use his imperial title once it had been recognized by Emperor Francis II and the Empire.[70]

Austrian ministers immediately recognized that refusal would mean renewed war, but like their Prussian counterparts, they deluded themselves in thinking that Napoleon's conversion of the revolutionary republic into a monarchy would make France more predictable. Although the leading minister, Count Cobenzl, acknowledged that Francis II's status 'has shrivelled to little more than an honorific title', it had to be upheld lest Russia claim parity and Britain assume its own imperial crown.[71] Conversion of the Holy Roman imperial title into a hereditary one was rejected as breaching the Empire's constitution. Instead, the vague status of the Habsburg lands as a separate monarchy provided the basis for Francis II to assume a new, additional and hereditary title of 'emperor of Austria'. The title was intended to maintain Austria's formal parity with France since 1757, whilst still allowing Francis to trump Napoleon through his additional Holy Roman dignity. In December 1804 the new status was announced along with a fanfare of trumpets and kettledrums to crowds assembled before specially constructed wooden tribunes in Vienna's six suburbs.[72] No coronation was considered necessary, because Francis had already been crowned as the (last) Holy Roman emperor in 1792: there was never an Austrian imperial coronation throughout the entire life of the Austrian empire, between 1804 and 1918.

The conservative publicist Friedrich von Gentz wrote to the future chief minister Metternich that Francis might as well call himself emperor of Salzburg, Frankfurt or Passau.[73] His critique reflected the widespread belief that the proliferation of imperial titles diminished them all.

Sweden lodged a formal protest in its capacity as guarantor of the Peace of Westphalia, claiming Francis had exceeded his powers by unilaterally assuming the title rather than securing agreement from the Reichstag.[74] Criticism was rendered irrelevant by relentless French pressure, which frustrated any remaining hope of reforming the Empire. Napoleon crowned himself king of Italy on 26 May 1805 using the Lombard iron crown, thus usurping one of the Empire's three core kingdoms. Further friction produced renewed war, culminating in Napoleon's decisive victory over Austria and Russia at Austerlitz on 2 December 1805. Napoleon soon abandoned ideas of assuming the Holy Roman imperial title, partly because this would hinder peace with Britain and Russia, while Austria still had the original regalia, but mainly because its associations were incompatible with his style of imperial rule (see Plate 3).[75] He now sought to undermine the remnants of the old order to break Austria's remaining influence over the smaller German territories. Faced with the threat of renewed war, Francis II reluctantly abdicated on 6 August 1806, hoping that by dissolving the Empire he would undermine the legitimacy of Napoleon's reorganization of Germany.

The events of 1804–6 signalled a new age for European empire. Although Napoleon's Grand Empire collapsed in 1814, his nephew ruled a Second French Empire between 1852 and 1870, while the subsequent republican regime expanded the country's overseas possessions into a large colonial empire from the 1880s. Prussia's victory over the Second French Empire led to the foundation of the German Second Empire in 1871. Queen Victoria finally formalized British imperialism by assuming the title 'empress of India' in 1876. Throughout, Austria, Russia and the Ottomans remained imperial states. There were now six empires on one continent. 'Empire' ceased to mean a singular 'world order' and became the title accorded a monarch ruling a large state.

NEW WORLDS

Imperial Spain

The hegemonic aspects of late nineteenth-century European imperialism were clearest in the global dominance in which even the continent's smaller countries shared – notably Belgium's notorious rule in the

Congo. This new imperial age had begun with Portuguese and Spanish conquests in the later fifteenth century and differed fundamentally from the imperial ideal embodied by the Empire. Spain is the most interesting case here, because it acquired the largest European empire (prior to the British) while its king was also Holy Roman Emperor Charles V.

Medieval Iberia was governed by multiple rival kingdoms. Documents for the king of Asturias used terms like *basileus* and *rex magnus* in the tenth century. These kingdoms were imperialist in the hegemonic sense, based on the victories of Asturias over the Moors and other Spanish kingdoms. The same impulse explains the intermittent use of the title *totius Hispaniae imperator* in the late eleventh and twelfth centuries. By 1200, Spanish writers rejected ideas that their country had ever been part of the Carolingian empire, citing Charlemagne's defeat in the Pyrenees in 778. Unlike their role in the Crusades, Holy Roman emperors played no part in the Reconquista of Iberia from the Moors.

Already prior to the Staufers' collapse, Vincentius Hispanus wrote 'the Germans have lost the Empire by their own stupidity', suggesting Spanish kings had demonstrated better credentials by battling Muslims.[76] Such claims received some attention outside Spain, assisting the election of Alfonso X of Castile as German king in 1257. Although 'foreign' like his rival for the royal title, Richard, earl of Cornwall, Alfonso was nonetheless the grandson of the German king Philip of Swabia and a Staufer ally. His election to the imperial office was also backed by Pisa and Marseille (then part of Burgundy), reflecting the wider Mediterranean connections of these parts of the Empire. Unlike Richard, who was elected simultaneously by a rival faction, Alfonso never went to the Empire, though he initially acted as German king by issuing charters to the dukes of Brabant and Lorraine, as well as petitioning the pope to prepare an imperial coronation.[77]

Alfonso's nominal rule ended in 1273 and remained an isolated interlude. Meanwhile, individual Spanish kingdoms acquired their own Mediterranean dominions. Catalonia briefly held the duchy of Athens, a fragment of the crumbling Byzantine empire in the fourteenth century. Aragon acquired Sicily (1282) and Sardinia (1297), whilst also absorbing neighbouring Catalonia and Valencia, before finally joining Castile in 1469 to create a united Spain. Spain joined the Italian Wars after 1494 to press claims to Naples. Potential conflict with imperial interests was defused through dynastic marriage with the Habsburgs, leading to Charles V's accession in Spain in 1516, three years ahead of his election as emperor. At that point, Charles ruled 40 per cent of all Europeans, controlled the continent's major financial and economic centres (Castile, Antwerp, Genoa, Augsburg), and enjoyed access to Spain's seemingly unlimited colonial wealth (Map 8).[78]

The combination of Europe's last Christian empire and foremost New World one proved an unsteady mix lasting only for Charles's reign. Charles was the last and greatest of the travelling emperors. Whereas none (except the three crusading emperors) had ventured far beyond imperial frontiers, Charles visited England and Africa both twice, France four times, Spain six, Italy seven and Germany nine. Meanwhile, conquistadors claimed Mexico, Peru, Chile and Florida in his name. As the French philosopher and jurist Jean Bodin already noted in 1566, the association with the rapidly expanding New World made the old Empire appear smaller, not greater.[79]

Antoine de Granvelle advised Charles V to designate his son Philip as successor rather than his younger brother Ferdinand I, because effective exercise of the imperial office clearly required considerable wealth. Charles had planned to nominate Philip as his brother's successor in a bid to establish alternating emperors from Austria and Spain, but was thwarted by Ferdinand's opposition in 1548.[80] Instead, Philip was assigned Burgundy, thus retaining a place within the Empire at the partition of the Spanish and Austrian branches in 1558. By that point it appeared that Spain had a better claim to represent the universal Christian mission. Sebastian Münster's *Cosmographia* included a map devised in 1537 by Johannes Putsch showing Europe as a monarch: Germania was merely the torso, whereas Iberia represented the head (see Plate 17).[81] This appeared still more justified once Philip annexed Portugal in 1580 after its king disappeared in battle against the Moors: now Spain held the other European world empire.

Philip had lived in Germany from 1548 to 1551, knew many princes personally, and still considered himself an imperial prince even after succeeding his father as king of Spain in 1556. These Hispano-German contacts would be largely broken by his death in 1598, while concessions to Protestants at the Peace of Augsburg (1555) reinforced Spanish perceptions of the Empire as in decline.[82] Spaniards increasingly articulated their own universalist claims based on victories over the Ottomans and heretics – the success of their arguments is demonstrated by the way history remembers their naval victory over the Turks at Lepanto (1571), rather than the more substantial conflicts fought by Austria in defence of Hungary. Spain's ruler, it was claimed, was Europe's premier king, because he was the most godly.[83] This allowed Spain to assume self-appointed leadership without directly antagonizing their Austrian cousins, who still held the imperial title. Considering himself the senior Habsburg, Philip III felt entitled to succeed Rudolf II, but also grand enough already to dispense with doing so. In 1617 he traded support for Ferdinand II's election as next emperor in return for territorial concessions from Austria intended to improve Spain's strategic position. Spain backed Austria during the Thirty Years War in the expectation that Ferdinand II would help it against the Dutch rebels and France on the grounds that Spanish possessions in Burgundy and northern Italy were still part of the Empire.

Biology overtook strategy after 1646 as the Spanish Habsburgs faced extinction, precipitating a decline that was more personal than structural.[84] Spain increasingly relied on Austria, especially to defend its north Italian possessions against France. Nonetheless, there was considerable Spanish resistance to the prospect of Austria inheriting their empire at the death of the last Spanish Habsburg, Charles II, in 1700. Britain and the Dutch Republic backed a continuation of existing arrangements using the Austrian Archduke Charles to found a new Spanish Habsburg line. Emperor Leopold I cooperated, but clearly intended securing Spain's possessions in Italy for Austria.[85] Austrian biological failure in turn undid these arrangements. The deaths of Leopold (1705) and his eldest son and successor Joseph I (1711) left Archduke Charles as the sole Habsburg candidate for the imperial title (as Charles VI). Britain and the Dutch opposed the resurrection of Charles V's combined Old and New World empire, forcing Charles VI reluctantly to renounce Spain and its overseas possessions by 1714.

No Place in the Sun

Although Austria recovered direct control of Burgundy and northern Italy, it remained excluded from Spain's colonial riches. This was compounded by Anglo-Dutch confirmation (in 1713) of the closure of the river Scheldt to international commerce, conceded by Spain as part of its peace with the Dutch in 1648. These arrangements secured Amsterdam's supremacy over Antwerp, which had been Europe's principal Atlantic entrepôt under Charles V. Such exclusion from lucrative global trade has long been part of the charge sheet cited by German nationalist historians for the Empire's supposed weakness. Even more recent, balanced accounts blame Charles V for denying Germany a chance to participate in early European colonialism through assigning Burgundy's maritime towns to Spain in 1548. 'Defeats' in the Thirty Years War a century later allegedly compounded this by transferring many North Sea and Baltic ports to Sweden. Germans were supposedly unable to engage effectively in colonial trade, retarding economic and social development, which had to be pushed through at great political cost during the later nineteenth century when Kaiser Wilhelm II vociferously demanded his 'place in the sun' of European imperialism.[86]

Quite apart from ignoring the extensive commercial activity of Italians who still lived within the Empire during this period, these arguments underestimate German involvement in colonial trade. Maximilian I and his family used the south German merchants like the Fugger, Welser, Herwart and Imhoff firms to procure precious stones from the Far East and New World. Germans, Netherlanders and Italians from the Empire were heavily involved in Portuguese colonial and trading ventures in India, and later in Dutch activity in Brazil, Africa and Indonesia. For instance, Count Johann Moritz of Nassau-Siegen was a key figure in disseminating scientific knowledge to Europe while he was governor of Dutch Brazil from 1636 to 1644. Thousands of German soldiers served the Portuguese, Dutch and British in the Indies and Americas, most notoriously in the failed attempt to suppress the American Revolution (1775–83).[87]

The absence of a strong, centralized monarchy did not inhibit direct colonial ventures from the Empire. Despite the outbreak of the Thirty Years War in 1618, Duke Friedrich III of Holstein-Gottorp founded the port of Friedrichstadt as a North Sea base for colonial commerce in 1621. Having secured imperial privileges, the duke also despatched a trade mission to Russia and Persia (1633–6). Opposition from other Holstein towns and a peasant insurrection frustrated these ventures.[88] Colonial activity was promoted as a panacea to the problems of economic development after the end of the Thirty Years War in 1648. As many other Europeans discovered, the actual costs generally outweighed the benefits: In 1669 Count Friedrich Casimir of Hanau-Münzenberg was deposed by his relations after losing his money buying a large tract of Dutch Guiana.

Brandenburg-Prussia undertook the largest of these ventures. Having failed to buy Tranquebar on the Bay of Bengal from Denmark, the elector founded the Brandenburg African Company in 1682, directly modelled on its much larger and better-financed Dutch rivals. This engaged in the Atlantic triangular trade, transporting 30,000 African slaves to the Americas and importing sugar, wood, cocoa, indigo and tobacco through its base at Emden. The Brandenburg navy never exceeded 34 warships and proved too small to overcome Dutch and French hostility. The main post was sold to the Dutch in 1717, with the last transferred to France four years later.[89] In 1667 Austria founded an Oriental Company to trade with Persia and the Ottomans. Disrupted by the Turkish Wars (1683–1718), this resumed in a new form in 1719 at Trieste, which Charles VI designated a free port. A new Austrian navy was established under an English admiral, while conscripted peasants built a road over the mountains linking Trieste to Vienna. Its subsequent bankruptcy in 1734 was due to its being tied to the Austrian state lottery, which went bust. A separate Ostend Company was founded in 1722 to circumvent the embargo on the Scheldt and open trade with India and China. This was abandoned in 1731 to purchase Anglo-Dutch support for Austrian interests in Europe. Prussia also briefly operated an Asiatic Company trading with China during the 1750s.

Adverse circumstances precipitated all these failures. The Empire also lacked the central focus present in the combination of government support and financial capital available in Iberia, England, France and the Dutch Republic. However, the primary reason was that such activity was never a priority for any of the Empire's multiple authorities. Eighteenth-century German territorial governments were more concerned to attract migrants than see valuable taxpayers and potential recruits emigrate to distant colonies. Numerous Germans indeed sought better lives in British North America, providing the origins of the 'Pennsylvania Dutch' (*Deutsch*) and the word 'dollar' (deriving from the German silver coin *Taler*). Nonetheless, Brandenburg-Prussia attracted 74,000 immigrants between 1640 and 1740, including 20,000 French Huguenots, followed by another 285,000 people by

1800. A further 200,000 migrants were enticed by the Habsburgs to settle in Hungary, while Catherine II induced 100,000 to settle in Russia. In all, 740,000 Germans moved east compared to 150,000 heading for North America during the eighteenth century.[90]

The Hanoverian succession in Britain in 1714 did not change the Empire's relationship to European colonialism. Concerned that his electorate might become a British dependency, George I kept Hanoverian government, armed forces and laws entirely separate. Britain-Hanover remained a purely personal union that fragmented in 1837 with the accession of Queen Victoria, who, as a woman, was disbarred from succeeding in Hanover, which went its brief, separate way under its own kings until annexed by Prussia in 1866.[91] The British crown played a prominent role in promoting what became the world's largest empire, but private capital also loomed large in the chartered companies active in North America, the Caribbean, Africa and especially India. Queen Victoria's assumption of an imperial title 18 years after the dissolution of the Mughul empire remained confined only to India. Likewise, republics such as France and (from 1898) the USA acquired colonies without assuming the formal trappings of empire. The mission and intent of these New World empires were very different from those of the Old World's Holy Roman Empire.

FIFTH MONARCHY

Emperors in their own Kingdoms

Europeans developed their own critique of empire long before they began subjugating non-Europeans. European anti-imperialism originated in papal propaganda during the Investiture Dispute and especially with the onset of renewed conflict against the Staufer emperors from the mid-twelfth century. Responding to renewed papal schism after 1159, John of Salisbury posed the rhetorical question to Frederick I: 'Who is he that subjugates the universal church to a particular church? Who has appointed the Germans the judges of nations? Who has granted such a coarse and violent folk the power to install a prince above humanity?'[92]

However, the papacy's own actions simultaneously invalidated its claims to supplant the emperor as universal judge. Increasingly, legal scholars rewrote imperialism from a benevolent common Christian order to present it as unwarranted hegemony of one power over another. Initially, these arguments were directed primarily at strengthening royal authority within each kingdom, rather than challenging the Holy Roman emperor's pre-eminence. The early thirteenth-century Italian lawyer Azo of Bologna claimed each king was 'an emperor in his own kingdom' (*rex imperator in regno suo est*), defining sovereignty at this point as freedom from internal constraints on royal power. England's King John claimed in 1202 that 'the kingdom of the English can be compared to an empire' for the same reason, though through Magna Carta his barons compelled him to acknowledge there were indeed limits.[93] Unlike in the Empire, sacralization of monarchy continued in the west, where it was used to elevate kings above fractious nobles. The crime of *lèse-majesté*, previously reserved to protect the emperor, was increasingly employed to defend kings. Even criticizing the king was now equated with sacrilege. These arguments were employed nationally, with each set of scholars claiming them exclusively for their own king whilst still acknowledging the emperor's authority as extending over other European kingdoms.[94]

The early Renaissance added impetus to this debate by disseminating a new understanding of Aristotle's political categories, and with attempts to write national histories, all of which encouraged the view that Europe was composed of distinct countries each claiming descent from 'free' peoples. French monarchs found these arguments especially useful in their struggles for influence against early fourteenth-century popes and emperors. The organization of the Council of Constance (1414–18) into 'national' groups of bishops is widely acknowledged as marking the general acceptance of Europe as composed of distinct sovereign jurisdictions.[95]

Gradual disenchantment with the ideal of a singular Christian order raised the question of how the various kingdoms should interact peacefully. It proved hard to conceive of anything other than some kind of hierarchy. Christian doctrine maintained the imperfection of earthly existence and divinely ordained socio-political inequality. The new theories of monarchy elevated each king above his own lords, making it difficult to accept that he was not also superior to other monarchs. Unfortunately, this intensified competition between monarchs, since precedence had to be actively asserted.[96]

These developments encouraged new interest in the emperor as arbiter of this potentially violent new order, not least because the Reformation removed the pope as an acceptable alternative, while the rapid accumulation of territories in direct Habsburg possession at last gave the emperor the means to intervene effectively in European affairs. French opposition and Charles V's inability to defuse the religious controversy swiftly closed this opportunity.[97] Spanish power and pretensions after 1558 attracted growing criticism that it was usurping the traditional imperial role through seeking an illegitimate 'fifth monarchy'. Although drawing on the traditional 'four world monarchies' ideology, this predominantly French and Protestant critique was implicitly hostile to the Empire, not least because its proponents usually saw Austria as Spain's willing spear carrier.[98] Imperialism now meant the illegitimate subordination of sovereign monarchies and their peoples.

Meanwhile, sovereignty assumed its modern definition through the response of Jean Bodin to the civil wars in his native France after 1562. Bodin expounded the view that sovereignty was indivisible and could not be shared either with groups or individuals within a country or those outside it. This idea formed the basis of the modern definition of the state, as articulated by Max Weber and others much later. Sovereignty becomes a monopoly of legitimate authority over a clearly demarcated area and its inhabitants. The sovereign state is responsible for internal order and can command its population's resources. External relations were redefined accordingly as the central government's exclusive prerogative. The earlier concern for loyalty was replaced by an insistence on authority. Medieval vassals had usually been free to act independently provided they did not breach good faith with their overlord. Such action was increasingly regarded as treasonable disobedience, and mercenary service and other 'extraterritorial violence' were gradually criminalized between about 1520 and 1856 by states insisting on an exclusive power to make war.[99]

The Empire as International Actor

Europe's shift from a medieval to a modern sovereign state order co-incided with the Empire's own reforms, consolidating it as a mixed monarchy where the emperor shared power with a complex hierarchy of imperial Estates.[100] Sovereignty remained fragmented and shared, rather than becoming concentrated in a single, 'national' government. To many later commentators, this merely appears further evidence of the Empire's 'decline'. However, medieval emperors had never monopolized powers of war and peace. Rather, imperial reform constructed new, collectively shared powers in response to the changing international circumstances and new methods of warfare.[101] Crucially for the Empire's subsequent history, these constitutional changes were made while the shape of the wider European order remained open and Charles V's accession in 1519 lent new substance to traditional claims of imperial pre-eminence.

Measures adopted between 1495 and 1519 distinguished between wars against non-Christians and those against other Christians. The former were still understood in established terms as repelling the Ottoman menace, rather than the colonial conflicts waged by conquistadors and others in the New World. As we have seen (see pp. 149–51), peace with Muslims was considered impossible, so no formal declaration of war was necessary. The imperial Estates were only allowed from the 1520s to debate the level of 'Turkish assistance' (*Türkenhilfe*), not the emperor's right to demand it. By contrast, conflicts with Christians were handled as judicial rather than military issues, because the emperor was expected to remain at peace with his fellow monarchs. The emperor could not demand assistance, though his obligation to consult the Reichstag since 1495 before making war in the Empire's name was lightened in 1519 to discussing this only with the electors. Moreover, like his medieval counterparts he was still free to wage war using his own resources.[102]

As a collective actor, the Empire approached war with Christian neighbours on a similar basis to breaches of its own internal 'public peace' declared in 1495. Rather than escalating conflict through an imperative to mobilize, imperial law sought to minimize violence by forbidding imperial Estates to assist those disturbing the peace. Acting through the Empire's new supreme courts, the emperor could issue 'advocates' mandates', identifying lawbreakers as 'enemies of the Empire' (*Reichsfeinde*). Although imperial Estates were required to assist in restoring peace, this system effectively ruled out mobilization for offensive war. Moreover, it drew on established medieval practices by requiring incremental action proceeding first with public warnings to desist, before force could be used. This process has often been mistaken for wilful inaction and has made it hard to identify if and when the Empire moved from peace to war in particular circumstances.

The Reichstag at Speyer declared France an enemy of the Empire in 1544, but this exceptional act rested on that country's temporary alliance with the Ottomans and was not repeated.[103] The emperor continued to use advocates' mandates against Christian enemies, including during the Thirty Years War and the conflicts against Louis XIV after 1672. The declaration of 'imperial war' (*Reichskrieg*) by the Reichstag against France on 11 February 1689 represented a significant innovation. The Empire had already mobilized to repel the French invasion of the Palatinate in 1688, but by expressly drawing on the 1544 precedent the new declaration sought to rally moral and material support by placing France on a par with the Ottomans. The practice was repeated in 1702, 1733, 1793 and 1799, in each case following actual mobilization through advocates' mandates and other, more decentralized constitutional mechanisms.

Formal 'imperial war' was a useful tool for the Habsburgs in steering the imperial Estates to support their objectives, but as a powerful symbol of collective action for the Empire's 'conservation, security and well-being' it also stood in stark contrast to the search for personal *gloire* exemplified by Louis XIV's belligerence.[104] Military action was also collective. Rather than create a single, permanent army, the Empire raised forces when needed by drawing on troops provided by the imperial Estates. Imperial law thus sanctioned the militarization of the Empire's principalities, giving their rulers a vested interest in preserving the overall constitutional framework as the legal basis for their own military power.

However, the authority to raise troops and taxes from their own subjects also allowed princes to engage as individual actors in the new European politics. Other monarchs always needed troops and were often prepared to pay for German assistance by promising money and influence to help princes achieve their own objectives. This created considerable public-order problems during the early sixteenth century as soldiers were discharged at the end of each campaign, often subsisting as marauders through the winter until hired again in the following spring. The provision of troops to both sides in the French and Dutch civil wars from the 1560s also threatened to drag the Empire into these conflicts. The Reichstag legislated through the 1560s and 1570s to assert control through the imperial Estates, who were empowered to restrict their subjects' service as mercenaries and to coordinate police action against marauders. These changes entrenched the monopoly of 'extraterritorial violence' in the hands of the imperial Estates as part of their 'German freedom', whilst preserving the collective structure by banning any military action harmful to the emperor or Empire.[105]

As with the right of Reformation from 1555, the Peace of Westphalia in 1648 simply incorporated this military authority in modified form rather than granting new powers. The principal change was to explicitly deny military authority to mediate nobles, towns and territorial assemblies. This has been widely misunderstood. The standard verdict was that 'the Empire in its old sense had ceased to exist' because 'every authority was emperor in its own territory'.[106] In fact, the princes did not receive new powers to make alliances; their dealings with outside powers remained constrained by the obligation not to harm the emperor or Empire. In practice, their engagement in European relations varied according to their inclination, material resources, geographical location and status within the Empire's constitutional order. The really significant change was that this order was increasingly at odds with the evolving sovereign state system. The gradual acceptance of Bodin's idea of indivisible sovereignty detached it from social status, shrinking the circle of legitimate public actors from all lords to just mutually recognized states. By contrast, princely status remained both social and political within the Empire's internal hierarchy. As imperial Estates, princes possessed only shares of the Empire's fragmented sovereignty, expressed as 'territorial sovereignty' (*Landeshoheit*), which remained circumscribed by imperial law and the emperor's formal position as their feudal overlord. Thus, in an international order increasingly characterized by independent states, princes occupied an anomalous position of being neither fully sovereign yet clearly something more than the aristocrats of western countries.

This explains the intensity of princely involvement in European wars and diplomacy from the late seventeenth century when all the larger principalities developed permanent armies and maintained envoys in major European capitals. There was 'an epidemic of desires and aspirations for a royal title', since this alone was now equated with sovereignty: being an elector or duke was no longer enough.[107] Arguably this contributed to international instability, either indirectly through the provision of auxiliaries, or through direct intervention as belligerents like Saxony, Prussia and Hanover in the Great Northern War. However, even more centralized European states were scarcely better at curbing autonomous violence by their subjects, whether in the form of the English and Dutch armed trading companies or the colonial militias which, for example, triggered the French and Indian War in 1754. Perhaps more remarkable still was the fact that, despite being the most heavily armed part of Europe, the Empire did not fragment into the kind of warlordism characterizing China after 1911.[108]

The Empire and European Peace

A Holy Roman emperor was no longer expected to act as Europe's policeman by the later sixteenth century, but there was still scope for the emperor as peacemaker. Such action was often in the Empire's interests, as well as in tune with the traditional imperial ideal. Although repeated efforts to resolve the Dutch civil wars failed, Maximilian II brokered an end to the Danish-Swedish War of 1563–70, securing 50 years of peace for northern Germany.[109]

The Westphalian settlement explicitly linked the Empire's internal equilibrium to wider European peace through its combination of constitutional changes within an international settlement.[110] The 'German freedom' of the imperial Estates was formalized to prevent the emperor converting the Empire into a centralized state capable of threatening its neighbours. Immediate practical conditions shaped this more than theoretical considerations. The Peace of Westphalia forbade Austria from assisting Spain, which remained at war with France until 1659. The unsettled conditions along the Empire's western frontier encouraged Elector Johann Philipp von Schönborn of Mainz and like-minded princes to seek a wider international alliance to guarantee the Westphalian settlement and secure permanent peace. When these efforts faltered around 1672, Schönborn and others tried interposing themselves as a neutral 'third party' to prevent the Empire being dragged into the wars against France.[111]

These efforts generally ran counter to the interests of the Habsburgs, who managed to scupper them by presenting the princes as dupes of the deceitful French. Nonetheless, the option of formal *Reichsmediation* collectively through the Reichstag retained considerable moral weight since it was first proposed in 1524 as a way of ending Charles V's war with France. Ferdinand III recovered Habsburg influence lost earlier in the Thirty Years War by inviting the imperial Estates to participate in the Westphalian peace congress. The Reichstag's permanence after 1663 offered further possibilities, because the presence of envoys from most European states gave it the character of an international congress.[112] Offers to mediate were made in each subsequent major war, but were always frustrated by Habsburg opposition and the growing ceremonial difficulties posed by the discrepancies between imperial Estates and European sovereigns.

The Empire's limitations as an active peacemaker did not diminish interest in its place in the continent's tranquillity, especially amongst those dissatisfied with the free-market approach to peace that relied on a supposedly self-regulating 'balance of power'. Because the Empire had represented an idealized universal order during the Middle Ages, it should not surprise us that writers after the sixteenth century also saw the Empire as a model for a common European system. Prominent exponents included the political philosopher Samuel von Pufendorf, the Abbé St Pierre, William Penn, Jean-Jacques Rousseau and Immanuel Kant. Their proposals involved states surrendering at least part of their sovereignty to one or more common institutions inspired by the Reichstag and the Empire's supreme courts. They offered a positive assessment of the Empire at a time when others felt it was in terminal decline.[113] Yet their idealized discussions bore little resemblance to the Empire's political and social realities. Peace in the Empire remained rooted in pre-modern methods of consensus-seeking and the defence of corporate rights, in contrast to the new ideals of sovereignty, individual rights and (after 1789) popular control of hegemonic state power.

PART II

Belonging

4

Lands

THE EMPIRE AND ITS LANDS

Core and Periphery

The Empire was never a unitary state with a homogeneous population, but instead a patchwork of lands and peoples under an uneven and changing imperial jurisdiction. This chapter outlines how and when different parts of Europe were associated with the Empire, arguing that its political core was not necessarily its geographical one. Empires and imperial expansion are usually explained through the core–periphery model. The Roman, Ottoman, Russian and British empires are presented as expanding outwards through the conquest or control of other lands. An empire is thus defined by the dominance of a core over more peripheral territory that is only loosely integrated or kept entirely separate. The core is usually considered more highly organized, economically developed and militarily superior to the often less densely populated periphery. This relationship also appears to explain collapse through the law of diminishing returns, with further conquests bringing additional administrative and security costs that outweigh gains in resources.

The Empire only loosely fits this model, contributing to the speculation already noted in the introduction of whether it was really imperial. The Franks were not, in fact, unusual in appearing more 'backward' than the late Roman societies they conquered in Gaul and parts of Italy. The same has been said of the Mongols during the thirteenth century or the Manchus in China after 1644. However, the Carolingians and their successors (with the partial exception of the Ottonians) generally disdained the more urbanized, densely populated Italy in favour of remaining north of the Alps. Aachen and Rome were only two of several important sites in a realm that remained characterized by multiple centres rather than a single core. The original Frankish heartland had stretched from the Loire valley eastwards to Frankfurt, and from Aachen in the north southwards into Provence and (later) Lombardy. This region was fragmented three ways by the ninth-century partitions, while the imperial title migrated among the Frankish successor kingdoms before finally coming to rest in Germany under Otto I. Ottonian rule shifted political geography northwards into Saxony without entirely displacing the significance of earlier centres. The focus moved south-west to the Middle Rhine under the Salians and then also to Italy with the Staufers, before shifting back to the Rhineland in the later thirteenth century. Luxembourg rule moved the imperial title to Bohemia, before it came to reside in Austria under the Habsburgs, though again without completely overshadowing established centres like Aachen, Frankfurt, Nuremberg and Regensburg.

This movement suggests we should re-imagine the interrelationship of the Empire's territories according to their degree of openness to the emperor's authority, rather than as a fixed pattern of control.[1] We can label 'king's country' the areas which elsewhere correspond to a core, provided we recognize that their identity changed during the Empire's history. The Franks merged relatively quickly with other elites and thereafter the Empire never had a single 'imperial people' akin to the position of the Manchus in China or Anglo-Saxons in the British empire. Instead, king's country was defined legally through prerogatives allowing the emperor to exploit particular resources to sustain his rule. While these properties were concentrated in certain regions, there were always some scattered elsewhere to enable him to roam more widely. Personal royal possessions assumed greater importance, becoming what can be called more properly 'dynastic territories' from the fourteenth century. These ultimately replaced properties associated with imperial prerogatives and constituted the king's country of late medieval and early modern emperors. Throughout, king's country was never contiguous, as a glance at a map of Habsburg possessions will readily show.

A second category of land 'close to the king' was also defined politically rather than geographically or ethnically and comprised areas on which the monarch could normally rely, but which were controlled indirectly through vassals. Initially, these lands were usually held by men who were related by blood or marriage to the royal family, but their support was contingent on how far they could persuade their own dependants to cooperate. These hierarchical ties of kinship and dependency become more formal, especially after the twelfth century, and were codified through the imperial reforms around 1500. Dynastic ties retained significance even into the eighteenth century, including the role of Habsburg archdukes as prince-bishops in the imperial church.

Areas 'open to the king' formed a third category, also mediated by vassalage and other jurisdictions, but held by people who would not necessarily fully honour formal obligations. The success of individual monarchs was often determined by their ability to maximize support from these areas. The constitutional changes around 1500 essentially involved the Habsburgs' acceptance of more formal power-sharing in return for binding the 'open' and 'close' areas within a system of more enforceable obligations. 'Distant' regions formed a fourth category and were the more peripheral politically, sharing some of the characteristics with the classic core–periphery model. The frontier zones of northern and eastern Germany remained peripheral for most of the Middle Ages. This relationship could change, however. Austria, established as a border zone in the tenth century, became the imperial core from the mid-fifteenth century. Conversely, Brandenburg shifted from open to the king under the Luxembourgs to become the Habsburgs' chief opponent after 1740.

Hierarchy

The four categories just discussed varied in their political proximity to the emperor, but did not necessarily relate hierarchically to each other. For example, distant regions were rarely subordinate to any of the other categories, but instead enjoyed the same immediacy under the emperor as much of the king's country. Hierarchy was a central feature of the Empire throughout its existence, and some important aspects require discussion here.

The Empire was neither a single command chain nor a neat pyramid with the emperor at the pinnacle. Instead, the Empire was an idealized overarching framework encompassing multiple elements that were both

internally hierarchical and that interrelated in complex patterns characterized by inequality. The most significant of these components were
already identified as kingdoms (*regna*) in the ninth century. However,
what actually constituted a kingdom was not constant. Similarly, not
all the places which contemporaries called *regna* were actually ruled by
men titled 'kings'. The Carolingians accorded Aquitaine and Bavaria
semi-regal status, without either of them becoming full kingdoms at
that point. It was generally accepted that a kingdom should be large,
but there was no agreed minimum size defined by either territory or
population. Ecclesiastical autonomy was significant early on, with the
creation of separate archdioceses important to the recognition of Hungary, Poland and Bohemia as kingdoms during the eleventh century.
This tied regal status to Christianization, especially manifested through
cathedral-building and recognition of a patron saint. Heathen barbarians never could be fully regal, no matter what they might themselves
claim. Political autonomy lagged considerably behind, since kingship
was not equated with sovereign independence until early modernity.
Despite being ruled by their own kings, Burgundy and Bohemia
remained parts of the Empire.

The interrelationship of the Carolingian kingdoms remained
unstable while the imperial title passed between them. Otto I's coronation in 962 permanently associated the imperial prerogatives and
status with the position of German king, making Germany the Empire's
premier kingdom (see Plate 15).[2] Italy slipped into second place after
having been primarily associated with the imperial title between
840 and 924. Otto's defeat of Berengar II ended the sequence of separate Italian kings. Henceforth, whoever was German king was also
king of Italy, even without a separate coronation. Burgundy emerged
from the Carolingian middle kingdom (Lotharingia) in 879 and maintained a distinct existence despite being considered subordinate to the
Empire from the late tenth century. After 1032, Burgundy passed to the
German king, who assumed authority directly, as in Italy. Italian and
Burgundian lords were not always prepared to accept this unless the
German king had also been crowned emperor, but they no longer
sought to raise one of their own number as king.[3]

Germany's premier status was demonstrated by the use of its royal
insignia for imperial coronations. Those of Italy and Burgundy only
assumed significance during the fourteenth century with international

challenges to the German king's pre-eminence. The title 'king of Italy' replaced that of 'the Lombards' used by Charlemagne, though it was still associated with the Lombard iron crown said to have belonged to Theodoric. Italian coronations were generally held after 844, though many German kings dispensed with one. When Henry VII arrived in Milan in 1311 the iron crown could not be found; it was believed to have been pawned but in fact had never existed. By then, however, it was thought that the German king received a silver crown, before being crowned with an iron one in Italy and finally the golden imperial crown at his imperial coronation in Rome. Siena goldsmiths were accordingly instructed to make an iron crown for Henry. Within two centuries this was so rusty that it was replaced by an ancient diadem preserved in the church of San Giovanni in Monza, which contained an iron hoop said to have been made from a nail from the Holy Cross. This was used to crown Charles V as king of Italy at Bologna in 1530 – the last emperor to go through a formal Italian coronation.[4] Burgundy lacked any enduring royal insignia. When it re-emerged as a separate state in the fifteenth century, its ruler was only a duke and he established the heraldic Order of the Golden Fleece to assert his prestige instead.

THE OLD KINGDOMS

Demarcation and Integration

The Empire's principal kingdoms were not clearly delineated before the eleventh century. Their inhabitants lacked maps and regarded geography differently from later generations. For example, rivers like the Rhine were medieval expressways rather than potential frontiers. Politics involved networks and chains of obligations and responsibilities, not uniform control of clearly bounded territories. Internal subdivisions within the three kingdoms of West Francia, East Francia and Lotharingia also remained in flux, in contrast to the wider European pattern of gradual integration of regions within a recognizable 'national' whole. Italian and German history has generally been written as if it ran in the opposite direction: as stories of national *disintegration* only redressed violently through nineteenth-century unification. Meanwhile, Burgundy largely disappears, because it is no longer a single country, instead being absorbed into France, Germany, Italy and the smaller 'nations' of Belgium, the Netherlands and Luxembourg.

The picture becomes clearer when we accept that 'integration' and 'demarcation' are not necessarily opposites. The integration of autonomous or conquered regions into more obviously centralized monarchies like France also required fixing boundaries and defining jurisdictions, especially where distinct legal arrangements were allowed to persist. The situation in the Empire had unique features, but was not wholly dissimilar. Demarcation here has been labelled 'territorialization' (see pp. 365–77) and entailed clearer spatial divisions, around 35 of which ultimately emerged as sovereign states after 1806. However, this process was neither one of progressive fragmentation into ever-smaller territories, nor the steady evolution of existing subdivisions towards sovereign statehood. Rather, the components changed their size and character throughout the Empire's existence. Some territories indeed fragmented, or became more distinct. Others appeared at some point, only to be subsumed later within neighbouring territories. Moreover, this process was not an expression of declining central power. Rather, spatial demarcation co-evolved with how the Empire was governed. In particular, demographic and economic expansion around 1000 opened new possibilities to expand the lordly elite through subdividing existing jurisdictions. In short, integration proceeded through demarcating more jurisdictions, rather than trying to bind those already established under tighter central supervision.

Germany

The standard fragmentation narrative sees Germany as already composed of several distinct tribal regions prior to 800. The Frankish conquests advanced through several stages from the sixth century as the Merovingians recognized certain tribal chiefs as 'dukes', or military leaders, in return for tribute and submission. Full conquest from the late eighth century integrated these duchies more closely within the Carolingian system, whilst demarcating them more clearly through, for instance, new law codes (see pp. 238–9) and diocesan boundaries (see pp. 84–6). This process occurred relatively rapidly in about four decades after 780 and gave shape to what later historians claimed were authentic ancient Germanic tribal 'stem-duchies' (Map 1).

Germany came to be defined through the association of a specific royal title with rule over these duchies. The Carolingian succession disputes from 829 kept this definition in flux – and likewise for Italy and Burgundy – since duchies were switched between the competing kings, or were truncated or extended as part of unstable partition agreements. The term *regnum teutonicorum* only emerged during the eleventh century, replacing a more diffuse sense of 'German lands' associated with the imperial title since Otto I's coronation in 962. Few authors identified these lands explicitly. As late as 1240, Bartholomaeus Anglicus included *Brabantia, Belgica, Bohemica, Burgundia, Flandria, Lotharingia, Ollandia* (Holland), *Sclavia* (the Slav lands) and *Selandia* (Zeeland), whilst omitting the perhaps more obvious Austria and Bavaria from his list.[5]

Bavaria, Saxony and Swabia were the most prominent tribal regions alongside Franconia, which identified the Frankish homeland in Charlemagne's day. None of these was clearly delineated in 800, and all were considerably larger than later regions bearing these names. Franconia originally encompassed the key Carolingian sites along the Rhine–Main nexus, including Frankfurt and Mainz. It also incorporated Thuringia around the upper Saale river since 533, though this region was still recognized as distinct. Thuringia gravitated towards Saxony under the Ottonians, before re-emerging in the thirteenth century as a regional designation for a group of separate territories (see pp. 374–5). The western half of Franconia meanwhile acquired its own identity as the Upper Rhineland, in turn subdividing into territories that included Mainz, Hessen and the Palatinate. The duchy of Franconia was formally dissolved in 1196, but the ducal title was revived under different circumstances in 1441 and held thereafter by the bishop of Würzburg until 1802, when most of the Franconian territories were absorbed into Bavaria.

Swabia emerged from the region known as Alemania after the tribal confederacy of the 'All-Men' (*Alemanni*), who occupied what would later be Alsace, Baden, Württemberg and most of Switzerland, which was then still often referred to by its Roman name of Rhetia. Swabia also underwent significant changes, including the separation of Alsace in 1079 and the demise of the Swabian ducal title around 1290 as the region reshaped itself into numerous, more distinct territories.[6]

Saxony was even larger in 800, stretching across the entire area north of Franconia from the North Sea coast to the middle Elbe. It was from here that the Saxons departed to settle in England during the fifth and sixth centuries. The Saxons also provided the Franks with one of their toughest opponents, resisting both them and Christianity longer than other German tribes, perhaps because they were a loose confederacy without a capital that could be captured.[7] Three main subdivisions within Saxony were apparent by 900, which provided spaces for later, more numerous territories to emerge. Westphalia to the west covered north-west Germany without yet being entirely distinct from Frisia along the North Sea coast or the areas that would later become Holland, Zeeland and the other Dutch provinces. The Frisians are often hard to distinguish from Saxons in early sources, but they acquired their own identity thanks largely to the particular topography of their low-lying region blending into the sea through marshes and islands. Westphalia was elevated to a duchy in 1180, but like Thuringia's re-emergence, this occurred while sharper demarcation generally meant contraction in size as other, new territories were also identified, albeit through association with counts and other lesser lords. Central Saxony was originally known as Engern and straddled the Weser river, but it was known by early modernity as Lower Saxony, which included the principalities of Brunswick and Hanover. The eastern part (Eastphalia) along the Elbe remained vulnerable to raiding and interaction with Slavic peoples beyond the river. Eastphalia expanded and contracted several times across the ninth and tenth centuries, but was particularly promoted by the Ottonians, who founded the archbishopric of Magdeburg. Imperial favour cemented the lasting identification of 'Saxony' with this region, and it was here that the duchy and the later Saxon electorate emerged.

Bavaria is identifiable from the mid-sixth century as distinct from the eastern part of the former Roman province of Rhetia beyond the river Lech, north of the Alps and south of the Danube. The Bavarians also resisted Frankish attacks, but they faced simultaneous pressure from the Avars in what is now Hungary to the east, and were forced to submit in 788.[8] Bavaria remained politically 'distant from the king' throughout the ninth and into the tenth century. The Ottonians were careful not to combine Bavaria and Swabia under the same lord, who might block the best Alpine routes to Italy. Bavaria's eastwards expansion was characterized by the creation of a succession of 'marcher lordships', or militarized frontier regions, like those also established along the Elbe (see pp. 200–202). The Ottonians used the opportunity of a victory over a Bavarian rebellion in 976 to separate the eastern marches, or *Ostarrichi*, which eventually became Austria.[9] Simultaneously, the southern Alpine region was detached as the march of Verona, neutralizing the chances of Bavarian lords extending their influence in Italy. These moves effectively ended earlier possibilities that Bavaria might emerge as a distinct sub-kingdom in the manner of Bohemia.

The Ottonians' victory over the Magyars at Lechfeld in 955 stabilized the Empire's south-east frontier, enabling Austria to develop from a thinly populated frontier region to become a firm part of the German kingdom by the eleventh century. Austria continued to expand south and east through the creation of new march lordships, notably Carinthia and Krain, as well as Tirol in the Alps to the west. All these jurisdictions were eventually raised to ducal status during the later Middle Ages.

Eastwards migration after 1140 transformed the northern march lordships along the Elbe originally established by the Ottonians to protect Saxony during the tenth century. Meissen at the exit through the mountains between Bohemia and Saxony was eventually absorbed into the electorate of Saxony around 1500. By contrast, Brandenburg, emerging around what would become Berlin, acquired distinct status as an electorate in the mid-fourteenth century. The Slavic principalities of Mecklenburg and Pomerania were Christianized in the eleventh and twelfth centuries, facilitating their incorporation into the Empire under their indigenous rulers despite counter-claims from Denmark and Poland (see pp. 213–14).

Italy

Charlemagne preserved Lombardy as a separate kingdom when he conquered it in 774, but it was known as the kingdom of Italy from 817. Having been the object of struggles between the main Carolingian kings from 875 to 888, the Italian royal title passed to local Carolingian lords, initially the margraves of Friaul and then the dukes of Spoleto. This succession of Italian kings had sufficient influence to be crowned emperors by the popes. A new round of competition after 924 saw the intrusion of Burgundian lords, chiefly the counts of Arles

(Provence) who secured the Italian title but not the imperial crown, which fell vacant until 962. The Provencials were in turn being displaced by the margraves of Ivrea after 945. Otto I's invasion secured control of northern Italy for the German kings by 966, ending 78 years of instability during which there had only been 18 years with a single, unchallenged Italian king.[10]

The settlement did not go entirely unchallenged thereafter, especially as the later Ottonians were often absent in Germany. The imperial position was weakened by a crushing defeat by the Saracens at Cotrone on the Calabrian coast (13 July 982). After further setbacks, the situation was deemed so precarious that Otto III's death in Italy on 23 January 1002 was concealed until reinforcements arrived to collect his corpse. Discontented Italian aristocrats elected Margrave Arduin of Ivrea as their king on 15 February. The new German king, Henry II, needed two major expeditions in 1003–4 to neutralize Arduin, who only formally abdicated in 1015. Problems resurfaced at Henry's death in 1024 when it took his successor, Conrad II, three years to remove another Italian rival. Conrad foiled a final conspiracy by Italian bishops to depose him in 1037, and there was no opposition on his death in 1039 to Henry III's succession or subsequently against later German kings.[11]

The Italian kingdom changed considerably across these three centuries. Charlemagne continued the recovery of royal power begun under the Lombards around 740, defeating a lordly revolt in 794. Although the actual realm remained restricted to the original Langobardia (Lombardy) in the north, it had a relatively well-organized core around Pavia and access to the wealth of the Po valley with its numerous towns. Pavia remained the capital of Italian kings from 888 to 962, kings who, like later emperors, always found relations with Rome difficult.[12] The Carolingians appropriated parcels of former Lombard royal land, including the former Byzantine outpost at Ravenna that remained a key imperial base into the early thirteenth century, as well as the area around Cremona and a strip from Vercelli south to Genoa. The king also possessed palaces in the towns plus considerable influence over most of the senior clergy, including the archbishop of Milan.

The rest of the kingdom was already divided into numerous fairly small jurisdictions reorganized as counties by Charlemagne, in contrast to the large German duchies. Additional marcher lordships (marquisates) were established on the frontiers: Ivrea covering Piedmont and Liguria in the north-west; Tuscany to the south securing access to Rome; and four created in 828 from the former Lombardy duchy of Friaul to block Magyar raids from the north-east. The counties remained fairly stable, but the marquisates fragmented during the tenth century, except Tuscany, which developed under the Attoni family based at their castle of Canossa after 940. The Attoni benefited by backing Otto I and Conrad II before it was clear that either would be victorious in Italy. Rich rewards followed, expanding Tuscany north to the Po and south over the Apennines almost to Rome itself, making it the largest feudal conglomeration in Italy.[13]

The patriarchate of Aquileia, which lay along the Isonzo river at the head of the Adriatic, was detached from Byzantium by Charlemagne. Existing since the third century, the see of Aquileia exercised superior spiritual jurisdiction west along the Alps to Lake Como. Although declining, the city still offered a potential counterweight to the secular lords. Having consolidated his hold over Italy by 1027, Conrad II gave Aquileia its own secular jurisdiction, which was later expanded by Henry IV after his difficulties in reaching Canossa in 1077 to secure an alternative route over the mountains. These changes underscore how medieval rulers saw physical geography in terms of access rather than 'natural frontiers'. Neighbouring Venice developed from refugees who escaped the Lombard invasion of 568 by fleeing to the lagoons, and thereafter it secured autonomy by recognizing papal spiritual jurisdiction whilst leaning politically towards Byzantium. Medieval emperors tolerated this, because Venice provided a useful commercial and diplomatic intermediary between the Empire and Byzantium. Venice rapidly conquered Aquileia's secular jurisdiction after 1418 and this was recognized by Emperor Sigismund as Venice's Terra Firma in 1437. Although Friaul was seized by Austria in 1516, the rest of the Terra Firma was essentially independent of the Empire after 1523. Aquileia's spiritual jurisdiction was dissolved in favour of its subordinate bishoprics in 1752.[14]

The pope had the largest secular jurisdiction of any western cleric, having acquired property across Italy, Sicily and Sardinia during late antiquity. These possessions were known as St Peter's Patrimony (*Patrimonium Petri*) by the sixth century, but contracted to the area around Rome during the Lombard era of the late sixth to late eighth century. As part of his alliance with the pope in 754, Pippin promised to restore the lost lands, adding some precision to what these were by identifying Ravenna and five towns known as the Pentapolis. Their acquisition promised to push papal jurisdiction across the Apennines to the Adriatic and establish control of all north–south movement. The reluctance of later emperors actually to relinquish these lands added a geo-strategic element to papal-imperial disputes.

Otto I renewed Carolingian arrangements whereby the pope held the Patrimonium under imperial suzerainty as part of the Empire.[15] Pope Leo IX began to widen his autonomy and this was finally conceded by the emperor in the Concordat of Worms in 1122. From 1115, popes claimed the huge Tuscan inheritance bequeathed them by their faithful ally, Matilda of Canossa. Lothar III and Henry VI temporarily reasserted imperial jurisdiction over this, but the Staufers' demise allowed the papacy to consolidate its claims after 1254.[16] A key factor in this was the post of imperial vicar, developed during the eleventh century to provide a guardian of imperial prerogatives in Italy during the emperor's absence. By the early thirteenth century, popes claimed this position as part of a wider imperial authority they now asserted as their own. However, such claims meant that Tuscany never entirely lost its association with the Empire, allowing its reintegration within it during the late fourteenth century.

The Frankish conquest interrupted the revival of Lombard royal power over the central and southern Italian duchies, which had enjoyed an autonomous existence since the sixth century. The Carolingians largely abandoned efforts to conquer the south, concentrating instead on subduing Spoleto, straddling the Apennines halfway down the peninsula. Their concern to retain Ravenna and the Pentapolis stemmed from the access they gave from Lombardy to Spoleto, which in turn covered the route southwards, as well as offering a good post from which to supervise the pope. Spoleto's strategic significance led to it being entrusted in 842 to the (then) loyal Widonen family, who were sufficiently powerful by the 880s to challenge the later Carolingians for the Italian title. The Ottonians would also give Spoleto to trusted vassals, as well as carving out the marquisate of Ancona in 972 as a check against Spoleto becoming too powerful. Again, this shows how fragmentation could serve royal interests rather than simply being an indication of weakness.

The south remained distant to the kings of Italy throughout the

Middle Ages. The large Lombard duchy of Benevento controlled most of the south in 800, except for the Byzantine outposts of Calabria (Italy's toe), Apulia (the heel), along with Naples, Gaeta and Amalfi.[17] The entire south was raided by the Arabs, who had conquered Sardinia and Sicily from Byzantium by 827. The later Carolingian emperors briefly established authority between 867 and 876, but lost this to a Byzantine rival amidst the disorders of the later ninth century. Otto I recovered influence a century later, but Benevento fragmented in the process, adding new duchies at Salerno and Capua ruled by lords claiming Lombard descent. Otto tried to integrate these into the Empire by enfeoffing Pandulf Ironhead, the ruler of Capua and Benevento, with Spoleto.[18] Pandulf's death in 981 was followed a year later by the disaster at Cotrone, in which his two sons died, eliminating the emperor's most reliable southern partners.

Weak imperial and Byzantine influence cancelled each other out, creating a vacuum filled by the Normans, who arrived from the west around 1000 as pilgrims and adventurers on their way to the Holy Land. Originally the 'north men' (i.e. Vikings), the Normans had conquered north-west France during the early tenth century. A century later, Normandy was too crowded to accommodate ambitious nobles who also saw rich pickings in southern Italy, which (thanks partly to Byzantine influence) was one of the few places in the west where gold coins still circulated. The Norman conquest of southern Italy was even more impressive than their better-known invasion of England in 1066. Whereas that expedition was backed by the full apparatus of the duchy of Normandy and comprised 8,000 well-armed troops, there were rarely more than a few hundred Norman freebooters in southern Italy. They were not inherently militarily superior to the locals, but proved skilful in adapting to circumstances and gained ground through intermarriage with Lombard and Byzantine elites. Something of their ruthless opportunism can be gauged from the contemporary nicknames for their leader, Robert d'Hauteville: 'the Weasel' and 'the Terror of the World'.[19]

Renewed Byzantine-imperial conflict over southern Italy in the 1020s allowed the Normans to gain a foothold by playing both sides. They controlled the entire south by 1077, conquering Sicily within another 20 years, ending nearly three centuries of a four-cornered contest between the Empire, Byzantium, Lombard dukes and Saracens.

The Salians persisted in futile efforts to subdue the newcomers. By contrast, the papacy copied the traditional imperial response to assertive barbarians and legitimated their possession of the south in 1054 in return for accepting papal suzerainty, establishing an uneasy but mutually beneficial alliance lasting into the late twelfth century.[20] The high point came in 1130 when the pope recognized the Normans as kings in return for formal vassalage to the papacy on behalf of Sicily and the southern mainland, which became known as Naples after its capital.

The Investiture Dispute disturbed the political balance within the kingdom of Italy, enabling numerous towns to escape lordly control and acquire jurisdiction over their own hinterlands, often with papal backing (see pp. 512–15). Civic emancipation was temporarily interrupted by an imperial resurgence under the Staufers, who benefited from the Normans' heavy involvement in the Crusades after 1095. Henry VI acquired a claim to Sicily by marrying the Norman heiress Constanza and asserted this after hard fighting in 1194.[21] Henry's programme of uniting Sicily and Naples to the Empire (*unio regni ad imperium*) was symbolized in the choice of Staufer and Norman names for his son born in 1194: Frederick Roger, the future Emperor Frederick II. Henry's bold stroke simultaneously deprived the pope of his main ally and placed Staufer territory on three sides of the Papal States. Determination to prevent the union drove papal policy throughout the next fifty years, including Innocent III's intervention in the double election and subsequent Staufer–Welf civil war of 1198–1214.[22]

A new balance emerged as the pope sanctioned the liquidation of the Staufers through the Anjou (Angevin) family, an offshoot of French royalty who conquered Sicily and Naples in the 1260s. The papacy re-established the indirect influence it had enjoyed with the Normans by recognizing the Angevins as kings in return for their acceptance of papal suzerainty. Sicily fell to the king of Aragon in 1282 and through him eventually to Spain along with Sardinia, but an Angevin line persisted in mainland Naples till 1442, before that too passed via Aragon to Spain.[23] Feudal jurisdiction over Sicily and Naples bolstered the pope's international standing, but never amounted to effective control of either territory, the rulers of which occasionally used their obligation to protect the papacy as cover for unwelcome intrusion into its affairs. The real Papal State remained much as it had been during the earlier Middle Ages. In 1274 Rudolf I accepted his predecessors' transfer of imperial rights, effectively emancipating the Patrimonium from the Empire and extending it to include Spoleto, Ancona and (finally) Ravenna and its surrounding region known as the Romagna. In practice, the pope governed these possessions indirectly through lesser secular lords who were often heavily involved in papal politics. After two decades of renewed consolidation, the Papal States were rocked by a massive popular revolt involving over 60 towns and 1,577 villages between 1375 and 1378. Although order was restored, in the process Tuscany was lost for good.

The defeat of Staufer ambitions confirmed the kingdom of Italy as confined to Lombardy and Tuscany and composed of city states that had usurped the secular powers of the bishops and earlier lay lords by the mid-thirteenth century. Other than a few notable exceptions like Genoa and Florence, civic government slipped via oligarchy into the hands of single families, in turn creating the basis for new duchies to emerge as regional centres extended dominance over surrounding lesser towns and lordships. These leading families, known as *signori*, became hereditary rulers from the 1260s. Their authority rested on jurisdictions sold or otherwise transferred to the town councils by emperors since the twelfth century, as well as counties bought or conquered from local lords.[24] This process completed a fundamental shift in Italy's relationship to the Empire. The old lords were gone, extinguishing kinship and other personal bonds between the German and Italian elites, while the prolonged conflicts with the papacy drastically reduced the emperor's influence over Italian bishops, who were no longer fully part of the imperial church.

All this changed rather than ended northern Italy's place in the Empire. As new men, the signori generally craved recognition and legitimacy, especially as they faced numerous local rivals. They looked to the emperor rather than the pope to provide this, because ties to the Empire remained much stronger in the north than elsewhere in Italy, while the papacy's 'captivity' in Avignon after 1309 reduced its attractions as a political partner. Fourteenth- and fifteenth-century emperors were generally willing to recognize powerful signori in return for their acceptance of the new city states as imperial fiefs. Although largely absent from Italy throughout this period, emperors nonetheless remained the sole recognized fount of all honours. They retained indirect influence by rewarding cooperative signori with successive elevation to higher titles, whilst withholding this from those who proved difficult. The larger of the new city states thereby progressed from counties to duchies by the late fifteenth century. Although Ferrara (emerging from Tuscany) and Urbino (which replaced Spoleto) were subsequently incorporated within the Papal States, Modena, Gonzaga and Milan all remained imperial fiefs alongside older jurisdictions like Genoa and the rump of Tuscany.

The new Italian princely elite differed considerably from that in Germany. Assemblies of Italian lords were already rare in the twelfth century and disappeared during the prolonged absence of the emperors after 1250. The signori had no tradition of direct personal relations with their monarch. Their emergence in a highly competitive environment further discouraged any corporate identity, while German kings saw no reason to foster anything that might threaten their ability to retain influence by playing off Italian rivalries. Finally, the desire to exclude papal interference in German royal elections encouraged a sharper demarcation of politics through new charters after the 1220s. Consequently, the Italian princes were excluded from the more formalized structures created in Germany during the fourteenth century – notably the Golden Bull, which restricted the German election to Bohemia and six German princes (see pp. 306–7). Italians rarely attended royal assemblies north of the Alps and Charles V refused to summon them to the Reichstag after 1548.

The significance of this is demonstrated by the anomalous position of Savoy, which assumed such significance in the process of Italian unification in the nineteenth century, yet remained the one Italian lordship formally integrated within 'German' imperial structures. Unlike the rest of imperial Italy, Savoy remained in the hands of an old lordly family, the Humbertines, who were originally Burgundian counts. Conrad II rewarded the Humbertiner for their help in securing Burgundy in 1032 with the gift of Alpine lordships. Further grants followed their support during the Investiture Dispute, developing Savoy as a secure anchor at the intersection of the Empire's three main kingdoms in the western Alps. Its strategic position prompted Charles IV to incorporate it within the kingdom of Germany in 1361, where it formally remained until 1797.[25]

Burgundy

Burgundy was the least coherent of the Empire's principal kingdoms and has often been viewed as an unstable frontier zone between France and Germany. It was also medieval Europe's main north–south route, containing the Rhine, Moselle and Rhône rivers, as well as the western Alpine passes and many of the most important towns of the Carolingian era. These factors explain why Lothar I chose Burgundy together with Italy as his middle kingdom of Lotharingia in the 843 partition. It was certainly difficult to forge a common identity across this long strip of territory.[26] Fragmentation was not inevitable, but the proximity of the West and East Frankish kings did offer alternative patronage for local lords, while the initial abundance of Lotharingian heirs encouraged partitions into separate royal lines that soon became extinct, frustrating possible reunifications. The result was a territory of extreme complexity, which over the longer term looks appallingly tangled, but would have appeared to contemporaries much more solid and coherent, with the seemingly endless changes of ownership and territorial size in practice carried out only at intervals of a century or more.

The most important partitions were those at Lothar's death in 855 and that enacted in the Treaty of Mersen in 870. These definitively detached Italy and split the rest of Lotharingia into a southern kingdom (Burgundy) and northern duchy (Lotharingia, usually known under its French label 'Lorraine'). The southern kingdom was initially based at Arles, north of the Rhône's mouth, hence its other name as Arelat. It stretched northwards to the headwaters of the Saône and Doubs rivers. It had been settled by the Burgundians, a tribe originating on the river Oder, during the fifth century and had been incorporated into the Frankish realm in 534.[27]

A further partition in 888, this time east–west, definitively detached the old core area around Mâcon and Châlons west of the upper Saône. Forming a third of the original Burgundian kingdom, this had already been assigned to West Francia in 843 and now became the duchy of Burgundy (Bourgogne) thanks to the permanent involvement of its ruling lords in French politics. Ducal Burgundy passed to a junior branch of the Capetians between 1002 and 1361. The remaining two-thirds also split roughly equally, but north–south. The northern part became a second, semi-regal duchy called Upper Burgundy and included the western half of what would later be Switzerland. The southern part, comprising the former Roman *provincia Gallia Transalpina*, became Lower Burgundy, later known as the county of Provence.

Upper and Lower Burgundy acquired considerable autonomy during the conflicts of the later Carolingian era. They were reunited by 948 as a single kingdom of Burgundy, also known as the *regnum Arelatense* (Arelat) after its capital, Arles. Between 888 and 1032 the Burgundian kings came from the Rudolfinger branch of the Welfs, an extensive Carolingian lordly family. Dynastic continuity did not translate into a strong monarchy, because the succession of partitions and reunifications had reduced the Burgundian kings' core areas to that around Lake Geneva and a few outlying castles and monasteries. Meanwhile, the counts of Provence effectively became independent to the south-west, while the lords of Maurienne established themselves in the part of the western Alps that eventually became Savoy. To the north, yet another part detached as the 'free county' (*Franche Comté*). German commentators like Thietmar of Merseburg regarded Burgundian kings as in thrall to their nobles.[28] The Rudolfinger sought protection by placing themselves under Ottonian suzerainty in 926, and agreed 80 years later to make Henry II their direct heir.

However, the Rudolfinger outlived the Ottonians, whose line ended with Henry II's death in 1024, and the relations of the current Burgundian king felt they had better claims to succeed him. They joined a loose coalition of Italian, Lorrainer, Swabian and Burgundian nobles in rejecting the authority of the Salian Conrad II, who succeeded Henry II as German king. Briefly, it appeared that much of old Lotharingia might be reunited by Conrad's principal challenger, William V of Aquitaine. Throughout, however, Conrad retained solid backing in Germany, while his opponents failed to combine effectively and were defeated in swift succession between 1027 and 1032. A short winter campaign concluded with Conrad's coronation as king of Burgundy in January 1033, a few months after the death of the last Rudolfinger.[29] Conrad asserted *royal*, not dynastic, claims. He had to, because he lacked any personal connections to Burgundy, unlike Henry II, whose mother was a Burgundian princess. Although probably an expedient, Conrad's decision to emphasize the continuity of royal claims contributed to acceptance that the Empire endured beyond the lives of its individual monarchs and even entire royal dynasties.

The bulk of the Burgundian crown lands had long since disappeared into the hands of local nobles who enjoyed considerable autonomy – indeed, this aided Conrad's victory, because many Burgundian lords defected to him, recognizing he would be a more hands-off ruler than Odo of Champagne, who had replaced the deceased William of Aquitaine as his main local opponent.[30] Nonetheless, Burgundy's acquisition cemented the Empire as a union of three major kingdoms, adding to its premier status in Christian Europe. It also improved access to Italy, whilst constricting French influence in the same direction. Control was consolidated in 1044 by Henry III's marriage to Agnes of Poitou, daughter of William of Aquitaine.[31]

Burgundy had even less of a royal tradition than Italy. There was no royal election and rarely a coronation. The Burgundian nobility comprised only counts and lesser lords, all of whom remained outside the Empire's elite, removing another reason why the emperor should visit often. In short, its internal fragmentation and politically distant character meant it could largely be left alone. Frederick I 'Barbarossa' renewed authority in 1156 through his marriage to Beatrix, heiress of Franche Comté, and had himself crowned king of Burgundy at Arles in 1178; all these moves were largely intended to secure Burgundy while he pursued his main interests in Italy. Otherwise, Burgundy was generally entrusted to royal governors, notably the Zähringen family, which amassed lands in what later became Baden on the Upper Rhine.

Barbarossa detached the free county again in 1169, while Savoy became an immediate imperial fief separate from Burgundy in 1310. Provence left the Empire after it was acquired by the Angevins in 1246, and Avignon (until then associated with Provence) was ceded to the papacy in 1348. France's repeated internal problems indicate that there was nothing inevitable about its gradual encroachment into what had once been the western and southern reaches of the Burgundian kingdom. Charles IV was the last emperor to be crowned Burgundian kings, in Arles in 1365. Having backed France in its war with England (and fought at Crécy in 1346), Charles did not see French royalty as his natural enemy. He entrusted the Viennois (the northern end of old Provence) to the future Charles VI of France, who was simultaneously named imperial vicar over Arles in 1378. This area became the Dauphiné, the land traditionally given to the French king's eldest son prior to his own succession. However, it was only through Charles VI's own longevity as French king after 1380 and coincidental internal problems in Germany that the Dauphiné became permanently detached from the Empire.[32] Consequently, the old Burgundian kingdom had largely disappeared by the fifteenth century.

Lorraine

Lorraine meanwhile followed a broadly similar trajectory through the emergence of smaller, more coherent territories from an ill-defined set of loose jurisdictions. The absence of any distinct royal tradition made it more obviously a border zone between East and West Francia, whose kings were more concerned to assert prestige than delineate a clear frontier. Lorraine and the entire Lower Rhine basin remained largely distant from both the French and German kings into the high Middle Ages. The leading Lorraine lord assumed the status of prince (*princeps*) in 911 to assert parity with the East Frankish dukes, but decided against following them in accepting the Ottonians eight years later. Instead, Lorraine remained associated with the West Frankish Carolingians, becoming embroiled in their civil war after 922. This allowed the Ottonians to assert suzerainty in 925, but the episode reinforced the sense of a separate Lotharingian heritage distinguishing the Lorraine lords from their German counterparts.[33]

French kings continued to dispute possession into the eleventh century. German kings intervened repeatedly during the tenth and eleventh centuries to prevent the duke of Lorraine acting independently. Otto I partitioned the duchy into Upper (southern) and Lower (northern) halves in 959 to make it more manageable. As with Burgundy, such partitions were not irreversible and both parts were rejoined between 1033 and 1046. Henry III interpreted this as threatening his authority, not least because the ambitious duke, Gottfried the Bearded, married the Tuscan heiress Beatrix in 1054, simultaneously challenging imperial power in Italy. Henry achieved his objective of separating the two halves of Lorraine through a long, if intermittent conflict from 1044 to 1055.[34]

Upper Lorraine was entrusted to Salian loyalists after 1047, but the king gradually promoted the local bishops of Metz, Toul and Verdun by assigning them neighbouring counties to balance ducal power. Meanwhile, the counts of Luxembourg and Bar escaped ducal supervision by establishing direct subordination under the emperor. Royal influence waned with the end of the Staufers in 1254, but any potential resurgence of ducal authority was checked by the complex pattern of overlapping jurisdictions developing across the thirteenth and fourteenth centuries. Lords throughout the Rhineland accepted lucrative fiefs providing additional rents in return for recognizing the French king as their exclusive 'liege lord' (*dominus ligius*). However, the attractions of remaining within the Empire encouraged them to retain their existing possessions within imperial jurisdiction. Thus, the dukes of Lorraine, archbishop of Trier, bishop of Liège, counts of Flanders, Hainault (Hennegau) and others now had two feudal overlords: the emperor for their immediate imperial fiefs, and the French king for specific fiefs outside imperial jurisdiction.

Lorraine's dukes continued to participate in imperial politics in the century after the Staufers' demise, but French kings exerted growing pressure, for example giving Duke Raoul a house in Paris in 1336 to bind him closer to their court. Charles IV released the duke from his obligations to the Empire in 1361, but like many such acts, this was not definitive, especially as the duke was still tied to the Empire through his possession of the town of Pont-à-Mousson. The extinction of the ruling Alsatian line of dukes in 1431 gave Sigismund the opportunity to reassert Lorraine's full obligations to the Empire and the duchy was included in the new infrastructure developed by imperial reform to distribute fiscal and military burdens in the fifteenth century.[35]

Flanders was detached from Lower Lorraine in 1007, while the rump duchy fragmented during the Investiture Wars and was replaced by the new duchies of Geldern, Limburg and Brabant by 1138. The new configuration was confirmed by Brabant's victory over the archbishop of Cologne at Worringen in 1288, ending over 120 years of Cologne expansion across the Lower Rhine and Westphalia. Brabant acquired Limburg, but in turn was defeated by Geldern and Jülich in 1371, thus stabilizing the region as a patchwork of medium-sized duchies. Meanwhile, the old rights of the German kings in Lorraine had been assigned to the count Palatine of the Rhine (*comes palatinus Rheni*), who was given princely status in 1155, later consolidated as one of the secular prince-electors.

Ducal Burgundy

The last and greatest of the new minor powers to emerge from the former Lotharingian lands was ducal (French) Burgundy, which passed in 1363 to a junior branch of the Valois family ruling France since 1328. Beginning with Philip the Bold, within sixty years the new Burgundian dukes escaped French suzerainty and acquired Europe's most heavily urbanized area north of the Alps. In addition to their own ability, key factors in their success included their intervention in France's civil war between 1420 and 1435 and an alliance with Charles IV's son and successor, King Wenzel, in 1378, which brought the eventual acquisition of Luxembourg, completed in 1443. Dynastic marriages netted Flanders, Artois, Franche Comté (all 1383) and Brabant (1430), while Hainault, Holland and Zeeland were conquered in 1433, and Charolais (1390) and Namur (1421) were purchased (Map 15).

Burgundian power peaked under Charles 'the Bold', who bought Alsace (1469) and conquered Geldern, Limburg and Zütphen (all 1473). Charles came closest to resurrecting the old middle kingdom, but under radically altered circumstances. Burgundy's rapid ascent alarmed France and also Lorraine and the Swiss, who combined in the 1440s to resist its eastwards expansion. Frederick III declined Charles's petition to be recognized as king. Any chance of realizing this dream ended with Charles's death in battle against the Swiss at Nancy in January 1477. The subsequent Franco-Habsburg war over the Burgundian succession ended in compromise in 1493, confirming French possession of the original ducal Burgundy (Bourgogne), while the Habsburgs scooped all the duke's other lands.

THE NEW KINGDOMS

The Northern and Eastern Marches

The Empire was bounded to the north and east by peoples who had remained outside both the Frankish realm and Latin Christianity and who imparted very different characteristics than those present along the western and southern frontiers. To understand how these areas developed, we need to jettison the interpretations of Germanic conquest and various struggles for national self-determination that have since the nineteenth century so often been projected onto the history of this part of Europe. For most of the early Middle Ages, German kings intervened along these frontiers primarily to meet the expectations of their *existing* subjects, rather than conquer new ones.[36]

The Carolingians were beset by skilful, ruthless raiders after 800: Vikings ravaged West Francia and Frisia, Saracens plundered southern France and Italy, Avars and later Magyars raided deep into northern Italy and southern Germany, while the Slavs were a constant threat along the Elbe. All these peoples used unconventional tactics and often locally superior numbers. The Vikings and Saracens used the rivers to penetrate the hinterland – the former reaching as far as Lorraine in 891. Their own homes were either distant, or almost entirely absent in the case of the Magyars, who remained nomadic into the later tenth century.[37] Infighting amongst the Carolingians simply widened the opportunities to plunder during the 880s.

Payments of the so-called 'Danish money' (*Danegeld*) to the Vikings by the relatively wealthy West Frankish kings after 845 could be quite successful in curbing violent raiding. However, such tribute was also considered unkingly and contributed to growing criticism of the western Carolingians. Where possible, kings preferred military action, which could also satisfy their own lords' expectations of plunder.[38] Such ideas were paramount in the development of the marcher lordships once the Carolingian Empire stopped expanding in 814. These militarized zones were partly outside the duchy structure and were entrusted to margraves (marquises) whose jurisdictions were often quite large and were endowed with important royal benefices to sustain them.[39] Some margraves became powerful figures in imperial politics, despite their location on the Empire's geographic periphery. The Ekkehardiner family rose to prominence in charge of the Saxon marches of Meissen and Merseburg after 985. A measure of their influence is that they persuaded Pope John XIX to move the bishopric of Zeitz to their castle of Naumburg in 1028. They were already considered potential contenders for the German royal title in 1002, but preferred to obtain further land in return for loyal service until their line was extinguished in 1046 (Map 4).

Sections of the marches included fixed defences, notably the *Limes Saxoniae* built in 810 from Kiel south to the Elbe, and the Danewerk earth wall extended between the Schlei and Treene rivers in 929 to stop

Danish raiders heading south. Such extensive works were difficult to build and maintain. Elsewhere, defence relied mainly on fortified monasteries and castles; initially wooden palisades and towers were replaced by stone constructions in the eleventh century. Strongpoints offered places of refuge, but could have the perverse effect of attracting raiders hoping to take the booty stored in them. There is some controversy whether the Ottonians settled armed farmers on the south-east frontier in the 930s; the Habsburgs certainly did this six centuries later to oppose the Ottomans. Nonetheless, it is clear that the Ottonians developed defence in depth, with castles and posts covering important river crossings and intended to delay mounted raiders who rarely had the capacity for a prolonged siege. Such positions were not merely defensive, since they provided bases to launch raids in the other direction. Henry I and his successors repeatedly led expeditions to extort tribute from the Slavs, partly to redistribute amongst their lords, but also to assert prestige and signal their retention of divine favour.[40]

Slavs and Magyars

Interaction with the Slavs and Magyars along the Empire's eastern frontier helped create the new kingdom of Bohemia, which became part of the Empire, and those of Poland, Hungary and Croatia, all of which ultimately remained outside it. Like their western European counterparts, these kingdoms subsequently claimed distinct identities based on myths of origins. These stories convey something of the tangled relationship between all these new states and the Empire. It was understood that Kievan Russia, Poland and Bohemia derived a shared heritage from three Slavic brothers. Rus travelled the least, stopping at Kiev to found the Ruthene peoples who eventually spread to the Carpathian Mountains. Lech settled in Gniezno between the Wartha and Vistula rivers and became the progenitor of the Poles, while Czech pushed on to discover *terra Boemia* – the land of honey (Bohemia).[41]

The Slavs to the north formed numerous powerful confederacies rather than kingdoms. Collectively known as the Wends, they in fact numbered several peoples. The Abodrites controlled the area between the Elbe and Denmark under their own duke. The Havelians along the Havel river occupied what became Brandenburg. The Veleti, or Liutians (*Lutici*), were a looser confederation emerging during the tenth century in what later became Pomerania along the Baltic coast. They were the principal force behind the rising that also drew Abodrite support and swept away much of the Ottonian presence along the lower Elbe in 983. The importance of restoring Ottonian prestige is demonstrated by the fact that the six-year-old Otto III accompanied the first retaliatory expedition (986), while another four major campaigns were launched between 991 and 997.[42] These were all punitive expeditions intended to reassert prestige, especially in Germany, rather than serious efforts to reconquer the area. The Sorbs were an important group who refused to join the rising. They lived just north of Bohemia in Lusatia, deriving its name from their word for marsh, and were the first to be Christianized permanently. By contrast, the Ranians refused Christianity and though restricted to Rügen Island off Pomerania, they remained significant through their influence on Baltic trade.

Other Slav confederacies occupied areas south of Bohemia. Ironically, it was Charlemagne's victory over the Avars controlling Pannonia (the Hungarian Plain) by 800 that allowed several of these groups to expand.[43] The Carinthians occupied the eastern Alps above the Drava river, while the Croats emerged from other, looser groupings on the Adriatic coast during the late ninth century.

All these peoples underwent a similar demarcation of power and territory between the ninth and thirteenth centuries. Like the Carolingians and Ottonians they built castles, making their lands harder to conquer. Relations could be violent, notably with the second major rising along the Elbe in 1066, and the Wendish Crusade after 1147. However, gradual acceptance of Christianity from the tenth century offered a route to more peaceful engagement with the Empire. It remained unclear prior to the thirteenth century whether this interaction would end with a people's incorporation within the Empire, or recognition as a separate realm beyond it.

The Frankish eastward expansion had the largest impact in the south, where the Carinthian Slavs were incorporated as a border march in 828. Elsewhere, the imposition of tribute was not necessarily a precursor to subjugation – especially as its purpose was usually prestige rather than annexation. The Bohemians and Moravians used the Carolingian civil wars to escape their tributary status imposed around 800. The Moravians established their own 'Great Empire' in the later ninth century in the vacuum left by Charlemagne's destruction of the Avar

Confederacy, while the Bohemians resumed raiding in 869.[44] Both were soon under pressure from the Magyars, a Finno-Ugric people from the Volga who themselves were being pushed westwards by the Turkic Pechenegs sponsored by Byzantium. The Franks called them *Ungari* (Hungarians) after their 'Confederation of Ten Arrows' (*On-Ogur*), a name which, in turn, reflects their military organization as swift mounted archers skilled in hit-and-run tactics. Overrunning Pannonia within a few years of their arrival in 895, the Magyars soon controlled the lucrative east–west trade in slaves, food and livestock, supplementing this with plunder from raids deep into southern Germany and Italy after 899. By 926, Henry I paid tribute to secure a temporary end to their depredations.

Although the Moravian empire collapsed in 906, the Magyar intrusion indirectly benefited the Bohemians and Poles by pushing trade northwards to follow the Cracow–Prague route, safe on the other side of the Carpathians. The new wealth promoted greater political centralization favouring the Premyslids controlling Prague, who were recognized by the Franks as counts in 871. The discovery of silver at Jihlava (Iglau) in Moravia and then at Kutná Hora in Bohemia increased Premyslid influence, and gave them an advantage over their poorer German counterparts. Having lost ground mid-century, Christianity was again accepted in Bohemia during the 890s, and over the next four centuries the Premyslids married 19 German princesses, becoming a prominent part of the Empire's elite.[45] The Premyslids were already recognized as hereditary dukes in 895 and ruled Bohemia until their extinction in 1306. The emperor had no crown lands, monasteries or castles in Bohemia, and never visited it on the customary royal progression prior to the fourteenth century.[46] Bohemia developed its own identity focused on the martyrdom of Prince Wenceslas I and it served as an important conduit for Latin Christianity's penetration further south and east. Nonetheless, Bohemia remained within the imperial church with its bishops at Prague and Olmütz initially under Mainz jurisdiction.

Poland and Hungary

The Piasts occupied a similar position in Cracow to the Premyslids in Prague, becoming the dominant Polish lordly family between 842 and 1370. They embraced new ideas transmitted from the Empire through

Bohemia, including the status of duke adopted by Mieszko I, who married a Premyslid princess and accepted baptism in 966, an act still celebrated as the birth of Polish Catholicism.[47] The Piasts were not trying to create an independent Poland – a concept entirely alien to the early Middle Ages. However, they were prepared to work with the Empire as a means of securing and enhancing their own status relative to local and neighbouring lords. Not only did they have the Premyslids as an example, but the Croat elite secured recognition as a separate kingdom in 925 in return for recognizing Latin rather than Byzantine Christianity. Mieszko established a bishopric based in Gniezno, the Piast capital until 1039, and in 990 dedicated his land to the papacy as a means of asserting autonomy whilst joining Christendom's princely elite.

Piast-imperial cooperation peaked with Otto III's long pilgrimage in 999–1000 to Poland, which had complex motives but included a desire to cement alliances with Slav princes. Mieszko and his son and successor Boleslav I Chrobry had backed Otto's punitive expeditions against the Wends during the 990s. Otto now recognized Gniezno as an archbishopric, securing Poland's ecclesiastical autonomy, as well as establishing a suffragan bishop in Breslau (Wroclaw) for Silesia, which was within imperial jurisdiction but held by the Piasts from 990 to 1353. These measures also advanced Otto's Christianizing agenda, because the new archbishop of Gniezno was better placed to promote missionary activity than his counterpart way to the west in Mainz, who had lost influence during the 983 Slav rising. Otto recognized Boleslav as the Empire's 'brother and helper' (*fratrem et cooperatorem imperii*) and, according to some accounts, placed a crown on his head.[48]

Otto III certainly sent another crown to Stephen, who thereby became king of Hungary in 1001. Christianity gained ground amongst the Magyars following the shock of their defeat at Lechfeld to Otto I in 955, which suggested easier riches lay in adopting a settled existence. Although Byzantine influence remained potent, the Ottonians offered military aid and recognition from the 970s, backing the Arpad family against those Magyars who wanted to continue the traditional life as nomadic raiders. Prince Vaik adopted the Christian name Stephen (Istvan) at his conversion in 985, soon importing western political ideas like the Empire's administrative structure of counties under sheriffs, and converting the enslaved population into freer, but still dependent serfs. Hungary's elevation to a kingdom in 1001 was underpinned by a new ecclesiastical structure with two archbishops and ten bishops. This process was slow, and twelfth-century travellers reported the Hungarians still lived in tents during the summer and autumn months.[49]

Otto III was subsequently criticized for converting tribute-paying princelings into independent kings. It is more likely that Boleslav and Istvan considered themselves the emperor's primary allies, while Otto regarded himself as king of kings. The relationship remained fluid because of internal changes in the Empire, Poland and Hungary. Bole-slav's successors were not crowned kings, and his son Mieszko II returned the royal insignia to the Empire in 1031. A royal title could mark temporary ascendency over domestic foes, while submission to the Empire was a favoured tactic of weaker rulers seeking external backing. In practice, Poland remained a tributary of the Empire from the 960s until the late twelfth century without this infringing its internal autonomy or requiring its ruler to participate in German polit-ics. In this sense, it remained more distinct than Bohemia, which was clearly an imperial fief by 1002.[50]

The emperor retained two additional forms of influence. Istvan's marriage to Gisela, daughter of the duke of Bavaria, associated him with the Ottonian elite and was a significant factor in his conversion. Boleslav was related by marriage to the Ekkehardiner of Meissen and to the Billung family, who were dukes of Saxony. The Piasts continued to marry into the Empire's elite for the next fifty years, but from the mid-eleventh century their choice of brides became more international, reflecting their desire for wider recognition.

The second option of military intervention remained possible into the twelfth century, but proved increasingly difficult. Boleslav seized Meissen following Otto III's death in 1002 in what was both a land grab and a blow against Henry II, who was less willing to recognize him as king and demanded a resumption of tribute.[51] A three-way fight developed between the emperor and the Polish and Bohemian dukes after 1003, joined by the Hungarians in 1030. Multiple issues were at stake. Each sought to assert prestige relative to the others, while the Polish, Bohe-mian and Hungarian rulers faced internal challenges, including from those unwilling to accept Christianity or embrace new socio-economic arrangements. Meanwhile, imperial intervention depended on cooper-ation from Bavaria and the eastern march lords like the Ekkehardiner who had their own regional interests. Conrad II's difficulties in Burgundy and Italy were an added distraction between 1024 and 1033. The Veleti used the chance to launch a series of increasingly destructive raids over the Elbe from 1033 to 1066. The Premyslids removed the relics of the martyred Ottonian missionary Vojtech from Gniezno in 1039 to promote Prague's elevation to an archdiocese independent from Mainz and secure ecclesiastical autonomy similar to that already enjoyed by Poland and Hungary.

Nonetheless, Conrad's successor Henry III skilfully reasserted imperial pre-eminence in a series of campaigns culminating in a great victory in support of the Arpads over Hungarian rebels at Menfö in 1044. The problems that confronted his son Henry IV hindered further intervention after 1073, while the Arpads and Piasts reasserted a more independent royal status by supporting the Gregorian reform papacy during the Investiture Dispute. With his customary ingenuity, Gregory VII reinterpreted Henry III's earlier gift of insignia captured at Menfö to argue that Hungary was subordinate to the papacy, not the Empire. The last serious efforts to enforce imperial suzerainty over Hungary and Poland failed by 1109, but infighting amongst the Piasts ensured some tribute was paid until 1184.

Bohemia

The Premyslids chose the opposite course of securing elevation as kings by backing the Salians. Henry IV granted Wratislav II a personal royal title in 1085 as thanks for defeating his German enemies at Mailberg three years earlier. This elevation underscores the significance of the imperial title, since Henry delayed the reward until after his own coronation as emperor in 1084, thereby maintaining his superior status. Only an emperor (or more controversially, a pope) could make a king. Kings could not make other kings, nor could royal titles simply be assumed: those attempting this failed to secure recognition from existing monarchs. As with the earlier example of the Piasts, the Premyslids' own infighting prevented them from making their royalty permanent. Vladislav II received another personal title from Frederick I in 1158. Ottokar I secured confirmation of this as hereditary by trading his support for the Staufers during the Empire's civil war after 1198. Frederick II's subsequent problems obliged him to confirm this in 1212 and 1231, as well as recognize Prague's autonomy from the imperial church. The 'lands of the Bohemian crown' (*corona regni Bohemiae*) were increasingly accepted as a distinct unit separate from the German kingdom. Frederick II issued a charter in 1212, agreeing to accept whoever the Bohemians chose as their king.

In future, each new Bohemian king automatically succeeded to the 'lands of the Bohemian crown', but his political rights in the Empire depended on being enfeoffed with the new title of Arch Cup Bearer (*Erzmundschenk*), created in 1212, which entitled him to participate in German royal elections. These changes consolidated Bohemia's autonomy, but it would be wrong to interpret them simply as a 'decline' in imperial authority, since they reflected a new understanding of feudal vassalage developed by the Staufers to ease management of the Empire.[52]

German lords periodically criticized this arrangement, which placed Bohemia outside their king's jurisdiction, yet still allowed it to help elect their king. The famous thirteenth-century legal treatise the *Sachsenspiegel* added ethnic arguments by claiming the Bohemians were a different people. Such criticism generally only surfaced in moments of tension and many Germans regarded Bohemians positively. Perhaps one in six of Bohemia's inhabitants were German-speaking by the late Middle Ages, following large-scale immigration encouraged by Bohemia's kings who valued Germans for their skills and labour. Although outside the imperial church, Bohemia was still involved in the major monastic movements like the Cistercians and Premonstratensians, while Bohemian lords built German-style stone castles like their Polish and Hungarian counterparts.[53]

The Premyslids made serious bids to secure election in Germany from the 1270s, only to be blocked by their Habsburg rivals in Austria. The struggle thwarted Rudolf I's efforts to reverse the 1212 arrangement and reduce Bohemia to the status of an immediate fief again. In an entirely unpredictable sequence of events, the Luxembourg family, previously based in north-western Europe, inherited Bohemia in 1310 after the Premyslids' extinction. They expanded the Bohemian crown lands by acquiring Silesia in stages between 1327 and 1353 through marriage with the local dukes, as well as the Sorb region of Lusatia by 1370 – in both cases at the Piasts' expense. Various junior Piast branches survived as Bohemian vassals in Silesia until 1653.[54] Where the Premyslids had failed, the Luxembourgs succeeded in using Bohemia as a base from which to rule the Empire, between 1346 and 1438. Bohemia now became 'king's country' as its autonomy was consolidated to secure it as a large territorial base from which to govern the Empire (see pp. 389–96).

Prussia

The Salians' efforts to assert suzerainty over Poland and Hungary failed just as demographic and economic growth in the Empire gathered momentum, prompting a resumption of eastward expansion suspended since the 980s. The subsequent Wendish Crusade after 1147 involved Bohemians, Danes and Poles, but is associated in the popular memory primarily with the Teutonic Order. This was a self-consciously Germanic organization, but was highly unusual in the much wider process of migration and in fact did not require its knights to be born Germans and made little effort to Germanize its multi-ethnic subjects 'beyond enforcing the most perfunctory Christianization'.[55]

The Order kept its relationship to the Empire deliberately ambiguous. Grand Master Hermann von Salza negotiated purposely contradictory agreements with Emperor Frederick II, Pope Gregory IX and the Piast Prince Conrad of Masovia in return for agreeing to assist the northern crusading effort in 1226. His agreement with Frederick secured the emperor's sanction and protection, whilst guaranteeing the Order's independence as only the Empire's 'associate' rather than vassal.[56] Utterly ruthless, the Order continued its aggressive expansion long after achieving its original goal of defeating the pagan Prussians. It exploited Poland's internal divisions into the 1320s to expand at the expense of fellow Christians, including capturing Gdansk in 1308, as well as buying Estonia in 1345 from Denmark, which had conquered it during the 1220s. Suzerainty was extended over the archbishopric of Riga in 1395, reducing the parallel Livonian Order to a subordinate branch (Map 21).

Thereafter the Order contracted in the face of a resurgent Poland, which inflicted a crushing defeat at Tannenberg in 1410 and by 1466 had captured western Prussia, including Gdansk. The prolonged conflicts with the Order after 1409 encouraged Polish intellectuals to embrace the western concept of monarchical sovereignty and argue their kingdom was fully independent. This was symbolized by Polish monarchs' adoption of a closed 'imperial' crown rather than the open

diadems worn previously.[57] Renewed war with Poland after 1519 precipitated the Order's collapse. Seeking to escape total defeat, Grand
Master Albrecht von Hohenzollern secularized the remaining, eastern,
half of Prussia as a hereditary duchy under Polish suzerainty in 1525,
parting ways with the rest of the Order that remained based in southern Germany.

The Livonian Order refused to follow suit and emancipated itself as
an independent military order still controlling 113,000 square kilometres inhabited by a million people.[58] Still beset by enemies, the Livonian
Order reinterpreted its thirteenth-century charter to claim its grand
master was an imperial prince entitled to the Empire's protection. The
Habsburgs had more pressing matters in western Europe, obliging
Grand Master Gottfried Kettler to follow the Teutonic example and
secularize his remaining territory as the duchy of Courland under Polish suzerainty in 1561. The Reichstag continued to debate Livonia's and
Prussia's relationship to the Empire into the 1570s before accepting that
both lay outside its frontiers. Courland remained an autonomous part
of the Polish-Lithuanian Commonwealth until falling to Russia in the
third and final Polish partition in 1795.

Ducal Prussia remained more closely connected to the Empire,
having been inherited in 1618 by the main Hohenzollern line ruling
Brandenburg since 1415. The Teutonic connection persisted in the
Hohenzollerns' use of black and white as two of their heraldic colours,
as well as the Order's iron cross that first appeared on Prussian battle
flags after 1701. Ducal Prussia remained underpopulated and strategically vulnerable, often more of a liability than an asset to Brandenburg's
rulers who were yoked through it as Polish vassals until 1660. Adroit
intervention in the Swedish–Polish war of 1655–60 secured international
recognition of ducal Prussia as a sovereign possession. The Hohenzollerns thereby joined the Habsburgs as the only German dynasties ruling
sovereign land beyond imperial frontiers. Hohenzollern Prussia was
raised to a kingdom by Emperor Leopold I in November 1700 to buy
military support for the impending War of the Spanish Succession. The
lavish coronation in Königsberg (Kaliningrad) in January 1701 was
intended simply to win international recognition and was never
repeated – Prussian kings assumed authority like Austrian emperors
after 1804 without coronations. Poland-Lithuania only recognized
Prussia's royal status in 1764, while the Teutonic Order always refused.

Later pro-Prussian historians dismissed these protests as irrelevant, yet Hohenzollern monarchs remained extraordinarily touchy about their new status and felt obliged to assert it through aggressive policies later in the eighteenth century.[59]

Poland, Hungary and Bohemia in the Later Middle Ages

Poland and Hungary underwent considerable internal change, accelerated by the devastation wrought by the brief but terrible Mongol invasions during the 1240s, which claimed the lives of a third of all Hungarians. Hungary already adopted a more formal form of mixed monarchy in 1220. This included significant political rights to the nobles, who, by now, exercised hereditary control of the counties, and established regular diets, or assemblies, where they and representatives from leading towns discussed policy with the king. On the Arpads' extinction, Hungary passed to a branch of the extensive Angevin family between 1308 and 1387, which made similar concessions to secure their acceptance in Poland where the Piasts died out in 1370.[60]

Polish nobles asserted new powers to escape Angevin rule in 1386, giving their crown to Prince Jogaila, who ruled Lithuania, Europe's largest surviving pagan country, on the condition he accept Christianity. Jogaila's family, the Jagiellons, ruled until 1572, but the union between Poland and Lithuania persisted beyond until the state was partitioned off Europe's map by Austria, Prussia and Russia between 1772 and 1795. Renewal of the union at Lublin in 1569 gave the Commonwealth its definitive shape as an elective monarchy. This was much broader than that in the Empire, while the Polish nobles (the *szlachta*) had a far more coherent and integrative ideology than their more hierarchically organized German counterparts, whose electoral rights were restricted to a tiny elite. The number of Polish noble electors rose from 6,000 in 1573 to 20,000 by 1587. Very few of them had landed titles like German nobles; instead they derived status from possession of hereditary royal offices with provincial responsibility. This bound them to the monarchy and helped ensure that the otherwise unwieldy Commonwealth remained a significant European power into the later seventeenth century.[61]

Hungarian nobles rejected a possible union with Poland in 1387, instead choosing Emperor Charles IV's younger son, Sigismund, as their king, thereby associating their kingdom with the Luxembourgs, who had ruled Bohemia since 1310 and the Empire as a whole since 1346. Sigismund's problems with his elder brother Wenzel delayed his succession in Bohemia until 1419, by which time it had become ungovernable through the Hussite insurrection. Although designated Sigismund's heirs in 1438, the Habsburgs soon lost both Hungary and Bohemia, opening a three-way struggle after 1468 that meshed with a revolt of the Austrian nobility. Hungarian influence in eastern Austria was not broken until 1490.[62]

The growing Ottoman threat encouraged east-central European nobles to accept monarchical unions as offering prospects for a more coordinated response. Hungary and Poland were linked by personal union from 1370 to 1387 and 1440 to 1444, as were Hungary and Bohemia from 1444 to 1457 and 1490 to 1526. The multiplicity of these connections and the frequency with which they changed reveals the relative openness of the situation immediately east of the Empire, as well as how Bohemian, Austrian and Silesian nobles had political and familial interests stretching across east-central Europe, and also west into Germany. The coincidence of Habsburg rule in the Empire, Bohemia and Hungary with the arrival of the Ottomans in the 1520s did not end these connections, but nonetheless radically altered the wider context, as we shall see shortly.

Denmark

Before we follow developments into early modernity, we need to conclude coverage of the Middle Ages by examining the situation to the north and north-west of the Empire. Denmark and the rest of Scandinavia remained beyond the Frankish world, though contacts deepened as the Saxons embraced Christianity from the 780s, allowing missionary work to extend northwards. The Franks and early Ottonians cooperated with the Abodrites along the lower Elbe to contain Viking raiding, while Henry I established a bridgehead to the north by conquering Schleswig in 934. The conversion of the Danish chieftain Harald Bluetooth then stabilized the northern frontier and opened possible cooperation to Christianize the Wends through the Hamburg-Bremen missions. Cooperation peaked in negotiations from 1025 to 1027 between Conrad II and Knut, the last and greatest of the Viking kings who temporarily united Denmark and England and extended control into Norway and the Vistula estuary. Knut sealed the alliance by attending Conrad's coronation in Rome in March 1027. Like the earlier agreements made by Otto III around 1000, this was sufficiently ambiguous to allow both parties to interpret it to suit their domestic audiences. Conrad ceded Schleswig to Denmark in 1036, but by then Knut's empire was already fragmenting following his death the previous year.

Knut's successors abandoned their cooperation with the Hamburg-Bremen mission and established their own ecclesiastical and dynastic ties to France, Hungary and Poland during the mid-eleventh century. However, the Danish monarchy's status as first among equals left it vulnerable to succession disputes. Thus, like those of east-central Europe, Danish rulers were often prepared to trade nominal submission to imperial suzerainty in return for the political capital of imperial recognition as kings.[63] Unfortunately, this could also bring risks for the Empire, demonstrated after 1146 when renewed Danish civil war spilled south across the Elbe as the rival claimants sought recognition and support in Germany.

The resulting prolonged, if intermittent, conflict eventually demarcated the Danish-imperial frontier, not along geographical or ethnic lines, but according to which master local lords eventually recognized. The Staufers relied heavily on the cooperation of their marcher lords, notably Frederick I, who gave Henry 'the Lion', duke of Saxony, a free hand to intervene in the Danish conflict. Henry promoted his own vassals, like the count of Holstein, who secured control of the North Sea coast between the Elbe and Schleswig. These political ambitions were a further factor adding to the violence of German migration into this region, as well as fuelling the Wendish Crusade after 1147. The situation grew more complex still with Henry's rebellion against Frederick after 1180. Frederick sought to regain control by awarding ducal titles to the remaining Abodrite and Veletian princes, thereby integrating their possessions of Mecklenburg and Pomerania within the Empire as imperial fiefs in 1181. The Staufer–Welf civil war interrupted this after 1198 by allowing Denmark to displace imperial influence across Mecklenburg and most of Pomerania and Holstein. Eventually, an alliance of north German and Wendish princes and towns defeated the Danes at Bornhöved in July 1227, forcing them to return the area north of the Elbe. Thereafter, Denmark remained confined to its peninsula and islands, allowing Lübeck and other newly founded towns to expand as the Hanseatic League.[64] The newly minted Wendish dukes re-emerged as imperial vassals, with the Abodrite line ruling Mecklenburg until 1918, while the Veletians survived in Pomerania until 1637 (acquiring Rügen in 1325).

England

Many German and English writers were fond of expressing a common Anglo-Saxon-Germanic heritage prior to 1914, but in fact this largely disappeared after the Saxon migrations of late antiquity. Important contacts remained, especially with the renewed missionary activity promoted by the Carolingians, who often relied on qualified monks from the British Isles, like St Boniface, but otherwise England and the Empire evolved separately. While a sense of Saxon heritage may have played a part, both countries were sufficiently distant not to be immediate competitors. Ironically, this opened possibilities for royal marriages which, like Byzantine-imperial matches, were intended mainly to impress a domestic audience and avoid antagonizing a king's nobles by tying him to one local family. Otto I married Alfred the Great's granddaughter, Edith of Wessex, while Henry III married Gunhild, daughter of Knut of Denmark-England. Edith's and Knut's deaths ended any chances of a lasting alliance in both cases.[65]

By contrast, connections in the high Middle Ages were more significant, if less celebrated in the nineteenth century. Emperor Henry V married Matilda, daughter of Henry I of England, in 1114 as a deliberate attempt to forge an alliance with the Anglo-Norman dynasty ruling much of Britain since 1066. It was hoped this would outflank a Franco-papal alliance threatening the Empire towards the end of the Investiture Dispute. A huge dowry of 10,000 pounds of silver was an added inducement, especially as this was paid upfront and financed Henry's Italian expedition in 1111. Matilda was accorded the rare honour of being crowned German queen ahead of her marriage. Despite the Investiture Dispute, the Empire's prestige was sufficient to attract English interest. After her husband's death in 1125, Matilda returned to England, where she was known as 'the Empress'. She triumphed over her English opponents and, through her second marriage to Geoffrey of Anjou, established the Plantagenet dynasty that ruled England-Normandy until 1399.[66]

Matilda's namesake and granddaughter married Henry 'the Lion' in 1168, forging a lasting alliance with the powerful Welf family based in Saxony and drawing English and imperial politics into closer contact. Henry sought shelter with his in-laws after his defeat by Frederick I in 1180 and found strong backing from his brother-in-law, Richard the Lionheart, who became English king in 1189. Richard used his crusading expedition to support Welf and Sicilian opposition to the Staufers in Italy. Having been shipwrecked on his return journey, Richard was apprehended in 1192 by the duke of Austria, whom he had offended in the Holy Land; allegedly he was disguised as a kitchen servant and caught holding a roast chicken. The duke handed him over to Emperor Henry VI in what was the first meeting of English and German monarchs. Henry extorted a huge ransom, racking up the price when he received a counter-offer from Richard's rival brother John, who was willing to pay to have him remain imprisoned. Eventually, Richard transferred 150,000 silver marks (weighing nearly 16 tons) and accepted imperial suzerainty over England in February 1194. The latter concession has caused some speculation, but Henry VI received several such nominal submissions from distant kingdoms without ever being in a position to convert these into effective control. The act's significance lay in the prestige accruing to Henry and the fact that Richard was bound not to assist his enemies. More practically, the huge ransom financed Henry's successful conquest of Sicily.[67]

Unsurprisingly, the Plantagenets financed Otto IV, son of Henry the Lion and grandson of England's Henry II, in his bid to displace the Staufers through the double election of 1198. In addition to kinship with the Welfs, the Plantagenets wanted to halt the French, who were now Staufer allies and busy conquering most of Normandy. The Anglo-Welf alliance came to grief in the Welfs' ignominious flight from the victorious French at Bouvines in 1214. As was becoming common practice, international tensions were defused by another dynastic marriage: Frederick II took Isabella, sister of England's Henry III, as his third wife in 1235 as part of a general reconciliation extending to rehabilitation of the Welfs in northern Germany. England was thus linked to the Staufers at the height of their final conflict with the papacy.

The marriage enabled Henry III's younger brother, Richard, earl of Cornwall, to present himself as the Staufer's successor. His bid for the German throne has often been dismissed as quixotic, while his bribes and concessions to secure election in January 1257 make him appear weak. In fact, Richard was both serious and quite successful. By 1258 he was prepared to abandon Plantagenet claims to Normandy if this would secure his German throne.[68] England remained an attractive ally after Richard's death in 1272, thanks to its growing trade with north-west Europe and its potential to hold France in check. England's more centralized monarchy also enjoyed significant tax revenues, enabling it to pay subsidies in 1294 and offer them in 1338. Four electors picked Edward III as anti-king against Charles IV in January 1348, but they had failed to consult Edward and he wisely declined to become involved. Thereafter, English relations with the Empire conformed to the emerging European pattern of interacting as nascent sovereign states, apart from Henry VIII's brief candidacy in the 1519 imperial election.

CONVERGENCE AND DISTINCTION AFTER 1490

The Centre

Two related processes transformed the Empire's internal composition around 1490. Constitutional reforms arranged the different levels of authority more clearly along a single, hierarchical order, distinguishing some spatial jurisdictions as superior to others. The superior jurisdictions associated with the status of imperial Estate now emerged as distinct territories. Lesser, mediate jurisdictions were subordinated as subdivisions within these territories. This process of greater distinction has been labelled 'territorialization' and will be discussed at greater length later (pp. 365–77 and 408–16). It simultaneously embedded the territories more deeply within the Empire, because each owed its rights and status through recognition from the other territorial authorities. In short, status was mutually agreed rather than self-determined, and thus tied to continued membership of the Empire rather than offering the basis for sovereign independence. Consequently, both processes contributed towards delineating the Empire's outer frontiers by distinguishing those lordships and towns embedded within the status hierarchy more clearly from those under the suzerainty of other European monarchs.

These processes of convergence and distinction proceeded unevenly across the Empire's three principal kingdoms, Germany, Italy and Burgundy. Crucially, they coincided with the new form of imperial rule perfected by the Habsburgs, which relied on an expanded territorial base under the emperor's direct control. Territorialization was significantly boosted by the Habsburgs' desire to insulate their possessions from the new common institutions being created by the parallel process of imperial reform (see pp. 396–408).

The developments around 1490 have largely been interpreted in national terms as the secession of Italy, Burgundy and Switzerland from the Empire, reducing it to a 'German Reich'.[69] Austria has also often been regarded at this time as distinct, either by those seeking to trace that country's 'origins' or by nineteenth-century critics accusing the Habsburgs of pursuing their own interests to the detriment of alleged common 'German' ones. Prussia's rise as a second German great power from the mid-eighteenth century appears to confirm this perspective. However, it would be wrong to reduce the Empire's later history to that of 'Reichstag Germany': the mass of smaller principalities and imperial cities with little or no chance of a separate existence in a Europe now more obviously composed of independent national states. Rather than seeing early modernity solely as the origins of later nations, it is better to interpret it as a significant reordering of how the Empire's different components interacted.

Imperial reform greatly strengthened the coherence of what had been the kingdom of Germany. Increasingly, this was now called 'the Empire', especially by outsiders who indeed viewed the Italian and Burgundian lands as separate Habsburg personal possessions. A major factor in this shift was the absence of German coronations after 1486, removing the separate significance of the German royal title since whoever was elected automatically became emperor (see pp. 69–70 and 301–7). The institutions created through imperial reform were primarily intended to regulate how the German kingdom was governed, not the wider Empire, since the Burgundian and Italian lords had already been excluded from the process of choosing the German king by the mid-fourteenth century. Thus, constitutional change combined with the distribution and management of Habsburg possessions to sharpen the distinctions between Germany, Italy and Burgundy.

The reforms delineated the extent of what had been the German kingdom by identifying which imperial fiefs enjoyed the status of imperial Estate, allowing them to participate in common institutions, notably the Reichstag, whilst also requiring them to contribute men and money through now more formalized systems for distributing shared burdens. A new intermediary layer of authority was interposed from 1500 to 1512 between territories and central institutions by grouping the imperial Estates on a regional basis in ten *Kreise* (imperial circles) to improve peace-keeping, law enforcement and defence coordination (Map 7).[70] Habsburg possessions were deliberately separated as the Austrian and Burgundian Kreise, while Bohemia (which only became a Habsburg possession in 1526) was excluded as still suspect after the Hussite insurrection. The Swiss also opted out, though still remaining within some aspects of imperial jurisdiction. The new structures were consolidated through the package of constitutional measures passed by the Reichstag meeting in Augsburg in 1555. As we have seen (pp. 115–28), this also adjusted the ecclesiastical structure within the former German kingdom, determining the future size and character of the imperial church and confirming which ecclesiastical territories survived as imperial Estates.

The North

These changes had their greatest impact in northern Germany, which had largely been 'distant from the king' since the Ottonians. Few northern territories played significant roles in late medieval imperial politics in contrast to those on the Middle and Upper Rhine and, from the fourteenth century, also Bavaria, Austria and Bohemia. Identification as imperial Estates and inclusion within the Kreis structure now integrated northern territories like Holstein, Mecklenburg and Pomerania fully within the Empire. Conversely, the exclusion of the former Teutonic lands of Prussia and Livonia from these structures placed them clearly outside the Empire.

While this clarified the northern frontiers, it did not exclude all external influence. German princes could still hold land outside the Empire, as exemplified by the Brandenburg Hohenzollerns in Prussia after 1618. Foreign rulers could also become imperial princes through the possession of imperial fiefs. Such interconnections already existed during the Middle Ages, but assumed a different character with the

Empire's constitutional reform and the new definition of sovereignty and conceptions of Europe as composed of independent states. The Empire remained defined by fragmented sovereignty where the emperor shared power with the semi-sovereign imperial Estates, whereas sovereignty was increasingly regarded as indivisible in other European states. The anomalous position is exemplified by the way George III and Frederick William III each felt obliged to send two letters of congratulations on Francis II's adoption of a hereditary Austrian imperial title in 1804: one in their character as sovereign monarchs of Britain and Prussia, the other in their capacity as imperial Estates in Hanover and Brandenburg.[71]

Other such personal unions existed. The oldest began in 1448 when the count of Holstein secured the election of his nephew Christian of Oldenburg as Danish king, establishing a dynasty still ruling today. Christian inherited Holstein on the extinction of its counts in 1459, but Emperor Frederick III raised it to a duchy in 1474 to ensure it remained an imperial fief within the Empire. The Oldenburgs were thus imperial princes in Holstein and kings in Denmark (and Norway, linked to Denmark from 1387 to 1814). They accepted their dual status, because it brought influence in the Empire and assisted long-standing Danish ambitions to control the entire Elbe estuary. The connections affected political behaviour, since Danish policy adopted the methods customarily employed elsewhere in the Empire to achieve objections. Although force was occasionally employed, Denmark generally used its influence in imperial institutions as it tried to acquire additional imperial fiefs along the Elbe. Repeated failure did not cause it to change its tactics or disengage from the Empire.[72]

The duchies of Holstein and Oldenburg remained convenient accommodation for junior branches of the main Oldenburg family, but further subdivisions created rival branches by the seventeenth century that tried to escape Danish tutelage. The most important of these were the Holstein-Gottorps, who forged their own connections to Swedish and Russian royalty. Duke Karl Peter Ulrich of Holstein-Gottorp briefly and disastrously ruled Russia as Tsar Peter III in 1762. Tensions were eased by an agreement in 1773 whereby Denmark assigned Oldenburg to the junior Holstein line (surviving there until 1918), while Russia relinquished claims to Holstein to the Danes. Such dynastic swops were no longer acceptable with the rise of more virulent nationalism during the nineteenth century. Two wars (1848–51, 1864) eventually obliged Denmark to cede both Holstein and Schleswig to Prussia.[73] Meanwhile, the former Frisian lordship of Jever (330 square kilometres) inherited from Oldenburg by Anhalt-Zerbst in 1667 passed to Russia at the death of Catherine II in 1796. Resembling a miniature version of modern-day Kaliningrad, this remained a Russian enclave until Tsar Alexander I gave it to his Oldenburg relations in 1818.

Sweden acquired western Pomerania, Bremen and other parts of northern Germany as spoils from the Thirty Years War (1618–48). Like Denmark, Sweden accepted the formal status as imperial vassal on behalf of these possessions, despite the rest of its lands constituting a sovereign kingdom. Denmark's and Sweden's German possessions remained imperial fiefs subject to imperial law. Both Scandinavian monarchies generally honoured their obligations to assist the Empire in later seventeenth- and early eighteenth-century wars. Sweden's monarchy was also closely related to German princely families. Following the abdication of Queen Christina (herself half-German) in 1654, Sweden was ruled by her Zweibrücken relations until 1720, thereafter by the landgrave of Hessen-Kassel, followed between 1751 and 1818 by a branch of the Holstein-Gottorps.[74] As in Denmark's case, this succession of 'German' rulers did not forge a direct union, since the German possessions remained governed by relations throughout, in contrast to Hanover's personal union with Britain between 1714 and 1837 where the succession of four Georges and a William were simultaneously electors and kings.

The East

Connections across the Empire's eastern frontiers were also direct personal unions similar to that with Hungary under Sigismund between 1410 and 1437. Neither he nor the Habsburgs tried to integrate their other kingdoms within the Empire as the Staufers had attempted with Sicily after 1194. The Habsburgs acquired Bohemia and Hungary in 1526 after several decades of relying on their own possessions to sustain their control of the Empire. They had no incentive to include Bohemia or Hungary in the framework created since the 1490s, because this would have exposed them to interference from the other imperial Estates. Instead, they developed their own institutions to manage what was, effectively, a parallel dynastic-territorial empire and which gave them an overwhelming superiority of resources, in turn allowing them to retain an almost unbroken grip on the imperial title over the next three centuries.

This Habsburg monarchy (see pp. 427–39) remained closely entwined with the Empire, even if some important elements were also sovereign states. Habsburg imperial rule depended on holding these additional extensive lands as independent sources of wealth and prestige. There were also extensive economic links, such as those along the Danube: Hungary, for instance, sent 100,000 cattle annually upriver into the Empire during the sixteenth century.[75] In the early 1520s the Reichstag hesitated to vote aid for Hungary's King Louis II, because it regarded him as a foreign prince. This changed once Hungary passed to the Habsburgs on Louis' death in battle in 1526 and the main objective of imperial taxation across the next 90 years was to subsidize the cost of defending the Hungarian frontier against the Ottomans. The bulk of the weaponry and other military materiel was supplied by firms based in the Empire and financed by German banks. The same is true of the troops who eventually evicted the Ottomans from Hungary between 1683 and 1699.

The imperial law code of 1532 was used in parts of Hungary until the mid-seventeenth century, but otherwise Hungary had its own legal system and did not import Austrian ones. Hungarian nobles resisted the use of Germanic titles like *Graf* for count until 1606, and very few acquired the personal status of imperial prince. However, the Habsburgs were often accompanied by Hungarians at imperial ceremonies, reminiscent of the Saracen bodyguard escorting Frederick II to Germany in 1235. Elements of imperial court ceremonial were imported into that used for Hungarian kings, while acceptance of imperial princely titles spread as the Habsburgs used their imperial prerogatives to reward loyal followers and to integrate them within a common system centred on their court in Vienna.[76]

Ferdinand I's accession in Bohemia in 1526 was not universally popular and he faced a serious revolt in 1547. Conscious of the earlier difficulties with the Hussites, the imperial Estates refused to assist him, on the grounds that Bohemia was a separate kingdom.[77] In response, he and his Habsburg successors rejected repeated calls that Bohemia should contribute to imperial taxes. The exercise of Bohemian electoral rights remained controversial, not least because Habsburg possession after 1526 meant they could vote for themselves. Although the vote was suspended in 1648, it was readmitted 60 years later.[78] Bohemia remained connected to the Empire through the arch-office associated with its electoral status. Ferdinand I initiated the practice of ensuring the family's chosen successor was crowned Bohemian and Hungarian king to give him royal status ahead of election as king of the Romans or emperor. Joseph I's unexpectedly early death in 1711 necessitated his younger brother Charles VI assuming the responsibility of becoming emperor. Charles's daughter Maria Theresa ruled as queen of Bohemia and Hungary whilst consort of Emperor Francis I. Thereafter, the Bohemian and Hungarian titles were assumed by the last three emperors after their imperial coronations. Throughout, the imperial title remained important to the Habsburgs' management of their own kingdoms, since its traditional universal associations elevated the dynasty above all components of their personal, territorial empire.

Like Hungarians, Bohemian lords were reluctant to accept imperial aristocratic titles, regarding themselves as vassals of their own king, not the emperor. As in Hungary, this crumbled in the face of the Habsburgs' Counter-Reformation policy of restricting employment to loyal Catholics. Bohemia's already multilingual nobility became even more cosmopolitan following the influx of Austrian, German, Italian and Burgundian families who received lands confiscated from rebels during the Thirty Years War. Restrictions on imperial prerogatives in 1654 meant that most imperial princely titles granted after that date remained purely personal, since they were not associated with land qualifying the beneficiary as an imperial Estate (see pp. 409–14).

The Habsburgs made serious efforts to secure election as kings of Poland in 1572, 1573 and 1586–8. Although these failed, they established dynastic ties to the Catholic branch of Sweden's Vasa family, which ruled Poland from 1587 to 1668.[79] The Habsburgs backed the royal ambitions of the Saxon elector, Friedrich August, who was elected Polish king in 1697 establishing another personal union lasting until 1763. The Saxon-Polish union did not create the common institutions that had developed to sustain the Habsburg union of Austria, Bohemia and Hungary, but was nonetheless closer than those between various German principalities and the Scandinavian monarchies.

The political relationship in the Saxon-Polish and Hanoverian-

British unions was the reverse of that in the Habsburg union, since in both cases the ruler's new royal status outranked his position as an electoral prince of the Empire. Both Poland and Britain were larger and richer than the electorates and their own internal politics and international interests soon became their new rulers' primary concern. The Saxon union was extinguished in the political realignment following the Seven Years War, but the Hanoverian-British one continued until 1837. Neither union was popular amongst its inhabitants. Most Britons regarded Hanover as a strategic liability, while Poles suspected the Saxons of pursuing separate interests. Britons and Poles travelled to Germany on grand tours and to study at the numerous German universities in the eighteenth century. Most professed a dislike of the Empire's society as hierarchical and exclusive in contrast to their own (idealized) inclusive participatory culture and distinctive liberties. Britain and Hanover developed important scientific, artistic and cultural links during the eighteenth century, but Hanoverians did not feel 'British', nor vice versa. Hanover's economy remained agrarian and failed to benefit from Britain's industrial take-off in the nineteenth century.

The South

Italy is often assumed to have 'played no active or meaningful role in the early modern Reich'.[80] Habsburg intervention south of the Alps is presented as selfish manipulation of residual imperial prerogatives to advance purely dynastic territorial goals.[81] Important connections were certainly severed by 1530: there were no more imperial coronation journeys to Rome, while the title of 'king of Italy' was dropped during the sixteenth century, though emperors continued to list royal titles for Germany, Bohemia, Hungary, Dalmatia, Croatia, Slavonia and (after 1700) Spain. The Habsburgs certainly used every opportunity to strengthen their own territorial possessions in Italy and this periodically caused disquiet amongst the imperial Estates north of the Alps who felt they were being dragged into unwanted conflicts. As we have seen (pp. 194), except for Savoy, Italian territories were excluded from most of the new institutions created by imperial reform around 1490.

The sense of separation is reinforced by the standard interpretation of Italian history from the Renaissance to the nineteenth-century process of national unification known as the *Risorgimento*. Like its German equivalent, this historiography presents a story of national fragmentation into separate states like Milan, Savoy-Piedmont, Tuscany and Venice. Fragmentation is likewise blamed for social and cultural stagnation and the aristocratization of urban life, the retreat of the *popolo* (middling burghers) from civic government, and the debilitating effects of factionalism – something already noted by outsiders, exemplified by Shakespeare's *Romeo and Juliet*. While German historians blamed German disunity on the Empire, Italians attributed theirs to foreign domination, beginning in the Italian Wars of 1494–1559. Any remaining connections to the Empire are subsumed within this narrative as manifestations of notionally alien, self-serving Austrian and Spanish Habsburg rule.

Later writers generally interpreted fragmentation in dynastic terms, seeing hereditary possession as the prime determinant of political order. In fact, imperial Italy remained a land of fiefs like Germany. In this sense, the Empire really did represent a barrier to the kind of national unification desired by many Italians after 1815. This explains their celebration of Napoleon, who might otherwise have been condemned as a foreign oppressor yet laid the preconditions for later unity by sweeping away the old imperial order.[82]

Late fifteenth-century Italy possessed two feudal networks that had grown with the Empire. The oldest contained the 'Latin fiefs' (*feuda Latina*) across northern and central Italy and defined the limits of imperial Italy. There were six large crown fiefs, of which five (Milan, Mantua, Savoy-Piedmont, Genoa and Tuscany) were products of the Luxembourgs' recognition of urban oligarchs as imperial princes during the fourteenth century. Charles V reasserted imperial jurisdiction over Tuscany in 1530, retrieving it from the pope, who had generally held it since the death of Matilda of Canossa in 1115. Parma-Piacenza was a product of the Italian Wars, only established in 1545 for a branch of the Farnese family. There were another 200 to 250 lesser fiefs (*feuda minora*) in four thick belts around Genoa: Liguria, Langhe, Lunigiana and Valle di Pregola. These were held by 50 to 70 families, including the Gonzaga, Carretto, Malaspina, Scarampi, Pico, Pallavicino, Doria and Spinola, whose names read like a roll call of some of the Habsburgs' most important courtiers.[83]

The second network was that of the papacy, which emerged during the twelfth century in competition to the imperial system: Habsburg officials claimed in 1709 that two-thirds of the pope's 296 fiefs had been usurped from the Empire. Most indeed originated in the jurisdictions established by the Carolingians and Ottonians. Concentrated in central Italy, most were small with a total population of only 223,000 in about 1700.[84] In addition, the pope claimed feudal jurisdiction over Naples and Sicily since his recognition of the Normans in 1054, confirmed when Sicily-Naples was elevated as a kingdom in 1130. Spain accepted these arrangements when it acquired Naples during the Italian Wars, continuing the tradition of presenting a white horse to the pope each year as a sign of submission.[85]

The partition of the Habsburg lands in 1558 created a third, Spanish, network by assigning Milan to Spain. King Wenzel had already granted Milan superiority over several surrounding fiefs in 1396. Spain exploited this to secure the supply route known as the Spanish Road linking Iberia by sea to Genoa and thence through Lombardy, across the Alps and down the Rhine to its battlefront in the Netherlands against the Dutch rebels after 1566.[86]

The persistence of the imperial feudal network ensured that Italian lords remained the emperor's vassals, even though they were excluded from the Reichstag, the Kreise and other institutions emerging around 1500. They were, however, subordinate to the Reichshofrat, the new supreme court established to safeguard imperial prerogatives. A special Italian section was created once the court became fully operational after 1559. The 1,500 cases from Italy were only a fraction of the 140,000 handled between then and 1806, but the number of Italian applicants nonetheless rose across this period.[87] Many cases involved jurisdictional disputes, but others involved a wide range of issues and allowed the Reichshofrat to check local abuses of power.

The transition to Habsburg imperial rule did not change the practice of naming local lords as imperial vicars to safeguard the emperor's interests and enforce court verdicts. Maximilian II reluctantly empowered his cousin Philip II of Spain as duke of Milan to implement Reichshofrat decisions across imperial Italy. Philip took this responsibility seriously, for he still regarded himself as an imperial prince, but his son Philip III was more concerned with purely Spanish interests and abused his position as commissioner in a long-running case involving abuses in Finale, Liguria, by the marquis of Carretto. Concerned to protect the Spanish Road, Philip III occupied Finale in 1602 and was eventually enfeoffed with it by Emperor Matthias in 1617. However, Spain was not prepared to challenge imperial jurisdiction openly, because it legitimated its own superior position in Lombardy. A decade later, Ferdinand II ignored Spanish interests in order to uphold his prerogative as feudal overlord in the disputed Mantuan Succession (1627–31).[88]

In 1545 Italian vassals were removed from the register developed during imperial reform to distribute fiscal and military obligations. However, this simply reflected their general exclusion from the German kingdom's new institutions, not from the wider imperial framework. They were disadvantaged relative to the Germans in lacking an assembly through which they could debate and possibly control assistance. Instead, each vassal was directly required to assist when summoned by the emperor. Italian vassals provided substantial support in all of Austria's conflicts until 1797, notably the Long Turkish War of 1593–1606 when Mantua's contingent included Claudio Monteverdi.[89] Such assistance is generally ignored when assessing the Empire, because it bypassed the Reichstag and other institutions and went directly to the Habsburg army and treasury. Yet its legal basis rested on the network of imperial fiefs and it was additional to the recruits and taxes sent by the Habsburgs' own Italian territories.

The acquisition of Milan from the disputed Spanish succession in 1714 eliminated the irritant of the separate Spanish feudal jurisdiction and led to the appointment of a new commissioner based in Milan to uphold the emperor's prerogatives throughout imperial Italy. The absence of an Italian equivalent to the Reichstag gave the emperor greater scope to use his prerogatives to suit himself. Charles VI retained Tuscany as a Habsburg possession at the extinction of the Medici dynasty in 1737. Titles and even small fiefs were traded or sold to obtain political and military support, with Torriglia in Liguria being raised as an additional crown fief in 1761.[90]

In one of history's lesser known ironies, Savoy, champion of Italian unification, in fact emerged from the kingdom of Burgundy and between 1361 and 1797 was formally part of Germany. This, of course, did not prevent its ruling family, the Humbertines, from pursuing territorial ambitions south of the Alps. Later national perspectives make little sense given that Savoy also encroached on what is now

Switzerland, held land that is now part of France, and claimed royal status through tenuous links to Cyprus.[91] The Savoyard use of the slogan 'Liberty of Italy' was similar to calls for 'German freedom' in that it was anti-Habsburg rather than directly anti-imperial. Savoy used its position as imperial vicar in Italy since the late sixteenth century to create its own suzerainty over surrounding minor lordships, similar to Spain's exploitation of Milan's superior jurisdiction. The need to prevent Savoy defecting to France during the Nine Years War (1688–97) obliged Leopold I to confer the semi-regal status of grand duke in 1696. The House of Savoy became full royalty in the settlement ending the War of the Spanish Succession, which awarded it Sicily in 1713. Subsequent Austrian pressure forced the Humbertines to trade this for Sardinia in 1720, placing them in a position roughly equivalent to the Hohenzollerns in holding land within the Empire but also a sovereign kingdom beyond it.

Savoy's position within the former German kingdom was not entirely meaningless, since it sustained influence within the Empire. Cooperation with Charles V was instrumental in Duke Emanuel Filiberto's recovery of his possessions in 1559 after 23 years of French occupation. Savoy's dukes either attended in person or sent a representative to every Reichstag between 1541 and 1714, and they accepted jurisdiction of the Empire's other supreme court, the Reichskammergericht, over themselves as imperial Estates. Even after their elevation as sovereign kings, Savoy's rulers continued to pay feudal dues on behalf of their imperial fiefs. They remained interested in imperial politics. Duke Charles Emanuel I was a serious candidate for the Bohemian crown in 1619, while the family pushed after 1788 to receive a new electoral title, securing Prussian backing for this ambition. The overall situation of imperial Italy and Savoy thus remained relatively stable until the shock of the French Revolutionary Wars saw both severed from the Empire in 1797. Now styled the House of Savoy, the Humbertines were restored in 1814 and eventually became monarchs of united Italy between 1861 and 1946.[92]

The West

The Empire's western frontier lacks a single national story to give it coherence, as no modern state chose to claim the old Lotharingian-Burgundian heritage. As with Italy, ties between this area and the

Empire are generally written from the perspective of Habsburg rather than imperial history. This is understandable since the Habsburgs secured the bulk of ducal Burgundy by 1493 and appropriated elements of its culture, notably the heraldic Order of the Golden Fleece. Unlike the acquisition of Hungary, the Burgundian inheritance expanded the Empire, because Frederick III enfeoffed his son Maximilian with all the Burgundian lands in 1478, including those recently acquired like Flanders and Artois, which were formerly French fiefs. Charles V, himself born in Ghent, continued Burgundy's expansion by adding seven Lower Rhenish and Frisian fiefs, creating a complex of 17 provinces by 1536 stretching from the North Sea to Switzerland.

Charles's action integrated the far north-west, a long-standing region 'distant from the king', more firmly within the Empire. Moreover, the entire Burgundian lands were included in the institutions created by imperial reform, including coming under Reichskammergericht jurisdiction and inclusion in the Kreis structure by 1512. Accordingly, Burgundians paid imperial taxes and were included in the imperial register of obligations compiled in 1521. Ulterior motives operated throughout, because the Habsburgs were concerned to include their new possessions within the Empire's new collective security system to defend them against further French attacks. However, they also sought to insulate Burgundy like other direct Habsburg possessions from the imperial Estates' influence. These policies also pandered to local interests, which the Habsburgs were keen to cultivate to consolidate their authority as Burgundy's rulers. Burgundians already resented the heavy taxes introduced by their own dukes before 1477 and had little interest in additional obligations towards the Empire.

Charles adjusted Burgundy's relationship in the Burgundian Treaty agreed on 26 June 1548 as part of the wide-ranging measures passed at his controversial Armoured Reichstag at Augsburg. The treaty was endorsed by the Reichstag and ratified by all 17 Burgundian provinces. It secured Burgundy's autonomy on Habsburg terms. Kreis boundaries were adjusted to remove the provinces of Utrecht, Overijssel and Drenthe (all acquired after 1524) from Westphalia and include them within the Burgundian Kreis instead, consolidating that region as exclusively Habsburg territory. Nonetheless, Burgundy remained an imperial Estate, but with only three votes in the Reichstag, because the Habsburgs chose not to claim additional votes for all 17 provinces. Burgundy was removed from the Reichskammergericht's jurisdiction, but Burgundians still had to contribute taxes towards its maintenance. Additionally, Burgundy was assessed for other imperial taxes at three times the rate paid by the electorates. Although sounding impressive, this was actually modest considering Burgundy contained Europe's richest cities.[93]

Spain would later claim that the Burgundian Treaty obliged the Empire to defend Burgundy, including against the northern (Dutch) provinces, which rebelled in 1566. The Austrian Habsburgs, however, generally excused themselves by referring to an adjustment in the Empire's defence structure in 1555 which had made any such assistance dependent on the agreement of the Reichstag: neither Austria nor the other German princes had any enthusiasm for being drawn into Spain's problems. The German princes were concerned involvement would unpick their own compromise laboriously agreed only a few years before in the Religious Peace of Augsburg. Spanish military efforts stalled by 1579, leading to the secession of the seven northern provinces as a Protestant republic. The Dutch negotiated international alliances and acted like a fully independent state. Renewed efforts to crush their revolt failed after 1621, prompting Spain to recognize Dutch independence as part of the Westphalian peace settlement in 1648. In practice, full separation from the Empire took longer, since Spain simply renounced its authority over the seven Dutch provinces in a separate treaty not signed by either the emperor or the other imperial Estates. The emperor recognized Dutch neutrality in 1653, meaning exemption from any obligation to assist the Empire in future wars. This was ratified by the Reichstag only in 1728. In practice, the Dutch Republic maintained its own garrisons in strategic lower Rhenish towns until 1679. It was also a close ally of Austria for much of the eighteenth century, while its leading political family, the House of Orange, was closely related to German imperial princes, notably in Nassau and Brandenburg-Prussia.[94] The truncated Burgundian Kreis remained part of the Empire, passing from Spain to Austria in 1714, which held it under the same terms as agreed in 1548 until it was overrun by revolutionary France in 1794.

The southern section of Burgundy, known as Franche Comté, was conquered by France in 1679 in what was one of the largest territorial losses suffered by the Empire during early modernity. France meanwhile encroached on Lorraine, which lay between Franche Comté and the rest of the Burgundian Netherlands. The three bishoprics of Metz, Toul and Verdun were weakened by the emancipation of their episcopal towns and the loss of imperial patronage following the Staufers' demise in 1254. Metz already accepted French vassalage in 1296. France assumed protectorate rights over the other two bishoprics during the fourteenth century, annexing them in 1552. As we have seen, Charles was unable to reverse this despite his costly siege of Metz, and the Empire acknowledged their loss in 1648.

All three bishoprics had land scattered across Lorraine, allowing France to increase pressure on Lorraine's dukes to accept vassalage. Charles V and France agreed the Treaty of Nuremberg in August 1542, accepting that Lorraine was 'free and unincorporated' in either of their realms. Henceforth, the duchy was exempt from any of the fiscal and military obligations created by imperial reform. However, the treaty also declared it under the Empire's eternal protection, while the duke remained an imperial vassal through his possession of Pont-à-Mousson, as well as subordinate to the French king on account of the duchy of Bar. Lorraine's dukes sought prestige and autonomy by engaging in both French and imperial politics since – like Savoy – their possessions were too small for a fully independent existence in an international environment still governed by hierarchical political thinking. The emperor raised the minor fief of Nomeny to a margraviate in 1567 to give the duke of Lorraine a full vote in the Reichstag. Growing French pressure in the 1630s and again after 1679 appeared a far greater threat than the relatively light constraints imposed by membership of the Empire. Lorraine's dukes accordingly allied themselves primarily with the Habsburgs and sought places for their sons in the imperial church. Lorraine was denied the recognition as royalty accorded Prussia and Savoy at the Utrecht congress ending the War of the Spanish Succession. In response, its dukes merged their family with the Habsburgs through the marriage of Maria Theresa and Francis Stephen in 1736, though Austria was then obliged to sacrifice Lorraine itself as part of a wider peace settlement with France in 1738. Lorraine's formal representation in the Empire was transferred from Nomeny to the tiny lordship of Falkenstein, partly to secure Habsburg influence but also reflecting a wider reluctance within the Empire to accept the consequences of real political changes.[95]

The process of Swiss independence was even longer than that of the Dutch. Most of what became Switzerland originated in Carolingian Burgundy, but the three future cantons of Uri, Schwyz and Unterwalden (whose alliance of 1291 is usually considered the country's birthday) initially belonged to the duchy of Swabia. There was never a single Switzerland before the nineteenth century, but instead a multitude of towns, lordships and rural communities bound through a complex web of alliances (see pp. 585–91). Medieval emperors visited fairly frequently on their way between the Empire's three main kingdoms. Most Swiss communities secured exemption from the Reichskammergericht's jurisdiction in 1499, but nonetheless remained part of the Empire and were still summoned to the Reichstag during the early sixteenth century. They continued to pay fees for the confirmation of their privileges at the accession of each new emperor. As late as 1644, Bern completed a new city gate adorned with the imperial coat of arms, while the emperor addressed the Swiss as his 'loyal subjects'. The Swiss were proud of their privileged autonomy, which they did not express in terms of modern sovereignty.

Despite the widespread belief to the contrary, the Peace of Westphalia did not confirm Swiss independence, but merely extended the privileges of 1499 to the city of Basel, which only joined the Confederation in 1501.[96] Austria renounced jurisdiction over some Alpine communities in 1652, but retained some rights, as well as over Konstanz, which it had annexed in 1548. Change was gradual and was hindered by the difficulties in deciding whether sovereignty lay with the individual communities, the cantons or the Confederation as a whole. Solothurn stopped requiring its citizens to swear loyalty to the Empire only in 1681. Other symbolic ties like coats of arms were not removed until around 1700. Meanwhile, the incorporation of the French-speaking areas of Fribourg (1454) and Solothurn (1481) diluted Germanness. The spread of French culture, exemplified by Jean-Jacques Rousseau, contributed to this in the eighteenth century. Whereas sixteenth-century Swiss had tended to see themselves as one of several German 'nations' within the Empire, their descendants two centuries later voiced a more distinct identity around the concept of Helvetica: the ideal of the moral and unpretentious Swiss in contrast to the petty and immoral German princely courts.

The French Revolutionary Wars saw the Confederation reorganized as the French-backed Helvetic Republic in 1798. Nonetheless, it was still considered necessary five years later for France to compel the Empire to acknowledge formally that Switzerland was an independent state.[97] The difficulty in identifying an exact date for Swiss independence is typical of the Empire's relations with what eventually became separate European states. Although conquest had played a significant part in many cases during the early Middle Ages, for most of the Empire's existence imperial jurisdiction had not meant 'foreign domination', but a relatively benign association with what was still regarded as a common political order composed of many communities. It is to the question of identities within that order that we turn in the next chapter.

5

Identities

IDENTITY AND BELONGING

Nations and Nationalism

The Empire disappeared at the point in European history generally considered to be the birth of modern nationalism. This coincidence is often related in older accounts arguing that the Empire's demise was barely registered by its inhabitants, who had long since transferred their loyalties to national states. The classic conservative interpretation of European history presented the continent's peoples as predetermined by language, ethnicity and culture. Archaeology, ethnology, linguistics and other specialist disciplines emerging after 1800 all provided corroborating evidence in the form of distinctive pottery, customs and root words. Political history was written as a story of each people's search for a viable framework to claim their place as a distinct country. States ruling 'mixed' populations were viewed suspiciously and apt to be condemned as 'artificial', unless they were imperial states ruling supposedly inferior non-European peoples elsewhere. German historians were convinced of the continuous existence of *Deutschtum* since antiquity, but usually believed the Empire had failed to provide the necessary framework for this to flourish.[1]

Later twentieth-century historians were more aware how previous generations had, with terrible results, manipulated evidence to convey false continuities and to claim parts of Europe as 'historic' homelands. Several influential writers dismissed the entire idea of pre-modern national identities, arguing that nationalism is a modern, 'artificial' ideology associated with mass politics of the industrial age.[2] Evidence advanced previously for continuity was now dismissed as marginal or exceptional. The most that was conceded was that a tiny military and clerical elite articulated a narrow view of themselves as a 'people' to bind warlord and followers through a common myth of origins.

Regnal Identities and the Empire

Such insights have been developed to argue that pre-modern identity was 'regnal', focused on a monarchy, rather than defined by the essentialist 'blood and soil' criteria advanced by nineteenth-century nationalists.[3] It is certainly easier to research the process of identification through the symbols and arguments employed to foster identity than to reconstruct individuals' subjective self-definition.[4] The medieval French monarchy made considerable efforts to foster loyalty, already projecting the family's own patron saint as a model for all subjects in the eleventh century – a strategy also employed in Bohemia, Hungary, Poland and Kievan Rus. Central holy places were endowed to assist this, like Westminster Abbey in England, or St Denis in France. Royal institutions, like the court, justice, taxes and war-making, also all focused attention on a common political centre.[5] The argument that pre-modern identities were regnal shares much with older arguments that Europe's states were products of centralizing processes largely driven by kings. As we have seen, such interpretations have distorted the Empire's history, because later generations have looked for centres and institutions that did not exist.

The Empire's inhabitants did not lack elements that could encourage a shared identity. While the actual Roman legacy was confined to the south and south-west, it was spread in its revised Holy Roman form by Charlemagne and his successors. For much of the early Middle Ages the Empire was simply the *regnum*, whereas all other kingdoms required some qualification limiting them to a specific people, as in the kingdom of the Lombards.[6] In this sense, the Empire was a more elastic and inclusive concept than more centralized monarchies like France. Latin served as a single elite language transcending vernacular dialects. Roman Christianity provided a common belief system, as well as much of the conceptual language required to discuss morality, politics and justice. Migration, especially after the eleventh century, spread people and ideas across the Empire. The political elite often travelled great distances to attend assemblies or participate in coronations and military campaigns. Distance was no barrier to the spread of other common institutions like monastic orders or the imperial church. There was great variety in socio-economic forms, but this was scarcely unique in medieval Europe, while there were no fundamental divisions between ethnic groups, such as those between steppe nomads and settled populations found in Russia or China.

These factors suggest there was nothing inevitable about the Empire's peoples eventually building multiple, distinct 'national' identities around notions of language, culture and ethnicity, most of which were indeed constructed precisely for this purpose only much later. The real difference between the Empire and more centralized monarchies was certainly political, but not how 'political' is customarily understood. Centralized monarchies fostered 'national' identities by selecting elements that made their regnal identity plausible and desirable. This always entailed excluding aspects hindering this, hence the use of language, culture and (after the Reformation) religion to distinguish 'loyal subjects' from 'suspect foreigners'. The Empire never attempted this, because it was always superior to any one kingdom and hence always contained more than one 'people'. The story of identification within the Empire was never one of failed efforts to forge a single (German) national identity. Rather, it was always a process through which communities and groups formed their own particular identities through securing a legally recognized autonomous position within the wider imperial framework.

PEOPLES

Tribes

The belief in the existence of different peoples is very old and can be found in the writings of ancient historians such as Herodotus, as well as in the Bible. The problem is to understand what this meant to those involved, because the words employed have acquired additional associations over time. This is especially true of the parts of Europe occupied by the Empire and which were the subject of intense study by nineteenth- and twentieth-century German ethnographers and archaeologists who used the terms 'tribe' (*Stamm*) and 'people' (*Volk*). Tribes were usually regarded as subdivisions of a common people, with the Franks, Saxons, Bavarians, Frisians and Alemanni all being considered 'Germanic'.[7] The writers generally romanticized their subjects as repositories of 'authentic' national culture, regarding history as a constant struggle to preserve cultural 'purity' in the face of foreign intrusions, as well as expansion through the merger of tribes on the basis of alleged common characteristics. Most argued that this process culminated in a national 'awakening' around 1800 as people became more self-aware of their commonalities. A typical example is the way in which linguists traced the history of their 'national' language by identifying common root words and describing how tribal tongues were gradually reduced to dialects before these too were eradicated through standardized spelling and pronunciation facilitated by printing and universal schooling.

The German word *Volk* was in fact rarely used before the eighteenth century, and then only to denote a specific group, particularly soldiers (*Kriegsvolk*).[8] Early writers like the etymologist Isidore of Seville and the Frankish historian Regino, abbot of Prüm, used Latin terms. *Populus* meant 'people' in the general sense of humans or inhabitants, especially the politically active section. *Gens* were people related by common descent, while *natio* usually denoted common origins more narrowly defined by birth. Nonetheless, medieval commentators – like their present-day counterparts – were often imprecise and ambiguous in their employment of such terms. Identity was usually multilayered and frequently expressed differently according to the situation, despite most writers' conviction that geography and climate imparted 'fixed' characteristics.

The term *natio* could be employed to identify a group that later writers called a 'tribe'. 'Nations' were originally 'barbarians', those who lay beyond Roman civilization, and it was not until the thirteenth century that the term acquired more positive attributes with the growing acceptance that Christendom was split into different sovereign peoples. Initially it was foreign students studying in Paris or Bologna who were identified as 'nations' according to common origins. The delegates at church councils were grouped this way after 1215, but the designations changed frequently and were inconsistent with later ideas. For example, 'Bohemians' at Prague University after 1348 included not just Czechs, but Hungarians, southern Slavs and German-speakers from Bohemia, while 'Bavarians' encompassed all central, western and southern Germans, with northern Germans and all Scandinavians being called 'Saxons'.[9] Even in the eighteenth century, 'nation' continued to be used flexibly, with the Viennese and Prussian soldiers variously constituting 'nations' according to some authors. However, from the sixteenth century, 'nation' assumed many of the characteristics once associated with *populus*, especially in the mouths of those claiming to represent the nation politically, whereas *populus* became more debased as the 'common' sort.

Identity Markers

Early writers already recognized the need for criteria to distinguish between tribes and peoples, but – like the terms used – these categories also shifted over time. Language (*lingua*) was already widely touted in the ninth century as an important distinguishing mark, but in practice the huge variance amongst vernaculars hindered actual understanding. Customs (*mores*) were also cited and often expanded into generalized characteristics. Thietmar of Merseburg identified cunning Swabians, greedy Bavarians who lived in poverty, quarrelsome Lorrainers prone to rebellion, and loyal Saxons who allowed their ruler to abuse their trust – the latter comment clearly motivated by his own dissatisfaction at Otto II's dissolution of his beloved bishopric. Common descent (*genus*) proved equally vague in practice, as it was applied variously to kinship groups and entire populations.

Myths of origins often proved more attractive because they combined various elements within a story that could serve many, especially political, agendas. Most myths identified one or more founding figures usually associated with victory or conquest, especially of the area their people currently inhabited. The martial aspect was important during the development of these stories in the early Middle Ages, an era when most of the population was enslaved. The myths thus legitimated the elite of free warriors and their self-identification with alleged characteristics like prowess, moral fibre and their supposedly unique political institutions. Myths were portable; indeed many contained stories of a shared migration, or that the current people emerged from the mingling of earlier groups including conquered and conquerors. The Franks considered themselves descended from Priam, the last king of Troy, who wandered westwards into central Europe, but they also believed they were a fusion of many tribes, initially each under its own king, before united by Clovis in the late fifth century. They distinguished themselves as an imperial *populus*, carrying a general civilization, rather than simply an individual *gente* (tribe), and – thanks to Clovis's conversion – they considered themselves 'God's people' (*populus Dei*).[10]

However, even in their core homeland, the Franks formed only 15–25 per cent of the population and were too few to establish themselves exclusively as a ruling class throughout the Carolingian realm. They generally merged with other elites through marriage or expropriation of land, with assimilation working in both directions depending on circumstances: some conquered elites considered themselves Franks, while elsewhere Frankish conquerors identified themselves at least partly with the areas they now controlled. The Franks sought to preserve their distinctiveness by continuing the late Roman practice of expressing separated identities through law codes. This aspect should not be over-exaggerated as most laws remained unwritten, while the distinction between law and custom was far from clear. Nonetheless, law assumed significance as a defining marker of identity when combined with other factors encouraging a sense of community; hence the significance of the use of expulsion as punishment for major transgressions, since this cast the wrongdoer from the tribe or people.[11]

The Franks wrote laws for each subject people incorporated within their realm from the late eighth century, often fabricating tradition by claiming these derived from earlier ones. The Alemanni, Bavarians, Frisians, Lombards, Saxons and Thuringians all had (or acquired) their own *Lex* distinct from the *Lex Francorum* (Salic law) reserved for the Franks. Paradoxically, this eroded the Franks' own self-belief as an imperial people, since they became just one group among many, even if their elite remained primarily the group in charge. In turn, this imparted the lasting sense of the Empire as inhabited by a variety of peoples, rather than as an exclusive, superior people standing apart and above those they ruled, as in the case of the British and Ottoman empires.

Other Frankish policies further eroded any sense of their being the Empire's exclusive rulers.[12] Rapid Christianization of the elites between 780 and 820 removed religion as a potential marker of difference – another contrast with British and Ottoman experience. Old power structures broke up, at least outside Saxony, southern Italy and, to an extent, also Bavaria. Continued redistribution of land and offices by later monarchs further reduced the differences amongst the elites – differences that were now socially and politically far less significant than those between the free and unfree populations.[13] Population growth from the eleventh century, together with migration after about 1100, eroded old identities whilst adding new ones.

Belief in tribal identities nonetheless persisted, because their original lack of clarity allowed later generations to shape them to suit their own purposes. For example, there was no direct link between the *Lex Saxonum* of 802 and the *Sachsenspiegel* of about 1224, but the existence of these two law codes served to substantiate claims of a continuous Saxon identity.[14] Identities were still sufficiently sharp in the early tenth century for some to criticize the Saxon Ottonians as being the 'wrong' people to replace the Frankish Carolingians as German kings in 919. The Ottonian chronicler Widukind of Corvey placed great emphasis on the story of the dying Conrad I, the last Carolingian, symbolically passing the Empire to the Saxons by allegedly designating Henry I, the first Ottonian, as his successor. By this point, Conrad and Henry were clan or family leaders, rather than tribal chiefs.[15] The sense of distinct peoples increasingly mattered less than other, more focused identities.

ESTATES, CLASSES AND FAMILIES

Estates Society

Tribes were never regarded as composed of equals. There was already a sense of the individual during the early Middle Ages. Each person had specific duties and was responsible for their own actions and salvation. However, prior to the eighteenth century, most commentators were more concerned with how horizontal and vertical divisions stratified society internally. Personal aspects, like interests, abilities or appearance, were all considered less important in identifying an individual than their membership of one or more of society's subgroups. The Empire was not unique in how social stratification reinforced political hierarchies, but the specific form of this interaction nonetheless contributed to its governance becoming increasingly multilayered and territorialized. A key factor in this development was that social distinctions were never fully transportable, at least partly rooting an individual's identity to place as well as person.

Frankish society recognized two fundamental social distinctions. The first identified free people, whom most writers considered the *populus*, and a much larger number of unfree people, mainly slaves born as such or obtained by raiding or conquering pagans. The second distinguished laity from clergy, the latter drawn overwhelmingly from the free population. However, a more complex, three-way functional division was also recognized, especially by 1000. Morality remained a key determinant, but writers were less bound by references to specific biblical passages and more interested in adapting earlier social categories to keep pace with the demographic and economic expansion experienced from the eleventh century.[16] These wider changes eroded the earlier Christian idea of freedom as a natural state, with servitude as the consequence of sin. New forms of agricultural production resulted in around 85 per cent of the population living as *laboratores* in some form of servitude as the 'commons', or third social Estate, whose function was to provide for the material needs of others. Whereas previously all free male laity had been considered warriors, *bellatores* were now restricted to the second Estate, which was evolving as hereditary nobility more concerned with controlling and exploiting land than fighting. Nonetheless, their programmatic function as society's defenders was used to legitimate their special privileges. The clergy (*oratores*) formed the senior Estate, placed first thanks to their function of praying for everyone's salvation.

All commentators were convinced that social structure was hierarchical as a necessary and fundamental feature of human existence. How hierarchy was rationalized changed over time, but always included the argument that humans possessed varying qualities and abilities. Those in authority developed lengthy justifications for their elevated status, generally emphasizing some form of asymmetrical reciprocity whereby duties and obligations were distributed unevenly throughout society. However, hierarchy was neither absolute nor fully clear. The sharp dividing line between free and unfree had been replaced by more complex graduations. All, including those in servitude, possessed rights relating to their Estate's function. The ideal was an interlocking system in which all should accept their allotted place, because all derived benefits from the functions performed by others on their behalf.

The reality was necessarily messier and less consensual. Status was neither exclusively self-determined nor simply imposed from above according to a rational blueprint, but instead depended heavily on how far individuals and groups could secure recognition from others. Although the ideal was presented as stable, status remained a process of constant negotiation. It was accepted that each Estate was internally stratified into various subgroups, but their precise interrelationship was often unclear. For example, the Latin term *milites* (soldiers) had associations with personal freedom during the early Middle Ages, but by the eleventh century it applied to a new group of unfree knights also known as *ministeriales*. A century later it had become inconceivable for a knight not to be both free and on the lower rung of hereditary nobility. Frederick I 'Barbarossa' promoted the knightly ideal after 1180, drawing on the new ethos of chivalry imported from France to bridge the widening gulf amongst the nobility caused by the emergence of a princely elite. Later, the nobility's continued and growing internal stratification raised questions whether its senior ranks could still be considered knights. Individuals could subvert conventions, as long as they enjoyed unimpeachable social credentials. Emperor Maximilian I placed himself in the front rank of his mercenary infantry (the *Landsknechte*) in an effort to raise their social status as warriors. Two centuries later, Prussia's king Frederick William I banned the use of the word *Miliz* (deriving from *miles*) for professional soldiers, because he wanted to distinguish his army from part-time militiamen.[17]

Theorists and rulers never resolved the contradictions inherent in their descriptions of Estates society, but their continued efforts embedded these categories deeply within social consciousness and legal practice.[18] A further factor was that the three Estates were largely self-recruiting. Even the clergy, who were expected to be celibate, were often not in practice for much of the Middle Ages, while the Reformation endorsed marriage for Protestant clerics and led to the emergence of dynasties of pastors where son followed father into the calling.[19] This pattern was still more pronounced for the nobility and commons, where a father's status determined that of his family. Vertical social mobility was generally much more restricted than geographical mobility through migration. Peter Eppelmann (aka Melander), a peasant from Nassau, became Count Holzapfel and commander of the imperial army during the Thirty Years War, but such examples were both rare and often perceived as transgressive. Melander was unusually well educated and many of his relations were pastors or public officials, while he enjoyed aristocratic patronage from an early age.[20] Generally, upwards mobility required several generations to achieve, delayed of course by the reluctance of superior groups to accept newcomers.

Status and Place

Around 5–10 per cent of the population fell outside the boundaries of Estates society by early modernity, because they lacked a fixed abode. The linkage of status to domicile was common throughout Latin Europe, but assumed a distinct form in the Empire thanks to its specific social and political developments during the high and later Middle Ages. Consequently, the identity of social groups became irretrievably entwined with the Empire's political and legal fabric. This was most pronounced in Germany thanks to the greater integration of territorialized authority within the overarching legal framework. As a result there were profound political and social consequences for the Empire and for the identity of its inhabitants.

Estates were not national, in the sense that there was no single 'imperial' clergy, nobility or commons. Instead, there were Paderborn clergy, Hessian nobles, Bavarian peasants, and a multitude of other groups defined by both place and social status, often subdividing further as, for example, not just Saxon burghers, but those of Leipzig, Dresden and other towns. In each case, their identity came to be expressed through shared rights incorporated in law and anchored in turn through their recognition in other charters or privileges associated with their community's relationship to the Empire.

This relationship was mutually reinforcing thanks to the difficulties each group experienced in defining and defending its identity. For example, late fifteenth-century German nobles tried to define their own status more clearly by emphasizing their ancestry, marriage and record of participation in tournaments, rather than be defined by privileges granted by their prince, such as tax exemptions, tithes and hunting rights. Self-determination was employed because nobles could not prevent their prince granting similar privileges to other groups. However, princes could also prove long and illustrious pedigrees, possessed superior resources, and were able to transform tournaments into lavish baroque spectacles that by 1600 were focused on their own courts and carefully choreographed to emphasize their own superior status and political agendas. The Empire's multilayered political structure offered alternative security for distinct privileges, since groups and communities could obtain recognition of their status from those superior to their own immediate lords. For example, the inhabitants of numerous towns during the high Middle Ages obtained charters from the emperor granting them corporate privileges that their own lords were unable to revoke.[21] The diffuse distribution of authority through the Empire thus reflected and reinforced decentralized, multilayered social distinctions. The social hierarchy was complex and fragmented, like the political structure that offered multiple sources to legitimate corporate rights.

The emergence of burghers as legally distinct, privileged inhabitants of towns was the most important change in the third Estate across the Middle Ages. This process also underscores the significance of place in the wider elaboration of social distinctions, because burgher status was encouraged by aspects of communal living unrelated to the socio-economic functions of commoners, as well as being an expression of political self-assertion and people's desire for greater control of their own destinies. Although burghers were collectively recognized as a distinct Estate by early modernity, they shared the late medieval characteristic of the other Estates in being fragmented by place, with each community having its own local and specific rights. These were not portable; therefore if someone moved to another town, they had to apply (and usually pay) for recognition as a burgher there.

While burghers were generally considered socially superior to peasants, their exact relationship to both the commons and to the other two traditional Estates remained unclear. The politicized slogan of the 'common man' (*gemeiner Mann*) emerged around 1500, embracing peasants and burghers without removing all distinctions between them.[22] Throughout the later Middle Ages and early modernity, individuals sought special marks of distinction through forms of address or the right to wear particular clothes, often usurping the privileges of more prestigious groups that in turn would then invent new ways of elevating themselves.[23] The spread of writing encouraged greater efforts to fix distinctions through elaborate laws, tables of ranks regulating hierarchies of titles, and sumptuary legislation defining what each corporate group should wear. Gender differences added complexity. A burgher's wife was socially superior to a man from a status group below burgher's rank, like a day labourer. If she was his employer, she might also exercise authority over him. Yet, as a woman, she was decidedly inferior in other respects, notably her ability to represent herself in a law court – something denied Saxon women until 1838 for instance.[24] Even perceptive commentators chose to ignore these contradictions. As late as 1795, the lawyer Johann Pütter wrote 'people of the same Estate can differ in rank and status without the Estate thereby losing its unity'.[25]

Classes?

By the late eighteenth century, the subdivision of Estates into corporate groups had assumed greater significance than the overall conception of a tripartite social order. Communities and groups cherished their corporate privileges because these offered time-hallowed protections for distinctive identities increasingly threatened by new forces of homogenization during this period.

Social mobility increased through the employment opportunities provided by expanding state administration. Governments possessed greater ability to revise established legal arrangements in the interests of fiscal-military efficiency, and to intrude into previously autonomous social spheres, establishing more direct relationships with all inhabitants regardless of their social status. Princely taxation increasingly targeted wealth rather than exempting status. Brandenburg-Prussia, for instance, experimented with graduated poll taxes in 1677 and 1679. Civil and military hierarchies were restructured according to their members' seniority of service in official ranks, rather than status determined by their birth. Many German territories issued patents of nobility rewarding commoners, who could then insert the predicative *von* ('of') into their names even without owning a landed estate. The Austrian army automatically ennobled any officer awarded the Maria Theresa medal instituted in 1757, while commoners with 30 years' service were invited to apply for ennoblement.[26] Meanwhile, economic changes and the proletarianization of many tasks through the spread of wage labour also levelled old distinctions whilst forging new ones. Elements of a class society were certainly emerging as people were marked by their relationship to production rather than social function.[27]

New arguments emerged that could serve to legitimate the removal of hallowed status distinctions. Social criticism was scarcely new. Medieval clerics already attacked noble privileges and their basis in violence as immoral, while the twelfth to early sixteenth centuries saw repeated bursts of popular anticlericalism fuelled by resentment at the often stark contrast between the lifestyle of clergy and their Christian ideals. However, the popular basis of such criticism broadened during the sixteenth century and focused more sharply on the obstacles to upward social mobility. For example, burghers tried to claim nobility on the basis of education and other achievements.[28] The criticism gradually shifted from this or that group being unworthy of its privileges to a more fundamental critique of Estates society. The growing emphasis on human reason in philosophical arguments from the late seventeenth century undermined faith in a divinely ordained human order. By the late eighteenth century, burghers increasingly renounced efforts to join the nobility and instead claimed moral superiority for their own 'bourgeois' culture. Political attitudes changed in line with this. Whereas authorities had been regarded as guardians of an idealized static social order into the eighteenth century, increasingly they were seen by some as motors of potentially beneficial changes through their ability to revise or overturn existing legal arrangements. As we shall see (pp. 639–45), such demands for change clashed with those who saw the Empire as a legal order protecting entrenched rights.

Family

Much of the late medieval and early modern legislation in the Empire focused on delineating rights associated with marriage, parenthood, legitimacy, property-ownership and inheritance. Changes in these aspects of social structure were also to have profound implications for the Empire's political order. The predominant form amongst the free population in 800 was the kindred or clan comprising a fairly large group of relations cooperating for mutual support and protection. Clan ties overrode those of marriage and nuclear families. For example, a wife could seek support from her kindred if her husband abused her or wanted a divorce.

These kindreds have entered history by the names of their 'founder', whose first name was applied by later genealogists as a family name for an age when such things were unknown. Thus, the Carolingians are Charlemagne's descendants, while the Liudolfinger (in turn ancestors of the Ottonians) are traced from Liudolf, who founded Gandersheim abbey in the ninth century (see pp. 82 and 86). Kindreds were indeed distinguished by common naming patterns – all the males in the Salian family were called Conrad or Henry.[29] Nonetheless, kindreds in fact operated through consanguinity and not patrilinear descent. Property could be bequeathed to any legitimate son or brother or even to more distant relations. Individual prestige, reputation and influence were all more important than immediate descent, though the latter was certainly important amongst royalty. There was little sense of an ancestral home, as royal service required the elite to move throughout the Frankish realm, while conquests and royal gifts gave them land scattered across wide areas.

The word 'family' (*familia*) was not determined primarily by blood or marriage ties before the twelfth century. Instead, it was most frequently used to denote the unfree workers and others economically dependent on a manor for whom the lord was legally responsible.[30] Monogamous marriage was already a church ideal by the ninth century and praised as an indissoluble union of two consenting adults. Changes in the twelfth century made it a sacrament requiring clerical involvement to be legally binding and therefore easier for the authorities to regulate. The proportion of the population married officially in church remained small prior to a renewed emphasis on marriage as the basis for a godly household following the Reformation. It was at this point that the German word *Familie* gained common currency to denote the nucleated family of parents and children as the social ideal.

The changing attitudes towards marriage reflected its growing social and political importance. More distinct patrilineal families emerged around 1000, as tracing a single line of descent through fathers and sons assumed greater significance than consanguinity. This process took at least two more centuries to complete. Matrilineal descent remained significant into the twelfth century. For example, the chronicler Wipo regarded Henry III's connections through his mother to Charlemagne as more significant than his more immediate relationship to his father, Conrad II. Likewise, it was politically important for Conrad III to be able to demonstrate ties to the former Salian line of kings through his mother Agnes, daughter of Henry IV. Consanguinity also served aristocratic political interests into the late twelfth century. Brothers and sisters could be pulled from church careers and redeployed in the wider interests of the kindred to breed sufficient heirs when required. In an age of deficient medicine and the frequent violent premature death of males, this made perfect evolutionary sense. The larger group had better overall survival chances than narrower strategies based on nucleated families.[31]

Frederick II used the expression 'House of Staufer' (*domus Stoffensis*) only once (1247) in over two thousand surviving documents.[32] However, things were already beginning to shift by then and cooperation between siblings declined noticeably from the 1230s. While kindreds had the advantage of numbers, they often suffered from indiscipline as each member pursued his own ambitions. Internal rivalries could be destructive, as the Carolingians' civil wars demonstrated from the 840s. Discipline could be imposed through subordinating individual interests to an ideal of the family as dynasty transcending the generations. This entailed acceptance of a stricter hierarchy of loyalties through a culture of self-restraint and deference to a paterfamilias. Patrilinealism and the seniority of the firstborn son provided a way to regulate subordination and determine the options each family member would be allowed to pursue. This explains the continued importance of the imperial church in providing suitable accommodation for the aristocracy's unmarried children. Paternalism was supposed to compensate for individuals' self-sacrifice as the senior head of the family employed his influence and connections to safeguard the material well-being and status of junior family members.

One sign of the spread of dynasticism was how twelfth- and thirteenth-century chroniclers began tracing royal genealogies to structure their accounts. The line of Saxon aristocrats ruling as kings after 919 was dubbed Ottonians from the succession of three Ottos by 1002. Early twelfth-century chroniclers named the next line of kings as the Salians (*reges Salici*) from their origins amongst the *Salfranken*, the Franks living in the Rhineland, once forming the western part of the original Franconia, which was distinguished through its use of Salic law. The family were already known locally as the Wormsers by 982 after their main possessions in the diocese of Worms.[33]

Association of family and place was partly a reflection of much wider trends. The growth in population since the eleventh century encouraged the use of more stable 'family' names to help identify people more easily. Another factor was a significant reduction in the diversity of first names after about 1100 as parents chose from a fairly restricted repertoire of those of well-known saints and monarchs. The transition from one to two names was completed between the thirteenth and fourteenth centuries amongst the urban population and adopted by the early fifteenth century in the countryside. Initially, individuals took either their father's or mother's first name as their surname, but increasingly geographic origins or occupation were used instead.[34] Aristocrats and nobles were always associated with place. Common patronage of monasteries already provided a focal point for kindreds, serving as a common burial place and way to preserve collective memory. The Salians initially used Worms Cathedral before shifting to Speyer, which they expanded after 1024 with the accession of their first Holy Roman emperor, Conrad II. Swabian nobles established family monasteries after the mid-eleventh century, followed by those in Bavaria around fifty years later.

The cause of 'church liberty' weakened some of these associations during the later eleventh century, while the practice of replacing earth and timber castles with more durable and expensive stone constructions provided alternative, secular sites.[35] Count Lothar, the future Lothar III, was known as von Supplinburg after his castle in Saxony. The Staufers derived their name from the Hohenstaufen castle built in 1079 to consolidate their new position as dukes of Swabia. The Habsburgs assumed their name around 1090 from their castle Habichtsburg built about seventy years earlier in what is now the Swiss canton of Aargau. Over time, these locations assumed almost mystical status as ancestral homes, though by the end of the Empire few nobles could actually trace such long lineages directly.

PLACE

Boundaries

The assumption of a castle or town name to identify a family linked its members with a specific location. However, people also identified with larger geographical areas. These were always human constructs, as there is nothing 'natural' about frontiers. The choice of markers like rivers or mountain ranges always involved the demarcation of power and the desire to control resources, as well as emotional attachment and feelings that can affect someone who has left a place or perhaps never even been there.[36] Place can assume significance beyond material considerations, notably through identification as a holy site. Size is not predetermined as it depends on how far the balance between population and space is socially and politically viable. Exactly how much space a community feels is justified depends on not only what they actually require, but how much they feel entitled to and can maintain without too much cost.

As Chapter 4 has indicated, the Empire's external and internal boundaries changed considerably across its history. The internal changes were probably more significant than the external expansion and contraction, since they reflected how power and identity became increasingly concentrated in more numerous hierarchically ordered and territorially bounded units. Whereas medieval travellers encountered the Empire as they moved between the fixed points of human settlement, those during the eighteenth century experienced it as they crossed clear internal boundaries marked by customs posts and sentry boxes.

To an extent this simply reflected broader European trends. Frontiers remained open transitional zones into the thirteenth century, which allowed inhabitants to identify with powers either side according to circumstances. Given the absence of mutually recognized sovereignty, central authorities viewed frontiers as one-sided limits where their own power finished without paying too much attention to arrangements beyond.[37]

Hierarchy mattered more politically than geographical boundaries. Authority was defined as chains of vassalage primarily linking people rather than places. This reflects the higher value placed on controlling people rather than land, which remained relatively plentiful into the eleventh century. Without machinery, command over people represented the only way to exploit land. Huge areas of forest, marsh and unfertile upland remained largely uninhabited into the eleventh century and often beyond.

Nonetheless, people were already associated with specific places by the ninth century. The Lombards believed their name derived from Wotan, but their control of the Po valley since the late sixth century gave that region its lasting designation as Lombardy. The Pomeranians were the 'People from the Sea' whose presence named the southern Baltic shore between the Elbe and Oder rivers. Likewise, all the major German regions derive their names from association with a tribal identity around 800: Bavaria, Franconia, Frisia, Swabia, Saxony, Swabia and Thuringia. Their inhabitants distinguished both ethnic and political (jurisdictional) boundaries by the tenth century, with the latter being more important in marking identity.[38]

Community

Identification with these larger units remained relatively weak into the late Middle Ages, at least outside the elites, whereas attachment to smaller communities was already strong much earlier. Pre-modern Europe contained many communities, both real and imagined, and varying in size from Christendom through kingdoms, towns, villages to monasteries, manors and castles.[39] Some communities were itinerant, but most were defined through the permanent concentration of people in a specific place.

Even isolated communities were connected somehow to others, so that all should be considered porous rather than fully closed. Nonetheless, common needs and activities focused collective identity. Many communities had an economic function, such as the manors of the early Middle Ages, or the towns of Italy and those founded in Germany from the eleventh century as market centres. Most forms of production required people to work together. Communal living brought numerous practical problems requiring people to collaborate; for example, fire safety or maintenance of drainage ditches. Christian worship was a communal activity. Already in the eighth century the church fostered the belief that individual sins endangered the wider community.[40] Other theological developments strengthened this, notably the concept of purgatory, which required the living to pray to speed the passage of souls to heaven. The development of more robust parish structures by the twelfth century provided a framework to engage the community in the maintenance of their church and participation in its activities. The pace accelerated considerably with the Reformation, which sharpened the distinctiveness of local religious practices, particularly in Germany, where different confessional groups often lived in relative proximity.

The form of rituals, use of prayer, internal decoration of churches and the timing and sound of their bells all became important markers of community.

Identity was expressed through symbols, flags, coats of arms and civic colours, adopted with increasing elaboration from the high Middle Ages. Early chronicles are largely by clerics recounting the deeds of kings with varying levels of approval. However, it was common by the eleventh century for monks to compile lists of abbots or bishops to demonstrate the continuity and purity of local religious practice. They were joined by secular chroniclers during the later Middle Ages who traced the origins of their home town, often in considerable detail. Most were commoners, but they proclaimed the 'nobility' of their own town, boasting a lineage equal to that of any aristocrat. Other, more personal documents also testify to individuals' identification with specific places, such as nuns writing for the edification of their community, or Jewish memory books of local martyrs.[41]

The growing size and density of settlements also helped sharpen their identities, as did the way they became embedded in wider political jurisdictions. Most of the Empire's settlements had acquired some form of self-government by the high Middle Ages. Pressure on resources contributed to sharper internal and external demarcation. Fences and walls served practical defensive purposes, but also marked each community's outer extent and the internal subdivision of its assets. These changes were accompanied by new conceptions of property, distinguishing that owned collectively from that belonging to individuals.[42]

Individuals' identity followed the generally hierarchical structure of all social, political and religious organization in the Empire. Each person had multiple identities. Exactly what these meant cannot be determined except in the rare cases where we have personal testimony, but their general shape can be discerned. There were the familial and social identities already discussed. Larger towns had craft guilds, lay spiritual fraternities and neighbourhoods all providing more local foci for identity within the wider sense of community. Horizontal solidarity was more prominent in some circumstances, such as within guilds engaged in friendly competition in civic sports, or during periods of political or economic tension. However, many communal activities were also designed to stress internal hierarchies, such as the social distinctions displayed in seating arrangements in churches, or through the processional order employed during religious festivals. Community might be celebrated as a special homely place (*Heimat*) offering warmth, security, familiarity and rootedness, but it was not open to everyone on equal terms. Merely being born in a specific place did not automatically guarantee full membership, since this often rested on the kind of privileges associated with the social Estates. Possession of such privileges was no guarantee of their continued enjoyment, since membership of a community also depended on observing its rules.[43]

Multilayered Identities

Higher authorities viewed communal identity with ambivalence. Internal solidarity could prompt a community to combine against its lord, such as the German episcopal towns of Bremen and Cologne, which threw off their bishops' jurisdiction during the twelfth and thirteenth centuries. However, it also enhanced cohesion and enabled communities to discharge their obligations, such as providing taxes or soldiers. Communal identity coalesced during the twelfth century as other spatial distinctions sharpened in the Empire through the gradual territorialization of lordly jurisdictions.

This process will be explored at greater length later (pp. 365–77), but for now it is important to note that only one side of it usually receives attention in histories of the Empire. The demarcation of clearer territorial jurisdictions indeed fragmented power, yet this was never solely a centrifugal process inevitably replacing the Empire with smaller, sovereign principalities after 1806. Rather, the demarcation of clearer jurisdictions within the Empire was accompanied by their greater integration within a common legal and political framework.

The Empire's significance is demonstrated by how its internal political hierarchy enabled people to relate themselves and their community to their wider environment. Writing in the early eleventh century, Hermann the Lame used the first-person plural 'our' for his own abbey in relation to others in the region, for his fellow Swabians when dealing with the rest of the Empire, and for Germans in discussing interaction with outsiders.[44] The monks who compiled lists of local bishops and abbots often combined these with parallel sequences of emperors, increasingly using both to write histories of their diocese as part of the Empire (See Plate 16).[45] The growing clarity of secular jurisdictions and their increasing significance for daily life provided another focus that displaced attachment to the larger, less clear, old 'tribal' areas as a secondary, more distant regional identity.

Secular jurisdictions were increasingly territorialized in the sense that specific powers and prerogatives came to rest in hereditary rule over an area and its inhabitants. The Franks already had a sense of *patria* as their Christian kingdom providing a common homeland for distinct groups of inhabitants.[46] This persisted in a general sense throughout the Middle Ages, but assumed a new form during the sixteenth century as territorial identities sharpened rapidly. The growing use of *patria* for territory helped transform the idea of *terra* (territory) from a bundle of sometimes disparate possessions held by a common ruler into a distinct and geographically bounded entity. All levels of society engaged in this, because all used a similar language of the 'common good' to claim the moral high ground when expressing their objectives (see pp. 498–503). Confessionalization reinforced this by associating each German territory with a specific form of Christianity, considerably widening the earlier regnal identity built around saints patronized by the ruling family to include other specific religious practices. Humanist scholars recovered or invented tribal identities to buttress what were in fact often spatially much smaller territorial identities. For example, writers serving the Hohenzollerns tried to appropriate the Teutonic past as a way of fostering an anti-Polish Prussian identity.[47] Territorial coats of arms and army uniforms provided further markers during the eighteenth century.

The rapid development of cartography from the fifteenth century made a profound impact by providing a ready image of territorially defined political power. Maps now showed political boundaries as well as natural features and towns. The members of the House of Savoy celebrated its elevation to ducal rank in 1416 with a huge cake in the shape of their territory.[48] Maps became increasingly detailed as cartographers struggled to meet their governments' desire to survey and quantify. From 1763 to 1787 the Austrian army prepared a 5,400-sheet map of all Habsburg territory. Although this was never published, the government issued a single-sheet map to all primary schools in 1781.[49]

Such maps greatly influenced how the Empire appeared in later historical atlases. Nothing underscores the nineteenth-century interpretation

more clearly: the Empire is a multicoloured patchwork of dynastic territories compared to the solid blocks of colour used for other, supposedly
more centralized states. Yet most maps produced prior to 1806 showed
the Empire with clear outer boundaries divided into the Kreise, its official regional subdivisions. Territories were often named and sometimes
also marked, but did not dominate. Written descriptions followed these
conventions.[50] The Empire remained a common fatherland composed of
numerous, lesser homelands.

6

Nation

OF THE GERMAN NATION

Political Influences

Italians and Burgundians identified with the Empire to varying degrees, but only the Germans associated it with their nation. Much has been made of the addition of the words 'of the German Nation' to the title 'Holy Roman Empire'.[1] Appearing in 1474, this combination was used more frequently after 1512 without becoming the Empire's official title – despite numerous later claims to the contrary. Protestants were far more likely than Catholics to add 'of the German Nation' when discussing the Empire, but even their use was inconsistent. Only one in nine official documents issued after 1560 included any reference to Germany, usually referring simply to 'the Empire'.

This chapter argues that the absence of a single political centre in the Empire complicated the definition of German national identity, encouraging several, often antagonistic versions of Germanness by the eighteenth century. This contributed to the richness of German identity, which was not restricted by linguistic or artistic criteria but instead was defined primarily politically. Later sections explore how the Empire was represented symbolically and how far its other, non-German-speaking inhabitants identified with it, as well as demonstrating the continued strength of older, broader political identities relative to narrower, more essentialist concepts of nationalism emerging around 1800.

The subsequent description of the Empire as simply 'Germany' stems from attempts to trace German history in national terms. Various national birthdays have been suggested, with the events surrounding the first partition of the Carolingian realm being the favourite. The chronicler Nithard recorded the Strasbourg oath sworn by Carolingian nobles in 842 in both Old High German and Old French versions. The tripartite division (East Francia, West Francia, Lotharingia) enacted the following year through the Treaty of Verdun appears to confirm the end of Charlemagne's Empire and its replacement by French and German kingdoms (Map 2). Other historians favour the Treaty of Mersen from 870 since this redrew the map in a more modern form by dividing most of Lotharingia between the East and West Frankish kingdoms. The extinction of the eastern Carolingians and their replacement in 919 by the Ottonians was also interpreted later as the true birth of the German monarchy. In this narrative, Otto I's coronation in 962 becomes the start of an entirely new, greater German empire.[2]

All these claims work by projecting later developments deep into the past. For example, Louis the Pious's son Louis II, who ruled East Francia after 843, only received the sobriquet 'the German' in Heinrich von Bünau's history of the Empire published in 1739.[3] Louis II was certainly known to contemporaries as *rex Germaniae* (king of Germany) while his brother Charles 'the Bald' was *rex Galliae* (king of Gaul), but it is unclear what these meant beyond distinguishing different parts of what many believed was still a common Frankish realm. The West Frankish king Lothar, the penultimate western Carolingian, attacked Aachen in the summer of 978. Otto II and his wife only just managed to escape. Lothar celebrated his coup by having the imperial eagle on the palace roof turned to face east instead of west. Writers either side of the Rhine interpreted this in partisan terms, displaying a sense of cultural differences, but nonetheless still focusing these on 'their' king in the form of the regnal identities discussed in the previous chapter.[4] The sense of difference did not end references to a broader Frankish heritage, which was invoked by emperors into the twelfth century and remained part of most discussions of the Empire's identity long after that.

The terms *Germani* (Germans) and *Teutonici* (Teutons) were not original self-designations, but labels applied by outsiders to the inhabitants of what later became known as Germany. The Romans used *Germani* to refer to all those northern peoples they did not want to conquer. The term gained renewed currency through its employment by (Latin-trained) missionaries entering this area from the seventh century. Missionaries also spread the use of the term *Teutonici*, derived from *lingua Theodisca*, which in turn stemmed from the Old German *thiot*, meaning 'people'; hence those who spoke a local vernacular rather than Latin. In reality, the inhabitants spoke a variety of Indo-European languages, while they saw themselves as distinct tribes or peoples.[5] By then, western writers were also employing the term *Alemanni* from the name of the tribe closest to them. In time, this evolved into the French and Spanish words for Germany (*Allemagne, Alemania*), while the Alemanni themselves became 'Swabians'.

The renewed engagement of northerners in Italian affairs from the mid-tenth century, after around 60 years' relative absence, embedded these designations. By 1000, Italians were likely to generalize all north-erners as *Teutonici*. The Ottonians appear to have embraced the label and carried it back over the Alps where it contributed to the gradual use of the term *regnum teutonicorum*.[6] The concept was politically expedient, enabling both the Ottonians and their Salian successors to disarm potential criticism that they were not really Carolingian Franks by presenting themselves as rulers of all peoples inhabiting the realm north of the Alps and east of the Rhine. To them, the 'German king-dom' was not synonymous with the Empire, which remained greater and included other kingdoms in Italy, Burgundy and Bohemia. The reduction of the Empire to Germany came from the Salians' papal opponents, as Gregory VII sought to belittle Henry IV by reducing him to merely a German king. Without abandoning claims to be emper-ors of a far greater realm, both the later Salians and the Staufers found identification with Germany also useful in countering papal actions. The 'German' king and his subjects were equal sufferers at the hands of a perfidious pope whose excommunication and interdict affected them all. This helps explain why John XXII went a step further in his attempts to belittle Louis IV by calling him 'the Bavarian'.

The multicentred character of imperial governance inhibited the kind of focused regnal identities forming around English, French, Pol-ish or Hungarian monarchs. Henry II and Charlemagne were canonized in 1146 and 1165 respectively without either of them gaining universal recognition as German or imperial patron saints. Writers in the Empire favoured strength in numbers, with the Empire's numerous saints and political centres as its distinguishing characteristic. Nonetheless, the wider sense of the Empire continued to become more closely associated with German identity after 1250. This requires qualification before proceeding, since it should not be misconstrued as arguing there was a single, wider 'Germanic' civilization based either politically on the Empire or on alleged commonalities of language, law or economic forms.[7]

It is also a paradox that the decades between 1251 and 1311, when German kings were not crowned emperors, were those of the growing association between the Empire and German identity. The Staufers' demise stimulated discussions of German identity at a time when it was also becoming clearer that Europe was subdividing into kingdoms each associated with a distinct people.[8] Writers were concerned that Germans should not lose imperial prestige while their kings were unwilling or unable to be crowned emperor. What later generations interpreted as weakness actually strengthened the ideological associations between German identity and the Empire. A relatively distant king-emperor could be attractive as a monarch who did not impose heavy burdens on his subjects. The absence of a single, stable political core freed the monarchy from being tied to any one part of Germany, enabling all regions to identify with it. This explains the growing interest in ideas of imperial translation of the Empire as inheritor of ancient Rome, ideas that were disentangled from papal critique and employed to assert that Germans were distinct from Europeans through their association with the imperial title and its pan-Christian mission. These discussions already elaborated all the tropes that found full expression two centuries later in Humanist writings: Germans demonstrated their virtues through their martial prowess, amply justifying their claim to be Christendom's defenders. In this way, the concept of imperial translation became the Empire's myth of origins, substituting for the more focused stories elsewhere, like the myths around the Goths in Sweden or the Sarmatians in Poland.

Language

Association with the Empire defined 'Germany' and 'German identity' politically, enabling both to continue including peoples of other languages and cultures. Likewise, electoral status made the archbishops of Mainz, Cologne and Trier all Germans despite their possessions being located in what was, historically, ancient Gaul. The Humanist Sebastian Münster's *Cosmographia*, published in Basel in 1544, presented a historical-geographical description of Germany in which the word *Teütschland* was synonymous throughout with the Empire regardless of the language on the ground. Johann Jacob Moser argued that French- and Italian-speaking Savoy 'belongs to Germany' through its incorporation within the German kingdom dating back to 1361, and he also used 'German' as shorthand for imperial.[9]

Germany remained a land of many languages, while political and linguistic boundaries never aligned. Some ninth-century texts were written in Frankish, like the Fulda translation of the Gospel that became the basis of the 6,000-line *Heiland* poem recounting Jesus's life in Old Saxon. Nonetheless, Latin remained the dominant written language until the emergence of Middle High German in the twelfth century. Eastward migration and conquest greatly complicated matters, with the number of dialects identified subsequently rising from 12 between 1150 and 1250 to 18 across the following 250 years. Notably, the spread of New High German northwards from southern Germany after 1350 displaced northern Low German, which developed subsequently in the north-west as Dutch, a word itself of course deriving from *Deutsch*.[10]

The linkage between Germany and the Empire was reinforced by the gradual displacement of Latin by German as an administrative language from the thirteenth century, about two centuries before English replaced either Latin or French for political and administrative communication in England.[11] The public peace proclaimed at Mainz in 1235 was the first significant constitutional document issued for the entire Empire in German. By 1300 German was increasingly used for charters, reflecting the larger number of laity holding office rather than clergy proficient in Latin. German accounted for half the documents produced by the Upper Bavarian chancellery across the first 25 years after its adoption in 1290. The use of Latin was reduced to technical and legal terms, except in Habsburg administration, where it continued to be used to communicate with Hungarians for the next four centuries. The administrative use of German helped to standardize it well ahead of the language reforms promoted by eighteenth-century intellectuals. The numerous lordly and civic authorities between Nuremberg, Eger, Würzburg and Regensburg began corresponding in a common, south German form after the mid-fourteenth century. This was adopted by the imperial chancellery in 1464 and thereafter by territorial governments like that of electoral Saxony. The advent of printing around 1450 accelerated this, because imperial institutions rapidly exploited the new media to distribute laws, decisions and information across the Empire. Luther's famous German Bible had to be retranslated into Low German to reach Baltic coast readers, but the imperial chancellery style was already adopted by north German territorial administrations around 1500 thanks to their communication with the Reichstag and other institutions. This contrasts with the problems of standardizing Italian. Despite the identification of the Tuscan dialect with Italian high culture since the Renaissance and its subsequent dissemination through printed literature, it failed to establish itself as the predominant form until official measures imposed after Italian unification in 1861.

Other languages in the Empire withered through failing to establish a written form. Prussian, Kashubian and Polabian all died out by 1700, though Sorbian continues to the present day thanks to its use by the Lusatian Estates, which adopted it as the official language of Protestant education in their territory. Romansh disappeared in the Vorarlberg, but survived in neighbouring Rhetia. Likewise, Slovene died out in Styria, but developed a written form in parts of Hungary, as had Yiddish already much earlier. Czech was written from the thirteenth century and thrived from the 1390s thanks to its use in imperial administration under the Luxembourgs and subsequent place within Hussitism. Thus, while German was linked to the Empire, the Empire itself was multilingual. The Golden Bull of 1356 specified German, Latin, Upper Italian and Czech as imperial administrative languages. The imperial chancellery used the language of the intended recipients from about 1370. Although German became the primary language after 1620, the Reichshofrat continued using Italian in its dealings with imperial Italy.[12]

Language was already politically sensitive before the Empire standardized official communication. Migration since the twelfth century sharpened language and ethnicity as factors shaping identity and demarcating access to resources in the areas of recent western settlement beyond the Elbe. Subsequent population growth added pressure by the 1320s when north German towns like Brunswick revised their guild regulations to exclude Wends and other non-German speakers.[13] These distinctions continued to matter in daily life in these regions, but dissipated as use of the Slavic languages decreased.

Culture

It was not until the 'culture wars' of the high Renaissance that language moved closer to its modern role as a key determinant of national identity. Renewed tensions with the papacy around 1400 contributed to this, as did the renegotiation of imperial-papal relations through the concordats of the later fifteenth century (see pp. 72–3). Critiques of papal corruption blended with the interests of Humanists in articulating national origins and identity, because words and other outward manifestations like clothing were regarded as indicative of inner morality and character. Tropes that had already appeared in the thirteenth century emerged now in more virulent form. German was supposedly the most ancient and purest language and a general marker of cultural superiority over the *Welsch*; this was a blanket pejorative term for all 'Latin' foreigners, chiefly French and Italians, but also including on occasion Poles, Hungarians and others.

Criticism of cultural and sartorial values was an expression of deeper anxieties stirred by greater social mobility and the perceived erosion of the status distinctions delineating corporate groups. These pressures were most acute in towns. One manifestation was the series of sumptuary laws regulating clothing, such as that issued in Leipzig in 1452 which restricted the use of styles and fabrics in an attempt to stop servants being mistaken for masters. Another ordinance, from 1431, targeted an unauthorized group counterculture by forbidding journeymen to wear shoes of a common distinctive colour.[14] Efforts to regulate appearance stimulated the discussion of whether there was – or should be – a distinctive national dress. Conrad Celtis called for imperial legislation to encourage a more 'German' appearance. Germans allegedly wore smart, restrained and simple clothes reflecting their honesty and integrity. By contrast, the *Welsch* were slovenly and promiscuous, especially – of course – their women, who sported low-cut, garish dresses, jewellery and ridiculous hairstyles. Hans Weigel's illustrated *Costume Book* published in 1577 depicted a soberly dressed woman from Metz in contrast to a brightly attired French woman in a deliberate attempt to demonstrate that Metz was still 'German' despite having been captured by France in 1552 (see Plate 18).

The discussion of national costume reveals the difficulties that Germans encountered in trying to define their identity through culture and ethnicity. Intellectuals could not agree whether they should don allegedly authentic Germanic garb or current fashions more in line with their present needs. In short, there was no actual national dress. As the Leipzig city council remarked in 1595, 'the clothes the people of the German nation wear almost always change from one year to the next'.[15] The same was true for other aspects of culture like painting, music, literature and architecture, all of which exhibited regional more than national characteristics. Beyond trumpeting the invention of printing as the Germans' gift to humanity, there was little else intellectuals agreed on as distinctly national about German culture.[16] All these efforts missed the point. It was the Empire's inclusive diversity that made it distinctive and enabled its numerous inhabitants to identify with it.

Nowhere is this clearer than in attitudes to German-speakers beyond the Empire. In early modernity there was a wider German-speaking cultural community, which extended along the Baltic shore through Polish Prussia and Courland into Estonia and beyond. However, none of these peoples were considered politically German, despite some of them living in places once associated with the Empire that in no way was considered a 'Greater Germany'. The Baltic Germans likewise found it easier and more expedient to identify with their home province, while those in Poland regarded the Polish-Lithuanian Commonwealth as guarantor of their own identity and rights.[17]

Humanism

The Humanist discussion of national identity raised consciousness of the distinction between the Empire's traditional transnational character and its more specific association with Germany. Central to this debate was the rediscovery of Tacitus's *Germania*, written in AD 98. Few in the Empire had read it before a manuscript copy was taken to Rome in 1451 and then rapidly disseminated through Humanist intellectual exchange. A Latin printed edition appeared in 1470, followed by a German translation in 1526. The book's impact was magnified by the dearth of information on the early Germans. Tacitus in fact never visited Germania, but wrote an informed, fairly even-handed description of the German tribes, including the sensational story of Arminius (Hermann), who defeated Quinctilius Varus's Roman legions in the Teutoburg Forest in AD 9.[18]

Like all sophisticated texts, *Germania* could be read in multiple ways. Italian Humanists seized on Tacitus's description of German vices of excessive eating and drinking as corroborating existing stereotypes. The German response was mixed. One strand took an anti-Roman course, exemplified by Ulrich von Hutten, who played on Tacitus' depiction of Germans as noble savages defeating decadent Romans in his own anti-papal polemics of the early sixteenth century. Combined with those advocating linguistic and cultural purity, this line of argument rapidly developed the trend to articulate a distinct German national identity in opposition to similar identities voiced elsewhere in Europe. The experience of the church council at Constance (1414–18) already fostered a sense of a *Germania nacio*, which grew as a rallying cry against both papal tax demands and the Ottoman threat. The Reformation added impetus, but Hutten's critique was much broader than Luther's better-known *Appeal to the Christian Nobility of the German Nation* (1520), which was limited to church reform.[19]

These discussions made a lasting impact through providing concepts and images to express the new national idea. The female figure of Germania had appeared as a captive Amazon on Roman coins, but was reinvented by Maximilian I 'as mother of the Holy Roman Empire of the German Nation' in the early sixteenth century. She remained the embodiment of the Empire as virtuous and pacific, reappearing as a symbol of Liberty during the 1848 Revolution before becoming militarized as a bloodthirsty Fury in the late nineteenth century.[20]

Meanwhile, thanks to Tacitus, German Humanists were able to remind their Italian counterparts that the Romans had never conquered Germany, whereas the Germans had plundered Rome. The coincidence of this discussion with the renewed sack of that city by Charles V's army in 1527 seemed to underscore their point, but it was not until 1643 that Hermann Conring drew the full, logical conclusions and rejected any connection between Rome and the Empire, arguing that the ancient Roman empire had collapsed long before Charlemagne was crowned emperor. However, for most people Tacitus simply proved the long-standing argument of imperial translation that the Germans, as conquerors of Rome, were its worthy imperial successors.

These arguments caused considerable problems for Protestants, who realized that the logic of anti-Romanism opened them to charges of being unpatriotic. The Roman Catholic Humanist Johannes Cochlaeus directly accused Luther of this, because his depiction of the pope as Anti-Christ challenged the legitimacy of imperial rule and its glorious tradition of defending the church. The Protestant theologian Philipp Melanchthon and the historian Johannes Schleiden responded by explicitly embracing imperial translation to support their calls for the emperor to renew the church by embracing the Reformation. The ideal-ization of medieval emperors continued to serve Protestant agendas into the mid-seventeenth century by implying criticism of the current Habsburg emperors as beholden to the pope. In short, the Empire was too much part of Protestant Germans' identity to be jettisoned in their break with Rome. Instead, Protestant intellectuals and princes tried to appropriate 'German' language and culture as their own and to present Catholics as unpatriotic. In practice, their efforts fell far short of what later generations expected of true Germans. The Fruitful Society (*Fruchtbringende Gesellschaft*), established in 1617, was the most fam-ous of these national cultural endeavours. Although dedicated to the purity of the German language, it accepted Scots, Swedes, Italians and others as members and published most of its works in Latin.[21]

German Freedom

Mutual accusations of lack of patriotism peaked during the Thirty Years War, with Protestants accusing Catholics of selling the Empire to Spanish Jesuits and the pope, while Catholics blamed Protestants for inviting in Danish, Swedish and French invaders. The fact that both sides claimed to be upholding the imperial constitution drew attention to this as a possible bridge between them. The funeral sermon for Archbishop-Elector Anselm Casimir of Mainz in 1647 noted that it would have been politically advantageous for him to have accepted an alliance offer from France, yet he had remained steadfastly loyal to the emperor and Empire. The elector's Lutheran neighbour, the landgrave of Hessen-Darmstadt, praised him as a 'true patriot' for his efforts at the Westphalian peace congress to persuade Catholic hardliners to offer Protestants more acceptable terms to end the war.[22]

While it might require modification, all believed the constitution offered the best protection for their 'German freedom'. This was broadly similar to other aristocratic expressions of freedom such as Polish and Hungarian 'liberty', 'free-born Englishmen' and *la liberté de*

la France. All combined demands for autonomy with claims to participate in politics. Those constituting the political 'nation' should be free
to pursue their lives without undue royal interference, yet were entitled
to share government with the king. There were other concepts of freedom, but it would be wrong to divide these into rival 'elite' and 'popular'
forms.[23] Neither was inherently more progressive or democratic. Civic
freedom often led to oligarchy, while supposedly 'aristocratic' arguments
could promote republican government (see pp. 519–22, 533–62 and
594–602). Symbols and arguments remained open to a variety of uses
prior to the emergence of a more rigid left–right ideological spectrum
after the French Revolution of 1789.

The Humanist articulation of German identity extrapolated 'liberties' from Tacitus's account of the Germans as an unconquered, free
people. The parallel process of imperial reform provided a new institutional framework to embed these into the imperial constitution.
Crucially, this entailed that German freedom depended on belonging
to the Empire rather than emancipation from it. This was a major factor blunting any potential for Protestantism to become a separatist
political movement. Furthermore, it ensured that freedom was
expressed as specific *liberties*, not uniform, equal and universal *Liberty*. Finally, it bound together the imperial Estates and the corporate
social groups, since all were mutually dependent in maintaining the
Empire as the collective guarantor of their own special status.

It was this combination that made German freedom distinct from its
equivalents in other countries, where writers claimed or invented broader
underlying 'common' liberties, such as 'national law' (*ius patrium*) in
France or 'the common custom of the realm' emerging in early
seventeenth-century England. Some German writers embraced elements
of this, like Conring in the early seventeenth century, or the historian
Jacob Paul von Gundling around one hundred years later. However,
they still inverted the standard pattern: rather than championing an
underlying set of universal freedoms, they celebrated the Empire as an
overarching system protecting numerous local and specific liberties. To
most Germans, a universal system of freedoms was equated with
tyranny since it threatened their cherished distinctiveness.[24]

THE EMPIRE SPEAKS

Multiple Voices

The Empire's polycentric structure necessitated different ways of communicating identity to those in more centralized states. Without a single capital, the Empire always lacked the cultural synergies produced by the concentration of creative, political and financial resources in a single, dominant city like Paris or London. This, however, also brought with it unique strengths. The Empire avoided the cultural tensions between capital and province, court and country, found in other monarchies. Instead, cultural production and the expression of attachment diffused more evenly throughout the Empire, extending a sense of 'ownership' more broadly both geographically and socially.

It is perhaps doubtful that these conditions encouraged greater artistic creativity, as has been claimed.[25] Nonetheless, the Empire produced the two innovations of the early modern 'communications revolution': printing and a regular postal network. Political decentralization frustrated censorship and control, while the absence of a single capital distributed cultural activity, patronage and educational opportunities more evenly.[26] Modern Germany still benefits from having more theatres and opera houses than any other European country, while cultural life is also still fairly evenly spread in Austria and Italy. However, we should not exaggerate the level of activity nor its impact on the broader population. It is always easier to analyse images and symbols than to understand how they were received by their audiences.

Both Carolingian and Ottonian rule are associated with a Renaissance, or revival and reinterpretation of classical antiquity, while similar, less extensive developments have been identified during the Staufer era. The Carolingian Renaissance was particularly important as the primary transmitter of ancient Roman imperial models and for the articulation of a Christian moralized politics. This gave Charlemagne and his successors an idea of what an imperial court should look like, but theirs was never a carbon copy of ancient Rome. Moreover, the Carolingian Renaissance did not penetrate far beyond the clergy; indeed, many of the clergy implicitly criticized the emperor for failing to match their ideal of a Christian Roman monarch.[27]

The Carolingians made a lasting adaptation of imperial Rome to Frankish sensibilities in that their political-cultural practice was about *presentation*, not *representation*. The emperor needed to be present among a select, immediate audience of great lords, rather than be represented through a coherent strategy of images and propaganda intended for a wider but physically distant audience. Much of medieval imperial politics was about creating and managing opportunities for the emperor to engage personally with the political elite. This was a permanent structural characteristic, because the Empire's monarchs remained itinerant into early modernity. Consequently, the earliest imperial symbols needed to be portable, and it was only under much-changed circumstances that the Luxembourgs and especially the Habsburgs developed a representational court culture closer in essential form to both ancient Rome and their European monarchical contemporaries.

Signs

The imperial crown was the Empire's most obvious and enduring symbol. As in so many ways, Charlemagne set an important precedent in using a crown denoting divine reward for true faith, rather than the ancient Roman practice of a laurel wreath symbolizing military victory. Custom maintained that the 'Charles Crown' (*Karlskrone*) was always used after 800. The surviving imperial crown is certainly very old, but even by the fifteenth century some doubted it was actually Charlemagne's. Multiple detailed studies by art historians have failed to establish exactly when it was made, as it was clearly modified several times. The general consensus remains that it was produced for either Otto I's coronation in 962 or that of his son (Otto II) as co-emperor in 967.[28] The octagonal design is said to represent Jerusalem, while each plate is richly decorated with images of Christ and Old Testament kings. The crown is 'closed' by an arch from front to back denoting its imperial status, in contrast to 'open' diadems of mere kings. It was reserved for imperial coronations by the twelfth century, with separate royal crowns used in German, Italian and Burgundian coronations. These secondary crowns never attained the same semi-sacral quality and were often melted down or pawned. There were additional 'private' crowns symbolizing purely secular authority. These were scarcely royal day wear – Rudolf II's gold crown from 1602 weighs 3.9 kilo-grams. Although not the last to be made, Rudolf's crown survived to become the Habsburgs' dynastic symbol and was used on a revised coat of arms to denote their new Austrian imperial status in 1804 (see Plate 14).[29]

Many other treasures accumulated by the thirteenth century. Like the crown, several existed in multiple copies, or were replaced or altered. Byzantine influence was strong, thanks to Constantinople's association with ancient Rome and its significance as a source of holy relics. However, the Empire's rulers and craftsmen displayed innovation of their own. The Ottonians invented the crowned cross combining secular and spiritual images to underscore their holy mission. Otto I added a cross to the imperial orb (*Reichsapfel*), which, by the eleventh century, had replaced the staff as the symbol of earthly rule.[30]

The Holy Lance (*Sacra Lancea*) contained the 'victory-bringing nail' said to have come from Christ's cross; it had been acquired around 925 by Henry I from Rudolf II of Burgundy. Its potency as a symbol of divinely ordained rule was heightened through association with the Ottonian victory over the Magyars at Lechfeld in 955 and over the Roman rebels in 1001. Around 1000, Otto III sent copies to Boleslav Chrobry and (possibly) Stephen of Hungary as part of his recognition of them as the Empire's junior partners.[31] Three swords became part of the imperial insignia, including the *Gladius Caroli Magni* that was said to be part of Charlemagne's booty taken from the Avars, having previously belonged to Attila the Hun, though it was most likely made a century later using an east European sabre. It was worn by emperors at their coronation.[32]

The Imperial Cross is a spectacular item allegedly containing a piece of Christ's cross once belonging to Charlemagne. Again, its provenance is controversial, but it certainly played an important part in religious processions by the eleventh century. Other important relics included an (alleged) thorn from Christ's crown, a tooth from John the Baptist, a chip from Christ's crib, a piece from his carpenter's apron, the table-cloth from the Last Supper and – for once genuine – Charlemagne's own Bible, as well as St Stephen's Purse, containing that saint's blood, which was placed on a table during royal coronations in Aachen. The sacral significance of these items emphasized the emperor's position as Christendom's pre-eminent ruler and his holy mission. However, some items from other cultures were incorporated, notably the spectacular coronation robes with their palm-tree and camel motifs made by Islamic craftsmen in Sicily, which were acquired by the Staufers, and the red Chinese silk Eagle Dalmatic embroidered with 68 eagle medallions, probably made for Louis IV. By that point, the imperial insignia formed a recognized collection recorded in inventories that did not question them as both authentic and timeless objects. Albrecht Dürer's painting of Charlemagne from 1510 shows the emperor wearing the imperial crown, the Eagle Dalmatic and the Islamic robes (see Plate 2).

Seals were another potent symbol, used to authenticate charters and other documents issued by the imperial chancellery. Carolingian seals and coins followed ancient Roman practice in showing the ruler's head in profile. This practice continued in West Francia until the end of the Carolingian era, but had already shifted in the east by 899 to show the monarch's whole body posed in profile as a triumphant warrior. The Ottonians invented a new form in 962 showing the emperor frontally, enthroned, crowned and holding a sceptre and orb as symbols of majesty. Later Ottonian seals got bigger, thicker and more imposing, while after 998 the Ottonian emperors began issuing metallic seals like popes, thereby elevating important charters to 'Golden Bulls'. The Ottonian style became the model for royal seals across Europe.[33]

Ottonian seals and court liturgy reflected the changed, more elevated and sacral monarchical ideal, adding images emphasizing the ruler's proximity to God alongside the more traditional prayers for divine protection. Whereas Carolingian images often showed the emperor surrounded by nobles or intellectuals, those of the Salian era reflected the more command-style monarchy by placing the emperor apart, often as a significantly larger figure than his retinue. The sacral element waned after the 1070s and monarchs appeared more obviously as mortals, especially in regnal and dynastic sequences of miniature portraits. Images became increasingly lifelike after 1300, perhaps in reaction to the imposters claiming to be the long-dead Frederick II, as well as reflecting new ideas of the self. Charles IV had over seventy portraits of himself distributed systematically across the Empire. Again, this reflected a fundamental political shift. As imperial rule came to rest in hereditary territorial possessions under the Luxembourgs, emperors no longer showed themselves so often directly to their important subjects through the traditional royal progress.

Portraits offered an easily portable substitute. Charles is presented rec-
ognizably with large eyes, a high forehead and high cheekbones. His
son Sigismund was also shown distinctively in portraiture with a mass
of blond hair and a forked beard. Presentation as individuals heightened the significance of the 'authentic', unchanging insignia symbolizing
the Empire's enduring character: all the Luxembourg portraits, like
those by Dürer, show each emperor wearing the same imperial crown.[34]

While the crown and royal portraits identified the monarch, the
Empire increasingly became associated with the image of an eagle.
Eagles already symbolized empires and armies in the ancient world and
formed part of Byzantine iconography. An imperial eagle adorned the
palace in Aachen at least by the time of the humiliating raid by the
West Frankish king Lothar in 978, and also appeared atop Otto III's
orb. It is clearly associated with the emperor from Frederick I 'Barbarossa'
onwards, appearing on all important items associated with the emperor
like his coat of arms, insignia, coins, tents and battle flag. The eagle
remained single-headed until the later twelfth century, when double-
headed versions appeared on civic coats of arms and devices associated
with the emperor. By the mid-fourteenth century, the double eagle was
firmly fixed as an imperial bird distinguishing it from single-headed
royal or princely eagles. Sigismund used a single-headed eagle as king
before adopting a double-headed one at his imperial coronation in
1433, but this practice ceased with Maximilian I's adoption of the
elected imperial title in 1508. Maximilian fixed the double eagle to the
Habsburg coat of arms, making it a dynastic symbol as well – this was
briefly contested in the 1740s by Charles VII, the one non-Habsburg
emperor of early modernity, who had the double eagle painted onto
Bavarian army flags. Sigismund added halos for the eagle's heads in
1433 to symbolize the Empire's holy character, as well as a crown.
After 1612, the imperial vicars used an uncrowned double eagle in their
periods of office during imperial interregna.[35]

The double-eagle image spread rapidly throughout the fifteenth
century, being embraced by groups as diverse as German students at
Bologna University to members of the Hanseatic League, as well as
being disseminated in print as broadsheets or illustrations in books
about the Empire. The rise of the imperial princes proliferated other,
single-headed eagles. In most cases, the eagle changed from the original
imperial black to red (Brandenburg, Tirol), or red-and-white-striped

(Hessen, Thuringia). The Teutonic Order adopted a black eagle before this bird became the Empire's primary symbol, and the black eagle was carried over to Prussia once the Hohenzollerns were raised as kings in 1701. Savoy also retained a black eagle into the nineteenth century, while Tuscany adopted a black double eagle combined with the Tuscan arms during the era of Habsburg rule.[36]

The eagle had originally been golden until the late thirteenth century, when gold became the most common colour for any background field, for example on flags or coats of arms. The papacy adopted the purple of ancient Rome, but the Empire favoured gold, black, red and white, although in no firm combination. The Staufer imperial battle flag was red with a white cross, persisting today as the Swiss flag. The red-white combination was also adopted by numerous princely dynasties and imperial cities.

The century after 1450 saw rapid change in imperial imagery, reflecting both the transition to a more formalized mixed monarchy, the establishment of Habsburg imperial rule, and the invention of new media like printing. Older elements like the Christian hero persisted into Maximilian I's reign, but were joined by revived classical images, notably the emperor as Hercules or as Jupiter presiding over a new Olympus. Although pagan, such symbols acquired new value through Renaissance Humanism, which cemented their association with political virtues like justice, clemency and peace. These symbols were also attractive after the Reformation, which made some Christian imagery politically problematic in a state with two recognized faiths. The classical world also supplied numerous non-human motifs that could be employed to symbolize the Empire's more collective character extending beyond just its monarch. For example, the electors were already described in the Golden Bull of 1356 as the 'pillars of the Empire'. Pillars, obelisks and columns all symbolized solidity, peace and justice. Other images conveyed more partisan interpretations, reflecting the imperial constitution's contested character through the sixteenth and seventeenth centuries. For example, presenting the Empire as a ship suggested it required a strong emperor as helmsman.[37]

Images of the emperor diverged under the Habsburgs. Their status as dynasts ruling their own extensive hereditary possessions was represented in magnificent portraits showing them generally full length, but almost always alone, except for collective family portraits. When shown in their imperial role they were surrounded by the electors or representatives of all the imperial Estates.[38] The political changes are further reflected in attempts to fix the increasingly complex status hierarchy in a new device known as the *Quaternionen*, showing the imperial Estates as figures or heraldic devices and first appearing in a fresco created in Frankfurt for Sigismund around 1414. Written descriptions soon spread, followed by printed engravings from the mid-fifteenth century that generally displayed the Estates against a background of a black double eagle. The electors were either omitted or shown as a rank of seven figures at the top. The other status groups followed in sequence below: dukes, margraves, landgraves, burgraves, counts, lords, knights, imperial cities, villages and peasants (see Plate 19). The *Quaternionen* were always schematic. There were invariably more in reality than the four members displayed for each group, while the locations presented as villages and peasants were often actually additional towns. Nonetheless, these images remained very popular until about 1600 when they were displaced by more accurate information on the actual composition of the imperial Estates, especially the printed lists of those summoned to the Reichstag, as well as by published maps and descriptions of the Empire.[39]

Symbolic innovation declined after the mid-sixteenth century, again reflecting the end of imperial reform and the broadly stable character of the Empire's constitution thereafter. The triumphal arches used by Maximilian II (1570) and Matthias (1612) for their entries into Nuremberg were virtually identical to that erected for Charles V in 1541.[40] The scale and scope of artistic patronage certainly broadened under Rudolf II, but much of it was too highbrow and esoteric to serve as effective propaganda. The most enduring creation was a heightened image of the emperor as victorious conqueror of the Turks and defender of the peace, an image that returned with the renewed wars against the Ottomans in the later seventeenth century.[41] Habsburg imperial imagery became more overtly Catholic around 1600, leaving no doubt of the emperor's own faith. However, Ferdinand III already sought to recover the more neutral, cross-confessional position that had been occupied by his predecessors in the mid to late sixteenth century, presenting himself as Solomon symbolizing wisdom and virtue rather than zealotry. Piety was increasingly turned outwards against external enemies, notably Louis XIV, who was criticized as disturbing Christendom's peace in contrast to the emperor as guarantor of order. Ferdinand also embraced the new artistic forms associated with the baroque, notably opera, and displayed some talent as a musician and composer himself. However, these innovations increasingly reflected changing taste and Habsburg dynastic objectives but produced no new representations of the Empire.

Locations

Places also acquired symbolic importance through events like royal elections, coronations and assemblies, as well as more permanently as palaces or tombs. It was characteristic of the Empire's political order that it used multiple locations rather than a single capital. The number of places with imperial associations grew over time, especially with the changes of ruling dynasty into early modernity since each royal family had a different geographical power base. Although some locations fell out of use, many never lost their significance entirely, while others like monasteries or towns unilaterally expressed their attachment to the Empire through furnishing 'emperor's halls' (*Kaisersäle*) and imperial portrait galleries.

Locations of symbolic importance were used throughout the Empire, but the preference for Germany was already obvious under the Carolingians. Aachen in the extreme west of Germany was the favoured royal palace and place of royal coronations for most of the Middle Ages. Charlemagne's stone throne, as well as the rather more portable Imperial Bible and St Stephen's Purse, were stored here, while the rest of the insignia travelled with the emperor. After the renewed civil wars around 1100, Henry V stored the insignia in his strong castle of Trifels in the Palatinate. They resumed their travels under the Staufers, before being entrusted to the Cistercian monks at Eussertal monastery until 1273 when they were scattered to various castles except for coronations. The move to more territorially based imperial rule under Charles IV was reflected in the concentration of the insignia, first in St Vitus Cathedral in Prague and then in the Karlstein castle between 1356 and 1421. The Hussite insurrection prompted their removal to Nuremberg, which remained the official repository until the French Revolutionary Wars.

The absence of a permanent capital discouraged the construction of the kind of representational buildings found in other European monarchies.[42] An itinerant emperor needed lots of palaces and could not invest heavily in a single site. Some medieval construction was nevertheless very impressive. Charlemagne and Otto III commissioned deliberately imposing buildings at Aachen, while the Ottonians developed Goslar and the Salians constructed Speyer's huge cathedral as their royal tomb. The difference only really became noticeable in early modernity when other monarchies built lavish palaces like the Escorial in Spain and Versailles in France or, in Russia's case, an entirely new capital at St Petersburg. The contrast grew more obvious with the proliferation of fashionable new princely residences at Ludwigsburg, Herrenhausen, Nymphenburg, and elsewhere across Germany. From 1663 the permanent Reichstag continued to meet in Regensburg's old Gothic town hall, suggesting to some visitors that the Empire was stuck in the distant past (see Plate 20). The city's construction of a new hall immediately next door at the beginning of the eighteenth century accentuated the distinction between old and new.

Print Culture

The early modern media revolution greatly extended the audience for imperial imagery, facilitating the shift from a culture of presentation to one of representation. Elements of presentation continued into the late eighteenth century, but performative acts like coronations and assemblies now reached far more people through their dissemination in the printed word and image. These developments coincided with the Empire's consolidation as a mixed monarchy, entrenching the decentralization of expressions of identity and inhibiting the emergence of a single, coherent representational culture.

Print culture spread rapidly. Within fifty years of its introduction around 1450 into western Europe by Johannes Gutenberg, 62 German cities operated about two hundred presses and within another 25 years over 11 million books and prints were in circulation. Contrary to received views of Germany as a land of poets and thinkers before the nineteenth century, print played a central role in politics from the outset. Frederick III immediately appreciated the new media's potential, commissioning 37 works before his death in 1493. His son Maximilian I was a master of spin, publishing a further 129 works within the first seven years of his accession alone.[43] A talented writer himself,

Maximilian revived the practice of crowning imperial poets laureate that had previously featured only fitfully in Italy, thereby expanding patronage of Humanist intellectuals and associating imperial power with fashionable art forms. The new imperial institutions matched the emperor's rush to print. The first printed report from a Reichstag appeared after the 1486 meeting, giving précis of the speeches. A semi-official record of all decisions appeared as the *Corpus Recessum Imperii* after 1501, well ahead of Hansard, which only began recording British parliamentary proceedings in 1774. Well before then, the Reichstag had emerged as a key political information hub, publishing far more information about its deliberations than any other European representative institution.[44] These developments demonstrated the Empire's shift from a presentational culture based on the personal presence of the emperor to one of representation mediated through print and images. To late eighteenth-century observers this appeared to render the Empire lifeless as its envoys at the Reichstag communicated through letters and memoranda, rarely gathering in the hall for speeches. From a twenty-first-century perspective this virtual political reality appears almost post-modern.

However, it was already obvious that the authorities could not monopolize the new media. The papacy had already attempted censorship in 1487 by ordering all printed works to be submitted to the approval of the archbishops of Mainz, Cologne, Trier and Magdeburg prior to sale. Maximilian swiftly excluded papal influence by asserting that censorship was an imperial prerogative, which itself was a demonstration of the Empire's ability to respond to circumstances. Publishers initially cooperated because an imperial licence offered copyright protection, enabling them to prosecute pirate printers through the new imperial supreme court, or Reichskammergericht. Johannes Reuchlin's discussion of Judaism was the first book to be banned, in 1512, but censorship only really became an issue once Luther had been outlawed by the Edict of Worms in 1521. By then it was too late in his case, as 700,000 copies of his works were in circulation.

The Empire adapted, abandoning the unrealistic goal of total control in favour of measures intended to influence content. The Imperial Book Commission was established in Frankfurt in 1569, reflecting that city's status as the centre of Europe's book trade. Additional legislation was intended to curb scandal, libel and polemic rather than stifle debate. Like the other sixteenth-century institutional changes, these measures contributed to the Empire's complementary structure by providing a regulatory framework to be enforced by imperial Estates in their own territories.[45] Regional differences in practice reflected the decentralization. Prussia was perceived as the state most tolerant of religious works (something that was not entirely true), while Austria and Bavaria were regarded as reactionary. Saxony was the most liberal overall, because it wanted to promote Leipzig as a rival centre of the book trade. In practice, censorship was often haphazard and handled variously by courtiers, librarians and university rectors.[46] Goethe, Schiller, Herder, Lessing and other leading authors used pseudonyms to avoid unpleasant repercussions as territorial governments tried to extend control during the later eighteenth century. Meeting resistance from the increasingly politicized reading classes, many territories then relaxed or abandoned censorship around 1800. Throughout, the Empire's decentralized structure facilitated relatively free expression, in contrast to France, where 183 people were imprisoned in the Bastille between 1760 and 1789 for breaching censorship laws.[47] Censorship resumed after the dissolution of the Empire in 1806, because consolidation into fewer states made it easier to oversee, while the spectre of French revolutionary terror increased its acceptance amongst readers.

Decentralization contributed to an equally diverse educational landscape, as each principality and even large city wanted to have its own university. The Empire's first university was founded in Prague in 1348, relatively late compared to Bologna (1088) or Paris (1170). However, the Empire had 45 universities by 1800, compared to 22 in France and 2 in England. The absence of a national church was another stimulus, since each territory wanted the full range of educational opportunities aligned to its own faith. Provision in Protestant territories was generally better and included even girls' elementary education in some Calvinist territories by the late sixteenth century. Nonetheless, many Catholic villages also had basic schooling, with the proportion of them providing it in the duchy of Jülich rising from a quarter in the sixteenth century to 90 per cent in the eighteenth century. Attendance was already mandatory in many territories by 1700, with provision in smaller principalities often far ahead of larger ones like Austria and Prussia. By the late eighteenth century, the two German great powers controlled half of the Empire's territory, yet they had only 10 universities between them, compared to 35 across the other principalities and imperial cities. The Empire's demise saw 20 of these universities closed by 1826, including Rinteln and Herborn, largely through the process of territorial consolidation. By 1500, literacy already stood at 5 per cent, with a peak of 20 per cent in large cities, while the overall rate reached 25 per cent by 1806, better than in France but behind parts of Britain.[48]

Education and literacy were relatively evenly spread, with almost every town having its own lending library by the eighteenth century.[49] The educated public were served by the world's first postal network, deliberately promoted through the grant of imperial privileges in 1490, creating a communications system transcending both geography and political decentralization. Already open to private customers in 1516, the network of post horses and coach routes connected most of the Empire within a century, allowing Europe's first regular newspapers to develop through a commercially viable distribution network, 26 years ahead of France.[50] The Empire had its first daily paper from 1635, some 67 years ahead of England. The expansion of territorial governments created additional markets for specialist journals on agriculture, economics, health, finance and military affairs. There were over two hundred commercial publishers in the Empire by the 1770s, while the number of authors tripled across 1760–91 to reach 8,000, or twice as many as in France, which had roughly the same population. Although this period was celebrated as the great age of German literature, luminaries like Goethe and Schiller sold only 2,000–3,000 copies of each new book, whereas Zacharias Becker's *Advice Booklet for Peasants* sold over a million. This reflected the primarily practical orientation of public communication in the Empire as earlier religious and political controversies gave way to an interest in problem-solving.[51]

Constitutional Commentary

The advent of print both encouraged and facilitated public discussion of the Empire. Known as *Reichspublizistik*, this constitutional commentary reflected a central character of imperial politics by remaining an endless dialogue without a universally accepted conclusion. Not only was the constitution never codified, but the mountains of official documents and public commentary added to the difficulty of defining it by providing evidence for endless exceptions to supposed general rules. The indefatigable Johann Jakob Moser wrote around one hundred volumes only to conclude that 'Germany is governed the German way'.[52]

Careful examination of these publications reveals that, while attitudes changed towards the Empire across early modernity, mainstream opinion remained broadly favourable. Disagreements were fiercest between the 1570s and 1640s, while some aspects were increasingly criticized after 1750, but no major thinker advocated substantial change. Even during the most heated exchanges the situation was broadly similar to that in Britain after 1689, when Whigs and Tories worked within the same constitution whilst disagreeing over details. Both Germany and Britain contrasted with late eighteenth-century France, where many leading intellectuals concluded that the Bourbon monarchy was no longer fit for purpose.

The fundamental issues were already articulated in 1458 by Enea Silvio Piccolomini, future Pope Pius II, who posed a rhetorical address to the Empire's princes: 'Of course you recognize the emperor as your king and lord, but he clearly exercises his authority like a beggar, and his power is effectively nothing. You only obey him as far as it pleases you and it pleases you as little as possible.'[53] Imperial politics appear here as a zero-sum game where the growth of princely power erodes that of the emperor, casting doubt whether the Empire was even still a monarchy. The Reformation intensified discussions by broadening 'German freedom' to include religious liberties. Faced with a seemingly implacably Catholic emperor, many Protestants argued that the Empire was really an aristocratic republic, or a commonwealth, in which the emperor was merely first among equals, like the Venetian doge. The concept of indivisible sovereignty advocated in the 1560s by the French philosopher and jurist Jean Bodin pushed discussions towards sharper categorization through his distinction between the outward form of government and its legal power (sovereignty). Thus, he argued, while the Empire might have the trappings of monarchy with regal symbols, it was in fact a commonwealth, because real power rested with the princes and was exercised through the Reichstag.

Catholics and also moderate Lutherans like Gottfried Antonius and Dietrich Reinkingk mounted a spirited defence of the Empire as monarchy; Reinkingk was even ennobled by Ferdinand III for arguing in 1655 that the emperor had supreme power once elected. Reinkingk was the monarchists' last hurrah, because the Thirty Years War revealed both the emperor's lack of supreme power and the dangers should he ever obtain it. The aristocratic counterblast was restated in an influential tract by Bogislav von Chemnitz, writing under the pseudonym Hippolithus a Lapide in 1643. Chemnitz was working for the Swedes and his book was symbolically burned by the imperial executioner. Not surprisingly, Prussia reissued Chemnitz's work in 1761 at the height of the Seven Years War when it also challenged Habsburg imperial authority.[54]

In fact, Chemnitz's interpretation was already politically unacceptable to most imperial Estates once Ferdinand III accepted revisions to the imperial constitution in the Peace of Westphalia (1648). This rejected both the monarchical and aristocratic interpretations in favour of a middle course advocated by writers like Dominicus Arumaeus and Johannes Limnaeus, who, in turn, reworked ideas already voiced around 1500 that the Empire was a mixed monarchy in which the emperor held the initiative, but shared important powers with the imperial Estates. Westphalia's main significance was to widen the circle sharing governance beyond the electors to include all imperial Estates. Moreover, it was clear by the 1680s that shares would remain unevenly distributed along the status hierarchy, limiting how far the junior Estates could influence policy, but equally ensuring they were not excluded altogether. This countered Bodin's either/or approach with its insistence that sovereignty was either wholly wielded by the emperor or exercised through the Reichstag, Instead, power was diffused through the Empire's different authorities, making them interdependent.

Samuel Pufendorf pushed the mixed-monarchy interpretation further through comparative analysis with other European states. Pufendorf's views gained currency thanks to his subsequent fame as Germany's first professor of natural law and his status as a leading intellectual. Like Chemnitz, he published his *De statu imperii Germanici* in 1667 under a pseudonym (the fantastically titled Severini de Monzambano). Pufendorf rejected attempts since Bodin to fit the Empire into the standard categories of states, arguing instead it was an 'irregular body'. His choice of the term 'monstrosity' to express this was immediately controversial and he deleted it from later editions of his book.[55] Pufendorf profoundly influenced how the Empire came to be interpreted after 1806, because he argued it had *declined* from a regular monarchy into an irregular one during the Middle Ages. He also revived Piccolomini's sharp dualist interpretation by arguing that while the Empire was an *irregulare Corpus*, its component principalities were regular monarchies. Pufendorf believed this was the root of all its political problems, because the princes were trying to break free, while the emperor was trying to reassert monarchical authority. Finally, his comparison with other European states presented the Empire as weak, because it lacked the central institutions found in France and elsewhere.

However, numerous other writers disputed that an 'irregular body' should necessarily be an inferior one and continued Pufendorf's historical analysis with more positive conclusions. Alongside Moser, Johann Pütter also contributed around one hundred volumes on the constitution, while Johann von Ludewig published a German translation of the Golden Bull with 2,500 pages of commentary. The verbosity of these authors represented the Empire through words in the way other states were projected in the timber, brick and stone of their royal palaces and parliaments. Their inability to suggest any alternative to existing conditions underlines the broad contentment with what Arch-chancellor Dalberg described as 'a permanent Gothic structure that might not conform to all the building regulations, but in which one lives securely'.[56]

IMPERIAL PATRIOTISM

German Attachment to the Empire

The concept of attachment to a fatherland (*patria*) gained currency with Humanist discourse and first appeared in the German form *Vaterland* in relation to the Empire in 1507.[57] Humanists' interest in civic engagement refashioned the patriot as someone actively promoting the common good, and further elaboration of this idea extended it later to encompass all inhabitants. Imperial patriotism varied considerably, as did its equivalents in other countries, but it has usually been considerably underestimated.[58]

The Empire's sense of itself was filtered through how it saw its place in Europe. As earlier sections of this work have shown, the ideal of the Empire as a Christian pan-national order persisted into early modernity, weakening any trend to more essentialist definitions of its inhabitants as a single nation determined by narrow criteria like language or ethnicity. Attitudes to outsiders were filtered through perceptions of the threat they posed to Christianity and 'German freedom'. This complicated relations with countries like France, Denmark and Sweden, all of which embraced varieties of Christianity regarded with hostility by at least some of the Empire's inhabitants after 1517, and all of whom invaded, claiming to uphold controversial interpretations of the imperial constitution. This ambivalence only disappeared as French expansionist policies under Louis XIV after 1667 were perceived as a general threat transcending religion and political status. Louis was accused of seeking an illegal 'fifth monarchy' that would displace the Empire's pre-eminent position and threaten its subjects' liberties. Francophobia incorporated earlier tropes associated with the Turks as an existential threat to Christian civilization.[59]

The extent to which Austrians and Czechs identified with the Empire is hard to assess, partly through a lack of research, but also because their loyalty to the emperor during the Habsburg era was indistinguishable from allegiance as his direct subjects. There was a distinct Czech identity by early modernity, but this was clearly neither fixed nor always opposed to 'German', 'European' or many other possible identities.[60] Patriotism was understandably strongest in Germany, which for many eighteenth-century writers was synonymous with the Empire. Recourse to the imperial supreme courts offers one quantitative measurement of the intensity and regional spread of engagement with the Empire. The two supreme courts – the Reichshofrat and Reichskammergericht – received 220,000 cases between 1495 and 1806, with the majority coming from the areas with the greatest political fragmentation. This is not entirely surprising. Since the courts were designed to resolve disputes between imperial Estates, it is natural that their business would reflect how these were concentrated, in the south and west. Rather more surprising is that after several centuries on the margins of imperial politics, the north German principalities and cities chose to use the courts as soon as they were established.[61]

Italian Views

Italians were conscious of *Italia* as a distinct country, but the idea of the Empire as 'foreign' stems largely from the nineteenth-century Risorgimento and from German nationalists condemning medieval emperors for pursuing the 'illusion' of power south of the Alps. The emperor's status as king of kings made him appear less immediately 'German' to Italians. Many did oppose imperial expeditions and protested at the *furor teutonicus*, but all emperors attracted at least some local support. Contemporaries did not view the choice as between 'native' and 'foreign' rule, but as about who could best deliver peace and justice. Otto I's intervention in Italy in 951 was not a conquest of a 'foreign' country, but the deposition of Berengar II, whom Pope John XII condemned as a tyrant.[62] The root problem was that the intermittent character of the emperor's presence in Italy inhibited the kind of working relationship that usually existed north of the Alps. The tendency to resort to force undermined claims to provide peace and justice. This deepened with the reception of Gregorian anti-imperial propaganda during the Investiture Dispute (1070s–1122), and the articulation of Ghibelline and Guelph sentiment during the Staufer era (1138–1254). Nonetheless, calls for the *libertas Italiae* voiced by the Lombard League were not campaigns for national independence, but protests against Staufer 'tyranny'.

Ghibelline sentiment persisted during the prolonged imperial absences after 1250 amongst those like Dante and Petrarch who believed only a strong imperial presence could provide the order that Italy so urgently needed. The papacy's 'Babylonian Captivity' in Avignon after 1309 increased interest, while many opposition groups within Italian towns hoped the emperor could liberate them from their local opponents. Given such unrealistic expectations, most imperial visits inevitably disappointed. Charles IV was criticized for appearing more concerned to extort money than address local problems. Moreover, Italian cities were accustomed to self-governance and resented paying for the expensive imperial entourage. The Pisans rioted in May 1355, setting fire to the palace where Charles and his wife were staying. The imperial couple were forced to flee naked into the street and order was restored only after considerable bloodshed.[63]

Guelph and Ghibelline sentiment gradually converged during the fourteenth century with all agreeing that politics were about asserting local civic autonomy relative to immediate neighbours, whilst still admitting the emperor had some role as suzerain. Emperors continued to visit Italy on average once a decade across the fourteenth and fifteenth centuries, but made only one appearance between 1452 and 1496 (in 1469), before returning amidst the very different circumstances of Habsburg imperial rule and the Italian Wars. The assignment of the Habsburgs' Italian possessions to Spain after 1558 also made the emperor appear more distant. By the eighteenth century, Genoese authors advocating their republic's sovereignty criticized the Empire as an *Imperio di Germania* that should stay north of the Alps. Other, lesser communities and lords continued to look to the emperor and Reichshofrat to protect their privileges in ways similar to their German counterparts. However, its strong associations with Germany and the fact that it only encompassed northern Italy rendered the Empire suspect in the eyes of later Italian nationalists. The same appears broadly true for Burgundy and the countries that emerged from it after 1797.

Only Aristocrats?

If the results of this regional survey are perhaps not so surprising, the social spread of imperial patriotism proves more unexpected. The general conclusion has been that the Empire mattered little outside the small elite of petty princes who depended on it to preserve their autonomy.[64] There is no doubt that the imperial princes identified their prestige and autonomy with the Empire's continued well-being. They often wanted to improve their own position, but only relative to their rivals. As Duke Ernst August of Hanover expressed it in 1682: 'It is not in the interests of this House to detach itself from the emperor and Empire, but on the contrary to remain firmly bound to them, since there is no more reliable security than in the Empire. And if the Empire were to go under, I do not see how this House can maintain its liberty and dignity.'[65]

His contemporary, Georg Friedrich of Waldeck, asked 'Where outside the Empire can one find such freedom as is customary within it?' While leading princes sought crowns elsewhere in Europe, they continued to engage in imperial politics. The elector Palatine commissioned two copies of the imperial crown in 1653 to give substance to his new title of Arch-Treasurer, awarded as part of the Westphalian settlement.[66] As the emperor's immediate vassals, the imperial knights also identified closely with the Empire. Although territorial nobles were encouraged to be loyal to their prince as immediate lord, they also looked to the emperor, because only he could grant the coveted status of full immediacy. The close juxtaposition of the different territorial nobilities combined with their relatively small size to encourage individuals to seek careers across the Empire. Often criticized by contemporaries as provincial hicks, most German nobles were at least aware of wider intellectual, educational, scientific, military and political networks. They saw themselves as a distinct 'nation' within a broader European aristocracy. Many families had branches in Burgundy, Italy, Bohemia and outside the Empire. Like educated commoners, they saw no contradiction between cosmopolitanism and multiple, more focused loyalties.[67]

The Empire's decentralized structure never employed a large staff. For most of the Middle Ages the 'imperial personnel' barely extended beyond the imperial chapel and the emperor's immediate household. Ruprecht gave the post of councillor to just 107 men across his reign (1400–1410). The establishment of permanent central institutions increased numbers somewhat after the 1490s. At least seven hundred people were employed at the Reichstag in the 1780s, with another 150 at the Reichskammergericht; but even adding the Reichshofrat, the chancellery and other agencies, the total is unlikely to have been more than 1,500.[68] Unlike other large states in early modernity, the Empire lacked permanent armed forces that might otherwise have served to encourage 'national' loyalty.

However, to look for such institutions would miss how the decentralized structure created numerous layers of engagement and identification. All imperial Estates sent envoys and agents not just to the Reichstag but to each other. The Empire defined their world. Only a few of the larger principalities maintained representatives at foreign courts by the eighteenth century. These roles had been performed by clergy during the Middle Ages, providing another example of the imperial church's significance to the Empire. The spread of educational opportunities from the high Middle Ages led to the rise of the 'learned' (*Gelehrten*), recruited largely from patrician families, who formed the backbone of most territorial administrations throughout early modernity. Like their noble counterparts, they were often highly mobile, working in several courts and imperial cities across their careers, which often included stints at the Reichstag or other institutions – like Goethe, who was a legal trainee at the Reichskammergericht before becoming a minister in Sachsen-Weimar. The experience of these men was as much imperial as territorial.[69] Some, like Goethe, were ambivalent about the Empire, while others, like Moser, were enthusiasts. Those serving larger territories could be more critical, but the Hohenzollerns' Reichstag envoy, Count Görtz, lamented the Empire's demise and chose to retire in Regensburg rather than return to Prussia.[70]

Rather more significantly, identification with the Empire stretched far deeper than the political and administrative elite. Despite their problematic relationship with many emperors, the Empire's Jews continued to pray for their welfare until 1806. Evidence that attachment extended beyond such official acts is provided by the blessings to the emperor recorded in family memory books (see Plate 9). Although Frankfurt Jews were confined to their ghetto on election days, they were included after 1711 in the homage ceremonies to new emperors. Jews performed homage ceremonies in four other imperial cities, though Worms council successfully petitioned to have the one there stopped. The episode perfectly demonstrates how identification with the Empire worked. The Jews saw their participation in such ceremonies as a way to assert their own corporate identity, while Christian city councillors sought to prevent this to achieve the opposite. Individual communities could also see the Empire as a framework for common action, exemplified by the Franconian Jews who in 1617 prosecuted the bishop of Bamberg on behalf of all their co-religionists to prevent him from requiring them to wear a star badge. Far from heralding a new dawn, many Jews perceived the Empire's demise as a disaster, since it removed the legal protections that had been corporate in line with their own visions of community, unlike the individual freedoms granted by post-1806 states.[71]

The imperial cities also found emperors to be problematic patrons and so already during the twelfth century these cities emphasized their relationship to the Empire as transpersonal. Later medieval emperors relied on the cities to accommodate them during their royal progresses, and their entry was always a cause for lavish celebration. Frederick II's third wife, Isabella Plantagenet, was greeted by 10,000 people when she arrived in Cologne in 1235. Royal entrées became increasingly elaborate around 1500 as the Habsburgs fused Italian and Burgundian ideas with classical examples supplied by Humanist scholars. Emperors' arrivals were now marked with elaborate triumphal arches, decorated floats and obelisks. The practice continued into the late eighteenth century, though modified in line with changing styles to include processions of state coaches and military parades. Arrivals for imperial elections, coronations and (until 1663) Reichstag openings were on an especially grand scale: 18,000 people participated in the procession of the electors into Frankfurt for the 1742 imperial election, equivalent to half the city's population.[72]

Imperial cities replaced palaces as the Empire's political venues during the fifteenth century, not just for events involving the emperor, but also for the numerous gatherings of imperial Estates, either in official gatherings, like the regional (Kreis) assemblies, or for their own alliances and congresses. Accommodating these activities could be burdensome, especially with the additional security costs during periods of tension, but such events also brought valuable business into the city and offered communities opportunities to express their own identity and place in the Empire.[73] Augsburg built an imposing new city hall from 1618 to 1622 prominently displaying the imperial double eagle on the portico in the hope of encouraging the Reichstag to choose it as a venue, as well as a statue of Emperor Augustus to stress its origins as a Roman imperial city.[74] Nuremberg was another city proud of its imperial traditions, which had been cemented in 1424 when Sigismund entrusted it with conserving the insignia. These had been displayed publicly since 1315, becoming an annual event each Easter from 1350. Nuremberg's conversion to Protestantism ended this tradition in 1524, because of the Lutheran critique of relics, but the city council refused to release the insignia to the still-Catholic Aachen, which repeatedly petitioned to replace Nuremberg as custodian.[75]

Attachment to the Empire extended to ordinary, rural inhabitants as well, despite the growth of numerous intervening layers of lordship between them and the emperor. Indeed, the emperor's relative distance and absence from daily life appears to have heightened the sense of reverence, and his rare appearances were a source of great curiosity and celebration. This extended even in death: Otto I's corpse took 30 days to travel the relatively short distance (130 kilometres) from Memleben for burial in Magdeburg so that it could be seen by the crowds along the route. The bishop of Speyer refused to bury Henry IV in his

1. The two swords theory: St Peter presenting a pallium to Pope Leo III and a flag to Charlemagne (Lateran palace).

2. Charlemagne as portrayed by Albrecht Dürer in about 1512, wearing the imperial crown and holding the sword and sceptre.

3. Napoleon contemplates Charlemagne's crown and stone throne in Aachen. The real crown had in fact been removed by the Austrians (late nineteenth-century painting).

4. Carolingian troops besieging towns (ninth-century manuscript).

5. The act of Canossa 1077. Henry IV kneels in front of Matilda of Tuscany to seek her mediation, while Abbot Hugh of Cluny looks on from the left.

REX ROGAT ABBATEM / MATHILDIM SUPPLICAT ATQ;

6. The *furor teutonicus*. Archbishop Balduin of Trier splits the skull of an Italian opponent during Henry VII's Roman expedition of 1312.

7. The last papal coronation of an emperor. Charles V and Clement VII in the coronation procession at Bologna in 1530.

8. Charles V as victor at the battle of Mühlberg, 1547, by Titian. The armour shown in the portrait is preserved in the royal palace in Madrid.

9. Identification with the Empire. A bag made by a Jewish craftsman around 1700 displaying the imperial eagle.

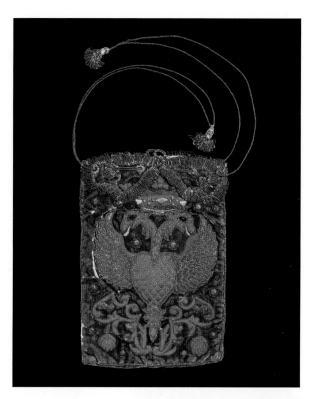

10. Charles V flanked by the Pillars of Hercules and the imperial eagle adorned with the Habsburg Order of the Golden Fleece, c.1532.

11. Charles VI points to Charlemagne's crown, showing the continued significance of the Empire for the Habsburgs in the eighteenth century.

12. The banquet for Joseph II's coronation as king of the Romans in Frankfurt, 1764. Note the place settings for the princes who failed to attend in person.

13. The three
ecclesiastical electors
officiating at Joseph II's
coronation in 1764.

14. Francis II depicted as
emperor of Austria in 1832,
wearing the Habsburg
imperial crown made for
Rudolf II in 1602.

15. Figures representing the Slavs, Germans, Gauls and Romans pay homage to Emperor Otto III.

16. The link between locality and Empire. A sequence of three Salian monarchs stands above a corresponding row of abbots of St Emmeram monastery.

cathedral in 1106, because the king died under papal excommunication. However, peasants stole the earth from atop his grave outside to scatter on their fields, believing it would improve fertility. Sigismund's corpse was allegedly left seated on a stool for three days when he died at Znaim in 1437 to enable the crowds to file past.[76]

The popular enthusiasm to celebrate Francis II's coronation in 1792 was doubtless heightened by the closure of all the inns and a ban on alcohol sales until his election was completed. However, an analysis of south German sermon texts shows real concern for the welfare of the imperial family.[77] One reason was the widespread identification of the emperor as the peasants' protector. A collection of popular stories from 1519 recounted how German peasants had aided Frederick I 'Barbarossa' in a mythical siege of Jerusalem, while six years later within days of the peasant rebels' bloody defeat at Frankenhausen at the foot of the Kyffhäuser Mountain there were rumours that Barbarossa would awake to avenge their innocent blood.[78]

Changes in judicial practice after the peasants' defeat opened access to the Empire's supreme courts, and one quarter of the Reichshofrat's cases were brought by ordinary inhabitants. So many peasant delegations arrived to petition the emperor that some Viennese inns specialized in accommodating them. Although the Habsburgs tried to restrict direct access in favour of official judicial channels in the eighteenth century, in 1711 three hundred peasants managed to accost the newly elected Charles VI and were delighted at his promise of action. They were still hopeful seven years later, but the likelihood of disappointment was high. One faction in a long-running dispute in Hauenstein in south-west Germany came close to repudiating allegiance to the Habsburgs in 1745. Nonetheless, Hauenstein peasant leaders who had petitioned the emperor gained personal prestige, encouraging several to invent stories of audiences and promises of help. Faith in imperial justice persisted, with unfavourable verdicts blamed on unsympathetic judges rather than on either the emperor or the system.[79]

Imperial court records reveal that ordinary folk possessed a relatively sophisticated understanding of the Empire's complex constitution and their place within it. The two supreme courts were often called to arbitrate jurisdictional disputes and sent commissioners to gather evidence, including questioning peasants. Those in larger principalities were less certain of details, but still regarded the Empire as the collective home of many communities, while the inhabitants of smaller territories frequently displayed detailed knowledge of how their lord related to the wider constitutional order. Peasants were prepared to send delegations to the Reichstag to see whether their ruler was overcharging them on imperial taxes. The literate recorded events like Reichstag meetings and electoral congresses in their diaries. Imperial mandates were publicly posted or announced by pastors at Sunday service, while other news travelled by word of mouth and until 1739 the Turkish Bells rang out during wars against the Ottomans.[80]

ROMANTIC NATIONALISM

Germany's Double Fatherland

The growth of princely dynasties provided additional foci for identity by early modernity. As rulers of the second largest territorial bloc in the Empire, the Hohenzollerns offered a potential alternative to attachment to the Habsburgs. King Frederick the Great deliberately promoted an image of Prussia's 'power and splendour' to other Germans whilst actively curtailing his own subjects' identification with the Empire. The traditional prayers for the emperor were banned throughout Prussia after June 1750, while Berlin city centre was remodelled as an imposing European-class capital. However, Frederick's direct military challenge to Habsburg pre-eminence after 1740 placed him in the awkward position of instigating civil war within the Empire after a century of internal peace. His propaganda ignored his own blatant disregard for the liberties of neighbouring Lutheran principalities to present Prussia as defending Protestant German liberties. However, he refrained from returning to the full-blown confessional polemic of the Reformation era. Instead, Protestant Prussia was associated with progressive government and true German values, whilst the Catholic Habsburgs were castigated for mismanagement, Ultramontanism and the suppression of German freedoms. The obvious inability of Austria and its powerful international allies to defeat Prussia in 1740–45 and 1756–63 appeared to corroborate these arguments.[81]

However, Frederick and his immediate successors did not seek a 'national' role and had no idea of the 'historic mission' attributed to them by later pro-Prussian historians. Frederick disdained German literature and culture, corresponded in French, and regarded himself as belonging to a cosmopolitan elite of Enlightened monarchs and thinkers. Yet his prominence made him a pan-German figure and, by default, associated Prussia with arguments for national renewal: his victory over a combined French and imperial army at Rossbach in 1757 was celebrated by some as a 'national' triumph.[82]

Count Pergen, the man in charge of Joseph II's coronation as king of the Romans in 1764, covertly hired Friedrich Carl von Moser to counter Prussian propaganda and help rebuild Austrian influence after the Seven Years War. Like many intellectuals, Moser was already disillusioned with Frederick's obvious cynicism and set about his task with energy to match that of his father, Johann Jacob. Four important works appeared between 1765 and 1767, of which *Of the German National Spirit* and *Patriotic Letters* were deservedly the best known. These attacked the 'double fatherland' of distinct Protestant and Catholic Germanies fostered by Prussian propaganda, arguing instead that German national identity was best served by the Empire's constitution. Moser believed this was now endangered by princely despotism and disregard of imperial law, and he called on all Germans to unite behind the emperor. The Habsburgs were so pleased that they considered the rare step of raising Moser's salary, but soon abandoned this once they spotted he had included them in his critique by distinguishing between 'good imperial' (*gut Kayserlich*) and 'good Austrian' policies. The Habsburgs also realized that Moser's attempt to cast Prussia as an 'imperial enemy' akin to France or the Ottomans was proving divisive. Moser was quietly removed and he was assigned instead a minor administrative post in 1770.[83]

Moser proved so troubling because he clarified the questions facing the Empire in the later eighteenth century. In addressing what constituted the true nation, Moser was quite conservative in emphasizing the imperial constitution nearly thirty years after Prussia's open challenge to Austria forced people to confront the gulf between formal status and the actual distribution of power. This made it impossible to discuss national identity without addressing the issue of imperial reform, which in turn raised the question whether freedom was best safeguarded by the current constitution, princely territorial states or greater individual rights and political participation.

The Politics of Sensibility

Possible alternative forms of attachment were exemplified by Joseph II's coronation, the event that prompted Moser's secret contract. Joseph's entry into Frankfurt on 29 March 1764 surpassed all previous entrées and his cavalcade included 95 six-horse coaches processing to the din of a 300-gun salute and two hours of continuous bell-ringing.[84] Writing in 1811, Goethe recalled feeling 'that the whole affair took on a motley, unsatisfactory, often tasteless appearance', especially the empty tables at the coronation banquet, attended by only three electors and one prince, in contrast to the nearly sixty princes and counts present for Charles VII's coronation in 1742 (see Plate 12). The troops employed in crowd control at Joseph's coronation used excessive force, at one point opening fire and killing a 19-year-old girl. Before his arrival, Joseph had written to his mother dismissing the event as 'une vraie comédie'. His view was undoubtedly coloured by grief at his wife's death only four months before, though this did not stop him eyeing up the princesses in attendance. Afterwards, he wrote again to his mother: 'Yesterday's ceremony, I must confess, is superb and august. I tried to carry it off decently, but without embarrassment. His Majesty the Emperor [Francis I] has admitted to us that he could not keep back his tears; they say the same thing happened to almost the whole congregation.'

Joseph's experience indicates the Empire's potential to appeal to the new politics of sensibility, which added programmatic 'nationalism' to the previously largely descriptive 'nation' identifying a distinct people. Nationalism required emotional and active engagement to promote the nation as the supreme form of social organization. The debate moved beyond the Humanists' 'culture wars' over which nation had the best claim to a classical pedigree, to promote new forms of distinctiveness based on allegedly innate social and ethnic characteristics. Nationalism assumed several partly contradictory forms, but can be labelled 'Romantic' due to the emphasis on sentiment and the essentialist articulation of the nation as a superior transcendental force – what has aptly been called 'a secular religion'.[85] One of the earliest German advocates of this passionate engagement was Thomas Abbt, whose poem *Death for the Fatherland* (1761) said it all, radically reordering traditional virtues to place sacrifice for the nation ahead of saintliness. Romantic nationalists considered it unacceptable to discuss identity in a language other than German and they began constructing a national history and literary canon to exclude people, events and works that did not fit their essentialist criteria. This entailed rejecting the pre-modern tradition of the Germans as a collection of different tribes whose distinct cultures and freedoms were guaranteed by the imperial constitution. Cultural and linguistic uniformity became the only acceptable basis for a nation state or, as Johann Gottfried von Herder put it more poetically: each nation could only have one language as the true expression of its soul. 'Foreign' forms had to be rejected as threatening national purity. These included not only the French and Italian influences that hitherto dominated elite musical and cultural life, but also the non-German customs and languages persisting across the Empire.[86] The closure of French theatre troupes began in 1757 as part of general economies in courtly expenditure during the Seven Years War, but continued from the 1760s with the foundation of new 'National', or German-speaking, theatres and opera houses in Hamburg, Vienna, Mannheim, Berlin and elsewhere.

The Romantic nationalists of the 'Sturm und Drang' era from the 1770s are now celebrated as Germany's literary giants, but in their day largely failed to find the employment they sought in territorial administrations and universities. Their calls for national renewal were undoubtedly sincere, but also influenced by their own experience of having to forge their networks outside established circles. Their distance from the traditional order was magnified in many cases by personal disappointment after placing unrealistic hopes in Joseph II or Frederick II of Prussia to lead their national revival. Those who did find official posts, like Goethe, were noticeably less hostile to the Empire. The broader population remained strongly attached to territorial and local identities, which appeared better served by the Empire's loose political order than by the kind of integral nation advocated by Romantics.[87]

Joseph's long reign (1765–90) meant there was no further imperial election until 1790, by which time the French Revolution was already transforming circumstances. Joseph preferred travelling incognito to the traditional pomp of an imperial progress, thereby further adding to perceptions of the old order's irrelevance. He missed the opportunity of attempting what the British monarchy would do under Queen Victoria to align itself with more populist nationalist sentiment by inventing new 'traditions'.

For all their limited appeal, the Romantic nationalists had made an important point: by 1800 the Empire indeed appeared antiquated and inadequate compared to their vision of a bright new national utopia. Acceptance of their critique rapidly gained ground once the Empire dissolved amidst the pressures of the Revolutionary and Napoleonic Wars, as the circumstances fitted the nationalists' calls for the old order to die in order for Germany to be reborn. The situation after 1815 witnessed repeated disappointments as it proved impossible to agree on what constituted the nation. The liberal ideal of a family of friendly nations was replaced by a competitive survival of the fittest. The acceptance of essentialist definitions of identity condemned Europeans to fruitless struggles over the optimal size of invented nation states. The creation and maintenance of larger states has entailed marginalizing or obliterating traits perceived as inimical to dominant national cultures, whereas the desire for self-determination has threatened to fragment parts of the European continent into ever smaller pieces. Seen from this perspective, the Empire's ability to accommodate different identities within a common framework assumes a new significance.

PART III

Governance

7

Kingship

KINGS AND THEIR QUALITIES

Governance not Government

Part III examines how the Empire was governed, while Part IV looks at how governance related to social developments. The emphasis on *governance* rather than *government* is deliberately intended to overcome earlier presentations of imperial politics as a succession of failed attempts to create a unitary state. 'Government' implies a centralized, institutionalized state with a clear chain of command and responsibility. Modern politics are largely about determining who controls such states and what policies they should pursue. 'Governance' more commonly denotes auto-politics and self-regulation, both of which are closer to the Empire's *regimen* of a broadly inclusive system relying more on consensus than command. This chapter begins by explaining how kings were chosen and the qualities they were expected to possess, before identifying their primary assistants and the resources at their disposal. The final section charts the main developments from the Carolingian to the Salian monarchs, thereby opening the chronological coverage continuing through the high and later Middle Ages in Chapter 8 and across early modernity under the Habsburgs in Chapter 9.

Imperial governance was programmatic in that it was guided by coherent ideals and goals. All kings and emperors – like modern governments – had to react to circumstances and improvise, but they were not simply at the mercy of events. The difference lies in what they were trying to achieve. 'State' and 'nation' were not yet clearly delineated concepts functioning as focused policy objectives. Kings and emperors were not state- or nation-builders, because no one felt either needed building. Medieval monarchs were expected to build churches and cathedrals. Otherwise, their role was primarily to uphold peace, justice and the honour of the Empire. Changing circumstances, like violence, rebellions, or invasions, were not seen as 'problems' to be 'solved' through new laws, better institutions, or more coherent frontiers. Most of the misunderstandings surrounding the Empire's political history stem from attempts to impose anachronistic expectations on its rulers' behaviour. For most of the Empire's existence, imperial governance was guided by the prevailing ideals of good kingship.

Imperial and royal powers were never explicitly delineated. It was accepted by the twelfth century that the emperor possessed exclusive prerogatives (*jura caesarea reservata*) largely relating to a clearer understanding of his position as feudal overlord. Subsidiary reserved powers (*jura caesarea reservata limitata*) could be exercised with the advice of great lords. These were identified more precisely from the mid-fourteenth century and included declarations of war and the imperial ban. A final set of shared powers (*jura comitialia*) were clarified during fifteenth-century imperial reform as being shared with all imperial Estates.[1] As later chapters will show, this gradual clarification of the Empire as mixed monarchy evolved with changing expectations of what authorities should do, rather than from a desire among princes to leave the Empire.

Ideal Kings

The collective element in governance was expressed most clearly in how kings were selected. The element of election was mixed with other forms and the monarchs should not be considered a kind of life president. Those involved never enjoyed an entirely free choice. The number of candidates was always limited to a select group considered *Caesarable*. Selection criteria were never formally specified, but can be extrapolated from discussions of ideal kings in contemporary chronicles, lives of saints, liturgical texts, and reflections on kingship known as the 'mirror of princes' (*Fürstenspiegel*), which existed under the Carolingians and became more common again from the twelfth century.

Religion and morality are central to these texts, which generally used biblical examples like Moses, David and Solomon.[2] As most authors were clergy prior to the fifteenth century, this emphasis is unsurprising. Kings were admonished to follow the clergy's advice, not to exceed their legitimate prerogatives and to display *humilitas* by acknowledging their own mortality and subordination to divine power.[3] Humility remained significant into the thirteenth century as a way to demonstrate purity of motives, accepting royal responsibilities as a duty to God rather than as a lust for power. Henry I was nick-named 'the Fowler' because he was supposedly busy setting bird nets rather than politicking during his election. Displaying humility was a good way to suggest that rivals were dangerously eager to be king.

Ninth- and tenth-century clerics often stressed purity of inner char-acter over material achievements. Pious 'failures' were preferable to sinning achievers, but even clerics like Thietmar of Merseburg expected tenth- and eleventh-century monarchs to act forcefully, considering cunning and anger to be appropriate manly virtues and necessary for political success.[4] The laity's views before the later Middle Ages can only really be discerned from how far royal actions met with approval or opposition. Core expectations remained stable: kings should defend the church, uphold the law, and be victorious in battle. However, the precise mix varied across time, while contemporaries often disagreed on how kings should achieve these goals.[5]

Not everyone was considered to possess these qualities from birth. Lineage remained an important element throughout the Empire's history and mostly the only viable candidates were those from what Tacitus called the *stirps regia* or royal kin. The modern German word *König* (king) derives from the older *kunja*, meaning both kinship and the warrior clan and its leader.[6] Real or fictive kinship was important in each transition in royal line until at least the thirteenth century. Challengers from outside the immediate circle still had to demonstrate royal blood. The first anti-king to be elected, Rudolf of Rheinfelden, was related to the former Burgundian royal family and had served as both governor of Burgundy and duke of Swabia from 1057. His first wife was Henry IV's sister Matilda, while his second spouse, Adelaide of Savoy, was also associated with royalty. The next anti-king, Hermann of Salm, headed the first line of Luxembourg counts (extinct 1198) and was thus grandson of Empress Kunigunde, wife of Henry II, and was related to the Ottonians and, distantly, the Salians. These connections made him appear an ideal compromise candidate to challenge Henry IV in 1081, but Hermann's lack of military success soon alienated his supporters.[7]

The ideal royal connections remained those with the Carolingians, especially Charlemagne. Berengar II and his son Adelbert claimed Carolingian descent while contesting Otto I's grab for Italy in the 950s. Associations with Charlemagne remained important into the sixteenth century, by which time royal apologists fitted the Empire's rulers into a seamless line stretching through the ancient Roman emperors back to the Trojans.

Lineage subsumed other aspects of heritage, including what would later be considered nationality. A sense of not being 'one of us' did not prevent the Saxon Ottonians replacing the Frankish Carolingians in 919, nor them in turn being followed by the Rhenish Salians, but the new lines nonetheless had to tread carefully at first in both cases. Otto I's coronation as Holy Roman emperor in 962 cemented the association of the imperial and German titles, but there was still no formal requirement that the German king actually be 'German'. Pope Innocent III asserted in his decree *Venerabilem* of 1202 that Leo III had 'transferred the Roman Empire in the person of Charlemagne from the Greeks to the Germans'. This statement was intended to historicize the papacy's claim to supremacy as 'translator' of the imperial title. It did not prevent the election of both English and Spanish candidates (respectively Richard of Cornwall and Alfonso X of Castile) as German king in 1257, nor was it a primary reason for the failure of several French candidacies around 1300. The papal decree assumed an unintended significance following renewed double election in 1314 as Innocent had unwittingly supplied an argument to exclude the papacy from interfering in the election of future German kings. However, it was only after the wider acceptance of new ideas of nationality that the decree's full impact was felt, enabling Charles V to win the 1519 imperial election against François I of France by depicting him as a 'foreigner'. Charles proved subsequently to be too 'Spanish' for many Germans, but this simply reinforced the consensus that only a 'German' should be emperor.[8]

Kings were expected to act kingly, imposing constraints both before and after accession. A bad man could not have divine favour. Henry IV was mercilessly attacked by his critics for his alleged debauchery and cruelty to his wife Praxedis. Acting regally ahead of an election could convince doubters, but it might also be perceived as haughty. Duke Friedrich II of Swabia was the Staufer candidate in 1125 and enjoyed Henry V's public endorsement as his successor, but he was criticized for being 'ready to be elected king, but not to elect a king'. His fellow dukes opted instead for Lothar III of Supplinburg, who had already kneeled before the assembled lords, exclaiming he would not accept the title. In this case, lack of lineage actually helped, because Lothar was unrelated to the Salians, whose command style of rule the dukes wanted to end.[9]

Kings were expected to show due regard for their senior vassals' sensibilities. Another of the many charges against Henry IV during his reign was that he kept the Saxon lords waiting all day to see him while he played dice with his cronies.[10] Displaying courage in battle and securing victory were also essential, not least because they provided evidence of true faith and divine favour. Henry I deliberately broke his truce with the Magyars in 932, securing his lords' support by arguing it would be better to devote their money to memorializing their heroic defence of Christendom than continuing paying tribute to pagans. The subsequent victory at Riade the following year was hugely significant in cementing acceptance of Ottonian rule. Much was made of the king's use of the Holy Lance in this battle, and again by his son Otto I at Lechfeld in 955, constructing a story of continued divine favour leading to Otto's imperial coronation in 962.[11]

Nonetheless, direct participation in warfare was very risky, as demonstrated by Otto II's defeat at Cotrone (982), which shook confidence in the Ottonians throughout the Empire. Personal courage at least could compensate for strategic failure. The two crusading emperors, Conrad III and Frederick I 'Barbarossa', are both associated with stories of having cleaved opponents in two with single sword blows.[12] Richard of Cornwall was a distinguished crusader prior to his election in 1257, while Sigismund managed to come out of the doomed Nicopolis crusade of 1396 with an enhanced reputation. Martial prowess remained important into early modernity. Maximilian I was famed as the 'last knight'. Charles V had a magnificent equestrian portrait of himself painted by Titian to celebrate his victory over the Schmalkaldic League at Mühlberg in 1547 (see Plate 8). Both Ferdinand III and Joseph I were praised for their coolness under fire.

By that point, good generalship was more expected of a king than a warrior's deeds. However, medieval kings were expected to look as if they might be mighty fighters. Several kings, including Henry IV, were said to measure up to Charlemagne's 1.8 metres, while Conrad II exceeded him at 2 metres as well as being celebrated for riding 150 kilometres in a single day. Henry VII was known as *Alto Arrigo* (Tall Harry) in Italy. Poise, gait, dexterity and general appearance were also important in this culture of personal presence. The fact that he had lost an eye was another factor against Duke Friedrich of Swabia compared to his younger brother, Conrad III. Ninth-century emperors and kings were expected to appear wearing silk robes with gold hems, golden sword belts and spurs. Items considered traditionally 'Frankish' remained important markers of legitimacy and continuity into the thirteenth century.[13]

Less stress was placed on intellectual ability. Conrad II was called *idiota* because he was illiterate. However, this reflected both the prejudice of the tiny clerical elite and the fact that he had not been raised in the expectation he would become king. Conrad gave his own son a much more rounded education. Conrad II's next three successors were all well educated; Otto III's main tutor was Gerbert of Aurillac, one of the leading intellectuals of his age and the future Pope Sylvester II. Henry III's Latin was sufficiently good for him to poke fun at Bishop Meinward of Paderborn's conduct of a church service.[14] Louis IV 'the Bavarian' was the last emperor to have only a nobleman's basic education. His successor, Charles IV, studied in Paris, wrote his own biography, spoke five languages and participated fully in Europe's high Gothic culture.[15] Later emperors also showed artistic flair, or at least patronized the arts, but this was scarcely unique amongst European royalty following the Renaissance.

As we have seen in the discussion of presentational culture (pp. 13 and 267), the politics of the medieval Empire emphasized direct, personal interaction; in short, a culture of personal presence. However, problems of distance and pressure of other concerns inhibited kings – and especially potential kings – from meeting everyone who might prove significant. Several prospective monarchs were relatively unknown quantities prior to their election. Under these conditions, it was important to adhere to other, accepted norms and to present oneself in accordance with expectations. Possession of the 'right' insignia was already an issue during the Carolingian civil wars of the 840s when rivals attempted to bolster claims through displaying allegedly 'authentic' items. Widukind of Corvey emphasized how the dying Conrad I allegedly legitimized the transition to Ottonian rule by giving Henry I the royal insignia. Henry II's widow, Kunigunde, played a similar role by entrusting the first Salian, Conrad II, with the insignia. Likewise, surrender of the insignia was interpreted as renunciation of kingship; unwillingly in Henry IV's case in 1105, but amicably by Frederick 'the Fair' in 1320.

Henry II intercepted Otto III's funeral cortège to seize the insignia in 1002, but this alone was insufficient: the lords initially rejected him on grounds of his weak physique and the absence of children despite a marriage of two years. However, Henry enjoyed the backing of Otto's sisters and reached Mainz ahead of his rival, Hermann II, duke of Swabia, to stage his own coronation first.[16] Similarly, Otto IV trumped Philip of Swabia, who had the insignia, by controlling Aachen and being crowned by the 'right' person – the archbishop of Cologne in 1198. In short, other elements were important in securing wider recognition of legitimacy. Another archbishop of Cologne insisted on there being only a single, recognized set of insignia in 1315 to consolidate his role in crowning kings. The desire to pre-empt potential rivals and anti-kings also influenced the Luxembourgs' efforts to concentrate all the items in a single treasury. However, as late as 1400 their rival Ruprecht was able to get away with a cheap imitation crown that he pawned three years later for just 150 florins.[17]

Election and Hereditary Succession

A variety of methods were used to decide the succession prior to their standardization in the Golden Bull of 1356. The elective element has long been blamed as a prime source of political weakness.[18] For the following, it is important to remember that until the late Middle Ages contemporaries did not regard 'elective' and 'hereditary' monarchies as sharply defined constitutional alternatives. Even English kingship contained elective elements in that the aristocracy's consent was required for a succession to be legitimate, while hereditary rule in France was achieved in practice by many kings crowning their sons as successors during their own lifetime.

As the participants in the Empire were well aware, hereditary succession was not inherently superior. Otto I, Henry IV and Frederick II all faced serious rebellions from their sons whom they had groomed as successors. The periods when the hereditary principle was strongest were also those of the longest royal minorities, notably for Otto III and Henry IV. While lineage was valued, direct descent was no guarantee of an ideal king. Aged 15, Wenzel succeeded his father Charles IV in 1378. Lavish preparations left the new king a spoiled teenager who soon took to drink. By contrast, election reduced the chances of an incompetent king. Five of the six monarchs elected in the century after 1254 were 'exceptionally able politicians'.[19] The exception, Adolf of Nassau, was deposed, something that was also easier to handle under an elective monarchy.

There were only four genuine 'double elections' across the millennium of imperial history (1198, 1257, 1314, 1410) when rival candidates were chosen very closely together, though never actually simultaneously. The others were all 'anti-kings' elected by their own supporters in opposition to a reigning monarch (see Table 2). Anti-kings were not a worse problem structurally than the 'pretenders' and 'wars of succession' affecting Europe's hereditary monarchies. Only two of the double elections triggered a serious civil war (1198, 1314). Altogether, the Empire fared far better than its ancient Roman predecessor, which had no system beyond nomination by the existing incumbent, combined with the nominee's ability to defeat rivals. Only two emperors were directly succeeded by their sons between 27 BC and AD 192, while over 80 gained power by usurping the throne between 235 and 284. Thereafter, there were only three years with a single, unchallenged emperor before 476.

The Empire got 'the best of both worlds', because its monarchy was theoretically elective but often hereditary in practice.[20] Nobles and the population generally preferred sons to follow fathers as this was interpreted as a sign of divine grace. Of the 24 German kings between 800 and 1254, 22 came from four families, with sons following fathers 12 times. However, while some later historians interpreted this as 'blood right', contemporaries used the looser 'hereditary right' (*ius hereditaria successio*), which did not specify an exact sequence and allowed lords some say in elections.[21] The Carolingians practised 'designation' whereby a reigning monarch already indicated which of his sons or relations should succeed him, providing the basis for co-kings

Table 2. Anti-Kings

Period Affected	Anti-King	Reigning Monarch
983–5	Heinrich II 'the Quarrelsome' of Bavaria	Otto III
1077–81	Rudolf of Rheinfelden	Henry IV
1081–88	Hermann of Salm	Henry IV
1088–90	Ekbert of Meißen	Henry IV
1093–1101	Conrad of Franconia (official co-king since 1087)	Henry IV
1106	Henry V (ruled uncontested from August 1106)	Henry IV
1127–35	Conrad III (ruled uncontested 1138–52)	Lothar III
1198–1218	Otto IV	Philip of Swabia
1212–18	Frederick II (ruled uncontested from 1218)	Otto IV
1246–7	Heinrich Raspe of Thuringia	Frederick II
1247–54	William of Holland (ruled uncontested 1254–6)	Frederick II till 1250, Conrad IV 1250–54
1257–73	Alfonso X of Castile	Richard of Cornwall
1314–25	Frederick 'the Fair' of Austria	Louis IV
1346–7	Charles IV (ruled uncontested from 1347)	Louis IV
1349	Günther von Schwarzenburg	Charles IV
1400	Friedrich of Brunswick	Wenzel
1400–1419	Wenzel (reigning king since 1378)	Ruprecht of the Palatinate
1410–11	Jobst of Moravia	Sigismund

(see Table 3, p. 312). Designation assumed particular importance during the change of royal families in 919 and 1024, with both Ottonian and Salian chroniclers claiming their line had received endorsement from the previous kings.

Only Henry VI tried to persuade the senior lords to accept a clearly hereditary Staufer monarchy in Germany along the lines of his newly acquired kingdom of Sicily. Despite his offer of concessions, the lords only took the conventional step of recognizing his two-year-old son Frederick II as successor, whilst leaving open the question of hereditary right. This episode assumed greater significance in twentieth-century writing than it probably deserves, since it was misinterpreted as an opportunity to have converted the Empire into a centralized monarchy supposedly cut short by Henry's unexpectedly early death.[22] Monarchs elsewhere certainly feared the Empire's conversion to hereditary rule. Pope Innocent III threatened in *Venerabilem* to deprive the Germans of their electoral rights if they chose another Staufer. Sweden and France tried to write into the Peace of Westphalia (1648) that no two consecutive emperors could come from the same dynasty. Such attempts were always rejected by the German princes as unwarranted interference in their free choice.

The actual process of election was far from transparent prior to the late Middle Ages. It did not rest on ideals of popular sovereignty, or notions that the great lords were the representatives of ordinary people. Instead, election was seen as an expression of a divine choice; it was precisely this aspect that contemporaries celebrated as making it superior to direct hereditary succession.[23] Although staged publicly as a spontaneous expression of divine will, selection always involved calculated assessments of the likely candidates' personal characteristics, military power and kinship networks. Outward unanimity was important to convey legitimacy. Dissenters either failed to participate or left before the outcome was publicly declared. Election thus blended to an extent with homage ceremonies, as the new king needed to secure public acceptance from those who had not been present. Both Henry II and Conrad II were obliged to seek the Saxons' agreement separately in ceremonies amounting almost to second elections in 1002 and 1024.[24] This practice was curbed thereafter, with election remaining a single event.

Dissenters could voice objections or absent themselves, but they could not veto a choice. Majority voting became clearly established during the fourteenth century as the previous desire for public unanimity waned.[25] Those who did leave risked handing the favoured candidate the appearance of being a unanimous choice. Usually, dissenters discreetly bargained concessions either just prior to the public acclamation of the new king or later in return for homage. Those who were irreconcilable generally retired to their lands and refused homage. This constituted the primary form of rebellion across the Empire's first two centuries.

The anti-Henrician faction expressly adopted the church reformers' call for 'free election' as expressing God's will when they elected Rudolf of Rheinfelden in 1077. Rudolf's promise not to designate any son as his successor was the first clear rejection of the hereditary principle in imperial politics.[26] However, it was not a decisive turning point, since Rudolf was defeated by Henry IV, who proceeded to get both his sons recognized as his successors through designation. Lothar III's election was 'free' in the sense that Henry V did not designate a successor, but exactly what happened is far from clear beyond that the proceedings did not constitute a break with past practice. Conrad III's accession in 1138 was 'a coup by only a few magnates'.[27] Sons followed fathers thereafter, though always with the approval of important lords, until the final emergence of 'free election' during the later thirteenth century.

The Electoral College

Exactly who participated in early elections remains unclear, though there was never a simple popular vote by warriors acting as a 'tribe'.[28] Elections were always elite affairs, and by 887 it was expected that the main regions would be represented by their dukes and other senior lords, though it is not certain how far these canvassed their own vassals before voicing an opinion. All major regions were expected to be represented by 911, and the absence of the Bavarians and Swabians in 919 required their subsequent coercion by Henry I. Burgundian and Italian lords paid homage, but were excluded from German elections, except in 983 when Otto II sought greater integration and had his son Otto III simultaneously elected German and Italian king at an assembly in Verona, and subsequently crowned in Aachen by the archbishops of Mainz and Ravenna.

The identity of the elections emerged slowly as contemporaries began distinguishing more sharply between deliberate 'choice' (*Kur*) and allegedly 'spontaneous' acclamation. Bishops appear not to have acted in Otto I's election, but clearly participated by the mid-eleventh century, having gained influence under Henry II. Abbots no longer participated after 1198, while bishops' involvement contracted to those in western Germany. Nonetheless, ecclesiastical lords still predominated into the thirteenth century, perhaps thanks to a greater sense of collegiality.[29] Meanwhile, any remaining regional grouping of secular representation disappeared with the emergence of smaller, more numerous duchies under the Staufers. Although the universal right of all lords to participate was still proclaimed in 1152, the number of electors had already narrowed. Counts were excluded after 1196, though the overall numbers of participants continued to fluctuate: the 1208, 1212 and 1220 elections were all large gatherings, while those of 1211, 1237, 1246 and 1247 were small, with only 11 princes appearing in Vienna to elect Conrad IV.[30]

The 1198 double election and those of anti-kings in 1246 and 1247 all revealed the dangers of faction. Both the Staufers and the papacy favoured reducing the electors to a clearly defined group, and their efforts were supported by writers like Eike of Repgow and Albert of Stade, whose influential treatise encouraged acceptance of a small group indirectly representing those who could no longer participate.[31] Practicalities compelled this. The civil war of the 1240s made it obvious that electors would have to support their candidate against any opposition, discouraging many from risking involvement. The extinction of the powerful Babenberg family in Austria (1246) and the Ludowingers in Thuringia (1247) further reduced the number of electors.

The identity of the ecclesiastical electors had stabilized at three by 1237. Mainz had already played a leading role since 936 and asserted the right of 'first vote' (*prima vox*) by 1002. Cologne's refusal to accept Mainz's status was a major factor behind the double election of 1198 as it backed Otto IV against the majority choice of Philip of Swabia.[32] Mainz's pre-eminence was confirmed by 1356, when it was charged with organizing each election. Cologne and Trier continued to bicker with Mainz over status, but all three combined to exclude Magdeburg and Salzburg definitively by 1237. Ecclesiastical votes were fixed in a transpersonal archdiocese, whereas secular power was family based, making it harder to identify which individual should exercise it. The decisive step came with the permanent association of electoral votes with ceremonial 'arch-offices' (*Erzämter*), named after functions performed at the royal court. The electors now narrowed rapidly as it was in the interest of those already within the privileged circle to exclude others.[33] Rudolf limited the secular recipients of arch-offices to his four sons-in-law: the count Palatine, the margrave of Brandenburg, the Askanier family in Saxony, and the king of Bohemia. A split in the Askanier complicated matters after 1273, but Charles IV fixed electoral votes to three ecclesiastical and four secular fiefs in the famous Golden Bull of 1356. Named after its imposing golden seal, this was deliberately intended as a definitive arrangement, consolidating the group as a corporate electoral college identified by special privileges beyond just their exclusive right to choose each king.[34]

The emergence of a clearly defined electoral college changed the practice of identifying a successor during the lifetime of an incumbent king. The last time this had occurred was in 1169 when the four-year-old Henry VI had been elected German king alongside his father, Emperor Frederick I Barbarossa, enabling him to succeed unchallenged in 1190. The next time was when Charles IV sought recognition of his son Wenzel as successor in 1376. This was the first election since the Golden Bull and established what became known as *vivente imperatore* ('during the emperor's life') elections, with the next election occurring in 1486 for Maximilian I. Maximilian's adoption of the title 'elected Roman Emperor' in 1508 led to the title 'king of the Romans' (*Römischer König*) being adopted for any successor elected during an emperor's lifetime. The Golden Bull permitted this practice but, like all important imperial documents, was open to differing interpretations. Emperors argued they could summon the electors when they chose, while the electors claimed their prior agreement was necessary, effectively adding another means to delay a *vivente imperatore* election. In practice, the Habsburgs waited until they were confident the electors would agree. They got this wrong in 1630 when the electors refused to accept Ferdinand III as king of the Romans, but otherwise the tactic was modestly successful and 7 of the 16 elections between 1519 and 1792 returned kings of the Romans, beginning with Ferdinand I in 1531.[35]

Electoral Promises

Clarification of election rules also separated that process more clearly from homage ceremonies, when subjects acknowledged a new monarch, promising loyalty in return for protection and respect for their liberties. Although medieval rulers only gave oral promises, these were considered binding and legitimized opposition should they be subsequently broken. Homage ceremonies spread to all major levels of authority within the Empire by early modernity, but they were particularly important for the medieval monarchy. Charlemagne's requirement in 802 that all males over 12 swear loyalty to him and his new imperial office continued under the later Carolingians, but the more intense personal bonds with senior lords always mattered more.[36] It became customary for each newly crowned monarch to undertake a royal progress (*Iter*) to win recognition from those lords absent from his election.

Homage extracted under coercion was considered invalid, opening the door to discreet bargaining to secure acceptance. This already appears to have been practised under the later Carolingians, though evidence is patchy before 1152 except for negotiations surrounding the election of co-kings (for these see Table 3, p. 312).[37] The issuing of diplomas soon after coronations suggests the delivery of pre-election promises, usually in the form of gifts of crown lands and immunities (privileges). All parties had an interest in discretion. The king's honour was at stake, while those expecting gifts risked humiliation if they petitioned openly for them.

The promises extracted from Rudolf of Rheinfelden in 1077 were exceptional and due to his status as anti-king: in addition to concessions to the pope over investiture, Rudolf had to promise not to name his own son as successor. Electoral pacts became a more obvious feature during the era of 'free election', being a feature of at least 11 of the 14 elections between 1198 and 1298. Adolf of Nassau made especially extensive gifts to secure support in 1292, with such rewards now being presented as reimbursement of the electors' expenses. However, the arrangements were mutual from at least 1273, when the electors were bound to assist the monarch in upholding imperial governance. The Golden Bull consolidated the electors' corporate identity by giving them a common set of privileges, including the right of self-assembly and considerable judicial autonomy in their own lands, for which they now sought confirmation from each new monarch. Charles V's election occurred under substantially altered circumstances. Not only was he already king of Spain, but the electors had absorbed new ideas emerging from imperial reform and demonstrated a greater sense of collective responsibility. The resulting 'electoral agreement' (*Wahlkapitulation*) was printed and publicly disseminated, becoming the basis for all future ones. The other princes demanded the right to participate in negotiating agreements after the Westphalian settlement of 1648, while there were also calls to stabilize the constitution by fixing the terms. A draft 'permanent agreement' (*capitulation perpetua*) was published in July 1711, but was never ratified by any emperor and, in practice, the 1519 text continued to be revised at each election, notably in 1742.[38]

Coronations

All Frankish kings had held coronations since Pippin in 754, involving changing into royal robes, receiving the insignia, an anointing and being crowned.[39] Variations in this sequence and the precise handling of each stage assumed great significance as political statements, especially of prevailing imperial-papal relations. The procedure was fixed in written documents known as *Ordines*. Twenty of these survive, including the oldest and most significant, dating from about 960, which was revised in 1309 and incorporated into the Golden Bull, remaining in force for the last coronation in 1792.

Anointing by a senior cleric was invented in 754 for Pippin to bolster his legitimacy after he had deposed the Merovingians. The practice became a permanent feature through its inclusion by Leo III in the ceremony created for Charlemagne in 800.[40] Anointing combined elements of baptism, priestly ordination and Old Testament kingship, allowing it to be interpreted variously as a consecration or merely a blessing. It was certainly understood as transforming the new king from mere mortal to God's instrument. The association of anointing with the imperial coronation probably led to its disuse amongst the East Frankish kings in the later ninth century. Henry I famously rejected it in 919, allegedly out of modesty.[41] Nonetheless, it was a feature of German coronations after 936 as a visible demonstration of the church's support and contributed to the sacralization of the monarchy under the Salians. English kings adopted anointing in imitation of the Empire. Scottish kings petitioned the pope for the right to do this, but were refused.

Coronations were supposed to follow immediately after elections, but could be delayed if the electoral site was deemed inappropriate. This was a feature of the twelfth and thirteenth centuries when elections were often held quickly to overawe potential rivals. Aachen remained the favoured site for royal coronations, with imperial ones held in Rome: 25 of the 30 emperors were crowned in Rome from 800 to 1530, including two by anti-popes (1084, 1328) and two by papal legates during the Avignon papacy (1312, 1355). St Peter's was used, except when rioting compelled relocation to the Lateran (1133, 1312). One coronation took place in Reims (816) and one in Bologna (1530), as well as two in Aachen without papal involvement (Louis I, 813; Lothar I, 817). The Golden Bull confirmed Aachen as the German coronation site, with Frankfurt for elections and Nuremberg for assemblies. The last rule was largely ignored, but Aachen continued in use until Ferdinand I's coronation there as king of the Romans in 1531. The end to papal involvement led to Frankfurt being used for both election and coronation from 1562, except for Rudolf II, who was crowned king of the Romans in Regensburg in 1575.

Timing was particularly important for medieval imperial coronations, since these usually involved adult males who were already German king and so could plan the event in advance: 15 of the 30 coronations took place on important holy days, including six at Easter and four at Christmas. The end to separate imperial coronations after 1530 reduced the liturgical element, since their timing was dictated more by the deaths of previous emperors and prevailing political circumstances.

Medieval imperial coronations began with a procession to St Peter's, where the emperor would be greeted by Roman senators and clergy; in Germany, the senior archbishops assumed this role in royal and early modern imperial coronations. Mainz and Cologne disputed this right in Germany, because it implied the power to legitimize the king. The Golden Bull ruled that Mainz would preside over coronations in Frankfurt, while Cologne officiated in Aachen (see Plate 13). This rule was broken only once, in 1742, when Charles VII was crowned by his brother who was archbishop of Cologne, because the current archbishop of Mainz remained loyal to the Habsburgs.[42]

Inside the church, the king or emperor would kneel on a carpet during prayers. He would then advance and prostrate himself before the altar while the liturgy was sung. The act of standing up physically demonstrated his transformation from mortal to monarch. In Germany he would then be questioned by the presiding archbishop, providing space to articulate expectations of good kingship. The anointing then usually followed. Early kings may have appeared already wearing a crown, but from 800 for emperors and from the tenth century for kings coronation took place as part of the ceremony. The electors played a more prominent role at this point, especially from the thirteenth century, as they handed over the crown and insignia. The monarch then donned vestments, buckled on Charlemagne's sword, put on his ring, received the orb and sceptre, and was crowned. Since the twelfth century, monarchs also swore an oath on Charlemagne's Bible.

Enthronement sometimes preceded either anointing or coronation in the Frankish era, but generally occurred afterwards. Timing was less important than location. By the tenth century, it had become essential to sit on Charlemagne's stone throne in Aachen, which was now recognized as the 'arch-throne of the entire realm' (*totius regni archisolium*). Early modern coronations in Frankfurt used a replica. It became customary at this stage in proceedings to dispense rewards, including ennobling knights. A coronation banquet followed, symbolizing shared joy but also demarcating status amongst the participants through the seating arrangements. Urbanization of the coronation sites created a larger number of participants, who by the high Middle Ages enjoyed free food and fountains of wine as visible displays of royal munificence.

Protestant writers minimized the coronation as part of their efforts to desacralize the Empire by 1600. Nonetheless, the coronation retained meaning and was necessary to complete the process of succession. After 1530 it was only required once for each monarch – those who had already been crowned king of the Romans did not have a separate imperial coronation. Seventeenth-century coronations remained lavish, and even those in the Empire's last century remained grand affairs.[43] They also remained unique to the emperor. German princes assumed office without coronations, though they acquired some symbols of office and held homage ceremonies. The lavish Prussian coronation of 1701 was an exception that was not even repeated in the nineteenth century. Otherwise, only the Bohemian king was crowned, and the Habsburgs' virtual monopoly of this title after 1526 further underscored their distinct status within the Empire.

INSTRUMENTS OF RULE

Co-Kings

Governance remained personal rather than institutional for much of the Empire's existence. The emperor's most important assistants were those closest to him, above all his own relations. Co-kings emerged as a way of promoting stability by resolving doubt over the succession ahead of the monarch's own death, but they also served to spread the burden of rule without delegating power outside the immediate royal circle. Securing recognition of a son as co-king was a favoured way of safeguarding control of Germany ahead of a coronation expedition to Rome. Initially, the title co-emperor was used, but it required papal involvement and was dropped after 967 in favour of co-king, which could be assumed once agreement had been secured from the German lords (see Table 3).[44]

Thereafter, once they had been crowned emperor, fathers distinguished themselves by only seeking recognition of their sons as co-kings. Since imperial trumped royal authority, the position of co-king could become difficult, especially given wider expectations of kings as dynamic

Table 3. Co-Kings and Emperors

Individual	Father	Co-King	Co-Emperor	Own Reign	Rebellion
Louis I	Charlemagne	–	813–14	814–40	–
Lothar I	Louis I	–	817/823–40	840–55	830, 833–4
Lambert II	Lambert I	–	892–4	894–8	–
Otto II	Otto I	961–73	967–73	973–83	–
Otto III	Otto II	983	–	983–1002	–
Henry III	Conrad II	1028–39	–	1039–56	–
Conrad (III)	Henry IV	1087–98	–	–	1093–1101
Henry V	Henry IV	1099–1106	–	1106–25	1105–6
Henry (VI)	Conrad III	1147–50	–	–	–
Henry VI	Frederick I	1169–90	–	1190–97	–
Frederick II	Henry VI	1196–8	–	1212–50	–
Henry (VII)	Frederick II	1220–35	–	–	1234–5
Conrad IV	Frederick II	1237–50*	–	1250–54	–

*not crowned

individuals, rather than passive executors of someone else's instructions. Both Henry IV's sons became the focus of wider discontent, prompting them to challenge their father in revolts. Frederick II's son, known as Henry (VII), was particularly unfortunate; so much so that his regnal number appears in parentheses as his royal status was not considered when a later Henry became king in 1308. Henry (VII)'s father left him in charge of Germany while he was away in Italy and Jerusalem from 1220 to 1235, but still tried to micro-manage him through letters, undercutting his personal authority and exacerbating his task of managing the lords. Meanwhile, Frederick received complaints his son was exceeding his authority by ignoring previous royal legislation, including actions complicating the emperor's already troubled relationship with the papacy. Henry was pushed into a position of open revolt by the autumn of 1234, but his support collapsed as soon as his father returned and Henry was compelled to surrender. Now a political embarrassment, he was imprisoned and died falling from a horse while being moved between castles in February 1242; many believed he had committed suicide.[45] The last co-king emerged from an ingenious solution to the civil war following the 1314 double election: Louis IV accepted his rival Frederick 'the Fair' as titular king in 1325, but in return for unchallenged rule of the Empire.

Queens and Empresses

The Empire and France were medieval Europe's only two major states where female rule was not recognized, though its exercise elsewhere was also limited to only 20 reigning queens between 1100 and 1600.[46] All the Empire's rulers were married, and their female partners played important roles in imperial governance. Clerical pressure forced the Carolingians to accept that formalized marriage was necessary to legitimize birth and inheritance claims by the late ninth century. Louis I's first wife, Irmingard, was crowned queen by Pope Stephen IV in 816 and all official consorts appear to have been crowned thereafter. Ageltrude, wife of Guido of Spoleto, was the first to be crowned empress, in February 891. The coronation Ordines of 960 provided for female coronation, and Otto I's second wife, Adelaide, became the second crowned empress, in 962. The Salians continued this practice. Frederick III's wife, Eleonora of Portugal, was the last to be crowned in the same ceremony as her husband, in 1452, until the practice was revived for Matthias and Anna of Tirol in 1612, though that for the empress was now staged two days after the emperor's coronation.[47]

The relatively inferior status of early queens is illustrated by the way Louis II's wife Emma was titled *coniunx* (wife) and not *regina* (queen) prior to the last two decades of his reign. The title shifted to *Romanorum regina* by the late ninth century for queens, and *imperatrix augusta* if her husband had been crowned emperor. An association with promoting spirituality and the patronage of family nunneries contributed to this improving status.[48] However, wives still faced repudiation if they failed to produce a male heir or if remarriage became politically expedient. Senior male clergy tended to divide women into virtuous Esthers and wicked Jezebels, providing the language that was exploited by hostile aristocratic factions to charge queens with adultery in the hope of getting them replaced by one of their own kin.

Empress Adelaide was fundamental in securing both the status and political influence of future queens. She was the first to be titled 'royal consort' (*consors regni*) in a deliberate revival of ancient Roman practice, implying a political role.[49] Later chroniclers called her 'mother of the realm' (*mater regnorum*), and she was certainly crucial in securing support from the Italian lords to Otto I's accession in Italy. Adelaide was canonized in 1097, indicating the continued importance of royal women in promoting the sanctity, piety and virtue underpinning their husband's political legitimacy. This peaked with Henry II's wife Kunigunde, who, perhaps to compensate for the couple's lack of children, played a leading part in developing the imperial church and became a cult figure after her canonization in 1200.[50] Patronage of convents also allowed queens to maintain family *memoria* through prayers for deceased kings and kin.

Although they could not rule in their own name, wives could play political roles. At least three empresses presided as judges over sessions of the royal court, especially in Italy: Adelaide, Matilda of England and Richenza, wife of Lothar III of Supplinburg. Henry I's widow Matilda brokered truces within the royal family during Otto I's reign, while Otto's own first wife, Edith of Wessex, patched up a feud between her husband and mother-in-law. A king could listen to his wife's calming advice without losing face. Accepting it could be presented as being gracious rather than weak. Thus, female mediation was an important element in moderating violence, something that appears to have been replicated at lower levels of the elite. Queens frequently acted as intercessors, promoting petitions from kin, friends and others seeking royal favour. One-third of Henry II's diplomas record his wife's interventions. Other female relations performed similar tasks, extending the reach of the royal family, even into other countries. Otto I's sisters Gerberga and Hadwig married the rival claimants to the West Frankish throne, enabling the emperor to broker peace there. His eldest daughter Liudgard married Conrad the Red in 944, helping to consolidate Ottonian control of Lorraine.

Royal women possessed agency and did not always do the bidding of male relatives. Engelberge greatly influenced her husband, Emperor Louis II, in his attempts to extend imperial control to southern Italy in the 870s. Matilda's favouritism for her younger son Heinrich caused Otto I considerable trouble, while Adelaide sided with her extended kin against her own son, Otto II, until he temporarily exiled her to Burgundy in 978.[51] Agency was clearest during regencies, because these lacked formal rules, offering scope for forceful personalities to assert themselves. The trend towards hereditary rule under the Ottonians necessitated regencies, because Otto III and Henry IV were both under 12, the Frankish age of majority, when they succeeded their father.[52]

Otto III was only three when he was elected co-king in June 983, just six months ahead of his father's death in the wake of the catastrophic defeat at Cotrone and amidst the Slav uprising. In an age of warriors, many found the idea of a boy-king wholly unacceptable and Heinrich 'the Quarrelsome', duke of Bavaria, attracted some support when he declared himself king in 984. The Empire's integrity was saved by Otto's mother, Empress Theophanu, who, in so many ways, occupied an exceptional position (see Plate 22). Several of Otto II's advisors urged him to send her packing back to Byzantium when it was discovered on her arrival in 972 that she was only the niece rather than daughter of the Byzantine emperor.[53] Nonetheless, her imperial lineage and the fact that she arrived with her weight in gold as a dowry ensured her marriage to Otto II went ahead. She became the only consort to receive the title 'co-empress' (*coimperatrix augusta*), and it was envisaged she would succeed as sole ruler if Otto II died without a son.[54]

Without question, Theophanu's special status owed much to her own ability and force of character. She was aided by Archbishop

Willigis of Mainz, who used the crisis of 983 to extract concessions consolidating his see's premier status. Heinrich the Quarrelsome was soon isolated and obliged to back down, allowing Theophanu to direct affairs without ever formally assuming a title as regent. On the contrary, she issued documents in her own name whilst in Italy, dating them like a reigning monarch from the year of her own coronation in 972 and on one occasion using the male form *imperator augustus*.

This was the closest the Empire came to Byzantine-style female imperial rule. The contemporary response was mixed. Critics combined traditional misogyny with xenophobia, accusing Theophanu of spreading a craving for luxury amongst the Empire's female inhabitants. Thietmar of Merseburg and others praised her for restoring stability after Cotrone. Theophanu's interests were personal and she showed no sense of female solidarity with her mother-in-law, Adelaide, whom she tried to banish. Adelaide continued the regency from 991 to 994 after Theophanu's death, while Otto III's aunt Matilda acted as 'matriarch' (*matricia*), looking after Germany during his Roman expedition in 999.

The last female regency was less successful. Empress Agnes acted as regent for her six-year-old son Henry IV, but was more obviously dependent on male advisors, notably Bishop Heinrich II of Augsburg, who was rumoured to be her lover. She made important errors, but also took an unfair share of the blame, with the monks of Niederalteich dismissively recording that she, 'as is often the case with women, was easily swayed by the advice of all sorts of people'.[55] Her retirement into pious widowhood in November 1061 was ostensibly to atone for her mistakes, but it also allowed her to regain autonomy and she retained some influence until her son's formal majority in March 1065.

Gregorian misogyny increased hostility towards female power soon thereafter, but the prime reason why no future consorts played such roles was that the exercise of clearer elective monarchy ended the possibility of minorities. The Habsburgs still relied on female relations as governors of their various hereditary possessions during the sixteenth and early seventeenth centuries, while empresses acquired new status with the development of dynastic, representative courts.[56] The revisions to Habsburg inheritance law known as the Pragmatic Sanction allowed Maria Theresa to rule her family's hereditary possessions herself after 1740, though the dispute over these changes caused the War of the

Austrian Succession (1740–48) and temporarily deprived the Habsburgs of the imperial title. Female regencies were fairly common in the German principalities where, usually, a widowed mother would rule jointly with a male relation until her son achieved his majority. Although women were personally ineligible from attending the Reichstag, this practice effectively widened female political influence in the Empire considerably beyond the remaining convents still recognized as imperial Estates, such as Essen and Quedlinburg (whose abbesses were likewise disbarred from attending in person and were represented instead by a male envoy). Women were disbarred from citizenship in imperial cities on the grounds they could not bear arms, but those in the countryside could still stand in for sick or absent husbands in village assemblies, or in some cases represent a household themselves as widows. In terms simply of female access to power, this situation contrasted favourably with that in supposedly more progressive western Europe.[57]

Imperial Vicars and Counts Palatine

The case of female regencies opens the question of how far others could substitute for an absent emperor. The position of imperial vicar emerged to exercise authority during the king's absence (*absente rege*), especially for Germany during Roman expeditions. The term 'vicar' derived from the Latin *vicarius*, meaning 'second hand' and thus designating an assistant and not an ecclesiastical office (though the modern title 'vicar' also originated as a bishop's assistant). The position of co-king generally fulfilled this function into the thirteenth century, but after the problems with Henry (VII), Frederick II planned to appoint vicars for Germany. Richard of Cornwall deliberately appointed the archbishops of Cologne and Mainz and the Count Palatine as vicars during his absences to ensure this important post was not held by a single person.[58] Few subsequent kings left Germany for long periods, reducing the need to make such arrangements except for interregna following an emperor's death without a king of the Romans having been elected. The Golden Bull established that in such situations the elector of Saxony would exercise imperial authority in northern Germany, while the elector Palatine was responsible for the south. The requirement to complete an imperial election within four months of an emperor's death was overshot on several occasions, but it was not in the other electors' interests to allow their Saxon and Palatine colleagues too long as vicars. Only in 1657–8 and 1740–42 were there prolonged interregna, in both cases deliberately and through external interference.[59]

Imperial vicars were more common in Italy where a count was already appointed in Spoleto in 972 to oversee imperial interests during the emperor's absence. Others were appointed temporarily for all or part of Italy with powers to issue decrees, collect imperial revenue, name magistrates, and deal with disputes. The pope increasingly tried to usurp these powers, claiming the right to exercise a 'general vicariate' over Italy and Arles during imperial interregna. Since the papacy defined an 'interregnum' as the absence of an emperor rather than a German king, it felt fully entitled to these powers after 1250 and named its new ally Charles d'Anjou as vicar for ten years in 1268. Rudolf I already reasserted claims in 1281, even without being crowned emperor, and this stance was continued by Henry VII and Louis IV, who appointed imperial vicars for specific territories and cities.[60] The count of Savoy was made general vicar by Charles IV in 1372 and his successors claimed this position as a hereditary right after 1422.[61] Charles V entrusted the position to his son Philip II as duke of Milan in 1548, but an administrative error in the imperial arch-chancellery upheld Savoy's objections in 1582. Despite the wide remit, actual powers remained curtailed by the emperor's prerogatives as suzerain over all Italian imperial fiefs and by the practical presence of real Habsburg power in northern Italy.

The formal delegation of lesser imperial powers also remained quite restricted. The main figure was the count Palatine, literally 'count of the palace' (comes palatinus, Pfalzgraf), emerging from the position of palace mayor, the highest official at the royal palace in Aachen. Having themselves used this position to usurp the Merovingian throne (as would the Capetians later in France), the Carolingians limited its powers, which became associated with jurisdiction of a fairly large county on the Lower Rhine by 916. The Ezzonid family held the position from 1023 to 1095, but were displaced through conflict with the pugnacious Archbishop Anno II of Cologne to the Middle Rhine during the 1060s, forming the basis of the later territory known as the Lower Palatinate.[62] Palatine powers included the ability to legitimize births and make other changes of status short of ennoblement. Such powers were increasingly also granted to other princes, for example Schwarzburg-Sondershausen in 1697. Nonetheless, the original count Palatine retained sufficient prestige to acquire both electoral status and the powers of imperial vicar in 1356.

The Royal Court and Arch-Chancellery

The itinerant character of imperial rule inhibited the growth of a fixed, institutionalized court to match that of the Byzantine emperor, which numbered 2,000 courtiers in the eleventh century. Nonetheless, the emperor's mobile entourage was both large and impressive, numbering 3,000–4,000 people, including servants and soldiers, during the Salian and Staufer eras.[63] Two primary functions already emerged under the Carolingians. One was the permanent, though itinerant, royal household charged with feeding, clothing and sheltering the king and his entourage. The second was an intermittent advisory role, which in turn divided into a confidential *curia minor* of trusted individuals and a wider *curia major* of larger assemblies of lords. Neither was institutionalized prior to the very late Middle Ages.

The boundaries between both advisory meetings and the royal household remained blurred, because assemblies required the king's presence. The ceremonial roles assigned lords at assemblies and coronation banquets were marks of favour and one-way participants could 'read' in them the current political balance. As part of the gradual transition from a culture of personal presence to more formalized political practice, these positions became fixed as the arch-offices associated with secular electoral titles. The Bohemian king was already distinguished as the arch-cupbearer (*Erzschenk*) around 1290, while the other titles were fixed by 1356: arch-steward (count Palatine), arch-marshal (Saxony), arch-chamberlain (Brandenburg).

The ecclesiastical electors were distinguished as imperial arch-chancellors. The arch-chancellery was the only permanent central administrative institution prior to early modernity, owing its origins to the notaries employed by Charles Martel to look after his documents. Louis I entrusted oversight of this to his arch-chaplain (*Archicapel-lanus*) in charge of his court chapel, which travelled with him, distinct from the clergy serving the royal palaces.[64] In the German kingdom Mainz secured control of both the chapel and chancellery, retaining the latter when the former was delegated to a more junior *capellarius* in 1040. Various senior clergy were appointed chancellors of Italy after 1012, though the post was eventually permanently associated with Cologne, despite the decline of actual business after the mid-thirteenth century. A Burgundian chancellery was established in 1042, initially under local archbishops before being transferred as an arch-office to Trier.

Only the Mainz chancellery developed as a functioning administrative body. It remained central to the city's political prestige and provided the basis for new functions during the late fifteenth century: chairmanship of the Reichstag, management of the imperial archive, and appointment of the secretariat servicing the Reichskammergericht.[65]

Written Culture

The relationship of writing to imperial governance is controversial, because written laws, instructions and other documents have long assumed hallowed status in historical scholarship as totems of political progress. They offer the most accessible route into the past and have proved especially attractive for historians living in an age dominated by formalized procedures. Surviving Carolingian administrative documents known as *capitularia* appear to present a command-style monarchy operating through a clear, hierarchical institutional structure in which lesser officials were closely supervised and required to submit regular written reports. The *capitulare de villis* of 771, for instance, specifies how royal lands are to be run and orders stewards to provide inventories of assets and revenue streams.[66] This has led to some extravagant claims for the Carolingians as conscious state-builders with a coherent grand strategy, allegedly capable of mobilizing 100,000 troops from a population of 20 million.[67]

There was certainly a surge in writing: 7,000 manuscripts survive across continental Europe from the ninth century, compared to 1,800 for the previous eight centuries combined.[68] Many of these documents are religious commentaries or chronicles. The primary use of writing prior to the twelfth century was to convey religious truth.[69] Even the most literate section of society, the clergy, did not possess a fully written administrative culture at this point. Writing itself lacked social prestige compared to martial prowess, horsemanship and other physical activities, as the earlier discussion of kingly virtues has illus-trated. Charlemagne issued only around 80 *capitularia* across his reign and they are largely absent from both the era before 780 and after 820, though there is some evidence that established administrative routines continued into the early tenth century.[70]

Regardless of the exact extent of written culture, it is unreasonable to expect that Charlemagne's subjects obeyed his sparse commands more completely than the Empire's inhabitants during the much better documented period after the fourteenth century, when it is clear that written official rules were often ignored or misunderstood by their intended recipients, or even unknown to them. Early modern authori-ties had to repeatedly issue the same instructions and often tolerated high levels of non-compliance on less important matters just to ensure the really serious ones were followed. Byzantium was far larger and enjoyed a continuous existence since late antiquity, but even its army was nominally 120,000 in the ninth and tenth centuries, of which no more than 12,000 could usually be concentrated in any one place.[71] Extrapolation of army size based on population estimates, or through calculating the number of men required to encircle the known extent of early medieval towns, are all highly speculative methods. The claims made for Carolingian capacity and efficiency would make even nineteenth-century German statesmen and generals 'green with envy'.[72]

The exaggeration of Carolingian capacity sharpens the contrast with the more unlettered Ottonian era, thereby contributing to the gen-eral sense of the Empire in terminal decline. If Carolingian structures derived directly from late antiquity and were as effective as has been claimed, one would have expected them to have easily survived the civil wars of the mid-ninth century, which pale in comparison with those of third- and fourth-century Rome.

The preceding suggests that Carolingian governance was probably already more like that of the Ottonians in relying heavily on personal presence, rituals and consensus. A more plausible estimate for Carolin-gian capacity is that a large army was around 5,000–12,000 warriors, providing less of a contrast with the 2,000–8,000 that the Ottonians could usually muster.[73] Practical difficulties of movement and supply inhibited large troop concentrations for long periods. A royal army would be composed from the king's own retinue and those of his lords who were close allies or who had answered his summons. The king's force would be supplemented by contingents provided by the lesser lords and communities of the immediate area where it was operating. Larger numbers of less-experienced and poorly trained men could be summoned locally for specific tasks, especially if major sieges were undertaken. These numbers grew largely thanks to the rise in population and production across the eleventh century. Frederick I's army on the Third Crusade in 1190 was considered huge by contemporaries; it probably numbered 15,000 including 3,000 knights – still far short of the hundreds of thousands some chroniclers claimed.[74]

It is unlikely that Ottonian commanders needed to read transcriptions of late Roman military manuals in order to know how to fight; their Slavic and Magyar opponents certainly did not, yet were frequently successful. It is highly speculative to blame Ottonian defeats on supposed failure to follow such advice, while attributing successes to allegedly having done so. Later graduates of European military academies could make elementary mistakes, despite their formal training. In addition to oral tradition and actual experience, tasks like economic management and the self-confidence that generally comes with elevated social status would all have prepared Ottonian nobles for command.[75] In short, change across the period from 800 to 1100 was by degrees rather than absolute. Written culture may have contracted around 900, but had never been widespread, while the level of contraction itself has been exaggerated.[76]

Few written documents were intended as universal laws. General laws were already considered fixed by moral and religious absolutes that could not be altered by mortals. Most documents issued in the name of German kings before early modernity were charters (*Urkunden*) regulating local, specific circumstances, and are better understood as 'privileges' rather than 'laws'. They illustrate how much royal activity was reactive, rather than planned: charters were usually issued at the request of their recipient. Written documentation had yet to assume precedence over other forms of legitimation like custom. Except for intellectual exchanges between scholars, during the Middle Ages most letters were destroyed after they had been read, in contrast to early modernity, when even mundane items such as bills and receipts were often preserved. When Frederick I wanted to know how to greet Pope Hadrian IV in 1155, he asked the oldest princes in his camp who had been present at the last imperial-papal meeting 22 years earlier. Their recollections carried equal weight with formal recorded protocols.[77] The relatively low volume of paperwork reduced the potential for conflict by making inconsistencies between claims and practice less obvious.

The Empire did not match the papacy's use of writing to document claims and extend influence; the papal chancery issued ten times as many documents as its imperial equivalent during the first half of the fourteenth century. Princely and civic representatives began keeping diaries of their negotiations at royal assemblies from the 1380s, and the practice became widespread by the 1420s when the imperial arch-chancellery was also maintaining an official transcript (see Plate 24). Written communication surged from the early fifteenth century, with the chancellery's output supplemented by additional letters sent directly by the emperor (see Table 4). Whereas only four personal letters survive for Henry III in the mid-eleventh century, Ruprecht in the early fifteenth sent 400 just to Frankfurt, Nuremberg, Cologne and Strasbourg. The transition to written culture was completed in the mid-sixteenth century under Charles V, who sent and received at least 120,000 letters, in addition to the vast number crossing his officials' desks.[78]

The Imperial Chancellery

The expanding paperwork necessitated the development of an imperial chancellery (*Reichskanzlei*) separate from the arch-office held by Mainz. Some kind of archive existed from at least the Salian era and continued under the Staufers, who likewise employed successive bishops of Speyer to oversee it. Speyer officials handled the actual paperwork, a further indication of the medieval Empire's reliance on the imperial church. They provided continuity into the later fifteenth century, with only a partial change of personnel under the later Luxembourgs, who enjoyed the additional services of the Bohemian royal chancellery. The original archive remained with Wenzel after his formal deposition in 1400, forcing his rival Ruprecht to develop a new one, but still relying on the bishop of Speyer and his staff. The new chancellery and some of its staff passed to Sigismund in 1410, indicating that the lack of dynastic continuity from 1254 to 1437 did not prevent the growth of an institutional memory.[79]

Sigismund's papers passed to Albert II in 1438 to form the basis of

Table 4. The Growth of Writing in Imperial Governance

Monarch	Timeframe	Documents and Charters	Annual Average
Charlemagne	768–814	100*	2
Louis I	814–40	500	19
Louis II	843–76	170	5
Charles II	843–77	500	15
Charles III	876–87	170	15
Otto I	962–73	200	18
Otto II	973–83	320	32
Otto III	983–96**	200	15
Henry II	1002–24	509	23
Conrad II	1024–39	245	16
Henry III	1039–56	351	21
Henry IV	1056–1106	550	11
Lothar III	1125–37	131	11
Frederick II	1196–1250	2,000+	37
Rudolf I	1273–91	2,500	139
Louis IV	1314–46	2,500	87
Charles IV	1346–76	10,000	313
Wenzel	1376–1400	3,200+	146
Ruprecht	1400–1410	4,800	480
Sigismund	1410–37	12,400	469
Albert II	1438–9++	413	310
Frederick III	1440–93	50,000	943
Maximilian I	1493–1519	100,000	3,846

*excluding 170 forgeries attributed to him

**The figures in the table refer to the period in which each monarch's documents have been counted. For most cases it is the entire reign, but for Otto III only the first 13 years.

+upper estimate

++16 months

the Habsburg imperial court chancellery (*Reichshofkanzlei*), run by the imperial vice chancellor, whose appointment had depended since 1356 on Mainz as arch-chancellor. In practice, the vice chancellor was a Habsburg official overseeing communication between the dynasty and the Empire. The actual business was channelled through the Reichshofrat, the second imperial supreme court, established in 1497 for this purpose as well as safeguarding imperial feudal prerogatives. Administration of the Habsburgs' hereditary possessions was detached to separate institutions during the 1520s, while the imperial court chancellery re-emerged as a distinct body in 1559 when the Reichshofrat was reorganized as a purely judicial court. These changes created a tripartite split: the Habsburgs separated administration of their own lands from the task of communicating with the Empire, while Mainz ran the separate imperial chancellery handling the paperwork associated with the Empire's common institutions, chiefly the Reichstag.[80]

The position of the imperial court chancellery remained ambiguous, since it was both a Habsburg and an imperial institution. Much depended on how far the vice chancellor was willing to subordinate himself to Habsburg interests. Most vice chancellors were senior aristocrats closely connected to the Habsburg court. They increasingly became the dynasty's expert advisors on imperial politics, reducing the imperial court chancellery to a clearing house for other Habsburg officials' correspondence with imperial Estates. Joseph II repeatedly tried to exclude any remaining Mainz influence after 1767, and while the archbishop successfully defended his formal privileges, the episode merely contributed to the alienation of the Habsburg government from the imperial church around 1800.[81]

RESOURCES

Key Characteristics in the Empire

Central financial institutions only emerged in the Empire around 1490 and looked very different from those in other European monarchies (see pp. 397–8). The general pattern in Europe was a shift from 'private' to 'public' finance as kings persuaded their subjects that their own resources were insufficient to meet rising expectations of royal governance. The king increasingly drew on his subjects' private means to finance 'public' purposes. The usual mechanism was some kind of representative assembly through which taxes were negotiated and legitimated.[82]

There are complex reasons why the Empire did not follow this path, the most significant of which was that the methods of resource mobilization established around 800 enabled it to meet the expectations of governance until well into the thirteenth century. Pressures for change emerged only slowly during the later thirteenth century, primarily through internal competition for control of the German crown. This changed how individual territories were governed, but impacted less on how resources were mobilized for common purposes. Major alterations only became necessary to meet new, external threats towards the end of the fifteenth century. Unlike the earlier competition for the crown, external dangers were recognized as common, and so legitimated broader changes in the overall imperial structure. The timing of this was important, because it occurred long after the Empire had begun to evolve as a more clearly delineated status hierarchy. Thus, the development of fiscal institutions reinforced the Empire as a mixed monarchy, rather than promoting the kind of centralization characterizing western European states.

For much of the Middle Ages men, consumables and services were all more useful than cash. The Carolingians levied annual general taxes on all free men, who paid in local produce or high-value items like fur pelts or honey, as well as in coin. Other occasional levies were raised for specific purposes, such as aiding Christians in the Holy Land. The Carolingians and Ottonians also extracted tribute from the Slavs. Louis II 'the German' received tribute worth at least 170 pounds in silver annually, enough to equip 68 mounted warriors.[83] Cash was imperishable and relatively portable, but always had to be converted into what was really needed (warriors, supplies, etc.) and which could not always be purchased easily when required. Thus, resource mobilization in the Empire involved developing legally enforceable claims to specific kinds of aid, rather than the fiscal institutions that feature so prominently in conventional accounts of European 'state-building'. The combination of assistance secured through legally enforceable obligations and direct extraction from the emperor's own possessions proved sufficient to sustain imperial rule so that both the limited taxation of the Carolingian era and the tribute along the eastern frontier could be allowed to lapse when their collection proved difficult.

The Carolingians created the basic framework for extraction by establishing different kinds of jurisdiction over land, material assets and people. Royal power was never solely limited to crown lands, and always extended over the entirety of the Empire. However, the monarch's ability to draw support from other areas was filtered through the different jurisdictions. The royal domain (*dominium*) encompassed possessions reserved to sustain the king's family and only ever accounted for a relatively small proportion of the total area. The bulk of the Empire was granted as benefices (*beneficia*), which remained royal possessions but were entrusted to dependants initially called both *fideles* (faithful) and *vassi*, the origins of the term 'vassal'. The later German word *Lehen* is usually translated as 'fief', but is also cognate with the English 'loan', which more easily conveys the original relationship. The system allowed the Carolingians and their successors to dispense with the need to raise taxes, which would have required permanent institutions and a large number of officials. Instead, beneficiaries used the resources from their fief directly to sustain themselves and carry out tasks on behalf of the monarch. This method was ideally suited for an economy where coins were not yet the principal means of exchange, since beneficiaries could draw resources directly in kind.

Allodial property comprised the private assets of the pre-Frankish elite as far as they had survived, plus that granted to or acquired by Carolingian lords, including the royal family. Contemporaries distinguished between royal allodial lands and domains, but historians disagree whether this had any practical significance prior to the eleventh century.[84] The Ottonians' extinction in 1024 raised the fate of their family possessions separate from the domains that were now associated with an enduring monarchy. This distinction became clearer in the transition from the Salians in 1125 when Lothar III fought the Staufers as private heirs to Henry V's personal possessions. Thereafter, family property was treated separately as hereditary dynastic assets separate from crown domains associated with the royal title. The same occurred with benefices, which were initially often assigned to lords who lacked private property in the same area, but frequently acquired it during their tenure as fief-holder. Possession of a fief by two or more generations of the same family swiftly encouraged ideas of hereditary ownership. Periodic royal efforts to stem or reverse this trend triggered relatively rare but nonetheless quite violent disputes with recalcitrant lords, as we shall see.

Feudalism

The distinctions between domains, benefices and allodial property remained fluid into the thirteenth century, because it was often not clear how individuals had acquired particular manors and other assets. The greater use of written documentation to record possession inevitably encouraged sharper distinctions and more coherent and exclusive concepts of personal property. Crucially, this occurred during the change from transpersonal kingship to enduring Empire. The exact nature of this process remains hotly debated.[85]

The root problem is semantics: a wide variety of terms were used well before they were defined in legal treatises in the twelfth century. The process of definition undoubtedly changed their meaning and use, complicating the interpretation of earlier evidence. The situation for the Empire was exacerbated by the excessive romanticization of the Germanic past, which reached new heights under the Nazis. Writing in the 1930s, Theodor Mayer presented the Empire as a *Personenverbandstaat*, or a state formed by ties of personal allegiance. This term proved very influential, yet it rested on imposing quite narrow and often anachronistic definitions on earlier medieval terms.[86] Mayer's model suggested the early Empire was organized with the king as leader of free warriors bound in personal allegiance. Finally, anglophone historiography brings its own problems, because the term 'feudalism' has been overloaded with other anachronistic interpretations implying a conscious system.[87] Variations were *part* of the reality, not aberrant discrepancies within an otherwise coherent system. Local arrangements were negotiated according to immediate needs. Renegotiation could involve exemptions and changes to the level of burdens associated with fief-holding.

Some viable generalizations can be made. Relations between monarch and fief-holders were always asymmetrical, based on reciprocity and constituting a form of vassalage that became more clearly defined as 'feudal' during the twelfth century (see pp. 356–65). Both parties were free men until the emergence of the ministeriales as a new group of unfree vassals in the eleventh century. Throughout, relations involved questions of loyalty and trust, because they were mediated primarily through oral rather than written agreements. General rules were not fully codified until early modernity. The Carolingians and Ottonians used the term *honores* for both benefice and the function associated with it.[88]

Vassalage could emerge from below as 'commendation' whereby a free man placed himself subordinate to a superior lord in return for 'protection and guardianship' (*Schütz und Schirm*). It could also come from being entrusted with a benefice to carry out a specific task. A sharper articulation of rights and responsibilities around the mid-twelfth century clarified this act as 'enfeoffment'. The term 'benefice' was simultaneously displaced by 'fief' (*feodum*).

Vassalage always included rights for the subordinate, especially excluding 'servile duties' (*opera servilia*) like manual labour, which remained a characteristic of the unfree population. Instead, vassals were expected to serve in 'word and deed' (*consilium et auxilium*). The former encompassed constructive advice, while the latter was understood primarily as military service and was driven by the introduction of the armoured cavalryman as a distinguishing feature of Carolingian warfare. The necessary equipment exceeded the resources of most free men, requiring assets to be grouped as benefices to sustain an elite of armoured knights. Although Carolingian and Ottonian lords expected royal campaigns to secure plunder, all accepted that benefice-holding would cover most of the costs of service. This freed the king from having to pay his army. Service was not fixed, but a period of six weeks became customary. Longer campaigns, like Roman expeditions, were restricted to exceptional circumstances agreed in advance at an assembly. The distribution of rich benefices to the imperial church resulted in this providing a substantial part of most emperors' forces: 15 bishops accompanied Otto II's ill-fated Italian campaign in 981–2, while twelfth-century archbishops could bring up to 1,700 troops, with 200 to 400 being the average size of an episcopal contingent.[89] Other duties could be expected, especially if these were tied to a particular benefice; for example, garrisoning castles or guarding frontier marches. Senior lords were also expected to attend the royal court, assist in passing judgements, uphold the law and provide advice. Failure to perform duties opened the culprit to charges of 'felony' (*felonia*), providing grounds for the king to escheat the fief (see pp. 613–17).

Vassalage already extended to chains of three of more lords and vassals by 800. A Carolingian capitulary of 799 allowed the church to assign its property as benefices to lay subvassals to circumvent the canon law restriction on clergy serving as warriors. Longer hierarchies benefited the king by creating denser networks capable of mobilizing more men. The trend to hereditary possession was already obvious and could be deliberately granted as an inducement. For example, Charles II 'the Bald' allowed those accompanying his Roman expedition of 877 to bequeath their benefices to their heirs. Hereditary possession could aid the king by stabilizing arrangements and giving benefice-holders greater incentive to promote economic development.

The rituals of vassalage changed in line with the shift from benefice to fief, but always remained personal even after written codification. Homage (Latin *homagium*, German *Huld*) was the more solemn ceremony in which the vassal became the 'man' of his lord; hence the derivation of 'homage' from the Latin *homo* for man. Homage had to be performed in person and was often tied to land or services. Fealty (*fidelitas*) was an expression of personal allegiance, which could be sworn in person or by proxy. Both types involved personal oaths, which played a prominent part in medieval political culture. The vassal 'commended' himself by placing his hands inside those of his lord. The solemn oath accompanying this 'joining hands' was sworn on a holy object, such as the portable imperial cross accompanying the king on his royal progress. 'Defiance' meant literally renouncing fidelity. Those doing so lost entitlement to their lord's protection and opened themselves to his punishment, including being deprived of their lands and offices.

Initially, the oath preceded investiture, which involved the lord handing the vassal an object symbolizing both the benefice and the vassal's status in a wider hierarchy. The Ottonians introduced the practice of handing over a flag to senior lords, which ritual came to characterize duchies, margraviates, counties palatine and landgraviates collectively as 'flag fiefs' (*Fahnenlehen*). Other objects included sceptres, swords, lances, gloves and even twigs.[90] The Salians' problems with the papacy led investiture to precede the oath under the Staufers, while the whole process came to be considered enfeoffment.

In line with its personal character, vassalage ended in the event of *Herren- und Mannfall*. At the death of a lord (*Herr*), all vassals were required to seek renewal of service from his successor, while the death of a vassal (*Mann*) obliged his heirs to request a fresh enfeoffment.[91] These requirements persisted after the Staufers formally accepted secular fiefs as hereditary. Hereditary fiefs meant that the king could not refuse to enfeoff a legitimate, able-bodied heir, but renewal was still required for the successor to exercise any rights or functions associated with the fief. Lordly families could choose one of their members as legitimate heir. This still required royal endorsement in the case of immediate imperial fiefs, creating additional opportunities for the king to intervene as arbiter of inheritance disputes.

Crown and Imperial Lands

Virtually any kind of property or right could be held as royal domains, fiefs or allodial possessions. Royal domains originally consisted of fairly extensive farmland worked largely by slave labour, as well as mills, fishponds and vast tracts of thinly populated forest reserved for hunting, notably the Dreieich Forest by Frankfurt and the Ardennes near Aachen.[92] These possessions were not managed through centrally planned extraction. Most of the produce was perishable, bulky or both. It was difficult to transport across a kingdom that even an unencumbered rider required a month to cross. Much was consumed locally, just maintaining the producers and those who administered individual assets like palaces. Some produce might be concentrated regionally, for example to support a military campaign. However, the main purpose was to feed the royal entourage on its endless tours of the realm.

It seems likely that the Merovingian monarchy was already partially itinerant and while the Carolingians had favoured sites, they never stayed at them for long. Royal progresses were common in medieval Europe, but itinerant monarchy became a distinguishing feature of the Empire, persisting long after other European kings had largely settled down, and in stark contrast to the self-exclusion of the Chinese emperor in his Forbidden City. The ability to travel extensively distinguished the king from his lords, since he alone could freely move throughout the entire realm.[93] Others would have to pay their way, unless they had strategically placed relations, and could find that prolonged absence weakened their local authority. The practice of royal progress continued well beyond the mid-thirteenth century, but gradually lost its significance as the formalization of elective monarchy by 1356 lessened each new king's need to show himself to lords absent at his accession. The institutionalization of assemblies in the form of the Reichstag by the late fifteenth century also provided a convenient way to meet everyone at once, while the parallel move to territorially based imperial governance established a new focus in the capital of the imperial family's hereditary lands.

The needs of itinerant monarchy dictated the extent and location of royal domains, which needed to be scattered to provide sustenance and accommodation along major routes and in areas of political and strategic significance. The Carolingians and Ottonians preferred travelling by river or lakes, given the lack of all-weather roads north of the Alps. Charlemagne had 25 major and 125 minor palaces sustained by 700 different royal estates (Map 14). Most of these were on or close to the Rhine, Main, Danube, Saale and Elbe.[94]

Aachen was the most important palace (*palatium*, *Pfalz*), used since the 760s as a winter residence because of its thermal springs. Other important sites included Cologne, Trier, Mainz, Worms, Strasbourg, Ingelheim and Frankfurt. Paderborn provided a base in Saxony, while Regensburg served the same purpose in Bavaria. Konstanz and Reichenau on an island in the same lake were key staging posts between Italy and Germany. These locations remained significant into the later Middle Ages. Subsequent royal lines added further sites around their own family properties. The Ottonians developed Magdeburg, Quedlinburg and Merseburg in the Elbe–Saale region. The Salians added Speyer near their own base on the Middle Rhine, but also Goslar in the rich mining region of the Harz in northern Germany.[95] Chapels were already present in Carolingian palaces, but the Ottonians developed closer connections between royal residences and religious sites, favouring royal abbeys and major cathedrals.

Most palaces were unfortified, except those near frontiers. There was no standard design, but the royal apartments were in an imposing building containing a great hall and chapel, while stables, servants' accommodation and storehouses completed the complex. Aachen became the model for Magdeburg and Goslar as the Ottonians and Salians stressed continuity with the Carolingians. The later Carolingians began fortifying palaces, and already allowed other lords to protect their own residences from the 870s, especially if these were in frontier areas or along rivers vulnerable to Viking raids. Fortifications generally consisted of wooded palisades, sometimes atop a hill (*Motte*). Henry IV broke tradition by embarking on extensive castle-building to assert tighter control over royal domains in the former Ottonian heartland of Saxony, which risked becoming a 'distant' region with the transition to Salian rule in 1024. Using new wealth and manpower from economic and demographic growth, Henry IV constructed at least eight stone castles perched on rocky crags. The most powerful was the Harzburg, built after 1067 on a high hill south-east of Goslar, only approachable along a narrow path. Unlike earlier fortifications that had been intended as refuges for the surrounding population, Henrician castles were only large enough to accommodate a royal garrison intended to dominate the surrounding area.

The Carolingians had already created a special jurisdiction called a *Burgwerk* surrounding fortifications, which allowed the commandant to draw the resources and labour required to construct and maintain defences. Similar rights were attached to palaces, but were also granted to bishops and abbots so they had the means to develop their churches. Henrician castles were held by the unfree vassals known as ministeriales. By the thirteenth century, castle commanders were called 'castellans' (*Burgmänner*) and were usually endowed with a fief sustaining themselves and their garrison of between 30 and 50 men.[96] These developments promoted the emergence of knights as a distinct group of vassals who were considered the lower echelon of the nobles.

The transfer of fiefs to support castellans was just part of a wider redistribution of resources under revised relationships throughout the Middle Ages. The Carolingians had already endowed monasteries and abbeys with additional royal assets, and the Ottonians extended this to enhance the ability of crown vassals to meet demands for royal service (*servitium regis*). The practice peaked under the Salians, who added few palaces, preferring instead to stay with abbots and bishops.[97] The difficulties created by repeated clashes with the papacy prompted the Staufers to promote imperial cities as alternative accommodation on crown domains (see pp. 505–7).

Resources were earmarked as *Tafelgüter*, literally 'table properties', supplying food and other consumables to sustain the royal court when it stayed in the associated palace, abbey or city. A rare surviving list from 968 records just one day's requirements: 1,000 pigs and sheep, 8 oxen, 10 barrels of wine, 1,000 bushels of grain, plus chickens, fish, eggs and vegetables. Information from the better-documented Staufer era indicates that an army of 4,800 troops needed 8,400 baggage attendants, 19,000 horses, mules and oxen pulling 500 wagons, together consuming 2.4 tons of food and 57 tons of fodder daily.[98]

The royal prerogatives included the right to *fodrum regis*, obliging communities to supply fodder, and to *Gistum* (hospitality). Various other rights existed, though their terms are not always clear. *Fodrum regis* retained its original meaning north of the Alps, but by the late Middle Ages meant accommodating the king in Italy where a separate term (*albergaria*) emerged by the eleventh century to denote obligations to house royal servants and troops.[99] Non-material services could also be required, as indicated by Henry V's charter removing legal and fiscal obligations from Speyer's inhabitants in 1111 in return for their performance of an annual mass to commemorate his father buried in the cathedral.[100] Royal service was commuted into cash in Italy during the eleventh century in a process that had become general across the Empire by the thirteenth century. As we shall see, however, indirect control of the Empire through vassalage remained the most important means of governance into early modernity, while the role of royal domains was taken by more extensive hereditary possessions directly held by the ruling dynasty.

FROM CONSENSUS TO COMMAND MONARCHY

Dukes and Counts

It is helpful to start our chronological examination of imperial governance by outlining the three main stages in development. The first three royal lines tried to control the Empire through a relatively flat hierarchy of functionaries bound to them through vassalage. Management of these vassals required constant personal engagement and was a major priority. Managerial style moved from a more consensual approach, most pronounced under the Ottonians, to a command style that reached its limits in the Salian period under Henry IV.

The Staufers' accession initiated a second stage around the mid-twelfth century based on revising relations to vassals along more obviously 'feudal' lines enshrined in general charters. This entailed the definitive acceptance of hereditary fief-holding, but also the deliberate fragmentation of the previously fairly large fiefs to create a larger, more hierarchically structured lordly hierarchy now headed by a princely elite. This hierarchy continued to evolve after the Staufers' demise around 1250 as jurisdictions gradually became more clearly delineated and territorially bounded. A fundamental division emerged between those holding full imperial fiefs immediately subject to the emperor, and lesser lords holding minor jurisdictions within these fiefs as vassals of at least one other layer of feudal authority between themselves and the monarch. Adapting imperial governance to these new conditions was delayed by the fact that all the realistic contenders to replace the Staufers were evenly matched materially and politically. The third stage opened as the Luxembourgs increasingly based imperial governance on extensive fiefs held as hereditary dynastic possessions rather than royal domains. This section explores the first of these stages, while the next two chapters examine the others in turn.

The Carolingians established the Empire's basic internal political structure by combining elements of their existing practice with those adapted from the Lombards and Germans they had defeated. Their principal achievement was to convert the political capital garnered from three generations of successful conquests into a revised relationship with their senior lords who had been only loosely subordinated to the Merovingian kings. The lords were now distinguished through their appointment to public offices, which assumed new prestige through the consolidation of the Frankish realm as the Empire.[101] Two parallel, partially overlapping secular and ecclesiastical hierarchies emerged; the latter was headed by archbishops and bishops endowed with benefices and collectively forming the imperial church already discussed in Chapter 2 (Maps 1 and 13).

The secular hierarchy comprised dukes and counts. The exact character of the early duchies remains controversial. The most likely conclusion is that the Carolingians initially distinguished between the title and function of 'duke' (*dux*) bestowed by the king, and the title and status of 'prince' (*princeps*), or tribal leader. The latter position only existed in recently conquered areas, especially Saxony, Bavaria, and, to an extent, Swabia, Lorraine and Lombard southern Italy. Princely power derived from below through recognition by lesser lords within the 'tribal' region. As with royal succession, contemporaries did not distinguish clearly between election and hereditary right. Kings affirmed 'electoral' rights in these regions into the eleventh century to curb the trend towards hereditary rule, which had, in practice, already become entrenched during the tenth century, notably in Saxony where the Billung family held sway from 961 to 1106.[102]

Ducal authority entailed military command, thereby providing the origins of the German word for duke (*Herzog*), as well as supervision of the counts. As with the royal selection of bishops, it is not clear how far the appointment of dukes was a free choice. Ducal titles appear to have been given to Saxon, Bavarian and Lombard princes to integrate them within Carolingian governance. Tribal structures were eroded through intermarriage and the transfer of land and influence across a broader elite. The title of 'duke' supplanted that of 'prince', which disappeared around 920, except in southern Italy, where it survived for another century. The attitude of local lords influenced the royal choice, not least because ducal authority was impossible to exercise without their cooperation. Developments across the tenth and eleventh centuries saw ducal positions fluctuate between royal appointments and hereditary possessions, with the overall trend in favour of the latter. Hereditary possession entailed the right to pass the title to a chosen successor, reducing the role of the king from one of appointment to confirmation, but this change was only possible through its parallel acceptance by the lesser lords. It should be remembered that for most of the Middle Ages what was being held hereditarily was a *title* and its associated functions and jurisdictions, and not a *territory* in the sense of a distinct area and its inhabitants.

There were only four duchies in the ninth-century German kingdom (Bavaria, Franconia, Swabia, Saxony), to which Lorraine was added in the early tenth century. Lorraine was divided into two in 959, while Carinthia was carved out of south-east Bavaria in 976. Burgundy contained no duchies, though its southern and western sections eventually acquired equivalent status as they broke away (Map 3). Likewise, ducal structures proved transitory in Italy prior to the thirteenth century (see pp. 187–94).

By contrast, there were perhaps 600–700 counties across the entire Frankish realm in the year 800, of which 400 were north of the Alps. Those west of the Rhine were created as secular subdivisions of a diocese and were called *pagi*, the origins of the French word *pays* (country).[103] Counties varied in size and were not fixed either in shape or numbers. The title 'count' (*comes*) literally meant the king's companion. Counts remained 'free', directly subject to the emperor, though they owed certain obligations to the dukes. Their main task was to maintain peace and uphold justice in cases of more serious crimes. Those in frontier areas had additional military functions as margraves, or marcher lords (see pp. 186–9 and 200–202). Counties were subdivided into 'hundreds' (*centenariae*) or 'vicarages' (*vicariae*), though neither these nor their associated subordinate officials seem to have survived for long. Charlemagne used emissaries (*missi*) to inspect counties and receive reports. Important missions were entrusted to pairs of bishops and counts. Neither of these control mechanisms survived for long into the ninth century, when monarchs instead relied on trusted abbots and bishops to undertake specific missions as required.

The distinction between function and person was never clear, and these figures should not be confused with modern civil servants. The king named them, but could do little to shape the pool of those considered worthy to hold these titles. There were no training schools prior to the development of the court chapel, which only performed this function for the imperial church. All relied on subvassals rather than salaried staffs. Local knowledge and connections were valued and they discouraged kings from rotating men from one post to another.

Seeking Consensus

Success under these conditions depended on securing acceptance and support for royal policies. Royal assemblies provided the main mechanism to achieve this. These had echoes of the much earlier Germanic tribal gatherings (*Thing*) of free warriors, but by 755 among the Franks they were fairly exclusive affairs meeting under a variety of labels: *placitum*, *synodus*, *conventus* and *Marchfeld*. The latter literally means 'March field', deriving from the practice of meeting between March and May as the grass grew long enough to make campaigning possible. Religious beliefs greatly influenced the timing of important meetings, with top-level encounters between the different Carolingian kings after 843 usually being held on prominent holy days like All Saints.

The combination of consultative assembly and military muster reinforced the personal element, since the king's presence was essential. It also reversed the relationship of the royal progress: rather than touring his kingdom, the king now made the 'kingdom' come to him, with some lords travelling hundreds of miles to meet him and participate in the assembly. Elite sociability was fostered through common activities like hunting, feasting and praying, which accompanied assemblies and provided additional opportunities for discussions, especially those that needed to be more private. Perhaps most importantly, they provided space for the king to present himself and display the virtues associated with good kingship, including leadership, justice, generosity and piety.[104]

Discussion of consensus requires some preliminary qualifications to avoid romanticizing it as some kind of manly, noble warrior culture with the king aided by reasonable, pragmatic and patriotic men. The sources are particularly difficult to interpret. There were no written rules, obliging us to infer these from how chroniclers recorded actual behaviour. Such writers were generally partisan, celebrating or criticizing kings, invoking idealized kingdoms, or airing grievances like Hinkmar, the ninth-century archbishop of Reims who wrote his *De ordine palatii* after his exclusion from the inner circle. His admonition to King Carlmann to follow the advice of wise old men like himself was clearly personally motivated, but Hinkmar's work, like similar pieces, is still instructive, because his arguments reflected broadly accepted norms.[105] Hinkmar urged the king to hold a general assembly of important men to test their response to his plans and to assist in determining general objectives. A meeting of 'seniors and principal advisors' should follow to agree the specifics. This more select gathering would have something of the character of a friendship group in which members would be freer to express opinions as there would be less risk of humiliation if the king rejected their advice.

The contemporary concept of 'friendship' (*amicitia*) allowed the king to widen his inner circle beyond his immediate relations, some of whom might be proving troublesome. Friendship could also shorten the formal hierarchy of vassalage, allowing the king to employ junior but able or materially useful men as his *familiares*. Hierarchy remained fluid, as the above description of Carolingian structures has illustrated, with dukes outranking counts, yet both still considered 'free' men directly subject to the king. The king's friends were already his vassals, but were bound by additional, ritualized activities staged deliberately to indicate a particular proximity. For instance, the king and his friends might alternate playing the roles of host and guest over different courses at a shared banquet. Gift-giving and exaggerated public displays of joy and sorrow were additional methods. Friends could extend royal influence by acting as brokers between the king and their own relations and clients. This was a major reason for seeking the king's friendship, since the broker gained prestige amongst his own clientele through his enhanced ability to secure favours and rewards. Those involved had a vested interest in keeping things in proportion. Excessive requests from either the king or his friends risked rejection and humiliating failure. Much of imperial governance thus relied on discreet negotiation, often via friends and other third parties, to find acceptable arrangements that were then presented publicly as if they were spontaneous decisions.[106]

This form of rule was facilitated by the relatively small size of the Carolingian and Ottonian elites. Widukind of Corvey, writing around 970, names 130 people in his chronicle, while even 40 years later Thietmar of Merseburg still only mentions 500, one-fifth of whom were women. The overall number of families was, of course, even smaller.[107] Moreover, the senior lords employed exactly the same methods to manage their own jurisdictions and wider networks. Social norms and ideals of justice and good kingship were also common currency. Finally, Frankish nobles also practised partible inheritance for their own allodial possessions so that, other than scale, there was no fundamental difference between the Carolingians who partitioned their empire into different kingdoms and their nobles who divided their lands amongst their sons. This sustained the hierarchy of power. What mattered to the lords was their personal proximity to the king, not their accumulation of hereditary possessions.

None of this meant that things necessarily ran smoothly. Admission to the *primores regni* was decided competitively, not consensually. This pinpoints the paradox of early medieval imperial politics. Governance was intended to achieve its goals amicably, but the actual process of seeking agreement was often disruptive and even violent. Consensus both shaped and reflected the shifting power balance, especially that between the king and his leading vassals. Disputes were personal, not constitutional, and generally stemmed from mismanaged expectations.

Carolingian Governance, 800–919

Having established the basic components to the governance of the early Empire, we can now turn to follow how it developed during the ninth century. The rapidity of Carolingian conquests from the 770s stoked expectations of rewards that could no longer be met after the 820s as imperial expansion halted amidst Arab, Viking and Slav incursions. The fratricidal wars after 829 were about dividing the spoils within what was still considered a common Frankish realm. Fighting was relatively brief and punctuated by frequent negotiations, often brokered discreetly by senior clergy. It was accepted that the internal strife differed from the earlier external wars of conquest in that the defeated side were still Christian Franks who could not be expropriated or enslaved. The particularly bloody battle of Fontenoy in June 841 shocked the elite and encouraged the collective lordly pressure that obliged the Carolingian royals to accept the first major partition of the Empire at the Treaty of Verdun (843) (Map 2).[108]

The partition into Lotharingia, East Francia and West Francia demonstrated the personal, rather than institutional, character to Carolingian rule in that it did not follow geographical, ethnic, linguistic or ecclesiastical boundaries. Instead, as eldest brother, Lothar went first, choosing to base his imperial authority in the middle kingdom anchored on Aachen and Rome, while Louis II received the lands to the east, and Charles II those to the west. There may be 'something of a "bargain basement" feel' to the later Carolingians, but they were neither as inept nor as indolent as both contemporary critics and later writers maintained.[109] Charles III only acquired his sobriquet 'the Fat' in the twelfth century. Their real problem was not irresistible centrifugal forces of dukes and kinglets seeking independence, but their own inability to produce legitimate heirs. This fuelled competition for possession of the different kingdoms created by their partitions. Charles III's deposition and death without legitimate heirs in 888 ended the last reunification and triggered a particularly vicious round of murderous quarrels amongst the Carolingian aristocracy.

Rivalry within the royal house stirred activism amongst the senior lords. Carolingian kings were obliged to consult their own vassals more often and to tolerate greater autonomy in return for military support. Meanwhile, many lords were left to shift for themselves in difficult circumstances, including threats from external raiders. Bishoprics and counties were now held successively by members of the same family, creating further vested interests and factions.[110] The Babenberg family, deriving their name from Bamberg, were promoted in Franconia by Charles III, but they lost out through the accession of Arnulf as king in East Francia in 887, since he promoted the rival Conradiner to counter their regional influence. The resulting 'Babenberger Feud' from 902 to 906 saw their defeat and the stabilization of the eastern monarchy under Conradiner influence.

Lotharingia broke up completely after 888, though as we have seen (pp. 47–8 and 187–8) the imperial title remained associated with the Italian kingdom until 924. Italian bishops like those in Modena and Reggio regained some of the autonomy they had lost under the Lombards, and acquired additional properties entrusted to their own subvassals in return for serving the Carolingians and their local successors based in Friaul, Spoleto and Ivrea. The bishops overshadowed the counts after the 880s, thanks to their control of Italy's still numerous towns, whereas comital jurisdiction was confined largely to the countryside. By the early tenth century, bishops began extending their jurisdiction over the suburban zones and acquired additional royal properties in return for backing the fairly weak Italian kings.[111]

West Francia had a larger and longer-established lordly hierarchy enjoying more stable local power. Around seven duchies emerged as the monarchy struggled to repel the Vikings who established themselves permanently in what would become Normandy. The Capetian family assumed a position equivalent to that held by the Carolingians' forebears at the Merovingian court by establishing a controlling influence in Paris after 885. This enabled the Capetians to eventually displace the Carolingians entirely and to become kings of France after 987.

Despite the Babenberger Feud, East Frankish lords remained appreciative of the positive role their king could play in coordinating defence of the long northern and eastern frontiers. Crucially, an inner group in East Francia had become accustomed to proximity to royal power and had no desire to share the associated benefits more widely. While they continued to bicker amongst themselves, they still wanted the monarchy to succeed, and took steps to avert a series of potential crises. Frankish custom maintained that boys could not be kings and that their lands should revert to the senior adult male of the dynasty. This situation occurred in 900 at the accession of Louis (IV) 'the Child', but the East Frankish lords refused to permit the West Frankish king to inherit and instead held four assemblies between 899 and 905 affirming their loyalty to the boy-king, who was guided by the archbishop of Mainz and other senior clergy.[112] Similar collective action ensured a transition to Conrad I, leader of the Conradiner family, as the first non-Carolingian king in 911, and again in 919 to recognize Henry I, head of the Liudolfinger (Ottonian) family.

Immediate circumstances and force of personality played a part. Conrad I was assisted by the lack of any viable local alternative candidate. Nonetheless, the same group of dukes and other senior lords cooperated throughout, not through any sense of 'national' consciousness, but because they recognized the East Frankish realm as a distinct political space guaranteeing their own regional clientele networks that had developed across the previous century. A general sense of shared Frankish heritage persisted into the 970s at least, but East and West Francia were both now more clearly defined as separate kingdoms organized around their own royal families and assemblies. Later chroniclers exaggerated the level of consensus. Conrad I faced a three-year revolt from the future Henry I, who demanded a greater share of the spoils, while the process of accepting Henry as king in 919 took five months, and required considerable force during 920–21 to obtain acquiescence in Swabia and especially Bavaria, which retained considerable autonomy.[113]

Ottonian Governance, 919–1024

The Ottonian remaking of the Empire in some ways resembled the earlier Carolingian achievement in that it followed a series of victories over the heathens (notably Lechfeld in 955), continued in an invasion of Italy to rescue the pope, and culminated in a carefully staged imperial coronation. The Ottonians were very conscious of Carolingian precedents and presented their rule as a revival of imperial authority, rather than a new beginning.[114] However, they emerged from within East Francia with a relatively restricted family powerbase in Saxony. Their rise to prominence was not accompanied by any significant redistribution of property, but rather rested on their acceptance of established lordly power and influence.

Ottonian rule confirmed a super elite of the original four dukes of Franconia, Swabia, Bavaria and Saxony, plus those of Lorraine, Bohemia and, more loosely, Burgundy, all of whom held quasi-viceregal powers over castles, royal monasteries and associated resources. They assumed some of the perquisites of royalty, notably 'by grace of God' titles and seals for their own documents, less to challenge their king than to elevate themselves from the more numerous counts and lesser lords. The king remained far more than first among equals. Otto I did not visit Swabia for a decade after 939, but its duke came to see him six times.[115] Although family possession of ducal status was more clearly hereditary, the original core duchy of Franconia was almost invariably held by the king directly until Henry IV gave it to the Staufers in 1079. The Ottonians also retained Saxony directly until 961 when it was passed to the Billungs, but the continued presence of extensive royal domains meant it was still known as 'the emperor's kitchen' into the eleventh century.[116]

Henry I's improved relations with Arnulf of Bavaria by 926 were an important factor in Otto I's election. Otto used the opportunity of Arnulf's death in 937 to assert firmer control over Bavaria before transferring it to his brother Heinrich in 948, who established the junior Ottonian branch that would provide Henry II as king after 1002. This arrangement was not unproblematic, because Heinrich's son and successor as duke, Heinrich II 'the Quarrelsome', conspired with Poland and Bohemia and had to be deposed in 976 by Otto II, who also weakened Bavaria by detaching Carinthia and Austria. Heinrich II subsequently disputed Otto III's succession, but was pacified by restoration to Bavaria in 985. Although occasionally turbulent, the existence of distinct duchies nonetheless allowed the Ottonians to contain the ambitions of close family members without having to resort to full partition of the kingdom.[117]

Indeed, the royal family dominated ducal ranks. The four primary duchies were held more frequently by the king or a close male relative than by other families between about 900 and the 1080s. Lorraine was in a different category, given its association with the now defunct Carolingian middle kingdom of Lotharingia. Unlike the four 'German' duchies, Lorraine was consistently ruled by indigenous dukes, though these were sometimes connected by marriage to the Ottonians. Although Swabia, Carinthia and, to an extent, Bavaria, were held by other families, sons rarely followed fathers. The continued significance of ducal offices is further illustrated by the fact that the Ottonians and Salians never suppressed those duchies they held directly, nor incorporated their jurisdictions within the royal domains. In short, duchies remained the principal 'institution' through which the king ruled the regions.

The Ottonians successfully distanced themselves from the violence of the later Carolingian era. Conrad I had crushed the Swabian revolt in 915 by beheading the opposing nobles, and two years later he decapitated his brothers-in-law Erchanger and Berthold for rebellion. By contrast, the Ottonians were prepared to pardon opponents where this appeared both safe and expedient, as their treatment of Heinrich the Quarrelsome indicates. Meanwhile, their tacit acceptance of the counties as hereditary removed them from often messy local politics, and allowed them to assume the status of superior, seemingly impartial judge.

Conflicts followed generally recognized lines. The king was rarely attacked directly, since most disputes were over the pecking order within the ducal elite. Malcontents would protest by leaving the royal presence and use their own kinship and clientele networks to mobilize support against their rival. They might add pressure by devastating crops or plundering, generally targeting their rival's adherents rather than risking a battle that would considerably raise the stakes. Participants in the dispute minimized risks by opposing particular royal decisions, not the king himself, in contrast to the late ninth-century civil wars fought to control the throne. Military action was about demonstrating potency while friends and other intermediaries discreetly sought a settlement. Negotiations were especially important where the malcontents opposed royal actions, since peace depended on finding a way they could submit without losing face. The Ottonians generally preferred magnanimity to harsh punishment, pardoning rebels and restoring at least most of their lands.

The Ottonians drew additional strength from the imperial church. Otto I entrusted the governance of Mainz and Cologne to close relatives, but the family's growing confidence is illustrated by his grandson's ability to appoint bishops from a much wider social circle. Although plunder could still be won in campaigns against the Slavs and Magyars, the Ottonians also used royal prerogatives to create new rights that could be given as rewards to loyalty and service. Market, mint and toll rights were granted to bishops, enabling them to exploit new economic opportunities (see pp. 486–93). The conquest of Italy and imperial coronation dramatically improved Ottonian prestige and widened their political opportunities. Elevation to imperial status clearly placed Otto I far above the dukes, enabling him to relinquish Saxony, his original family homeland.

However, Italy also expanded an already large realm, adding to the difficulties of governing through personal presence. Not all German lords were happy to see their king assume the ambitions and responsibilities associated with the imperial mission, especially as this required his presence south of the Alps. Otto I spent 10 of his last 12 years in Italy, finally returning in triumph to hold a succession of assemblies in 972–3 that conveyed a sense of solid support. However, many of the men he had known whilst German king were now dead, and it took his son Otto II until 980 to assert his own authority. Meanwhile, those Ottonian methods developed in Germany were not entirely transferable to the very different political landscape in Italy where there were no large duchies other than Spoleto. Otto I relied heavily on Pandulf Ironhead, one of the last of the old Lombard elite, who was allowed to add Spoleto and Benevento to his original duchy of Capua.[118]

Pandulf's death in 981 created a power vacuum in southern Italy just as Otto II was blockading Venice to force it to renounce ties to Byzantium. Otto expanded his actions, elevating Salerno to an archbishopric to counter the Byzantine one in Otranto. He then marched south with perhaps the largest ever Ottonian army, including 4,000 armoured cavalry, intending to demonstrate his imperial credentials by succeeding where the Byzantines had recently failed and drive the Saracens out of Calabria. He was lured into a trap and decisively defeated at Cotrone on the east Calabrian coast on 13 July 982. The dukes of Bavaria and Swabia died along with 16 counts and several bishops and abbots. Otto only escaped by riding out to sea where he was rescued by a Greek ship whose crew tried to kidnap him once they realized who he was.[119] The disaster shook confidence in the Ottonians, who appeared to have lost divine favour. The heavy casualties amongst the elite intensified competition to fill the vacancies. Otto took the exceptional step of holding a joint Italian-German lordly assembly at Verona on Whitsun 983, rallying support and securing endorsement of his three-year-old son as co-king.

Otto II's unexpected death in December 983 added to the crisis of the Slav revolt along the Elbe. Yet the situation demonstrated the inherent strengths of Ottonian rule. The years spent patiently cultivating the 'friendship' of key lords now paid off, as most remained loyal, despite now serving a boy king, Otto III, under the female regency of his mother Theophanu (see pp. 315–16). Heinrich the Quarrelsome's support was restricted to the political (and geographical) periphery: the dukes of Poland and Bohemia, the Abodrites, some Lorraine lords, and the western archbishops of Trier and Cologne. By acting as if he were already king, Heinrich alienated potential Saxon support. Careful negotiations gave him a face-saving way out and removed the need for Theophanu and her supporters to fight.[120]

Otto III's death in 1002 ended his family's main line and allowed Heinrich the Quarrelsome's son, Henry II, to seek recognition. He only gained acceptance after some violence in which a rival candidate, Margrave Ekkehard of Meissen, was murdered and Strasbourg was plundered.[121] Henry is usually presented as stepping back from the supposedly more expansive ambitions of his two immediate predecessors, but the change was mainly one of style as he intensified the sacral element of kingship and toured the Empire more extensively.

Salian Command Monarchy, 1024–1137

Henry II's lack of children raised concern during his reign over the succession. The response was similar to that at the end of the Carolingian line: a meeting was organized at Kamba on the Rhine opposite Oppenheim in the summer of 1024 by the inner circle comprising Henry's widow, Kunigunde, her brothers the duke of Bavaria and counts of Luxembourg and Mainz, and key bishops. The Salians were the only viable candidates. They were favoured by Kunigunde and her relations, and were backed by the Lorraine aristocracy, perhaps because of their shared roots in the Rhineland. There was currently no duke of Franconia since this post had been retained directly by the king since 939, while Swabia was held by a minor at that point. The Saxons, Italians and Slavs appear to have stayed away. Consequently, the proceedings became a discreet test of how much support the two Salian branches could muster. Conrad (II) the Elder, heading the junior Salian branch based at Speyer, emerged as the favourite allegedly because he already had a son. Conrad the Younger of the senior (older) Worms branch left Kamba with his supporters before the result was announced publicly, thereby preserving the appearance of unanimity. The Saxons continued to maintain their distance as in 1002, requiring Conrad II to secure their acceptance separately at Minden in December. Conrad encountered difficulties broadly similar to Henry I a century previously, but on a far wider scale because he succeeded to Italy as well as Germany, and inherited Henry II's claims to Burgundy. Opposition in Swabia only ended when its duke, Ernst, was killed in 1030, and it took a further two years for Conrad to secure both Italy and Burgundy (Map 4).[122]

Conrad's success confirmed the Empire as a hierarchy of three principal kingdoms headed by Germany, Italy and Burgundy. The challenge of governance was now even greater than under the Ottonians. The expanded size of the realm added to the difficulties of governing through personal presence. Meanwhile, the lordly hierarchy had lengthened and its members had become more numerous. There were now several pushy new families who had the power though not yet the status of dukes, achieved by acquiring several counties and placing relations in the imperial church. In addition to the Salians themselves, these included the Ekkehardiner at Meissen, the Luxembourgs, Ezzonids, Babenbergs and Welfs. There were also more numerous and distinct lesser nobles, plus the class of servile ministeriales emerging about 1020. These were not, as once thought, a royal creation to free the king from dependency on the great lords, but instead ministeriales were promoted by the imperial clergy.[123] Bishops and abbots selected able men of unfree status and enfeoffed them with resources to enable them to serve as knights or administrators. The Salians also began employing ministeriales to administer royal domains and garrison the new castles built in the 1060s. The ministeriales gradually acquired other privileges, embraced an aristocratic ethos, and eventually converted their relationship based on servitude into one of more conventional vassalage to fuse with other lesser nobles as knights and barons by about 1300.

It would be wrong to interpret the ministeriales as the potential staff required to create a centralized monarchy. They were indeed used to oversee more intensive management of royal domains, notably in

Saxony. However, the Salians were themselves a product of the same political culture as their lords. There was no blueprint for a centralized state to follow, nor evidence that anyone thought such a structure was superior. Instead, Conrad and his successors tried to improve established methods by making it harder for lords to refuse royal commands. Conrad's well-known articulation of the Empire as 'an enduring crown' was one element in this, as was the increasing emphasis on royal authority, underpinned by a more elevated, sacral monarchical image.

Conrad remained in the late Ottonian mould of an emperor touring the Empire to meet lordly expectations of good kingship. One-fifth of his trips were to Saxony, where the local lords clearly resented the Salian accession and their displacement to the outer circle.[124] This paid off, and Henry III's accession in 1039 resembled a triumphal progress. Conrad also returned to the earlier policy of concentrating duchies in royal hands as they became vacant: Bavaria in 1027, Swabia in 1038 and Carinthia in 1039. All three passed along with Franconia to Henry III on his accession, but he broke past practice by giving them away, keeping only Bavaria. Bavaria was held by a king or his son for 46 years between 1002 and 1125, with the other six individuals chosen from close allies, though four had to be deposed after brief periods by the king. Meanwhile, the Salians continued Henry II's practice of promoting Bamberg, Eichstätt and other Bavarian bishops as counterweights. This seems to have worked well and Henry IV had little difficulty retaining their loyalty after 1075, unlike Saxony, where the policy of backing the archbishop of Bremen simply antagonized local lords further and contributed to the Saxon revolt in 1073.[125]

This policy represented a fundamental shift from using ducal jurisdictions directly to a more indirect management of the ducal elite. It reduced friction by accepting the trend to hereditary possession, which was already clearly established in Lorraine and soon also Swabia. The king retained powers of confirmation, but local 'elections' were now far more like homage ceremonies where the new duke sought acceptance from the lesser lords. Ducal power rested on possession of significant allodial property, much of it often former royal domains, as well as clearer political jurisdiction over the lesser nobles.[126]

However, the ducal elite faced harsher punishments if they abused their new autonomy. The Ottonians had operated what was, essentially, a 'two strikes' policy with only repeat offenders facing serious consequences, though even here exceptions were made, as in the case of Heinrich the Quarrelsome. This was no longer possible under the more elevated concept of monarchy cultivated by the Salians. Rebellion ceased to be a personal dispute over status and became an affront to divine order. It was harder to forgive wrongdoers who were now considered sinners. Using the Roman law concept of *crimen laesae maiestatis*, revived by Henry III, Salians no longer simply removed offenders from office, but also confiscated their allodial property.

The difficulties of the new course were already exposed in 1035 when Conrad II deposed Adalbero Eppensteiner as duke of Carinthia for pursuing a policy towards the Hungarians contrary to royal wishes. Conrad clearly intended an assembly of lords as a pliant court to endorse his verdict, but many of those present expressed disquiet, including the king's son, Henry (III), who, as duke of Bavaria, had sworn friendship with Adalbero. Conrad secured consent by falling to the floor crying, a move that could easily have backfired and damaged his prestige.[127] Although Henry III appears to have curried favour by reversing many of his father's decisions, he continued the same methods, encountering even greater difficulties when he tried to enforce a new partition in Lorraine after 1044. He eventually achieved his goal, but alienated the duke's relations in Tuscany.

Long the beneficiary of Ottonian patronage, the Tuscans had proved crucial in Conrad II's victory over Italian opposition to his succession from 1024 to 1027. Tuscany's defection to Pope Gregory VII after 1077 was a serious blow to the imperial position in Italy. The absence of other large jurisdictions necessitated a different approach to governing south of the Alps. The Salians spent only 22 of their 101 years of rule in Italy, and half of that was Henry IV's largely unwilling presence during the Investiture wars. Their preferred method was to rely on the Italian bishops, both by appointing loyalists trained in the royal chapel, and by strengthening the episcopate by extending their control over their cathedral towns and surrounding area. This made some sense, given that demographic and economic growth began earlier in Italy than in Germany, eroding the old county structure and fuelling popular demands for greater civic autonomy. The Salians were not necessarily hostile to these developments, for instance extending their patronage by giving the post of royal judge to wealthy townsmen, some of whom subsequently rose to become counts or bishops. Conrad II also intervened to settle what became known as the Valvassores' Revolt between 1035 and 1037. The *valvassores* were the subvassals of the 'captains' (*capitanei*) who held both urban property and church fiefs in the surrounding countryside. Conrad's *Constitutio de feudis* of 28 May 1037 extended the benefits of hereditary possession of fiefs to the lesser lords, whilst continuing to assert the king as final judge of all disputes.[128]

These policies were unintentionally conflictual, because they weakened episcopal authority over the valvassores and captains, notably in Milan, where a complex dispute developed over popular demands for autonomy and conflicting claims from the emperor and pope to intervene. When aligned with the difficulties encountered over Lorraine, this suggests the Salians were already encountering serious structural problems ahead of Henry IV's minority following his father's death in 1056.[129]

The Saxon and Investiture Wars, 1073–1122

Discontent amongst east Saxon lords coincided with the first stages of what would become the Investiture Dispute around 1073. Neither of these problems was immediately life-threatening for the Salian monarchy. Henry IV continued to enjoy considerable support amongst the German and Italian episcopates, as well as many lay lords. However, his inability to find quick solutions to these problems fuelled underlying discontent at Salian methods and gave credence to charges of misrule. A more exalted style of monarchy inhibited the cultivation of 'friends' and made it difficult to compromise without losing face, and Henry rebuffed several attempts by lay and secular lords to broker settlements. Royal prestige was now defined by power and victory, not consensus and clemency. Unfortunately, open defiance, as in Saxony, left the king no choice but to employ force. The Salians were thus in the same bind in Germany as the Ottonians had been in earlier disputes with the papacy: violent methods conflicted with most people's ideal of good kingship. The German lords provided Henry with an opportunity to restore politics to the earlier consensual course by summoning him to their assembly at Trebur in October 1076. Yet acceptance would have entailed an unacceptable humiliation, and so Henry undertook his extraordinary journey to Canossa in an attempt to outflank his opponents by reaching a deal with Pope Gregory.[130]

The move failed to stop the malcontents electing Rudolf of Rheinfelden as the first real anti-king in March 1077. Rudolf was backed by the leading Saxons, the dukes of Bavaria and Carinthia, and around eight middling secular lords, plus the archbishops of Mainz, Salzburg, Magdeburg and their suffragan bishops. The majority of lay and ecclesiastical lords were still loyal to the emperor or at least neutral. However, the combination of civil war in Germany and the open struggle with the Gregorian papacy intensified the divisions. Both Henry and the Gregorians deposed each other's supporters from the episcopate, while the king replaced the rebellious southern dukes with loyalists in 1079, including the Staufers, who received Swabia. There were now rival kings, popes, dukes and bishops, entrenching the conflict in the localities and widening the numbers of those involved with vested interests. The relatively even balance prevented either side from achieving sufficient preponderance to force their opponents to accept peace.

Although obstinate, Henry was sufficiently astute to seize the collapse of the Welf-Tuscan alliance in 1095 not merely to escape from northern Italy but to offer significant concessions across the next three years. This confirmed one of the two main political outcomes of this turbulent period: the demise of the old ducal elite and its replacement by a more numerous group controlling more modest jurisdictions. This group was recruited from the middling families who had amassed allodial property and county jurisdictions and were now accommodated by the creation of new jurisdictions associated with ducal rank. Henry reconciled the Zähringer, whom he had deposed from Carinthia in 1078, by raising their allodial property in the Black Forest to a new duchy 20 years later. This was rounded out by transferring Zürich, the richest royal domain in the region, as well as other jurisdictions formerly associated with Swabia. Meanwhile, the counts Palatine emerged as equivalent to dukes on the Middle Rhine by 1156. Henry V continued this policy after his accession in 1106, which coincided with the extinction of the Saxon Billungs. Although Saxony was not partitioned, Henry gave the Billung allodial property to the rising Askanier and Welf families. Other jurisdictions in Saxony were consolidated as a distinct landgraviate of Thuringia by 1131, while the remnants of what had been the Saxon North March (*Nordmark*) were detached in 1134, becoming the margraviate of Brandenburg after 1157.[131]

The tentative return to consensual politics unravelled as Henry V sought to supplant his father after 1105, leading to renewed war until the latter's death the following year. Henry V's heavy handling of his former favourite, Lothar von Supplinburg, triggered another revolt in 1112–15 during which the king lost control of northern Germany and only survived thanks to continued Staufer support. Antagonism resurfaced at Henry V's death in 1125. The leading Welf, Heinrich 'the Black' of Bavaria, defected from his former Staufer allies and backed the election of Lothar von Supplinburg. Conrad Staufer of Franconia was proclaimed king by his own supporters, including his elder brother in Swabia, splitting Germany north–south. He only accepted defeat in 1135 in return for a pardon, finally allowing Lothar III to tour the south.[132]

The outcome confirmed the second lasting consequence from the troubles since 1073: command monarchy was discredited and defeated. The Trebur meeting of 1076 was the first of what historians have called 'kingless assemblies' (*königlose Tage*), as senior lords convened on their own initiative. Other meetings followed in 1105, 1121 and 1122, the latter compelling Henry V to settle the Investiture Dispute with the Worms Concordat. Although further collective action failed to avert violence in 1125, Lothar III nonetheless returned to a more consensual style. However, this did not restore Ottonian conditions. Instead, the restructured elite now saw themselves as sharing responsibility for the Empire's welfare. This was expressed as 'emperor and Empire' (*imperator et regnum*), first voiced at the 1122 assembly and signifying that lords expected to participate in important decisions rather than merely offer advice. It remained for the Staufers to adapt governance to meet these expectations.[133]

8

Territory

FEUDALIZATION

Change and Continuity under the Staufers

This chapter explores the Empire's governance from the start of the Staufers in 1138 to the era of imperial reform around 1500. These three and a half centuries are not normally considered together. Rather than continuity, most accounts stress a break around 1250, usually presenting this as the end of royal state-building and the onset of political decentralization under a succession of 'weak' kings. The narrative of 'decline' rests on treating the Empire as a conventional 'national monarchy' undermined by the Staufers' alleged disregard for 'German' interests in favour of 'unrealistic' ambitions in Italy.[1]

The usual interpretation places undue emphasis on aspects that were relatively unimportant to Staufer governance outside their Sicilian possessions and misses the lines of continuity both backwards to the Salian era and forwards beyond 1250. The Staufers' real importance lies not in their *failure* to centralize, but their *success* in revising and recombining earlier methods into a new, more collective form of imperial governance by the emperor and a more self-conscious princely elite. Far from representing decline, the feudalization of the Empire's lords and the territorialization of their authority actually preserved the Empire once the Staufers themselves imploded after 1250.

Sicily and the Crown Lands

The Staufers' conquest of Norman Sicily in 1195 certainly appears to signal a new direction (Map 5). Sicily was a rich prize, with over 500,000 inhabitants; the island was the Mediterranean's grain basket and, together with its associated lands around Naples, it added 100,000 square kilometres to the Staufers' personal possessions. The Normans had already established a command monarchy, supported by a powerful judiciary using codified law, and an administration where written culture was routine. These structures were retained by Henry VI and Frederick II, who used them to consolidate their authority across the former Norman possessions, confiscating castles from recalcitrant nobles and redistributing them to loyal followers like Conrad von Urslingen, who already administered Spoleto after 1177 and now became governor of Sicily. Markward von Annweiler, a former minis-teriale, was entrusted with Ancona, Romagna, Ravenna and the Abruzzi to secure the vital corridor linking northern Italy to the new southern possessions around Naples.[2]

However, most of the Norman treasures were distributed to reward Staufer supporters, while the invasion had literally cost a king's ran-som: Henry VI financed the operation using the 16 tons of silver that England paid to free Richard the Lionheart. The Staufers also inherited the problem of split-site management from the Normans, who already had problems controlling the mainland barons from Sicily. These difficulties grew when Henry's unexpectedly early death at 32 was followed by papal interference and the double election of 1198, which destabilized Staufer rule in Germany and Italy. The Norman lords seized the opportunity to revolt and their unrest continued into the 1240s with papal encouragement. In short, Sicily proved never suffi-ciently stable to be a base from which to reorganize imperial governance. Nor did the experience of ruling Sicily provide compelling evidence that its style of kingship was inherently superior to the methods developed over past centuries in Germany. The pro-Staufer lords clearly thought not, since they chose Frederick II's uncle, Philip of Swabia, in 1198 rather than renewing their endorsement of him as Henry VI's successor made only 18 months earlier.

The Staufers' engagement in Italy was more prolonged than that of the Salians. Henry IV spent only a quarter of his reign there, compared to a third under Frederick I 'Barbarossa' and three-quarters under Frederick II. Nonetheless, the family powerbase remained Swabia, which they had held since 1079 along with allodial possessions in Alsace. These lands were close to those of their Salian patrons. Thus, Conrad III's accession in 1138 shifted the Empire's core region back to south-west Germany from the north, to which it had briefly moved under Lothar III. Barbarossa and Henry VI bought or inherited additional lands across southern and east-central Germany after 1160, increasing the number of individual crown properties to 4,300.[3] Existing palaces were renovated and expanded, while new, fortified ones were built in their core region: Wimpfen, Gelnhausen, Hagenau and Kaiserslautern. Altenburg and Eger were constructed in central Germany to secure access to Bohemia.

While scarcely 'a catastrophe for Germany',[4] Henry VI's death in 1197 was a serious setback for the Staufers, because it triggered the double election and civil war after 1198. The county Palatine on the Middle Rhine was seized by their Welf rivals, while the newly acquired properties in east-central Germany were lost. However, Frederick II recovered royal lands which, by 1241, were almost as extensive as at their peak in 1197, while the family's own possessions expanded considerably with the (temporary) acquisition of Austria and Styria in 1237. Royal possessions were managed more intensively through methods such as clearance of wastes and greater engagement in the commercializing economy. Royal officials, recruited from ministeriales, were posted to oversee crown lands, castles, and the growing number of imperial towns that the Staufers also actively promoted.

Governance followed a broadly similar path in Italy, though with far greater emphasis on reclaiming regalia rather than lands. Thanks to the new understanding fostered by the Worms Concordat of 1122, regalia were now more clearly understood as legal rights to exploit particular resources and to exercise certain kinds of jurisdiction, especially in Italy's numerous towns. Barbarossa convened an assembly of Italian lords at Roncaglia near Piacenza in November 1158 and demanded the return of all regalia allegedly usurped since the 1070s. Contemporaries estimated these were worth 30,000 pounds of silver annually.[5] This was not simply an attempt to set the clock back. Barbarossa accepted greater demands for civic self-government, but insisted that the new elected officials swear loyalty to him as emperor. He also demanded that all towns maintain a royal palace, though he agreed these could now be placed outside their walls. Overall, he aimed to forge a more direct relationship with Italian towns, similar to that in Germany. Strong opposition in the form of the Lombard League forced him to compromise in 1183. Over the next 12 years many of the recently recovered regalia were transferred to the cities in return for cash and political support, notably during the conquest of Sicily in 1194–5. Henry VI renewed efforts at tighter control, appointing royal castellans in castles to curb civic influence in their rural hinterlands, but also continued to pawn Italian crown lands.[6]

Previous emperors had promoted tighter supervision of crown lands, notably Henry IV. Like their predecessors, the Staufers' development of crown and family possessions was simply part of a wider range of royal strategies and certainly should not be interpreted as an *alternative* to feudalization, especially as the Roncaglia assembly also saw efforts to foster tighter political loyalty based on clearer reciprocal obligations between king and vassals.[7]

The New Feudal Order

Staufer policies become clearer when we recognize they were not seeking a unitary state, but instead employed different methods in their various lands. In Sicily they regarded themselves as the legitimate heirs to Norman hereditary kingship, whereas they tried to manage the Empire by reworking relations with their vassals. This process has been labelled the 'Feudalization of the Empire' and represented the definitive abandonment of attempts to prevent fiefs becoming hereditary in favour of trying to turn this to the emperor's advantage.[8]

Lothar III had already attempted to reorder relations with his vassals by defining a longer and clearer status hierarchy in 1136. Conrad III continued this, as did Barbarossa after 1157 when he encouraged the use of Roman law, which was being studied at the new university of Bologna. Bologna lawyers helped define vassalage in more obviously feudal terms, but their influence should not be exaggerated, as the disassociation of public functions from aristocratic titles was already accelerating since the early eleventh century. All lords were assuming broadly similar responsibilities as, for example, bishops acquired counties and thus superior criminal jurisdictions. Meanwhile, the Investiture

Dispute encouraged superior lords to fix their vassals' obligations more precisely in writing to be sure of their support.[9]

The process of feudalization involved identifying the scope of fiefs and their associated rights and obligations more clearly in written charters. This established a sharper hierarchy. The feudal lord retained superior powers over the fief, variously termed *dominium directum*, *dominium feodale* or *dominium superius*, but always consisting of reserve rights expressed practically as the power to confirm the vassal's possession. The vassal enjoyed rights of usage (*dominium utile*), often defined expansively to include powers to develop the fief economically and to oversee the lives of its inhabitants.

These distinctions were standard throughout Latin Christendom, but assumed a particular form in the Empire thanks to the deliberate elaboration of a complex status hierarchy after the mid-twelfth century. The more intensive management of crown lands reflected how the Staufers no longer saw these as assets to be distributed as rewards for loyalty and support. Instead, they used their undefined imperial reserve powers to distinguish additional ranks of lords. Moreover, as suzerains of the entire Empire, the Staufers retained existing powers to confirm or withhold recognition of individual lords' inheritance of what were now accepted as hereditary fiefs.

Feudalization emerged ad hoc from the practical problems of managing the senior lords, notably the Welf family, whose rise demonstrated the problems associated with established methods. The Welfs were an old, well-connected family with several branches. The one established in 1055 around Ravensburg in Swabia rose to prominence through its appointment as dukes of Bavaria in 1070. Although the Welfs lost this in 1077 after opposing Henry IV, they changed sides and were reinstated in 1096. Ten years later they were allowed to inherit part of the Billungs' private property in Saxony and were rewarded with the Saxon ducal title in 1127 after their defection from the Staufers helped secure Lothar III's election. Heinrich 'the Proud', the leading Welf, was designated the successor by Lothar only to be defeated by Conrad III in the 1138 election. The Welfs were punished through the loss of both duchies at Heinrich's death in 1139, but his only son, Henry 'the Lion', was compensated with the county of Brunswick and eventually recovered Saxony in return for recognizing Conrad III.[10] This sequence of reward, punishment and partial reinstatement was entirely in line with Salian

and Ottonian practice, and reflected the importance of personal friend-
ships and animosities within the Empire's lordly elite. However, these
changes depended heavily on circumstance, like the opportunity provided by Heinrich the Proud's death, which allowed Conrad to block
Henry the Lion's inheritance.

Barbarossa took a different course by following Henry IV's example
of splitting larger ducal jurisdictions to facilitate more subtle management of the senior lords. Barbarossa needed to reward Henry the Lion
for his invaluable assistance in securing the royal election in March
1152, but did not want to make him too powerful.[11] Accordingly, when
he gave the now vacant duchy of Bavaria back to Henry in 1156, he
simultaneously detached its eastern marches as a new duchy of Austria,
which he gave to the Babenberg family. The Babenberg ally, Duke
Vladislav of Bohemia, was granted royal status in return for renouncing claims to Austria and for accepting the incorporation of the Piast
duchy of Silesia into the Empire in 1163. Meanwhile, a new duchy of
Merania was created in 1152 from various lordships on the Croatian
and Dalmatian coast and given to Count Conrad of Dachau.

Henry the Lion was left as de facto royal governor of northern Germany during Barbarossa's prolonged absences in Italy. However, he
used this to pursue a feud with the archbishop of Cologne after
1166 over possession of Westphalia, the western part of the old duchy
of Saxony. He developed his own court which, unlike the emperor's,
was fixed in Brunswick. Henry became the first German lord to assume
the prerogative of issuing his own charters, while his marriage to
Matilda, daughter of the English king Henry II, appeared to confirm
his regal aspirations. The deciding factor in the ensuing conflict was
the relative willingness of the participants to accept obligations to the
Empire. Cologne's archbishop, Count Philipp von Heinsberg, won Barbarossa's favour by agreeing to provide additional troops just as Henry
refused to assist the imperial campaign of 1176 unless he received the
royal lands at Goslar. The dispute deepened as Henry refused a personal summons to participate in another campaign.[12]

Barbarossa returned to Germany in 1177 having been defeated in
Italy. He needed to reassert his authority and rally support, while Count
Philipp saw an opportunity to defeat his regional rival. Henry the Lion's
trial in 1178 followed the conventional pattern of prolonged consultation amongst interested parties, allowing counts like the Askanier and

Bogislav of Stettin a chance to complain about his overbearing management of northern Germany. The verdict was passed as the Gelnhausen Act on 13 April 1180. Henry was exiled and Westphalia was given to Cologne as a distinct duchy, while the rest of Saxony passed to the Askanier Count Bernhard of Anhalt. Five months later Bavaria was transferred to Count Palatine Otto of Wittelsbach, another of Barbarossa's partisans. However, the process of 1156 was repeated with the margraviate of Styria being detached as a separate duchy under the Traungau family. A year later, Bogislav was freed from Saxon jurisdiction as duke of Pomerania, while the archbishop of Aquileia was given ducal rank based on the former margraviate of Friaul.[13] These changes doubled the number of ducal titles since 1098.

Henry the Lion returned from exile in 1185, but found little support for his efforts to reverse the Gelnhausen Act before his death in 1195.[14] Henry VI's unexpected death in 1197 allowed Henry the Lion's son, Otto IV, to challenge the Staufers, resulting in the 1198 double election. The Staufer candidate, Philip of Swabia, was backed by the beneficiaries of the 1180–81 redistribution, plus Mainz and the bulk of the imperial church and ministeriales. Only Cologne broke ranks, hoping to displace Mainz as the premier archbishopric by staging Otto's election. Otto also drew support from those alarmed by Staufer absenteeism in Italy and Henry VI's proposal for a hereditary monarchy.[15] Most of the fighting was in Italy, where it seriously damaged imperial prestige, but the war was already settled before Otto's defeat at Bouvines in 1214, since most of his supporters had defected to Frederick II, who replaced the murdered Philip of Swabia as Staufer candidate in 1208.

The Emergence of the Princes

Frederick II confirmed Wittelsbach possession of the Palatinate and Bohemia's royal status after being elected king by his own supporters in 1212. Once his victory was secure, he formalized what until then had been a temporary expedient and granted uniform privileges in two charters to the spiritual (1220) and lay lords (1231).[16] Other European monarchs issued similar general charters: England's Magna Carta (1215), the Aragonese Privileges (1283, 1287), the *Joyeuse Entrée* of Brabant (1356). Those in the Empire codified ideas of princely status (*principatus*) evolving since the tenth century, which suggested that all senior lords were collectively 'princes' regardless of their precise titles or lay or spiritual characters. Scholars in Bologna and elsewhere encouraged this with a new interpretation of ancient Rome's military and political elite as combining judicial powers (*jurisdictio*) with governance (*regimen*).[17] In short, the charters did not *devolve* royal powers to the princes, but applied new terminology to distinguish them as a political elite above other lords.

Already after 1180, Barbarossa distinguished more sharply between *princeps* and *nobiles*. Both were noble in the sense of socially distinct from commoners thanks to their military function, but the former were now clearly politically superior. Frederick II's charters confirmed this by relating princely status directly to holding immediate imperial fiefs (*Reichslehen*). He retained the traditional position as suzerain, entitling him to confirm each new vassal in possession of his fief and to adjudicate internal family inheritance disputes. However, the changes also brought significant new advantages. Confirmation of the new duchies enlarged the number of senior vassals immediately subordinate to the emperor. The grant of broadly similar charters to both spiritual and lay princes ensured a more uniform set of obligations towards the Empire. Separate legislation since 1136 meanwhile strengthened the authority of the nascent princes over their own vassals, while continuing demographic and economic development ensured that, although smaller than the old duchies, the new ones could now be asked to provide more assistance. Finally, the Staufers' parallel articulation of a collective imperial honour helped instil a sense of their obligations as binding on all in 'service to the Empire' (*Reichsdienst*).[18]

A new fundamental division between immediate and mediate vassals emerged as politically more significant than the earlier distinction between lay and spiritual lords. The charters identified the princes as a corporate group collectively enjoying the status of 'imperial immediacy' (*Reichsunmittelbarkeit*) directly under the emperor. Other lords were 'mediate' (*mittelbar*) under at least one intervening layer of authority between them and the emperor. Ecclesiastical princely fiefs remained more defined than their secular counterparts, because they were clearly transpersonal, whereas secular ones depended on the size and biological survival of princely families. The duchy of Merania on the Adriatic coast created in 1152 passed on the extinction of the counts of Dachau in 1180 to the counts of Andechs, but was broken up when they died out in 1248 and was absorbed into Istria. In addition to Merania, there were 16 secular princes in 1200, including the dukes holding the rumps of Bavaria, Saxony, Swabia and Lorraine, as well as Carinthia and the new duchies of Austria, Brabant, Styria and Zähringen. The others comprised Bohemia (now a kingdom), the count Palatine, the margraves of Brandenburg, Lusatia and Meissen, the landgrave of Thuringia and the count of Anhalt. Collectively, these princes held jurisdictions covering a third of the German kingdom. Another third was held by the 47 archbishops and bishops, 27 abbots and 18 abbesses comprising the imperial church. All archbishops and bishops now held secular powers in their lands comparable to dukes. The remaining third comprised royal domains and the possessions of around 80 counts and several thousand free nobles, all of whom were still immediate under the emperor, but lacked the princes' corporate privileges. Another 14 ducal titles were created across the next two centuries, compared to only two dissolutions following family extinctions (Merania, Zähringen) (Table 5). The Swabian title was also defunct following the death of the last Staufer in 1268 when the bulk of its associated possessions passed to the count of Württemberg. The Franconian title had been transferred to the bishop of Würzburg in 1168, but effectively ceased to exist outside the bishopric itself.[19]

Twelve of the new titles involved the elevation of loyal counts by grateful monarchs who used their prerogatives to adjust the status of existing counties to duchies. Brunswick's elevation was an exception that proves the marginal role played by personal possessions in the formation of German territories. Having returned to Germany and imprisoned his own son in 1235, Frederick II was at the height of his power and finally persuaded the Welfs to accept peace on his terms. They surrendered their allodial possessions around Brunswick and received them back as an imperial fief augmented by the income from the crown lands at Goslar. This established Frederick's own claim on Brunswick's resources through vassalage, and confined the Welfs to a relatively minor role until the family's dramatic resurgence during the seventeenth century. It also confirmed the three-way division of the old Saxon duchy into Westphalia (associated with Cologne), Brunswick in the centre, and Sachsen-Lauenburg in the east, held by the Askanier until their extinction in 1689.

The emergence of this princely elite around 1200 incorporated the

Table 5. New Ducal Titles

1235	Brunswick
1310	Henneberg
1310/13	Savoy
1317/39	Geldern
1348	Mecklenburg
1354	Luxembourg
1354	Bar*
1356	Jülich (margraves since 1336)
c.1358	Austria**
1363	The Burgrave of Nuremberg received permission to use the personal title of prince
1366	The Count of Nassau received permission to use the personal title of prince
1380	Berg
1394	Krain (used a ducal title already since 1364)
1417	Cleves
1430/36	Cilli (title of prince; incorporated into Styria after 1456)
1474	Holstein
1495	Württemberg (last of the medieval elevations to ducal status)

*raised to a margraviate, though its later lords claimed ducal status

**new title of 'archduke' invented by Duke Rudolf IV

more successful of the pushy new lordly families emerging since the later tenth century who had acquired titles of margrave or landgrave, as well as the count Palatine and the Askanier counts of Anhalt. Similarly, the counts of Cilli acquired princely status without receiving a ducal title. Baden's rulers originated as a distant branch of the Zähringen family installed as margraves of Verona in 1061. They kept their margrave title when they transferred to possessions on the Upper Rhine in 1112. The territories known later as Ansbach and Bayreuth became margraviates through their acquisition by the burgrave of Nuremberg around 1415. Brabant and Limburg became duchies around the beginning of the twelfth century as Henry IV and Henry V temporarily transferred the disputed Lorraine ducal title to their counts during the Salian civil war. Likewise, the lordship of Bouillon became a duchy in 1330 through its acquisition by later dukes of Lorraine. What became

known as the Saxon duchies emerged from the defunct landgraviate
of Thuringia, which passed to the Wettin family during the thirteenth
century. Later partitions amongst the Wettins created separate duchies in Altenberg, Coburg, Eisenach, Gotha, Meiningen and Weimar
from fragments of Thuringia. Likewise, partitions within the Palatine and Welf families by the seventeenth century attached princely
status to many of their counties and lordships as these were parcelled
out among different heirs. In all cases, the emperor's permission was
required, providing further opportunities to extract concessions from
the beneficiaries.[20]

Hierarchy and Status

The last of the medieval elevations occurred in 1495 when the count of
Württemberg was made duke, legitimated through his possession of Teck,
which had once been held by the defunct dukes of Zähringen. Thereafter,
counts who were promoted simply received the title of 'prince' (*Fürst*),
adding a subtle, yet significant distinction between themselves as 'new
princes' and the 'old princely houses' holding electoral, ducal, margravial or landgravial rank. Titles served as fine distinctions within an
otherwise common corporate group and became the focus of often
intense competition during early modernity.

All immediate fiefs were linked to the emperor through the obligations of vassalage. Women acquired the status of duchess, margravine
or princess through marriage or kinship, but were generally disbarred
from fief-holding. This had obvious disadvantages as families adopted
more dynastic inheritance strategies. Since around 1037, emperors had
designated some fiefs as *Weiberlehen*, permitting women to inherit if
the vassal died without a son.[21] The most important of these 'women's
fiefs' was Austria, which was designated as such in 1156. The emperor
benefited from continuity of service since, though the female fief-holder
could not serve herself, she was obliged to send male warriors to
fulfil her duties. There were at least ten female imperial fiefs by the
eighteenth century, while Charles VI effectively converted the entire
Habsburg hereditary possessions into one through the Pragmatic Sanction in 1713 to allow his daughter, Maria Theresa, to inherit.[22] The
idea of *Leihezwang* expressed in the thirteenth-century *Sachsenspiegel*
suggested the emperor had to redistribute any fief that fell vacant. This

was never formally adopted and was rendered irrelevant by the flexibility of inheritance arrangements that ensured there were always heirs. In practice, the emperor had to buy off or defeat claimants if he wanted to retain a vacant fief. The difficulties are illustrated by the long and ultimately fruitless attempts by thirteenth-century kings to retain the landgraviate of Thuringia after the death of Heinrich Raspe in 1247.

Many immediate fiefs were small and not associated with princely titles. Some were parcels of royal domains that remained in the hands of former ministeriales during the later thirteenth century. Others belonged to knights who only secured recognition of immediacy in the sixteenth century (see pp. 553–62). However, the vast majority were classed as mediate fiefs following the Staufer legislation and in turn fell into two main categories. The first, known as 'knight's fiefs' (*Ritter-* or *Schildlehen*), obliged their holders to act as armed retainers for their lord and provided the primary way in which princes discharged their own obligations to the Empire prior to early modernity. The second category emerged through the extension of vassalage as a means of profiting from the new forms of wealth being created by commoners. 'Wallet fiefs' developed in late medieval Austria and Bavaria as peasants agreed to pay dues into their lord's wallet (*Beutel*) rather than perform various services in person. In fourteenth-century Brandenburg and elsewhere, burghers acquired fiefs and even towns held them collectively. The commercialization of fief-holding and lordship generally allowed this to spread as lords sold or pawned fiefs. By 1596, 54 of Württemberg's 181 lesser fiefs were held by commoners.[23]

Contemporaries responded to the growing complexity of feudal arrangements by trying after 1200 to fix their overall structure in what was known as the 'military shield order' (*Heerschildordnung*). This envisaged a hierarchy descending from the king through ecclesiastical princes, secular princes, counts and barons, subvassals of these, further subvassals or ministeriales and finally the commoner 'passive vassals'. Authors accepted some regional variations, but such schemes remained an idealized representation of reality and were abandoned by 1500.[24] There was never a single continuous feudal chain from king to peasant. All secular princes and most counts and barons were in fact immediately subordinate to the king, and not through other intermediaries.

More meaningful distinctions were expressed in new forms of homage and investiture rituals developed during the thirteenth century. Princes received enfeoffment in person from the enthroned king to symbolize their proximity to majesty. Counts and knights were summoned to receive enfeoffment from their nearest prince acting as the emperor's proxy, while citizens swore homage through their magistrates in the imperial cities. Princely investitures assumed increasingly elaborate forms in the high Middle Ages. A prince would arrive at the emperor's camp with hundreds of followers. He would then ride round the king three times while his nearest relations kneeled as petitioners before the monarch. The prince then dismounted and knelt to receive investiture (see Plate 23). The development of heraldry added to the display. Electors received flags emblazoned with the badge of their arch-office, while senior immediate vassals were given red flags symbolizing their superior 'bloody jurisdiction' (*Blutsgerichtsbarkeit*) over capital crimes.[25] Elements of written culture crept in; for instance, the counts were summoned by letter rather than imperial heralds by the fifteenth century. However, the rituals demonstrated the continued importance of the personal element in these arrangements, which, like those during the earlier Middle Ages, were agreed discreetly in advance to avoid public humiliation for the participants.

TERRITORIALIZATION

Territories in Imperial History

Territorialization denotes how the status and rights associated with fiefs became fixed in specific lands. The term derives from Leopold von Ranke in 1839 who distinguished political development at the level of the principalities from that at national level. Like 'feudalization', the term is both useful and problematic. Ranke's distinction proved fundamental in entrenching the dualist interpretation of the Empire being eaten from within as the principalities supposedly usurped the emperor's powers. It implies that territorialization was 'unwanted', driven instead by princes who placed their own interests above those of the nation. The customary linkage of 'territory' to 'state' adds to this, suggesting a federalization of the Empire as a loose association of what became de facto independent states. Similar problems stem from the strong contemporary tradition of regional history, which traces the development of the modern German federal states (*Bundesländer*) from the various principalities, counties and cities once occupying their current space.[26]

Territorialization was a feature of the entire Empire and not just those principalities large enough to appear on the pages of historical atlases. The process emerged from the wider adjustments of power outlined in the preceding section and which represented a division of labour within the elite's collective responsibility for the Empire. The emperor upheld the Empire's overall integrity, pursued the imperial mission, and offered 'leadership' along the lines of idealized kingship. The princely elite exercised more local responsibilities for order and justice through their 'political self-sufficiency'.[27] They were expected to carry out their tasks without the emperor's supervision or assistance. Territorialization developed to enable them to achieve this, thus complementing rather than contradicting imperial authority. The late medieval and early modern conflicts between emperors and princes remained largely personal, not constitutional.

The exercise of jurisdiction had always entailed some sense of spatial limits, though this was complicated by the fact that authority was often over people, not places. As earlier chapters have indicated, the original duchies were not understood by their inhabitants as having precise frontiers. The feudalization of vassalage helped change conceptions of space and authority, encouraging the reconfiguration of the Empire's internal order as a hierarchy of spatial divisions defined by the feudal order. These divisions gradually acquired solidity, crystallizing between about 1480 and 1580. While they could be combined into larger units, they could no longer be merged or dissolved into each other. New administrative subdivisions emerged that became equally rigid. These boundaries persisted well beyond 1806, in some cases to the present.

Social and Economic Factors

Territorialization is associated with princes, but was only possible thanks to the demographic and economic growth since the eleventh century that enabled lords to exploit land more intensively and extensively. Much of the Empire remained covered in forest and twelfth-century lords acquired more exclusive rights over these and other 'empty' areas, and used the prerogatives granted by the emperor to command the labour needed to clear woodland, drain marshes and plant wastes. The internal migration discussed in Chapter 2 was also part of this general situation. Changes in land use necessitated clearer boundaries to demarcate lordly authority and secure exclusive claims to labour and resources. Meanwhile, the greater concentration of wealth and people provided support for a larger and denser lordly hierarchy, especially in south and west Germany.

The Staufer charters of 1220 and 1231 accelerated an existing trend to fix authority in writing. The nascent princely elite began creating their own chancelleries from their personal chapel staff, like the emperor had done three centuries earlier. Cologne, the Palatinate and Upper Bavaria all did this during the thirteenth century, being joined by Austria (1299) and Württemberg (1350). Most others only followed in the fifteenth century, including Saxony (1428), Lower Hessen (1469), and all larger territories after the 1480s.[28] These bodies developed their own internal hierarchies and demarcation of function as their advisory role was transferred to separate 'court councils', which also assumed greater permanence around the mid-fourteenth century. The chancelleries' initial primary task was to maintain the feudal registers (*Lehensbücher*) appearing from 1220 and listing subordinate vassals and their obligations. The registers were expanded from the mid-fourteenth century to record the issuing of charters and other key documents and were soon supplemented by correspondence ledgers. These developments were rarely consistent, nor planned. Tirol maintained financial accounts from 1288, but stopped this when it passed to the Habsburgs in 1363 and only resumed the practice in 1415.

Territorialization was also related to the broader social transformation from aristocratic kindreds to patrilinear families, because the greater wealth both reduced mutual dependency whilst increasing the desire to demarcate exclusive shares. Like the emperors, princely families developed identities around castles, monasteries and family tombs. The margraves of Baden developed the Cistercian monastery of Lichtenfeld in 1248, which they used to bury their dead for the next 150 years as a focal point for their self-identity.[29] One family's misfortune was often a boon to others and the margraves were fortunate to acquire additional territory through inheritance. Natural extinction ended the rise of the Ebersbergers in Bavaria, Conradiners in the Wetterau and

Ezzonids on the Lower Rhine by the mid-eleventh century, dispersing their carefully accumulated lands to others. Indeed, the development of patrilinear families created smaller breeding groups, increasing the chances of extinction, though those chances were now usually only limited to individual branches. The demise of the Zähringer in 1218 halted the growth of a potentially powerful south-west German duchy, which was split between what became Baden, Fürstenberg and the Swiss confederation. Conversely, the longevity of individual rulers often contributed to territorialization. Count Eberhard I ruled Württemberg for 46 years after 1279, enabling him to exploit four changes of king to recover lands lost at the start of his reign to Rudolf I. Count Eberhard II's 48-year rule after 1344 then consolidated Württemberg and provided the basis for its subsequent elevation to a duchy.[30]

Unlike the emperor, lords holding immediate fiefs enjoyed greater powers to escheat lesser, mediate fiefs, enabling them to block potential local rivals by preventing anyone accumulating too many holdings. Meanwhile, the recovery of vacant mediate fiefs allowed lords to reward loyal clients by enfeoffing them. As a result, access to higher status grew more restricted, since it was difficult for lesser nobles to accumulate their own powerbase, which could support their personal elevation. The difficulty in securing sufficient land contributed to biological extinction. Only 10 of the 25 Styrian lordly (*Herren*) families in 1300 survived a century later, while those in Carinthia declined from 12 to two across 1286–1446. The number of Austrian lordly families fell from 33 in 1200 to nine by 1450. Changes in the lower ranks were even greater: 118 Lower Austrian knightly families died out between 1524 and 1574, followed by another 92 by 1625. Only 83 of the 259 Brandenburg noble families in 1540 were still represented in 1800. This reflected a 'natural' process in pre-industrial Europe because richer families fared better as they produced more children. Thus, while a status group might preserve its overall wealth, its composition could change significantly as the poorer families died out. Unless it opened its ranks to new members, such a group could face gradual extinction. The top stratum of the bishop of Würzburg's vassals was the only one to grow (from 12 families in 1303 to 51 by 1519), whereas the total number of vassal families declined from 421 to 182 in the same period.[31]

Although the Würzburg mediate elite prospered, they and their equivalents elsewhere had no prospect of forming their own territories without first acquiring the status of immediacy through their own personal elevation, or the purchase or inheritance of an existing immediate fief. However, even counties offered only a restricted basis, since most of the large ones had already been raised as new principalities. Most of the counties that remained in the fourteenth century only comprised a castle, small town or large village, and some parcels of land. Rule here was more direct, since few counts had many mediate vassals of their own. Dynastic partitions eroded the potential of many counts' families on the Rhine, Main and Danube. For instance, the county of Löwenstein was sold to the Palatinate in the mid-fifteenth century only to re-emerge after 1611 to accommodate junior lines of the Wittelsbachs. Counts declined in prestige as a group because many counties passed into the hands of princes whose ranks were also growing. The counts of Görz sold all their possessions to the Habsburgs between 1335 and 1500. By 1400, few of the families of counts had held that rank for more than a century and none were viable contenders to be German king in contrast to the position around 1300 (see pp. 377–96).

Growing commercialization contributed to territorialization by eroding the original military function of vassalage and providing a way that additional fiefs could be acquired. Fiefs could be assessed in terms of cash values, derived from revenue streams or land prices, rather than in disparate forms of produce and bundles of rights and obligations. It became easier to transfer fiefs, because it was clearer what was being sold and how much it should cost. This also helped resolve inheritance disputes without involving the emperor as arbitrator. Large fiefs were very expensive. Albrecht III sold his share of the Habsburg lands to his brother Leopold for 100,000 florins in 1379, while Sigismund transferred Brandenburg to Friedrich IV of Hohenzollern for four times that sum in 1415.[32] Those with cash could develop and expand their territories. The Württemberg counts founded only seven towns, but bought three in the thirteenth century, 47 in the fourteenth and 10 more in the fifteenth century. This example illustrates another general point in that the counts bought land and lordships wherever these became available as a means to amass wealth and influence, rather than to create a neat, compact territory. For example, they made extensive purchases in the 1320s in Alsace, a considerable distance across the Rhine from their county; safeguarding these enclaves would haunt Württemberg rulers until they were finally lost in the French Revolutionary Wars.[33] Although families generally tried to concentrate their acquisitions from the late fourteenth century, territorialization continued to follow the logic of the imperial status hierarchy, not modern geopolitical thinking.

The intensification of vassalage and commercialization of fief-holding combined to create new subdivisions within princely jurisdictions. These, in turn, slowly gave fiefs greater geographical coherence. Dependent vassals became more closely associated with these subdivisions after the mid-thirteenth century. Other factors assisted this, including the shift to patrilinear families based in castles where the eldest male assumed responsibility for discharging obligations to the lord. The emergence of a more fixed parish structure also provided a handy means to define the shape of the subdivisions, which increasingly became known as 'districts' (*Ämter*). This process was neither rational nor planned. Most princely jurisdictions remained a collection of subordinate fiefs. Large chunks of land often remained unincorporated within the district structure – in some cases into the eighteenth century. Districts were generally small, mostly only three or four parishes, but they never replaced villages and towns as the primary foci for inhabitants' identities.

Nonetheless, districts slowly acquired greater coherence, especially as they developed more clearly as administrative units under district officials (*Amtleute* or *Amtmänner*). Larger territories like Bavaria, Saxony, Styria and the Palatinate created superior districts (*Oberämter*) as an additional coordinating layer between the centre and localities. Again, variations remained. Officials in only 13 of the 40 to 45 districts in sixteenth-century Brandenburg were directly appointed by the elector, with the rest comprising his subvassals serving in that capacity under feudal obligations.[34] By then, the district was the chief administrative unit in most territories and its official received new powers in line with the expanding ambitions of princes to regulate ordinary life and to meet the new obligations imposed by imperial reform (see pp. 396–408 and 445–62). Above all, districts provided the infrastructure required to collect taxes. Geldern in north-west Germany was unusual in already establishing a central treasury with its own accounts in 1290 in addition to the ledgers maintained by the districts. The other small Rhenish territories followed suit by 1350, but Austria and Bavaria were more typical in only doing this around 1500.

Ecclesiastical Territorialization

Ecclesiastical lords were initially ahead of their secular counterparts in developing the elements that eventually fused as territorialization. Bishops and abbots already lived apart from other clergy in their own residences by 900, followed by abbesses during the twelfth century, adding to their sense of being by various definitions 'superior'.[35] The task of church-building, together with the higher burdens imposed by medieval kings on the imperial church, encouraged the development of taxes well before these appeared in most secular fiefs. As we have seen (pp. 347–8), ecclesiastical lords were the first to employ ministeriales, circa 1020. Around a century later, these lords were building their own stone castles, like Aschaffenburg (1122) and Erfurt (1123) that were constructed to protect the archbishop of Mainz's key possessions. Ecclesiastical lords also benefited from being based in towns, whereas few secular lordships possessed sizable towns prior to the later Middle Ages. Senior clerics had already developed traditions of being buried in their main church before most secular lords cultivated family tombs.

However, ecclesiastical territorialization gathered pace precisely at a time when many cathedral towns escaped episcopal jurisdiction by securing recognition of their self-governance. Bishops retained control of the cathedral and usually some other important buildings, but otherwise lost the ability to command the inhabitants' wealth and labour (see pp. 512–15). Although senior clergy developed a sense of transpersonal office, they were not hereditary rulers. The Investiture Dispute and papal schisms proved particularly disruptive, because rival popes frequently appointed their own bishops to the same see. Even under normal conditions, a new bishop often had to find his feet and cultivate local clients. Cathedrals and abbeys had their own administrations known as 'chapters' staffed by canons supported by benefices attached to the church. Chapters acquired additional resources and rights. For example, Henry IV allowed the chapter in Speyer to own property after 1101. Chapters considered themselves representatives of their church and had displaced lesser clergy and lay inhabitants from any role in selecting new bishops and abbots by the high Middle Ages. The position of chapters was strengthened by the outcome of the Investiture Dispute, which confirmed the principle of 'free election'. The chapters developed along broadly similar lines to the Empire's electoral college and entrenched their position by bargaining 'electoral agreements' from prospective bishops and abbots from the fourteenth century. Innocent XII forbade further agreements after 1695 and though such contracts continued to be made, bishops were generally backed by the pope and emperor in the event of disputes. Moreover, canons frequently hoped to become bishops themselves, and so refrained from undermining episcopal powers too far. Ecclesiastical princes thus broadly followed their secular counterparts in adopting a more command-style of governance from the later seventeenth century, complete with magnificent new palaces to display their status.[36]

Spiritual boundaries remained fairly stable, since they could only be altered with papal agreement, unlike the frequent partitions and changes in secular jurisdictions. However, the actual territory of bishops and abbots was always much smaller than their spiritual jurisdictions. Since it originated in gifts of crown land to the church, ecclesiastical territory was considered inalienable. Pieces were sold or pawned, but never on the scale witnessed with secular possessions, especially as the chapters always opposed alienation as threatening to their church. The Salians transferred numerous counties to church lords, while, as we have seen, Frederick II confirmed the bishops' possession of ducal powers entailing judicial and military privileges equivalent to the secular princes. The Staufers' demise ended the growth of ecclesiastical lands and jurisdictions, since no future monarchs were able to be so generous, while the spiritual character of abbots and bishops ensured that they could not accumulate further lands through inheritance. The subsequent viability of ecclesiastical territories therefore depended on how far they had been favoured by earlier medieval rulers. Paderborn and Eichstätt remained poor, as did bishoprics and abbeys north of the Elbe, which were mostly later foundations which had had less time to acquire land than the longer-established ones in the old core regions along the Rhine and Main. The relative vulnerability of many northern and eastern ecclesiastical territories also helps explain why they were already on their way to being secularized ahead of the Reformation.

Ecclesiastical lords also appeared to be less potent patrons than their secular counterparts after 1250 and were often unable to prevent their vassals escaping their jurisdiction. Cologne is a prominent example. Since the 1060s, successive archbishops had amassed the extensive *terra coloniensis* across north-west Germany, consolidated by the grant of their new title as duke of Westphalia in 1180. However, the counts took the opportunity of the Staufer's demise to emancipate themselves during the later thirteenth century. The defeat of Archbishop Siegfried von Westerburg of Cologne in the battle of Worringen in 1288 proved a major setback and though he continued to oppose his counts' desires, those in Geldern, Jülich, Berg and Cleves all eventually secured their autonomy through the acquisition of ducal titles in the fourteenth century. A similar process occurred in the archbishopric of Trier where the counts of Luxembourg and Nassau escaped jurisdiction, while the bishop of Würzburg found his acquisition of the old Franconian ducal title did not improve his position relative to neighbouring secular lords.[37]

Mainz became hemmed in through the expansion of secular neighbours (Map 17). The acquisition by the lords of Hessen of the landgraviate of Thuringia in 1247 enabled them to develop a distinct territory, cutting that of Mainz in two by isolating the section around Erfurt from the main strip at the Rhine–Main nexus. Hessen was able to stop Mainz from summoning its inhabitants before episcopal courts after 1370. Mainz's refusal to grant similar concessions to the neighbouring Palatinate led to a long and debilitating dispute that lasted from the fifteenth century into the 1660s. However, ecclesiastical lords were not invariably the losers. Margrave Albrecht Achilles of Bayreuth overreached himself in the mid-fifteenth century when he tried to coerce local monasteries into accepting his protection, but fell deeply into debt when he was then blocked by the bishop of Bamberg.[38]

Secular Territorialization

The examples of Mainz, Hessen and the Palatinate suggest we should not interpret territorialization as a linear process driven by a succession of rulers all working to the same plan. The Palatinate remained one of the most powerful 'territories' of the later Middle Ages by relying on its electoral and Palatine status and rights, rather than through amassing land. It owed its later influence to Barbarossa's transfer of the count Palatine title to his half-brother Conrad of Staufen in 1156, and the subsequent grant of former Salian estates in the Rhineland and, especially, protectorates over Worms, Speyer and Lorsch ecclesiastical properties. The royal estates at Alzey were transferred to the Palatinate in 1214, followed by fiefs acquired from Speyer and Worms; the latter included Heidelberg in 1225, which became the administrative seat. The Staufers' demise ended these donations, ensuring that Palatine territorialization was closer to that of the ecclesiastical territories rather than hereditary secular duchies. Subsequent growth remained largely restricted to efforts at converting the Palatinate's bundles of jurisdictions over knights, towns and monasteries into more immediate forms of control.[39]

Thuringia's example also illustrates how territorialization was never a simple process of consolidation. Originally the area of the Toringi, who had been conquered by the Franks in 534, Thuringia was bounded by the Harz mountains and the Unstrut, Werra and Saale rivers. In addition to Erfurt, which belonged to Mainz, the region contained the important imperial abbeys of Fulda and Hersfeld. The accession of the Ottonians in 919 transformed it from a border zone to a core region soon endowed with important palaces. The Ludowinger family of counts based at Schauenburg became the dominant local presence under the Salians and were awarded the title of landgrave in 1130. Barbarossa rewarded Ludowinger support by giving them the Palatine powers formerly associated with ducal Saxony, which he stripped from Henry the Lion in 1180. These powers were similar to those of the counts Palatine on the Rhine, and gave the Thuringian landgrave opportunities to cultivate his own clientele. The Ludowinger family inherited additional property in Hessen protected by the castle of Marburg, as well as the castles of Neuburg on the Unstrut and the Wartburg, the latter made famous in 1517 when Luther nailed his *Ninety-Five Theses* on its chapel door. So far, Thuringia's development fitted the classic pattern of gradual accumulation and consolidation. It was sufficiently advanced for Landgrave Heinrich Raspe to be considered worthy of election as anti-Staufer king in 1246. However, Thuringia was not coherent enough to survive his death a year later, as this opened a prolonged inheritance dispute that eventually pulled it apart. Hessen passed as a separate territory to the counts of Brabant, who were awarded a landgrave title in 1292. The rest passed to the Wettin family as counts of Meissen, who managed to repel royal efforts to escheat it as a vacant fief between 1294 and 1307. The Wettins resumed the earlier consolidation, but were unable to reassert control over the lords of

Gleichen, Henneberg, Reuss and Schwarzburg, who had meanwhile gained autonomy. The Wettins acquired the Saxon ducal title from the defunct Wittenberg branch of the Askanier in 1423, but split their possessions in 1485, separating the electorate of Saxony to the east from the rump of Thuringia, which was subsequently partitioned as the 'Saxon duchies' of Weimar, Gotha and Coburg after 1572, followed by further subdivisions during the next two centuries.[40]

Partitions were a constant feature, indicating the very slow acceptance of dynasticism as a political principle. The Welfs split in 1267, barely three decades after the establishment of their new duchy at Brunswick, and multiple lines persisted until 1918. Hessen repeatedly split into Upper and Lower sections after 1308, with this division becoming permanent with the establishment of separate lines based in Kassel and Darmstadt in 1567. Baden's initial expansion stalled in repeated partitions after 1190, with only a brief reunification from 1475 to 1536 until the various sections were finally concentrated in 1771. Other families divided their lands without such serious repercussions for their subsequent influence: the Habsburgs, Wittelsbachs, Hohenzollerns and (to an extent) the Wettins.

Jülich's steady expansion on the Lower Rhine was thus highly unusual. Its dukes successively acquired Geldern, Berg, Ravensberg, Cleves and Mark between 1393 and 1521. Its demise was rather more typical. Biological extinction of the ruling line opened what proved the last inheritance dispute accompanied by serious violence, between 1609 and 1614, other than that over the Austrian succession (1740–48), which was an altogether different affair.[41] Jülich's example also demonstrates the growing rigidity of fiefs, since its expansion occurred after feudal jurisdictions had acquired more stable identities and boundaries. Each fief retained its own laws and institutions as it was acquired by the duke of Jülich, who held fiefs as a personal union rather than integrated territory.

The Growing Significance of Mediate Fiefs

The inheritance or transfer of immediate fiefs affected their mediate, dependent vassals as well. Territories thus remained composites, comprising three elements: 1) the allodial possessions of the ruling family in secular principalities or lands attached to the cathedral and chapter in ecclesiastical ones; 2) the possessions of territorial subjects subject to their prince's legal and fiscal jurisdiction; and 3) the mediate vassals' fiefs. The exact mix varied considerably, while jurisdictions frequently did not entirely align with land ownership. For example, ecclesiastical princes exercised spiritual jurisdiction across the lands of their secular neighbours, while princes might share rights or hold different levels of criminal jurisdiction over parts of their possessions.

Crucially, fief-holding retained political and military significance across the fourteenth and fifteenth centuries and did not simply become another form of landownership, unlike in France and England where lords responded to the new economic pressures by converting many of their obligations into cash payments. Instead, the periodic struggles to control the German crown required that princes and their vassals remain armed.[42] Armed retaliation through feuds remained a legal way to seek redress under imperial law, while lordship over mediate vassals offered an effective way to expand influence in the conditions of the later thirteenth century. The Staufers' last decade saw serious fighting in much of the Empire, while the kings after 1257 were rarely able to help their lesser vassals. The ministeriales and knights charged with administering crown lands and protecting imperial abbeys were usually too weak to fend for themselves. Many placed themselves under the protection of neighbouring bishops or secular princes, notably the count Palatine and the dukes of Bavaria.

This process continued even as the general political situation stabilized after 1273, because the agrarian depression setting in around 1300 adversely affected the lesser vassals. Many of those who were still 'free' (i.e. immediate under the king) now voluntarily placed themselves under princely protection and became mediate vassals. The new understanding of property greatly facilitated this, because the knights retained 'rights of usage' of their fiefs. Often, these arrangements included princely confirmation of new forms of inheritance allowing the knight to exclude daughters and other relations in future. Overall, these developments hastened the merger of the ministeriales within the lesser nobility, either as knights who remained free under the king or as a new social Estate of 'territorial nobles' (*Landadel*) under a prince.

These changes were often accompanied by considerable violence at the local level, because they involved clarifying exactly who was subordinate to whom and what rights and land each noble held. Princes also used the new powers acquired in the 1220 and 1231 charters, which allowed them to decide who was allowed to build castles and to oblige their vassals to 'open' their own castles to them. Princes often deliberately manipulated personal and material animosities to extend lordship over a rival's mediate vassals. Nobles responded by forming associations to defend their status and autonomy. Princes could offer cash subsidies to cover the cost of service as inducements to entice vassals to switch allegiance. They also broke up their own allodial property to form new fiefs that could be granted to clients.[43]

Although still useful, the term 'territorialization' is thus in many ways a misnomer. Rather than the coloured patches shown on later historical atlases, princely territories expanded largely as webs of jurisdictions. Coalescence was often interrupted by the extinction of families or their partition into different branches, as well as more fundamentally by the economic and demographic upheavals of the first half of the fourteenth century. True 'territorialization' as conceived by later historians only really commenced with the political and institutional changes of imperial reform during the later fifteenth and sixteenth centuries, as we shall see (pp. 396–406 and 524–38).

FROM LITTLE KINGS TO BIG DYNASTIES

The End of the Staufers

Territorialization advanced further and faster in Bavaria, Austria, Tirol, Bohemia and parts of west and north-west Germany. These were neither necessarily the richest nor most populous parts of the Empire. The prolonged royal presence in Franconia, Swabia, the Upper Rhine and parts of Thuringia contributed to the number of small fiefs emerging from the crown lands, while the concentration of people and wealth in the south-west also helped sustain a larger number of relatively small lordships. The Staufers' demise after 1250 saw the monarchy shift to the more territorialized parts of Germany. At first glance, this appears to corroborate the old view of the Empire as being undermined by princely autonomy. However, the Staufers' end was more personal than structural. After a 15-year absence in Italy and the Holy Land,

Frederick II had returned to Germany in 1235 accompanied by lavishly dressed Muslim bodyguards, camels and elephants – the ultimate symbol of pre-modern imperialism. Despite not recruiting additional troops, he crushed a rebellion without a fight, deposed his son Henry (VII) and Duke Friedrich II Babenberg of Austria, and settled the long-running dispute with the Welfs.[44]

The real problem was legitimacy, not autonomy. The princes certainly desired autonomy, but this is what the Staufers had been giving them since the 1180s. Individual princes might prove uncooperative, like Duke Friedrich II, who recovered Austria by force in 1237 and obliged the emperor to accept this three years later as the price of his support.[45] However, it was Frederick's mishandling of the situation in Italy and his second excommunication after 1239 that undermined his authority and made it harder to compel the princes to honour their commitments to the Empire.

The Survival of the Monarchy

The period from the death of Frederick II's son Conrad IV in 1254 and Rudolf I's accession in 1273 appears as an 'interregnum' in traditional accounts.[46] The papacy certainly regarded the imperial title as vacant until Henry VII's coronation in 1312. However, there was no break in German kings who throughout also claimed to rule over Burgundy and Italy. Indeed, there were often too many kings. The anti-king William of Holland outlived Conrad IV to enjoy two years' uncontested rule. The double election after his death returned both Alfonso X of Castile and Richard, earl of Cornwall, who had Staufer credentials through being Frederick II's brother-in-law. Unlike Alfonso, who never visited Germany, Richard came to be crowned king in Aachen in May 1257. He distributed privileges to his supporters, but also used force against those who had backed Alfonso. He was obliged in 1259 to return to England where deteriorating relations between his brother King Henry III and the barons threatened the flow of funds financing his rule. He came back briefly to Germany in 1260, before leaving to support his brother in the Barons' War, in which he was captured. German princes continued to visit him in England, while his supporters successfully repelled an incursion of Conradin, the last Staufer, from Italy into Swabia in 1262. The Angevins' execution of Conradin in 1268 eased

Richard's position just as he was at last able to return to Germany where he spent around a year enjoying uncontested rule, before being obliged to leave for England again where he died in April 1272. Richard retained the feudal relations developed by the Staufers, as well as several key officials who had served William of Holland. The idea of Richard's reign as an interregnum only developed after 1273 as Rudolf I's supporters presented him as 'restoring' the monarchy.[47]

The 75 years after Richard's death proved an era of 'leaping elections' (*springenden Wahlen*) with five successive kings from different families until greater continuity emerged under the Luxembourgs. In contrast to previous monarchs, these were all 'little kings' unrelated to earlier royal lines and they came instead mainly from the ranks of the counts. Their low status should not mislead us into underestimating the continued power and prestige of the Empire's monarchy. Apparent royal weakness was scarcely unusual. In Richard's homeland, Edward I was the sole king to rule uncontested during the twelfth and thirteenth centuries, while only three English kings were succeeded directly by their sons, and just one ruled without an assassination attempt. Above all, the royal office never became a worthless prize in the manner of, say, the Chinese presidency in the warlord era of 1911–30, and those possessing it were able to achieve tangible goals.

One reason for the monarchy's continued significance was that it was part of a wider framework in which the other participants still believed and valued. The king symbolized the proper order. Individual details might be disputed, but no one doubted that a proper order was *monarchical*. Aachen and Frankfurt remained the key political sites. The Empire did not fragment. Duke Friedrich II's attempt to secure recognition of Austria as a kingdom failed in the mid-1240s.[48] Bohemia remained a kingdom, but also firmly within the Empire. Continued subordination to the king was not simply out of habit, but because the Empire's survival had become part of the princes' self-consciousness. Individuals might acquire crown lands, but no one could usurp royal prerogatives without threatening the rights and autonomy of all princes as the monarch's immediate vassals.

Despite the absence of a crowned emperor, the princes still saw themselves as part of the wider Empire rather than simply lords of what were, still, relatively small territories. They embraced the Staufers' concept of collective *honor imperii*, because feudalization had heightened their sense of being stakeholders in the established order. This explains why they were prepared to cooperate with the resumption of the Staufers' public-peace activities by Richard and Rudolf (see pp. 620–22). New ideas of the princes' roles were carried by men educated at Italian universities who were now entering royal and princely service. Princes were not simply royal agents following commands, but members of a corporate elite expected to act on their own initiative to secure peace within their jurisdictions. Although still subordinate, princes were thus co-constituents of monarchy, not counterweights to potential monarchical tyranny as elsewhere. This explains why the Empire's princes did not develop a right of resistance like Polish or Hungarian aristocrats, nor did they seek to limit royal power through more institutional forms like a House of Lords in the English, Polish or Hungarian parliaments.

Another major reason was that the three senior princes were all ecclesiastical: Mainz, Cologne and Trier. As clergy, they could not stand as candidates in royal elections, and yet their own prestige derived from their arch-offices and roles in elections and coronations. Apart from 1257 when Trier broke ranks, contributing to the double election, the three ecclesiastical electors worked to preserve the collective order. Meanwhile, the deliberate partition of the old duchies after Henry the Lion's defeat in 1180 prevented the emergence of an obvious candidate to follow the Staufers after 1254, since none of the secular princes held a commanding position. The situation embedded as a lasting characteristic of imperial politics. All the main actors wanted to preserve the overall structure whilst adjusting their own position within it. They tended to combine against anyone threatening this system's basic stability. While self-correcting, the internal balance was far from harmonious. It was now much harder to pick a winner in royal elections, as no contender appeared much stronger than his rivals after 1250. This widened the political possibilities as different factions coalesced in the hope of security and reward. The absence of firm electoral rules prior to 1356 also encouraged this and contributed to the double elections of 1257 and 1314.

Each new king exploited his reign to reward his most reliable supporters, but particularly himself by enhancing the autonomy of his own territory.[49] This naturally fuelled resentment amongst those who had backed defeated candidates and contributed to their refusal to repeat the practice before 1250 of recognizing a successor during the lifetime of an incumbent king. This explains the succession of kings from different families after 1254. However, there was no free-for-all. The situation worked to narrow rather than widen the number of viable candidates. Despite their expansion under the Staufers, the princes remained a small elite within a much larger aristocracy (Map 6). Most were simply too weak to stand for election, especially as potential electors did not want to become obliged to bail out their candidate should he encounter difficulties, and so they still sought able men with considerable resources. Although they failed to secure a direct successor, each incumbent generally strengthened his own family's position during his reign, thus elevating it further from those who had not yet provided a king.

Royal Candidates

Politics thus resembled a game of musical chairs, with each successive reign reducing the number of 'players'. Moreover, not everyone wanted to 'play' as personal interests and local concerns discouraged individual princes from standing. Only Bavaria remained from the original duchies by the thirteenth century as a substantial principality. Since 1180 it had been held by the Wittelsbachs, who originated from the counts of Scheyern in the eleventh century and took their name from their new castle south-west of Pfaffenhofen in 1115. Their influence really began once they acquired the more prestigious county Palatine on the Rhine in 1214, and they saw themselves as the Staufers' natural successor after 1250.[50] However, the family provides another illustration of how territorialization and dynasticism were not planned or desired historical outcomes. Bavaria was partitioned into Upper and Lower duchies in 1255 to accommodate two brothers as heirs. Both lines experienced further splits before a brief reunification from 1340 to 1349, with renewed partition only being resolved through a bloody inheritance dispute in 1504–5. Bavaria and the Palatinate were held combined until 1317 when a separate Palatine Wittelsbach line emerged before itself splitting four ways in 1410. Further partitions followed a brief reunion between 1449 and 1470. Bavaria and the Palatinate were not recombined until 1779, with a final reunification of all other possessions taking a further twenty years.

The Askanier also split with individual branches offering candidates in royal elections: the margrave of Brandenburg stood in 1257, followed by the count of Anhalt in 1273. The division of the line ruling Saxony in 1288 into rival Wittenberg and Lauenburg branches frustrated the family's efforts to claim Thuringia and complicated royal elections, since both claimed the Saxon vote until this was definitively awarded to Wittenberg in 1356.

With Wittelsbach and Askanier influence dissipated, only Bohemia and the Habsburgs appeared plausible candidates to succeed Richard of Cornwall in 1273. Bohemia was now by far the most prestigious territory in the Empire, thanks to its royal title, relative size and annual revenues of 100,000 silver marks – five times that enjoyed by the duke of Bavaria.[51] King Ottokar II voted twice in 1257 deliberately to force Richard to allow him to claim the vast Babenberg inheritance of Austria, Carinthia, Krain and Styria left vacant by that family's extinction in 1246. However, Ottokar's growing power alarmed the other electors, who chose Rudolf I of Habsburg instead in 1273.

Rudolf I

Rudolf is often presented as attempting to reset the monarchy on a centralizing course by initiating a policy of 'Revindication' in December 1273. Named from the Latin verb *revindicare* ('to demand back'), this was intended to recover crown lands dissipated since the 1240s. The losses were indeed severe: only a tenth of mints remained in royal hands, while the crown now only held rights over one in ten towns compared to one in three at the start of the thirteenth century.[52] Rudolf had to compromise, allowing politically important princes to retain some areas they had acquired, though he often reworked the basis to weaken their absolute ownership. Overall, the results were impressive: Rudolf revived crown control over imperial church fiefs to 66 per cent of the level under the Staufers, whilst recovering crown lands to 73 per cent and Staufer family property to an impressive 68 per cent considering this had been almost completely lost. The bulk of Staufer allodial possessions were thus added to the crown lands. Thanks to intervening economic development, the combined value of crown possessions was now higher than under the Staufers. Rudolf's success further underscores the argument that the monarchy did not unduly suffer during the 'interregnum'.

The main changes included an end to the expansion of the crown lands and their concentration in south-west Germany combined with a considerable contraction in Saxony and the Lower Rhine. Less obviously, management also changed in response to the continuing emancipation of the ministeriales as knights, as well as further immunities for royal monasteries. Some of these developments were long term. Already in the eleventh century, kings stopped drawing supplies from the economically weaker monasteries and instead granted these exemptions or assigned them to supplement the resources of larger abbeys or bishoprics. Meanwhile, obligations to provide food and accommodation for the royal entourage were increasingly converted into cash taxes from the early twelfth century – well ahead of similar developments in France. Taxation was extended to royal towns that had developed on crown lands under the Staufers. The obligation to feed and accommodate the king was frequently commuted into cash but, unlike the situation in Italy, German royal towns remained more directly subordinate to the king. Rudolf also developed structures already initiated by Richard of Cornwall by establishing jurisdictions called 'bailiwicks' (*Landvogteien*) to oversee the towns and recovered crown assets. Bailiffs were selected from loyal counts and knights who were charged with safeguarding royal prerogatives and upholding peace within their jurisdictions. The network was renewed in 1292 and continued into the first half of the fourteenth century. However, it only encompassed the crown lands and not the immediate fiefs of the lay and spiritual princes, who remained subordinate to the king through the feudal hierarchy developed under the Staufers.

The bailiwicks reflected the geographic spread of royal influence by being concentrated in the south and west.[53] Bohemia was temporarily compelled to return the former Staufer crown land of Eger in 1276, but Rudolf encountered serious difficulties when he tried to recover Austria, Carinthia, Styria, Krain and Thuringia on the grounds these were vacant imperial fiefs since the deaths of the last Babenberg (1246) and Heinrich Raspe (1247). Repeated efforts to obtain these fiefs were a central feature of imperial politics until finally abandoned in the mid-fourteenth century. Virtually the entire north, constituting a third of the German kingdom, was 'distant from the king'. Only 3 per cent of Rudolf's charters were issued from locations in this area, while he never ventured further north-west than Aachen.[54] The last royal visit to

Goslar was in 1253. Political gravity shifted south-west, despite isolated later incidents like Charles IV's visit to Lübeck in 1375. The regions 'close to the king' were now Swabia, Franconia, the Middle and Upper Rhineland and parts of Thuringia. These provided most of the resources sustaining the monarchy into the early fourteenth century. The reliance of kings on these regions helped sustain the still large numbers of free minor lords, several of whom benefited from elevations in status, like the Zollerns, who became burgraves of the Nuremberg bailiwick and later rose to prominence as the Hohenzollerns. Not everyone was prepared to cooperate. The Württemberg counts showed how it was still possible to prosper despite generally refusing to serve the king. They rallied support in the south-west from those who saw Rudolf's plans as threatening the autonomy they had won since 1250. Count Eberhard I led a revolt in 1285–7 that blocked Rudolf's attempt to re-establish the duchy of Swabia.[55]

The bulk of the assets recovered through Revindication were alienated again in the century following Rudolf's death in 1291. The form of alienation differed from that prior to 1273, because many were now pawned either for cash mortgages or under new service agreements binding the mortgagee to provide support over long periods. Pawning became more common from the late thirteenth century, because mortgages circumvented canonical prohibitions on usury by transferring assets rather than contracting loans against interest. Only 13 imperial cities were never pawned between 1273 and 1438.[56] Unlike transfer by gift or enfeoffment, the king retained the option of recovering the property by redeeming the mortgage. However, the mortgages were often so high as to make redemption unlikely: Louis IV mortgaged Eger for 20,000 pounds of silver in 1322 back to Bohemia, which retained it permanently. Eger is still today the westernmost point of the Czech Republic. Meanwhile, mortgages cut the king off from the real value of the land since the mortgagee drew the revenue and other benefits in the meantime. Lucrative assets like Rhine tolls, mints, and ore and salt mining rights were repeatedly mortgaged until they were effectively permanently alienated.[57]

All this might suggest that Rudolf's reign indeed represents a lost opportunity to centralize. However, the bailiwicks never represented the basis for a new royal bureaucracy, but instead relied on using established prerogatives to entrust minor lords with supervision of royal assets. The dissipation of these assets through mortgages and other forms of alienation effectively removed the crown lands as a significant resource by the late fourteenth century. Rather than constituting 'decline', this instead reflected a fundamental shift in the basis of imperial rule to rest on the king's direct possession of immediate fiefs as hereditary family lands.

This was already apparent under Rudolf. He owed his election to appearing less of a threat to princely liberties than Ottokar, because Rudolf only held modest possessions in Switzerland and on the Upper Rhine. These produced an annual revenue of just 7,000 pounds in silver; hence the Revindication policy begun soon after his coronation. However, his use of the royal office to contest Ottokar's claims to the Babenberg inheritance proved far more significant in the longer term. Rudolf's methods also illustrate the potential of the new feudal structures developed under the Staufers. Rudolf held an assembly at Nuremberg in November 1274 when he confirmed the princes in possession of their immediate imperial fiefs. However, this act explicitly asserted the monarch as suzerain, requiring all to seek formal re-enfeoffment within a year under the practice of *Herren- und Mannfall* (see p. 300). Rudolf used Ottokar's failure to do this as an excuse to employ force to resolve the disputed Babenberg inheritance in his own favour after 1276. Rudolf's strategy entailed high risks, because few of the princes were prepared to see Ottokar fully divested of his lands. However, this problem was solved by Ottokar's death amidst defeat at Dürnkrut, north-east of Vienna, on 26 August 1278. The electors eventually agreed in 1282 that Rudolf could enfeoff his sons as dukes of Austria and Styria. These acquisitions added 18,000 pounds of silver in annual revenue for the Habsburgs, compared to only 8,000 pounds now flowing from all the imperial cities after Revindication.[58]

Rudolf's victory signalled the new direction, but not yet the definitive turning point. The leading princes still expected the king to live from what were increasingly termed the imperial lands (*Reichsgut*) and, for this reason, had backed Revindication in principle if not always in practice. They remained suspicious of a king who wanted to acquire too many large fiefs directly as family property (*Hausgut*). A transitional pattern set in for the next century. Kings continued to use imperial lands, though increasingly as objects to pawn. Meanwhile, they used their royal office to secure vacant fiefs for their immediate relations. Henry VII was able to enfeoff his son Johann with Bohemia in 1310, while Louis IV gave Holland, Zeeland and Hainault to his son Wilhelm in 1345. By keeping his gains split between his sons in 1282, Rudolf allayed the electors' fears that either would be too powerful. Unfortunately, two of his sons predeceased him, leaving only Albert as sole heir when Rudolf died in July 1291. Albert's curt manner further discouraged the electors, while he was simultaneously distracted by a revolt against Habsburg rule in Switzerland.[59]

Adolf and Albert

The electors eventually chose Count Adolf of Nassau as king in May 1292. Adolf's family was one of the success stories from the previous two centuries, having risen from bailiffs serving the archbishop of Mainz. They amassed a large conglomerate of fiefs and jurisdictions on the Lower Rhine after 1080, securing comital rank when these were grouped into the new county of Nassau in 1160, permitting their emancipation from both Mainz and Trier overlordship. Like so many noble families in this period, their good fortune encouraged partitions after 1255, because their relative wealth allowed them to provide for more of their children through inheritance. Further partitions followed and the Nassau lands were not reunited until the very different circumstances of 1814.

Adolf was the weakest of the 'little kings'. Again, circumstances played a role, because Archbishop Siegfried von Westerburg of Cologne wanted a pliant king to reverse his earlier defeat at Worringen in 1288.[60] Adolf was obliged to grant Cologne and the other electors significant concessions, but otherwise continued Rudolf's Revindication and baili-wick policy. Adolf used the windfall of English subsidies – intended to finance a joint war against France in 1294 – to buy off claims to Thur-ingia and Meissen, enabling him temporarily to incorporate these into the imperial lands in 1296.[61] This proved his undoing, because Bohe-mia, Saxony and Brandenburg still coveted Thuringia and now combined to oppose Adolf, winning support from Mainz and Austria, but not Trier. The dispute gathered momentum as Adolf refused to compromise. Mainz secured agreement from Saxony, Brandenburg and the count Palatine to depose Adolf on 23 June 1298 in the first of what proved to be only two depositions undertaken exclusively by the electors without papal involvement. The action was highly controversial, because the legality of Adolf's election and coronation were uncontested and it was hard to find a convincing argument against him.

The situation demonstrated the relative strength of the monarchy as an institution, even if the current incumbent was weak. Moreover, the decision not to involve the papacy showed how the leading princes shared a sense of collective responsibility for the Empire, despite their ulterior motives. It is likely that they already chose Albert of Austria as successor at this point, though details are sparse.[62] Adolf was killed in the rout of his forces by Albert at Göllheim near Worms on 2 July 1298. His death contributed to the lasting image of him as a failure, yet he had proved surprisingly successful, despite starting from an even weaker base than Rudolf. The outcome demonstrates the continued significance of agency in events: things would have been quite different if Albert had died instead.

Albert ascended the throne tainted by Adolf's death.[63] A new election was staged in a deliberate show of unity and probity. Albert soon proved the electors' original fears from 1292 as correct, swiftly outwitting them to consolidate possession of Thuringia and moving to secure Bohemia, left vacant by the death of the last Premyslid in 1306. He was undone by his own family's lack of dynastic discipline when he was murdered on 1 May 1308 by his nephew Johann, who wanted a larger share of the spoils.

Luxembourgs and Wittelsbachs

The Habsburgs again appeared too strong and the electors rejected Albert's eldest son, Frederick 'the Fair', and instead chose the count of Luxembourg as King Henry VII in 1308. The Luxembourgs' emergence broadly mirrored that of their Nassau neighbours, except that military defeat rather than family partition stalled an otherwise rapid rise to prominence. Luxembourg developed as a large county that eventually became detached from Lorraine by the twelfth century. Attempts by the family to acquire the duchy of Limburg in 1283 triggered the dispute that ended in Cologne's defeat at Worringen in 1288. Luxembourg backed the losing side and lost Limburg. However, Count Henry's brother Balduin was archbishop of Trier and persuaded his electoral colleagues to back Henry.[64] Like Adolf, his initial weakness obliged Henry to make concessions at his accession. He is considered an unrealistic dreamer for being the first monarch since Frederick II to go to Rome and be crowned emperor. However, this move made perfect sense in helping to raise Henry's personal prestige over the other princes. He also continued the trend begun under Rudolf I by renouncing further attempts to incorporate Thuringia within the imperial lands. This bought the necessary support for Henry to escheat Bohemia as a vacant fief and transfer it to his son in 1310, laying the basis of future Luxembourg power, like Rudolf I's acquisition of Austria for the Habsburgs in 1278.

Henry VII's unexpectedly early death from malaria in August 1313 necessitated what unintentionally proved the first double election since 1257. The incremental growth of hereditary fief-holding across the previous forty years made the Luxembourgs and Habsburgs evenly matched frontrunners. Hoping to break the deadlock, Johann of Bohemia's supporters agreed on the Wittelsbach Duke Louis of Upper Bavaria as a compromise candidate. However, Habsburg partisans pre-empted them by electing Frederick the Fair at Frankfurt on 19 October 1314. The Luxembourgs camped at Sachsenhausen on the opposite side of the Main belatedly proclaimed their candidate as Louis IV the next day. Frederick had been elected first, held the correct insignia, and was crowned by the archbishop of Cologne, traditionally considered the 'right' person to do so. However, Louis got to the 'right' location at Aachen first and was crowned by the archbishop of Mainz with substitute insignia. These moves aptly symbolized the underlying political stalemate that opened the Empire to renewed papal interference. Relatively low-level skirmishing shifted the balance gradually in Louis' favour after 1315, culminating in a convincing victory at Mühldorf on the Inn on 28 September 1322 when Frederick was captured. As in 1278 at Dürnkrut and 1298 at Göllheim, the Empire's fate was decided in battle.[65]

Louis defused the dispute by recognizing Frederick as nominal co-king in 1325, the last time this arrangement was used. Louis also distributed some of the remaining south German imperial lands to Frederick's relations and allowed them to inherit Carinthia when this fell vacant in 1335. However, Johann of Bohemia now openly opposed Louis over conflicting claims to Brandenburg, which had fallen vacant on the extinction of the Askanier line there in 1320. A further dispute erupted over rival claims to the Tirol in 1346. These problems illustrated both the growing importance of hereditary possessions in the competition for the monarchy and the dangers for kings who insisted on trying to claim vacant fiefs themselves, rather than standing above disputes as impartial judges. France and the papacy backed the Luxembourgs, while renewed excommunication weakened Louis' legitimacy. In April 1346 five of the seven electors chose Johann's son Charles (IV) as anti-king. Louis remained politically powerful, but died of a heart attack whilst hunting in October 1347.

Shift of Emphasis under Charles IV

Charles IV was an unscrupulous opportunist, dividing contemporary opinion as sharply as Frederick II had in his day.[66] He skilfully held the political balance in the mid-fourteenth century, managing to curb both Habsburg and Wittelsbach influence without driving either into open opposition. Wittelsbach supporters belatedly elected Count Günther von Schwarzenburg as anti-king in January 1349, but he was defeated at Eltville on the Rhine in the third case of the succession being decided in battle, and renounced his title on 29 May in return for an amnesty for his followers. Charles's confirmation of Wittelsbach possession of Brandenburg reconciled the family to his rule, while their continued partitions hindered any real chance of challenging him later. Both Bavaria and Austria were excluded from the electoral college when this was given definitive shape in the Golden Bull of 1356. The secular votes all went to Charles's close allies, including the Wittenberg Askanier rather than the Lauenburg branch that had backed Schwarzenburg. However, Charles reconciled Austria by agreeing a hereditary pact in 1364 that eventually provided the basis for the Habsburgs to succeed the Luxembourgs in 1438. However, like Bavaria, in the meantime convenient deaths and further family partitions prevented the Habsburgs from challenging Luxembourg rule.[67]

Charles's long reign (1346–78) allowed time to consolidate Luxembourg rule and to shift imperial governance decisively to its new basis in hereditary possessions rather than the imperial lands and church. This was not obvious at the start of his reign when he resumed the Revindication policy with particular intensity to recover assets pawned by Louis IV, only to abandon it for good after 1371. Immediate circumstances provided one reason for this decision. Charles pawned four towns and associated lands, together forming what became known as the Upper Palatinate, to the Wittelsbachs in 1373 in return for their renunciation of claims to Brandenburg, allowing him finally to escheat this as a vacant fief that he granted to his second son, Sigismund. In this way, Charles swopped imperial land to expand his family's hereditary possessions. He then extended this to other imperial assets, raising 2 million florins, or 48 per cent of all the cash he received from Germany during his reign.[68] Although the money was useful, it was simply an added bonus from what was now a long-term strategy to wreck the traditional basis for imperial rule. By stripping the royal title of the means to sustain itself, Charles ensured that his family were the only viable candidates as kings, since only they now had the necessary resources. To this end, he also deliberately alienated the infrastructure built up since 1273 to administer imperial lands. The bailiff rights were pawned or sold to the counts exercising them. In one sense, this continued the Staufers' policy of expanding the princely elite as a way of ensuring no single family had too much regional power. For example, the Nuremberg bailiwick was sold to that imperial city, but the criminal jurisdiction was detached and sold to the Hohenzollern burgraves, who were also raised to princely status by a special charter in 1363.[69]

The much-reduced imperial lands remained formally in being, though subsequent emperors accepted the de facto conversion of the earlier mortgages into outright sale. The remnants of the Alsatian, Ortenau and Swabian bailiwicks eventually passed to the Habsburgs, leaving only three villages as 'free' directly under the emperor. Old-style itinerant kingship was now clearly impossible.

Meanwhile, Charles developed his family's lands to a far greater extent than any of his predecessors. Central to his policy was his family's possession of Bohemia since 1310, because this gave the Luxembourgs royal status, considerable resources and a privileged position within the Empire. Charles deliberately widened Bohemian autonomy, elevating Prague as a distinct archdiocese in 1344, underpinned by the construction of St Vitus Cathedral after 1347 in the Gothic style. Having secured the German throne, he issued 12 charters in April 1348 confirming and extending Bohemian privileges, notably 'incorporation' of the kingdom's various lands together under the *corona Bohemiae.*[70] This allowed Charles to break the practice pursued since Rudolf of partitioning family possessions to accommodate younger sons and thus make the elder appear less threatening to the electors. Silesia, Lusatia and Moravia were all fully integrated within Bohemia, rather than as separate imperial fiefs. Charles's younger brother Johann Heinrich and his third son Johann were given Moravia and Görlitz respectively in 1373, providing them with both status and resources, whilst keeping them under Bohemian overlordship. Brandenburg had to remain a separate imperial fief, because it had been confirmed as an electorate in 1356, and was needed to maintain Luxembourg influence in the electoral college.[71] A separate Bohemian chancellery was established to free Charles from dependence on the imperial chancelleries associated with the ecclesiastical electors. Royal prerogatives were manipulated to redirect east–west trade away from the Danube to the Nuremberg–Prague–Pressburg route, benefiting Bohemia and undercutting his Habsburg rivals. Charles's measures had their limits: the Bohemian nobles defeated his attempt to revise their country's law code in 1355. However, his rule there was secure and enabled him to draw on considerable tax revenues.

The Empire's governance now finally came to rest in a truly magnificent capital. The 41,000-square metres Wenceslas Square was laid out to beautify Prague and promote the cult of Bohemia's patron saint. The new Charles Square was nearly twice as large, dwarfing anything else in the Empire: Nuremberg's main square was only 8,500 square metres. The new Prague University – central Europe's first – was also part of a deliberate attempt to establish the city as a truly European capital.[72] The old relationship was now reversed: German princes were expected to come to his new court.

The imperial insignia were gathered together in the new *Karlstein* (Charles's Stone) castle, built 30 kilometres from Prague between 1348 and 1365, further underlining how Bohemia was now intended as the basis for permanent Luxembourg imperial rule. The Golden Bull of 1356 fixed Bohemia as the senior secular electorate. Charles's two-year-old son Wenzel was crowned Bohemian king in 1363 as a preliminary step to securing his recognition as Charles's successor in the Empire. The new title 'king of the Romans' deliberately transformed the election from the choice of the German king to deciding the fate of the Empire. This allowed Charles to overcome potential objections that

Bohemia should be excluded from the electoral college on the grounds it was not 'German'.[73] Wenzel's election in 1376 was the first time a successor had been chosen during an emperor's lifetime since Conrad IV in 1237.

Traditional practices were not abandoned entirely. Charles retained influence within the imperial church and continued cultivating contacts amongst counts and nobles in regions close to the king since the 1270s. These areas still provided 44 per cent of royal servants, compared to 33 per cent from his hereditary possessions, and they likewise received 38 per cent of royal charters, compared to the 20 per cent issued to his direct subjects.[74] While Charles now had a fixed capital, he still spent long periods in Franconia, as well as making two extended tours of the western frontier (1356, 1365) and a prolonged progress across the Empire as part of his state visit to France in 1377–8.

Governance of Imperial Italy

Charles also continued the modest revival of imperial governance in Italy begun by Henry VII in 1311–13 and Louis IV in 1327–8 by undertaking his own Roman expeditions in 1354–5 and 1368–9. All three monarchs went primarily to be crowned emperor, but also to defend imperial prerogatives against papal and growing French influence.[75] Their reception depended on circumstances, but only Henry encountered serious opposition. Despite local difficulties, Louis and Charles enjoyed greater support and benefited from the papacy's absence in Avignon (1309–77). Italians generally preferred the emperor as a more distant overlord to more immediate alternatives like the pope or the Angevin kings of Naples.

The situation had changed considerably since the late Staufer era. The major Italian cities had mostly slipped from being republics to oligarchic regimes. These still sought confirmation of their autonomy, but their leaders now also wanted recognition as hereditary princes and were prepared to pay handsomely. The Visconti in Milan gave Charles 150,000 florins in return for recognition as imperial vicars in 1355, as well as contributing another 50,000 to his coronation expenses. Florence paid 100,000 florins that year, and agreed an annual tax of 4,000 florins that it paid until 1378. Altogether, Charles received an average of 34,000 florins from Italy each year of his 32-year reign, constituting 21 per cent of all the money he obtained from the Empire.[76]

Charles sold confirmation of civic autonomy and other privileges, but he refrained from the wholesale alienation he practised in Germany. Moreover, like his two predecessors, he was generally careful to distribute his favours fairly evenly. Charles gained prestige from making peace with the Visconti rather than using force to secure Milan as the vital entry point into northern Italy. Wenzel continued his father's practice of rewarding the Visconti, who were elevated as dukes of Milan in May 1395, repaying the favour four years later when they blocked Wenzel's rival Ruprecht from entering Italy. However, Charles balanced this by appointing the counts of Savoy as general vicars in Italy in 1372 and integrating their possessions within Germany to secure an alternative route. Sigismund later conferred margravial rank on the Gonzaga, whom Louis had favoured in the 1320s to secure access through their strategic town of Mantua.

No Italian lord felt sufficiently confident to ignore the emperor, who might otherwise favour their local rival. Imperial displeasure could be expressed by placing a city under the ban that could legitimate attacks by its neighbours. Princely ranks bolstered urban despots against their internal opponents, while grants of vicar's powers enabled them to extend control over their city's hinterland. Although he did not appear often nor bring many troops, the emperor remained the sole recognized fount of honours. Charles conferred knighthoods on 1,500 Italians at his coronation in 1355.[77] Italian cities depended on imperial protection for their merchants trading north of the Alps. The emperor was still seen as someone who could resolve local problems: Genoa voluntarily relinquished autonomy and placed itself directly under imperial authority for 20 years after 1311, because 'self-rule no longer worked'.[78]

Structural Problems under Wenzel and Ruprecht

Charles achieved much, but he died in 1378 before completing the transition to imperial governance based on large hereditary possessions. Although far more substantial than those of any previous emperor, Charles's lands were insufficient to meet all his costs and he was heading towards financial crisis. Meanwhile, his practice of pawning imperial cities, especially smaller ones like Friedberg, was stirring opposition from their inhabitants, who felt their patron was betraying them to rapacious princes.

Wenzel was not the man to meet these challenges. A typical spoilt child of a family on the make, Wenzel was overindulged and inexperienced. He tended to dodge responsibility by going hunting, while his ill health after 1388 was exacerbated by alcoholism. Character flaws were still significant in this period, because personal presence remained an important aspect of imperial governance. Charles's changes to the feudal hierarchy clearly established the electors as the new super-elite whose support had to be constantly cultivated and managed. Wenzel spent only three years of his 22-year reign outside Bohemia and a third of this time was in Nuremberg, being the imperial city easiest to reach from his kingdom. He failed to visit Germany at all in the critical decade after 1387 and altogether held only four assemblies with the electors and princes. Although he sent representatives to another five assemblies, these were considered poor substitutes by men whose own prestige still rested on their personal proximity to the monarch.

Meanwhile, Wenzel's own position in Bohemia imploded after 1393. Having already antagonized the senior lords by favouring the lesser knights, Wenzel sanctioned the murder of Prague's vicar general, John Nepomuk, who had opposed royal interference in the Bohemian church. The lords allied with the Habsburgs and Wenzel's brother Sigismund and cousin Jobst in May 1394, imposing the latter as governor of Bohemia. The kingdom descended into civil war between Wenzel and Jobst after 1395. Although Wenzel eventually recovered control by 1397, the episode alarmed the electors, who had already convened independently in Frankfurt in July 1394, reviving the practice developed during the later Salian era of meeting without royal permission (see pp. 406–7). Wenzel squandered opportunities for compromise, prompting the electors to name Sigismund as general vicar for the Empire on 13 March 1396. This act challenged Wenzel, who, as king, alone held the right to make such an appointment, but it fell short of deposing him, because general vicars were intended simply to exercise imperial authority in the monarch's absence from the kingdom. Sigismund had meanwhile become king of Hungary. His defeat by the Turks at Nicopolis in September 1396 prevented him from assuming the position and obliged the electors to move independently towards the full deposition of Wenzel.

The experience of deposing Adolf in 1298 revealed the risks of such a step. The electors demonstrated how imperial political culture had changed since then by carefully choreographing their actions to conform to the new sense of collective responsibility. Further electoral congresses in 1397 and 1399 emboldened the electors to summon Wenzel to meet them in May 1400 to explain his actions. When he failed to appear, the four Rhenish electors assembled at Oberlahnstein on the Rhine on 20 August in the presence of numerous princes and lords. In contrast to the moral arguments used in earlier elections of anti-kings (and the absence of any real case in 1298), the electors cited constitutional grounds for deposing Wenzel because he had failed to fulfil his duties according to the Golden Bull. The four electors convened the next day in nearby Rhense and elected Ruprecht, count Palatine, as German king, leaving Wenzel as king of Bohemia.[79]

As in 1298, the electors had ulterior motives, since they resented the shift of political gravity after 1348 away from their own region to Bohemia and which they clearly sought to reverse through the choice of one of their own number as king. Ruprecht had the precedent of Louis IV and felt that the Wittelsbachs were rightfully the Empire's first family. He was also conscious that the Habsburgs were growing stronger and wanted to seize the opportunity to pre-empt them as potential kings. The lengthy, peaceful process of deposing Wenzel contrasted with Henry IV's violent usurpation of the English throne in 1399 in which he imprisoned and subsequently starved his rival, Richard II.

Contemporaries predicted failure from the start of Ruprecht's reign. He clung on until his death in 1410, but his authority was restricted to the Middle Rhine, south-west Germany and Bavaria, while Wenzel held Bohemia and enjoyed some support in Germany and Italy. Ruprecht's reign demonstrates the significance of Charles's changes to the basis of imperial governance. The Palatinate was too small to sustain royal rule, providing 50,000–60,000 florins annually, whilst revenue from the imperial lands was only 25,000 florins, down from the average of 164,000 florins under Charles. Ruprecht was the first monarch to use the new financial services provided by the banks being founded in Italian and Burgundian cities, borrowing 500,000 florins during his reign. While this kept him afloat, he had little to offer potential supporters. His relative isolation is demonstrated by the fact that two-thirds of his lay advisors were his own subjects or vassals, while no senior imperial nobles sought employment at his court.[80]

Sigismund: Old Practices in New Circumstances

Charles's strategy paid off, and the Luxembourgs were able to ride out Ruprecht's challenge despite being led by the incompetent Wenzel. They were the only candidates at Ruprecht's death in 1410. Wenzel was ignored, but rivalry between Sigismund and Jobst produced the Empire's last double election.[81] The ongoing papal schism contributed to this, since rival popes backed different candidates. However, Jobst's death within a few months enabled Sigismund to stage a second, unanimous election in July 1411.

Sigismund represents an exception to the general trend since 1273.[82] He was forced to rely on more traditional methods of fostering consensus, because he lacked a territorial base within the Empire. Although Sigismund had ruled Hungary since 1387, that kingdom's resources were fully committed to battling the Ottoman advance through the Balkans. Wenzel's death in 1419 at last gave him Bohemia, but precisely at the point when this kingdom descended into renewed civil war during the Hussite insurrection. Brandenburg was recovered at Jobst's death, but it had been ruined by the prolonged struggles to control it since 1373 and was transferred to Burgrave Friedrich IV of Hohenzollern in 1415, partly because of the high fees he was prepared to pay, but also to secure the friendship of one of the few important princes associated with Ruprecht's regime. The Wettin margraves of Meissen were won over by enfeoffing them with electoral Saxony, left vacant by the extinction of the Wittenberg branch of the Askanier in 1422. These deals indicate the growing importance of Brandenburg and Saxony as electorates and helped integrate them with the previously more dominant four Rhenish electors. Finally, Sigismund revived closer ties with the Empire's remaining free lesser nobility by allowing them to form leagues and so counterbalance growing princely influence in the regions (see pp. 553–7).

IMPERIAL REFORM

Beginnings

Sigismund's reign saw the beginnings of what later historians called 'imperial reform', which culminated in the establishment of new institutions between around 1480 and 1530 collectively giving the Empire its definitive early modern form. This process is difficult to date precisely, because it changed character as it progressed. Like the Ottonians and Salians, Sigismund and his contemporaries conceived *reformation* largely as *renovation*, or restoration of an idealized, lost former political order.[83] The immediate issues were those that had already loomed large since the Staufers, especially how best to uphold justice and public order, while the trigger was also familiar: helping the papacy put its house in order (see pp. 70–73). However, Sigismund's intervention to end the Great Schism already differed substantially from early medieval emperors in that he collaborated with the new movement arguing that the church was a collective represented by a general council of bishops. Meanwhile, broader discussions of 'proper order' involved new, often radical views on the relationship between society, religion and politics. These desires would erupt violently around 1520, prompting further constitutional revisions to stabilize the Empire.

The timing of reform and especially its shift from renewal to innovation stems from the intrusion of new problems, forcing the Empire's elite to accept new ways of coping with common threats. These problems were generally similar to those facing other European monarchies: how to overcome civil strife and protect the kingdom against external enemies. The usual response involved concentrating more power in royal hands, backed by a more extensive and efficient network of royal officials. These changes were underpinned by the reworked ideas of Roman law circulating within most of Europe since the twelfth century, which provided arguments favouring royal authority. The Empire did not take this course, despite participating in the discussion of Roman law ideas. One reason was that the changes made since the Staufers had enabled it to retain a lightweight, low-cost form of royal government which no important participant saw any reason to abandon now. Princes and cities enjoyed considerable individual autonomy, but discharged 'public' functions at their own expense, freeing the emperor from having to organize and pay for this. The other reason was that the emperor's main task was considered to be maintaining internal peace, not waging external war. Peace was intended to be permanent, whereas war was always presented as a necessary exception. This meant that apologists for greater royal power in the Empire could not use the fiction employed in France, England and Spain that new taxes were short-term emergency measures. Instead, it remained politically unacceptable to develop centralized institutions capable of sustaining the king's permanent interference in his subjects' lives. Regular taxation was equated with 'eternal servitude' inimical to 'German freedom'.[84]

Pressures for Reform

In contrast to fifteenth-century England, Castile and France, there had been no civil wars in the Empire since Charles IV's swift victory over Günther von Schwarzenburg in 1349. The subsequent succession disputes in 1400 and 1410 were more sullen stand-offs than full-blown conflicts. Yet serious violence erupted at local and regional level from tensions arising from feudalization and territorialization. The imperial church lands were often the worst affected, because mounting debts forced bishops to alienate property, leading to disputes with their chapters and entanglements with often aggressive secular neighbours. A notable example was the Mainz dispute from 1459 to 1463 triggered by the newly elected archbishop's refusal to pay an exorbitant fee demanded by the pope to confirm him in office. The pope deposed him and invited the chapter to elect a rival, thus opening the electorate to interference from neighbouring princes who saw an opportunity to seize its property. Unrest continued into the 1470s as the disorder added to social and economic problems, stirring popular protest. Elector Palatine Friedrich I 'the Victorious' widened the conflict through additional disputes with other south-west princes and cities.[85]

The south and west were particularly prone to disorder, thanks to their dense and complex feudal hierarchy that fragmented jurisdictions, creating numerous points for potential friction. The disputes were not 'private' wars, but recognized legal practice, since the Empire permitted subjects to seek redress through feuding. This practice had been contained in the past, because feuds generally remained small scale, involving seizure or destruction of property, rather than full military operations. However, feuding increased in intensity and scale as princes waged multiple conflicts using their mediate vassals as surrogates, while many lesser vassals acted on their own initiative to preserve or widen their autonomy. Franconia saw 278 noble feuds between 1440 and 1570, with a peak from 1460 to 1479, followed by a second, lesser one from 1500 to 1509. The proportion of feuds pitting nobles against princes rose from 40 per cent during the first peak to 53 per cent in the second, compared to feuds amongst nobles accounting for only 15 per cent.[86] Most feuds involved intimidation, arson, looting, cattle rustling and kidnapping, with killings rarely being premeditated since an opponent's death negated the feud's purpose of compelling him to admit publicly to being in the wrong. The numerous cases of peaceful resolution are easily forgotten. The cliché of the rapacious 'robber barons' was an urban myth, fostered from this period onwards as part of a wider critique of nobility. Burghers themselves waged feuds, also burning villages and destroying crops belonging to hostile lords. Moreover, aristocratic concepts of honour were being embraced by others, spreading the use of the feud: 258 feuds were waged by Bavarian peasants and other commoners between 1450 and 1500.[87]

However, the overall level of violence did rise during the first half of the fifteenth century, when the disputes among princes in the Rhineland and south-west destroyed 1,200 villages. A further 1,500 villages were destroyed during the Hussite insurrection, which added to an overall perception of mounting disorder.[88] The sense of danger was magnified by the emergence of the first serious external threat since the Mongols in the 1240s. The western frontier was disturbed by mercenaries temporarily displaced from the French civil wars in 1444–5, followed by ducal Burgundy's aggressive expansion after 1468 and the subsequent dispute over its inheritance between the Habsburgs and French kings lasting from 1477 to 1493. Meanwhile, the 'Turkish menace' grew after the failure of the last old-style crusade in 1444. The Turks launched their first raid into Krain in 1469, followed by almost annual attacks on Styria after 1471.

Like the feuding, these wars were on an unprecedented scale. Henry VII's Roman expedition of 1311 involved a royal army of 5,000 men, entirely in line with forces over the previous five centuries. By 1483, the French monarchy could mobilize 50,000, at a point when even the Habsburgs only mustered 18,000 in their campaigns in Hungary. New forms of warfare required a higher proportion of disciplined mercenary infantry fighting in regular formations. By the early sixteenth century, one year's campaign against the Ottomans was reckoned to cost between 1.8 and 3.6 million florins, while the Habsburgs' wars against France proved even more expensive, with costs doubling between 1530 and 1550 to reach 5.4 million florins annually.[89] Established methods could not cope. Sigismund and Frederick III received occasional substantial one-off payments from their immediate vassals, but the total annual revenue from imperial prerogatives had flat-lined at 25,000 florins since 1400. Several knights declared feuds against Frederick III for failing to pay their salaries, and he was not even safe from his own creditors who, in 1473, seized his horses, temporarily stranding him in Augsburg.

There was a growing recognition that change was necessary. One reason was that many of the enemies were now heretics (Hussites) and infidels (Turks), posing an existential threat that demanded real action. Princes also realized that feuding was undermining their authority. They relied on lesser nobles and mediate vassals both to administer their lands and as surrogates to wage war on their rivals. Unsurprisingly, their subjects found it hard to distinguish between tax-collecting and robbery, and often experienced territorial justice as arbitrary, responding with their own feuds against princely officials.[90]

It was indicative of the gradual underlying shift to written political culture that reform proposals began circulating as manuscripts from the early fifteenth century. By the 1440s these were becoming longer, more detailed and more practical.[91] The most famous is the *Reformatio Sigismundi*, which appeared during the church council at Basel around 1439, and was first printed in 1476, with three more editions by 1497. Although the author remains unknown, the proposal's association with the emperor raised its profile. It was the first such text in German and is one of the earliest lengthy political discussions in that language. It is often difficult to follow, because German still lacked the vocabulary to discuss the kind of constitutional issues that had traditionally been debated only in Latin. The choice of German clearly signalled a desire to reach a wider audience, unlike the texts produced during the earlier conflicts with the papacy, which had been position statements intended only to help envoys engaged in face-to-face negotiations. Its concrete proposals were clearly partisan: the author advocated abolishing the imperial church and redistributing its resources to the knights, who were also to be protected from rapacious princes through further constitutional changes.

Leadership of Reform

Despite his association with the document, Sigismund was in no position to lead reform, being distracted by the church councils, the Hussite emergency and Hungary's defence.[92] His death in 1437 ended the Luxembourg royal line and finally opened the door to the Habsburgs, whom Charles IV had recognized as potential heirs in 1364. The recent marriage of Sigismund's daughter Elisabeth to the Austrian Duke Albrecht V strengthened the duke's position as sole candidate and he was accepted as King Albert II after an interregnum of only four months in 1437–8. Although not averse to reform, Albert was determined to secure his inheritance in Bohemia and Hungary. He never visited the core parts of the Empire after his election and died of dysentery in 1439 while campaigning in Hungary after a reign of 19 months, aged just 42.[93]

The Habsburgs' position as the only viable candidates was confirmed by the acceptance of Albert's cousin as Frederick III in 1440, despite his not being present at his own election. It was two years before Frederick left Austria to be crowned king at Aachen, and he again stayed in his own lands between 1444 and 1471, except for his imperial coronation journey to Rome in 1452. Understandably, this led to criticism of his being the 'imperial arch-nightcap', a pun on the electoral arch-titles suggesting Frederick was asleep on the job.[94] In fact he clearly thought of himself as emperor, choosing to style himself as 'Frederick III' in sequence after the Staufer emperor, rather than after his own Habsburg predecessor Frederick the Fair, whom Louis IV accepted as co-king. Frederick also retained many of the former Luxembourg imperial servants, but he also conformed to the new pattern of imperial rule that required he secure his own lands before he could see to the rest of the Empire. Unfortunately, he faced considerable opposition from Austrian and Bohemian nobles and had to abandon claims to Bohemia in 1458, only to become embroiled in a dispute with his brother Albrecht VI over Austria between 1461 and 1463, which ruined that land's finances. Frederick was then distracted by a prolonged dispute with Hungary, which now had its own king and invaded Austria in the 1480s.[95]

The experience of Wenzel's deposition in 1400 and Sigismund's reassignment of the Saxon and Brandenburg titles together contributed to a stronger corporate identity amongst the electors by the 1420s. Taking their cue from the church councils, the electors already proposed themselves as a permanent advisory body for the Empire in 1438–9. This suggestion was not followed up, but their sense of responsibility for the Empire's welfare grew with Frederick's apparent uninterest in imperial affairs during the mid-fifteenth century. Trier, Bohemia and Mainz all submitted their own reform proposals, as did other princes like the duke of Bavaria from the 1460s. Count Berthold von Henneberg emerged as the spokesman for reform after becoming elector of Mainz in 1484 and he exploited Frederick III's desire to secure recognition of his son, Maximilian, as successor to compel greater action on reform. Like many previous Mainz archbishops, Henneberg wanted to cement his diocese's premier status within the Empire. However, his arguments carried weight because he shared a broad desire to enact viable reforms.[96]

Frederick III opposed reform as threatening to impose formal restrictions on his prerogatives. He avoided direct confrontation, which risked humiliation if the princes refused to give way, and instead spun out discussions until the electors accepted Maximilian I as king of the Romans in 1486, the first successor to be chosen during an emperor's lifetime for 110 years and a sign that Henneberg and others genuinely wanted to work with the Habsburgs. Frederick retired to Linz in 1488, leaving Maximilian to manage the Empire. This opened the door to compromise, since Maximilian could now pose as mediator between the princes and his father. Despite misgivings over some aspects of reform, Maximilian continued this policy of brokerage after Frederick's death in 1493 when he posed as the impartial judge seeking the best solution to the Empire's problems from amongst the various options suggested by the princes.[97]

Judicial Reform

Maximilian achieved real success by accepting judicial reform as the price for a viable system of military and fiscal aid at the Reichstag meeting in Worms in 1495. This declared a new imperial public peace which, unlike its medieval predecessors, was expressed as both universal and eternal. Crucially, this consolidated the evolving status hierarchy by charging all holders of immediate fiefs to forswear violence as a means of conflict resolution and instead to combine against all those breaching the Empire's peace. This reduced mediate vassals clearly to being the assistants of the emperor's immediate vassals, thus identifying how resources should be controlled and who was to provide them. The new Reichskammergericht of 1495 was created as a joint supreme court of both emperor and Empire, replacing feuding with judicial arbitration. Maximilian developed the Reichshofrat as a separate court solely dependent on him as emperor to resolve disputes involving imperial prerogatives (see pp. 625–32).

The new judiciary obliged the realization of long-held plans for a regional infrastructure to coordinate peace enforcement. This had first been envisaged in Rudolf I's public peace of 1287 and had been re-emphasized in Wenzel's peace of 1383. It addressed the demise of the old, large duchies by creating new regions called *Kreise* ('circles') to group the German immediate fief-holders and identify their area of collective responsibility. Unlike the old duchies, the Kreise were collective institutions without a single prince as head. They remained only proposals until 1500, when the smaller fiefs were grouped into six Kreise, with a further four added in 1512 to incorporate the electorates and Habsburg lands. Bohemia and Italy remained outside this structure. The princes accepted incorporation, because they realized their relatively modest resources prevented their playing as prominent a role in imperial politics as the electors, whereas regional politics touched their immediate interests. The Kreise were identified in all imperial legislation after 1507 as the framework for implementing common decisions, including selecting Reichskammergericht judges, enforcing that court's verdicts, organizing military contingents and regulating exchange rates. These tasks promoted their development, compelling their members to convene their own assemblies and establish their own practices and conventions, all guided by general legislation issued through the Reichstag.[98]

Fiscal Reform

No real effort had been made since the Carolingian capitularies to fix what the Empire's inhabitants were supposed to contribute fiscally to common tasks. Medieval emperors maintained registers of royal lands, but otherwise charters specified only the obligations of individual vassals. Peer pressure and the desire to impress helped sustain the size of military contingents assembled for Roman expeditions. The Salians attempted general taxes in 1084, 1114 and 1124–5, but did so amidst civil war, which immediately undermined their legitimacy. Although they received some money from imperial cities, they lacked an infrastructure to collect taxes elsewhere. Likewise, Frederick II's general tax project of 1241 failed, whereas he was able to collect regular sums from the imperial cities and especially their Jewish minorities.[99] As we have seen (pp. 356–65), this was not unduly problematic, because the reworking of feudal obligations around 1230 continued to ensure vassals responded in sufficient numbers for later medieval kings to achieve real objectives.

The rapidly escalating costs and scale of warfare forced the Empire to confront its inherent 'free rider' problem caused by numerous vassals avoiding or only partially fulfilling obligations. This proved the most innovative aspect of reform, because it forced those involved to redefine their relationship to the Empire more precisely. Crucially, this occurred as all concerned were rapidly embracing writing in their own territorial administrations and as a means of regulating relations with outsiders. It was quickly agreed that it would be impossible to revive the old imperial lands, and that all fief-holders should assume new obligations expressed in cash terms. The first general tax was agreed in 1422 to combat the Hussites, but foundered amidst opposition from the clergy and cities. Another tax for the same purpose in 1427 proved more successful, thanks to energetic backing from a papal legate who secured clerical support. About 38,000 florins had been raised by late 1429, but compliance was still patchy and no one fully mastered the practical problem of collecting money across such a numerous and socially differentiated population.[100]

Despite prolonged discussions, this problem was not resolved until the 1495 Reichstag when the establishment of the Reichskammergericht forced those present to agree the new 'Common Penny' tax to be collected by the immediate fief-holders and magistrates of the imperial cities. The initial levy raised over 136,000 florins between 1495 and 1499.[101] The Common Penny was levied another five times between 1512 and 1551 but was increasingly displaced by the matricular system, which eventually supplanted it as the principal way all common burdens were assessed both at imperial and Kreis level. Introduced in 1422, the matricular system was used a further five times by 1480 to raise troops and money against the Hussites and Turks. Each immediate fief and imperial city received an obligation to provide a fixed quota of soldiers or, from 1486, their cash equivalent calculated according to monthly wages. The quotas were recorded in an official register (*Matrikel*), with that prepared in 1521 becoming a benchmark for all future assessments.[102]

The matricular system was preferred because it enabled fief-holders and magistrates to conceal their true wealth. The initial Common Penny proved difficult, because hardly any territories possessed adequate tax registers, as they had few direct levies of their own. Registers were time-consuming to prepare, but their real problem was how they revealed personal and communal wealth to outsiders. Cities were particularly concerned that sensitive financial information would simply add to the desire of neighbouring princes to intrude on their autonomy. Quotas were only loosely related to actual wealth, because they were assigned in roughly descending order according to the titular status of each fief. For example, from 1486 all electors were assessed the same despite their considerable disparities in wealth. Quotas had additional political advantages, since the amounts in the registers were only ever intended as a basic guide and could be summoned as multiples or fractions as the case demanded. The fief-holders and magistrates had to meet the emperor to agree the size and duration of the grant, allowing them the opportunity to influence its use as well. Quotas eased military planning by fixing contingent sizes and also enabled the emperor to see more clearly who was dodging their responsibilities.

Vassals were responsible for raising, equipping, training and maintaining their troops, ensuring that the Empire's central bureaucracy remained small compared to those of western European monarchies. Frankfurt's city treasurer was sworn in as *Reichspfennigmeister* in 1495 to receive Common Penny payments remitted by fief-holders and magistrates. The post remained temporary, limited to individual tax grants authorized by the Reichstag, until made permanent in 1543. The Frankfurt treasurer's responsibility was limited to south Germany in 1557 when a second official was appointed in Leipzig to receive payments from the north. Augsburg and Regensburg were identified as additional 'towns of deposit' (*Legstädte*). The role of Reichspfennigmeister peaked under Zacharias Geizkofler, who expanded it in the late sixteenth century to become the emperor's chief banker and financial advisor. The remit contracted rapidly after his resignation in 1603 and the post was essentially replaced by the creation of the new position of 'Receiver of the Imperial Operations Fund' in 1713, who handled funds voted to support the imperial army.[103] A Fiscal's Office (*Fiskalamt*) was established in Speyer in 1507 to help the Reichskammergericht prosecute those failing to pay imperial taxes, while a separate branch was established in 1596 to assist the Reichshofrat perform the same function in Italy.[104]

THE STATUS HIERARCHY

From Royal Assembly to Reichstag

Displacing the difficult administrative tasks to the territories allowed imperial reform to concentrate on formalizing how the Empire reached collective decisions. This cemented it as a mixed monarchy in which the emperor shared powers with the imperial Estates according to an increasingly rigid status hierarchy. The principal institution was the Reichstag, which combined two previously separate forms of assembly to become the Empire's main forum for legitimating policies and reaching binding agreements.

As we have seen (pp. 337–9), the Carolingians already held assemblies with important vassals. These are now called 'court assemblies' (*Hoftage*), a term invented in 1980, to distinguish meetings that contemporaries understood as *curia*, or advisory royal courts, rather than *dieta* (diets), which generally implied a greater sense of rights for the participants.[105] While certain conventions applied over timing and location, assemblies depended on the king to summon them and had no fixed membership. Feudalization contributed to the narrowing of participants to senior vassals and by the fourteenth century only around 20 people attended such assemblies. Meetings were fairly frequent though, with 40 held between 1314 and 1410 together with another 15 between 1381 and 1407 chaired by a royal envoy in the king's absence.[106]

The other form comprised meetings held on the initiative of senior vassals. The oldest of these were the assemblies held after the death of kings who left no previously recognized heir. Other so-called 'kingless assemblies' were held after 1076, notably to elect anti-kings (see pp. 302–3). The electors held 18 meetings separate from elections between 1273 and 1409, reflecting their growing corporate identity. Sigismund formally recognized the electors as 'pillars of the Empire' in 1424, signalling a greater willingness to consult them on common matters. However, tensions resurfaced after 1480 between the four Rhenish electors and their northern and eastern colleagues in Brandenburg, Saxony and Bohemia. These problems frustrated their efforts to exclude others from the right to share decisions with the monarch.[107]

Development was also slowed after the 1420s by the emperor's reluctance to attend assemblies himself. Despite the accelerating transition to written communication, participants interpreted the emperor's absence as undermining the legitimacy of any decisions they might reach, which was, of course, precisely why Frederick III often stayed away. However, the pressure to agree reform encouraged Frederick or his son Maximilian to attend after 1471, while the growing urgency saw nine assemblies between 1486 and 1498.[108] The meeting in Worms in 1495 was widely recognized by participants as a milestone and was the first to call itself a Reichstag (imperial diet). The choice of term was deliberate, recognizing the change from the old royal assembly to a new kind of institution, transforming vassals' *duty* to offer advice and aid into a *right* to share in common decisions. While they remained the emperor's vassals, they now also became imperial Estates (*Reichsstände*) collectively constituting the Empire with the emperor.[109]

Frequency and Location

Ten further meetings followed between 1500 and 1518, but institutional development slowed due to Maximilian's growing preference for more informal meetings with key individuals. The Habsburgs' need for assistance against the Turks renewed development during the nine meetings between 1521 and 1532. Growing confessional tension prevented the Reichstag reconvening from 1533 to 1540, but eight more meetings were held between 1541 and 1548, entrenching the earlier developments that were consolidated and extended in the session held in Augsburg in 1555 which agreed the Religious Peace.[110] In all, 40 to 45 Reichstags were held between 1495 and 1654, depending on the definition of a full meeting, compared to 40 assemblies between 1356 and

1493. Meetings varied in length from five weeks (Nuremberg, 1522) to 10 months (Augsburg, 1547–8).

Meetings under Maximilian I were still linked to the royal itinerary which that emperor resumed in order to engage more fully with the old core areas of Germany, holding 20 assemblies in 15 locations between 1486 and 1518, including four in towns that were not imperial cities.[111] Thereafter, Reichstags always met in an imperial city, which was obliged to provide its town hall for the event. Nuremberg was the favoured venue, hosting 15 meetings, followed by Regensburg with 14, ahead of the others by some margin. Nuremberg's growing embrace of Protestantism encouraged the Habsburgs to favour Regensburg, which was also easier to reach along the Danube from Vienna. All meetings convened there after 1594, except for a brief relocation to Frankfurt in 1742–4 under Charles VII. The Empire was unique in Europe in convening its representative assembly away from the royal capital, contributing to the permanent separation of the ceremonial and representational functions of the monarch's court from formal political negotiations with his vassals and subjects.

Form of Representation

Unlike the medieval assemblies, the Reichstag acquired a fixed membership by 1521, which proved fundamental in determining the status hierarchy. This provided another important contrast with virtually all European parliaments, where representation was tied to social Estates like lords, clergy and commons generally meeting in separate 'houses'. Representation in the Empire derived instead from the formalization of feudal obligations and consequently was tied to holding immediate imperial fiefs. The decisive factor was how far fief-holders and city magistrates were prepared to accept the new burdens imposed by the matricular system. These could be considerable. Lübeck's matricular assessment in 1486 was four to six times higher than what it had previously paid in dues to the emperor as an imperial city. Lübeck chose to accept this and was consequently invited to subsequent assemblies, allowing its representatives to assert its new status as an imperial Estate. By contrast, Trier was regularly invited at first because it was a large and rich city, yet its refusal to contribute led to its exclusion later. The rapidity of developments between 1480 and 1520 was not immediately obvious, and many of those involved did not appreciate the consequences of refusal. Yet by 1521 it became clear that acceptance of official burdens confirmed both representation in the Reichstag and the status of immediacy, whereas refusal denied the former and jeopardized the latter. In Trier's case, the archbishop used the city's refusal to argue it was no longer 'free' but directly subordinate to him and, consequently, should assist him in paying the electorate's share of imperial taxes.

Tax collection methods further reinforced the hierarchy. Immediate fief-holders and magistrates were already identified in 1427 as responsible for collection, and from 1475 were allowed to recoup their expenses from their subjects. Arrangements introduced in 1507 clarified this further, requiring mediate vassals and subjects to pay to immediate ones, who in turn remitted the money to the Reichspfennigmeister. Finally, the 1543 Reichstag exempted princes from personal obligations to pay.[112]

In addition to hierarchy, the Reichstag reflected the associational, corporative element in the Empire's society by grouping the imperial Estates into three colleges, or *corpora* (bodies), of electors, princes and cities. Religious divisions added two confessional corpora of Protestants and Catholics cutting across all three status groups by the 1520s (see pp. 128–31). Membership was determined by the status of imperial fiefs, so that families holding more than one kind of fief might be represented more than once. Both the electoral and princely corpora were additionally subdivided into lay and spiritual 'benches', meaning the clergy did not meet together in a separate house, but were split hierarchically between the three ecclesiastical electors and the other church lords sitting with the princes.

Corporatism was strongest amongst the electors, whose corpus was both the smallest and oldest. Already in 1424 the seven electors agreed not to admit further members, but instead to maintain an exclusive pre-eminence over all other princes. However, they were still acutely conscious of their own internal ranking order, which had been fixed in 1356 and appeared frequently around this time in prints showing the emperor in the middle, with the three ecclesiastical electors to his right as seniors, with Mainz closest, then Cologne followed by Trier, and their four secular colleagues to his left in rank order of Bohemia, the Palatinate, Saxony and Brandenburg (see Plate 21). Despite their determination to exclude others, the electors had to accept changes imposed by the Habsburgs. First, the Ernestine Wettins were punished for leading the Protestant Schmalkaldic League by having the Saxon title transferred to their Albertine relations who had backed Charles V in 1547. The Bavarian Wittelsbachs received the Palatine title under similar circumstances during the Thirty Years War in 1623, though the Palatinate was compensated by a new title ranked eighth in 1648. The Bohemian vote was simultaneously suspended to keep the number of electors to the original seven and ensure there was no possibility of a tied vote in imperial elections. Leopold I rewarded the duke of Calenberg (Hanover) with a further new, ninth title in 1692, prompting an angry response from other old princely houses like those in Hessen, Württemberg, Gotha and Brunswick, who all felt unfairly passed over.[113] The Habsburgs skilfully manipulated princely rivalries to secure not only recognition of the new Hanoverian title, but readmission of the Bohemian vote in 1708 to ensure there remained an uneven number of electors. The Palatinate recovered its original fifth title when it inherited Bavaria in 1778, while the eighth title was abandoned. Later adjustments were made as part of the readjustments accompanying the Empire's demise around 1803–6 (Table 6).

Table 6. Changes in the Electoral College

Date	Joining	Leaving
1547	Albertine Saxony	Ernestine Saxony
1623	Bavaria (receiving the 5th title)	The Palatinate
1648	The Palatinate (new, 8th title)	Bohemia (vote suspended)
1692	Hanover (vote recognized 1708)	
1708	Bohemia (vote readmitted)	
1778		Bavaria (as 8th title)
1803	Salzburg	Mainz (vote transferred to the Arch-Chancellor)
	Württemberg	Cologne + Trier (titles abolished)
	Hessen-Kassel	
	Baden	
1805	Würzburg*	Salzburg (title transferred to Würzburg)

*as a new secular grand duchy

The princes consistently resented electoral pre-eminence. Already in 1498, Duke Georg of Lower Bavaria successfully led his peers in obliging the electors to lower their dais at the end of the hall so that they would not sit too far above the princes. The cities were even more obviously inferior, as their envoys were always commoners who were confined to the back of the hall and were obliged to stand during parts of the proceedings whereas the others remained seated (see Plate 26).[114]

Only 281 of the 402 fiefs and cities listed in the 1521 register actually participated in a Reichstag. The others were already slipping into mediate status through their unwillingness or inability to meet the associated fiscal and military burdens (Table 7). The reductions were greatest amongst the numerous minor ecclesiastical and secular fiefs, which were obliged to share collective votes (*Kurialstimmen*) rather than exercising full, individual votes (*Virilstimmen*). Although six prelates 'turned Swiss', leaving imperial politics to participate in the Swiss Confederation, including those of Einsiedeln and St Gallen, the others eventually secured two votes, one for the Swabians in 1575 and one for all the rest lumped together as 'Rhenish' in 1654. Their numbers remained stable, except for the few who were 'promoted' to prince-abbots or prince-bishops with individual votes. Two-thirds of the 143 counts listed in 1521 subsequently disappeared, with half of these through the extinction of their family and the inheritance or sale of their fief to another count. Only eight secured elevation to full prince, but around 50 new counts were created, largely through the Habsburgs

Table 7. Reichstag Participation Rates, 1521

Status Group	Listed in 1521 Register	Participated
Electors	7	7*
Ecclesiastical Princes	51	45
Secular Princes	32	29
Prelates	83	48
Counts	143	93
Imperial Cities	86	59
Total	402	281

*The Bohemian vote was de facto suspended following the Hussite insurrection until the kingdom was acquired by the Habsburgs in 1526.

granting imperial titles to their own loyal nobles.[115] Most remained titular counts without representation, though several like the Kaunitz family bought or inherited counties or imperial knights' fiefs. The Swabian and Wetterau counts were already well organized by 1500, securing votes soon after, whereas the Franconians, who were the least numerous, secured theirs in 1640, and the Westphalians were finally admitted in 1654.[116]

The representation of ecclesiastical princes stabilized with the effective end of their territorialization in the fifteenth century, since they neither acquired additional fiefs nor partitioned their existing ones. Changes prior to 1802 were limited to the two waves of secularizations sanctioned in 1555 and 1648. The former confirmed the mediatization of some bishoprics already under way before the Reformation, while the latter transferred eight senior ecclesiastical fiefs and their associated full votes directly to secular princes. Civic votes declined only marginally through further mediatization. Senior secular votes experienced greater volatility prior to 1582, when the Reichstag fixed the status of imperial Estates permanently with specific fiefs (Map 9). Henceforth, this status would not be extinguished with the end of a princely family, nor could partition create additional votes.[117]

It remained possible to accumulate votes through acquiring other recognized fiefs, or if the emperor raised a county to a principality. Like the electors, existing princes tried to preserve corporate exclusivity by blocking new members. The emperor remained free to confer the personal status of imperial prince, raising 160 individuals to this rank between 1582 and 1806. However, the status of imperial Estate now clearly depended on possession of a qualifying fief. Of the five counts promoted to prince between 1579 and 1623, only Arenberg received a full princely vote. Thirteen of the 15 new princes created after 1623 secured full votes in 1654, but simultaneously the Reichstag obliged the emperor to agree that further admissions required consent from the princely corpus. Thereafter, only eight new princes acquired full votes, often waiting decades like Liechtenstein, which was only accepted in 1715, while 23 titular princes still sat on the counts' benches in the late eighteenth century because their fiefs had not been upgraded to principalities.[118]

Rigidity and Concentration of Power

One reason for this long discussion of the Empire's status hierarchy is to show both its persistence and growing rigidity by the late eighteenth century. Another is to underscore how the formal structure did not match the territorial distribution of power. Most general discussions of the Empire confuse imperial Estates with 'territories', enumerating the latter according to the formal registers of Reichstag votes to suggest there were around three hundred. The formal structure was based on imperial Estates and in fact never recognized 'territories'. The latter evolved through the accumulation of fiefs in the hands of individual princely families who gradually developed their own administrative structures cutting across the old feudal jurisdictions. However, they never abolished the formal distinctions since their status and representation rested on these, and not their 'territory'. The actual distribution of power within the imperial church was more closely aligned to the formal structure than amongst the secular Estates, because ecclesiastical fiefs could never be permanently combined. Individual archbishops or bishops might exercise two or more votes through their possession of more than one diocese, but this always remained a purely personal union and did not fuse the fiefs together as a single territory. By contrast, the Habsburgs, Hohenzollerns, Welfs, Wittelsbachs, Wettins and other princely families developed permanent territories combining various levels of representation in the formal structure.

By 1792, the 8 electors held 24 princely votes, including the Habsburgs with 1 electoral vote (Bohemia) and 3 princely votes (Austria, Burgundy, Nomeny), while the kings of Denmark and Sweden each held a princely vote. The 12 old princely families like those in Hessen, Baden and Württemberg together held 25 princely votes, while the 12 new princely families had 13 (Nassau held 2). This contrasted with the more even spread across the imperial church where the three ecclesiastical electors currently also held 6 bishoprics, while the other 18 archbishops and bishops together had 24 sees with full votes. There were 99 counties, but many of these were held by electors or princes. Thus, most of the land and formal representation was concentrated with Austria and Prussia, the 6 other electors and 13 princely families holding 81 per cent of the Empire, plus all electoral and 56 of the

100 princely votes. They formed two large territories (Austria, Prussia) and around 23 medium-sized territories. Another 16.4 per cent of the Empire was split between 151 ecclesiastical and secular lords, generally lacking princely status. Even here, 3 secular new princes, 1 archbishop and 12 bishops held over half of these possessions. The remaining 2.6 per cent of the Empire was split between 51 imperial cities (of which only 45 still sent envoys to the Reichstag) and 400 families of imperial knights, who were excluded from all the Empire's representative institutions (Table 8).

Table 8. Territory and Formal Status in 1792

Status Group	Dynastic Lines	Territorial Share (%)	Reichstag Votes
Austria	1	31.4	1 e, 3 p, 2 cc
Prussia	1	19.2	1 e, 8 p, 1 cc
Denmark	1	1.2	1 p
Sweden	1	0.7	1 p
3 Secular Electors*	3	17.6	3 e, 15 to 16 p, 1 cc
13 Old Princes	17	9.1	23 p
12 New Princes	15	1.8	12 p
48 Counts	72	2.9	4 cc
3 Ecclesiastical Electors	–	3.6	3 e
30 Ecclesiastical Princes	–	9.1	30 p
40 Prelates	–	0.8	2 pp
51 Imperial Cities	–	1.1	51 c
400 Knights, Families	–	1.5	–
3 Imperial Villages	–	–	–

Key:
c   civic vote
cc   share in counts' vote
e   electoral vote
p   princely vote
pp   share in prelates' vote

*Saxony, Palatinate-Bavaria, Hanover

The Kreis Assemblies

The development of the Kreise created a second, regional level of representation as their growing responsibilities required their members to meet frequently by the mid-sixteenth century (Map 7). The status of Kreis Estate was always wider than that of imperial Estate, ensuring that more fiefs were represented in the Kreis Assemblies (*Kreistage*) than at the Reichstag. The assemblies reflected the differing composition and regional politics of each Kreis. The Bavarian Assembly met as a unified plenary body, whereas that in Swabia began with three benches, adding two more when the minor ecclesiastical and secular fiefs were admitted with full votes – in contrast to their marginalization in the Reichstag. Kreis membership continued to fluctuate, especially through the admission of counts who gained votes for minor lordships not represented in the Reichstag. The emperor could not require a Kreis to admit new members. Status exclusivity also played a role at this level, but generally existing members were willing to admit new ones because this increased the number of overall contributors to common burdens: Westphalia admitted five new members between 1667 and 1786.

The southern and western Kreise were the most vibrant, because of the French threat and because they had the largest memberships, who relied on the assemblies to resolve disputes and organize peace, security and defence. Eighteenth-century Franconia had 23 qualifying fiefs and cities, but 33 actual members because several minor counties and lordships were shared by different princely houses. Its assembly met 322 times between 1517 and 1791, before remaining in permanent session until dissolved in 1806. Bavaria's material power was balanced by the more numerous smaller members all with full votes in the Bavarian Assembly, which met 85 times between 1521 and 1793. The Lower and Upper Saxon Kreise were dominated by Hanover, Brandenburg and Saxony, whose assemblies no longer convened after 1682 and 1683 respectively, though other forms of consultation continued.[119]

The Reichstag and Kreis Assemblies were the main forms in what was a wider representational culture that produced other forms during the sixteenth century. The Kreis Assemblies could meet together as a *Reichskreistag*, while both they and the Reichstag developed committee structures to handle specific judicial, military and financial affairs.

Reichstag committees were reorganized as more formalized Imperial Deputations after 1555. The electors enjoyed uncontested rights of self-assembly and convened their own congresses into the mid-seventeenth century, but the Reichstag's permanence after 1663 rendered most of these other forms superfluous (see pp. 443–5).

Reichstag Procedure

The emperor held the Right of Proposition, allowing him to open the Reichstag by presenting proposals to be discussed. In practice, imperial Estates and even private individuals could petition the directors of the three corpora to place items on the agenda.[120] Each corpus debated in a separate room, consulting periodically through a process known as 'correlation' with the intention of reaching a consensus to be presented as a recommendation (*Reichsgutachten*) for the emperor's approval. In practice, envoys often met separately outside the meeting hall. The emperor was free to veto a proposal, request further debate, or approve it as a full decision (*Reichsschluß*) to be included in the printed 'recess' (*Reichsabschluß*) issued at the close of each Reichstag.

The majority principle evolved separately within each corpus, beginning with the electors, followed by the cities in 1471, and finally for all decisions following Maximilian's recommendation in 1495. However, reaching a decision was often arduous, because each corpus followed a practice known as *Umfrage*, inviting each member in strict hierarchical sequence to respond to the imperial proposition. A simple 'yes' or 'no' was not permitted; each member had to voice an opinion and these were often long or deliberately ambiguous. There was no show of hands or other method that might have allowed precise counting. Instead, the corpus's director had leeway in deciding what the majority was. The process of correlation also lacked firm rules, especially as the overall majority was not decided simply by counting votes across all three colleges. The civic corpus was disadvantaged by the convention that the electors and princes only consulted it once they had agreed between themselves, though the Peace of Westphalia (1648) confirmed their right to participate in correlation.

The 1424 assembly in Nuremberg agreed that decisions were binding even on those who failed to attend and this spread to the later Reichstag and Kreis Assemblies. The rule had to be repeated, notably in 1512, because it broke the earlier convention allowing lords to demonstrate disagreement by absenting themselves or leaving an assembly early. Insistence on binding decisions encouraged a new form of delaying tactic, also facilitated by the transition to written political communication. Whereas the spiritual and lay lords were individuals expected to represent themselves, the imperial cities were communes that already provided written instructions for their envoys in the fifteenth century. Likewise, the imperial abbesses were excluded on gender grounds from attending in person and had to send a male official. Indirect representation opened the door to *Hintersichbringen*, or referring back to absentee masters on the grounds of inadequate instructions, allowing an imperial Estate to dodge awkward issues without openly opposing them. The practice was already criticized in 1495 when it was tacitly agreed to restrict referring back to genuinely important issues. The imperial proposition was generally now published in advance to force Estates to provide effective instructions. However, envoys remained bound to their masters, unlike the Reichskammergericht judges, who swore loyalty to the court, and referring back remained justifiable if circumstances changed during a Reichstag session, as occurred relatively often.

These practices help explain the slow pace of imperial politics, which later generations have often been quick to censure. The primary function of the Reichstag and the Kreis Assemblies was to legitimate political action. Imperial reform created a mass of documented decisions and recorded precedents, translating what had often been customs into written laws that remained uncodified and that might offer several potentially competing arguments.[121] Participants were concerned to find the 'right' basis for common action, since this would encourage more effective compliance with decisions. There was a tendency to leave difficult matters unresolved to allow time to chivvy dissenters, rather than risk the disruption that might ensue if they were coerced. As with justice, politics in the Empire was more about managing than resolving problems and was in many ways more realistic and often more humane than methods employed in other countries. It was not necessarily less 'modern' than the practices of some later systems: the practice of shunting difficult matters to committees where they might be hijacked by special interests is, for example, just as characteristic of contemporary US politics. Like Congress, the Reichstag was also a venue for political theatre, offering the opportunity to address a wider public, rally support, and legitimate what were initially merely opinions and claims.

Attendance and Status

Changes in the form of attendance at the Reichstag is one of the most visible manifestations of the broader shift from medieval to early modern political culture in the Empire. Emperor Frederick III appeared before the royal assembly in Augsburg in May 1474 dressed in full imperial robes, enthroned, with a drawn sword of justice to pronounce a verdict condemning the elector Palatine for breaching the peace.[122] The emperor or a close male relative generally attended at least the opening of each Reichstag until 1653. Leopold I appeared in Regensburg in 1664, a year after the opening of what proved to be a permanent or 'eternal' Reichstag. Thereafter, emperors were represented by an official known as the 'principal commissar': 4 of the 13 men holding this post between 1663 and 1806 were prince-bishops, with the others all being secular princes, though usually from the 'new' houses. Commissars maintained large staffs to reflect their status as the emperor's representative. The last, Carl Alexander von Thurn und Taxis, was accompanied by in 1806 307 people, compared to the ten or so assisting most other envoys.[123]

Princely attendance was already patchy in the fifteenth century. Even at the well-attended 1471 assembly, 36 of the 81 invited princes failed to show up, while 37 of the 89 cities did not send representatives. Around 15 to 30 of the 60 to 70 princes attended the Reichstags held from the 1480s to 1550s.[124] Confessional tensions caused Protestants to stay away from the 1520s, reflecting the persistence of the earlier practice of voicing disagreement through absence. However, the Reichstag was too important to be ignored, and absentees now sent envoys instead. Although the 1608 session was famously disrupted by a walk-out orchestrated by the elector Palatine, all Protestant princes sent representatives to the next meeting in 1613, while the Lutheran but pro-imperial rulers of Hessen-Darmstadt and Pfalz-Neuburg attended in person.[125] Practicalities also encouraged a shift to indirect participation. It was expensive and often inconvenient to attend in person, especially now that the Reichstag remained in session far longer than medieval assemblies. The general acceptance of the validity of written communication and the development of the reliable imperial postal service were added incentives to rely on envoys instead.

The shift to the new forms of representation increased general identification with the Empire since discussions and decisions were transmitted to wider audiences through written and printed material, in contrast to medieval royal assemblies where decisions were often reached discreetly beforehand and then ritually enacted by a relatively small number of participants (see pp. 337–9). However, in contrast to the relatively loose procedural rules, writing fixed status with ever greater precision. Whereas feudalization identified different status groups, the matricular registers now ranked their individual members in sequence. The practice of Umfrage acted this out in the assembly rooms. The ranking order was already ossifying by the 1480s, but despite the reams of lists, protocols and other documents, the complex feudal and institutional order defied neat classification. The different character of representation in the Reichstag and Kreis Assemblies created anomalies, while faulty record-keeping could provide arguments to make changes. This accelerated the erosion of presence culture, since it was often easier to remain absent and pretend that a status dispute did not exist.[126]

Thus, the Reichstag and Kreis Assemblies displayed the fundamental paradox of the early modern Empire. They assumed institutional shape with 'modern' practices like recognized procedure, written records and published outcomes, but their development was accompanied by appeals to 'old custom' (*Alte Herkommen*) to defend privileges and immunities based on past precedent.[127] This makes it hard to draw general conclusions about imperial reform. Older scholarship is predictably negative, arguing that dualism between the Habsburgs and princes stalemated reform, leaving development only 'partially modernized' by 1555.[128] This critique has some substance. Attempts to fix the status order more precisely merely made its discrepancies more obvious. For example, both Brandenburg and Pomerania insisted on the Pomeranian ducal title and coat of arms. Lorraine was recorded in the matricular register, but never paid and was also a vassal of the French king. Imperial political culture relied on accepting rather than rationalizing these anomalies. Over time, though, friction from the numerous inconsistencies hindered collective action by providing excuses for non-compliance. For this reason we should not mistake status disputes as trivial. Yet their persistence to the very end also belies the traditional interpretation of the Empire as moribund, since the issues still mattered. Nor did they prevent hard work. Even the supposedly lethargic Frederick III remained locked in debate for 12 hours without food or drink at the 1471 assembly. Sessions frequently began at 4 a.m. and continued till the evening. The Reichstag's permanence after 1663 allowed for shorter formal working days, but envoys remained busy outside these hours with informal negotiations, correspondence, and what would be termed today 'public relations' like entertaining diplomats and writing memoranda for publication.[129] As we shall see (pp. 445–69), these activities produced real change, shifting imperial politics from symbolic gestures like mandates against blasphemy or injustice to concrete action over defence, crime, religious controversy and economic affairs.

Moreover, the remit of the Reichstag and Kreis Assemblies was far broader than those of most European assemblies, which were limited to debating royal policy and deciding how far to back it with taxes. In addition to indeed doing this, the Empire's institutions worked out policy implementation, including specialist tasks like military regulations, exchange rates and law codes.[130] They also proved sufficiently robust to absorb the shocks from the Reformation without the violence experienced in France and the Netherlands. Although unable to prevent the Bohemian Revolt that caused a devastating civil war between 1618 and 1648, the same framework ultimately still provided the means to resolve that conflict and stabilize the Empire.

Nonetheless, the Empire merely modified existing institutions rather than developing new ones after the mid-sixteenth century. It failed to combine the legitimacy of governance with political power to forge a modern government. Instead, power and legitimacy remained separate. The emperor, Reichstag and other institutions remained accepted as legitimate, but lacked the means to implement decisions, leading some historians to categorize the Empire as a 'political system' rather than a state.[131] However, others have drawn attention to the complementary character of the Empire's development, which grew much more pronounced with imperial reform.[132] The territories did not develop in opposition to the emperor, but as part of the Empire's overall evolution. Rather than seeking to displace the territories, imperial reform incorporated them as the Empire's infrastructure. Thus, imperial institutions served to find and legitimate common policies, while the territorial administrations implemented them. The system cohered, because no element could dispense entirely with the others. It is the task of the next chapter to see how these structures fared during the three centuries of Habsburg imperial rule.

9
Dynasty

DYNASTICISM

Dynasticism not Dualism

Imperial reform had rebalanced the Empire's governance to accommodate territory as the basis of both imperial and princely power. As the Empire entered the sixteenth century, it remained at the heart of European politics, culture and economic activity. Its flexibility and creativity enabled it to survive early modern Europe's two greatest challenges: the Reformation and the Thirty Years War. Meanwhile, the era also saw the accession of Charles V, a truly pan-European monarch and arguably the best-remembered Holy Roman emperor after Charlemagne. Charles had already ruled Spain for three years prior to his election as emperor in 1519. His reign saw the co-existence of the Holy Roman Empire, rooted in Europe's medieval past, and Spain's expanding colonial empire, suggestive of Europe's future global dominance. Charles's decisions in 1558 to partition his possessions and retire to Spain to die both appear to mark the end of an epoch. This is certainly how many historians have chosen to present it, writing subsequent European history as that of nation states, many of which had extra-European colonial empires. The Empire almost disappears in this story, featuring at best as a kind of German adjunct to Habsburg Austria and, after 1648, as the supposed passive object of Austria's rivalry with the ascending power of the Prussian Hohenzollerns.

This standard narrative discusses the Empire's governance in terms of a double dualism. The tension between emperor and princes as imperial Estates at the 'national level' was supposedly mirrored in each territory by similar conflicts between each prince and his territorial Estates (*Landstände*), composed of representatives from the mediate nobles, towns and (sometimes) clergy.[1] Dualism at the territorial level is generally regarded as ending with the triumph of princely absolutism in 1648, something which was celebrated in Prussian history because it enabled the Hohenzollerns to emerge as the family that would eventually supplant the Habsburgs in Germany. Growing princely power is presented as fuelling centrifugal forces, draining the imperial office and formal structure of any meaning by the mid-eighteenth century, if not before.

This standard narrative reflects its roots in conventional ideas of state-building as a process of centralization, usually attributed to heroic and far-sighted monarchs and statesmen. Earlier chapters have already established that this perspective grossly oversimplifies and distorts the Empire's richer political development. Likewise, the common understanding of eighteenth-century politics as an Austro-Prussian dualism ignores the lesser territories collectively constituting a larger 'third Germany', as well as underestimating the continued significance of the imperial constitution as a common framework – something that the final section of this chapter will return to. Dualism makes more sense when applied to the Habsburgs, whose renewed, rapid territorial expansion between 1683 and 1718 – likewise explored below – expanded their hereditary possessions into a second, dynastic-territorial empire only partially overlapping with the Holy Roman Empire. The increase in Habsburg resources exposed another duality: the growing discrepancy between the constitution and the actual distribution of material power. However, as we shall see both here and on pp. 637–54, this did not render the formal structure wholly irrelevant. On the contrary, the status hierarchy continued to matter a great deal, as already indicated in the discussion of the imperial title (pp. 159–63). The real problem was that no one seemed able to bring the formal constitutional order and current politics back into alignment.

Interpretations emphasizing dualism stress tensions and discrepancies. The usual verdict is that territorialization was propelling the Empire inevitably from a loose monarchy towards a federation of principalities. Having failed to reassert stronger monarchy in the 1540s and 1620s, the Habsburgs allegedly lost interest in the Empire beyond the men and money they could extort for their own purposes. This view misses important continuities across time, as well as underestimating how all elements along the status hierarchy remained within a common political culture. The presence of such commonalities should not blind us to the Empire's serious problems, but nonetheless the commonalities help explain why it functioned amidst wider changes and why it retained meaning for its inhabitants.

Dynasticism was perhaps one of the strongest common practices within early modern imperial politics. One of the most striking aspects of imperial governance at this point is the unprecedented continuity in the imperial office. The period from 1254 to 1437 saw 16 kings and anti-kings from 11 families, while son followed father only once (1378). After 1438, there were no more anti-kings and the Habsburgs provided all but one (Charles VII, 1742–5) of the 18 monarchs. Not only did the Habsburgs last three times longer than any previous royal family (the Staufers, 116 years), but now there was greater continuity with sons following fathers directly eight times, with a further four successions of younger brothers following the premature deaths of reigning older siblings. The succession of a cousin or a nephew, more common in the Middle Ages, now only occurred twice (Frederick III after Albert II; Ferdinand II after Matthias), while the resumption of Habsburg imperial rule in 1745 came through the early modern innovation of dynastic continuity in the female line with the election as emperor of Maria Theresa's husband, Francis I, former duke of Lorraine.

The Politics of Inheritance

Greater continuity stemmed from the acceptance of male primogeniture as the primary form of inheritance across all levels of the Empire's society. As we have seen (pp. 356–70), male primogeniture was encouraged through the feudalization of vassalage and had been explicitly endorsed by Frederick I 'Barbarossa' in 1158 before being confirmed for the secular electorates in 1356. However, we have already noted (pp. 381–2) its slow acceptance and the continuation of partitions that eased the problems of ruling non-contiguous lands by dividing them between relations. This also reduced family tensions by providing for younger sons, improving their marriage prospects. Within princely families, all members continued to share the status of immediacy. The spread of Roman civil law reinforced this from the late twelfth century, because wives gained their husband's rank and a claim to the means required to sustain this, including during widowhood. The Reformation not only increased the significance of marriage throughout society, but encouraged a return to Old Testament traditions amongst Protestant princes. As family patriarchs, fathers were expected to provide for all children. Duke Ernst 'the Pious' of Gotha expressly rejected primogeniture on these grounds in 1654.[2]

Ernst's was a relatively late example of partible inheritance. Many families adopted primogeniture between the thirteenth and fifteenth centuries, even if they subsequently temporarily suspended it, or made exceptions. It was not adopted as a 'modernizing' measure, but as a practical response to late medieval imperial politics, demonstrating the advantages of preserving large territorial blocs. Additionally, the leading mediate vassals and subjects increasingly lobbied against partition in order to preserve the tax base and limit princely debt; for example, the count of Württemberg was forced to forgo a planned partition in 1473. Crucially, aristocratic families could adopt the tighter family discipline required by dynasticism, because younger sons and unmarried daughters could still be accommodated in the imperial church. This explains why the closing of this option to Protestants in 1555 proved so explosive (see pp. 122–3). The definitive shift to territorially based imperial governance under the Habsburgs provided a further means to absorb the consequences of primogeniture. Territorial administration relied increasingly on salaried officials, not mediate vassals. Serving the imperial family had always been prestigious, while the Habsburgs' possession of the most extensive territories also meant they were the Empire's largest employers, constantly seeking new courtiers, officials and army officers.

The multilayered feudal structure also allowed families to adopt different inheritance practices simultaneously. Immediate fiefs became indivisible by 1582, when the Reichstag ruled that partitions could not be used to create additional votes. Some families continued to divide their lands internally but shared exercise of their associated imperial rights as a condominium. Others assigned or created mediate fiefs within their jurisdictions, as for example Charles IV, who granted Moravia and Görlitz to his younger sons in 1373 (see p. 391). Likewise, Frederick William the 'Great Elector' of Brandenburg established a junior Hohenzollern line in 1688 for the eldest son from his second marriage by granting him the former lordship of Schwedt. Surviving for a century, this secondary line provided the senior branch with a useful pool of additional marriage partners to offer other German princes, whilst reserving its own offspring for more prestigious alliances. King Frederick II 'the Great', though personally remaining childless, proved skilful in promoting marriages for his relations, whilst ruthlessly refusing to grant them the means to be autonomous princes: he only left two horses in his will to his brother Heinrich.[3]

Many early modern German princes not only married but kept numerous mistresses. The most notorious womanizer was Augustus 'the Strong' of Saxony, who reputedly fathered 355 children.[4] Such activities fuelled the contemporary critique of the seventeenth- and eighteenth-century baroque princely courts, but also reflected reduced sexual options following the Reformation's restriction of marriage to church-sanctioned liaisons. Meanwhile, the formalization of the feudal hierarchy through imperial reform heightened status-consciousness amongst the Empire's elite. Pressure increased within families to marry only within or (ideally) above their current status as delineated by their formal princely titles. Here we can see just one of the many connections between the Empire's politics and wider society, an issue that will be explored further in the next chapter. Late sixteenth-century German lawyers developed earlier Italian ideas into the concept of 'morganatic' marriage, which conformed to ecclesiastical requirements but was based on a contract circumventing Roman civil law. The bride received gifts and an income, but was denied equal socio-political status. She could not assume her husband's rank and title, but instead received a new title linked to a real or fictive property granted her. Children from such unions lacked full rights, but remained a 'dynastic reserve' like the secondary family lines that could be called upon in the absence of other legitimate heirs to prevent family extinction.

Morganatic marriages became increasingly common with the adoption of primogeniture. Younger sons who were unlikely to inherit the family's imperial fief often had to accept a bride of lower status. Arrangements were generally flexible, but serious problems usually emerged if the main heir or ruling prince made such a match, since this was regarded as damaging the family's *lustre* and hence endangering its position within the imperial status hierarchy. Relations often claimed that as unequal marriage invalidated the prince's right to inherit, and that could lead to acrimonious disputes, such as that between relations of the prince of Sachsen-Meiningen in 1763. Princes accordingly petitioned the emperor to elevate their wife's status. The emperor's powers to do this were restricted by the electoral agreement (see p. 478) of 1742, but remained a way he could influence imperial politics. For example, the already scandal-ridden Duke Carl Eugen of Württemberg fell in love with Franziska Theresia von Bernhardin, daughter of a mere baron and already married to one of his chamberlains, whom she later divorced. Carl Eugen petitioned Joseph II, who eventually raised Franziska as imperial countess of Hohenheim in 1774. The affair continued until the duke's own estranged wife died in 1780. Although the couple married morganatically in 1785 and the duchy's Lutheran church even agreed to include her in their prayers, Carl never managed to persuade the emperor to raise her as full duchess.[5]

The *Casa d'Austria*

The Habsburgs were not more virtuous than the Empire's other senior families. Many had illegitimate children, including Rudolf II, whose refusal to take a legitimate wife created a succession crisis after 1600.[6] Neither, as we shall see, did they exhibit greater family discipline, partitioning their lands with serious consequences on several occasions. These considerations force us to consider why the Habsburgs came to dominate the early modern Empire. There is no simple answer. Rather, their success derived from dynastic and individual biological good fortune (longevity, fecundity, ability), together with favourable circumstances.

Like the other great families of the late medieval Empire, the Habsburgs began as counts who amassed sufficient resources to be serious contenders for the royal title by the mid-thirteenth century. Their relative wealth encouraged them to partition their possessions, with the bulk of their original holdings at the junction of Alsace, Switzerland and Swabia being held by the senior, Laufenburg, line until its extinction in 1415. Count Rudolf, who represented the dynasty's political breakthrough thanks to his election as king in 1273, in fact came from the junior line. His real contribution to his family's subsequent success was to use his position as king to secure the Babenbergs' old duchy of Austria (see pp. 385 and 338). Crucially, Emperor Frederick II had endorsed the Babenbergs' introduction of a single law code for all Austria in 1237, which reduced the prospect of partition as a way to resolve the long inheritance dispute, lasting from 1246 to 1282, unlike Thuringia, where a parallel contest ended with its being split into pieces between claimants by the early fourteenth century.

Although the Habsburgs were displaced as kings by the Luxembourgs in 1308 and the Wittelsbachs in 1314, they were now in the front rank and were able to consolidate and expand their possessions in return for cooperating with the current monarch (Map 6). Louis IV's settlement with Frederick 'the Fair' saw the family acquire Carinthia and Krain by 1335 despite opposition from rivals, as well as the Tirol in 1363, which rounded out Austria as a large territory between the Alps and the Danube. As with the Luxembourgs, Wittelsbachs and others, the accumulation of fiefs made partition easier since there was more to distribute and Austria split into Albertine and Leopoldine lines from 1379 to 1490 despite a family agreement against this in 1355.[7] The Albertine line benefited from the 1364 inheritance pact with the Luxembourgs and provided King Albert II in 1438. His death in turn benefited the Leopoldine line, which provided the emperors after 1440, as well as inheriting the south-west German possessions from the now defunct Laufenburg branch after 1415, though the Swiss areas were definitively lost in 1499. Finally, Maximilian I's inheritance of the Tirol from another junior line in 1490 provided a significant boost, since this territory had become the main area of silver mining in the Empire, literally allowing the emperor to dig money from the ground.[8]

At 53 years, Frederick III's reign was the longest of any emperor and entrenched Habsburg imperial rule despite his many difficulties. His son Maximilian used his position as emperor to intervene in the Wittelsbach inheritance dispute in 1504–5, playing the Palatine and Bavarian lines off against each other to keep both from becoming potential challengers. The fruits of dynastic strategies soon rendered such late medieval practices unnecessary to the Habsburgs' retention of the imperial title. The web of dynastic marriages spun by Frederick pulled in their spoils as the successive extinctions of the ruling families in ducal Burgundy (1477), Spain (1516), Bohemia and Hungary (both 1526) left Maximilian's grandsons, Charles V and Ferdinand I, as the heirs to vast additional territories (Map 8). Contemporaries remarked:

'Let others wage war, but thou, O happy Austria, marry; for those kingdoms Mars gives to others, Venus gives to thee.'

Dynastic good fortune gave the Habsburgs far more territory than any of their possible rivals at a time when the electors appreciated the need for the emperor to possess the means to defend the Empire from the Turkish menace. However, the additional territory increased Habsburg liabilities, especially as Burgundy was contested by France, whom most of the princes were reluctant to consider a general enemy of the Empire. These tensions contributed to what became the greatest ever dynastic partition: Charles V's division of Habsburg possessions into Spanish and Austrian branches (see pp. 438–9). The loss of scale was compounded by his brother Ferdinand I's own tripartite subdivision of the Austrian line in 1564. The main Austrian line extinguished with Matthias in 1619, passing to Ferdinand II as head of the junior Styrian branch. The third, Tirolean, line died out in 1595, but was revived twice to accommodate junior relatives, before being definitively reabsorbed into Austria in 1665.

Throughout, however, Austria itself remained undivided, its special status having been enhanced by Duke Rudolf IV's forgery of the *Privilegium maius* around 1358 to expand the genuine privileges granted when Austria was elevated to a duchy in 1156. Responding to his exclusion from the electoral college, Rudolf invented the entirely new title of 'archduke' with semi-regal powers, including ennoblement, and appropriately kingly insignia like a crown and sceptre. The symbols angered Charles IV the most, but his rapprochement with the Habsburgs in the 1360s helped entrench Austria's special status, which Frederick III confirmed in 1453, shortly after his imperial coronation.[9] Already Rudolf used his archducal powers to found Vienna University, the Empire's second and a deliberate response to Charles's new university in Prague. Austria's distinct status persisted and the Habsburgs never used their powers as emperor to award themselves electoral rights. Instead, they fostered a sense that Austria was already somehow superior, though the precise ceremonial distinctions were never clarified. Despite considering raising it as a kingdom in the 1620s, they likewise rejected this, not least because they were now already royal thanks to their possession of Bohemia and Hungary, which stayed with Austria in the 1558 partition. The Bohemian and Hungarian constitutions were revised in 1627 and 1687 respectively, asserting that these were hereditary rather than elective kingdoms. The unity of all possessions within and beyond imperial frontiers was expressed in 1703 as the *Monarchia Austriaca* (see pp. 159 and 162).

Matthias had a new archducal crown made in 1616 and it was used in all Austrian homage ceremonies until 1835.[10] The crown bore an image of St Leopold, the Babenberg margrave of Austria who was canonized in 1485 and became the monarchy's patron saint. The choice of image was part of a wider strategy to assert a divine right to rule. A family legend maintained that when Rudolf I was out riding in 1264, he gave his horse to a priest whom he saw carrying a Eucharist. By 1640, this had been rewritten to claim that God had given the Eucharist to the universal church while entrusting the divine right to rule the Empire to the Habsburgs.[11] Efforts to forge a common identity based on saints associated with the dynasty failed, as Hungary and Bohemia already had their own traditions.[12] However, a consistently dynastic ideology took root under Frederick III and developed with the lavish artistic patronage of Maximilian I and Charles V propagating a sense of a single, common *Casa d'Austria*, which survived all subsequent partitions.

This ideology was simultaneously imperial and dynastic. Rudolf I was celebrated not just for acquiring Austria but as the king who allegedly restored the Empire after the 'interregnum' following the end of the Staufers. Stories repeated the Rudolf motif for later Habsburgs, like Ferdinand II and Ferdinand III, who both supposedly also gave their horses to priests. Meanwhile, ingenious genealogists traced the Habsburgs as descendants of Aeneas, son of Venus and a Trojan royal who led the survivors of the fall of Troy via Carthage to Rome. Thanks to the idea of imperial translation, the line could be continued forward through the ancient Roman emperors, Christian Merovingians, Carolingians, and all the Empire's other subsequent illustrious rulers.[13] The skilful blending of family stories and imperial tradition trumped anything offered by their rivals to present the Habsburgs as the only ones worthy to be emperors.

The relative absence of serious challengers contrasts with the situation in the late Middle Ages. The Reformation opened speculation of a Protestant alternative once Lutherans secured full political rights in 1555. Rumours identified the Danish and Swedish kings as possible candidates, as well as the Protestant electors of Saxony, Brandenburg and the Palatinate. In practice, only Gustavus Adolphus of Sweden represented a serious threat, and he never considered standing in a conventional election, but instead sought to subvert Habsburg rule by forcing his German allies to accept their fiefs as dependent on him rather than the emperor. Any plans to usurp the imperial title died with him in the battle of Lützen in November 1632. Discussion revived as the Saxon, Brandenburg and Hanoverian electors acquired foreign crowns around 1700. While they considered themselves personally worthy of the imperial title, all refrained from seeking it because of the risks this would involve. Prussia's subsequent development undermined Habsburg imperial management, but none of the Hohenzollern monarchs wanted to be emperor. Only the Bavarian Wittelsbachs attempted this, with disastrous results for themselves and the Empire.[14]

HABSBURG IMPERIAL GOVERNANCE

Governing the Habsburg Lands

The period between Maximilian I's accession in 1493 and Leopold I's death in 1705 saw the consolidation and peak of the Habsburg system of imperial governance based on dynastic hereditary possessions. The family's territorial expansion coincided with the high point of imperial reform around 1520, accelerating and transforming that process. The material power that made the dynasty the obvious choice as emperors, also threatened German liberties. The emperor assumed a Janus-faced position as the Empire's sovereign and its most powerful prince. The imperial Estates appreciated a strong emperor capable of repelling the Ottomans, and were prepared to relinquish some of their cherished liberties to institutions they believed would bind the Habsburgs to performing their imperial duties. The Habsburgs accepted greater constitutional checks on prerogatives as the price for a more potent infrastructure to mobilize the additional resources from the imperial Estates needed to meet their own ambitions and commitments. The material results of these constitutional adjustments will be explored in the next section, after the discussion here of how the Habsburgs managed the Empire and their own extensive possessions.[15]

The Habsburgs had no thought of 'building' a state or creating a separate Austria. Nonetheless, their actions did distinguish their own territories more clearly as they followed the practice of kings since 1273 by enhancing the autonomy of their own possessions as a base from which to govern the Empire. Their court exemplifies this as it underwent a fundamental transformation under Maximilian I. The consultative functions were detached to the Reichstag, which now provided the main forum for the emperor to negotiate with the Empire's political elite. Meanwhile, Maximilian greatly expanded the representational aspects along the lines of Charles IV by establishing his dynastic court as a glittering institution projecting his family's power. Although it continued to accompany the emperor on his travels, the Habsburg court generally remained within the hereditary lands, especially Vienna, except for a prolonged stay in Prague under Rudolf II from 1576 to 1612. While the emperor or his representative attended at least the opening of each Reichstag, his itinerary was also now dictated by meetings of the various provincial Estates, or assemblies, in his Austrian, Bohemian and Hungarian lands.[16]

Elector August of Saxony was the last prince to be enfeoffed with the traditional rituals in the open air in 1566. Thereafter, princes travelled to Vienna to pay homage in ceremonies now held behind closed doors. The symbols were Habsburg rather than imperial. The emperor no longer wore his traditional robes, but instead all participants dressed in black after the fashion of the Spanish court of Philip II. Increasingly, princes sent representatives as proxies, further eroding the old personal feudal nexus in favour of more formalized constitutional relations.[17]

The court remained a centre for brokerage that was still largely personal, but geared primarily to managing the Habsburgs' own nobility. Recent studies have demolished the idea of early modern kings as puppet-masters, entangling their nobles in a golden honey trap that disarmed them and rendered them politically harmless.[18] Most nobles never attended court, which always contained several competing power centres around the monarch's consort, relations and other important figures. Nonetheless, the court did focus power and act as a hub for patronage networks linking the royal centre to the localities. It gave firmer form to the kind of politics existing more generally in the Empire since the Carolingians, because the court was now permanent and fixed. Proximity to the king enhanced the prestige of individual nobles and allowed them to cultivate their own clientele. The Habsburgs used this to restructure how they ruled their own lands between 1579 and the mid-seventeenth century. Court and administrative posts were restricted to men who proved their loyalty by either remaining Catholic or converting from Protestantism. The Habsburgs employed their archducal rights and imperial prerogatives to ennoble faithful servants and to confer the prestigious status of imperial nobility on loyal subjects from their Bohemian, Italian and Hungarian lands, as well as from across the Empire. Around fifteen thousand individuals were granted the status of imperial noble between 1500 and 1800, peaking during the crisis years of the 1620s when up to six hundred were ennobled annually, or five times the average across early modernity.[19]

The Habsburgs also granted titles and positions associated with their own court and institutions. Ferdinand III gave the title 'court councillor' (*Hofrat*) to 400 men across his reign. The court expanded from 400 courtiers in the late fifteenth century to 1,500 people by 1735, while the Habsburg army and administration offered employment to many thousands. Only the Wittelsbachs came close to matching the Habsburg court, briefly, in the 1550s and again around 1700. Most princely courts comprised a couple of hundred people, few of whom were nobles. For example, that in Wolfenbüttel numbered 381 in 1747, but only 20 of these posts were considered suitable for nobles, in addition to the 26 pageboys and 15 ladies-in-waiting. The largest groups were the 81 stable hands and 52 lackeys and messengers.[20] Viennese etiquette and architectural styles remained the models throughout the Empire and only Cologne's electoral palace at Bonn followed the internal layout of rooms used in Versailles. Despite his rivalry with the Habsburgs, Frederick the Great of Prussia used Viennese examples when he remodelled Berlin in the mid-eighteenth century. The Prussian state library, completed in 1786, was a direct copy of plans prepared by the Habsburgs' leading architect 80 years previously.[21]

Palatine rights allowed only princes to create lesser 'patent nobles' (*Briefadel*), which permitted commoners to insert the coveted 'von' before their surname. The Habsburgs' possession of Bohemia consolidated their monopoly on creating more prestigious titles, since no other prince had royal status until the Saxon elector became king of Poland. While the Saxons used this to ennoble some of their own subjects, the Hanoverians were relatively sparing in their use of British royal powers after 1714. Only the Hohenzollerns sought to compete seriously with the Habsburgs once they gained a royal title for Prussia in 1700. In 1742 Frederick the Great forced the short-lived Wittelsbach emperor, Charles VII, to declare the validity of Prussian noble titles throughout the Empire, thus adding to their attraction.[22]

Habsburg administrative institutions grew from their court to handle the expanding business and the family's desire to demarcate their lands more clearly. Albert II had already separated the Austrian and 'Roman' (i.e. imperial) chancelleries in 1438. Maximilian I established his own treasury (*Hofkammer*) in Innsbruck in 1496 rather than pay Austria's share of the Common Penny to the imperial receiver at Frankfurt. Further distinctions emerged when Charles V transferred control of the hereditary lands to his younger brother Ferdinand I between 1522 and 1525.[23] As with so much of his reign, Charles's action illustrates the transition to early modernity. Sharing power with Ferdinand as his designated successor resembled the medieval management of the Empire through a co-king. However, Ferdinand's position was geographically fixed and underpinned by both imperial and Habsburg institutions, whereas Charles remained itinerant, making 40 separate journeys during his reign, half of which was spent outside the Empire, while most of his time within it saw him in Italy or Burgundy rather than Germany.

Charles's status as king of Spain had already raised concern at his election that he would prove an absentee emperor, especially given previous experience with Frederick III's reluctance to leave Austria and with Maximilian I, who was accused of spending too much time campaigning in Burgundy and northern Italy. The Reichstag had already imposed a regency council (*Reichsregiment*) on Maximilian in July 1500 to enable selected imperial Estates to help implement the agenda of imperial reform: uphold the public peace, dispense justice, administer finances and regulate social behaviour. Maximilian managed to get the council disbanded early in 1502, but Charles's departure for Spain in 1521 led to its re-establishment to share responsibility with Ferdinand I, who made a more serious effort to work with it. The imperial Estates soon tired of their own creation. Its membership was supposed to rotate, but it was always dominated by the electors. Concerned for their own status and 'freedom', princes were prepared to accept their traditional subordination to the emperor, but not to their peers. They seized the opportunity of Charles's return to Germany in 1530 to disband the council. Ferdinand's election as king of the Romans the next year gave him quasi-regal authority sufficient to act on his own initiative. Meanwhile, the institutionalization of the Reichstag appeared a more suitable forum with which to share power than the narrower council, which was never revived.[24]

Habsburg administration was reorganized while the imperial and dynastic roles were split between Charles and Ferdinand. In 1527 Ferdinand created an advisory privy council separate from the old *Hofrat*, which retained judicial functions: a separation of powers enacted around five decades ahead of that in princely territories. Hungary and Bohemia retained their own institutions once they passed to Ferdinand in 1526.[25] Ferdinand expanded the remit of the new Austrian institutions once he himself became emperor at Charles's death in 1558. The Habsburg treasury now received imperial taxes remitted by the Reichspfennigmeister. The Reichshofrat founded by Maximilian in 1497 was revived as a supreme court for cases involving imperial prerogatives, especially those relating to feudal relations. This temporarily absorbed the Austrian Hofrat, while the imperial and Austrian chancelleries also merged, handling correspondence with both the Empire and Habsburg lands. These changes reflected a return to past practice and were intended to save money rather than centralize imperial governance. Now that Ferdinand I combined both imperial and Habsburg authority, there seemed no need for separate institutions. However, the underlying trend was still to distinguish between Habsburg and imperial functions. For example, the 1566 chancellery ordinance separated imperial and dynastic business between two sets of officials in the same institution.

Dynastic and imperial institutions were formally separated by Ferdinand II in 1620, while the Bohemian chancellery was moved to Vienna four years later in an effort partially to centralize management of the Habsburg lands.[26] Tensions persisted between the Habsburg and imperial chancelleries and much depended on the personal relations between the emperor and imperial vice chancellor. Like other princes, the Habsburgs found their own institutions often became unwieldy talking shops incapable of swift decision-making, yet staffed by people too important to dismiss. They consequently created a succession of new, initially smaller advisory bodies intended to formulate policy and coordinate the other departments. These inner councils frequently bypassed the imperial chancellery and dealt with important imperial Estates directly, simply through expediency. Miscommunication and duplication of function were common elsewhere in Europe, but they certainly contributed markedly to slow decision-making and poor administration in the Habsburg monarchy into the mid-eighteenth century.

Habsburg Lands and the Empire

The rapid accumulation of dynastic possessions between 1477 and 1526 did not expand the Empire. Those lands already within the Empire remained so: Burgundy, Milan, Bohemia. Those outside were not incorporated within imperial jurisdiction: Hungary, Spain, Sicily, Naples. Meanwhile, Habsburg possessions within the Empire were grouped separately into the Austrian and Burgundian Kreise in 1512, while Bohemia was omitted entirely from the new regional structure. The princes had insisted on incorporation, hoping to extend scrutiny and control over the financial and military contributions from the Habsburg lands through the new common structures. The Habsburg lands always contributed the lion's share, far in excess of their formal assessments, but Maximilian I and his successors were determined not to allow the princes to direct how they spent their own subjects' money.

Over time, the Habsburgs came to appreciate the benefits of having incorporated their Austrian and Burgundian lands within the Kreise, since this allowed them to engage in regional politics as imperial Estates as well as emperor.[27] After 1558 it also allowed the Austrian branch to retain a hold over Burgundy despite Charles V assigning it to Spain in 1548. Charles had agreed that Burgundy should pay double tax rates (triple if assisting against the Turks), and Spain initially honoured this, though it paid Austria directly rather than remitting the money through the Reichspfennigmeister. Austria's refusal to treat the Dutch Revolt after 1566 as a breach of the public peace soured relations and led to Spain suspending further payments.[28] Nonetheless, Spain also appreciated the utility of retaining its Burgundian territories as part of the Empire, since this allowed it to act as an imperial Estate rather than a 'foreign power'. Spanish intervention in support of Austria during the Thirty Years War was presented this way to undercut anti-Habsburg Protestant propaganda.

Both Burgundy and Austria only existed as Kreise on paper; neither held an assembly, despite both containing a few minor non-Habsburg members.[29] Meanwhile, the imperial police ordinances of 1530 and 1548 exempted Austria from a wide range of laws passed by the Reichstag. The imperial currency ordinance of 1559 granted similar exemptions, while Habsburg subjects were prevented from appealing cases to the imperial supreme courts after 1637. The Peace of Westphalia allowed the Habsburgs to claim all their possessions as officially Catholic, denying their still substantial Protestant minority the rights granted minorities elsewhere by that treaty, except for six 'peace churches' established in Silesia.

Although they isolated their lands, the Habsburgs still needed to deal with the rest of the Empire to foster legitimacy and solicit aid. Traditional methods were employed alongside the new institutions developing across the era of imperial reform. Swabia emerged as the area 'closest to the king' during the late fifteenth century, because this region was next to the Habsburgs' original possessions in Alsace and around the Black Forest. Dealings with Swabia showed how the family skilfully employed the opportunities offered by the lengthening status hierarchy. As local lords themselves, the Habsburgs deliberately engaged with their neighbours more as equals to win their cooperation through the Swabian League, founded in 1488, which constituted the cornerstone of what has been termed the 'Maximilian System'.[30] Their methods show how the Empire's internal structure was still fluid at this point. Frederick III and Maximilian I not only negotiated with those lords and cities who were being invited to the new Reichstag, but also with mediate nobles and towns in the process of forming assemblies (*Landstände*) in territories that themselves were still taking shape. Although they preferred to cooperate with senior nobles, both emperors were prepared to work with burghers where necessary, and offered cash, privileges, appointments and favourable judicial verdicts to cultivate useful clients.

These methods worked best where the emperor could appeal to a broad cross section of inhabitants, as in the south-west, but they were harder to employ in regions physically further from Habsburg possessions, which were also usually those with fewer lordships or inhabitants. The development of the Kreise gave the imperial Estates an alternative framework for regional cooperation independent of the emperor.

Nonetheless, the Habsburgs continued to see a league as a way to forge binding ties to imperial Estates outside the increasingly formalized imperial institutions. This became harder following the Reformation when Lutheran princes and cities combined in the Schmalkaldic League to demand religious autonomy, thereby hastening the demise of the pro-imperial Swabian League, which failed to renew its charter in 1534.

Charles's victory over the Schmalkaldic League in 1547 at the battle of Mühlberg appeared to offer an opportunity for him to attempt a significant reorganization of imperial governance at the 'Armoured Reichstag' in Augsburg the following year. Milan and the western Habsburg possessions were transferred to Spain under the Burgundian Treaty. Meanwhile, Ferdinand remained responsible for Austria, Bohemia and Hungary. All princely alliances were formally annulled, except the defunct Swabian League, which was revived as a new Imperial League (*Reichsbund*), intended to bind the imperial Estates to the Habsburgs. All imperial Estates were now to pay funds into a central Imperial Military Chest to support an army under Habsburg control. Rather than centralizing the Empire, these measures were intended to provide a clearer division of responsibility, with Ferdinand and Charles's son Philip looking after the two blocs of Habsburg territory, while the German lands were grouped within the League to manage them more easily. All three elements remained under Charles's suzerainty as emperor.[31]

The scheme failed, because Charles tried to move too far too fast. By trying to include all electors in his new league, Charles allowed them to combine against it, using the Reichstag, which was now too well established to be ignored. Charles's decision to push the measures in person at the Armoured Reichstag made it difficult to compromise without losing prestige. Resistance gathered into the Princes Revolt of 1552, forcing the Habsburgs not only to abandon the Imperial League but eventually to agree the Religious Peace of Augsburg in 1555.

This outcome exposed the difficulties of managing such an extensive collection of lands, prompting Charles to partition Habsburg possessions through a series of measures between 1556 and 1558. Whereas Frankish nobles retained a sense of a wider empire after the partition in the Treaty of Verdun (843), the connections after 1558 were now only dynastic, with the two Habsburg branches considering themselves a common Casa d'Austria. Spain was imperial through its extensive possessions stretching to the New World, while Austria owed its status to retaining the imperial title in the person of Ferdinand I.

Ferdinand also tried to manage the German lands through a pro-imperial league called the Landsberg Alliance. Formed in 1556, this persisted until 1598, but never included more than nine imperial Estates confined to the south-east.[32] The league's significance lay in its deliberately cross-confessional membership of both Protestants and Catholics. By leading it, Ferdinand signalled the future direction of Habsburg imperial governance: the family justified its continued hold on the imperial title by presenting itself as trustworthy guardian of the common good and the Empire's internal peace and external security. Ferdinand and his three immediate successors now accepted the Reichstag as the primary forum to negotiate with the imperial Estates, securing substantial financial backing by holding 12 Reichstags between 1556 and 1613.

However, the sheer number of imperial Estates complicated the process of finding a consensus, encouraging a parallel trend to consult the electors, either ahead of a Reichstag or instead of it, as occurred during Ferdinand II's reign. Charles V's unprecedented abdication on 3 August 1556 greatly enhanced the electors' influence, since Ferdinand I depended on their continued support to secure the imperial title ahead of his elder brother's actual death in September 1558.[33] Ferdinand won them over by opposing Charles's plan to make the title hereditary (see p.165), and by confirming their right of self-assembly. Cooperation continued despite the conversion of the elector Palatine to Calvinism around 1560. The electors accepted Ferdinand I's son Maximilian II and grandson Rudolf II as kings of the Romans in 1562 and 1575 respectively, on each occasion ensuring the seamless continuity of Habsburg imperial rule.[34]

Imperial Governance during the Thirty Years War

Rudolf II's refusal to marry precipitated a succession crisis that deepened with the Habsburgs' financial and political bankruptcy following the Long Turkish War (1593–1606). Unlike the previous deposition of Wenzel in 1400 orchestrated by the electors, the Habsburgs kept their problems to themselves. Spain backed Matthias as a safer pair of hands than the depressive and reclusive Rudolf. Matthias's attempt to force

Rudolf to transfer power triggered the Brothers' Quarrel after 1608, which saw both make damaging concessions to the Protestant nobles who dominated their provincial Estates. By May 1611, Rudolf had been deprived of all Habsburg lands and remained under virtual house arrest in his castle in Prague. His death in 1612 allowed Matthias to secure election as emperor, but he was himself childless and ill, and the whole episode seriously damaged Habsburg prestige and influence.[35]

As we have seen (pp. 121–5; also pp. 564–5), the distraction created a partial political vacuum in the German lands that was filled by the Protestant Union and Catholic League, formed respectively in 1608 and 1609 by the rival Wittelsbach branches of the Palatinate and Bavaria (Map 19). By 1617, Matthias had neutralized the League by compelling Bavaria to admit new members, rendering the organization no longer suitable as a vehicle for its own interests. Meanwhile, the Palatinate's deliberate disruption of the Reichstag in 1608 encouraged the trend to consult only the three ecclesiastical electors (Cologne, Mainz and Trier) and the generally pro-imperial Saxony.[36] The group widened to include Bavaria once that prince received the Palatine lands and electoral title in 1623 as a reward for helping to crush the Bohemian Revolt (1618–20) at the start of the Thirty Years War. Electoral congresses convened in 1627, 1630 and 1636–7. Saxony temporarily defected to the Swedes between 1631 and 1634 to pressure Ferdinand II into reversing his ill-judged Edict of Restitution. Although limited, Ferdinand's concessions were sufficient to entice Saxony back in the Peace of Prague in May 1635.

Saxony was allowed to annex the former Habsburg provinces of Upper and Lower Lusatia, which it had occupied since 1620 as a pledge that the cash-strapped Habsburgs would refund the cost of its military assistance in crushing the Bohemian Revolt. In return, it accepted Ferdinand's interpretation of the war as a rebellion, thereby legitimating his expropriation of his opponents' lands and titles whenever he could defeat them, like the Palatinate. Whereas the Religious Peace of Augsburg had been negotiated openly at a Reichstag, the Peace of Prague was agreed between Saxony and the emperor and then presented to the imperial Estates, who could only accept or reject it. Only Bavaria and, to a lesser extent, Cologne and Brandenburg were able to negotiate special concessions. The exclusion of the lesser imperial Estates fuelled their sense of disenfranchisement. Already, many minor lords and cities had joined the Protestant Union and Catholic League because they believed the existing institutions no longer guaranteed their autonomy amidst the political and confessional tension. The Palatinate especially had played on their resentment, presenting a more aristocratic interpretation of the constitution in the guise of religious parity, since meeting in two confessional corpora offered to level the Reichstag's hierarchy of three colleges: electors, princes and imperial cities.[37]

Ferdinand III addressed these concerns after his accession in 1637 in the hope of rallying broad support to end the Thirty Years War on the basis of the Peace of Prague. He held the first Reichstag for 27 years in Regensburg between 1640 and 1641, restoring some trust in Habsburg leadership despite the deteriorating military situation now that France had intervened to support Sweden, while Spain was no longer able to assist Austria.[38] Ferdinand's move inhibited the formation of a clear anti-Habsburg bloc among the imperial Estates, despite the willingness of France and Sweden to support constitutional changes that would indeed have converted the Empire into something more resembling an aristocracy. He avoided his father's mistake at the Peace of Prague and invited all imperial Estates to the Westphalian peace congress in 1645, rallying most of them to block the more radical revisions proposed by France and Sweden.[39]

Stabilization of the Empire, 1648–58

The Peace of Westphalia of 1648 is usually seen as one of the 'greatest catastrophes' in German history.[40] Supposedly, the Empire was reduced to a loose federation under the emperor's nominal presidency, emancipating the principalities from the constitution, now allegedly 'preserved in aspic'.[41] The terms referred to 'territorial rights' (*ius territorii*) and 'alliance rights' (*ius foedera*), but did not in fact grant new powers. Exercise of such rights remained curtailed by imperial law and duty to the Empire, as had been the case before 1618. Awkward constitutional questions were simply postponed until the next Reichstag. Imperial prerogatives remained broadly intact, though the exercise of some of them now clearly depended on consultation through the Reichstag. The repeated reference throughout the treaty to 'imperial Estates' further eroded the personal character of imperial politics, best symbolized by the princes' loss of their earlier right (since Augsburg in 1555) to change their subjects' religion, which was now fixed by identifying each territory as officially either Protestant or Catholic.[42]

The presence of France and Sweden as foreign guarantors was probably the least significant of the main set of changes (see pp. 127–8 and 174). Saxony, Bavaria and above all Brandenburg obtained additional land at a point when the war had demonstrated the military potential of the larger territories (Map 9). The Habsburgs secured their core goals, including acceptance of the sweeping redistribution of private property within Austria and Bohemia in the 1620s, which rebalanced the Habsburg monarchy as an alliance between the ruling dynasty and major aristocratic landowners. The consolidation of Habsburg power preserved the Empire as a hierarchy, since no other prince was able to challenge their leadership. Likewise, the electors combined to ensure their continued pre-eminence over the other princes, regardless of the actual distribution of material resources.[43]

Austrian policy after 1648 was preoccupied with retaining the imperial title and asserting claims to the Spanish succession, given the increasing likelihood of that branch's extinction, which grew after the accession of the childless and feeble-minded Charles II in 1665. Engagement with the Empire was necessary to both goals, especially as acquisition of Spain's Italian lands was prioritized. Ferdinand carefully cultivated broad support amongst the imperial Estates, securing the election of his son Ferdinand IV as king of the Romans. Ferdinand III staged a lavish entry into Regensburg in 1653 for his son's coronation and the opening of a new Reichstag amidst fireworks and opera performances, all demonstrating his family's continued power despite the recent harrowing war. Additional limits were placed on his ability to create new princes, but more radical attempts to revise the constitution were defeated, and Ferdinand won new support from north German Protestant territories alarmed by Sweden's ambitions in their region.[44]

Imperial politics remained open, with various routes for the emperor and imperial Estates to achieve their goals. These options gradually narrowed after the early 1680s without the constitution ever reaching total gridlock. A sense of uncertainty continued with the Franco-Spanish war, which only ended in 1659, as well as Ferdinand IV's death at just 20 in July 1654, followed by that of his father aged only 48 in April 1657. Ferdinand III had not had sufficient time to secure the election of his second son, Leopold I, as king of the Romans, leading to an interregnum prolonged to 14 months by French interference. The electors not only rejected Louis XIV's candidacy, but refrained from imposing anything more than minor additional restrictions on imperial prerogatives in return for electing Leopold in July 1658.[45]

The Permanent Reichstag

Leopold was only 18 when elected emperor and what proved to be his longevity (1658–1705) gave the Habsburgs the stability they needed to achieve their objectives.[46] Crucial to Leopold's success was his willingness to work within rather than against the post-1648 constitutional order. Various attempts to negotiate with the electors and a small Imperial Deputation failed to resolve outstanding security and reform questions, obliging Leopold to summon a new Reichstag when confronted with a Turkish attack on Hungary in 1662.[47] Having opened on 20 January 1663, the Reichstag remained permanently in session until the end of the Empire. This was not planned: there were four serious attempts to wind it up before 1741, while no formal sessions were held during 1692–7, 1747–50 and 1780–85 due to political tensions, notably Austro-Prussian rivalry.

Nonetheless, the Reichstag's permanence exceeded the annual meetings agreed in 1495 and also began much earlier than Britain's 'mother of parliaments', which only became permanent after 1717. England's Triennial Act (1694) restricted each Parliament to no more than three years, because a permanent assembly was regarded like a 'standing army', as a mark of tyranny. This pinpoints the key distinction between Britain's Parliament and the Empire's Reichstag. British parliamentarians were representatives elected by enfranchised inhabitants who would lose their rights and influence if the same people remained MPs indefinitely.

The Reichstag was not a parliament, because it represented the imperial Estates, not their populations. There was no prospect of its evolving into a democratic institution without fundamentally altering the Empire's character as a mixed monarchy and enfranchising inhabitants rather than territories.

The Reichstag remained permanent simply because it proved the most effective forum within which all imperial Estates and the emperor could negotiate, thereby rendering most other consultative institutions

redundant. This set the basic pattern for Habsburg imperial governance until 1806. The emperor would seek formal ratification for
important measures like declarations of war by negotiating with the
Reichstag and, in many cases, also the Kreis Assemblies, especially
those in the south and west that enabled him to contact numerous
smaller territories. Meanwhile, more informal channels were used to
achieve more localized goals, or to speed up formal ratification, by
negotiating directly with influential individual imperial Estates through
envoys or correspondence. Bilateral and occasionally multilateral alliances were forged with princes, usually to secure additional military
support above official obligations. These methods further eroded the
personal element in imperial politics, which increasingly assumed the
character of multiple written agreements between its different actors.

Politics remained asymmetrical, rather than equal as we would have
expected if the Empire had truly become a federation after 1648.
Princes appeared as petitioners, seeking the emperor's backing for an
elevated status for themselves, their morganatic wives or mistresses, or
revisions to their territory's formal position within the Empire, or other
benefits like favourable verdicts in disputes with their neighbours. The
goals of princes thus remained specific, and they did not seek generalized constitutional change; indeed, they often protested when other
princes received the same kind of favours they sought themselves. Participation in wider European warfare was generally driven by similar
desires. Princes overwhelmingly sought connections with other states
that were already the emperor's allies, like Britain and the Dutch
Republic, in the hope these would pressure him on their behalf.[48]

Although the Habsburgs occupied the position of strength, theirs
was a difficult hand to play. They remained perennially short of money,
and were often unable to pay for the additional military assistance that
princes provided. More importantly, the reservoir of desirable honours
in their gift was finite. Minor ennoblements and local political backing
cost the Habsburgs little, but direct interference in imperial justice
risked undermining their prestige and, ultimately, their ability to manage the Empire. Habsburg support was usually limited to applying
pressure on the parties involved to reach the desired settlement. Significant status elevations were harder to achieve after 1654 when they
needed the Reichstag's agreement. Leopold became adept at dangling
promises that were rarely delivered, at least not in full.

He secured the election of his eldest son, Joseph I, as king of the Romans in January 1690, safeguarding the continuity of Habsburg rule. The election was actively promoted by the archbishop of Mainz, who appeared with five other electors in person to cast unanimous votes. This was a strong endorsement of Habsburg rule amidst a two-front war against both France and the Ottomans.[49] However, the constant conflicts after 1672 accelerated the internationalization of imperial politics by widening the number of European powers keen to hire German auxiliaries. France was prepared to pay handsomely for key princes to refrain from participating in imperial defence, adding to the pressure on Leopold as the Spanish succession loomed in the 1690s. He was forced to deliver on promises and elevate the duke of Calenberg (Hanover) to electoral status in 1692, intensifying competition amongst the other 'old princely houses'. Savoy had to be granted grand-ducal status in 1696, while Austria assisted the Saxon elector, whom the Poles chose as their king the following year. Finally, and fatefully, Leopold agreed to recognize the Brandenburg elector as 'king in Prussia' in November 1700 in return for military backing in what became the War of the Spanish Succession within a few months. Each time, he alienated other Habsburg clients and stoked problems for the future.

COLLECTIVE ACTION

Imperial Taxation

Wars such as that over the Spanish succession required a level of resource mobilization far in excess of anything undertaken by the medieval Empire. The overall size of European armies rose by 1,000 per cent across the sixteenth to eighteenth centuries, or more than three times the rate of population growth.[50] Contrary to the received view, the Empire responded quite effectively to this challenge. This is not obvious from the level of revenue accruing from imperial prerogatives, which remained minimal after Charles IV's dissipation of the crown lands in the late fourteenth century and despite efforts to revive income during the early eighteenth century (Table 9).[51]

After the initial problems with the Common Penny to fund the

Table 9. Annual Revenue Derived from Imperial Prerogatives, c.1780

Source	Amount (florins)
Fines and dues levied by the imperial courts	60,000
'Voluntary contribution' paid by the imperial knights	30,000
Dues from imperial cities (13 still paid these)	10,384
'Jewish Tax' from the Frankfurt Ghetto	3,100
Total	103,484

Reichskammergericht, the 1507 Reichstag introduced a new tax, called the *Zieler* because it was to be paid in two annual instalments timed to coincide with the Frankfurt *Zielen*, or spring and autumn trade fairs. The imperial Estates were assigned quotas, but they were left to themselves how to find the money. Many fell into arrears, but the problem was magnified by the practice throughout the Empire's population of recording debts long after any realistic prospect of payment. Tax rates were raised in 1720 when the salaries of judges and staff were doubled as part of a wider reform of the court's administration. The official annual total of the Zieler was now 120,000 florins, or 25 per cent above what was required for salaries. Receipts varied between 78,000 and 139,500 florins annually from 1742 to 1770. Another reform increased the Zieler again in 1776, and within six years the tax was running a healthy surplus, while Brandenburg, which had not paid anything since 1713, resumed payments after 1790 and soon cleared its entire arrears.[52]

Far more money was raised on an ad hoc basis for defence using the matricular system introduced by imperial reform (see pp. 404–6). The system could be used to levy troops and/or their cash equivalents, which had been calculated since 1521 using a unit of account called a Roman Month (RM) based on the pay bill of the armed escort envisaged for Charles V's coronation journey. The nominal value of an RM was reckoned initially at 128,000 florins, but it had already fallen to 68,700 florins by 1576, and to around 50,000 by the eighteenth century.[53] Like the Zieler arrears, these reductions reflect flaws in how assessments were assigned. Several imperial Estates already protested in 1524 at their assessments, eventually securing revisions for the period 1545–51 that collectively reduced the official RM by 6 per cent.

Further problems crept in as some territories received temporary remissions, such as imperial cities hit by major fires. They often failed to resume paying the higher rates. Meanwhile, the Kreise developed their own registers to raise funds at the regional level. Although based on the 1521 imperial register, the Kreis rates often differed, offering further scope for unauthorized 'self-moderation' as individual Estates adjusted their payments to whichever rate was lowest.

These problems were in fact common in Old Europe where taxes relied on registers assigning assessments only loosely correlated with actual wealth. Once compiled, such registers were hard to revise, not least thanks to the vested interest of those who were under-assessed in resisting change. In fact, imperial political culture constrained self-moderation. Smaller Estates were particularly reluctant to challenge the Empire by unilaterally revising their quotas, and by the mid-eighteenth century many accepted that if they wanted a reduction, they would have to submit to a full investigation of their economic and financial circumstances by an imperial commission.[54] Even combined with territories leaving the register through French annexation, like Metz, Toul and Verdun, self-moderation only accounted for 15,900 florins, or a quarter of the losses by 1600. Twice that amount disappeared through the removal of minor Estates listed in the 1521 register, which avoided payment by forgoing the status of imperial Estate and accepting mediatization by another territory, such as the town of Lemgo, absorbed into the principality of Lippe. All attempts to persuade the beneficiaries to make up the missing payments were abandoned by 1577, but at least fixing the status of imperial Estate five years later entailed firm acceptance of the assigned burdens. The remaining quarter of the losses derived from the special status of the Austrian and Burgundian Kreise, since these never remitted taxes through the imperial receiver.

In fact, maintenance of the Habsburgs' imperial role cost their own subjects far more than their official quotas. Maximilian I spent 25 million florins across his reign, mainly to recover Milan as an escheated imperial fief in the Italian Wars. Austrian taxes provided the Habsburgs with between 500,000 and 1 million florins a year, while the Netherlands contributed a further million annually from 1507. Despite these sums, assistance from the Empire was essential and the 2 million florins voted for 1495–1518 represented an important additional source, even if only half the promised amount was actually paid.[55]

Significantly, Maximilian's 6 million florins of debt were contracted as Habsburg liabilities, reflecting his separation of Habsburg administration from that of the rest of the Empire. Rather than seek amortization through the Reichstag, he and his successors chose to negotiate agreements with their provincial Estates, who raised taxes from Habsburg subjects to pay the creditors. While this necessitated concessions to these assemblies, including religious toleration in the later sixteenth century, it freed the emperor from exposing his own finances to Reichstag scrutiny.

More substantial assistance came in response to the rapid Ottoman advance through Serbia and Hungary after 1521, establishing a pattern persisting into the early seventeenth century. The Habsburgs petitioned each Reichstag for 'emergency aid' to cope with the immediate threat, plus 'permanent aid' on an extended basis to maintain frontier defences in Hungary. Like other early modern European assemblies, the Reichstag initially refused the latter, recognizing that permanent tax grants would reduce the emperor's need to summon it again. Instead, it voted fixed grants, which could be drawn on as cash or troops until the allocated amount had been consumed. The total raised during Charles V's reign is difficult to calculate, because individual Estates often paid after considerable delay, but overall the imperial treasury had received around 4.3 million florins by 1555 (Table 10).[56]

Although far above what previous emperors had received, this amount still fell far short of Charles's burgeoning expenses. The 1544 grant provided only 3.7 per cent of the emperor's war funding across 1543–52, with the bulk raised largely from German and Netherlands bank loans.[57] However, the seemingly meagre amount reflected the division of labour within Habsburg governance and the Empire's international orientation in the interests of peace. The Reichstag only assigned Charles half its 1544 grant and even this was an exceptional case, because it did not feel obliged to back what it regarded as his private war with France. Instead, most imperial aid was directed to Ferdinand, who had been tasked with repelling the Ottomans. The actual scale of assistance was far greater than the official amounts, because it was largely provided as troops were raised, equipped and maintained at the expense of the individual imperial Estates.

Ferdinand's administrative and financial reforms doubled the revenue he could extract from Austria, Bohemia and his part of Hungary

Table 10. Imperial Taxation, 1521–1613

Voted	Sum	Duration	Purpose	Actual Payment
1521	6 RMs	1521–30	Turkish Aid	Troops sent in lieu 1522–6, 1529
1530	48 RMs	1530–33	Turkish Aid	Troops sent in lieu 1532
1541	1.5 RMs	1541	Turkish Aid	
1542	Common Penny	1542	Turkish Aid	
1543	Common Penny	1543	Turkish Aid	
1544	Common Penny	1544	½ for Charles, ½ Turkish Aid, equivalent to 12 RMs	
1545	Common Penny	1545		
1548–51	Cash (0.5m fl)	1548–52	Fortifications	0.35m fl paid (70%)
1551	Common Penny			0.4m fl paid (57%)
1556–7	16 RMs	1557–8	Fortifications	⎫
1559	0.5m fl cash*	1560–62	Fortifications	⎬ 1.141m fl paid (69.1%)
1566	48 RMs	1566–9	Turkish War	2.922m fl paid (77%)
1570	12 RMs	1572–5	Fortifications	0.7m fl paid (81.2%)
1576	60 RMs	1578–82	Fortifications	3.77m fl paid (82.2%)
1582	40 RMs	1583–7	Fortifications	2.12m fl paid (85%)
1594	80 RMs	1594–7	Turkish War	⎫
1597–8	60 RMs	1598–1602	Turkish War	⎬ 16.57m fl paid (88%)
1603	86 RMs	1604–6	Turkish War	
1613	30 RMs	1614–18	Border Defence	⎭

*equivalent to 7 RMs

to reach about 2.2 million florins annually by 1560, still far less than the average of 14.2 million that his brother had enjoyed from all his domains, including 6.9 million from the Burgundian lands. Ferdinand spent at least 530,000 florins on his court and administration annually, and between 540,000 and over 1 million on fortifying and defending the Hungarian frontier.[58] His debts quintupled to 10 million florins by his death in 1564, excluding another 1.5 million of private debt. The three-way division of Habsburg lands between his sons after 1564 robbed them of any economies of scale, forcing each branch to trade concessions to their provincial Estates in return for taxes amortizing over 10.6 million florins of debts by 1615. Despite being a noted art patron, Rudolf II in fact cut court expenditure, channelling the savings into border defence. Yet despite the provincial Estates doubling their tax grants, Habsburg debts tripled to 32 million florins by 1612, by which time annual revenue had reached only 5.4 million.[59]

This summary of the Habsburgs' deteriorating financial situation underscores the growing importance of aid from the Empire across the second half of the sixteenth century. The 409 RMs voted for 1556–1603 represented well over five times the sums granted during Charles V's reign. Despite confessional tension, payment rates rose from around 70 per cent at mid-century to 88 per cent during the last quarter. Additional aid worth 7.5 million florins was secured by approaching the Kreise directly during the Long Turkish War. Altogether, the Habsburgs received 31 million florins for the period 1556–1607, equivalent to 600,000 annually, adding considerably to regular revenue.[60] The Reichstag was most generous during the Long Turkish War, but more than a quarter of the money was voted when there were no active hostilities against the Ottomans, thereby coming close to the Habsburgs' demand for permanent funding (Table 11).

Only the 1608 Reichstag closed without agreeing fresh assistance, while that voted in 1613 together with late payments from earlier grants added another 2 million florins received across 1608–31.[61] Arrears totalled 5.3 million florins by 1619, but the regularity of grants before 1608 gave the Habsburgs better credit as emperors than as territorial rulers. The Reichspfennigmeister was able to raise an additional 3.8 million florins as 'anticipations' against future imperial taxes, plus a further 1.9 million in long-term loans at only 5 per cent, or way below the extortionate rates that bankers charged French and Spanish kings.[62]

Table 11. War Funding Raised during the Long Turkish War, 1593–1606

Source	Amount (million fl)	Percentage
Austrian and Bohemian Estates taxes	40	59.6
Reichstag and Kreis Assembly grants	20	29.8
Grants from imperial Italy	0.5	0.7
Spanish subsidies	3.75	5.6
Papal	2.85	4.3
Total	67.1	100

The problem of arrears should also be set against the fact that several territories voluntarily paid extra contributions, which could be considerable: such payments totalled 553,784 florins during 1592–4.[63] Above all, the system demonstrated the strength of the collective political culture. The Reichstag voted money for specific purposes, but its accounting system was restricted to recording how far individual imperial Estates met their obligations and it had no control over actual expenditure. Yet, despite their faults, the Habsburgs honoured their promise to spend the money on defending Hungary from the Ottomans.

It is against this background that the financial problems of the Thirty Years War become clear. The controversy surrounding the Bohemian Revolt dissuaded Ferdinand II from summoning a Reichstag, relying instead on requesting support from the Kreis Assemblies and individual imperial Estates, especially the cities, some of which paid considerable sums: Cologne provided 82,830 florins for 1619–31, equivalent to 110 RMs of its matricular quota.[64] In an effort to lend these measures greater legitimacy, the emperor obtained the electors' agreement to a general levy of 96 RMs annually from 1630 to confront the Swedish invasion. A further 240 RMs were sanctioned this way for 1635–8, before Ferdinand III finally recognized that Reichstag approval was essential if these measures were to stand any chance of acceptance, securing another 240 RMs in 1641. Direct approaches to the Kreis Assemblies covered the gap between 1638 and 1640. The payment rate fell far below what had been achieved in the late sixteenth century, because the emperor was compelled to assign receipts from different regions directly to units of the imperial army in their vicinity. This eroded the already fragile distinction between official war taxes and the numerous other exactions imposed by commanders. Already in February 1638, the Franconians complained that these additional costs were two to five times what they owed in RMs and asked to off-set further war taxes against what they were paying directly to the emperor's troops. Nonetheless, payments could still be significant. Official demands on the archbishopric of Salzburg totalled 1,137 RMs across 1635–48, of which 1,334,420 florins or 64 per cent was paid. Given that these sums were far above previous taxes and considering the conditions in which they were paid, this was simultaneously a remarkable achievement and a quantitative indication of the immense misery inflicted by the war.[65]

The real strength of the imperial fiscal system was demonstrated during 1648–54 when it was used to raise the money to disband both sides' armies as agreed in the Peace of Westphalia. Despite 30 years of terrible war, seven of the ten Kreise had paid 7.8 million florins to Sweden by 1654, as well as maintaining its army in the meantime at a cost of a further 20.5 million. The Bavarian Kreis raised 753,300 florins to pay off the Bavarian elector's army, while Mainz, Cologne and parts of the Westphalian Kreis raised 1.2 million to pay off Hessen-Kassel's soldiers, as well as 375,000 to pay Spain in exchange for its return of the Frankenthal fortress in 1652. The emperor was promised 100 RMs to disband his troops, but other than his lands being exempted from the payments to Sweden and Bavaria, he received little, forcing the cost onto his own subjects. Altogether, the official fiscal structure raised about 30.25 million florins in just six years to disband around 170,000 soldiers and bring peace to the Empire after 30 years of devastating warfare.[66]

The experience of the war rendered continuation of these methods politically impossible, as the imperial Estates were no longer prepared simply to grant money without being able to control its expenditure. Instead, they returned to the methods employed in the 1520s of providing military contingents in lieu of tax. Any cash grants were now geared to supporting collective defence by providing money through a new Imperial Operations Fund (*Reichsoperationskasse*) to pay the general staff, transport and other centrally incurred costs, while the contingents were maintained directly by the territories that fielded them (Table 12).[67]

Table 12. Tax Grants during the Permanent Reichstag, 1663–1742

Voted	Sum	Purpose	Payment
1663	50 RMs	Turkish Aid	troops sent in lieu,1663–4
1669	50 RMs	Hungarian border defence	payments from some Estates
1686	50 RMs	Turkish Aid	largely offset by troops in lieu
1687	50 RMs	Turkish Aid	largely offset by troops in lieu
1707	0.3m fl	Imperial Operations Fund	
1708	1.5m fl	Imperial Operations Fund	
1710	0.3m fl	Imperial Operations Fund	at least 6.52m fl paid (71.7%)
1712	1m fl	Imperial Operations Fund	
1713	6m fl	Imperial Operations Fund	
1714	7.5m fl	Imperial Operations Fund	largely offset by troops in lieu
1716	50 RMs	Turkish Aid	1.77m fl paid by 1736 (56.5%)
1732	6 RMs	Repair of Philippsburg and Kehl	0.29m fl paid (79.6%)
1733	3 RMs	Munitions for Philippsburg and Kehl	0.04m fl paid (38%)
1734	30 RMs	Imperial Operations Fund	0.35m paid by Jan. 1735
1735	50 RMs	Imperial Operations Fund	less than 50% paid
1737	50 RMs	Turkish Aid	1.3m fl paid by March 1739 (48.6%)
1740	50 RMs	Turkish Aid	little paid
1742	50 RMs	Gift to Charles VII	1.82m fl paid (68%)

The increasingly complementary distribution of functions across the Empire's different levels saw growing fiscal activity through the Kreis Assemblies, which raised additional sums, including for their own operations funds. The almost continual warfare between 1672 and 1714 led to these sums becoming virtually permanent additional taxes. Historians are only now grappling with the full scale of this activity, which is recorded in hundreds of account books scattered throughout Germany's numerous regional archives. The Upper Rhine Assembly voted 1,000 RMs across 1681–1714. Although the value of its Kreis RM declined from 8,900 florins (1681) to 4,100 florins (1704), the amounts were still substantial, especially considering the actual payment rate was about 90 per cent.[68] Indeed, payments received centrally by the Reichspfennigmeister, or the Imperial Operations Fund, give no indication of the true scale of the Empire's fiscal-military effort, especially as most of the non-payment was often offset by much heavier expenditure incurred directly by the territories. Indeed, official grants became a way of leveraging more money from territorial subjects, since the Reichstag made payment of imperial taxes binding on all inhabitants in 1654.

This is best illustrated by the War of the Spanish Succession (1701–14), which also saw the Empire's largest military effort after 1648. The central funds amounted to 9.1 million florins, of which about three-quarters were paid, including this time also by the Habsburgs, who contributed 32 per cent above their official assessment as a political gesture to encourage support for what was largely a war in their private interest. Additional voluntary contributions from the imperial knights, three Hanseatic cities and some clergy netted a further 3.24 million florins.[69] By contrast, Austrian military expenditure averaged 20 million annually. However, total expenditure was 650 million across 1701–14, including the cost of the official contingents and additional auxiliaries provided by the imperial Estates, as well as their other directly incurred war expenditure. Only 90 million of this was covered by subsidies from the emperor's British and Dutch allies. The remainder was divided roughly one-third for the Habsburgs and two-thirds for the remaining imperial Estates, indicating that the latter bore a disproportionately heavy burden. The Empire's overall effort exceeded Britain's military and naval expenditure by about 237.5 million florins.[70]

This effort was not matched subsequently, though the imperial Estates still provided substantial financial and direct military aid during the wars against France and the Ottomans in the 1730s. No further Turkish Aid was paid after 1740, reflecting the declining significance of the original imperial mission. The Reichstag voted 330 RMs to combat revolutionary France during 1793–9, but the strained circumstances meant that only about 5 million florins, or around a third, of the initial 230 RMs were paid.[71]

Imperial Defence

The Empire's military effort is perhaps the most commonly derided aspect of its early modern existence. Most nineteenth- and twentieth-century historians measured state effectiveness by martial prowess. The Empire's apparent incapacity is usually illustrated by its mobilization against Prussia during the Seven Years War. At the battle of Rossbach on 5 November 1757, Frederick the Great crushed a much larger combined Franco-imperial army, inflicting losses of 5,000 compared to 548 of his own troops. The rout and subsequent disintegration of the imperial army (*Reichsarmee*) led to its being mocked as the 'run-away army' (*Reiß-aus Armee*). In fact, imperial troops made up only one-quarter of the combined army, and a third of them were actually the Austrian contingent. The causes of the defeat were multiple and cannot be attributed simply to any supposed deficiencies of the Empire.[72]

The Empire as a whole never possessed a permanent army, but instead imperial reform created a mechanism to mobilize troops when required for collective defence and internal peace enforcement. Burdens were apportioned between the imperial Estates using the matricular quota system. Legislation issued between 1495 and 1555 established the process by which mobilization could be authorized by the Reichstag for the entire Empire, or by the Kreis Assemblies for their own regions. Further adjustments in 1570 rejected tentative moves across the previous decade towards funding a permanent cadre in peacetime.[73] The accumulative effect of these measures was to link official military activity firmly to upholding the eternal public peace. This associated 'military authority' (*Militärhoheit*) with the imperial Estates, since these had been charged since 1495 with maintaining the peace, thus denying such powers to mediate lords and communities whose martial activities came under growing supervision from the territorial authorities. Imperial Estates were identified with powers of command, able to name officers for their own forces, just as they had led forces in person under the previous, more personal, feudal obligations. Nominal supreme command remained reserved for the emperor, but in practice he named several generals. From the mid-seventeenth century the emperor consulted the Reichstag when appointing commanders of common imperial forces, but retained exclusive control of his own Habsburg troops. Princes recruited for foreign powers, most famously Hessen-Kassel during the American Revolution, claiming this as a 'German freedom', but that activity remained formally restricted by the proviso that it should not harm the Empire or emperor. Failure to observe this gave Joseph I an excuse to sequestrate Bavaria, Cologne and Mantua during the War of the Spanish Succession.[74]

Except for financial support in 1544, the Empire refrained from backing Charles V's wars against France, compelling him to use his own forces and those he secured by appealing to individual princes. The large numbers of German mercenaries serving him in Italy and the Low Countries were paid for by his own revenues and borrowing. Formal collective action remained limited to policing the western frontiers, especially after 1562, to insulate Germany from the civil wars raging in France and the Netherlands. Measures agreed at Reichstags between 1555 and 1570 failed to prevent either side from recruiting German and Italian troops, but otherwise successfully prevented these conflicts spreading into the Empire, except for Spanish and Dutch incursions in north-west Germany after 1585.

Like taxation, the main military effort was directed eastwards as Turkish Aid, reflecting the common expectation that the Empire should remain at peace with Christians whilst fulfilling its duty to repel the Ottomans. Substantial contingents were despatched five times from 1532, culminating in a sustained effort during the Long Turkish War, ending in 1606.[75] These were field forces raised for specific campaigns, augmenting troops from the Habsburg lands and much smaller numbers of volunteers from across Europe. Rudolf II opened the Long Turkish War in 1593 with a field army of around 12,000 men from his own lands and 8,000–10,000 from the Empire.[76] The only permanent force comprised 20,000 garrison troops guarding the Hungarian frontier after the 1520s, as well as a gunboat flotilla on the Danube.[77]

Military organization at the territorial level conformed to the imperial structure. Princes and imperial cities maintained small guard units, primarily for status and public order. These provided a professional cadre for contingents sent against the Turks. Peasants were enrolled in territorial militias legitimized by reference to imperial legislation requiring princes to maintain public order and assist the Empire. The militias underwent periodic reorganizations, especially from the 1570s when more systematic drilling was introduced, but they remained comparatively ineffective. Major operations always required professionals, hence the significance of the Empire's fiscal system to pay them. The Schmalkaldic League and other alliances formed during the sixteenth and early seventeenth centuries all borrowed directly from the Empire's quota system in their own mobilization structures.

The Habsburgs tried to fight the Thirty Years War using these structures by claiming that the Bohemian Revolt was a breach of the public peace, while presenting Swedish intervention as a foreign invasion. Throughout, they legitimated their operations by issuing mandates summoning their opponents to lay down their arms and negotiate. Those who failed to respond were branded outlaws to be targeted with punitive action. Habsburg supporters like Bavaria conformed to this approach, since it legitimated their own seizure of lands and titles from the emperor's enemies.[78] Initially, all belligerents tried to fund war from regular taxes, supplemented by foreign subsidies, forced loans and coinage debasement, the latter causing rampant inflation between 1621 and 1623. Most of the emperor's early opponents were relatively minor princes who lacked either large territories or reliable foreign backers, and were forced to subsist by extorting money and supplies from the areas where their armies were operating. General Albrecht von Wallenstein's 'contribution system', adopted by the emperor's forces after 1625, attempted to regularize this and extended it on an unprecedented scale. Wallenstein hoped to win the war by awe rather than shock, assembling such overwhelming numbers that further fighting would become unnecessary. Drawing on imperial legislation since 1570, Wallenstein issued ordinances regulating what his troops could demand from local communities, thus entirely bypassing regular tax systems. Subsidies and taxes from the Habsburg lands were now reserved to buy military hardware and other items that could not be sourced locally, as well as servicing the loans on which the entire system increasingly depended.[79]

Wallenstein's system suffered from several major flaws, not least the excessively high pay rates he allowed his senior officers and the rudimentary checks on graft and corruption. The numerous abuses feature prominently in contemporary criticism and subsequent historical discussion, but it was their political implications that made his methods so controversial. Wallenstein's army tapped the Empire's resources directly without reference to the Reichstag or the Kreis Assemblies. He gave the emperor an army funded by the Empire, but under Habsburg control and used to wage what was really a highly contentious civil war. Whilst contributions sustained the ordinary soldiers, their officers expected larger rewards, not least because they generally raised and equipped their units at their own expense. Wallenstein was already a major beneficiary of the redistribution of property confiscated from Bohemian nobles in the wake of the imperial victory at White Mountain in 1620. Confiscations were rolled out across the rest of Germany following further victories from 1623, with Wallenstein receiving the duchy of Mecklenburg in 1628, sequestrated from its dukes, who had unwisely backed Danish intervention three years before.

Alarmed, the electors combined to force Ferdinand II to dismiss Wallenstein in 1630, reduce the army, and switch to regular imperial taxes that allowed greater scrutiny and control. Sweden's invasion of the Empire prevented the full implementation of these changes, and prompted Ferdinand to reinstate Wallenstein. Wallenstein failed to defeat the Swedes and was increasingly regarded as a liability in Ferdinand's efforts to persuade Sweden's German partners to defect. Wallenstein's judicial murder in February 1634 demonstrated that the emperor retained control over the army and the loyalty of most of its personnel, but the problem of organizing war remained. Temporary military ascendency allowed Ferdinand to order all imperial Estates to combine their own troops with his as a single imperial army funded by regular imperial taxes. This arrangement was enshrined in the Peace of Prague in 1635, but it failed because the prevailing conditions rendered its financial arrangements untenable. In practice, the emperor had to allow Bavaria, Saxony, Cologne and – to an extent – Brandenburg considerable military autonomy. France and Sweden evolved an effective strategy after 1641, successively targeting pro-imperial territories, like Brandenburg and Bamberg, until they agreed neutrality. This gradually reduced the areas supporting imperial troops, forcing them onto the defensive. Nonetheless, Ferdinand III and his German allies still mustered over 76,000 men in 1648, compared to the 84,000 of his opponents, a significant factor in the emperor's ability to extract reasonably favourable terms in the Peace of Westphalia.

The overwhelming desire for peace after 1648 led to the disbandment of virtually all forces in the Empire. Only the Habsburgs retained a small permanent army, which they redeployed in Hungary.[80] However, the wider international situation compelled further discussion of defence. The emperor's preferred solution was to return to the late sixteenth-century practice of extended Reichstag grants subsidizing the cost of the Habsburgs' own army. This was politically unacceptable after the experience with Wallenstein. The electorates and several medium-sized principalities established their own permanent forces during the later 1650s and 1660s. The earlier militias were sometimes revived and adapted as a limited form of conscription providing cheap recruits to augment the professionals. The outbreak of almost permanent warfare on the Empire's western frontier after 1672 saw these forces expand considerably, creating the first true 'standing armies' alongside that of the emperor.[81]

This forged a new divide in the Empire between the 'armed Estates' (*Armierten Stände*) and their unarmed neighbours. Leopold I relied heavily on the armed Estates who could supply troops fairly quickly during both the Turkish War of 1662–4 and especially in the Dutch War of 1672–9 to defend the Rhine against French attacks. Collective defence became a modified version of Wallenstein's system as Leopold assigned unarmed territories and cities to provide funds and supplies to support the troops of the armed Estates. Unarmed territories now risked slipping into mediate status under powerful territories like Brandenburg, Saxony, Hanover and the heavily armed bishopric of Münster, all of which tried to formalize their predominance by establishing protectorates. By 1679 it was obvious that the armed Estates intended to deprive unarmed ones of the right to participate in the Reichstag and Kreis Assemblies on the grounds they were no longer meeting their obligations to the Empire directly. This threatened to federalize the Empire through the mediatization of smaller territories, shortening the status hierarchy to a collection of large and medium-sized militarized principalities.

Leopold realized this would undermine his ability to manage the Empire and he sided with the lesser imperial Estates at the Reichstag to force through a compromise defence reform in 1681–2, establishing a system of collective security lasting until 1806.[82] The matricular quotas were revised more clearly on a regional basis, retaining the 1521 register for cash contributions, but assigning new manpower contingents to give a basic rate (*Simplum*) totalling 12,000 cavalry and 28,000 infantry. As before, these could be mobilized as a fraction or multiple of the basic quota. The reform succeeded, because it stabilized the status hierarchy without preventing any further change. The *right* as well as the *duty* of all Estates to contribute was confirmed. The role of the Kreise expanded to organize contingents from the smaller territories who could combine their soldiers into regiments of broadly uniform size. The smaller territories could still opt to pay cash in lieu, but the money was now to go through the Reichspfennigmeister (later the Imperial Operations Fund) to prevent them being bullied into unequal local arrangements by more powerful neighbours. All imperial Estates were free to maintain additional troops above what they should provide for the Empire, especially as such obligations were on a sliding scale with no theoretical upper limit. However, this did not amount to the 'law of the gun' (*Canonen-Recht*) as some critics maintained, because in 1671 Leopold prevented the armed princes from securing the Reichstag's sanction for unlimited war taxes. Consequently, the legal position remained the one agreed in 1654 that subjects were only obliged to pay for 'necessary fortresses and garrisons', thus still allowing some scope for territorial Estates to decide what these amounted to, as well as for the emperor to intervene when they could not agree.[83] The armed Estates were also still free to provide additional auxiliaries through private arrangements with the emperor that might advance their dynastic goals. Finally, collective defence remained tied to the established constitutional framework governing decisions for war and peace, thus anchored on the ideal of a defensive war, since only this was likely to secure the necessary approval through the Reichstag.

The collective structure was capable of substantial, sustained effort (Table 13).[84] Although the actual Kreis contingents (*Kreistruppen*) were always lower than the totals agreed by the Reichstag, it should be remembered that the Habsburgs always subsumed their own contribution within their own army, thus accounting for another 30 per cent above the numbers supplied by the smaller territories. Many of the auxiliaries also included men serving in lieu of Kreis contingents, because many princes wanted to keep all their soldiers together in a single force to increase their weight within the grand coalitions against France. For example, such forces accounted for 28 per cent of the auxiliaries provided during the War of the Spanish Succession.

The continuous warfare saw the total number of soldiers maintained by the emperor and imperial Estates rise from 192,000 in 1683 to peak at 343,300 in 1710. The most significant and surprising aspect of this rapid militarization was the disproportionate growth amongst the smaller territories, whose total strength grew by 95 per cent to reach

Table 13. Imperial Defence, 1664–1714 (annual averages)

Conflict	Kreistruppen	Auxiliaries	Total	Habsburg Army	Total
Turkish War 1662–4	15,100	16,600	31,700	51,000	82,700
Dutch War 1672–9	12,680	53,830	66,510	65,840	132,350
Great Turkish War 1683–99	7,670	10,430	18,100	70,000	88,100
Nine Years War 1688–97	31,340	26,070	57,410	70,000	127,410
War of Spanish Succession 1701–14	37,950	96,140	134,090	126,000	260,090

170,000 men, compared to a 75 per cent increase in the Prussian army to 43,500, and a 62 per cent rise in Habsburg strength to 129,000.[85] Thus, imperial defence imposed a heavy burden on the Empire's weakest elements, but this simultaneously ensured their political survival. The Westphalian and Upper Saxon minor territories used the Kreis structure to organize their own contingents, enabling them after 1702 to break free from onerous arrangements imposed by Prussia, Saxony and the Palatinate, which had previously provided troops to the imperial army on their behalf. In contrast to the almost universal disbandment in 1648, the Westphalian, Upper Rhenish, Electoral Rhenish, Swabian, Franconian and Bavarian Kreise agreed in 1714 to remain armed in peacetime by maintaining contingents at one and a half times the basic quota. Perhaps more surprising still is that militarization remained contained by a highly legalistic political culture (unlike, say, China in the 1920s where warlords created their own provincial armies with little regard to the republic's formal order). Despite their lands being the most heavily armed part of Europe, the German princes continued to submit their disputes to judicial arbitration through the imperial courts, rather than make war on their neighbours.

The collective system mobilized 34,200 Kreis troops for the 1735 campaign during the War of the Polish Succession (1733–5) against France, while at least 112,000 recruits and auxiliaries were supplied to the Habsburg army across 1733–9.[86] The disappointing outcome of this campaign and the parallel Turkish War (1736–9) combined with political disillusionment with the Habsburgs and the disaster of Wittelsbach imperial rule between 1742 and 1745 to weaken collective defence. Most territories reduced their peacetime forces and several withdrew from military cooperation at Kreis level. This trend was compounded by the underlying shift in the Empire's internal military balance as the combined strength of the Austrian and Prussian armies expanded from 185,000 men in 1740 to 692,700 fifty years later, compared to the combined total of all other forces that dropped by around 9,000 men to 106,000 by 1790. As we shall see (pp. 637–48), this growing military imbalance seriously threatened the Empire's continued viability.

Economic Measures

The standard model of European history sees centralized monarchies as incubators of social and economic development. Royal capitals emerged as political, economic and cultural hubs, concentrating wealth and fostering dynamic innovation. Royal authority helped spread uniform systems of law, coinage, tariffs, weights and measures, helping to integrate local and regional economic activity. Localities and groups lost local protection and were compelled to innovate in order to survive within larger market networks. Monarchies reduced the 'transaction costs' of doing business by providing a safe environment under the rule of law.[87] While there is certainly plenty of evidence supporting this interpretation, it does not mean that other kinds of political order were invariably inferior in fostering economic developments.

For most of the Empire's history, its most dynamic economic regions were those of the greatest political fragmentation, like Flanders, Brabant and the Rhineland, rather than the larger territories such as those of the north and east. The reasons are complex. A major factor was that the more productive areas were clustered along the major transport route of the Rhine and its tributaries. While this concentration of wealth facilitated a dense, more complex lordly hierarchy, the resulting political diversity did not inhibit further demographic and economic growth. The proximity of different authorities could also encourage innovation and experimentation, such as the founding of luxury goods manufacturing during the later seventeenth and eighteenth centuries.[88] The real test was how far the Empire could mitigate the constraining consequences of its internal structure, whilst not stifling the potentially innovative economic aspects.

Economic coordination remained conventional throughout the Middle Ages. Like other monarchs, the emperor's main task was guaranteeing peace and justice for moral reasons, with any benefits for prosperity remaining secondary considerations. Direct intervention was restricted to what would now be termed investment incentives: privileging particular lords and communities through grants of market, mint, mining, and toll rights, all of which proved significant in promoting urban development. The number of settlements with market rights doubled to 90 across the tenth century, rising to 140 in the eleventh century and reaching 250 in the next. Politics shaped this as much as economics, since episcopal towns were the principal beneficiaries, reflecting the emperor's reliance on the imperial church. Only 25 mints were active in the Empire before 1140, but the Staufers' use of regalia as rewards increased this number to 250 by 1197, of which only 28 were under royal control, while 106 were held by spiritual and 81 by lay lords. The total nearly doubled again to 456 by 1270, with the balance shifting to the secular lords, who now operated 277 mints, compared to 152 spiritual and 37 royal ones. This expansion was partly in response to the growing money economy and demand for small change, but largely reflects the shift from the Staufers to the 'little kings' who bought support. It also underscores a point to be made in the following chapter that the Empire had a tangible impact on the lives of ordinary inhabitants.[89] As we have seen (pp. 369–70), changes in vassalage from the twelfth century contributed to commercialization by opening fiefs and jurisdictions to sale and mortgages.

Royal privileges frequently contradicted each other. One charter might grant toll rights to one lord, whereas another exempted individuals or communities. Only trade-fair rights followed a more coherent development. The Frankfurt fair received special privileges in 1330, followed in 1466 by that of Leipzig, which received 15 more confirmations and extensions by 1770. The imperial charters guaranteed free trade by exempting merchants from tolls and providing special protection for themselves and their wares as they travelled to and from a fair. These competitive advantages enabled them to undercut other markets, in turn attracting further business to Frankfurt and Leipzig. The effective establishment of the eternal public peace by 1525 enabled the Empire to deliver the promised security. The more sophisticated early modern legal culture brought additional benefits. For instance, Leipzig secured a Reichshofrat ruling against its own prince, the elector of Saxony, who was promoting a rival trade fair in Naumburg. Leipzig and Frankfurt both secured injunctions to limit the development of Brunswick as an alternative venue. The two imperial trade fairs complemented each other. Leipzig mainly served the north and east with links to the North Sea and Baltic, while Frankfurt was orientated south and west with connections to Italy and the Mediterranean. Both serviced more regionally focused networks based around subsidiary fairs in other towns, thus providing an economic network mirroring the Empire's political structure.[90]

Territorialization provided an additional layer of economic regulation and coordination from the fourteenth century as authorities increasingly assumed the initiative within their jurisdictions and also issued privileges and exemptions. The Reformation added a heightened moral imperative, boosting existing efforts to regulate daily life through 'police measures' (see pp. 534–8). Imperial reform strengthened the Empire's capacity to guarantee general peace and defuse socio-economic tensions. The Reichstag issued general normative legislation in the sixteenth century, providing guidelines that were adapted to local circumstances through incorporation in territorial law codes and regulations. This allowed for diversity of practice within a common system, enabling serious disputes to be resolved through the imperial courts. In this way, imperial institutions maintained a partially free market encompassing a quarter of all Europeans around 1500. Most of the population was legally free to move, though some territories imposed restrictions, notably Brandenburg-Prussia, where in the eighteenth century emigration was equated with military desertion.

Charles V's dependency on south German and Italian bankers prompted him to oppose the anti-monopoly legislation promoted by electors and princes at the Reichstag after 1519. However, the Reichstag gradually dismantled the canon law prohibition on usury after 1530, extending 5 per cent as the ceiling for all credit arrangements in 1654. Territorial authorities and local communities frequently borrowed at higher rates, but imperial law did curb excessive charges since creditors could not use the courts to enforce them. The 1653–4 Reichstag tackled the lack of credit following the Thirty Years War by giving all debtors a three-year moratorium whilst cutting interest arrears by three-quarters. Special arrangements were made for the devastated Palatinate, which received a ten-year moratorium. These measures protected debtors, but upheld the integrity of the capital market by rejecting calls for repudiation of all liabilities. However, the system remained conservative. Although reduced, old obligations retained their validity and continued to burden future generations – in some cases into the nineteenth century.[91]

Currency regulation provides a similar picture of partial success on its own terms, but at the cost of sustaining conservative practices. The Reichstag asserted loose overall supervision of mints by making currency debasement a capital offence in 1532, and issuing the imperial currency ordinance (*Reichsmünzordnung*) in 1524 to regulate exchange rates by establishing an official relationship between the south German gold florin and the north German silver taler. The two coins became official units of account to which all territorial currencies could be related according to their precious-metal content. Politics hampered these arrangements from the start, since the northern territories felt that their currencies were undervalued. Three revisions to the ordinance failed to solve this by 1571, because territories issued coins called 'florins' and 'talers' but containing varying quantities of precious metal. Regulation was devolved in 1566 to the Kreise, which were considered to stand a better chance of managing the situation closer to the ground and to punish deviations from the rules. Maximilian II undermined collective efforts by unilaterally removing the Habsburg lands from the common framework in 1573 as part of the wider effort to insulate the dynasty's possessions from scrutiny by the imperial Estates.[92]

However, the real problem was the conservative attitude to money. All levels of authority clung to the belief that wealth was finite and expressed through bullion. Yet precious metal was both a medium of exchange and an object itself, for example for use in making jewellery. The cost of minting coins could rise above their face value, encouraging their debasement through mixing in inferior-value metal. The regulations were devised before the spread of copper coins as small change in the later sixteenth century. Above all, official rates bore little relation to economic value defined through productivity. Meanwhile, the need for reliable exchange rates grew with the development of deposit banks in Amsterdam (1609), Hamburg (1619) and Nuremberg (1621), which used 'imaginary' units of account to facilitate international money transfers.[93]

The proliferation of mints during the high Middle Ages hindered control. The Reichstag tried in 1603 to limit their number to three or four per Kreis, but in Lower Saxony alone there were 30 in 1617, 12 of which were condemned by the Kreis currency meeting that year for breaching official rules.[94] Debasement, or lowering the value of currency, appeared a quick fix to the pressing need to pay soldiers after 1618. The economically weaker belligerents resorted to this in 1619, followed by the Habsburgs two years later. The most notorious operator was the Prague Mint Consortium, composed of politically influential Habsburg officials, including Wallenstein, which issued 40 million florins of largely nominal coin in an operation considered by modern economists to be far worse than the quantitative easing by the European Central Bank in response to the 2008 Eurozone crisis, and precipitating what has been termed the Western world's first financial crash.[95] Bread prices rose 400 per cent in 1621–2, triggering riots and military mutinies.

Like the wider Thirty Years War of which it was part, the financial crisis had been caused in part by deficiencies in the Empire, yet that same structure helped resolve it. Imperial currency regulations provided a recognized framework for concerted action that worked, because most of those involved recognized that debasement was counter-productive. Imperial cities already acted in 1620, followed by more coordinated efforts through the Kreise in 1622–3 that prompted territorial authorities to devalue their currencies by up to 90 per cent whilst recalling debased coins and reminting them at official rates. Most territories had returned to the silver standard by 1623, including for their small change, while copper coins were largely driven from the Empire.

The relatively successful outcome discouraged innovation and the pre-war system remained in place, with territories issuing their own coinage and monitoring entrusted to the Kreise, guided by the existing imperial currency ordinances. Some lessons had been learned, and the resumption of prolonged warfare after 1672 saw swift action from the Kreise against the few territories attempting debasement.[96] The

Reichstag last adjusted exchange rates in 1738, but again official values did not match market rates, prompting Austria to devalue its own currency. Thereafter, Austro-Prussian rivalry hindered coordination, especially once Prussia followed Austria's example and devalued below the official rate in 1750. It then issued large quantities of debased coins to subsidize the cost of the Seven Years War (1756–63), while Austria resorted to central Europe's first paper money by issuing 12 million florins in 'coupons' in 1761. Prussia revalued in 1764, but not to the official rate. With both German great powers outside the official exchange-rate mechanism, Bavaria and others left after 1765, leading to the breakdown of cross-regional cooperation through the Kreise. The overall consequences were not too grave. The outcome was the end of efforts to fix rates permanently through imperial law, allowing currencies to fluctuate according to market values. The official legislation continued to offer opportunities to cooperate and to prosecute fraudsters.[97]

Toll and tariff regulation followed a similar course. Like mints, tolls and tariffs proliferated through royal charters to individual lords and towns, most of whom interpreted the terms fairly broadly to develop a range of income streams. Richard of Cornwall tried to reduce their number in 1269, while Rudolf I banned all 'unjust tolls' five years later.[98] By that point, numerous authorities possessed such rights without anyone, the emperor included, having universally recognized powers to revoke them. Tolls and tariffs continued to develop in response to locally changing circumstances and the growing need to raise cash rather than just labour and produce from inhabitants. The emergence of the Reichstag and Kreise provided a framework for more effective management at a time when many believed tolls were strangling trade. As part of his election agreement, Charles V promised not to grant further toll rights without the electors' consent, while the Reichstag added in 1576 that territories required their neighbours' consent before establishing new toll posts. Financial imperatives led to this being ignored, especially after 1618. Wartime tolls were formally abolished by the Peace of Westphalia, and the peace implementation congress in Nuremberg charged the Kreise with enforcing this. Action failed in some regions, like Lower Saxony and the Electoral Rhine, because no one wanted to be the first to lower tariffs. Elsewhere, leading territories set an example, because they realized tolls were harming lucrative transit trade. Total abolition of internal tolls was rejected, and in 1658 Leopold confirmed the 1576 arrangements. Thereafter, central coordination was limited to official trade embargoes against France during the wars after 1672.

A common toll and tariff policy was hindered throughout by the complexity of the Empire's internal structure, not only within Germany but between it and Burgundy and Italy. However, later imperial Germany also lacked a uniform customs system before 1904, while internal tariffs were scarcely uncommon in pre-modern Europe. England's unified system was exceptional. France's internal toll stations employed 20,000 revenue officers, who still treated Lorraine as a separate country after its formal annexation in 1766.[99] The real problem lay not with imperial institutions, but how the larger territories embraced fashionable economic thought known as 'cameralism', which encouraged economic autarky. Local producers were to be protected by tariffs and promoted by state subsidies, while other measures attempted to shape social behaviour and encourage greater thrift, piety and obedience. Some aspects of cameralism advocated greater centralization at the territorial level. However, a major goal remained to preserve the corporate social order and resolve its problems. Thus, toll policy also reflected this. For example, only five of the nine toll posts on the Elbe river in Bohemia were state operated, with three run by municipalities and one controlled by nobles.

Cameralist measures were frequently counter-productive, but they appeared to work better in larger territories, raising anxiety amongst their smaller neighbours that they were economically as well as politically disadvantaged. The Kreis structure offered opportunities for micro-territories to coordinate activities, especially because many economic issues directly affected public order. For example, the Swabian Kreis organized police sweeps against vagrants, control measures during epidemics, and price regulation in times of dearth. Its 1749 road ordinance allowed it to compel cooperation from landowners who were not Kreis members to help maintain highways across the region.[100]

Overall, imperial and Kreis coordination remained only partially effective, while the positive aspects of political diversity did not apply to all economic sectors. For example, cameralism intensified competition where territories in close proximity produced and sold similar goods. This could stimulate innovation, while fear of losing business might curb the desire to raise tariffs. However, many activities were largely fixed, like water transport, forestry, mining and their associated capital equipment. For example, barges developed for one river trade could not necessarily be used to transport goods on another waterway. Much of the Rhine and Elbe trade relied on transporting heavy bulk goods, especially timber, which remained the main item in both quantity and value into the 1820s, but also iron ore, stone and agricultural produce like grain, wine, fruit, hemp and wool. All these items were unsuited for road transport, making it hard to use alternative routes to waterways.

Consequently, by the eighteenth century there were 32 toll stations on the Rhine and 35 on the Elbe, most of which were operated by different lords. Their owners had little incentive to reduce rates to boost trade, because they already enjoyed a captive market. Tolls added nearly 60 per cent to the cost of salt just travelling between Cologne and Frankfurt, while it was cheaper to take wine up the Main to Frankfurt and overland to Kassel for shipment down the Weser instead.[101] It was precisely these kinds of problems that the imperial framework should have resolved by providing the forum to reach a mutually beneficial solution, yet all talks failed, because too few authorities were prepared to forgo local advantages, and there was no mechanism to compel them. Only thanks to French pressure after 1795 were the Rhine toll stations reduced to 12 with published rates within a common system called the *Octroi* under Franco-German administration. Simultaneously, a start was at last made on dredging and straightening the river. The successor states retained the Octroi after 1815 until the last Rhine toll was abolished in 1868.

NEW CHALLENGES AFTER 1705

A Second Habsburg Empire

The Empire's last century is often written of as a prelude to the 'struggle for mastery in Germany' between Austria and Prussia.[102] This story of rivalry often marginalizes the other German territories as bystanders or victims. Imperial institutions seem powerless or irrelevant. Yet the century began with unprecedented imperial power.[103] By the time of

Leopold I's death in 1705, the Habsburgs had surmounted the financial and military crisis triggered by Bavaria's and Cologne's defection to France in 1703 during the opening stages of the War of the Spanish Succession. Imperial authority had been reasserted through the sequestration of Bavaria and Cologne, as well as Mantua, Mirandola and various other Italian fiefs that had also ill-advisedly sided with the French candidate for the Spanish throne, Philip V. The electors not only confirmed this, but readmitted the suspended Bohemian electoral vote in 1708. The new emperor, Joseph I, pursued a separate war against the papacy in 1708–9, ignoring the electors' protests.[104] More significantly, the Habsburgs seemed on the cusp of securing the entire Spanish inheritance as Leopold's younger son was installed as Charles III in July 1705 with British, Dutch and Portuguese backing.

The situation began to unravel as the allied powers wrecked the opportunity of a negotiated settlement by insisting France help them evict Philip V from the part of Spain he still controlled. Joseph I's premature death in April 1711 raised the prospect of the reunification of Spanish and Austrian lands under a single Habsburg once his younger brother was elected Emperor Charles VI. Britain and the Dutch Republic opposed this, cutting a separate deal with France at Utrecht in 1713 to abandon the costly war on compromise terms. Philip V received Spain and its overseas possessions, but surrendered Burgundy and most of its Italian lands to Austria. Although Charles received Reichstag backing for another campaign, he was compelled to accept these conditions at the Peace of Rastatt in 1714.

The outcome was a deep personal disappointment for Charles, but in fact completed the dramatic transformation of Habsburg power under way since the successful relief of the Turkish siege of Vienna in 1683. Sensing a chance to recover all of Hungary, Leopold had continued fighting the Ottomans despite the opening of a separate western front with the outbreak of the Nine Years War (1688–97). By 1699, he had captured Transylvania as well as Hungary, while Serbia was also conquered during a further Turkish War (1716–18). Habsburg control was also now more secure, as Joseph's forces crushed the extensive Hungarian revolt of 1703–11 at the extraordinary cost of 500,000 dead.[105] Total Habsburg hereditary possessions more than doubled by 1720 to reach 739,500 square kilometres, shifting political gravity as two-thirds of this lay outside the Empire. The Habsburgs now had two and a half times as many subjects as in 1648, with their Italian lands populated by twice as many people as in Austria. Overall, Habsburg possessions equalled the Empire's entire extent, making them a European great power in their own right.[106]

As with the earlier expansion of 1477–1526, the new acquisitions were not incorporated within the Empire, heightening the dualist character of Habsburg rule and reflected in a sharper separation in 1709 of the imperial chancellery from its Austrian counterpart, which was now clearly the superior institution. It took several decades for the implications of this to become fully apparent. The Habsburgs were already the imperial family, so their territorial acquisitions did not immediately challenge the Empire's status hierarchy. Their additional resources allowed them to expand patronage of princely and aristocratic houses in the Empire. The career of Carl Alexander of Württemberg provides a good example. From a junior branch of the Lutheran family ruling Württemberg, Carl Alexander had little chance of inheriting the ducal title. He converted to Catholicism in 1712 whilst in Habsburg military service, thereby firmly identifying himself with the dynasty, which appointed him governor of newly conquered Serbia seven years later. Having unexpectedly inherited Württemberg in 1733, he repaid Habsburg patronage by providing substantial military support during the War of the Polish Succession. However, Carl Alexander also expected to be rewarded with minor territorial concessions and the long-standing Württemberg goal of elevation to electoral status.[107]

His demands reflected the growing competition amongst the princes stoked by Leopold's distribution of favours in return for support over the Spanish succession. By 1720, the Empire contained four royal families alongside the Habsburgs: the Saxon Wettins (Poland), Hanoverian Welfs (Britain), Brandenburg Hohenzollerns (Prussia) and Savoy (Sardinia). Although French pressure obliged Charles VI to restore the Wittelsbachs in Bavaria, none of that family's branches acquired a crown despite their heavy involvement in the War of the Spanish Succession. The Utrecht conference completed the trend initiated at Westphalia in the 1640s of excluding non-sovereign entities from international diplomacy. Of the imperial Estates, only Prussia and Savoy were allowed to participate. Post-1713 Europe consisted primarily of the winners who mutually recognized the sovereign status of one another.

The Empire meanwhile preserved those who failed to secure

recognition, including relatively weak elements like the imperial cities, alongside much larger entities such as Bavaria and the Palatinate. All elements remained bound within a common order guaranteeing their autonomy and status, which would evaporate if the Empire were dissolved. They paid at least lip service to formal norms, since to do otherwise would discredit their own position and hand advantages to local rivals.[108]

Prussia and the Empire

The power of established norms is demonstrated by Prussia's behaviour after its elevation to a kingdom in 1700. Prussia's emergence as the emperor's most dangerous vassal is usually explained by reference to the continuous line of healthy, able rulers since the 'Great Elector' Frederick William. His son and successor was dismissed by his own grandson, King Frederick II, as a 'theatre king' whose elevation as King Frederick I was simply part of an alleged obsession with irrelevant ceremony.[109] In fact, Frederick I increased the army by a third to total 40,000 men by his death in 1713, making the accession of Frederick William I less of a 'break in style' than commonly assumed. Nonetheless, Frederick William I's cuts in court expenditure and ruthless military expansion are generally interpreted as creating the tools employed aggressively against Austria by his son Frederick II after 1740.

Military power was crucial to Prussia's influence, but any explanation is incomplete without reference also to its place in the Empire. Even after the inheritance of ducal Prussia in 1618, two-thirds of Hohenzollern land was within the Empire, as were all further gains until 1740. The Hohenzollerns were major beneficiaries from the Peace of Westphalia, which secured them half the disputed Jülich-Cleves inheritance, half of Pomerania, and several secularized imperial church lands. Although individually small, these territories were more densely populated and produced higher per-capita tax revenues than ducal Prussia: by 1740, three-quarters of the Hohenzollerns' 2.4 million subjects were also inhabitants of the Empire.[110]

These possessions were already over twice as large as Bavaria or Saxony by 1648, but their full potential remained to be developed. Brandenburg's soil was poor, while much Hohenzollern territory remained in relatively isolated parcels scattered across northern Germany. The

Great Elector applied considerable pressure on the Estates of each territory to grant higher taxes during the 1650s, but this became harder to achieve from the 1670s as Leopold I vetoed unlimited war taxes and the imperial courts threatened to intervene.[111] Subsequent Hohenzollern rulers preferred to leave the tax structure unchanged rather than unpick the bargains they had struck with their various provincial nobilities and towns. Significant reform was continually postponed until Prussia's defeat by Napoleon in 1806 made change unavoidable. Bavaria, Saxony, Hanover and to a lesser extent the Palatinate and even Münster all enjoyed similar revenues and maintained large armies roughly comparable to Prussia's until 1700. The Bavarian and Saxon courts continued to outshine Prussia's, further concealing the growing discrepancy in real power that developed after 1700.

The real significance of ducal Prussia lay in its position outside imperial jurisdiction. Skilful diplomatic and military manoeuvres during the Northern War (1655–60) secured international recognition of Prussia's full independence from Poland, though it took some time for its provincial Estates to accept this.[112] It placed the Hohenzollerns alongside the Habsburgs as the only imperial princes with sovereign land outside the Empire, and provided the basis for the Hohenzollerns' subsequent elevation to royalty. However, their political gravity remained in northern Germany. Frederick I was crowned king in the Prussian capital Königsberg, but Berlin remained the centre of Hohenzollern government. Frederick and his next two successors continued developing Berlin as a city of European importance. Their behaviour was identical to that of the House of Savoy, which remained based in Turin in Piedmont rather than relocating to Sardinia; this provided the basis for its royal title after 1720. Prussia and Sardinia remained subordinate adjuncts in contrast to the other German princes who acquired crowns, including the Hanoverians and Saxon Wettins, whose electorates assumed secondary status to Britain and Poland. Savoy's ambitions lay south of the Alps, so its royal status did not disrupt the hierarchical order in Germany, especially as the Savoyards deliberately disengaged from the Reichstag to avoid ceremonial difficulties after 1714. Additionally, Savoy was underpowered compared to Prussia and was not in a position to challenge Austria until well into the nineteenth century.[113]

By contrast, the Hohenzollerns were deeply embedded in the Empire both geographically and constitutionally. Moreover, their royal status was less certain: they were only kings 'in' Prussia, whereas the Savoyards were kings *of* Sardinia, which had long been recognized as a kingdom. Considerable doubt existed whether Leopold I really possessed the authority to raise Prussia to a kingdom, especially since that territory's incorporation into Poland had been both more recent and more secure than its earlier ties to the Empire. Unlike over-mighty vassals during the Middle Ages, the Hohenzollerns were not challenging the Habsburgs for the imperial title, but instead sought recognition as a second powerful dynastic-territorial monarchy with equivalent status and autonomy to Austria.

Frederick I immediately pushed for ceremonial changes to assert this, quickly souring relations with Austria. Already in 1705, Habsburg ministers regretted the award of royal status to the Hohenzollerns, and diplomatic relations were temporarily broken off after 1707, despite the continuing military alliance against France.[114] Despite the problems, Frederick secured a partial exemption for all Hohenzollern fiefs from Reichskammergericht jurisdiction in 1702. Such privileges were not uncommon, as we shall see (pp. 626–7). What is more significant is that the Hohenzollerns did not push for more uniform autonomy like the Habsburg lands, but instead continued to treat each of their possessions as distinct so as not to forgo even comparatively minor rights and influence associated with them. The Austrian lands were far larger than Hohenzollern territory before 1715, but they only had a single vote in the Reichstag, while the Habsburgs exercised a further vote for Burgundy, plus Lorraine's vote until 1738. The Hohenzollerns instead kept their possessions distinct to maximize representation both in the Reichstag and in the Westphalian and Upper and Lower Saxon Kreis Assemblies.

Formal political influence was important, because the Hohenzollerns could not compete with Habsburg informal patronage. Although large, the Hohenzollern army and court lacked the prestige and the number of well-paid appointments the Habsburgs could offer, while the emperor had much wider powers of ennoblement. The Hohenzollerns also remained second-class participants in the dynastic marriage market, with their choice of partners largely restricted to middling Protestant princely families, such as the Brunswick Welfs. Representation in the Reichstag provided a platform to rally support to block uncongenial Habsburg measures, as well as to legitimate Hohenzollern policy on a wider stage. This proved particularly important to Prussia's military expansion during the wars after 1672 when its involvement was sanctioned through the system of imperial defence, allowing it to forge ties with numerous minor territories that paid Prussia to field their contingents to the imperial army. These opportunities ended with peace in 1714, which also cut off Anglo-Dutch subsidies precisely as Frederick William I was expanding his army further, forcing him to introduce conscription by 1733 to reduce military expenses.[115] Although now more than twice as large as the army of any other German principality, Prussia's forces remained within the system of collective security, contributing a contingent during the War of the Polish Succession. Prussia also adhered to the constitutional requirement to notify other imperial Estates when shifting units from one part of its scattered possessions to another, and generally complied more closely with the obligation to pay for accommodation and transport during transit than either Austria or Saxony.

Prussia deliberately encouraged the immigration of Huguenot and other Protestant refugees after the 1680s to increase its population. Although on a far larger scale, such measures were not unusual in the Empire. The Hohenzollerns meanwhile remained within the Empire's broader religious order. Attempts to rally support against the Habsburgs by fanning Protestant fears failed to enable the Hohenzollerns to displace Saxony as leader of the Corpus Evangelicorum and instead temporarily discredited the Prussian king as a troublemaker (see p. 130).

Likewise, numerous territories were earmarked as potential future acquisitions by Frederick William I and his son, but selection was guided by dynastic claims and, before 1740, mainly targeted minor principalities that would increase Prussian influence in south Germany. No attempt was made to seize these by force. Instead, Prussia tried to tighten its grip through protectorate rights and buying out rival claimants. Its first two kings were obliged to accept several setbacks, notably in 1722 when Charles VI annulled a favourable inheritance treaty painstakingly negotiated with Prussia's Hohenzollern relations in Bayreuth.[116] Even comparatively minor imperial Estates withstood Prussian bullying before 1740. That changed in June of that year with the accession of Frederick II, a man who held the Empire in contempt and – unlike his predecessors – was prepared to use force to achieve his goals.

The War of the Austrian Succession

Frederick did not have long to wait for an opportunity. Charles VI's death on 20 October 1740 extinguished the Habsburg male line and opened the question of the Austrian succession. Powers hostile to the Habsburgs ignored their earlier recognition of the Pragmatic Sanction revising Habsburg inheritance law in favour of Charles's daughter, Maria Theresa. With a large army and full treasury, Frederick was able to act first, already deciding just nine days after Charles's death to attack, despite having no claims on Habsburg territory beyond largely lapsed rights to small parts of Silesia. Silesia was not only large, populous and industrious, but its capture would prevent Saxony establishing a land bridge to Poland.[117] Prussian troops crossed the frontier on 16 December 1740, deliberately confusing the local Habsburg authorities by claiming they were occupying Silesia to safeguard it for Maria Theresa.

This step determined Frederick's policy for the rest of his reign. It is important not to read subsequent events with the benefit of hindsight, especially as Frederick fostered an image of himself and his kingdom as 'great'.[118] Despite Austria's near bankruptcy, demoralized army and elderly statesmen, Frederick's action was extremely risky. The Habsburgs had defeated every challenger since the sixteenth century. Frederick's ambitions nearly came to an end just a few months into his invasion when he fled the battle of Mollwitz in April 1741, narrowly avoiding capture by the Austrians. Although his army went on to win, he came close to capture or death in several later battles. Had this been the case, it is almost certain that his relations would have made peace on disadvantageous terms, just as Sweden had done when a bullet ended its great power status by killing King Charles XII at the siege of Frederiksten in 1718. The actual outcome for Frederick proved very different. By December 1745, Prussia had compelled Austria to cede Silesia and Glatz, increasing its territory to over 161,000 square kilometres with 4 million inhabitants. Prussia now had nearly a third more territory than Bavaria, Saxony, Hanover and the Palatinate combined, and the equivalent to four-fifths of their total population. Already apparent before 1740, the material discrepancy now carried real political weight, as Austria had meanwhile defeated Bavaria by 1745.

Wittelsbach Imperial Rule, 1742–5

Whereas Frederick sought additional territory to bolster Prussia's European status, Bavaria's elector Carl Albrecht made a bid for the imperial crown in the manner of the late medieval struggles to rule the Empire (pp. 377–96). Bavarian intervention paradoxically demonstrated the success of Habsburg methods since 1438. Although able to secure election as Charles VII on 24 January 1742, the Bavarian elector was unable to establish stable imperial rule. Meanwhile, Maria Theresa and her husband, Francis Stephen, were able to survive on the considerable resources of the Habsburg lands, supplemented by Anglo-Dutch support.[119] Bavaria was already weak and only managed to launch its bid for Habsburg possessions eight months after Prussia's invasion of Silesia, a move that caused considerable disquiet amongst the other electors and contributed to a 15-month interregnum. Loyalty to the Habsburgs remained strong amongst some middling and many minor imperial Estates. The Bavarian elector eventually triumphed over Francis as the Habsburg candidate thanks to massive French and Prussian pressure combined with discontent over the last decade of Charles VI's reign and concern at Austria's great power interests.[120] The Austrian army entered Munich two days after Charles VII's election, amply demonstrating Bavaria's incapacity to sustain imperial rule. Bavarian revenue in 1742 was only 1.9 million florins compared to expenditure of 6.48 million, of which 4.5 million went to the army, which still totalled only 25,000 soldiers, many of whom were hastily pressed militiamen. France supplied 8.8 million florins in aid, but Bavaria's debts had climbed to over 32 million by the time of Charles's death in 1745.[121]

Despite his deteriorating military situation, Charles VII's initial reception was fairly favourable. Fifty princes and counts attended his coronation in person on 12 February 1742, while representation at the Reichstag improved as several Estates sent envoys after long absences. The Reichstag voted assistance which, when combined with contributions from the imperial knights, provided 3 to 3.5 million florins across Charles's reign.[122] This did not, however, constitute formal endorsement of his war with Austria, which was regarded as a private matter, with the Reichstag adopting a position of official neutrality. The south and western Kreise mobilized troops to uphold this until 1748. Charles was forced to make concessions to win support. Fifteen counts were raised to princely status, with some of them providing troops for the Bavarian army. More significantly, Charles granted Prussia ceremonial distinctions matching Austria's status, including according Frederick II the title of 'majesty', enabling him to become king *of* rather than merely *in* Prussia. Prussian support was retained by recognizing its possession of Silesia as a sovereign duchy, raising doubts as to whether it still belonged to the Empire, while Spanish cooperation was purchased through conceding plans for a new kingdom to be created from Austria's possessions in northern Italy.

Meanwhile, the other electors were mollified by revisions to the emperor's electoral agreement in 1742, confirming that they were no longer personally obliged to seek confirmation of their fiefs at the start of each reign. More damaging still, Charles offered to renounce claims to Austria and Bohemia if Bavaria was recognized as a kingdom. When that failed, he proposed ending the war at the expense of the imperial church in a new wave of secularization. Although intended as secret, details of these negotiations were soon leaked by his enemies, exposing Charles's inability to deliver his promise to be the 'small man's emperor' favouring the minor imperial Estates against the two German great powers.[123] By 1744 it was clear that Charles's fortunes depended on how far Frederick II was willing to back him. Charles's death on 20 January 1745 enabled his son, Maximilian III Joseph, to cut a deal with Austria, supplying troops in its ongoing war with France in return for an Austrian withdrawal from Bavaria.[124]

Austro-Prussian Rivalry

Frederick II secured international recognition of his possession of Silesia as the price for accepting Maria Theresa's husband as Emperor Francis I in 1745 and refraining from opposing Austria in the remaining three years of war against France and Spain. Contemporaries perceived the period 1740–45 as a significant break with the past. Francis was only Habsburg by marriage and appeared the junior partner to Maria Theresa, who retained exclusive control of her hereditary lands. The division between imperial and Habsburg rule continued when Joseph II succeeded his father as emperor in 1765. Although Maria Theresa conceded co-rule to her son, he granted her ceremonial precedence ahead of his own wife at the Habsburg court, symbolizing how imperial affairs had slipped into a secondary consideration in Habsburg policy, and sharpening the distinction between *kaiserlich* referring to the emperor and *reichisch* relating to the Empire. Already, Austrians talked of travelling 'to the Empire' as if it were a foreign country. The importance of the Habsburg lands is expressed by the imbalance in paperwork, with the Austrian state chancellery producing 259 volumes of records in the period 1745–1806, compared to only 25 for its imperial counterpart.[125]

Nonetheless, all senior Habsburg figures, including Maria Theresa, were convinced that the loss of the imperial title in 1740 had been a disaster and were determined to rebuild their influence in the Empire.[126] They found some support, because the experience of 1740–45 had exposed the dangers of a weak emperor (Charles VII) and confirmed there was no viable alternative to Habsburg rule. Austria and Prussia together held half the Empire, excluding imperial Italy. Even when combined with the earlier loss of Naples and Sicily to Spain in 1735, Austria possessed a substantial empire of its own (Map 10). The disparity with other German principalities widened with the damage inflicted on Bavaria and Saxony during the War of the Austrian Succession. Contemporaries were increasingly aware of these material differences through a better understanding of statistics and more accurate information.

Austrian policy was governed by the desire to punish Prussia and recover Silesia, both considered necessary to restore the Habsburgs' international standing. Diplomacy constructed a powerful coalition that included France and Sweden as guarantors of the Peace of Westphalia, as well as Russia, which hoped to annex Prussia itself. Fearing attack, Frederick the Great launched a pre-emptive strike in August 1756, planning to seize Saxony as a base from which to fight. Prussian troops also moved into Mecklenburg during 1757 to block a potential Swedish advance. Both actions played into Habsburg hands, since Frederick's invasion of two Lutheran territories undermined his propaganda that he was defending constitutional liberties against Catholic Habsburg tyranny. His clear breach of the public peace appeared to provide Austria with the legal basis to sequestrate his lands, as it had done with its opponents during the Thirty Years War.[127]

The majority of imperial Estates were prepared to back collective military action to restore peace, but not to achieve Austria's goal of dismembering Prussia. Frederick's successful defence against years of poorly coordinated attacks enabled him to make peace in 1763 on the basis of the pre-war status quo. The Empire was the only belligerent to achieve its official war aim, forcing Prussia to evacuate Saxony and Mecklenburg.[128] Yet Prussia was the real victor, since its survival against seemingly impossible odds confirmed its status as a great power. Frederick built the huge showpiece Neues Palais in Potsdam to prove his country's potency despite having just fought a costly war.

However, Prussia remained vulnerable, having only escaped defeat thanks to British aid and the fortuitous change of ruler in Russia leading to that country's exit from the war early in 1762.[129] Although allied to Russia after 1764, Frederick was conscious how quickly Russian troops had conquered east Prussia itself in 1757, holding it until peace was established six years later. Aware that he could not rely on international allies, Frederick refined his dealings with the Empire. His criticism of the Empire was only published long after his death, whereas his policies after 1763 show skilful use of the constitution to disrupt Habsburg imperial management and prevent Austria mobilizing the still considerable resources of the minor territories against Prussia.[130] Prussia now presented itself as defender of German liberties against Habsburg tyranny as a way to block Joseph II's attempts to reform imperial justice after 1765.

However, dynasticism proved the most explosive issue. Prussia had long-standing claims to the lands of the Franconian Hohenzollerns that merged into the margraviate of Ansbach-Bayreuth in 1769. Meanwhile, a Bavarian succession crisis loomed as Maximilian III Joseph had no son to succeed him. Dynasticism had shifted since the early eighteenth century in line with the generally more materialist approach to imperial politics. Although his father and grandfather had expended considerable effort to secure Ansbach-Bayreuth, Frederick was prepared to swop his claims if Saxony would cede the more strategically located Lusatia to strengthen his hold on Silesia. Meanwhile, Joseph II tried to persuade the Palatine Wittelsbachs to cede their claims to Bavaria in return for having the far richer, but from an Austrian perspective strategically vulnerable, Netherlands instead.[131]

Towards a Polish Future

The prolonged negotiations from the mid-1760s saw these territories assessed in terms of size, revenue and population, rather than their formal status as imperial fiefs. The discussions were interrupted by a civil war in Poland that led to the First Partition of that country, by Austria, Prussia and Russia.[132] Frederick II gained Polish Prussia, thereby finally linking Hohenzollern Prussia to Brandenburg, while Austria seized Galicia. Poland's fate exposed the risks for the Empire if Austria and Prussia continued their collaboration. Henceforth, the third Germany of smaller territories was stalked by the spectre of a 'Polish future'.

Both great powers needed time to digest their Polish gains, while Maximilian III Joseph's sudden death in December 1777 opened the Bavarian succession issue before Joseph II had clinched a deal with the Palatine Wittelsbachs. Emperor Joseph overplayed his hand, bullying Elector Carl Theodor into accepting poor terms without securing prior support from his French allies, who preferred to fight Britain in the American War of Independence. Frederick rejected Austrian proposals in April 1778, instead forgoing the Ansbach-Bayreuth inheritance since this would not balance Joseph's potential gains in Bavaria. Prussia rallied Saxony to fight under the banner of defending the Empire's constitutional order in the brief War of the Bavarian Succession (1778–9). Both Prussia and Austria made great efforts to secure wider support in the Empire, without success. The war exposed serious deficiencies in both the Austrian and Prussian armies, but Frederick managed to do sufficient damage to oblige Joseph to abandon his exchange plans beyond annexing a small slice of eastern Bavaria.[133]

Joseph then outflanked Frederick by forging an alliance with Russia, which abandoned cooperation with Prussia in return for a freer hand in dealing with the Ottomans in south-east Europe. Isolated without an international ally, Frederick returned to leading an obstructive opposition in imperial institutions. He was greatly assisted by Joseph's many mistakes, including continuing Austria's insistence that princes follow the old enfeoffment ceremonial. Joseph quietly dropped this in 1788, allowing princes to seek confirmation by letter like the electors. Joseph caused another minor scandal by issuing 140 so-called *Panisbriefe* during 1781–3, entitling Habsburg officials to free accommodation in the remaining imperial monasteries. This allowed Frederick to attack him for misusing imperial prerogatives, especially as these 'meal tickets' were issued unsystematically, while it was far from clear whether they could still be applied to religious houses that no longer had full immediacy or had become Protestant institutions. Meanwhile, Joseph alienated many ecclesiastical princes by curtailing their spiritual jurisdiction over Habsburg lands, and by aggressively promoting his siblings within the imperial church.[134]

Frederick corralled several medium-sized and minor territories into the League of Princes (*Fürstenbund*) on 23 July 1785, which eventually grew to 18 members.[135] This was certainly not part of any Prussian mission to unify Germany, but was simply a tactical device to hinder Habsburg management of the Empire. His nephew and successor, Frederick William II, abandoned the League once Prussia escaped international isolation through an alliance with Britain in 1788. Within a year, France had descended into revolution, while one year later Joseph was dead and had been succeeded by his younger brother, Leopold II. The Empire's last 16 years would be dominated by the difficulties of attempting reform amidst an existential war. Before we can assess how far it stood any chance of success, we need to turn to the broader question of how its constitutional order was anchored in its social structures.

PART IV

Society

10

Authority

LORDSHIP

The Empire and Social History

Holy Roman emperors have often proved strange figures in European history. They do not seem to 'belong' anywhere. They are constantly moving about, appearing here and there, only to disappear again, often for decades at a time. It is thus scarcely surprising that the relationship between the Empire's governance and the lives of its inhabitants has remained the largest gap in its history. This relationship has often been overlooked, because it was widely assumed throughout the nineteenth and much of the twentieth century that the Empire was irrelevant to its inhabitants' daily existence.[1] The Empire's transnational character has not helped, since much social history takes the nation state as its framework, with, for example, medieval and early modern 'German' population calculated according to 1930s frontiers and omitting political units like Burgundy that subsequently disappeared. Local and regional history also often focuses on later boundaries as if earlier political structures had little or no impact, while the recent fashion for micro-studies has added to the difficulties of drawing general conclusions over time and space. A full social history is beyond the scope of this book. The following will not claim that the Empire was some kind of cradle of European civilization deriving from a Frankish legacy. Difference and divergence are major themes, because the Empire never constituted a single, homogeneous society, nor did it have a unified economy. Instead, the next three chapters will argue that the Empire's political institutions and practices were rooted in society and shared its strengths and weaknesses.

Political structures both expressed and conserved a society that became stratified hierarchically and structured horizontally along corporate lines. The Empire held and retained meaning as the framework protecting political and social diversity. Spatial and chronological variations in the political order reflected social and economic differences. One example is the higher concentration of lords in south-west Germany and old Carolingian heartlands along the Rhine. Another example is illustrated in the differences between east and west, which owe much to the timing of migration and settlement beyond the Elbe, and the relative weakness of the intermediary level of princely authority at the point of demographic and economic change in the fifteenth century. Variations in the emergence of towns also relate to regional differences in political authority, as well as the readiness of emperors and lords to grant privileges. The timing of political changes was often influenced by socio-economic factors, such as the demographic growth and economic innovation facilitating the shift from extensive to intensive lordship around 1200.

The Empire and Society

Throughout, the social role of political authority was to legitimate and regulate access to and control of resources as well as the interaction between individuals and groups. As we shall see, how this was done changed considerably during the Empire's existence. The key difference between the Empire and European countries was that the former emerged as multicentred, not just politically, but also socially, economically and culturally. This left a lasting legacy, especially in the German lands, where these developments reached their fullest extent with imperial reform and its consequences at the local and territorial level. The result was the idea that a proper social order was composed of distinct groups and communities, each with local and specific rights. The role of authorities was to protect and nurture this society and to resolve its difficulties.

The most potent form of authority in the Empire was lordship (*Herrschaft*). Like 'feudalism' (see pp. 328–31), 'lordship' is a highly contentious term with almost as many definitions as there are historians.[2] The debate reflects the real problems of the sources, which reveal that medieval and early modern Europeans used a variety of words for what historians call 'lordship', and did so in multiple ways. The term remains useful, provided it is understood as a set of powers that could be concentrated in the hands of a single lord, but equally might become distributed between several lords, or exercised by corporate institutions or groups like city councils, religious houses and even peasant communes.[3] The following offers a brief chronological survey of the main socio-economic developments throughout the Empire into the eighteenth century, while the remainder of the chapter examines the tensions between the hierarchical and associational aspects of the Empire's socio-political order.

Carolingian and Ottonian Society

We have already seen (pp. 179–99) how the Empire encompassed more Romanized areas to the south and west, as well as large regions that had escaped incorporation within the ancient Roman empire. Information on the latter regions is sparse, but it seems unlikely that what became the German kingdom was inhabited by a free warrior people holding the land in common.[4] The majority of people during late antiquity lived in hamlets, with the few towns and larger villages restricted to the more Romanized areas like Italy. Isolated farms existed, but they belonged to the elite rather than crofters. The population relied on stock-rearing. Fields were tilled individually, because land was plentiful, while the small, dispersed population rendered common ownership unnecessary. The few large estates worked by dependent labour were mainly in Italy. Markets were underdeveloped compared to later eras, with most activities concentrating on subsistence rather than exchange. Social difference was expressed legally in terms of free or unfree populations, rather than primarily economically.

Europe's population grew by a third in the fifty years before 700 to reach 24 million, providing a powerful factor promoting the rise of the Franks, who developed a system known as 'villication', establishing the manorial economy to harness the greater labour power. This coincided with the development of more coherent, centralized political structures, since these could draw on the surplus production to sustain larger numbers of warriors and clergy freed from the necessity to feed themselves. In turn, these structures provided the legal framework to command and coordinate dependent labour, since market forces alone were too weak to achieve this.[5] Villication involved a shift to a three-field system. Instead of rotating fields annually between grass and grain, the Franks introduced a three-year cycle of winter planting, summer planting and laying fallow. This enabled the still-small population to exploit the land more intensively, because they could work on different fields throughout the year. The manor developed to coordinate the workforce. Manors could be crown possessions (*villae*) entrusted to stewards (*villici* or *maiores*), or could be granted as a benefice to a lay or spiritual lord, or they might be developed by lords on their own property.[6]

Each manor was centred on the lord's house, including barns and assets like mills, or specialist workshops on large manors like that at Staffelsee abbey employing 24 female textile workers in the early ninth century. The lord or his steward lived in the house together with servile domestics (*servi dominici*, or *Gesinde*), who were maintained at the lord's expense from produce from the manor and were employed to maintain it and work the 'domains', or land reserved for the lord. A typical Carolingian manor might also have 50 tenants or 'live-out servants' (*servi casati*) with farmsteads known as 'hides' (*mansi*, or *Hufe*), each with 30 'rods' or 'yokes' (*Morgen*) of land.[7] The exact size of hides varied with soil quality, but each one generally encompassed 24 to 26 hectares. The tenants used this land to support themselves and their families, whilst also working three days a week to assist the domestics farming the domains (see Plate 27). Common land (*Allmende*) formed the third part of the system, consisting of meadows, ponds and woods used by all the manor's inhabitants. The manorial system thus rested on the medieval concept of lordship and usage: the lord retained jurisdiction over all land associated with the manor, but only worked the domains directly, allowing tenants and others varying access to the remainder.

This system spread through Carolingian conquest into Germany and, to a lesser extent, parts of Italy. Developments were interrupted by Viking, Slav and Magyar incursions, but resumed during the late tenth century and consolidated across the next, when they also spread eastwards amongst the Slavs and Magyars through interaction with Ottonian society. Even in the tenth and eleventh centuries, the bulk of production was consumed locally, with trade limited primarily to imports. Political needs remained broadly constant, as the Ottonians continued to require a socio-economic order able to supply sufficient mounted warriors for them to fight their enemies and campaign in Italy.

The manorial system eroded sharp distinctions between free and unfree, creating a more complex social structure. The peasantry emerged as a hybrid group with rights associated with hides, but still dependent on a lord. Given the small population, lords were keen to retain workers and granted hereditary tenure to their peasants, but they also imposed restrictions on the sale or partition of hides to maintain them as viable subunits of the manor. Domains remained important, for example producing four times the income derived from tenures at Cluny abbey in the mid-twelfth century.[8] Live-in domestics remained slaves into the eleventh century, their numbers sustained partly by slave-raiding until the late tenth century, together with requisitioning children from tenants whose own family growth remained constrained by the number of hides available. The earlier free peasantry survived better in Saxony (especially Westphalia) into the Ottonian era, but declined elsewhere in Germany with the spread of dependency, and by 1100 perhaps only 10 per cent of the population remained legally free.[9] The military obligations established by the Carolingians might take free men away from their farms for months. Accepting dependency offered a way to escape this. The church was especially keen to attract labour for its large construction projects, as well as to work its lands, and frequently extended protection in return for service and a share in produce.

A functional division gradually emerged to structure society into Estates, or corporate social groups. The clergy and nobility were exempt from manual labour, performing spiritual and military tasks instead. The commons, or third Estate, comprised the bulk of the population providing society's material needs. Society stratified along lines of protection and service, with a clearly lordly elite sustained by peasant production. Lordship continued to develop as the legal framework to regulate this relationship through structures like manors, law courts, dioceses and parishes.

Salian and Staufer Society

The mid-eleventh century marks a significant watershed, ending the expansion and consolidation of Frankish-Ottonian socio-economic forms, and the emergence of more diversified patterns. One reason was the success of the manorial economy in raising productivity. Hunger crises persisted into the eleventh century, but not on the scale of those in the ninth century, or again during the twelfth. Bread had become the staple food, as evidenced by the rapid spread of water mills during the eleventh century after their slow development since the Carolingian era. The more intensive field use allowed for the cultivation of more diverse crops, including vegetables that improved diet. Already the invention of the deep-bladed plough had allowed the Franks to work the heavier northern European soil. New forms of harnessing draught animals, together with the invention of the horseshoe, improved ploughing in the eleventh century, while iron axes and scythes now replaced wooden implements.[10]

Change not only came 'from below', but was also stimulated by lordly pressures, such as the building of stone castles and cathedrals like that at Paderborn under Bishop Meinward. The bishop had peasants beaten for laziness, and once had one woman dragged on her bottom across her garden until it was clear of weeds.[11] Most lords, including counts, found the rising costs of military service could not be met from existing means, and not only pushed their peasants to be more product-ive but also sought privileges like market and mint rights to help develop their lands and to gain access to cash as well as produce and labour.

Europe's population rose from 38.5 million in 1000 to 73.5 million in 1340, experiencing the fastest growth in France, England and Germany. The population of the German kingdom tripled between 1000 and 1237, rising even faster in some areas like eastern Saxony, which saw tenfold growth.[12] The German population grew from 8 mil-lion in the twelfth century to peak at 14 million around 1300, while the number of Italians rose from around 5 million in 950 to between 7 and 8 million by 1300, at which point Hungary and the Slav areas to the east had perhaps 9.5 to 13 million inhabitants. For the most part, popu-lation growth encouraged a virtuous circle, providing more labour to boost production further. Forests were cleared in the Vosges, south-west Germany, the Palatinate, Franconia, Thuringia, Bohemia and other upland areas during the eleventh century. Improved drainage and dyke construction reclaimed land along the Elbe and North Sea coasts around the early twelfth century, thanks largely to the influx of migrants to these regions.[13]

Despite this, population growth increased pressure on land and so fuelled urban growth, initially in Italy where the former Roman settlements had revived already in the tenth century, and it encouraged the foundation of new towns north of the Alps after 1100 (see pp. 504–8). Towns stimulated more specialized production and market networks, including expanding long-distance trade. More stable relations between the Empire and Denmark and other Baltic powers encouraged such trade and contributed to a north–south division in Germany. The north was integrated within Baltic and North Sea networks through new towns founded on the coasts and along major rivers, while the south remained linked through more established towns to Mediterranean trade. Expanding markets meanwhile yoked north Italian towns closer to their immediate hinterlands, contributing substantially to their growing political supremacy over rural lords. In turn, towns acted as catalysts for their surrounding area, which developed market gardening and viticulture to serve the urban population, many of whom were not primarily engaged in food production. Growing commercialization increased the demand for secular, vernacular literacy, as well as sharper divisions of labour and a shift from subsistence to profit.[14]

Producing for the market required new divisions of labour and more sophisticated land management than could be provided through the manorial economy. Migration to towns and further east across the Elbe caused temporary labour shortages. This added pressure on lords to offer their peasants better terms so as to encourage them to remain on their land. The process began first in Italy where the manorial economy was never as widespread as north of the Alps, and where greater urbanization and better roads had facilitated commercialization already in the tenth century. The trend spread north during the eleventh century, accelerating after 1100 and peaking around 1300.[15] Lords moved from taking income in the form of peasants' labour to extracting it as shares of their produce through varieties of sharecropping. Italian lords soon revised this to extracting cash rents, because their tenants had greater access to urban markets to sell their produce. This became widespread during the twelfth century, transforming hides into leaseholds. Meanwhile, most of the lordly domains were broken up to create additional tenancies. Short-term leases developed in Italy from the twelfth century, often only lasting until the next harvest. Major operators like

Cistercian monasteries, which had worked their land directly with dependent labour, also converted to leaseholds by the fourteenth century. Meanwhile, many peasants sublet parts of their plots to cottagers.[16]

Combined, these developments propelled further social stratification. The need for slaves evaporated with the dwindling domains, consolidating peasants as a social group commanding their own labour. However, new distinctions emerged between the rural and urban population, as well as within both. Other variations emerged through different inheritance patterns, themselves anchored in agreements with lords. Partible inheritance remained the dominant form in the German south-west, Rhineland and parts of Franconia, but primogeniture spread elsewhere, protecting peasants from the impoverishment that often followed multiple partitions, but also distinguishing them from new groups of land-poor or landless inhabitants. More fortunate peasants used their relative wealth to buy further exemptions, for example by paying lords with candle wax rather than their labour. Lords frequently encouraged the commutation of labour services into cash dues and rents. Meanwhile, peasants acquired an incentive to develop their plots, because they were free to keep any surpluses once they had paid their fixed obligations to their lord.

Rents allowed more flexible forms of lordship. The lord's presence was no longer required to coordinate manorial labour, enabling him not merely to be absent, but to draw income from scattered possessions not grouped into manors. Manors became centres of lordly jurisdiction rather than economic production. Jurisdictions themselves fragmented after 1300 with the general commercialization of fiefs, since individual elements could be sold or transferred. One important element was mastery of serfs (*Leibherrschaft*), which declined with the contraction of directly worked estates, but persisted in some areas as the power to command labour. Even tenants and leaseholders usually remained subject to some kind of residual obligation, such as maintaining walls and roads, or providing a few days' portage each year. Other feudal elements also persisted, such as lordly restrictions on individual choice, for example marriage or freedom of movement.

A second important element of lordship comprised seigniorial authority deriving from the *dominium directum*, or underlying ownership of land used by tenants and leaseholders. This ensured that lord–peasant relations were never entirely dictated by economic factors. Seigniorial authority provided the legal framework to negotiate the terms of the lease, determining how far peasants could control and use their plots, as well as their protection from eviction. These powers were increasingly articulated from the thirteenth century as 'landlordship' (*dominus fundi, Grundherrschaft*).[17] This aspect was far more significant north of the Alps than in Italy, which largely bypassed this form through a shift directly to private written contracts with leaseholders. These contracts remained asymmetrical, especially as cities acquired jurisdiction over their rural hinterlands and imposed restrictions on the rights of leaseholders to renounce their contracts. Political interests drove these changes, because magistrates recognized that their own power depended on their ability to ensure that sufficient food reached their city's market.

Judicial authority (*Gerichtsherrschaft*) constituted the third major form of lordly power. Population growth and economic commercialization brought overall benefits, but often at considerable individual cost, straining customary legal arrangements.[18] The longer feudal hierarchy and the shift to patrilinear families and more territorially based power all added to the need to demarcate jurisdictions more clearly. Jurisdiction stratified up and down the lordly hierarchy into higher and lesser authority, with important cases reserved for the former (see pp. 622–3). Jurisdiction also allowed lords to maintain military authority over a population that was often no longer economically dependent upon them directly, for example enabling senior lords to summon their vassal tenants to help fulfil their own obligations, including those to the emperor.

The Fourteenth-Century Crisis

The trends of the Salian and Staufer eras continued into the early fourteenth century, further underscoring the point made earlier (pp. 66–7 and 377–9) that the Staufers' demise was personal rather than structural. Nonetheless, high politics continued to make a social impact. The rivals for the German crown after 1250 granted immunities and privileges to lords and towns to win their support, while relative royal weakness provided more scope for local initiatives in revising existing legal and social arrangements. Meanwhile, economic growth slowed during the late thirteenth century as rising lordly demands on peasants combined with the still-growing population to encourage renewed subdivision of tenancies in many areas. Between half and three-quarters of peasant farms in northern Burgundy and south-west Germany were reduced to only 3–5 hectares.[19]

Unfortunately, adverse climatic conditions set in with colder, wetter weather around 1300, damaging harvests and causing famine in parts of Germany between 1309 and 1311, with further problems thereafter.[20] All normal activities and concerns were suspended as the malnourished population fell victim to the Black Death, which killed around 60 per cent of inhabitants from 1348 to 1350. This was not a solitary cataclysm. The plague returned with virtually every subsequent generation into the fifteenth century, with some outbreaks actually even worse, such as that in Bohemia in 1379–80. This slowed the recovery, so that the total population around 1470 was still a quarter below that in 1347. The mortality crisis triggered the fourteenth-century recession, characterized by the rapid contraction in settled areas, with, for example, 1,000 square kilometres lost to the North Sea where flood defences were no longer maintained. Less fertile or accessible areas were either abandoned or given over to meadows, pasturage, or the steady spread of reforestation. Those areas with better soil were now worked even more intensively, since this offered the best returns on the available labour.

The result was accelerated market specialization and exchange, since localities were less able to provide all their needs directly. A more diversified economic landscape emerged. Mixed husbandry and arable farming predominated, because animal manure increased and prolonged soil fertility. Such areas often clustered around towns, which provided markets for meat. Meanwhile, population decline reduced the demand for grain and left more for animal feed. Viticulture expanded along the Moselle, Rhine, Main, Saale, Unstrut, Rhône and Po rivers, and in other parts of Italy. The population recovery accelerated this by providing the labour required by viticulture. Some areas developed crops for manufacturing, notably wool in Saxony and flax in Swabia. Rural industry also grew where there were good mineral deposits, notably salt mining in Austria, Bavaria and parts of the Alps, as well as silver and other ore extraction in the Tirol, Harz and parts of Saxony. Bohemian glass manufacture also acquired an international reputation in this period.[21]

The relative rapidity of these changes proved deeply disturbing, though their exact connection with heightened violence in the fourteenth and fifteenth centuries remains controversial.[22] Lordship was certainly hard hit as land values crashed, for instance falling in the county of Namur by between a quarter and a half. Population decline increased labour's scarcity and bargaining power. Tenants negotiated lower rents and dues, while those in Bavaria and Franconia secured hereditary tenure. The trend towards a landless proletariat was now reversed as former day labourers gained access to tenancies. The few lords still farming with dependent serfs now stopped this practice, while wages became more widely available to attract and retain workers. Weaker lords generally fared worst, like the knights and mediate vassals with small fiefs, who often sought alternative employment as princely retainers and administrators, thereby consolidating both the longer lordly hierarchy and the territorialization of princely power. Where possible, lords used existing elements of servitude to invent new taxes, such as emigration fees, marriage licences and death duties, though their overall burden eased with the economic recovery after 1470.[23]

Thanks to accumulated capital, towns and individual burghers were often well placed to profit in these conditions, buying land or investing in viticulture around their town. Urban artisans also benefited from higher wages. Towns and burghers bought or mortgaged lordly rights, accelerating the fragmentation of lordship into different kinds of jurisdiction that could be shared or held by multiple owners. Overall, this process prevented the development of a uniform society of subjects sharing a common relationship to authority in the Empire.

Growth and Diversity in Early Modernity

The initial recovery paradoxically produced the 'late medieval agrarian depression' around 1350 until 1470.[24] Land was slowly reoccupied after 1370 and production increased, especially as harvest yields also improved. Despite periodic famine years like 1437–8, grain prices fell to a long-term low in the mid-fifteenth century. Social and geographic mobility resumed in the mid-fourteenth century, but slowed again around 1400 until the rapid and sustained demographic recovery between 1470 and 1530. By 1560 the population in most areas matched early fourteenth-century levels, and in some places continued to rise until a renewed slowdown around 1580 with the onset of the renewed colder, wetter weather of the 'Little Ice Age'. The Thirty Years War (1618–48) reduced the Empire's population by a fifth, primarily by magnifying the impact of renewed plague.[25] The rate of recovery was slowed by renewed warfare after 1672 but restored to 1618 levels around 1710, while renewed and sustained growth set in around 1730. Middling principalities like Brunswick and Württemberg now saw annual growth rates of 6 to 7 per cent, rising to 10 per cent in Brandenburg. Bavaria was the only major territory to experience marginal population decline across the eighteenth century. The total for the Empire (including Burgundy, but excluding imperial Italy) rose from around 20 million in 1700 to over 29 million in 1800, with perhaps another 5 million in imperial Italy. Population density was far higher than in Habsburg and Hohenzollern territory outside the Empire, which together held another 12.6 million people in 1800.[26]

Food prices rose 250 per cent across 1500–1800, whereas real wages fell by up to a half. The discrepancy worsened in the second half of the eighteenth century when rising population caused food prices to rise up to six times faster than wages. Crop failures precipitated serious subsistence crises during 1755–62, 1770–74 and 1787–9. Systemic underemployment set in by the later eighteenth century, with a quarter of the population living precariously and 5 to 10 per cent displaced to a life on the roads.[27]

The extent to which development diverged along the river Elbe remains one of the most controversial aspects of European history, since it lent itself to ideological distinctions between western democracy and eastern autocracy.[28] It is clear that different trends set in during the fifteenth century, producing what has been labelled a 'second serfdom' east of the Elbe. This entailed the re-emergence of bonded, dependent labour working large manorial estates. Its roots lay in the impact of the fourteenth-century crisis, which proved far more serious in the east, because peasants had fewer opportunities to profit from their temporarily increased labour value. There were fewer towns and market networks were less well developed compared to those in the west. As grain prices continued to fall, only large-scale production remained profitable, especially where it had access along rivers to ports able to ship bulk cargoes to feed the more urbanized markets of north-western Europe. Lesser lords in the east were also better placed relative to princes than their western counterparts, given the less dense and flatter lordly hierarchy. Princes east of the Elbe relied on knights and mediate vassals to govern the more dispersed rural population and had granted more land as mediate fiefs. Compared to that in the west, the imperial church was a smaller and more recent creation east of the Elbe and less able to provide alternative employment to lesser lords, or to act as a possible support for princes. Altogether, the eastern regions remained distant from the king, who played a less significant role in promoting local developments through charters and immunities.

Consequently, knights in the east of the Empire had greater opportunities to acquire concentrated and extensive jurisdictions. In particular, they were often able to use the institutions of the nascent territorial administrations to their advantage, for example through imposing wage limits and tighter supervision of the rural population.[29] Mastery of serfs was revived to secure labour for a new form of manorial economy (*Gutswirtschaft*) based on a large, landed estate (*Gut*) operating a monoculture of grain production for export. This developed in Schleswig, Holstein, Mecklenburg, Pomerania, Brandenburg, Bohemia, and to a lesser extent in parts of Austria, as well as outside the Empire in Poland and Hungary. In fact, relatively few eastern lords truly fit the model of the *Junker* 'agrarian capitalist', while perhaps only 10 per cent of grain production was exported through long-distance Baltic trade. Other forms of production and land use continued. Nonetheless, the development of the new manorial economy helped to distinguish regions east of the Elbe as one of several major socio-economic areas in the early modern Empire.

Likewise, political as well as economic factors provided particular characteristics in the western Empire. As we shall see (pp. 534–8), territorial authorities expanded their regulation of daily life in the interest of moral, religious and fiscal agendas. Farms became fiscal as well as economic units, with mid-fifteenth century Bavarian edicts already distinguishing core plots that could not be partitioned at inheritance.[30] Leases generally became hereditary, while labour service continued to decline relative to cash rents and increasingly also taxes. Sharecropping persisted in Italy, though better conditions emerged in the Po valley. In contrast to France and elsewhere, German lords west of the Elbe retained very little land under their direct control, allowing peasants access to the bulk of the cultivated area. Princely domains already only accounted for 15 per cent of cultivated land in Austria and Lower Bavaria in the later Middle Ages. The proportion in Bavaria shrank to 13.2 per cent by the late eighteenth century, while nobles owned 34 per cent, clergy 56 per cent, urban corporations 0.4 per cent and freeholding peasants only 4 per cent. However, these rates refer to underlying *dominium directum*, not rights of usage that allowed Bavarian peasants access to over 90 per cent of land through leases. Even east of the Elbe the situation was not wholly unfavourable. The Prussian king held only 4.5 per cent of the agricultural land, with nobles owning and directly managing 11 per cent, and cities and foundations a further 4.5 per cent. Peasants had access to the remaining 80 per cent as plots tied to manors or through leases. Control remained political, rather than immediately economic. The Bavarian elector was direct lord of only 10.6 per cent of peasants, but held lesser as well as superior legal jurisdiction over a further 55.9 per cent, while the clergy and nobility were lords of the rest.[31]

DEFINING THE COMMON GOOD

Fellowship and Lordship

The social changes around 1100 contributed to the slow emergence of horizontal associational fellowship (*Genossenschaft*) alongside vertical lordship. These two forms of social organization need to be treated carefully as it is easy to assign them clear ideological distinctions. Much of German history has been seen as a struggle between the two before (depending on the viewpoint) either their synthesis in modern society or the triumph of authoritarianism.[32] The Empire often takes the blame for the outcome, as apparently weak central power supposedly allowed the population to be oppressed by a multitude of petty princes (*Duodezfürsten*), who were already satirized in the eighteenth century: Friedrich Schiller's play *Kabale und Liebe* depicts a prince selling his subjects as mercenaries to fund a luxurious lifestyle. The standard contrast with powerful monarchs like Louis XIV or Prussia's Frederick II 'the Great' makes these princes appear even more ridiculous. The polemical potential was not lost on nineteenth-century German liberals, who regarded the principalities surviving beyond 1806 as the primary obstacles to national unification.

We need to remove the moral signs, and not simplify the situation as a clash between progressive, proto-democratic fellowship and reactionary lordship. Associational and communal forms were not exclusive to peasants and burghers, but were important to clergy and nobles, as we shall see (pp. 553–62), while communes could also be lords (pp. 516–18 and 579–91). Lordship and fellowship did not merely co-exist but were closely interdependent. Above all, the ideology of the common good, like government techniques, was not simply pioneered by citizens only to be stolen later by princes. Instead, hierarchical and horizontal forms worked in 'creative tension',[33] producing new ideas and practices.

Communities contained associational and hierarchical elements, and not all inhabitants regarded lords as outsiders. Most recognized that communities require leaders. These were not temporary 'faces in the crowd', striding forward at the right moment, but were generally established figures with the social and political capital necessary for leadership.[34] Arguments rarely divided people purely according to wealth, and instead provided an extensive political vocabulary employed across the social spectrum. What united rulers and ruled was their engagement in the same debate over the ideal community.

Core values like peace, justice and harmony were related to morality and Christianity, and were thus considered timeless and 'authentic'.[35] Although all three were contested in practice, a fourth, *Notdurft*, proved the most controversial. Its ambiguities are revealed by its two possible translations of 'sustenance' and 'necessity'. The former implied entitlement to the material means of existence, potentially including social levelling to ensure at least minimum shares for all. This could operate as a kind of 'moral economy' criticizing exploitation, hoarding and price rigging, thereby providing a basis to reject 'excessive' lordly demands. However, it also suggested a moral obligation to ensure sustenance, adding force to the idea of necessity overriding established arrangements in the name of the greater good.

The distinction between 'common good' (*salus publica*, or *Gemeinnutz*) and 'self-interest' (*Eigennutz*) was already well established during the early Middle Ages, and it sharpened with the wider appreciation of the contribution of the third Estate to general well-being. The term 'common man' emerged by 1280 as a largely positive appellation, while ordinary folk were celebrated in illuminated manuscript books and cathedral carvings and windows, all depicting the Christian ideal of serving the community. The basic antithesis between common and private good persisted into the late eighteenth century and in many ways beyond, despite subtle changes in how it was expressed. The development of Natural Law from the seventeenth century argued that authority rested on a social contract in which the population surrendered some of their 'natural' freedoms in return for the benefits of living in an orderly society.[36]

Questions of Authority

The crucial question remained who was entitled to define the common good and thus to set the normative measures intended to foster and preserve it? Additionally, what limits could be imposed on that authority and what recourse did the subordinate population have against its abuse? Medieval writers remained fixed on the person of the king, rather than princes or lesser lords, but the articulation of good kingship was easily transferable to other authorities, especially as these acquired clearer public functions during the period of imperial reform. Numerous texts identified the prince as responsible for the *bonum commune*. These retained the earlier moral emphasis, but now devoted more space to judging policies rather than personal characteristics. They contributed to the growing articulation around 1500 of the imperial Estates as authorities (*Obrigkeiten*) governing subjects (*Untertanen*).[37] Attempts during the Reformation to re-theologize the language of the common good failed, especially as the political outcome expanded the powers of imperial Estates to supervise church and religious life.

The Peace of Westphalia and subsequent political discussion defined the imperial Estates more clearly as possessing 'territorial sovereignty' (*Landeshoheit*), which became the collective term for the bundle of accumulated rights sanctioned by imperial law.[38] Clearer ideas of authority gained ground with the fiscal and military needs of the later seventeenth and eighteenth centuries, which encouraged further intervention in daily life to promote thrift, obedience and productivity. It was accompanied by a change in style, most noticeable among the princes, but also apparent in the imperial cities, where the magistrates became more patrician and aristocratic. Already around the mid-sixteenth century, princes remodelled their castles or built new residences to present carefully crafted images of power. Whereas the castles of medieval lords might suggest they feared attack from their subjects, the unfortified baroque palace exuded confident authority. Language changed too, as the word 'common' became more ambiguous. 'Common man' lost its positive associations in the wake of the violence of the Peasants War (1524–6) and became the antithesis of 'noble' (*Edel*), while 'common woman' denoted a prostitute.[39] The language of consensus persisted into the sixteenth century, with rulers being 'gracious' (*gnädig*) in negotiating with their 'loyal subjects' (*getreue Untertanen*). However, these terms were increasingly displaced in the ruler's discourse by words emphasizing his power to command: *Befehl, Gehorsam, Respekt, Hoheit, Autorität*. Princes simultaneously stressed their personal 'honour' and 'reputation', which were now measured by the prince's place in the imperial hierarchy and his international standing.[40]

The experience of the Thirty Years War allowed princes to employ the argument of necessity to justify emergency measures. The official commemoration of the war through annual religious services and processions gave thanks for deliverance from horror, but simultaneously blamed the calamity on the sins of the pre-war population, who had allegedly incurred God's wrath. Religious services and government mandates repeatedly admonished subjects to be pious, dutiful, thrifty and obedient, all as means to ensure the horrors of war would not return.[41] The cumulative result was a more absolutist style and conception of rule, elevating the prince above his subjects. Only he, it was claimed, could see beyond individual selfish interests to govern in the common good. Thanks to its roots in the public functions defining the status of imperial Estate, absolutism developed at this level, including for Austria and Prussia, rather than for the Empire overall in the person of the emperor. 'Imperial absolutism' remained only a spectre conjured through the rhetoric of 'German liberties' to oppose tighter Habsburg management of the Empire.[42] Absolutism was distinguished from arbitrary rule by the restriction of absolute authority to within certain limits. All discussions of princely power acknowledged imperial law and the Empire as part of these limits (see pp. 538–46).

The spread of Enlightened ideas provided new arguments to support official direction of public life, especially through the utilitarian critique of received traditions, adding weight to the language of necessity to disregard existing arrangements if deemed obsolete. Historians dispute how far such ideas actually changed princely rule.[43] Style certainly changed, as rulers consciously distanced themselves from the Renaissance and baroque celebration of the prince as a semi-divine, heroic ruler, in favour of appearing more modestly as the state's 'first servant', signally by the fashion for wearing simple military uniform rather than the pearl-buttoned silk coats and giant wigs of the recent past. In some respects rule became even more personal than before. Despite presenting himself as Prussia's first *servant*, Frederick the Great tried to *master* all business himself, conducting government from his 'cabinet' or writing desk, rather than like other princes through formal meetings with councillors. Overall, however, government became more impersonal. Emperor Joseph II, himself a near parody of the pre-Revolutionary cult of the 'first servant', established in his law code of 1787 that crimes were now understood to be 'against the state', allowing the authorities to prosecute even if no plaintiff came forward.

Individual Interest

This opened possibilities for a new relationship between rulers and ruled, whereby an impersonal state related equally to individual inhabitants regardless of rank. Changes in theology, science and art had articulated new ideas of the individual since the later thirteenth century. Moral hostility to 'singularity' persisted and was reinforced by the Reformation, which emphasized confessional conformity, including lifestyle as well as belief. Nonetheless, well before anglophone writers like Bernard Mandeville or Adam Smith, Germans expressed positive interpretations of self-interest. Leonhart Fronsperger, a military clerk and noted writer, argued in 1564 that divergent individual needs actually created harmony by encouraging mutual interdependence.[44] The development of imperial taxation meanwhile encouraged the relaxation of earlier restrictions on private wealth creation, since this could help meet obligations to the Empire.

However, German discussions took a different path from those among English-speaking philosophers like John Locke who developed the idea of rights relating directly to individuals, rather than deriving indirectly through association with a household, community or other corporate group. Adam Smith subsequently extended this into liberal economic theory by arguing that individual wealth creation would add to overall prosperity, rather than simply representing the theft of someone else's share of supposedly finite wealth. The market, not the state, should regulate society. The state was reduced to being a 'night watchman' guaranteeing only minimal order and security. The position remained reversed in most discussions in the Empire, where territorial authority was itself a product of corporate rights and could not be so easily disentangled from the social order. The state, not the individual, retained the initiative. In practice, new ideas of individualism simply added to existing arguments for state intervention to micro-manage lives and make people happy, if necessary by force. Attempts by writers like Heinrich Justi to reduce the state's role, merely envisaged the ideal of a well-oiled machine entangling rather than liberating individuals.[45] The basic contradictions in these arguments carried over into nineteenth-century German liberalism: the state was to remove barriers to individual happiness by dismantling protectionism and facilitating a free market, yet to do so required ever greater powers to overcome the considerable popular opposition to such measures.

COMMUNITY

Villages

The continued identification of the individual with collective happiness owed much to the strength of communal social organization. This developed in Scandinavia, France and elsewhere, so the differences between these countries and the Empire are a matter of degrees rather than absolutes, but their specific expression in a corporate socio-political order was nonetheless significant.[46] Communal political forms emerged relatively early in the Empire as a defining element alongside lordship. They were weakest during the early Middle Ages, but grew stronger around the eleventh century, expanding rapidly during the fourteenth century to peak around 1500. If their subsequent development was checked by the expansion of princely governments, both urban and rural communes remained generally stronger than in other countries, and persisted well beyond 1806.

The vast majority of the Empire's inhabitants lived in scattered hamlets into the tenth century. The 200–300 people living on a typical Carolingian manor were described as a single *familia*, but their structure was not communal since important decisions were reserved for the lord or his steward, while a significant proportion lived segregated as slaves. The few, more genuine communities that existed were all religious houses like monasteries and convents, though again these usually also contained subordinate dependents. Several different kinds of settlement might be combined in one place, notably royal palaces that also functioned as farms and often had attached religious houses.[47]

True villages only emerged with the economic changes of the mid-eleventh century, coupled with the contraction of domains and the disappearance of the entirely servile population. They were given focus through the spread of church-building and incorporation of more rural areas into parishes. Parishes were not corporations, because they depended on the church hierarchy, but their development helped forge communal identity, especially as Gregorian reform stressed their role in selecting clergy. Even if clerical appointments remained largely in the control of lords and (later) patricians, other subsequent theological developments periodically reinforced parish identity, notably the spread of more formalized communal worship after 1215. Various forms of village developed, but nucleated settlements were fairly typical and consisted of houses grouped around a church, surrounded by gardens and often an outer perimeter demarcated by an earth wall or wooden palisade to protect against strangers and wild animals. Beyond this lay land organized in the three-field system, plus common assets like meadows and woods.[48]

Towns

Towns contracted in the Romanized areas during late antiquity as the dwindling population could no longer defend settlements that remained tempting targets for raiders. Many bishops abandoned their diocesan towns to escape the Vikings during the ninth century, further hastening urban decline. In Italy, this process accelerated the *incastellamento*, or construction of castles in more defensible sites, proliferating the fortified places that made it so difficult for later emperors to establish firm control there.[49] Nonetheless, all 107 Italian episcopal towns in the twelfth century could claim continuous occupation since ancient Rome, while the presence of a bishop also ensured continuity in Germany's oldest urban settlements: Mainz, Trier, Cologne, Worms, Speyer and Strasbourg. Kings and lords often appear in annals as 'founders' of medieval towns, though of course the real work was done by the inhabitants. Nonetheless, political factors need to be added to purely materialist and functionalist explanations for urban development: for example, Pavia, Ravenna and Rome all owed their importance in part to continuous favour by the Lombards, Byzantines and Carolingians respectively.

Thanks to their continuous existence, Italian towns already enjoyed considerable advantages over their equivalents north of the Alps, especially once their populations began to grow during the tenth century after four centuries of stagnation. These towns were both larger and had a higher proportion of legally free inhabitants, who were able to use their relative wealth to acquire rights and property in the surrounding countryside. Politics also favoured this process, because Carolingian rule had established fewer powerful lords, compared to Germany. This established a lasting distinction between the town and its surrounding area, now identified as the 'count's land' (*contado*). The extension of urban control over the hinterland was checked during the reign of Hugo of Arles, who won the support of the Italian episcopate by selling them many of the counts' rights over both town and countryside around 940. Although bishops generally held both jurisdictions for the next century, the upper strata of the urban population were emerging as their lesser vassals. Gregorian reform accelerated this trend by reinforcing this group's claims to participate in selecting bishops and generally to exercise greater influence over their own affairs.

Carolingian expansion saw the foundation of new towns north of the Alps around important monasteries to serve as bases for the expanding ecclesiastical structure. The new settlements formed around a cathedral, sometimes with other religious buildings sited to structure the town in the shape of a cross. Defensive palisades and ditches demarcated town from country by the tenth century. Ottonian patronage provided an additional spur with the grant of toll and market rights to many bishops, enabling episcopal towns to develop as regional economic centres. This trend peaked in the mid-eleventh century as the Salians granted exemptions from servitude to attract additional inhabitants. The Salians and especially their Staufer successors also increasingly favoured towns on their royal progresses rather than rural palaces or monasteries. Towns expanded to incorporate a market square with merchants' and artisans' houses within an expanded fortified ring. Speyer, for instance, already grew tenfold during the Ottonian era, while in total 130 new market towns developed along the Rhine and Danube across this period.[50]

Although generally newer than Italian towns, those north of the Alps were often more advanced economically at this point. Middle and Lower Rhenish towns engaged in long-distance trade, while those in Flanders and Brabant were already centres of cloth manufacturing from 1020. Most Italian towns remained only regional centres into the twelfth century, apart from Genoa and Venice, which grew rapidly through the trade opportunities opened by the Crusades after 1096. Meanwhile, a new type of urban foundation spread east from Lorraine in the twelfth century as secular lords now also established towns endowed with immunities directly from their foundation in a deliberate attempt to attract wealth and labour by offering an attractive new settlement. The Zähringer founded Freiburg (literally 'free town') in the Breisgau in 1120, while other early examples include Lübeck (1143), Munich (1158) and Leipzig (1161). Whereas there were only 200 German towns in 1025, there were over 600 by 1150, and 1,500 by 1250; of these, 150 were in royal lands, 38 controlled by bishops and the rest under lordly jurisdiction. By contrast, very few new towns were founded in Italy, with the most famous being Alessandria, established collectively by the Lombard League in 1168 and named after their ally Pope Alexander III. This is not surprising, since Italy already had around 300 large towns, whose population was expanding four times faster than anywhere else in Europe. By 1300, there were 20 cities in north and central Italy with at least 20,000 inhabitants, while Florence had 100,000 and Milan 175,000.[51]

By contrast, rural settlements expanded in numbers, but rarely significantly in size across 1000–1300. Colonization and migration transformed the east European countryside from scattered hamlets to villages during the twelfth century, when many Slavic villages were also reorganized through new legal codes. Migration drew off population from the west, where settlement size and numbers stabilized both overall and in the relation between the number of people and the area of land that could be worked without having to travel too far each day.

Less favourably sited settlements were now abandoned, though lords continued to offer inducements to attract migrants to more difficult areas like the Black Forest. The number of new towns peaked along with eastern colonization in the period 1220–1320, with the foundation of Berlin, Frankfurt an der Oder, Breslau, Gdansk and Königsberg. Many of the towns established at this point were not entirely new, like Stuttgart, which expanded from a village under the patronage of the Württemberg counts. New foundations continued across 1320–1450, but on a much reduced scale.

Early towns often encountered significant difficulties through being endowed with insufficient land or access to water. Later efforts granted more land to enable the first settlers to grow their own food. Twelfth-century foundations also addressed social questions through charters regulating relations to lords. Many of the new towns beyond the Elbe deliberately copied charters from so-called 'mother towns' to the west. Although new itself, Lübeck served as the exemplar for 100 other towns after the thirteenth century, while Magdeburg law was used from east central Europe to Russia, and Nuremberg and Vienna were copied across Bohemia, Moravia and the Balkans. Elsewhere, cities like Frankfurt served as models for smaller towns in their region.

Growth ended abruptly with the Black Death. The total number of German settlements fell by 40,000 to 130,000 across 1340–1470, with contraction reaching 40 per cent in upland areas like Hessen, Thuringia and the Austrian Alps, compared to 10 per cent in more favourable lowland regions, especially between the Lower Rhine and Weser and on the middle Elbe. Around 4,500 settlements were also abandoned in Bohemia and Moravia. Yet losses in Italy were only 10 to 25 per cent.[52] Towns suffered badly during the plague itself, but fared better overall in retaining their size. By 1450, the Empire had around 2,500 towns, including 88 Swiss and 150 Austrian ones, but excluding those in Italy. Whereas there was one town per 400 square kilometres in south-west Germany, the ratio in the north-east was one per 1,000 square kilometres. Most had fewer than 2,000 inhabitants, while only 5 per cent had over 5,000 and just 30 towns had more than 10,000. Cologne was the largest with 40,000 inhabitants. Pre-modern urban settlement was now essentially complete, with only 200 more towns added by 1800, largely as princely residences, garrisons or refugee settlements like

Mannheim, Potsdam and Erlangen. The urban proportion of the population also remained broadly constant, rising only from 20 to 25 per cent across 1300–1800, with the highest density in Holland and Brabant, where the proportion was already 40 to 50 per cent in 1514. Further development remained constrained by agricultural productivity: a medium-sized village produced only sufficient surplus to feed 25 town dwellers in the late sixteenth century, meaning that at least 10,000 villages were required to sustain the German urban population.[53] Despite differences between Germany, Italy and the Low Countries, urban development in the Empire broadly conformed to a western and central European pattern influenced by how politics and agriculture were organized. Growth during the high Middle Ages had created a multitude of individually modest towns, compared to the pattern in south-east Europe and the Islamic world, which was dominated by far fewer but individually larger cities: fourteenth-century Cairo already had 600,000 inhabitants, a figure not reached in Germany or Italy until well into the nineteenth century.

The Emergence of the Household

More obviously communal self-government only emerged from the eleventh century, beginning in Italian towns and becoming general by 1200. This complex process frequently pitted lords and commons against each other, and many of the concessions were only won through violent protest. However, civic emancipation was never a singular, glorious act, but instead developed incrementally, often over several centuries, with some rights acquiring new meaning with changed circumstances. Most privileges were intended to promote a town's development, not free its inhabitants, while lords often retained residual rights.[54] The new freedoms were never equal or universal *Liberty*, but instead local and particular *liberties* that bound the community and its inhabitants within the wider web of rights constituting the Empire's legal order. Communal government in rural areas involved the transfer of decision-making power from a lord or steward to villagers, especially through the demarcation of access rights to specific resources. The village assumed an identity as a collective actor, but not all its inhabitants could participate in decisions.

Communal government rested on households, which became the

fundamental socio-political unit in the Empire and the primary site for production, consumption and (for non-clerical houses) reproduction. Households originated in the Frankish development of the hide as a family package of rights and resources. Villages developed around these households by 1200, manifest by the spread of more solid house-building techniques employing a sturdy timber-frame or even stone construction. The house assumed a semi-sacred character with special rituals surrounding its construction and especially in setting the roof.[55] Door keys symbolized the power to control entry. Biblical examples encouraged a potent household ideology resting on the ideal of a married couple. This ideal underwent subtle shifts, especially in how gender roles were defined, as well as the rediscovery during the Renaissance of ancient ideas of good farm management (*oeconomia*), and later this received heightened religious-moral emphasis with the Reformation.[56]

Throughout, the household was celebrated as a place of safety and warmth, symbolized by its hearth, now solidified with stone or brick chimneys. The household was supposed to provide materially for all its members, hence the internal moral economy. However, it was also hierarchical under the patriarchal *pater familias* or *Hausvater*, responsible for economic coordination and maintenance of the 'peace of the house' (*Hausfrieden*). It is scarcely surprising that the household became a potent political metaphor and a key element in the debates over the common good from the high Middle Ages. Household members were expected to behave responsibly, so as not to damage their collective reputation and, with that, access to valuable resources. External peer pressure encouraged this, through criticism of drunken and other 'bad' householders as undermining overall communal well-being. Marriage remained restricted until at least one of the prospective partners could inherit or otherwise obtain the property necessary for a viable autonomous existence. The development of taxation increased the emphasis on maintaining individual household viability, since the most usual way to collect direct levies was to apportion quotas to towns and villages, which were expected to find the money themselves by requiring all householders to contribute. Moreover, as we have seen (pp. 245–8, 367–9 and 427–31), households featured at all levels of society from humble peasants to the Casa d'Austria. Although households were also sites for 'private' emotions, it was their public aspect that was idealized until the emergence in the 1770s in some places of the 'bourgeois family' as a private domestic sphere.[57]

Rural Self-Government

The development of communal government involved enfranchising male householders according to their property value in towns, or whether they leased or owned larger farms in villages. This established a link between taxation and representation, but at the communal level rather than higher up in any representative assembly. Those who were not economically independent were generally excluded from enfranchisement in the communal institutions: cottagers, landless labourers, unmarried younger men and generally the entire female population, though widows were allowed to represent households in some areas.

Rural self-government initially emerged around 1130 on the Empire's periphery in areas where there were both fewer lords and fewer people generally: along the Lower Austrian frontier and in the North Sea marshes and those of the Weser and Elbe.[58] These were all areas of recent settlement where pioneers were rewarded with corporate rights. Subsequent waves of migrants carried these arrangements across the Elbe, as well as into upland areas. The problems of starting a new life in often difficult circumstances undoubtedly contributed to a more collaborative approach, at least initially. Meanwhile, existing Alpine communities along transit routes bargained better terms by cooperating to keep passes free from obstacles by clearing rocks and maintaining bridges.

Many lords were happy to promote self-government, because this freed them from having to manage local affairs, which were now handled by village mayors assisted by selected householders. Criminal jurisdiction usually remained in the lord's hands, while the inhabitants generally still leased his land. Territorialization extended other forms of jurisdiction during the fourteenth century, including powers to levy taxes and later also militiamen and conscripts. Thus, the process through which communes acquired rights was part of the wider development of the Empire and territories, and not in opposition to this. The commune 'was at one and the same time a corporate association of agrarian producers and an instrument of feudal lordship to ensure the functioning of feudal exploitation and maintenance of feudal order'.[59]

These developments continued in the west into early modernity, and though interrupted by 'second serfdom' east of the Elbe, villages remained important in that region too. Hereditary mayors developed in Brandenburg villages by the fourteenth century under the margrave's jurisdiction. The margrave transferred his supervisory rights to his nobles around 1500 in return for tax grants collected by the communes at their inhabitants' expense. As the old mayoral families died out, lords replaced them with their own appointees. Saxony and other areas east of the Elbe saw similar developments. However, even mayors appointed by lords were still members of their village community. Lords relied on them and the family patriarchs to organize serf labour from the village's younger sons. Inhabitants retained rights of appeal to princely courts and successfully challenged excessive lordly demands, because princes wanted to protect households as their primary tax unit. Princely intervention rarely lightened the overall burden, but did generally shift it from lordly exactions to territorial taxes.

Brandenburg-Prussia went further by 1733 and established the state's right to conscript peasants as soldiers, only releasing them back as agricultural labourers on its own terms. The Hohenzollerns converted their own domains into hereditary leases in 1702, allowing their new tenants to elect village officials. Many Junkers subsequently commuted labour service into paid employment, recognizing this as more productive. Some Brandenburg communities benefited from rising grain prices, accumulating sufficient wealth to buy their own knight's fiefs by the late eighteenth century. The Prussian General Law Code of 1794 confirmed communal autonomy, integrating villages as the lowest echelon of state administration.[60]

The situation was different in Bohemia, where the areas under Czech law gave fewer rights to communal institutions like village headmen and courts. Although the actual implementation of Czech law converged with German practice during early modernity, this was not always for the better. In practice, Bohemian lords were able to remove troublesome headmen, despite their hereditary tenure of office, in those parts of Bohemia under German law, such as Friedland (Frydland). Headmen remained heavily dependent on lords for their economic livelihoods, since their incomes derived from lordly privileges like brewing rights, rather than wages. Nonetheless, communal institutions were just too useful for lords to ignore. As elsewhere, most lords were absentees and relied on the headmen chairing village courts to keep order and ensure the smooth running of the manorial economy. This necessitated a flexible response to peasant complaints, effectively granting headmen wide discretionary powers. The primary difference with the rest of the Empire is instructive as it demonstrates how local legal arrangements elsewhere were connected to the wider constitutional framework. Bohemia approximated more closely to the western unitary kingdoms with a flatter hierarchy of jurisdictions. Its villages remained largely outside state administration, which depended heavily on the noble-dominated provincial Estates to raise taxes and recruits. Unlike most of Germany, Bohemian villagers did not have access to a separate hierarchy of princely and imperial law courts to obtain independent redress prior to Joseph II's emancipation patent in 1781.[61]

Civic Emancipation

The trend towards civic self-government resumed in Italy around 1000 after its interruption by the royal sponsorship of bishops during the previous century. As with its rural equivalent, towns often acquired greater autonomy through cooperation rather than conflict with lords, including the emperor. None of the Empire's medieval royal families pursued a coherent policy of favouring towns to win burghers as alternative political partners to balance the lords. The royal families did not think in class terms but instead responded to local circumstances, their main concern being to match general expectations for royal justice and morality. Their thinking also remained hierarchical, with senior lords already known to them personally as their 'natural' partners. The emergence of the civic communal movement thus represents the failure not just of the monarch, but of all lords to widen the Empire's consensual politics to accommodate new socio-economic forces. Imperial favour remained purely tactical. For example, Henry IV generally supported the Italian episcopate, not least because his Gregorian opponents usually backed those in episcopal towns who were already trying to unseat local bishops. However, Henry sided with the communal movement in Tuscan towns, because these generally opposed Matilda of Canossa.[62] Meanwhile, most burghers had no desire to assert their voice in managing the realm, but instead simply wanted more control over their own lives.

The crucial step in civic emancipation was the acquisition of the count's rights over a town when these had passed into the hands of the local bishop. Some bishops were happy to be free from the responsibility of protecting their town and becoming dragged into the innumerable problems arising from rapid urbanization. Towns thus 'communalized' these jurisdictions by assuming responsibility for protecting themselves and handling internal justice and other public functions. This explains why civic autonomy began earlier in Italian than in German towns, which were generally smaller and so more dependent on lordly protection. It also explains why relations quickly soured in many Italian towns as citizens discovered that the bishop's or count's continued presence conflicted with their internal self-regulation. Cremona's inhabitants ejected their bishop in 1036 and extended the city walls to enclose the episcopal compound. Likewise, towns resented the presence of royal palaces and garrisons as extra-territorial enclaves disrupting their jurisdiction. As we have seen (pp. 45–6), the Pavians famously tore down the royal palace for this reason in 1024. Over the next two centuries, citizens used their growing collective wealth to buy out royal rights to exercise justice or demand accommodation in their city.

Gregorian reform stimulated civic emancipation through its sustained critique of allegedly corrupt and immoral senior clergy and the secular lords accused of protecting them. Burghers increasingly asserted themselves as morally superior to both lords and clergy, notably in Milan, where the urban Patarenes movement temporarily expelled the archbishop between 1042 and 1044. The Patarenes had specific local roots, but also exemplified a general belief amongst townsfolk that self-government was essential to ensuring a peaceful, godly community.[63] The ideal of the sworn godly community was often central to many towns' myth of origins – that they had been founded as a single collective act of the population gathering together to pledge a 'solemn association' (coniuratis) (see Plate 28). For example, Bremen's city hall is supposedly the size of its original inhabitants standing in a solid rectangle.

This process was well under way before the Investiture Dispute gave it a significant impetus by the fragmentation of local power through the presence of schismatic bishops, as well as the higher-level contest between emperor and pope. The competing authorities often granted concessions in return for financial and military backing from cities. Henry IV and his son renounced claims for accommodation (*albergaria*) to persuade Mantua and Verona to abandon Matilda of Canossa. The success of north Italian towns in freeing themselves from such obligations is demonstrated by the fact that none of their imperial palaces survived the high Middle Ages.[64]

A similar pattern set in north of the Alps, though a few decades later. Worms was the first German town to expel its bishop, when it sheltered Henry IV from his Saxon opponents in 1073. Henry rewarded it by exempting it from royal tolls in January 1074 in a move that was significant since he gave this privilege to the inhabitants collectively rather than just to favoured individuals or merchants.[65] As with all royal privileges in this era, it is important not to misconstrue this as simply the dissipation of central authority. Through his action, Henry demonstrated to his opponents that only he had the power to make such changes. Nonetheless, the corrosive impact of the Investiture wars accelerated the grant of further privileges, increasingly also by other senior lords. Mainz's archbishop rewarded his burghers for rescuing him from Henry V in 1115 by granting them management of their own city. Other important episcopal towns emancipated themselves around the same time, including Cologne, Trier, Speyer, Cambrai and Valenciennes.[66]

Changing legal practice gave civic autonomy a firmer shape. The twelfth century saw a change from economic privileges associated with market rights (*Marktrecht*) to more general civic rights (*ius civitas*, or *Stadtrecht*), making the town and its inhabitants a legal corporation. For example, Strasbourg's bishop granted his city a 112-article civic law around 1131.[67] An important element was the power to raise the taxes and labour needed to sustain self-rule and carry out tasks ranging from street cleaning to building new city walls. Towns could now make up their own rules without reference to a lord, even if he might retain some elements of jurisdiction or, as was often the case in German episcopal cities, still possessed his own enclave around the cathedral, such as in Strasbourg and Bremen. Towns could also own property and assets, like a city hall, brewery, mills, smithy, poorhouse, plus land and woods beyond their walls. Increasingly, a town was called a *Stadt*, rather than a *Burg* (burgh, borough), the latter deriving from the word for their lord's castle, though its inhabitants were still called 'burghers' (*burgenses*, or *Bürger*). The term 'commune' (*Gemeinde*) had emerged already during the twelfth century as an abstract of its individual members, enabling them to interact in a world of lords as if they were a collective person.

The initial transition to self-government after 1080 saw the establishment of consular regimes in which individuals were enfeoffed with lordly rights on behalf of the commune, for example in Asti and Milan. Consuls were drawn from the urban elite and were often already vassals of the local bishop or count, making the transfer of power easier since they were men whom the lord trusted. Consular government had spread to many Italian cities by 1130 and was adopted north of the Alps around 1200, for example in Cologne, Lübeck and Utrecht.[68]

Consuls were soon counterbalanced by broader-based councils to stop what Napoleon, as consul of the French Republic, would do much later when he made himself dictator. A two-tier system emerged as the basic form of councils both sides of the Alps. Government was headed by a senior council (*Rat*) of 12 members or multiples thereof, led by one or often two mayors simultaneously as a further check on personal rule. Members served fixed periods, usually with a prohibition on an immediate second term, and assumed the functions previously performed by the consul or the lord's steward. The second tier was intended to control the first and consisted of a much larger citizens' assembly.

Italian and German Cities Compared

The process of emancipation accelerated under the Staufers, coinciding with feudalization and thus forming part of a more general development of autonomous management of more clearly defined local jurisdictions. However, the specific form of emancipation took different directions in Germany and Italy thanks to the interaction of these countries with imperial politics, as well as their social and economic conditions. Whereas Italian towns pre-dated the Empire, most of those north of the Alps were not founded until after 1120 and were consequently much more closely tied to lordly jurisdictions precisely at the time when these were being redefined along feudal lines. This highlighted some specific instances of the process of German civic emancipation. Some towns owed their freedoms to the privileges granted to attract their first inhabitants as settlers, such as Freiburg in the Breisgau. In other cases, lords lost control, because their jurisdiction was over the land where the town was built, not the houses within it. Although the inhabitants initially paid ground rent, the value of their buildings soon outstripped that of the land. It became impossible for the lord to recover the ground, because he could not compensate the inhabitants for their 'improvements' to it. This helped establish the rule that residence in a town for a year and a day made a person free, greatly encouraging further immigration.[69]

The larger Italian and German towns shared a common experience as episcopal seats, and hence their connection to the imperial church and its accommodation of emperors touring the Empire. In Italy this accelerated the transfer of regalia to major cities as the Staufers hoped to secure these against often pro-papal bishops from the 1150s. Frederick Barbarossa received 2,000 silver marks annually from the Lombard League cities in the late twelfth century.[70] Commutation of royal regalia into taxation or sale transformed a relationship based on protection and subordination into a more commercial arrangement. Renewed imperial weakness with the civil war between 1198 and 1214 provided more opportunities to wring concessions, while the dense urban landscape made it hard for either of the contending kings to find a firm footing in northern Italy. One consequence was that most cities escaped from the obligation to continue paying regular taxes.

Another was that the emperor's efforts to win allies accelerated the differentiation amongst Italian cities as the larger ones increasingly dominated their smaller neighbours. Whereas in Germany towns generally fought against the influence of princes, large Italian centres like Milan, Cremona, Florence and Siena competed to assert influence not only over their own hinterlands, but over smaller towns further afield. This helps explain the volatility of north Italian politics, as cities changed sides, while leagues formed and fragmented depending on the prevailing military balance and the arrival and departure of imperial armies. Larger cities also benefited from the collapse of land prices following the Black Death when their citizens were able to buy more land and rights in the *contado* (the region surrounding a city). Thus, political centralization and the extension of a city's political control over its hinterland served many of its inhabitants' economic interests by protecting their investments and increasing the favourable trade relations with surrounding small towns and villages. By the late fourteenth century, Siena's citizens owned over 70 per cent of the land around their city. Venice and Genoa were exceptional in enjoying secure, protected locations with good access to the sea, allowing them to refrain initially from competition for land, and instead engage in long-distance trade with their eastern Mediterranean and Black Sea partners.[71]

Many German episcopal towns also acquired self-government in the twelfth century, but their bishops still controlled their hinterlands, unlike in Italy, where these had already passed under civic jurisdiction. Well served by ministeriales, German bishops had no need to enfeoff richer townsmen as mediate vassals. Moreover, the German episcopate retained closer ties to the emperor. The Staufers and their immediate successors had no need to turn to burgher lawyers like the French kings, because the imperial church continued to supply literate clergy for royal service. The proportion of non-nobles as recipients of royal charters rose only from 2 per cent in the twelfth century to 10 per cent by about 1250. Having temporarily favoured some cities in the early thirteenth century, the Staufers swung more consistently behind lay and spiritual princes with their general charters in 1220 and 1231.[72] Thereafter, the bishops of Würzburg, Bamberg, Passau and Halberstadt reasserted more direct authority over their towns, stunting their economies in the process.

This explains the growing division between territorial towns and those that the Staufers had developed on their own lands, which ultimately became imperial cities (civitae imperialis, or Reichsstädte). Episcopal towns only acquired the lesser status of 'free', obliging their bishop, sometimes after considerable violence, to move to a palace outside their walls.[73] This promoted the development of some smaller towns as episcopal residences, for example Bruchsal (for Speyer), Brühl (for Cologne), Eutin (for Lübeck) and Meersburg (for Konstanz). Bishops retained legally protected compounds in their episcopal towns, these themselves often leading to tension, and explaining why these towns played a prominent role in the German civic leagues of the thirteenth and fourteenth centuries (see pp. 570–79). Cologne managed to secure full immediacy as an imperial city in 1288, though its shut-out archbishop continued to contest this for some time. The situation remained fluid into the later fifteenth century, because monarchs frequently pawned imperial cities, some of which slid under princely jurisdiction, such as Dortmund and Regensburg, until their status was stabilized through imperial reform and representation in the Reichstag.

Nonetheless, imperial patronage enabled many German towns to achieve their primary goal of safe access to the outside world for trade and food. They had less incentive to conquer or acquire territory, unlike in Italy, where around 25 cities each controlled at least 1,000 square kilometres, with Florence possessing 12,000 square kilometres by 1400, while Venice amassed nearly three times that across 1339–1428. By contrast, only Nuremberg came close, with 1,650 square kilometres, while Ulm had 930 square kilometres and all other German towns only 100 square kilometres or less.[74] Despite the disparity in size between Italian and German towns, the process of asserting dominance broadly followed a similar pattern. Economic influence generally preceded political control, but was always assisted by manipulation of lordly jurisdictions and other legal privileges. For example, Nuremberg bought the castle and jurisdictions of its former imperial castellan in 1427, and within 15 years controlled 442 dependent villages and hamlets.[75] Townsfolk also used their self-government to assert lordship over their hinterland. Affluent Italian citizens exploited their control of consular positions and city councils after 1200 to raise resources and build roads, canals and new suburbs, thus further revising relations with the countryside in their favour. They also extended credit to surrounding peasants and lords, thereby establishing an 'informal empire' similar to that created by nineteenth-century European financiers in Latin America, North Africa and Asia. All this was generally followed by establishing the right to name or confirm village officials and to levy taxes and recruits.

German towns did this on a smaller scale, for example extending influence by granting citizenship to people living outside their walls to create networks of dependants to rival those of the lords. The princes persuaded the emperor to prohibit these so-called 'false citizens' (*cives falsi*, or *Pfahlbürger*) in 1231, though the ban had to be renewed in 1356. The generally sparser rural population made territorial acquisition a less attractive proposition in Germany, where it could often be controlled commercially instead, for example by persuading the surrounding area to adopt the city's currency and weights and measures. Rather than control space, German towns concentrated on securing access routes, for example buying castles guarding important roads or river crossings.

The Growth of Oligarchy

Italian, Burgundian and German cities shared the same tendency towards oligarchy, which was also manifest in villages to a lesser degree. The communal slogan was freedom, not equality. Freedoms were acquired as 'immunities', meaning exemptions from lordly exactions and jurisdictions. The commune emerged as a collective, corporate 'lord'. Its members were personally free, but only through their association with a specific community. Their freedoms vanished if they emigrated or were expelled. Status was guarded jealously, and citizens had little incentive to extend it to others outside, except as a means of extending their own security and economic dominance. For example, in 1256–7 Bologna paid 379 masters to renounce jurisdiction over 6,000 of its inhabitants, who had to pay new taxes to the city instead.[76] Access to citizenship remained closely controlled by each city's council, just as equivalent bodies restricted the franchise in villages. The authorities in power remained concerned for their community's viability, and tried to exclude those who it was felt exhausted communal resources such as meadows. This often provided another source of friction with lords, who sometimes promoted the interests of the poor or landless as a useful pool of cheap labour, whereas richer inhabitants feared them as a potential burden. Urban populations were thus highly stratified, consisting of a group of enfranchised citizens, who did not necessarily form the majority, together with an intermediary layer of tolerated 'residents' without full privileges, and a proletariat with few rights. All three groups were further divided, for example between established families and newcomers.

Cologne's government was already in the hands of the 'guild of the rich' (*Richerzeche*) by the 1130s.[77] Oligarchy emerged 'naturally' through the growing complexity and volume of business that communal institutions had to handle. Office-holding had become time-consuming and often difficult by the twelfth century, obliging towns to revise their constitutions and allow longer terms of office. Their administrations became divided between lower functionaries who were now paid and higher posts that remained honorific, supposedly in line with the public ideal of self-sacrifice, but in practice a way of restricting them to men of means. Cooption increasingly replaced direct election in selecting councillors, partly because those in power saw their friends as 'safe pairs of hands', but also to discourage populism, which so often led to violence, especially in Italy. Growing social stratification and economic diversification encouraged faction and 'party' interests during the thirteenth century.[78] Rival groups competed for power, attempting to exclude their rivals if they held it. Florence contained 150 fortified towers in 1200, reflecting the sense of anxiety amidst often bloody violence and vendettas. In part, the greater strife in Italian towns derived from the larger number of nobles holding property both inside their walls and outside in the contado, who transferred their feuds to civic politics. German nobles had fewer economic or political interests in towns and their urban mansions remained unfortified. However, the violence also reflected the more advanced state of Italian communal development where the stakes were often higher, as well as the greater distance from external agencies who might mediate or defuse tension, such as the emperor and imperial courts.

The trend towards oligarchy in Italian and German towns was periodically checked by popular revolts in the late thirteenth century and again during the fourteenth. Constitutions were rewritten to widen participation, especially through guilds as new corporate interest groups. Oligarchy generally soon returned, because towns remained legally as well as economically stratified, and their enfranchised population generally refused to extend citizenship to residents or the proletariat. There was little further change after the mid-sixteenth century, with most German and Swiss towns now controlled by a few families related by kinship and business interests. By the end of the eighteenth century, only 250 families in Bern were still eligible for senior public office, while just 13 held half the seats on Zürich's city council. The pattern was generally repeated in the countryside: 29 peasants in one Swabian village held 143 public offices between them around 1580. Wealth, rank and power had become concentrated in the hands of small elites whose cooperation was sought by lords and princes.[79]

The situation in Italy was more extreme, as a few ruthless families rose from urban despots to become a new princely elite. The trend towards aristocracy was always more pronounced here than north of the Alps. Richer Italian burghers advanced towards noble status by becoming the subvassals of bishops and counts by the early eleventh century, continuing to serve as mounted retainers into the thirteenth century, when they were increasingly subjected to taxation by more powerful city councils. Paradoxically, because rural lords posed less of a threat to civic liberties than in Germany, Italian cities found it easier to accept them within their walls. Intermarriage with richer burghers further blurred distinctions, creating an elite known as the *signori*, who used vassalage and control of small rural fiefs to underpin their power in both the city and its contado. Constitutions were rewritten allowing signori to hold positions as civic captains and other offices for life. Holding on to power often proved difficult in this violent, highly competitive environment, and most signori were content with dominating their own city, though the Visconti in Milan continued that city's expansion at the expense of weaker neighbours. As we have seen (pp. 193–4 and 393–4), successful despots secured their authority by trading support for Roman expeditions in return for the emperor's grant of hereditary princely status. Florence was relatively exceptional as one of the few large cities retaining a more republican regime, largely because its wealth allowed for a more elaborate bureaucracy and for the mercenaries necessary to defend its regional influence.[80] Venice and Genoa likewise remained republics, but with relatively large yet exclusive patriciates that in any event assumed the outward symbols of nobility such as coats of arms.

No German or Burgundian burgher rose from councillor to become the prince of his home town. The only German principality based directly on a town was Brunswick, created under the special circumstances of the Welfs' reconciliation with the Staufers in 1235 (see p. 361). Nobles and lords were part of urban life, but did not merge to the same extent with patriciates, which instead were distinguished from their fellow citizens by lifestyle, marriage patterns and, from the fourteenth century, a self-conscious projection of themselves as their community's leading families. Unlike in Italy, the presence of so many powerful princes offered sufficient employment opportunities for knights and other lesser nobles, together with a route to social mobility for burghers, who could rise through employment in the expanding princely territorial administrations rather than serve their home town. All German and Burgundian cities already had lords, being either their bishop, prince or the emperor, who was a much closer presence for the imperial cities than for Italian towns. Additionally, the tendency towards oligarchy was checked by imperial intervention. Although Charles V revised numerous civic constitutions to strengthen patrician powers, he nonetheless ensured these remained communal rather than princely regimes.

The Empire's Bourgeoisie

The relatively small size of most German towns was a further factor ensuring oligarchy did not develop into despotism. For example, the Württemberg territorial town of Wildberg comprised 1,328 inhabitants in 300 households in 1717. These shared 95 public offices, including the three mayoral positions, 15 members of two councils, and 25 inspectors of roads, buildings, bread, fish, cattle and meat.[81] One fifth of male householders thus held at least one public office, ensuring that authority remained fairly well distributed and a significant proportion of the population retained a meaningful stake in communal affairs. Towns retained a vitality and cohesion based on fairly broad daily interaction between people who generally knew each other well.

This point has wider significance, given the general impression of German towns as declining economically and politically after 1648. This negative interpretation rests on a contrast with their cultural and economic dynamism around 1500, as well as unfavourable comparisons with cities in other countries, especially those in western Europe that benefited from colonial trade and early industrialization during the eighteenth century. Whereas cities like Nuremberg had been at the forefront of the German Renaissance and Reformation, and had played a major role in institutionalizing the Reichstag, they appear sleepy backwaters by the late eighteenth century, when most had static or even declining populations and all were hemmed in by principalities that outweighed them culturally as well as politically. Eighteenth-century Germany appears a land of princely courts, dotted with small 'residence towns' (*Residenzstadte*) dominated by imposing baroque palaces, opera houses and court theatres. The general impression is that princes and nobles dominated German society, retarding both economic development and the emergence of a politically conscious bourgeoisie. This situation has been blamed for the lack of a genuine revolution and the late start for German industrialization.[82] In short, the imperial cities and, by extension the Empire, appear backward because they failed to develop as industrial and commercial centres like London or Amsterdam.

Things look different when viewed from the perspective of the Empire's urban population. Political conditions were far more stable in the eighteenth century than in the urban heyday around 1500. The last imperial city to be deprived of its autonomy was Donauwörth, annexed by Bavaria in 1607, while in 1671 Brunswick became the last territorial town bombarded into accepting greater princely control.[83] Both cases were exceptional. Although individually small, German towns were numerous and fairly evenly distributed, at least west and south of the Elbe. Their inhabitants already represented 13.5 per cent of the German population in 1450, remaining roughly at this level for 250 years before doubling by 1800. Only Vienna, Berlin and Hamburg had over 100,000 inhabitants and so did not compare to London, which at around 1 million contained a tenth of England's population. However, there were only two other English towns with over 15,000 inhabitants, whereas this size was exceeded by 7 imperial cities and 27 territorial towns, indicating that the Empire's experience was not unduly at variance with supposedly more progressive parts of Europe.[84]

The relatively even distribution of the German urban population in multiple, middle-sized centres persisted well into modernity, while the country still today lacks a single, dominant metropolis. This has brought economic and cultural benefits. Certainly, most early modern imperial cities succeeded on their own terms by providing stable and safe environments for the majority of their inhabitants. Most cities had relatively high levels of small-scale manufacture and commerce, with even fairly minor cities like Heilbronn and Lindau serving as regional economic centres. Wealth discrepancies were indeed very considerable, but urban growth did not produce large slums, while inhabitants remained cohesive and identified strongly with their 'home town' and with the Empire.[85]

The majority of the Empire's most passionate advocates came from the urban elite, like Johann Jacob Moser, who grew up in Herrenberg and Stuttgart in Württemberg. After graduating from Württemberg's local university of Tübingen, Moser eventually entered the duchy's civil administration, then spent four years as a law professor at his alma mater. After that, he successively worked in the Reichskammergericht, the Württemberg civil service (again), the Prussian university of Frankfurt an der Oder, as a freelance legal consultant to Emperor Charles VII, and director of the Hessen-Homburg privy council. Finally, and tumultuously, he served the Württemberg Estates during their long dispute with their duke.[86] Moser's career demonstrates the relative ease with which educated burghers moved between civic, princely and imperial employment. The Empire's multicentred politics thus offered numerous chances for social mobility largely independent from broader economic developments.

REPRESENTATION AND REGULATION

Princely Administrations and their Staff

Medieval kingship was primarily about the morality rather than the scope of action. Social engagement was limited to largely symbolic acts like helping individual widows and other 'defenceless' inhabitants. According to the chronicler Wipo, Conrad II brushed aside his courtiers' advice to hasten to his coronation and instead stopped to listen to petitions from a peasant, an orphan and a widow, and thereby 'prepared himself that day the way to the remaining affairs of government'. Wipo stressed that Conrad 'responded like a vicar of Christ', yet there was nothing particularly 'imperial' about his actions.[87] Similar stories are recounted for other medieval kings. However, subjects increasingly expected their kings to respond to their concerns in a more sustained and systematic way. Through petitions, protests and representation in parliaments, subjects compelled monarchs to legislate and eventually to develop centrally directed institutions to ameliorate society's concerns.

At first sight, the Empire appears to move in the opposite direction as its central authority seemingly becomes more distant from the lives of ordinary inhabitants after the mid-thirteenth century. However, the difference is less pronounced when all layers of authority are viewed together. Social and economic regulation developed at the level of princely territories and imperial cities, rather than through central institutions, in a process that remained mutually interdependent into the eighteenth century and that established additional layers of representation within most of the Empire's component territories, complementing the representation of the imperial Estates in the Reichstag.

These provincial and territorial Estates (*Landstände*) were the princes' allies *and* rivals. Their ambiguous role explains why historical interpretations have often diverged widely, with some regarding the Estates as champions of popular liberty against princely despotism, whereas others condemned them as vested interests frustrating beneficial changes.[88] The Estates were a product of the general changes within the Empire from the late Middle Ages into early modernity as local and territorial authorities expanded their functions to cope with rising population, economic change, and the growing complexity of daily life.

Princely administration remained rudimentary into the fourteenth century compared to the towns, but also to some other European authorities, notably the papacy. Towns were the first to be confronted by the complexities of mass communal living and developed new methods to cope, including adopting writing in routine administration. However, the contrast with princely and imperial administration should not be pushed too far. Lords and kings benefited from their long association with the church, whose monasteries and abbeys also pioneered new techniques early on, while manorial administration could also be quite complex, especially as jurisdictions fragmented and economic relations were commercialized. Italian and later also German and Burgundian lords were perfectly able to master the requirements of commercial leases and new forms of asset management.

Nonetheless, princely and royal administration remained small, because outside war-making its primary tasks were limited to demonstrative acts of justice and good kingship. The growing hierarchy of vassalage enabled those higher up the social scale to concentrate on these affairs, considered their 'proper' business, whilst devolving more mundane issues to their inferiors. These continued the existing face-to-face methods, because as the population grew, it supported more lordships whose authority remained restricted to roughly the same number of people. The overarching imperial framework continued to legitimate princely and lordly authority through the charters associated with feudalization, and new coordinating legislation like that of the public peace (pp. 402–3 and 620–27). Meanwhile, princes and cities increasingly assumed greater responsibilities as their jurisdictions coalesced into more distinct territories.

Territorial administration acquired a firmer institutional footing in the fourteenth century, several centuries after the establishment of the imperial chancellery that undoubtedly provided a model. Clergy predominated, given the scarcity of educated literate staff, which persisted due to the paucity of university graduates. Clerics were also cheaper, since they lived off their benefices, whereas laity required salaries. Cologne's chancellery employed 12 clerics in the 1340s, while its Palatine equivalent still managed with just four to five scribes some ninety years later. Most administration was handled by lesser nobles, either directly as vassals or as paid officials, for example serving as castellans and bailiffs as the district structure took shape. Princes meanwhile followed the emperor's example, touring their lands with a cavalcade of servants, baggage wagons, kitchen utensils and carpets to make each stopover more comfortable. After the mid-fourteenth century, they began camping for longer periods near good resources, like lucrative toll posts, or copying Staufer practice by staying in their territorial towns. The focus on fewer but increasingly substantial palaces accelerated in the fifteenth century and developed into the norm during the next century when each principality became firmly associated with a residence town. The significance of such towns is illustrated by the way that Hanover gave its name to an entire territory originally formally known as the duchy of Calenberg. The greater stability increased the pressure on resource management, since supplies were no longer consumed close to source, but had to be provided in a form capable of sustaining what had become a permanent princely court at a fixed location. This coincided with imperial reform, which itself placed additional demands on the princes and cities.

Princely administration expanded to cope, and its staff acquired higher social status. Commoners regarded councillors and other senior staff as effectively nobles, opening a new route to social mobility alongside the church. Even comparatively small principalities and imperial cities founded universities and grammar schools to meet the growing demand for suitable candidates. Huge differences in pay persisted between noble and 'learned' officials into the late eighteenth century, though education became a prerequisite for many posts.[89] Overall numbers remained modest. A typically middling principality in the eighteenth century might have 100–300 officials from senior councillors to messengers in its central agencies, and up to 800 officials of all ranks in its districts, together serving 200,000–400,000 inhabitants. Even in Prussia, the central agencies grew from 300 officials in 1680 to 640 by the 1750s, by which point there were still only 14,000 officials altogether, of whom 4,500 were excise collectors. Many officials were employed by the localities or the Estates, rather than directly by the prince. For example, in 1762 Austria and Bohemia had 7,421 public officials employed by the Habsburgs, 1,494 by the provincial Estates, and 11,669 by nobles and towns.[90]

The emergence of princely administrations generated demands to share in the benefits of social mobility, wealth, status and influence. Criticism of 'foreign advisors' (*fremde Räte*) had already surfaced in the fourteenth century as locals accused their prince of unduly favouring outsiders to their disadvantage. Late examples include Dr Wolfgang Günther in Hessen-Kassel and Joseph Süss Oppenheimer (who was Jewish as well as an outsider) in Württemberg, who were both blamed for unpopular policies and executed as soon as their princely patrons died.[91] The insistence on *Indigenatsrecht*, or binding requirements only to employ 'natives', was a major factor behind the coalescence of territorial elites, thereby contributing to the multilayered identities we have already encountered (pp. 252–4). The latter was also promoted by the growth of territorial Estates.

The Emergence of Territorial Estates

The Empire's culture of seeking consensus to legitimate action was a major influence on the development of representation at the provincial and territorial level. The 1231 statute not only granted princes greater powers in their jurisdictions, but obliged them to consult 'the better and greater men' (*meliores et majors*) to help them carry out their responsibilities. This provided the basis for Estates in the Austrian and Bohemian provinces.[92] Homage ceremonies offered another impulse by providing opportunities for leading subjects to bargain for corporate rights and press grievances. In most cases, Estates emerged well ahead of their first actual plenary diet (*Landtag*). For example, those in Bavaria were already involved in the duchy's financial affairs in the late fourteenth century, but only held their first diet in 1453. The presence of cathedral chapters could inhibit developments in ecclesiastical territories, because the clerical elite already found these effective platforms for their interests and had little incentive to include lay nobles or urban magistrates in negotiations with their prince-bishop. However, the latter often wanted to include his secular vassals and towns, either to balance his chapter politically or to harness their resources as well. The meeting of the Magdeburg diet in 1400 is generally accepted as the first to convene in a German territory. This also highlights a more fundamental point that territorial Estates could be actively promoted by rulers, rather than simply emerging in opposition to them.

Estates existed in virtually every German, Bohemian and Burgundian territory and province by 1500, but not in Italy, where political development at this level had diverged, with the formation of territorial states based on the dominance of large cities over their hinterlands. Representation in Italy remained restricted to city councils, which denied their rural subjects a voice. Only Savoy followed the pattern elsewhere in the Empire, again underscoring the significance of its origins in Burgundy and subsequent association with the German kingdom. Village assemblies emerged together with Estates for the various Savoyard provinces by the late fourteenth century, though these lost significance after 1560, except in outlying areas.[93]

Estates represented corporate status groups, not inhabitants as equal citizens. Clergy were usually represented through mediate religious houses, which sent their abbots or priors. In some cases, like Salzburg, the cathedral chapter formed part of the territory's Estates.[94] Nobles participated on the basis of their mediate fiefs, provided rulers recognized that these qualified. In some territories, like Saxony, holders of all such fiefs could attend, even where these were held by towns. Elsewhere, nobles elected representatives from those holding qualifying property. Town magistrates and village headmen had already gained representation in the Tirolean Estates in 1363, and soon in many other Alpine territories, including Salzburg, Basel, Chur, Brixen, Sitten and Vorarlberg, as well as across parts of the south-west like Baden and a few other special cases like East Frisia. In most cases, the commons were restricted to the mayors of leading territorial towns. The tripartite division into clergy, nobles and commons was relatively rare: Bavaria, Upper Palatinate, Breisgau, Sundgau, Cologne, Salzburg, Basel, Liège, and the Ernestine and Welf duchies. North and east German Estates generally had two noble curia of lords and knights, alongside one for the leading territorial towns: electoral Saxony, Brandenburg, and most of the Habsburg provinces.

All representatives claimed to speak on behalf of their wider communities. In the case of nobles, this meant their tenants or serfs. Like envoys at the Reichstag and Kreis Assemblies, representatives held imperative mandates binding them to instructions agreed in advance within their communities. This inhibited the development of more ideological factions or parties by limiting the opportunities for representatives to appeal to others beyond their own constituents. Also like the Empire's higher assemblies, the Estates followed late medieval practice in taking decisions by majority vote in corporate groups and then bargaining to reach an overall consensus. Meetings thus provided opportunities to assert social, corporate and (later) confessional status, as well as decide material issues.[95]

The Estates in Austria and Bohemia owed their relative strength to emerging between the late thirteenth and mid-fourteenth centuries, well ahead of other parts of the Empire.[96] They also represented large provinces that developed taxation relatively early, thanks to economic assets such as silver mines and a vigorous transit trade, and especially because their rulers needed to fund defence against external threats, notably the Hungarians and Turks from the fifteenth century. In line with their territorially based imperial management, the Habsburgs dealt with their provincial Estates directly, and ensured that leading nobles and towns did not gain representation in the Reichstag. The Habsburgs also negotiated with each in turn on the basis of divide and rule. This proved difficult for them in Bohemia, where general diets of all five provinces together remained relatively common into the seventeenth century and, indeed, provided the institutional underpinning of the Bohemian Revolt (1618–20). The Burgundian dukes actively promoted general diets, called States General, in the 1430s to integrate the provinces accumulated through their rapid expansion since the 1380s. The Habsburgs were obliged to retain the States General when they acquired most of the Burgundian provinces after 1477, especially as the States General had become indispensable to raising taxes. The States General convened on average twice a year until the 1570s, when they split, with those in the seven northern provinces meeting separately in what eventually became the Dutch Republic.[97] Maximilian I experimented with a similar General Diet for his Austrian provinces, but as in Bohemia this never developed as a permanent body, unlike the Burgundian States General. His successors largely eschewed general meetings, but the fundamental restructuring of the Habsburg nobility in the 1620s removed the need for substantial revisions to the Estates, since these were now dominated by families who owed their status and wealth to having backed the emperor in the Thirty Years War.[98] The Hohenzollerns, Wettins and Hanoverian Welfs also refrained from establishing General Diets as they accumulated additional imperial fiefs, each with their own Estates.

Estates without any noble representatives were known as *Landschaften*, literally 'the countryside'. These are often interpreted as emerging more democratically 'from below' in contrast to Estates that appear more as an outgrowth of elite politics.[99] In fact, the Zweibrücken and Palatine Landschaften were initially convened on the initiative of their princes. Others emerged because nobles opted out of territorial politics to secure immediacy as imperial knights, reducing representation to clergy and commons, for instance in Württemberg, Würzburg, Bamberg, Bayreuth, Ansbach, Trier and Fulda. Around 20 Swabian and Franconian territories developed full Landschaften composed only of mayors and village headmen, but these were all bishoprics, counties and lordships without indigenous nobles other than their lord. A few imperial cities also created similar institutions in order to negotiate more effectively with their dependent villages. There was no clear correlation between political vitality and social composition: the noble-dominated Mecklenburg assembly survived until 1918, whereas those assemblies in Bamberg and Würzburg that lacked nobles largely ceased functioning in the eighteenth century.

Provincial and territorial Estates adopted broadly similar rhetoric, as in the Reichstag, with their members presenting themselves as loyal subjects whose role was to assist in ensuring moral governance, peace, justice and the common good. Like the emperor, princes held the initiative, choosing if and when to summon their Estates and to set the agenda. A few Estates claimed the right of self-assembly, but this was formally prohibited in 1658. Estates responded with petitions and lists of grievances, using these to bargain collective rights entrenching their position within each territory. However, Estates could also become vehicles for sectional interests, as in the Habsburg lands, where Protestants used them in the 1560s and 1570s to secure limited toleration despite the opposition of Catholic members. Towns and nobles frequently clashed over economic questions and relative shares of taxation. Negotiations were characterized by greater proximity between ruler and ruled than discussions in the Reichstag and Kreis Assemblies. Moral questions were expressed more openly, including criticism of princes' personal failings, of their mistresses and courtly extravagance. A major reason for the difference in style from Reichstag proceedings was that territorial taxes paid for the prince's household and his other policies, whereas imperial taxation funded only a narrow range of activities more clearly related to peace and justice.

The Estates' criticism had real force, because the self-interest of their members frequently converged with the moral conviction that the established social order should be preserved and that any changes were to restore an idealized harmony by addressing perceived abuses rather than altering essentials. The Estates consciously distanced themselves from the princely court and administration, claiming they alone offered impartial advice, not the servile flattery of courtiers and hired lackeys. However, the Estates did not seek to replace princes with republics, or to extend political participation to ordinary inhabitants. Even Johannes Althusius, one of the Empire's more radical early modern thinkers, saw the Estates' chief function as a check on monarchical power, rather than its replacement.[100]

Most Estates established standing committees of selected members to represent their interests between full diets. Rulers often found these more congenial to deal with, especially as their smaller membership was more open to the usual forms of princely patronage involving honours, favours and bribes. Many territories held their last plenary diet between the 1650s and 1680s, though a few reconvened, sometimes after many decades. This trend towards oligarchy certainly restricted representation to a narrow elite that often acquired close ties to princely administrations, even where plenary diets continued to meet intermittently, as in Württemberg.[101] However, this was not simply a case of princely absolutism muzzling the people's representatives, but rather reflected a consensus amongst influential sections of society that good governance rested on orderly administration and the rule of law, rather than democracy.

Territorial Taxation

Most Estates owed their origins to the financial problems of late medieval territories. Like the emperor, princes found that traditional means of resource extraction were unable to sustain either their ambitions or

the new understanding of their proper function. They had also dissipated their domains and now derived most of their income from the
jurisdictions and privileges originally granted by past monarchs, such
as toll, market and tariff rights. Tolls could be significant if a prince
possessed land across a major transit route. Mainz raised as much from
its Rhine levies in 1400 as from dues paid by 30 territorial towns.
Silver-mining provided three-quarters of Tirolean and half of Saxon
revenue in the first half of the sixteenth century. However, these were
all exceptional cases and the general picture was one of rising debt
(Table 14).[102]

Estates emerged partly through the protest of those affected by the
expedients that princes adopted to cope, for example townsfolk who
did not want to be pawned to another lord. Rulers also appreciated that
broader consultation would allow them to draw on their own subjects'
personal resources. The result was to create a new set of taxes alongside those deriving from privileges and feudal dues. These new levies

Table 14. Revenue and Debt in Selected
Principalities c.1500 (in florins)

Territory	Annual Revenue	Debt
Austria and Tirol	364,000	1,720,000
Bavaria (both branches)	132,200	741,900
The Palatinate	90,000	500,000
Electoral Cologne	90,000	?
Salzburg	90,000	?
Saxon Duchies	73,000	240,000
Electoral Saxony	63,000	200,000
Mainz	60,000	?
Brandenburg	60,000	?
Nuremberg	51,000	?
Württemberg	48,400	213,400
Trier	40,000	?
Ansbach-Bayreuth	30,000	233,500
Swabian cities (combined)	133,600	?
Swabian counts, prelates, knights	104,100	?

became known as 'territorial taxes' (*Landsteuer*) since they applied more broadly to most or all inhabitants and were raised for an agreed common purpose. Such taxes were already levied ten times in Bavaria in the fourteenth century, and were introduced in the Palatinate after 1395. Rulers found that cooperation with Estates not only reduced opposition, but was essential for tax collection. This explains why community leaders and leading clergy and nobles were summoned in the first place, since these were often the same people overseeing collection in the absence of any other local administration. The Münster Estates helped their bishop collect taxes after 1359, while a joint ducal-Estates tax commission was established in Upper Bavaria in 1396. By the sixteenth century, Estates taxes provided half to four-fifths of most territories' revenue. Estates were so useful that those princes who lacked them often now tried to form them, for example in Baden in 1558.

Estates used their power of the purse to influence policy. As leading property owners themselves, their representatives had a lot to lose from reckless actions, notably war. This provided a major break on violence and helped ensure that the growth of princely power did not produce an endless series of inter-territorial wars. For example, the Württemberg Estates forced their duke to agree to consult them after 1514 on major issues affecting the duchy. However, the Empire's fiscal structure meanwhile identified princes along with the magistrates of imperial cities as responsible for collecting imperial taxes (see pp. 403–6). Imperial taxes immediately assumed the status of higher obligations overriding local concerns. Princes excluded their own territorial Estates from any say in the matter beyond helping to decide how to raise the money. Many deliberately concealed the true scale of their official obligations in order to demand far higher sums than they actually owed the Empire, hoping to keep the balance.[103] Imperial legislation strengthened the princes' hand, for example by ruling in 1566 that subjects failing to pay imperial obligations could be fined twice the amount. Military expenditure could also be presented as an imperial obligation, because all princes were obliged to assist upholding the public peace and defending the Empire. The almost continual imperial mobilization after 1672 ended any peace dividend following the Thirty Years War and established military taxation as permanent in virtually all territories, especially as the smaller ones decided to maintain their imperial contingents in peacetime after 1714. This process also helps explain the decline of plenary diets, since rulers now usually only consulted Estates' standing committees on tax levels, not their existence or purpose, which had become fixed.

As a result, Estates assumed the character of a branch of territorial administration with their own infrastructure of officials, treasuries and account books. Estates' members frequently sat with princely officials on joint commissions overseeing the management and repayment of territorial debts. The Estates' credit-worthiness was closely tied to that of their prince, who benefited from lower interest rates thanks to his ability to borrow against future taxes. Debt amortization opened up large areas of princely policy to the Estates' scrutiny, if only retrospectively. Their officials also jointly audited military and other accounts. Of course, actual practice was far from perfect. One duke of Württemberg deliberately presented false accounts to his Estates to conceal the fact that he was receiving French subsidies, with the extent of the deception only becoming clear over two centuries later. Another duke was deceived by an envoy he sent to The Hague who spun out his time at government expense by sending misleadingly optimistic reports on his negotiations. Meanwhile, the envoy's brother in the Württemberg administration altered a ducal decree, doubling his salary, without this being discovered for 14 years.[104] Nonetheless, while Estates were scarcely representative in a modern democratic sense, they did encourage greater probity and discourage venality in a manner similar to that noted for Britain's Parliament.[105] All this contrasted with France, where the monarchy's reluctance to consult its subjects after 1614 undermined its credit-worthiness and ultimately frustrated financial reform.

Police Measures and Social Discipline

Like taxation, social regulation is usually associated with the rise of centralized states. In the standard account, states first disciplined their own staffs and then used these to encourage the ideal of obedient, pious and thrifty subjects. In doing so, it is claimed, this instilled the work ethic that made the Industrial Revolution possible, as well as allegedly instilling Germanic subservience to militarized authority.[106] Social regulation in the Empire was known as 'police measures' (*Policey*, *Polizei*), from the thirteenth-century translation of Aristotle's *Politeia*.

This meant both 'polity', or state, and good order, suggesting that the authorities had both the right and duty to regulate social behaviour in the interests of the common good. The Reformation certainly influenced how these ideas were implemented in the Empire. Lutheranism in particular contributed to the belief that all moral and rational action should be judged according to its capacity to promote personal happiness and well-being. Humans, it was widely believed, would naturally incline towards sin, unless checked by a properly informed clergy, good education and a strong secular authority.

It is important not to simplify police regulation as state repression. Police measures emerged to fill a legal void by ordering aspects of life not already governed by customary law and traditional rights, such as the new problems arising from urbanization and economic changes in the high Middle Ages. These measures attempted to prevent competing interests from disrupting social harmony. For example, rural producers wanted high prices to maximize profits, whereas townsfolk wanted cheap food. Growth in both settlement size and overall population rendered traditional means like church charity ineffective against problems such as famine and plague.

The French monarchy responded to similar difficulties by assuming new powers and functions centrally and issuing royal legislation from the 1370s. Central legislation in the Empire remained restricted to providing a framework for public order prior to early modernity. Instead, police measures were allowed to develop from within communities from the thirteenth century onwards. Most of the early measures tried to control access to scarce resources, for example by setting criteria for membership of an urban or a rural commune, and by regulating marriage and inheritance. Others measures included food-safety inspections, building regulations, fire safety, rubbish collection, sanitation, public health, and Bavaria's famous 1516 purity law that was really an attempt simply to control beer prices.

Regulation increased the importance of writing in public life. Before the twelfth century, books were usually only about religion. Thereafter, others appeared on law and as bound volumes of parchment used to record accounts, marriages, property ownership, licences and a host of other secular matters.[107] This emerged broadly simultaneously at all levels of what would become territorial administration, from the village to the prince's chancellery, during the thirteenth century. It laid the basis for the modern 'surveillance society' as local authorities increasingly recorded their inhabitants' lives in detail, and began issuing them with identification papers and passes that could be checked as they moved across the territory and beyond.

Higher lords and princes played relatively minor roles in these agendas before the emergence of their own self-consciousness as public authorities in the fifteenth century. Imperial reform accelerated this process by charging princes and other territorial authorities with a wider range of public functions relating to peace, justice, security and mobilization of resources to discharge these tasks. The Reichstag issued a wide range of general legislation between about 1500 and 1577, including the economic measures we have already seen (pp. 462–9) and three imperial police ordinances (1530, 1548, 1577). These reinforced the distinctions between imperial Italy, where they did not apply, and the rest of the Empire. They provided general guidelines that could either be implemented directly or modified to suit local laws and circumstances. Imperial legislation directly stimulated territorial activity: the number of territorial police ordinances doubled in the 52 years after the 1548 imperial ordinance, compared to the previous century and a half.[108] The quality of territorial measures also changed as existing codes and measures were rewritten, rationalized and standardized along imperial guidelines.

Many of the measures reflected the heightened morality and anxieties of the Reformation era in which they were issued. The imperial police ordinances targeted card-playing, gambling and drinking, both to curb these as potential public-order issues and to encourage greater thrift and productivity. Other clauses were aimed at spies, arsonists, witches, conspirators and subversives in general. The aim was to achieve a well-regulated society by eliminating or at least minimizing risks and threats, thus shifting the ideal from peace to security. Later measures targeted beggars and vagrants for similar reasons. Overall, territorial legislation moved in the seventeenth century from stabilizing measures that simply corrected immorality towards those intended actively to change attitudes and behaviour. Some of the accompanying rhetoric was genuinely heartfelt, and many measures were in direct response to perceived changes and new 'problems', such as the population growth and costly wars from the 1730s to early 1760s.[109] However, a ruthless fiscal drive was there from the sixteenth century, and it grew with the new arguments of cameralism in the seventeenth century that productivity could be raised by punishing 'idleness' and encouraging thrift. Measures that could be classed as 'economic' formed 40 per cent of all police regulation in eighteenth-century Baden-Durlach, whereas regulation involving social order, including religion, now formed only 25 per cent, with 15 per cent covering public order and safety, 12 per cent health, education and culture, and 8 per cent land and building regulations.[110]

Innovation remained within limits set by corporate social and political structures, as all authorities were reluctant to take steps that might disturb public order or disrupt established revenue streams. For example, many territories did promote the commercialization of common assets, either for sale or by taking them into central state control, but none adopted the wholesale 'enclosures' that broke up common lands in early modern England. Instead, the authorities sought to stabilize existing households by giving farms access to commons in proportion to their existing size, not according to their need or the requirements of a commercial land market.[111] In short, the Empire's authorities disadvantaged both the poor and the enterprising.

Cameralism remained very much a 'baroque science', often creating additional problems through contradictory, inadequate and unnecessary measures.[112] Cameralist writers were certainly frequently self-serving, obscuring defects and advancing their careers by peddling panaceas or visions of utopian, benevolent, impartial states. However, the Empire's territorial authorities were far from all-powerful. Numerous measures were unenforceable, or were only implemented with difficulty, because they contravened popular values or expectations. Official regulation was also adapted to popular pressure and often originated in demands for action from ordinary inhabitants.[113] The result was an 'empowering interaction' in which engagement with ordinary people allowed the latter at least some chance to shape policy.[114] Paradoxically, this encouraged acceptance of established authority by ensuring the territorial state served genuine needs. Throughout, the authorities retained the upper hand. Although governance at the local level still relied heavily on the cooperation and compliance of community leaders and ordinary people, overall direction remained reserved to higher levels. Petitions and protests might achieve meaningful specific changes, but usually only if they conformed to official norms. For example, wives might secure court verdicts against violent spouses by convincing the judges their husbands were bad householders rather than male abusers.[115]

The process developed its own logic and momentum through centre–local interactions and through the administration's 'inner dynamism' as officials continually expanded their remit.[116] For example, Württemberg village courts increasingly referred cases over access to forests to the ducal superior court; the latter thereby became the ultimate authority in such matters, in which it previously had no great interest. In short, the state unintentionally encouraged its inhabitants to widen its functions and responsibilities. Regulation of one aspect of life frequently prompted intervention in another, especially as individual mandates often served multiple goals. Both the governed and governing came to see the authorities' role no longer as merely divinely ordained stewardship of humanity, but as a body duty-bound to promote positive improvements. Overall, the integration of society and authority reinforced the belief that the common good was best advanced by benevolent administration and the adherence to agreements and laws, rather than through expanding forms of direct representation.

SOCIETY, TERRITORY AND EMPIRE

Absolutism and its Limits

These developments are usually interpreted as measures that sustained more absolutist princely power, which is the flipside of the customary presentation of the Empire as a loose federation after 1648. This section will argue that not only were the territories still formally within the Empire, but that they and imperial institutions remained entangled in a common corporate social order that persisted beyond 1806. Contemporaries were well aware of the growth in princely power and pretensions. Johann Jacob Moser observed in 1773:

> More and more the desire to be sovereign is mastering electoral and princely courts: how many soldiers does one have? As many as one wants; how many taxes does one decree? As many as one wants; how many excises and other duties does one impose? As many as one wants. In short, one does what one wants, and the territorial Estates

and subjects, if they are still alright, can howl; or one brooks no contradiction ... [and] they are driven to numerous crimes, disobedience and rebellion.[117]

Moser wrote from bitter personal experience, having been consigned to a dungeon for five years after protesting at the duke of Württemberg's illegal taxation during the Seven Years War.[118] However, he owed his eventual release to a case brought by the duchy's Estates, who successfully prosecuted the duke in the imperial courts, culminating in the imposition of tight fiscal constraints in 1770.[119] Thus, Moser was also able to remind princes that their powers 'did not make their land into their own free state, but only part of the entire state-body of the German Empire'.[120] Some princes agreed wholeheartedly. Max Franz, Emperor Joseph II's younger brother and archbishop-elector of Cologne and prince-bishop of Münster, regarded his cathedral chapters and Estates as guardians of his territories' constitutions, quite properly preventing him from interfering with the rule of law. The laws that bound Max Franz's subjects applied equally to himself and his officials.

Most historians have remained sceptical, doubting how far imperial institutions could constrain Austria and Prussia, whilst also noting how territorialization invested ideological power in princely governments to act on their own initiative. To some, the late eighteenth century saw a growing tension between dynamism at the territorial level and a rigid and seemingly increasingly irrelevant imperial framework.[121] The most obvious manifestations of dynamism were the 'enlightened' reforms implemented in Austria, Prussia and many middling and even smaller secular and ecclesiastical territories after about 1770.[122] These measures changed the substance and not just the style of territorial governance. Promotion of the common good expanded more explicitly to include subjects' happiness, as well as security and order. Happiness was now defined by material welfare and physical well-being, rather than in moral-religious terms. Practical examples included the secular-inspired welfare measures and the changed and expanded provision of education. A second area of activity entailed the dismantling of the confessional state through greater toleration, widening the individual and corporate liberties already provided through imperial law since 1648. In the late eighteenth century, Catholic territories such as Austria expropriated huge quantities of 'useless' church property in the manner of the earlier Protestant secularization, but they used the resources obtained to support state-controlled welfare and education, rather than to improve clerical instruction or advance religious goals. Such changes were legitimated by reference to the concept of utility central to much Enlightened thought and which supported the alteration or removal of 'traditional' privileges in the name of the common good.

The contradictions inherent in the reforms were most obvious in efforts to codify territorial laws, because these entailed rationalization and systematization at odds with the fudges critical to sustaining the Empire and its corporate social order.[123] Codification accelerated trends already present in cameralist regulation by levelling social distinctions in the name of common progress. Society was being pushed from an order based on legally distinct corporate Estates and towards one composed of legally equal individuals sharing a uniform relationship to the state. Socio-legal distinctions gave way to stratification defined more obviously economically by class. The ultimate direction of these developments was still far from clear in the late eighteenth century, while the authorities lacked a coherent plan beyond a still largely traditional concern for the common good and fiscal efficiency. Codification and other efforts at standardization proceeded quite slowly. It took 52 years to dismantle the tariff barriers between Austrian provinces after 1775, while even after the impact of Napoleon, Baden in 1810 still used 112 different measurements of length, 92 measurements for square measures, 65 for dry goods, 163 for fruit, 123 for liquids, 65 for alcohol, and 80 separate definitions of a pound weight.[124]

Public Debt

The real problem was not any sclerosis in imperial institutions, but the general reluctance to tamper with the corporate socio-political order. This is best illustrated by the growing problems of debt as the Empire's larger and smaller territories emerged from the wars of 1672–1714. Unlike the aftermath of the Thirty Years War (see pp. 464–5), the imperial Estates did not work through the Reichstag to tackle this problem collectively. Some territories were able to reduce their liabilities, but all suffered from renewed costly warfare between 1733 and 1763. The Habsburgs alone spent 404.85 million florins fighting three wars from 1733 to 1748. Significant administrative and fiscal reforms from the mid-1740s enabled the monarchy to weather the Seven Years War, which cost around 40 million florins a year. Further post-war measures helped boost net annual revenue to 65 million by 1790, around three times higher than that in 1740. However, debts rose almost as fast, from 118 million (1756) to 291 million florins (1781), while the Turkish War of 1787–91 cost 220.4 million, pushing total liabilities to over 400 million by the outbreak of the French Revolutionary Wars in 1792.[125]

No other territory matched the Habsburgs' revenue, expenditure or debts. While their exposure to debt varied, abstinence from warfare was no guarantee for healthy finances since princely expenses were often proportionately far higher in smaller than larger territories. Maintenance of a princely court consumed one-fifth to one-quarter of peacetime expenditure in most medium-sized and smaller territories compared to 1.7 per cent of Habsburg outgoings in 1784. Minor princes often lived well beyond their means, compensating for their relative lack of real political influence by spending lavishly to assert their status. Ernst Friedrich III of Sachsen-Hildburghausen dined daily with 100 guests while his debts piled up, reaching an astonishing 1.3 million florins by 1769, equivalent to 23 years of his principality's revenue.[126] Prussia's freedom from state debt was misleading, because this derived from ruthless parsimony, while in all other respects the Hohenzollern monarchy shared the same structural problems common throughout the Empire.

By the later eighteenth century, all German (and also Italian) principalities found themselves with fiscal structures that had failed to keep pace with demographic and economic growth. Practicalities partly explain this. Despite improved surveillance and accounting procedures, it remained difficult to assess individual wealth accurately. Since their inception in the fourteenth century, general taxes attempted to target individuals rather than households or communities, but efforts were frustrated by the desire to fix assessment rather than accept that change itself was inevitable and devise more flexible methods instead. Reluctance to divulge details also hindered the compilation of reliable tax registers, while officials entrusted with this task were obliged to respect corporate immunities, though these were never as extensive nor as extreme as in Spain or Hungary. For instance, clergy and nobles rarely possessed complete exemption, even from direct taxes. Indirect taxes proved so attractive because they could be levied on goods in flow without requiring detailed registers of individual or communal wealth. This explains the reluctance to dismantle internal and frontier tolls and tariffs. However, indirect levies were only really lucrative in countries with expanding economies and substantial long-distance, external trade, like Britain and the Dutch Republic.

Consequently, German governments relied on quota systems similar to the Empire's matricular register, apportioning tax burdens amongst communities and in turn within these to households. Quotas generally reinforced corporate distinctions, with clergy, nobles and commons being assigned distinct shares, especially in the case of taxes agreed by territorial Estates. For example, the bishopric of Paderborn used a land tax called the *Schatzung* (Assessment), levied in multiples of a basic quota that was worth about 6,800 talers in 1590. The cathedral canons and the territorial nobles were exempt, leaving the basic quota to be divided amongst the remaining status groups, with the lesser clergy paying about 10 per cent of it, the burghers of the bishopric's 23 towns 40 per cent, and the peasants the remaining half. Subsequent adjustments altered this distribution, notably through the extension of exemption to all clergy by 1700. This reduced the value of a basic quota to only 5,000 talers, obliging the authorities to increase the number of multiple quotas levied each time to maintain overall revenue.[127]

Naturally, favoured groups lobbied hard to defend their corporate advantages. The most significant event in crown–noble relations in Brandenburg-Prussia after 1648 and prior to the emancipation of serfs in 1807 was the widespread protest in 1717 against the king's attempt to commute his vassals' personal military service into taxation. The nobles' appeal to the Reichshofrat only increased the determination of the Hohenzollerns to secure further exemption from imperial jurisdiction. However, the Hohenzollerns' Pomeranian nobles only accepted conversion of their fiefs into allodial property in 1787, thus opening them to taxation, long after Brandenburg-Prussia secured exemption from the jurisdiction of the imperial courts around 1750.[128] Despite securing considerable autonomy, the Hohenzollerns refrained from tampering with the composite character of their monarchy, which remained composed of different provinces still defined by their formal boundaries as imperial fiefs. Each province had its own Estates, even if these now rarely met in plenary diets. While the basic fiscal structure was uniform across the monarchy, its actual implementation rested on agreements with these Estates that no Hohenzollern king dared to disturb.

More fundamentally, throughout the Empire both rulers and ruled refused to accept the true cost of government. Virtually every territorial government, except Prussia's, regularly overspent, with the Habsburg annual deficit fluctuating between 4 million and 80 million florins across 1787–1800.[129] Borrowing had long become an established part of government finance, further illustrating how backward Prussia was in still hoarding a reserve of coins packed into barrels in the palace vault. Princely and civic finances were geared to debt servicing and repayment, rather than tapping rising wealth. Accounting remained primarily legal rather than fiscal, recording liabilities and obligations between governments, their subjects and creditors, rather than attuned to administering budgets.[130] Even though cost estimates and planning had become routine aspects of financial management by the early eighteenth century, governments still operated along late medieval lines by tying individual revenue streams to specific purposes like maintaining the princely household or military expenditure. Each major branch of government had its own treasury, receiving revenue, making expenditure and contracting debts. Money could be switched between accounts, but clear oversight generally remained elusive. The desire to conceal military expenditure from the Estates in some territories simply added to this problem.

Debts were modernized in the sense of becoming eternal, attached to an impersonal state, rather than extinguishing at each ruler's death. However, they remained legal contracts and were personal rather than commercial. The state and the urban and rural corporations comprising it acted like individuals, linked by a multitude of separate contracts to their creditors. Default was difficult, especially as most credit was raised through personal connections between individual officials and lenders. Borrowing on international money markets remained limited, as did attempts in Austria, the Palatinate and elsewhere to establish state banks, especially as these were invariably undercapitalized. Thus, territorial nobles and religious houses remained the principal lenders. Church and charitable institutions owned two-thirds of Bavarian state debt in 1790, compared to only a tenth held by private individuals.

The problem was so intractable because it affected all levels of public institutions, except, ironically, the Empire, which was virtually debt-free (see pp. 405–6). Towns and villages contracted debts not simply for their own purposes, but to meet tax quotas imposed by princes and territorial Estates. Inhabitants also fell into debt as tax arrears were often converted into local debts while their community paid on their behalf. The 6,000 subjects of Ochsenhausen abbey in Swabia owed 584,000 florins in tax arrears by the end of the eighteenth century.[131] Unlike those of Britain and the Dutch Republic, German governments did not make the transition to commercialized debt by issuing tradable bonds. Indeed, most governments were lagging behind their subjects. Before 1618, landlords extended credit to tenants without requiring interest, instead extracting 'payment' in the form of continued subordination. The experience of the Thirty Years War encouraged many to commercialize these arrangements, shifting from social investment and material reward to purely monetary transactions despite official cameralist measures intended to preserve peasants as taxpayers.[132]

Stability and Reluctance to Change

Continued membership of the Empire cushioned territories against the need for radical change by providing a safety value for popular protest through judicial arbitration and administrative review (see pp. 631–7). Imperial institutions also intervened directly to stabilize smaller territories when they got into difficulties. The Reichshofrat handled at least 131 cases involving debts of the imperial knights during the eighteenth century, as well as intervening in imperial cities, counties and small principalities. Württemberg alone acted as imperial debt commissioner in 120 cases in Swabia between 1648 and 1806. Commissioners could be tough: those in Sachsen-Hildburghausen called in military assistance from neighbouring territories in 1769 when the local prince refused to accept their reforms, which included disbanding the principality's oversized army. Moreover, commissions achieved real successes. That sent to the imperial city of Nördlingen reduced its debt from 696,176 florins in 1750 to 84,408 in 1793.[133]

Such action sustained weaker micro-territories like Waldeck-Pyrmont, which Prince Friedrich Karl August was forced to pawn to Hessen-Kassel in 1784 for 1.2 million talers just to cover his most pressing debts, after his own Estates refused to accept further liabilities. With Hessen-Kassel already the prince's main creditor along with the Dutch Republic, it seemed likely that the next step would be full annexation, but Waldeck's autonomy was saved by intervention from the Reichshofrat in 1804, which appointed Prussia as its commissioner. Even at this late stage in the Empire formal processes still functioned. In January 1805 the prince abdicated in favour of his younger brother, who accepted drastic economies proposed by Prussia, which refrained from abusing its position to annex Waldeck itself. The commission dissolved along with the Empire in August 1806, but Waldeck saved itself by joining Napoleon's new Confederation of the Rhine, weathering the subsequent storms of German political history to survive as a separate entity until 1922.[134]

These examples could be multiplied, but the general point is that intervention stabilized cities and principalities by adjusting existing constitutional and fiscal arrangements. Further, more radical changes were considered not merely undesirable but unnecessary. The overriding impression gained from reading accounts of these individual cases is that those involved did not believe that their socio-political order was 'broken'. While one-third of Mainz knights were involved in debt cases, they remained wealthy as a group, especially the Catholics, who enjoyed access to plum positions in the imperial church. Whereas the imperial city of Wimpfen was crippled by the 1770–72 famine, others like Aalen and Zell am Hammersbach remained debt-free despite their small size and other problems. The imperial prelates on average held only 138 square kilometres with 2,400 subjects each – some had no taxpayers at all. They deliberately avoided modernization by keeping their administration simple to reduce overheads, yet they were hugely successful on their own terms, and able to embark on costly baroque church-building using income from donations and pilgrims. Some were even able to purchase autonomy, like Neresheim abbey, which bought out Öttingen's protectorate rights to join the ranks of Swabian prelates in 1764.[135]

There was likewise no sense of impending crisis in the larger territories. Despite its rocketing debts, interest payments consumed only 30 per cent of Habsburg expenditure, as opposed to 60 per cent in France. The resilience of the existing order was further demonstrated by its ability to manage the renewed burden of major war after 1792.

Baden raised 13 loans totalling 8 million florins between 1794 and 1805, against a pre-war debt of just 65,000 florins, whereas Bavaria, despite 20 million florins of debts, was still able to raise 31 loans totalling 14 million across the same period.[136] The Empire's political components and corporate groups generally achieved what mattered to them: preserving their autonomy and sustaining their material existence. While the Empire's constitutional order did not prevent adjustments, it certainly made radical changes less likely.

I I

Association

LEAGUES AND ASSOCIATIONS

Political Tendencies and Common Features

The creative tension between lordship and fellowship characterizing relations between lords and communities was present in all forms of association. Exploring these underscores the previous chapter's argument that political and social orders were mutually reinforcing. Associations were almost invariably based on members of a similar socio-political status and were formed to advance corporate goals. They provided a means to transcend localism by providing a framework for individuals or communities of similar status to combine for mutual benefit. Most associations were formed to preserve existing status and privileges, but they could also seek to expand their members' influence and bargain new rights. Emperors often viewed princely alliances with suspicion, while peasant and artisan movements generally appeared subversive, and have certainly been presented as such by many historians. Associational forms emerged alongside Estates society, which they reinforced rather than challenged. Their relationship to the Empire was broadly similar, and only two leagues, albeit important ones, led to the formation of independent states (Switzerland and the Dutch Republic).

Regardless of their different status, all corporate groups combined in similar ways. Until well into early modernity, all associations were at heart sworn alliances (*coniurationes*, or *Einungen*). These had already appeared amongst the Frankish clergy in the eighth century and spread to laity in the eleventh as a way to secure aid and protection on a mutual and more symmetrical basis than through subordination to a lord. As we have seen (pp. 513–15), sworn associations were import-ant to the foundation of new towns and the urban communal movements. Townsfolk agreed to treat each other as brothers, creating a larger and formalized extended kinship. Oaths gave alliances a sacral character, heightened by the culture of personal presence. Members gathered together and signalled their participation by holding up the first two fingers of their right hand as their 'oath fingers' (*Schwur-finger*); hence the punishment of cutting off these fingers for those accused of breaking their promises.

The sacral element was strengthened by common religious activities like celebrating mass and venerating specific saints as patrons of an organization. Guilds, for instance, often maintained their own chapel and marched together in civic religious processions. This aspect peaked between the thirteenth and fifteenth centuries when many associations were specifically founded for prayer or charitable purposes. The theo-logical aspect lessened in Protestant areas with the Reformation, which undermined the basis for 'good works', but the Counter-Reformation gave renewed impetus in Catholic regions, notably with the establish-ment of Marian cults.[1] Written culture contributed to lessening the religious element by allowing members to communicate across greater distances. Alliances were now enshrined in treaties, often signed and sealed by representatives acting for absent masters, though nobles clung to the practice of swearing personal oaths longer than did cities. The overlap between presence and written culture was strongest during the sixteenth and seventeenth centuries when common activities remained important elements in fostering solidarity. For example, Strasbourg's guilds were known after the taverns where they met rather than by their trades. Princes and lords shared these changes of culture. For example, weddings and funerals provided important opportunities for political discussions and were a major feature of Protestant alliances.[2]

Oaths and charters were generally fixed in purpose and scope. Most associations were time-limited, though some were hereditary pacts binding on heirs and descendants. Exceptions were usually made so that individual members did not contravene any existing obligations to non-members. This became routine for all alliances between imperial Estates during early modernity, which usually stated they were not directed against the emperor or Empire. Members were nominally equal, unless the alliance combined several status groups. Equality was understood in terms of law, status and honour, but could take on a broader meaning in the more radical forms of association emerging in the high Middle Ages. Such trends were not restricted to those movements later historians have labelled as 'popular'. For example, nobles also advocated openness and transparency, encouraging each member to declare his wealth under oath to ensure fair distribution of common burdens. Princes placed the least emphasis on equality, and were reluctant to enter blanket, open-ended arrangements that might threaten their autonomy. However, internal stratification was apparent in all associations, including those of the 'common man' (see pp. 579–94).

Regardless of their social composition, virtually all associations at least nominally elected their leaders, even if in practice it was often clear who the successful candidates would be. Nobles preferred small advisory committees, regarding plenary meetings as inconvenient and expensive. Towns preferred full meetings, since their own governments already included citizens' assemblies balancing city councils, and alliances combining more than one status group adopted a similar approach.

Lay Associations

The spread of associations to laity in the eleventh century was part of the general disappearance of older forms of servitude and the adoption of more communal forms of living. As we have seen (pp. 240–42 and 487–9), both processes were related to the emergence of Estates society and thus also to hierarchy and the political order. The freedom to associate was never entirely autonomous and all alliances were concerned to assert their legitimacy. Most alliances appearing between 1100 and 1300 were local and related to specific economic activities and aspects of urban life. Merchants' guilds were already appearing in northern Germany during the eleventh century, because individual lords were unable to protect long-distance traders. By combining, merchants were able to bargain for recognition and security from lords along their trade routes. Artisans' and traders' guilds emerged during the twelfth century to protect specific economic interests, such as fish-sellers in Worms (1106), Würzburg cobblers (1128) and Mainz weavers (1175). Such groups were always more than purely economic organizations.

They certainly acted as closed shops, demanding high qualifications as barriers to new entrants, and imposing self-regulation and quality controls to discriminate against others seeking to engage in their trade. However, they also operated an internal moral economy to ensure all members had reasonable opportunities to make a living, and sustained collegiality by helping each other in the event of personal or family misfortune, and through various social and religious activities. Guilds proved potent platforms from which to bargain for rights and demand a share in communal government. Frederick II issued decrees banning them as subversive in 1219 and 1231, but their utility as a means of organizing and controlling trades ensured they continued.[3]

Apprentices' and journeymen's brotherhoods appeared during the economic depression of the 1330s and spread following the Black Death in reaction to the guilds' increasing exclusivity. The practice of restricting masters' titles to the sons of existing guild members excluded journeymen economically and politically. Craft guilds and journeymen's associations survived into the nineteenth century, long after the merchants' organizations had lost their function as international trade developed during the seventeenth century with greater legal protection from territorial governments. Journeymen followed craftsmen by making membership selective rather than voluntary, despite their continued outward assertions of freedom.

Lay organizations had already assumed their definitive form by the later fourteenth century, with further development restricted largely to consolidating existing practices. These organizations had become a permanent feature of towns and also rural crafts in many areas. As urban society matured, it spawned other associations, notably shooting clubs (*Schützengesellschaften*) between the thirteenth and sixteenth centuries. Their members were initially armed with crossbows, and, though they updated their weaponry to firearms as these developed, the shooting clubs remained primarily expressions of neighbourhood identity rather than practical military organizations.[4] Humanist debating societies developed in the fifteenth century, such as the *Societas Rhenania*, founded in Heidelberg in 1495. These rarely had over 30 members each and declined during the confessional tension of the Reformation era, only to re-emerge around 1600 with a new focus on language and science. The Empire lagged behind Britain and France in developing coffee-house culture from the late seventeenth century, partly because it lacked such easy access to imported coffee, while the modest size of most towns restricted the market for what remained a luxury product. Vienna had only 80 cafés in the 1780s compared to 900 in Paris. However, the Empire's polycentric socio-political structure encouraged a much more evenly distributed intellectual culture, especially given the equally broad spread of literacy and media outlets. There were 50 to 60 'patriotic' and economic societies by the late eighteenth century, whose 4,500 members debated practical aspects of public life ranging from political economy to bee-keeping, and often published their own journals. In addition, there were 430 reading societies, with up to 20,000 members, and 250 to 300 freemasons' lodges, with a similar membership.[5]

Unlike monastic orders that operated internationally, the Empire's lay organizations remained local. The craftsmen's and journeymen's associations did not seek to federate between towns or across territories on the basis of common trades. Very few of the intellectual societies recruited members beyond their home region, though the relatively free flow of information allowed them to communicate with each other. Social life in the new universities established in Germany during the late fifteenth century was initially organized around their academic structure of four faculties: theology, law, medicine and philosophy. However, by 1600, student societies had formed around young men on the basis of their home region rather than subject of study. For instance, Rostock University, which only admitted around 200 students annually in the 1640s, had separate societies for Pomeranians, Westphalians, Brandenburgers, Silesians, Thuringians, Brunswickers, Prussians, Frisians, Holsteiners and Scandinavians, in addition to local boys from Mecklenburg.[6]

NOBLES AND PRINCES

The Electors' League

Associations between nobles and princes lacked the basis in physical proximity underpinning organizations like guilds within individual communities, but otherwise they shared many common features. They claimed to be free associations of legally empowered individuals, like those joining groups within communities, but unlike civic leagues, where communities combined as collective actors. Despite their more elevated socio-political status, combinations of nobles and princes were likewise often regarded as subversive by their superiors, notably during Henry IV's reign. Princes initially had little interest in alliances, operating instead as kinship groups rather than as dynastic families needing allies. By contrast, collegiality developed much earlier among the electors, who shared an interest (like guildsmen) in excluding others from their organization.

The seven electors held 18 meetings independent of royal elections between 1273 and 1409, demonstrating a sense of corporate identity and responsibility for the Empire.[7] The process of excluding papal interference encouraged the formation of the Electors' League (*Kurverein*) in 1338, which became their main vehicle to assert collective pre-eminence over other princes through an exclusive, direct relationship to the emperor.[8] Their identity was enshrined in the Golden Bull of 1356, which confirmed their right of free assembly. The four Rhenish electors of Mainz, Cologne, Trier and the Palatinate remained more influential than those in Bohemia, Saxony or Brandenburg throughout the later Middle Ages, partly because the latter three were held by the ruling Luxembourg family or its close allies. It was this Rhenish group that deposed Wenzel in 1400 and planned to do the same with Sigismund in 1424. However, the Hussite emergency encouraged Brandenburg and Saxony to cooperate more closely with their Rhenish colleagues, while the parallel decline of the three ecclesiastical electors relative to neighbouring secular princes prompted them to welcome greater collaboration. The Luxembourgs' demise in 1437 ended the direct possession of an electorate by the monarch until the Habsburgs acquired Bohemia in 1526, further encouraging collegiality.

However, tensions continually resurfaced, especially between Mainz and the Palatinate, and prevented the electors dominating the Reichstag as it emerged around 1495. The four Rhenish electors remained the active core, leading the process of electing Charles V and holding at least 15 meetings separate from their other three colleagues during his reign. Their attempt to assert exclusive leadership had failed by 1567, ensuring the electors remained a single college, despite new tensions following the conversion of the elector Palatine (1560) and his Brandenburg colleague (1613) to Calvinism. The Electors' League was confirmed in 1558 and 1635, but the development of the permanent Reichstag after 1663 removed the need for separate meetings.[9] This brief survey already reveals a pattern that will reappear throughout this chapter. Collaboration developed along corporate-status lines in the late Middle Ages, assumed more institutional form around 1500, and was ultimately rendered superfluous by the Reichstag's permanence after 1663, leading to a decline in most forms of political associations.

Aristocratic Associations

Aristocratic associations developed in response to the adverse circumstances affecting many nobles from the mid-thirteenth century, including the growth of more coherent principalities and more potent towns, as well as economic fluctuations. While many lesser lords thrived by exploiting the new opportunities, there were always large numbers who found themselves squeezed between assertive peasants and aggressive princes. Princes and other titled aristocrats like counts were emerging as clearly superior to knights and other untitled lords, who were simultaneously losing their immediate relationship to the emperor (see pp. 375–7). Charles IV's wholesale dissipation of the crown lands accelerated this trend from the 1370s and princes replaced the emperor as lord over many of the Empire's lesser fiefs.

The knights and other lesser nobles were not doomed feudal reactionaries, nor is there evidence of any general 'crisis of the aristocracy'.[10] Götz von Berlichingen was the most famous of the 'robber barons', immortalized in Goethe's play of 1773, which presents his predicament as exemplifying a clash between old and new orders. As the fifth and youngest son of a family of Swabian knights, Götz's options indeed appeared limited and he pursued 15 separate feuds that eventually made his name as both a troublemaker and a skilled commander. In fact, he adapted well to the changing circumstances, amassing considerable wealth and writing his autobiography, which eventually served as Goethe's source material. Götz's knightly contemporary, Ulrich von Hutten, was one of the Empire's leading intellectuals. Franz von Sickingen, who died leading the Knights Revolt in 1523, exemplified the many former ministeriales who rose in princely service. Sickingen's own family secured the status of immediacy in 1488, while he acquired land, castles and considerable wealth through controlling the Palatinate's mercury mines. Like other knights, he both fought princes and served them as a mercenary commander and moneylender.

Thus, we should see the associations of the lesser lords and knights both as means to defend their autonomy amidst often threatening circumstances and as vehicles for individuals to profit from those same circumstances. Knights were not averse to serving princes, but they generally wished to preserve or acquire immediacy. The counts of the Harz region in north Germany attempted this by forming a sworn association based on kinship to manage their possessions collectively as a condominium. Like townsfolk and guildsmen, they hoped to minimize internal discord, because this threatened to expose them to potentially dangerous neighbours. To this end, they forswore feuding and agreed to submit disputes to common arbitration, as well as to cooperate in exploiting their mines and to ransom any member captured in disputes with outsiders.[11] The Harz region failed to develop as a coherent territory when the individual counties were acquired by neighbouring princes. However, princely families also found similar arrangements useful to preserve collective weight if dynastic partition had created several branches sharing relatively small areas, as was the case among the Welfs, the Askanier in Anhalt and the Ernestine Saxons into the seventeenth century. The spread of primogeniture and the development of a clearer status hierarchy discouraged this practice by identifying princely rank and constitutional rights more precisely with individual imperial fiefs by the 1580s.

Lesser lords also collaborated by pooling resources to build and maintain 'co-heirship castles' (*Ganerbenburgen*) like Burg Friedberg on the Middle Rhine founded in 1337 by 12 families who elected a common castellan. Such groups were quite common in Hessen, Baden, Württemberg, Alsace, Lower Saxony and the Palatinate, where the knights were more common than in eastern Germany. Like the Harz counts' condominium, this form of co-proprietorship was binding on heirs and linked to internal discipline and self-sacrifice. For example, members who engaged in unsanctioned feuds were to be expelled for endangering the collective. The Friedberg group demonstrated considerable potential, acquiring the mortgage to the imperial city of the same name in 1455, and buying the county of Kaichen 20 years later. This enabled the Friedberg group to play an influential role in both the Wetterau counts' group after 1492 and the Rhenish imperial knights' canton, securing survival as a miniature aristocratic republic until annexed by Hessen-Darmstadt at the Empire's dissolution in 1806.[12]

While such groups based on kinship and co-ownership were tolerated, associations between unrelated noblemen were viewed with suspicion after the formation of the first such league in 1331. The Golden Bull condemned such organizations as conspiratorial, but the prevailing circumstances continued to compel lesser lords to band together and so new leagues emerged after 1360. Faced with the Hussite insurrection and lacking his own territory within the Empire, Sigismund saw advantages in cooperating with the nobles and granted privileges to all knights, including those lacking immediacy, endorsing the formation of knights' unions in 1422.

While their social character was broadly uniform, the political direction of knights' unions diverged according to local circumstances. Those formed in less-populated areas were generally obliged to define themselves relative to only one locally dominant prince and so had less room to manoeuvre than organizations that could bargain with several powerful lords. Violence could erupt if the local princely family split internally, as occurred amongst the Habsburgs in the fourteenth century, or if the prince accumulated large debts or pursued dangerous external policies. Frederick III did both in the 1450s, prompting 39 Austrian nobles to establish the Mailberg League in October 1451. This soon expanded to 500 members, including Bohemians and Hungarians, and ultimately the League besieged him in Wiener Neustadt. Frederick clashed again with his nobles in 1461–3 and 1469–71, and while he prevented them from emancipating themselves as free knights, he had to allow them a greater say in managing Austria through the provincial Estates.[13]

A broadly similar pattern emerged in Bavaria, where the duke slowly persuaded his knights after 1311 that their status and privileges derived from him, rather than from some ancient right. Although this undercut claims to be immediate, it offered the Bavarian knights improved protection against other nobles during feuds, as well as opening employment opportunities in the duchy's expanding administration. The Württemberg counts employed similar methods to encourage dependency and secure a ready pool of armed retainers. However, the Bavarian knights saw disputes within the ducal family after 1489 as an opportunity to escape its jurisdiction and established a league known as the *Löwler-bund*. Within five years they were obliged to accept submission in return for improved local corporate rights, which expanded in 1557 to representation in the Bavarian Estates. As in Austria, Estates representation enabled the nobles to oblige their prince to negotiate how much their tenants should pay in territorial taxes. Their position was consolidated through their employment as tax collectors and district officials.[14]

The chances to preserve autonomy were better in regions with more people and resources, like Swabia, Franconia and the Rhineland. The greater proximity of nobles encouraged cooperation, while princely jurisdictions were split, opening niches for more autonomy. Additionally, these regions were heartlands of the imperial church, which provided nobles with alternative employment, income and influence, lessening their dependency on secular masters. For example, princely power was split in Franconia by the fifteenth century between the margraves of Ansbach and Bayreuth and the bishops of Bamberg and Würzburg, together with a number of counts and other more modest lords. Württemberg's influence in Swabia was balanced by the Habsburgs, whose possessions in nearby Alsace and the Breisgau allowed them to intervene as local princes as well as in their capacity after 1438 as the imperial family. This already proved significant during the events in Bavaria between 1489 and 1494 when the emperor initially backed the Löwler League to force Bavaria's duke to relinquish his grip on the heavily indebted imperial city of Regensburg.

Swabia saw the formation in 1408 of the most important knights' organization, the League of St George's Shield (*St Georgenschild*). This soon encompassed all Swabian free nobles and many of those in Franconia who joined to defend their autonomy against powerful princes. Although the League declined after 1468, it revived two decades later when it was given greater coherence through regional subdivision into four 'quarters' and the creation of a court to regulate internal disputes. By that point, 29 prelates and 26 counts and barons were members along with 531 knights. The decision to back the Habsburgs in the Swiss War of 1499 overstretched the League. Many found membership too costly and numbers plummeted to 27 prelates, 10 counts and barons and just 60 knights. Attempts to revive it in 1512 foundered on growing status tensions, especially as the counts and prelates were better placed to participate in the new institutions created by imperial reform and no longer wanted such close ties to people they regarded as socially inferior.[15]

The Knights Revolt, 1522–3

As we have seen (pp. 408–9), the introduction of imperial taxes forced those claiming 'free' status to decide whether to pay to retain this, or risk losing immediacy by avoiding the new burdens. The knights had already resisted attempts by princes to include them in the new territorial taxes developed after the mid-fourteenth century (see pp. 531–4). Many opted out of the territorial Estates that emerged at this point by claiming they were 'free' and thus exempt from such burdens. Although the knights were usually personally exempt, they realized that the new taxes would take a significant proportion of their tenants' rents, thereby reducing their own incomes just as it was becoming more expensive to fund an aristocratic lifestyle. When the Franconian princes convened in 1495 to discuss collecting the new Common Penny agreed by the Reichstag, the local knights responded with the classic argument that they were exempt because they already paid a 'blood tax' as society's warriors.[16]

It is here that we can see another example of how society and politics interacted in the Empire. Unlike territorial taxes, the Common Penny and subsequent imperial levies enjoyed a higher legitimacy through being sanctioned by the Reichstag and through their purpose in upholding justice and repelling the Turks. Simultaneously, imperial reform disadvantaged the knights relative to the princes, who were now clearly identified as the prime guardians of the eternal public peace that had outlawed feuding. Princely dignity and status were anchored constitutionally, whereas knights had lost an important means of defending their autonomy, rank and honour. The new order was underlined by the deposition of Duke Ulrich of Württemberg for murdering a love rival and annexing the imperial city of Esslingen, which led to the imperial sequestration of his duchy between 1519 and 1534.[17] The message was clear: princes had nothing to gain from defying the new order and everything to lose.

The situation was more complicated for the knights, who lacked both resources and a firm role in the new institutions. Although individually weak, they retained potential through cooperation. Franz von Sickingen and Götz von Berlichingen demonstrated this in 1515 when they drew on their personal contacts to recruit 7,000 mercenaries for their feud with the city of Worms. Seven years later they mustered 2,000 cavalry and 10,000 infantry against the elector of Trier. Unfortunately, at the time this made the knights appear an even greater threat to the Empire's peace and the newly institutionalized status hierarchy. Matters deteriorated as Sickingen convened a series of congresses in 1521–2 culminating in the formation of the Landau League of Swabian and Rhenish knights. There was nothing unusual about this organization, which displayed all the features of previous knightly associations, as well as those being formed among the counts to assert collective influence in the Reichstag. The Landau members promised mutual aid and forswore internal feuds. However, the wider circumstances, combined with the knights' continued refusal to pay imperial taxes, made their organization immediately subversive.

The response also showed how much had been changed by imperial reform. Charles V's brother Ferdinand mobilized support through the Empire's new legal and peacekeeping mechanisms. Sickingen and his fellow knights were branded outlaws, making them fair game for the south-western princes who mobilized against them. Sickingen died as his castle of Landstuhl was pummelled by princely artillery on 7 May 1523. The princes went on to demolish a further 23 castles.[18] Already suffering from the advanced stages of syphilis, Ulrich von Hutten fled to an island on Lake Zürich where he died three months later, while the surviving knights submitted to princely authority.

Imperial Knighthood

The Franconian knights largely abstained from backing Sickingen, already adopting a less confrontational course after 1507 by stressing subordination to the emperor. By 1532, they and their Swabian counterparts accepted the logic of their own argument and paid a 'voluntary subsidy' (*subsidium charitativum*) direct to Ferdinand.[19] This decision to contribute directly secured the hybrid status of imperial knighthood (*Reichsritterschaft*). The knights remained personally free under the emperor and distinct from mediate territorial nobles solely under a prince. Imperial knights thus did not participate in territorial Estates, causing those still doing so in Swabia and Franconia to opt out. However, the knights were not full imperial Estates since their earlier refusal to pay imperial taxes had led to their exclusion from the Reichstag and the Kreis Assemblies. For this reason, they were excluded from the religious settlement of 1555 and denied the right of Reformation to manage their own churches. Lacking full imperial fiefs, the knights also only possessed lesser criminal jurisdiction, meaning their tenants were subject to princely courts for more serious offences. In fact, though their possessions were immediate, they were also frequently bound in vassalage to local princes and generally followed their lead in religious matters.[20]

However, additional imperial privileges in 1559 exempted the knights and their tenants from being taxed or conscripted by princes, who were obliged to accept the knights' fiefs as 'freer' than ordinary mediate fiefs. The situation remained in flux as the pace of imperial reform slowed in the later sixteenth century. Many knights pushed for allodification of their fiefs, meaning their conversion to direct personal possessions, which would have removed princely jurisdiction entirely and left them only with the emperor as direct overlord.

The ambiguities were exposed by another, more localized revolt, instigated by Wilhelm von Grumbach, a knight who played king-maker in the bishopric of Würzburg by securing the election of his preferred candidate, Konrad von Bibra, in 1540. Bibra's death three years later exposed Grumbach to the revenge of the man he had originally defeated, Melchior Zobel von Giebelstadt. Grumbach skilfully exploited all the Empire's mid-sixteenth century problems, which provides a further reason to explore this incident in detail. The backdrop was the aftermath of Charles V's victory over the Schmalkaldic League and his attempt to reorganize imperial management, which eventually led to the Princes Revolt of 1552. As elsewhere, Franconian lords were entangled in a myriad of local disputes over churches, landownership, territorial and criminal jurisdictions, and the pressures resulting from attempts to forge more centrally steered fiscal and administrative systems at the territorial level. All lords from prince to knight were also struggling to accommodate younger sons amidst changing forms of inheritance.

Like Sickingen, Grumbach was no reactionary throwback, and he exploited opportunities provided by the new institutions, including

winning a case in the Reichskammergericht against Zobel over possession of his Würzburg knight's fief. Grumbach secured the backing of
princes who had been punished by the Habsburgs for picking the wrong
side in the larger conflicts in the Empire between 1546 and 1553, notably the notoriously unruly Margrave Albrecht Alcibiades, who had
been his pupil, and the Ernestine Saxon Johann Friedrich II, who had
lost his electoral title to his Albertine cousin following defeat in the
Schmalkaldic War. However, Grumbach also deliberately played the
theme of the 'good old days' of knightly autonomy to rally support.
Without his knowledge, one of his supporters murdered Zobel in 1558.
The new bishop blamed Grumbach and confiscated his fief. Grumbach's decision in 1563 to retaliate by declaring a feud transformed a
complex case in which no party was entirely innocent, into a clear
breach of imperial law.

Crucially, the new emperor, Maximilian II, decided to work through
the institutional framework to restore peace, rather than accept the
offer of an alliance with the knights against the princes. Efforts to
defuse the situation in 1566 through talks in the Reichstag failed when
Johann Friedrich II declared for Grumbach in the hope of recovering
his lost electoral title. Maximilian branded the unfortunate Grumbach
and his allies outlaws, thus sanctioning a repeat of 1523 as the south
German princes combined to restore order by force. Grumbach was
captured and executed to make an example in 1567.[21]

The 'Grumbach Affair' attracted attention across the Empire, not
least for wild rumours of conspiracies involving Calvinists and the
French. However, its real importance was in demonstrating both the
effectiveness of imperial reform and how it had created a new constitutional order. By 1566 it was already obvious that there was little
enthusiasm amongst the knights and territorial nobles for aristocratic
associations as alternatives to accommodation with the Empire and
princes. The latter worked to defuse tension by accepting the knights as
junior, but nonetheless legitimate, partners in the Empire's status hierarchy. The 1566 Reichstag confirmed that knights could incorporate
their fiefs into 'cantons' on a regional basis, thereby giving them a
distinct, common organization to secure autonomy whilst they still
remained vassals of princes. The knights united as a common corporate group in 1570, agreeing to pay contributions to the emperor to
subsidize defence against the Turks, and establishing a permanent

infrastructure of five Swabian, six Franconian and three Rhenish cantons, plus a further, autonomous Alsatian canton. Although they held common congresses after 1577, cantonal organization remained restricted to membership fees that supported a small staff handling correspondence with imperial institutions. The most important attribute of self-regulation was the ability to decide collectively on applications from outsiders for membership.[22]

Internal solidarity remained heavily influenced by long-established family alliances, kinship and communal property ownership, like that at Friedberg. Cronyism and nepotism prevailed over confessional differences, except for increased tensions during the period 1590–1640. Knights established a firm grip on the cathedral chapters in Mainz, Bamberg, Würzburg and several other important church lands, enabling individual families like the Schönborns to exercise considerable influence in seventeenth- and eighteenth-century imperial politics.[23]

Princes broadly accepted the consolidation of imperial knighthood since this contained the knights as a distinct group, thus reducing the likelihood that their own territorial nobles would gain similar freedoms. There were some 1,600 to 1,700 imperial knights' fiefs in the late eighteenth-century Empire. Together, these encompassed 10,455 square kilometres with 450,000 inhabitants, making them collectively equivalent to one of the larger principalities such as Hessen-Kassel or Salzburg. However, these fiefs were split between around 400 families and were scattered across south and west Germany. By contrast there were 1,400 mediate church and knightly fiefs in Bavaria alone, and perhaps around 50,000 noble families in Germany, with many more in the Habsburg and Hohenzollern lands outside the Empire.[24]

Residual jurisdiction still allowed princes to mediatize knights' fiefs, for example if families died out or broke the law. The Franconian margraves recovered 99 fiefs in this way between 1618 and 1730, while the bishop of Würzburg suppressed 29. The dukes of Württemberg simply bought 21 fiefs between 1545 and 1724. Other forms of pressure could be applied, such as damming crucial streams or restricting the movement of goods and people. Württemberg, Hessen, Ansbach and the Palatinate were the most aggressive towards the knights, notably during Charles VII's weak imperial rule (1742–5).[25]

The knights responded by seeking to upgrade their status from 'members of the Empire' (*membra imperii*) to full imperial Estates, but they continually undermined their case by refusing to accept additional burdens. The Wetterau counts had already accepted these in 1495 and secured a collective vote in the Reichstag's princely college. The formalization of a clearer status hierarchy through imperial reform encouraged the counts to break ranks with the knights. The Wetterau counts had already separated from the local imperial knights in 1511, while the acquisition of similar collective votes by the Swabian, Franconian and Westphalian counts reduced cooperation in these regions too.[26] The knights further wrecked their chances by recklessly insisting on precedence ahead of the imperial cities during negotiations to include them in the Reichstag in the 1640s. Further attempts later in the seventeenth century and again in the 1770s foundered on similar problems. The knights' relationship to the Empire remained largely personal and direct to the emperor. They continued to pay significant voluntary contributions in wartime, while many validated their status by serving in the Habsburg army; over 80 knights held the rank of general or colonel in the Thirty Years War alone.[27]

Cross-Status Alliances

The knights' relationship to the counts points to the difficulties encountered during early modernity in forming alliances across different status groups. A coincidence of interests could overcome this at regional level, especially in the south-west, which had the highest concentration of cities, knights, lords and princes. Most of these combined with Frederick III to form the Swabian League on 14 February 1488 (Map 18). The most potent of all late medieval regional alliances, the League absorbed the smaller Lower Union, founded in 1474, as well as the St George's Shield association. Frederick joined in his capacity as Austrian archduke, allowing him to cooperate with a wide range of his socio-political inferiors without compromising his personal authority as emperor.

The League mixed elements of late medieval associations, like forswearing feuds and promising mutual aid, with new ideas deriving from imperial reform, including a quota system for military and financial contributions, and a coordinating council composed of representatives from all status groups. The members deliberately reconstituted their organization in 1500 as a formal league, dropping the earlier label 'union' (*Einung*) with its roots in looser, sworn associations.[28] Despite its failure against the Swiss in 1499, the League prevailed over Bavaria in freeing Regensburg in 1492, liberated Esslingen from Ulrich of Württemberg in 1519, crushed the Knights Revolt in 1523, and surmounted the far greater challenge of the Peasants War in 1524–6. Importantly, cross-status solidarity proved stronger than cooperation in separate groups. Württemberg left the League in 1512, because its duke refused to work with the cities, yet his attempt to found an alternative, exclusively princely alliance collapsed amidst mutual recriminations. Similarly, the knightly St George's Shield association withered because the League appeared to offer better security.

A major factor in the League's success was its firm basis in imperial law, which had encouraged regional collaboration to uphold the public peace since the twelfth century. This became more complicated as the League expanded to include members across the Rhineland and central and south-east Germany, notably during the suppression of the peasants in 1524–6. By then, however, the League was already being rendered redundant by the parallel development of institutions created through imperial reform (see pp. 402–12). These appeared more attractive, partly thanks to their broader constitutional basis and closer relationship to the emperor, but also because they were more clearly organized hierarchically along status lines. The north German princes had already refused to join the League because, like Württemberg, they did not want to share power so evenly with the cities. The League's court dealt with an average of five cases annually, whereas the number of cases brought by Swabians to the Reichskammergericht rose from 20 in 1500 to between 30 and 40 after 1515, prompting the League to subordinate its own judiciary to the new imperial court.[29] Finally, the Habsburgs realized that imperial institutions were more useful, because they offered a way to engage with all imperial Estates, whereas the League's members remained primarily concerned with their own region and, for instance, refused to back Maximilian I in his war with Venice in 1508. Whereas the Empire was eternal, the League was time-limited, requiring periodic negotiations to renew it. Habsburg-Bavarian tension further eroded cohesion and the last charter was allowed to expire on 2 February 1534.

Confessional Leagues

Confessional tension was a further factor undermining the Swabian League and a new element in imperial politics. Confession appeared to offer an alternative to regionalism as a way of uniting different status groups across a much wider area. The Schmalkaldic League emerged in 1531 from a northern group of Lutheran imperial Estates led by Saxony, and a southern group organized by Hessen.[30] The Protestant Union (1608), Catholic League (1609) and Heilbronn League (1633) also demonstrated confession's ability to foster solidarity across social and geographical distance. All four organizations included electors, princes, counts and cities from across the Empire (Map 19).

Apart from their confessional character, all resembled the Swabian League in combining traditional mutual aid and internal peace with the more formalized structures emerging from imperial reform, including written charters, governing councils balanced by plenary congresses, and the quota system to distribute burdens. The alliances, like the Empire, thus possessed mechanisms to mobilize forces when required, rather than permanent armies. They also copied the new regional framework of the Kreise. The Schmalkaldic and Catholic leagues had northern and southern 'directories', while a further south-western directory was briefly added to the Catholic League in 1615–17. The Protestant Union had a more geographically restricted membership consisting mainly of western and central German territories. Its successor, the Heilbronn League, was formed by Sweden to coordinate its German allies during the Thirty Years War and expressly used the Kreis structure to group the smaller Protestant and occupied territories of Swabia, Franconia, the Upper and the Electoral Rhine. Negotiations failed to include the larger principalities from the two Saxon Kreise. The Heilbronn League convened only two congresses and collapsed soon after Sweden's defeat to the Habsburgs at Nördlingen in 1634. Although also weak, the Protestant Union nonetheless held 25 plenary congresses across its 13-year existence, matching the activity of its Schmalkaldic predecessor. The Catholic League also met frequently, both during its first incarnation from 1609 to 1617, and again once it was revived with imperial permission between 1619 and 1634. All four mobilized substantial armed forces, especially the Schmalkalders, who fought Charles V in 1546–7, and the Catholic League, which backed Ferdinand II during the Thirty Years War.

Yet it is going too far to claim that any of these organizations possessed 'true state-like qualities'.[31] None added to the range of institutional forms already pioneered by the Swabian League and imperial reform. All struggled to legitimate themselves, since appeals to confession could – and did – contradict loyalty to the emperor. The Schmalkalders already suffered severe internal tensions, because not all of them were willing to accept the more radical Protestant resistance theories (see pp. 109–10). Their comprehensive defeat in 1547 rendered purely confessional arguments doubly suspect thereafter. The Protestant Union laboured to present itself instead as a temporary auxiliary to the formal imperial institutions which it claimed had broken down, arguments that its own leadership undermined through their part in disrupting the Reichstag and imperial courts. Individual members fought the Habsburgs during the Thirty Years War, but the Union dissolved itself rather than break openly with the emperor. The Catholic League faced similar problems and was pushed into dissolving itself by Emperor Matthias in 1617. Its revival two years later owed much to the skills of its founder, Duke Maximilian I of Bavaria, who presented his organization merely as an auxiliary to official efforts at restoring peace on the emperor's terms. Maximilian delayed military operations until he received mandates authorizing action against the emperor's enemies.[32]

Concern over legitimacy deterred many potential members. The Schmalkaldic League had only recruited 23 imperial Estates by 1535, while the Union peaked at around 30 members, or barely half of all Protestant territories. Only three of the larger principalities joined the Heilbronn League, restricting its membership to the weaker counts and cities. The Catholic League was essentially a Bavarian-led alliance of the imperial church lands, with a few associated counts and cities. The Union and Catholic League were primarily vehicles for the interests of the rival Palatine and Bavarian branches of the Wittelsbachs. Apart from the Heilbronn League, which was formed in wartime, the other alliances were split between a majority who saw membership as insurance should sectarianism descend into violence, and a conspiratorial minority who secretly relished the prospect of confrontation. Like the Swabian League, all found it difficult to hold their leadership to account, especially as princes used personal meetings to hatch plans outside the formal framework of councils and congresses.

Kreis Associations

The Swabian League's vitality inhibited the activation of the Kreis structure in that region. The first Swabian Kreis assembly only convened in 1542, eight years after the League's charter expired.[33] Thereafter, Swabia became the most active and effective of all ten Kreise, because its collective institutions repeatedly proved their worth in resolving common problems in this, the most territorially fragmented of the Empire's regions. The more inclusive character of Kreis representation made the assemblies especially useful for the Empire's weakest territories, which lacked full votes in the Reichstag. Confessional tension periodically disrupted the Swabian Assembly, which met in separate Protestant and Catholic congresses on several occasions during the seventeenth century. These were always 'a crisis rather than a break', as the overall Kreis structure survived throughout and ensured the two parties still talked to each other.[34]

The Kreise had been assigned a wide range of functions by the imperial legislation between 1500 and 1570, establishing them as legitimate platforms for regional and cross-regional collaboration. Their assemblies convened common congresses between 1544 and 1577, but these were rendered redundant by the Reichstag's supremacy as the 'national' forum; this was something that the electors actively promoted to secure their own political pre-eminence. However, the Kreis Assemblies demonstrated their utility during the Thirty Years War when they provided confessionally neutral venues for the Empire's weaker political elements to coordinate their response to the crisis.[35] Security concerns after 1648 encouraged continued efforts to base regional and cross-regional defence on the Kreis structure. This gained momentum as mutual rivalries revealed the fragility of purely princely alliances, which proved unable to outlast the temporary coincidence of interest prompting their formation. The most significant was the Rhenish Alliance of 1658–68, which was the only princely group to have a broader agenda of stabilizing the post-1648 political balance in the Empire.[36] Led by Mainz, the Alliance eventually encompassed around 20 Protestant and Catholic secular and ecclesiastical princes. Yet it was fatally compromised by its association with France, a power clearly intending its sponsorship of the group as a means to disrupt Habsburg management of the Empire.

As part of the imperial constitution, the Kreise offered a framework capable of sustaining broad cross-status alliances through formal 'associations' agreed by two or more Kreis Assemblies, which were binding on all their members. The more inclusive representation through the assemblies reassured the weaker Estates that they had a reliable mechanism to control their more powerful neighbours. The new responsibilities assigned the Kreise by the Empire's defence reform in 1681–2 prevented the electors from frustrating such cooperation as they had done in the late sixteenth century. In fact, Mainz emerged as the main promoter of Kreis Associations, because its electors took their responsibilities towards the Empire seriously, and saw leadership of the smaller imperial Estates as a way of sustaining their traditional status as arch-chancellors.[37] Swabian-Franconian collaboration expanded after 1691 into an association with the Bavaria, Westphalian, Upper and Electoral Rhenish Kreise, thus encompassing the majority of the Empire's weakest territories. The association greatly assisted defence coordination, but suffered from the polarization of imperial politics through Austro-Prussian rivalry. Although renewed indefinitely on 1 March 1748, the association's stipulation that its members be allowed to remain neutral rendered it useless for Habsburg policy and it effectively ceased to exist.[38]

Underlying the demise of the Kreis Association was a much broader factor that rendered all princely and noble leagues redundant: the Reichstag's permanence after 1663 gave all imperial Estates an effective forum to debate policy and assert status. Eighteenth-century princely alliances were primarily expressions of clientele politics as princes sought to advance their dynastic goals by allying with the emperor or major international partners like France, Britain or the Dutch Republic.[39] The pattern only changed in the 1770s as middling princes discussed how to preserve their autonomy amidst Austro-Prussian tension. However, they no longer saw the cities, counts, prelates or knights as useful partners and, indeed, harboured designs to annex them to make their own lands more viable. This direction assumed its logical conclusion in the ultimate of all princely leagues, the Confederation of the Rhine of 16 middling princes with Napoleon in July 1806, which precipitated the Empire's collapse a month later (see pp. 653–4).

CITIES

The Lombard League

Civic leagues were a response to the threats posed by lords and princes. Like aristocratic associations, they were ultimately rendered redundant by the growth of a variety of imperial institutions that proved a more attractive means to maintain their members' identity and autonomy. Townsfolk were jealous of their freedoms, which they rarely wished to extend to their rural neighbours, whom they frequently derided as bumpkins or as servile followers of lords. The latter were also regarded as part of the rural world separate from urban sophistication, though this distinction was less pronounced in Italy than in Germany. Lords were resented for their demands for taxes and, later, soldiers and artillery. The development of effective gunpowder weaponry from the mid-fifteenth century prompted many towns to rebuild their fortifications and to store artillery and ammunition, placing them at the forefront of military developments. Even in the eighteenth century, imperial cities were expected to provide most of the imperial army's artillery train.

For their part, lords saw towns as dangerous havens of equality, responsible for subverting their tenants and encouraging a land-flight that denuded them of workers. New ideas of knighthood partly transcended lordly and princely hierarchies from the thirteenth century to forge a common sense of themselves as noble warriors embodying true freedom in contrast to grubby towns filled with greedy merchants and wage slaves. However, lords and cities were not necessarily antagonistic. Lords were often involved in founding and promoting urban development and benefited from civic amenities. Townsfolk could see advantages in lordly protection, while the trend to more oligarchical urban government created an upper stratum whose members were often keen to acquire noble status.[40]

These ambiguities are manifest in the history of the Empire's civic leagues, which was never a simple clash between progressive citizens and reactionary aristocrats. Lordly-civic relations were always part of a wider matrix that could see cooperation or conflict depending on circumstances. As we have seen (pp. 519–222), most towns experienced internal tensions between those holding power and others seeking to supplant them. The situation in Italy was further complicated by the attempts of major cities to control their surrounding regions, and by the papal-imperial conflicts of the high Middle Ages. Many Italian burghers, including the Romans, preferred the emperor to the pope, but as we have seen (pp. 34–6 and 512–14), the Empire's rulers did not view politics in class terms and their alliances with individual towns were contingent on circumstances.

Frederick I 'Barbarossa' demanded that Italian lords and cities return imperial regalia at the assembly in Roncaglia in November 1158. However, he was prepared to transfer privileges back to those cities that supported him, like Pavia, Cremona, Como and Lodi. Local tensions between these cities and their own rivals prompted Milan to establish an alliance with Piacenza, Brescia and Tortona in 1159, which proved the precursor to Italy's most powerful civic group, the Lombard League (*Lega Lombarda*). Events fitted the pattern of imperial intervention in Italy since 1077 with the emperor becoming mired in local and regional disputes. Conflict escalated as he had to reward allies, defend his honour and avenge setbacks. Milan was besieged at the instigation of the archbishop of Cologne, Rainald of Dassel, whom Barbarossa had appointed as legate in Italy. Once captured in March 1162, Milan was razed and even its churches were demolished, their holy relics being carried off in triumph to Cologne.[41]

With Milan temporarily eliminated, the emperor's civic partners had little reason to continue their collaboration and soon resented his tax demands. In March 1167 Cremona and Pavia formed the Lombard League, which swiftly expanded to include Bergamo, Brescia, Mantua, Padua, Venice, Verona, Vicenza, and Romagnol towns such as Bologna and Ferrara. The organization was backed by Pope Alexander III, who gave his name to the League's new fortress of Alessandria, built in 1168 to block imperial control of the Po valley. However, the League never encompassed all Lombard cities, as local rivalries drove many into the imperial camp, including Milan, which was rebuilt in 1167. Verona formed its own, generally anti-imperial group to the east, while the Tuscan towns combined on a similar basis to the south.

Barbarossa accepted the impossibility of defeating the League by agreeing a six-year truce in 1177, which was extended as the compromise Peace of Konstanz in June 1183. The cities accepted continued imperial overlordship in return for confirmation of their communal autonomy and recognition of their League. The good working relationship persisted until the imperial civil war following the double election of 1198. Self-interest trumped corporate solidarity as Milan and its allies backed Otto IV, while Cremona and its associates supported the Staufers. Milan established a new Lombard League in March 1226, which became a significant factor in the renewed round of imperial-papal conflicts lasting into the 1250s. However, centrifugal forces grew with the rise of the signori, who saw control of communal government as a means to extend local hegemony. The Staufers' demise removed the emperor as a factor in north Italian politics for nearly three-quarters of a century, during which civic solidarity was further eroded by the continued growth of more despotic governments.

German Civic Leagues

Few German cities matched their Italian counterparts' control of their immediate hinterlands, and they were much more dependent on good relations with lords and other neighbours to secure the free flow of food and trade. Meanwhile, the Staufers' promotion of a more numerous princely elite created a different political environment in which many German towns felt acutely vulnerable. Most towns were clustered in the Rhineland, Wetterau and Swabia, the areas where lordly jurisdiction was most fragmented and complex. This was both an opportunity and a threat. Fragmented jurisdictions could open possibilities for greater civic autonomy, especially for episcopal towns to escape their bishops' control. However, proximity to multiple lords increased the chances for friction and antagonism. North German towns faced different challenges. Although there were fewer lords in their immediate vicinity, the long-distance trade required by these towns crossed multiple lordly jurisdictions and brought them into contact with powers outside the Empire, like Sweden and Russia. The Staufers' preoccupation with Italy and south-west Germany forced northern towns to find alternative ways to protect their interests.

The result was a diverging pattern of civic alliances. The northern towns gradually combined as the Hanseatic League (*Hansa*), the largest civic alliance anywhere in medieval Europe (Map 21). Centred on Lübeck, which itself had only been founded 17 years earlier, the Hansa developed after 1160 as a means to protect specific trade routes, such as that between Lübeck and Novgorod. It broadened in the thirteenth century into a federated network as trade criss-crossed between cities establishing closer ties, like that between Hamburg and Lübeck after 1241.[42] Writing at a time of heightened global competition with Britain, nineteenth- and early twentieth-century German historians presented the Hansa as the economic and cultural representatives of their nation, while more recent writers by contrast consider the League as offering an alternative to centralized state formation.[43]

The Hansa's reach was certainly impressive, for it absorbed the Westphalian and Lower Saxon civic leagues (both formed 1246), as well as the Wendish alliance of south Baltic towns. By 1300, its trade network encompassed 2 million square kilometres and 15 million people, half of whom were outside the Empire. The core area extended for 1,500 kilometres of coastline from Flanders to Finland, with links up major rivers to inland cities like Cologne, Goslar and Magdeburg.[44] The Hansa began using its collective weight after 1277 to force kings and princes to grant favourable trading concessions, leading to a series of struggles after 1388 with England, Russia and the count of Flanders. The core group of Wendish cities around Lübeck were foremost in promoting these conflicts, often against the wishes of other members. Meanwhile, individual cities used their new wealth to buy out local lords, who sold their jurisdictions to the city councils. For example, in 1392 Hamburg bought out the count of Schauenburg, who claimed the old rights over the city once exercised by the archbishop of Bremen. This enabled Hamburg, Lübeck and some other cities to become 'free' like episcopal cities that had escaped their bishops' control.

Lübeck was relatively unusual in securing the additional status of an imperial city in 1226, though it did not attend imperial assemblies at this point.[45] The emperor rarely appeared in the north and was not regarded as a natural partner. Although still part of the Empire, the Hanseatic towns did not participate in its politics or contribute to imperial reform. However, they did not create much of an alternative either, remaining only a loose alliance until the 1470s, when they belatedly established more formal structures, including an assembly. The extended membership and diverse trading interests made it difficult to find common ground. Few members were prepared to help others engaged in what usually appeared to be distant, local disputes.

Civic leagues emerged elsewhere in Germany around the same time as the Hansa, but with different characteristics. The initial catalyst was Frederick II's absence in Italy, which saw the formation of the first Rhenish League in 1226 around Mainz, Bingen, Worms and Speyer, all episcopal towns seeking to widen their autonomy. The royal towns of Frankfurt, Gelnhausen and Friedberg also joined, giving the organization a compact geographical focus on the Rhine–Main nexus.[46] The emperor's initial response was broadly hostile, and civic leagues were banned by the charter granted to princes in 1231. However, in practice leagues were still tolerated and even encouraged as ways of securing the public peace through regional cooperation. The Wetterau urban league was established on this basis in 1232, comprising Wetzlar and the three royal towns from the first Rhenish League. The promulgation of an imperial public peace three years later gave such organizations firmer legal footing, while the growing disorder following the appearance of anti-kings in 1246–7 encouraged cooperation for mutual protection.[47]

A second Rhenish League was established by Mainz and Worms in February 1254 with a ten-year charter (Map 20). Within a year it had been joined by over 100 towns across the Rhineland, Westphalia, and southern, central and northern Germany, including territorial towns that joined with lordly permission; Ladenburg was even ordered to by the bishop of Worms. Eight ecclesiastical and 12 secular princes also joined, while William of Holland endorsed the organization in 1255, hoping to bolster his relatively weak royal rule. Richard of Cornwall followed his example after his election in 1257, enhancing the organization's legitimacy and imparting something of the cross-status character displayed later by the Swabian League. Unlike that organization, the Rhenish League remained dominated by the cities and failed to establish a formal infrastructure. Indeed, it exemplified the weaknesses inherent in all the Empire's civic leagues, whose rapid initial expansion diluted coherence and undermined unity.[48] Nonetheless, the Rhenish League demonstrated that such organizations could prove potent, at least when faced with common threats. Already in September 1254 it besieged Ingelheim castle to punish Werner von Bolanden, a knight who had broken the public peace, and in October 1256 it inflicted similar treatment on Count Dieter of Katzenelnbogen.

Like the Staufers, Richard of Cornwall chose his allies according to their respect for established socio-political norms and their support for specific royal policies, and his collaboration with the cities was not an attempt to escape dependency on the princes (see pp. 378–9). More- over, unlike in Italy, there were 105 royal towns on crown lands by the 1270s, which provided the monarch with more immediate urban part- ners. Here, Richard acted just like other lords, expecting his towns to back him in return for protection and sanctions for communal freedoms. Subsequently, Rudolf I's reorganization of the crown lands threatened some towns which did not want to exchange their previous direct rela- tionship to the monarch for the supervision of a bailiff appointed from amongst local lords who might have their own, more threatening agen- das. The rapid succession of kings after 1291 undermined stable royal patronage further, as well as creating a generally more disturbed polit- ical environment. The result was a wave of new regional civic alliances, all formally identified with upholding the public peace: Thuringian (1303), Swabian (1312), Upper Lusatian (1346), Alsatian (1354), Rhen- ish (1381) and Lower Saxon (1382).[49] The greatest of these was the Swabian Civic League established by Ulm on 4 July 1376. By 1385, some 40 mainly royal towns had joined the League.

The leagues offered a practical way to preserve the peace on which their members' trade and food supplies depended. However, they could lead to problems for the emperor, who was forced to decide between his continued support for their efforts and the backing of strong princes opposed to the cities. Württemberg's defeat of the Swabian towns at Altheim in February 1372 was both a catalyst for the Swabian Civic League and a factor behind Charles IV's reappraisal of his efforts to recover the crown lands.[50] The final break came in 1377 when the royal cities refused to pay homage to Charles's son Wenzel, the newly elected king of the Romans, in protest against the imposition of new taxes and the pawning of four towns to Bavaria. Charles could not ignore such open defiance and began hostilities by devastating the area around Ulm. Despite backing from Bavaria and Württemberg, royal forces were defeated at Reutlingen later in 1377, forcing Charles to promise not to pawn further towns. Relations soon broke down again after Wenzel's accession in 1378, because he continued to insist on the new taxes, and failed to restrain the knightly Lion's Society (*Löwengesellschaft*), which had emerged from the former royal bailiwick in the Wetterau and had attacked Frankfurt.

In response, the Swabians strengthened their organization by adopting the classic elements of a late medieval union: regular assemblies taking decisions by majority vote and acting as a court. They also mirrored the electors' alliance in expressing allegiance to the Empire as a transpersonal monarchy whilst opposing Wenzel as king. This was a potentially powerful ideology, since it offered a way to transcend localism and regionalism by linking the welfare of individual communities with that of the Empire. The Swabians prefigured the later Kreis Associations by forging alliances en bloc with the Rhenish (1381) and Lower Saxon (1382) civic leagues, as well as with the Swiss Confederates (1385). These developments appeared doubly threatening to lords, because they occurred during the aftermath of the Black Death, which saw peasants threatening to migrate to towns unless they were granted greater social and economic freedoms. Renewed fighting had already developed after 1381 between individual towns and the weaker, minor lords. The unrest was a major factor in the growing resentment of Wenzel's perceived misgovernment of the Empire. Wenzel attempted to resolve this by promulgating another public peace, at Nuremberg in 1383. The towns objected to the king's insistence that they join this individually, rather than collectively, and they forced the princes to recognize the Swabian Civic League as a formal partner in 1384.

Two City Wars

As with the second Rhenish Civic League in the mid-thirteenth century, the potency of the Swabian Civic League attracted some princes, notably the archbishop of Salzburg. The archbishop secretly became its ally to protect himself while he pursued his own policy of incorporating rich religious houses, like Berchtesgaden priory, leading to war with the Bavarian duke in 1387. Emboldened by the recent victory of their Swiss allies over a Habsburg army at Sempach (July 1386), the Swabians felt obliged to back the archbishop, opening what became the First City War (*Städtekrieg*) in 1388–9.[51] This was waged in the typical late medieval manner. None of the belligerents were able to sustain large forces for long, restricting most operations to raids against economic assets, such as sorties by citizens to burn a lord's villages. The townsfolk's willingness to meet the princes in battle proved their undoing: they were defeated by Count Eberhard II of Württemberg at Döffingen

(August 1388) and by Count Palatine Ruprecht II at Worms (November 1388). A new, general public peace was proclaimed at Eger in May 1389, obliging the disbandment of the Swabian and Rhenish civic leagues and banning such organizations in future.

The episode confirmed what many citizens already knew: princes were unreliable allies liable to wreck civic harmony. However, the complexity of local-regional-imperial interactions inhibited political polarization along status lines. Cities continued to cooperate during Wenzel's last decade and the reign of his successor, Ruprecht, but they refrained from further formal alliances. However, they also joined forces with princes against local common threats. The Swabians even combined with Eberhard II of Württemberg, despite his earlier role as royal tax collector, when they felt threatened by the local knights. Meanwhile, the Wetterau, Swabian and Alsatian towns joined Mainz and various south German princes in the Marbach League against Ruprecht in September 1405.[52]

Open alliances became possible again with the accession in 1410 of Sigismund, who saw civic and knightly associations as substitutes for a territorial base in the Empire. However, the emperor still appeared a fairly distant and unreliable partner for towns that faced continued encroachment from powerful princes like those in the Palatinate, Württemberg and Ansbach, who were consolidating their jurisdictions more clearly along territorial lines. The 1440s saw the establishment of a new Swabian Civic League, along with a separate alliance of Lake Constance towns and a Franconian group led by Nuremberg. The result was another City War in Swabia in 1449–50, leading to the collapse of the civic league in that region in 1454, while the Franconians fought slightly more successfully against Margrave Albrecht Achilles of Bayreuth from 1449 to 1453.[53] The short-term consequence was renewed burgher–noble antagonism. In the medium term, the violence helped propel imperial reform to find a more effective way of resolving conflict. This, in turn, ultimately ended civic emancipation and princely encroachment by stabilizing the identity and jurisdictions of the imperial cities and principalities that were collectively recognized as imperial Estates.

Integration in Imperial Institutions

The Second City War already indicated that a balance was emerging between the princes and the royal cities. Albrecht Achilles was unable to breach Nuremberg's impressive new fortified ring studded with 123 towers.[54] Perhaps more significantly, Bavaria refrained from joining the margrave, preferring instead more peaceful means to extend its influence by negotiating treaties of protection with several towns. Increasingly, princes realized that their own territorial towns could replace the credit and consumer facilities offered by the imperial cities, making these less attractive targets. The improving agrarian situation eased tensions by discouraging land flight. With a few exceptions like Württemberg, princes abandoned attempts to subdue free and imperial towns in favour of developing those on their own lands, consolidating the Empire's diversified urban landscape.

Meanwhile, the gathering pace of imperial reform provided royal towns with an alternative to civic leagues. A key factor in Nuremberg's defiance of the Bayreuth margrave was that its annual revenue was far higher than his. Already in the 1420s, Sigismund and the electors looked to cities as valuable contributors to the common military effort against the Hussites and continued to do so as the Ottoman menace loomed throughout the century. By 1471, most royal towns sent representatives to each royal assembly, holding their own civic congress (*Städtetag*) as part of the proceedings. This provided the nucleus of what became the civic corpus as the Reichstag took shape around 1495, by which point the stronger monarchy of the Habsburgs appeared to offer cities a much more reliable partner. By participating in the common institutions, the royal towns now fully became *imperial cities*, as well as imperial Estates.

Their imperial status now trumped residual solidarity with other towns, which were now more firmly reduced to mediate elements of princely territories. The process remained in flux between about 1480 and 1555 as the status of individual cities like Trier fluctuated until they clearly accepted or rejected the burdens associated with Reichstag representation. Many city councils had doubts about embracing the new institutions, especially as they felt the official distribution of tax quotas favoured the electors and princes. In fact, the assessments were a reasonable reflection of the underdeveloped state of many principalities' finances relative to those of leading cities. The cities were unable to prevent the princes using the Reichstag to force through anti-monopoly legislation in 1512 contrary to the interests of their leading merchants. Religious differences added to the tensions once 60 of the 65 active imperial cities embraced Protestantism after 1524, renewing lordly suspicions of townsfolk as subversives.[55]

Although these trends temporarily forged renewed solidarity with the inhabitants of territorial towns, they also opened new rifts amongst the burghers of the imperial cities. The Reformation often split populations along socio-economic lines, with the poor converting in Augsburg, Biberach, Ravensburg and Dinkelsbühl, while the patricians remained Catholic. The resultant unrest provided Charles V with the excuse to annex Konstanz and rewrite the constitutions of 27 other imperial cities between 1548 and 1552. Article 27 of the 1555 Religious Peace denied imperial cities the full right of Reformation, fixing their confessional character whilst providing some safeguards for dissenting minorities. By 1618, 35 were largely Protestant, while 20 were predominantly Catholic, but virtually all had significant minorities. Sectarianism fused with socio-economic problems to cause public disorder in Augsburg, Aachen, Kaufbeuren, Dinkelsbühl and, most notoriously, Donauwörth, where Bavarian intervention to restore peace became one of the incidents cited by the Palatinate to justify establishing the Protestant Union. The problems of the late sixteenth century encouraged an introspective conservatism intended to reduce the risks of further intervention. Meanwhile, the improved effectiveness of the imperial courts during the later seventeenth and eighteenth centuries provided cities with more peaceful ways to defuse their internal problems whilst preserving their autonomy.

Continued attachment to the Empire was reinforced by the absence of any viable alternative. The Hansa failed to match either the political centralization of their royal trading partners like Denmark and England or the institutional integration provided by imperial reform. Their loose federation was unable to prevent the stronger members stealing economic opportunities from their weaker neighbours. The Flanders towns transferred with most of Burgundy to the Habsburgs in 1477. Leading north German members like Hamburg, Cologne and Goslar participated in the new imperial institutions emerging around 1500. Notably, the Kreis structure offered a new way of regulating relations with neighbouring princes in northern Germany, while the Reichstag's development also served to integrate this region into the Empire. Although 63 Hanseatic towns agreed to federate with the Empire in 1557, full integration was delayed by their reluctance to accept the burdens of Turkish defence, which grew significantly during the second half of the sixteenth century (see pp. 445–62). Meanwhile, Russian and Swedish expansion along the southern Baltic shore both exposed the dangers and reduced the Hansa towns to those in the Empire.

Several leading towns advocated closer involvement with imperial institutions, especially as Rudolf II's political alignment with Spain served their economic interests, which were suffering from English competition. In 1597 Rudolf banned the English Merchant Adventurers from trading in the Empire. England retaliated by no longer recognizing the Hansa after 1602, causing a split as Hamburg and other cities wanted to continue trading with the Merchant Adventurers. By 1604, only 14 cities still paid Hanseatic membership dues. The downward spiral reduced collective weight, further encouraging engagement with the Empire as an alternative. The Hansa attempted to remain neutral during the Thirty Years War, but only the heavily fortified cities of Hamburg, Bremen and Lübeck managed this, thanks also to their importance as financial and diplomatic centres for all sides. The Hansa were confirmed as a legal corporation in 1648, but were now viewed suspiciously by other imperial cities. Growing threats from Denmark and Sweden encouraged Hamburg and Bremen to secure their autonomy by formal recognition as imperial cities after 1654. They were simply too important to fall under the jurisdiction of a foreign power. By contrast, applications from other Hansa towns were all rejected in the 1640s, and these were allowed to slip into the status of territorial towns. Münster, Erfurt, Magdeburg and Brunswick were all bombarded into submission when they refused. By 1667 the Hansa was essentially defunct.[56]

The imperial cities stabilized as 13 Catholic, 34 Protestant and 4 bi-confessional cities, of which 31 were in the old imperial heartland of south-west Germany. The Peace of Westphalia (1648) consolidated their position as imperial Estates, while reform of collective defence and the development of Kreis Associations removed any incentive for separate civic leagues. Rather than seeking independence as sovereign republics, imperial cities asserted their corporate status as 'noble', meaning free and elevated above both their own subjects and other, territorial towns.[57]

PEASANTS AND THE 'COMMON MAN'

Communalism

The cities' rejection of a broader alliance with rural inhabitants was another factor in the integration of the former within the Empire's status hierarchy. The construction of a broader socio-political order based on the horizontal, associative aspects of communities has been labelled 'communalism' and has been claimed as late medieval Germany's 'third way' to modernity between absolutist territorial state-building and the construction of a homogeneous national state.[58] Communalism was a specifically late medieval–early modern form of egalitarianism that was collective in that it focused on the community, rather than the individual. Freedom was expressed and celebrated collectively through communal gatherings and festivals, and by verbal and visual reminders of the community's traditions and identity. All this originated in the communal self-government emerging in the Empire's towns and villages during the high Middle Ages. It was a movement of ordinary folk seeking a better life amidst often harsh and adverse circumstances, and it emerged pragmatically and well before the rediscovery of classical Greek civic democracy by Humanist scholars during the Renaissance. Communalism extended individual communal self-government by using the same practices to federate multiple communities, effectively building state-like organizations from the ground up.

As with all aspects of communal development, it is important not to romanticize or exaggerate communalism. As we have seen (pp. 510–22), communal government contained vertical as well as horizontal elements through its basis in the enfranchisement of (largely male) householders and its exclusion or marginalization of the poor, unmarried and recently arrived. Communities might indeed unite in the face of external threats, but these could also divide them. Harmony was often fabricated, or achieved through peer pressure and the punishment of 'deviance'. Moreover, the communal ideal of freedom remained one of emancipation rather than empowerment: it was freedom *from* dependency and threat.[59] Communal freedom was often voiced in antagonistic terms similar to what later ages would term the rhetoric of class war. Yet it lacked the abstract concepts of liberty and equality used by, for example, the American and French revolutionaries in the late eighteenth century. Although capable of innovation, communal movements were not seeking to build a brave new society according to a grand blueprint, but instead defended an idealized version of their existing order against perceived threats.

Communal forms derived strength from face-to-face interaction within communities. This restricted wider structures to federal forms, since only these allowed each community to preserve its own identity and purpose. The preceding examination of civic leagues has already revealed the free-rider problem inhibiting their development into more durable political forms. Cities might be vulnerable, but they were usually better protected, larger and wealthier than villages. Standing alone did not appear as daunting as it might for rural inhabitants. This generally restricted communalism to the areas of non-nucleated settlement, like hamlets and scattered farmsteads. The formation of some overarching governance in such areas was often the only way their inhabitants could combat natural hazards and external threats. Non-nucleated settlement tended to be located in regions where other geographic features also favoured communalism rather than lordship. Communalism thrived on the Empire's economic and political periphery amongst communities sufficiently wealthy to be viable, but not rich enough to attract raiders or encourage involvement in wider politics.

Dithmarschen

One such region was the coastal strip from Flanders to the Danish peninsula (Map 22). Unlike the areas further east along the Baltic, the North Sea coast was incorporated relatively early into the Empire, but remained politically peripheral and underpopulated. It was included in the county and, later, parish structures, but was never a major area of interest to the lay or spiritual elite. A mix of lordly and communal elements emerged, with the former predominating in Flanders in the west and the latter to the east in Frisia.[60] While towns developed in Flanders, the more northerly and easterly areas saw smaller self-governing communities emerge through lordly absenteeism. Lords were few and more interested in affairs elsewhere. They delegated supervision to stewards and other intermediaries. Over time, these supervisory powers were transferred to locals, or lapsed altogether. Local people wanted autonomy, not the absence of all protection or recognition from existing authorities. The Empire's multilayered structure allowed them to achieve their goals through securing imperial sanction for their special status.

The region was not unfavourable. The marshy soil proved quite fertile, especially in the area of Dithmarschen north of the Elbe estuary, which supported 40,000 inhabitants by the mid-sixteenth century or twice the population density of central Switzerland.[61] Dithmarschen had already been made a county in the Carolingian era, but lordly control was always weak, even after the count's rights were transferred to the archbishop of Bremen in 1180. The inhabitants were only obliged to pay a small fee on the accession of each archbishop. Communal self-government had already emerged by the eleventh century thanks to the need to cooperate to maintain the dykes and other flood defences. The introduction of a parish structure during the thirteenth century provided a framework to construct more effective common institutions. Each parish sent representatives to a common assembly, codified in the charter of 1447, which confirmed a typically communal form of a 48-member council balanced by a general assembly representing a federation of around 20 parishes. Already termed *Universitas terrae Dithmarciae* by its inhabitants in 1283, this peasant republic demonstrated its potency by repelling attempts by the count of Holstein to assert lordly authority in 1319 and 1404.

Dithmarschen's influence peaked in the century after consolidating its government in 1447. The emperor treated it as an imperial fief, summoning the peasants to send representatives to royal assemblies in the 1430s and again to the Reichstag in 1496. However, like the royal towns, the peasants found that the Empire's growing status hierarchy made interaction with formal institutions difficult. Moreover, Frederick III wanted to extend his influence into northern Germany and saw the region's lords as more obvious partners who could be integrated more closely within the Empire by elevation as imperial princes. To this end, he elevated Holstein's count to a duke and recognized his territorial ambitions by formally enfeoffing him with Dithmarschen in 1474.

The peasants demonstrated a sophisticated understanding of the complexities of imperial politics by protesting to Pope Sixtus IV that the emperor was undermining the imperial church, on the grounds that their county belonged to the archbishopric of Bremen. Frederick was forced to rescind his enfeoffment in 1481. The Danish king had inherited Holstein's claim and now saw an opportunity to advance his territory to the Elbe, which would allow him to tax the lucrative river trade. Employing a ruthless mercenary band, the Black Guard, he invaded, only to be routed at the battle of Hemmingstedt on 17 February 1500 by the peasants, who exploited their local knowledge to pole-vault across the marshes and trap the invaders.[62] However, what had been advantageous turned to Dithmarschen's detriment by the mid-sixteenth century. Their relative isolation left them without natural allies, unlike either the Swiss or Dutch. In particular, the absence of any indigenous town deprived them of connections to the Empire's urban networks. Neighbours resented them as wreckers and pirates, luring coastal shipping into their treacherous shallows. The Hansa accordingly rejected their application for membership. A renewed Danish invasion triumphed in 1559, though the king was obliged to leave the inhabitants considerable autonomy.

Frisia

Frisia, immediately to the west of Dithmarschen, shared similar origins, but exhibited less coherence, despite articulating an identity around 'Frisian freedom'. The region had been conquered by the Franks around the mid-eighth century, but was granted its own laws and largely left to look after itself. It was not until the Staufer era that a concerted effort was made to integrate the region more firmly within the Empire, a move encouraged by the general migration north and east into previously underpopulated areas. The Staufers' first choice of ruler, the bishop of Utrecht, was killed by the Frisians in battle in 1227. The region was then assigned to Holland, whose Count William became one of the contenders for the German crown after 1247. His attempt – and his reign – ended when his horse crashed through the ice and he was captured and killed by the Frisians in January 1256. His successor as count managed to conquer West Frisia by 1289. Control remained difficult into the fourteenth century, and West Frisia passed along with Holland to Burgundy in 1433.

Frisia's fragmentation was part of the gradual process of demarcating clearer territorial jurisdictions across the late medieval Empire. Regions without lords either had to find their own place in the hierarchy or risked incorporation within another territory. Frisia's eastern edge became the county of Oldenburg, whose ruler benefited from kinship with the Danish king after the mid-fifteenth century. While Oldenburg evolved as a conventional lordship, several other communities were settled by colonists between the lower Weser and the mouth of the Elbe, and they, like Dithmarschen's peasants, were able to secure greater self-governance under the loose superior jurisdiction of Bremen's archbishop. The community of Stedingen was the most westerly, sited on the Weser north of Bremen and inhabited by around 12,000–15,000 people who were personally free but under the archbishop's suzerainty. The need to cooperate to maintain flood defences forged this community around 1200, but its attempt to escape the archbishop entirely foundered after 1207 as he was not prepared to grant the same freedoms as those secured in Dithmarschen. Lordly control was asserted using a crusade after 1232, the same method then being employed further east along the Baltic shore. Stedingen's inhabitants were defeated in 1234 and their community was divided by Oldenburg and the archbishopric of Bremen. The fate of the remaining four communities was mixed. Rüstingen was physically split asunder by an inundation in 1314, with half subsequently absorbed into Oldenburg, while the western part became the lordship of Jever. Wursten on the marshes north of Bremerhaven fell under the archbishop's control during the 1520s. Kehdingen was a 47-kilometre long marsh along the lower Elbe, which passed to Bremen along with the rest of the county of Stade in 1236. Four campaigns finally forced its inhabitants to accept the bishop's rule, though he allowed them to retain considerable autonomy. Along with the other marsh communities, Kehdingen became the fourth (peasant) Estate in Bremen's territorial assembly in 1397. Although excluded from representation during the 1590s, the peasants continued to claim rights to participate. Hadeln differed from the other communities in that it had been settled much earlier and was part of Saxony. Like the others, it asserted greater autonomy during the thirteenth century, but more successfully because the old Saxon duchy fragmented. Hadeln was a 300-square-kilometre self-governing peasant republic with its own law and assembly by the fifteenth century, and it preserved this directly under the emperor after 1689. Charles VI ceded Hadeln in 1731 to Hanover in return for Hanoverian recognition of the Pragmatic Sanction changing Habsburg inheritance law.[63]

Only East Frisia retained communal government into the eighteenth century. As with other peasant communities, there was a tendency for village leaders to emerge as hereditary chiefs and gradually acquire the status of lesser nobility from the thirteenth century. Although they feuded amongst themselves, the Frisian chiefs accepted the Brok family as pre-eminent from the mid-fourteenth century until 1464, when they were succeeded by the Cirksena, who ruled until 1744. The Cirksena had likewise risen from village leaders, but benefited from Frederick III's policy of integrating the northern periphery by granting titles to local notables. The Cirksena were made imperial counts (1464) and later princes (1654), but the bulk of the population remained free house-holders enfranchised through possession of qualifying farmsteads. Householders dominated the East Frisian Estates, which also included the port of Emden, the small towns of Aurich and Norden, and a handful of knights who, unlike those elsewhere, were independent landowners rather than the count's feudatories. The Estates bargained for constitutional guarantees in 1595 and 1611. Mirroring Frederick III's policy, Rudolf II endorsed these treaties to tie East Frisia's own constitution to that of the Empire and so stopped it slipping under Dutch influence.[64]

The Cirksena periodically tried to expand their influence by espousing the cause of the villagers who were disenfranchised by lacking qualifying property. Confessional differences added to political tensions as Emden embraced Calvinism while the rest of the population adhered to Lutheranism. Problems grew after 1665 as the Cirksena adopted a different lifestyle and political behaviour in an attempt to join other imperial princes as social equals. Imperial intervention barely held the balance between the competing interests, including renewed external interference from the Dutch, Danes and neighbouring Welf dukes, and the bishop of Münster. Brandenburg-Prussia exploited these difficulties to establish a permanent military presence in Emden after 1682. Tension spilled over into civil war between 1725 and 1727, splitting the Estates before the radical Emden faction was defeated and the previous status quo restored. Prussia accepted this situation when it annexed East Frisia in 1744 following an inheritance pact with the last Cirksena. The friction seriously impaired functioning governance, rendering the Estates incapable of effective action and thereby essentially disempowering the communes, which had lost their main forum for action.[65]

The Swiss Confederation

The Swiss Confederation went further than any of these examples by separating from the Empire as an independent state (Map 16). Like the peasant communities of the north-west, those of the Empire's long Alpine strip were also favoured by geography, though of a very different kind. The mountains allowed varied forms of agriculture and animal husbandry, sustaining a modest population that did not need to move since others travelled through their lands, which lay across the routes between Burgundy, Germany and Italy. Control of vital passes made the Alpine communities strategically important to all medieval monarchs and helps explain the rich ecclesiastical endowments in this region, which included the archbishopric of Salzburg, the bishoprics of Basel, Chur, Brixen and Trent, and important abbeys like St Gallen and Einsiedeln.

The mountain ridges made lateral communications often very difficult and encouraged a wide variety of communities, including numerous small and medium-sized towns and different kinds of villages, as well as lay and spiritual lordships. Apart from the local bishops, the senior lords tended to be busy elsewhere, creating scope for local self-rule, similar to that encountered in the North Sea marshes. Like the Frisians, local communities developed a myth of ancient freedoms that were in fact quite new, dating mainly to the twelfth century. Jurisdiction followed natural features like valleys, helping to shape how communities engaged with each other. Central and western Switzerland saw the development of incorporated valleys (*Talschaften*), which in turn formed the basis of what were later called 'cantons'.[66] By contrast, communal forms developed within lordly lesser jurisdictions in Rhetia, Vorarlberg and the Tirol in the eastern Alps, where judges' circuits formed the basis for districts. Both the cantons and districts established management committees to coordinate common activities and represent the inhabitants in dealings with outsiders.

There is a tendency to lose sight of this diversity in favour of the stirring story of hardy Swiss mountaineers, such as William Tell, overthrowing Habsburg lordship and establishing what is widely interpreted as one of the modern world's first democracies.[67] In fact, the William Tell story only surfaced around 1470, long after Swiss communities acquired self-governance. The process of emancipation involved some communities asserting their own control over others, broadly similar to the dominance of Italian cities over their hinterlands. Meanwhile, the complexity of settlement patterns led to differing forms of engagement with local and more distant lords, including the emperor, any one of whom might be an ally rather than an enemy under some circumstances.

Moreover, the formation of communal governance in the Alps needs to be placed in the wider context of the Empire's reorganization along feudal and territorial lines, which, by the thirteenth century, increasingly compelled previously 'peripheral' areas to define their own status and relationship to more distant communities. In particular, the fragmentation of the old duchy of Swabia ended the political unit previously containing much of the Alps, including the former Roman province of Rhetia. The extinction of the Zähringen dukes in 1218 led to the emancipation of Bern and Zürich as imperial cities, especially as the Staufers saw the granting of political immediacy as a way to prevent key Alpine routes falling into the hands of potential rivals amongst the Empire's princely elite. To this end, Henry (VII) bought up the Habsburgs' claims from the Zähringen inheritance to exercise jurisdiction over the Uri and Schwyz valleys in 1231 and 1240, since these gave access to the newly pioneered St Gotthard Pass, opened in 1230. Like Bern and Zürich, the valleys became part of the royal lands under direct Staufer protection, but with communal self-government.

Much of the conflict that emerged by the late thirteenth century was not against feudalism, but involved disputes over the exercise of stewardship rights (*Vogteirechte*) associated with management of the crown lands in the wake of the Staufers' demise. These disputes often pitted local nobles against more powerful outsiders like the Habsburgs who wanted to control the powerful abbeys of Einsiedeln and Engelberg. The abbeys and towns pursued their own interests in these conflicts, such as Zürich and Bern, which asserted control over their own hinterlands. Meanwhile, the economic transformation of the Alpine valleys across 1200–1400 involved smallholders being dispossessed by cattle ranchers expanding their operations to feed populations in the growing Lombard cities.[68]

Rudolf I's election as king in 1273 transformed the situation by adding royal power to the Habsburgs' already considerable regional influence thanks to his family's existing possession of the county jurisdiction around Zürich. Rudolf's policy of Revindication (see pp. 382–6) appeared particularly threatening to many Swiss lords and communities who perceived it as a bid to consolidate Habsburg power along the Upper Rhine and western Alps. The famous 'oath comradeship' (*Eidgenossenschaft*) between the three incorporated valleys of Uri, Schwyz and Unterwalden was made in August 1291, two weeks after Rudolf's death, because they feared the election of another Habsburg as king.[69] Such associations were not uncommon, and that of 1291 was not celebrated as the foundation of Swiss independence until 1891. It was directed against a perceived lordly threat, and was not a bid to leave the Empire. Indeed, Alpine communities generally looked to the emperor to consolidate their autonomy by enshrining it in legal charters. Henry VII granted a privilege in 1309 endorsing the three valleys as self-governing rural feudatories forming their own imperial bailiwick directly under him.

Imperial politics again intervened to push this development, since the double election of 1314 raised the possibility of another Habsburg, Frederick 'the Fair', as king. Frederick's relation, Duke Leopold of Austria, intervened to punish the Schwyz peasants who had plundered Einsiedeln abbey, which was under his protection. His punitive expedition was defeated at Morgarten on 15 November 1315, though only around 100 of his troops were killed, and not the thousands claimed by some later historians. Nonetheless, it was a significant reverse, precipitating the collapse of Habsburg influence in the area based on possession of the rights of imperial bailiff. The three valleys renewed their confederation, which was increasingly known to outsiders as the *Schwyzer*, or Swiss. Their status of imperial immediacy elevated the confederates above other rural communities and made them acceptable partners for cities like Bern and Zürich, enabling the Confederation to expand between 1332 and 1353 through additional alliances with other cantons.

Habsburg regional influence, however, grew simultaneously with the acquisition of the Breisgau (1368) immediately to the north and the Tirol (1363) to the east, while their competition with the Luxembourgs encouraged redoubled efforts to reassert authority over the Swiss. Habsburg defeats at Sempach (1386) and Nüfels (1388) coincided with the First Civic War (see pp. 574–5 above) and the general backdrop of protest following the Black Death. The Alpine communities further east responded to Habsburg encroachment from the Tirol by forming the God's House League (Chadé, 1367), Rhetia, or the 'Grey League' (Grisons, 1395) and the Ten Parish League (1436). They combined in 1471 as a federation known as the 'Three Leagues' (*Drei Bünde*), which encompassed 52 communities with a total population of 76,000 by the eighteenth century.[70] A further 'League above the Lake' emerged among communities south of Lake Constance during a revolt by the Appenzell region against the abbot of St Gallen in 1405. Although joined by communities in the Vorarlberg, Upper (southern) Swabia and the imperial city of St Gallen, this league was crushed by the local knights combining as the League of St George's Shield in 1408.

Despite the sharper social tension, localism and conflicting interests prevented a broad alliance between the different Alpine leagues. The Swiss allied with Appenzell in 1411, but only admitted it as a member of their Confederation in 1513. Each of the Three Leagues allied separately with the Confederation in 1497–9, but reaffirmed their own federation in 1524. Meanwhile, the Swiss pursued their own policy of expansion, conquering the rural communities of the Aargau (1415) and Thurgau (1460) from the Habsburgs. The growing military reputation of the Swiss allowed their leaders to sign lucrative contracts with the French king and Italian princes to supply mercenaries, entangling the Confederation in more distant politics, notably the wars against ducal Burgundy from the 1440s to 1477, and the Italian Wars after 1494.[71] The Swiss also responded to Burgundian and Savoyard pressure from the west and south by accepting the imperial cities of Fribourg (1478) and Solothurn (1481) as members. The Valtelline and other parts of Milan were conquered by the Swiss in 1512.

These conflicts were frequently brutal: Swiss and German troops waged 'bad war', meaning the normal rules governing the taking of prisoners were suspended. However, the wider context remained strategic rather than ideological. France's intrusion into Italy after 1494 heightened the significance of the Alpine passes to the Empire's integrity. Crucially, this coincided with the peak of imperial reform, forcing the Alpine communities to define their relationship to the Empire. Their earlier conflicts with the Habsburgs had left them suspicious of the new Reichstag, and they refused the summons to attend meetings after 1471, in contrast with the German cities who used this opportunity to integrate themselves in the Empire as full imperial

Estates. The Swiss held their own assemblies (*Tagsetzungen*) after 1471. These drew in Basel, Zürich and other local towns like Luzern, which might otherwise have participated in the Reichstag, while the Three Leagues held separate meetings, especially after renewing their federation in 1524.

The introduction of the Common Penny tax in 1495 forced a decision. For the first time, the Empire was asking the Alpine communities for a substantial financial contribution, yet appeared to offer little in return, having largely left the Swiss on their own to repel the Burgundians before 1477. Moreover, the Swiss did not feel the need for the new imperial public peace, because they had already agreed a version of this through their own confederation. The Swiss refusal compelled Maximilian I to respond with force to assert both his imperial and Habsburg regional authority. The resulting conflict was known (depending on perspective) as the Swiss or Swabian War.[72] Maximilian mobilized the Swabian League on the basis of his membership as ruler of Austria and the Tirol in January 1499. The Swiss won three victories, but failed to cross the Rhine northwards into Swabia, and so accepted the compromise Peace of Basel on 22 September.

It would be premature to call the treaty the birth of Swiss independence. The Swiss were granted exemption from the taxes and institutions agreed at the 1495 Reichstag, but otherwise remained within imperial jurisdiction. Both the Confederation and the Three Leagues continued to display their roots in the Empire's socio-political order. They remained networks of separate alliances between distinct communities that retained their own identity, laws and self-government. In this respect, the Confederation failed to match the Dithmarschen peasants who already had a codified constitution and common legal system by the mid-fifteenth century. Neither the Confederation nor the Three Leagues had a capital. A few communities remained apart, notably Gersau, which effectively acquired imperial immediacy when its local lord sold his rights to the parishioners in 1390. As with the other places, Gersau's inhabitants secured imperial confirmation of their immediacy (in 1418 and 1433). Although they had cooperated with the Swiss since 1332, the fact that their tiny community was only accessible by boat across Lake Luzern enabled them to remain fully autonomous until 1798, when they were forced by France to join the Swiss Confederation and the Three Leagues in the new Helvetic Republic.[73]

The Confederation eventually encompassed 13 cantons with 940,000 inhabitants by 1600.[74] Basel, Bern, Luzern and Zürich were civic republics that had extended economic and political dominance over their rural hinterlands similar to the pattern in northern Italy. Tensions from this process erupted periodically into civil war, notably between 1440 and 1446 when Zürich was temporarily expelled from the Confederation. Confessional differences following the Reformation exacerbated existing rivalries. Renewed conflict prompted a compromise in 1531 that prefigured the Empire's Peace of Augsburg (1555) by fixing the confessional identity of each canton. The six Protestant cantons were especially concerned not to push their seven Catholic neighbours into a closer alliance with the Habsburgs.

The Swiss rejected the formalized status hierarchy entrenched in the Empire by imperial reform, and instead did not differentiate between the more urbanized and the rural cantons, each of which had two votes in the federal assembly. However, canton boundaries reflected their origins as imperial fiefs, meaning they varied considerably in size and wealth. Protestant wealth and population grew faster, adding to the resentment that the Catholics had two more votes. The Peace of Aargau stabilized the Confederation after renewed civil war in 1712, but without resolving the underlying problems. Meanwhile, both the Confederation and the Three Leagues controlled subordinate dependencies conquered collectively during their period of territorial expansion between 1415 and 1512. These areas retained self-government, but were denied representation in the federal assemblies. The Italian-speaking Catholic inhabitants of the Valtelline especially resented domination by the Protestant German-speakers of Rhetia, leading to prolonged unrest between 1620 and 1639.[75] In short, the exclusion of superior lords did not bring peace, but was followed by serious socio-economic and religious divisions.

Social practice remained hierarchical, and only outsiders believed the Swiss were all 'peasants'.[76] Swiss equality involved the assertion that they were equal to any noble, opening the door to a noble lifestyle for those who could afford it. Lordly jurisdictions were converted into property rights that generally passed to a class of powerful, rich families like the Salis, Planta, Guler and Schauensteins in Rhetia, for instance. These displayed their status through coats of arms, and used their near monopoly on communal posts like district judges or military commanders

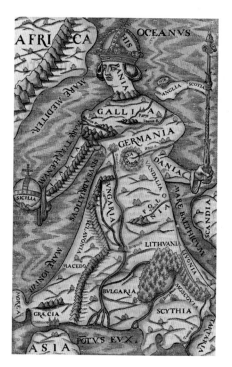

17. Johannes Patsch's 1537 map
of Europe as a single Empire, with
Habsburg Spain as its crowned head.

18. The sober woman from Metz, from
Hans Weigel's *Trachtenbuch* of 1577.

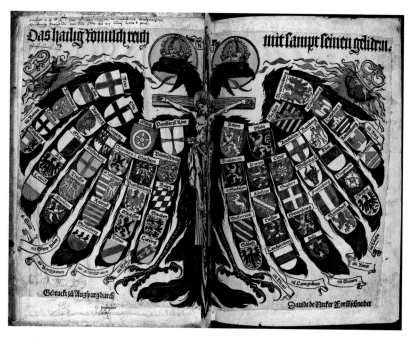

19. Hans Burgkmaier's 1510 version of the *Quaternionenadler*, showing
the Empire's corporate order in groups of four locations identified by their
heraldic device, topped by the seven electors and the papacy.

20. Regensburg's old town hall (*left*), where the Reichstag met, is flanked to the right by the city's new hall, built for its own council.

21. Imperial majesty. The collective character of imperial politics is symbolized through the widely reproduced image of the emperor surrounded by the seven electors.

22. Christ crowning and blessing Otto II (*left*) and his wife Theophanu (*right*), from an ivory relief c.982.

23. The rituals of enfeoffment. Emperor Sigismund (*seated*) enfeoffs Friedrich I with the electorate of Brandenburg in 1417.

24. The power of writing. The intellectual Nicholas of Cusa, portrayed by Dr Winard von Steeg (1371–1453).

25. The so-called 'Cappenburger Barbarossa Head', widely interpreted as a contemporary portrait of Emperor Frederick I.

26. The Reichstag in plenary session in 1653. The ecclesiastical rulers are to the left, the secular to the right, with the emperor's commissioner and the electors at the far end.

27. Carolingian peasants engaged in seasonal tasks, as depicted in a ninth-century calendar.

28. The community as a sworn association. The citizens of Ulm gather for their annual ceremony at their city hall in 1650.

29. The emperor and the law. Title page of a ninth-century collection of capitularies showing Charlemagne (*left*), his son Pippin and a scribe.

30. The Reichskammergericht in session. Note how the general layout resembles that of the Reichstag (plate 26).

31. The end of the Empire. Carl von Dalberg receives Napoleon in front of the archiepiscopal palace at Aschaffenburg in September 1806.

32. The Kyffhäuser myth. Emperor Barbarossa awakes from his slumbers, in a late nineteenth-century mural in the rebuilt Imperial palace at Goslar.

33. Heinrich Himmler laying a wreath at the tomb of Henry the Fowler in Quedlinburg Abbey, 1 July 1936. This first *Heinrichsfeier* was an attempt to fit Henry into the Nazi version of history.

34. Sergeant Ivan Babcock photographed on 13 June 1945 wearing the Aachen copy of the imperial crown (made for Wilhelm II in 1912), which had been hidden in a mine near Siegen during the Second World War.

35. A modern statue in Konstanz harbour by Peter Lenk, of Imperia holding aloft the diminutive forms of Emperor Sigismund and Pope Martin V.

to secure access to the best meadows and take control of lucrative transit trade. Rhetian politics became particularly nasty during the later sixteenth century when unscrupulous leaders exploited mass assemblies of enfranchised citizens to promote their own agendas, which could culminate in armed intimidation, kangaroo courts or, in the worst case, the sectarian massacre of 1620. Populist politics exposed communalism's dark side and was, unfortunately, the one area where the Alpine communities deviated substantially in political culture from the Empire.

The German Peasants War

Otherwise, Alpine communal self-government was similar to that found in many rural areas across the Empire. The crown lands not only included towns and abbeys, but at least 120 autonomous villages immediately under the emperor's jurisdiction.[77] These 'imperial villages' (*Reichsdörfer*) were sold off fairly quickly once the dissipation of crown lands began in the late fourteenth century, because they were considered less valuable assets than the towns. The Free People of the Leutkirch Heath near Ravensburg were repeatedly pawned, but survived thanks to their having been attached to the imperial bailiwick of Swabia since the 1270s and in 1541 were eventually redeemed by the Habsburgs, who saw the jurisdiction as useful in managing their scattered south-west German possessions. Leutkirch retained its autonomy until 1802, when the Habsburgs were obliged to cede it to Bavaria. Another four villages survived through similar quirks.[78]

The bulk of the German rural population still enjoyed communal self-government, having bargained improved rights following the Black Death (see pp. 494–8). Alliances between communes already served as a platform for large-scale revolts in the Rhineland and Swabia during the late fifteenth and early sixteenth centuries. Foremost amongst these was the *Bundschuh* movement, so-called after its symbol of an unlaced boot. The Poor Conrad rising of 1514 proved fundamental in consolidating the Württemberg Estates as a check on ducal authority.[79] The revolts were a response to the intensification of lordship, as lords used the economic and demographic recovery after 1470 to try to regain the influence they had lost a century earlier. Peasants objected to new restrictions on their access to woods and streams, as well as tax demands that grew with the Common Penny and other imperial taxes.

Existing lordly structures were poorly placed to handle large-scale protest, which soon overwhelmed the system of lesser jurisdiction with its village and district courts. The highly fragmented jurisdiction in south-west Germany left peasants without clear opportunities to appeal against unfavourable verdicts. A new rising began in May 1524 as a protest against taxation, but became radicalized within six months under the rapid diffusion of Reformation evangelism and the media revolution: 25,000 copies of the Upper Swabian peasants' Twelve Articles were printed within two months of their appearance in Memmingen. The Articles were the most famous of several sets of demands. Only 13 per cent of the programmes included the demand that communities should elect their own pastors, meaning the freedom to adopt the Reformation, whereas 90 per cent attacked serfdom and lordly exactions. References to religion were part of a broader call for a fairer society. The third of the Twelve Articles claimed 'it is demonstrated by Scripture that we are free and wish to be free', but qualified this by saying: 'not that we wish to be completely free and to have no authority, for God does not teach us that'. What the peasants really wanted is not always clear, because their programmes were usually drawn up with the assistance of burgher lawyers. Many clearly thought their villages were, or should be, directly subordinate to the emperor. All expressed loyalty to the emperor, who was a conveniently distant authority. Their main concern was securing real improvements in their daily lives. The murder of lords and princes was very rare and most hoped the authorities would become their Christian brothers in an idealized harmony. Rebels in larger territories like Bamberg and the Tirol envisaged forming assemblies exclusively composed of commoners (*Landschaften*) to govern alongside their prince, while those in Württemberg, Baden and Salzburg planned to use similar institutions as the sole form of territorial government. Rebels in more fragmented areas attempted something closer to the organization of the Swiss and Dithmarschen peasants by forming sworn associations of autonomous communities. Few of these plans were realized, owing to the violence and to rapidly changing events.[80]

The rising developed its own momentum as the German Peasants War, with around 300,000 under arms by 1525 in a clear demonstration of the potency of communal government. Peasant organization was often quite sophisticated, with villages sending men on rotation to spread the burden and minimize social and economic disruption. However, peer pressure was also often necessary, with participation enforced by the threat of expulsion from the community.[81] The initial spread was facilitated by the inability of the authorities to coordinate a response. Individual lords often conceded local demands, emboldening neighbouring communities to voice demands as well. Mühlhausen in Thuringia was one of the few imperial cities openly to join the peasants; solidarity elsewhere was fragile at best and peasants often resented burghers almost as much as lords. The cities' decision to back the princes in the Swabian League proved a major factor in the peasants' eventual defeat. Working through the League, the authorities made further tactical concessions to isolate radicals from moderates while they gathered their forces to restore order in the name of the Empire's public peace. Around 75,000–100,000 ordinary folk were killed, amounting to 10 to 15 per cent of able-bodied males in the worst-affected regions.[82]

The outcome has widely been interpreted as a failure, condemning Germany to an authoritarian future.[83] In fact, it stabilized the Empire's corporate social order. Many communities secured real improvements: even the Swabian League's commander, Georg Truchsess von Waldburg, granted most of his own peasants' demands. Peasant representation was incorporated into the Estates in the Tirol, Salzburg, Baden and several smaller territories. Social regulation was tightened, partly to address perceived injustice, but also to win the loyalty of householders whose position relative to other community members was strengthened through new legislation. Finally, the system of imperial justice was substantially revised in 1526 to extend the right of appeal and channel future grievances towards peaceful arbitration.[84]

Turning Swiss

It took some time for these changes to ease tensions, especially as economic conditions worsened for many people during the last third of the sixteenth century. Meanwhile, the Swiss Confederation appeared to offer an alternative, encouraging a desire among peasants and burghers to 'turn Swiss'. Although the Hegau and Sundgau communities applied to join during the Peasants War, most were too far away for this to be an immediate option, while the Confederation had no desire to become involved. South-west German peasants continued to voice this aspiration occasionally during disputes with lords into the eighteenth century.[85] Imperial cities had greater prospects, since they enjoyed the same immediacy as the Swiss cantons. The Confederation extended special protection to favoured allies as 'associated places' (*Zugewandte Orte*) after 1475.[86]

The issue became pressing during the 1530s as Zwinglianism, the Swiss brand of Protestantism, gained ground in several Swabian, Alsatian and Rhenish cities, while princes like Philipp of Hessen saw the Swiss as potential allies of the Schmalkaldic League.[87] The Schmalkalders' defeat in 1547 exposed the risks of confessionally based alliances, while the Swiss were increasingly reluctant to accept the liabilities that came with additional associates. Even existing associates were neglected. For example, Rottweil allowed its associate status to lapse during the later sixteenth century when, like many other imperial cities, it saw greater advantages in cooperating with more immediate neighbours in the Kreis Assembly, and with other cities in the Reichstag. It tried to reactivate the link when threatened by the duke of Württemberg during the Thirty Years War. That conflict threatened to reopen confessional tensions within the Confederation, which struggled to maintain neutrality. The Swiss only lodged an ineffectual protest when Württemberg captured Rottweil in 1632, and instead it was the imperial army that liberated the city two years later.[88] The Swiss opt-out of imperial institutions meant their voice carried no weight within the Empire's legal system, preventing them from aiding their associates.

ESTATES

The Dutch and Bohemian Revolts

The incorporated assemblies that emerged in virtually all territories from the late fourteenth century were another form of association. They enjoyed a stronger legal basis than peasant communes, whose rights were more local, while their involvement in territorial taxation and politics had encouraged a higher level of institutional development, with committees, archives, fiscal systems and, often, involvement in militia organization. They also combined several status groups, unlike rural and urban communes, which generally excluded clergy and nobility, the two wealthiest social Estates. Estates offered two possible alternatives to princely led territorialization. They could develop trans-territorial federations similar to the larger Alpine leagues, but based on agreements between Estates assemblies rather than among towns and incorporated valleys. Alternatively, they might remain within territorial boundaries, but transform government along more republican lines.

Both possibilities were early modern phenomena, the first peaking between about 1560 and 1620 with the emergence of the Dutch Republic and the outbreak of the Bohemian Revolt. The Estates of the seven northern Burgundian provinces formed a union in 1579 following their rebellion against Spanish rule around a decade earlier. The union established its own common institutions in 1585, effectively becoming an independent republic by 1609, though a further 27 years of renewed fighting after 1621 were necessary to secure definitive recognition from Spain.[89] The republic's official name was the United Provinces, each of which was governed by its own States, or assembly, composed of representatives from towns and landowning knights. The seven States sent delegates to a common States General to coordinate defence and represent the republic to outsiders.

The Dutch initially struggled to govern without a king, briefly raising the prospect, between 1577 and 1581, that they might accept Archduke Matthias, the future emperor, as a constitutional monarch. He was followed by François d'Anjou as *prince et seigneur* until the latter's death in 1584 coincided with more favourable military circumstances that enabled radicals to consolidate a more republican form of government.[90] A serious monarchical element was nonetheless retained in the position of 'stadholder', or governor appointed by the States of each province. These positions could be combined by one person, enabling the influential princes of Orange to assume political leadership of the republic for long periods.[91]

The Dutch were thus well on their way to establishing an Estates-based republic when the Protestant nobility of the Austrian monarchy sought to use similar institutions to underpin their bid for constitutional and religious liberties after 1618. The Bohemian and Austrian Estates were well established and accustomed to cooperating across provincial boundaries to coordinate taxes and defence against the Turks. They also had strong ties to their Polish and Hungarian equivalents thanks to the legacy of common rule under the Jagiellon family. Many

Humanists considered Polish and Czech as dialects of a common language, while aristocrats of all four countries were frequently multilingual, or could at least converse with each other in Latin. Study at German and Italian universities provided further common bonds, as did military service against the Turks. Above all, they shared concepts of corporate rights (*libertates*), conceiving themselves as a *societas civilis* sustained by individual engagement for the public good through office-holding, representation in provincial diets and general opposition to *dominium absolutum*, or unrestrained royal rule, considered dangerous to all inhabitants.[92]

The ideology of the Estates as public guardians gained ground with the Habsburg failures and dynastic infighting after 1606, while concessions from the rival archdukes added to each province's store of privileges. The famous Letter of Majesty extorted from Rudolf II allowed the Protestant members of the Bohemian Estates to establish what amounted to a parallel government after 1609. However, the dynasty's renewed confidence enticed many key figures to signal renewed loyalty by converting to Catholicism. Skilful management ensured that the Bohemian diet accepted Archduke Ferdinand, the future emperor, as their king in June 1617.[93] The Bohemian elite was thus far from united when the radical malcontents staged the Defenestration of Prague in May 1618, precipitating a full-scale revolt.

However, it would be wrong to see the revolt in the Austrian Habsburg lands as doomed on account of its largely aristocratic leadership, compared to their supposedly more progressive, bourgeois Dutch equivalents. The Dutch provinces were already Europe's most economically advanced region. The rebels benefited from continued economic growth, enabling them to develop permanent, disciplined armed forces whose loyalty was secured through regular pay.[94] This enabled the Dutch to win independence with the conventional military methods of a regular army under state control, despite the significance of both their civic militia and maritime piracy to republican ideology. Theirs was not a people's war. The Bohemian and Austrian rebels attempted the same, even preferring to negotiate for Ottoman military aid rather than arm their peasants. However, they never solved their financial problems, and their army's discontent at its pay arrears was a major factor in its catastrophic defeat at White Mountain in 1620.[95]

The Bohemian rebels formally deposed Ferdinand and established the *Confoederatio Bohemica* on 31 July 1619.[96] The five Bohemian provinces established a Confederation, whilst retaining self-government like the Dutch provinces. Although in many ways still conservative, the Confederation's leadership adopted new institutions, like a general diet of all five provinces and a common supreme court. In an effort to make the union work, Bohemia accepted parity of status and rights with the other four provinces. The Confederation was extended on 16 August through a federation with the Protestant rebel factions in Upper and Lower Austria, while later an alliance was formed with the prince of Transylvania, who had instigated renewed revolt in Habsburg Hungary. The Confederates designed their constitution ahead of offering the Bohemian crown to Frederick V, the elector Palatine, who unwisely accepted, thereby widening the revolt into the Thirty Years War (see pp. 123–6). Whilst following a broadly similar trajectory to the Dutch, the Bohemian rebels moved faster in rejecting the Habsburgs, thanks to their stronger identity as a distinct country.

Like the Dutch, they faced considerable problems in rallying the support of the wider population. There were still substantial Catholic minorities, who were discriminated against under the new constitution and whose presence increased the Habsburgs' incentive to continue fighting. The leading rebels were largely Calvinists, whereas the majority of Bohemians were Utraquists or Lutherans. The obviously Calvinist bias of Frederick V and his courtiers alienated many Bohemians.[97] Religious diversity was both greater and more problematic than during the Dutch Revolt. Despite their common bonds, there were also significant divisions between Austria, Bohemia and Hungary, as well as amongst their component provinces, while the tradition of general diets was less established than that of the Burgundian States General. Concern for provincial liberties frustrated military and fiscal coordination, seriously undermining the Confederation's war effort.

Wider circumstances were also against the Bohemians and their allies. Their uprising was broadly regarded as a repeat of the earlier Dutch Revolt, which had been marked by sectarian violence and civil war. The Defenestration immediately rebounded on the rebels. Their preferred choice as leader, the Lutheran Saxon elector, Johann Georg I, refused to have anything to do with them and eventually aided Ferdinand II in crushing the rebellion. International assistance was less forthcoming or effective than that received by the Dutch, with the

Dutch themselves aiding the Bohemians only as a means to keep both Habsburg branches distracted.[98]

The Jülich-Cleves Estates Union

The historical prominence of the Dutch and Bohemian revolts has over-shadowed another example of Estates-based federalism: the union of the Cleves, Mark, Jülich and Berg Estates in 1521. This was formed to match the acquisition of all four principalities by a single family previ-ously ruling just Cleves and Mark. All four assemblies retained their own administration and laws, but the previous two pairings of Cleves-Mark and Jülich-Berg forged closer ties. Further consolidation was inhibited by the spread of Protestantism, which failed to convert all inhabitants, leaving the four principalities confessionally mixed. The Estates also suffered from the usual tensions between nobles and towns over the subdivision of tax burdens. However, the duke was also unable to forge a more unitary administration, not least due to his defeat by Charles V in 1542–3 over rival claims to Geldern, which left him with 633,000 talers in debt. The duke was then forced to allow the four Estates a greater role in governance.

The Estates retained influence throughout the sixteenth century, thanks to further problems. The Dutch Revolt after 1566 threatened to destabilize the entire Lower Rhine, while the accession of the mentally ill Duke Johann Wilhelm in 1592 opened the question of succession as he had no direct heirs. The ducal government regularly dealt with a combined committee representing the four Estates from the 1580s, especially to promote an irenic form of Christianity intended to reduce sectarianism and deny outsiders excuses for intervention. A month ahead of Johann Wilhelm's death in May 1609, the Estates agreed to remain united and not to favour either of the two main claimants, Brandenburg or Pfalz-Neuburg. They failed to prevent a short war in 1609–10 that led to de facto partition, with Brandenburg holding Cleves and Mark, and Pfalz-Neuburg occupying Jülich and Berg. Nonetheless, Estates' envoys continued to work for an amicable settle-ment, and they were included collectively in the Treaty of Xanten (1614), by which Spain and the Dutch avoided open war by mutually accepting continued partition of this strategic area.[99]

The Estates renewed their union in 1647 as it was feared the partition might become permanent. They hoped to preserve the integrity of the four principalities and their associated dependencies in Ravenstein and Ravensberg. These goals were traditional and the Estates did not seek to usurp princely powers and form a republic. However, the princes suspected them of wanting to 'turn Dutch' through a federation with the United Provinces. Dutch commercial and religious influence was strong across the Lower Rhine and Westphalia, and was underpinned between 1614 and 1679 by the occupation of strategic small towns.[100] Charges of seeking to join the Dutch were also levelled against the Estates of both East Frisia and the bishopric of Münster. The princes' criticism reflected genuine fears for their own authority, but was also good propaganda since it presented the Estates as trying to leave the Empire. The Estates were also disadvantaged by the Peace of Westphalia, which firmly identified them as belonging to the mediate political sphere, thus clearly denying them the right to negotiate with external powers.

Elector Frederick William of Brandenburg was particularly aggressive, refusing to allow a general diet of the united Estates and attempting to isolate them by dealing with each individually. However, the elector overplayed his hand by invading Jülich-Berg in a bid to seize the entire inheritance in 1651. Although they lacked formal representation in the Reichstag, the Estates sent envoys to the meeting in 1653–4, causing Frederick William to fear that Emperor Ferdinand III might respond to their petition by depriving him of Cleves and Mark. However, the outcome indicated that the days of Estates unions were over. Ferdinand III preferred to deal with the elector, who, as an imperial prince, was party to much wider political issues, notably resolving Sweden's relationship to the Empire following the Thirty Years War. Brandenburg's compromise with Pfalz-Neuburg in 1666 removed the Estates' last hope as both princes agreed that the partition was permanent and forbade further unions between the assemblies.[101]

Republicanism

Republican ideas were rarely involved in these struggles, except for the Dutch once they decided to reject Spanish rule entirely. Dutch republicanism was inspired by the late Humanist reading of ancient Greek and Roman history and philosophy that presented an idealized society of sober, patriotic citizens.[102] This aspect of the classical legacy was largely rejected in the Empire, which drew inspiration instead from imperial Rome. Later sixteenth-century observers interpreted the French and Netherlands civil wars as the direct consequence of 'Monarchomachs', or self-appointed 'king-makers' who had usurped divine authority and overturned all proper order. These beliefs were reinforced by the experience of the Bohemian Revolt and subsequent Thirty Years War, as well as the parallel British civil wars, which culminated in the execution of Charles I in January 1649 and Cromwell's military dictatorship. By the late seventeenth century, German thinkers even criticized their few predecessors, like Johannes Althusius, who had advocated a greater role for territorial Estates in governance.[103] Most commentators interpreted republicanism as moral rather than constitutional, relating it to the early modern ideal of a *res publica*, or a commonwealth where liberties were safeguarded by orderly government and the rule of law. This accorded Estates their traditional role as part of the broader multilayered legal structure protecting German liberties in the Empire.

Gottlieb Samuel Treuer was the first to link despotism explicitly with tyranny, in 1719, thereby encouraging a trend to discuss politics in binary abstract terms like freedom *or* slavery, rather than as remedies for specific problems. However, the Empire's political pluralism encouraged most writers to focus on finding the right balance among existing institutions rather than present politics as a stark choice between diverging alternatives.[104] The century after the Thirty Years War saw the slow acceptance of the idea of the impersonal state at the level of the Empire's territories, defining these as public entities embodied less by their princes than by charters, laws and legal agreements belonging to all inhabitants. This adversely affected how many intellectuals viewed the Estates, which were increasingly criticized as sectional, corporate interest groups, rather than benevolent guardians of inhabitants' liberties. Authors now assigned civil freedoms to a new conception of the private sphere, in which individuals were entitled to act as they pleased within the law, sheltered from arbitrary state intervention.

Debates increasingly hinged on what form of government could best guarantee such freedoms. The outbreak of the American Revolutionary War in 1775 attracted wide attention, not least because America's last king, George III, was also elector of Hanover and hired 30,000 Germans to suppress the kind of liberties many intellectuals desired for the

Empire. The war placed a 'German' monarch clearly in a despotic, even tyrannical role. The debate widened during the 1780s as intellectuals deliberately addressed wider audiences through the burgeoning periodicals and regular press, leading to calls for 'people's representation' by 1790. These advocated replacing assemblies based on corporate social status, with gender and wealth criteria, simultaneously opening direct representation to all richer males, whilst still denying it to the poor and more clearly excluding all females.[105]

Although some writers now envisaged states without princes, debates in the Empire still differed from those in the anglophone world. English-speaking writers since the late seventeenth century had linked political organization to property. The primary purpose of the social contract believed to underpin civil society was the preservation of property. Consequently, property-owners should have a say in government, an argument that the Americans expressed in 1775 as 'no taxation without representation'. By contrast, German writers generally continued to define the state as the rule of law, arguing that good laws protected rights and property. Justi still saw the Estates, like Althusius had, as guardians of laws, rather than law-makers. Most Germans regarded fully republican government as dangerous, citing the examples of Britain and Poland-Lithuania to argue that disassociating representation from corporate groups and incorporated communities gave too much scope for divisive 'parties' and 'factions'. Without imperative mandates, representatives would be free to pursue their own self-interests. These arguments gained a new lease of life as news arrived after 1789 of the horrifying excesses of the French revolutionaries, while the final two Polish partitions (1793 and 1795) suggested that factionalism could lead to political extinction.[106]

Actual practice remained in the established pattern, as exemplified by the discussions since 1762 of how to revive Saxony, which had been devastated during the Seven Years War. The need to finance reform raised the question of taxation and representation, but proposals concentrated on detailed tinkering with existing structures, for example by suggesting the nobles should assume a greater share of common burdens and allow commoners holding knights' fiefs to exercise the associated rights to participate in diets. The pace of change accelerated slightly following large-scale peasant protest between August and October 1790. The Saxon Estates were modified in 1805, but it was not until 1831 that they were replaced by a two-chamber parliament that finally abolished the nobles' patrimonial jurisdiction in 1855.[107]

The Saxon unrest encompassed 50 parishes and was the largest popular protest in the Empire outside the Habsburg lands since the Peasants War. It was caused by frustration at the local courts' inability to clear a backlog of 230 cases against lordly exactions and abuses. Contemporaries stressed the differences between Saxony and France, including the resolution of the former's problems through the established methods of administrative and judicial review, rather than mass bloodshed. The Saxons were not seeking a new form of government, but to make the existing one work properly. Where peasants did criticize Estates as unrepresentative, it was simply to reinforce demands that they be included as a corporate group.[108] Association was thus a way in which different social groups could secure specific identities and rights within a hierarchical corporate legal and political order. The next chapter examines how this order attempted to regulate disputes between these groups and how far it could accommodate further change by the late eighteenth century.

12

Justice

FINDING THE LAW

Justice in the Empire

Peace and justice were considered essential to any community throughout the Middle Ages and early modernity, as they are today. The
authorities' capacity to maintain law and order was central to how they
were perceived. As in many other respects, the Empire has often been
judged as ineffectual, because it favoured arbitration rather than swift
and unambiguous verdicts.[1] There has also been a tendency to see protest as an intrusion threatening political stability, rather than as a form
of negotiation and a check on arbitrary power. Investigating how the
Empire handled conflict and disorder reinforces the findings of the two
previous two chapters that its social and political structures were
closely interwoven. This section examines the conventions guiding
conflict resolution across all levels of the Empire's society. The second
section argues that legal and judicial arrangements were primarily
intended to find and sustain workable compromises, ideally through
reconciliation rather than exemplary punishment. The chapter con-
cludes by questioning how far the Empire remained a viable social and
political order by the later eighteenth century.

Justice developed in line with the Empire's decentralized structure
and was influenced by what would later be called 'public opinion'. Consensus was an ideal throughout medieval Europe, but assumed an
unusually significant place in the Empire, because enforcement mechanisms remained weak, necessitating broad acceptance beyond those
immediately involved to ensure verdicts were not ignored. The general

European pattern saw judicial institutions evolve as part of political centralization, placing them under more obvious central (usually royal) control. The degree of judicial independence thus determined how far justice was politicized. The Empire's judicial structures were more genuinely independent of central authority, though we will see that this did not mean they were necessarily 'modern'. Politicization was far less a matter of royal interference than of how far those charged with settling a case were influenced by wider interests.

Justice involved finding laws appropriate to circumstances. From its foundation, the Empire used an eclectic combination of written and unwritten laws. The latter, often labelled as 'customs', were not necessarily inferior to written systems, which themselves should not be interpreted as direct precursors to later practice. Medieval lawyers distinguished between *lex* as law deriving from contracts between rulers and subjects over (usually) specific matters, and *ius* as law in general expressed variously in statutes, court verdicts, and broader concepts of fairness and justice. These distinctions did not always survive in practice over time, while the situation was further complicated by the fact that written laws remained largely uncodified; even the largest German territories had not completed codification of their own legal systems by 1806, while imperial law existed separately as a bundle of charters, legislation and recorded precedents. The Empire was scarcely unique in this respect: eighteenth-century France had 800,000 laws in 300 separate regional codes.[2]

Law thus had multiple sources. All were identified with tradition, but this could be (re)invented, allowing considerable flexibility whilst appearing to remain rooted in an idealized past. The disadvantage was the obvious lack of clarity and the almost inevitable delays, especially as both law and judicial procedure adopted written forms during early modernity. Delay could soften the process, at least outside criminal proceedings, by allowing more time for compromise. Consensus also had theological roots. Final judgement was reserved for God, while the perceived imperfections of earthly existence encouraged an emphasis on 'fairness' (*Billigkeit*), rather than abstract justice according to unambiguous law (*Gerechtigkeit*). In short, participants usually accepted that human life was complex and that both parties shared the blame in many disputes.[3]

Forms of Law

Much of the Frankish legal system appears superficially modern. It derived in part from ninth-century readings of ancient Roman practice encouraging Carolingian kings to assert the authoritarian ideal of themselves as chief magistrate and law-giver, and to issue written capitularies (see Plate 29). In fact, these were legally binding guidelines relating to specific activities like managing royal farms, rather than comprehensive codes. They were usually issued after consultation with bishops, and (often) counts, and they mixed elements of secular law with moral injunctions for good behaviour.[4] They sat alongside a variety of tribal law codes written down by Frankish officials and supposedly embodying the distinctive customs of each of the Empire's peoples (see pp. 238–9). The codes dealt with major moral and social issues, especially relating to property and its uses, and to crimes against people and objects. They listed compensation in the form of fines to be paid to victims and their relatives, as well as punishments for more grievous offences, especially those against the king or church. For example, a code from 797 imposed the death penalty for those resisting conversion or who cremated their dead according to pagan rites. The capitularies and tribal codes stood in loose relationship to manorial law (*Hofrecht*), which governed the manorial economy by upholding lordly control over the manor's management and its dependent labour. Like the capitularies, manorial law was largely a set of guidelines specifying the choice of crops and timing of planting and harvesting. The natural annual cycle of decisions gradually accumulated further precedents as local 'wisdoms' (*Weistümer*) providing further guidance.[5]

There were two further forms of institutional law. One comprised the rules governing the core activities of the elite and their relations to the monarch: homage, vassalage, fealty, right of counsel, fief-holding and its military and material obligations. As we have seen (pp. 356–65), these rules would be interpreted from the twelfth century as feudal law (*Lehensrecht*). Some elements originated in Carolingian capitularies, but much derived from royal diplomas and charters issued by the Ottonians and Salians, conferring special legal privileges outlining the rights, benefits and obligations of the recipients, and more generally by extension also the inhabitants of particular fiefs. Like manorial law, much accumulated over time as recorded precedents, for example the verdicts (*sententiae*) of royal courts in individual cases. The second form was canon law, comprising the body of written laws and accepted practices governing the structure and operation of the church. Thanks to its greater standardization and wider dissemination, this was the most widely available form of written law. As such, it was the primary focus of legal study and commentary, and it influenced decisions well beyond ecclesiastical matters. Canon law was given greater coherence by a twelfth-century Italian monk called Gratian, but the reception of his *Decretum* was slowed in Germany by the absence of recognized law schools prior to the founding of Prague University in 1348.[6]

The growth in written law from the eleventh century stemmed from the desire to fix rules and encourage greater consistency of treatment, as well as to accommodate urban growth and the transition from manors to tenancies. Civic law (*Stadtrecht*) developed to enable towns to manage their own affairs as legal corporations. Village law (*Dorfrecht*) followed more slowly by the later fourteenth century for the same purpose. Both forms were linked to written charters regulating specific arrangements applying to each community and its relationship to local lords. Emperors issued four general statutes between 1037 and 1158 regulating vassalage and other aspects of feudal relations. Frederick II's charters of 1220 and 1231 for the ecclesiastical and secular princes were also part of this development.[7] Emperors continued to issue specific laws in response to particular cases, such as Henry III, who imposed the death penalty for poisoning and assassination in Italy, and disinherited children from marriages involving underaged brides.[8]

Ancient Roman law had never been entirely forgotten, but existed only in limited compendia compiled in the early Middle Ages. Scholars began piecing these together in the 1090s, and their efforts received wider attention with the growing significance of Italian and French law schools across the next century. The main impact was procedural: law did not have to be 'found' in each case according to local wisdom, but instead already existed as a universally applicable code. The task of identifying the relevant parts and applying these to the specifics of each case was entrusted to lawyers, in turn further accelerating the expansion of higher education to train these experts. This fundamentally transformed individuals' relationship to the judicial process. Litigants no longer confronted each other directly, but through their legal representatives, while the position of judge shifted from arbiter to someone charged with determining guilt and setting appropriate punishment. The growing acceptance of these principles created 'common law' (*ius commune*) as a secular competitor to canon law as a universally applicable legal system. Common law gained ground thanks to the need for common rules to allow individual communities to decide cases involving outsiders whose local laws were different to their own. This created a tension between common or Roman law and local custom, especially because the growing practice of recording all kinds of guidelines and decisions made changes and discrepancies increasingly obvious. However, written law long remained primarily a tool against 'bad custom' rather than a challenge to tradition.[9]

The political impact of these changes remained ambiguous. They did not necessarily promote centralization, because judges were required at multiple levels within the nascent corporate society. For example, Italian cities quickly incorporated Roman law into their own judicial systems. The parallel development of civic and village law encouraged the acceptance of communities as possessing the right of self-regulation (*ius statuendi*), which in turn gave shape to the police measures in towns and territories issued to cover activities and situations not legislated for in existing written law (see pp. 534–8). Meanwhile, the complementary character of the imperial hierarchy encouraged princely innovation guided by the public-peace legislation from the thirteenth century.

The famous *Mirror of the Saxons* (*Sachsenspiegel*) was written around 1224 by Eike von Repkow, a judge from the Magdeburg area, who compiled a wide-ranging set of precedents, customs and pieces of written law. His text was translated into the south German dialect and influenced a similar Swabian compendium (*Schwabenspiegel*) appearing in 1275. Both attracted considerable historical attention, but they were really partisan attempts to describe how the Empire worked rather than actual law codes. These only appeared at the start of the fifteenth century, for example in the Tirol in 1404, and represented a new, territorial form of law (*Landrecht*) drawn up by princes in consultation with their Estates in response to complaints at abuses and inconsistencies. The spread of law codes was facilitated by the growing number of advisors trained in secular, especially Roman, law, who increasingly displaced the clerics previously staffing princely chancelleries. The process of fixing practice in writing accelerated with the advent of printing, which allowed the swift dissemination of multiple copies throughout a territory. Territorial legislation became increasingly ambitious, merging with police measures to cover wider aspects of daily life. For example, the bishopric of Bamberg adopted a uniform criminal code across its territory in 1506. The framers of these codes clung to their original intention of producing a definitive document based on principles considered timeless and unchanging, whilst still protecting local and particular rights. These conflicting aims were never satisfactorily reconciled, while new circumstances added to pressures for revisions. Tirol had replaced its first general code three times by 1474.

The Impact of Written Law

The Reformation renewed the moral impulse behind legislation and encouraged attempts to derive scriptural law (*ius scripturae*) from the Bible as a blueprint for a godly society. Luther and other Protestant theologians abandoned this after radicalization of the project during the Peasants War (see pp. 592–4). So-called 'Godly Law' persisted, but was slowly absorbed within more secular ideas of Natural Law as common underlying aspects of human existence, exemplified by appeals to 'natural justice'. This process intensified the engagement with Roman law, already gathering pace in Germany since the late fifteenth century when Humanists rejected the earlier, twelfth-century articulation of ancient codes as incomplete, whilst simultaneously abandoning the medieval scholastic practice of trying to harmonize Roman precepts with Christianity. Instead, Humanists now sought to reconstruct the 'pure' original Roman version.[10]

Their scholarly project had direct practical application, because the growth of territorial law codes increased the attraction of a single benchmark to resolve anomalies and to judge complex cases involving different communities. Roman legal concepts were adopted in the procedural ordinances prepared for the two supreme courts established by imperial reform in the 1490s, as well as the *Carolina* penal code of 1532, and the imperial police ordinances of 1530, 1548 and 1577. Meanwhile, the legally binding decisions of the Reichstag and other imperial institutions were published after 1501 in a semi-official series that ran to over 40 editions. Together, these printed codes and ordinances influenced widespread revision of territorial laws and judicial practice, while the norms and procedures of imperial law were further disseminated through their place in the curricula of the new universities established to train territorial and local officials. In practice, there was still considerable scope for custom to plug gaps in territorial and imperial law, especially as popular ideals of 'fairness' enabled custom to be invoked to justify what were often innovatory measures responding to new circumstances.[11]

The eighteenth century saw the abandonment of earlier attempts to reconcile positive written law with idealized underlying systems of Godly or Natural Law. Instead, law was to be rationalized according to the Enlightened belief in human reason, primarily by removing inconsistencies between local and territorial practice. This explicitly centralized both law and judicial practice, since it involved curbing local initiative to ensure that such inconsistencies did not re-emerge. Enlightened codification was potentially revolutionary, because it moved legitimacy from theology and towards secular ideals of citizenship. The purpose of law was increasingly understood as guaranteeing individual human rights to life and property. Progress was slow, because rationalization encountered the same difficulties as earlier attempts at standardization. For example, Frederick William I abandoned initial attempts to codify Prussia's laws. His son renewed the attempt in 1746, but work stalled when Prussia's chief justice died in 1755. A third attempt was made after 1780, culminating in the promulgation of the famous General Law of the Prussian Lands (*Allgemeines Landrecht*) in 1794. The use of the plural 'lands' for the components of the Prussian monarchy indicates the continued force of tradition, which extended to preserving the nobility's corporate status.[12]

Austria separated its administration and judiciary only in 1749, but each province continued to use different laws. General criminal codes were issued in 1768 and 1787, but the process of codifying the monarchy's legal systems was abandoned in 1766 after 13 years of work, because Joseph II realized a uniform code would require a similarly uniform judicial structure, which, at that point, seemed beyond the realm of possibility. Work resumed once he changed his mind in 1780, but it took another 31 years to complete.[13] Similar initiatives in other territories either failed, halted after partial codification, or simply drew together existing practice in a single document without addressing inconsistencies. In short, the development of law mirrored that of the Empire generally in that it created multiple, partially conflicting and overlapping systems arranged in a complex hierarchy that defied rational logic.[14]

JURIDIFICATION

Conflict Resolution

It is characteristic of the Empire that the transition to written law consolidated a decentralized form of conflict resolution, rather than a centralized judiciary deciding right from wrong according to abstract principles. In doing so, it 'juridified' much earlier forms of conflict resolution by reshaping them along more bureaucratic and institutional lines without losing the emphasis on preserving peace through workable compromises. Like other aspects of the Empire's corporate society, these practices were found across the socio-political hierarchy, establishing attitudes and behaviours that persisted even after individual territories slipped beyond the direct reach of most imperial institutions.

Our sources are sparse for much of the Empire's medieval legal history, and mostly present what their writers thought justice *should* be rather than how it was actually applied. For its first five centuries, the Empire's inhabitants were less concerned with identifying which law had been broken than determining who had been wronged and how. Judgements might refer to specific documents, like the charters cited in Otto II's ruling on a property dispute in favour of the abbot of San Vincenzo on the Volturno in 981.[15] The authorities also recognized that writing was necessary to record decisions and could be produced to challenge earlier verdicts. However, decisions usually invoked law only as a generality underpinning their authority. The key questions remained the status of those involved and the jurisdiction they fell under, while practical issues predominated over learned legal debate.

Medieval chronicles record so many disputes that it is easy to get lost in the detail of individual cases. Nonetheless, it is possible to detect three recurring issues. One concerned perceived failures relating to the hierarchy of rights and responsibilities, including the duty of those of higher status to protect the powerless, and the especially grievous charge of felony, defined as a vassal's improper behaviour towards a superior lord. A key element in the latter was infidelity, which involved a breach of loyalty, such as abandoning a lord in battle or failing to follow a summons, especially if called repeatedly. Other serious felonies included disturbing the peace through excessive force, or entering into relations injurious or offensive to one's overlord, for instance by accepting vassalage from another lord without permission. Rebellion was defined as open defiance or attacks on a lord's friends or clients. Felony amongst immediate lords included actions undermining the *honor imperii*, such as those of Balderich, who was removed from his post as margrave of Friaul in 828 for neglecting frontier defence against the Bulgarians.[16]

A second category involved disputes about status and honour, which defined the relationship of individuals and communities to the broader socio-political order. This type of conflict was pronounced in periods of rapid socio-economic change, notably the later eleventh to twelfth century, and again in the later fourteenth and later fifteenth centuries. Disagreements over jurisdictions formed the third category and were endemic to the growth of a denser, more complex hierarchy of lords and communities. Such disputes involved access to resources, the exercise of mint, toll and tax rights, as well as judicial powers themselves. These last two categories of dispute reflected the local and personal character of justice for most of the Empire's history. Jurisdiction was determined by the social-legal status of the parties involved, varying not just between major corporate social groups like clergy, nobility and commons, but also according to the specific character of the litigants' local rights. Late medieval police regulation and early modern territorial law incorporated military personnel, courtiers, palace servants, public officials, university staff and a host of others as groups enjoying distinct legal status. The nature of the offence provided another variable, determining whether a case should be heard before civil, ecclesiastical, feudal or some other kind of tribunal. Complex cases often made it difficult to decide which court or law applied.

The Empire's legal history is essentially a story of delineating these responsibilities and aligning them with the evolving status hierarchy, whilst sustaining consultative processes and collective enforcement of decisions. Justice was already decentralized and local under the

Carolingians, something that is scarcely surprising given the population's dispersal over a wide area with poor communications. In the ninth century, counts handled secular cases within their counties, acting as judges (*Schöffen*) who both passed and enforced verdicts (*placita*). The counts' judicial function declined as their authority shifted towards hereditary lordship from the tenth century, and there was no direct continuity between the Carolingian county structure and the territorial superior jurisdictions that emerged in the thirteenth century (see pp. 365–77). One factor in this change was the Ottonians' grant of immunities from comital jurisdiction to the inhabitants of episcopal towns. Another was the practice of abbots and bishops to issue their own guidelines for the dependent populations of their benefices.

The Ottonians continued the Carolingian ideal of the king as chief magistrate and their law court continued to take precedence wherever it went during the monarch's progress around the realm. However, local jurisdiction was permanent and (increasingly) hereditary, whereas royal judicial authority remained itinerant and by the twelfth century related to a monarchy which was clearly elective.[17] The king's real role was to embody idealized justice through exemplary action in serious cases, with a secondary function to intervene if lesser authorities failed to resolve problems satisfactorily. Kings retained considerable initiative, especially over deciding how and when to intervene, as well as the prestige to annul local decisions by, for example, claiming they were based on 'bad custom'. Kings could also transfer custom from one area to another: Henry III rejected a complaint from some Bohemians that he was breaking agreements made by one of his predecessors by arguing that every king added new laws.

However, kings were rarely able to decide weighty matters unilaterally, because they were expected to be guided by 'good counsel'. Occasionally, tenth- and early eleventh-century kings overruled grumbling lords, but usually they favoured consensus, since verdicts generally considered just stood a better chance of being accepted and enforced.[18] For this reason, royal court verdicts were signed by all who had participated in making them. This practice was replicated in courts chaired by dukes, counts and other lesser magistrates. Wrongdoers were expected to provide *satisfactio* commensurate with the *offensio* they had caused. For much of the early Middle Ages, redress was often in the form of material *compensatio*. The authorities' role was to oversee and adjudicate this process, ensuring that perpetrator and victim agreed 'reasonable' terms. Morality provided certain guidelines, notably that the 'poor and defenceless' were not to suffer, nor should a weaker party be crushed entirely, even if in the wrong. How this applied in practice was another matter.

Felony and Infidelity

Cases involving felony and infidelity were the ones that really mattered to the Empire's highly competitive elite, because no lord could allow affronts to go unpunished without losing face. Prior to the emergence of Estates society in the eleventh century, honour was reserved to the free minority who alone were considered fully responsible for their actions, entitling them both to be rewarded with respect for good behaviour and to be punished for misdemeanours. However, contemporaries recognized that a free person's disobedience could be a reasonable protest at a perceived injustice, for example a lord's neglect of his vassals' legal rights. This imparted a similar dynamic to medieval disputes within the elite as would be displayed in popular unrest after the high Middle Ages: protest was a way to oblige authorities to change their behaviour or provide redress. At all social levels, most disputes involved posturing, as the interested parties mixed symbolic assertions of the legitimacy of their case with demonstrations of their material power, including the controlled use of violence. The aim was to rally support whilst undermining their opponent's position. There were broadly understood stages of escalation, with higher authorities usually only becoming involved once a cycle of reprisals had deepened into a longer-running feud, by which time it was often difficult to distinguish 'right' from 'wrong'.[19]

The king or senior lord usually acted cautiously. If he was not immediately party to the dispute, he could encourage those involved to accept his mediation. If the case concerned him directly, he would invite a relative or other influential figure to act as a discreet broker. These practices are fundamental to the Empire's character as a mixed system. Rebellions were not about lords resisting the creation of a centralized monarchy, but personal disputes amongst the Empire's ruling elite. Royal justice was thus not 'neutral', but part of a dynamic process by which the elite resolved contentious issues.

Leading vassals could be summoned to form what would later be called a 'feudal court' (*Lehenshof*), composed of the peers of those involved in the dispute. The king could preside or deputize the role of judge. The accused would be summoned to account for their actions. During the Ottonian era such courts generally refrained from formulating clear charges, allowing those involved to compromise without losing face by presenting the dispute as a misunderstanding. The Carolingians and Salians tended to act more clearly as judges from the outset. Nonetheless, judicial authority remained primarily moral rather than institutional, encouraging compromise by stigmatizing those flouting the rules. Excessive violence or failure to appear before the court was construed as placing that party automatically in the wrong, enabling the authorities to dispense with a formal hearing and proceed immediately to punishment. This practice became enshrined by early modernity as the concept of 'notoriety', whereby an individual demonstrated their guilt through wanton disregard for accepted norms. Those identified as guilty this way could be branded in absentia as a public enemy (*hostis publicus*) in a practice that had become known by early modernity as the 'imperial ban' (*Reichsacht*): they were declared outlaws, suspending any rights or legal protection, voiding any contracts and freeing any dependants, servants or subjects from any obligations. The purpose of this process was to isolate the accused, depriving them of support, and thus reducing the need for violence to apprehend and punish them.[20]

The dispute between Otto I and his son Liudolf illustrates these methods. As always, the causes were complex and included disagreements between father and son over intervention in Italy, and Liudolf's anxiety for his inheritance following his father's second marriage in 951. Liudolf signalled his protest by boycotting the family's Easter celebrations in 952, an action intended to undermine Otto's standing among the aristocracy. The latter, however, largely rallied to Otto, showing their support by attending his court. Bolstered by their presence, Otto issued an ultimatum to Liudolf and his principal ally, Conrad the Red, duke of Lorraine (who was also Otto's son-in-law): both were to attend the royal court to answer for their actions, or face the consequences. Following their failure to appear, Otto deprived Conrad of his duchy, but initially refrained from issuing a verdict against Liudolf. Both sides rallied their vassals and began a series of raids and other military operations intended to demonstrate strength and lend weight to negotiations discreetly brokered by the archbishops of Mainz and Cologne. Conrad eventually accepted the loss of Lorraine in return for a royal pardon. Increasingly isolated, Liudolf pre-empted another summons from his father by seeking him out whilst hunting near Weimar in 954. Having begged for mercy, Liudolf was pardoned, partly as a public show of family solidarity in the face of a renewed Magyar invasion.[21]

Conrad the Red's removal from office (*Absetzung*) represented the standard punishment for serious felony cases. The evolution of the Empire's elite into hereditary lords made this quite complicated. The Ottonians distinguished between revoking a fief (and its associated title and jurisdictions) and the fate of the culprit's own property. Whereas they generally spared the latter, the Salians were more likely to confiscate allodial possessions as well as revoking a fief, and in extreme cases extended expropriation to the assets of wives and relations. Early medieval kings imprisoned some felons by entrusting them to the supervision of loyal abbots or bishops. Wayward royal relatives could find themselves shut up in isolated monasteries. Banishment was often preferred, removing an individual from their local networks without the cost of imprisoning them. Excommunication could supplement banishment by excluding the culprit from the community of believers. Death was possible, but was rarely used for senior lords, though lesser vassals were executed for perceived serious offences. Death sentences were passed far more frequently than they were implemented, because medieval kings could gain prestige by commuting them as an act of clemency, though this became less common under the Salians and Staufers. Lesser lords and commoners were always treated less favourably. Louis II 'the German' hanged so many criminals that the archbishop of Mainz was forced to institute special measures to stop the corpses becoming a health hazard.[22]

There was no fixed scale of punishments, partly due to the secondary and incomplete character of written law at this point, but also because cases were judged according to circumstances. Repeat offenders were treated more severely, but the authorities were also conscious that continued punishment of the same family over several generations could stoke dangerous resentment. Above all, the outcome had to be enforceable, otherwise those involved would lose face. Harsh verdicts might tip opinion against the king and possibly encourage wider protest. However, the Empire's monarchs remained more than first among equals and, contrary to the standard interpretation of decline, there was no reduction in their ability to depose truculent vassals (Table 15).[23] Emperors deposed twice as many vassals as the kings of West Francia (27 cases from 844 to 958) and three times the number in Lotharingia (17 cases from 843 to 958).

Ottonian and Early Salian Arbitration

The later Carolingians' continued assertion of themselves as supreme judge stemmed from their relative weakness and direct involvement in many of the disputes they claimed to adjudicate. By contrast, the Ottonians' greater stability allowed them to adopt a more open-ended form of conflict resolution relying more on mediation than confrontation. A key element in this was the practice of ritual submission known as *deditio* whereby the wrongdoer publicly acknowledged his guilt by prostrating himself before the king and begging for mercy, as Liudolf did with his father in 954. Charlemagne had pardoned enemies, but only as a mitigation of their punishment. For example, the rebellious Bavarian duke Tassilo III was forgiven at an assembly in Frankfurt in

Table 15. The Removal of Immediate Vassals

Monarch	Reign	Number of Depositions
Charlemagne	768–814	10
Louis 'the Pious'	814–40	20
Louis 'the German'	843–76	9
Carloman and Arnulf	876–99	11
Zwentibold and Louis 'the Child'	899–911	9
Conrad I	911–18	3
Henry I	919–36	0
Otto I	936–73	27
Otto II	973–83	6
Otto III	983–1002	5
Henry II	1002–24	13
Conrad II	1024–39	9
Henry III	1039–56	6

794, but still deposed and imprisoned in a monastery. On other occasions, death sentences were reduced to blinding. Charlemagne's son Louis the Pious appears to have been the first to alter this practice by inventing a new ceremony of ritual humiliation when faced by a rebellion of his own son, Lothar, in 834. Louis needed to reverse his own humiliation at the hands of his three sons who had forced him to do public penance the previous year. Having gained the military upper hand, Louis forced Lothar to prostrate himself, in return for being forgiven and accepted back into the political elite.[24]

The ritual of deditio was ostentatiously emotional, with tears of contrition both signalling submission and calculated to encourage a formal pardon from a king who risked losing face by failing to show clemency. Likewise, a king's public rage was not necessarily anger or a childish inability to control emotions, but a public signal that an opponent had overstepped the mark. The risks for both sides encouraged discreet negotiations to arrange terms in advance, which were performed in a carefully choreographed ceremony symbolizing the restoration of a harmonious order. This practice was unusual in medieval Europe, with only one case being identified for England prior to the Norman Conquest.[25] However, it remained restricted to the elite, and lesser vassals were likely to be treated harshly, as exemplified in 998 by Otto III's execution of Crescentius and his ritual humiliation and imprisonment of the anti-pope John XVI (see pp. 50–51).

Harsher Justice

Two anecdotes exemplify a shift to a harsher justice after the mid-eleventh century. As we have seen (p. 524), Conrad II delayed his journey from his election to his coronation in 1024 to hear petitions from a peasant, a widow and an orphan, despite the advice from his entourage to hurry on. Contemporary commentators used (or invented) this episode to praise Conrad for being more interested in justice than his own dignity. The newly crowned Frederick Barbarossa was accosted in 1152 by a retainer who hoped for a pardon for a past fault. Despite throwing himself on the floor, the plaintiff was ignored by the king, who was praised by Otto of Freising for his 'constancy of opinion' in not allowing himself to be swayed from the proper application of the law by special pleading.[26]

One of the reasons for this change was the risky character of the deditio. Henry IV's experience at Canossa in 1077 appears to have dissuaded him from using this practice again.[27] The collapse of trust between Henry and his senior lords was another factor, particularly as the breach deepened into prolonged civil war, making it difficult for individuals to serve as neutral mediators. The adoption of a more sacral style of kingship after 1002 widened the political distance between the monarch and senior lords and encouraged a shift from Christian mercy to Old Testament severity. Behaviour changed as well, and it became politically unacceptable for a king to cry in public. Further factors included eleventh-century church reform and a papacy that now insisted on unconditional obedience, and the accompanying heightened morality that shifted general judicial practice from compensating victims to punishing the guilty.

Henry VI's cruel punishments were not a personal quirk, but a consequence of this longer-term trend that inhibited the earlier acts of clemency. Faced with widespread opposition soon after his arrival in Sicily in 1194, Henry had his opponents tortured and executed, or deported to Germany. His rival, William III, was blinded and castrated, ritually rendering him unfit to be king. After a rebellion in the Norman mainland in 1197, Henry had prisoners sawn in half or drowned at sea. Frederick II employed similar methods to reassert authority after the civil war of 1198–1214, and again after the Apulian revolt of 1230. His assizes court convened at Capua in 1220 banned feuds, requiring all disputes to be adjudicated by royal judges. The 219-paragraph Constitution of Melfi, promulgated in August 1231, was Europe's first comprehensive secular law code. Based on Roman law, it applied only to Sicily and Naples. While aspects of Staufer practice appear modern relative to the Empire, they also reflect the particular circumstances of their rule over the former Norman kingdom. Norman rule was itself only a few generations old, while that of the Staufer rested on a conquest that remained contested into the mid-1230s.[28]

The trend to harsher justice was not universally welcomed. Otloh, a Regensburg monk, attributed Henry III's death to divine punishment for ignoring the petitions of the poor. The poor certainly felt the growing severity, as lords regarded any opposition as an affront to their status. Archbishop Anno II of Cologne provoked a revolt by requisitioning a merchant ship without prior consultation in 1074. He allowed his soldiers to pillage the merchants' houses as a reprisal. Anyone resisting was killed or bound in chains. The ringleaders were blinded, while others were whipped and shorn. Finally, the entire population was required to perform ritual penance as an admission of their 'guilt'.[29]

Pacifying the Empire

The Salians' concept of themselves as Christ's vicars encouraged an ambitious goal of what commentators in the 1040s already called a 'general pacification' (*magna pacificato*) of the Empire. The impulse came from the monarch, unlike the Peace of God (*Pax Dei*) movement that spread through France from Aquitaine after 975 as bishops responded to increasing violence. Having tried to persuade secular lords to renounce force, the bishops switched after 1027 to a more pragmatic Truce of God (*Treuga Dei*), requiring participants to forswear violence from Thursdays to Monday mornings.[30] These ideas only reached the Empire in the 1080s when they were largely rejected by bishops along the western frontier who refused to participate in regional truces organized by their French counterparts.

Henry III's project appears to have been entirely independent, even if some of its methods were similar to the Truce of God. Henry's peace was royal and central, not episcopal and local. Embracing sacral kingship, Henry demonstrated his commitment to peace as a good Christian by praying and admonishing his subjects to live in harmony. However, this was backed by royal power through harsher, exemplary punishments for those breaching the peace. Pardons were still possible, for example for Gottfried 'the Bearded' during the 1040s, but his partial restoration as duke of Lorraine after a rebellion was as a special indulgence issued by Henry on his exclusive authority as king, and not through a symbolic submission brokered by other lords. This explains why some clergy accused Henry of vanity on the grounds that true peace was only obtainable in heaven, while others condemned the royal peace as a *pax perniciosa*, because it had not been arranged with the bishops.[31]

Henry's initiative stalled, since his death in 1056 was followed by his son's long minority and subsequent problems. Henry IV did use his authority to broker regional, temporary peace pacts in Saxony (1084), Bavaria and Swabia (both 1093), while bishops made similar arrangements through synods in their diocese: Liège (1082), Cologne (1083) and Mainz (1095). None of these measures was particularly effective given the cycle of civil wars throughout the later stages of Henry's reign. Lack of success fuelled the anti-Henrician propaganda of royal failure.

The Public Peace

Henry responded by promulgating the first 'public peace' (*Landfrieden*) at Mainz in 1103 with the backing of the dukes of Bavaria, Zähringen and Swabia. Intended to last four years, this was already broken by renewed rebellion early in 1105. However, it would be wrong to dismiss it as a failure. Henry had resumed his father's peace policy, but adapted it to the Empire's new political balance, initiating a form of peace-keeping that would shape imperial political and judicial practice until 1806. His successors promulgated similar measures, though no copies survive before Barbarossa's public peace of 1152. The preservation of this text was due to a major effort to disseminate its terms in writing to all bishops, counts and margraves. It was renewed in 1179, and followed by further, more restricted versions in 1186 and 1223, before Frederick II issued another general peace in 1235.[32]

All these measures intended a general pacification of the Empire rather than the local truces attempted in France. Each measure was agreed by the king at a general assembly of major lords who swore to uphold it. The impulse was the widespread desire to surmount the cycle of civil wars between 1073 and 1106 by replacing violence with more peaceful arbitration. Crucially, the king now submitted to the peace himself, rather than trying to stand above it like Henry III. Henry IV's experience demonstrated that reliance on force merely lent credence to his opponents' charges of royal tyranny. The last two Salians and their Staufer successors wanted to place opponents in the wrong as potential peace-breakers. Meanwhile, promulgation through an assembly obliged those present to assist in upholding it. Crusading ideology preached since 1095 also played a part for both Conrad III and Barbarossa, who embraced the pope's call for peace amongst Christians to enable warriors to go to the Holy Land. Finally, the measures reflected new concepts of peace itself. In the early Middle Ages, it was believed that peace was best established by allowing each social group and community to be left undisturbed in possession of its rights. This legitimated the feud that was intended to assert rights against those who ignored or usurped such rights. By the twelfth century, peace was understood more in terms of right and wrong, with all violence perceived as a direct threat to tranquillity.[33]

However, this development did not mitigate the trend towards harsher justice. The 1103 public peace incorporated bloody punishments, including blinding or amputation of a hand for theft, robbery and extortion, while those directly breaching the peace were to be maimed and deprived of their property and fief. These penalties were not simply for deterrent effect; they were considered fairer than the earlier system of fines, which the poor found harder to pay.[34] While the public-peace legislation reinforced the emperor as supreme judge, this was not a role he was either willing or able to perform often. The emperor was involved in settling at least 150 cases in royal towns across 1101–1254, including 80 in the last 30 years of that period.[35] This gives a small indication of the potential total volume of business across the Empire, which was clearly beyond the capacity of any medieval king to handle. The public peace was intended to free the king from the burden of lesser cases, whilst reserving to him those involving princes and other immediate lords.

Worldly imperfections were fully recognized in the temporary nature of each public peace. A king was not expected to enforce verdicts, leaving those involved free to accept his judgement or find their own settlement. For this reason, the public peace retained the option to feud. This approach was pragmatic, encouraging peaceful resolution, whilst recognizing this was not always possible given that disputes involved not just the pride and 'face' of those immediately concerned, but that of their clients and supporters.[36] Violence was permitted, but contained and channelled through measures intended to ensure that those using 'excessive' force forfeited the legitimacy of their case. For example, the 1235 peace contained clauses to protect economic activity by guaranteeing the safety of royal highways even during a feud.

The idea of the public peace survived the Staufers' demise, because it represented a practical way to confront violence whilst protecting the interests of those charged with enforcing it. King William issued one in 1255 as part of his alliance with the Rhenish Civic League, while Richard of Cornwall promulgated another in 1268.[37] Rudolf I and his successors renewed these measures, either for the entire Empire (1287, 1290, 1298), or for specific regions (1276, 1281, 1289). Renewed conflict after 1298 interrupted these developments, which resumed under Charles IV, who renewed the general peace in 1354 prior to his Roman coronation journey. The Golden Bull consolidated existing practice by charging the electors with upholding the peace and making peace maintenance the primary task of future leagues and unions in the Empire.[38]

The Emergence of a Judicial Hierarchy

Royal peace initiatives helped realign judicial practices with the emerging status hierarchy and the needs of a society structured more obviously into corporate Estates. The 1231 charter to princes gave dukes, bishops, counts and margraves expanded magisterial powers, not only over their own vassals and servants, but over virtually all the inhabitants in their jurisdiction. In the longer term, this represented an important step in territorializing princely power. More immediately, it adjusted conflict management and resolution to the new division of labour, since the princes were now charged with judging infractions according to the definition of crimes and scale of punishments agreed in the public peace. This change clearly identified princes as exercising powers of corporal punishment (*Blutsgerichtsbarkeit*), and helped identify their courts as superior, since such cases had to be referred to them from the localities. Combined with mint, toll, tax and other rights, these new powers were important elements in marking the princes as a distinct status group. Concern for status helped make the system work, because the desire to deny outsiders excuses to intervene was a powerful incentive for princes to keep their own jurisdictions in order.[39]

Generally, a two-tier judicial hierarchy developed within these princely jurisdictions by 1300. The lowest tier emerged as lords retreated from direct management of towns and villages, which established local courts chaired by mayors. These usually met four times a year to judge a broad range of disputes and crimes punishable mainly by fines.[40] A second, higher tier emerged with the development of districts as administrative subdivisions within princely fiefs. District courts were chaired by officials representing the prince, and usually had a circuit (*Gerichtsprengel*) of up to ten villages that they toured to hear more serious cases. A third tier appeared around 1500 as superior territorial courts were established, either as a *Hofgericht* chaired by the prince, or as a 'territorial court' (*Landgericht*) under an appointed judge. These central courts institutionalized the central exercise of 'bloody jurisdiction' across an entire territory, regardless of its formal division into different fiefs. The establishment of these superior courts was usually underpinned by additional imperial privileges, such as those granted to Trier in 1458. The hierarchical structure was mirrored in the imperial and free cities where a lesser magistrates' court (*Ratsgericht*) handled minor transgressions like breaches of civic ordinances or building regulations, while a superior 'city court' (*Stadtgericht*) judged serious crimes like murder, arson, theft or rape, and could impose corporal punishment.[41]

While varying considerably in detail, all courts adhered to broadly similar norms and procedures. Judgement by peers had already been part of Ottonian practice and continued as trial by 7 to 12 jurors selected from upstanding members of the community. The judge was assisted by a clerk, while by the fifteenth century cases could be brought by an official prosecutor as well as by a plaintiff. Despite the trend to more formalized, written procedures, the emphasis remained more on mediation than determining guilt and punishment. In some regions, jurors were required to seek an amicable settlement prior to a case coming to court. Cases involving insult or slander used a process called 'sending' (*Beschickung*) in which a third party was delegated to ask what the offender had really intended. Neighbours were expected to engage in 'saving' (*Retten*), intervening to break up fights and prevent serious harm.[42]

Appellate Justice

The development of a longer judicial hierarchy extended the open-ended character of justice by enabling cases to be appealed against or referred to superior courts for additional adjudication. Already from the twelfth century, the new towns founded east of the Elbe would call on their 'mother cities' for legal advice, while the spread of universities after 1348 led to difficult cases being referred to law faculties, which functioned by 1530 as a kind of appeals court.[43] These practices evolved in consequence of the division of judicial labour intended to free the emperor to concentrate on disputes among the princely elite. Appeals to the emperor became a special, restricted privilege already in the Staufer era. Frederick II appointed a royal *Justiciar* in 1235 to relieve him of the burden of judging cases himself. Although this post lapsed during the 1250s, it was revived in February 1274 as permanent, yet with a more restricted remit for cities and counts but no longer princes, whose disputes were still judged by the monarch.[44] The advisory council developed into the *Kammergericht* (cameral court), which accompanied the king on his royal progress and had its own chancellery (*Kanzlei*) to record proceedings.

The limited remit of royal justice encouraged additional local initiatives, particularly in response to the greater social unrest and political disorder of the fourteenth and fifteenth centuries. The most notorious were the freelance courts called *Veme* operating between 1300 and 1450 in Westphalia and sometimes beyond in areas rarely visited by the king. These were largely self-appointed courts, but were protected by the archbishop of Cologne and sometimes enjoyed royal sanction to uphold the public peace. They met openly if the accused appeared voluntarily, but otherwise convened in secret and in practice served as vehicles for Westphalia's nobles to consolidate their local and regional power. Their potential was limited and they disappeared once open opposition from Frederick III dissuaded local princes from allowing them to hear further cases.[45]

The public-peace measures of 1383 and 1389 adjusted to the development of more clearly delineated territorial judicial systems by grouping these on a regional basis prefiguring the Kreis structure adopted after 1500. In contrast to thirteenth-century practice binding princes to uphold the peace through their feudal obligations, the 1383 measures envisaged associations of all immediate lords acting more autonomously to maintain order in their own region. This development was backed by the princes, because they, rather than the knights and towns, were primarily responsible for judging serious cases in their region. These measures could be effective: Count Dietrich von Wernigerode was executed by his peers in 1386 for breaking the peace.[46] After the efforts at a general peace in the 1380s, similar measures continued to be made on a regional basis after 1400, but were hindered by princes' growing reluctance to submit their disputes to arbitration. As we have seen (pp. 398–9), the result was an escalation in violent feuding that spread from the elite to other sections of society.

However, all late medieval associations continued the culture of collective conflict resolution and peace enforcement. The Swabian League's court handled 250 cases across 1488–1534, three-quarters of which involved disputes between different status groups, like towns and princes.[47] Cases involving disputes with non-members often proved difficult if these refused to acknowledge the court's jurisdiction. Consequently, demands for more effective royal justice became a central element in imperial reform. Initial efforts in 1442 faltered, but Frederick III secured successive extensions of a new general public peace after 1465. Following 1467, breaches of the peace were treated as *crimen laesae maiestatis*, effectively stigmatizing them as rebellion and allowing those responsible to be placed under the imperial ban. The Turkish menace was invoked to enjoin Christians to stop fighting each other and combine against the infidel.

The prospect of more severe punishment added pressure to establish a more effective appellate court as a final tribunal ensuring that public-peace cases were handled fairly. The Kammergericht had suffered from the general dissipation of regalia rights since the 1370s, when the post of judge was often pawned to princes allied to individual emperors. For example, Frederick III transferred it to successive bishops of Passau between 1461 and 1470, and then to Archbishop Adolf II of Mainz. Like the modern practice of entrusting public functions to semi-private agencies, operators had an incentive to improve efficiency by reducing costs and boosting receipts through fees and fines. Calls for a permanent, independent court grew louder from 1471, but serious problems only emerged when no one was willing to assume the franchise after Adolf's death in 1475.[48]

The Reform of Imperial Justice

Negotiations at royal assemblies after 1486 led to the promulgation of the eternal public peace in 1495. Like the rest of imperial reform, this was a compromise combining past practice with genuine innovation. The peace's eternal character was less significant than the ban on feuds and all forms of violent self-help as a legal means of redress, shifting debate away from the legitimacy of individual feuds to condemning the entire practice. A second innovation was the creation of a new permanent supreme tribunal officially called the 'Emperor's and Empire's cameral court', but generally shortened to Reichskammergericht (see Plate 33).[49] The court was given a printed procedural ordinance, completed on 7 August 1495. Personnel were sworn in on 31 October and they heard the first case three days later, indicating that the Empire could act swiftly when the necessary consensus was there.

Several additional features make the Reichskammergericht appear more modern than its equivalents in other European countries. It was independent from the royal household, moving instead between various imperial cities before settling in Speyer after 1527 until that city was sacked by French troops in 1689. The court reopened four years later in Wetzlar, where it stayed until the Empire's demise.[50] The court's independence was enhanced by how its judges were selected. The emperor named the presiding *Kammerrichter*, but the other *Assessoren* were nominated by the imperial Estates, who were obliged to cooperate through the new Kreis structure to present candidates to the court, which, after the very first appointments, made the final choice itself. Personnel swore loyalty to the court, not to the lords or cities that had nominated them, and there is considerable evidence that they acted genuinely independently and collectively.[51]

The Reichskammergericht's jurisdiction covered Germany and initially also Burgundy, but not Switzerland (see pp. 588–9) or Italy. One task was to uphold the eternal peace by adjudicating disputes amongst all individuals and communities enjoying the status of imperial immediacy, thereby largely rendering regional peace leagues redundant. As previously, each immediate authority was charged with keeping order within its own jurisdiction through the hierarchy of local, district and territorial courts. The Reichskammergericht's second task was as a final court of appeal for cases from these territorial judiciaries. This aspect operated unevenly across the Empire according to the varying degrees with which each territory had secured the Privilege of Not Appealing (*Privilegium de non appellando*) since 1356 when the Golden Bull exempted the electors' subjects from the jurisdiction of the royal Kammergericht in return for their establishment of territorial courts of appeal.

Other princes' claims for exemption on customary grounds were rejected, and they had to negotiate their own separate privileges with the emperor, creating a new concession that could be traded for political support. Usually, only limited privileges were granted, still reserving important cases for the Reichskammergericht. Privileges were important mainly for prestige reasons, and required princes to establish their own appeals structures. Some princes acquired so-called 'unlimited privileges' in the eighteenth century, but prior to 1803 even these did not exclude all appeals, while the Reichskammergericht could intervene regardless if territorial courts broke their own procedures or denied subjects justice.[52] The most extensive immunity was the exemption of the entire Burgundian lands as part of the wider demarcation of Habsburg possessions in 1548, and based on the existence of a permanent Burgundian appellate court in Mechelen after 1504. Immunities could be revoked, most notably those of Mecklenburg following an appeal by the duchy's Estates against the duke in 1785. This case is particularly significant, because the ruling denied the duke's claims that his privileges rested on the Peace of Teschen (1779), which had been guaranteed by France and Russia.[53]

The Reichskammergericht was joined by the Reichshofrat as a second supreme court established in Vienna by Maximilian I in December 1497 to safeguard the judicial aspects of his imperial prerogatives. The new court was not universally welcomed and effectively disappeared with Maximilian's death in 1519. Ferdinand I reconstituted it by detaching responsibility for imperial prerogatives from the Habsburgs' own territorial superior court in 1559. Unlike the Reichskammergericht, the Reichshofrat was entirely staffed by Habsburg appointees and had jurisdiction across the Empire, including Italy, on the basis that the emperor was feudal lord of all those with imperial immediacy. It was not intended to compete with the Reichskammergericht, but soon strayed into its business because issues arising from fief-holding, like inheritance disputes, could become breaches of the peace. Additionally, the court exercised the emperor's prerogatives of grace and pardon, allowing it to expand its remit to include appeals from territorial subjects by the later sixteenth century. Its closer relationship to the emperor encouraged plaintiffs who hoped verdicts in their favour would be backed by the full weight of Habsburg power.[54] To reduce friction, cases could not be transferred between the two courts by litigants seeking more favourable verdicts. In practice, disputes were often so complex that several parallel proceedings ran simultaneously.

The Impact on Judicial Practice

The Reichskammergericht profoundly influenced judicial practice throughout the Empire, as did the Reichshofrat once it caught up by adopting written procedures in 1559. At both courts, the presiding judge assigned cases to 'senates' (panels) of legally trained 'assessors', who received written memoranda and arguments submitted by lawyers representing the contending parties, in a complete contrast to the oral, face-to-face confrontational process prior to 1495. Both courts could empower commissioners to gather additional evidence, including taking witness statements. These methods were copied by territorial courts, which also changed their procedures in criminal cases to follow the 1532 Carolina code in standardizing inquisitorial methods and shifting the obligation to prove guilt from the accuser to a prosecutor.

The changes were not universally beneficial, for example making it far easier to level accusations of witchcraft without fear of punishment if they could not be proved. The greater emphasis on establishing guilt encouraged the widespread use of torture to extract confessions, directly contributing to the 'witch craze' as prosecutors sought to identify others involved in what were believed to be communal deviant practices. Neither the Carolina code nor the territorial codes derived from it offered much protection against arbitrary arrest and often a denunciation was sufficient, especially if the accused belonged to rootless or marginal social groups. German territorial courts executed 22,500 alleged witches during the sixteenth and early seventeenth centuries, mostly through the failure of local authorities to follow official inquisitorial procedures or to restrain over-zealous prosecutors. Since witchcraft was defined as a crime and so was reserved to territorial 'bloody jurisdiction', the imperial courts could only intervene on grounds of procedural irregularities, but they managed to curb prosecutions in some areas.[55]

As inquisitorial practice became more sophisticated, the need for torture decreased well ahead of its official abolition in most territories during the eighteenth century. The authorities still used harsh measures, such as locking up suspects until they confessed, but also undertook detailed investigations, especially in complex cases. The Sachsen-Hildburghausen contractor Moses Schimmel was asked 1,500 questions during his interrogation on corruption charges between

1771 and 1775, with his answers carefully recorded in six volumes of court documents.[56]

The 1495 Reichskammergericht ordinance was revised in 1521 and 1555, but subsequent changes remained administrative and financial, not legal, because confessional controversy made it politically difficult to alter judicial procedures. New procedural rules were ready by 1613 only to founder on lack of agreement in the Reichstag, though they were unofficially adopted in 1654 when the Reichshofrat also received a revised ordinance. Consequently, the imperial courts remained guided by the sixteenth-century understanding of Roman law and failed to match new legal thinking that increasingly shaped how territorial courts operated. This was not as serious as it might first appear, because both imperial courts remained primarily tasked with brokering viable compromises rather than reaching definitive verdicts. More problematic was their adherence to secret hearings and decisions published without explanations, because it was feared transparency might undermine their authority. This helps explain why Reichskammergericht verdicts in the sixteenth-century 'religious cases' encountered so much opposition, fuelling the controversy that hamstrung the 'visitation', or monitoring, process through the Reichstag after 1588. The next visitations were not conducted until 1707–14 and 1767–76, and were primarily concerned with the court's internal administration and finance. The Prussian judiciary began explaining its verdicts after 1793, and some imperial judges soon copied this unofficially.[57]

Neither court was well staffed, considering they served over 20 million people by the eighteenth century. The Reichshofrat had 14 to 20 judges at any one time in the sixteenth century, rising to 25, backed by 34 chancery staff, after 1600. These met three to four times a week, considering up to 20 cases each session. The Reichskammergericht was likewise overburdened, and its staffing levels were a constant issue at the Reichstag. It was at or close to full complement between 1566 and 1610, falling to a low point between 1648 and 1713 when there were never more than 13 judges in post, forcing its temporary closure from 1704 to 1709. Official staff levels were halved in 1720, but individual pay was doubled and a real effort was made to avoid future vacancies; something that was achieved consistently after 1782 (Table 16). Total staff numbers were larger at around 150, with an additional 50 legal trainees and solicitors helping with the paperwork.

Table 16. Official Reichskammergericht Staff Levels

Date	Kammerrichter	Presidents	Assessors
1495	1	–	16
1555	1	2	24
1566	1	2	32
1570	1	2	38
1648	1	2	50
1720	1	2	25

Case Load

Given the staffing problems, the case load is astonishing. Details survive for about 80,000 Reichskammergericht cases, but the total was probably higher, while the Reichshofrat handled around 140,000 cases, of which files still exist for about half. The overall volume of cases was greater still, because each court also dealt with revisions and renewals of existing cases, for instance tripling the Reichshofrat's total business. The relative balance fluctuated, with the Reichshofrat generally receiving more cases each time the Reichskammergericht was in difficulties. The extension of immunities reduced the proportion of new cases reaching the Reichskammergericht from four-fifths to half or less of its business, but it was still handling more cases annually in the early 1800s than it had around 1500, while the Reichshofrat managed a threefold increase across the same period.[58]

Inevitably, a considerable backlog developed, drawing hostile comment, especially after 1806. According to Goethe, there were 50,000 unresolved cases and a further 20,000 pending before the Reichskammergericht in 1771, but these figures are wildly inflated. Although the actual total cannot be reconstructed, the court had cleared the entire backlog by 1780. Around 4,000 Reichshofrat cases built up by the mid-1760s, mainly due to the Seven Years War, but these had been resolved by the end of the decade, during which time it handled 10,000 new ones. (By contrast, the backlog before the European Court of Human Rights reached 150,000 in 2012.)[59] Some cases took years to resolve: 4 per cent of those introduced at the Reichskammergericht in the late sixteenth century were still ongoing a century later. Again, this requires interpretation, because the task was not to 'solve' them, but to encourage peaceful settlement, with prolonged engagement in practice being successive adjustments according to changed circumstances.

Both courts could appoint commissioners who could act quickly and forcefully if life was endangered. Court mandates could be backed by troops mobilized through the Kreise. Brokerage was more common, with mediation accounting for 42 per cent of all Reichshofrat commissions under Ferdinand III, while 54 per cent of those handled by Württemberg across 1648–1806 were for the same purpose, compared to just 15 per cent to enforce verdicts. Enforcement relied on the cooperation and compliance of the imperial Estates, both those entrusted with this task and those affected by the case. The difficulties this entailed increased the desire for workable solutions, which were generally achieved, and probably no more than a hundred decisions of both courts combined remained unenforced across the Empire's last 150 years.[60]

Preserving the Peace

Most of the cases involving those with immediacy stemmed from dynasticism, which changed princely inheritance practices. For example, attempts to divide the possessions of the Ernestine Saxons in 1680 produced 61 Reichshofrat cases across 1699–1730 just involving the Sachsen-Coburg branch, while disputes amongst Lippe-Detmold's ruling family contributed 65 Reichskammergericht cases between 1613 and 1783. Questions of inheritance, marriage, guardianship and maintaining relatives accounted for 30 per cent of all Reichshofrat commissions from 1637 to 1657, or twice the number of cases over territorial rights, and six times more than those about feudal rights. Again, imperial judicial practice reflected wider social characteristics: ordinary inhabitants made increasing use of the lesser courts to resolve similar status and inheritance disputes.[61]

Only a tiny minority of cases resulted in the imposition of the imperial ban. The 1495 Reichstag authorized the Reichskammergericht to ban those breaking the peace, but in practice the emperor always insisted on doing this through the Reichshofrat. The 1559 Reichstag abandoned earlier efforts to assert the imperial Estates' involvement, and allowed the emperor to issue a ban without a prior hearing on the basis of notoriety. This proved unproblematic when employed against individuals like the knight Wilhelm von Grumbach, who appeared a public menace (see pp. 559–60), but Ferdinand II's use of these powers as a political weapon during the Thirty Years War caused considerable disquiet.[62] Nonetheless, later emperors continued to ban opponents, notably during the War of the Spanish Succession, until Charles VI agreed at his accession in 1711 that he would consult the Reichstag in future. Prussia's invasion of Saxony in August 1756 put this to the test, because Austria hoped to use this clear breach of the peace to ban Frederick II, thereby providing grounds to deprive him of his possessions in the event of victory. Prussian sympathizers blocked the motion in the Reichstag, which simply sanctioned peacekeeping mobilization.[63] This was an exceptional case. The Reichshofrat threatened the ban on 160 occasions after 1559, but only imposed it nine times, five of which were at the start of the Thirty Years War.[64]

The ban was rarely necessary, because open rebellion was extremely unusual in the early modern Empire, while the Reichshofrat was able to impose meaningful sanctions through its normal judicial process, for example deposing at least six princes between 1684 and 1727. Charles VII agreed at his accession in 1742 to consult the Reichstag before deposing further princes, but both imperial courts continued to remove princes on criminal charges on the basis of their 'bloody jurisdiction' over immediate vassals, deposing four princes this way between 1770 and 1793.[65]

Defusing Social Tension

The courts' remit was expanded considerably by the 1526 Reichstag's ruling that complaints from ordinary subjects could be appealed provided certain procedures were observed. Passed in response to the Peasants War, this measure achieved its goal of channelling protest away from open violence and towards resolution through judicial and administrative review. This process has been labelled 'juridification' and involved a fundamental change in behaviour at all social levels.[66] Lords had previously used violence to assert authority and status. Feuding had been criminalized in 1495 and now repression was likely to be condemned in the courts. For example, the duke of Württemberg was obliged to return his troops to barracks after his subjects protested in 1701 and 1765, while the prince of Nassau-Siegen (1707) and the duke of Mecklenburg (1728) were both deposed after they used their soldiers to seize their subjects' property in disputes over taxation and religious freedom.[67]

The authorities generally perceived that the new practices were in their own interests, since the wider imperial framework allowed them to call on their neighbours' military assistance should their own subjects fail to restrict their protests to judicial channels. These principles were incorporated into territorial judicial procedures. For example, despite Austria's effective exemption from Reichskammergericht jurisdiction, its legislation extended rights of appeal through its own courts to common inhabitants in 1579. Thus, both the Empire and its constituent territories practised a form of 'peasant protection' (*Bauernschutz*) by inserting the courts between ordinary folk and lordly exploitation.

These changes were not universally welcome. Recourse to the courts often appeared part of the problem, not the solution, thanks to the costs, time and uncertainty involved. It also contradicted the faith that a benevolent ruler should respond promptly and positively once informed of his subjects' distress. Access to appellate justice was accompanied by curbs on direct petitioning, making the courts appear to be new barriers between inhabitants and princes. Courts were also staffed by nobles and educated commoners, both same groups wielding socio-economic power. Although the imperial courts operated on the principle of 'presumed liberty', considering people to be free unless proven otherwise, it was often difficult for ordinary folk to provide written evidence to refute lordly claims on their labour and produce.[68]

The appeals system did not eliminate violence, particularly as frustration could build through delay and explode if the courts did not produce the expected justice, as we have observed in Saxony in 1790 (pp. 601–2). While nothing matched the Peasants War, there were major revolts in Upper Austria in 1594–7, 1626 and 1632–6, as well as in Bavaria in 1633–4 and 1705–6. All but the first of these events were exacerbated by war. Otherwise, protest was largely confined to five waves of unrest in smaller territories broadly correlating with hunger crises and wartime taxation: 1650–60, 1700–1716, 1725–33, 1752–66 and 1767–77. Beyond these, there were at least 30 major disturbances in imperial cities after the sixteenth century, as well as numerous smaller incidents, including 55 in Hessen and 380 in Ansbach-Bayreuth from the mid-seventeenth to the late eighteenth century.[69] These all paled in comparison to the general revolts in Bohemia (1679, 1775), Hungary (1660s, 1671–81, 1703–11) and Transylvania (1784) under Habsburg rule.

Outside the Habsburg lands, violence was generally contained. Peasants and burghers used strikes, petitions and bluster, often alongside court cases, in carefully coordinated strategies to pressure the authorities into conceding demands. The significance of juridification lay in opening formal channels of communication, and encouraging acceptance that clear, simple answers were unlikely to resolve complex problems. The courts recognized that absolute verdicts could escalate violence. For example, the Reichshofrat rejected the bishop of Basel's appeals for a final verdict in his favour against his Estates in 1730–33, because this would have made his subjects desperate.[70] This helps explain the length of many cases, in which the imperial and territorial superior courts acted more as mediators than as institutions seeking to determine guilt or innocence.

Neither this nor the enlightened reforms of the later eighteenth century were a conscious strategy of 'defensive modernization' intended to reform from above to avert revolution from below.[71] None of the Empire's numerous authorities predicted what was coming after 1789, but many were certainly anxious. The prince of Hohenzollern-Hechingen was at loggerheads with his subjects over feudal demands after 1584 in what became one of the Empire's longest-running disputes. Disagreement increasingly focused on his attempts to use forced labour to extend and maintain his hunting grounds, a move that simultaneously curtailed peasants' access to the territory's forest. Efforts to confiscate the peasants' hunting guns stirred such opposition that the prince feared revolt and called in Württemberg troops during the 1730s. However, repeated recourse to the Reichskammergericht managed the situation, upholding the prince's feudal jurisdiction, but halting his repressive measures. Württemberg was obliged to recall its troops, and future intervention only proceeded with official sanction as peacekeepers organized through the Swabian Kreis. Violence was largely avoided and a new prince ended the dispute in 1798 by renouncing feudal jurisdiction over all but one particularly recalcitrant village.[72]

The emphasis on the local and particular was thus double-edged. It provided all the Empire's social groups and communities with opportunities to achieve real gains by basing their demands on specific, identifiable rights. For example, the Reichshofrat imprisoned Count Karl Magnus of Grehweiler for ten years after he had forged his subjects' consent to huge loans for his building projects.[73] More powerful rulers, including those in Mecklenburg, Württemberg, Bavaria, Sachsen-Weimar and Reuss, also lost cases in the second half of the eighteenth century. However, the aversion to abstract, absolute ideals fragmented protest, preventing both politicization and thus the likelihood of violence, but also isolating those involved from potential allies. The Hechingen peasants failed to obtain support from inhabitants in neighbouring territories, despite often similar problems there. Differences over strategy also weakened popular movements, contributing to factionalism within communities.[74]

The Hechingen case illustrates a second general point: popular unrest and court intervention were both most frequent in the Empire's smaller territories. Kornelimünster abbey, with just 5,000 subjects, produced 200 Reichskammergericht cases, while nearly a fifth of the 1,100 cases from Lippe-Detmold to the same court across 1522–1806 were brought by subjects against the prince or his officials.[75] Like the intervention of imperial debt commissions (see pp. 544–5), court involvement was a consequence of these territories' underdevelopment. The small scale of such territories placed ruler and ruled in close proximity, leaving few intervening administrative layers to defuse tension. Above all, the absence of appellate courts necessitated direct recourse to imperial justice: 833 of Lippe's cases were appeals.

Peasants generally developed a favourable view of the Empire's supreme courts, whose adherence to standardized procedures often contrasted with seemingly capricious seigniorial justice. Lords, especially in smaller territories, had tried to assert social distance by manipulating their judicial powers, placing themselves above the law, whilst dispensing clemency periodically to win acceptance of their elevated position. Juridification after 1526 bound them within a system beyond their personal control. It objectified justice, removing or at least lessening the impact of individual circumstances, especially as imperial law applied to all and was widely disseminated through print.[76] Although governance still involved brokerage, this was now less personalized and blatant since it ran through institutionalized channels, rather than through vassalage and patrimonialism. Territorial authorities were represented more by public officials than the prince. Official claims to impartiality gained some credence when real results were obtained, and individual officials rejected prevailing prejudices about peasants as naturally unruly. Adherence to common core values enabled even elementary differences to be fought out without straining the existing order, which all parties recognized as legitimate.

The Rule of Law

The famous German 'state under the rule of law' (*Rechtsstaat*) was thus a product of the Empire's long evolution, and not a reaction to the French Revolution. The existence of the Rechtsstaat explains why most inhabitants felt French-style revolution was unnecessary or even harmful. The imperial courts safeguarded access to law and equal treatment in the judicial process, but not full legal equality. Most people continued to regard injustice as an unwarranted disruption of a harmonious order, refusing to accept that conflict was inherent in all unequal socio-economic power relations. Judicial intervention stabilized the Empire, both curbing violence and perpetuating gross inequality. Society remained local, corporate and hierarchical. In fact, the courts were increasingly called upon by ordinary people in the later eighteenth century to defend local privileges against the rationalizing, levelling ambitions of territorial governments seeking more equal, but also more intrusive, relationships with their inhabitants.[77]

Late eighteenth-century critics condemned the Empire's judicial framework as confusing, and incapable of effective protection through its lack of a single, uniformly applicable legal code. However, as we have seen (pp. 608–10), territorial codification was slow and failed to improve individual security. On the contrary, the wider protection of imperial appellate justice was removed in 1806 without any alternative safeguards being installed.[78] Writing in May 1806 on the eve of the Empire's dissolution, the Habsburg official Joseph Haas praised 'the judicial power [which] was, until now, the shining jewel of our constitution. Two imperial courts, whose counsellors were appointed with great care and were free of external influence, competed with each other in the impartial administration of justice, and gave even the lowest subject right against the most powerful prince.' Haas predicted that once this system was removed, there would be nothing to protect individual and corporate liberties from the relentless drive for fiscal-military efficiency: 'there is no doubt [that] canals will be dug, roads laid, avenues and parks, theatres and pools created, cities illuminated, [and] we will shine and starve. The only robbers threatening the subjects' property will be the tax collector and the French and German soldiers.'[79]

BETWEEN EQUILIBRIUM AND INSTABILITY

Corpses and Funeral Pyres

By the time Haas submitted his memorandum, many felt the Empire was nearing its end. However, when this came just three months later, it was no *Götterdämmerung*, with a redemptive leap into the funeral pyre involving a final battle to forge a bright new future. Instead, the Empire fractured incrementally under relentless French battering. Contemporaries were fully aware that internal weaknesses hastened this process, if not directly causing it. In the subsequent search for explanations for central Europe's subjugation to French imperialism, it was easy to blame the Empire that had disappeared rather than the princes who survived as rulers of larger, fully sovereign states and who, as Haas predicted, were free to silence their critics.

The overwhelming conclusion after 1806 has been that the Empire had been dead already since at least 1648, if not 1250, and now 'stood like a corpse ... ready to crumble at a touch'.[80] This interpretation usually contrasts a supposedly moribund imperial structure with the alleged dynamism of the larger German territories, notably Austria and Prussia. The recent, more positive reappraisal of the Empire has the advantage of reflecting the lack of any sense of impending crisis prior to 1790, but has pushed revisionism too far in the opposite direction. Both approaches still view the Empire in dualist terms, underestimating how far social and political structures were entwined. Although substantially altered, much of the Empire's pre-modern social structures outlived it for several decades at least. This historical debate exists precisely because the situation remained open in the late eighteenth century. Many problems were surfacing, but they were not immediately life-threatening. Some institutions were no longer compatible with circumstances, or were too inflexible, while others gained new momentum as they tackled immediate problems. This section explains why it proved so hard for those with a vested interest in the Empire to envisage any other political structure for central Europe.

The German State Sickness

Many commentators believed the Empire's form had outlived its substance by the mid-eighteenth century. Whereas princely governments were housed in palaces built in the fashionable baroque or rococo styles, the Reichstag still met in Regensburg's gothic town hall. The contrast was not lost on contemporary visitors: the publicist Friedrich Nicolai remarked that the hall 'is like the German Empire itself, old, rambling and decayed' (see Plate 20).[81] Whereas mid-seventeenth-century engravings depicted the hall full of people, later eighteenth-century illustrations showed it empty, reflecting the demise of a culture of personal meetings as the imperial Estates preferred written communication. Even the bishop of Regensburg, who lived a few streets away, was represented by an envoy, while many smaller territories entrusted their mandate to others to save paying diplomats. Six of the 51 imperial cities no longer even did this, while already in 1764 the 161 votes were collectively exercised by just 35 envoys.[82]

The same applied to other imperial institutions. One Reichskammergericht judge dismissed his own court's decisions as 'nothing more than worthless pieces of paper', while Joseph II felt that 'justice always gives way to politics; a wrongdoer, provided he is sustained by force, can go unpunished and be notorious without incurring disrepute.'[83] Even the indefatigable Johann Jacob Moser, who devoted virtually his entire life to studying the Empire, abandoned his original project of describing the constitution because of the blatant discrepancy between theory and practice.[84]

The most influential criticism was that in Johann Heinrich Zedler's article 'German State Sickness, or the State Sickness of the Holy Roman Empire of the German Nation', published in 1745.[85] Zedler's claim that the Empire displayed 'unconventional forms of governance' essentially continued Samuel Pufendorf's earlier term 'monstrosity' (see pp. 279–80). Nonetheless, Zedler's article exemplified the growing trend to describe the Empire by listing what it lacked compared to a centralized state: a permanent army, swift justice, uniform fiscal and legal structures. Moreover, Zedler's biological metaphor chimed with philosophical currents that increasingly saw the world in organic terms, rather than the mechanical universe popular in seventeenth-century thought. By 1806, some leading intellectuals expressed the sense that the Empire had been sick for a long time and that its doctors had long given up hope. Goethe's mother wrote two weeks after Francis II's abdication that the news was not unexpected, 'as when an old friend is very ill'. Later historians have expressed similar views that the Empire died 'a "natural" death' from old age, rather than having been murdered by Napoleon.[86]

Criticism of the imperial constitution was boosted by Prussian propaganda during the Seven Years War, which included a new edition of Chemnitz's tract from the 1640s presenting the Empire as an aristocratic federation. A tract entitled *Why Should Germany Have an Emperor?* (1787) advocated abolishing the imperial office as a relic of medieval barbarism and a barrier to enlightened progress.[87] Although exceptional, its anonymous author nonetheless represented the new perception of historical time, involving a sharper and generally hostile characterization of the 'Middle Ages' between the flowering of classical civilization and its revival in the Renaissance. Enlightened thought expressed renewed faith in human progress provided it could be unshackled from the fetters of tradition.

The Reform Debate

The implications of these ideas only became obvious during the French Revolution and Napoleonic Wars. Before then, most commentators found it difficult to see beyond the established order that still guided all reform plans. Corporate rights and local identities were still anchored in the imperial constitution, which remained the underlying source of legitimacy for the entire socio-political order. As we have seen (pp. 599–602), there was little enthusiasm for alternatives, like popular sovereignty, or equality as a new basis for liberty. The relatively open and vibrant public sphere provided opportunities for thousands of contributors to discuss all kinds of reform, the sheer volume itself being a sign of the Empire's continued importance.[88] The debate was conducted across the Empire and involved all confessional groups and was generally constructive. Criticism usually focused on specific faults, in contrast to debates in France that increasingly attacked the entire monarchical system. The absence of radical suggestions was not due to ignorance of other political systems, because the open and extensive press and periodical literature disseminated information fairly freely. For example, Germans were informed about England through Hanover and its influential university at Göttingen, but few advocated reforming the Empire along the lines of the English constitutional monarchy. Friedrich Carl von Moser and Prince Leopold Friedrich Franz of Anhalt-Dessau simply suggested adding an elected lower house to the Reichstag, while Hegel proposed converting the existing civic corpus along similar lines.[89]

The more realistic proposals all envisaged some kind of princely league as a vehicle for renewed imperial reform. Interest was strongest amongst the middling territories like Mainz, Sachsen-Weimar, Baden, and smaller secular principalities like Anhalt-Dessau or Zweibrücken, who all felt increasingly powerless in the face of Austrian and Prussian expansion. Leagues were not seen as alternatives to the Empire, but as ways to improve coordination and prevent status disputes from undermining the weaker principalities' collective weight in existing institutions. For example, the Reichstag's princely corpus temporarily suspended its work in February 1780 after a dispute over who should exercise the votes for the duchies of Westphalia and Franconia, even though these no longer really existed as territories. League proposals after 1770 drew on new ideals of friendship emerging from late Enlightenment and early Romantic thought, which blurred earlier distinctions between political, literary and scientific activity, and advocated freer forms of interaction outside the now rigid status hierarchy. The League of Princes (*Fürstenbund*) emerged from a personal meeting between Leopold Friedrich Franz of Anhalt-Dessau and Carl Friedrich of Baden in July 1782.[90]

Leopold Friedrich Franz expressed the reform programme through laying out a 100-square-kilometre park at Wörlitz. Opened to the public, this was intended to appeal to both the senses and the intellect by mixing English-style landscaped gardens with 'scientific' model farms into a composite without any specific focal point, in deliberate contrast to the baroque formal gardens designed to present a centralized order. Wörlitz thus expressed the smaller princes' argument that regional diversity, not standardization, was the best route to progress.[91] Other measures were more immediately practical and were intended to present smaller principalities as model states to disarm arguments for annexation on grounds of efficiency that were voiced during the First Partition of Poland (1772). The ecclesiastical territories were often at the forefront of such reforms, because they felt most vulnerable. Following serious fires in 1781, the bishopic of Paderborn combined various insurance schemes into a single society backed by the government to cover property worth 2.3 million florins. Mainz replaced charity with state welfare in 1785, providing free maternity cover for unmarried mothers and other enlightened measures not seen in many other Catholic states until the late twentieth century.[92]

Concrete proposals for wider reform of the entire Empire were rather thin, and the potential of the League of Princes has been overestimated since it suggested nothing beyond tinkering with existing arrangements.[93] The Reichskammergericht was to be overhauled by another visitation, while the Kreise were to be rationalized by adjusting membership, revising quotas to align more closely with actual wealth, and to incorporate Bohemia and Silesia as additional Kreise to force Austria and Prussia to contribute more. Other ideas included imposing additional curbs on imperial prerogatives at the next election, or backing Prince Max Joseph of Zweibrücken-Birkenfeld as next king of the Romans, a suggestion that was not totally far-fetched given that he was heir to both Bavaria and the Palatinate, which he had inherited in 1799.

Some proposals would have weakened existing structures by widening princely autonomy, for instance by transferring responsibility for imperial debt commissions from the Reichshofrat to committees of princes. A few proposals involved more fundamental reform in specific areas. Carl Theodor von Dalberg, the future imperial arch-chancellor, started revising the 1532 Carolina penal code as a National Law Book after 1787, and advocated abolishing serfdom, customs barriers and guild restrictions, all of which would have struck at the heart of corporate society.[94] Most were reluctant to go that far. Saxony only joined the League of Princes to preserve its existing status, while Justus Möser and other writers struggled to reconcile enlightened ideals with corporatist hierarchical structures.[95] The new princely sociability was still exclusive, indeed more so than some earlier forms. Unlike the fifteenth-century reform era, the middling princes did not cooperate with counts, knights or imperial cities in their proposals, justifiably raising suspicions about their true motives. Several proposals simply ignored the right of ecclesiastical princes to their fiefs, and proceeded immediately to considering how to legitimate their expropriation.

It hardly inspired confidence that Landgrave Wilhelm IX of Hessen-Kassel asserted inheritance claims by invading the tiny principality of Schaumburg-Lippe in 1787, a year after joining the League of Princes. A Reichshofrat verdict, backed by Prussian, Hanoverian and Cologne diplomatic pressure, secured a bloodless withdrawal and obliged the landgrave to pay reparations.[96] While this appeared to demonstrate the efficacy of existing institutions, unrest in Liège between 1789 and 1791 revealed serious defects in the Empire's peacekeeping system, as neither the courts nor the Kreis Assemblies could compel Austria and Prussia to cooperate. Prussia recognized the Belgian revolutionaries' declaration of independence in January 1790, making it hard for Austria to call on the Empire to restore order.[97]

By then, princely reform efforts were losing momentum. They faced the same problems as Luther and the other reformers in the early sixteenth century who were unable to reform the Catholic church without papal cooperation. None of the princes wanted to leave the Empire, but equally none could interest the Habsburgs in imperial reform. Unlike Maximilian I or Charles V, neither Joseph II after 1780 nor his two successors had any incentive to change existing arrangements. Reform was more likely to make the Empire harder to manage, rather than increase its material benefit to Austria. Despite Joseph's sometimes rough treatment of the ecclesiastical princes and other minor Estates, Austria still appeared their more natural ally than Prussia or the middling princes. Austria could count on 65 votes in the electoral and princely colleges between 1785 and 1792 compared to 43 likely to side with Prussia, while the cities overwhelmingly backed the Habsburgs.[98] Any chance of princely sponsored reform ended with the Convention of Reichenbach on 27 July 1790, which established an Austro-Prussian alliance of convenience lasting until April 1795. Another separate league of middling princes was proposed at a meeting in Wilhelmsbad in September 1794, when it was hoped this might attract British financial backing, but the scheme was soon scotched by Austrian diplomacy.[99]

The Absence of Revolution

The lack of popular pressure for change was a significant factor behind the conservatism of the reform proposals. Burghers made growing use of the Reichshofrat to resolve disputes in their cities, while 28 per cent of all cases brought by peasants to the Reichskammergericht were initiated after 1750. Increased recourse to the supreme courts indicates greater acceptance of their role in conflict resolution, rather than evidence of a mounting crisis. Baron Knigge, organizer of the conspiratorial Bavarian secret society known as the Illuminati and a revolutionary sympathizer, wrote in 1793 that the long duration of Reichskammergericht cases allowed passions to subside, while ordinary people retained faith in eventual redress. This, he felt, was why 'we in Germany probably should not expect a dangerous political revolution'.[100]

The Empire's inhabitants viewed the French Revolution with a mixture of complacency, panic and, for a few, admiration. Many mistook the Liège, Belgian and Saxon revolts in 1789–90 for the spread of revolution to the Empire – not surprisingly, since protesters sometimes copied French slogans and symbols. A 'liberty tree' mysteriously appeared in Paderborn town square one night in 1792 with a notice exhorting the inhabitants to throw off the yoke of their aristocratic oppressors. Two years later, rioting peasants demolished the prison in Gesmold, Lower Saxony, as if it were a local Bastille and demanded 'freedom and equality like in France'. French émigrés deliberately fanned the authorities' fears, hoping to enlist the German princes for a counter-revolutionary crusade.[101] In fact, there was little enthusiasm for the kind of changes enacted in France: no one heeded the notice in Paderborn, while the Gesmold peasants dispersed once they felt they had made their point. Protesters' aims remained conventional, and the level of unrest did not increase despite the rapidly escalating burdens of war after 1792.

'German Jacobins', or open supporters of revolution, were a 'tiny minority within a small minority' of French sympathizers.[102] The absence of support is not surprising given the prevailing hostility to republicanism and individualism. French bourgeois equality with its inviolability of property suggested the horrors of an unfettered free market strongly at odds with the moral economy of the Empire's regulated corporate society. A republic was briefly established in Mainz after French troops captured the city in 1792. Some German Jacobins envisaged extending this to the whole of the Empire, or reorganizing the Empire to exclude Austria and Prussia. Although they embraced French centralist ideas, some were still guided by elements of the imperial constitution. Christoph Friedrich Cotta, a former imperial publicist turned Jacobin, advocated converting the Reichstag into an elected parliament.[103] French ideas were soon discredited by news of the accompanying violence and escalating terror. The French occupation of the Rhineland after 1792 made their freedom appear even more despotic than the rule of Louis XIV, whose troops had devastated the same region a century before. Animosity deepened with forced requisitioning and other demands across the next 20 years, cementing anti-French stereotypes that persisted into the mid-twentieth century.[104]

Most believed that a combination of imperial justice and progressive reforms by territorial governments had made revolution unnecessary. Although the Reichstag adjourned for its summer recess a few weeks after the storming of the Bastille on 14 July 1789, the Empire's multi-layered structure enabled effective coordination of security measures through the Kreise, which established a military cordon on the western frontier and tightened censorship after August 1789.[105] It took war to force change on the Empire. The French revolutionaries abolished feudalism on 4 August 1789, though full implementation was delayed until 1838 by the difficulties of defining exactly what 'feudalism' was.[106] The decree affected various Rhenish princes like the bishop of Speyer and landgrave of Hanau-Lichtenberg, who still possessed extensive jurisdictions and property in Alsace and Lorraine. The peace treaties transferring these territories to France in 1648 and 1738 had remained within the spirit of early modern European relations by leaving these rights intact. The French revolutionaries now asserted the modern notion of absolute sovereignty to argue their decree applied everywhere in France, whereas the princes clung to older ideals of fragmented sovereignty to defend their extra-territorial rights. Preoccupied with domestic problems, the revolutionaries initially offered financial compensation, but the Rhenish princes unwisely insisted on full restitution.

The other imperial Estates were reluctant to risk war over the issue, while Prussia manipulated the controversy as part of its general policy of causing trouble for Austria. By the time Leopold II offered to negotiate in December 1791, it was too late, as leadership of the revolution had passed to men who saw it as their duty to export their ideas and who regarded war as a solution to the mounting problems in France.[107]

Prussia Stands Alone

France initially only declared war on Austria on 20 April 1792, planning to conquer the Austrian Netherlands, which was still in ferment over opposition to local Habsburg administrative reforms. Austria bought Prussian support for a counter-offensive by agreeing to its annexation of Ansbach-Bayreuth (the childless prince of which retired to live with his English mistress on a Prussian pension). The joint invasion of France stalled at Valmy in September, a battle celebrated as a great revolutionary victory, but which consisted principally of the French army not fleeing from the Prussians, who retreated after losing only 184 men.[108] This famous failure of nerve broke the Austro-Prussian offensive, but there had never been a real chance that the invaders could have crushed the Revolution. War resumed after the French regicide on 21 January 1793, with Austria and Prussia on the defensive and distracted by continued mutual rivalry over Poland's fate. The two German great powers combined in March 1793 to force the Reichstag to declare war on France, thus legitimating their exploitation of collective security to bolster their own flagging military effort.[109] Thereafter, the Empire's fate depended to a considerable extent on Austrian and Prussian policy.

Prussian ministers were inhibited by personal rivalries from formulating a consistent policy, something that merely heightened Austrian suspicions.[110] The Hohenzollerns' advisors were profoundly unsettled by events, but their yearning to restore politics to a more predictable course compelled them to confront Prussia's relationship to the Empire. They concluded that 'old German liberty' and the Empire's 'decrepit constitution' were creating the same weaknesses which they were busy exploiting in Poland to carve up that country. Although their proposals went further than those voiced in the earlier reform debate, they still only envisaged streamlining rather than dissolving the Empire. The ecclesiastical and minor territories were to be distributed amongst the secular principalities, while the territorial Estates were to be abolished to remove them as constraints on the ability of rulers to raise taxes and reshape society. The most famous of these proposals was submitted by Carl von Hardenberg on 5 February 1806 and was intended to simplify imperial politics by reorganizing the Empire into six, more geographically logical, Kreise, in turn grouped into three federations led by Austria, Prussia and Bavaria under the emperor's overall leadership.[111]

Prussia's ministers hoped to salvage something of the old order, not create a German nation state. They wanted a viable Empire that could contain Austria and ensure Prussia's security, especially given the unreliability of allies like Britain and Russia. Prussia even restored autonomy to Nuremberg in September 1796 after briefly annexing the city without permission.[112] The ministers were aware of the contradictions between what they thought best for the Empire and their own desire to aggrandize Prussia, but were reluctant to choose between these goals until compelled by military failure and state bankruptcy to make a separate peace with France at Basel in April 1795.[113] Prussia was thrust into a semi-imperial role by agreeing with France to convert northern Germany into a neutrality zone. Unable to pay its own troops, Prussia fell back on imperial structures to corral the northern imperial Estates into funding an 'army of observation' to uphold neutrality, including convening a combined Upper and Lower Saxon Kreis Assembly at Hildesheim in 1796. Northern Germany experienced Prussia's presence as a foreign occupation, and longed for a restoration of pre-war conditions.[114]

Meanwhile, Prussia had reduced its debt by 22 million talers to 33 million by 1806, while making considerable territorial gains during the reorganization of 1801–3, appearing 'to have achieved the dream of every gambler: to win without betting'.[115] The establishment of a more stable French government, known as the Directory, in 1795 did not bring the expected normalization of relations, and Prussian envoys still found the situation in Paris confusing. Even after 1803, ministers hoped that continued Habsburg imperial rule would prevent Napoleon establishing vassalage over southern Germany, and so rejected a French offer in October 1804 to convert the neutrality zone into a Prussian north German empire.[116]

Austria and the Empire

Many later German historians quietly ignored the catastrophic impact of Prussia's withdrawal into neutrality after 1795, arguing instead that the Empire was already dead and criticizing Francis II and his chief minister Baron Thurgut for placing Austrian above 'German' interests.[117] Like his Prussian counterparts, Thurgut already contemplated major changes, including secularizing the three ecclesiastical electorates. Similarly, he struggled to reconcile saving the Empire with advancing Habsburg objectives. His successors after 1800 were even more determined to save the old order, especially Johann Philipp Stadion, who became foreign minister on 25 December 1805. Like his brother Friedrich Lothar, who was Habsburg envoy for Bohemia at the Reichstag after 1803, Johann Philipp was an imperial knight with a deep attachment to corporate society. Baron Hügel, Austria's primary Reichstag envoy after 1793 and an ennobled burgher, shared this sentiment and oversaw the crucial effort to save the imperial insignia from advancing French troops in 1796.[118]

France's revolution was a serious setback for Austria, robbing it of its principal ally since 1756; cementing that alliance had been the reason Francis II's daughter Marie-Antoinette had married the future Louis XVI in 1770. Meanwhile, Austria engaged in a costly and largely unsuccessful war against the Ottoman empire between 1788 and 1791, mainly to please Russia, whose friendship was vital in holding Prussia in check. The failure of the Austro-Prussian offensive in 1792 convinced Thurgut that Austria was engaged in an existential struggle requiring an entirely new approach. As war resumed early in 1793, he wrote: 'the Empire is lost and can only hope to be rescued by Austria and Prussia. Consequently, these powers are entitled to establish a permanent order in the Empire even without asking the imperial Estates.'[119] Austria's temporary understanding with Prussia after 1790 gave Thurgut a unique opportunity to dispense with the customary wrangling to secure half measures, and instead force policies through the Reichstag against opposition from the weaker Estates.

Faced with French invasion after 1793, many of these backed the declaration of war, hoping that this would keep the military effort within the framework of collective security. Imperial mobilization was impressive. The lesser territories provided three-quarters of their official quotas, together with additional auxiliaries and militia more than making up the difference. The weakest elements often contributed disproportionately. The imperial knights paid 5.7 million florins in voluntary contributions between 1793 and 1801, while Prussia failed to pay its war taxes. Prussia provided 12,000 troops as its imperial contingent, plus another 10,000 in return for cash in lieu from weaker Estates and another 20,000 subsidized by Austria. Yet Prussia retained over 160,000 men at home, because it did not want to antagonize its own subjects by raising taxes.[120]

The Refusal to Sacrifice Liberties

Consequently, the principal burden fell to Austria, which had spent 500 million florins fighting France by 1798, pushing its debt to 542.5 million.[121] Efforts to raise further resources proved counterproductive. The south-western Estates mobilized militia in 1793–4, but service was soon seen as another burden. Military setbacks and Prussia's withdrawal spread disillusionment, as did the growing acceptance that France could not be defeated by conventional means.[122] Two anecdotes illustrate the general reluctance to sacrifice what was being fought for just to achieve victory. The Reichshofrat upheld an appeal in 1794 from an official who had been dismissed by the Hanoverian government after he had lodged his own court case opposing the war against France as unconstitutional. Three years later, when challenged by Napoleon to defend the imperial church's wealth in the light of Christ's poverty, Friedrich Lothar Stadion argued simply that it was sanctioned by imperial law.[123]

Austria was unable to make peace in 1795, because it was bound by alliances with Britain and Russia. The Peace of Basel concentrated the war in south Germany and north Italy, but Austria fought on hoping to decide the Empire's fate without consulting Prussia.[124] Austrian forces held their own during 1796, but increasingly distrusted the remaining south German contingents. The Swabian Kreis troops were forcibly disarmed in July 1796, but Austria was unable to prevent Württemberg and Baden from concluding separate armistices the following month. As in 1740, Austria regarded refusal to cooperate as betrayal, and consequently felt even less compunction to adhere to constitutional norms. Imperial reform was now dictated by military circumstances.

Renewed defeats in 1797 obliged Austria to agree preliminary peace terms at Campo Formio on 18 October, ceding the Rhineland to France and renouncing imperial jurisdiction over north Italy. Crucially, Campo Formio introduced the principle of compensation whereby secular rulers losing possessions through these changes were to be compensated east of the Rhine at the expense of the weaker imperial Estates, with Austria already secretly planning to annex Salzburg.

The public outcry deterred immediate implementation of the terms, while Austrian ministers still hoped to salvage key elements of the old order that they knew would limit Prussia's potential gains. A congress convened in Rastatt at the end of 1797 to work out the details, but negotiations were delayed by Napoleon's expedition to Egypt. The next 18 months made it abundantly clear that the fate of the lesser Estates was at stake and they rallied behind Austria when a renewed Russian alliance prompted Francis II to resume the war in 1799. Napoleon returned from Egypt and established himself as First Consul governing France in November. New French victories at Hohenlinden and Marengo in 1800 obliged Austria to sue for peace.

Reorganization of the Empire, 1801–4

Terms agreed at Lunéville in February 1801 broadly repeated those of Campo Formio, allowing France to annex 26,000 square kilometres and 1.8 million people west of the Rhine, as well as confirming that the Austrian Netherlands, Savoy and imperial Italy were no longer part of the Empire. The question of compensation was entrusted to an Imperial Deputation, but in practice was driven by power politics. Prussia already occupied Hanover with French permission in April 1801, setting a precedent for the middling princes who now dealt directly with France and Russia using the fig-leaf argument that these were guarantors of the Peace of Westphalia. France wanted to reorganize much of the Empire into larger territories that might be future allies, while Russia tried to preserve a more traditional balance whilst promoting the interests of dynasties like Württemberg and Hessen-Darmstadt who were related to the Romanovs. Along with Bavaria and Baden, these princes now began occupying neighbouring territories during 1801–2. The changes were belatedly endorsed with minor amendments by the Deputation in a document known as the

Final Decision (*Reichsdeputationshauptschluß*), which was ratified by the Reichstag on 24 March 1803 and accepted by the emperor, the Reichskammergericht and imperial lawyers (Map 11).[125]

Compensation far exceeded the losses west of the Rhine. Prussia got the lion's share, gaining 10,010 square kilometres with 431,000 inhabitants and nearly 2.5 million talers in annual revenue more than it lost to France. The other principal beneficiaries were Bavaria, Württemberg, Baden, Hessen-Kassel, Hessen-Darmstadt and Hanover, which was restored to Britain and given land, even though it lost nothing west of the Rhine. Austria annexed the bishoprics of Trent and Brixen, while Salzburg, Eichstätt and part of Passau went as a new electorate to Francis II's younger brother, Ferdinand Joseph, who had been forced to cede Tuscany to France.[126] In all, 112 imperial Estates were mediatized or lost to France, including virtually the entire church lands east of the Rhine, totalling 71,225 square kilometres with 2.36 million subjects and 12.72 million florins in annual revenue.

The historical verdict has been the repetitive refrain that the Empire 'was now as good as dead'.[127] This prognosis was still premature, because the majority of the Empire's inhabitants did not experience 1801 as a total defeat, unlike 1918 or 1945. The territorial reorganization revealed both the strengths and weaknesses of the constitutional order, and it achieved the substance if not the spirit of many of the earlier reform plans through consolidating the Empire into a smaller number of individually larger principalities. Most regarded secularization as rationalization and not as a sin, as had been the case for many Catholics in 1555 and 1648.[128] The Final Decision softened the blow by guaranteeing the free exercise of religion as Catholic lands passed to Protestant princes. While burghers mourned the loss of autonomy, some hoped that mediatization would rescue their home towns from the growing burden of debts.[129]

The assessment was surprisingly upbeat because the changes were thought to be limited to a redistribution of imperial fiefs rather than indicating a repudiation of corporate society. The mediatized authorities and populations only lost their constitutional autonomy, not their other rights. All the beneficiaries accepted binding responsibilities towards the victims, especially the imperial clergy, agreeing to pay annual pensions varying from up to 60,000 florins for former bishops to a tenth of that for former abbesses, while former canons were allowed a generous nine-tenths of their former incomes.[130] Meanwhile, the new governments assumed all liabilities, which could be considerable: Bavaria acquired additional debts of 93 million florins. The lively reform debate continued, still concentrating on technicalities like adjusting the Reichstag and other institutions to align with the recent territorial redistribution.

However, the wider international situation ensured that the Empire no longer controlled its own destiny. All were acutely conscious of Poland's recent fate when a new constitution intended to secure independence merely hastened external efforts to partition the country out of existence after 1793. Reformers rightly feared that vigorous measures to strengthen the Empire would prompt France to resume the war. Austria was unable to capitalize on renewed imperial patriotism for the same reason, as its forces were in no condition to fight. Deeper, more fundamental factors also inhibited reform. Territorial redistribution had not been a 'clean sweep' (*Flurbereinigung*), because formal power was still related to the status hierarchy. Reorganization of the electorates did nothing to reduce Austrian and Prussian influence and merely added to disputes over precedence. The princely college was restructured, giving the counts 53 full votes based on their acquisition of imperial cities and abbeys. The latter were often relatively rich, thus also briefly solving the counts' debt problems. However, the electors were the primary beneficiaries since they simultaneously received the full votes of the former bishoprics, increasing their share of princely votes to 78 out of the new total of 131. Meanwhile, the consolidation of all Wittelsbach lands through inheritance meant that Bavaria had three times as much land as all counts combined. It was obvious that simply elevating someone like the count of Bretzenheim to princely status did not bring any real influence. Meanwhile, the annexation of four imperial cities by France and the mediatization of a further 41 by German counts and princes reduced the civic corpus to just six, rendering it little more than an adjunct to the Reichstag. The redistribution of votes made Austrian management of the Reichstag more difficult. Francis hesitated to confirm the new order, thereby undermining the assembly's vitality.[131] The Kreise were likewise affected, with Baden and Württemberg insisting on exercising the votes of the imperial cities they had annexed, alienating the remaining, weaker members, who were already concerned at being marginalized.

The real problem concerned the position of the middling princes.

These had gained considerably in both real and formal influence, yet still had no prospect of using the imperial constitution to hold Austria and Prussia to account. They drew the lessons of events since 1796 and concentrated on developing their military potential to trade this, when necessary, for French recognition of their continued autonomy. The reality was not lost on the former counts, who resorted to the conventional practice of combining after August 1803 in two regionally based unions. Some still hoped to make the old order work through improved cooperation in the Reichstag and Kreis Assemblies, while Prince Karl of Isenburg-Birstein tried to militarize the Frankfurt Union as a possible partner for Napoleon. However, status consciousness was too deeply ingrained. The two unions failed to collaborate, and individual counts joined the middling princes in 'mediatizing' the imperial knights: in some cases, castles were besieged and the knights dragged away in chains.[132] Austrian ministers recognized that the assault on the knights presaged the end of the emperor's prerogatives and issued a legal injunction backed by the Reichstag in January 1804.[133] Fear of France, which was now allied to several of the princes, prevented the injunction being enforced.

The Decisive Blow, 1805

Napoleon meanwhile forced the pace of events, proclaiming himself emperor (1804) and creating a new kingdom of Italy (1805). Austria sought refuge in renewed alliances with Britain and Russia. Unlike in the wars of 1793–7 and 1799–1801, there was no attempt to appeal to the Empire. Dalberg clung to the illusion that neutrality would preserve the Empire, but open support for France from Bavaria, Baden and Württemberg revealed how things were changing. Napoleon initiated hostilities, defeating the Austrians at Ulm in October 1805 and entering Vienna a month later, succeeding where the Ottomans had twice failed. A further Austro-Russian defeat at Austerlitz on 2 December broke all resistance. Austria agreed an armistice with France, the Russians retreated, and Prussia, which had mobilized, now backed down in return for renewed French permission to annex Hanover. Through this, Napoleon turned Prussia into 'an accomplice' in his destruction of the Empire.[134]

New treaties bound Baden, Bavaria and Württemberg closer to France, paving the way for Napoleon to dictate terms to Austria in the

Peace of Pressburg on 26 December 1805. Austria accepted further territorial redistribution benefiting France's German allies, and recognized Bavaria and Württemberg as sovereign kingdoms, and Baden as a sovereign grand duchy (Map 12).[135] Pressburg was universally received as a hammer blow, crushing whatever optimism remained. Habsburg ministers recognized that the independence of Baden, Bavaria and Württemberg meant that little was left of the Empire. Sweden already declared in January 1806 that it would no longer participate in the Reichstag, which it regarded as dominated by usurpation and egoism.[136] Napoleon created the new grand duchy of Cleves-Berg for his brother-in-law Murat, who acted as independent prince. The French emperor then forced Dalberg to accept another distant Bonaparte relation, Cardinal Fesch, as successor designate to the imperial arch-chancellorship in May 1806.[137]

Austria still struggled to preserve what remained of the Empire, disputing Napoleon's interpretation of Pressburg to claim that the Swabian, Bavarian and Franconian Kreise still existed. The reluctance to face facts extended to Baden, Bavaria and Württemberg. Napoleon pressed the three sovereigns to renounce the Empire entirely. Württemberg did withdraw from the imperial postal network, but otherwise all hesitated to take the final step. Each felt uneasy about the circumstances in which they acquired their new status and wondered what value it had if the old hierarchical order was collapsing. Baden and Württemberg still paid their levy to maintain the Reichskammergericht, which continued to function into July 1806.[138]

The Final Act, 1806

Napoleon pressed on with plans to bind the militarily potent principalities to France and told his foreign minister at the end of May 1806 that he no longer recognized the Empire's existence.[139] The bitter atmosphere has coloured subsequent accounts of the final act, with virtually every German-speaking author into the late twentieth century criticizing Francis II for not doing more to save the Empire. Certainly, the emperor demeaned his position by trying to bargain territorial concessions from France in return for relinquishing the title.[140] Francis himself blamed Prussia for not supporting him, while later commentators anachronistically bemoaned the lack of German nationalism.

Sixteen German princes hastened the end by agreeing the Confederation of the Rhine on French terms on 12 July 1806. In addition to Murat, the signatories comprised Dalberg, Bavaria, Württemberg, Baden, Hessen-Darmstadt, and 11 lesser princes, including Karl of Isenburg-Birstein, who used his carefully cultivated personal contacts with Napoleon to ensure he was included.[141] Napoleon gave them until 25 July to ratify it, and on 22 July told Francis to abdicate by 10 August or face war. Only Bavaria, Württemberg, Hessen-Darmstadt and Isenburg publicly declared they were leaving the Empire. The Confederation Act included Napoleon's permission to mediatize the remaining counties, which Württemberg immediately proceeded to do. The princes belatedly apologized to the Reichstag that adverse circumstances since 1795 had left them no choice, trying to excuse their actions by claiming the Empire had already ceased to exist. The next day, Habsburg officials feverishly prepared legal documents to enable Francis not merely to abdicate, but to remove the Empire entirely from Napoleon's grasp by dissolving it.

Having been twice reminded by his ministers, Francis reluctantly signed the papers. On the morning of 6 August an imperial herald in full regalia rode through Vienna to the Jesuit church of the Nine Choirs of Angels. After climbing to the balcony, he summoned the inhabitants with a silver fanfare to announce the end of the Empire. The Reichstag was formally informed on 11 August, while letters were sent to foreign diplomats over the following week.[142]

The Empire was certainly not dead by the late eighteenth century, and if it was sick, as Zedler and others suggested, it was not yet on life support. If revolutionary France had not intervened, the most likely prognosis was that the Empire's socio-political order would have persisted further into the nineteenth century, but it is unlikely that this could have been sustained against the levelling and homogenizing forces unleashed by capitalism and industrialization around 1830. Attempts to preserve the corporate order beyond 1806 will be addressed in this book's final chapter, which also assesses the Empire's longer-term significance for Germany and Europe.

13

Afterlife

DISMANTLING THE EMPIRE, 1806–15

Public Dismay

Despite the widespread awareness of changing circumstances, news of the Empire's dissolution caused consternation. The idea that the general population were indifferent is a myth elaborated by later historians, usually by taking a few quotations from Goethe and others out of context.[1] Some intellectuals and artists indeed welcomed its demise and looked to Napoleon as the herald of a new age. However, many were deeply affected, like the painter Caspar David Friedrich, who fell ill as a result.[2] On 20 July 1806 the French envoy in Bavaria already reported waves of 'nostalgia' at the Empire's imminent end, and noted the widespread concern at losing a system that protected the weak against the strong.[3] The remaining envoys at the Reichstag received the formal announcement with dismay.[4] The newly minted elector of Hessen-Kassel, with tears in his eyes, told an Austrian envoy that he regretted the loss of 'a constitution from which Germany has long derived its happiness and freedom'.[5] Even those who directly benefited were upset. Von Dalberg was close to tears when he signed the Confederation Act, while the dour, authoritarian Friedrich I, who had just become Württemberg's first king, privately mourned the Empire's end.[6]

With Germany full of Napoleon's troops, few dared to protest. Johann Palm, a Nuremberg book dealer, was executed on 26 August for writing an anonymous 150-page pamphlet criticizing French policy.[7] Hans von Gagern wrote that, as a government minister in Nassau, he could take no action, because the French occupied the principality, yet he deeply regretted the division of 'my general fatherland'. Many others noted how, in contrast to 1801–3, people were now too frightened to discuss political reform.[8]

Public discussion of the Empire's end was thus delayed until 1813 when allied troops began liberating Germany after Napoleon's defeat in Russia the year before. The period immediately following Napoleon's final defeat in 1815 was profoundly conservative and saw debate constrained by tight censorship laws. These circumstances affected those who published memoirs, especially the last 'imperial generation' who reached later middle age around 1820. Their accounts reflected how their careers had fared after 1806. Predictably, those who had suffered most expressed the deepest regret, notably the old aristocratic and legal elite, and the princes mediatized after 1801.

Continuity amidst Change

Hegel famously described the imperial constitution as constructed of round stones that would roll away if pushed. Many historians have followed him in depicting 1806 as 'zero hour', deliberately using the term 'old Empire' (*Altes Reich*) to consign the imperial socio-political order to history and to present modern Germany as a product of nineteenth-century war and economic developments. 'In the beginning was Napoleon,' writes Thomas Nipperdey at the start of his general history.[9] Many of Hegel's stones in fact proved immovable boulders, because it took several years to dismantle the constitutional order and many more to remove underlying socio-legal arrangements.

The legality of Francis II's abdication was the most immediate issue since the majority of central Europeans remained governed by rulers who, till then, had been imperial vassals. Austrian ministers carefully phrased the abdication patent to blame the new Confederation of the Rhine for having already wrecked the Empire, reducing Francis's act to simply releasing his vassals from their feudal ties. For this reason, Austria's representative told the later German Federal Assembly on 5 November 1816 that the Empire had ceased to exist when the Confederation princes ratified their alliance with Napoleon on 1 August 1806.[10] Legalism still guided behaviour. Austrian ministers seriously debated whether the imperial insignia belonged to the Habsburgs or the Empire collectively, and strove to avoid the impression that Francis had simply stolen them. As in 1803, there was a continued sense of duty towards those who had served the Empire, and Austria provided pensions for the Reichshofrat staff who found themselves unemployed.

Sweden issued an official protest on 22 August 1806, arguing that the Empire still existed but was merely under French occupation. Britain took a similar line, even briefly going to war with Prussia for having annexed Hanover. Most imperial lawyers concluded that, though Francis was entitled to abdicate, he could not unilaterally dissolve the Empire, which was a collective order of emperor and imperial Estates.[11] The sense of uncertainty was heightened by the continued existence of the Prussian-controlled northern neutrality zone, which still adhered to the constitutional order established in 1803 and whose princes had refrained from joining the Confederation of the Rhine.

Prussia used the opportunity to increase pressure on the northern princes from July onwards, presenting them with a stark choice of either accepting closer cooperation on its terms or becoming French vassals. Prussian ministers envisaged annexing the three wealthy cities of Hamburg, Bremen and Lübeck, whilst allowing Hanover and Saxony to assume royal titles and permitting Hessen-Kassel to take the remaining smaller north-western territories. Hessen-Kassel and Saxony were prepared to accept a *Kayßer von Preußen*, but wanted to retain more of the old structures, including the Westphalian and Lower and Upper Saxon Kreise. Even Prussia wanted to preserve a Danish presence in Holstein and accept Russian possession of the tiny lordship of Jever. Russia rejected this, refusing to respond to official notification of Francis's abdication and acting as if the Empire still existed. However, Austria was prepared to accept Prussian plans, because it saw these as the only way to restrict the Confederation of the Rhine to the south and west. France did not have to do much to block Prussia's belated imperial project. Minor north German princes like those of Waldeck and Lippe-Detmold had already joined the Confederation in August 1806 to escape annexation. Prussia failed to secure more than defensive treaties with Saxony and Hessen-Kassel, leaving it isolated when Napoleon decided to settle matters by war in October.[12]

Liquidating the Empire

The imperial postal service was already in difficulties during the 1790s and fragmented into 30 rival territorial networks during 1806, though the Thurn und Taxis family would continue to operate a reduced business until forced by Prussia to sell this in July 1867.[13] Otherwise, the deeply engrained legalism persisted, smoothing the new territorial reorganization, as it had done in 1801–3. However, this time there was no longer a single, superior constitutional order, and it was not clear where formal responsibility lay. In practice, the Imperial Deputation's Final Decision from March 1803 continued to operate and its guidelines were incorporated in the Confederation Act of July 1806 by obliging members to look after the employees and debts of the territories Napoleon permitted them to annex.[14]

For example, the 300-square-kilometre Westphalian county of Rietberg had been elevated to a principality in 1803 and survived into 1806 through its incorporation within the neutrality zone. It was assigned to the Department of Fulda, an administrative subdivision of the new kingdom of Westphalia, created in 1807 by Napoleon for his brother Jérôme, using the Hessen-Kassel and former Westphalian and Lower Saxon bishoprics recently annexed by Prussia. The new district official reported on the fate of Rietberg's 'army' of one lieutenant and 23 men 'that these soldiers are not National Guards, but were a real and long-standing military force, maintained partly to discharge obligations to the Empire and partly for police and public-order duties'. Accordingly, the new government ruled that they were entitled to pensions at public expense.[15]

Meanwhile, the grand duchy of Berg, another Napoleonic creation, inherited responsibility for liquidating the affairs of the Westphalian Kreis on the grounds that the former duke of Berg had been the Kreis convenor. It took until 1811 to wind up business and arrange pensions for former officials. Liquidation of the Swabian Kreis fell to Württemberg and was completed in 1809. Austria did what it could to disrupt this, entrusting the former Reichshofrat president Count Philipp Öttingen-Wallerstein with heading a commission in February 1807 to divide the court's cases between those still ongoing and a historic archive. The work was incomplete when renewed French occupation of Vienna forced Austria to surrender the documents in 1809. Napoleon planned a central archive for all Europe and had the court papers, along with some other Habsburg material, carted off in 2,500 chests to Paris. After Napoleon's defeat, the Treaty of Paris (May 1814) compelled France to return to Austria all documents relating to *l'ancien Empire Germanique*.[16]

The Reichskammergericht staff fared less well than those of the Reichshofrat, because no one wanted to take responsibility for what had been a common institution maintained by all imperial Estates. Nonetheless, thanks to their prestige and competence, over half the former judges found posts in the successor states, including Karl Albert von Kamptz, who became Prussian minister of justice.[17] The court's base, the former imperial city of Wetzlar, had already been assigned in 1803 to Dalberg's new arch-chancellor principality. He established a new law school there in 1808 ostensibly modelled on French examples, but in practice continuing the Reichskammergericht's function to train jurists for all Germany. Former staff were employed as teachers. The German Confederation confirmed the employment of Reichskammergericht archivists to look after the court's documents in 1816. Prussia, which had received Wetzlar within the renewed redistribution of territory after Napoleon's final defeat the year before, forced the Confederation to establish a commission in 1821 to disperse the documents. It is a measure of the complexity of the Empire's legal history that it took 24 years to work out where to send them, since it was far from clear which of the successor states 'owned' individual cases. The papers were sent across Germany between 1847 and 1852, much to the frustration of modern historians, who ever since have had to search numerous regional archives to reconstruct imperial legal history.[18]

The Persistence of Corporate Society

The continuity of personnel encouraged that of practice, contributing to the uneven experience in the Empire's former territories across 1806–15. Full French-style legal and administrative reforms were limited to Berg and Westphalia, the two states governed by Napoleon's relations, as well as the Rhineland directly annexed to France, and to the grand duchy of Würzburg and Dalberg's grand duchy of Frankfurt, established in 1806. Elsewhere, change was largely an acceleration of earlier rationalization and codification, driven now by the need to incorporate mediatized territories and to meet Napoleon's demands for military support. Württemberg more than doubled in size between 1802 and 1810, annexing 78 smaller territories, while its population changed from being solidly Lutheran to nearly one-third Catholic.[19] The situation was similar in Baden, Bavaria, Hessen-Darmstadt and

Nassau, which all made significant gains. Existing administrations could not cope, and were hastily overhauled using prevailing enlightened ideas, French models and pure expediency. Saxony, Mecklenburg and the surviving smaller principalities were more stable, because they were given little or no additional territory after 1806.

Much of the socio-legal order survived even multiple territorial re-organizations. Mecklenburg retained its 1755 constitution until 1918. The Saxon Estates survived until 1831, Hadeln's peasant assembly met until 1884, while corporatism continued to shape Prussia's internal politics long after that. The mediatized princes retained privileged legal status, and control of their own domains and over clerical appointments, plus lesser jurisdiction, hunting and fishing rights within the boundaries of their former imperial fiefs, until 1848. Prussian manors enjoyed tax exemption until 1861, police authority up to 1872, and favourable control over servants until 1918, with lordly influence over local churches persisting even after that. Manorial districts remained the primary units of state administration in Prussia until 1927, all despite the fact that reforms between 1807 and 1821 emancipated serfs from the manorial economy.[20] Hamburg's Jewish Ordinance from 1710 remained in force into the later nineteenth century, while Bavaria's partially codified civil code from 1754 persisted until 1900. Prussia lacked a uniform commercial code before 1861, while a supreme court for the German states was not established again until 1879. Codification of civil law across the states of the Second German Empire took from 1879 until 1900 to complete. Some cultural elements of the old order displayed still greater longevity: Buchenbach parish near Freiburg assumed the spiritual responsibilities of the Swabian monasteries secularized in 1803 and continued to say prayers in memory of Emperor Frederick I 'Barbarossa' until after the First World War.[21]

The Confederation of the Rhine

Political fragmentation was in some ways greater after 1806, because dissolution of imperial structures removed the common framework, leaving central Europe divided into the Austrian Empire, Prussia and the sovereign states grouped into Napoleon's Confederation of the Rhine. Fragments of the Empire persisted alongside these larger entities. West Pomerania remained Swedish until 1815, Jever was still

Russian up to 1818, while Denmark held Holstein until forced to relinquish this in 1864. All three enclaves owed their survival to Napoleon's reluctance to antagonize the powers that owned them. The Teutonic Order commandery at Mergentheim was reserved to Austria by the Peace of Pressburg. Austrian troops guarded this outpost in Swabia until the 1809 war with France, which saw Mergentheim annexed by Württemberg as Napoleon's ally.[22] Although Hanover disappeared in the territorial redistribution after 1806, it retained a shadowy existence through the service of most of its former army as the King's German Legion with the British from 1803 to 1815.

Dynastic continuity was still more striking. Not only did the Habsburgs and Hohenzollerns remain rulers of large states, but 39 princely families and dynastic branches survived as sovereigns in the Confederation of the Rhine. These included the rulers of tiny Schaumburg-Lippe, which had only just escaped Hessian annexation, thanks to the imperial courts in 1787 (see p. 642). The von der Leyen family, elevated from imperial knights to counts as recently as 1711, became princes in 1803 and survived after 1806 thanks to kinship with both Dalberg and Josephine Bonaparte. Their possessions were only mediatized in 1815, passing first to Austria and then Baden after 1819. The Liechtensteins made it all the way from former ministeriales to twenty-first-century sovereigns, having acquired huge estates in Styria, Moravia, Bohemia and Silesia after the twelfth century to become imperial princes in 1623. They finally obtained a Reichstag vote a century later for their lordship of Vaduz, comprising a mere 165 square kilometres, which they bought in 1712. The Liechtensteins secured independence by joining the Confederation of the Rhine in 1806, though their real wealth lay in the estates they retained in the Austrian empire. They escaped integration within Bismarck's Germany by forging a customs union between Vaduz and Austria in 1866. A similar relationship with Switzerland then ensured the continued survival of the Liechtensteins after 1919.

The Confederation developed in four stages, with the initial 16 members leaving the Empire in July 1806. Electoral Saxony joined the Confederation in December, becoming a kingdom, as did the Ernestine Saxon dukes, all of whom sought a closer relationship with Napoleon after his comprehensive victory over Prussia that October. The third phase began in April 1807 when 12 northern and central German principalities from the former neutrality zone joined the Confederation, and ended when Napoleon created the new kingdom of Westphalia in December. Finally, Oldenburg and the two branches of Mecklenburg joined in 1808. Napoleon deliberately preserved some of the smaller states as thorns in the sides of their larger neighbours like Bavaria and Württemberg to hold these in check. Although fully sovereign, all were vulnerable. Napoleon was the Confederation's 'protector', but annexed Oldenburg, Salm-Salm, Salm-Kyrburg and Arenberg, as well as truncating the grand duchy of Berg to expand French territory to the North Sea coast in December 1810. Simultaneously, he seized the cities of Hamburg, Bremen and Lübeck, which had survived since 1806 without joining the Confederation.

Many continued to draw inspiration from the Empire in their efforts to make the Confederation more viable and less vulnerable to Napoleonic whim. Franz Joseph von Albini, Dalberg's chief minister, persuaded Dalberg not to resign, but instead to lay down his imperial arch-chancellorship on 31 July 1806 and accept Napoleon's offer to become the Confederation's 'prince-premier' (*Fürstprimus*).[23] Dalberg hoped the position would allow him to shape the Confederation as a modernized, streamlined, federal version of the Empire. Napoleon indulged him, allowing him to submit various draft constitutions, all of which envisaged the French emperor as 'protector' with the position of prince-premier as substitute arch-chancellor. A 'federal assembly' (*Bundestag*) would convene in Regensburg in place of the Reichstag. Votes were to be distributed roughly according to size, with Bavaria receiving six, Württemberg four, the prince-premier and all grand dukes three each, Nassau two and the rest one apiece. Status thinking persisted in the idea of dividing the assembly into a college of kings and one of princes.

The plans attracted some interest, especially as the weaker Confederation princes hoped a constitution would silence the legal debate as to whether the Empire had been dissolved or was merely currently occupied by France and its allies.[24] However, all princes clung to their new sovereignty and feared that, like today's opponents of the EU, common institutions would cramp their independence. Napoleon had no interest in federal structures that might provide a platform to oppose his military and political demands. Dalberg persisted, remaining loyal to the Confederation till the end and refusing to open negotiations with the

Allies once it became obvious that Napoleon was losing the war. Instead, Dalberg abdicated on 28 October 1813 in favour of Eugène de Beauharnais, Napoleon's stepson, who had been designated next prince-premier in 1810. After temporary exile in Konstanz, Dalberg was allowed by Bavaria to return as the new, purely clerical, archbishop of Regensburg in 1814.

Confirming the End

Compared to the Empire, the Confederation offered very little to its inhabitants who experienced it, much as the Habsburg official Joseph Haas predicted, now simply as Napoleon's recruiting sergeant and tax collector. After France's defeat, there was a strong desire to return to normality, which most still associated with the Empire. Many expected that the Congress of Vienna (1814–15), convened to agree the post-Napoleonic settlement, would restore the Empire. The future Prussian king, Frederick William IV, felt the Empire had simply been in 'abeyance' since 1806 and wanted to revive as much of it as possible.[25] The prince regent and future king George IV and his ministers saw restoring the Empire as a way to recover Hanover. George only assumed the title of king of Hanover in October 1814 when it became obvious the Empire would not be resurrected, making it necessary to match Bavarian, Saxon and Württemberg royal status.[26]

Others persisted further, notably Count Friedrich Ludwig of Solms-Laubach, who had been a prime mover in Prince Karl of Isenburg-Birstein's Frankfurt Union of 1803. Unlike his fellow princes after 1806, Count Friedrich wanted to reverse the mediatization of minor rulers like those in Erbach and Leiningen and he lobbied Napoleon on their behalf – unsurprisingly without effect. He adapted the older rhetoric of imperial patriotism to the new language of German nationalism voiced during the 1813 campaign to present the aristocrats as fighting for their fatherland. At the end of the year he formed an association reminiscent of those of the early modern counts to mobilize minor princes who had lost their autonomy since 1803 or were likely to do so now. He won some sympathy from the influential Prussian minister Baron Stein, but merely managed to secure an extension of the mediatized rulers' existing privileges when the German Confederation was established in June 1815.[27] Rather more surprising was the desire among many ordinary inhabitants for a reversal of the changes since 1803, particularly for their communities to recover autonomy or to be returned to their previous rulers. Baden and Württemberg arrested pro-Austrian sympathizers to scotch a movement calling for a restoration of Habsburg rule in Swabian lands they had acquired in 1806.[28]

The process of defeating Napoleon had already rendered such hopes illusory by the autumn of 1813 when the Allies confirmed that Bavaria and Württemberg could keep their new territories in return for changing sides against France. By then, a decade of near-continuous warfare had demonstrated the military potential of the enlarged principalities, ensuring that the interests of their sovereigns could not be ignored by Austria and Prussia. With partition between the two great powers now off the agenda for the moment, the Congress of Vienna defaulted to the Empire for inspiration as how to organize central Europe. Taking their cue from Dalberg – though without saying so – all proposals presented a rationalized, federal version of the old order. Despite his famous advocacy of a 'national monarchy', Stein's proposal was really a romanticized version of medieval emperorship presiding over a federalized Empire including enlarged Austrian and Prussian monarchies.[29] The past shaped discussions directly. For example, the agreements from the last two imperial elections in 1790 and 1792 were used to guide what powers any new emperor might have. Most proposals envisaged some kind of Kreis structure to group the smaller states. All proposed a federal congress based on the Reichstag. No one seriously considered a republic.

The result was the German Confederation of Austria, Prussia, 4 kingdoms, 18 grand duchies, 11 principalities and 4 free cities. All were considered sovereign, yet combined within elements of a federal state. The new Federal Diet (*Bundestag*) opened in November 1816 in the Thurn und Taxis palace in Frankfurt, establishing a symbolic link to the Empire, because princes from that family had been the Habsburgs' principal commissioners to the Reichstag during the later eighteenth century. The Confederation shared much of the Empire's imprecision and fudge. Its constitution was drawn up hastily during the Hundred Days campaign after Napoleon's surprise return from Elba in February 1815. Many elements were little more than vague suggestions, leaving future developments open, though convergence along federal lines was clearly an option.

Lacking precision, the Confederation partly defaulted to old imperial practice. Austria's emperors were formally hereditary Confederation presidents, but were still treated with a general deference owing more to the Holy Roman imperial legacy than the Austrian imperial title assumed only in 1804. The Habsburgs were still the only German imperial family. They fared no worse than the Hohenzollerns, who had been humiliatingly defeated in 1806 and had to be pushed by their generals into changing sides against Napoleon at the end of 1812. Austria's further defeat in 1809 had at least burnished the Habsburgs' patriotic credentials, since they had assumed the challenge of liberating Germany without support from other German rulers. All the new German princes gathered at Schönbrunn Palace when Ferdinand succeeded Francis II in 1835 as the first Habsburg emperor who had not also once held the Holy Roman title. Frankfurt city council embarked on a 15-year project after 1838 to decorate the 'emperor's room' in their city hall with portraits of every monarch from Charlemagne to Francis II. The Habsburgs attracted considerable sympathy when Austria fought alone and lost against France and Piedmont in the War of Italian Unification in 1859. Only the Hohenzollerns contested their leadership role and even then not consistently before mid-century. Prussia's king was the only Confederation sovereign absent when Austria's new emperor, Franz Joseph, convened a summit in Frankfurt in 1863 to debate political reforms.

The Confederation Act of 1815 established the judicial sovereignty of each member state, instructing them to create their own courts of appeal. Article 12 allowed the four free cities to refer cases to courts in other states to ensure impartiality, rather like the practice of seeking judicial advice used in the early modern Empire (see pp. 628–36). Similarly, the Federal Diet acted as an informal supreme court, in the same manner as the Reichstag, which had performed this function without its being specified constitutionally. As with so many other early liberal aspirations, these vague arrangements proved incapable of preventing arbitrary justice in some Confederation members.[30]

Article 14 declared some previous laws null and void in an effort to prevent conflict between the legal systems of Confederation members and those of the mediatized territories within their new borders. However, it was unclear whether Francis's abdication in 1806 had ended the validity of imperial law, especially as territorial law largely derived from this and often incorporated it verbatim. Only Berg and Westphalia had adopted the Napoleonic Code. Austria, Bavaria and Oldenburg had reformed their codes by 1814, but the process was slow elsewhere, lasting between 1769 and 1820 in Hessen-Darmstadt. Holstein already declared in September 1806 that the Carolina penal code and other imperial laws remained valid unless they explicitly contradicted its own law. Most followed this expedient, and it was adopted in Article 23 of the Vienna Congress Final Accord of 1820, which endorsed the continued validity of all imperial laws and norms that were still useful in the successor states.[31] The difficulties encountered in changing existing legal arrangements help explain the survival of corporate society beyond 1806.

THE EMPIRE IN EUROPEAN HISTORY AFTER 1815

Attitudes outside Germany

Dealing with the Empire's historical legacy took far longer. The viability of the German Confederation was compromised by Austria's dual role as its president and as guarantor of the settlement imposed on Italy by the Vienna Congress. This superficially mirrored the geographic extent of the Empire, but the circumstances were very different, because the former princely houses and civic republics of imperial Italy had been swept away by the French after 1796. Only the House of Savoy was restored (to Piedmont in 1814), but was considered too weak to defend Italy against possible future French aggression. Austria now ruled Lombardy and Venetia as possessions outside the German Confederation. Three of the other remaining four north Italian states were governed by the Habsburgs' relations. Meanwhile, the papacy was restored in central Italy and the Bourbons resumed as kings of Naples-Sicily. As neither were interested in Italian unity, Piedmont emerged as Italy's champion, assuming a place equivalent to Prussia for many German nationalists.

In these circumstances, the Empire appeared either irrelevant to 'true' Italian history or as a symbol of 'German oppression'. Giuseppe Verdi's opera *La battaglia di Legnano* premiered in Rome on 27 January

1849, two months after Pope Pius IX had fled a liberal-nationalist revolution. Its theme of the victory of the Lombard League over Emperor Barbarossa and his 'German' knights in 1176 was a clear inspiration to the revolutionaries battling to eject the Austrians from Italy. Although the opera was suppressed by Austrian censors following the defeat of Piedmont and the Roman Republic that summer, a reference to Legnano was inserted into the Italian national anthem after unification and independence had been achieved in the 1860s. The Empire has remained associated with hegemony, with, for example, Umberto Bossi's *Lega Nord* also claiming the Lombard League's legacy in its campaign against the national government in Rome during the 1990s.[32]

Other than claiming Charlemagne exclusively for themselves, French observers broadly agreed with the generally negative view of the Empire propagated by Leopold von Ranke and his fellow German historians. The Empire, it was believed, belonged only to the medieval past, when 'the weight of Christian universalism' crushed any potential for a viable nation state. Having apparently disappeared completely in the 840s, its revival under Otto I merely created a 'true colossus with feet of clay'.[33] This weakness was a constant source of anxiety, since French statesmen and historians believed that any attempt to forge a truly national German state would involve aggressive expansion at the expense of Germany's current neighbours – a view amply reinforced by the experience of 1870–71, 1914–18 and 1938–45.[34]

Non-Germans still within the Confederation's frontiers were less hostile, because the post-1815 political and legal arrangements preserved something of their old autonomy. This acquired political significance during the 1848–9 revolutions, which forced the Confederation to confront the discrepancy between its political framework and the new, more militant and essentialist nationalist ideas. By 1851, the option of incorporating all Habsburg and Hohenzollern land within the Confederation was off the table due to opposition from other powers, who feared it would create a central European superstate. Discussions, therefore, increasingly narrowed to a Greater German solution incorporating German-speakers beyond existing frontiers, or a Lesser German variant excluding Austria if it did not want to detach itself from the other Habsburg lands.

The controversy greatly accelerated ethnic nationalism within non-German parts of the Habsburg monarchy. The Czechs were particularly anxious to avoid marginalization if incorporated within a unified Germany. Czech liberals rejected an offer to participate in the Frankfurt Parliament during 1848–9, preferring to remain within the multilingual Habsburg monarchy. Czech historians grew more interested in the Empire, which they presented positively, as it had not threatened Bohemian autonomy. Views only became more hostile in the later nineteenth century when nationalists struggled to assert a more distinct identity, sucking historical interpretations of the Empire into general anti-German sentiment. German historians conveniently supplied ammunition with their studies detailing the Empire's numerous failings.[35]

German Perspectives

Many Germans were initially more sympathetic to the Empire. The new liberal-nationalist ideals attracted limited popular support. Only 468 students participated in the famous Wartburg Festival on 18 October 1817, held on the fourth anniversary of the allied victory over Napoleon at Leipzig in a location also befitting the tercentenary just two weeks later of Luther's *Ninety-Five Theses* that sparked the Reformation. Even the Hambach Festival in 1832 drew fewer than 30,000 liberals, compared to the 1.1 million pilgrims visiting Trier in 1844 to see what was believed to be Christ's Holy Robe.[36] For most, identity remained multilayered. Wilhelm von Humboldt, writing in 1813, argued that living in a particular land within a wider community was what defined the German character.[37] Incremental identification from community through state to nation was in tune with the Confederation's political structure and has been labelled 'federal nationalism'.[38] It contrasted with the situation in Italy after 1815 where there was no federal political structure and where fragmentation was associated with foreign (Habsburg) oppression.

However, it still left many dissatisfied. Only Austria and Prussia were still decentralized, with strong provincial as well as communal and state identities. Military necessity had produced more strongly centralized political systems in the other German states, whose rulers had no desire to foster separate identities for the areas they had mediatized between 1803 and 1815.[39] Meanwhile, the process of mediatization raised false hopes amongst intellectuals for more progressive socio-economic and political change, whereas actual reforms were primarily limited to improving fiscal-military efficiency. Many of the post-1815 states failed to introduce more democratic representation. Increasingly, progressive intellectuals saw the Third Germany of smaller principalities as a reactionary holdover from what was now understood as the pre-revolutionary 'old regime'.[40] The experience of 1792–1815 transformed the understanding of 'the people', with many calling for the segregated society of Estates to be replaced by a more equal relationship amongst inhabitants, and between them and the state. The 'nation' was increasingly viewed as composed of 'the people', rather than defined by legal and constitutional arrangements. Nationalism became an oppositional strategy for those critical of the established order, rather than an endorsement of existing structures.[41]

Encouraged by the spread of Romanticism, nationalists looked to the past for inspiration to shape Germany's future. The Empire's more recent history appeared only a tale of decline towards inglorious demise. While many liberals remained uncomfortable with earlier emperors' close associations with the papacy, the medieval Empire appeared more promising. The Middle Ages were sufficiently distant to be romanticized as a lost harmonious society. Conveniently, liberal and conservative agendas chimed with the prevailing historical scholarship, which distinguished a powerful German national monarchy until 1250 from a supposedly long period of terminal decline. This interpretation was popularized by the spread of local-history societies after 1819. Some served the agendas of small-state patriotism by focusing on the local dynasty, perhaps most successfully in Bavaria, where the reign of Louis IV 'the Bavarian' was used to underpin the new Wittelsbach kingdom.[42] However, others took a broader view, notably the *Monumenta Germaniae Historica*, dedicated to publishing documents on the medieval German church.

Artists and writers attractively packaged the Middle Ages for a wider audience. Johann Jakob Bodmer's rediscovery of the *Nibelungenlied* in 1757 was popularized from the early nineteenth century through new collections of German literature and folk tales. Another influential example was Goethe's play about Götz von Berlichingen, the sixteenth-century 'robber baron', which he published in 1773. Casting 62 characters in addition to supporting masses, it is almost impossible to perform, and often departs from history: Götz dies at the end of the

Peasants War in 1525, rather than in reality from old age in 1562. How-ever, Goethe's Götz is a powerful symbol of martial 'German freedom' who deals directly with the emperor, rather than through a lordly hier-archy.[43] The idea was taken up by many others in an attempt to reconnect with a supposedly more authentic and less corrupt age. For instance, Friedrich de la Motte Fouqué's story *Die Zauberring* (1812) is a courtly romance of knights, damsels and swordplay set in a landscape of dark forests and castles on rocky crags.

The past was also physically invoked. Cologne Cathedral had been begun in 1248 but was still unfinished when work was abandoned in 1560. A local initiative in 1808 to restart it won the support of Prussian Crown Prince Frederick William, who laid the foundation stone for the new work in 1842, explicitly linking construction to the task of build-ing national unity.[44] Max von Schenkendorf's poem *The German Cities* stimulated interest in Albrecht Dürer and Hans Sachs, and offered a way to reclaim some of the early modern past without engaging with Reformation history and its still-difficult legacy for nineteenth-century Germany, where religious divisions assumed new political significance.[45] The first monuments to Dürer and Sachs were unveiled in the early 1840s, while Sachs was celebrated at the Pan-German Song Festival in 1861, in turn inspiring Richard Wagner's *Die Meistersinger von Nürn-berg*. Hans von Aufseß's collection of medieval German art became the basis of the German National Museum, which opened in Nuremberg in 1852 and was adopted the following year as a 'national undertaking' by the German Confederation.

Romanticism's 'back to the future' vision was open to both conser-vative and liberal interpretations. Many celebrated medieval society as an organic, harmonious social order, and claimed that corporatism would render formal constitutions unnecessary. This was a politicized version of Richard Wagner's ideal of a complete synthesis of the arts (*Gesamtkunstwerk*), fusing all elements into a common whole. The appeal through metaphors, stories and images often found greater popular resonance than abstract arguments and political programmes. Above all, it suggested a distinctly Germanic solution to the problems of modernity superior to what many perceived as the excesses of British liberalism or mechanistic French Revolutionary ideology. Francopho-bia was a convenient way to gloss over current tensions within Germany, and the official commemoration of the 'Wars of Liberation' (1813–15) ignored the fact that German troops had fought on both sides in 1806, 1809 and 1813.[46]

The search for a more authentically 'German' past involved a rejection of ancient Rome, not least because liberal nationalists increasingly pinned their hopes on Protestant Prussia in opposition to Catholic Austria. The earlier celebration of imperial translation was reversed in favour of interpreting Roman culture as passing through Charlemagne to France, bypassing Germany almost entirely. Ancient Greece supplanted Rome as the classical model, boosted by German involvement in Greek independence in 1829. Ludwig I of Bavaria, father of modern Greece's first king, built Valhalla (1830–42) overlooking the Danube near Regensburg as a pantheon fusing Greek and Germanic influences.[47] The eaves of one side were decorated with personifications of the German states and Germania, while Arminius – now Germanified as 'Hermann' – looked out from the other, typifying the broader trend to celebrate the ancient Germans' resistance to the Romans. The emergence of archaeology as a specialist discipline in Germany from the 1780s saw virtually any non-Roman object labelled as 'Germanic' in a bid to demonstrate the superiority of *Kultur* over Western, Frenchified 'civilization'. Fund-raising for the Hermann Memorial in the Teutoberg forest began in 1841, attracting sponsorship from the British, Austrian and Dutch royal families – demonstrating the portability of the story, which was also construed as a victory for freedom over (Napoleonic-French) oppression. Things had changed somewhat by the time the monument was actually built in 1871–5, with Hermann now overtly linked to Kaiser Wilhelm I in an attempt to root the new Second Empire in the ancient past.[48]

The 1848 Revolution exposed the difficulties of combining these disparate elements within the desired harmony. The revolutionary parliament convened in Frankfurt, partly as the location of the Federal Diet, but also thanks to its earlier imperial associations. Unable to meet in the unfinished *Kaisersaal* in the town hall, the envoys convened in the nearby Paulskirche. The parliament adopted black, red and gold as the new national colours in an attempt to forge a further connection with the Middle Ages. Although all three colours were associated with the medieval Empire, they were only combined as a tricolour by the Lützow rifle corps during the Napoleonic Wars and were used subsequently by liberals from 1817. The parliament added a black double eagle on a gold shield, though without the halos, and this remained the Confederation's symbol until 1866.[49] Prussia was obliged to find a different set of colours once it defeated Austria and formed its own North German Confederation in 1867. Hanseatic red and white were combined with the black of Prussia's royal eagle and became the official colours from 1871, appearing as a new tricolour belatedly adopted as a national flag in 1892. Although both were intended to root new states in the past, the two sets of colours had acquired distinct ideological associations by 1919 that had nothing to do with the pre-1806 Empire. The Weimar Republic compromised by using democratic black, red and gold as the national flag, and conservative black, white and red for the mercantile marine.

The Second Empire

Italian and German unification between 1859 and 1871 was a disaster for Europe's small states, 12 of which lost their independence.[50] The Habsburgs were compelled to grant Hungary equal political status, creating the Dual Monarchy of Austria-Hungary in 1867. This failed to resolve whether this was still an empire or a personal union, with the Habsburgs continuing the early modern fudge already characteristic in their adoption of a hereditary imperial title in 1804.[51] It proved difficult to decide when Austrian history began. Actual separation from Germany sprang from the defeat of 1866, which hardly offered a suitably patriotic starting point. Consequently, Austrian history only became a compulsory subject at the country's universities in 1893 when it adopted the wider scholarly convention of tracing the country's development as part of wider 'imperial history' (*Reichsgeschichte*), until the reign of Charles V, when Habsburg emperors subtly morphed into good Austrians who dealt with the Empire almost as if it was a separate, fairly minor country.

Prussia's victory over France in 1870–71 allowed it to convert the expedient of the North German Confederation into the Second Empire by absorbing the south German states of Baden, Bavaria, Hessen-Darmstadt and Württemberg. The new empire was proclaimed on 18 January 1871 in the Hall of Mirrors in Versailles in a ceremony staged deliberately not only to demonstrate victory over France, but to echo selected elements of the Holy Roman past in an effort to base the new state on something broader than military triumph. Otto von Bismarck persuaded Ludwig II of Bavaria to lead the surviving German princes to acclaim Wilhelm I as emperor in an act drawing directly on what was believed to be early medieval practice. The proclamation explicitly referred to the 'German imperial title dormant for over 60 years'.[52] Holy Roman connections continued as Wilhelm sat on the Ottonian Goslar throne rather than his royal Prussian one when he opened the new Reichstag on 21 March. The early modern formulation 'emperor and empire' (*Kaiser und Reich*) was also used to accommodate the fact that the Second Empire consisted of a much-enlarged Prussia (itself still a kingdom), 21 kingdoms and principalities and three free cities.

These actions derived from expediency rather than genuine commitment to the Holy Roman past. The Goslar throne was used because the Habsburgs still held the Aachen treasures and imperial insignia. Bismarck needed to mask the fact that creating the Second Empire had involved severing historic ties to Austria, suppressing six sovereign German states and asserting Prussian dominance over the remainder. A vague association with the earlier imperial title avoided calling Wilhelm I 'federal president', which sounded dangerously republican after the experiences of 1848. The interim imperial coat of arms devised for January 1871 used the Prussian eagle with a shield emblazoned with Hohenzollern devices underneath Charlemagne's crown. The latter appeared on the 1871 commemorative medal and on major historical monuments built between the 1870s and 1890s to evoke a common German past, but it was embarrassing that the real crown was still in the Habsburg treasury.[53] New official arms were soon devised combining a fantasy crown with the Prussian Order of the Black Eagle. Prussian traditions became clearer when Wilhelm I's son Frederick numbered himself third at his succession in 1888 following the sequence from Frederick II 'the Great' rather than the fifteenth-century Emperor Frederick III. The popular historian Gustav Freytag had already written in 1870 that a new emperor should wear an army officer's helmet and coat, not an imperial crown and robes, and indeed Anton von Werner's famous 1885 painting of the January 1871 ceremony shows the assembled German royalty dressed in military uniforms.

After 1871, Holy Roman traditions were discarded in favour of a romanticized medieval German past that existed in artificial detachment from its actual historical context. The Thuringian poet Friedrich Rückert had popularized the local Kyffhäuser legend that Emperor Barbarossa had been sleeping under a mountain until Germany was reborn. The story attracted growing attention after it appeared in the second part of the Grimm brothers' folk-tale collection in 1817. This chimed with Romantic ideas of rebirth that were popular in the wake of the Napoleonic Wars. Meanwhile, Friedrich Raumer began what became a six-volume history of the Staufers under the immediate influence of Francis's abdication in 1806. Raumer presented the Staufers as a dramatic story of rise and fall, cementing the popular view of them as representing the last age of German greatness. Subsequent governments invoked the Staufers to suggest the birth of a new Germany. *Barbarossa* was the name chosen for the first flagship of the new Federal Navy established by the Frankfurt parliament in 1848.[54] The elderly Wilhelm I was already dubbed *Barbablanca* ('White Beard') at his acclamation in 1871. Veterans from the wars of 1866 and 1871 petitioned to erect a national monument at Kyffhäuser. As soon as scholars pronounced that the mountain had once been sacred to Wotan, the idea seemed doubly appropriate and the new emperor, Wilhelm II, laid the foundation stone in 1892. The grandiose structure was formally inaugurated on 18 June 1896 with a march-past of 30,000 veterans. It combines an equestrian statue of Wilhelm I with a second showing Barbarossa waking at the foot of the plinth.[55] Rückert's poem remained on the school curriculum into the twentieth century.

Meanwhile, the decaying Goslar imperial palace was restored as a national monument between 1868 and 1897 and decorated with paintings depicting selected aspects of imperial history, including the waking Barbarossa (see Plate 32). Otherwise, national monuments were not built at sites associated with the Holy Roman Empire but at ahistorical locations like the junction of the Mosel and Rhine, which was dubbed the 'German Corner' (*Deutsches Eck*) and adorned in 1897 with another grandiose monument to Wilhelm I.[56] A huge statue of Germania was constructed between 1871 and 1883 outside Rüdesheim on the Rhine to present the Second Empire as cementing German unity. The 500 'Bismarck Towers' built across Germany from 1900 to 1910 celebrating that statesman were modelled on Theodoric's tomb at Ravenna to claim a common Gothic past. Meanwhile, the Hanseatic League was reinvented as a purely German enterprise to lend legitimacy to Wilhelmine naval and colonial policy.[57]

The Empire and the 'German Problem'

Both Austria-Hungary and the Second Empire collapsed at the end of the First World War as revolutions forced all German monarchs to abdicate. Both empires had been successful in many respects, especially Germany, which had become the world's fourth largest economy by 1914. Their imperialism was contemporary, a product of the highly competitive environment of the late nineteenth-century world, rather than the pre-1806 imperial past. Neither empire solved the question of belonging. Official policy in Austria-Hungary had continued to place dynastic loyalty above local or national identity, inadvertently creating a situation similar to that in earlier nineteenth-century Germany as nationalism became an ideology of those opposed to the government. Austria-Hungary was broken up in the Versailles Settlement of 1919, which left Austria as a small republic shorn of empire. Even with the Habsburgs gone, it proved difficult to historicize the imperial past. Conservative writers tried to claim it as a civilizing mission, to allow Austria to escape its much-reduced frontiers by suggesting that the country might once again provide order for an otherwise fragmented and chaotic central Europe. Hugo Hantsch emphasized Catholicism as a unifying element, while Heinrich Ritter von Srbik stressed a common *Germantum*, though without racial overtones. Friedrich Heer did both in his romanticized presentation of the Empire as a benign force.[58]

Imperial Germany's initial toleration of multilayered identities angered those who felt that the process of unification had not gone far enough in 1871. A variety of groups agitated for a more homogeneous cultural identity and for the incorporation German-speakers still outside the Empire.[59] The declaration of German as the state language throughout Prussia proved counter-productive, stirring a Polish nationalist backlash. The targeting of Catholics, Jews and Socialists as unpatriotic was equally divisive. Disagreement over German nationality was one of many factors undermining the Weimar Republic established amidst revolution and civil war in 1919. Article 127 of the Weimar constitution provided communal autonomy and self-regulation within a wider legal framework, drawing directly on historical studies of communal forms in the Holy Roman Empire and broader German past. However, many rejected republican government as 'un-German', regarding the Weimar regime as another 'interregnum' like 1250–73. Again, it seemed that a weakened and divided Germany was waiting for its Barbarossa to awake and provide leadership. A new generation of historians, including Ernst Kantorowicz, who – ironically – was Jewish, repeated Raumer's earlier rehabilitation of the Staufers, who were celebrated as far-sighted empire-builders. Kantorowicz's biography of Frederick II inspired Heinrich Himmler, while Hermann Goering sent Mussolini a copy. The Hitler Youth staged their flag-dedication ceremony amidst the ruins of Hohenstaufen castle in June 1933.[60]

Most professional historians were deeply conservative and their studies of the Empire's elective monarchy lent weight to the popular critique of Weimar democracy as pointless and divisive. The anti-Roman interpretation of the German past was consolidated in the so-called New Constitutional History pursued between the 1930s and 1970s by Theodor Mayer, Otto Brunner, Walter Schlesinger and others, who tried to identify a specifically Germanic medieval socio-political organization, supposedly based on the personal elements of lordship, to define the pre-modern state as an aristocratic association of kings and nobles (*Herrschaftsverband*).[61] Although adhering to the professional standards of German scholarship, their studies romanticized warrior nobles and provided ideal material for less scrupulous writers to extrapolate a theory of Germanic leader–follower society.

Having seized power, the Nazis abolished the separate identities of Bavaria, Saxony, Württemberg and other regions, replacing these on 5 February 1934 with a unitary nationality derived from racist criteria. The old political units, which often still used boundaries deriving from imperial fiefs, were replaced by new subdivisions called *Gaue*, a name associated with Germanic tribal homelands. Many Nazis found the Holy Roman past unusable. Joseph Goebbels planned an exhibition in Münster to demonstrate how the Peace of Westphalia had supposedly divided Germany, but abandoned this after the fall of France in 1940 eradicated the Nazis' sense of shame at their country's 'weak' past. Hitler repeatedly used the Holy Roman Empire as a rhetorical counterpoint to his united Germany, parroting decades of conservative historical critique by, for instance, claiming that 'if the German feudal princes had been loyal to the German emperors, the Holy Roman

Empire of the German Nation would have become a mega-empire'.[62] The Second Empire was commended for having briefly achieved national unity, but was otherwise condemned as a missed opportunity. A circular was sent to all Nazi Party organizations on 13 June 1939 banning further use of the adjective 'third' in reference to the Reich, since Hitler wished to avoid any comparisons with the two previous empires.[63] The Nazi ideologue Alfred Rosenberg was outspokenly hostile, dismissing the Holy Roman Empire as a tool of the papacy and trying to claim that the 4,500 Saxons executed by Charlemagne for refusing to convert to Christianity were precursors to Nazi fighters; for this he was reprimanded by Hitler, who had a more heroic image of the Frankish king (who was, of course, a *German*).[64]

Hitler's intervention indicated the difficulties of ignoring the Holy Roman Empire altogether, if for no other reason than it encompassed so much of Germany's past. After the *Anschluss* with Austria in 1938, an SS honour guard was sent to fetch the imperial insignia from Vienna and escort them to Nuremberg, which had both been their location during early modernity and was now home to the Nazi Party headquarters. Although staged to symbolize the return of Austria (now dubbed the *Ostmark*) to Germany, the enterprise was problematic since Charlemagne's crown was decorated with images of the Jewish kings David, Solomon and Hezekiah.[65] Himmler was perhaps the most enthusiastic of the senior leadership in appropriating the medieval Empire to legitimate the 'new order'. He chose July 1936, the thousandth anniversary of the death of his Ottonian namesake Henry I, to inaugurate an annual *Heinrichsfeier* at Quedlinburg castle for the SS (see Plate 33). Like many of his contemporaries, Himmler was influenced by the nineteenth-century misinterpretation of Henry as 'founder' of a 'German empire'. An SS division was named 'Hohenstaufen', while French SS volunteers formed another called 'Charlemagne' in 1944.

Karl Richard Ganzer, the head of the Nazified national historical institute, celebrated a continuous Germanic imperial mission from Charlemagne to the present in a book that sold 850,000 copies soon after its appearance at the height of the German *Blitzkrieg*. Ganzer's work appealed because it was simply a cruder version of what many Austrian historians and others like Fredrich Wilhelm Foerster had claimed since the 1920s, that the Empire had provided order for Europe.[66] The misuse and misunderstanding of history are perhaps best exemplified in the naming of the invasion of Russia. The general staff intended the banal code name 'Fritz' or 'Otto', but Hitler insisted on calling it Operation Barbarossa, probably because he regarded the emperor's crusading credentials as suitable for a mission to eradicate Bolshevism.[67]

Later Twentieth-Century Perspectives

Nazi distortions had relatively little impact on the historical understanding of most Germans, who remained wedded to the conservative interpretations deriving from Ranke and later nineteenth-century scholarship. They continued to believe a medieval Empire had existed until 1250 or possibly the reign of Charles V, and thought this had been a stabilizing Christian order, whereas the early modern Empire was condemned as weak and responsible for delaying national greatness.[68] These now traditional views survived Germany's total defeat in 1945, because they were shared by the victorious Allied powers. British, American and French scholarship drew on the same detailed studies by nineteenth-century German historians for their interpretative framework, not least because this had been transplanted by the numerous intellectuals fleeing Germany in the 1930s who now held influential teaching posts in US universities.

The new German Democratic Republic established in 1949 had little interest in the Empire, simply continuing nineteenth-century interpretations repackaged within Marxist stadial history as the 'feudal age'. Princely power supposedly triumphed over 'universal imperial policy' by 1550, condemning Germany to political weakness and retarding economic development, which Marxist historiography attributed to centralizing national states.[69] Meanwhile, the GDR government continued the Nazis' centralized state in a new form, reorganizing its territory into new 'districts' (*Bezirke*) in a deliberate attempt to break lingering regional identities.

Germany's partition between 1945 and 1990 assisted the Western Allies' project of de-Prussifying Germany, since the former Hohenzollern lands conveniently lay in the Soviet zone, including the rump of old Prussia that survives today as the Russian enclave of Kaliningrad. Cold War historiography distinguished sharply between Western liberal traditions and alleged Eastern European authoritarianism. The standard interpretation of agrarian relations underpinned this with its model of a 'second serfdom' developing east of the Elbe from the late Middle Ages (see pp. 496–7). This political project did not challenge received wisdom about the Holy Roman Empire, since the conservative reading of German history unwittingly provided evidence to support Anglo-American interpretations of that country deviating from a Western liberal norm along its own 'special path' to Hitler (see p. 3).

Meanwhile, the West German republic's federal structure reinvigorated regional history, as each of the new federal states (*Bundesländer*) established or revived historical commissions and journals dedicated to its area's history. Heraldic devices were borrowed from those of the leading principalities that had once existed within the boundary of each federal state, for example modern Lower Saxony's use of the white horse of Hanover. Detailed historical atlases and multivolume regional studies all reinforced long-standing popular perceptions of the German past as consisting of a multitude of fragmented local histories in which medieval emperors might occasionally put in an appearance, but for which otherwise the Empire was largely irrelevant.

The word 'Reich' was now indelibly tainted with Nazism, inhibiting the wider reception of the more positive scholarly reappraisal of the early modern Empire under way since the late 1960s. Organizers of an exhibition on early modern Germany in Regensburg in 2000 deliberately avoided it, because they thought the public would confuse a reference to the Holy Roman Empire with Hitler's Germany or Bismarck's Second Empire.[70] Exhibitions concentrated on displaying glittering medieval treasures and artworks, rather than explaining how the Empire had functioned. Already in 1946 the Allies returned the imperial insignia to Vienna from Nuremberg, where they had survived the war hidden in a bunker (see Plate 34). West Germany's new Federal Parliament considered appealing in 1952 for their return, while Aachen's cathedral chapter insisted that the three items removed by Austrian troops in 1794 were holy relics that should be restored.[71] Individual emperors remained fixed in public consciousness through their place in the school curriculum and depiction in popular TV dramas and documentaries, but perspectives remained stubbornly those of the nineteenth century.

At best, the Empire seemed harmless compared to Germany's more recent past. A 9-metre high, 18-ton concrete figure was erected secretly one night in April 1993 on the stump of an old lighthouse in Konstanz's lakeside harbour (see Plate 35). Designed by sculptor Peter Lenz, the figure is named 'Imperia', but unlike the pompous monuments of the Second Empire, this does not refer to the Empire, but to a character in a story by Balzac, in turn loosely based on a courtesan who lived around a century after Konstanz hosted the famous church council. Probably the world's largest monument to a prostitute, Imperia is also representative of the 700 real courtesans who actually serviced the council. Turning every three minutes on her own axis, the voluptuous figure holds diminutive naked figures of Pope Martin V and Emperor Sigismund – identifiable primarily by their headgear – in the palm of each upturned hand, while her tiara resembles a medieval fool's hat, adding to the mockery of power. She remains the subject of continual objections from the diocese of Freiburg and local conservative politicians. Yet the council is powerless to remove Imperia, because her location belongs to German Federal Railways, which part-financed her erection, while she has become a major tourist attraction. Throughout, controversy has focused on the apparent mockery of the papacy, whereas no one complains about a naked emperor.[72]

THE EMPIRE AND THE EU

The Europeanization of Imperial History

The scholarly reappraisal of the Empire since the late 1960s is representative of a broader Europeanization of German history, reconnecting with traditions till then denigrated as inferior to Teutonic *Kultur*. One aspect has involved examining previously neglected themes, especially in German political history, and has tended to view the Empire through the lens of the post-1949 German Federal Republic and its place in European integration.[73] Another element has been to reinterpret the history of Europe's current states in less national terms. This has not progressed very far for the history of the Empire, which German historians are far more likely to refer to as 'of the German nation' than were its actual inhabitants.

In some respects the Europeanization of the imperial past resembles the nineteenth-century nationalist projects, especially in the way medieval history has been plundered for personalities and images that could be appropriated to articulate present-day agendas. Since 1977, several exhibitions have promoted the Staufers as transnational European rulers whose Empire incorporated 'regions of innovation' transmitting culture, trade and ideas between Germany and Italy.[74] Above all, Charlemagne has come to personify the links between the Empire and post-1945 aspirations for a united Europe, whereas other emperors, notably Charles V, remain viewed in national terms, even if these perspectives might now appear together in the same volume.[75] Charlemagne's new European status owes much to the superficial coincidence between his actual empire and the space occupied by France, West Germany, Italy and the Benelux countries behind initial post-war European integration. At a press conference in 1950, Charles de Gaulle presented Franco-German cooperation as 'picking up Charlemagne's project, this time on modern economic, social, strategic and cultural grounds'.[76] Nationalists had found Charlemagne problematic by the 1870s, as he appeared too French for the Germans and too German for the French. Already in the 1840s, the French historian François Guizot seized on a ninth-century source's presentation of Charlemagne as the 'Father of Europe' to claim the Franks were 'European'. The annual Charlemagne Prize, inaugurated in Aachen in December 1949 as the new German Federal Republic's first political award, is explicitly intended to promote European integration.[77] Aachen Cathedral was the first German monument to be designated a UNESCO World Heritage Site (1978).

The Empire as Model

Conservative politicians favouring European integration found the Empire an attractive model with which to underpin their arguments. The heir to the Habsburg throne, Otto von Habsburg, in his speeches and writings during the 1970s drew on Austrian historiography of the 1920s and 1930s, which had already presented the medieval Empire as a positive factor in ordering Europe, and which chimed with his contrast between democratic Western European countries and the godless Communist Eastern Bloc: 'the imperial idea will rise again in the form of European unity'.[78] Although several leading historians of the Empire have explicitly rejected such arguments,[79] others openly present the early modern Empire as a blueprint 'to create a Europe of the regions'.[80] These claims draw on the positive reappraisal of the early modern

Empire emerging from specialist studies published since 1967 and which some use to interpret it as polycentric, federal, and embodying the complementary division of responsibility between regions and the centre that the European Commission calls 'subsidiarity'. Further alleged parallels include the Empire's conciliatory tendencies, its internal rule of law, and its tolerance of differing identities, which provided 'an ideal framework for flourishing and diverse cultures' whilst inhibiting the development of a modern nationalism 'that has spread so much evil across Europe and the world'.[81] The Council of Europe sponsored a major exhibition in Berlin and Magdeburg in 2006 to mark the bicentenary of the Empire's dissolution. Opening the exhibition, the German culture minister Bernd Neumann presented the medieval Empire as a 'model of a functioning supra-state order'. In the run-up to the fiftieth anniversary of the Treaty of Rome the following year, Neumann referred to the Empire as a model for the EU. Pope Benedict XVI drew similar parallels based on an oddly upbeat reading of medieval church–state relations.[82]

At least such statements have the merit of presenting the Empire in terms that make it intelligible to a wider public, by contrast with the stress on complexity, exceptions and qualifications that otherwise characterizes modern scholarship. Making a subject 'relevant' to the contemporary world is increasingly important as public funding becomes restricted to research that can demonstrate practical 'impact'. However, two significant problems emerge. Despite record attendances at the recent exhibitions, the older negative narratives retain their grip on the broader public understanding of the Empire. Europeans still generally conceive their past through the prism of nineteenth-century nation states, and are often encouraged to do so by conservative governments and education policies. The past remains a 'road to modernity', with some routes rated better than others according to a common yardstick still largely defined by the national sovereign state. This can have direct political repercussions, as the German foreign minister Joschka Fischer discovered in spring 2000 when he compared an 'expanded EU without institutional reform' to the 'late phase of the Holy Roman Empire'. Fischer's understanding of the Empire was still the weak structure presented by older historiography, but the French interior minister Jean-Pierre Chevènement read the reference to 'Reich' to mean that Germans wanted to remove European nation states in order to

establish a new imperial dominance over the continent.[83] Several leading German historians have also expressed alarm at their colleagues'
equation of the Empire with the EU, believing this could stir 'latent
fears of German hegemonic ambitions', and mean that 'German enthusiasm for Europe will be misinterpreted as a cloak for German national
interests'.[84]

Beyond the potential for misunderstanding, there is a second problem of how the Empire's history might actually help understand some
of the problems facing today's Europe. Since the 2004 enlargement and
2008 economic crisis, opinion on the EU has divided ever more sharply
into two camps. One advocates forging a closer political union, including making the European Parliament a more effective democratic body.
Older, negative assessments of the Empire provide ammunition for
these arguments. Like Fischer, the British historian Brendan Simms has
compared the unreformed EU to the Empire, claiming both 'are characterized by interminable and inconclusive debate'. Echoing Hamilton
and Madison's equally dim assessment of 1787 (see pp. 1–2 and 8),
Simms argues that the EU should become 'The United States of Europe' along Anglo-American lines, subordinating its member states to a
fully federal system, whilst reforming the European Parliament to
provide a democratic mandate for a new common government.[85] The
counter-argument is provided by nationalists like those in the UK Independence Party (UKIP) who believe that the EU can never match the
vitality of sovereign states, both as governments and as foci for identity.
For them, current problems can only be solved by reducing the union
to a free trade area, or dissolving it entirely.

Although arriving at opposite conclusions, both perspectives are
bound by the same understanding of the state as a single, centralized
monopoly of legitimate power over a recognized territory. This definition is a European invention, retrospectively backdated to the Peace of
Westphalia and used to articulate an international order based on
mutually recognized sovereign states. Such states are supposedly
hermetically sealed containers, with their populations free to decide
internally how they are governed, whilst acting internationally with
one voice through their national government. While this still underpins
organizations like the United Nations, it is increasingly unlikely that
such states are political history's final destination: wide aspects of daily
and national life are clearly beyond the effective control of most

governments, which are increasingly vulnerable to global economic, popular, technological and environmental forces.[86]

Imperial History as Guide for Today's Issues

EU enlargement has been interpreted as hegemonic imperialism, acting in the manner of nineteenth-century European colonialism by imposing its own norms and standards of civilization on those it admits as new members.[87] This perspective is close to the nationalist critique of the EU as a union that imposes an unwelcome uniformity on its citizens, smothering rather than liberating them. However, many Europeans regard their own national governments as more immediately oppressive than the European Commission, and feel they would be better off without them. In September 2014 the United Kingdom only narrowly avoided fragmentation when the Scots voted in a referendum against independence. It is far from clear that recovery of 'national sovereignty' along the lines advocated by UKIP and its equivalents in other countries would restore citizens' confidence in national governments controlled largely by colourless politicians widely criticized for being out of touch with local and individual needs. There is considerable concern at a 'democracy deficit' throughout the Western world, where disillusionment with the political process is leading to self-disenfranchisement, manifest through dwindling voter turnout and widespread cynicism.

Several attempts to address this have described the EU as a 'neo-medieval empire', arguing that it is not converging along the Westphalian model into a federal superstate, but is evolving instead as a complex structure of fragmented sovereignty and 'plurilateral' governance.[88] The concept of neo-medievalism is an analytical construct that would benefit from closer engagement with the actual history of the Holy Roman Empire, at least during its last three centuries. Comparisons can be instructive, if not necessarily flattering to either the EU or the Empire. First, the Empire's history is a reminder that decentralized political systems are not necessarily peaceful in their intentions. Like the Empire, the EU does not possess its own armed forces, nor has it waged wars, yet decentralization ensures a significant proportion of wealth continues to be spent on defence as each member remains fully armed. The EU has remained at peace, but individual member states such as France and the

UK have been involved in several wars and other substantial military operations, not all of them clearly sanctioned by the UN or any other multilateral organization. Although celebrated in the more positive scholarly interpretations as having peaceful intentions, the eighteenth-century Empire was the most heavily armed part of Europe, and it proved incapable of preventing individual members, such as Austria or Saxony, from waging their own wars outside its frontiers.[89]

Both the EU and the Empire have lacked a single capital or a clear political core. Although individual elements have enjoyed more influence than others, this did not result in subjugation – except in the final stages of the Empire after 1801. The EU displays clear differences from the Empire in that its members retain the formal legal equality accorded to sovereign states. This extends to special cultural provisions, such as ensuring official documentation is prepared in all national languages, as well as equal freedom of movement for citizens, goods and capital. By contrast, autonomy in the Empire was embedded in a hierarchy defined by status and differing constitutional rights. However, the EU struggles to reconcile formal equality with the considerable diversity in population, wealth and economic potential across its membership, as evidenced by the repeated revisions to voting arrangements in its central institutions. It also shares the Empire's imprecision around frontiers, which remain only superficially defined by national boundaries. Member states are combined in different overlapping levels of jurisdiction, such as the Schengen border agreement, the Eurozone and the EU itself. Additionally, individual members have binding commitments to states outside the union, such as the UK's leadership of the Commonwealth, just as early modern Austria and Prussia had extensive hereditary possessions outside the Empire.

The EU further resembles the Empire in lacking an organized uniform body of citizens. Its relationship to its inhabitants is indirect and mediated by autonomous political levels, such as the member states, which can still set their own criteria for citizenship, yet issue passports conferring rights extending across the entire union. The Empire appears to have done rather better than the EU in fostering attachment amongst its inhabitants, who valued it as a framework sustaining local and particular liberties, and in respecting diversity, autonomy and difference. It is here that perhaps the most interesting comparisons can be made. Sovereignty is fragmented in the EU, as it was in the Empire. In both, policy implementation depends on members' cooperation, allowing scope for local adaptation and initiative. These arrangements require consensus to a far higher extent than in centralized sovereign polities, including federal ones like the United States where central institutions (for example Congress) act directly on citizens through their ability to pass laws affecting their lives, tax their wealth, or conscript them as soldiers. It is precisely this arrangement that appears threatened by voter apathy and disenchantment, because citizens risk losing control of the institutions of government. By contrast, decentralized, fragmented political structures do not lend themselves to common direct democratic control, as evidenced by the European Parliament's struggle to find a meaningful role within the EU and in the minds of European voters.

Some political scientists now argue that decentralized, fragmented systems might offer different, perhaps even better ways to forge consensus by 'legitimation through deliberation'.[90] Decentralized structures can spread authority, creating multiple, more local and thereby perhaps more meaningful arenas for decisions to be reached. Consensus becomes a more open-ended, ongoing process of bargaining between interested parties, rather than a periodic assignment of mandates to elected representatives expected to agree definitive decisions. Democratic legitimacy derives from the openness of debate, not the practice of voting. Citizenship is about involvement in and access to discussion through civil society and a free media, not simply formal rights and institutions.

It seems likely that, for such ideas to work, participants must accept that politics can no longer be guided by absolutes, rather in the manner that conflict resolution in the Empire was about workable compromises, not questions of 'right' or 'wrong'. Like current practice within the EU, the Empire relied on peer pressure, which was often more effective and less costly than coercion, and which functioned thanks to the broad acceptance of the wider framework and a common political culture. However, our review of the Empire has also revealed that these structures were far from perfect and could fail, even catastrophically. Success usually depended on compromise and fudge. Although outwardly stressing unity and harmony, the Empire in fact functioned by accepting disagreement and disgruntlement as permanent elements of its internal politics. Rather than providing a blueprint for today's Europe, the history of the Empire suggests ways in which we might understand current problems more clearly.

Glossary

Abschied see *Recess*.

Allodial property Land and other assets belonging to a family, separate from any legal jurisdictions they might possess. Often held collectively, in common, and distinct from individual personal possessions.

Amt Dual meaning as either a public post held by an official or an administrative district within a territory.

Arch-offices The ceremonial titles assumed by the electors during the high Middle Ages and associated permanently by the Golden Bull (q.v.) with particular electorates.

Armed Estate A territory possessing a permanent military establishment beyond that required to fulfil imperial obligations.

Benefice Land or other assets conferred as a reward or to facilitate service (see *Fief*). The term derived from the Old High German *lîhan* (*Lehen*), Latinized as *Beneficium* and meaning to lend, award or confer. It was used widely in the early Middle Ages and did not necessarily entail vassalage until 1166. Its usage during the later Middle Ages was increasingly restricted to denote property and assets endowed to support clergy (see also *Fief*).

Canton A territorial division for administrative or governing purposes. Its most prominent usage is to denote the self-governing areas combining after 1291 as the Swiss Confederation, though these were actually called 'places' (*Orte*) until the official adoption of the term 'canton' in 1798. 'Canton' was already the official designation of the regional associations of the imperial knights from the mid-sixteenth century, and was also the label for the recruiting districts introduced into the Prussian monarchy in 1733.

Capitularies Legally binding, written administrative guidelines issued by the Carolingians.

Communalism Collective political action through communal institutions embodying the associative principle binding neighbours together.

Confessionalization The demarcation of religious belief according to confessional orthodoxy, identifying an area and its inhabitants firmly with one variety of Christianity.

Contado Originally 'the counts' land', this term came to mean the hinterland dominated by a town in medieval Italy.

Deditio Ritualized submission to royal (or lordly) authority, primarily used during the Ottonian and Salian eras and usually brokered by third parties to end a dispute in return for a full or partial restitution of lands and titles.

Dienstherrschaft The feudal right to claim labour service from dependent peasants.

Electoral capitulation or *Wahlkapitulation* Agreements between an emperor, or a spiritual prince, and their electors made prior to the final confirmation of their election, confirming corporate rights and privileges.

Electors The princes entitled to participate in the selection of each emperor. Their privileges were codified by the Golden Bull (q.v.).

Estates A set of complex terms related to the corporate structure of early modern society that was divided into privileged orders of clergy, nobility and commons. Each of these orders was considered an Estate (*Stand*), as were the recognized subgroups within them. Representative institutions drawing on these groups were also called Estates. Territorial Estates (*Landstände*) were composed of representatives of the corporate groups from a particular territory. As constituent elements of the Empire, each territory (with certain exceptions) was both an 'imperial Estate' (*Reichsstand*) with a place in the Reichstag, and a *Kreisstand* with a seat in the relevant Kreis Assembly (q.v.).

Fief The terms *feudum* and *feodum* were Latin versions of Old High German words for movable property. Emerging in the ninth century, they were increasingly equated with benefices (q.v.), displacing that term after the mid-twelfth century, though usage was uneven and only became established in north-east Germany a century later. From 1166, both fief and benefice were understood as involving vassalage and were tied to homage.

Gerichtsherrschaft The right of feudal jurisdiction over a given area.

Ghibelline A term coined in the twelfth century to designate imperial supporters, especially in Italy. It derived from Waiblingen in Swabia, then (erroneously) believed to be the Salians' family home (see also *Guelph*).

Golden Bull The imperial charter of 1356 codifying the privileges of the electors, or *Kurfürsten*, who chose each emperor. These rights included the indivisibility of the electorates and their exemption from some forms of imperial jurisdiction.

Gravamina Petitions, especially those from Estates to a ruler.

Grundherrschaft The form of landownership whereby tenants rented plots from their feudal lord.

Guelph A term coined in the twelfth century to designate the emperor's opponents in Italy. It derived from the Welf family, which had land in Italy and Germany and which played a significant role in opposing Henry IV in the 1080s (see also *Ghibelline*).

Gutswirtschaft The manorial economy characterizing the area east of the Elbe where lordly estates were worked by dependent serfs and hired labourers producing bulk crops traded on the international market.

Immediacy The status of *Reichsunmittelbarkeit*, indicating a relationship to the emperor that was direct and not mediated by any intermediate authority or lord.

Imperial church The collective term for the *Reichskirche*, or ecclesiastical territories.

Imperial city or *Reichsstadt* A city with the status of immediacy (q.v.), as distinct from a territorial town. The same applied to other terms employing the prefix *Reich*: imperial knights, imperial counts, imperial prelates.

Imperial Italy The part of northern Italy under the emperor's feudal jurisdiction that included Milan, Savoy, Genoa, Parma, Tuscany, Mantua, Solferino and other smaller principalities.

Imperial vicar An individual charged with exercising imperial authority during the emperor's absence, either in a specific locality or across an entire kingdom.

Investiture The Latin terms *vestitura* and *investitura* denoted the act of legalizing possession of assets or jurisdictions. The term derived from the papal practice since the seventh century of sending vestments (the *pallium*) to a new archbishop.

Iter Royal progress through the Empire to seek homage from those not present at the coronation.

Itio in partes The constitutional amendment introduced by the Peace of Westphalia in 1648 that permitted the imperial Estates assembled in the Reichstag to discuss contentious religious issues in two separate confessional blocs, or *corpora*.

Kreis Formally *Reichskreis*, or imperial circle. One of the ten regional subdivisions of the Empire into which most territories were grouped.

Kreis Assembly or *Kreistag* Containing the members of that Kreis to debate common concerns.

Kreis Association A formal alliance between two or more Kreise that had been ratified by the assemblies.

Kreis convenor or *Kreisausschreibender Fürst* One who coordinated the meetings of the Kreis Assembly and dealt with formal correspondence with the emperor and imperial institutions.

Kurfürsten see *Electors*.

Landeshoheit see *Territorial sovereignty*.

Landschaft A form of Estates where commoners predominated.

Landtag Territorial diet, or plenary meeting of the Estates.

Latest Imperial Recess The last concluding document issued by the Reichstag session of 1653–4. The next meeting, of 1663, remained in permanent session and issued legislation as necessary.

Matricular system The system for distributing fiscal and military burdens to the territories based on a list (*Matrikel*) recording their obligations.

Mediatization The loss of the status of immediacy (q.v.), usually through annexation by another territory.

Ministeriales A term used from the later eleventh century, replacing *servientes*, which appeared around 1020. Ministeriales were unfree knights bound in servitude to a feudal lord in return for a fief (q.v.), thereby owing military service on the basis of their birth (unfreedom) rather than voluntary submission. Some were also employed as administrators. The ministeriales were unique to Germany, Brabant and Lorraine, and were not found elsewhere in the Empire or Europe. They gradually embraced an aristocratic ethos, converting a relationship based on servitude into more conventional vassalage by 1500.

Ordines Coronation protocols specifying the form and sequence of ceremonial elements.

Police regulation or *Polizei*, originally spelt *Policey* Normative legislation issued by established authorities to sustain corporate society by guiding behaviour and addressing social and economic problems.

Privilege of not appealing The *privilegium de non appellando* exempted territories from the jurisdiction of the two imperial courts. It was usually granted in limited form, though the electors acquired greater exemption.

Public peace The *Landfrieden* declared permanent in 1495 that required all territories to renounce violence and submit disputes to arbitration through the imperial courts. Further legislation, especially between 1555 and 1570, strengthened these arrangements.

Recess The concluding document of an assembly that listed all agreements and legislation decided at that session.

Reich As a prefix, denoted 'imperial', as in *Reichsfürst* or imperial prince.

Reichsdeputation The Imperial Deputation or special standing committee selected by the Reichstag to discuss important business. The ordinary (*ordentliche*) Imperial Deputation was established by the public peace legislation to oversee the operation of imperial justice and other measures when the Reichstag was not in session. It was effectively superseded once the Reichstag remained in permanent session after 1663. Extraordinary deputations could still be selected to discuss other business, such as the territorial redistribution of 1801–3.

Reichshofrat The imperial aulic council established in 1497 to safeguard the emperor's prerogatives. It developed after 1558 as a second supreme court alongside the *Reichskammergericht* (q.v.).

Reichskammergericht The imperial cameral court created in 1495 and charged with upholding the public peace and acting as a supreme court of appeal. Its judges were mainly appointed by the imperial Estates through the Kreis structure.

Reichsstandschaft The quality of being an imperial Estate (q.v.), entitling representation in the Reichstag.

Reichstag The imperial diet, or assembly of the emperor and imperial Estates.

Revindication Deriving from *revindicare* ('to demand back') and denoting a policy first introduced by Rudolf I in 1273 to recover crown assets alienated since the 1240s and continued intermittently until definitively abandoned in the 1370s.

Roman expedition The journey from Germany to Rome for coronation as emperor by the pope. The practice was initiated by Otto I in 962 and often had the character of a military campaign.

Roman Month The unit of account measuring the financial contributions from the territories paid according to the matricular system (q.v.) for common purposes, usually defence. The term came from the monthly wage bill of the troops intended to escort the emperor to his coronation in Rome.

Romans, king of the The title *Römischer König* was created in 1376 and given to the successor designate chosen by the electors to succeed an incumbent emperor on his death.

Servitium regis 'Serving the king' through counsel, military and material support. The term used for the obligations imposed by vassalage, especially during the early Middle Ages.

Signoria The *signoria* emerged from the patricians in thirteenth-century Italy to dominate civic government everywhere except in Umbria and Tuscany. The most successful included the Este, Montefeltro, Gonzaga and Visconti families, who all eventually secured the status of imperial prince.

Social discipline The interpretation suggesting that society was transformed by state regulation, encouraging individuals to behave as obedient, thrifty subjects.

Stand, Stände see *Estates*.

Strator service Acting as ceremonial groom to the pope, involving some or all of the following elements: prostrating oneself before the pontiff, kissing the papal stirrups, and helping the pope to dismount. Allegedly first performed by Pippin on meeting Pope Stephen II in 753, the ceremony was subsequently claimed by popes as a means of asserting superiority over emperors. Last performed by Frederick III, in 1452.

Territorial sovereignty or *Landeshoheit* Denoting the powers accumulated and developed by the imperial Estates (q.v.) to act on their own initiative in territorial and imperial politics. These powers rested on imperial law and included the right to reform religion, maintain troops, negotiate with foreign governments and issue legislation within the relevant territory, provided these actions were not directed against the integrity and well-being of the emperor and Empire.

Territorialization The process of identifying political power and representation in imperial institutions with a given area.

Umfrage The practice of voicing opinion at the Reichstag and Kreis Assemblies in strict order of precedence determined by formal status.

Appendix 1: Emperors, 800–1806

Reigns dated from imperial coronation.

800–814	Charlemagne
814–40	Louis I 'the Pious' (co-emperor from 813)
840–55	Lothar I (co-emperor from 817)
855–75	Louis II (co-emperor from 850)
875–7	Charles II 'the Bald' (king of West Francia 843–77)
[878–80]	
881–8	Charles III 'the Fat'
[889–90]	
891–4	Guido, duke of Spoleto
894–8	Lambert II, duke of Spoleto (co-emperor from 892)
896–9	Arnulf of Carinthia
[900]	
901–5/34	Louis III (king of Lower Burgundy 887–905/28; blinded 905, died 934)
916–24	Berengar I, margrave of Friaul
[925–61]	
962–73	Otto I 'the Great'
973–83	Otto II (co-emperor 967)
[984–95]	
996–1002	Otto III
[1003–13]	
1014–24	Henry II
[1025–6]	
1027–39	Conrad II
[1040–45]	
1046–56	Henry III
[1057–83]	
1084–1106	Henry IV
[1107–10]	

1111–25	Henry V
[1126–32]	
1133–7	Lothar III of Supplinburg, duke of Saxony
[1138–54]	
1155–90	Frederick I 'Barbarossa'
1191–7	Henry VI
[1198–1208]	
1209–18	Otto IV
[1219]	
1220–50	Frederick II
[1251–1311]	
1312–13	Henry VII
[1314–27]	
1328–47	Louis IV 'the Bavarian'
[1348–54]	
1355–78	Charles IV
[1379–1432]	
1433–7	Sigismund
[1438–51]	
1452–93	Frederick III
[1494–1507]	
1508–19	Maximilian I (king of the Romans from 1486)
1519–56	Charles V (crowned by Pope Clement VII in 1530)
1558–64	Ferdinand I
1564–76	Maximilian II
1576–1612	Rudolf II
1612–19	Matthias
1619–37	Ferdinand II
1637–57	Ferdinand III
[1657–8]	interregnum
1658–1705	Leopold I
1705–11	Joseph I
1711–40	Charles VI
[1740–42]	interregnum
1742–5	Charles VII (the Wittelsbach Carl Albrecht of Bavaria)
1745–65	Francis I
1765–90	Joseph II
1790–92	Leopold II
1792–1806	Francis II (assumed a distinct Austrian imperial title in 1804 and ruled till 1835)

Appendix 2: German Kings

For anti-kings, see Table 2 (p. 303).

Carolingians

768–814	Charlemagne (as king of the Franks)
814–40	Louis I 'the Pious' (as king of the Franks)
840–43	Lothar I
843–76	Louis II 'the German'
876–87	Charles III 'the Fat'
887–99	Arnulf of Carinthia
900–911	Louis 'the Child'
911–18	Conrad I of Franconia

Ottonians

919–36	Henry I
936–73	Otto I 'the Great'
973–83	Otto II
983–1002	Otto III
1002–24	Henry II

Salians

1024–39	Conrad II
1039–56	Henry III
1056–1106	Henry IV
1106–25	Henry V
1125–37	Lothar III of Supplinburg

Staufers

1138–52	Conrad III
1152–90	Frederick I 'Barbarossa'

Staufers (cont.)

1190–97	Henry VI
1198–1208	Philip of Swabia
[1198–1218	Otto IV]
1215–50	Frederick II
1250–54	Conrad IV

'Little Kings'

1254–6	William of Holland (anti-king from 1247)
1257–72	Richard of Cornwall
[1257–73	Alfonso X of Castile]
1273–91	Rudolf I of Habsburg
1292–8	Adolf of Nassau
1298–1308	Albert I of Austria (Habsburg)
1308–13	Henry VII of Luxembourg
1314–47	Louis IV 'the Bavarian' (Wittelsbach)
[1314–30	Frederick 'the Fair' (Habsburg)]

Luxembourgs

1347–78	Charles IV (anti-king from 1346)
1378–1400	Wenzel (deposed 1400)
1400–1410	Ruprecht of the Palatinate
1410–37	Sigismund (Luxembourg)

Habsburgs

1438–9	Albert II
1440–93	Frederick III
1493–1519	Maximilian I

Thereafter, as the emperors.

Appendix 3: Kings of Italy

774–814	Charlemagne
[781–810	Pippin as co-king]
813–17	Bernhard (Pippin's son; blinded and deposed)
817–40	Louis I 'the Pious'
840–55	Lothar I
855–75	Louis II
875–6	Charles II 'the Bald' (king of West Francia 843–77)
877–79	Carloman
879–88	Charles III 'the Fat'
889–924	Berengar I, margrave of Friaul
889–94	Guido, duke of Spoleto
894–7	Lambert, duke of Spoleto
894–9	Arnulf of Carinthia
900–905	Louis III 'the Blind' (king of Lower Burgundy)
922–34	Rudolf, king of Upper Burgundy
926–47	Hugo, count of Arles (Provence)
[945–50	Lothar of Arles, co-king]
945–64	Berengar II, margrave of Ivrea
[950–64	Adalbert, co-king]

Title assumed automatically by German kings after 962/83.

Chronology

3rd Century

Germanic tribes raid the Roman empire and some begin to settle and become assimilated.

313

Conversion of Emperor Constantine. Christianity spread to become the official religion of the Roman empire by 391 when all other cults were banned. The Christian church developed an infrastructure mapped onto the Roman provinces across the empire, with five patriarchs, or leaders, based in Rome, Constantinople (former Greek town of Byzantium), Jerusalem, Antioch and Alexandria.

395

The intermittent splits in the Roman empire since 286 became permanent with the continuous existence of a western emperor in Rome and an eastern one in Constantinople.

5th Century

Age of migrations. The arrival of Slavs and Huns in central Europe by the mid-fourth century displaced some Germanic peoples south and west, adding to the pressure on the Roman empire. The invaders founded their own kingdoms inside the Roman empire, including the Visigoths in Spain and southern France, the Burgundians along the Rhône, the Alemanni on the Upper Rhine, the Franks between the Loire and the Main, the Bavarians south of the Danube, and the Lombards in northern Italy. The invading Visigoths sacked the city of Rome (410), shaking confidence in the Roman imperial order, which was now clearly in decline. The Germanic tribes resented the Huns as competitors and were often happy to cooperate with the Romanized population against them. The Huns were defeated at Troyes (451), and subsequently retreated after decimation by plague and the death of Attila (453).

476

Augustulus, the last western Roman emperor, was deposed by Odovacar, leader of the Goths invading Italy. Eastern imperial rule continued as the Byzantine empire, which saw itself as the direct continuation of ancient Rome and entered a period of revival and expansion. The Byzantine emperor sponsored Theodoric (454–526), leader of the Ostrogoths (another tribe displaced by the Huns), to recover Italy. Theodoric invaded in 489, defeating and killing Odovacar four years later, and was recognized by the emperor as ruler of Italy (497).

481

Accession of Clovis, of the Merovingian clan of the Franks, as king. Within 20 years, Clovis had united all the Frankish lordships in former Roman Gaul into a single kingdom (Francia), adopting Roman Christianity and the remnants of Roman administrative and ecclesiastical institutions. Clovis and his successors repeatedly partitioned their kingdom between their sons, but it nonetheless continued to grow through reunifications and new conquests. By 730, the Franks ruled most of the Germanic tribes north of the Alps, including the Burgundians, Alemanni, Thuringians and Frisians. To the north and east, the Saxons and Bavarians remained outside Frankish influence.

535–62

Gothic War. The new Byzantine emperor, Justinian I, was not content to rule Italy indirectly through the Ostrogoths. Having already recovered north Africa and parts of southern Spain by 534, Justinian invaded and eventually conquered Italy. The Byzantine administrative structure was introduced, with military districts (themes), each with its own commander (*dux*, or duke), mapped onto the old Roman provinces. A command base (exarchate) was established in Ravenna in 540 as the seat of Byzantine government in Italy.

568

The Lombards, who had previously cooperated with the Byzantines against the Ostrogoths, crossed the Alps and swiftly overran much of Italy. The Lombards intermarried with local elites and established a stable kingdom (Langobardia) based initially (584) in Milan, and later at Pavia (616). Refugees fleeing the Lombards established Venice in the safety of the lagoons (569). The Byzantine presence was reduced to the 'Roman part' (Romagna) based around Ravenna.

590

Accession of Pope Gregory I the Great whose rule laid the groundwork for the papacy to fill the void left by the contraction of Byzantine influence in Italy.

610

Emergence of Islam. Within two decades Mohammed's followers had overrun Arabia, and between 634 and 640 they had conquered Palestine, Syria, Armenia and western Anatolia, removing them from the Byzantine empire. Byzantine Egypt fell two years later as the Arabs advanced westwards across north Africa, completing their conquest by 709. The last Visigoth kingdom in Spain fell to them in 711. Although Constantinople repulsed three Arab attacks, the Byzantine empire remained on the defensive and was unable to oppose the Lombard advance in Italy. The Arab capture of Jerusalem, Antioch and Alexandria by 642 increased the significance of the two surviving Christian patriarchs based in Rome and Constantinople.

663

Constans II became the last Byzantine emperor to visit Rome. The brief Byzantine revival in Italy subsided after his murder in 668. Lombard lords established semi-autonomous duchies in the former Byzantine districts at Benevento, Spoleto and Capua in central-southern Italy.

680

The Byzantine empire recognized the existence of the Lombard kingdom in Italy, while around this point the papacy effectively usurped the administrative powers associated with the Byzantine *dux* around Rome, thereby establishing itself as a temporal as well as spiritual power. The area of papal political jurisdiction became known as the *Patrimonium* and provided the material underpinning for the pope's claims to lead the western Christian church, as well as enabling him to maintain his independence from the Lombards.

717

The Lombards exploited deteriorating papal-Byzantine relations to expand their influence in Italy at the expense of both, capturing Ravenna (751) and effectively ending Byzantine influence in mainland Italy. Rather than attempt to recover Italy, Byzantium exploited the collapse of the Arab caliphate in Damascus (750) to recover its lost territories in the eastern Mediterranean.

732

Victory of a Frankish army under Charles Martel over the Arabs at Poitiers. The Arabs were confined to Spain, and Martel enhanced the influence of his clan (the Pippinids, later called the Carolingians) at the Merovingian court.

751

Martel's son, Pippin the Short, deposed the Merovingians and made himself king of the Franks with papal assistance. Pippin formally sanctioned papal territorial jurisdiction over the Patrimonium and promised to protect the pope. Following two papal visits, Pippin intervened against the Lombards in Italy in 754–6 without securing a definitive settlement there. The Franks were then distracted by a succession dispute amongst Pippin's sons after 768, from which Charlemagne emerged as sole heir by 771.

773–4

Charlemagne defeated the Lombards and asserted himself as their king, thereby combining Langobardia with Francia. The Lombard duchies in Spoleto and Benevento retained their autonomy in return for accepting this outcome.

775–94

Charlemagne subdued the Saxons and Bavarians, whom the Franks regarded as vassals, but who had in fact remained independent until this point. This was accompanied by a significant intensification of Christianization measures amongst the Germanic tribes, with new archbishoprics founded at Cologne, Trier, Mainz, Salzburg and Hamburg-Bremen. Carolingian administration expanded along lines broadly similar to that used by the Byzantines in Italy from the sixth century, with the establishment of military-judicial districts (duchies) subdivided into counties. This process accelerated the cooption and assimilation of Germanic and Lombard elites with the Franks.

791–6

Major Frankish victory over the Avars, a nomadic tribe who had overrun what is now Hungary and were raiding Germany and Italy.

796

Emperor Constantine VI was blinded by his mother, Irene, who became the first woman openly to rule Byzantium in 797 until she was deposed by another coup in 802. These events allowed Pope Leo III to claim that the ancient Roman imperial title was vacant and could be 'translated' to Charlemagne.

CAROLINGIANS, 800–919

800

Charlemagne crowned emperor on Christmas Day by Leo III in Rome.

809

Arab conquest of Sardinia (held until 1003).

814

Death of Charlemagne and reign of his son Louis 'the Pious' (died 840). Tensions within the ruling elite and clergy over the distribution of power and role of the emperor.

827

Arab invasion of Sicily, completed by the capture of Syracuse (878). Meanwhile, Arab raiding of mainland Italy intensifies, including an audacious attack on Rome itself (846) and the conquest of Bari and Apulia by 840. The latter were reconquered for the kingdom of Italy in 871–6 by Louis II, but the continued Arab threat sustained the papacy's interest in having an emperor as protector.

830

Start of Viking raids along the North Sea and Channel coasts into the Empire, especially up French rivers, becoming a serious problem by the later ninth century.

840–43

A succession dispute within the Carolingians led to the Treaty of Verdun (843), which divided the Empire into three kingdoms: West Francia (roughly France, under Charles 'the Bald'), East Francia (roughly Germany, under Louis 'the German') and Lotharingia (a middle kingdom from the North Sea up the Rhine and into Italy, under Lothar I, who also received the imperial title). The Carolingians retained a sense of common kinship and a single Frankish empire, but continued rivalry frustrated cooperation.

855

The subdivision of the middle kingdom on Lothar I's death into a smaller Lotharingia, Italy (whose king held the imperial title until 875) and Provence (until 863). Borders remained fluid even after further adjustments through the Treaties of Meersen (870) and Ribemont (880), which transferred northern Lotharingia (Lorraine and Brabant) to East Francia, reducing Lotharingia to Italy and Burgundy.

862

Onset of raiding into East Francia by the Magyars, who had supplanted the Avars in Hungary. Raids extended into Italy after 899.

875–7

Succession dispute between the East and West Frankish kings triggered by the extinction of the Carolingian line holding Italy and the imperial title. The East Frankish kingdom was temporarily partitioned, 876–82.

885–7

Brief reunification of all three main Frankish kingdoms under Charles III 'the Fat', East Frankish king since 876 and emperor since 881.

887

Definitive split of the Frankish lands into (initially) five successor kingdoms:

1. East Francia, evolving into Germany, ruled by a Carolingian line until 911
2. West Francia, evolving into France, and afflicted by a long struggle between a Carolingian royal line and the Capetian clan, who displaced them as kings in 987
3. Burgundy, ruled 888–1032 by the Guelphs (Welfs), who had risen from knights in Carolingian service
4. Italy, under a succession of local nobles chosen as king and who were usually able to persuade the pope to crown them emperor between 891 and 924
5. Lorraine, which re-emerged as a separate duchy in 895. This passed to West Francia in 911, but to East Francia in 925.

887–99

Reign of Arnulf, an illegitimate son of the East Frankish royal line. Arnulf intervened in Italy, becoming its king (894) and was crowned emperor (896), but had difficulty controlling the four duchies of his kingdom: Franconia, Saxony, Bavaria and Alemania (Swabia). These problems grew during the reign of his son, Louis (IV) 'the Child' (900–11). Magyar raiding intensified in 907–11. Meanwhile, the Italian royal title passed to Margrave Berengar I of Friaul after Arnulf's death. Berengar was made emperor by Pope John X in 916, partly in recognition of his role in curbing Magyar incursions. His successors after 924 won sufficient support among Italian lords to retain the royal title, but the imperial one remained vacant until 962.

891

Guido of Spoleto became the first non-Carolingian to be crowned emperor. His wife, Ageltrude, also became the first empress to be crowned.

895

The Premyslid family became recognized as dukes of Bohemia (title hereditary from 950).

910

Byzantium temporarily recovered its former possessions in Apulia, which had been lost to the Carolingian kingdom of Italy in 876.

911–18

The East Frankish Carolingian royal line died with Louis 'the Child' in 911. Conrad I, duke of Franconia, became king, but had no heirs, opening the transition to Ottonian rule.

OTTONIANS, 919–1024

919

The East Frankish lords decided against partition and accepted Henry I, duke of Saxony, as king. Henry was from the Ottonian clan (also known as the Liudolfinger). Ottonian rule was accepted by the West Frankish Carolingians in 921 and the kingdom was declared indivisible (929). Henry stemmed the Magyar raids by organizing defences in eastern Bavaria and by buying a truce through tribute, 926–32, before attacking and defeating a Magyar force at Riade (May 933).

936–73

The reign of Henry's son, Otto I 'the Great', saw the consolidation of Ottonian rule and the permanent association of the imperial title with East Francia. As the second king from his line, Otto was able to act more forcefully than his father in managing his kingdom. He cemented the techniques used to govern the Empire for the next century or more, ruling by a combination of decisive acts to assert authority, whilst otherwise seeking a consensus amongst the lordly elite. The duchies were distributed to close royal relations, and could be revoked as punishment for rebellion. Greater use was made of educated clergy as advisors and to train future bishops, who were given sees as they fell vacant as a means to counterbalance the secular lords and to promote Christianization and royal influence. Bishoprics and monasteries that cooperated were favoured with charters granting immunities and privileges. In return, the church provided accommodation for the royal court, and military assistance in the form of warriors when needed. New bishoprics were founded along the eastern Saxon frontier at the Elbe, together with militarized 'march' lordships, to curb raids from the Moravian and Elbian Slavs. These policies were broadly successful, but could provoke jealousies, notably when Otto insisted on depriving some new bishoprics of resources to found a new archbishopric at Magdeburg (960s).

940–55

Renewed warfare with the Magyars in Bavaria culminated in Otto's decisive victory at Lechfeld (August 955), ending further raiding and stabilizing the south-eastern frontier.

951

Intervention in Italy. The former Frankish kingdom of Italy was combined with Otto's German kingdom. Access to Italy was secured by creating a new march lordship at Verona, which was initially attached to Bavaria.

951–4

Rebellion of Liudolf and Conrad the Red against Otto I.

962

Coronation of Otto I as emperor in Rome. Otto issued the *Pactum Ottonianum* regulating relations with the papacy, by accepting the pope's continued rule over territory around Rome. Negotiations for recognition by Byzantium led to Otto II's marriage to the Byzantine princess Theophanu in 972.

963

John XII became the first pope to be deposed by an emperor, as punishment for opposing Otto I (4 December).

973–1002

The reigns of Otto II and Otto III saw repeated attempts to sustain a more active imperial presence in Italy, including campaigns to assert overlordship over the south Italian duchies and to repel Arab raids from Sicily.

981

Otto II's suppression of the bishopric of Merseburg created a rift amongst the imperial family and the Saxon bishops, which lasted until 1004 when Merseburg was restored.

982

Otto II was decisively defeated by the Arabs at Cotrone in his attempt to conquer southern Italy.

983

A massive Slav invasion swept away many of the Ottonian castles and missions along the Elbe. Otto II's death coincided with this crisis, but Ottonian rule was sufficiently robust to continue, despite the need for an unprecedented female regency of the late king's wife and mother for the young Otto III.

999–1000

Otto III signalled a more sacral monarchy with an extended pilgrimage to Gniezno in Poland. The eastern frontier was secured by renewed campaigning along the Elbe (996), and (more temporarily) through agreements with the Polish and Hungarian rulers (1000).

1002–24

The reign of Henry II, duke of Bavaria and great-grandson of Henry I, who succeeded because Otto III died childless. Otto's death exposed the weakness of imperial rule in Italy where leading nobles elected Margrave Arduin of Ivrea as king, with French and Burgundian backing. Henry reasserted authority with two military campaigns (1003, 1004), which rallied supporters and isolated Arduin, who eventually abdicated (1015). Henry continued the trend towards a more sacral monarchy, founding the new bishopric of Bamberg and relying heavily on the imperial clergy to assist his rule.

1003–44

An intermittent three-way conflict between the Empire, Bohemia and Poland over jurisdictions and imperial claims to overlordship. The struggle broadened after Henry II's death (1024) with additional conflicts with Hungary, and Hungarian intervention in Bohemia (1030–31, 1039–44).

1009–29

A rebellion in the Byzantine parts of southern Italy (Apulia, 1009–18) triggered a long conflict ultimately benefiting the newly arrived Normans, whose growing power was recognized by their enfeoffment with the county of Aversa (1029).

SALIANS, 1024–1138

1024

Henry II's death ended the Ottonian royal line. Conrad II from the Salian royal family was accepted as German king, but had to fight to assert his authority over Italy and Burgundy, famously articulating the view of impersonal monarchy enduring 'like a ship whose helmsman has died'. This completed the process begun under Otto I of consolidating the Empire as led by the German king who automatically acceded to the Italian and Burgundian crowns without separate elections or coronations.

1025–8

Conrad II imposed his authority on those German dukes who had failed to pay homage. Although continuing Ottonian methods of seeking face-saving compromises, Conrad also moved towards a more commanding style of monarchy that would characterize Salian rule. Repeated offenders were now punished by losing hereditary family property, as well as their ducal or comital titles. The number of duchies increased with the elevation of the march of Carinthia (976) and the permanent partition of Lorraine into two (1044). The centre of political gravity shifted from Saxony (under the Ottonians) to the Rhineland, though the Salian base around Worms only briefly enjoyed ducal status.

1038–40

A final Byzantine expedition failed to reverse the Norman advance in southern Italy. Meanwhile, the growing power of the Seljuk Turks threatened the Byzantine heartlands in Anatolia.

1039–56

The reign of Henry III, variously interpreted as the peak of Salian rule or the origins of later problems. A series of military campaigns ended the intermittent conflicts since 1003 along the eastern frontier as Henry bound Bohemia more closely to the Empire (1041) and defeated the Hungarians at Menfö on the Raab (1044), ending their interference in imperial politics. Repeated problems between the papacy and the Roman clans increased calls for imperial intervention, culminating in the Synod of Sutri (1046) when Henry deposed three rival pontiffs and imposed his own.

1056–65

Henry IV was only six at his father's death, necessitating the first regency since 983–94. Rivalry between Archbishop Anno of Cologne and his opponents prevented coherent policy and led to renewed intervention in the papacy under much less favourable circumstances than in 1046. This damaged royal prestige, especially among reform-minded clergy, though the situation was not irretrievable.

1057–91

The Normans took the remaining Lombard duchies of Capua (1057), Salerno (1076) and Benevento (1077), as well as the last Byzantine outposts of Bari (1071) and Brindisi (1072). Sicily was meanwhile conquered and taken from its Arab masters (1061–91).

1066

The last major Slav (Wendish) rising along the lower Elbe destroyed Christian churches north of the river and definitively ended the ambitions of Hamburg-Bremen's archbishop to exercise spiritual jurisdiction over all of Scandinavia (which acquired its own archbishop at Lund in 1103).

1073–5

The Saxon War caused by discontent at Henry IV's assertion of royal authority through a castle-building programme and use of unfree knights (*ministeriales*).

1075

A dispute since 1071 over the appointment of the archbishop of Milan escalated into the Investiture Dispute as Pope Gregory VII refused to allow the king to choose and confirm senior clergy. This threatened royal influence in the German and Italian imperial church that had become an essential support of imperial rule since Otto I. The controversy began to polarize German and Italian clergy and nobility, adding theological weight to those discontented with other aspects of royal policy.

1076

The Investiture Dispute deepened as Henry IV rallied loyal bishops to depose Pope Gregory, who retaliated by excommunicating the king and his supporters. The pope was backed in Italy by Matilda of Canossa, who had inherited the extensive Tuscan lands guarding access to papal territory from the north. Gregory opened contact with discontented German lords, who began contemplating deposing Henry.

1077

Henry pre-empted a coup by a dramatic winter crossing of the Alps to meet Gregory at Canossa, where the king compromised on some issues to secure a release from excommunication. The German malcontents pushed ahead regardless and elected Rudolf of Rheinfelden as the first German anti-king (March 1077). Gregory initially withheld recognition from Rudolf in the hope of pressurizing Henry to abandon royal claims to investiture.

1077–1106

The Investiture Wars. Henry and his German and Italian supporters waged a series of campaigns against two sets of opponents who only loosely cooperated against him. In Germany, Henry faced those who backed Rudolf of Rheinfelden and, after Rudolf's defeat and death (1080), his successor as anti-king, Hermann of Salm. Although Salm eventually abandoned the struggle, Henry faced rebellions from his two sons, each of whom declared against him after he had named them his successor. Henry retained support in Germany, notably from the Staufer family, to whom he entrusted Swabia and Franconia in 1079 to guard access between Germany, Italy and Burgundy. In Italy, Henry fought the reform papacy under Gregory VII and his successors. Henry relied on pro-imperial Italian bishops, nobles and towns, and appointed his own popes, who only briefly controlled Rome. The reform papacy was backed strongly by

Matilda of Tuscany, as well as the Normans, who used the confusion to consolidate their hold over southern Italy and Sicily. The conflict spawned numerous, more local struggles, because both sides appointed their own bishops to the same dioceses. This situation allowed many Italian and some German towns, already growing thanks to increasing population and economic activity, to bargain greater autonomy from royal and episcopal control.

1106–11

Henry V seized control of the German crown from his father, who died shortly afterwards. Henry restored royal authority throughout most of Germany and was crowned emperor by the reform papacy. Abandoned by the king, the rival papacy established by Henry IV soon collapsed. A military campaign in 1108 failed to reassert overlordship over Poland and Hungary, which had lapsed during the Investiture Dispute.

1111–22

Long negotiations between Henry V and the reform papacy and its supporters in Italy and Germany culminated in the Concordat of Worms (1122), whereby the emperor accepted canonical election of clergy, while the pope permitted imperial/royal investiture for bishops' temporal jurisdiction and allowed the monarchy to retain considerable influence over appointments in the German bishoprics and imperial abbeys. This agreement ended the Investiture Dispute without resolving the underlying disagreement over the relationship between papal and imperial authority.

1120s

An increase in migration north and especially eastwards across the Elbe into Slav lands prompted a resumption of the Ottonian practice of naming marcher lords to control and extend the frontier, and to promote Christianization. New lords were named for Holstein (1110), Meissen (1123), Lusatia (1134) and Brandenburg (by 1157).

1125–37

The reign of Lothar III of Supplinburg and transition from Salian to Staufer rule. Henry V died childless, but the leading German lords and clergy rejected his nephew, Duke Frederick of Swabia, who headed the Staufer family, in favour of the seemingly more malleable Lothar, a count from Saxony.

1127–35

Civil war erupted as Staufer supporters proclaimed Frederick's younger brother Conrad as anti-king after Lothar tried to deprive the Staufers of lands they had acquired under the Salians. Conrad crossed the Alps and was accepted as Italian king, but he failed to secure the important Tuscan lands, left without a clear ruler after Matilda's death in 1115, and retired to Germany in 1130. Lothar wore down Staufer resistance from 1132, assisted by his coronation as emperor in 1133. Papal support was purchased by revising Tuscany's status so that the emperor retained possession, but accepted it as a dependency of the pope. The Staufers accepted defeat in 1135, recognizing Lothar in return for retaining their principal possessions in Swabia, Alsace and eastern Franconia. Lothar had benefited from support from the Welf (Guelph) family based in Bavaria. The Welf duke of Bavaria was allowed to consolidate his hold over Austria and Carinthia, and to have his son (and Lothar's son-in-law), Henry the Proud, be enfeoffed with Saxony and designated the future king.

1130

Pope Anacletus II raised Norman Sicily to a kingdom under nominal papal suzerainty.

1131

Thuringia was detached from Saxony as a separate landgraviate.

STAUFERS, 1138–1250

1138

The Staufers rallied German lords who felt Lothar's designation of Henry the Proud threatened their role in choosing a king. The former anti-king was now accepted as Conrad III and promptly sequestrated Bavaria and Saxony. An immediate Welf response was thwarted by the death of Henry the Proud (1139), leaving his ten-year-old son, Henry the Lion, as head of the family. Conrad continued the methods developed under the Salians of seeking a consensus amongst leading lords, provided this did not compromise royal authority. Saxony and Bavaria were returned to Henry the Lion by 1147 as part of a general settlement intended to pacify Germany. However, Conrad also signalled new directions by accepting a growth in the numbers and autonomy of the leading secular lords, notably promoting the influence of the Babenberg family holding Austria.

1147

Start of the Wendish, or Northern, Crusade.

1147–8

Conrad III led a contingent from the Empire in the Second Crusade, but failed to capture Damascus or establish a workable relationship with Byzantium, despite their common hostility to the Normans in the Mediterranean.

1152–90

The reign of Frederick I 'Barbarossa', nephew of Conrad III and cousin to Henry the Lion. Frederick greatly expanded and accelerated his predecessor's policies, partly in response to rapid demographic growth and new legal concepts, and partly as a deliberate strategy to rebalance governance in the Empire. The number of senior secular lords was deliberately increased by elevating counties and marcher lordships to ducal status (Austria 1156, Würzburg 1168), and by recognizing Slav chiefdoms as imperial fiefs (Mecklenburg and Pomerania). Other lordships were created by detaching land from existing duchies. The duke of Bohemia, the most powerful Slav lord, accepted definitive incorporation in the Empire in return for his own royal title and considerable autonomy (1158). Meanwhile, the emperor and secular lords promoted urban development by granting charters to new towns (e.g. Freiburg 1120, Lübeck 1143, Leipzig 1161, Brunswick 1166) and extending the autonomy of existing ones (e.g. Deventer, Speyer and Worms).

1154–86

Frederick made seven attempts to extend these policies to Italy, which no German king had visited since 1137. He adapted to the changing conditions in Italy where civic emancipation from episcopal and lordly control was further advanced than in Germany, and where a resurgent papacy controlled the central lands, while the Normans, now recognized as kings, ruled the south (Naples) and Sicily. The emergence of the Normans as a third force in Italian politics altered the previous pattern of papal-imperial relations. Strong popes sought enhanced influence by playing the Empire and Normans off against each other, but circumstances often changed quickly, and weak popes (of which there were several) were compelled to make concessions to one in order to escape a dangerous dependency on the other. Fear of the Normans prompted a pro-imperial policy that saw Frederick crowned emperor in 1155.

Frederick used the opportunity to reorganize imperial rule in the old royal heartlands of northern Italy. The most controversial issue was the control of royal and imperial rights known as regalia. New ideas had emerged in the wake of the Investiture Dispute, which defined regalia more clearly as legal entitlements to material benefits like cash, labour and free accommodation, as well as rights to fortify settlements and appoint officials. Frederick asserted an exclusive monopoly of such rights at an assembly at Roncaglia (1158), and demanded the return of those he considered had been usurped by lords and communities over the last decades. However, he had no intention of exercising these rights directly, and was prepared to devolve them to lords and cities in return for cooperation and (from the cities) cash taxes. Implementation depended on local circumstances, since many cities saw advantages in cooperating, not least if their political and economic rivals currently opposed the emperor.

The result was a complex four-way struggle between the emperor, papacy, Normans and an increasingly autonomous group of cities that combined as the Lombard League (1167). The papacy was split from 1159 with rival pro-Norman and pro-imperial popes, prompting Frederick to emphasize the Holy Roman aspects of the Empire and its ideological mission. Measures included Charlemagne's canonization by the pro-imperial papacy (1165). Frederick also astutely manipulated rivalries between the Italian cities, capturing many and destroying their castles. However, his enemies proved too numerous for the forces at his disposal, especially once the pro-Norman papacy cooperated with the Lombard League.

1177

Frederick broke the hostile alliance by abandoning the pro-imperial papacy and ending the schism. A compromise with the Lombard League in 1183 was followed three years later by the marriage of Frederick's 19-year-old son Henry to the 30-year-old Constanza, heiress to the Norman kingdom. Frederick continued to face opposition from individual north Italian cities, while he and the papacy still disagreed over their respective rights in Tuscany.

1178–80

The rebellion of Henry the Lion, who had alienated many Saxon lords during Frederick's absence in Italy. Henry was forced to flee to England. Western Saxony was detached as a new duchy of Westphalia, which was given to the archbishop of Cologne, who had been steadily amassing lands on the Lower Rhine since the later eleventh century. Ducal Saxony contracted eastwards, and lost its influence over the new march lordships that were being established north of the Elbe in former Slav territory. Meanwhile Styria was detached from Bavaria as a new duchy. The rest of Bavaria was given as a duchy to the

Wittelsbach family, which now joined the ranks of the senior lords. The outcome consolidated the trend since Frederick's accession towards a new, more obviously feudal relationship between the monarch and the lords, who now held their duchies and counties more clearly as hereditary fiefs. However, Frederick's deliberate policy of breaking up the remaining large duchies and distributing the new ones to different families reduced the likelihood of any single lord amassing lands as substantial as those previously held by the Guelphs.

1189–90

Frederick embarked on the Third Crusade (1189–92), launched in response to the Saracen victory over Christian forces at Hattin (1187), which led to the Muslim conquest of Jerusalem. Frederick's decision also reflected his desire to sustain a working relationship with the papacy.

1190–97

Henry VI succeeded his father, Frederick I 'Barbarossa', who died during the Third Crusade. Henry successfully neutralized opposition to his accession in Germany and obtained a fortune extorted from the English King Richard I 'the Lionheart', who had conspired with Staufer enemies and was captured as he returned from the crusades in 1192. Richard was released in February 1194, having placed his kingdom (nominally) as a vassal of the Empire. The ransom financed Henry's successful invasion of Sicily in December 1194. Sicily was formally joined to the Empire and Henry began steps towards a more hereditary form of succession for all his kingdoms. The annexation of Sicily transformed the strategic balance in Italy, leaving the papacy alone to face a much more powerful emperor who now insisted that papal possessions were imperial fiefs. Henry VI died unexpectedly at 31 amidst preparations for a new crusade and before his plans for his succession had received universal acceptance.

1198–1208

A double election and civil war. Henry VI had died leaving a very young son, Frederick II. Although Frederick had already been accepted in 1196 as the future German king, Staufer supporters decided instead in 1198 to back Henry's uncle, Philip of Swabia. Staufer opponents elected Henry the Lion's son as Otto IV, signalling a revival of Welf family fortunes, but entailing civil war for the Empire. Pope Innocent III seized the opportunity to reassert papal independence by proclaiming himself adjudicator and deciding in favour of Otto IV, who appeared less threatening than the Staufers. Philip was excommunicated. Meanwhile, Innocent dropped the earlier papal opposition to Staufer rule in Sicily in return for guardianship of the young Frederick II after 1198. Otto confirmed this by accepting papal overlordship over Sicily and disputed areas on the mainland like Tuscany. Many lords considered these concessions were damaging the Empire and defected to Philip, whose forces had largely defeated Otto's remaining supporters by 1206. A settlement in Philip's favour with papal support looked likely when he was unexpectedly murdered in a private quarrel in 1208.

1202

Pope Innocent III issued the decretal *Venerabilem* articulating the theory that his predecessor Leo III had 'translated' the ancient Roman imperial title from Byzantium to the 'Germans' in the person of Charlemagne in 800 (*translatio imperii*).

1209–14

Renewed civil war. Pope Innocent had no choice but to crown Otto IV emperor (1209). Otto immediately resumed Staufer policies to reassert imperial authority in northern Italy, as well as backing a rebellion against the young Frederick II of Sicily which broke out among the Norman lords in Naples (October 1210). This rebellion continued intermittently into the 1220s and spread to Sicily, where many resented the influx of German lords as Staufer advisors. Pope Innocent excommunicated Otto (November 1210), whose support collapsed again as German lords invited Frederick to become their king. Frederick won the race to reach Germany ahead of Otto in 1212 and was crowned king in Mainz. He secured papal backing through the Golden Bull of Eger (1213), confirming Otto's earlier concessions to the papacy that now exercised feudal jurisdiction over central and southern Italy, as well as (nominally) Sicily. Otto supported an English invasion of France in order to retain the English support that his family had enjoyed since 1180. The invaders were crushed by Philip II of France at Bouvines (July 1214), effectively ending Otto's attempt to be a serious force. The incident demonstrated how imperial politics were becoming enmeshed with wider European affairs.

1215

Frederick II was crowned again at Aachen to legitimize his new power. Otto retired to his family's hereditary possessions at Brunswick, where he died, childless, in 1218. Having initially sequestrated their possessions, Frederick forged a definitive settlement with the Welf family by detaching Brunswick from Saxony as a new duchy and imperial fief (1235).

1220–31

Frederick resumed the earlier Staufer policy of feudalizing relations with the German lords, who received clearer local autonomy in return for accepting their lands as direct fiefs of the Empire. This arrangement was consolidated by a general charter (1220) for all senior German clergy, who now emerged as ecclesiastical princes. Many bishoprics and even abbeys had acquired counties and other secular jurisdictions, which were now demarcated more clearly as ecclesiastical fiefs dependent directly on the Empire. The charter also strengthened bishops' powers over their cathedral towns, though this did not stop many cities emancipating themselves from episcopal authority as 'free cities' under direct imperial jurisdiction. A broadly similar charter was issued for the senior secular lords (1231).

1226

The Golden Bull of Rimini granted secular jurisdiction to the Teutonic Order for lands it was conquering in the Northern Crusade against pagan Slavs along the south-eastern Baltic shore. This established the basis for the future Teutonic Order state in Prussia, which was considered part of the Empire but not an active part of the German kingdom.

1227–50

Prolonged papal-imperial conflict. Frederick II desired good relations with the papacy and needed papal support to help legitimize his rule. He was also susceptible to pressure to answer papal calls for a new crusade to free Jerusalem. However, he was equally determined to reassert Staufer authority in both Sicily and Naples, as well as resume the earlier policy of establishing the emperor as direct overlord of all Italy. Frederick alienated the papacy by breaking his earlier promises (including the Golden Bull of Eger, 1213), and in 1220 by returning to Henry VI's policy of linking Sicily directly to the Empire. Frederick's brutal suppression of the Norman rebels in Sicily and Naples by 1225 also suggested his growing power. The pope excommunicated him (1227), having rejected his excuses for delaying his departure on the crusade.

1228–9

The kingdom of Jerusalem. Frederick launched his own expedition to Jerusalem, having married its Christian queen, Isabella II of Brienne, as his second wife (1225). Jerusalem had been constituted as a crusader kingdom (1099) and maintained a shadowy existence during the Saracen occupation after 1187.

Currently divided and facing the Mongols to the east, the Saracens granted the Christians access for ten years (1229). Frederick accepted rather than fight unnecessarily and returned to Italy after his coronation as nominal king of Jerusalem.

1230

The Treaty of San Germano (23 July): the pope reluctantly abandoned support for a renewed Neapolitan rebellion and released Frederick from excommunication in return for renewed recognition that Sicily was a papal, not an imperial, fief.

1232

Papal-imperial relations collapsed again when the pope refused to back Frederick against the Lombard League, which had re-formed in 1226 to defend civic autonomy,

1234-5

The rebellion of Henry (VII), who had been left in charge of Germany during Frederick's absence. Frederick returned to Germany in 1235 after an absence of 15 years. Henry's support collapsed and he was deposed and imprisoned, dying accidentally in 1242.

1235

Frederick asserted imperial protection for Jews in return for regular taxes.

1235-7

Frederick regulated affairs in Germany in cooperation with the lay and spiritual princes, who agreed a public peace (1235) and in 1237 accepted his other son, Conrad IV, as the eventual successor.

1237-50

War in Italy. Frederick's efforts to suppress the Lombard League prompted his second and permanent excommunication by the pope (1239). Despite individual successes, Frederick was unable to gain a decisive preponderance. Meanwhile the pope escaped to Lyons, where he formally deposed the emperor (1245), emboldening Frederick's German enemies to elect a succession of anti-kings:

first the Thuringian landgrave Heinrich Raspe (1246), and after his death, Count William of Holland (1247). The war damaged both imperial and papal prestige and remained undecided at Frederick's death in 1250.

1246

The extinction of the Babenberg family ruling Austria since 976 opened a long dispute between the Bohemian Premyslid family and the Habsburgs, who eventually emerged as dukes of Austria in 1273.

1250–68

The Staufer collapse. Although named as Frederick II's successor, Conrad IV had not been crowned and quickly lost ground. The pope used his claims to feudal jurisdiction over Sicily-Naples to reassign this kingdom to Charles of Anjou, brother of the French king. The Anjou line lost Sicily to Aragon in 1282, but retained Naples until 1442. Charles's execution of Conrad's son Conradin (1268) definitively ended Staufer attempts to recover their Italian possessions.

'LITTLE KINGS', 1250–1347

1250–73

The so-called Interregnum as rule of the Empire remained contested between several relatively weak monarchs. Meanwhile, the papacy refrained from crowning another emperor until 1312.

1254

The first Rhenish Civic League spread rapidly to encompass 70 towns and enjoyed some backing from King Richard, earl of Cornwall, after 1257, who hoped it would counterbalance princely influence.

1257

Rivalry among the leading princes led to another double election, which was also the first in which 'foreign' candidates were successful. Richard of Cornwall, the second son of the English King John, at least visited the Empire four times during his reign (1257–72). Alfonso X of Castile was a grandson of Philip of Swabia and thus a Staufer ally, but never came to the Empire or exercised any real influence before the end of his reign (1273).

1273

The election of Rudolf I. The leading princes were now emerging as electors who saw their role in choosing kings as a way to elevate themselves over the other ecclesiastical and secular lords. The electors recognized the dangers of a double election, while the papacy also urged a single choice, because it wanted help against the growing power of the Anjou kingdom of Sicily-Naples. These circumstances broadly repeated themselves in the next three elections (1292, 1298, 1308), as the electors compromised on candidates who lacked a substantial territorial base, like Count Rudolf of Habsburg in 1273. This frustrated the imperial ambitions of the Premyslid family ruling Bohemia, since all electors regarded the Premyslids as already too powerful. However, the process of so-called 'leaping elections', or successively choosing monarchs from different families, simply intensified the interaction between imperial and territorial politics. The rival families increasingly saw larger and more consolidated territorial possessions as a springboard to a royal candidacy, while those that were successful used their reigns to favour their own families to improve their chances at the next contest. Ambitions for the imperial title and rule in Italy persisted, but were frustrated by unfavourable circumstances and the imperative of building up strength in Germany.

1273–91

The reign of Rudolf I. Rudolf combined efforts to recover crown lands with a consolidation of Habsburg family power. Imperial vassals were ordered to restore rights and properties illegally usurped since 1250. This was used against King Ottokar II of Bohemia, Rudolf's main rival in the 1273 election, who refused to return former crown lands. Rudolf's high-risk strategy culminated in his victory at Dürnkrut on the Marchfeld, north-east of Vienna, where Ottokar was killed (August 1278). The Premsylids were left with Bohemia and Moravia, but had to surrender Austria and Styria to Rudolf, who enfeoffed his sons as imperial princes (1282). The Habsburgs emerged considerably stronger, but, like many families, they did not yet practise primogeniture and continued to experience internal divisions and even open conflicts. Rudolf's deliberate choice of Speyer, the burial place of Salian kings, as his own deathbed, also showed how traditional ideals of kingship remained important alongside the growing significance of dynasticism.

The policy of recovery ('Revindication') of crown assets achieved mixed results elsewhere. Loyal counts were appointed as bailiffs to safeguard imperial rights in a new regional network of 'bailiwicks' (*Landvogteien*) across southern Germany. Rudolf cultivated good relations with the free and imperial cities to underpin this network and counterbalance the local and regional influence of ecclesiastical and secular princes. However, the increasingly powerful counts of Württemberg thwarted efforts to restore the duchy of Swabia through consolidation of imperial rights in that region (1285–7). Protests at Habsburg and imperial policy further south stimulated the communal movement amongst Swiss villagers, leading to the first cantonal alliance (1291). Rudolf's death (July 1291) frustrated initially promising steps towards securing tighter royal control of Thuringia, which had passed to the Wettin family (based in Meissen) on the extinction of its previous rulers in 1247. Rudolf's relatively long reign assisted the success of his measures. His next three successors continued his programme, but began afresh each time and died before they made much progress.

1277

The Visconti family seized power in Milan, which they subsequently expanded at the expense of neighbouring lordships and cities, including the old Italian royal capital of Pavia (1359). The Visconti's growing influence exemplified broader changes in northern Italy as the communal regimes, which had emerged since the late eleventh century, were transformed via despotic city states into new duchies during the fourteenth and early fifteenth centuries.

1292–1313

The reigns of Adolf of Nassau (1292–8), Albert I of Austria (1298–1308) and Henry VII of Luxembourg (1308–13). Three issues divided the Empire's ruling elite during this period. The first was the growing influence and self-consciousness among the electors, who were determined to assert their collective pre-eminence over all other princes and aristocrats. This encouraged the electors to avoid mutual disagreements that might undermine their exclusive control of royal elections. Building on their experience in 1273, the electors agreed their candidate in advance and extracted financial and political concessions in return for their endorsement of him as king. This impacted on imperial-papal relations, since the electors rejected any papal interference in their deliberations. However, it also increased the importance of the electors' own interests in imperial politics, notably Cologne's ultimately unsuccessful efforts to reverse its defeat at Wörringen (1288) where a local coalition of lords had broken its domination of north-western Germany. The Empire's centre of political gravity shifted to the Rhine, where the four leading electors were based: Mainz, Cologne, Trier and the increasingly influential secular elector Palatine. Bohemia's influence declined after the Premyslids' defeat at Dürnkrut, while Saxony and Brandenburg remained only junior partners.

The second issue concerned the continuing Habsburg–Premyslid rivalry, as the Bohemian royal family tried to recover Austria and Styria. This conflict hindered Habsburg efforts to retain the German royal title after Rudolf I's death. Any chances of profiting from the natural extinction of the Premyslids (1306) was thwarted by Albert I's murder (1308) by his own nephew, Johann, who felt aggrieved at the division of Habsburg property after 1291. The beneficiaries of this dispute were the Luxembourg family, since their patriarch, Henry VII, used his position as king to award Bohemia to his son, Johann (1310).

Thuringia provided the third issue, since all three kings continued Rudolf I's policy of opposing Wettin claims to inherit this landgraviate. Again, the brevity of each reign negated royal successes, notably that of Adolf of Nassau, who persuaded the Wettin heir to sell his rights in 1294. Albert I's military solution failed in his defeat at Lueka (1307), confirming the Wettin in possession of Thuringia as well as Meissen, and thus their influence in east-central Germany.

1298

Deposition of Adolf of Nassau. Adolf's success in Thuringia was perceived as a threat by the Saxon, Brandenburg and Bohemian electors, who secured the support of three of their four Rhenish colleagues to confront the king. Although it is unlikely they planned initially to depose him, their action gained its own dynamic, culminating on 23 June 1298 in the first deposition of a reigning monarch by the electors (earlier depositions had been by popes). Adolf's attempt to reverse this ended in his death in the battle of Göllheim (2 July 1298). The electors had no choice but to elect the Habsburg duke Albert I (whom they had rejected in 1292), as both a supporter of their Thuringian policy and the only viable candidate as king.

1309–77

The 'Babylonian Captivity' of the papacy resulted from French pressure on the pope, who was obliged to leave Rome and live in Avignon.

1312

The coronation of Henry VII as emperor (29 June). All German kings since 1273 wanted to be crowned emperor and had continued to assert imperial rights in northern Italy, notably disputing papal claims to Tuscany. Plans for a Roman expedition (notably under Rudolf I) had been repeatedly shelved due to adverse circumstances. The situation changed as the papacy sought to free itself from French influence and invited Henry to Rome. Henry received substantial German support, partly in the prospect of plundering Italian cities. Italian opposition delayed the march, and thus the coronation, by over four months. Henry planned to recover Naples from the Angevins, but died from malaria (August 1313).

1314

The double election of Louis IV and Frederick 'the Fair'. Electoral collegiality collapsed in the face of lobbying from the Luxembourg and Habsburg families, which intersected with disputes between the Luxembourgs and the duke of Carinthia over exercise of the Bohemian vote, and between rival branches of the Askanier family over the Saxon vote. The Luxembourgs accepted the compromise election of Duke Louis of Upper Bavaria (from the Wittelsbach family), but Habsburg supporters chose Frederick the Fair, Albert I's eldest son, as king the day before (19 October 1314). This was the first double election since 1257, and the first since 1198 to lead directly to civil war.

1314–25

A civil war erupted between Louis IV and Frederick the Fair, waged largely through intermittent skirmishing. The Swiss victory at Morgarten (1315) had no direct bearing on the royal contest, but it did confirm Swiss autonomy from Habsburg jurisdiction. The dispute triggered renewed papal-imperial tension, because Pope John XXII saw intervention as an opportunity to assert a more prominent European role and thus a way of loosening French influence over the papacy. Rather than choose between the rival candidates, Pope John argued that imperial prerogatives reverted to the papacy on the grounds that the German throne was vacant. Coinciding with the controversy surrounding the Franciscans' critique of church wealth, papal intervention attracted considerable comment, much of it providing the basis for arguments about spiritual-secular relations and church governance that would emerge again during the Great Schism (1378–1417). Pope John's excommunication of Louis IV (1324) merely increased resentment in the Empire against papal interference. Louis captured Frederick the Fair at the battle of Mühldorf am Inn (1322), but Frederick's younger brother continued resistance until both Habsburgs accepted the Treaty of Munich (September 1325). In return for renouncing their royal claims, Frederick was left with the courtesy title of king and the Habsburgs retained their possessions.

1328

Louis IV crowned emperor. After Pope John XXII had repeatedly rebuffed his peace overtures, Louis invaded Italy (1327), where pro-imperial (Ghibelline) sentiment had grown through resentment at the pope's continued absence in Avignon. Having been crowned by two pro-imperial bishops, Louis formally deposed Pope John and installed a Franciscan as rival, Pope Nicholas V, who promptly repeated the imperial coronation in more lavish style (May 1328).

Nicholas's resignation ended the papal schism (1330), but Louis was unable to reconcile with Pope John or his successors, still based in Avignon.

1338

The Electors' League (*Kurverein*). Louis endorsed electoral pre-eminence and recognized the electors' right of self-assembly. This event represented the breakthrough of the idea that the papacy had no influence on German royal elections and that a king could exercise authority without requiring papal recognition of his election. Louis remained excommunicated, but the papal interdict was soon ignored in the Empire.

1340

Louis inherited Lower Bavaria, reuniting the duchy and consolidating Wittelsbach influence in the Empire. A further inheritance added the counties of Holland, Zeeland and Hainault (1345, held by the Wittelsbachs until 1433).

1346–7

Louis IV's deposition and renewed civil war. Louis had struggled throughout his reign to balance the Habsburgs and Luxembourgs, the two powerful families whose rivalry had prompted his election as king in 1314. Compromise with the Habsburgs in 1325 alienated the Luxembourgs (now based in Bohemia). The Habsburgs backed Louis against King Johann of Bohemia in 1335 over rival claims to the inheritance of the counts of Tirol (who had acquired Carinthia in 1276). However, Louis was powerless to prevent a separate deal that saw the Habsburgs take Carinthia while Tirol went to the Luxembourgs. Charles, Johann of Bohemia's son, had carefully cultivated the support of the Avignon papacy. Pope Benedict XII declared Louis deposed (13 April 1346) and called upon the electors to choose a successor. With two votes already in the hands of his relations (Bohemia, Trier), Charles secured the backing of another three electors on 11 July 1346. His claims remained in doubt until Louis died of a heart attack (11 October 1347).

LUXEMBOURGS, 1347–1437

1347–78

Reign of Charles IV, grandson of Henry VII and the most important of the late medieval emperors.

1348

Consolidation of Bohemian autonomy as the 'lands of the Bohemian crown' (*corona regni Bohemiae*). This marked a significant shift in the methods of imperial rule away from reliance on imperial prerogatives and crown lands in favour of amassing a hereditary power base. The Bohemian lands (now including Silesia and Lusatia) were given firmer legal and administrative structures, while a lavish cultural and building programme raised Prague to a capital of European significance, complete with the Empire's first university (1348). However, Luxembourg dynasticism stopped short of integrating Tirol and Luxembourg itself. The latter remained in the hands of a junior branch, while the former was transferred to the Habsburgs by 1363. Charles IV meanwhile transferred numerous imperial rights to the princes and lords to win acceptance of his rule after 1346, including the imperial bailiwicks established in the 1270s by Rudolf I, though Charles initially continued to buy back former alienated crown lands where possible.

1348–54

The Black Death reduced the Empire's population by around a third, and ended the high medieval economic boom and migration to lands east of the Elbe. The socio-economic dislocation heightened anxiety, contributing to violent anti-Jewish pogroms that Charles IV actively encouraged.

1349

The election of Count Günther von Schwarzenburg as anti-king, as a belated and ill-coordinated Wittelsbach response to Charles's usurpation of Louis IV. Schwarzenburg was defeated and renounced his title, dying a few months later as opposition to Charles collapsed.

1355

Charles IV crowned emperor. The subsidence of the plague permitted Charles to go to Italy (1354), where his march was unopposed and he was crowned emperor. Charles returned briefly to Italy in 1368. The relative success of both interventions was contingent on his good relations with the papacy, and his avoidance of violent efforts to recover imperial rights.

1356

The Golden Bull. Charles cemented his imperial rule through an accommodation with the electors which built on that reached by Louis IV in 1338. This document reflected the prevailing balance of power and Charles's desire to consolidate Luxembourg dynastic influence. The electors were confirmed as a privileged elite above other princes. The dispute over the Saxon electoral title was resolved in favour of the Wittenberg branch of the Askanier family, which had backed the Luxembourgs. Electoral titles were henceforth permanently fixed in Mainz, Cologne, Trier, Bohemia, the Palatinate, Saxony and Brandenburg, whose lands were declared indivisible to prevent further disputes over these rights.

The Habsburgs and Bavarian Wittelsbachs were excluded. The latter had temporarily neutralized themselves through further family partitions after 1348, but the Habsburgs responded by forging the *Privilegium maius* (1358) based on the real *Privilegium minus* (1156) to claim the entirely new status of 'archdukes', asserting ceremonial (though not political) parity with the electors. Charles ignored this, forcing the Habsburgs to swear loyalty. However, his acceptance of their claims to the Tirol (1363) paved the way for a Habsburg–Luxembourg family pact (1364), easing tensions. Luxembourg influence was consolidated when Charles bought off rival claims to Brandenburg on the extinction of its ruling Askanier electors (1373).

The rest of the Golden Bull codified arrangements for choosing the German king along lines already emerging by 1338. The electors were empowered to choose a king of the Romans as successor designate during a monarch's lifetime, subject to his approval. Papal claims were rejected in favour of explicit claims that the German king was 'emperor elect' from his own election, and could exercise imperial prerogatives regardless of whether he was crowned emperor by the pope.

1361–72

The adjustment of the western frontier. Charles asserted his authority as king of Burgundy, whilst adjusting actual control to the realities of growing French influence. The county of Savoy, the 'free county' (Franche Comté) of Burgundy and the bishopric of Basel were transferred from Burgundy to the German kingdom (1361). The count of Savoy was named imperial vicar for Italy with responsibility for upholding imperial rights in the emperor's absence (1372). Meanwhile, the establishment of a new ducal line in the French part of Burgundy (1363) saw the growth of a dangerous regional power on the Empire's western frontier.

1371

Charles IV definitively abandoned the 'Revindication' policy, which had been initiated by Rudolf I in 1273 to recover crown lands, and instead switched to basing imperial rule on his extensive family possessions.

1376

The election of Charles's son Wenzel as king of the Romans, in return for privileges and the transfer of further crown assets to the electors.

1376–7

Swabian Civic League. The cost of acquiring Brandenburg (1373) and buying Wenzel's election was offset by new taxes on the imperial cities. Those in Swabia retaliated by forming a league that was also directed against encroachment by local princes. The cities defeated Charles and his Bavarian and Württemberg allies, forcing the emperor to agree not to pawn cities to princes. Further civic leagues were formed in Alsace (1376), the Rhineland (1381) and Lower Saxony (1382).

1378–1400

The reign of Wenzel exposed the contingencies upon which Charles had built his successes. Wenzel was barely 18 at his father's death, and his overindulgent upbringing failed to prepare him for the task of kingship. Luxembourg resources were substantial, and grew as his younger brother Sigismund became king of Hungary (1387) through marrying the Hungarian heiress. However, Wenzel controlled only Bohemia directly, as he was forced to allow his relations to govern Luxembourg and Moravia. Brandenburg had to be pawned to finance Sigismund's accession in Hungary. With the imperial crown lands dissipated by his father, Wenzel had few alternative resources with which to confront the many problems emerging in the aftermath of the Black Death and the progressive territorialization of princely power.

1378–1417

The Great Schism. An attempt by the papacy to escape French influence by returning to Rome was cut short by the pope's death shortly afterwards. Pro- and anti-French factions amongst the cardinals elected rival successors who appealed to European kings for recognition and support. Wenzel continued his father's policy of recognizing the anti-French pope, but was too weak to intervene.

1388–9

The First (Swabian) City War. South-western Germany had the highest population density, supporting a more fragmented and complex hierarchy of lordly jurisdictions than elsewhere in the Empire. Cities, knights and lords were not necessarily enemies, but often had conflicts over rights as they struggled to adjust and profit from the changes following the Black Death. The Swiss towns and villages drew closer together, defeating Habsburg efforts to reassert lordly jurisdiction (battle of Sempach, 1386). The knights occupied an ambiguous position, by serving as officials helping to consolidate princely jurisdictions as more distinct territories, whilst simultaneously being threatened by these same processes. The formation of knightly leagues (1370s) threatened both princely authority and the cities that were sometimes the targets of 'robber barons'. The Swabian cities defeated the local knightly associations (1381–2). Their growing power provoked retaliation from the princes, who defeated the Swabians at Döfflingen and the Rhenish League near Worms.

1389

The Public Peace of Eger. The violence prompted growing calls for Wenzel to intervene, but he preferred to stay in Bohemia and extort cash from the cities in return for recognizing their leagues and allowing them and the princes to plunder their Jewish populations. The collapse of the civic leagues paved the way for imperial representatives to agree a comprehensive peace across the Empire. This involved recognizing the involvement of princes and towns in upholding peace in each region, and it has been interpreted as a step towards the structures that emerged in the era of imperial reform. At the time it diminished Wenzel's authority.

1394–1400

The deposition of Wenzel. Wenzel's reluctance to leave Bohemia encouraged the electors to hold their own meetings without him. Wenzel's reliance on the Bohemian knights alienated the Bohemian lords, including his own Luxembourg relations, starting an open civil war in Bohemia by 1395. The Turkish advance towards Hungary fully occupied Sigismund, who was unable to respond to the elector's pleas to act as regent in the Empire. After considerable deliberation, the four Rhenish electors deposed Wenzel on grounds of incapacity (20 August 1400). Wenzel remained king of Bohemia until his death (1419).

1400–1410

The reign of Ruprecht, elector Palatine, who was elected king the day after Wenzel's deposition. Ruprecht's reign was compromised from the start by the refusal of many lords and cities to recognize his authority. The Palatinate was too small to support royal rule, while dissipation of crown assets not only reduced income but meant that Ruprecht had little with which he could reward potential supporters. His weakness was exposed by his unsuccessful campaign in Italy in 1401–2, where he failed both to obtain an imperial coronation and to defeat the powerful Visconti family that now ruled Milan.

1410

The last double election. The Luxembourgs had no serious rivals, but were split themselves between Sigismund and his cousin, Jobst of Moravia. The rivalry was deepened through its connection to the papal schism, as each candidate was backed by a different pope. Jobst's death a few months later (1411) resolved the situation.

1410–37

The reign of Sigismund, the last Luxembourg monarch. Sigismund remained king of Hungary, but held no land in the Empire, because Luxembourg had been transferred to ducal Burgundy (1409), while Wenzel remained king of Bohemia until 1419. Sigismund accepted he could never recover Brandenburg, which had been pawned to finance his acquisition of Hungary, and so transferred it to Friedrick IV of Hohenzollern, burgrave of Nuremberg (1415); this move initiated the slow rise of the Hohenzollern family to international prominence. The Wettin family also increased its influence with Sigismund's sanction of their acquisition of Saxony-Wittenberg on the extinction of the Askanier line there.

1414–18

The Council of Constance. Sigismund assumed the traditional imperial role as guardian of the church by intervening to end the Great Schism, deposing the now three rival popes and naming a new, generally recognized pontiff. He legitimized his action by backing the conciliar movement of senior clergy who wanted regular church councils to balance papal authority. Although reunited and back in Rome, the papacy underwent four decades of renewed tension between successive pontiffs and opposing church councils, which eventually elected Duke Amadeus VIII of Savoy (1383–1451) as the last anti-pope, Felix V (1439–49).

1419–34

The Hussite War in Bohemia. One factor in Sigismund's intervention to end the Great Schism was to secure church backing against the Hussite fundamentalist movement in Bohemia. The Hussite movement was already fragmenting, but some strands became associated after Wenzel's death with opposition to Sigismund's succession in Bohemia. The pope sanctioned war against the Hussites as a crusade. Repeated campaigns were repulsed, but the failures did force many German princes to cooperate more closely with Sigismund, who was also calling for assistance to stop the Ottoman Turkish advance through the Balkans towards Hungary. Sigismund compromised to be free to go to Hungary, extending toleration to moderate Hussites in return for an end to the war and acceptance of his rule in Bohemia (1434).

1422

The first imperial matricular list (*Reichsmatrikel*) agreed by a general assembly of electors, princes and cities at Nuremberg to provide a way of sharing military and financial assistance. Although the actual aid failed to defeat the Hussites, the meeting set an important precedent for the Empire's future development, and can be seen as part of the beginnings of imperial reform. This reform was stimulated by the parallel discussions about church reform emerging from the Great Schism, but it likewise dissipated without firm results around the mid-fifteenth century.

1433

Sigismund crowned emperor in Rome.

1438–9

The reign of Albert II and the transition from Luxembourg to Habsburg rule. Sigismund had no son, and honoured the Luxembourg–Habsburg family pact of 1364 by marrying his daughter to Archduke Albert II of Austria and promoting him as his successor. Albert was accepted as king in Hungary, Bohemia and, in the absence of another viable candidate, in the Empire. His brief reign was consumed defending Bohemia against Polish claims, and Hungary against a Turkish invasion.

IMPERIAL REFORM, 1440–1555

1440–93

The reign of Frederick III, Albert II's cousin, who was unanimously elected German king. Frederick was condemned at the time and subsequently for neglecting the Empire in favour of Habsburg interests, and it is true that the tension between dynastic and 'imperial' interests did become a more obvious political component at this point. However, his reign was the longest of any king/emperor and also saw the acceleration of those processes that have been labelled 'imperial reform' and that gave the Empire its early modern form. These processes were closely connected to the growing political significance of written culture, itself assisted by the invention of printing (c.1450). Imperial reform involved institutionalizing political arrangements through fixing rights and responsibilities in constitutional documents. This process transformed the Empire more visibly into a mixed monarchy where the emperor shared powers with a hierarchy of princes, lords and cities. These emerged more clearly now as imperial Estates (*Reichsstände*); a process that was largely mirrored by parallel developments within many of the Empire's territories where princes only consolidated their jurisdictions by recognizing that their own vassals and towns could share the exercise of some powers (e.g. Magdeburg 1400, Bavaria 1453, Württemberg 1457). There was a growing consolidation of territorial jurisdictions through the delineation of districts (*Ämter*) as administrative subdivisions, together with the creation of central organs (advisory councils and law courts) and more codified territorial law (now issued in multiple printed copies).

1444

An Ottoman victory over Christian crusaders at Varna, Bulgaria, signalled the end for the Byzantine empire, which disappeared with the fall of Constantinople (1453). The sultan incorporated the Byzantine Roman imperial tradition into Ottoman ceremonial, challenging the Empire's claims to monopolize this tradition. Continued Ottoman expansion established their empire as a permanent threat by 1471 when raiding parties could reach into Austria.

1448

The Concordat of Vienna provided a definitive settlement of imperial-papal relations lasting until 1803. In return for acknowledging the emperor's influence over the award of clerical benefices in the imperial church, the papacy secured the right to tax minor benefices and obtained the emperor's recognition of the pope's superiority over any church council in matters of ecclesiastical reform. This broad agreement was supplemented over the next three decades through further concordats with individual princes, sanctioning greater princely authority over local churches. Secular territorial jurisdiction was consolidated, notably in several north-eastern principalities where the process of incorporating imperial bishoprics was already far advanced: Brandenburg (involving the bishoprics of Brandenburg, Havelberg, Lebus); Saxony (involving Meissen, Naumburg, Merseburg); and Mecklenburg (involving Schwerin and Ratzeburg). In each case, the bishops retained spiritual jurisdiction, but lost their status as imperial princes, along with many secular rights and assets. The Habsburgs acquired a similar position in their own lands, ensuring the local clergy and religious houses did not obtain the status of imperial immediacy.

The Concordat contributed to causing the Reformation in three ways. First, imperial recognition of papal supremacy over church councils renewed debates over reform, since the measures passed by the conciliar movement since 1414 were declared invalid. The conciliar movement collapsed with the death of Felix V (1451), history's last anti-pope. Second, papal powers to tax benefices stimulated resentment amongst German clergy, who drew up the first 'Complaints of the German Nation' (*Gravamina nationis Germanicae*) in 1455, which was followed by many other critiques of ultramontane influence. Third, papal sanction of the incipient 'secularization' of several bishoprics prefigured that during the Reformation and indicated how secular authorities might take charge of church management in their own territories.

1452

Frederick III crowned emperor by Pope Nicholas V. This was the last imperial coronation to take place in Rome. Frederick used his position as emperor to confirm and extend the *Privilegium maius*, which had been forged by Duke Rudolf IV in 1358 to assert Austria's parity with the electors. Frederick now granted powers of ennoblement, normally reserved for the emperor, to his own family as hereditary rulers of Austria.

1457

The death of Ladislas Posthumous, the son of Albert II born after the latter's death in 1439. Frederick had tried to control Albert's kingdoms of Bohemia and Hungary through his guardianship of Ladislas, but the nobility of both countries elected their own kings after the boy's death. Tensions escalated through Hungarian ties to Austrian nobles opposed to Frederick, especially during the 1460s, leading to full war with Hungary (1482–90).

1459–63

The Princes War as the elector Palatine tried to recover regional influence his family had lost since 1410. Fighting remained confined to south-west Germany, but contributed to criticism of Frederick and to calls for imperial reform.

1474–7

The Burgundian War. The violent and rapid expansion of ducal Burgundy came to an abrupt end with Charles the Bold's death in battle against a hostile coalition of west German lords and the Swiss. Habsburg claims to the Burgundian inheritance led to war with France (1477–93), and provided a root cause of subsequent Habsburg-French rivalry.

1486

The election of Frederick's son, Maximilian I, as king of the Romans. This both secured Habsburg succession in the Empire and marked a new stage in imperial reform, because Maximilian was both more prepared than his father to accept changes and henceforth largely replaced him in dealings with princes, lords and cities.

1488

The formation of the Swabian League (lasted till 1534) between the emperor and south-western cities, knights, lords and – increasingly – also princes. The League was a response to security concerns, but also provided a framework for the Habsburgs to manage a particularly complex part of the Empire where they had direct territorial interests. It also showed how constitutional developments remained open at this stage of imperial reform, because the League had the potential of being both a supplement for other institutions (such as the Reichstag) and an alternative to them for emperor–Empire interaction.

1493–1519

The reign of Maximilian I. This saw the consolidation of the Habsburgs' core territories through the acquisition of the silver-rich Tirol by the main line, and the creation of a more robust administrative structure similar to those emerging in some other German territories. Dynasticism became more coherent and potent, especially through the network of marriage alliances spun by Frederick III and Maximilian that saw the Habsburgs acquire Burgundy (1477), Spain and its dependencies (1516), Bohemia and Hungary (both 1526).

1494–1559

The Italian Wars started with a French invasion of Italy to contest Spanish (Aragonese) claims to Naples, as well as imperial influence in Milan. Maximilian intervened to uphold imperial jurisdiction in northern Italy. A cycle of wars ensued, simplifying somewhat after 1516 as the Habsburg inheritance of Spain removed that country as an independent belligerent. Franco-Habsburg antagonism provided a common thread throughout and spread the conflict to the Franco-Netherlands frontier as France renewed claims to Burgundy. The larger Italian principalities like Tuscany and Modena emerged more clearly as independent, though still minor, actors alongside the papacy and Venice, which also became more prominent at this point.

1495

The Reichstag at Worms, generally regarded as marking the division between the Middle Ages and early modernity for the Empire. The general assemblies (known as *Reichstage*) of emperor, princes, lords and cities had grown more frequent from the 1470s, helping to consolidate the Empire as a mixed monarchy by providing a viable forum for collective decision-making. The meeting in Worms proved of lasting significance in establishing the Reichstag's membership, procedures and powers. The meeting approved the new Common Penny (*Gemeiner Pfennig*) tax levied directly on all inhabitants, adding a second way of raising money to the matricular system available since 1422. Grants under both systems were dependent on the Reichstag's agreement. Although the matricular system had essentially displaced the Common Penny by the mid-sixteenth century, the decisions taken in 1495 proved decisive in confronting all princes, lords and cities with a fundamental choice. By accepting responsibility for paying their agreed share of imperial taxes, they secured their place in the Reichstag as 'imperial Estates' (*Reichsstände*) sharing governance with the emperor. Refusal to participate led to exclusion from the Reichstag and, generally, the other institutions being created through imperial reform. Exclusion threatened the status of immediacy directly under the emperor. Those cities and lords who refused to participate slipped into mediate status, whereby their relationship to the emperor was mediated by subordination, like other territorial towns and lords, to one of the imperial Estates. This process was accelerated by the preparation of a new matricular list at the 1521 Reichstag, which served as the basis for all future revisions to tax and military quotas assigned to imperial Estates.

The Reichstag's procedural arrangements and financial measures entrenched the Empire's internal political hierarchy by grouping the imperial Estates into three 'colleges' of electors, princes and cities, and ensuring that even within these bodies, interaction was guided by individual status in strict order of precedence. Status was fixed ever more precisely through its articulation in written privileges and procedures.

The Worms meeting also established new peace-keeping and judicial arrangements, declaring a permanent public peace to end feuding, whilst establishing the *Reichskammergericht* as a new supreme court to arbitrate disputes between imperial Estates. The new court symbolized the Empire's mixed character through the court's formation jointly by the emperor and imperial Estates, all of whom assumed responsibility for maintaining it, nominating judges and implementing verdicts. By being independent, the court also symbolized how the Empire and its new institutions were greater than the sum of their parts. The Empire, through its constitution, was emerging more clearly as a legal framework with its own dynamic. It legitimized the status of the individual imperial Estates and, more generally, all groups, communities and entities were recognized somewhere in the growing body of imperial law.

1499

The Swiss or Swabian War. Maximilian I attempted to curb Swiss expansion and force them to accept the burdens and responsibilities associated with imperial reform. His defeat marked the definitive end of Habsburg efforts to assert lordship over Switzerland, but though the Swiss were exempted from the new institutions created by imperial reform, they nonetheless remained within the Empire.

1500–1512

The Reichstag in Augsburg (1500) established six 'imperial circles' (*Reichskreise*) to facilitate implementation of the measures agreed at Worms five years earlier. This Kreis structure was extended by bringing most of the remaining German territories within the system through the establishment of four additional circles. The Habsburgs deliberately enhanced their autonomy within the Empire by drawing the boundaries of the Austrian and Burgundian Kreise to ensure that both were almost entirely composed of their own possessions. Switzerland, imperial Italy and the Bohemian lands all remained outside this framework. The Kreis structure developed unevenly, but all ten Kreise were functioning by the 1540s, because their members appreciated the advantages of regional cooperation. The Kreise were another lasting achievement of imperial reform. By contrast, efforts to impose a permanent advisory council (*Reichsregiment*) on the emperor failed by 1530, partly through Habsburg opposition, but also because the imperial Estates came to realize that the Reichstag was a better vehicle for their interests.

1508

The papacy recognized Maximilian I as 'elected Roman emperor', thereby accepting the arguments advanced since the fourteenth century that the German king exercised imperial prerogatives from his election. Papal involvement diminished, conveniently at a time when the military situation in Italy made a coronation journey more difficult.

1517

The start of the Reformation with Martin Luther's publication of his 95 Theses. Critically, the religious controversy began while imperial reform was still underway. Debates over the correct form of Christianity became entangled with disputes over the Empire's proper political order.

1519–56

The reign of Charles V, grandson of Maximilian I and already king of Spain since 1516. Even more than Maximilian, Charles embodied both old and new, reinforcing the sense that the early sixteenth century marked an important stage in the Empire's development.

1521

The Reichstag in Worms consolidated imperial reform through the new matricular list, and initiated a series of increasingly substantial grants in taxes and military aid, enabling the Habsburgs to defend the Empire's eastern frontier against the Ottomans. Charles's declaration of Luther as an outlaw further politicized the Reformation, which was now, formally, treated as a public-order matter. Those princes embracing Lutheranism subsequently became known as Protestants through their objections to the Catholic majority's insistence on enforcing the imperial ban. The political history of the Reformation essentially became a sequence of Protestant efforts to suspend or reverse the legal measures initiated in 1521, most notably the Catholics' use of the public-peace legislation from 1495 to prosecute Lutherans for theft when they took over church property and spiritual jurisdictions.

1521–2

Charles transferred responsibility for Austria to his younger brother Ferdinand I, who subsequently became king of Bohemia and Hungary after the death of those countries' monarch at the battle of Mohács against the Ottomans (1526).

Ferdinand reorganized administration for his possessions (1527), consolidating their distinct status within the Empire as the Habsburg hereditary lands (*Erbländer*).

1522–6

The Knights Revolt (1522–3) was followed by the German Peasants War (1524–6), as both groups sought to realize social and political aims within their embrace of the Reformation. The Empire provided a framework for a coordinated princely response, notably in the south-west through the Swabian League. The princes' triumph ensured their subsequent leadership of the Reformation. However, the imperial constitution was changed to adjust how the defeated parties related to the Empire. Although still excluded from most of the new imperial institutions, the knights largely escaped incorporation within princely territories, because the emperor affirmed their immediate status as 'imperial knights' (*Reichsritter*) in return for cash taxes. Both they and the peasants were also granted access to the *Reichskammergericht* (supreme court) to resolve disputes with lords and to protect their rights (1526). The imperial cities, some of which had backed the peasants, were recognized more clearly as imperial Estates to prevent them 'turning Swiss' by joining the Swiss Confederation. This option remained into mid-century, but grew progressively less attractive with mounting differences between Swiss and German Protestantism, and a clearer appreciation of the effectiveness of imperial institutions as vehicles for civic interests.

1527

Unable to pay his army, Charles V encouraged it to sack Rome after Pope Clement VII had sided with France. Up to 10,000 civilians were killed and the event severely damaged Charles's reputation.

1529–41

The peak of Ottoman-Habsburg conflict. Having conquered most of Hungary (1526), the sultan besieged Vienna (1529) in an attempt to eliminate Charles V as a rival to his imperial claims. Although repulsed from Vienna, Ottoman forces retained Hungary and forced Charles's brother Ferdinand to pay cash tribute (1541, annual from 1547). Despite a major military effort in 1565–7, the Habsburgs were unable to conquer the Turkish part of Hungary, and had to continue their tribute in return for an extension of the truce.

1530

The coronation of Charles V as emperor by Pope Clement VII in Bologna was the last imperial coronation by a pontiff; thereafter all future emperors were crowned by a German archbishop, usually in Frankfurt. There were no more separate royal and imperial coronations. Monarchs were crowned either when they were elected king of the Romans during the lifetime of an incumbent emperor (*vivente imperatore*), or when they were elected after the death of an emperor who died without a prearranged successor. The German royal title had become progressively less distinct since the fourteenth century and was now subsumed within the imperial one, without being formally abolished.

1530–45

The consolidation of both the Reformation and imperial reform. Lutheranism emerged more clearly as a permanent alternative to Catholicism, complete with its own statement of faith (Augsburg Confession, 1530) and church structures established in those cities and principalities that had embraced it. These Protestant imperial Estates formed the Schmalkaldic League (1531) to oppose Catholic attempts to use the Empire's legal machinery to reverse these developments. Despite religious tensions, the imperial Estates continued cooperation through the Reichstag, which passed wide-ranging regulations for public order, morality, economic management and defence, all of which influenced similar measures in the German principalities and cities. Charles's younger brother, Ferdinand I, was elected king of the Romans (1531) and increasingly assumed responsibility for the Empire's affairs.

1546–7

The Schmalkaldic War. Charles V used a temporary ascendancy over France in the Italian Wars as an opportunity for a military solution to the religious deadlock in the Empire. The Schmalkaldic League was decisively defeated (battle of Mühlberg, 1547). Charles removed lands and the electoral title from the Ernestine branch of the Saxon Wettins who had led the League, and gave these to the Protestant Duke Moritz of the Albertine branch, who had backed him during the war. This was the first change amongst the electors since 1356, and demonstrated Charles's imperial power.

1547–8

The 'Armoured Reichstag' at Augsburg, so named by the presence of Charles's troops as he attempted a definitive settlement of all important issues in his favour. Religious observance was to follow guidelines set out in the 'Interim', a pro-Catholic statement to remain in force pending a final decision from the Council of Trent (1545–63), chaired by the pope. Management of the Habsburg lands was reorganized through the Burgundian Treaty, assigning the family's possessions in the Burgundian Kreis and Italy to Charles's eldest son Philip II, who was also designated his successor in Spain with its dependencies in Naples, Sicily and the New World. Philip's uncle Ferdinand I was accepted as Charles's successor in the Empire and the family's hereditary lands. Relations with the rest of the Empire were to run through a pact (the *Reichsbund*) between the emperor and leading imperial Estates.

1552

The Princes Revolt. An alliance of Protestant princes emerged amidst mounting violent disorder in Franconia and parts of Saxony. Moritz of Saxony secured French support for the revolt by allowing France to extend jurisdiction over the imperial cities (and de facto the associated bishoprics) of Metz, Toul and Verdun. The princes forced Ferdinand to agree the Peace of Passau, suspending much of the settlement reached four years earlier in Augsburg.

1555

The Religious and Profane Peace of Augsburg. Prolonged negotiations since 1553 produced a comprehensive settlement at a Reichstag in Augsburg to the religious and political problems of the first half of the sixteenth century. The religious clauses were deliberately ambiguous to allow parties of different faiths to agree on a common document. Lutherans received legal recognition alongside Catholics in the Empire. All imperial Estates were declared to possess the right of Reformation (*ius Reformandi*), embodying the secular supervision of church affairs in their territorial jurisdictions. The Peace of Passau was recognized as a normative year for the possession of church property, meaning the Lutherans could keep what they had taken from the Catholic church up to that point. Dissenting minorities received certain safeguards, but the treaty made contradictory provisions regarding the status of the imperial church. Catholics believed the Peace reserved all imperial church jurisdictions and offices exclusively for them, giving Catholics an in-built majority in the new imperial institutions, because there were more ecclesiastical than secular imperial Estates. Lutherans believed special guarantees issued by Ferdinand I allowed them to acquire such lands despite the recognition of 1552 as a normative year elsewhere in the Peace.

The more lengthy secular clauses codified and extended the imperial reform measures for defence, public order, coinage and economic coordination. The Kreise received enhanced powers, increasing the scope for regional collaboration and initiatives. Other than Austria and Burgundy, all Kreise developed assemblies as platforms to coordinate implementation of imperial laws and Reichstag decisions, as well as to introduce regional measures of their own. Representation amongst immediate lords was much broader in the Kreis Assemblies than at the Reichstag, where the majority of minor princes and counts lacked full votes in the princely college. These measures mark the high point of imperial reform. Further important legislation passed by subsequent Reichstag meetings into the 1570s modified and consolidated existing constitutional arrangements without fundamentally altering them.

HABSBURG STABILIZATION AND EXPANSION, 1556–1739

1556–8

The abdication of Charles V and partition of the Habsburg monarchy. Charles interpreted the events of 1552–5 as a defeat of his measures imposed in 1548. He accelerated the transfer of power already underway to his brother Ferdinand, formally abdicating (3 August 1556) and returning to Spain, where he died (21 September 1558). Ferdinand I was recognized as Roman emperor a few weeks later in 1556, but the full transfer of power was not completed until a formal ceremony on 15 March 1558 once he secured agreement from the electors. The process further consolidated the Empire as a mixed monarchy: the emperor remained pre-eminent (the Habsburgs had initiated the transfer), but ruled only through agreement from leading imperial Estates (the transfer was only completed through the electors' agreement). The transfer also completed the separation of the Habsburgs into separate Austrian and Spanish branches, which persisted until the extinction of the latter in 1700.

1556–76

The reigns of Ferdinand I (to 1564) and his son Maximilian II (1564–76). The administration of the Austrian lands was strengthened, but structural problems emerged following Ferdinand I's allocation of the Tirol and Inner Austria (Styria, Carinthia and Krain) to his younger sons, creating junior Habsburg branches. The *Reichshofrat*, established under Maximilian I, was reorganized and placed on a firm footing (1559) as a second imperial supreme court to safeguard imperial prerogatives, including feudal jurisdiction across imperial Italy. Good relations with individual important princes ensured the maintenance of the 1555 Augsburg Peace, despite the emergence of Calvinism as a major third religion without clear sanction in imperial law, and despite the onset of Catholic 'Counter-Reformation' measures, including the activities of the Jesuits in Germany.

1559–68

The Peace of Cateau-Cambrésis (1559) ended the Italian Wars in the Habsburgs' favour, with France renouncing its claims to Spain's Italian possessions, including Milan. Unlike earlier treaties, the Peace held because the death of Henry II (at a tournament celebrating the peace) plunged France into a crisis, which deepened into the French Wars of Religion (1562–98). Discontent over the cost of the Italian Wars, plus exclusion from influence and religious grievances amongst the Netherlands nobility, escalated during the mid-1560s into open opposition to Spanish rule, culminating in the Dutch Revolt after 1568 (also known as the Eighty Years War). The Revolt also assumed the character of a civil war, with most of the Catholic population backing Spain against the largely Calvinist Dutch rebel leadership.

1576–1612

The reign of Rudolf II. Habsburg management of imperial politics gradually lost direction amidst considerable problems. The deepening of the French and Dutch civil wars threatened the Empire's western territorial integrity as all parties sought to recruit German troops. Rudolf refused to back Spain against the Dutch rebels, whose territory effectively became an independent republic after 1585. Disputes over the religious terms of the Augsburg Peace sharpened around 1583 when Rudolf refused to allow Protestants who had become imperial bishops to exercise the prerogatives of imperial Estates.

1583–7

The Cologne War. The open conversion of the archbishop of Cologne to Calvinism triggered Spanish military intervention, which installed a member of the Bavarian Wittelsbachs instead. The episode exposed Rudolf's inability to resolve problems himself whilst greatly extending the influence of Bavaria, which emerged as the political leader of the more militant German Catholics.

1590s

The rival Wittelsbach branch in the Palatinate definitively converted to Calvinism, having previously switched between this and Lutheranism. The elector Palatine promoted an agenda of constitutional reform intended to secure recognition of Calvinism and dismantle the Catholic majority in imperial institutions, by levelling some of the status differences between imperial Estates in favour of his supporters amongst the partially disenfranchised imperial counts and minor princes. As the rival Wittelsbach branches associated with diverging interpretations of the Augsburg Peace, politics began polarizing more sharply along confessional lines. The elector Palatine manipulated controversies over church property to undermine confidence in existing institutions and rally support for a new Protestant league.

1593–1606

The Long Turkish War. Rudolf capitalized on continued cross-confessional support against the Ottoman threat to escalate problems on the Hungarian frontier into full-scale war. The Habsburgs compelled the sultan to accept the validity of their Roman imperial title, but were bankrupted by the war and bought a renewal of the 1541 truce by ceding some Hungarian territory and renewing their tribute. The 1606 truce was renewed five times by 1642, ensuring that the Ottomans did not challenge the Habsburgs during the crisis of the Thirty Years War.

1606–12

The Habsburg Brothers' Quarrel. The unsatisfactory outcome of the Turkish war fuelled resentment of Rudolf amongst his Austrian and Spanish relations. Habsburg authority eroded as Rudolf and his rival brothers made political and religious concessions to their provincial Estates in return for backing in their own quarrel (notably, Rudolf's 'Letters of Majesty', granting privileges to Bohemian and Silesian Protestant nobles in 1609).

1608–9

The formation of the Palatine-led Protestant Union (1608) and its rival, the Catholic League (1609) under Bavaria, in the wake of grandstanding by both Wittelsbach dynasties following the inconclusive Reichstag at Regensburg (1608). The Palatinate capitalized on Rudolf's mishandling of the Donauwörth incident (involving religious riots) to argue that existing institutions were impaired.

1609–14

The Jülich succession dispute exposed weaknesses in the Catholic League and especially the Protestant Union, as well as the general aversion to major war amongst most powers in and outside the Empire.

1612–19

The reign of Matthias, who progressively usurped control of the Habsburg lands from Rudolf, before succeeding him as emperor after his death. Political and confessional tensions persisted, but there was no inevitable slide towards major war. The League was dissolved (1617), while the Union lost members.

1618–48

The Thirty Years War ran in parallel with a resumption of the Spanish-Dutch conflict (1621–48) after a 12-year truce, and a new Franco-Spanish war (1635–59). The Thirty Years War escalated through the failure to contain a revolt of disaffected Protestant Bohemian nobles against Habsburg efforts to reassert authority on the basis of equating Catholicism with political loyalty. The decision of the elector Palatine to accept the Bohemian crown from the rebels (1619) spread the conflict into southern and western Germany. Despite repeated imperial victories, the war was prolonged by Danish (1625–9), Swedish (1630–48) and French (1635–48) interventions, as well as Habsburg miscalculations. Despite the foreign intervention, war in the Empire remained distinct from conflicts elsewhere in Europe.

1619–37

The reign of Ferdinand II, from the Inner Austrian branch of the Habsburgs.

1628–31

The War of Mantuan Succession. Spain's concern for the security of its north Italian possessions frustrated imperial efforts for a peaceful solution to disputed claims to the duchy of Mantua, and eventually compelled Austria to back France in a limited war. France secured its candidate in Mantua, but lost influence in northern Italy once open Franco-Spanish war began in 1635.

1629

The Edict of Restitution. Ferdinand II capitalized on a commanding military position to issue what was intended as a definitive verdict to end disputed interpretations of the religious clauses of the Peace of Augsburg (1555). This imposed a narrow Catholic interpretation, alienating most Protestants, who, like some Catholics, also felt the emperor had exceeded his powers by issuing such a verdict unilaterally.

1635

The Peace of Prague. Ferdinand II suspended the Edict as part of a wider settlement aimed at isolating Sweden by detaching its German supporters. The Peace still favoured Catholics, since these formed the majority of the emperor's supporters, but included important concessions, notably to Saxony. The Peace is widely interpreted as the high point of imperial influence, but any advantage was soon squandered by Habsburg mismanagement of the war.

1637–57

The reign of Ferdinand III, who took a more pragmatic approach than his father, Ferdinand II.

1648

The Peace of Westphalia, involving three treaties. Spain recognized Dutch independence in a treaty signed at Münster in January. The southern provinces remained part of the Empire as the Spanish Netherlands, still formally constituting the Burgundian Kreis. A second Treaty of Münster (24 October) settled peace between France and the Empire at the cost of Austria ceding its rights in Alsace. The Treaty of Osnabrück (24 October) ended war between Sweden and the emperor. The settlement stabilized the Empire as a mixed monarchy in which the emperor shared power with the imperial Estates, and confirmed the autonomy of the Habsburg hereditary lands, which were now more firmly under the dynasty's control.

1649–50

The Nuremberg 'execution congress' implemented the peace terms. Demobilization was completed successfully by 1654, ensuring the lasting success of the Westphalian settlement.

1653–4

The Reichstag in Regensburg convened to settle the remaining constitutional issues postponed by the Westphalian peace congress. Ferdinand III's management of the Reichstag signalled the Habsburg strategy of rebuilding influence in the Empire by working within the new constitutional framework. Rather than produce a definitive settlement, the Reichstag contributed to the evolution of the imperial constitution as a framework for continuing discussion of common problems. These discussions continued in various forms until the end of the Empire, though successive minor amendments had eroded much of the constitutional flexibility by the mid-eighteenth century.

1654

The publication of the 'Latest Imperial Recess' (*Jüngster Reichsabschied*). The 1653–4 meeting was the last time the Reichstag concluded by publishing a 'recess', or list of its decisions, which had been customary since the later fifteenth century. This was because the next meeting (1663) remained permanently in session and published decisions as they were made.

1657–8

The interregnum caused by the death of Ferdinand IV (king of the Romans since 1653) before his father, Ferdinand III. Louis XIV's possible candidacy in the ensuing imperial election was the first attempt by a French monarch to become emperor since François I in 1519, and the last time a foreign monarch considered standing.

1658–1705

The reign of Leopold I, younger son of Ferdinand III, who continued his father's policy of managing the Empire by presenting Habsburg objectives as common, imperial interests.

1662–4

A renewed Turkish war followed the breakdown of the earlier truce. Leopold I received substantial military assistance from the Empire, Sweden and France, enabling his forces to repel an Ottoman attack. The Treaty of Vasvár (1664) renewed the truce, but ended the humiliating tribute paid to the sultan.

1663

The Reichstag summoned to Regensburg to discuss military aid remained permanently in session, becoming the Eternal Diet (*Immerwährender Reichstag*) and lasting until 1806.

1667–1714

A sequence of wars in western Europe: War of Devolution (1667–8), Dutch War (1672–9), Nine Years War (1688–97), War of the Spanish Succession (1701–14). These conflicts threatened the integrity of the Empire's western frontier through French territorial ambitions and the growing involvement of German princes.

The demographic and economic recovery from the Thirty Years War slowed as princes created new, permanent armies maintained from territorial taxation. Although partly defensive, these measures were also a response to the wider changes in the Empire and Europe generally since from mid-century, as the international order became more obviously based on the new concept of indivisible sovereignty (articulated since the 1570s). Imperial princes lacked full sovereignty, yet many refused to consider themselves merely the Empire's aristocracy. Involvement in international conflict allowed them to seek recognition and elevation in status in what can be termed the 'monarchization' of princely ambition. Internally, militarization fuelled longer-term trends that have been labelled 'absolutism', as princes asserted a more exclusive style of government in their territories, refusing to share power with their nobles through formal bodies like territorial assemblies. For the Empire, it meant a new status division between larger and richer 'armed Estates' with their own forces, and those without permanent troops.

1681–2

Imperial defence reform. Mobilization against France during the Dutch War (1672–9) had exposed the dangers of reliance on the armed Estates, who compelled Leopold I to assign them the resources of the unarmed territories in return for substantial military assistance. These pressures continued after 1679 with further French encroachment on the Empire's western frontier (the 'Reunions' culminating in the annexation of Strasbourg in 1681). Leopold responded to the concerns of the smaller imperial Estates by incorporating them within a reformed system of collective security agreed at the Reichstag. Defence henceforth relied on a mixed system of collective imperial forces raised through the matricular quota system, and large contingents fielded by Austria and the other armed principalities.

1683–99

The Great Turkish War, precipitated by the Ottoman attack on Vienna. Although Polish assistance played a vital role in relieving the city, the reformed defence structure proved its worth and enabled Leopold to begin a reconquest of Turkish Hungary, which expanded to include the annexation of Transylvania by 1698. The outbreak of the Nine Years War on the Empire's western frontier (1688) threatened Leopold's chances of securing all of Hungary and obliged him to trade particular privileges in return for substantial military support from powerful German princes. The duke of Calenberg (Hanover) was given a new electoral title in 1692, triggering a controversy not settled until 1708. Leopold also backed the Saxon elector, who became the first prince to secure a royal title, through his election as king of Poland (1697), establishing a personal union between Saxony-Poland lasting until 1763. Meanwhile, the semi-regal title of grand duke was conferred on the ruler of Savoy (1696) to retain his cooperation in keeping France out of imperial Italy. The Ottomans conceded Habsburg control of all Hungary and Transylvania in the Treaty of Karlowitz (1699), for the first time replacing the previous temporary truce with a settlement intended as a permanent peace.

1697

The conversion of the Saxon elector to Catholicism to further his Polish ambitions coincided with the conclusion of the Nine Years War in the Peace of Rijswijk, which contained a special clause permitting the now Catholic Wittelsbach line ruling the Palatinate to breach the 1624 normative year fixed at Westphalia. The controversy partially re-confessionalized imperial politics until the early 1730s, without polarizing them along the lines experienced around 1600.

1700

The death of Charles II extinguished the Spanish Habsburgs. The issue of the Spanish succession had become ever more pressing since 1665 as it emerged that Charles would not have a direct heir. It was already a factor behind Leopold I's concessions to Hanover and Saxony in the 1690s, and now prompted him to grant the title of 'king in Prussia' to the Hohenzollern elector of Brandenburg, who crowned himself in a lavish ceremony in January 1701.

1701

Leopold I precipitated the War of the Spanish Succession by disputing last-minute arrangements that assigned all of Spain to Louis XIV's younger grandson, Philip V. Britain and the Dutch Republic backed Austria from 1702, while Leopold used the formal framework of the Reichstag to sanction full imperial mobilization against France. The conflict overlapped with the Great Northern War (1700–1721), in which Denmark, Russia and Saxony-Poland challenged Sweden's status as the dominant Baltic power. Bavaria and Cologne (held since 1583 by Bavarian Wittelsbach archbishops) backed France in the hope of securing a kingdom to be carved out of the Spanish Netherlands. The rival Palatine branch backed Austria for the same reason. Bavaria and Cologne were declared outlaws following the allied victory at the battle of Blenheim (1704).

1705–11

The reign of Joseph I, elder son of Leopold I, represented the peak of the Habs-burgs' recovery of imperial influence since 1648.

1711–40

The reign of Charles VI, younger brother of Joseph I. Joseph's unexpectedly early death wrecked Leopold's arrangement with his British and Dutch allies, who had insisted on the continued separation of the Spanish and Austrian pos-sessions and refused to accept Charles as ruler of both. Charles was obliged to agree peace with France, ending the War of the Spanish Succession in the trea-ties of Utrecht (1713) and Rastatt and Baden (both 1714). Philip V received Spain and its colonies, while Naples, Sicily, Milan and the Spanish Netherlands were recognized as Austrian possessions.

1714

The Hanoverian accession in Britain added another German prince with a royal crown. Bavaria and Cologne were released from the imperial ban, but, like their Palatine relations, the Bavarian Wittelsbachs had failed to secure a kingdom from the War of the Spanish Succession. The Grand Duke of Savoy became a full king, initially in Sicily, and then Sardinia (from 1720).

1716–18

The Austrian conquest of Serbia in a renewed war with the Ottomans. Follow-ing the other Habsburg gains since 1699, this made Austria a European great power, reducing the significance of its association with the imperial title.

1726

Austria recognized the tsar as Russian emperor to secure the continued friend-ship of this increasingly powerful eastern neighbour.

1733–5

The War of the Polish Succession saw a revision of the 1713–14 settlement in Spain's favour, forcing Austria to cede Naples and Sicily to a junior line of the Spanish Bourbons. Lorraine was detached from the Empire to compensate the defeated can-didate in the Polish succession dispute. It transferred fully to France in 1766.

1736–9

The renewed Turkish war, in support of Russia, cost Austria its gains from 1716–18 and compounded the financial and political crisis following the Polish succession conflict.

AUSTRO-PRUSSIAN RIVALRY, 1740–92

1740

The death of Charles VI ended the main Habsburg male line ruling since 1440 and precipitated another interregnum (the first since 1657–8) as the electors rejected Francis, former duke of Lorraine and husband to Charles's daughter Maria Theresa.

1740–48

The War of the Austrian Succession began due to the unprovoked Prussian invasion of Silesia by Frederick the Great, who sought to profit from the crisis to enlarge his lands at Austria's expense. The war expanded through the merger of the Austro-Prussian conflict with renewed Spanish efforts to recover the remaining possessions lost in 1714, as well as a new Anglo-French War.

1742–5

The reign of Charles VII, elector of Bavaria (the Wittelsbach Carl Albrecht), who contested Maria Theresa's inheritance of Austria and Bohemia (but not Hungary) since 1741. Although initially welcomed by many minor imperial Estates and those disillusioned with the last years of Habsburg rule, Charles's obvious dependency on French and Prussian support weakened imperial authority and prestige.

1745

The death of Charles VII and election of Maria Theresa's husband as Francis I. The electors recognized that only the Habsburgs had sufficient direct possessions to sustain an imperial role. Prussia accepted Francis's accession and withdrew from the war in return for Austria's reluctant acknowledgement of its retention of Silesia.

1756–63

The Seven Years War, started by Prussia to break a coalition forming to deprive it of Silesia. Like the War of the Austrian Succession, this was an imperial civil war, but this time the Empire was formally mobilized against Prussia. Prussia survived with its territory intact, demonstrating its influence as a second great power alongside Austria. Although the Empire achieved its official aim of restoring peace, the war discredited its system of collective security and encouraged a growing debate on renewed imperial reform.

1765–90

The reign of Joseph II, eldest son of Francis I and king of the Romans since 1764. Joseph accelerated internal reforms initiated after 1748 and intended to match Prussia's military efficiency. These reforms not only consolidated Austrian power distinct from its imperial status, but increasingly impinged on its position in the Empire by alienating traditional imperial supporters, notably amongst the imperial church by 1781. This allowed Prussia to assume the mantle of constitutional champion, rallying anti-Austrian sentiment to hinder both Habsburg imperial management and the reform agenda.

1772

The First Partition of Poland, by Austria, Prussia and Russia, raised the possibility of a 'Polish Future' for the Empire should the two German great powers ever decide to settle their rivalry at the expense of the weaker imperial Estates. This stimulated the reform debate, which was boosted further by the brief Austro-Prussian War of the Bavarian Succession (1778–9).

1790–92

The reign of Leopold II, Joseph II's brother, dominated by the difficulty of responding to rapidly changing circumstances: the French Revolution (1789), revolt in the Austrian Netherlands (1790), and the growing power of Russia in Poland and the Balkans.

THE END, 1792–1806

April 1792

The French declaration of war on Austria began the French Revolutionary Wars. Austria bought Prussian support (recognition of Hohenzollern inheritance of

Ansbach and Bayreuth), and both pressured the imperial Estates to declare imperial war (1793).

July 1792

The accession of Francis II in the last imperial election and coronation.

1793, 1795

The Second and Third Partitions removed Poland from the map, and distracted Prussia, which had difficulty digesting its new gains.

1795

The Peace of Basel. Prussia withdrew from the war against France, taking the whole of northern Germany into neutrality (until 1806). Several other princes began negotiating with France. French annexation of the Austrian Netherlands removed the Burgundian Kreis and shifted the imperial frontier east to the Rhine.

1797

The Peace of Campo Formio. Austria accepted French annexations west of the Rhine and opened a congress at Rastatt to settle peace between France and the Empire.

1799–1801

The failure of the Rastatt Congress led to renewed imperial war with France. Without aid from Prussia and the north, Austria and the rump Empire were defeated.

1801

The Peace of Lunéville. The Empire accepted peace on the basis of Campo Formio. Imperial Italy was ceded to France, but Austria took Venice. Those princes who had lost territory west of the Rhine were to be compensated east of that river at the expense of the imperial church and cities. Powerful armed princes forced the pace, occupying land ahead of formal sanction, but with the backing of international allies, especially France and Russia.

1803

An Imperial Deputation decision sanctioned the redistribution of territory, radically altering the Empire's internal balance and status hierarchy. Reform discussions intensified, but little could be achieved in the face of Austrian and Prussian opposition.

1804

Francis II responded to Napoleon Bonaparte's self-coronation as 'emperor of the French' by assuming an hereditary Austrian imperial title distinct from the Holy Roman one.

1805

Napoleon forced the pace of events by assuming the title of 'king of Italy', and forging closer alliances with German princes. Austrian efforts to resist were crushed at the battle of Austerlitz, leading to the Peace of Pressburg, which declared France's German allies to be sovereign states.

July 1806

Sixteen princes renounced allegiance to the Empire and formed the Confederation of the Rhine in alliance with Napoleon.

August 1806

Francis II abdicated to prevent Napoleon usurping the Holy Roman imperial title and its associations.

Abbreviations

AHR	*American Historical Review*
AKG	*Archiv für Kulturgeschichte*
ARG	*Archiv für Reformationsgeschichte*
BDLG	*Blätter für deutsche Landesgeschichte*
CEH	*Central European History*
DA	*Deutsches Archiv für Erforschung des Mittelalters*
EHR	*English Historical Review*
EME	*Early Medieval Europe*
EU	European Union
fl	florin
FMS	*Frühmittelalterliche Studien*
GH	*German History*
GHIL	*German Historical Institute London Bulletin*
GWU	*Geschichte in Wissenschaft und Unterricht*
HHStA	*Haus-, Hof- und Staatsarchiv Vienna*
HJ	*Historical Journal*
HJb	*Historisches Jahrbuch*
HZ	*Historische Zeitschrift*
IHR	*International History Review*
IPM	*Instrumentum Pacis Monasteriense* (Peace of Münster)
IPO	*Instrumentum Pacis Osnabrugense* (Peace of Osnabrück)
JMH	*Journal of Modern History*
MIÖG	*Mitteilungen des Instituts für Österreichische Geschichtsforschung*
MÖSA	*Mitteilungen des Österreichischen Staatsarchivs*
NA	*Nassauische Annalen*
NJLG	*Niedersächsisches Jahrbuch für Landesgeschichte*
NTSR	*Neues Teutsches Staats-Recht*, by J. J. Moser (20 vols., Frankfurt, 1766–75)
PER	*Parliaments, Estates and Representation*

P&P	*Past & Present*
RM	Roman Month
RVJB	*Rheinische Vierteljahrsblätter*
tlr	taler
TRHS	*Transactions of the Royal Historical Society*
VSWG	*Vierteljahrschrift für Sozial- und Wirtschaftsgeschichte*
WZ	*Westfälische Zeitschrift*
ZBLG	*Zeitschrift für bayerische Landesgeschichte*
ZGO	*Zeitschrift für die Geschichte des Oberrheins*
ZHF	*Zeitschrift für Historische Forschung*
ZNRG	*Zeitschrift für Neuere Rechtsgeschichte*
ZSRG GA	*Zeitschrift der Savigny-Stiftung für Rechtsgeschichte. Germanistische Abteilung*
ZSRG KA	*Zeitschrift der Savigny-Stiftung für Rechtsgeschichte. Kanonistische Abteilung*
ZWLG	*Zeitschrift für Württembergische Landesgeschichte*

Notes

INTRODUCTION

1. James Madison writing in *The Federalist*, 19 (8 Dec. 1787), in E. H. Scott (ed.), *The Federalist and Other Constitutional Papers by Hamilton, Jay, Madison* (Chicago, 1898), pp.103–8 at 105. For a critical reading, see Helmut Neuhaus, 'The federal principle and the Holy Roman Empire', in Hermann Wellenreuther (ed.), *German and American Constitutional Thought* (New York, 1990), pp.27–49. For a more positive comparison between the Empire and the US, see also W. Burgdorf, 'Amerikaner schreiben ihre Verfassung von den Deutschen ab', *Focus-Online* (23 May 2014), http://www.focus.de/wissen/experten/burgdorf (accessed 27 June 2014).

2. S. Pufendorf, *Die Verfassung des deutschen Reiches* [1667], ed. Horst Denzer (2nd ed. Stuttgart, 1994). Madison had clearly read this, referring to 'the deformities of this political monster': Scott (ed.), *The Federalist*, p.106. Voltaire's comments appeared in 1761 in his *Essai sur les moeurs et l'esprit des nations*, ed. R. Pomeau (Paris, 1963), I, p.683.

3. B. Schneidmüller, 'Konsens – Territorialisierung – Eigennutz. Vom Umgang mit spätmittelalterlicher Geschichte', *FMS*, 39 (2005), 225–46 at 236–8. For recent examples of its persistence, see H. A. Winkler, *Germany: The Long Road West* (2 vols., Oxford, 2006–7), and H. Myers, *Medieval Kingship* (Chicago,1982), pp.120–21. For further discussion, see E. Wolgast, 'Die Sicht des Alten Reiches bei Treitschke und Erdmannsdörffer', in M. Schnettger (ed.), *Imperium Romanum – irregulare corpus – Teutscher Reichs-Staat* (Mainz, 2002), pp.169–88.

4. Again, this view is deeply entrenched in the general and specialist literature: H. Plessner, *Die verspätete Nation* (Stuttgart, 1959); F. Meinecke, *Weltbürgertum und Nationalstaat* (Munich, 1908). The term 'consolation prize' comes from Len Scales' insightful essay 'Late medieval Germany: An under-Stated nation?', in L. Scales and O. Zimmer (eds.), *Power and the Nation in European History* (Cambridge, 2005), pp.166–91 at 167.

5. An influential example of this approach is G. Barraclough, *The Origins of Modern Germany* (Oxford, 1946). Further discussion in W. W. Hagen, *German History in Modern Times* (Cambridge, 2012), pp.6–20, and his 'Descent of the Sonderweg: Hans Rosenberg's history of old-regime Prussia', *CEH*, 24 (1991), 24–50; T. Reuter, 'The origins of the German Sonderweg? The Empire and its rulers in the high Middle Ages', in A. J. Duggan (ed.), *Kings and Kingship in Medieval Europe* (London, 1993), pp.179–211.

6. F. Frensdorff, 'Reich und Reichstag. Ein Beitrag zur Geschichte der deutschen Rechtssprache', *Hansische Geschichtsblätter*, 16 (1910), 1–43; E. Schubert, *König und Reich* (Göttingen, 1979), pp.245–54.

7. The literature on this is appropriately imperial in scope. Useful contributions include: H. Münkler, *Empires: The Logic of World Domination from Ancient Rome to the United States* (Cambridge, 2007); S. N. Eisenstadt, *The Political Systems of Empires* (Glencoe, IL, 1963); J. Burbank and F. Cooper, *Empires in World History* (Princeton, 2010), pp.1–22.

8. For example, at 1.2 million square kilometres, Charlemagne's original empire just makes it into one influential list of empires, but thereafter the Empire disappears from the list by falling below the arbitrary threshold of 1 million square kilometres minimum: P. Turchin, 'A theory for formation of large empires', *Journal of Global History*, 4 (2009), 191–217.

9. M. W. Doyle, *Empires* (Ithaca, 1986).

10. E.g. N. Ferguson, *Empire: How Britain Made the Modern World* (London, 2003). For a critique, see D. H. Nexon and T. Wright, 'What's at stake in the American empire debate', *American Political Science Review*, 101 (2007), 253–71.

11. E.g. M. Mazower, *Hitler's Empire: Nazi Rule in Occupied Europe* (London, 2008).

12. D. H. Nexon, *The Struggle for Power in Early Modern Europe* (Princeton, 2009); A. J. Motyl, 'Thinking about empire', in K. Barkey and M. von Hagen (eds.), *After Empire: Multiethnic Societies and Nation-building* (Boulder, CO, 1997), pp.19–29; S. Kettering, 'The historical development of political clientelism', *Journal of Interdisciplinary History*, 18 (1988), 419–47.

13. I owe this insight to Johannes Burkhardt's stimulating essay 'Die Friedlosigkeit der frühen Neuzeit', *ZHF*, 24 (1997), 509–74.

14. Münkler, *Empires*, p.85.

15. Historical periodization is yet another contested field. For convenience, this work uses the convention that late antiquity lasted into the mid-seventh century, followed by the early Middle Ages to about 1000, the high Middle Ages until around 1200, the late Middle Ages to around 1400, and then 'early modernity' into the late eighteenth century.

16. B. Bowden, *The Empire of Civilisation* (Chicago, 2009).

17. Cited from H. H. Gerth and C. Wright Mills (eds.), *From Max Weber: Essays in Sociology* (London, 1948), p.78. Useful further discussion is in S. Reynolds, 'There were states in medieval Europe', *Journal of Historical Sociology*, 16 (2003), 550–55.

18. Notable examples include S. Rokkan, *State Formation, Nation-Building, and Mass Politics in Europe* (Oxford, 1999), pp.209–11; G. Benecke, *Society and Politics in Germany, 1500–1750* (London, 1974); G. Schmidt, *Geschichte des Alten Reiches. Staat und Nation in der Frühen Neuzeit 1495–1806* (Munich, 1999); M. Umbach (ed.), *German Federalism* (Basingstoke, 2002); J. Whaley, *Germany and the Holy Roman Empire, 1493–1806* (2 vols., Oxford, 2012). Critique in A. Kohler, 'Das Heilige Römische Reich – ein Föderativsystem?', in T. Fröschl (ed.), *Föderationsmodelle und Unionsstrukturen* (Munich, 1994), pp.119–26. For the discussion of federal ideas by early modern writers, see H. H. F. Eulau, 'Theories of federalism under the Holy Roman Empire', *American Political Science Review*, 35 (1941), 643–64.

19. Scott (ed.), *The Federalist*, p.106.

20. R. L. Watts, *Comparing Federal Systems* (2nd ed., Montreal, 1999), esp. pp.6–9. For the following, see also the extremely interesting comparison of the Empire and the US by R. C. Binkley, 'The Holy Roman Empire versus the United States', in C. Read (ed.), *The Constitution Reconsidered* (2nd ed., New York, 1968), pp.271–84.

21. Much of this literature is cited in Chapter 7. See also Barbara Stollberg-Rilinger's introduction to her (ed.), *Vormoderne politische Verfahren* (Berlin, 2001), pp.11–23; K. Rohe, 'Politische Kultur und ihre Analyse', *HZ*, 250 (1990), 321–46.

22. B. Schneidmüller, 'Konsensuale Herrschaft', in P.-J. Heinig et al. (eds.), *Reich, Regionen und Europain in Mittelalter und Neuzeit* (Berlin, 2000), pp.53–87, and his 'Zwischen Gott und den Getreuen. Vier Skizzen zu den Fundamenten der mittelalterlichen Monarchie', *FMS*, 36 (2002), 193–224; G. Althoff, *Die Macht der Rituale: Symbolik und Herrschaft im Mittelalter* (Darmstadt, 2003).

23. C. Tilly, 'How empires end', in Barkey and von Hagen (eds.), *After Empire*, pp.1–11 at 4. Here, the Empire is similar to other empires, for example China, where the effectiveness of the imperial authority 'depended on the minimization of formal governmental intervention in the affairs of local communities': R. A. Kapp, *Szechwan and the Chinese Republic: Provincial Militarism and Central Power, 1911–1938* (New Haven, CT, 1973), p.2.

24. K. Epstein, *The Genesis of German Conservatism* (Princeton, 1966); L. Krieger, *The German Idea of Freedom* (Chicago, 1957); P. Blickle, *Obedient Germans? A Rebuttal* (Charlottesville, VA, 1997).

25. A. Lüdtke, *Police and State in Prussia, 1815–1850* (Cambridge, 1989); H.-U. Wehler, *Deutsche Gesellschaftsgeschichte* (5 vols., Munich, 2008).

Further discussion in D. Langewiesche, *Liberalism in Germany* (Basingstoke, 2000).

26. K. H. Wegert, *German Radicals Confront the Common People: Revolutionary Politics and Popular Politics, 1789–1849* (Mainz, 1992).
27. As claimed by P. C. Hartmann, *Das Heilige Römische Reich deutscher Nation in der Neuzeit 1486–1806* (Stuttgart, 2005), esp. pp.163–4. Further discussion of this point on pp.680–86.
28. B. M. Bedos-Rezak, 'Medieval identity: A sign and a concept', *AHR*, 105 (2000), 1489–533.
29. Some have interpreted this as the origins of 'spin': A. Wakefield, *The Disordered Police State: German Cameralism as Science and Practice* (Chicago, 2009), pp.9–13, 136–8. See more generally A. Gestrich, *Absolutismus und Öffentlichkeit. Politische Kommunikation in Deutschland zu beginn des 18. Jahrhunderts* (Göttingen, 1994), pp.34–56.

CHAPTER I: TWO SWORDS

1. G. Koch, *Auf dem Wege zum Sacrum Imperium. Studien zur ideologischen Herrschaftsbegründung der deutschen Zentralgewalt im 11. und 12. Jahrhundert* (Vienna, 1972), p.273; E. Müller-Mertens, 'Imperium und Regnum im Verhältnis zwischen Wormser Konkordat und Goldener Bulle', *HZ*, 284 (2007), 561–95 at 573–5. For the various titles and their use, see H. Weisert, 'Der Reichstitel bis 1806', *Archiv für Diplomatik*, 40 (1994), 441–513.
2. P. Heather, *The Goths* (Oxford, 1996).
3. M. Todd, *The Early Germans* (2nd ed., Oxford, 2004), pp.225–38; R. Collins, *Early Medieval Europe, 300–1000* (Basingstoke, 1991).
4. H. J. Mierau, *Kaiser und Papst im Mittelalter* (Cologne, 2010), pp.26–39.
5. T. F. X. Noble, *The Republic of St Peter: The Birth of the Papal State, 680–825* (Philadelphia, 1984). Further discussion of the Patrimonium on pp.189–93.
6. D. A. Bullough, 'Empire and emperordom from late antiquity to 799', *EME*, 12 (2003), 377–87 at 384–5.
7. R. McKitterick, *The Frankish Kingdoms under the Carolingians* (Harlow, 1983), pp.16–76; M. Costambeys et al., *The Carolingian World* (Cambridge, 2011), pp.31–79.
8. R. Schieffer, *Der Karolinger* (4th ed., Stuttgart, 2006).
9. A. T. Hack, *Das Empfangszeremoniell bei mittelalterlichen Papst-Kaiser-Treffen* (Cologne, 1999), pp.409–64.
10. Among the numerous biographies the most useful include R. Collins, *Charlemagne* (Basingstoke, 1998); M. Becher, *Charlemagne* (New Haven,

CT, 2003); A. Barbero, *Karl der Grosse. Vater Europas* (Stuttgart, 2007); H. Williams, *Emperor of the West: Charlemagne and the Carolingian Empire* (London, 2010).

11. R. McKitterick, *Charlemagne: The Formation of a European Identity* (Cambridge, 2008), esp. pp.103, 378.

12. Collins, *Charlemagne*, pp.141–50; Costambeys et al., *Carolingian World*, pp.160–70; Becher, *Charlemagne*, pp.7–17; R. Folz, *The Coronation of Charlemagne* (London, 1974).

13. Collins, *Early Medieval Europe*, p.269.

14. The circumstances were clearly more complex than they are often portrayed in accounts of the Empire's foundation as simply the pope's attempt to replace Byzantium with a more reliable partner: e.g. W. Ullmann, 'Reflections on the medieval Empire', *TRHS*, 5th series, 14 (1964), 89–108; J. Muldoon, *Empire and Order: The Concept of Empire, 800–1800* (Basingstoke, 1999), pp.64–86.

15. H. Beumann, 'Nomen imperatoris. Studien zur Kaiseridee Karls des Großen', *HZ*, 185 (1958), 515–49.

16. B. Schneidmüller, *Die Kaiser des Mittelalters* (2nd ed., Munich, 2007), p.30. For the coronation, see Folz, *Coronation of Charlemagne*, pp.132–50.

17. As argued by H. Mayr-Harting, 'Charlemagne, the Saxons and the imperial coronation of 800', *EHR*, 111 (1996), 1113–33.

18. Collins, *Charlemagne*, p.148; and his 'Charlemagne's imperial coronation and the Annals of Lorsch', in J. Story (ed.), *Charlemagne: Empire and Society* (Manchester, 2005), pp.52–70.

19. Bullough, 'Empire and emperordom', 385–7; D. van Espelo, 'A testimony of Carolingian rule? The *Codex epistolaris carolinus*, its historical context and the meaning of *imperium*', *EME*, 21 (2013), 254–82.

20. J. L. Nelson, 'Women at the court of Charlemagne: A case of monstrous regiment?', in J. C. Parsons (ed.), *Medieval Queenship* (Stroud, 1994), pp.43–61 at 47–9.

21. A good overview of these problems can be found in K. F. Morrison's introduction to T. E. Mommsen and K. F. Morrison (eds.), *Imperial Lives and Letters of the Eleventh Century* (New York, 2000), pp.3–40. For the contemporary understanding of the legal position, see Mierau, *Kaiser und Papst*, pp.163–220.

22. L. Knabe, *Die gelasianische Zweigewaltentheorie bis zum Ende des Investiturstreits* (Berlin, 1936); W. Levison , 'Die mittelalterliche Lehre von den beiden Schwertern', *DA*, 9 (1952), 14–42.

23. As acknowledged by Emperor Henry IV in his encyclical to the Empire's bishops, Whitsun 1076, in Mommsen and Morrison (eds.), *Imperial Lives and Letters*, pp.151–4.

24. M. Suchan, *Königsherrschaft im Streit. Konfliktaustragung in der Regierungszeit Heinrichs IV. zwischen Gewalt, Gespräch und Schriftlichkeit* (Stuttgart, 1997).

25. R. W. Southern, *Western Society and the Church in the Middle Ages* (Harmondsworth, 1970), pp.91–100.

26. J. Schatz, *Imperium, Pax et Iustitia. Das Reich–Friedensstiftung zwischen Ordo, Regnum und Staatlichkeit* (Berlin, 2000), pp.134–54.

27. The former view is held by C. M. Booker, *Past Convictions: The Penance of Louis the Pious and the Decline of the Carolingians* (Philadelphia, 2009). The latter by M. de Jong, *The Penitential State: Authority and Atonement in the Age of Louis the Pious, 814–840* (Cambridge, 2009).

28. G. Althoff, *Die Ottonen. Königsherrschaft ohne Staat* (2nd ed., Stuttgart, 2005), p.187.

29. J. Laudage, *Die Salier. Das erste deutsche Königshaus* (2nd ed., Munich, 2007), pp.34–47.

30. A. Coreth, *Pietas Austriaca* (West Lafayette, IN, 2004); M. Hengerer, 'The funerals of the Habsburg emperors in the eighteenth century', in M. Schaich (ed.), *Monarchy and Religion: The Transformation of Royal Culture in Eighteenth-Century Europe* (Oxford, 2007), pp.366–94. See also p.431.

31. E. Boshof, *Königtum und Königsherrschaft im 10. und 11. Jahrhundert* (3rd ed., Munich, 2010), pp.101–8.

32. Count Otto of Lomello's account cited by G. Althoff, *Otto III* (Philadelphia, 2003), p.105. Althoff downplays the penitential aspect of this act. See also J. W. Bernhardt, 'Concepts and practice of empire in Ottonian Germany (950–1024)', in B. Weiler and S. MacLean (eds.), *Representations of Power in Medieval Germany, 800–1500* (Turnhout, 2006), pp.141–63 at 154–8; H. Helbig, 'Fideles Dei et regis. Zur Bedeutungsentwicklung von Glaube und Treue im hohen Mittelalter', *AKG*, 33 (1951), 275–306. For the Gniezno leg of the trip, see pp.83, 206–7.

33. Henry IV claimed he had been called to kingship by Christ and ruled 'by the pious ordination of God': letter to Pope Gregory VII in 1076, in Mommsen and Morrison (eds.), *Imperial Lives and Letters*, pp.150–51.

34. H. Keller, *Ottonische Königsherrschaft: Organisation und Legitimation königlicher* Macht (Darmstadt, 2002), pp.168–71. For the insignia, see pp.267–9.

35. A. Schulte, 'Deutsche Könige, Kaiser, Päpste als Kanoniker in deutschen und römischen Kirchen', *HJb*, 54 (1934), 137–77.

36. Koch, *Auf dem Wege*, pp.61–99.

37. M. Bloch, *The Royal Touch* (New York, 1989). The Royal Touch was said to cure scrofula.

38. R. Morrissey, *Charlemagne and France: A Thousand Years of Mythology* (Notre Dame, IN, 2003), pp.96–7.

39. J. Miethke, 'Geschichtsprozess und zeitgenössisches Bewusstsein – Die Theorie des monarchischen Papsts im hohen und späteren Mittelalter', *HZ*, 226 (1978), 564–99; A. Hof, ' "Plenitudo potestatis" und "imitatio imperii" zur Zeit Innozenz III.', *Zeitschrift für Kirchengeschichte*, 66 (1954/55), 39–71.

40. R. McKitterick (ed.), *Carolingian Culture: Emulation and Innovation* (Cambridge, 1994); E. E. Stengel, *Abhandlungen und Untersuchungen zur Geschichte des Kaisergedankens im Mittelalter* (Cologne, 1965), pp.17–30.

41. S. Coupland, 'Charlemagne's coinage: Ideology and economy', in Story (ed.), *Charlemagne*, pp.211–29.

42. For the transition from late antiquity to the early Middle Ages generally, see C. Wickham, *The Inheritance of Rome: A History of Europe from 400 to 1000* (London, 2009). The socio-economic dimension is discussed further on pp.485–98.

43. Todd, *Early Germans*, pp.233–4.

44. Stengel, *Abhandlungen*, pp.65–74; Bernhardt, 'Concepts and practice', 144–7; J. A. Brundage, 'Widukind of Corvey and the "non-Roman" imperial idea', *Mediaeval Studies*, 22 (1960), 15–26.

45. A good summary of this debate is in Althoff, *Otto III*, pp.81–9. See also G. Althoff and H. Keller, *Heinrich I. und Otto der Grosse. Neubeginn und karolingisches Erbe* (Göttingen, 1985).

46. H. A. Myers, *Medieval Kingship* (Chicago, 1982), pp.9–12, 121–2; Stengel, *Abhandlungen*, esp. pp.17–30.

47. Koch, *Auf dem Wege*, pp.128, 230–45, 277–8. The relative balance of elective and hereditary monarchy in the Empire is discussed further on pp.301–5.

48. Koch, *Auf dem Wege*, pp.200–215; F. Seibt, *Karl IV. Ein Kaiser in Europa 1346 bis 1378* (Munich, 1978), pp.207–15.

49. S. Epperlein, 'Über das romfreie Kaisertum im frühen Mittelalter', *Jahrbuch für Geschichte*, 2 (1967), 307–42.

50. S. Weinfurter, *The Salian Century* (Philadelphia, 1999), pp.27–8.

51. W. Eggert and B. Pätzold, *Wir-Gefühl und Regnum Saxonum bei frühmittelalterlichen Geschichtsschreibern* (Cologne, 1984); E. Müller-Mertens, *Regnum Teutonicum. Aufkommen und Verbreitung der deutschen Reichs- und Königsauffassung im früheren Mittelalter* (Vienna, 1970). The title king of the Romans had already been used briefly by Henry II. See also pp.179–200.

52. W. Goez, *Translatio imperii. Ein Beitrag zur Geschichte des Geschichtsdenkens und der politischen Theorie im Mittelalter und in der frühen Neuzeit* (Tübingen, 1958); E. Müller-Mertens, 'Römisches Reich im Besitz der Deutschen, der König an Stelle des Augustus', *HZ*, 282 (2006), 1–58.

53. H. Thomas, 'Julius Caesar und die Deutschen', in S. Weinfurter (ed.), *Die Salier und das Reich* (3 vols., Sigmaringen, 1991), III, pp.245–77.

54. M. Gabriele, *An Empire of Memory: The Legend of Charlemagne, the Franks, and Jerusalem before the First Crusade* (Oxford, 2011); A. A. Latowsky, *Emperor of the World: Charlemagne and the Construction of Imperial Authority, 800–1229* (Ithaca, NY, 2013).

55. B. Töpfer, *Das kommende Reich des Friedens. Zur Entwicklung chiliastischer Zukunftshoffnungen im Hochmittelalter* (Berlin, 1964); L. Roach, 'Emperor Otto III and the end of time', *TRHS*, 6th series, 23 (2013), 75–102.

56. H. Löwe, 'Kaisertum und Abendland in ottonischer und frühsalischer Zeit', *HZ*, 196 (1963), 529–62 at 547.

57. C. Morris, *The Papal Monarchy: The Western Church from 1050 to 1250* (Oxford, 1989), pp.518–26; Schatz, *Imperium*, pp.198–203.

58. F. Shaw, 'Friedrich II as the "last emperor"', *GH*, 19 (2001), 321–39; P. Munz, *Frederick Barbarossa* (London, 1969), pp.3–21; J. M. Headley, 'The Habsburg world empire and the revival of Ghibellinism', *Medieval and Renaissance Studies*, 7 (1978), 93–127.

59. L. Scales, *The Shaping of German Identity: Authority and Crisis, 1245–1414* (Cambridge, 2012), p.210.

60. Muldoon, *Empire and Order*, pp.18–19; A. Colas, *Empire* (Cambridge, 2007), esp. pp.7–9, 18–19, 32–3; J. H. Burns, *Lordship, Kingship and Empire: The Idea of Monarchy, 1400–1525* (Oxford, 1992), pp.97–100; L. E. Scales, 'France and the Empire: The viewpoint of Alexander of Roes', *French History*, 9 (1995), 394–416. More detail in J. Kirchberg, *Kaiseridee und Mission unter den Sachsenkaiser und den ersten Saliern von Otto I. bis Heinrich III.* (Berlin, 1934). The challenge of royal sovereignty is explored further on pp.169–76.

61. According to M. Innes, 'Charlemagne's will: Piety, politics and the imperial succession', *EHR*, 112 (1997), 833–55, Charlemagne had probably envisaged a collegiate style of rule with close relatives sharing power under a common patriarch.

62. J. L. Nelson, *The Frankish World, 750–900* (London, 1996), pp.89–98; Costambeys et al., *Carolingian World*, pp.208–13.

63. C. Brühl, *Deutschland – Frankreich. Die Geburt zweier Völker* (Cologne, 1990), pp.359–62; F.-R. Erkens, '*Divisio legitima* und *unitas imperii*. Teilungspraxis und Einheitsstreben bei der Thronfolge im Frankenreich', *DA*, 52 (1996), 423–85; W. Brown, 'The idea of empire in Carolingian Bavaria', in Weiler and MacLean (eds.), *Representations of Power*, pp.37–55.

64. E.g. P. Riché, *The Carolingians: A Family who Forged Europe* (Philadelphia, 1993), p.168; J.-F. Noël, *Le Saint-Empire* (Paris, 1976), pp.7–11.

65. Schatz, *Imperium*, pp.33, 55–68, 100–113; W. Blockmans, 'The fascination of the Empire', in E. Bussière et al. (eds.), *Europa* (Antwerp, 2001), pp.51–68 at 54. Further discussion on pp.603–4.

66. G. Claeys, *Searching for Utopia: The History of an Idea* (London, 2011).

67. This is a particular problem with the otherwise useful work by Schatz, *Imperium*.

68. Wipo of Burgundy's chronicle, in Mommsen and Morrison (eds.), *Imperial Lives and Letters*, p.82.

69. H.-W. Goetz, 'Regnum. Zum politischen Denken der Karolingerzeit', *ZSRG GA*, 104 (1987), 110–89 at 117–24.

70. E. Karpf, *Herrscherlegitimation und Reichsbegriff in der ottonischen Geschichtsschreibung des 10. Jahrhundert* (Stuttgart, 1985).

71. Mommsen and Morrison (eds.), *Imperial Lives and Letters*, p.72. Dynasticism is discussed further on pp.422–31.

72. T. Zotz, 'Carolingian tradition and Ottonian-Salian innovation', in A. J. Duggan (ed.), *Kings and Kingship in Medieval Europe* (London, 1993), pp.69–100 at 70–71; H. Keller, 'Die Ottonen und Karl der Große', *FMS*, 34 (2000), 112–31; M. Gabriele and J. Stuckey (eds.), *The Legend of Charlemagne in the Middle Ages* (Basingstoke, 2008).

73. P. Classen, 'Corona imperii. Die Krone als Inbegriff des römisch-deutschen Reiches im 12. Jahrhundert', in P. Classen and P. Scheibert (eds.), *Festschrift für Percy Ernst Schramm* (2 vols., Wiesbaden, 1964), I, pp.90–101. See pp.267–8 for the imperial crown.

74. Mommsen and Morrison (eds.), *Imperial Lives and Letters*, p.73. Though this famous passage was penned by Wipo, it nonetheless reflected Conrad's own thinking: H. Wolfram, *Conrad II, 990–1039* (University Park, PA, 2006), pp.324–6.

75. J. Petersohn, 'Rom und der Reichstitel "Sacrum Romanum Imperium"', *Sitzungsbericht der wissenschaftlichen Gesellschaft an der Johann Wolfgang Goethe-Universität Frankfurt am Main*, 32 (1994), 71–101; Koch, *Auf dem Wege*, pp.253–75.

76. H. Conring, *New Discourse on the Roman-German Emperor* [1641] (Tempe, AZ, 2005).

77. Examples of this range from popular accounts like G. H. Perris, *Germany and the German Emperor* (London, 1912), p.33, to scholarly works like Myers, *Medieval Kingship*, pp.120–21, 218–22.

78. This compares to six Greeks, five Syrians, five Romans and one Italian, 654–752: Southern, *Western Society and the Church*, pp.54, 65.

79. Hack, *Das Empfangszeremoniell*, pp.605–25.

80. H. Zimmermann, 'Imperatores Italiae', in H. Beumann (ed.), *Historische Forschungen für Walter Schlesinger* (Cologne, 1974), pp.379–99.

81. T. Reuter (ed.), *The Annals of Fulda* (Manchester, 1992), p.135; Mierau, *Kaiser und Papst*, pp.53–5.

82. P. Partner, *The Lands of St Peter: The Papal State in the Middle Ages and the Early Renaissance* (London, 1972), pp.77–102.

83. H. Keller, 'Entscheidungssituationen und Lernprozesse in der "Anfängen der deutschen Geschichte". Die "Italien- und Kaiserpolitik" Ottos des Großen', *FMS*, 33 (1999), 20–48; H. Zielinski, 'Der Weg nach Rom: Otto der Große und die Anfänge der ottonischen Italienpolitik', in W. Hartmann and K. Herkbers (eds.), *Die Faszination der Papstgeschichte* (Cologne, 2008), pp.97–107.

84. The best contemporary account is F. A. Wright (ed.), *The Works of Liudprand of Cremona* (London, 1930), pp.215–32. For the events, see T. Reuter, *Germany in the Early Middle Ages, c.800–1056* (Harlow, 1991), pp.169–73; M. Becher, *Otto der Große. Kaiser und Reich* (Munich, 2012), pp.215–30.

85. The *Ottonianum* is printed in B. H. Hill Jr, *Medieval Monarchy in Action: The German Empire from Henry I to Henry IV* (London, 1972), pp.149–52. See also H. Zimmermann, 'Das Privilegium Ottonianum von 962 und seine Problemgeschichte', *MIÖG*, supplement 20 (1962), 147–90.

86. Collins, *Early Medieval Europe*, p.347.

87. Althoff, *Die Ottonen*, p.123.

88. Althoff, *Otto III*, pp.61–2, 72–81. The Empire's judicial practice is discussed on pp.610–37.

89. The latter is argued by Weinfurter, *Salian Century*, pp.91–6, on the grounds Suitger remained bishop of Bamberg whilst pope. See also G. Frech, 'Die deutschen Päpste', in Weinfurter (ed.), *Die Salier*, II, pp.303–32.

90. For the debate whether these changes constitute the 'first European revolution', see R. I. Moore, *The First European Revolution c.970–1215* (Oxford, 2000); K. Leyser, 'Am Vorabend der ersten europäischen Revolution', *HZ*, 257 (1993), 1–28. The concept is disputed by R. Schieffer, ' "The papal revolution in law"?', *Bulletin of Medieval Canon Law*, new series, 22 (1998), 19–30. For the impact of these changes on the Empire, see pp.488–93, 504–8.

91. C. H. Lawrence, *Medieval Monasticism* (2nd ed., London, 1989); H. J. Hummer, *Politics and Power in Early Medieval Europe: Alsace and the Frankish Realm, 600–1000* (Cambridge, 2005), pp.227–49.

92. J. Howe, *Church Reform and Social Change in Eleventh-Century Italy* (Philadelphia, 1997); K. G. Cushing, *Reform and the Papacy in the Eleventh Century* (Manchester, 2005), pp.34–7, 91–5; M. Rubin (ed.), *Medieval Christianity in Practice* (Princeton, 2009).

93. J. Howe, 'The nobility's reform of the medieval church', *AHR*, 93 (1988), 317–39; N. Kruppa (ed.), *Adlige – Stifter – Mönche. Zum Verhältnis zwischen Klöstern und mittelalterlichem Adel* (Göttingen, 2007).

94. More detail on these obligations on pp.333–4.

95. J. Miethke and A. Bühler, *Kaiser und Papst im Konflikt* (Düsseldorf, 1988), pp.17–23; J. T. Gilchrist, *Canon Law in the Age of Reform, 11th–12th Centuries* (Aldershot, 1993).

96. J. Laudage, *Priesterbild und Reformpapsttum im 11. Jahrhundert* (Cologne, 1985).

97. The rules were revised again in 1179, expanding the number of cardinals and establishing the requirement of a two-thirds majority: F. J. Baumgartner, *Behind Locked Doors: A History of the Papal Elections* (Basingstoke, 2003). See more generally I. S. Robinson, *The Papacy, 1073–1198* (Cambridge, 1990); Morris, *Papal Monarchy*, pp.79–108.

98. D. J. Hay, *The Military Leadership of Matilda of Canossa, 1046–1115* (Manchester, 2008); M. K. Spike, *Tuscan Countess: The Life and Extraordinary Times of Matilda of Canossa* (New York, 2004).

99. The arrival of the Normans is covered in greater depth on pp.191–2.

100. E. Boshof, 'Das Reich in der Krise. Überlegungen zum Regierungsausgang Heinrichs III.', *HZ*, 228 (1979), 265–87. For the regency, see pp.315–16.

101. H. E. J. Cowdrey, *Pope Gregory VII, 1073–1085* (Oxford, 1998); G. Tellenbach, *Die westliche Kirche vom 10. bis zum frühen 12. Jahrhundert* (Göttingen, 1988); W. Hartmann, *Der Investiturstreit* (3rd ed., Munich, 2007).

102. M. Suchan, 'Publizistik im Zeitalter Heinrichs IV.', in K. Hruza (ed.), *Propaganda, Kommunikation und Öffentlichkeit (11.–16.Jahrhundert)* (Vienna, 2003), pp.29–45, and her *Königsherrschaft im Streit* (Stuttgart, 1997); I. S. Robinson, *Henry IV of Germany, 1056–1106* (Cambridge, 1999), and his *Authority and Resistance in the Investiture Contest: The Polemical Literature of the Late Eleventh Century* (Manchester, 1978).

103. The term *investiturae controversia* dates from 1123: B. Schilling, 'Ist das Wormser Konkordat überhaupt nicht geschlossen worden?', *DA*, 58 (2002), 123–91 at 187–8.

104. R. Schieffer, *Die Entstehung des päpstlichen Investiturverbots für den deutschen König* (Stuttgart, 1981); H. Keller, 'Die Investitur', *FMS*, 27 (1993), 51–86, and his 'Ritual, Symbolik und Visualisierung in der Kultur des ottonischen Reiches', *FMS*, 35 (2001), 23–59 at 26–7.

105. R. Pauler, *Die deutschen Könige und Italien im 14. Jahrhundert von Heinrich VII. bis Karl IV.* (Darmstadt, 1997), pp.10–11. For the following, see T. Struve, *Salierzeit im Wandel. Zur Geschichte Heinrichs IV. und des Investiturstreites* (Cologne, 2006), esp. pp.26, 227–40.

106. J. Eldevik, *Episcopal Power and Ecclesiastical Reform in the German Empire: Tithes, Lordship and Community, 950–1150* (Cambridge, 2012), pp.103–255.

107. C. Zey, 'Im Zentrum des Streits. Mailand und die oberitalienischen Kommunen zwischen *regnum* und *sacerdotium*', in J. Jarnut and M. Wemhoff (eds.), *Vom Umbruch zur Erneuerung?* (Munich, 2006), pp.595–611; H. Keller, 'Die soziale und politische Verfassung Mailands in den Angfängen des kommunalen Lebens', *HZ*, 211 (1970), 34–64. For a contemporary

pro-Gregorian account, see I. S. Robinson (ed.), *Eleventh-Century Germany: The Swabian Chronicles* (Manchester, 2008), pp.132–244. The imperial perspective appears in Mommsen and Morrison (eds.), *Imperial Lives and Letters*, pp.108–77.

108. Berthold of Reichenau's account in Robinson (ed.), *Eleventh-Century Germany*, p.160. See also S. Weinfurter, *Canossa. Die Entzauberung der Welt* (Munich, 2006).

109. J. Fried, *Canossa. Entlarvung einer Legende* (Berlin, 2012); T. Reuter, *Medieval Polities and Modern Mentalities* (Cambridge, 2006), pp.147–66.

110. Cowdrey, *Gregory VII*, pp.167–98; I. S. Robinson, 'Pope Gregory VII, the princes and the *Pactum* 1077–1080', *EHR*, 94 (1979), 721–56.

111. E. Goez, 'Der Thronerbe als Rivale. König Konrad, Kaiser Heinrichs IV. älterer Sohn', *HJb*, 116 (1996), 1–49.

112. G. Althoff, *Heinrich IV.* (Darmstadt, 2006), pp.213–19, 269–73; Hay, *Military Leadership of Matilda*, pp.145–6.

113. Details in Morris, *Papal Monarchy*, pp.154–64; Robinson, *The Papacy*, pp.421–41; Laudage, *Die Salier*, pp.98–107.

114. J. Fried, 'Der Regalienbegriff im 11. und 12. Jahrhundert', *DA*, 29 (1973), 450–528.

115. Laudage, *Die Salier*, p.9; Weinfurter, *Canossa*, p.207. More cautious assessments in H. Hoffmann, 'Canossa – eine Wende?', *DA*, 66 (2010), 535–68; L. Körntgen, *Königsherrschaft und Gottes Gnade. Zu Kontext und Funktion sakraler Vorstellungen in Historiographie und Bildzeugnissen der ottonisch-frühsalischen Zeit* (Berlin, 2001), pp.435–45.

116. Weinfurter, *Salian Century*, pp.173–4.

117. R. I. Moore, *The Formation of a Persecuting Society: Power and Deviance in Western Europe, 950–1250* (Oxford, 1990); J. A. F. Thomson, *The Western Church in the Middle Ages* (London, 1998), pp.119–29; Lawrence, *Medieval Monasticism*, pp.244–70; Morris, *Papal Monarchy*, pp.339–57, 442–504.

118. M. Kintzinger, 'Der weiße Reiter. Formen internationaler Politik im Spätmittelalter', *FMS*, 37 (2003), 315–53. Frederick I 'Barbarossa' reluctantly performed Strator service in 1154, but presented this as a mere compliment to the pope.

119. K. Görich, *Die Staufer. Herrscher und Reich* (2nd ed., Munich, 2008), p.34.

120. Koch, *Auf dem Wege*, pp.149–77, 191–9, 248–53; N. Rubinstein, 'Political rhetoric in the imperial chancery', *Medium Aevum*, 14 (1945), 21–43; K. Görich, 'Die "Ehre des Reichs" (*honor imperii*)', in J. Laudage and Y. Leiverkus (eds.), *Rittertum und höfische Kultur der Stauferzeit* (Cologne, 2006), pp.36–74.

121. K. Görich, *Friedrich Barbarossa* (Munich, 2011), pp.231, 283. See also F. Opll, *Friedrich Barbarossa* (4th ed., Darmstadt, 2009); Munz, *Frederick Barbarossa*.

122. The strategic problems are illuminated by H. Berwinkel, *Verwüsten und Belagern. Friedrich Barbarossas Krieg gegen Mailand (1158–1162)* (Tübingen, 2007). For the Lombard League, see pp.568–70.

123. P. Csendes, 'Die Doppelwahl von 1198 und ihre europäischen Dimensionen', in W. Hechberger and F. Schuller (eds.), *Staufer & Welfen* (Regensburg, 2009), pp.157–71.

124. Pauler, *Die deutschen Könige*, pp.12–13, 230–31. See generally J. C. Moore, *Pope Innocent III (1160/61–1216)* (Notre Dame, IN, 2009).

125. He was murdered by Otto of Wittelsbach in a private feud in June 1208: Görich, *Die Staufer*, p.85.

126. After a succession of largely negative views, Ernst Kantorowicz offered an overly positive portrayal in *The Emperor Frederick the Second, 1194–1250* (London, 1957, first published in German, 1927). Good modern biographies include E. Horst, *Friedrich II., der Staufer* (5th ed., Düsseldorf, 1986), and the monumental W. Stürner, *Friedrich II.* (2 vols., Darmstadt, 2009).

127. The final stage is recounted in H. U. Ullrich, *Konradin von Hohenstaufen. Die Tragödie von Neapel* (Munich, 2004).

128. Schneidmüller, *Die Kaiser*, p.86.

129. Partner, *Lands of St Peter*, pp.263–70; D. Matthew, *The Norman Kingdom of Sicily* (Cambridge, 1992), pp.362–80.

130. Pauler, *Die deutschen Könige*, pp.13–16; F. Trautz, 'Die Reichsgewalt in Italien im Spätmittelalter', *Heidelberger Jahrbücher*, 7 (1963), 45–81 at 48–50.

131. Pauler, *Die deutschen Könige*, pp.43–114; W. M. Bowsky, *Henry VII in Italy: The Conflict of Empire and City-State, 1310–1313* (Lincoln, NB, 1960). A contemporary account of Henry's expedition appears in M. Margue et al. (eds.), *Der Weg zur Kaiserkrone. Der Romzug von Heinrichs VII. in der Darstellung von Erzbischof Balduins von Trier* (Trier, 2009).

132. Bowsky, *Henry VII*, p.167.

133. F. Baethgen, 'Der Anspruch des Papsttums auf das Reichsvikariat', *ZSRG KA*, 10 (1920), 168–268.

134. J. Miethke, 'Kaiser und Papst im Spätmittelalter. Zu den Ausgleichsbemühungen zwischen Ludwig dem Bayern und der Kurie in Avignon', *ZHF*, 10 (1983), 421–46; Mierau, *Kaiser und Papst*, pp.115–28; Pauler, *Die deutschen Könige*, pp.117–64.

135. A. Fößel, 'Die deutsche Tradition von Imperium im späten Mittelalter', in F. Bosbach and H. Hiery (eds.), *Imperium / Empire / Reich* (Munich, 1999), pp.17–30; E. L. Wittneben, 'Lupold von Bebenburg und Wilhelm von Ockham im Dialog über die Rechte am Römischen Reich des Spätmittelalters', *DA*, 53 (1997), 567–86.

136. R. Pauler, *Die Auseinandersetzungen zwischen Kaiser Karl IV. und den Päpsten* (Neuried, 1996).

137. J. Whaley, *Germany and the Holy Roman Empire 1493–1806* (2 vols., Cambridge, 2012), I, pp.103, 503.

138. J. M. Levine, 'Reginald Pecock and Lorenzo Valla on the *Donation of Constantine*', *Studies in the Renaissance*, 20 (1973), 118–43.

139. F. Escher and H. Kühne (eds.), *Die Wilsnackfahrt. Ein Wallfahrts- und Kommunikationszentrum Nord- und Mitteleuropas im Spätmittelalter* (Frankfurt am Main, 2006).

140. F. Welsh, *The Battle for Christendom: The Council of Constance, 1415, and the Struggle to Unite against Islam* (London, 2008).

141. Whaley, *Germany*, I, pp.86–7.

142. W. Zanetti, *Der Friedenskaiser. Friedrich III. und seine Zeit, 1440–1493* (Herford, 1985), pp.107–23.

143. E. Meuthen (ed.), *Reichstage und Kirche* (Göttingen, 1991).

144. J. Hook, *The Sack of Rome, 1527* (London, 1972).

145. M. F. Alvarez, *Charles V: Elected Emperor and Hereditary Ruler* (London, 1975), pp.83–8; H. Kleinschmidt, *Charles V: The World Emperor* (Stroud, 2004), pp.129–32.

146. G. Kleinheyer, *Die kaiserlichen Wahlkapitulationen* (Karlsruhe, 1968), pp.72–6; T. Brockmann, *Dynastie, Kaiseramt und Konfession. Politik und Ordnungsvorstellungen Ferdinands II. im Dreißigjährigen Krieg* (Paderborn, 2011), pp.386–9. A sentence was inserted in 1653 that the emperor had to respect the Peace of Augsburg while protecting the church.

147. R. Staats, *Die Reichskrone. Geschichte und Bedeutung eines europäischen Symbols* (2nd ed., Kiel, 2008), pp.116–17.

148. T. J. Dandelet, *Spanish Rome, 1500–1700* (New Haven, CT, 2001).

149. M. Hengerer, *Kaiser Ferdinand III. (1608–1657)* (Cologne, 2012), pp. 173–6, 297–8; K. Repgen, *Dreißigjähriger Krieg und Westfälischer Friede* (Paderborn, 1998), pp.539–61, 597–642; A Koller, *Imperator und Pontifex. Forschungen zum Verhältnis von Kaiserhof und römischer Kurie im Zeitalter der Konfessionalisierung (1555–1648)* (Münster, 2012), pp.157–210.

150. C. W. Ingrao, *In Quest and Crisis: Emperor Joseph I and the Habsburg Monarchy* (West Lafayette, IN, 1979), pp.96–121; D. Beales, *Joseph II* (2 vols., Cambridge, 1987–2009), II, pp.214–38, 353–4.

151. G. F.-H. and J. Berkeley, *Italy in the Making* (3 vols., Cambridge, 1932–40), vol. III; J. Haslip, *Imperial Adventurer: Emperor Maximilian of Mexico and his Empress* (London, 1974); M. Stickler, 'Reichsvorstellungen in Preußen-Deutschland und der Habsburgermonarchie in der Bismarckzeit', in Bosbach and Hiery (eds.), *Imperium*, pp.133–54 at 139–40.

CHAPTER 2: CHRISTENDOM

1. D. Hay, *Europe: The Emergence of an Idea* (2nd ed., Edinburgh, 1968), pp.16–36, 52; B. Guenée, *States and Rulers in Later Medieval Europe* (Oxford, 1985), pp.1–9; R. Bartlett, *The Making of Europe: Conquest, Colonization and Cultural Change, 950–1350* (London, 1993), esp. pp.250–55, 292–314.

2. L. Scales, *The Shaping of German Identity* (Cambridge, 2012), pp.396, 414–15.

3. The sense of difference is clear from contemporary Christian accounts of Slavic beliefs, e.g. Thietmar of Merseburg, *Ottonian Germany: The Chronicon of Thietmar of Merseburg*, ed. D. A. Warner (Manchester, 2001), pp.252–4. See also A. Angenendt, *Liudger. Missionar – Abt – Bischof im frühen Mittelalter* (Münster, 2005), pp.32–46; D. Třeštík, 'The baptism of the Czech princes in 845 and the Christianization of the Slavs', in *Historica: Historical Sciences in the Czech Republic* (Prague, 1995), pp.7–59.

4. K. Barkey, *Empire of Difference: The Ottomans in Comparative Perspective* (Cambridge, 2008), pp.109–53.

5. S. P. Huntington, *The Clash of Civilizations and the Remaking of World Order* (London, 1996).

6. J. van Engen, 'The Christian Middle Ages as an historiographical problem', *AHR*, 91 (1986), 519–52.

7. As claimed by R. McKitterick, *Charlemagne* (Cambridge, 2008), Chapter 5.

8. T. Reuter, 'Plunder and tribute in the Carolingian empire', *TRHS*, 5th series, 35 (1985), 75–94; J. Laudage et al., *Die Zeit der Karolinger* (Darmstadt, 2006), pp.166–72.

9. R. Collins, *Early Medieval Europe, 300–1000* (Basingstoke, 1991), pp.321–2.

10. T. Reuter, 'Carolingian and Ottonian warfare', in M. Keen (ed.), *Medieval Warfare* (Oxford, 1999), pp.13–35 at 31.

11. C. H. Lawrence, *Medieval Monasticism* (2nd ed., London, 1989), p.71.

12. See the account of Hermann's friend and biographer, Berthold, in I. S. Robinson (ed.), *Eleventh-Century Germany* (Manchester, 2008), pp.108–12.

13. M. Innes, 'Franks and Slavs c.700–1000', *EME*, 6 (1997), 201–16; S. Coupland, 'From poachers to gamekeepers: Scandinavian warlords and Carolingian kings', *EME*, 7 (1998), 85–114. See more generally T. Reuter, 'Charlemagne and the world beyond the Rhine', in J. Story (ed.), *Charlemagne* (Manchester, 2005), pp.183–94; M. Costambeys et al., *The Carolingian World* (Cambridge, 2011), pp.80–153.

14. R. McKitterick, *The Frankish Kingdoms under the Carolingians* (Harlow, 1983), pp.109–24; Lawrence, *Medieval Monasticism*, pp.22, 74–82.

15. C. I. Hammer Jr, 'Country churches, clerical inventories and the Carolingian Renaissance in Bavaria', *Church History*, 49 (1980), 5–17.

16. I. Wood, *The Missionary Life: Saints and the Evangelisation of Europe, 400–1050* (Harlow, 2001).

17. A. Angenendt (ed.), *Geschichte des Bistums Münster* (5 vols., Münster, 1998), I, pp.131–43.

18. W. Kohl (ed.), *Bistum Münster* (Berlin, 2000), pp.1–24; H.-J. Weiers, *Studien zur Geschichte des Bistums Münster im Mittelalter* (Cologne, 1984), pp.3–19. In addition to Angenendt's biography of Liudger, see also B. Senger, *Liudger. Leben und Werk* (Münster, 1984); G. Isenberg and R. Rommé (eds.), *805: Liudger wird Bischof* (Münster, 2005).

19. G. Althoff, *Die Ottonen* (2nd ed., Stuttgart, 2005), pp.17–18.

20. For Otto I's requisitioning of Roman relics to support German missions, see Thietmar of Merseburg, *Chronicon*, pp.103–4.

21. Althoff, *Die Ottonen*, p.151. The destruction of the Slav rising is recounted by Thietmar of Merseburg, *Chronicon*, pp.141–3. For Cotrone see pp.191–345.

22. The political dimensions of this and Hungary's parallel experience are covered on pp.204–7.

23. C. Stiegemann and M. Wemhoff (eds.), *799: Kunst und Kultur der Karolingerzeit. Karl der Große und Papst Leo III. in Paderborn* (3 vols., Mainz, 1999).

24. Bohemia had been assigned since 950 to the bishopric of Regensburg. For Otto's creation of Magdeburg, see Althoff, *Die Ottonen*, pp.119–22, 128–33; M. Becher, *Otto der Große* (Munich, 2012), pp.197–203, 242–5, 252–3.

25. Thietmar of Merseburg, *Chronicon*, pp.140–42.

26. G. Althoff, *Otto III* (Philadelphia, 2003), pp.62–5, and his *Die Ottonen*, pp.179–89, 210–11.

27. R. W. Southern, *Western Society and the Church in the Middle Ages* (Harmondsworth, 1970), p.171; Costambeys et al., *Carolingian World*, p.172. Most archbishops oversaw four to six bishoprics, except the archbishop of Mainz, whose archdiocese contained 16 bishoprics by the eleventh century.

28. R. Morrissey, *Charlemagne and France* (Notre Dame, IN, 2003), p.305.

29. J. W. Bernhardt, *Itinerant Kingship and Royal Monasteries in Early Medieval Germany, c.936–1075* (Cambridge, 1993), pp.149–61.

30. H. Lorenz, *Werdegang von Stift und Stadt Quedlinburg* (Quedlinburg, 1922).

31. I. Wood, 'Entrusting western Europe to the church, 400–750', *TRHS*, 6th series, 23 (2013), 37–74.

32. S. MacLean (ed.), *History and Politics in Late Carolingian and Ottonian Europ: The Chronicle of Regino of Prüm and Adalbert of Magdeburg* (Manchester, 2009), p.5; W. Rösener, *The Peasantry of Europe* (Oxford, 1994), p.39; B. H. Hill Jr, *Medieval Monarchy in Action* (London, 1972), p.164.

33. J. Eldevik, *Episcopal Power and Ecclesiastical Reform in the German Empire: Tithes, Lordship and Community, 950–1150* (Cambridge, 2012).

34. Althoff, *Die Ottonen*, p.235.

35. M. Innes, *State and Society in the Early Middle Ages: The Middle Rhine Valley, 400–1000* (Cambridge, 2000), pp.18–30; H. J. Hummer, *Politics and Power in Early Medieval Europe: Alsace and the Frankish Realm, 600–1000* (Cambridge, 2005), pp.38–55.

36. F.-R. Erkens, 'Die Bistumsorganisation in den Diözesen Trier und Köln', in S. Weinfurter (ed.), *Die Salier und das Reich* (3 vols., Sigmaringen, 1991), II, pp.267–302; Innes, *State and Society*, p.43; Hummer, *Politics and Power*, pp.72–6. See generally S. Reynolds, *Kingdoms and Communities in Western Europe, 900–1300* (2nd ed., Oxford, 1997), pp.79–90.

37. P. Blickle, *Das Alte Europa. Vom Hochmittelalter bis zur Moderne* (Munich, 2008), p.92; B. Kümin, *The Communal Age in Western Europe, c.1100–1800* (Basingstoke, 2013), pp.51, 55.

38. R. Schieffer, 'Der ottonische Reichsepiskopat zwischen Königtum und Adel', *FMS*, 23 (1989), 291–301; L. Santifaller, *Zur Geschichte des ottonisch-salischen Reichskirchensystems* (2nd ed., Vienna, 1964).

39. T. Reuter, 'The "imperial church system" of the Ottonian and Salian rulers: A reconsideration', *Journal of Ecclesiastical History*, 33 (1982), 347–74.

40. O. Engels, 'Das Reich der Salier – Entwicklungslinien', in Weinfurter (ed.), *Die Salier und das Reich*, III, pp.479–541 at 516–33.

41. H. L. Mikoletzky, *Kaiser Heinrich II. und die Kirche* (Vienna, 1946), pp.41ff.

42. H. Zielinski, *Der Reichsepiskopat in spätottonischer und salischer Zeit (1002–1125)* (Stuttgart, 1984), esp. p.243. For the church under the Salians, see also Weinfurter (ed.), *Die Salier und das Reich*, II, and H. Wolfram, *Conrad II, 990–1039* (University Park, PA, 2006), pp.249–307. The *ministeriales* are discussed on pp.347–8.

43. For Meinward, see W. Leesch and P. Schubert, *Heimatchronik des Kreises Höxter* (Cologne, 1966), p.170. See also Althoff, *Die Ottonen*, pp.234–5; S. Weinfurter, *The Salian Century* (Philadelphia, 1999), p.57.

44. Weinfurter, *The Salian Century*, pp.63–7.

45. S. Weinfurter, 'Herrschaftslegitimation und Königsautorität im Wandel: Die Salier und ihr Dom zu Speyer', in Weinfurter (ed.), *Die Salier und das Reich*, I, pp.55–96.

46. G. Jenel, *Erzbischof Anno II. von Köln (1056–75) und sein politische Wirken* (2 vols., Stuttgart, 1974–5), I, pp.175–95; I. S. Robinson, *Henry IV of Germany, 1056–1106* (Cambridge, 1999), pp.43–4.

47. Jenel, *Erzbischof Anno*, II, pp.303–11.

48. B. Schütte, *König Konrad III. und der deutschen Reichsepiskopat* (Hamburg, 2004), p.102. For an example of the chapters' development, see L. G. Duggan, *Bishop and Chapter: The Governance of the Bishopric of Speyer to 1552* (New Brunswick, NJ, 1978), pp.11–83, and the discussion on pp.371–2. For France, see J. Bergin, *Crown, Church and Episcopate under Louis XIV* (New Haven, CT, 2004).

49. K. Zeumer (ed.), *Quellensammlung zur Geschichte der deutschen Reichsverfassung in Mittelalter und Neuzeit* (Tübingen, 1913), pp.42–4. See also pp.359–60.

50. U. Andermann, 'Die unsittlichen und disziplinlosen Kanonissen. Ein Topos und seine Hintergründe, aufgezeigt an Beispielen sächsischer Frauenstifte (11.–13. Jh.)', *WZ*, 146 (1996), 39–63. For the wider trends, see also pp.356–77.

51. M. Burleigh, *Germany Turns Eastwards: A Study of Ostforschung in the Third Reich* (Cambridge, 1988). For early colonization, see M. Rady, 'The German settlement in central and eastern Europe during the high Middle Ages', in R. Bartlett and K. Schönwälder (eds.), *The German Lands and Eastern Europe* (London, 1999), pp.11–47.

52. Bartlett, *Making of Europe*, pp.106–96.

53. K. Blaschke, *Bevölkerungsgeschichte von Sachsen bis zur industriellen Revolution* (Weimar, 1967), pp.65–6, 70, 77–8.

54. These connections are nicely illustrated in P. R. Magocsi, *Historical Atlas of Central Europe* (2nd ed., Seattle, 2002), pp.37–41. See also Bartlett, *Making of Europe*, pp.172–7.

55. Quoted in J. M. Piskorski, 'The medieval colonization of central Europe as a problem of world history and historiography', *GH*, 22 (2004), 323–43 at 340.

56. N. Davies, *God's Playground: A History of Poland* (2nd ed., 2 vols., Oxford, 2005), I, pp.64–5; Rösener, *The Peasantry*, pp.50–52.

57. Scales, *German Identity*, pp.402–5; Piskorski, 'Medieval colonization', p.338.

58. F. Kämpfer, 'Über den Anteil Osteuropas an der Geschichte des Mittelalters', in M. Borgolte (ed.), *Unaufhebbare Pluralität der Kulturen?* (Munich, 2001), p.58.

59. N. Jaspert, 'Religiöse Institutionen am Niederrhein zum Ende des Mittelalters', in M. Groten et al. (eds.), *Der Jülich-Klevische Erbstreit 1609* (Düsseldorf, 2011), pp.267–88 at 268–76; B. Demel, 'Der Deutsche Orden und seine Besitzungen im südwestdeutschen Sprachraum vom 13. bis 19. Jahrhundert', *ZWLG*, 31 (1972), 16–77. The Templars established a few houses in Saxony and parts of northern Italy. After their suppression in 1312, most of their German possessions were transferred to the Knights of St John.

60. J. Riley-Smith, *What Were the Crusades?* (3rd ed., Basingstoke, 2002); C. Tyerman, *God's War: A New History of the Crusades* (Cambridge, MA, 2006).

61. N. Morton, '*In subsidium*: The declining contribution of Germany and eastern Europe to the crusades to the Holy Land, 1221–91', *GHIL*, 33 (2011), 38–66 at 46. See generally E. Christiansen, *The Northern Crusades* (London, 1997).

62. I. Fonnesberg-Schmidt, *The Popes and the Baltic Crusades, 1147–1254* (Leiden, 2007); W. Urban, *The Teutonic Knights: A Military History* (London, 2003); and the contributions by E. Mugurevics, M. Starnawska, L. Pósán and K. Górski in A. V. Murray (ed.), *The North-Eastern Frontiers of Medieval Europe* (Farnham, 2014).

63. *NTSR*, VIII, pp.317–79.

64. R. Kieckhefer, *Repression of Heresy in Medieval Germany* (Liverpool, 1979), pp.83–96; P. Hilsch, 'Die Hussitenkriege als spätmittelalterlicher Ketzerkrieg', in F. Brendle and A. Schindling (eds.), *Religionskriege im Alten Reich und in Alteuropa* (Münster, 2006), pp.59–69; O. Odložilík, *The Hussite King: Bohemia in European Affairs, 1440–1471* (New Brunswick, NJ, 1965). For Utraquism, see Z. V. David, *Finding the Middle Way: The Utraquists' Liberal Challenge to Rome and Luther* (Washington DC, 2003).

65. A. Haverkamp, *Medieval Germany, 1056–1273* (Oxford, 1988), p.212.

66. E. J. Goldberg, *Struggle for Empire: Kingship and Conflict under Louis the German, 817–876* (Ithaca, NY, 2006), p.36.

67. T. Reuter, *Germany in the Early Middle Ages, c.800–1056* (Harlow, 1991), p.235.

68. I. Heidrich, 'Bischöfe und Bischofskirche von Speyer', in Weinfurter (ed.), *Die Salier und das Reich*, II, pp.187–224 at 205–6; Haverkamp, *Medieval Germany*, pp.213–15.

69. Quoted in R. Chazan, 'Emperor Frederick I, the Third Crusade and the Jews', *Viator*, 8 (1977), 83–93 at 89.

70. A. Sommerlechner, 'Das Judenmassaker von Fulda 1235 in der Geschichtsschreibung um Kaiser Friedrich II.', *Römische Historische Mitteilungen*, 44 (2002), 121–50; A. Patschovsky, 'The relationship between the Jews of Germany and the king (11th–14th centuries)', in A. Haverkamp and H. Vollrath (eds.), *England and Germany in the High Middle Ages* (Oxford, 1996), pp.193–218 at 201–3.

71. D. P. Bell, *Jewish Identity in Early Modern Germany* (Aldershot, 2007), p.57; Haverkamp, *Medieval Germany*, p.343.

72. F. Seibt, *Karl IV. Ein Kaiser in Europa 1346 bis 1378* (Munich, 1978), pp.192–200; J. K. Hoensch, *Die Luxemburger* (Stuttgart, 2000), pp.132–4.

73. For example in Austria: A. Niederstätter, *Österreichische Geschichte, 1400–1522* (Vienna, 1996), pp.103–4.

74. Bell, *Jewish Identity*, p.58.

75. G. Hödl, *Albrecht II. Königtum, Reichsregierung und Reichsreform, 1438–1439* (Vienna, 1978), pp.82–99.

76. Niederstätter, *Österreichische Geschichte*, pp.105–7.

77. R. J. W. Evans, *Rudolf II and his World* (2nd ed., London, 1997), pp.236–42.

78. *NTSR*, V, part I, 223–9; S. Ehrenpreis et al., 'Probing the legal history of the Jews in the Holy Roman Empire', *Jahrbuch des Simon-Dubnow-Instituts*, 2 (2003), 409–87; H. J. Cohn, 'Jewish self-governing assemblies in early modern central Europe', in M. H. de Cruz Coelho and M. M. Tavares Ribeiro (eds.), *Parlamentos. A lei, a prática e as representações* (Lisbon, 2010), pp.88–95.

79. B. A. Tlusty, *The Martial Ethic in Early Modern Germany* (Basingstoke, 2011), pp.175–85; S. Westphal, 'Der Umgang mit kultureller Differenz am Beispiel von Haftbedingungen für Juden in der Frühen Neuzeit', in A. Gotzmann and S. Wendehorst (eds.), *Juden im Recht. Neue Zugänge zur Rechtsgeschichte der Juden im Alten Reich* (Berlin, 2007), pp.139–61.

80. R. P. Hsia, 'The Jews and the emperors', in C. W. Ingrao (ed.), *State and Society in Early Modern Austria* (West Lafayette, IN, 1994), pp.71–80 at 76–7. For the new supreme courts, see pp.625–32.

81. The new supreme courts appear to have largely avoided the discriminatory practices that characterized the legal process at the level of individual cities where many Jews lived: M. R. Boes, 'Jews in the criminal-justice system of early modern Germany', *Journal of Interdisciplinary History*, 30 (1999), 407–35.

82. C. R. Friedrichs, 'Politics or pogrom? The Fettmilch uprising in German and Jewish history', *CEH*, 19 (1986), 186–228, and his 'Anti-Jewish politics in early modern Germany: The uprising in Worms, 1613–17', *CEH*, 23 (1990), 91–152.

83. Ehrenpreis et al., 'Probing the legal history', p.479 n.15; T. Schenk, 'Reichsgeschichte als Landesgeschichte. Eine Einführung in die Akten des kaiserlichen Reichshofrats', *Westfalen*, 90 (2012), 107–61, at 126–7.

84. J. I. Israel, 'Central European Jewry during the Thirty Years' War', *CEH*, 16 (1983), 3–30; J. P. Spielman, *The City and the Crown: Vienna and the Imperial Court, 1600–1740* (West Lafayette, IN, 1993), pp.123–35; A. Rutz, 'Territoriale Integration durch Bildung und Erziehung?', in Groten et al. (eds.), *Der Jülich-Klevische Erbstreit*, pp.337–57 at 344.

85. K. Müller, 'Das "Reichscamerale" im 18. Jahrhundert', *Wiener Beiträge zur Geschichte der Neuzeit*, 20 (1993), 152–77; W. Kohl (ed.), *Westfälische Geschichte* (3 vols., Düsseldorf, 1983–4), I, pp.655–7.

86. P. C. Hartmann, 'Bevölkerungszahlen und Konfessionsverhältnisse des Heiligen Römischen Reiches deutscher Nation und der Reichskreise am Ende des 18. Jahrhunderts', *ZHF*, 22 (1995), 345–69.

87. K. A. Roider Jr, *Austria's Eastern Question, 1700–1790* (Princeton, 1982), pp.95–9.

88. J. H. Schoeps, ' "Ein jeder soll vor alle und alle vor ein stehn". Die Judenpolitik in Preußen in der Regierungszeit König Friedrich Wilhelms I.', in F. Beck and J. Schoeps (eds.), *Der Soldatenkönig* (Potsdam, 2003), pp.141–60; T. Schenk, 'Friedrich und die Juden', in *Friederisiko* (2 vols., Stiftung Preussische Schlöer und Gärten, 2012), I, pp.160–74.

89. P. H. Wilson, 'Der Favorit als Sündenbock. Joseph Süß Oppenheimer (1698–1738)', in M. Kaiser and A. Pečar (eds.), *Der zweite Mann im Staat* (Berlin, 2003), pp.155–76. Oppenheimer became the subject of several later novels and films as 'Jew Süß'.

90. Friedrichs, 'Anti-Jewish politics', 151.

91. G. Schmidt-von Rhein and A. Cordes (eds.), *Altes Reich und neues Recht* (Wetzlar, 2006), pp.267–72.

92. Good introductions to this substantial topic include L. P. Wandel, *The Reformation* (Cambridge, 2011); D. MacCulloch, *Reformation: Europe's House Divided, 1490–1700* (London, 2003).

93. B. Stollberg-Rilinger, *Des Kaisers alte Kleider. Verfassungsgeschichte und Symbolsprache des Alten Reiches* (Munich, 2008), pp.99–135.

94. R. R. Benert, 'Lutheran resistance theory and the imperial constitution', *Il pensiero politico*, 6 (1973), 17–36; R. von Friedeburg, *Self-Defence and Religious Strife in Early Modern Europe: England and Germany, 1530–1680* (Aldershot, 2002); A. Strohmeyer, *Konfessionskonflikt und Herrschaftsordnung. Widerstandsrecht bei den österreichischen Ständen (1550–1650)* (Mainz, 2006).

95. J. Whaley, *Germany and the Holy Roman Empire, 1493–1806* (2 vols., Oxford, 2012), I, pp.168–82, provides an excellent summary of the events.

96. The leading example was Leopold von Ranke, *Deutsche Geschichte im Zeitalter der Reformation* (Vienna, 1934), esp. pp.305–20. Echoes of this approach are still voiced today, e.g. T. A. Brady Jr, *German Histories in the Age of Reformations, 1400–1650* (Cambridge, 2009).

97. H. Duchhardt, *Protestantisches Kaisertum und Altes Reich* (Wiesbaden, 1977), pp.8–51.

98. H. Lutz, 'Friedensideen und Friedensprobleme in der Frühen Neuzeit', in G. Heiss and H. Lutz (eds.), *Friedensbewegungen, Bedingungen und Wirkungen* (Munich, 1984), pp.28–54.

99. U. Andermann, 'Säkularisation von der Säkularisation', in his (ed.), *Die geistlichen Staaten am Ende des Alten Reiches* (Epfendorf, 2004), 13–30 at 15–21. See p.194 for the suppression of bishoprics.

100. C. Ocker, *Church Robbers and Reformers in Germany, 1525–1547* (Leiden, 2006); H. Kellenbenz and P. Prodi (eds.), *Fiskus, Kirche und Staat im konfessionellen Zeitalter* (Berlin, 1994).

101. E.g. between Mainz, Hessen and Saxony: A. Schindling and W. Ziegler (eds.), *Die Territorien des Reichs im Zeitalter der Reformation und die Konfessionalisierung* (7 vols., Münster, 1989–97), IV, pp.75–6. This work provides the most comprehensive account of the Reformation outcomes in the Empire's German territories.

102. M. Heckel, 'Die Religionsprozesse des Reichskammergerichts im konfessionell gespaltenen Reichskirchenrecht', *ZSRG KA*, 77 (1991), 283–350; G. Dolezalek, 'Die juristische Argumentation der Assessoren am Reichskammergericht zu den Reformationsprozessen 1532–1538', in B. Diestelkamp (ed.), *Das Reichskammergericht in der deutschen Geschichte* (Cologne, 1990), pp.25–58.

103. Schindling and Ziegler (eds.), *Die Territorien des Reichs*, I, pp.59–61.

104. R. Bireley, *The Refashioning of Catholicism, 1450–1700* (Basingstoke, 1999); M. R. Forster, *Catholic Germany from the Reformation to the Enlightenment* (Basingstoke, 2007), pp.1–37.

105. Quotation from Whaley, *Germany*, I, p.323. See also L. Schorn-Schütte (ed.), *Das Interim 1548/50* (Heidelberg, 2005). On Charles's other measures at this point, see pp.228–9, 436–9.

106. N. Rein, *The Chancery of God: Protestant Print, Polemic and Propaganda against the Empire, Magdeburg 1546–1551* (Aldershot, 2008); K. Schäfer, *Der Fürstenaufstand gegen Karl V. im Jahr 1552* (Taunusstein, 2009); M. Fuchs and R. Rebitsch (eds.), *Kaiser und Kurfürst. Aspekte des Fürstenaufstandes 1552* (Münster, 2010).

107. A. Kohler, *Ferdinand I, 1503–1564* (Munich, 2003), pp.225–51; E. Wolgast, 'Religionsfrieden als politisches Problem der frühen Neuzeit', *HZ*, 282 (2006), 59–96.

108. The most substantial of the many works on the Peace is A. Gotthard, *Der Augsburger Religionsfrieden* (Münster, 2004), which in some respects returns to older, more pessimistic interpretations. A more positive corrective is provided by M. Heckel, 'Politischer Friede und geistliche Freiheit im Ringen um die Wahrheit. Zur Historiographie des Augsburger Religionsfriedens von 1555', *HZ*, 282 (2006), 391–425. For the deliberate ambiguities and dissimulation in the text, see M. Heckel, 'Autonomia und Pacis Compositio', *ZSRG KA*, 45 (1959), 141–248.

109. K. Schlaich, 'Maioritas – protestatio – itio in partes – corpus Evangelicorum', *ZSRG KA*, 63 (1977), 264–99 at 288–9.

110. Wolgast, 'Religionsfrieden', pp.63–4. See also H. Louthan, *Converting Bohemia: Force and Persuasion in the Catholic Reformation* (Cambridge, 2009), and pp.28–9.

111. G. R. Potter, *Zwingli* (Cambridge, 1976); M. Taplin, 'Switzerland', in A. Pettegree (ed.), *The Reformation World* (London, 2000), pp.169–89. The emergence of the Swiss Confederation is covered on pp.585–91.

112. B. Gordon, 'Italy', in Pettegree (ed.), *Reformation World*, pp.277–95; M. Firpo, 'The Italian Reformation', in R. Po-chia Hsia (ed.), *A Companion to the Reformation World* (Oxford, 2004), pp.169–84.

113. E. Cameron, *The Reformation of the Heretics: The Waldenses of the Alps, 1480–1580* (Oxford, 1984), pp.163–6.

114. W. Reinhard, 'Pressures towards confessionalization? Prolegomena to a theory of the confessional age', in C. Scott Dixon (ed.), *The German Reformation* (Oxford, 1999), pp.169–92. Detailed coverage in Schindling and Ziegler (eds.), *Die Territorien des Reichs*.

115. The literature on these topics is now extensive. For a summary see S. R. Boettcher, 'Confessionalization: Reformation, religion, absolutism and modernity', *History Compass*, 2 (2004), 1–10. Good case studies include M. R. Forster, *Catholic Revival in the Age of the Baroque: Religious Identity in Southwest Germany, 1550–1750* (Cambridge, 2001); W. B. Smith, *Reformation and the German Territorial State: Upper Franconia, 1300–1630* (Rochester, NY, 2008).

116. H. T. Gräf, *Konfession und internationales System. Die Außenpolitik Hessen-Kassels im konfessionellen Zeitalter* (Darmstadt, 1993), pp.108–11. This period of imperial politics is covered in more detail by A. P. Luttenberger, *Kurfürsten, Kaiser und Reich. Politische Führung und Friedenssicherung unter Ferdinand I. und Maximilian II.* (Mainz, 1994); Whaley, *Germany*, I, pp.339–474.

117. J. Engelbrecht, 'Staat, Recht und Konfession. Krieg und Frieden im Rechtsdenken des Reiches', in H. Lademacher and S. Groenveld (eds.), *Krieg und Kultur* (Münster, 1998), pp.113–28; A. Schmidt, 'Irenic patriotism in sixteenth- and seventeenth-century German political discourse', *HJ*, 53 (2010), 243–69.

118. G. Murdock, *Beyond Calvin: The Intellectual, Political and Cultural World of Europe's Reformed Churches* (Basingstoke, 2004).

119. O. Chadwick, 'The making of a reforming prince: Frederick III, elector Palatine', in R. B. Knox (ed.), *Reformation Conformity and Dissent* (London, 1977), pp.44–69; B. Nischan, *Prince, People and Confession: The Second Reformation in Brandenburg* (Philadelphia, 1994). Emden's exceptional character owed much to the presence of Dutch exiles: A. Pettegree, *Emden and the Dutch Revolt* (Oxford, 1992).

120. T. Sarx, 'Heidelberger Irenik am Vorabend des Dreißigjährigen Krieges', in A. Ernst and A. Schindling (eds.), *Union und Liga, 1608/09* (Stuttgart, 2010), pp.167–96; V. Press, *Calvinismus und Territorialstaat* (Stuttgart, 1970).

121. Palatine-Bavarian rivalry is neglected in many general accounts of this period. Further coverage in A. L. Thomas, *A House Divided: Wittelsbach*

Confessional Court Cultures in the Holy Roman Empire, c.1550–1650 (Leiden, 2010).

122. The issues are summarized effectively by M. Heckel, 'Die Krise der Religionsverfassung des Reiches und die Anfänge des Dreißigjährigen Krieges', in K. Repgen (ed.), *Krieg und Politik, 1618–1648* (Munich, 1988), pp. 107–31. See also P. H. Wilson, 'The Thirty Years War as the Empire's constitutional crisis', in R. J. W. Evans et al. (eds.), *The Holy Roman Empire, 1495–1806* (Oxford, 2011), pp.95–114.

123. R. Pörtner, *The Counter-Reformation in Central Europe: Styria 1580–1630* (Oxford, 2001); H. Louthan, *The Quest for Compromise: Peacemakers in Counter-Reformation Vienna* (Cambridge, 1997); J. F. Patrouch, *A Negotiated Settlement: The Counter-Reformation in Upper Austria under the Habsburgs* (Boston, 2000); K. J. MacHardy, *War, Religion and Court Patronage in Habsburg Austria: The Social and Cultural Dimensions of Political Interaction, 1521–1622* (Basingstoke, 2003).

124. For the debate on this point see P. H. Wilson, 'The causes of the Thirty Years war, 1618–48', *EHR*, 123 (2008), 554–86; W. Schulze (ed.), *Friedliche Intentionen – Kriegerische Effekte. War der Ausbruch des Dreißigjährigen Krieges unvermeidlich?* (St Katharinen, 2002). For the following see P. H. Wilson, *Europe's Tragedy: A History of the Thirty Years War* (London, 2009); O. Asbach and P. Schröder (eds.), *The Ashgate Research Companion to the Thirty Years' War* (Farnham, 2014). The Union and the League are discussed further on pp.564–5.

125. J. Polišenský, *Tragic Triangle: The Netherlands, Spain and Bohemia, 1617–1621* (Prague, 1991). For an account by one of the Defenestrators' victims, see P. H. Wilson (ed.), *The Thirty Years War: A Sourcebook* (Basingstoke, 2010), pp.35–7. All three survived their fall.

126. P. H. Wilson, 'Dynasty, constitution and confession: The role of religion in the Thirty Years War', *International History Review*, 30 (2008), 473–514; H. Schilling (ed.), *Konfessioneller Fundamentalismus* (Munich, 2007); F. Brendle and A. Schindling (eds.), *Religionskriege im Alten Reich und in Alteuropa* (Münster, 2006). See also the informative case study by H. Berg, *Military Occupation under the Eyes of the Lord: Studies in Erfurt during the Thirty Years War* (Göttingen, 2010).

127. Further elaboration of these points in P. H. Wilson, 'Meaningless conflict? The character of the Thirty Years War', in F. C. Schneid (ed.), *The Projection and Limitations of Imperial Powers, 1618–1850* (Leiden, 2012), pp.12–33, and 'Was the Thirty Years War a "total war"?', in E. Charters et al. (eds.), *Civilians and War in Europe, 1618–1815* (Liverpool, 2012), pp.21–35.

128. R. Bireley, *Ferdinand II, Counter-Reformation Emperor, 1578–1637* (Cambridge, 2014), esp. pp.91–166; T. Brockmann, *Dynastie, Kaiseramt und Konfession. Politik und Ordnungsvorstellungen Ferdinands II. im*

Dreißigjährigen Krieg (Paderborn, 2011); D. Albrecht, *Maximilian I. von Bayern 1573–1651* (Munich, 1998); P. D. Lockhart, *Denmark in the Thirty Years, War, 1618–1648* (Selinsgrove, 1996).

129. H. Urban, *Das Restitutionsedikt* (Munich, 1968); M. Frisch, *Das Restitutionsedikt Kaiser Ferdinands II. vom 6. März 1629* (Tübingen, 1993). See also pp.457–8.

130. I. Schuberth, *Lützen – på spaning efter ett minne* (Stockholm, 2007); M. Reichel and I. Schuberth (eds.), *Gustav Adolf* (Dößel, 2007); K. Cramer, *The Thirty Years' War and German Memory in the Nineteenth Century* (Lincoln, NB, 2007). For the presentation of Sweden's motives during the war, see E. Ringmar, *Identity, Interest and Action: A Cultural Explanation of Sweden's Intervention in the Thirty Years War* (Cambridge, 1996).

131. J. Öhman, *Der Kampf um den Frieden. Schweden und der Kaiser im Dreißigjährigen Krieg* (Vienna, 2005). For the following see also D. Croxton, *Peacemaking in Early Modern Europe: Cardinal Mazarin and the Congress of Westphalia, 1643–1648* (Selinsgrove, 1999), and his *Westphalia: The Last Christian Peace* (New York, 2013).

132. The full texts of both are available in various translations at www.pax-westphalica.de/ipmipo/index.html. The territorial redistribution is discussed on pp.220–29, while pp.441–3 cover the impact on the imperial constitution in greater depth.

133. R.-P. Fuchs, *Ein 'Medium zum Frieden'. Die Normaljahrsregel und die Beendigung des Dreißigjährigen Krieges* (Munich, 2010).

134. Schlaich, 'Majoritas'.

135. J. Luh, *Unheiliges Römisches Reich. Der konfessionelle Gegensatz 1648 bis 1806* (Potsdam, 1995), pp.17–43. For the debate on the place of religion in politics after 1648, see D. Stievermann, 'Politik und Konfession im 18. Jahrhundert', *ZHF*, 18 (1991), 177–99.

136. Whaley, *Germany*, II, p.63.

137. M. Fulbrook, *Piety and Politics* (Cambridge, 1983); R. L. Gawthrop, *Pietism and the Making of Eighteenth-Century Prussia* (Cambridge, 1993).

138. E.-O. Mader, 'Fürstenkonversionen zum Katholizismus in Mitteleuropa im 17. Jahrhundert', *ZHF*, 34 (2007), 403–440; I. Peper, *Konversionen im Umkreis des Wiener Hofes um 1700* (Vienna, 2010).

139. For a detailed example, see G. Haug-Moritz, *Württembergischer Ständekonflikt und deutscher Dualismus* (Stuttgart, 1992).

140. G. Haug-Moritz, 'Corpus Evangelicorum und deutscher Dualismus', in V. Press (ed.), *Alternativen zur Reichsverfassung in der Frühen Neuzeit?* (Munich, 1995), pp.189–207; P. H. Wilson, 'Prussia and the Holy Roman Empire, 1700–40', *GHIL*, 36 (2014), 3–48.

141. This is claimed for Augsburg: E. François, *Die unsichtbare Grenze. Protestanten und Katholiken in Augsburg, 1648–1806* (Sigmaringen, 1991).

The other three bi-confessional cities were Biberach, Dinkelsbühl and Ravensburg. See also J. Whaley, 'A tolerant society? Religious toleration in the Holy Roman Empire, 1648–1806', in O. P. Grell and R. Porter (eds.), *Toleration in Enlightenment Europe* (Cambridge, 2000), pp.175–95.

142. The changes are listed in more detail in H. Neuhaus, *Das Reich in der Frühen Neuzeit* (Munich, 1997), pp.30–31. See also W. Ziegler, 'Die Hochstifte des Reiches im konfessionellen Zeitalter 1520–1618', *Römische Quartalschrift*, 87 (1992), 252–81. Only seven imperial abbeys disappeared through direct secularization during the Reformation. Six left the Empire through incorporation within the Swiss Confederation. See also pp.409–14.

143. The last to do this was Isny in 1782.

144. H. Brück, *Geschichte der katholische Kirche in Deutschland im neunzehnten Jahrhundert* (4 vols., Mainz, 1887–1901), I, p.3.

145. S. Schraut, *Das Haus Schönborn. Eine Familienbiographie. Katholischer Reichsadel, 1640–1840* (Paderborn, 2005).

146. L. G. Duggan, 'The church as an institution of the Reich', in J. A. Vann and S. Rowan (eds.), *The Old Reich* (Brussels, 1974), pp.149–64 at 154–5. The proportion of commoners in the medieval church was probably higher, since the social background of 421 bishops is unknown. See also B. Blisch, 'Kurfürsten und Domherren', in F. Dumont et al. (eds.), *Mainz. Die Geschichte der Stadt* (Mainz, 1998), pp.879–97; G. Christ, 'Selbstverständnis und Rolle der Domkapitel in den geistlichen Territorien des alten deutschen Reiches in der Frühneuzeit', *ZHF*, 16 (1989), 257–328.

147. E. Gatz (ed.), *Die Bischöfe des Heiligen Römischen Reiches 1448 bis 1648* (Berlin, 1996), pp.163–71; G. Bönisch, *Clemens August* (Bergisch Gladbach, 2000).

148. E.g. K. Epstein, *The Genesis of German Conservatism* (Princeton, 1966), pp.276–85, 605–15.

149. T. C. W. Blanning, *Reform and Revolution in Mainz, 1743–1803* (Cambridge, 1974); P. H. Wilson, *German Armies: War and German Politics, 1648–1806* (London, 1998); J. Nowosadtko, *Stehendes Heer im Ständestaat. Das Zusammenleben von Militär- und Zivilbevölkerung im Fürstbistum Münster 1650–1803* (Paderborn, 2011).

150. D. Beales, *Prosperity and Plunder: European Catholic Monasteries in the Age of Revolution, 1650–1815* (Cambridge, 2003); M. Printy, *Enlightenment and the Creation of German Catholicism* (Cambridge, 2009).

151. Febronism's place in imperial politics is discussed in more detail by K. O. Frhr. v. Aretin, *Das Alte Reich, 1648–1806* (4 vols., Stuttgart, 1993–2000), III, pp.237–97. For the League of Princes see also pp.482, 640–42.

152. E.g. Dalberg held a mass to celebrate Napoleon's victories over Prussia at Jena and Auerstädt in 1806. For this and the following see K. Hausberger (ed.), *Carl von Dalberg* (Regensburg, 1995); K. M. Färber, *Kaiser und Erzkanzler. Carl von Dalberg und Napoleon am Ende des Alten Reiches* (Regensburg,

1988); G. Menzel, 'Franz Joseph von Albini, 1748–1816', *Mainzer Zeitschrift*, 69 (1974), 1–126; R. Decot (ed.), *Säkularisation der Reichskirche, 1803* (Mainz, 2002); K. Härter, 'Zweihundert Jahre nach dem europäischen Umbruch von 1803', *ZHF*, 33 (2006), 89–115. See also pp.641–54, and the coverage of the Confederation of the Rhine on pp.660–63.

153. W. H. B. Smith, *Mauser Rifles and Pistols* (Harrisburg, PA, 1947), pp.12–13.

154. Detailed example in E. Klueting, ' "Damenstifter sind zufluchtsörter, wo sich Fräuleins von adel schicklich aufhalten können". Zur Säkularisation von Frauengemeinschaften in Westfalen und im Rheinland 1773–1812', in T. Schilp (ed.), *Reform – Reformation – Säkularisation. Frauenstifte in Krisenzeiten* (Essen, 2004), pp.177–200.

155. Aretin, *Alte Reich*, III, pp.518–21.

CHAPTER 3: SOVEREIGNTY

1. J. D. Tracy, *Emperor Charles V, Impresario of War: Campaign Strategy, International Finance, and Domestic Politics* (Cambridge, 2002), pp. 239–40. For the following see also J. M. Headley, 'The Habsburg world empire and the revival of Ghibellinism', *Medieval and Renaissance Studies*, 7 (1978), 93–127 esp. 116; E. Rosenthal, '*Plus ultra, non plus ultra*, and the columnar device of Emperor Charles V', *Journal of the Warburg and Courtauld Institutes*, 34 (1971), 204–28.

2. G. Dagron, *Emperor and Priest: The Imperial Office in Byzantium* (Cambridge, 2003); F. Dvornik, *Early Christian and Byzantine Political Philosophy* (2 vols., Washington DC, 1966); D. M. Nicol, 'Byzantine political thought', in J. H. Burns (ed.), *The Cambridge History of Medieval Political Thought c.350–c.1450* (Cambridge, 1988), pp.51–79.

3. E. N. Luttwak, *The Grand Strategy of the Byzantine Empire* (Cambridge, MA, 2009).

4. The theological differences are summarized in R. Collins, *Early Medieval Europe, 300–1000* (Basingstoke, 1991), pp.266–8; R. W. Southern, *Western Society and the Church in the Middle Ages* (Harmondsworth, 1970), pp.62–5.

5. Ottonian engagement with Poland and Hungary is explored in more depth on pp.204–7. For the following see C. A. Frazee, 'The Christian church in Cilician Armenia: Its relations with Rome and Constantinople to 1198', *Church History*, 45 (1976), 166–84; David R. Stokes, 'A failed alliance and expanding horizons: Relations between the Austrian Habsburgs and the Safavid Persians in the sixteenth and seventeenth centuries' (University of St Andrews PhD thesis, 2014), 156–61.

6. K. Müller, 'Kurfürst Johann Wilhelm und die europäische Politik seiner Zeit', *Düsseldorfer Jahrbuch*, 60 (1986), 1–23 at 13–14.

7. W. Ohnsorge, *Das Zweikaiserproblem im früheren Mittelalter* (Hildesheim, 1947). For imperial-Byzantine conflicts in Italy, see pp.187–92.

8. L. H. Nelson and M. V. Shirk (eds.), *Liutprand of Cremona: Mission to Constantinople (968 AD)* (Lawrence, KS, 1972); G. Koch, *Auf dem Wege zum Sacrum Imperium* (Vienna, 1972), pp.218–30; A. A. Latowsky, *Emperor of the World: Charlemagne and the Construction of Imperial Authority, 800–1229* (Ithaca, NY, 2013), pp.44–51.

9. M. Becher, *Otto der Große* (Munich, 2012), pp.245–51; S. Weinfurter, *The Salian Century* (Philadelphia, 1999), pp.28–9. For tenth-century imperial-Byzantine contacts generally, see K. Leyser, *Medieval Germany and its Neighbours, 900–1250* (London, 1982), pp.103–37. On Theophanu see also pp.315–16.

10. P. Frankopan, *The First Crusade: The Call from the East* (Cambridge, MA, 2012).

11. W. Treadgold, *A Concise History of Byzantium* (Basingstoke, 2001), pp. 215–16, 236.

12. M. Angold, *The Fall of Constantinople to the Ottomans* (New York, 2012).

13. Koch, *Auf dem Wege*, pp.227–9.

14. A. Cameron, *The Byzantines* (Oxford, 2010), pp.163–6; P. Burke, 'Did Europe exist before 1700?', *History of European Ideas*, 1 (1980), 21–9; J. Hale, *The Civilisation of Europe in the Renaissance* (London, 1993), pp. 3–50; L. Wolff, *Inventing Eastern Europe: The Map of Civilization in the Mind of the Enlightenment* (Stanford, 1994), and the contributions of J. G. A. Pocock and W. C. Jordan in A. Pagden (ed.), *The Idea of Europe from Antiquity to the European Union* (Cambridge, 2002).

15. A. Çirakman, *From the 'Terror of the World' to the 'Sick Man of Europe': European Images of Ottoman Empire and Society from the Sixteenth Century to the Nineteenth* (New York, 2002); A. Höfert, *Den Feind beschreiben: 'Türkengefahr' und europäisches Wissen über das Osmanische Reich, 1450–1600* (Frankfurt, 2003); S. Faroqhi, *The Ottoman Empire and the World around It* (London, 2007); M. Wrede, *Das Reich und seine Feinde. Politische Feindbilder in der Reichspatriotischen Publizistik zwischen Westfälischem Frieden und Siebenjährigem Krieg* (Mainz, 2004), pp.66–216; P. Sutter Fichtner, *Terror and Toleration: The Habsburg Empire Confronts Islam, 1526–1850* (London, 2008), pp.21–53.

16. S. F. Dale, *The Muslim Empires of the Ottomans, Safavids and Mughals* (Cambridge, 2010).

17. C. Finkel, *Osman's Dream: The Story of the Ottoman Empire, 1300–1923* (London, 2005).

18. K. Barkey, *Empire of Difference: The Ottomans in Comparative Perspective* (Cambridge, 2008), pp.101–8; I. Almond, *Two Faiths One Banner:*

When Muslims Marched with Christians across Europe's Battlegrounds (Cambridge, MA, 2009), pp.134–6.

19. J. Darwin, *After Tamerlane: The Global History of Empire since 1405* (New York, 2008), pp.37–8; J. Burbank and F. Cooper, *Empires in World History* (Princeton, 2010), pp.70–78.

20. G. Althoff, *Die Ottonen* (2nd ed., Stuttgart, 2005), pp.111–12.

21. C. Kostick, 'Social unrest and the failure of Conrad III's march through Anatolia, 1147', *GH*, 28 (2010), 125–42; G. A. Loud (ed.), *The Crusade of Frederick Barbarossa: The History of the Expedition of the Emperor Frederick and Related Texts* (Farnham, 2013), pp.48–55. See also the sources cited on p.775.

22. W. Stürner, *Friedrich II.* (2 vols., Darmstadt, 2009), II, pp.68–74, 85–98, 130–69; Almond, *Two Faiths*, pp.49–74.

23. L. Scales, *The Shaping of German Identity: Authority and Crisis, 1245–1414* (Cambridge, 2012), pp.221–4.

24. G. Hödl, *Albrecht II. Königtum, Reichsregierung und Reichsreform, 1438–1439* (Vienna, 1978), p.195.

25. J. H. Elliott, *Imperial Spain, 1469–1716* (London, 1963), pp.45–76. Poland had its own tradition as 'Christendom's bulwark': see N. Davies, *God's Playground: A History of Poland* (2nd ed., 2 vols., Oxford, 2005), I, pp.125–30.

26. S. Vryonis Jr, 'The Byzantine legacy and Ottoman forms', *Dumbarton Oaks Papers*, 23/24 (1969/70), 251–308.

27. M. S. Birdal, *The Holy Roman Empire and the Ottomans: From Global Imperial Power to Absolutist States* (London, 2011), pp.59–85 esp. p.84. For the rule of law in the Empire, see pp.631–7.

28. Finkel, *Osman's Dream*, pp.48, 53–4; Barkey, *Empire of Difference*, pp.82–3.

29. M. F. Alvarez, *Charles V* (London, 1975), pp.82–8. For the following see G. Necipoğlu, 'Süleyman the Magnificent and the representation of power in the context of Ottoman-Hapsburg-papal rivalry', *The Art Bulletin*, 71 (1989), 401–27.

30. J. Reston Jr, *Defenders of the Faith: Charles V, Suleyman the Magnificent and the Battle for Europe, 1520–1536* (London, 2009); Tracy, *Emperor Charles V*, pp.141–9, 154–9, 170–82.

31. P. S. Fichtner, *Emperor Maximilian II* (New Haven, CT, 2001), pp.119–34; J. P. Niederkorn, *Die europäischen Mächte und der 'Lange Türkenkrieg' Kaiser Rudolfs II. (1593–1606)* (Vienna, 1993).

32. J. F. Pichler, 'Captain John Smith in the light of Styrian sources', *The Virginia Magazine of History and Biography*, 65 (1957), 332–54.

33. Stokes, 'A failed alliance and expanding horizons'; J. P. Niederkorn, 'Zweifrontenkrieg gegen die Osmanen. Iranisch-christliche Bündnispläne in der Zeit des "Langen Türkenkrieges", 1593–1606', *MIÖG*, 104 (1996), 310–23.

34. Quoted in K.-H. Ziegler, 'The peace treaties of the Ottoman empire with European Christian powers', in R. C. H. Lesaffer (ed.), *Peace Treaties and International Law in European History* (Cambridge, 2004), pp.338–64 at 345. For the following see also G. Wagner, 'Österreich und die Osmanen im Dreißigjährigen Krieg', *Mitteilungen des Oberösterreichischen Landesarchivs*, 14 (1984), 325–92; I. Hiller, 'Feind im Frieden. Die Rolle des Osmanischen Reiches in der europäischen Politik zur Zeit des Westfälischen Friedens', in H. Duchhardt (ed.), *Der Westfälische Friede* (Munich, 1998), pp.393–404; R. R. Heinisch, 'Habsburg, die Pforte und der Böhmische Aufstand (1618–1620)', *Südost-Forschungen*, 33 (1974), 125–65, and 34 (1975), 79–124.

35. E. Eickhoff, *Venedig, Wien und die Osmanen. Umbruch in Südosteuropa, 1645–1700* (Munich, 1970), pp.179–227. See also pp.443–62.

36. E. Petrasch et al. (eds.), *Die Karlsruher Türkenbeute* (Munich, 1991). For the siege and relief, see J. Stoye, *The Siege of Vienna* (London, 1964); P. H. Wilson, *German Armies: War and German Politics, 1648–1806* (London, 1998), pp.68–100.

37. Fichtner, *Terror and Toleration*, pp.61–76; K. A. Roider Jr, *Austria's Eastern Question, 1700–1790* (Princeton, 1982), pp.77–8.

38. M. Cherniavsky, *Tsar and People: Studies in Russian Myths* (New Haven, CT, 1961), pp.6–43; S. Franklin and J. Shepard, *The Emergence of Rus, 750–1200* (London, 1996).

39. I. de Madariaga, 'Tsar into emperor: The title of Peter the Great', in R. Oresko et al. (eds.), *Royal and Republican Sovereignty in Early Modern Europe* (Cambridge, 1997), pp.351–81.

40. L. Hughes, *Russia in the Age of Peter the Great* (New Haven, CT, 1998), p.352; W. Baumgart, *The Crimean War, 1853–1856* (London, 1999), pp.10–12. See generally H. Schraeder, *Moskau das dritte Rom. Studien zur Geschichte der politischen Theorien in der slawischen Welt* (Darmstadt, 1957).

41. It reappeared on the Russian president's flag in 1994. It is also used by the self-governing theocracy of Mount Athos, which persists under Greek protection. Further discussion of the double-eagle image on pp.270–72.

42. A. Knobler, 'Holy wars, empires and the portability of the past: The modern uses of medieval crusades', *Comparative Studies in Society and History*, 48 (2006), 293–325 at 302–3.

43. C. Roll, 'Hatten die Moskowiter einen Begriff vom Reich?', in M. Schnettger (ed.), *Imperium Romanum – irregulare corpus – Teutscher Reichs-Staat* (Mainz, 2002), pp.135–65.

44. For the wedding see R. K. Massie, *Peter the Great and his World* (London, 1981), pp.625–6. The dynastic ties are explored at length in C. Scharf, *Katharina II., Deutschland und die Deutschen* (Mainz, 1995), pp.272–346, which has excellent genealogical tables. For the context see

W. Mediger, *Mecklenburg, Rußland und England-Hannover, 1706–1721* (2 vols., Hildesheim, 1967).

45. Madariaga, 'Tsar into emperor', pp.358–9, 374–5; Hughes, *Russia*, p.97.
46. A. H. Benna, 'Das Kaisertum Österreich und die römische Liturgie', *MÖSA*, 9 (1956), 118–36 at 118–19.
47. K. O. Frhr. v. Aretin, *Das Reich. Friedensordnung und europäisches Gleichgewicht, 1648–1806* (Stuttgart, 1986), pp.337–52. Further coverage of late imperial politics on pp.469–82.
48. Fuller discussion in C. Brühl, *Deutschland – Frankreich. Die Geburt zweier Völker* (Cologne, 1990).
49. R. Morrissey, *Charlemagne and France* (Notre Dame, IN, 2003), pp.49–85; K. F. Werner, 'Das hochmittelalterliche Imperium im politischen Bewusstsein Frankreichs (10.–12. Jahrhundert)', *HZ*, 200 (1965), 1–60; H. Löwe, 'Kaisertum und Abendland in ottonischer und frühsalischer Zeit', *HZ*, 196 (1963), 529–62 at 544–8.
50. G. Duby, *The Legend of Bouvines* (Berkeley, 1990), p.136..
51. C. Jones, *Eclipse of Empire? Perceptions of the Western Empire and its Rulers in Late-Medieval France* (Turnhout, 2007), esp. pp.357–61.
52. G. Zeller, *Aspects de la politique française sous l'Ancien Régime* (Paris, 1964), pp.12–98; J.-M. Moeglin, 'Der Blick von Frankreich auf das mittelalterlichen Reich', in B. Schneidmüller and S. Weinfurter (eds.), *Heilig – Römisch – Deutsch. Das Reich im mittelalterlichen Europa* (Dresden, 2006), pp.251–65. Rigord's 'Deeds of Philip Augustus' can be found in H.-F. Delaborde (ed.), *Oeuvres de Rigord et de Guillaume le Breton* (2 vol., Paris, 1882–5), II. Thanks to Colin Veach for drawing my attention to this source.
53. This point is made by C. Jones, 'Understanding political conceptions in the later Middle Ages: The French imperial candidatures and the idea of the nation-state', *Viator*, 42 (2011), 83–114 at 113–14.
54. Morrissey, *Charlemagne and France*, pp.108–9; Zeller, *Aspects de la politique française*, pp.55–9. Henry VIII of England was also a candidate, but withdrew once he realized that election would prove expensive.
55. Zeller, *Aspects de la politique française*, pp.76–82.
56. M. Wrede, 'L'état de l'Empire empire? Die französische Historiographie und das Reich im Zeitalter Ludwigs XIV', in Schnettger (ed.), *Imperium Romanum*, pp.89–110; R. L. John, *Reich und Kirche im Spiegel französischen Denkens. Das Rombild von Caesar bis Napoleon* (Vienna, 1953), pp.156–208; Morrissey, *Charlemagne and France*, pp.152–9, 206–8; C. Kampmann, *Arbiter und Friedenstiftung. Die Auseinandersetzung um den politischen Schiedsrichter im Europa der Frühen Neuzeit* (Paderborn, 2001), pp.66–241.
57. P. C. Hartmann, *Geld als Instrument europäischer Machtpolitik im Zeitalter des Merkantilismus* (Munich, 1978). Further discussion of Charles VII on pp.477–8.

58. K. O. Frhr. v. Aretin, *Das Alte Reich, 1648–1806* (4 vols., Stuttgart, 1993–2000), III, pp.458–67.

59. G. Wagner, 'Pläne und Versuche der Erhebung Österreichs zum König-reich', in idem (ed.), *Österreich von der Staatsidee zum Nationalbewußtsein* (Vienna, 1982), pp.394–432; G. Klingenstein, 'Was bedeuten "Österreich" und "österreichisch" im 18. Jahrhundert?', in R. G. Plaschka et al. (eds.), *Was heißt Österreich?* (Vienna, 1995), pp.149–220.

60. K. O. Frhr. v. Aretin, 'The Old Reich: A federation or hierarchical sys-tem?', in R. J. W. Evans et al. (eds.), *The Holy Roman Empire, 1495–1806* (Oxford, 2011), pp.27–42 at 36; D. Beales, *Joseph II* (2 vols., Cambridge, 1987–2009), II, p.148. Joseph's assessment of the Empire has been edited by H. Conrad as 'Verfassung und politische Lage des Reiches in einer Denkschrift Josephs II. von 1767/68', in L. Carlen and F. Steineg-ger (eds.), *Festschrift Nikolaus Grass* (2 vols., Innsbruck, 1974), I, pp.161–85.

61. Quoted by A. Schmid, 'Franz I. und Maria Theresia (1745–1765)', in A. Schindling and W. Ziegler (eds.), *Die Kaiser der Neuzeit 1519–1918* (Munich, 1990), pp.232–48 at 239–40. For the following see also P. H. Wilson, 'Bolstering the prestige of the Habsburgs: The end of the Holy Roman Empire in 1806', *IHR*, 28 (2006), 709–36.

62. A. H. Benna, 'Kaiser und Reich, Staat und Nation in der Geschichte Österreichs', in Wagner (ed.), *Österreich*, pp.377–93 at 381–3, and her 'Das Kaisertum Österreich', *MÖSA*, 9 (1956), 122–5. See also P. H. Wil-son, 'The meaning of empire in central Europe around 1800', in A. Forrest and P. H. Wilson (eds.), *The Bee and the Eagle: Napoleonic France and the End of the Holy Roman Empire, 1806* (Basingstoke, 2009), pp.22–41.

63. S. Externbrink, *Friedrich der Große, Maria Theresia und das Alte Reich. Deutschlandbild und Diplomatie Frankreichs im Siebenjährigen Krieg* (Berlin, 2006); E. Buddruss, *Die französische Deutschlandpolitik, 1756–1789* (Mainz, 1995).

64. R. Dufraise, 'Das Reich aus der Sicht der Encyclopédie méthodique 1784–1788', in R. A. Müller (ed.), *Bilder des Reiches* (Sigmaringen, 1997), pp.123–54.

65. S. S. Biro, *The German Policy of Revolutionary France: A Study in French Diplomacy during the War of the First Coalition, 1792–1797* (2 vols., Cambridge, MA, 1957).

66. R. Wohlfeil, 'Untersuchungen zur Geschichte des Rheinbundes, 1806–13. Das Verhältnis Dalbergs zu Napoleon', *ZGO*, 108 (1960), 85–108 at 95; K. O. Frhr. v. Aretin, 'Das Reich und Napoleon', in W. D. Gruner and K. J. Müller (eds.), *Über Frankreich nach Europa* (Hamburg, 1996), pp.183–200 at 198–9. Dalberg's motives are discussed on pp.134–6. P. Dwyer gives more attention to Napoleon's attitudes towards the Empire

than most biographers: *Napoleon: The Path to Power, 1769–1799* (London, 2007), and *Citizen Emperor: Napoleon in Power, 1799–1815* (London, 2013).

67. Napoleon I, *correspondance de Napoléon Ier* (32 vols., Paris, 1858–70), III, p.74. For the following see M. Pape, 'Der Karlskult an Wendepunkten der neueren deutschen Geschichte', *HJb*, 120 (2000), 138–81 at 142–61.

68. M. Lyons, *Napoleon Bonaparte and the Legacy of the French Revolution* (Basingstoke, 1994), pp.230–31; N. Aston, *The French Revolution, 1789–1804* (Basingstoke, 2004), pp.93–5; Morrissey, *Charlemagne and France*, pp.252–69; John, *Reich und Kirche*, pp.230–48. Napoleon told Pius VII 'Je suis Charlemagne' on 15 February 1806.

69. H. Rössler, *Napoleons Griff nach der Karlskrone. Das Ende des Alten Reiches, 1806* (Munich, 1957), pp.73–6; M. Broers, 'Napoleon, Charlemagne and Lotharingia: Acculturation and the boundaries of Napoleonic Europe', *HJ*, 44 (2001), 135–54.

70. *HHStA*, Staatskanzlei Vorträge, Kart.167, 20 May 1804.

71. *HHStA*, Staatskanzlei Vorträge, Kart.168, memorandum of 8 Aug. 1804. Cobenzl believed the recent union of the British and Irish parliaments presaged the assumption of a British imperial title. See also Prinzipalkommission Berichte Fasz.179b, decision of 11 Aug. 1804. Fuller discussion of these deliberations in G. Mraz, *Österreich und das Reich, 1804–1806* (Vienna, 1993).

72. *HHStA*, Titel und Wappen Kart.3.

73. Cited by K. O. Frhr. v. Aretin, *Heiliges Römisches Reich, 1776–1806* (2 vols., Wiesbaden, 1967), I, p.468 n.86.

74. *HHStA*, Prinzipalkommission Berichte Fasz.179b, report from 27 Aug. 1804. Several historians have agreed with Sweden: Aretin, *Heiliges Römisches Reich*, I, p.468; H. Ritter v. Srbik, *Das Österreichische Kaisertum und das Ende des Heiligen Römischen Reiches, 1804–1806* (Berlin, 1927), pp.24–5, 38.

75. K. M. Färber, *Kaiser und Erzkanzler. Carl von Dalberg und Napoleon am Ende des Alten Reiches* (Regensburg, 1988), pp.86–92; Rössler, *Napoleons Griff*, pp.21–2. The Empire's dissolution is discussed further on pp.644–59.

76. Cited by G. Post, 'Two notes on nationalism in the Middle Ages', *Traditio*, 9 (1953), 281–320 at 307–8. See also S. Epperlein, 'Über das romfreie Kaisertum im frühen Mittelalter', *Jahrbuch für Geschichte*, 2 (1967), 307–42 at 323–8; Löwe, 'Kaisertum und Abendland', pp.548–56.

77. H. Thomas, 'Die lehnrechtlichen Beziehungen des Herzogtums Lothringen zum Reich von der Mitte des 13. bis zum Ende des 14. Jahrhunderts', *RVJB*, 38 (1974), 166–202 at 167, 173–4. See also H. K. Schulze, *Grundstrukturen der Verfassung im Mittelalter* (3rd ed., 3 vols., Stuttgart, 1995–2000), III, pp.230–31.

78. Among the many works on Charles, that edited by H. Soly (Antwerp, 1998) gives the best overview of him as pan-European monarch.
79. J. M. Headley, ' "Ehe Türckisch als Bäpstisch": Lutheran reflections on the problem of Empire, 1623–28', *CEH*, 20 (1987), 3–28 at 5; F. Bosbach, *Monarchia universalis. Ein politischer Leitbegriff der Frühen Neuzeit* (Munich, 1988), pp.45–56.
80. Fichtner, *Emperor Maximilian II*, pp.24–6, 29–30.
81. *Cosmographia* first appeared in 1544 and included Putsch's map in the editions published after 1556. See also E. Straub, *Pax et Imperium. Spaniens Kampf et seine Friedensordnung in Europa zwischen 1617 und 1635* (Paderborn, 1980), pp.20–28.
82. F. Edelmayer, *Maximilian II., Philipp II. und Reichsitalien.* (Stuttgart, 1988), and his *Söldner und Pensionäre. Das Netzwerk Philipps II. im Heiligen Römischen Reich* (Munich, 2002), esp. pp.48–51.
83. L. Geevers, 'The conquistador and the phoenix: The Franco-Spanish precedence dispute (1564–1610) as a battle of kingship', *IHR*, 35 (2013), 23–41 at 34–7. For the following see H. Ernst, *Madrid und Wien, 1632–1637* (Münster, 1991); D. Maffi, *En defensa del imperio. Los ejércitos de Felipe IV y la Guerra por la hegemonía europea (1635–1659)* (Madrid, 2014).
84. C. Storrs, *The Resilience of the Spanish Monarchy, 1665–1700* (Oxford, 2006).
85. L. Auer, 'Zur Rolle Italiens in der österreichischen Politik um das spanischen Erbe', *MÖSA*, 31 (1978), 52–72; L. and M. Frey, *A Question of Empire: Leopold I and the War of Spanish Succession, 1701–1705* (Boulder, CO, 1983).
86. These claims are made by H. Schilling, *Höfe und Allianzen. Deutschland 1648–1763* (Münster, 1989), pp.61–70.
87. I. Hantsche (ed.), *Johann Moritz von Nassau-Siegen (1604–1679) als Vermittler* (Münster, 2005); K. Siebenhüner, 'Where did the jewels of the German imperial princes come from?', in R. J. W. Evans and P. H. Wilson (eds.), *The Holy Roman Empire, 1495–1806: A European Perspective* (Leiden, 2012), pp.333–48; P. Malekandathil, *The Germans, the Portuguese and India* (Hamburg, 1999); C. Tzoref-Ashkenazi, *German Soldiers in Colonial India* (London, 2014); R. Atwood, *The Hessians: Mercenaries from Hessen-Kassel in the American Revolution* (Cambridge, 1980); T. Biskup, 'German colonialism in the early modern period', in J. McKenzie (ed.), *The Encyclopedia of Empire* (Oxford, 2016), forthcoming.
88. G. H. Weiss, *In Search of Silk: Adam Olearius' Mission to Russia and Persia* (Minneapolis, 1983). For the following see P. H. Smith, *The Business of Alchemy: Science and Culture in the Holy Roman Empire* (Princeton, 1994), pp.141–72.

89. R. Schück, *Brandenburg-Preußens Kolonial-Politik unter dem Großen Kurfürsten und seinen Nachfolgern (1647–1721)* (2 vols., Leipzig, 1889). For the following see H. Hassinger, 'Die erste Wiener orientalische Handelskompagnie 1667–1683', *VSWG*, 35 (1942), 1–53; F. Schui, 'Prussia's "trans-oceanic moment": The creation of the Prussian Asiatic Trading Company in 1750', *HJ*, 49 (2008), 143–60.

90. R. Bartlett and B. Mitchell, 'State-sponsored immigration into eastern Europe in the eighteenth and nineteenth centuries', in R. Bartlett and K. Schönwälder (eds.), *The German Lands and Eastern Europe* (London, 1999), pp.91–114; C. Dipper, *Deutsche Geschichte, 1648–1789* (Frankfurt am Main, 1991), pp.23–6; G. Schmidt, *Wandel durch Vernunft. Deutsche Geschichte im 18. Jahrhundert* (Munich, 2009), p.256. For the 'Transylvanian Saxons' see R. J. W. Evans, *Austria, Hungary, and the Habsburgs: Central Europe c.1683–1867* (Oxford, 2006), pp.206–27.

91. Anglo-Hanoverian connections are discussed further on pp.219, 222–3.

92. W. J. Millor et al. (eds.), *The Letters of John of Salisbury* (London, 1955), I, p.206, letter no.124 to Ralph of Sarre in June/July 1160. For the schism see pp.63–4.

93. Quote from T. D. Hardy (ed.), *Rotuli litterarum patentium* (London, 1835), p.18. My thanks to Colin Veach for this reference.

94. W. Ullmann, 'The development of the medieval idea of sovereignty', *EHR*, 64 (1949), 1–33; E. E. Stengel, *Abhandlungen und Untersuchungen zur Geschichte des Kaisergedankens im Mittelalter* (Cologne, 1965), pp.239–86; W. Kienast, *Deutschland und Frankreich in der Kaiserzeit (900–1270): Weltkaiser und Einzelkönige* (3 vols., Stuttgart, 1974–5), II; Jones, *Eclipse of Empire?*, pp.355–6; J. Headley, 'The demise of universal monarchy as a meaningful political idea', in F. Bosbach and H. Hiery (eds.), *Imperium / Empire / Reich* (Munich, 1999), pp.41–58.

95. C. Hirschi, *The Origins of Nationalism: An Alternative History from Ancient Rome to Early Modern Germany* (Cambridge, 2012), pp.81–8.

96. B. Stollberg-Rilinger, 'Die Wissenschaft der feinen Unterschiede. Das Präzedenzrecht und die europäischen Monarchien vom 16. bis zum 18. Jahrhundert', *Majestas*, 10 (2002), 125–50.

97. Kampmann, *Arbiter und Friedenstiftung*, pp.26–64.

98. P. Schmidt, *Spanische Universalmonarchie oder 'teutsche Libertet'* (Stuttgart, 2001); D. Böttcher, 'Propaganda und öffentliche Meinung im protestantischen Deutschland 1628–1636', in H. U. Rudolf (ed.), *Der Dreissigjährige Krieg* (Darmstadt, 1977), pp.325–67.

99. J. E. Thomson, *Mercenaries, Pirates and Sovereigns: State-Building and Extraterritorial Violence in Early Modern Europe* (Princeton, 1994); C. Tilly, *Coercion, Capital and European States, AD 990–1992* (rev. ed., Oxford, 1992).

100. For overviews of the Empire's place in European relations at this point see D. Berg, *Deutschland und seine Nachbarn, 1200–1500* (Munich, 1997); H. Duchhardt, *Altes Reich und europäische Staatenwelt 1648–1806* (Munich, 1990).

101. For the general context see J. Black, *European Warfare, 1494–1660* (London, 2002).

102. J. C. Lünig, *Corpus juris militaris des Heiligen Römischen Reichs* (2 vols., Leipzig, 1723), I, pp.381–7; H. Steiger, 'Das ius belli ac pacis des Alten Reiches zwischen 1645 und 1801', *Der Staat*, 37 (1998), 493–520. The mechanisms of imperial collective security are discussed on pp.454–62.

103. K. Müller, 'Zur Reichskriegserklärung im 17. und 18. Jahrhundert', *ZSRG GA*, 90 (1973), 246–59 at 249. For the following see C. Kampmann, *Reichsrebellion und kaiserliche Acht. Politische Strafjustiz im Dreißigjährigen Krieg und das Verfahren gegen Wallenstein 1634* (Münster, 1992), and his 'Reichstag und Reichskriegserklärung im Zeitalter Ludwigs XIV.', *HJb*, 113 (1993), 41–59.

104. The opinion of the Swabian imperial Estates in 1705 cited by M. Plassmann, *Krieg und Defension am Oberrhein. Die Vorderen Reichskreise und Markgraf Ludwig Wilhelm von Baden (1693–1706)* (Berlin, 2000), p.595.

105. P. H. Wilson, 'The German "soldier trade" of the seventeenth and eighteenth centuries', *IHR*, 18 (1996), 757–92.

106. J. G. Droysen, *Geschichte der preußischen Politik* (5 parts in 14 vols., Leipzig, 1855–86), part 3, I, pp.338–40. Similar views are widely expressed throughout the twentieth century, e.g. A. Randelzhofer, *Völkerrechtliche Aspekte des Heiligen Römischen Reiches nach 1648* (Berlin, 1967). For recent and critical engagement with the question of sovereignty in the Westphalian settlement see: D. Croxton, 'The Peace of Westphalia of 1648 and the origins of sovereignty', *IHR*, 21 (1999), 569–91; A. Osiander, 'Sovereignty, international relations, and the Westphalian myth', *International Organization*, 55 (2001), 251–87; P. M. R. Stirk, 'The Westphalian model and sovereign equality', *Review of International Studies*, 38 (2012), 641–60.

107. A. Waddington, *L'acquisition de la couronne royale de Prusse par les Hohenzollern* (Paris, 1888), p.43. Further discussion of the context in H. Duchhardt, *Deutsche Verfassungsgeschichte, 1495–1806* (Stuttgart, 1991), pp.180–95, and in the present book pp.218–20.

108. P. H. Wilson, 'Das Heilige Römische Reich, die machtpolitisch schwache Mitte Europas – mehr Sicherheit oder eine Gefahr für den Frieden?', in M. Lanzinner (ed.), *Sicherheit in der Vormoderne und Gegenwart* (Paderborn, 2013), pp.25–34.

109. J. Arndt, 'Die kaiserlichen Friedensvermittlungen im spanisch-niederländischen Krieg 1568–1609', *RVJB*, 62 (1998), 161–83; Fichtner,

Emperor Maximilian II, pp.156–72; J. Lavery, *Germany's Northern Challenge: The Holy Roman Empire and the Scandinavian Struggle for the Baltic, 1563–1576* (Boston, 2002), pp.105–32.

110. H. Duchhardt, 'Westfälischer Friede und internationales System im ancien régime', *HZ*, 249 (1989), 529–43.

111. L. Auer, 'Konfliktverhütung und Sicherheit. Versuche zwischenstaatlicher Friedenswahrung in Europa zwischen den Friedensschlüssen von Oliva und Aachen 1660–1668', in H. Duchhardt (ed.), *Zwischenstaatliche Friedenswahrung in Mittelalter und Früher Neuzeit* (Cologne, 1991), pp.153–83; K. P. Decker, *Frankreich und die Reichsstände, 1672– 1675* (Bonn, 1981); A. Sinkoli, *Frankreich, das Reich und die Reichsstände, 1697–1702* (Frankfurt am Main, 1995).

112. K. Härter, 'The Permanent Imperial Diet in European context, 1663–1806', in Evans et al. (eds.), *Holy Roman Empire*, pp.115–35. The Empire's pacific character was presented positively in seventeenth- and eighteenth-century engravings: see J. Burkhardt, 'Reichskriege in der frühneuzeitlichen Bild-publizistik', in Müller (ed.), *Bilder des Reiches*, pp.51–95 at 72–80.

113. K. v. Raumer, *Ewiger Friede. Friedensrufe und Friedenspläne seit der Renaissance* (Munich, 1953); P. Schröder, 'The Holy Roman Empire as model for Saint-Pierre's *Projet pour rendre la paix perpétuelle en Europe*', in Evans and Wilson (eds.), *The Holy Roman Empire*, pp.35–50; M. Wrede, 'Frankreich, das Reich und die deutsche Nation im 17. und 18. Jahrhundert', in G. Schmidt (ed.), *Die deutsche Nation im frühneuzeitlichen Europa* (Munich, 2010), pp.157–77.

CHAPTER 4: LANDS

1. The following extends Peter Moraw's analysis of the later Middle Ages into a general model for the Empire's history: 'Landesgeschichte und Reichsgeschichte im 14. Jahrhundert', *Jahrbuch für westdeutsche Landes-geschichte*, 3 (1977), 175–91, and his 'Franken als königsnahe Landschaft im späten Mittelalter', *BDLG*, 112 (1976), 123–38. The relationship of geography to governance is explored further in Part III.

2. H. K. Schulze, *Grundstrukturen der Verfassung im Mittelalter* (3rd ed., 3 vols., Stuttgart, 1995–2000), III, pp.73–83.

3. F. Trautz, 'Die Reichsgewalt in Italien im Spätmittelalter', *Heidelberger Jahrbücher*, 7 (1963), 45–81 at 54–5.

4. R. Pauler, *Die deutschen Könige und Italien im 14. Jahrhundert von Heinrich VII. bis Karl IV.* (Darmstadt, 1997), pp.67–8; R. Elze, 'Die "Eis-erne Krone" in Monza', in P. E. Schramm, *Herrschaftszeichen und Staatssymbolik* (3 vols., Stuttgart, 1954–6), II, pp.450–79. Napoleon used the Monza crown in 1805, as did Ferdinand I of Austria in 1838. It was

also used in the funeral processions for the Italian kings Victor Emanuel II (1878) and Umberto I (1900). The German and imperial insignia are discussed on pp.267–9.

5. E. Schubert, *Fürstliche Herrschaft und Territorium im späten Mittelalter* (2nd ed., Munich, 2006), p.1. The emergence of a distinct German identity is discussed on pp.255–65. A detailed guide to the historical development of the German territories and regions is provided by G. Köbler, *Historisches Lexikon der deutschen Länder* (5th ed., Munich, 1995).

6. *Das Land Baden-Württemberg* (issued by the Staatliche Archivverwaltung Baden-Württembergs, Stuttgart, 1974), I, pp.109–66; T. Zotz, 'Ethnogenese und Herzogtum in Alemannien (9.–11. Jh.)', *MIÖG*, 108 (2000), 48–66.

7. M. Todd, *The Early Germans* (2nd ed., Oxford, 2004), pp.202–10.

8. M. Spindler (ed.), *Handbuch der bayerische Geschichte* (2nd ed., 2 vols., Munich, 1981), I, pp.101–245; S. Airlie, 'Narratives of triumph and rituals of submission: Charlemagne's mastering of Bavaria', *TRHS*, 6th series, 9 (1999), 93–119.

9. G. Scheibelreiter, 'Ostarrichi. Das Werden einer historischen Landschaft', in W. Brauneder and L. Höbelt (eds.), *Sacrum Imperium. Das Reich und Österreich, 996–1806* (Vienna, 1996), pp.9–70; H. Dienst, 'Ostarrîchi – Oriens–Austria. Probleme "österreichischer" Identität im Hochmittelalter', in R. G. Plaschka et al. (eds.), *Was heißt Österreich?* (Vienna, 1995), pp.35–50. The term 'Ostarrichi' has been documented since 996.

10. C. Wickham, *Early Medieval Italy: Central Power and Local Society, 400–1000* (Ann Arbor, MI, 1981), pp.47–63, 168–80; E. Hlawitschka, 'Die Widonen im Dukat von Spoleto', *Quellen und Forschungen aus italienischen Archiven und Bibliotheken*, 63 (1983), 20–92. Adalbert of Magdeburg's account of Otto's campaign can be found in S. MacLean (ed.), *History and Politics in Late Carolingian and Ottonian Europe* (Manchester, 2009), pp.251–71.

11. C. Brühl, *Deutschland – Frankreich* (Cologne, 1990), pp.677–8. More detail in H. Wolfram, *Conrad II, 990–1039: Emperor of Three Kingdoms* (University Park, PA, 2006), pp.95–113, 118–37.

12. A. Haverkamp, 'Die Städte im Herrschafts- und Sozialgefüge Reichsitaliens', in F. Vittinghoff (ed.), *Stadt und Herrschaft. Römische Kaiserzeit und hohes Mittelalter* (Munich, 1982), pp.149–245 at 159–66.

13. H. H. Anton, 'Bonifaz von Canossa, Markgraf von Tuszien, und die Italienpolitik der frühen Salier', *HZ*, 214 (1974), 529–56. See generally S. Reynolds, *Kingdoms and Communities in Western Europe, 900–1300* (2nd ed., Oxford, 1997), pp.240–49.

14. B. Guenée, *States and Rulers in Later Medieval Europe* (Oxford, 1985), pp.12–13; T. Scott, *The City-State in Europe, 1000–1600* (Oxford, 2012),

pp.78–91; D. Hay and J. Law, *Italy in the Age of the Renaissance, 1380–1530* (London, 1989), pp.225–6, 260–75.

15. P. Partner, *The Lands of St Peter: The Papal State in the Middle Ages and the Early Renaissance* (London, 1972). The Pentapolis were Rimini, Pesaro, Fano, Senigallia and Ancona.

16. T. Gross, *Lothar III. und die Mathildischen Güter* (Frankfurt am Main, 1990).

17. Wickham, *Early Medieval Italy*, pp.49, 146–63.

18. B. M. Kreutz, *Before the Normans: Southern Italy in the Ninth and Tenth Centuries* (Philadelphia, 1991), pp.37–47, 102–6, 119–25; T. Reuter, *Germany in the Early Middle Ages, c.800–1056* (Harlow, 1991), pp.173–4.

19. F. Neveux, *A Brief History of the Normans* (London, 2008); G. A. Loud, *The Age of Robert Guiscard: Southern Italy and the Norman Conquest* (Harlow, 2000); D. Matthew, *The Norman Kingdom of Sicily* (Cambridge, 1992).

20. I. S. Robinson, *The Papacy, 1073–1198* (Cambridge, 1990), pp.367–97.

21. T. Ertl, 'Der Regierungsantritt Heinrichs VI. im Königreich Sizilien (1194)', *FMS*, 37 (2003), 259–89. For the wider speculation about Henry's plans see pp.303–4.

22. T. Frenz, 'Das Papsttum als der lachende Dritte? Die Konsolidierung der weltlichen Herrschaft der Päpste unter Innozenz III.', in W. Hechberger and F. Schuller (eds.), *Staufer & Welfen* (Regensburg, 2009), pp.190–201.

23. Hay and Law, *Italy*, pp.149–58, 236–60. The pope also had more direct control over the duchy of Benevento, which had shrunk to the town of that name.

24. S. A. Epstein, *Genoa and the Genoese, 958–1528* (Chapel Hill, NC, 1996); J. Larner, *Italy in the Age of Dante and Petrarch, 1216–1380* (London, 1980), pp.128–52; Scott, *City-State*, pp.51–6, 64–78, 92–128. See also pp.512–22.

25. E. L. Cox, *The Eagles of Savoy: The House of Savoy in Thirteenth-Century Europe* (Princeton, 1974), and his *The Green Count of Savoy: Amadeus VI and Transalpine Savoy in the Fourteenth Century* (Princeton, 1967). Savoy was raised to a duchy in 1416. Its relationship to the Empire is discussed at length in *NTSR*, I, 46–52, 72–84.

26. As argued by J. Schneider, *Auf der Suche nach dem verlorenen Reich. Lotharingien im 9. und 10. Jahrhundert* (Cologne, 2010). For the following see also B. Schneidmüller, '*Regnum* und *ducatus*. Identität und Integration in der lotharingischen Geschichte des 9. bis 11. Jahrhunderts', *RVJB*, 51 (1987), 81–114; R. McKitterick, *The Frankish Kingdoms under the Carolingians* (Harlow, 1983), pp.258–75.

27. Todd, *The Early Germans*, pp.197–201.

28. Thietmar of Merseburg, *Ottonian Germany: The Chronicon of Thietmar of Merseburg*, ed. D. A. Warner (Manchester, 2001), pp.325–8.

29. E. Boshof, *Die Salier* (5th ed., Stuttgart, 2008), pp.63–70; T. Riches, 'The Peace of God, the "weakness" of Robert the Pious and the struggle for the German throne, 1023–5', *EME*, 18 (2010), 202–22 at 212–16; Wolfram, *Conrad II*, pp.239–46; Brühl, *Deutschland – Frankreich*, pp.672–9.

30. S. Weinfurter, *The Salian Century* (Philadelphia, 1999), p.50.

31. Boshof, *Die Salier*, pp.113–16.

32. F. Seibt, *Karl IV.* (Munich, 1978), pp.350–60.

33. G. Althoff, *Die Ottonen* (2nd ed., Stuttgart, 2005), pp.49–52, 92–3; M. Werner, 'Der Herzog von Lothringen in salischer Zeit', in S. Weinfurter (ed.), *Die Salier und das Reich* (3 vols., Sigmaringen, 1991), I, pp.367–473; Schneidmüller, '*Regnum* und *ducatus*', pp.89–91.

34. E. Boshof, 'Lothringen, Frankreich und das Reich in der Regierungszeit Heinrichs III.', *RVJB*, 42 (1978), 63–127.

35. H. Thomas, 'Die lehnrechtlichen Beziehungen des Herzogtums Lothringen zum Reich von der Mitte des 13. bis zum Ende des 14. Jahrhunderts', *RVJB*, 38 (1974), 166–202; H. Bogdan, *La Lorraine des ducs* (Condé-sur-l'Escaut, 2007), pp.47–62; F. Pesendorfer, *Lothringen und seine Herzöge* (Graz, 1994), pp.55–8. Pont-à-Mousson was acquired with the county (later duchy) of Bar to the north-west of Lorraine itself in the fourteenth century. Bar had owed feudal obligations to France since 1301, while Pont-à-Mousson had been an imperial fief since 1354. Although he released the duke from obligations owed by Lorraine, Charles reasserted suzerainty over Metz, Toul and Verdun in 1356. Lorraine eventually passed to the Vaudemont family in 1501.

36. M. Innes, 'Franks and Slavs c.700–1000: The problem of European expansion before the millennium', *EME*, 6 (1997), 201–16; H. Keller, 'Das "Erbe" Ottos des Großen', *FMS*, 41 (2007), 43–74 at 56–7.

37. C. R. Bowlus, *The Battle of Lechfeld and its Aftermath, August 955* (Aldershot, 2006), pp.19–44 (on Magyar tactics); T. Reuter (ed.), *The Annals of Fulda* (Manchester, 1992), pp.23, 88–98, 121–3 (on the Slavs); Neveux, *A Brief History of the Normans*, pp.24–37.

38. S. Coupland, 'The Frankish tribute payments to the Vikings and their consequences', *Francia*, 26 (1999), 57–75.

39. J. M. H. Smith, '*Fines imperii*: The marches', in R. McKitterick (ed.), *The New Cambridge Medieval History*, II, *c.700–c.900* (Cambridge, 1995), pp.169–89; H. Büttner, 'Die Ungarn, das Reich und Europa bis zur Lechfeldschlacht des Jahres 955', *ZBLG*, 19 (1956), 433–58.

40. Althoff, *Die Ottonen*, pp.53–5; M. Hardt, 'The *Limes Saxoniae* as part of the eastern borderlands of the Frankish and Ottonian-Salian Empire', in F. Curta (ed.), *Borders, Barriers and Ethnogenesis* (Turnhout, 2005), pp.35–50; D. S. Bachrach, *Warfare in Tenth-Century Germany* (Woodbridge, 2012), pp.23–36, 59–60, 92–101.

41. N. Davies, *God's Playground: A History of Poland* (2nd ed., 2 vols., Oxford, 2005), I, pp.54–5.

42. G. Althoff, *Otto III* (Philadelphia, 2003), pp.46–8; J. Petersohn, 'König Otto III. und die Slawen an Ostsee, Oder und Elbe um das Jahr 995', *FMS*, 37 (2003), 99–139.

43. C. R. Bowlus, *Franks, Moravians and Magyars: The Struggle for the Middle Danube, 788–907* (Philadelphia, 1995); F. Curta, *Southeastern Europe in the Middle Ages, 500–1250* (Cambridge, 2006); Reuter, *Germany in the Early Middle Ages*, pp.79–84.

44. Reuter (ed.), *The Annals of Fulda*, pp.58–61; Reuter, *Germany in the Early Middle Ages*, pp.82–4. The exact location of the Greater Moravian Empire remains a matter of some controversy.

45. L. Scales, *The Shaping of German Identity* (Cambridge, 2012), p.408; F. Prinz, 'Die Stellung Böhmens im mittelalterlichen deutschen Reich', *ZBLG*, 28 (1965), 99–113.

46. The exception was Eger (Cheb), acquired by the Staufer in the 1160s to secure access into western Bohemia, but pawned to that kingdom in 1322.

47. Davies, *God's Playground*, I, pp.52–8, 70.

48. H. Ludat, *An Elbe und Oder um das Jahr 1000. Skizzen zur Politik des Ottonenreiches und der slavischen Mächte in Mitteleuropa* (Vienna, 1995); J. Fried, *Otto III. und Boleslaw Chrobry* (Stuttgart, 1989); Althoff, *Otto III*, pp.97–107. The historical controversy surrounding Otto's actions is summarized by D. A. Warner's introduction to Thietmar of Merseburg, *Chronicon*, pp.21–6.

49. K. Leyser, 'The battle at the Lech, 955', *History*, 50 (1965), 1–25 at 4; J. Bérenger, *A History of the Habsburg Empire, 1273–1700* (Harlow, 194), pp.45–6.

50. S. Gawlas, 'Der Blick von Polen auf das mittelalterliche Reich', in B. Schneidmüller and S. Weinfurter (eds.), *Heilig – Römisch – Deutsch. Das Reich im mittelalterlichen Europa* (Dresden, 2006), pp.266–85. See generally N. Berend et al., *Central Europe in the High Middle Ages* (Cambridge, 2013).

51. Althoff, *Die Ottonen*, p.208. For the following see also Reuter, *Germany in the Early Middle Ages*, pp.260–64.

52. A. Begert, *Böhmen, die böhmische Kur und das Reich vom Hochmittelalter bis zum Ende des Alten Reiches* (Husum, 2003). The changes to vassalage are discussed on pp.356–65.

53. L. E. Scales, 'At the margin of community: Germans in pre-Hussite Bohemia', *TRHS*, 6th series, 9 (1999), 327–52.

54. H. Aubin et al. (eds.), *Geschichte Schlesiens*, I, *Von der Urzeit bis zum Jahre 1526* (3rd ed., Stuttgart, 1961).

55. Scales, *German Identity*, pp.431–7 (quote from p.436). Prussia's controversial historiography is discussed in M. Weber (ed.), *Preussen in*

Ostmitteleuropa (Munich, 2003). For the Order's foundation see pp.97–9.

56. H. Boockmann, *Ostpreußen und Westpreußen* (Berlin, 1992), pp.94–5; E. E. Stengel, *Abhandlungen und Untersuchungen zur Geschichte des Kaisergedankens im Mittelalter* (Cologne, 1965), pp.207–37.

57. Gawlas, 'Der Blick von Polen', 280–85. For Polish Prussia see K. Friedrich, *The Other Prussia: Royal Prussia, Poland and Liberty, 1569–1772* (Cambridge, 2000). For the following see W. Hubatsch, 'Albert of Brandenburg-Ansbach, Grand Master of the Order of Teutonic Knights and duke in Prussia, 1490–1568', in H. J. Cohn (ed.), *Government in Reformation Europe, 1520–1560* (London, 1971), pp.169–202; F. L. Carsten, *The Origins of Prussia* (Oxford, 1954), pp.1–100; D. Kirby, *Northern Europe in the Early Modern Period: The Baltic World, 1492–1772* (Harlow, 1990), pp.66–73.

58. A. V. Berkis, *The Reign of Duke James in Courland, 1638–1682* (Lincoln, NB, 1960), p.10. For the following see J. Lavery, *Germany's Northern Challenge: The Holy Roman Empire and the Scandinavian Struggle for the Baltic, 1563–1576* (Boston, 2002), pp.132–41.

59. K. Friedrich and S. Smart (eds.), *The Cultivation of Monarchy and the Rise of Berlin: Brandenburg-Prussia, 1700* (Farnham, 2010); C. Clark, 'When culture meets power: The Prussian coronation of 1701', in H. Scott and B. Simms (eds.), *Cultures of Power in Europe during the Long Eighteenth Century* (Cambridge, 2007), pp.14–35; *NTSR*, I, 111–32.

60. K.-U. Jäschke, *Europa und das römisch-deutsche Reich um 1300* (Stuttgart, 1999), pp.39–54; Davies, *God's Playground*, I, pp.86–92.

61. R. Butterwick (ed.), *The Polish-Lithuanian Monarchy in European Context, c.1500–1795* (Basingstoke, 2001).

62. A. Niederstätter, *Österreichische Geschichte, 1400–1522* (Vienna, 1996), pp.341–59; W. Zanetti, *Der Friedenskaiser. Friedrich III. und seine Zeit, 1440–1493* (Herford, 1985), pp.130–208, 275–338.

63. K. V. Jensen, 'The blue Baltic border of Denmark in the high Middle Ages', in D. Abulafia and N. Berend (eds.), *Medieval Frontiers: Concepts and Practices* (Aldershot, 2002), pp.173–93; K. Jordan, 'Heinrich der Löwe und Dänemark', in M. Göhring and A. Scharff (eds.), *Geschichtliche Kräfte und Entscheidungen* (Wiesbaden, 1954), pp.16–29 at 17–19.

64. E. Hoffmann, 'Die Bedeutung der Schlacht von Bornhöved für die deutsche und skandinavische Geschichte', *Zeitschrift des Vereins für Lübeckische Geschichte und Altertumskunde*, 57 (1977), 9–37. The Hansa are discussed on pp.570–71, 577–8.

65. A. Bihrer, *Begegnungen zwischen dem ostfränkisch-deutschen Reich und England (850–1100)* (Ostfildern, 2012); K. Leyser, 'Die Ottonen und Wessex', *FMS*, 17 (1983), 73–97; J. Sarnowsky, 'England und der Kontinent im 10. Jahrhundert', *HJb*, 114 (1994), 47–75.

66. K. Leyser, *Medieval Germany and its Neighbours, 900–1250* (London, 1982), pp.191–213.

67. K. Görich, 'Verletzte Ehre. König Richard Löwenherz als Gefanger Kaiser Heinrichs VI', *HJb*, 123 (2003), 65–91; J. Gillingham, 'The kidnapped king: Richard I in Germany, 1192–4', *GHIL*, 30 (2008), 5–34. The Staufer–Welf conflict is discussed further on pp.357–9.

68. B. K. U. Weiler, *Henry III of England and the Staufen Empire, 1216–1272* (Woodbridge, 2006), p.198. Richard's reign as German king is discussed further on pp.378–9.

69. J. Whaley, *Germany and the Holy Roman Empire, 1493–1806* (2 vols., Oxford, 2012), I, p.340. Some of these issues will be picked up in more detail on pp.255–65, 668–78.

70. For a geographical survey of the Kreise, see P. H. Wilson, *From Reich to Revolution: German History, 1558–1806* (Basingstoke, 2004), pp.185–90, with a full membership list of each on pp.364–77. Further discussion on p.403.

71. *HHStA*, Titel und Wappen, Kart.2.

72. P. D. Lockhart, *Frederick II and the Protestant Cause: Denmark's Role in the Wars of Religion, 1559–1596* (Leiden, 2004), and his *Denmark in the Thirty Years' War, 1618–1648* (Selinsgrove, 1996).

73. W. Carr, *Schleswig-Holstein, 1815–1848* (Manchester, 1963); G. Stolz, *Die Schleswig-holsteinische Erhebung. Die nationale Auseinandersetzung in und um Schleswig-Holstein von 1848/51* (Husum, 1996).

74. W. Buchholz, 'Schwedisch-Pommern als Territorium des deutschen Reichs 1648–1806', *ZNRG*, 12 (1990), 14–33; B. C. Fiedler, 'Schwedisch oder Deutsch? Die Herzogtümer Bremen und Verden in der Schwedenzeit (1645–1712)', *Niedersächsisches Jahrbuch für Landesgeschichte*, 67 (1995), 43–57; K. R. Böhme, 'Die Krone Schweden als Reichsstand 1648 bis 1720', in H. Duchhardt (ed.), *Europas Mitte* (Bonn, 1988), pp.33–9.

75. G. Pálffy, 'An "old empire" on the periphery of the Old Empire: The kingdom of Hungary and the Holy Roman Empire in the sixteenth and seventeenth centuries', in R. J. W. Evans and P. H. Wilson (eds.), *The Holy Roman Empire, 1495–1806: A European Perspective* (Leiden, 2012), pp.259–79 at 271. For Habsburg government and the Empire's financial and military involvement in Hungary's defence, see also pp.445–62.

76. M. Hengerer, *Kaiserhof und Adel in der Mitte des 17. Jahrhunderts* (Konstanz, 2004).

77. W. Eberhard, *Monarchie und Widerstand. Zur ständischen Oppositionsbildung im Herrschaftssystem Ferdinands I. in Böhmen* (Munich, 1985).

78. Begert, *Böhmen, die böhmische Kur und das Reich*, pp.442–76. For the following see also J. Pánek, 'Der böhmische Staat und das Reich in der Frühen Neuzeit', in V. Press (ed.), *Alternativen zur Reichsverfassung in*

der Frühen Neuzeit? (Munich, 1995), pp.169–78; P. Maťa, 'Der Adel aus den böhmischen Ländern am Kaiserhof 1620–1740', in V. Bůžek and P. Král (eds.), *Šlechta v habsburské monarchii a císařsky dvůr (1526– 1740)* (České Budějovice, 2003), pp.191–233, and his 'Bohemia, Silesia and the Empire: Negotiating princely dignity on the eastern periphery', in Evans and Wilson (eds.), *The Holy Roman Empire*, pp.143–65.

79. H. Noflascher, 'Deutschmeister und Regent der Vorlande. Maximilian von Österreich (1558–1618)', in H. Maier and V. Press (eds.), *Vorderöster-reich in der frühen Neuzeit* (Sigmaringen, 1989), pp.93–130 at 101–6. For the following see R. Rexheuser (ed.), *Die Personalunionen von Sachsen-Polen 1697–1763 und Hannover-England, 1714–1837* (Wiesbaden, 2005); B. Simms and T. Riotte (eds.), *The Hanoverian Dimension in British History, 1714–1837* (Cambridge, 2007); J. Black, *The British Abroad: The Grand Tour in the Eighteenth Century* (Stroud, 1992); N. Harding, *Hanover and the British Empire, 1700–1837* (Woodbridge, 2007); K. Lembke and C. Vogel (gen. eds.), *Als die Royals aus Hannover kamen* (4 vols., Dresden, 2014); D. Makiłła, 'Friedliche Nachbarschaft. Das Bild des Reiches in der polnischen Geschichtsschreibung', in M. Schnettger (ed.), *Imperium Romanum – irregulare corpus – Teutscher Reichs-Staat* (Mainz, 2002), pp.221–9; H.-J. Bömelburg, 'Polen und die deutsche Nation – Konfligierende Identitätszuschreibungen und antago-nistische Entwürfe politischer Ordnung', in G. Schmidt (ed.), *Die deutsche Nation im frühneuzeitlichen Europa* (Munich, 2010), pp.129–55.

80. Whaley, *Germany*, I, p.21.

81. C. W. Ingrao, *In Quest and Crisis: Emperor Joseph I and the Habsburg Monarchy* (West Lafayette, IN, 1979), pp.79–121 esp. 96–7; G. Schmidt, *Geschichte des Alten Reiches* (Munich, 1999), p.200.

82. L. Riall, *The Italian Risorgimento: State, Society and National Unifica-tion* (London, 1994).

83. B. Raviola, 'The imperial system in early modern northern Italy: A web of dukedoms, fiefs and enclaves along the Po', in Evans and Wilson (eds.), *The Holy Roman Empire*, pp.217–36, and the articles in the special issue of *Zeitenblicke*, 6 (2007), no.1, at http//www.zeitenblicke.de/2007/1 (accessed 22 October 2009).

84. K. O. Frhr. v. Aretin, *Das Reich. Friedensordnung und europäisches Gleichgewicht, 1648–1806* (Stuttgart, 1986), pp.84–5, 159, 281.

85. T. J. Dandelet, *Spanish Rome, 1500–1700* (New Haven, CT, 2001), pp.56–7.

86. For the strategic context see G. Parker, *The Army of Flanders and the Spanish Road, 1567–1659* (Cambridge, 1972); P. H. Wilson, *Europe's Tragedy: A History of the Thirty Years War* (London, 2009), pp.151–61.

87. M. Schnettger, '*Impero Romano – Impero Germanico*. Italienische Perspektiven auf das Reich in der Frühen Neuzeit', in Schnettger (ed.),

Imperium Romanum, pp.53–75 at 59–66; Aretin, *Das Reich*, pp.88–99. The Reichshofrat is discussed further on pp.627–31.

88. F. Edelmayer, *Maximilian II., Philipp II. und Reichsitalien. Die Auseinandersetzungen um das Reichslehen Finale in Ligurien* (Stuttgart, 1988); D. Parrott, 'The Mantuan Succession, 1627–31: A sovereignty dispute in early modern Europe', *EHR*, 112 (1997), 20–65.

89. J. P. Niederkorn, *Die europäischen Mächte und der 'Lange Türkenkrieg' Kaiser Rudolfs II. (1593–1606)* (Vienna, 1993), pp.386–448; C. Storrs, 'Imperial authority and the levy of contributions in "Reichsitalien" in the Nine Years War (1690–1696)', in M. Schnettger and M. Verga (eds.), *L'Impero e l'Italia nella prima età moderna* (Bologna, 2006), pp.241–73; M. Schnettger, 'Das Alte Reich und Italien in der Frühen Neuzeit', *Quellen und Forschungen aus italienischen Archiven und Bibliotheken*, 79 (1999), 344–420 at 359–64; G. Hanlon, *Twilight of a Military Tradition: Italian Aristocrats and European Conflicts, 1560–1800* (London, 1998).

90. K. Müller, 'Das "Reichskammerale" im 18. Jahrhundert', *Wiener Beiträge zur Geschichte der Neuzeit*, 30 (1993), 152–77 at 159–60.

91. R. Oresko, 'The House of Savoy in search for a royal crown in the seventeenth century', in R. Oresko et al. (eds.), *Royal and Republican Sovereignty in Early Modern Europe* (Cambridge, 1997), pp.272–350. For the following see also R. Oresko and R. Parrott, 'Reichsitalien and the Thirty Years' War', in K. Bussmann and H. Schilling (eds.), *1648: War and Peace in Europe* (3 vols., Münster, 1998), I, pp.141–60; C. Zwierlein, 'Savoyen-Piemonts Verhältnis zum Reich 1536 bis 1618', in Schnettger and Verga (eds.), *L'Impero*, pp.347–89; S. Externbrink, 'State-building within the Empire: The cases of Brandenburg-Prussia and Savoy-Sardinia', in Evans and Wilson (eds.), *The Holy Roman Empire*, pp.187–202.

92. R. Kleinman, 'Charles-Emmanuel I of Savoy and the Bohemian election of 1619', *European Studies Review*, 5 (1975), 3–29; L. Pelizaeus, *Der Aufstieg Württembergs und Hessens zur Kurwürde, 1692–1803* (Frankfurt am Main, 2000), pp.53–4.

93. N. Mout, 'Core and periphery: The Netherlands and the Empire from the late fifteenth to the early seventeenth century', in Evans and Wilson (eds.), *The Holy Roman Empire*, pp.203–15.

94. H. Gabel, 'Ein verkanntes System? Das Alte Reich im zeitgenössischen niederländischen Urteil', in Schnettger (ed.), *Imperium Romanum*, pp.111–34; A. C. Carter, *Neutrality or Commitment: The Evolution of Dutch Foreign Policy, 1667–1795* (London, 1975). See generally J. I. Israel, *The Dutch Republic: Its Rise, Greatness and Fall, 1477–1806* (Oxford, 1995).

95. R. Babel, *Zwischen Habsburg und Bourbon. Außenpolitik und europäische Stellung Herzog Karl IV. von Lothringen und Bar von Regierungsantritt*

bis zum Exil (1624–1634) (Sigmaringen, 1989); H. Wolf, *Die Reichskirchenpolitik des Hauses Lothringen (1680–1715)* (Stuttgart, 1994); Pesendorfer, *Lotharingen*, pp.99–177.

96. D. Croxton, 'The Peace of Westphalia of 1648 and the origins of sovereignty', *IHR*, 21 (1999), 569–91 at 576–7; F. Egger, 'Johann Rudolf Wettstein and the international recognition of Switzerland as a European nation', in Bussmann and Schilling (eds.), *1648: War and Peace*, I, pp.423–32; T. Maissen, 'Die Eidgenossen und die deutsche Nation in der Frühen Neuzeit', in Schmidt (ed.), *Die deutsche Nation*, pp.97–127.

97. M. Jorio, 'Der Nexus Imperii – Die Eidgenossenschaft und das Reich nach 1648', in idem (ed.), *1648: Die Schweiz und Europa* (Zurich, 1999), pp.133–46 at 133–4.

CHAPTER 5: IDENTITIES

1. For a lucid and comprehensive guide to these debates, see L. Scales, *The Shaping of German Identity* (Cambridge, 2012), pp.1–52, and the literature cited in the Introduction. Reactions to the Empire's dissolution are discussed on pp.655–7.

2. B. Anderson, *Imagined Communities: Reflections on the Origin of the Spread of Nationalism* (London, 1983); E. J. Hobsbawm, *Nations and Nationalism since 1780: Programme, Myth, Reality* (2nd ed., Cambridge, 1992). Further discussion in W. Pohl (ed.) with H. Reimitz, *Strategies of Distinction: The Construction of Ethnic Communities, 300–800* (Leiden, 1998); S. Forde et al. (eds.), *Concepts of National Identity in the Middle Ages* (Leeds, 1995).

3. S. Reynolds, *Kingdoms and Communities in Western Europe, 900–1300* (2nd ed., Oxford, 1997), pp.250–331; C. Brühl, *Deutschland – Frankreich* (Cologne, 1990), esp. p.714.

4. V. Groebner, *Who Are You? Identification, Deception, and Surveillance in Early Modern Europe* (New York, 2007), pp.26–7.

5. C. Beaune, *The Birth of an Ideology: Myths and Symbols of Nation in Late-Medieval France* (Berkeley, 1991); C. Lübke, *Fremde im östlichen Europa. Von Gesellschaften ohne Staat zu verstaatlichten Gesellschaften (9.–11. Jahrhundert)* (Cologne, 2001); F. Graus, *Die Nationenbildung der Westslawen im Mittelalter* (Sigmaringen, 1980), esp. p.142.

6. H.-W. Goetz, 'Regnum. Zum politischen Denken der Karolingerzeit', *ZSRG GA*, 104 (1987), 110–89 esp. 117, 171.

7. M. Todd, *The Early Germans* (2nd ed., Oxford, 2004), pp.1–11, 242–54; H. K. Schulze, *Grundstrukturen der Verfassung im Mittelalter* (3rd ed., 3 vols., Stuttgart, 1995–2000), I, pp.11–35.

8. P. Blickle, 'Untertanen in der Frühneuzeit', *VSWG*, 70 (1983), 483–522 at 484–8. For the following see J. Henderson, *The Medieval World of Isidore of Seville* (Cambridge, 2007); S. MacLean, 'Insinuation, censorship and the struggle for late Carolingian Lotharingia in Regino of Prüm's chronicle', *EHR*, 124 (2009), 1–28; R. Bartlett, 'Medieval and modern concepts of race and ethnicity', *Journal of Medieval and Early Modern Studies*, 31 (2001), 39–56.

9. C. Hirschi, *The Origins of Nationalism* (Cambridge, 2012), pp.62–82; U. Nonn, 'Heiliges Römisches Reich deutscher Nation. Zum Nationen-Begriff im 15. Jahrhundert', *ZHF*, 9 (1982), 129–42.

10. K. F. Werner, 'Das hochmittelalterliche Imperium im politischen Bewusstsein Frankreichs (10.–12. Jahrhundert)', *HZ*, 200 (1965), 1–60 at 16–17; Todd, *Early Germans*, pp.179–80.

11. B. Arnold, *Princes and Territories in Medieval Germany* (Cambridge, 1991), pp.66–7; R. Collins, *Early Medieval Europe, 300–1000* (Basingstoke, 1991), pp.274–7; R. Bartlett, *The Making of Europe* (London, 1993), pp.204–20; Schulze, *Grundstrukturen*, I, pp.23–5, 108.

12. J. Ehlers, 'Methodische Überlegungen zur Entstehung des deutschen Reiches im Mittelalter und zur nachwanderzeitlichen Nationenbildung', in C. Brühl and B. Schneidmüller (eds.), *Beiträge zur mittelalterlichen Reichs- und Nationsbildung in Deutschland und Frankreich* (Munich, 1997), pp.1–13.

13. K. Leyser, 'The German aristocracy from the ninth to the early twelfth century', *P&P*, 41 (1968), 25–53; K. F. Werner, 'Important noble families in the kingdom of Charlemagne', in T. Reuter (ed.), *The Medieval Nobility* (Amsterdam, 1978), pp.137–202.

14. H.-W. Goetz, 'Das Herzogtum im Spiegel der salierzeitlichen Geschichtsschreibung', in S. Weinfurter (ed.), *Die Salier und das Reich* (3 vols., Sigmaringen, 1991), I, pp.253–71, doubts the persistence of some kind of 'tribal' identity, but others present convincing evidence for regionally bounded identities: O. Engels, 'Der Reich der Salier', in ibid, III, pp.479–541 at 479–514.

15. L. Körntgen, *Ottonen und Salier* (3rd ed., Darmstadt, 2010), pp.1–3.

16. L. Gall, *Von der ständischen zur bürgerlichen Gesellschaft* (Munich, 1993); A. Haverkamp, *Medieval Germany, 1056–1273* (Oxford, 1988), pp.78–92, 198–211; G. Tellenbach, *The Church in Western Europe from the Tenth to the Early Twelfth Century* (Cambridge, 1993), pp.122–34; D. Saalfeld, 'Die ständische Gliederung der Gesellschaft Deutschlands im Zeitalter des Absolutismus', *VSWG*, 67 (1980), 457–83. For the European perspective see B. Guenée, *States and Rulers in Later Medieval Europe* (Oxford, 1985), pp.157–70. The demographic and economic changes are explored further on pp.487–98.

17. J. Laudage and Y. Leiverkus (eds.), *Rittertum und höfische Kultur der Stauferzeit* (Cologne, 2006), esp. the introduction; H. Wolfram, *Conrad II, 990–1039* (University Park, PA, 2006), pp.169–75; J. B. Freed, 'Nobles, ministerials and knights in the archdiocese of Salzburg', *Speculum*, 62 (1987), 575–611; J. Bumke, *The Concept of Knighthood in the Middle Ages* (New York, 1982); L. Silver, *Marketing Maximilian: The Visual Ideology of a Holy Roman Emperor* (Princeton, 2008), p.163; H. Wiesflecker, *Kaiser Maximilian I.* (5 vols., Vienna, 1971–86), I, p.176, V, p.518.

18. K. Leyser, *Medieval Germany and its Neighbours, 900–1250* (London, 1982), pp.161–89; H. Keller, 'Die soziale und politische Verfassung Mailands in den Anfängen des kommunalen Lebens', *HZ*, 211 (1970), 34–64 esp. 41–9.

19. B. Tolley, *Pastors and Parishioners in Württemberg during the Late Reformation, 1581–1621* (Stanford, 1995).

20. F. Geisthardt, 'Peter Melander, Graf zu Holzappel, 1589–1648', *Nassauische Lebensbilder*, 4 (1950), 36–53.

21. H. Zmora, *The Feud in Early Modern Germany* (Cambridge, 2011), pp.100–110, 133–4; H. Watanabe-O'Kelly, 'War and politics in early seventeenth-century Germany: The tournaments of the Protestant Union', in Centro di Studi Storici, Narni (ed.), *La civiltà del torneo (sec. XII–XVII)* (Rome, 1990), pp.231–45; and the chapters by L. Ognois and A. Seeliger-Zeiss in A. Ernst and A. Schindling (eds.), *Union und Liga 1608/09* (Stuttgart, 2010). Urban charters are discussed on pp.507, 513–14.

22. P. Blickle, *The Revolution of 1525* (2nd ed., Baltimore, 1985); J. G. Gagliardo, *From Pariah to Patriot: The Changing Image of the German Peasant, 1770–1840* (Lexington, KY, 1969). The identity of the 'common man' is discussed on pp.501, 579–80.

23. O. P. Clavadetscher, 'Nobilis, edel, fry', in H. Beumann (ed.), *Historische Forschungen für Walter Schlesinger* (Cologne, 1974), pp.242–51. Early modern examples of efforts to maintain status distinctions in *NTSR*, XIII, part I, 917–18, 920; XIV, 384–7.

24. H. Wunder, *He is the Sun, she is the Moon: Women in Early Modern Germany* (Cambridge, MA, 1998), p.188.

25. Quoted by Gall, *Von der ständischen zur bürgerlichen Gesellschaft*, p.7.

26. M. Hochedlinger, 'Mars ennobled: The ascent of the military and the creation of a military nobility in mid-eighteenth-century Austria', *GH*, 17 (1999), 141–76.

27. C. Dipper, *Deutsche Geschichte, 1648–1789* (Frankfurt am Main, 1991), pp.77–80; G. Schmidt, *Wandel durch Vernunft. Deutsche Geschichte im 18. Jahrhundert* (Munich, 2009), pp.291–325; O. Mörke, 'Social structure', in S. Ogilvie (ed.), *Germany: A New Social and Economic History*, II, *1630–1800* (London, 1996), pp.134–63 esp. 136–7, 148.

28. H. J. Cohn, 'Anticlericalism in the German Peasants' War 1525', *P&P*, 83 (1979), 3–31; K. Bleeck and J. Garber, 'Nobilitas. Standes- und Privilegienlegitimation in deutschen Adelstheorien des 16. und 17. Jahrhunderts', *Daphnis*, 11 (1982), 49–114; M. Kaiser, ' "Ist er vom adel? Ja. Id satis videtur". Adlige Standesqualität und militärische Leistung als Karrierefaktoren in der Epoche des Dreißigjährigen Krieges', in F. Bosbach et al. (eds.), *Geburt oder Leistung?* (Munich, 2003), pp.73–90; H. C. E. Midelfort, 'Adeliges Landleben und die Legitimationskrise des deutschen Adels im 16. Jahrhundert', in G. Schmidt (ed.), *Stände und Gesellschaft im Alten Reich* (Stuttgart, 1989), pp.245–64. For the following see also E. Schubert, 'Adel im ausgehenden 18. Jahrhundert', in J. Canning and H. Wellenreuther (eds.), *Britain and Germany Compared* (Göttingen, 2001), pp.141–229 at 144–9.

29. Wolfram, *Conrad II*, pp.322–4.

30. G. Franz, *Geschichte des deutschen Bauernstandes vom frühen Mittelalter bis zum 19. Jahrhundert* (Stuttgart, 1970), pp.26–7; M. Costambeys et al., *The Carolingian World* (Cambridge, 2011), pp.275–323. For the following see also J. A. Brundage, *Law, Sex and Christian Society in Medieval Europe* (Chicago, 1987); J. F. Harrington, *Reordering Marriage and Society in Reformation Germany* (Cambridge, 1995).

31. J. R. Lyon, *Princely Brothers and Sisters: The Sibling Bond in German Politics, 1100–1250* (Ithaca, NY, 2012); W. Störmer, *Früher Adel. Studien zur politischen Führungsschicht im fränkisch-deutschen Reich vom 8. bis 11. Jahrhundert* (2 vols., Stuttgart, 1973).

32. K. Görich, *Die Staufer. Herrscher und Reich* (2nd ed., Munich, 2008), p.20.

33. H. Keller, *Die Ottonen* (4th ed., Munich, 2008), pp.16–17; K. Schmid, 'Zum Haus- und Herrschaftsverständnis der Salier', in Weinfurter (ed.), *Die Salier*, I, pp.21–34.

34. N. Schindler, *Rebellion, Community and Custom in Early Modern Germany* (Cambridge, 2002), pp.51–84; Bartlett, *Making of Europe*, pp.270–80.

35. M. Innes, *State and Society in the Early Middle Ages: The Middle Rhine Valley, 400–1000* (Cambridge, 2000), pp.30–40; H. J. Hummer, *Politics and Power in Early Medieval Europe: Alsace and the Frankish Realm, 600–1000* (Cambridge, 2005), p.257; J. B. Freed, 'Reflections on the early medieval German nobility', *AHR*, 91 (1986), 553–75 at 563.

36. D. Abulafia, 'Introduction', in idem and N. Berend (eds.), *Medieval Frontiers* (Aldershot, 2002), pp.1–34; R. J. W. Evans, *Austria, Hungary, and the Habsburgs* (Oxford, 2006), pp.114–33.

37. F. Prinz, 'Die Grenzen des Reiches in frühsalischer Zeit', in Weinfurter (ed.), *Die Salier*, I, pp.159–73; G. Lubich, 'Früh- und hochmittelalterlicher

Adel zwischen Tauber und Neckar. Genese und Prägung adliger Herr-schaftsräume im fränkisch-schwäbischen Grenzgebiet', in S. Lorenz and S. Molitor (eds.), *Herrschaft und Legitimation* (Leinfelden-Echterdingen, 2002), pp.13–47.

38. H. Maurer, '*Confinium Alamannorum*. Über Wesen und Bedeutung hochmittelalterlicher "Stammesgrenzen"', in Beumann (ed.), *Historische Forschungen*, pp.150–61.

39. M. J. Halvorson and K. E. Spierling, *Defining Community in Early Modern Europe* (Aldershot, 2008). See also the literature cited in n.2 above and the discussion of communal ideals on pp.498–503.

40. R. Meens, 'Politics, mirrors of princes and the Bible: Sins, kings and the well-being of the realm', *EME*, 7 (1998), 345–57.

41. B. Arnold, 'Episcopal authority authenticated and fabricated: Form and function in medieval German bishops' catalogues', in T. Reuter (ed.), *Warriors and Churchmen in the High Middle Ages* (London, 1992), pp. 63–78; K. Graf, 'Feindbild und Vorbild. Bemerkungen zur städtischen Wahrnehmung des Adels', *ZGO*, 141 (1993), 121–54; C. Woodford, *Nuns as Historians in Early Modern Germany* (Oxford, 2002); D. P. Bell, *Jewish Identity in Early Modern Germany* (Aldershot, 2007), pp.72–98.

42. Y. Mintzker, *The Defortification of the German City, 1689–1866* (Cambridge, 2012), pp.11–41. See pp.508–22 for communal self-government.

43. M. Walker, *German Home Towns: Community, State and General Estate, 1648–1871* (2nd ed., Ithaca, NY, 1998); C. Applegate, *A Nation of Provincials: The German Idea of Heimat* (Berkeley, 1990).

44. I. S. Robinson (ed.), *Eleventh-Century Germany* (Manchester, 2008), p.14. Other examples include Wipo of Burgundy: T. E. Mommsen and K. F. Morrison (eds.), *Imperial Lives and Letters of the Eleventh Century* (New York, 2000), p.79, and Thietmar of Merseburg, *Ottonian Germany: The Chronicon of Thietmar of Merseburg*, ed. D. A. Warner (Manchester, 2001), esp. p.75.

45. Arnold, 'Episcopal authority', pp.77–8.

46. Goetz, 'Regnum', p.173.

47. K. Friedrich, *The Other Prussia: Royal Prussia, Poland and Liberty, 1569–1772* (Cambridge, 2000), pp.71–95.

48. F. Trautz, 'Die Reichsgewalt in Italien im Spätmittelalter', *Heidelberger Jahrbücher*, 7 (1963), 45–81 at 75. See generally B. Schmidt, '*Mappae Germaniae*. Das Alte Reich in der kartographischen Überlieferung der Frühen Neuzeit', in M. Schnettger (ed.), *Imperium Romanum – irregulare corpus – Teutscher Reichs-Staat* (Mainz, 2002), pp.3–25.

49. G. Klingenstein, 'Was bedeuten "Österreich" und "österreichisch" im 18. Jahrhundert?', in R. G. Plaschka et al. (eds.), *Was heißt Österreich?* (Vienna, 1995), pp.149–220 at 202–4.

50. E.g. M. Merian, *Topographia Germaniae* (14 vols., Frankfurt am Main, 1643–75).

CHAPTER 6: NATION

1. H. Weisert, 'Der Reichstitel bis 1806', *Archiv für Diplomatik*, 40 (1994), 441–513; H. K. Schulze, *Grundstrukturen der Verfassung im Mittelalter* (3rd ed., 3 vols., Stuttgart, 1995–2000), III, pp.50–64.

2. E. Hlawitschka, 'Vom Ausklingen der fränkischen und Einsetzen der deutschen Geschichte', in C. Brühl and B. Schneidmüller (eds.), *Beiträge zur mittelalterlichen Reichs- und Nationsbildung in Deutschland und Frankreich* (Munich, 1997), pp.53–81; M. Becher, *Otto der Große* (Munich, 2012), pp.257–64.

3. K. Herbers and H. Neuhaus, *Das Heilige Römische Reich* (Cologne, 2005), p.31.

4. T. Riches, 'The Carolingian capture of Aachen in 978 and its historiographical footprint', in P. Fouracre and D. Ganz (eds.), *Frankland: The Franks and the World of the Early Middle Ages* (Manchester, 2008), pp.191–20.

5. M. Todd, *The Early Germans* (2nd ed., Oxford, 2004), pp.8–14.

6. E. Müller-Mertens, *Regnum Teutonicum. Aufkommen und Verbreitung der deutschen Reichs- und Königsauffassung im früheren Mittelalter* (Vienna, 1970).

7. As claimed by D. Nicholas, *The Northern Lands: Germanic Europe, c.1270–c.1500* (Oxford, 2009). See the critical review by L. Scales, http://www.history.ac.uk/reviews/review/853 (accessed 1 Sept. 2010).

8. P. Geary, *The Myth of Nations: The Medieval Origins of Europe* (Princeton, 2002); L. Scales, *The Shaping of German Identity: Authority and Crisis, 1245–1414* (Cambridge, 2012), and his '*Germen militiae*: War and German identity in the later Middle Ages', *P&P*, 180 (2003), 41–82.

9. S. Wendehorst and S. Westphal (eds.), *Lesebuch Altes Reich* (Munich, 2006), pp.59–66; *NTSR*, I, 46.

10. C. J. Wells, *German: A Linguistic History to 1945* (Oxford, 1985), pp. 95–125; W. B. Lockwood, *An Informal History of the German Language* (2nd ed., London, 1976), pp.11–77; R. Bergmann, 'Deutsche Sprache und römisches Reich im Mittelalter', in B. Schneidmüller and S. Weinfurter (eds.), *Heilig – Römisch – Deutsch. Das Reich im mittelalterlichen Europa* (Dresden, 2006), pp.162–84. See generally R. Bartlett, *The Making of Europe* (London, 1993), pp.198–204.

11. L. Scales, 'Rose without thorn, eagle without feathers: Nation and power in late medieval England and Germany', *GHIL*, 31 (2009), 3–35 at 23–8.

12. M. Prietzel, *Das Heilige Römische Reich im Spätmittelalter* (2nd ed., Darmstadt, 2010), p.88; P. Burke, *Languages and Communities in Early Modern Europe* (Cambridge, 2004), esp. pp.79–84.

13. Scales, *German Identity*, pp.427–30.

14. U. Rublack, *Dressing Up: Cultural Identity in Renaissance Europe* (Oxford, 2010), pp.10, 265–70; T. Weller, *Theatrum Praecedentiae. Zeremonieller Rang und gesellschaftliche Ordnung in der frühneuzeitlichen Stadt: Leipzig, 1500–1800* (Darmstadt, 2006), pp.82–119. For the following see also C. Hirschi, *The Origins of Nationalism* (Cambridge, 2012), pp.99–118.

15. Quoted in Weller, *Theatrum Praecedentiae*, p.97.

16. M. von Engelberg, ' "Deutscher Barock" oder "Barock in Deutschland" – Nur ein Streit um Worte?', in G. Schmidt (ed.), *Die deutsche Nation im frühneuzeitlichen Europa* (Munich, 2010), pp.307–34; T. DaCosta Kaufmann, 'Centres or periphery? Art and architecture in the Empire', in R. J. W. Evans and P. H. Wilson (eds.), *The Holy Roman Empire, 1495–1806: A European Perspective* (Leiden, 2012), pp.315–32; P. C. Hartmann, *Kulturgeschichte des Heiligen Römischen Reiches 1648 bis 1806* (Vienna, 2001).

17. C. Scharf, *Katharina II., Deutschland und die Deutschen* (Mainz, 1995), pp.55–271; M. North, 'Nationale und kulturelle Selbstverortung in der Diaspora: Die Deutschen in den russischen Ostseeprovinzen des 18. Jahrhunderts', in Schmidt (ed.), *Die deutsche Nation*, pp.83–96; H.-J. Bömelburg, 'Polen und die deutsche Nation', in ibid, pp.129–55.

18. J. Whaley, *Germany and the Holy Roman Empire, 1493–1806* (2 vols., Oxford, 2012), I, pp.53–7; Todd, *Early Germans*, pp.4–7; Hirschi, *Origins of Nationalism*, pp.11, 119–79.

19. C. Sieber-Lehmann, ' "Teutsche Nation" und Eidgenossenschaft. Der Zusammenhang zwischen Türken- und Burgunderkriegen', *HZ*, 253 (1991), 561–602; T. Scott, 'The Reformation between deconstruction and reconstruction', *GH*, 26 (2008), 406–22.

20. B. Brandt, 'Germania in armor: The female representation of an endangered German nation', in S. Colvin and H. Watanabe-O'Kelly (eds.), *Warlike Women in the German Literary and Cultural Imagination since 1500* (Rochester, NY, 2009), pp.86–126; H. Watanabe-O'Kelly, *Beauty or Beast? The Woman Warrior in the German Imagination from the Renaissance to the Present* (Oxford, 2010), esp. pp.10–11.

21. D. V. N. Bagchi, ' "Teutschland über alle Welt": Nationalism and Catholicism in early Reformation Germany', *Archiv für Reformationsgeschichte*, 82 (1991), 39–58; K. Manger (ed.), *Die Fruchtbringer – eine Teutschherzige Gesellschaft* (Heidelberg, 2001).

22. F. Brendle, *Der Erzkanzler im Religionskrieg. Kurfürst Anselm Casimir von Mainz, die geistlichen Fürsten und das Reich 1629 bis 1647* (Mainz,

2011), pp.491–7. See generally A. Schmidt, *Vaterlandsliebe und Religions-konflikt. Politische Diskurse im Alten Reich (1555–1648)* (Leiden, 2007).

23. This is a common tendency, e.g. P. Blickle, *Das Alte Europa. Vom Hoch-mittelalter bis zur Moderne* (Munich, 2008), pp.160–62. See more generally W. te Brake, *Shaping History: Ordinary People in European Politics, 1500–1700* (Berkeley, 1998); E. Hölzle, *Die Idee einer altgerman-ischen Freiheit vor Montesquieu* (Munich, 1925); G. Schmidt, 'Die "deutsche Freiheit" und der Westfälische Friede', in R. G. Asch et al. (eds.), *Frieden und Krieg in der Frühen Neuzeit* (Munich, 2001), pp.323–47.

24. H. Dreitzel, *Absolutismus und ständische Verfassung in Deutschland* (Mainz, 1992), pp.17, 65–6, 74–5.

25. T. C. W. Blanning, *The Culture of Power and the Power of Culture: Old Regime Europe, 1660–1789* (Oxford, 2002), p.66. For the following see the three works by W. Behringer: *Im Zeichen des Merkur. Reichspost und Kommunikationsrevolution in der Frühen Neuzeit* (Göttingen, 2003); 'Communications revolutions: A historiographical concept', *GH*, 24 (2006), 333–74; 'Core and periphery: The Holy Roman Empire as a communication(s) universe', in R. J. W. Evans et al. (eds.), *The Holy Roman Empire, 1495–1806* (Oxford, 2011), pp.347–58.

26. W. Adam and S. Westphal (eds.), *Handbuch der kultureller Zentren der Frühen Neuzeit. Städte und Residenzen im alten deutschen Sprachraum* (3 vols., Berlin, 2012).

27. H. Schutz, *The Carolingians in Central Europe, their History, Arts and Architecture* (Leiden, 2004); R. McKitterick (ed.), *Carolingian Culture: Emulation and Innovation* (Cambridge, 1994), and her 'The Carolingian Renaissance of culture and learning', in J. Story (ed.), *Charlemagne* (Man-chester, 2005), pp.151–66.

28. R. Staats, *Die Reichskrone. Geschichte und Bedeutung eines euro-päischen Symbols* (2nd ed., Kiel, 2008); G. J. Kugler, *Die Reichskrone* (Vienna, 1968); G. G. Wolf, *Die Wiener Reichskrone* (Vienna, 1995); J. Ott, *Krone und Krönung. Die Verheißung und Verleihung von Kronen in der Kunst von der Spätantike bis um 1200 und die geistige Auslegung der Krone* (Mainz, 1998). It has also been suggested it was made for Conrad II in 1024, or even Conrad III around a century later: M. Schulze-Dörrlamm, *Die Kaiserkrone Konrads II. (1024–1039)* (Sigmaringen, 1991). The polit-ical significance of coronations and the insignia generally is discussed on pp.301–2, 309–11.

29. HHStA, Staatskanzlei Vorträge, Kart.168 (9 Aug. 1804).

30. M. Schulze-Dörrlamm, *Der Mainzer Schatz der Kaiserin Agnes aus dem mittleren 11. Jahrhundert* (Sigmaringen, 1991); H. Keller, *Ottonische Königsherrschaft* (Darmstadt, 2002), pp.30–32. For detailed discussions of all the insignia and possible meanings, see H. Fillitz, *Die Insig-nien und Kleinodien des Heiligen Römischen Reiches* (Vienna, 1954);

P. E. Schramm, *Herrschaftszeichen und Staatssymbolik* (3 vols., Stuttgart, 1954–6). Most of the items are displayed in the Imperial Treasury in Vienna and can be viewed in colour in M. Leithe-Jasper and R. Distelberger, *The Kunsthistorisches Museum Vienna: The Imperial and Ecclesiastical Treasury* (London, 2003).

31. H. L. Adelson, 'The Holy Lance and the hereditary German monarchy', *The Art Bulletin*, 48 (1966), 177–92. The Lance had several associations, including with the spear used by Roman legionary Longinus to pierce Christ's side, and with St Mauritius, patron saint of Burgundy. Recent research dismisses any association with Odin and a pagan Germanic tradition.

32. M. Schulze-Dörrlamm, *Das Reichsschwert* (Sigmaringen, 1995), discusses the various swords, again suggesting a much later date in line with her interpretation of the imperial crown.

33. Keller, *Ottonische Königsherrschaft*, pp.131–66.

34. J. Lowden, 'The royal/imperial book and the image or self-image of the medieval ruler', in A. J. Duggan (ed.), *Kings and Kingship in Medieval Europe* (London, 1993), pp.213–39; B. Schneidmüller, 'Zwischen Gott und den Getreuen', *FMS*, 36 (2002), 193–224 at 210–19; J. Laudage et al., *Die Zeit der Karolinger* (Darmstadt, 2006), pp.91–106; L. Scales, 'The illuminated Reich: Memory, crisis and the visibility of monarchy in late medieval Germany', in J. P. Coy et al. (eds.), *The Holy Roman Empire, Reconsidered* (New York, 2010), pp.73–92.

35. F.-H. Hye, 'Der Doppeladler als Symbol für Kaiser und Reich', *MIÖG*, 81 (1973), 63–100; C. D. Bleisteiner, 'Der Doppeladler von Kaiser und Reich im Mittelalter', *MIÖG*, 109 (2001), 4–52; B. Pferschy-Maleczek, 'Der Nimbus des Doppeladlers. Mystik und Allegorie im Siegelbild Kaiser Sigismunds', *ZHF*, 23 (1996), 433–71.

36. E. Ricchiardi, *La bandiere di Carlo Alberto (1814–1849)* (Turin, 2000).

37. R. A. Müller (ed.), *Bilder des Reiches* (Sigmaringen, 1997); M. Tanner, *The Last Descendant of Aeneas: The Hapsburgs and the Mythic Image of the Emperor* (New Haven, CT, 1993).

38. B. Stollberg-Rilinger, *Des Kaisers alte Kleider* (Munich, 2008), pp.55–60.

39. E. Schubert, 'Die Quaternionen. Entstehung, Sinngehalt und Folgen einer spätmittelalterlichen Deutung der Reichsverfassung', *ZHF*, 20 (1993), 1–63; H. J. Cohn, 'The electors and imperial rule at the end of the fifteenth century', in B. Weiler and S. MacLean (eds.), *Representations of Power in Medieval Germany, 800–1500* (Turnhout, 2006), pp.295–318 at 296, 300–303.

40. M. Goloubeva, *The Glorification of Emperor Leopold I in Image, Spectacle and Text* (Mainz, 2000), p.40.

41. R. J. W. Evans, *Rudolf II and his World* (2nd ed., London, 1997), pp.167–70. For the following see A. H. Weaver, *Sacred Music as Public Image for Holy Roman Emperor Ferdinand III* (Farnham, 2012); P. K. Monod, *The*

Power of Kings: Monarchy and Religion in Europe, 1589–1715 (New Haven, CT, 1999), pp.235–6; F. Matsche, *Die Kunst im Dienst der Staatsidee Kaiser Karl VI.* (2 vols., Berlin, 1981).

42. W. Braunfels, *Die Kunst im Heiligen Römischen Reich* (6 vols., Munich, 1979–89). Royal palaces are discussed on pp.332–4, while tombs are covered on pp.248, 274, 334, 367.

43. R. Hirsch, *Printing, Selling and Reading, 1450–1550* (Wiesbaden, 1967); L. Silver, *Marketing Maximilian: The Visual Ideology of a Holy Roman Emperor* (Princeton, 2008). For the debates on political communication within the Empire see A. Gestrich, *Absolutismus und Öffentlichkeit* (Göttingen, 1994). For the following see J. L. Flood, *Poets Laureate in the Holy Roman Empire* (4 vols., Berlin, 2006).

44. S. Friedrich, *Drehscheibe Regensburg. Das Informations- und Kommunikationssystem des Immerwährenden Reichstags um 1700* (Berlin, 2007); J. Feuchter and J. Helmrath (eds.), *Politische Redekultur in der Vormoderne* (Frankfurt am Main, 2008); K. Härter, 'War as political and constitutional discourse: Imperial warfare and the military constitution of the Holy Roman Empire in the politics of the Permanent Diet (1663–1806)', in A. de Benedictis and C. Magoni (eds.), *Teatri di guerra* (Bologna, 2010), pp.215–37.

45. P. S. Spalding, *Seize the Book, Jail the Author: Johann Lorenz Schmidt and Censorship in Eighteenth-Century Germany* (West Lafayette, IN, 1998); Wendehorst and Westphal (eds.), *Lesebuch Altes Reich*, pp.34–5.

46. P. E. Selwyn, *Everyday Life in the German Book Trade* (University Park, PA, 2000), pp.189–206; A. Strohmeyer, 'Zwischen Kaiserhof und französischem Hof', in J. Bahlcke and C. Kampmann (eds.), *Wallensteinbilder im Widerstreit* (Cologne, 2011), pp.51–74 at 70.

47. C. Dipper, *Deutsche Geschichte, 1648–1789* (Frankfurt am Main, 1991), pp.207–10.

48. Although focusing on two smaller institutions, Matthias Asche provides a good overview of higher education throughout the Empire's history: *Von der reichen hansischen Bürgeruniversität zur armen mecklenburgischen Landeshochschule* (Stuttgart, 2000). See also A. Rutz, 'Territoriale Integration durch Bildung und Erziehung?', in M. Grote et al. (eds.), *Der Jülich-Klevische Erbstreit 1609* (Düsseldorf, 2011), pp.337–57; J. V. H. Melton, *Absolutism and the Eighteenth-Century Origins of Compulsory Schooling in Prussia and Austria* (Cambridge, 1988); Hartmann, *Kulturgeschichte*, pp.327–46.

49. J. V. H. Melton, *The Rise of the Public in Enlightenment Europe* (Cambridge, 2001), pp.105–8.

50. J. Weber, 'Strassburg, 1605: The origins of the newspaper in Europe', *GH*, 24 (2006), 387–412. See also W. Behringer's publications cited

in n.25 above, and A. Pettegree's *The Invention of News: How the World Came to Know About Itself* (New Haven, CT, and London, 2014).

51. Melton, *Rise of the Public*, p.123; Selwyn, *Everyday Life*, p.96; Whaley, *Germany*, II, p.465.

52. M. Walker, *Johann Jakob Moser and the Holy Roman Empire of the German Nation* (Chapel Hill, NC, 1981); A. Gestrich and R. Lächele (eds.), *Johann Jacob Moser* (Karlsruhe, 2002).

53. Enea Silvio Piccolomini, *Deutschland*, ed. A. Schmidt (Cologne, 1962), p.122. For the following see M. Stolleis, *Geschichte des öffentlichen Rechts in Deutschland*, vol. I (Munich, 1988).

54. W. Burgdorf, *Reichskonstitution und Nation. Verfassungsreformprojekte für das Heilige Römische Reich deutscher Nation im politischen Schrifttum von 1648 bis 1806* (Mainz, 1998), pp.140–48.

55. B. Roeck, *Reichssystem und Reichsherkommen. Die Diskussion über die Staatlichkeit des Reiches in der politischen Publizistik des 17. und 18. Jahrhunderts* (Stuttgart, 1984), p.28; P. Schröder, 'The constitution of the Holy Roman Empire after 1648: Samuel Pufendorf's assessment in his *Monzambano*', *HJ*, 42 (1999), 961–83. For a good modern edition see H. Denzer (ed.), *Die Verfassung des deutschen Reiches* (Stuttgart, 1994).

56. Quoted in H. Schilling, *Höfe und Allianzen. Deutschland 1648–1763* (Berlin, 1989), p.125.

57. Weissert, 'Reichstitel', 468–70. For the following see M. Lindemann, *Patriots and Paupers: Hamburg, 1712–1830* (Oxford, 1990), esp. pp.78–83; M. Levinger, *Enlightened Nationalism: The Transformation of Prussian Political Culture, 1806–1848* (Oxford, 2000).

58. E.g. by H. A. Winkler, *Germany: The Long Road West* (2 vols., Oxford, 2006–7), I, pp.31–2.

59. M. Wrede, *Das Reich und seine Feinde* (Mainz, 2004).

60. L. Lisy-Wagner, *Islam, Christianity and the Making of Czech Identity, 1453–1683* (Farnham, 2013).

61. F. Ranieri, *Recht und Gesellschaft im Zeitalter der Rezeption. Eine rechts- und sozialgeschichtliche Analyse der Tätigkeit des Reichskammergerichts im 16. Jahrhundert* (2 vols., Cologne, 1985).

62. H. Keller, 'Der Blick von Italien auf das "römische" Imperium und seine "deutschen" Kaiser', in Schneidmüller and Weinfurter (eds.), *Heilig – Römisch – Deutsch*, pp.286–307.

63. S. K. Cohn Jr, *Lust for Liberty: The Politics of Social Revolt in Medieval Europe, 1200–1425* (Cambridge, MA, 2006), p.218. See also N. Rubenstein, 'The place of the Empire in fifteenth-century Florentine political opinion and diplomacy', *Bulletin of the Institute of Historical Research*, 30 (1957), 125–35; M. Schnettger, '*Impero Romano – Impero Germanico*. Italienische Perspektiven auf das Reich in der Frühen Neuzeit', in idem

(ed.), *Imperium Romanum – irregulare corpus – Teutsche Reichs-Staat* (Mainz, 2002), pp.53–75.

64. Recently, this interpretation has been given new life by those arguing that the Empire's political culture was essentially aristocratic and that its existence was purely 'virtual', devoid of any real meaning for daily existence. The social dimension of this discussion is explored in Part IV.

65. G. Schnath, *Geschichte Hannovers im Zeitalter der neunten Kur und der englischen Sukzession, 1674–1714* (5 vols., Hildesheim, 1938–82), I, p.166.

66. Quoted in W. Jannen Jr, ' "Das liebe Teutschland" in the seventeenth century – Count George Frederick von Waldeck', *European Studies Review*, 6 (1976), 165–95 at 178; Kugler, *Reichskrone*, pp.113–19.

67. P. H. Wilson, 'The nobility of the early modern Reich, 1495–1806', in H. M. Scott (ed.), *The European Nobilities in the Seventeenth and Eighteenth Centuries* (2nd ed., 2 vols., Basingstoke, 2007), II, pp.73–117; H. Carl, 'Europäische Adelsgesellschaft und deutsche Nation in der Frühen Neuzeit', in Schmidt (ed.), *Die deutsche Nation*, pp.181–99; B. Giesen, *Intellectuals and the Nation: Collective Identity in a German Axial Age* (Cambridge, 1998).

68. P. Moraw, 'Kanzlei und Kanzleipersonal König Ruprechts', *Archiv für Diplomatik*, 15 (1969), 428–531; G. Schmidt-von Rhein, 'Das Reichskammergericht in Wetzlar', *NA*, 100 (1989), 127–40 at 127–30; A. Baumann et al. (eds.), *Reichspersonal. Funktionsträger für Kaiser und Reich* (Cologne, 2003).

69. B. Koch, *Räte auf deutschen Reichsversammlungen. Zur Entwicklung der politischen Funktionselite im 15. Jahrhundert* (Frankfurt am Main, 1999); B. Wunder, 'Die Sozialstruktur der Geheimratskollegien in den süddeutschen protestantischen Fürstentümern (1660–1720)', *VSWG*, 58 (1971), 145–220.

70. *HHStA*, Prinzipalkommissar Berichte Fasz.182d, letter of 11 Aug. 1806.

71. W. Burgdorf, *Ein Weltbild verliert seine Welt. Der Untergang des Alten Reiches und die Generation 1806* (2nd ed., Munich, 2009), pp.211–17; S. Ehrenpreis et al., 'Probing the legal history of the Jews in the Holy Roman Empire', *Jahrbuch des Simon-Dubnow-Instituts*, 2 (2003), 409–87 at 443, 451–4; D. P. Bell, *Jewish Identity in Early Modern Germany* (Aldershot, 2007), p.80.

72. G. J. Schenk, *Zeremoniell und Politik. Herrschereinzüge im spätmittelalterlichen Reich* (Cologne, 2003); M. A. Bojcov, 'How one archbishop of Trier perambulated his lands', in Weiler and MacLean (eds.), *Representations of Power*, pp.319–48; H. J. Cohn, 'Representing political space at a political site: The imperial diets of the sixteenth century', in B. Kümin (ed.), *Political Space in Pre-industrial Europe* (Farnham, 2009), pp.19–42; L. E. Saurma-Jeltsch, 'Das mittelalterliche Reich in der Reichsstadt', in

Schneidmüller and Weinfurter (eds.), *Heilig – Römisch – Deutsch*, pp. 399–439. For the 1742 election see P. C. Hartmann, *Karl Albrecht – Karl VII*. (Regensburg, 1985), pp.218–43.

73. E.g. fifteenth-century Frankfurt: H. Boockmann, 'Geschäfte und Geschäftigkeit auf dem Reichstag im späten Mittelalter', *HZ*, 246 (1988), 297–325.

74. M. Merian, *Topographia Germaniae* (14 vols., Frankfurt am Main, 1643–75), volume covering Swabia, plate between pages 10 and 11. The city was to be disappointed: no Reichstag had been held there since 1582 except for briefly in 1713 when it temporarily relocated from Regensburg to avoid the plague.

75. H. J. Berbig, 'Der Krönungsritus im Alten Reich (1648–1806)', *ZBLG*, 38 (1975), 639–700.

76. H. Keller, *Die Ottonen* (4th ed., Munich, 2008), p.56; W. Hartmann, *Der Investiturstreit* (3rd ed., Munich, 2007), p.34; B. Schneidmüller, *Die Kaiser des Mittelalters* (2nd ed., Munich, 2007), p.107.

77. C. Hattenhauer, *Wahl und Krönung Franz II. AD 1792* (Frankfurt am Main, 1995), p.137; Gestrich, *Absolutismus und Öffentlichkeit*, pp.151–2.

78. P. Münz, *Frederick Barbarossa* (London, 1969), p.10. Further discussion of the peasants' political identification with the emperor on p.592.

79. W. Troßbach, 'Die Reichsgerichte in der Sicht bäuerlicher Untertanen', in B. Diestelkamp (ed.), *Das Reichskammergericht in der deutschen Geschichte* (Cologne, 1990), pp.129–42; D. M. Luebke, *His Majesty's Rebels: Communities, Factions and Rural Revolt in the Black Forest, 1725–1745* (Ithaca, NY, 1997).

80. Wendehorst and Westphal (eds.), *Lesebuch*, pp.48–51, 95–6.

81. T. Biskup, *Friedrichs Größe: Inszenierungen des Preußenkönigs in Fest und Zeremoniell, 1740–1815* (Frankfurt, 2012); S. Mazura, *Die preußische und österreichische Kriegspropaganda im Ersten und Zweiten Schlesischen Krieg* (Berlin, 1996); G. Schmidt, *Geschichte des Alten Reiches* (Munich, 1999), pp.271–89, 352; Blanning, *The Culture of Power*, pp.212–32.

82. J. W. von Archenholz, *Geschichte des Siebenjährigen Krieges in Deutschland* in Deutschland (Berlin, 1828), pp.76–80.

83. A. Green, 'Political institutions and nationhood in Germany', in L. Scales and O. Zimmer (eds.), *Power and the Nation in European History* (Cambridge, 2005), pp.315–32 at 317–18; Whaley, *Germany*, II, pp.410–12; Wendehorst and Westphal (eds.), *Lesebuch*, pp.16–18.

84. See Goethe's reminiscences: *Collected Works*, Vol. 12, ed. T. P. Saine and J. L. Sammons (Princeton, 1987), IV, *From my Life: Poetry and Truth*, pp.139–61. Further discussion in D. Beales, *Joseph II* (2 vols.,

Cambridge, 1987–2009), I, pp.111–15; Stollberg-Rilinger, *Des Kaisers alte Kleider*, pp.227–81.

85. Winkler, *Germany*, I, p.49. See also C. Wiedemann, 'Zwischen National-geist und Kosmopolitismus. Über die Schwierigkeiten der deutschen Klassiker, einen Nationalhelden zu finden', *Aufklärung*, 4 (1989), 75–101, and generally E. Kedourie, *Nationalism* (3rd ed., London, 1966).

86. D. Fulda, 'Zwischen Gelehrten- und Kulturnationalismus. Die "deutsche Nation" in der literaturpolitischen Publizistik Johann Christoph Gottscheds', in Schmidt (ed.), *Die deutsche Nation*, pp.267–91.

87. I. F. McNeely, *The Emancipation of Writing: German Civil Society in the Making, 1790s–1820s* (Berkeley, CA, 2003), pp.242–3.

CHAPTER 7: KINGSHIP

1. H. Neuhaus, *Das Reich in der Frühen Neuzeit* (Munich, 1997), pp.17–19, with more detail in *NTSR*, II.

2. H. Wolfram, *Conrad II, 990–1039* (University Park, PA, 2006), pp.150–53; H. Keller, *Ottonische Königsherrschaft* (Darmstadt, 2002), pp.30–32;.K. Leyser, *Medieval Germany and its Neighbours, 900–1250* (London, 1982), pp.241–67; K. Repgen (ed.), *Das Herrscherbild im 17. Jahrhundert* (Münster, 1991). Royal piety is discussed on pp.30–32.

3. See e.g. Wipo of Burgundy's comments on Conrad II: T. E. Mommsen and K. F. Morrison (eds.), *Imperial Lives and Letters of the Eleventh Century* (New York, 2000), pp.65–6. For the following: B. Weiler, 'The *rex renitens* and the medieval idea of kingship, ca. 900–ca. 1250', *Viator*, 31 (2000), 1–42.

4. Thietmar of Merseburg, *Ottonian Germany: The Chronicon of Thietmar of Merseburg*, ed. D. A. Warner (Manchester, 2001), pp.18–21. Also Regino of Prüm in S. MacLean (ed.), *History and Politics in Late Carolingian and Ottonian Europe* (Manchester, 2009), pp.45–6.

5. Useful discussion in K. Görich, *Friedrich Barbarossa* (Munich, 2011), pp.601–48.

6. H.-D. Kahl, 'Zum Ursprung von germ. *König*', *ZSRG GA*, 77 (1960), 198–240.

7. E. Hlawitschka, 'Zur Herkunft und zu den Seitenverwandten des Gegen-königs Rudolf von Rheinfelden', and M. Twellenkamp, 'Das Haus der Luxemburger', both in S. Weinfurter (ed.), *Die Salier und das Reich* (3 vols., Sigmaringen, 1991), I, pp.175–220, 475–502 at 492–6. See also D. Mertens, 'Von Rhein zur Rems' in ibid, I, pp.221–52, for Staufer claims of descent from the Salians.

8. C. Hirschi, *The Origins of Nationalism* (Cambridge, 2012), pp.180–95; H. J. Cohn, 'Did bribes induce the German electors to choose Charles

V as emperor in 1519?', *GH*, 19 (2001), 1–27; A. Schmidt, 'Ein französischer Kaiser? Die Diskussion um die Nationalität des Reichsoberhauptes im 17. Jahrhundert', *HJb*, 123 (2003), 149–77.

9. H. Stoob, 'Zur Königswahl Lothars von Sachsen im Jahre 1125', in H. Beumann (ed.), *Historische Forschungen für Walter Schlesinger* (Cologne, 1974), pp.438–61. For Lothar III's election, see also pp.357–8. For the importance of judging medieval kings according to their contemporaries' expectations, see G. Althoff, *Otto III* (Philadelphia, 2003), pp.132–46.

10. T. Reuter, 'The medieval German *Sonderweg*? The Empire and its rulers in the high Middle Ages', in A. J. Duggan (ed.), *Kings and Kingship in Medieval Europe* (London, 1993), pp.179–211 at 197.

11. G. Althoff, *Die Ottonen* (2nd ed., Stuttgart, 2005), pp.61–4.

12. K. Görich, *Die Staufer* (2nd ed., Munich, 2008), p.35.

13. Wolfram, *Conrad II*, p.25; G. Lubich, 'Beobachtungen zur Wahl Konrads III. und ihrem Umfeld', *HJb*, 117 (1997), 311–39 at 312; E. J. Goldberg, *Struggle for Empire: Kingship and Conflict under Louis the German, 817–876* (Ithaca, NY, 2006), pp.189–91.

14. H. Fuhrmann, *Germany in the High Middle Ages, c.1050–1200* (Cambridge, 1986), p.39.

15. J. K. Hoensch, *Die Luxemburger. Eine spätmittelalterliche Dynastie gesamteuropäischer Bedeutung, 1308–1437* (Stuttgart, 2000), p.108.

16. Thietmar of Merseburg, *Chronicon*, pp.187–90; Althoff, *Die Ottonen*, pp.202–7. See generally J. Petersohn, 'Über monarchische Insignien und ihre Funktion im mittelalterlichen Reich', *HZ*, 266 (1998), 47–96.

17. P. Moraw, 'Ruprecht von der Pfalz. Ein König aus Heidelberg', *ZGO*, 149 (2001), 97–110 at 98.

18. Typical of the older view is the belief that the emperor was reduced to a 'figurehead': G. H. Perris, *Germany and the German Emperor* (London, 1912), pp.34–5.

19. J. Gillingham, 'Elective kingship and the unity of medieval Germany', *GH*, 9 (1991), 124–35 at 128–9.

20. Ibid, 132.

21. The emphasis on 'blood right' is strongest in literature appearing in the Nazi era: H. Mitteis, *Die deutsche Königswahl. Ihre Rechtsgrundlagen bis zur Goldenen Bulle* (Darmstadt, 1975; 1st pub. 1938). Fuller discussion of these points in E. Hlawitschka, *Untersuchungen zu den Thronwechseln der ersten Hälfte des 11. Jahrhunderts und zur Adelsgeschichte Süddeutschlands* (Sigmaringen, 1987); R. Schneider, *Königswahl und Königserhebung im Frühmittelalter* (Stuttgart, 1972).

22. E. Perels, *Der Erbreichsplan Heinrichs VI.* (Berlin, 1927); U. Schmidt, *Königswahl und Thronfolge im 12. Jahrhundert* (Cologne, 1987), pp.225–60.

23. Schmidt, *Königswahl*, pp.145–66.

24. U. Reuling, *Die Kur in Deutschland und Frankreich. Untersuchungen zur Entwicklung des rechtsförmlichen Wahlaktes bei der Königserhebung im 11. und 12. Jahrhundert* (Göttingen, 1979), p.205; S. Patzold, 'Königserhebungen zwischen Erbrecht und Wahlrecht? Thronfolge und Rechtsmentalität um das Jahr 1000', *DA*, 58 (2002), 467-507.

25. A. Begert, *Die Entstehung und Entwicklung des Kurkollegs. Von den Anfängen bis zum frühen 15. Jahrhundert* (Berlin, 2010), pp.171-90.

26. Schmidt, *Königswahl*, p.33. For Rudolf see T. Struve, *Salierzeit im Wandel* (Cologne, 2006), pp.84-95. For his election see I. S. Robinson, *Henry IV of Germany, 1056-1106* (Cambridge, 1999), pp.167-70; H. E. J. Cowdrey, *Pope Gregory VII, 1073-1085* (Oxford, 1998), pp.167-71; Reuling, *Die Kur*, pp.104-16.

27. Schmidt, *Königswahl*, p.262. See also ibid, pp.34-59, 69-91; B. Schneidmüller, '1125 - Unruhe als politische Kraft im mittelalterlichen Reich', in W. Hechberger and F. Schuller (eds.), *Staufer & Welfen* (Regensburg, 2009), pp.31-49; S. Dick, 'Die Königserhebung Friedrich Barbarossas im Spiegel der Quellen', *ZSRG GA*, 121 (2004), 200-237.

28. The older interpretation is voiced by Mitteis, *Die deutsche Königswahl*, pp.95-8.

29. U. Reinhardt, *Untersuchungen zur Stellung der Geistlichkeit bei den Königswahlen im Fränkischen und Deutschen Reich (751-1250)* (Marburg, 1975), esp. pp.83-9; D. Waßenhoven, 'Bischöfe als Königsmacher? Selbstverständnis und Anspruch des Episkopats bei Herrscherwechseln im 10. und frühen 11. Jahrhundert', in L. Körntgen and D. Waßerhoven (eds.), *Religion and Politics in the Middle Ages: Germany and England by Comparison* (Berlin, 2013), pp.31-50; R. Reisinger, *Die römisch-deutschen Könige und ihre Wähler, 1198-1273* (Aalen, 1977), p.110.

30. H. C. Faußner, 'Die Thronerhebung des deutschen Königs im Hochmittelalter und die Entstehung des Kurfürstenkollegiums', *ZSRG GA*, 108 (1991), 1-60 at 34-8.

31. E. Boshof, 'Erstkurrecht und Erzämtertheorie im Sachsenspiegel', in T. Schieder (ed.), *Beiträge zur Geschichte des mittelalterlichen deutschen Königtums* (Munich, 1973), pp.84-121.

32. H. Stehkämper, 'Der Kölner Erzbischof Adolf von Altena und die deutsche Königswahl (1195-1205)', in Schieder (ed.), *Beiträge*, pp.5-83. See also Reinhardt, *Untersuchungen zur Stellung der Geistlichkeit*, pp.269-73.

33. Begert, *Die Entstehung und Entwicklung des Kurkollegs*, pp.149-70. The arch-offices are discussed on pp.319-20.

34. A. Wolf, *Die Entstehung des Kurfürstenkollegs, 1198-1298* (Idstein, 1998); W.-D. Mohrmann, *Lauenburg oder Wittenberg? Zum Problem des sächsischen Kurstreites bis zur Mitte des 14. Jahrhunderts* (Hildesheim, 1975); U. Hohensee et al. (eds.), *Die Goldene Bulle.*

Politik - Wahrnehmung - Rezeption (2 vols., Berlin, 2009). For Charles IV's motives, see pp.389-92.

35. A. Gotthard, *Säulen des Reiches. Die Kurfürsten im frühneuzeitlichen Reichsverband* (Husum, 1999), pp.609-11; T. Brockmann, *Dynastie, Kaiseramt und Konfession* (Paderborn, 2011), pp.320-25. The figures look a little better from the Habsburgs' perspective when we remember that two imperial elections were triggered by the unexpectedly early deaths of incumbent emperors (1711, 1792), while another election was held following the equally unanticipated premature death of a king of the Romans (1658).

36. Goldberg, *Struggle for Empire*, pp.220-21.

37. S. Haider, *Die Wahlversprechungen der römisch-deutschen Könige bis zum Ende des zwölften Jahrhunderts* (Vienna, 1968); G. Kleinheyer, *Die kaiserlichen Wahlkapitulationen* (Karlsruhe, 1968), pp.21-2.

38. The 1711 agreement is printed in K. Zeumer (ed.), *Quellensammlung zur Geschichte der deutschen Reichsverfassung in Mittelalter und Neuzeit* (Tübingen, 1913), pp.474-97. See also H.-M. Empell, 'De eligendo regis vivente imperatore. Die Regelung in der Beständigen Wahlkapitulation und ihre Interpretation in der Staatsrechtsliteratur des 18. Jahrhunderts', *ZNRG*, 16 (1994), 11-24.

39. E. Boshof, *Königtum und Königsherrschaft im 10. und 11. Jahrhundert* (3rd ed., Munich, 2010), pp.51-77; W. Goldinger, 'Das Zeremoniell der deutschen Königskrönung seit dem späten Mittelalter', *Mitteilungen des Oberösterreichischen Landesarchivs*, 5 (1957), 91-111; H. J. Berbig, 'Der Krönungsritus im Alten Reich (1648-1806)', *ZBLG*, 38 (1975), 639-700. For the following see also R. Elze (ed.), *Ordines coronationis imperialis* (MGH, vol.19, Hanover, 1960).

40. R. A. Jackson (ed.), *Ordines coronationis franciae: Texts and Ordines for the Coronation of Frankish and French Kings and Queens in the Middle Ages* (2 vols., Philadelphia, 1995-2000), I, pp.1-23. Charlemagne's coronation is discussed on pp.26-9.

41. Thietmar of Merseburg, *Chronicon*, pp.72-3. See also Reinhardt, *Untersuchungen zur Stellung der Geistlichkeit*, pp.83-4, 90-132; Keller, *Ottonische Königsherrschaft*, pp.91-130.

42. E. Boshof, 'Köln, Mainz, Trier. Die Auseinandersetzung um die Spitzenstellung im deutschen Episkopat in ottonisch-salischer Zeit', *Jahrbuch des Kölnischen Geschichtsvereins*, 49 (1978), 19-48.

43. See contemporary descriptions: C. Hattenhauer, *Wahl und Krönung Franz II. AD 1792* (Frankfurt am Main, 1995), pp.203-360; *NTSR*, II, 311-59.

44. R. Schieffer, 'Otto II. und sein Vater', *FMS*, 36 (2002), 255-69.

45. B. Weiler, 'Reasserting power: Frederick II in Germany (1235-1236)', in idem and S. MacLean (eds.), *Representations of Power in Medieval Germany, 800-1500* (Turnhout, 2006), pp.241-71. Henry is numbered (VII),

because his status was either unknown or not recognized at Henry VII's accession in 1308.

46. A. Wolf, 'Reigning queens in medieval Europe: When, where, and why', in J. C. Parsons (ed.), *Medieval Queenship* (Stroud, 1994), pp.169–88.

47. A. Fößel, *Die Königin im mittelalterlichen Reich* (Sigmaringen, 2000), pp.17–49; B. Stollberg-Rilinger, *Des Kaisers alte Kleider* (Munich, 2008), pp.190–93; *NTSR*, II, 642–57. For the position of Carolingian women see J. L. Nelson, 'Women at the court of Charlemagne: A case of monstrous regiment?', in Parsons (ed.), *Medieval Queenship*, pp.43–61; P. Stafford, *Queens, Concubines and Dowagers: The King's Wife in the Early Middle Ages* (London, 1983).

48. E. J. Goldberg, '*Regina nitens sanctissima Hemma*: Queen Emma (827–876), Bishop Witgar of Augsburg and the Witgar-Belt', in Weiler and MacLean (eds.), *Representations of Power*, pp.57–95; S. MacLean, 'Queenship, nunneries and royal widowhood in Carolingian Europe', *P&P*, 178 (2003), 3–38.

49. T. Vogelsang, *Die Frau als Herrscherin im hohen Mittelalter. Studien zur 'consors regni'-Formel* (Göttingen, 1954); G. Baumer, *Otto I. und Adelheid* (Tübingen, 1951).

50. P. Hamer, *Kunigunde von Luxemburg. Die Rettung des Reiches* (Luxembourg, 1985); S. Pflefka, 'Kunigunde und Heinrich II. Politische Wirkungsmöglichkeit einer Kaiserin an der Schwelle eines neuen Jahrtausends', *Historischer Verein Bamberg*, 135 (1999), 199–290.

51. C. E. Odegaard, 'The Empress Engelberge', *Speculum*, 26 (1951), 77–103 at 95; Althoff, *Die Ottonen*, pp.76, 138–9.

52. T. Offergeld, *Reges pueri. Das Königtum Minderjähriger im frühen Mittelalter* (Hanover, 2001).

53. Thietmar of Merseburg, *Chronicon*, p.103. See generally E. Eickhoff, *Theophanu und der König* (Stuttgart, 1996); A. Davids (ed.), *The Empress Theophano: Byzantium and the West at the Time of the First Millennium* (Cambridge, 1995). L. Wangerin, 'Empress Theophanu, sanctity, and memory in early medieval Saxony', *CEH*, 47 (2014), 716–36. For Heinrich the Quarrelsome see also pp.343–6.

54. J. W. Bernhardt, 'Concepts and practice of empire in Ottonian Germany (950–1024)', in Weiler and MacLean (eds.), *Representations of Power*, pp.141–63 at 150–51; Fößel, *Die Königin*, pp.51–4. For the following see also Althoff, *Otto III*, pp.40–51.

55. Cited by S. Weinfurter, *The Salian Century* (Philadelphia, 1999), p.114. See generally M. Black-Veldtrup, *Kaiserin Agnes (1043–1077)* (Cologne, 1995); G. Jenal, *Erzbischof Anno II. von Köln (1056–75) und sein politisches Wirken* (2 vols., Stuttgart, 1974–5), I, pp.155–95; G. Althoff, *Heinrich IV.* (Darmstadt, 2006), pp.41–66.

56. M. S. Sánchez, *The Empress, the Queen and the Nun: Women and Power at the Court of Philip III of Spain* (Baltimore, 1998); C. W. Ingrao

and A. L. Thomas, 'Piety and power: The empresses-consort of the high baroque', in C. C. Orr (ed.), *Queenship in Europe, 1660–1815* (Cambridge, 2004), pp.107–30.

57. P. H. Wilson, 'Women in imperial politics: The Württemberg consorts, 1674–1757', in Orr (ed.), *Queenship*, pp.221–51; P. Puppel, *Die Regentin. Vormundschaftliche Herrschaft in Hessen, 1500–1700* (Frankfurt am Main, 2004); H. Wunder, *He is the Sun, she is the Moon: Women in Early Modern Germany* (Cambridge, MA, 1998), pp.165–74.

58. B. Weiler, 'Image and reality in Richard of Cornwall's German career', *EHR*, 113 (1998), 1111–42 at 1125–6.

59. W. Hermkes, *Das Reichsvikariat in Deutschland* (Bonn, 1968).

60. F. Baethgen, 'Der Anspruch des Papsttums auf das Reichsvikariat', *ZSRG KA*, 10 (1920), 168–268; R. Pauler, *Die deutschen Könige und Italien im 14. Jahrhudert von Heinrich VII. bis Karl IV.* (Darmstadt, 1997), pp.13–14, 23–4.

61. R. Pauler, *Die Auseinandersetzungen zwischen Kaiser Karl IV. und den Päpsten* (Neuried, 1996), p.211. For the following: C. Zwierlein, 'Savoyen-Piemonts Verhältnis zum Reich 1536 bis 1618', in M. Schnettger and M. Verga (eds.), *L'Impero e l'Italia nella prima età moderna* (Bologna, 2006), pp.347–89 at 367–84.

62. G. Droege, 'Pfalzgrafschaft, Grafschaften und allodiale Herrschaften zwischen Maas und Rhein in salisch-staufischer Zeit', *RVJB*, 26 (1961), 1–21; Jenal, *Erzbischof Anno*, I, pp.110–54. For the following: J. Peltzer, *Der Rang der Pfalzgrafen bei Rhein. Die Gestaltung der politisch-sozialen Ordnung des Reichs im 13. und 14. Jahrhundert* (Ostfildern, 2013).

63. Fuhrmann, *Germany*, p.32. See also J. Laudage, 'Der Hof Friedrich Barbarossas', in idem and Y. Leiverkus (eds.), *Rittertum und Höfische Kultur der Stauferzeit* (Cologne, 2006), pp.75–92; Goldberg, *Struggle for Empire*, pp.191–8. For the Carolingian court see R. McKitterick, *The Frankish Kingdoms under the Carolingians* (Harlow, 1983), pp.78–80; J. Laudage et al., *Die Zeit der Karolinger* (Darmstadt, 2006), pp.146–62. Royal assemblies are discussed on pp.337–8.

64. McKitterick, *The Frankish Kingdoms*, pp.80–85.

65. P. C. Hartmann (ed.), *Der Mainzer Kurfürst als Reichserzkanzler* (Stuttgart, 1997); H. Duchhardt, 'Kurmainz und das Reichskammergericht', *BDLG*, 110 (1974), 181–217.

66. W. Metz, *Zur Erforschung des karolingischen Reichsgutes* (Darmstadt, 1971).

67. B. S. Bachrach, *Early Carolingian Warfare* (Philadelphia, 2001), pp.57–9; R. McKitterick, *Charlemagne* (Cambridge, 2008), Chapter 4; A. Barbero, *Karl der Grosse* (Stuttgart, 2007).

68. G. Brown, 'The Carolingian Renaissance', in R. McKitterick (ed.), *Carolingian Culture* (Cambridge, 1994), pp.1–51 at 34. See also R. McKitterick,

The Carolingians and the Written Word (Cambridge, 1989); A. Wenderhorst, 'Who could read and write in the Middle Ages?', in A. Haverkamp and H. Vollrath (eds.), *England and Germany in the High Middle Ages* (Oxford, 1996), pp.57–88.

69. H. Keller, 'Vom "heiligen Buch" zur "Buchführung". Lebensfunktionen der Schrift im Mittelalter', *FMS*, 26 (1992), 1–31.

70. M. Costambeys et al., *The Carolingian World* (Cambridge, 2011), pp. 182–9; D. S. Bachrach, 'The written word in Carolingian-style fiscal administration under King Henry I, 919–936', *GH*, 28 (2010), 399–423.

71. W. Treadgold, *A Concise History of Byzantium* (Basingstoke, 2001), esp. p.236.

72. Quote from R. Collins, 'Making sense of the early Middle Ages', *EHR*, 124 (2009), 641–65 at 650.

73. Ottonian emperors rarely fielded more than 2,000 armoured cavalry and 4,000–6,000 infantry and baggage personnel while in Italy: L. Auer, 'Der Kriegsdienst des Klerus unter den sächsischen Kaiser', *MIÖG*, 79 (1971), 316–407, and 80 (1972), 48–70.

74. J. France, 'The composition and raising of the armies of Charlemagne', *Journal of Medieval Military History*, 1 (2002), 61–82; T. Reuter, 'Carolingian and Ottonian warfare', in M. Keen (ed.), *Medieval Warfare* (Oxford, 1999), pp.13–35 at 28–9; Goldberg, *Struggle for Empire*, pp. 124–6; Althoff, *Die Ottonen*, pp.106, 148; G. Halsall, *Warfare and Society in the Barbarian West, 450–900* (London, 2003), pp.119–33; Leyser, *Medieval Germany*, pp.11–42; G. A. Loud (ed.), *The Crusade of Frederick Barbarossa* (Farnham, 2013), p.19. Far larger estimates for Ottonian forces appear in D. S. Bachrach, *Warfare in Tenth-Century Germany* (Woodbridge, 2012), pp.12, 177–8, 232–6.

75. Very few seventeenth- or early eighteenth-century Habsburg officers received formal training or read military books, yet they were accustomed by status and running landed estates to the tasks of man-management, animal care, and numerous other practical skills: E. A. Lund, *War for the Every Day: Generals, Knowledge and Warfare in Early Modern Europe, 1680–1740* (Westport, CT, 1999).

76. H. Schwarzmaier, 'Das "Salische Hausarchiv"', in Weinfurter (ed.), *Die Salier und das Reich*, I, pp.97–115. See also H. Keller, 'Ritual, Symbolik und Visualisierung in der Kultur des ottonischen Reiches', *FMS*, 35 (2001), 23–59 esp. 55–9; Leyser, *Medieval Germany*, pp.69–101.

77. A. T. Hack, *Das Empfangszeremoniell bei mittelalterlichen Papst-Kaiser-Treffen* (Cologne, 1999), pp.586–7; H. J. Cohn, 'The political culture of the Imperial Diet as reflected in Reformation-era diaries', in D. Repeto García (ed.), *Las Cortes de Cádiz y la historia parlamentaria* (Cadiz, 2012), pp.603–72, and his 'The protocols of the German imperial diet during the reign of Emperor Charles V', in J. Feuchter and J. Helmrath

(eds.), *Politische Redekultur in der Vormoderne* (Frankfurt am Main, 2008), pp.45–63.

78. G. Koch, *Auf dem Wege zum Sacrum Imperium* (Vienna, 1972), p.30; P. Moraw, 'Kanzlei und Kanzleipersonal König Ruprechts', *Archiv für Diplomatik*, 15 (1969), 428–531 at 438–9; W. Blockmans, *Emperor Charles V, 1500–1558* (London, 2002), p.133.

79. R. Schneider, 'Landeserschließung und Raumerfassung durch salische Herrscher', in Weinfurter (ed.), *Die Salier und das Reich*, I, pp.117–38 at 130–34; Moraw, 'Kanzlei'.

80. J. M. Headley, *The Emperor and his Chancellor: A Study of the Imperial Chancellery under Gattinara* (Cambridge, 1983); E. Ortlieb, 'Die Entstehung des Reichshofrats in der Regierungszeit der Kaiser Karl V. und Ferdinand I.', *Frühneuzeit-Info*, 17 (2006), 11–26.

81. B. Blisch, *Friedrich Carl Joseph von Erthal (1774–1802). Erzbischof – Kurfürst – Erzkanzler* (Frankfurt am Main, 2005), pp.32–3.

82. See the two collections edited by R. Bonney: *Economic Systems and State Finance* (Oxford, 1995); *The Rise of the Fiscal State in Europe c.1200–1815* (Oxford, 1999).

83. Goldberg, *Struggle for Empire*, pp.203–6.

84. Boshof, *Königtum und Königsherrschaft*, p.82.

85. E. A. R. Brown, 'The tyranny of a construct: Feudalism and the historians of medieval Europe', *AHR*, 79 (1974), 1063–88; S. Reynolds, *Fiefs and Vassals: The Medieval Evidence Reinterpreted* (Oxford, 1994), and her response to J. Fried, both in *GHIL*, 19 (1997), no.1, pp.28–41, no.2, pp. 30–34. Good overviews for the specific situation in the Empire: K.-H. Spiess, *Das Lehnswesen in Deutschland im hohen und späten Mittelalter* (2nd ed., Stuttgart, 2009); S. Patzold, *Das Lehnswesen* (Munich, 2012).

86. T. Mayer, 'Die Entstehung des "modernen" Staates im Mittelalter und die freien Bauern', *ZSRG GA*, 57 (1937), 210–88, and his 'Die Ausbildung der Grundlagen des modernen deutschen Staates im hohen Mittelalter', *HZ*, 159 (1939), 457–87. For critique: H.-W. Goetz, 'Regnum. Zum politischen Denken der Karolingerzeit', *ZSRG GA*, 104 (1987), 110–89; E. Schubert, *Fürstliche Herrschaft und Territorium im späten Mittelalter* (2nd ed., Munich, 2006), pp.222, 57–61.

87. Notably Marxist interpretations: R. H. Hilton, *Class Conflict and the Crisis of Feudalism* (London, 1985).

88. T. Zotz, 'In Amt und Würden. Zur Eigenart "offizieller" Positionen im früheren Mittelalter', *Tel Aviver Jahrbuch für deutsche Geschichte*, 22 (1993), 1–23.

89. L. Auer, 'Der Kriegsdienst des Klerus unter den sächsischen Kaisern', *MIÖG*, 79 (1971), 316–407, and 80 (1972), 48–70; T. Reuter, '*Episcopi cum sua militia*: The prelate as warrior in the early Staufer era', in idem (ed.), *Warriors and Churchmen in the High Middle Ages* (London, 1992),

pp.79–94; B. Arnold, 'German bishops and their military retinues in the medieval Empire', *GH*, 7 (1989), 161–83; K. L. Krieger, 'Obligatory military service and the use of mercenaries in imperial military campaigns under the Hohenstaufen emperors', in Haverkamp and Vollrath (eds.), *England and Germany*, pp.151–68.

90. C. E. Odegaard, 'Carolingian oaths of fidelity', *Speculum*, 16 (1941), 284–96, and his 'The concept of royal power in Carolingian oaths of fidelity', *Speculum*, 20 (1945), 279–89; H. Keller, 'Die Investitur. Ein Beitrag zum Problem der "Staatssymbolik" im Hochmittelalter', *FMS*, 27 (1993), 51–86.

91. H. K. Schulze, *Grundstrukturen der Verfassung im Mittelalter* (3rd ed., 3 vols., Stuttgart, 1995–2000), I, pp.56–9, 73–4.

92. C. Brühl, *Fodrum, Gistum, Servitium regis. Studien zu den wirtschaftlichen Grundlagen des Königtums im Frankenreich und in den fränkischen Nachfolgestaaten Deutschland, Frankreich und Italien vom 6. bis zur Mitte des 14. Jahrhunderts* (2 vols., Cologne, 1968); W. Metz, *Das Servitium regis. Zur Erforschung der wirtschaftlichen Grundlagen des hochmittelalterlichen deutschen Königtums* (Darmstadt, 1978).

93. K. Leyser, 'Ottonian government', *EHR*, 96 (1981), 721–53 at 746–7; E. Müller-Mertens, 'Reich und Hauptorte der Salier', in Weinfurter (ed.), *Die Salier und das Reich*, I, pp.139–58.

94. Costambeys et al., *The Carolingian World*, pp.122, 172–8.

95. T. Zotz, 'Carolingian tradition and Ottonian-Salian innovation: Comparative observations on palatine policy in the Empire', in Duggan (ed.), *Kings and Kingship*, pp.69–100; J. Dahlhaus, 'Zu den Anfängen von Pfalz und Stiften in Goslar', in Weinfurter (ed.), *Die Salier und das Reich*, II, pp.373–428.

96. Schulze, *Grundstrukturen*, II, pp.112–15.

97. J. W. Bernhardt, *Itinerant Kingship and Royal Monasteries in Early Medieval Germany, c.936–1075* (Cambridge, 1993), pp.75–135.

98. Keller, *Ottonische Königsherrschaft*, p.109; H. Jericke, 'Konradins Marsch von Rom zur palentinische Ebene im August 1268 und die Größe und Struktur seines Heeres', *Römische Historische Mitteilungen*, 44 (2002), 151–92.

99. D. J. Hay, *The Military Leadership of Matilda of Canossa, 1046–1115* (Manchester, 2008), p.184.

100. S. Weinfurter, 'Salisches Herrschaftsverständnis im Wandel. Heinrich V. und sein Privileg für die Bürger von Speyer', *FMS*, 36 (2002), 317–35.

101. M. Innes, 'Charlemagne's government', in J. Story (ed.), *Charlemagne* (Manchester, 2005), pp.71–89.

102. G. Althoff, 'Die Billunger in der Salierzeit', in Weinfurter (ed.), *Die Salier und das Reich*, I, pp.309–29; Wolfram, *Conrad II*, pp.177–90.

103. McKitterick, *The Frankish Kingdoms*, pp.87–97; Costambeys et al., *The Carolingian World*, pp.172–9.

104. J. L. Nelson, 'Kingship and empire in the Carolingian world', in McKitterick (ed.), *Carolingian Culture*, pp.52–87 esp. 52; Goldberg, *Struggle for Empire*, pp.226–9.

105. S. Patzold, 'Konsens und Konkurrenz. Überlegungen zu einem aktuellen Forschungskonzept der Mediävistik', *FMS*, 41 (2007), 75–103.

106. G. Althoff, *Verwandte, Freunde und Getreue. Zum politischen Stellenwert der Gruppenbindungen im früheren Mittelalter* (Darmstadt, 1990), pp.119–33, and his 'Friendship and political order', in J. Haseldine (ed.), *Friendship in Medieval Europe* (Stroud, 1999), pp.91–105; C. Garnier, *Die Kultur der Bitte. Herrschaft und Kommunikation im mittelalterlichen Reich* (Darmstadt, 2008).

107. B. Schneidmüller, 'Zwischen Gott und den Getreuen', *FMS*, 36 (2002), 193–224 at 212.

108. Costambeys et al., *The Carolingian World*, pp.213–22, 379–83; McKitterick, *The Frankish Kingdoms*, pp.169–73. For the high level of violence and its impact see G. Halsall (ed.), *Violence and Society in the Early Medieval West* (Woodbridge, 1998).

109. R. Collins, *Early Medieval Europe, 300–1000* (Basingstoke, 1991), p.309. See J. Nelson, *Charles the Bald* (London, 1992); S. MacLean, *Kingship and Politics in the Late Ninth Century: Charles the Fat and the End of the Carolingian Empire* (Cambridge, 2003).

110. Keller, *Ottonische Königsherrschaft*, pp.12–21.

111. A. Haverkamp, 'Die Städte im Herrschafts- und Sozialgefüge Reichsitaliens', in F. Vittinghoff (ed.), *Stadt und Herrschaft. Römische Kaiserzeit und hohes Mittelalter* (Munich, 1982), pp.149–245 at 166–9.

112. Goldberg, *Struggle for Empire*, pp.335–42; Althoff, *Die Ottonen*, p.15. See also R. Hiestand, 'Pressburg 907. Eine Wende in der Geschichte des ostfränkischen Reiches?', *ZBLG*, 57 (1994), 1–20.

113. J. Fried, 'Die Kunst der Aktualisierung in der oralen Gesellschaft. Die Königserhebung Heinrichs I. als Exempel', *GWU*, 44 (1993), 493–503; R. Deutinger, '"Königswahl" und Herzogserhebung Arnulfs von Bayern', *DA*, 58 (2002), 17–68; M. Becher, *Otto der Große* (Munich, 2012), pp.71–88.

114. E. Hlawitschka, 'Vom Ausklingen der fränkischen und Einsetzen der deutschen Geschichte', in C. Brühl and B. Schneidmüller (eds.), *Beiträge zur mittelalterlichen Reichs- und Nationsbildung in Deutschland und Frankreich* (Munich, 1997), pp.55–81 at 58–69; Althoff, *Die Ottonen*, pp.230–47.

115. Keller, *Ottonische Königsherrschaft*, p.61.

116. E. Boshof, *Die Salier* (5th ed., Stuttgart, 2008), p.98.

117. Keller, *Ottonische Königsherrschaft*, pp.65–72.

118. Becher, *Otto der Große*, pp.239–40, 249–50.

119. Thietmar of Merseburg, *Chronicon*, pp.143–6.

120. Ibid, pp.150–55; Althoff, *Otto III*, pp.30–40.

121. A. Wolf, 'Die Herkunft der Grafen von Northeim aus dem Hause Luxemburg und der Mord am Königskandidaten Ekkehard von Meißen 1002', *Niedersächsisches Jahrbuch für Landesgeschichte*, 69 (1997), 427–40. For the following: Althoff, *Otto III*, pp.146–8; Keller, *Ottonische Königsherrschaft*, pp.51–7, 92–4.

122. Wipo of Burgundy's account of Conrad's succession: T. E. Mommsen and K. F. Morrison (eds.), *Imperial Lives and Letters of the Eleventh Century* (New York, 2000), pp.57–65. See also Wolfram, *Conrad II*, pp. 42–5; Weinfurter, *Salian Century*, pp.18–24. See pp.189, 194 for Conrad's struggles over Italy and Burgundy.

123. B. Arnold, *German Knighthood, 1050–1300* (Oxford, 1985), pp.23–52, 100–139; W. Hechberger, *Adel, Ministerialität und Rittertum im Mittelalter* (2nd ed., Munich, 2010), pp.27–34, 91–9; T. Zotz, 'Die Formierung der Ministerialität', in Weinfurter (ed.), *Die Salier und das Reich*, III, pp.3–50; Wolfram, *Conrad II*, pp.169–77.

124. W. Giese, 'Reichsstrukturprobleme unter den Saliern – der Adel in Ostsachsen', in Weinfurter (ed.), *Die Salier und das Reich*, I, pp.273–308.

125. W. Störmer, 'Bayern und der bayerische Herzog im 11. Jahrhundert', in Weinfurter (ed.), *Die Salier und das Reich*, I, pp.503–47; P. Johanek, 'Die Erzbischöfe von Hamburg-Bremen und ihre Kirche im Reich der Salierzeit', in ibid, II, pp.79–112.

126. O. Engels, 'Das Reich der Salier – Entwicklungslinien', in Weinfurter (ed.), *Die Salier und das Reich*, III, pp.479–541.

127. I. Heidrich, 'Die Absetzung Herzog Adalberos von Kärnten durch Kaiser Konrad II. 1035', *HJb*, 91 (1971), 70–94. Further discussion of royal justice on pp.610–25.

128. Printed in B. H. Hill Jr, *Medieval Monarchy in Action* (London, 1972), pp.205–7. See also Haverkamp, 'Die Städte im Herrschafts- und Sozialgefüge Reichsitaliens', p. 169–84.

129. This argument was advanced by E. Boshof, 'Das Reich in der Krise', *HZ*, 228 (1979), 265–87, and has found general acceptance: J. Laudage, *Die Salier* (2nd ed., Munich, 2007), pp.35–7, 48; W. Hartmann, *Der Investiturstreit* (3rd ed., Munich, 2007), p.6; F. Prinz, 'Kaiser Heinrich III. Seine widersprüchliche Beurteilung und deren Gründe', *HZ*, 246 (1988), 529–48; Weinfurter, *Salian Century*, pp.110–11.

130. Patzold, 'Konsens und Konkurrenz', pp.89–97 and the discussion on pp.58–60.

131. B. Arnold, *Princes and Territories in Medieval Germany* (Cambridge, 1991), pp.95–6.

132. O. Hermann, *Lothar III. und sein Wirkungsbereich. Räumliche Bezüge königlichen Handelns im hochmittelalterlichen Reich (1125–1137)* (Bochum, 2000).

133. Although exaggerating the degree of consensus, J. Schlick provides a useful discussion of these changes: *König, Fürsten und Reich (1056–1159)* (Stuttgart, 2001), pp.11–48, 94–5. See also Weinfurter, *Salian Century*, pp.177–9; Boshof, *Die Salier*, pp.293–9.

CHAPTER 8: TERRITORY

1. For example, H. Fuhrmann, *Germany in the High Middle Ages, c.1050–1200* (Cambridge, 1986), pp.125–86; H. Boldt, *Deutsche Verfassungsgeschichte. I Von den Anfängen bis zum Ende des älteren deutschen Reiches 1806* (3rd ed., Munich, 1994), esp. p.249.

2. D. Matthew, *The Norman Kingdom of Sicily* (Cambridge, 1992), pp.306–62.

3. A. C. Schlunk, *Königsmacht und Krongut. Die Machtgrundlage des deutschen Königtums im 13. Jahrhundert* (Stuttgart, 1988), p.16.

4. Fuhrmann, *Germany*, p.186.

5. K. Görich, *Friedrich Barbarossa* (Munich, 2011), pp.301–11; F. Opll, *Friedrich Barbarossa* (4th ed., Darmstadt, 2009), pp.64–6; J. Laudage, *Friedrich Barbarossa (1152–1190)* (Regensburg, 2009), pp.124–34. According to Fuhrmann, *Germany*, p.23, annual revenue from Italy under the Staufers totalled 65,000 pounds in silver.

6. A. Haverkamp, 'Die Städte im Herrschafts- und Sozialgefüge Reichsitaliens', in F. Vittinghoff (ed.), *Stadt und Herrschaft. Römische Kaiserzeit und hohes Mittelalter* (Munich, 1982), pp.149–245 at 208–11, 221–3; G. Deibel, 'Die finanzielle Bedeutung Reichs-Italiens für die staufischen Herrscher des zwölften Jahrhunderts', *ZSRG GA*, 54 (1934), 134–77 esp. 143–5. The Lombard League is discussed on pp.569–70.

7. P. Schulte, 'Friedrich Barbarossa, die italienischen Kommunen und das politische Konzept der Treue', *FMS*, 38 (2004), 153–72.

8. H. K. Schulze, *Grundstrukturen der Verfassung im Mittelalter* (3rd ed., 3 vols., Stuttgart, 1995–2000), I, pp.63–7.

9. M. T. Fögen, 'Römisches Recht und Rombilder im östlichen und westlichen Mittelalter', in B. Schneidmüller and S. Weinfurter (eds.), *Heilig – Römisch – Deutsch* (Dresden, 2006), pp.57–83; J. Dendorfer and R. Deutinger (eds.), *Das Lehnswesen im Hochmittelalter* (Ostfildern, 2010).

10. J. Ehlers, *Heinrich der Löwe* (Munich, 2008), pp.21–46; K. Jordan, *Henry the Lion* (Oxford, 1986).

11. K. Görich, 'Jäger des Löwen oder Getriebener der Fürsten? Friedrich Barbarossa und die Entmachtung Heinrichs des Löwen', in W. Hechberger and F. Schuller (eds.), *Staufer & Welfen* (Regensburg, 2009), pp.99–117.

12. J.-P. Stöckel, 'Die Weigerung Heinrichs des Löwen zu Chiavenna (1176)', *Zeitschrift für Geschichtswissenschaft*, 42 (1994), 869–82.

13. B. Arnold, *Princes and Territories in Medieval Germany* (Cambridge, 1991), pp.96–111; Laudage, *Barbarossa*, pp.271–90.

14. Ehlers, *Heinrich der Löwe*, pp.375–87.

15. B. U. Hucker, *Otto IV. Der wiederentdeckte Kaiser* (Frankfurt am Main, 2003); H. Stehkämper, 'Der Kölner Erzbischof Adolf von Altena und die deutsche Königswahl (1195–1205)', in T. Schieder (ed.), *Beiträge zur Geschichte des mittelalterlichen deutschen Königtums* (Munich, 1973), pp.5–83.

16. The charter for the lay lords was initially issued by Henry (VII) in 1231 and confirmed by Frederick a year later. They are printed in K. Zeumer (ed.), *Quellensammlung zur Geschichte der deutschen Reichsverfassung in Mittelalter und Neuzeit* (Tübingen, 1913), pp.42–4, 51–2.

17. B. Arnold, *Medieval Germany, 500–1300* (Basingstoke, 1997), pp.188–9, and his *Princes and Territories*, pp.17–20.

18. S. Patzold, 'Konsens und Konkurrenz. Überlegungen zu einem aktuallen Forschungskonzept der Mediävistik', *FMS*, 41 (2007), 75–103 at 100–102.

19. E. Schubert, *Fürstliche Herrschaft und Territorium im späten Mittelalter* (2nd ed., Munich, 2006), p.10; Schulze, *Grundstrukturen*, I, p.66; Arnold, *Princes and Territories*, pp.88–9.

20. The main Palatine principalities were Birkenfeld, Neuburg, Simmern, Sulzbach, Veldenz and Zweibrücken. The Welf principalities were Calenberg (Hanover), Göttingen, Grubenhagen, Lüneburg and Wolfenbüttel.

21. Conrad II appears to have been the first to permit this: H. Wolfram, *Conrad II, 990–1039* (University Park, PA, 2006), p.192.

22. The others were the duchies of Limburg, Brunswick-Lüneburg, the margraviate of Baden, the counties of Battenberg, Mömpelgard and Reckheim, and the imperial lordships of Anholt, Landscron, Schauen and Wickrath.

23. A. L. Reyscher (ed.), *Vollständige, historisch und kritisch bearbeitete Sammlung der württembergischen Gesetze* (29 vols., Stuttgart, 1828–51), XIX, part I, p.x; A. Flügel, *Bürgerliche Rittergüter. Sozialer Wandel und politische Reform in Kursachsen (1680–1844)* (Göttingen, 2000).

24. J. Merz, 'Bistümer und weltliche Herrschaftsbildung im Westen und Süden des spätmittelalterlichen Reiches', *HJb*, 126 (2006), 65–89 at 68–9; Schulze, *Grundstrukturen*, I, pp.87–90.

25. B. Stollberg-Rilinger, *Des Kaisers alte Kleider* (Munich, 2008), pp.64–71.

26. Schubert, *Fürstliche Herrschaft*, pp.52–7. See also H. Patze (ed.), *Der deutsche Territorialstaat im 14 Jahrhundert* (2 vols., Sigmaringen, 1970–71); Boldt, *Deutsche Verfassungsgeschichte*, pp.149–246.

27. Arnold, *Princes and Territories*, p.281.

28. E. Schubert, 'Die Umformung spätmittelalterlicher Fürstenherrschaft im 16. Jahrhundert', *RVJB*, 63 (1999), 204–63 at 229–36; P. Rückert, 'Von der Stadt zum Amt. Zur Genese württembergischer Herrschafts- und Verwaltungsstrukturen', *ZWLG*, 72 (2013), 53–74 at 65. For territorialization generally see P. Moraw, *Von offener Verfassung zu gestalteter Verdichtung. Das Reich im späten Mittelalter 1250 bis 1490* (Berlin, 1985), pp.183–201; Arnold, *Princes and Territories*, pp.152–210.

29. H. Krieg, 'Die Markgrafen von Baden im Gebiet von Neckar und Murr (11. bis 13. Jh.)', *ZWLG*, 72 (2013), 13–32.

30. S. Lorenz, 'Von Baden zu Württemberg. Marbach – ein Objekt im herrschaftlichen Kräftespiel des ausgehenden 13. Jahrhunderts', *ZWLG*, 72 (2013), 33–52 at 48–9; E. Marquardt, *Geschichte Württembergs* (3rd ed., Stuttgart, 1985), pp.18–23.

31. J. B. Freed, 'Medieval German social history', *CEH*, 25 (1992), 1–26 at 1–2; H. Zmora, *The Feud in Early Modern Germany* (Cambridge, 2011), pp.82–99; K. J. MacHardy, *War, Religion and Court Patronage in Habsburg Austria* (Basingstoke, 2003), p.133.

32. A. Niederstätter, *Österreichische Geschichte, 1278–1411* (Vienna, 2004), pp.178–81; O. Hintze, *Die Hohenzollern und ihr Werk* (Berlin, 1915), p.75.

33. W. Grube, '400 Jahre Haus Württemberg in Mömpelgard', in R. Uhland (ed.), *900 Jahre Haus Württemberg* (Stuttgart, 1985), pp.438–58.

34. J. Whaley, *Germany and the Holy Roman Empire, 1493–1806* (2 vols., Oxford, 2012), I, p.490; Rückert, 'Von der Stadt zum Amt', pp.61–74; Schubert, 'Die Umformung spätmittelalterlicher Fürstenherrschaft', pp.209–15.

35. J. Gerchow, 'Äbtissinnen auf dem Weg zur Landesherrschaft im 13. Jahrhundert. Das Beispiel der Frauenstifte Essen und Herford', in T. Schilp (ed.), *Reform – Reformation – Säkularisation. Frauenstifte in Krisenzeiten* (Essen, 2004), pp.67–88 at 84–8.

36. H. E. Feine, *Die Besetzung der Reichsbistümer vom Westfälischen Frieden bis zur Säkularisation, 1648–1803* (Stuttgart, 1921); E. J. Greipl, 'Zur weltlichen Herrschaft der Fürstbischöfe in der Zeit vom Westfälischen Frieden bis zur Säkularisation', *Römische Quartalschrift*, 83 (1988), 252–69 esp.257–8.

37. W. Janssen, *Das Erzbistum Köln im späten Mittelalter, 1191–1515* (Cologne, 1995); Merz, 'Bistümer und weltliche Herrschaftsbildung', pp.75–7.

38. K. E. Demandt, *Geschichte des Landes Hessen* (2nd ed., Kassel, 1980); W. Dotzauer, 'Der kurpfälzische Wildfangstreit und seine Auswirkungen im rheinhessisch-pfälzischen Raum', *Geschichtliche Landeskunde*,

25 (1984), 81–105; W. B. Smith, *Reformation and the German Territorial State: Upper Franconia, 1300–1630* (Rochester, NY, 2008), pp.44–9.

39. H. J. Cohn, *The Government of the Rhine Palatinate in the Fifteenth Century* (Oxford, 1965); V. Press, *Calvinismus und Territorialstaat. Regierung und Zentralbehörden der Kurpfalz, 1559–1619* (Stuttgart, 1970).

40. H. Patze and W. Schlesinger (eds.), *Geschichte Thüringens* (5 vols., Cologne, 1982).

41. A. D. Anderson, *On the Verge of War: International Relations and the Jülich-Kleve Succession Crises (1609–1614)* (Boston, 1999). The Austrian succession is discussed on pp.476–9.

42. B. Arnold, *German Knighthood, 1050–1300* (Oxford, 1985), pp.17–20, and his *Princes and Territories*, pp.40–43.

43. Arnold, *German Knighthood*, pp.103–10, 140–61, 252–5; Moraw, *Von offener Verfassung*, pp.73–7; Zmora, *The Feud*, pp.86, 93–4. Aristocratic associations are discussed on pp.553–8.

44. D. Abulafia, *Frederick II: A Medieval Emperor* (London, 1988), pp.239–49; W. Stürner, *Friedrich II.* (2 vols., Darmstadt, 2009), II, pp.302–16.

45. H. Dopsch, *Österreichische Geschichte, 1122–1278* (Vienna, 2003), pp.189–98.

46. B. Schneidmüller, 'Konsens – Territorialisierung – Eigennutz. Vom Umgang mit spätmittelalterlichen Geschichte', *FMS*, 39 (2005), 225–46 at 236–8.

47. B. Weiler, *Henry III of England and the Staufen Empire, 1216–1272* (Woodbridge, 2006), pp.172–97, and his 'Image and reality in Richard of Cornwall's German career', *EHR*, 113 (1998), 1111–42.

48. G. Wagner, 'Pläne und Versuche der Erhebung Österreichs zum Königreich', in idem (ed.), *Österreich von der Staatsidee zum Nationalbewußtsein* (Vienna, 1982), pp.394–432; Dopsch, *Österreichische Geschichte*, pp.197–201.

49. T. Reuter, 'The medival German *Sonderweg*? The Empire and its rulers in the high Middle Ages', in A. J. Duggan (eds.), *Kings and Kingship in Medieval Europe* (London, 1993), pp.179–211 at 209.

50. M. Spindler (ed.), *Handbuch der bayerischen Geschichte* (2nd ed., 2 vols., Munich, 1981), I, p.409; P. Moraw, 'Ruprecht von der Pfalz', *ZGO*, 149 (2001), 97–110 at 102.

51. Revenue from B. Guenée, *States and Rulers in Later Medieval Europe* (Oxford, 1985), p.11.

52. A. Haverkamp, *Medieval Germany, 1056–1273* (Oxford, 1988), pp.285, 298. For the following see Schlunk, *Königsmacht und Krongut*.

53. There were nine: Upper and Lower Swabia, Upper and Lower Alsace, Ortenau, Speyergau, Wetterau, Rothenburg and Nuremberg.

54. M. Prietzel, *Das Heilige Römische Reich im Spätmittelalter* (2nd ed., Darmstadt, 2010), p.14.

55. P. Moraw, 'Franken als königsnahe Landschaft im späten Mittelalter', *BDLG*, 112 (1976), 123–38; *Das Land Baden-Württemberg* (issued by the Staatliche Archivverwaltung Baden-Württembergs, Stuttgart, 1974), I, pp.167–9.

56. Prietzel, *Reich im Spätmittelalter*, p.23.

57. E. Isenmann, 'Reichsfinanzen und Reichssteuern im 15. Jahrhundert', *ZHF*, 7 (1980), 1–76, 129–218 at 12–16.

58. Niederstätter, *Österreichische Geschichte, 1278–1411*, pp.71–86; K. Peball, *Die Schlacht bei Dürnkrut am 26. August 1278* (Vienna, 1992).

59. Niederstätter, *Österreichische Geschichte, 1278–1411*, pp.96–105. See pp.586–8 for the Swiss revolt.

60. E. Gatz (ed.), *Die Bischöfe des Heiligen Römischen Reiches 1198 bis 1448* (Berlin, 2001), pp.274–6.

61. A. Gerlich, 'König Adolf von Nassau im Bund mit Eduard I. von England', *NA*, 113 (2002), 1–57.

62. K.-U. Jäschke, *Europa und das römisch-deutsche Reich um 1300* (Stuttgart, 1999), pp.77–85; Prietzel, *Reich im Spätmittelalter*, pp.33–4.

63. Niederstätter, *Österreichische Geschichte, 1278–1411*, pp.105–13.

64. J. K. Hoensch, *Die Luxemburger* (Stuttgart, 2000), pp.11–30; Jäschke, *Europa*, pp.92–117; Gatz (ed.), *Bischöfe 1198 bis 1448*, pp.799–802.

65. Niederstätter, *Österreichische Geschichte, 1278–1411*, pp.113–32; Hoensch, *Die Luxemburger*, pp.71–104.

66. R. Schneider, 'Karls IV. Auffassung vom Herrscheramt', in Schieder (ed.), *Beiträge*, pp.122–50 at 122–3.

67. Niederstätter, *Österreichische Geschichte, 1278–1411*, pp.151–4.

68. Hoensch, *Die Luxemburger*, pp.166–8; Isenmann, 'Reichsfinanzen', p.17.

69. Hintze, *Die Hohenzollern*, pp.18–25.

70. F. Seibt, *Karl IV.* (Munich, 1978), pp.314–17; Hoensch, *Die Luxemburger*, pp.118–32; Moraw, *Von offener Verfassung*, pp.242–7.

71. Luxembourg itself had already been detached to a separate branch of the family and was pawned in 1388 to Charles IV's nephew Jobst, eventually passing to the new duchy of Burgundy in 1409. Sigismund pawned Brandenburg to Jobst in 1387 to finance his own election as Hungarian king.

72. B. D. Boehm and J. Fajt (eds.), *Prague, the Crown of Bohemia, 1347–1437* (New Haven, CT, 2005); M. V. Schwarz (ed.), *Grabmäler der Luxemburger. Image und Memoria eines Kaiserhauses* (Luxembourg, 1997), esp. pp.12–16.

73. J. Pánek, 'Der böhmische Staat und das Reich in der Frühen Neuzeit', in V. Press (ed.), *Alternativen zur Reichsverfassung in der Frühen Neuzeit?* (Munich, 1995), pp.169–78 at 170–71.

74. Prietzel, *Reich im Spätmittelalter*, p.74.

75. H. S. Offler, 'Empire and papacy: The last struggle', *TRHS*, 5th series, 6 (1956), 21–47. For a summary of the situation in Italy from 1250 to 1273, see J. Larner, *Italy in the Age of Dante and Petrarch, 1216–1380* (London, 1980), pp.38–45.

76. Isenmann, 'Reichsfinanzen', p.17. For Charles's Italian policy generally see R. Pauler, *Die Auseinandersetzungen zwischen Kaiser Karl IV. und den Päpsten* (Neuried, 1996).

77. G. Rill, 'Reichsvikar und Kommissar. Zur Geschichte der Verwaltung Reichsitaliens im Spätmittelalter und in der Frühen Neuzeit', *Annali della fondazione italiana per la storia amministrativa*, 2 (1965), 173–98; Hoensch, *Die Luxemburger*, p.142.

78. S. A. Epstein, *Genoa and the Genoese, 958–1528* (Chapel Hill, NC, 1996), p.184.

79. E. Schubert, *Königsabsetzung im deutschen Mittelalter* (Göttingen, 2005), esp. pp.362–4, 398–403; Moraw, 'Ruprecht', pp.100–104. Saxony refused to participate, while the Brandenburg and Bohemian votes were held by the Luxembourgs. For the wider context see F. Rexroth, 'Tyrannen und Taugenichtse. Beobachtungen zur Ritualität europäischer Königsabsetzungen im späten Mittelalter', *HZ*, 278 (2004), 27–53.

80. P. Moraw, 'Beamtentum und Rat König Ruprechts', *ZGO*, 116 (1968), 59–126; Isenmann, 'Reichsfinanzen', pp.17–18; Prietzel, *Reich im Spätmittelalter*, p.100.

81. A. Begert, *Die Enstehung und Entwicklung des Kurkollegs* (Berlin, 2010), pp.190–92.

82. S. Wefers, *Das politische System Kaiser Sigismunds* (Stuttgart, 1989); W. Baum, *Kaiser Sigismund* (Graz, 1993); J. K. Hoensch, *Kaiser Sigismund* (Munich, 1996).

83. Prietzel, *Reich im Spätmittelalter*, pp.114–19. See generally H. Angermeier, *Die Reichsreform, 1410–1555* (Munich, 1984).

84. Guenée, *States and Rulers*, pp.96–105; Isenmann, 'Reichsfinanzen', 9, 133–7.

85. A. Erler, *Die Mainzer Stiftsfehde, 1459–1463, im Spiegel mittelalterlicher Rechtsgutachten* (Frankfurt, 1963); D. Brosius, 'Zum Mainzer Bistumsstreit, 1459–1463', *Archiv für hessische Geschichte und Altertumskunde*, new series, 33 (1975), 111–36.

86. Zmora, *The Feud*, pp.78–80.

87. C. Reinle, *Bauernfehden* (Stuttgart, 2003), p.254.

88. W. Abel, *Agricultural Fluctuations in Europe from the Thirteenth to the Twentieth Centuries* (London, 1986), p.87.

89. F. Lot, *Recherches sur les effectifs des armées françaises des Guerres d'Italie aux Guerres de Religion, 1492–1562* (Paris, 1962); J. D. Tracy, *Emperor Charles V, Impresario of War* (Cambridge, 2002), esp. pp.247, 268.

90. S. Wefers, 'Versuch über die "Außenpolitik" des spätmittelalterlichen Reiches', *ZHF*, 22 (1995), 291–316 at 304–9; R. Görner, *Raubritter. Untersuchungen zur Lage des spätmittelalterlichen Niederadels, besonders im südlichen Westfalen* (Münster, 1987).

91. Angermeier, *Reichsreform*, pp.84–9.

92. Older historical scholarship was concerned to identify the question of leadership, since this allowed it to apportion blame for the supposed 'failure' of reform to create a unitary state.

93. G. Hödl, *Albrecht II. Königtum, Reichsregierung und Reichsreform, 1438–1439* (Vienna, 1978).

94. W. Zanetti, *Der Friedenskaiser. Friedrich III. und seine Zeit, 1440–1493* (Herford, 1985); Moraw, *Von offener Verfassung*, pp.379–85, 411–15.

95. A. Niederstätter, *Österreichische Geschichte, 1400–1522* (Vienna, 2004), pp.242–55, 348–57; P. Csendes, *Wien in den Fehden der Jahre 1461–1463* (Vienna, 1974).

96. K. S. Bader, *Ein Staatsmann vom Mittelrhein. Gestalt und Werk des Mainzer Kurfürsten und Erzbischofs Berthold von Henneberg* (Mainz, 1954–5); H. J. Cohn, 'The electors and imperial rule at the end of the fifteenth century', in B. Weiler and S. MacLean (eds.), *Representations of Power in Medieval Germany, 800–1500* (Turnhout, 2006), pp.295–318.

97. G. Benecke, *Maximilian I (1459–1519)* (London, 1982); H. Wiesflecker, *Kaiser Maximilian I.* (5 vols., Vienna, 1971–86). For Maximilian's negotiating style see H. Carl, *Der Schwäbische Bund, 1488–1534* (Leinfelden-Echterdingen, 2000), pp.503–5, 511.

98. W. Dotzauer, *Die deutschen Reichskreise (1383–1806)* (Stuttgart, 1998); W. Wüst (ed.), *Reichskreis und Territorium* (Stuttgart, 2000). The range of Kreise activities is enumerated in *NTSR*, X, 427–758. The Kreis Assemblies are discussed on pp.415–16.

99. R. Schneider, 'Landeserschließung und Raumerfassung durch salishe Herrscher', in S. Weinfurter (ed.), *Die Salier und das Reich* (3 vols., Sigmaringen, 1991), I, pp.117–38 at 128–30; Isenmann, 'Reichsfinanzen', 129–54.

100. S. Rowan, 'Imperial taxes and German politics in the fifteenth century', *CEH*, 13 (1980), 203–17.

101. P. Schmid, *Der Gemeine Pfennig von 1495* (Göttingen, 1989), p.564; Isenmann, 'Reichsfinanzen', 154–98. For the following see P. Rauscher, *Zwischen Ständen und Gläubigern. Die kaiserlichen Finanzen unter Ferdinand I. und Maximilian II. (1556–1576)* (Munich, 2004), esp. pp.83–93.

102. The 1521 register is printed in H. H. Hofmann (ed.), *Quellen zum Verfassungsorganismus des Heiligen Römischen Reiches deutscher Nation 1495–1815* (Darmstadt, 1976), pp.40–51. The money and troops raised under these arrangements are discussed on pp.446–62.

103. A. Sigelen, *Reichspfennigmeister Zacharias Geizkofler zwischen Fürstendienst und Familienpolitik* (Stuttgart, 2009); M. Schattkowsky, 'Reichspfennigmeister im Ober- und Niedersächsischen Reichskreis', *BDLG*, 137 (2001), 17–38.

104. B. A. Rautenberg, *Der Fiskal am Reichskammergericht* (Bern, 2008); M. Schnettger, 'Das Alte Reich und Italien in der Frühen Neuzeit', *Quellen und Forschungen aus italienischen Archiven und Bibliotheken*, 79 (1999), 344–420 at 375–7.

105. P. Moraw, 'Versuch über die Entstehung des Reichstags', in H. Weber (ed.), *Politische Ordnungen und soziale Kräfte im Alten Reich* (Wiesbaden, 1980), pp.1–36. Older scholarship frequently anachronistically applied the label 'Reichstag' to these earlier meetings.

106. T. M. Martin, *Auf dem Weg zum Reichstag, 1314–1410* (Göttingen, 1993).

107. A. Gotthard, *Säulen des Reiches. Die Kurfürsten im frühneuzeitlichen Reichsverband* (Husum, 1999); P. Moraw, 'Fürstentum, Königtum und "Reichsreform" im deutschen Spätmittelalter', *BDLG*, 122 (1986), 117–36.

108. H. Cohn, 'The German imperial diet at the end of the fifteenth century', in J. Sobrequés et al. (eds.), *Actes del 53è congrés de la Comissió Internacional per a l'Estudi de la Història de les Institucions Representatives i Parlementàries* (2 vols., Barcelona, 2005), I, pp.149–57.

109. G. Annas, *Hoftag – Gemeiner Tag – Reichstag. Studien zur strukturellen Entwicklung deutscher Reichsversammlungen des späten Mittelalters (1349–1471)* (2 vols., Göttingen, 2004), I, pp.77–97, 438; H. Angermeier, 'Der Wormser Reichstag 1495 – ein europäisches Ereignis', *HZ*, 261 (1995), 739–68. A more cautious assessment of the 1495 meeting's novelty is given by P. J. Heinig, 'Der Wormser Reichstag von 1495 als Hoftag', *ZHF*, 33 (2006), 337–57.

110. H. J. Cohn, 'The German imperial diets in the 1540s', *Parliaments, Estates and Representation*, 26 (2006), 19–33. The Religious Peace is discussed on pp.115–17.

111. Benecke, *Maximilian*, pp.138–9. For the following see H. J. Cohn, 'Representing political space at a political site: The imperial diets of the sixteenth century', in B. Kümin (ed.), *Political Space in Pre-Industrial Europe* (Farnham, 2009), pp.19–42.

112. F. Blaich, 'Die Bedeutung der Reichstage auf dem Gebiet der öffentlichen Finanzen im Spannungsfeld zwischen Kaiser, Territorialstaaten und Reichsstädten (1495–1670)', in A. De Maddalena and H. Kellenbenz (eds.), *Finanzen und Staatsräson in Italien und Deutschland in der frühen Neuzeit* (Berlin, 1992), pp.79–111 at 79–86; J. J. Schmauss and H. C. von Senckenberg (eds.), *Neue und vollständige Sammlung der Reichsabschiede* (4 vols., Frankfurt am Main, 1747), I, pp.482–92.

113. L. Pelizaeus, *Der Aufstieg Württembergs und Hessens zur Kurwürde, 1692–1803* (Frankfurt am Main, 2000).

114. S. W. Rowan, 'A Reichstag in the reform era: Freiburg im Breisgau, 1497–98', in J. A. Vann and S. W. Rowan (eds.), *The Old Reich* (Brussels, 1974), pp.31–57 at 49.

115. The eight elevations were: Hohenzollerns (Swabian line), Fürstenberg, East Frisia, Oldenburg, Nassau, Salm, Schwarzenberg, Schwarzburg. The most prominent of the Habsburg elevations included the Colloredo, Harrach, Khevenhüller, Neipperg, Pückler, Starhemberg, Windischgrätz and Wurmbrand families.

116. E. Böhme, *Das Fränkische Reichsgrafenkollegium im 16. und 17. Jahrhundert* (Stuttgart, 1989); J. Arndt, *Das Niederrheinisch-Westfälische Reichsgrafenkollegium und seine Mitglieder (1653–1806)* (Mainz, 1991).

117. H. Neuhaus, *Reichsständische Repräsentationsformen im 16. Jahrhundert* (Berlin, 1982).

118. T. Klein, 'Die Erhebungen in den weltlichen Reichsfürstenstand 1550–1806', *BDLG*, 122 (1986), 137–92. Those elevated without full votes included Waldeck (1719), Reuss (1778) and Lippe (1789).

119. B. Sicken, *Der Fränkische Reichskreis* (Würzburg, 1970); P. C. Hartmann, *Der Bayerische Reichskreis (1500 bis 1803)* (Berlin, 1997); T. Nicklas, *Macht oder Recht. Frühneuzeitliche Politik im obersächsischen Reichskreis* (Stuttgart, 2002).

120. Mainz chaired the electoral college, while the princely corpus was headed alternately by Austria and Salzburg, and chairmanship of the civic college fell to the city hosting the Reichstag. For the following see K. Schlaich, 'Maioritas – protestatio – itio in partes – corpus Evangelicorum', *ZSRG KA*, 63 (1977), 264–99; 64 (1978), 139–79, and his 'Die Mehrheitsabstimmung im Reichstag zwischen 1495 und 1613', *ZHF*, 10 (1983), 299–340. More extended coverage in *NTSR*, VI, part 1.

121. For a detailed example see S. Friedrich, 'Legitimationsprobleme von Kreisbündnissen', in W. E. J. Weber and R. Dauser (eds.), *Faszinierende Frühneuzeit. Reich, Frieden, Kultur und Kommunikation 1500–1800* (Berlin, 2008), pp.27–50.

122. K.-F. Krieger, 'Der Prozeß gegen Pfalzgraf Friedrich den Siegreichen auf dem Augsburger Reichstag vom Jahre 1474', *ZHF*, 12 (1985), 257–86 at 284–6.

123. W. Fürnrohr, 'Die Vertreter des habsburgischen Kaisertums auf dem Immerwährenden Reichstag', *Verhandlungen des Historischen Vereins für Oberpfalz und Regensburg*, 123 (1983), 71–139; 124 (1984), 99–148.

124. Cohn, 'The German imperial diet at the end of the fifteenth century', p.152 n.18.

125. B. Rill, *Kaiser Matthias* (Graz, 1999), pp.222–3.

126. Stollberg-Rilinger, *Des Kaisers alte Kleider*, pp.40–45, 204–66.

127. B. Roeck, *Reichssystem und Reichsherkommen* (Stuttgart, 1984).

128. For a recent and sophisticated restatement of this interpretation see H. Schilling, 'Reichs-Staat und frühneuzeitliche Nation der Deutschen oder teilmodernisiertes Reichssystem', *HZ*, 272 (2001), 377–95.

129. Cohn, 'The German imperial diet at the end of the fifteenth century', p.152.

130. K. Härter, 'The Permanent Imperial Diet in European context', in R. J. W. Evans et al. (eds.), *The Holy Roman Empire, 1495–1806* (Oxford, 2011), pp.115–35.

131. A. Gotthard, *Das Alte Reich, 1495–1806* (3rd ed., Darmstadt, 2006); W. Reinhard, 'Frühmoderner Staat und deutsches Monstrum', *ZHF*, 29 (2002), 339–57; and the work cited in n.127.

132. While there is some disagreement over terms, there is broad agreement on the Empire's complementary character: G. Schmidt, *Geschichte des Alten Reiches* (Munich, 1999), and his 'The Old Reich: The state and nation of the Germans', in Evans et al. (eds.), *Holy Roman Empire*, pp.43–62; J. Burkhardt, *Vollendung und Neuorientierung des frühmodernen Reiches, 1648–1763* (Stuttgart, 2006), pp.26–43, and his 'Europäischer Nachzügler oder institutioneller Vorreiter?', in M. Schnettger (ed.), *Imperium Romanum – irregulare corpus – Teutscher Reichs-Staat* (Mainz, 2002), pp.297–316. Further discussion in P. H. Wilson, *The Holy Roman Empire, 1495–1806* (2nd ed., Basingstoke, 2011), pp.3–11.

CHAPTER 9: DYNASTY

1. U. Lange, 'Der ständestaatliche Dualismus – Bemerkungen zu einem Problem der deutschen Verfassungsgeschichte', *BDLG*, 117 (1981), 311–34. The territorial Estates are discussed on pp.525–34.

2. P. S. Fichtner, *Protestantism and Primogeniture in Early Modern Germany* (New Haven, CT, 1989). For the long-running dispute over Ernst's will and the subsequent partition of Gotha, see S. Westphal, *Kaiserliche Rechtsprechung und herrschaftliche Stabilisierung. Reichsgerichtsbarkeit in den thüringischen Territorialstaaten, 1648–1806* (Cologne, 2002), pp.104–80.

3. P. H. Wilson, 'Prussia's relations with the Holy Roman Empire, 1740–1786', *HJ*, 51 (2008), 337–71; M. Kaiser, 'Regierende Fürsten und Prinzen von Geblüt. Der Bruderzwist als dynastisches Strukturprinzip', *Jahrbuch Stiftung Preussische Schlösser und Gärten Berlin-Brandenburg*, 4 (2001–2), 3–28.

4. T. Sharp, *Pleasure and Ambition: The Life, Loves and Wars of Augustus the Strong* (London, 2001). For princely mistresses generally see S. Oßwald-Bargende, *Die Mätresse, der Fürst und die Macht. Christina*

Wilhelmina von Grävenitz und die höfische Gesellschaft (Frankfurt am Main, 2000).

5. M. Sikora, 'Conflict and consensus around German princes' unequal marriages', in J. P. Coy et al. (eds.), *The Holy Roman Empire, Reconsidered* (New York, 2010), pp.177–90; U. Keppler, 'Franziska von Hohenheim', *Lebensbilder aus Schwaben und Franken*, 10 (1966), 157–85. Further examples of possible imperial influence in these affairs: S. Westphal, *Ehen vor Gericht – Scheidungen und ihre Folgen am Reichskammergericht* (Wetzlar, 2008).

6. K. Vocelka and L. Heller, *Die private Welt der Habsburger* (Graz, 1998).

7. A. Niederstätter, *Österreichische Geschichte, 1278–1411* (Vienna, 2004), pp.135–81.

8. A. Niederstätter, *Österreichische Geschichte, 1400–1522* (Vienna, 2004), pp.140–63.

9. P. Moraw, 'Das Reich und Österreich im Spätmittelalter', in W. Brauneder and L. Höbelt (eds.), *Sacrum Imperium. Das Reich und Österreich, 996–1806* (Vienna, 1996), pp.92–130 at 116–19. The *Privilegium maius* was only revealed as a forgery in 1852.

10. K. Vocelka and L. Heller, *Die Lebenswelt der Habsburger* (Graz, 1997), pp.161–3.

11. K. Brunner, *Leopold der Heilige* (Vienna, 2009); A. Coreth, *Pietas Austriaca* (West Lafayette, IN, 2004), pp.14–18. The date of 1264 is significant, because Urban IV established the feast of Corpus Christi that year.

12. S. Samerski, 'Hausheilige statt Staatspatrone. Der mißlungene Absolutismus in Österreichs Heiligenhimmel', in P. Mat'a and T. Winkelbauer (eds.), *Die Habsburgermonarchie 1620 bis 1740* (Stuttgart, 2006), pp.251–78.

13. M. Tanner, *The Last Descendant of Aeneas: The Hapsburgs and the Mythic Image of the Emperor* (New Haven, CT, 1993); G. Althoff, 'Studien zur habsburgischen Merowingersage', *MIÖG*, 87 (1979), 71–100; W. Seipel (ed.), *Wir sind Helden. Habsburgische Feste in der Renaissance* (Vienna, 2005). See also the sources cited in Chapter 6, notes 39 and 40.

14. H. Duchhardt, *Protestantisches Kaisertum und Altes Reich* (Wiesbaden, 1977). Bavaria already emerged as the only likely Catholic candidate in 1524: A. Kohler, *Antihabsburgische Politik in der Epoche Karls V.* (Göttingen, 1982), pp.82–97.

15. General overviews: P. S. Fichtner, *The Habsburg Monarchy, 1490–1848* (Basingstoke, 2003); C. W. Ingrao, *The Habsburg Monarchy, 1618–1815* (2nd ed., Cambridge, 2000).

16. For example, Ferdinand III's itinerary: M. Hengerer, *Kaiser Ferdinand III. (1608–1657)* (Cologne, 2012), pp.167–72.

17. B. Stollberg-Rilinger, *Des Kaisers alte Kleider* (Munich, 2008), pp.201–14.

18. For the debates see C. Opitz (ed.), *Höfische Gesellschaft und Zivilisationsprozeß* (Cologne, 2005); J. Duindam, *Myths of Power: Norbert Elias and*

the Early Modern European Court (Amsterdam, 1995), and his Vienna and Versailles: The Courts of Europe's Dynastic Rivals, 1550–1780 (Cambridge, 2003). For the following see also: M. Hengerer, Kaiserhof und Adel in der Mitte des 17. Jahrhunderts (Konstanz, 2004); P. Maťa, 'Bohemia, Silesia and the Empire: Negotiating princely dignity on the eastern periphery', in R. J. W. Evans and P. H. Wilson (eds.), The Holy Roman Empire, 1495–1806 (Leiden, 2012), pp.143–65; and the two important articles by V. Press, 'The Habsburg court as center of the imperial government', JMH, 58, supplement (1986), 23–45, and 'Österreichische Großmachtbildung und Reichsverfassung. Zur kaiserlichen Stellung nach 1648', MIÖG, 98 (1990), 131–54.

19. These statistics come from a paper presented by Klaus Margreiter at the Sixth Early Modern Workshop at the German Historical Institute London in 2007.

20. Breakdown in P. S. Spalding, Seize the Book, Jail the Author (West Lafayette, IN, 1998), p.205. For the Wittelsbach court see A. L. Thomas, A House Divided: Wittelsbach Confessional Court Cultures in the Holy Roman Empire, c.1550–1650 (Leiden, 2010); R. Babel, 'The courts of the Wittelsbachs c.1500–1750', in J. Adamson (ed.), The Princely Courts of Europe, 1500–1750 (London, 1999), pp.189–209.

21. This last example comes from a paper given by Eckhart Hellmuth at the Turin Academy of Sciences, April 2012.

22. T. Schenk, 'Das Alte Reich in der Mark Brandenburg', Jahrbuch für Brandenburgische Landesgeschichte, 63 (2012), 19–71 at 60–61; G. Benecke, 'Ennoblement and privilege in early modern Germany', History, 56 (1971), 360–70; NTSR, XIII, part I, 390, 923–4; XIV, part VII, 15–21.

23. M. Prietzel, Das Heilige Römische Reich im Spätmittelalter (2nd ed., Darmstadt, 2010), p.138; Kohler, Antihabsburgische Politik, pp.73–5.

24. C. Roll, Das zweite Reichsregiment, 1521–1530 (Cologne, 1996); H. Angermeier, 'Die Reichsregimenter und ihre Staatsidee', HZ, 211 (1970), 263–315.

25. P. S. Fichtner, Ferdinand I of Austria (New York, 1982); A. Kohler, Ferdinand I, 1503–1564 (Munich, 2003). For the Habsburg lands in this period see the comprehensive study by T. Winkelbauer, Österreichische Geschichte, 1522–1699 (2 vols., Vienna, 2003).

26. L. Groß, 'Der Kampf zwischen Reichskanzlei und österreichischer Hofkanzlei um die Führung der auswärtigen Geschäfte', Historische Vierteliahrschrift, 22 (1924–5), 279–312.

27. A. K. Mally, 'Der österreichische Reichskreis', in W. Wüst (ed.), Reichskreis und Territorium (Stuttgart, 2000), pp.313–31.

28. P. Rauscher, Zwischen Ständen und Gläubigern. Die kaiserlichen Finanzen unter Ferdinand I. und Maximilian II. (1556–1576) (Munich, 2004), esp. pp.337–40.

29. The city of Besançon was part of the Burgundian Kreis until its annexation by France in 1678. The Austrian Kreis contained the bishoprics of Trent, Brixen, Gurk, Seckau and Lavant, various Teutonic Order possessions, the counties of Schauenburg, Liechtenstein and Hardegg, and the lordships of Wolkenstein, Losenstein and Roggendorf. Incorporation within the Kreis accelerated the existing trend for most of these territories to slip under Austrian suzerainty.

30. T. A. Brady Jr, 'Phases and strategies of the Schmalkaldic League', *ARG*, 74 (1983), 162–81 at 175, 178–9. The Swabian League is discussed on pp.562–6. For the following see also A. Metz, *Der Stände oberster Herr. Königtum und Landstände im süddeutschen Raum zur Zeit Maximilians I.* (Stuttgart, 2009).

31. V. Press, *Das Alte Reich* (Berlin, 1997), pp.67–127; N. Mout, 'Die Niederlande und das Reich im 16. Jahrhundert (1512–1609)', in V. Press (ed.), *Alternativen zur Reichsverfassung in der Frühen Neuzeit?* (Munich, 1995), pp.143–68 at 151–5. For the Schmalkaldic War, 1546–7, and Armoured Reichstag, see pp.114–15.

32. F. Göttmann, 'Zur Entstehung des Landsberger Bundes im Kontext der Reichs-, Verfassungs- und regionalen Territorialpolitik des 16. Jahrhunderts', *ZHF*, 19 (1992), 415–44; M. Lanzinner, 'Der Landsberger Bund und seine Vorläufer', in Press (ed.), *Alternativen*, pp.65–80.

33. G. Kleinheyer, 'Die Abdankung des Kaisers', in G. Köbler (ed.), *Wege europäischer Rechtsgeschichte* (Frankfurt am Main, 1987), pp.124–44.

34. A. Gotthard, *Säulen des Reiches* (Husum, 1999), pp.199–475; A. P. Luttenberger, *Kurfürsten, Kaiser und Reich. Politische Führung und Friedenssicherung unter Ferdinand I. und Maximilian II.* (Mainz, 1994).

35. H. Sturmberger, *Land ob der Enns und Österreich* (Linz, 1979), pp.32–75; M. S. Sánchez, 'A house divided: Spain, Austria and the Bohemian and Hungarian successions', *Sixteenth Century Journal*, 25 (1994), 887–903.

36. Saxon policy is analyzed by D. Phelps, 'The triumph of unity over dualism: Saxony and the imperial elections 1559–1619', in R. J. W. Evans et al. (eds.), *The Holy Roman Empire, 1495–1806* (Oxford, 2011), pp.183–202.

37. P. H. Wilson, 'The Thirty Years War as the Empire's constitutional crisis', in Evans et al. (eds.), *Holy Roman Empire*, pp.95–114. Further discussion on pp.123–5.

38. K. Bierther, *Der Regensburger Reichstag von 1640/1641* (Kallmünz, 1971).

39. K. Ruppert, *Die kaiserliche Politik auf dem Westfälischen Friedenskongreß (1643–1648)* (Münster, 1979); P. H. Wilson, *Europe's Tragedy: A History of the Thirty Years War* (London, 2009), pp.716–78.

40. F. Dickmann, *Der Westfälische Frieden* (7th ed., Münster, 1998), p.494. Excellent overview of the negotiations and treaty terms in K. Repgen, 'Die

Hauptprobleme der Westfälischen Friedensverhandlungen von 1648 und ihre Lösungen', *ZBLG*, 62 (1999), 399–438.

41. D. Beales, *Joseph II* (2 vols., Cambridge, 1987–2009), II, pp.410–11.

42. J. Burkhardt, 'Das größte Friedenswerk der Neuzeit', *GWU*, 49 (1998), 592–612 esp. 600–601; G. Schmidt, 'The Peace of Westphalia as the fundamental law of the complementary Empire-State', in K. Bussmann and H. Schilling (eds.), *1648: War and Peace in Europe* (3 vols., Münster, 1998), I, pp.447–54.

43. W. Becker, *Der Kurfürstenrat. Grundzüge seiner Entwicklung in der Reichsverfassung und seine Stellung auf dem Westfälischen Friedenskongreß* (Münster, 1973).

44. A. Müller, *Der Regensburger Reichstag von 1653/54* (Frankfurt am Main, 1992). See generally K. O. Frhr. von Aretin, *Das Alte Reich, 1648–1806* (4 vols., Stuttgart, 1993–2000), I.

45. A. C. Bangert, 'Elector Ferdinand Maria of Bavaria and the imperial interregnum of 1657–58', (University of the West of England, PhD, 2006). Louis' candidacy is discussed on pp.157–8.

46. J. P. Spielman, *Leopold I of Austria* (London, 1977); L. and M. Frey, *A Question of Empire: Leopold I and the War of Spanish Succession, 1701–1705* (Boulder, CO, 1983).

47. M. Schnettger, *Der Reichsdeputationstag, 1655–1663* (Münster, 1996). For the following: A. Schindling, *Die Anfänge des Immerwährenden Reichstags zu Regensburg* (Mainz, 1991); C. Kampmann, 'Der Immerwährende Reichstag als "erstes stehendes Parlament"?', *GWU*, 55 (2004), 646–62.

48. P. H. Wilson, 'The German "soldier trade" of the seventeenth and eighteenth centuries', *IHR*, 18 (1996), 757–92.

49. Aretin, *Das Alte Reich*, II, p.55. For the following, see ibid, II, pp.54–73.

50. P. Wilson, 'Warfare in the Old Regime 1648–1789', in J. Black (ed.), *European Warfare, 1453–1815* (Basingstoke, 1999), pp.69–95 at 80.

51. K. Müller, 'Das "Reichskammerale" im 18. Jahrhundert', *Wiener Beiträge zur Geschichte der Neuzeit*, 30 (1993), 152–77; G. Walter, *Der Zusammenbruch des Heiligen Römischen Reichs deutscher Nation und die Problematik seiner Restauration in den Jahren 1814/15* (Heidelberg, 1980), pp.11–13.

52. G. Benecke, *Society and Politics in Germany, 1500–1750* (London, 1974), p.274. For the pay bill see J. J. Schmauss and H. C. von Senckenberg (eds.), *Neue und vollständige Sammlung der Reichsabschiede* (4 vols., Frankfurt am Main, 1747), III, pp.350–51, with Zieler quotas at IV, pp.109–14.

53. E. Heischmann, *Die Anfänge des stehenden Heeres in Österreich* (Vienna, 1925), p.63. The actual matricular register lists 4,202 cavalry and 20,063 infantry, equivalent to 130,676 florins, but the troop numbers

were usually rounded down. For the following see W. Schulze, 'Die Erträge der Reichssteuern zwischen 1576 und 1606', *Jahrbuch für die Geschichte Mittel- und Ostdeutschlands*, 27 (1978), 169–85.

54. R. Graf von Neipperg, *Kaiser und Schwäbischer Kreis (1714–1733)* (Stuttgart, 1991), pp.79–82.

55. Winkelbauer, *Österreichische Geschichte*, I, pp.481, 493.

56. W. Blockmans, *Emperor Charles V, 1500–1558* (London, 2002), p.155. This was equivalent to 2.2 million Castilian ducats. Between 3 and 3.5 million were paid in 1521–48 with the rest thereafter: Winkelbauer, *Österreichische Geschichte*, I, p.513. Arrears of the various Common Penny grants totalled 400,000 florins by the 1550s: Rauscher, *Zwischen Ständen und Gläubigern*, p.322. Main sources for Table 10: W. Steglich, 'Die Reichstürkenhilfe in der Zeit Karls V.', *Militärgeschichtliche Mitteilungen*, 11 (1972), 7–55; P. Rauscher, 'Kaiser und Reich. Die Reichstürkenhilfen von Ferdinand I. bis zum Beginn des "Langen Türkenkriegs" 1548–1593', in F. Edelmeyer et al. (eds.), *Finanzen und Herrschaft. Materielle Grundlagen fürstlicher Politik in den habsburgischen Ländern und im Heiligen Römischen Reich im 16. Jahrhundert* (Munich, 2003), pp.45–83.

57. Charles raised 9 million ducats (17.6 million florins) in taxes and loans for military expenses 1543–52: J. D. Tracy, *Emperor Charles V, Impresario of War* (Cambridge, 2002), p.247. Altogether he borrowed 58 million florins in 1520–56, costing 18 million florins in interest charges: W. Maltby, *The Reign of Charles V* (Basingstoke, 2002), pp.67–75.

58. P. Rauscher, 'Comparative evolution of the tax systems in the Habsburg monarchy, c.1526–1740', in S. Cavaciocchi (ed.), *La fiscalità nell'economia Europea secc. XIII–XVIII* (Florence, 2008), pp.291–320; O. Pickl, 'Fiskus, Kirche und Staat in Innerösterreich im Zeitalter der Reformation und Gegenreformation (16./17. Jahrhundert)', in H. Kellenbenz and P. Prodi (eds.), *Fiskus, Kirche und Staat im konfessionellen Zeitalter* (Berlin, 1994), pp.91–110; G. Pálffy, 'Türkenabwehr, Grenzsoldatentum und die Militärisierung der Gesellschaft in Ungarn in der Frühen Neuzeit', *HJb*, 123 (2003), 111–48, and his 'The origins and development of the border defence system against the Ottoman Empire in Hungary', in G. Dávid and P. Fodor (eds.), *Ottomans, Hungarians, and Habsburgs in Central Europe* (Leiden, 2000), pp.3–69.

59. Rauscher, *Zwischen Ständen und Gläubigern*, pp.269–71. Rudolf II's court cost 419,000 florins annually compared to 650,000 florins under Maximilian II.

60. W. Schulze, *Reich und Türkengefahr im späten 16. Jahrhundert* (Munich, 1978).

61. P. Rauscher, 'Nach den Türkenreichstagen. Der Beitrag des Heiligen Römischen Reichs zur kaiserlichen Kriegführung im 17. und frühen 18.

Jahrhundert', in idem (ed.), *Kriegführung und Staatsfinanzen. Die Habs-burgermonarchie und das Heilige Römische Reich vom Dreißigjährigen Krieg bis zum Ende des habsburgischen Kaisertums 1740* (Münster, 2010), pp.433–85 at 444.

62. A. Sigelen, *Reichspfennigmeister Zacharias Geizkofler zwischen Fürsten-dienst und Familienpolitik* (Stuttgart, 2009), pp.152–64, 602–7; Rauscher, 'Nach den Türkenreichstagen', 451.

63. Sigelen, *Reichspfennigmeister Zacharias Geizkofler*, p.141. This included money sent by Italian lords and the imperial knights.

64. H.-W. Bergerhausen, 'Die Stadt Köln im Dreißigjährigen Krieg', in S. Ehrenpreis (ed.), *Der Dreißigjährige Krieg im Herzogtum Berg und in seinen Nachbarregionen* (Neustadt an der Aisch, 2002), pp.102–31 at 110–11. Swabia and Franconia paid over 256,000 florins in 1626–30: Rauscher, 'Nach den Türkenreichstagen', 445.

65. R. R. Heinisch, *Paris Graf Lodron. Reichsfürst und Erzbischof von Salzburg* (Vienna, 1991), pp.254, 256–7; R. Weber, *Würzburg und Bam-berg im Dreißigjährigen Krieg. Die Regierungszeit des Bischofs Franz von Hatzfeldt, 1631–1642* (Würzburg, 1979), pp.268–86; J. F. Foerster, *Kurfürst Ferdinand von Köln. Die Politik seiner Stifter in den Jahren 1634–1650* (Münster, 1976), pp.164–7.

66. A. Oschmann, *Der Nürnberger Exekutionstag 1649–1650. Das Ende des Dreißigjährigen Krieges in Deutschland* (Münster, 1991); T. Lorentzen, *Die schwedische Armee im Dreißigjährigen Kriege und ihre Abdankung* (Leipzig, 1894), pp.184–92; D. Albrecht, *Maximilian I. von Bayern 1573–1651* (Mün-ster, 1998), pp.1087–90; Heinisch, *Paris Graf Lodron*, pp.289–302.

67. Sources for Table 12: Staatsarchiv Darmstadt, E1, C43 and 3; Rauscher, 'Nach den Türkenreichstagen', 465–82; *NTSR*, IV, 1125–8.

68. G. A. Süß, 'Geschichte des oberrheinischen Kreises und der Kreisassozia-tionen in der Zeit des Spanischen Erbfolgekrieges (1679–1714)', *ZGO*, 103 (1955), 317–425; 104 (1956), 145–224.

69. Rauscher, 'Nach den Türkenreichstagen', 477. These additional contribu-tions are excluded from Table 12.

70. P. H. Wilson, 'Financing the War of the Spanish Succession in the Holy Roman Empire', in M. Pohlig and M. Schaich (eds.), *The War of the Span-ish Succession: New Perspectives*, forthcoming.

71. K. Härter, *Reichstag und Revolution, 1789–1806* (Göttingen, 1992), pp.422–6, 435–6.

72. The traditional negative interpretation is discussed by H. Neuhaus, 'Das Problem der militärischen Exekutive in der Spätphase des Alten Reiches', in J. Kunisch and B. Stollberg-Rilinger (eds.), *Staatsverfassung und Heeresverfassung in der europäischen Geschichte der Frühen Neuzeit* (Berlin, 1986), pp.297–346. For a reappraisal of the imperial

army's performance in the battle, see P. H. Wilson, *German Armies: War and German Politics, 1648–1806* (London, 1998), pp.272–4.

73. H. Neuhaus, 'Reichskreise und Reichskriege in der Frühen Neuzeit', in Wüst (ed.), *Reichskreis und Territorium*, pp.71–88; M. Lanzinner, *Friedenssicherung und politische Einheit des Reiches unter Kaiser Maximilian II. (1564–1576)* (Göttingen, 1993); Luttenberger, *Kurfürsten, Kaiser und Reich*, pp.307–444.

74. D. Götschmann, 'Das Jus Armorum. Ausformung und politische Bedeutung der reichsständischen Militärhoheit bis zu ihrer definitiven Anerkennung im Westfälischen Frieden', *BDLG*, 129 (1993), 257–76.

75. Contingents were sent in 1532, 1542, 1552, 1566–7 and 1593–1606. For the latter see J. Müller, 'Der Anteil der schwäbischen Kreistruppen an dem Türkenkrieg Kaiser Rudolfs II. von 1595 bis 1597', *Zeitschrift des Historischen Vereins für Schwaben und Neuburg*, 28 (1901), 155–262; G. Tessin, 'Niedersachsen im Türkenkrieg, 1594–1597', *NJLG*, 36 (1964), 66–106; P. C. Hartmann, 'Der bayerische Reichskreis im Zeichen konfessioneller Spannungen und türkischer Bedrohung', *ZBLG*, 60 (1997), 599–616.

76. B. Rill, *Kaiser Matthias* (Graz, 1999), p.70.

77. G. E. Rothenberg, *The Austrian Military Border in Croatia, 1522–1747* (Urbana, IL, 1960); W. Aichelburg, *Kriegsschiffe auf der Donau* (2nd ed., Vienna, 1982).

78. For the following see: P. H. Wilson, 'Strategy and the conduct of war', in O. Asbach and P. Schröder (eds.), *The Ashgate Research Companion to the Thirty Years' War* (Farnham, 2014), pp.269–81, and Wilson, *Europe's Tragedy, passim*.

79. G. Mortimer, *Wallenstein: The Enigma of the Thirty Years War* (Basingstoke, 2010); A. Ernstberger, *Hans de Witte, Finanzmann Wallensteins* (Wiesbaden, 1954).

80. P. Hoyos, 'Die kaiserliche Armee, 1648–1650', in *Der Dreißigjährige Krieg* (issued by the Heeresgeschichtliches Museum, Vienna, 1976), pp.169–232.

81. Wilson, *German Armies*, pp.26–68, and the sources cited there.

82. H. Angermeier, 'Die Reichskriegsverfassung in der Politik der Jahre 1679–1681', *ZSRG GA*, 82 (1965), 190–222; H. J. Wunschel, *Die Außenpolitik des Bischofs von Bamberg und Würzburg Peter Philipps von Dernbach* (Neustadt an der Aisch, 1979).

83. Contemporary criticism in *NTSR*, vol.16, part 3, p.3. M. Hughes, 'Die Strafpreussen: Mecklenburg und der Bund der deutschen absolutistischen Fürsten, 1648–1719', *Parliaments, Estates and Representation*, 3 (1983), 101–13.

84. Sources for Table 13: P. H. Wilson, 'The Holy Roman Empire and the problem of the armed Estates', in Rauscher (ed.), *Kriegführung und*

Staatsfinanzen, pp.487–514 at 513, modified from additional data in Wilson, 'Financing', table 1. Note that the forces engaged in the Great Turkish War and Nine Years War need to be combined to give the overall average for the period 1688–97.

85. More detailed breakdown in P. H. Wilson, *From Reich to Revolution: German History, 1558–1806* (Basingstoke, 2004), p.226.

86. Wilson, *German Armies*, pp.226–41, and 'Armed Estates', 511–12.

87. S. R. Epstein, *Freedom and Growth: The Rise of States and Markets in Europe, 1300–1750* (London, 2000), pp.12–37, 173–4; A. Giddens, *The Nation-State and Violence* (Berkeley, 1985).

88. O. Volckart, 'Politische Zersplitterung und Wirtschaftswachstum im Alten Reich, ca. 1650–1800', *VSWG*, 86 (1999), 1–38.

89. Statistics from A. Haverkamp, *Medieval Germany, 1056–1273* (Oxford, 1988), pp.180, 288. Urban development is discussed on pp.504–24. See also G. Fouquet, 'Das Reich in den europäischen Wirtschaftsräumen des Mittelalters', in B. Schneidmüller and S. Weinfurter (eds.), *Heilig – Römisch – Deutsch* (Dresden, 2006), pp.323–44.

90. N. Brübach, *Die Reichsmessen von Frankfurt am Main, Leipzig und Braunschweig (14.–18.Jahrhundert.)* (Stuttgart, 1994).

91. F. Blaich, 'Die Bedeutung der Reichstage auf dem Gebiet der öffentlichen Finanzen im Spannungsfeld zwischen Kaiser, Territorialstaaten und Reichsstädten (1495–1670)', in A. De Maddalena and H. Kellenbenz (eds.), *Finanzen und Staatsräson in Italien und Deutschland in der Frühen Neuzeit* (Berlin, 1992), pp.79–111 at 100–110; C. Hattenhauer, *Schuldenregulierung nach dem Westfälischen Frieden* (Frankfurt am Main, 1998).

92. Rauscher, *Zwischen Ständen und Gläubigern*, pp.104–16. For the following see H.-J. Gerhard, 'Ein schöner Garten ohne Zaun. Die währungspolitische Situation des Deutschen Reiches um 1600', *VSWG*, 81 (1994), 156–77.

93. C. P. Kindelberger, 'The economic crisis of 1619 to 1623', *Journal of Economic History*, 51 (1991), 149–75.

94. J. O. Opel, 'Deutsche Finanznoth beim Beginn des dreißigjährigen Krieges', *HZ*, 16 (1866), 213–68 at 218–19.

95. *The Guardian*, 19 Sept. 2007; *Süddeutsche Zeitung*, 19 and 20 Jan. 2013. See also: S. Leins, *Das Prager Münzkonsortium 1622/23* (Münster, 2012); M. W. Paas, *The Kipper und Wipper Inflation, 1619–23: An Economic History with Contemporary German Broadsheets* (New Haven, CT, 2012).

96. J. A. Vann, *The Swabian Kreis: Institutional Growth in the Holy Roman Empire, 1648–1715* (Brussels, 1975), pp.229–39; Winkelbauer, *Österreichische Geschichte*, I, pp.483–4; Süß, 'Geschichte des oberrheinischen Kreises', pp.385–9.

97. W. Hubatsch, *Frederick the Great: Absolutism and Administration* (London, 1975), pp.138–9; E. Klein, *Geschichte der öffentlichen Finanzen in*

Deutschland (1500–1870) (Wiesbaden, 1974), pp.54–9; H.-G. Borck, *Der Schwäbische Reichskreis im Zeitalter der französischen Revolutions-kriege (1792–1806)* (Stuttgart, 1970).

98. B. Weiler, 'Image and reality in Richard of Cornwall's German career', *EHR*, 113 (1998), 1111–42 at 1120 and 1136. For the following: I. Bog, *Der Reichsmerkantilismus* (Stuttgart, 1959); Blaich, 'Die Bedeutung der Reichstage', 95–100.

99. E. F. Heckscher, *Mercantilism* (rev. ed., 2 vols., London, 1935), I, pp.78–109.

100. Vann, *Swabian Kreis*, pp.241–8.

101. T. C. W. Blanning, *Reform and Revolution in Mainz, 1743–1803* (Cambridge, 1974), p.71. For these arguments generally see R. M. Spaulding, 'Revolution-ary France and the transformation of the Rhine', *CEH*, 44 (2011), 203–26.

102. B. Simms, *The Struggle for Mastery in Germany, 1779–1850* (Basing-stoke, 1998); J. G. Gagliardo, *Germany under the Old Regime, 1600–1790* (London, 1991), pp.312–53.

103. For contrasting interpretations on whether Habsburg power had peaked before 1705, or did so under Joseph I, see C. W. Ingrao, *In Quest and Cri-sis: Emperor Joseph I and the Habsburg Monarchy* (West Lafayette, IN, 1979), pp.31–77; V. Press, 'Josef I. (1705–1711). Kaiserpolitik zwischen Erblanden, Reich und Dynastie', in R. Melville et al. (eds.), *Deutschland und Europa in der Neuzeit* (Stuttgart, 1988), pp.277–97.

104. Aretin, *Das Alte Reich*, II, pp.97–219.

105. Ingrao, *In Quest and Crisis*, p.158. For Charles see B. Rill, *Karl VI. Habs-burg als barocke Großmacht* (Graz, 1992).

106. Further discussion of these statistics in Wilson, *From Reich to Revolu-tion*, pp.308–10.

107. P. H. Wilson, *War, State and Society in Württemberg, 1677–1793* (Cam-bridge, 1995), pp.163–83; P. Sauer, *Ein kaiserlicher General auf dem württembergischen Herzogsthron. Herzog Carl Alexander von Würt-temberg, 1684–1737* (Filderstadt, 2006).

108. This has been termed 'organizational hypocrisy': Stollberg-Rilinger, *Des Kaisers alte Kleider*, p.280.

109. D. McKay, *The Great Elector* (Harlow, 2001). For attempts to reappraise Frederick I see L. and M. Frey, *Frederick I: The Man and His Times* (Boulder, CO, 1984); F. Göse, *Friedrich I. Ein König in Preußen* (Regensburg, 2012). For Prussia's emergence generally see K. Friedrich, *Brandenburg-Prussia, 1466–1806* (Basingstoke, 2012); C. Clark, *Iron Kingdom: The Rise and Downfall of Prussia, 1600–1947* (London, 2006); P. G. Dwyer (ed.), *The Rise of Prussia, 1700–1830* (Harlow, 2000).

110. Wilson, *From Reich to Revolution*, p.323.

111. Classic account in F. L. Carsten, *The Origins of Prussia* (Oxford, 1954), pp.179–277. For the following see also P. H. Wilson, 'Prussia as a

fiscal-military state, 1640–1806', in C. Storrs (ed.), *The Fiscal-Military State in Eighteenth-Century Europe* (Farnham, 2009), pp.95–124.

112. L. Hüttl, *Friedrich Wilhelm von Brandenburg, der Große Kurfürst, 1620–1688* (Munich, 1981), pp.201–95.

113. S. Externbrink, 'State-building within the Empire: The cases of Brandenburg-Prussia and Savoy-Sardinia', in R. J. W. Evans and P. H. Wilson (eds.), *The Holy Roman Empire, 1495–1806* (Leiden, 2012), pp.187–202.

114. A. Berney, *König Friedrich I. und das Haus Habsburg (1701–1707)* (Munich, 1927); A. Pečar, 'Symbolische Politik. Handlungsspielräume im politischen Umgang mit zeremoniellen Normen. Brandenburg-Preußen und der Kaiserhof im Vergleich (1700–1740)', in J. Luh et al. (eds.), *Preussen, Deutschland und Europa, 1701–2001* (Groningen, 2003), pp.280–95; P. H. Wilson, 'Prussia and the Holy Roman Empire, 1700–40', *GHIL*, 36 (2014), 3–48.

115. P. H. Wilson, 'Social militarization in eighteenth-century Germany', *GH*, 18 (2000), 1–39.

116. R. Endres, 'Preussens Griff nach Franken', in H. Duchhardt (ed.), *Friedrich der Große, Franken und das Reich* (Cologne, 1986), pp.57–79.

117. For Prussian-Saxon rivalry see F. Göse, 'Nachbarn, Partner und Rivalen: die kursächsische Sicht auf Preußen im ausgehenden 17. und 18. Jahrhundert', in J. Luh et al. (eds.), *Preussen*, pp.45–78. For Prussia's wars see D. E. Showalter, *The Wars of Frederick the Great* (Harlow, 1996). See also R. Browning, *The War of the Austrian Succession* (New York, 1993), and the similarly entitled book by M. S. Anderson (Harlow, 1995).

118. T. Biskup, *Friedrichs Größe. Inszenierungen des Preußenkönigs in Fest und Zeremoniell, 1740–1815* (Frankfurt, 2012). Among the many biographies the following are worth consulting: T. Schieder, *Frederick the Great* (Harlow, 2000); J. Kunisch, *Friedrich der Große. Der König und seine Zeit* (Munich, 2004). Briefer overviews incorporating the research produced for the Frederick tercentenary: J. Luh, *Der Große. Friedrich II. von Preußen* (Munich, 2011); W. Burgdorf, *Friedrich der Große* (Freiburg im Breisgau, 2011).

119. R. Zedinger, *Franz Stephen von Lothringen (1708–1765)* (Vienna, 2008).

120. Aretin, *Das Alte Reich*, II, pp.413–39.

121. P. C. Hartmann, *Karl Albrecht – Karl VII.* (Regensburg, 1985), p.95; Wilson, *German Armies*, pp.247–60.

122. Aretin, *Das Alte Reich*, II, pp.442–3.

123. Ibid, II, pp.449–58; Hartmann, *Karl Albrecht*, pp.194, 217–18, 238, 244–5, 254, 285–90; W. von Hofmann, 'Das Säkularisationsprojekt von 1743. Kaiser Karl VII. und die römische Kurie', in *Riezler-Festschrift* (Gotha, 1913), pp.213–59.

124. A. Schmid, *Max III. Joseph und die europäischen Mächte. Die Aussenpolitik des Kurfürstentums Bayern von 1745–1765* (Munich, 1987), pp.29–235.

125. Stollberg-Rilinger, *Des Kaisers alte Kleider*, pp.281–4; K. O. Frhr. v. Aretin, *Das Reich* (Stuttgart, 1986), pp.27–8.

126. Beales, *Joseph II*, I, p.119. See also pp.159–63.

127. The diplomatic background is covered by H. M. Scott, *The Birth of a Great Power System, 1740–1815* (Harlow, 2006), pp.72–116. See also F. A. J. Szabo, *The Seven Years War in Europe, 1756–1763* (Harlow, 2008); M. Persson, 'Mediating the enemy: Prussian representations of Austria, France and Sweden during the Seven Years War', *GH* 32 (2014), 181–200; Aretin, *Das Alte Reich*, III, pp.81–111.

128. As argued by J. Burkhardt, *Vollendung und Neuorientierung des frühmodernen Reiches, 1648–1763* (Stuttgart, 2006), pp.438–41. The war is considered from the Empire's perspective in Wilson, *German Armies*, pp. 264–80. For an Austrian perspective see M. Hochedlinger, *Austria's Wars of Emergence, 1683–1797* (Harlow, 2003), pp.330–48.

129. J. Kunisch, *Das Mirakel des Hauses Brandenburg. Studien zum Verhältnis von Kabinettspolitik und Kriegführung im Zeitalter des Siebenjährigen Krieges* (Munich, 1978).

130. V. Press, 'Friedrich der Große als Reichspolitiker', in Duchhardt (ed.), *Friedrich der Große*, pp.25–56; Wilson, 'Prussia's relations'.

131. M. Hanisch, 'Friedrich II. und die Preussische Sukzession in Franken in der internationalen Diskussion', in Duchhardt (ed.), *Friedrich der Große*, pp.81–91; P. P. Bernard, *Joseph II and Bavaria* (The Hague, 1965); Aretin, *Das Alte Reich*, III, pp.183–212.

132. J. Lukowski, *The Partitions of Poland, 1772, 1793, 1795* (Harlow, 1999); M. G. Müller, *Die Teilungen Polens 1772, 1793, 1795* (Munich, 1984); T. Cegielski, *Das Alte Reich und die erste Teilung Polens 1768–1774* (Stuttgart, 1988).

133. M. E. Thomas, *Karl Theodor and the Bavarian Succession, 1777–1778* (Lewiston, NY, 1989); D. Petschel, *Sächsische Außenpolitik unter Friedrich August I.* (Cologne, 2000), pp.47–56.

134. Stollberg-Rilinger, *Des Kaisers alte Kleider*, pp.288–97; Beales, *Joseph II*, II, pp.408–9.

135. K. O. Frhr. v. Aretin, *Heiliges Römisches Reich, 1776–1806* (2 vols., Wiesbaden, 1967), I, pp.164–85, and his *Das Alte Reich*, III, pp.299–333. Further discussion of this organization's aims on pp.640–41.

CHAPTER 10: AUTHORITY

1. J. B. Freed, 'Medieval German social history', *CEH*, 25 (1992), 1–26; S. C. Karant-Nunn, 'Is there a social history of the Holy Roman Empire?',

in R. J. W. Evans et al. (eds.), *The Holy Roman Empire, 1495–1806* (Oxford, 2011), pp.245–62.

2. A useful summary of these is in C. Veach, *Lordship in Four Realms* (Manchester, 2014), pp.6–10.

3. B. Arnold, *Princes and Territories in Medieval Germany* (Cambridge, 1991), pp.67–8.

4. For the debate on this point see H. K. Schulze, *Grundstrukturen der Verfassung im Mittelalter* (3rd ed., 3 vols., Stuttgart, 1995–2000), I, pp.102–6, II, pp.78–82. For the following see H. Wunder, 'Peasant communities in medieval and early modern Germany', *Recueils de la Société Jean Bodin pour l'histoire comparative des institutions*, 44 (1987), 9–52 esp. 22–3.

5. The literature on this is substantial. Good overviews include A. Verhulst, *The Carolingian Economy* (Cambridge, 2002); W. Rösener, *The Peasantry of Europe* (Oxford, 1994), pp.21, 33–44; W. Troßbach and C. Zimmermann, *Die Geschichte des Dorfs. Von den Anfängen im Frankenreich zur bundesdeutschen Gegenwart* (Stuttgart, 2006), pp.23–6; M. Costambeys et al., *The Carolingian World* (Cambridge, 2011), pp.234–5, 254–62; J. Laudage et al., *Die Zeit der Karolinger* (Darmstadt, 2006), pp.172–82.

6. For examples of Frankish landholding patterns, see M. Innes, *State and Society in the Early Middle Ages* (Cambridge, 2000), pp.51–68.

7. For the possible origins of the hide see W. Goffart, 'From Roman taxation to medieval seigneurie', *Speculum*, 47 (1972), 165–87, 373–94.

8. G. Duby, 'Medieval agriculture, 900–1500', in C. M. Cipolla (ed.), *The Fontana Economic History of Europe* (6 vols., Glasgow, 1972), I, pp.175–220.

9. H. Fuhrmann, *Germany in the High Middle Ages c.1050–1200* (Cambridge, 1986), p.37.

10. L. White Jr, 'The expansion of technology, 500–1500', in Cipolla (ed.), *Fontana Economic History*, I, pp.143–74.

11. W. Rösener, 'Bauern in der Salierzeit', in S. Weinfurter (ed.), *Die Salier und das Reich* (3 vols., Sigmaringen, 1991), III, pp.51–73. For Meinward see also H. Wolfram, *Conrad II, 990–1039* (University Park, PA, 2006), pp.285–6. For the following see W. Metz, 'Wesen und Struktur des Adels Althessens in der Salierzeit', in Weinfurter (ed.), *Die Salier und das Reich*, I, pp.331–66.

12. J. C. Russell, 'Population in Europe, 500–1500', in Cipolla (ed.), *Fontana Economic History*, I, pp.25–70 at 36; K. Blaschke, *Bevölkerungsgeschichte von Sachsen bis zur industriellen Revolution* (Weimar, 1967), p.71.

13. W. Abel, *Agricultural Fluctuations in Europe from the Thirteenth to the Twentieth Centuries* (London, 1986), pp.25–7.

14. G. Fouquet, 'Das Reich in den europäischen Wirtschaftsräumen des Mittelalters', in B. Schneidmüller and S. Weinfurter (eds.), *Heilig – Römisch – Deutsch* (Dresden, 2006), pp.323–44 at 329–30; R. S. Lopez, *The Commercial Revolution of the Middle Ages, 950–1350* (Cambridge, 1976).

15. W. Rösener, 'The decline of the classic manor in Germany during the high Middle Ages', in A. Haverkamp and H. Vollrath (eds.), *England and Germany in the High Middle Ages* (Oxford, 1996), pp.317–30; C. Wickham, *Early Medieval Italy* (Ann Arbor, MI, 1981), pp.111–14, 188.

16. Troßbach and Zimmermann, *Die Geschichte des Dorfs*, pp.42–3.

17. Schulze, *Grundstrukturen der Verfassung*, I, pp.95–6.

18. S. Weinfurter, *The Salian Century* (Philadelphia, 1999), pp.77–8.

19. Rösener, *Peasantry*, p.66.

20. W. C. Jordan, *The Great Famine: Northern Europe in the Early Fourteenth Century* (Princeton, 1996). For the following: O. J. Benedictow, *The Black Death, 1346–1353* (Woodbridge, 2004); Abel, *Agricultural Fluctuations*, pp.35–48, 102–4.

21. T. Scott, *Society and Economy in Germany, 1300–1600* (Basingstoke, 2002), pp.72–112.

22. See S. K. Cohn Jr, *Lust for Liberty: The Politics of Social Revolt in Medieval Europe, 1200–1425* (Cambridge, MA, 2006), pp.205–27.

23. Rösener, *Peasantry*, pp.64–82; Duby, 'Medieval agriculture', pp.212–15.

24. Abel, *Agricultural Fluctuations*, pp.45–95.

25. P. H. Wilson, *Europe's Tragedy* (London, 2009), pp.781–95; Q. Outram, 'The socio-economic relations of warfare and the military mortality crises of the Thirty Years' War', *Medical History*, 45 (2001), 151–84, and his 'The demographic impact of early modern warfare', *Social Science History*, 26 (2002), 245–72.

26. J. Whaley, *Germany and the Holy Roman Empire, 1493–1806* (2 vols., Oxford, 2012), II, p.454; P. H. Wilson, *From Reich to Revolution: German History, 1558–1806* (Basingstoke, 2004), pp.50, 310, 323.

27. C. Dipper, *Deutsche Geschichte, 1648–1789* (Frankfurt am Main, 1991), pp.10–75; C. Küther, *Menschen auf der Straße. Vagierende Unterschichten in Bayern, Franken und Schwaben in der zweiten Hälfte des 18. Jahrhunderts* (Göttingen, 1983).

28. Full discussion in M. Cerman, *Villagers and Lords in Eastern Europe, 1300–1800* (Basingstoke, 2012).

29. Rösener, *Peasantry*, pp.81, 104–24. For the following see H. Kaak, *Die Gutsherrschaft* (Berlin, 1991); J. Peters (ed.), *Gutsherrschaft als soziales Modell* (Munich, 1995).

30. Rösener, *Peasantry*, p.117.

31. E. Weis, 'Ergebnisse eines Vergleichs der grundherrschaftlichen Strukturen Deutschlands und Frankreichs vom 13. bis zum Ausgang des 18.

Jahrhunderts', *VSWG*, 57 (1970), 1–14; H. Schissler, 'The social and political power of the Prussian Junkers', in R. Gibson and M. Blinkhorn (eds.), *Landownership and Power in Modern Europe* (London, 1991), pp.99–110 at 104; R. Schlögl, 'Absolutismus im 17. Jahrhundert. Bayerischer Adel zwischen Disziplinierung und Integration', *ZHF*, 15 (1988), 151–86.

32. O. von Gierke, *Deutsche Genossenschaftsrecht* (reprint Graz, 1954; first published 1868); P. Blickle, *Obedient Germans? A Rebuttal* (Charlottesville, VA, 1997); O. Brunner, *Land and Lordship: Structures of Governance in Medieval Austria* (Philadelphia, 1992).

33. A term from Rösener, *Peasantry*, p.43. The idea that cities pioneered communal ideology and practice stems from Georg von Below in 1914, but is still often repeated: E. Schubert, *Fürstliche Herrschaft und Territorium im späten Mittelalter* (2nd ed., Munich, 2006), pp.75–7.

34. D. M. Luebke, *His Majesty's Rebels: Communities, Factions and Rural Revolt in the Black Forest, 1725–1745* (Ithaca, NY, 1997), pp.203–4. For the following see R. von Friedeburg, ' "Reiche", "geringe Leute" und "Beambte": Landesherrschaft, dörfliche "Factionen" und gemeindliche Partizipation, 1648–1806', *ZHF*, 23 (1996), 219–65; M. J. Halvorson and K. E. Spierling, *Defining Community in Early Modern Europe* (Aldershot, 2008).

35. H.-C. Rublack, 'Political and social norms in urban communities in the Holy Roman Empire', in K. von Greyerz (ed.), *Religion, Politics and Social Protest* (London, 1984), pp.24–60; P. Münch, 'Grundwerte der frühneuzeitlichen Ständegesellschaft?', and R. Blickle, 'Nahrung und Eigentum als Kategorien in der ständischen Gesellschaft', both in W. Schulze (ed.), *Ständische Gesellschaft und soziale Mobilität* (Munich, 1988), pp.53–72, 73–93.

36. I. Hunter, *Rival Enlightenments: Civil and Metaphysical Philosophy in Early Modern Germany* (Cambridge, 2001).

37. R. A. Müller, 'Die deutschen Fürstenspiegel des 17. Jahrhunderts', *HZ*, 240 (1985), 571–97; Schubert, *Fürstliche Herrschaft*, pp.81–6.

38. *NTSR*, vol.16, in nine parts.

39. B. Scribner, 'Communities and the nature of power', in idem (ed.), *Germany: A New Social and Economic History*, I, *1450–1630* (London, 1996), pp.291–326; L. Roper, ' "The common man", "the common good", "common women": Gender and meaning in the German Reformation commune', *Social History*, 12 (1987), 1–21.

40. V. Seresse, 'Schlüsselbegriffe der politischen Sprache in Jülich-Berg und Kleve-Mark um 1600', in M. Groten et al. (eds.), *Der Jülich-Klevische Erbstreit 1609* (Düsseldorf, 2011), pp.69–81; A. Gestrich, *Absolutismus und Öffentlichkeit* (Göttingen, 1994), pp.79–80.

41. C. Gantet, *La paix de Westphalie (1648). Une histoire sociale, XVIIᵉ–XVIIIᵉ siècles* (Paris, 2001).

42. A. Wandruszka, 'Zum "Absolutismus" Ferdinands II.', *Mitteilungen des Oberösterreichischen Landesarchivs*, 14 (1984), 261–8. For the debate on absolutism as a historical concept see L. Schilling (ed.), *Absolutismus, ein unersetzliches Forschungskonzept?* (Munich, 2008); P. H. Wilson, *Absolutism in Central Europe* (London, 2000).

43. H. M. Scott (ed.), *Enlightened Absolutism* (London, 1990); P. Baumgart, 'Absolutismus ein Mythos? Aufgeklärter Absolutismus ein Widerspruch?', *ZHF*, 27 (2000), 573–89.

44. W. Schulze, 'Vom Gemeinnutz zum Eigennutz', *HZ*, 243 (1986), 591–626.

45. D. Klippel, 'Reasonable aims of civil society: Concerns of the state in German political theory in the eighteenth and early nineteenth centuries', in J. Brewer and E. Hellmuth (eds.), *Rethinking Leviathan* (Oxford, 1999), pp.71–98; B. Stollberg-Rilinger, *Der Staat als Maschine. Zur politischen Metaphorik des absoluten Fürstenstaats* (Berlin, 1986).

46. P. Blickle (ed.), *Resistance, Representation and Community* (Oxford, 1997).

47. C. Loveluck, 'Rural settlement hierarchy in the age of Charlemagne', in J. Story (ed.), *Charlemagne* (Manchester, 2005), pp.230–58; Costambeys et al., *The Carolingian World*, pp.229–41.

48. S. Reynolds, *Kingdoms and Communities in Western Europe, 900–1300* (2nd ed., Oxford, 1997), pp.101–54; Troßbach and Zimmermann (eds.), *Die Geschichte des Dorfs*, pp.21–34. Nucleated villages may already have existed in parts of the Frankish world by the ninth century, but the evidence is ambiguous.

49. A. Haverkamp, 'Die Städte im Herrschafts- und Sozialgefüge Reichsitaliens', in F. Vittinghoff (ed.), *Stadt und Herrschaft. Römische Kaiserzeit und hohes Mittelalter* (Munich, 1982), pp.149–245 at 153–61.

50. Weinfurter, *Salian Century*, pp.78–80.

51. B. Diestelkamp, 'König und Städte in salischer und staufischer Zeit', in Vittinghoff (ed.), *Stadt und Herrschaft*, pp.247–97; H. Jakobs, 'Aspects of urban social history in Salian and Staufen Germany', in Haverkamp and Vollrath (eds.), *England and Germany*, pp.283–98; T. Scott, *The City-State in Europe, 1000–1600* (Oxford, 2012), pp.17–18.

52. C. Pfister, 'The population of late medieval and early modern Germany', in Scribner (ed.), *Germany*, pp.33–62 at 40–41; G. Franz, *Geschichte des deutschen Bauernstandes vom frühen Mittelalter bis zum 19. Jahrhundert* (Stuttgart, 1970), pp.120–22; Abel, *Agricultural Fluctuations*, pp.81–5.

53. J. de Vries, *European Urbanization, 1500–1800* (Cambridge, MA, 1984); T. Scott and B. Scribner, 'Urban networks', in Scribner (ed.), *Germany*, pp.113–44; Troßbach and Zimmermann (eds.), *Die Geschichte des Dorfs*, p.66.

54. For a specific example see G. Strauss, *Nuremberg in the Sixteenth Century* (2nd ed., Bloomington, IN, 1976), pp.39–56.

55. Troßbach and Zimmermann (eds.), *Die Geschichte des Dorfs*, pp.31–2.
56. P. Blickle, *Das Alte Europa* (Munich, 2008), pp.16–38; I. V. Hull, *Sexuality, State and Civil Society in Germany, 1700–1815* (Ithaca, NY, 1996), pp.29–51; T. Robisheaux, *Rural Society and the Search for Order in Early Modern Germany* (Cambridge, 1989), pp.68–146; D. W. Sabean, *Power in the Blood* (Cambridge, 1984), pp.199–211, and his *Property, Production and Family in Neckarhausen, 1700–1870* (Cambridge, 1990), pp.88–116.
57. For this see O. Mörke, 'Social structure', in S. Ogilvie (ed.), *Germany: A New Social and Economic History*, II, *1630–1800* (London, 1996), pp.134–63 at 156–7.
58. Franz, *Geschichte des deutschen Bauernstandes*, pp.49–71; Troßbach and Zimmermann (eds.), *Die Geschichte des Dorfs*, pp.36–43, 78–96.
59. Scribner, 'Communities', p.302.
60. L. Enders, 'Die Landgemeinde in Brandenburg. Grundzüge ihrer Funktion und Wirkungsweise vom 13. bis zum 18. Jahrhundert', *BDLG*, 129 (1993), 195–256; J. Peters (ed.), *Konflikt und Kontrolle in Gutsherrschaftsgesellschaften* (Göttingen, 1995); W. W. Hagen, *Ordinary Prussians: Brandenburg Junkers and Villagers, 1500–1840* (Cambridge, 2002).
61. S. Ogilvie, 'Village community and village headman in early modern Bohemia', *Bohemia*, 46 (2005), 402–51.
62. T. Struve, *Salierzeit im Wandel* (Cologne, 2006), pp.145–76.
63. H. Keller, 'Die soziale und politische Verfassung Mailands in den Angfängen des kommunalen Lebens', *HZ*, 211 (1970), 34–64 at 51–60; H.-W. Goetz, 'Gottesfriede und Gemeindebildung', *ZSRG GA*, 105 (1988), 122–44.
64. D. J. Hay, *The Military Leadership of Matilda of Canossa, 1046–1115* (Manchester, 2008), pp.171–84; C. Brühl, 'Königs-, Bischofs- und Stadtpfalz in den Städten des "Regnum Italiae" vom 9. bis zum 13. Jahrhundert', in H. Beumann (ed.), *Historische Forschungen für Walter Schlesinger* (Cologne, 1974), pp.400–419; C. Wickham, 'The "feudal revolution" and the origins of Italian city communes', *TRHS*, 6th series, 24 (2014), 29–55.
65. Printed in B. H. Hill Jr, *Medieval Monarchy in Action* (London, 1972), pp.235–6.
66. A. Haverkamp, *Medieval Germany, 1056–1273* (Oxford, 1988), pp.162–9, 283–90; H. Stehkämper, 'Die Stadt Köln in der Salierzeit', in Weinfurter (ed.), *Die Salier und das Reich*, III, pp.75–152 at 119–30; Fuhrmann, *Germany*, pp.77–81.
67. P. Dollinger, 'Straßburg in salischer Zeit', in Weinfurter (ed.), *Die Salier und das Reich*, III, pp.153–64. See generally Blickle, *Das Alte Europa*, pp.79–84.

68. E. Maschke, 'Stadt und Herrschaft in Deutschland und Reichsitalien (Salier- und Stauferzeit)', in Vittinghoff (ed.), *Stadt und Herrschaft*, pp. 299–330 at 304–11; L. Martines, *Power and Imagination: City-States in Renaissance Italy* (London, 1979), pp.14–17.

69. Blickle, *Das Alte Europa*, pp.164–5.

70. Haverkamp, 'Die Städte', pp.200, 219–21. For the following: D. Hay and J. Law, *Italy in the Age of the Renaissance, 1380–1530* (London, 1989), pp.47–74; Scott, *City-State*, pp.64–192; Diestelkamp, 'König und Städte', pp.268–78; Maschke, 'Stadt und Herrschaft', pp.300–304.

71. H. Maurer (ed.), *Kommunale Bündnisse Oberitaliens und Oberdeutschlands im Vergleich* (Sigmaringen, 1987).

72. Diestelkamp, 'König und Städte', pp.282–94. The charters are discussed on pp.359–60.

73. Leading examples include Mainz, Cologne, Speyer, Worms, Bremen, Lübeck, Hamburg, Strasbourg and Basel.

74. D. Waley, *The Italian City-Republics* (3rd ed., London, 1988); G. Chittolini, 'Cities, "city-states" and regional states in north-central Italy', *Theory and Society*, 18 (1989), 689–706; Wilson, *Reich to Revolution*, pp.378–9.

75. Strauss, *Nuremberg*, pp.45, 51.

76. Haverkamp, 'Die Städte', p.236; Scott, *City-State*, pp.47–51.

77. Stehkämper, 'Die Stadt Köln', pp.136–40.

78. J. Larner, *Italy in the Age of Dante and Petrarch, 1216–1380* (London, 1980), pp.106–27; Scott, *City-State*, pp.18–19.

79. Luebke, *His Majesty's Rebels*, pp.220–21.

80. Haverkamp, 'Die Städte', pp.204–8, 231; Scott, *City-State*, pp.51–6.

81. S. Ogilvie, *State Corporatism and Proto-Industry: The Württemberg Black Forest, 1580–1797* (Cambridge, 1997), pp.59–60.

82. H.-U. Wehler, *Deutsche Gesellschaftsgeschichte* (5 vols., Munich, 2008); M. Hughes, *Early Modern Germany, 1477–1806* (Basingstoke, 1992), pp.110–11; K. Epstein, *The Genesis of German Conservatism* (Princeton, 1966), pp.62–3, 285–9. For the question of economic decline see T. McIntosh, *Urban Decline in Early Modern Germany: Schwäbisch Hall and its Region, 1650–1750* (Chapel Hill, NC, 1997).

83. D. Albrecht, *Maximilian I. von Bayern, 1573–1651* (Munich, 1998), pp. 394–418; H. J. Querfurth, *Die Unterwerfung der Stadt Braunschweig im Jahre 1671* (Brunswick, 1953).

84. H. T. Gräf, 'Small towns in early modern Germany: The case of Hesse, 1500–1800', in P. Clark (ed.), *Small Towns in Early Modern Europe* (Cambridge, 1995), pp.184–205; Wilson, *Reich to Revolution*, pp.71, 378–9.

85. R. Endres, 'Zur wirtschaftlichen und sozialen Lage in Franken vor dem Dreißigjährigen Krieg', *Jahrbuch für fränkische Landesforschung*,

28 (1968), 5-52; M. Walker, *German Home Towns* (2nd ed., Ithaca, NY, 1998).

86. M. Walker, *Johann Jakob Moser and the Holy Roman Empire of the German Nation* (Chapel Hill, NC, 1981).

87. Wipo of Burgundy in T. E. Mommsen and K. F. Morrison (eds.), *Imperial Lives and Letters of the Eleventh Century* (New York, 2000), pp.70-71.

88. The classic liberal interpretation is presented by F. L. Carsten, *Princes and Parliaments in Germany: From the Fifteenth to the Eighteenth Century* (Oxford, 1959). The debate is summarized by R. Esser, 'Landstände im Alten Reich', *ZNRG*, 27 (2005), 254-71, with new perspectives in G. Ammerer et al. (eds.), *Bündnispartner und Konkurrenten der Landesfürsten? Die Stände in der Habsburgermonarchie* (Vienna, 2007).

89. K. H. Marcus, *The Politics of Power: Elites of an Early Modern State in Germany* (Mainz, 2000);

90. R. Straubel, 'Heer und höhere Beamtenschaft in (spät-)friderizianischer Zeit', in P. Baumgart et al. (eds.), *Die preußische Armee zwischen Ancien Régime und Reichsgründung* (Paderborn, 2008), pp.96-106; H. C. Johnson, *Frederick the Great and his Officials* (New Haven, CT, 1975); Whaley, *Germany*, II, p.468; Wilson, *Reich to Revolution*, p.241. The Habsburg statistics exclude clergy and schoolteachers.

91. Their stories are detailed in the contributions by H. T. Gräf and P. H. Wilson in M. Kaiser and A. Pečar (eds.), *Der zweite Mann im Staat* (Berlin, 2003).

92. K. J. MacHardy, *War, Religion and Court Patronage in Habsburg Austria* (Basingstoke, 2003), pp.33-4. For European comparisons see B. Guenée, *States and Rulers in Later Medieval Europe* (Oxford, 1985), pp.171-91.

93. D. Carpanetto and G. Ricuperati, *Italy in the Age of Reason, 1685-1789* (London, 1987), pp.54-75; E. L. Cox, *The Green Count of Savoy* (Princeton, 1967), pp.368-70; G. Symcox, *Victor Amadeus II : Absolutism in the Savoyard State, 1675-1730* (London, 1983), esp. pp.58-9.

94. R. Freiin von Oer, 'Estates and diets in ecclesiastical principalities of the Holy Roman Empire', *Liber memorialis Georges de Lagarde* (Louvain, 1970), pp.259-81. For the following see also V. Press, 'The system of Estates in the Austrian hereditary lands and in the Holy Roman Empire', in R. J. W. Evans and T. V. Thomas (eds.), *Crown, Church and Estates: Central European Politics in the Sixteenth and Seventeenth Centuries* (Basingstoke, 1991), pp.1-22.

95. See the contributions of E. Harding, T. Neu and D. M. Luebke in J. P. Coy et al. (eds.), *The Holy Roman Empire, Reconsidered* (New York, 2010).

96. A. Niederstätter, *Österreichische Geschichte, 1278-1411* (Vienna, 2004), pp.285-301.

97. H. G. Koenigsberger, *Monarchies, States Generals and Parliaments: The Netherlands in the Fifteenth and Sixteenth Centuries* (Cambridge, 2001).

98. T. Winkelbauer, 'Landhaus und Hofburg', in H. Manikowska and J. Pánek (eds.), *Political Culture in Central Europe* (Prague, 2005), pp.299–331.

99. As argued by P. Blickle, *Landschaften im Alten Reich* (Munich, 1973).

100. B. Stollberg-Rilinger, *Vormünder des Volkes? Konzepte landständischer Repräsentation in der Spätphase des Alten Reiches* (Berlin, 1999); H. Dreitzel, *Absolutismus und ständische Verfassung in Deutschland* (Mainz, 1992). The Estates' potential to become modern parliaments and form republics is discussed further on pp.594–602.

101. G. Haug-Moritz, *Die württembergische Ehrbarkeit. Annäherungen an eine bürgerliche Machtelite der Frühen Neuzeit* (Ostfildern, 2009). See also K. Vetter, 'Die Stände im absolutistischen Preußen', *Zeitschrift für Geschichtswissenschaft*, 24 (1976), 1290–306.

102. G. Droege, 'Die finanziellen Grundlagen des Territorialstaates in West- und Ostdeutschland an der Wende vom Mittelalter zur Neuzeit', *VSWG*, 53 (1966), 145–61; U. Schirmer, *Kursächsische Staatsfinanzen (1456–1656)* (Stuttgart, 2006).

103. W. Schulze, *Reich und Türkengefahr im späten 16. Jahrhundert* (Munich, 1978), pp.223–301.

104. P. H. Wilson, *War, State and Society in Württemberg, 1677–1793* (Cambridge, 1995), pp.37, 208.

105. J. Brewer, *The Sinews of Power: War, Money and the English State, 1688–1783* (New York, 1988). See also the useful survey across Europe by R. G. Asch, 'Kriegsfinanzierung, Staatsbildung und ständische Ordnung in Westeuropa im 17. und 18. Jahrhundert', *HZ*, 268 (1999), 635–71.

106. For these debates see G. Oestreich, *Neostoicism and the Early Modern State* (Cambridge, 1982); G. Lottes, 'Disziplin und Emanzipation. Das Sozialdisziplinierungskonzept und die Interpretation der frühneuzeitlichen Geschichte', *Westfälische Forschungen*, 42 (1992), 63–74. One variant of this approach adds Reformation theology into the mix: R. Po-chia Hsia, *Social Discipline in the Reformation: Central Europe, 1550–1750* (London, 1989); P. S. Gorski, *The Disciplinary Revolution: Calvinism and the Rise of the State in Early Modern Europe* (Chicago, 2003).

107. H. Keller, 'Vom "heiligen Buch" zur "Buchführung". Lebensfunktionen der Schrift im Mittelalter', *FMS*, 26 (1992), 1–31 at 21–9. For the following: V. Groebner, *Who Are You? Identification, Deception and Surveillance in Early Modern Europe* (New York, 2007); I. F. McNeely, *The Emancipation of Writing: German Civil Society in the Making, 1790s–1820s* (Berkeley, CA, 2003), esp. pp.35–48.

108. Whaley, *Germany*, I, p.493. Full coverage in K. Härter and M. Stolleis (eds.), *Repertorium der Policeyordnungen der Frühen Neuzeit* (10 vols., Frankfurt, 1996–2010). See also K. Härter, 'Security and "Gute Policey" in early modern Europe: Concepts, laws and instruments', *Historical Social Research*, 35 (2010), 41–65.

109. Dipper, *Deutsche Geschichte*, pp.70–73.
110. A. Holenstein, *'Gute Policey' und lokale Gesellschaft im Staat des Ancien Régime. Das Fallbeispiel der Markgrafschaft Baden(-Durlach)* (Epfendorf, 2003).
111. P. Warde, *Ecology, Economy and State Formation in Early Modern Germany* (Cambridge, 2006).
112. Quote from Walker, *German Home Towns*, p.145. There is an extensive literature highlighting the negative impact of cameralist and police measures: H. Rebel, *Peasant Classes: The Bureaucratization of Property and Family Relations under Early Habsburg Absolutism, 1511–1636* (Princeton, 1983); A. Wakefield, *The Disordered Police State: German Cameralism as Science and Practice* (Chicago, 2009); P. K. Taylor, *Indentured to Liberty: Peasant Life and the Hessian Military State, 1688–1815* (Ithaca, NY, 1994).
113. J. Schlumbohm, 'Gesetze, die nicht durchgesetzt werden – Ein Strukturmerkmal des frühneuzeitlichen Staates?', *Geschichte und Gesellschaft*, 23 (1997), 647–63; K. Wegert, *Popular Culture, Crime and Social Control in 18th-Century Württemberg* (Stuttgart, 1994).
114. A. Holenstein, 'Empowering interactions: Looking at statebuilding from below', in W. Blockmans et al. (eds.), *Empowering Interactions: Political Cultures and the Emergence of the State in Europe, 1300–1900* (Farnham, 2009), pp.1–31.
115. U. Rublack, *The Crimes of Women in Early Modern Germany* (Oxford, 1999); R. Blickle, 'Peasant protest and the language of women's petitions: Christina Vend's supplications of 1629', in U. Rublack (ed.), *Gender in Early Modern German History* (Cambridge, 2002), pp.177–99.
116. The term 'inner dynamism' comes from M. Raeff, *The Well-Ordered Police State: Social and Institutional Change through Law in the Germanies and Russia, 1600–1800* (New Haven, CT, 1983).
117. *NTSR*, XIV, 253.
118. P. H. Wilson, 'Johann Jacob Moser und die württembergische Politik', in A. Gestrich and R. Lächele (eds.), *Johann Jacob Moser. Politiker, Pietist und Publizist* (Karlsruhe, 2002), pp.1–25, and his *War, State and Society*, pp.213–33.
119. G. Haug-Moritz, *Württembergischer Ständekonflikt und deutscher Dualismus* (Stuttgart, 1992), pp.295–453.
120. *NTSR*, XIV, 249. For the following see W. Kohl (ed.), *Westfälische Geschichte* (3 vols., Düsseldorf, 1983–4), I, pp.620–21; *NTSR*, XVI, part 3, 31–96.
121. For a measured statement of this interpretation see J. J. Sheehan, *German History, 1770–1866* (Oxford, 1989), pp.11–71.
122. Useful contributions to the extensive literature on this topic include: C. W. Ingrao, *The Hessian Mercenary State: Ideas, Institutions and Reform under Frederick II, 1760–1785* (Cambridge, 1987); S. Mörz, *Aufgeklärter*

Absolutismus in der Kurpfalz während der Mannheimer Regierungszeit des Kurfürsten Karl Theodor (1742–1777) (Stuttgart, 1991); Scott (ed.), *Enlightened Absolutism*, and the special issue of *GH*, 20 (2002), no.3 on the electorates.

123. J. Q. Whitman, *The Legacy of Roman Law in the German Romantic Era* (Princeton, 1990), pp.41–65.

124. E. F. Heckscher, *Mercantilism* (rev. ed., 2 vols., London, 1935), I, pp.70, 118.

125. M. Hochedlinger, *Austria's Wars of Emergence, 1683–1797* (Harlow, 2003), pp.280–85; P. H. Wilson, *German Armies: War and German Politics, 1648–1806* (London, 1998), p.235. More detail in P. G. M. Dickson, *Finance and Government under Maria Theresia, 1740–1780* (2 vols., Oxford, 1987).

126. S. Westphal, *Kaiserliche Rechtsprechung und herrschaftliche Stabilisierung* (Cologne, 2002), p.315.

127. H. J. Brandt and K. Hengst, *Geschichte des Erzbistums Paderborn* (2 vols., Paderborn, 2002–7), II, pp.111–12.

128. F. Göse, 'Das Verhältnis Friedrich Wilhelms I. zum Adel', in F. Beck and J. H. Schoeps (eds.), *Der Soldatenkönig* (Potsdam, 2003), pp.99–138 at 101–8.

129. *Krieg gegen die französischen Revolution, 1792–7* (issued by the Austrian Kriegsarchiv, 2 vols., Vienna, 1905), I, p.189.

130. H.-P. Ullmann, 'The emergence of modern public debts in Bavaria and Baden between 1780 and 1820', in P.-C. Witt (ed.), *Wealth and Taxation in Central Europe* (Leamington Spa, 1987), pp.63–79.

131. Blickle, *Landschaften*, p.116.

132. H. Wunder, 'Finance in the "economy of Old Europe": The example of peasant credit from the late Middle Ages to the Thirty Years War', in Witt (ed.), *Wealth and Taxation*, pp.19–47; Robisheaux, *Rural Society*.

133. V. Press, 'Die Reichsstadt in der altständischen Gesellschaft', in J. Kunisch (ed.), *Neue Studien zur frühneuzeitlichen Reichsgeschichte* (Berlin, 1987), pp.9–42; W. D. Godsey Jr, *Nobles and Nation in Central Europe: Free Imperial Knights in the Age of Revolution, 1750–1850* (Cambridge, 2004), pp.22–46; M. Fimpel, *Reichsjustiz und Territorialstaat. Württemberg als Kommissar von Kaiser und Reich im Schwäbischen Kreis (1648–1806)* (Tübingen, 1999), pp.42–3; Westphal, *Kaiserliche Rechtsprechung*, pp.256–431; R. Hildebrandt, 'Rat contra Bürgerschaft. Die Verfassungskonflikte in den Reichsstädten des 17. und 18. Jahrhunderts', *Zeitschrift für Stadtgeschichte, Stadtsoziologie und Denkmalpflege*, 1 (1974), 221–41 at 230–34.

134. C. Cramer, 'Territoriale Entwicklung', in B. Martin and R. Wetekam (eds.), *Waldeckische Landeskunde* (Korbach, 1971), pp.171–262 at 249–50.

135. G. Kollmer, *Die schwäbische Reichsritterschaft zwischen Westfälischem Frieden und Reichsdeputationshauptschluß* (Stuttgart, 1979); K.-P. Schroeder, *Das Alte Reich und seine Städte. Untergang und Neubeginn.*

Die Mediatisierung der oberdeutschen Reichsstädte im Gefolge des Reichsdeputationshauptschlusses, 1802/03 (Munich, 1991); A. von Reden-Dohna, 'Problems of small Estates of the Empire: The example of the Swabian imperial prelates', *JMH*, 58, supplement (1986), 76–87.

136. Figures from Hochedlinger, *Austria's Wars*, p.284; Ullmann, 'The emergence of modern public debts', *passim*.

CHAPTER 11: ASSOCIATION

1. B. Heal, *The Cult of the Virgin Mary in Early Modern Germany* (Cambridge, 2007).

2. H. Carl, *Der Schwäbische Bund, 1488–1534* (Leinfelden-Echterdingen, 2000), pp.189–91; L. Ognois, 'Politische Instrumentalisierung eines christlichen Ereignisses? Die Festtaufe Friedrichs von Württemberg im Jahre 1616', in A. Ernst and A. Schindling (eds.), *Union und Liga 1608/09* (Stuttgart, 2010), pp.227–63.

3. Useful summaries of the extensive literature on this: S. Reynolds, *Kingdoms and Communities in Western Europe, 900–1300* (2nd ed., Oxford, 1997), pp.67–78, 165–8; H. K. Schulze, *Grundstrukturen der Verfassung im Mittelalter* (3rd ed., 3 vols., Stuttgart, 1995–2000), II, pp.184–98; T. A. Brady Jr, 'Economic and social institutions', in B. Scribner (ed.), *Germany: A New Social and Economic History*, I, *1450–1630* (London, 1996), pp. 259–90 at 266–70; O. Ogilvie, 'The beginnings of industrialization', in idem (ed.), *Germany: A New Social and Economic History*, II, *1630–1800* (London, 1996), pp.263–308 at 285–90.

4. B. A. Tlusty, *The Martial Ethic in Early Modern Germany: Civic Duty and the Right of Arms* (Basingstoke, 2011), pp.189–210.

5. Statistics from J. Whaley, *Germany and the Holy Roman Empire, 1493–1806* (2 vols., Oxford, 2012), II, p.466.

6. M. Asche, *Von der reichen hansischen Bürgeruniversität zur armen mecklenburgischen Landeshochschule* (Stuttgart, 2000), p.245.

7. T. M. Martin, *Auf dem Weg zum Reichstag, 1314–1410* (Göttingen, 1993), pp.172–213; E. Schubert, 'Die Stellung der Kurfürsten in der spätmittelalterlichen Reichsverfassung', *Jahrbuch für westdeutsche Landesgeschichte*, 1 (1975), 97–128.

8. Printed in L. Weinrich (ed.), *Quellen zur Verfassungsgeschichte des römisch-deutschen Reiches im Spätmittelalter (1250–1500)* (Darmstadt, 1983), no.88. For the following see H. Cohn, 'The electors and imperial rule at the end of the fifteenth century', in B. Weiler and S. MacLean (eds.), *Representations of Power in Medieval Germany, 800–1500* (Turnhout, 2006), pp.295–318.

9. A. Gotthard, ' "Als furnembsten Gliedern des Heiligen Reichs". Überlegungen zur Rolle der rheinischen Kurfürstengruppe in der Reichspolitik

des 16. Jahrhunderts', *RVJB*, 59 (1995), 31–78, and his *Säulen des Reiches. Die Kurfürsten im frühneuzeitlichen Reichsverband* (Husum, 1999), pp.35–197.

10. As suggested by older literature like W. R. Hitchcock, *The Background of the Knights' Revolt, 1522–1523* (Berkeley, 1958). For the following: H. Zmora, 'Princely state-making and the "crisis of the aristocracy" in late medieval Germany', *P&P*, 153 (1996), 37–63; W. Friedensburg, 'Franz von Sickingen', in J. von Pflugk-Harttung (ed.), *Im Morgenrot der Reformation* (Stuttgart, 1927), pp.557–666; E. Schubert, 'Ulrich von Hutten (1488–1523)', *Fränkische Lebensbilder*, 9 (1980), 93–123; H. Ulmschneider, *Götz von Berlichingen* (Sigmaringen, 1974).

11. E. Schubert, 'Die Harzgrafen im ausgehenden Mittelalter', in J. Rogge and U. Schirmer (eds.), *Hochadelige Herrschaft im mitteldeutschen Raum (1200 bis 1600)* (Leipzig, 2003), pp.13–115.

12. K. E. Demandt, *Geschichte des Landes Hessen* (2nd ed., Kassel, 1980), pp.469–70; Schulze, *Grundstrukturen*, II, pp.116–18.

13. A. Niederstätter, *Österreichische Geschichte, 1400–1522* (Vienna, 2004), pp.238–57.

14. M. Spindler (ed.), *Handbuch der bayerischen Geschichte* (2nd ed., 2 vols., Munich, 1981), II, pp.310–16, 556; M. J. LeGates, 'The knights and the problems of political organizing in sixteenth-century Germany', *CEH*, 7 (1974), 99–136; E. Pflichthofer, *Das württembergische Heerwesen am Ausgang des Mittelalters* (Tübingen, 1938), pp.13–15; Carl, *Der Schwäbische Bund*, pp.116–18.

15. F. R. H. Du Boulay, *Germany in the Later Middle Ages* (London, 1983), pp.74–6; Carl, *Der Schwäbische Bund*, pp.64–5, 99–111.

16. H. Zmora, *State and Nobility in Early Modern Germany: The Knightly Feud in Franconia, 1440–1567* (Cambridge, 1997), pp.129–30.

17. L. F. Heyd, *Ulrich, Herzog zu Württemberg* (3 vols., Stuttgart, 1841–4).

18. Succinct summary in Whaley, *Germany*, I, pp.209–19, with the events in J. Heilmann, *Kriegsgeschichte von Bayern, Franken, Pfalz und Schwaben von 1506–1651* (2 vols., Munich, 1868), I, pp.29–35.

19. H. Zmora, 'The formation of the imperial knighthood in Franconia', in R. J. W. Evans et al. (eds.), *The Holy Roman Empire, 1495–1806* (Oxford, 2011), pp.283–302, and his *State and Nobility*, pp.123–42.

20. See the three pieces by V. Press: 'Kaiser und Reichsritterschaft', in R. Endres (ed.), *Adel in der Frühneuzeit* (Cologne, 1991), pp.163–94; 'Die Reichsritterschaft im Reich der frühen Neuzeit', *NA*, 87 (1976), 101–22; 'Die Ritterschaft im Kraichgau zwischen Reich und Territorium, 1500–1623', *ZGO*, 122 (1974), 35–98.

21. Good overviews in H. Rabe, *Deutsche Geschichte, 1500–1600* (Munich, 1991), pp.476–8; P. S. Fichtner, *Emperor Maximilian II* (New Haven, CT, 2001), pp.141–4.

22. V. Press, 'Reichsritterschaften', in K. G. A. Jeserich et al. (eds.), *Deutsche Verwaltungsgeschichte*, I, *Vom Spätmittelalter bis zum Ende des Reiches* (Stuttgart, 1983), pp.679–89; *NTSR*, XVII, 386.

23. R. J. Ninness, *Between Opposition and Collaboration: Nobles, Bishops and the German Reformations in the Prince-Bishopric of Bamberg, 1555–1619* (Leiden, 2011); S. Schraut, *Das Haus Schönborn. Eine Familienbiographie. Katholischer Reichsadel, 1640–1840* (Paderborn, 2005).

24. G. Köbler, *Historisches Lexikon der deutschen Länder* (5th ed., Munich, 1995), p.xxii.

25. V. Press, 'Der württembergische Angriff auf die Reichsritterschaft 1749–1754 (1770)', in F. Quarthal (ed.), *Zwischen Schwarzwald und Schwäbischer Alb* (Sigmaringen, 1984), pp.329–48.

26. G. Schmidt, *Der Wetterauer Grafenverein* (Marburg, 1989).

27. R. Endres, 'Die Friedensziele der Reichsritterschaft', in H. Duchhardt (ed.), *Der Westfälische Friede* (Münster, 1998), pp.565–78.

28. E. Bock, *Der Schwäbische Bund und seine Verfassungen, 1488–1534* (Breslau, 1927). For the following see C. Greiner, 'Die Politik des Schwäbischen Bundes während des Bauernkrieges 1524 und 1525 bis zum Vertrag von Weingarten', *Zeitschrift des historischen Vereins für Schwaben und Neuburg*, 68 (1974), 7–94.

29. Carl, *Der Schwäbische Bund*, pp.33–4, 365–6, 370–86.

30. E. Fabian, *Die Entstehung des Schmalkaldischen Bundes und seiner Verfassung 1524/29–1531/35* (Tübingen, 1962); G. Haug-Moritz, *Der Schmalkaldische Bund 1530–1541/42* (Leinfelden-Echterdingen, 2002). For the other organizations see F. Neuer-Landfried, *Die Katholische Liga. Gründung, Neugründung und Organisation eines Sonderbundes, 1608–1620* (Kallmünz, 1968); T. Hölz, *Krummstab und Schwert. Die Liga und die geistlichen Reichsstände Schwabens, 1609–1635* (Leinfelden-Echterdingen, 2001); A. Gotthard, 'Protestantische "Union" und Katholische "Liga" – Subsidiäre Strukturelemente oder Alternativentwürfe?', and H. Langer, 'Der Heilbronner Bund (1633–35)', both in V. Press (ed.), *Alternativen zur Reichsverfassung in der Frühen Neuzeit?* (Munich, 1995), pp.81–112, 113–22, and the contributions to Ernst and Schindling (eds.), *Union und Liga*.

31. T. A. Brady Jr, 'Phases and strategies of the Schmalkaldic League', *ARG*, 74 (1983), 162–81 at 174.

32. M. Kaiser, *Politik und Kriegführung. Maximilian von Bayern, Tilly und die Katholische Liga im Dreißigjährigen Krieg* (Münster, 1999).

33. K. S. Bader, *Der deutsche Südwesten in seiner territorialstaatlichen Entwicklung* (2nd ed., Sigmaringen, 1978), pp.191–7.

34. Hölz, *Krummstab und Schwert*, p.140. See also J. A. Vann, *The Swabian Kreis* (Brussels, 1975), pp.97–131; P.-C. Storm, *Der Schwäbische Kreis als Feldherr* (Berlin, 1974), pp.71–111.

35. F. Magen, 'Die Reichskreise in der Epoche des Dreißigjährigen Krieges', *ZHF*, 9 (1982), 409–60; S. Friedrich, 'Legitimationsprobleme von Kreisbündnissen', in W. E. J. Weber and R. Dauser (eds.), *Faszinierende Frühneuzeit. Reich, Frieden, Kultur und Kommunikation, 1500–1800* (Berlin, 2008), pp.27–50.

36. R. Schnur, *Der Rheinbund von 1658 in der deutschen Verfassungsgeschichte* (Bonn, 1955). Further discussion of princely alliances in P. H. Wilson, *German Armies: War and German Politics, 1648–1806* (London, 1998), pp.150–78.

37. K. O. Frhr. v. Aretin (ed.), *Der Kurfürst von Mainz und die Kreisassoziationen, 1648–1746* (Wiesbaden, 1975); R. H. Thompson, *Lothar Franz von Schönborn and the Diplomacy of the Electorate of Mainz* (The Hague, 1973); Wilson, *German Armies*, pp.165–201.

38. B. Sicken, *Das Wehrwesen des fränkischen Reichskreises. Aufbau und Struktur (1681–1714)* (Nuremberg, 1967), esp. pp.87–92; M. Plassmann, *Krieg und Defension am Oberrhein* (Berlin, 2000).

39. P. H. Wilson, 'The German "soldier trade" of the seventeenth and eighteenth centuries', *IHR*, 18 (1996), 757–92, and his *German Armies*, pp.202–97.

40. K. Graf, 'Feindbild und Vorbild. Bemerkungen zur städtischen Wahrnehmung des Adels', *ZGO*, 141 (1993), 121–54; B. Arnold, *Princes and Territories in Medieval Germany* (Cambridge, 1991), pp.167–76.

41. Dassel's exact responsibility remains disputed, but is stressed by P. Munz, *Frederick Barbarossa* (London, 1969), pp.92–5, 180–83. See generally G. Raccagni, *The Lombard League, 1164–1225* (Oxford, 2010).

42. P. Dollinger, *The German Hansa* (London, 1970); J. Schildhauer, *The Hansa* (New York, 1988); M. Puhle, 'Die Hanse, Nordeuropa und das mittelalterliche Reich', in B. Schneidmüller and S. Weinfurter (eds.), *Heilig – Römisch – Deutsch* (Dresden, 2006), pp.308–22.

43. H. Spruyt, *The Sovereign State and its Competitors* (Princeton, 1994), esp. pp.109–29.

44. Statistics from P. Moraw, *Von offener Verfassung zu gestalteter Verdichtung. Das Reich im späten Mittelalter 1250 bis 1490* (Berlin, 1985), p.309.

45. Dortmund, Goslar, Nordhausen, Mühlhausen in Thuringia, and (from 1475) Cologne were the only northern cities to follow Lübeck's example and secure imperial city status during the Middle Ages.

46. Arnold, *Princes and Territories*, pp.57–8, 173–4.

47. A. Buschmann, 'Der Rheinische Bund von 1254–1257', in H. Maurer (ed.), *Kommunale Bündnisse Oberitaliens und Oberdeutschlands im Vergleich* (Sigmaringen, 1987), pp.167–212. For the context see M. Kaufhold, *Deutsches Interregnum und europäische Politik. Konfliktlösungen und Entscheidungsstrukturen, 1230–1280* (Hanover, 2000).

48. A. Haverkamp, *Medieval Germany, 1056–1273* (Oxford, 1988), p.26; Moraw, *Von offener Verfassung*, pp.208–9.

49. T. M. Martin, *Auf dem Weg zum Reichstag, 1314-1410* (Göttingen, 1993), pp.276-316.

50. Ibid, pp.295-6. Charles's change of course is also discussed on pp.389-90. For the following also: F. Seibt, *Karl IV.* (Munich, 1978), pp.332-5; Spindler (ed.), *Handbuch der bayerischen Geschichte*, II, pp.226-8.

51. E. Gatz (ed.), *Die Bischöfe des Heiligen Römischen Reiches 1198 bis 1448* (Berlin, 2001), pp.672-3; Spindler (ed.), *Handbuch der bayerischen Geschichte*, II, pp.230-32.

52. E. Marquardt, *Geschichte Württembergs* (3rd ed., Stuttgart, 1985), pp. 23-4; M. Prietzel, *Das Heilige Römische Reich im Spätmittelalter* (2nd ed., Darmstadt, 2010), p.98.

53. E. Schubert, 'Albrecht Achilles, Markgraf von Kulmbach und Kurfürst von Brandenburg, 1414-1486', *Fränkische Lebensbilder*, 4 (1971), 130-72; Moraw, *Von offener Verfassung*, pp.277-8. The Lake Constance group disintegrated amidst the war with ducal Burgundy in 1474.

54. G. Strauss, *Nuremberg in the Sixteenth Century* (2nd ed., Bloomington, IN, 1976), pp.12-17.

55. P. Blickle, *Communal Reformation: The Quest for Salvation in Sixteenth-Century Germany* (Atlantic Highlands, NJ, 1992); B. Moeller, *Imperial Cities and the Reformation* (Philadelphia, 1972); L. J. Abray, *The People's Reformation: Magistrates, Clergy and Commons in Strasbourg, 1500-1598* (Oxford, 1985).

56. G. Schmidt, 'Hanse, Hanseaten und Reich in der frühen Neuzeit', in I. Richefort and B. Schmidt (eds.), *Les relations entre la France et les villes Hanséatiques de Hambourg, Brême et Lübeck, Moyen Âge-XIXe siècle* (Brussels, 2006), pp.229-59; R. Postel, 'Hamburg at the time of the Peace of Westphalia', in K. Bussmann and H. Schilling (eds.), *1648: War and Peace in Europe* (3 vols., Münster, 1998), I, pp.337-43; U. Weiß, '"So were in puncto Jmmedietas civitatis das müglichste zu tun". Die Erfurt-Frage auf dem Westfälischen Friedenskongreß', in H. Duchhardt (ed.), *Der Westfälische Friede* (Munich, 1998), pp.541-64.

57. A. Krischer, 'Das diplomatische Zeremoniell der Reichsstädte, oder: Was heißt Stadtfreiheit in der Fürstengesellschaft?', *HZ*, 284 (2007), 1-30.

58. This argument is advanced in numerous works by Peter Blickle and summarized in 'Communalism, parliamentarism, republicanism', *Parliaments, Estates and Representation*, 6 (1986), 1-13.

59. R. von Friedeburg, '"Kommunalismus" und "Republikanismus" in der frühen Neuzeit?', *ZHF*, 21 (1994), 65-91; H. Rebel, *Peasant Classes* (Princeton, 1983), pp.10-20.

60. F. Petri, 'Zum Problem der herrschaftlichen und genossenschaftlichen Züge in der mittelalterlichen Marschensiedlung an der flämischen und niederländischen Nordseeküste', in H. Beumann (ed.), *Historische Forschungen für Walter Schlesinger* (Cologne, 1974), pp.226-41.

61. W. L. Urban, *Dithmarschen, a Medieval Peasant Republic* (Lewiston, NY, 1991); B. Kümin, 'Kirchgenossen an der Macht. Vormoderne politische Kultur in den "Pfarreirepubliken" von Gersau und Dithmarschen', *ZHF*, 41 (2014), 187–230.

62. W. Lammers, *Die Schlacht bei Hemmingstedt* (Neumünster, 1953).

63. G. Franz, *Geschichte des deutschen Bauernstandes vom frühen Mittelalter bis zum 19. Jahrhundert* (Stuttgart, 1970), pp.86–91. See ibid, pp.79–83, 94–5, for other small self-governing communities in the west of the Empire.

64. H. Wiemann, *Die Grundlagen der landständischen Verfassung Ostfrieslands. Die Verträge von 1595 bis 1611* (Aurich, 1974).

65. B. Kappelhoff, *Absolutisches Regiment oder Ständeherrschaft? Landesherr und Landstände in Ostfriesland im ersten Drittel des 18. Jahrhunderts* (Hildesheim, 1982); M. Hughes, *Law and Politics in 18th-Century Germany: The Imperial Aulic Council in the Reign of Charles VI* (Woodbridge, 1988); R. Tieben, 'Statebuilding with the participation of the Estates? East Frisia between territorial legislation and communalist ritual, 1611–1744', in W. Blockmans et al. (eds.), *Empowering Interactions: Political Cultures and the Emergence of the State in Europe, 1300–1900* (Farnham, 2009), pp.267–78.

66. The term 'canton' was only officially adopted in 1798 with the foundation of the Helvetic Republic, but will be used here for convenience in preference to the contemporary term 'place' (*Ort*). For the following see D. M. Luebke, *His Majesty's Rebels: Communities, Factions and Rural Revolt in the Black Forest, 1725–1745* (Ithaca, NY, 1997), esp. pp.19–20; P. Stadler, 'Die Schweiz und das Reich in der Frühen Neuzeit', in Press (ed.), *Alternativen*, pp.131–42.

67. For the debate on Swiss exceptionalism see J. Steinberg, *Why Switzerland?* (Cambridge, 1976).

68. R. Sablonier, *Gründungszeit ohne Eidgenossen. Politik und Gesellschaft in der Innerschweiz um 1300* (Baden, 2008).

69. J. Berenger, *A History of the Habsburg Empire, 1273–1700* (Harlow, 1994), pp.54–5. For the following see also A. Niederstätter, *Österreichische Geschichte, 1278–1411* (Vienna, 2004), pp.119–22.

70. R. C. Head, *Early Modern Democracy in the Grisons: Social Order and Political Language in a Swiss Mountain Canton, 1470–1620* (Cambridge, 1995); A. Wendland, *Der Nutzen der Pässe und die Gefährdung der Seelen. Spanien, Mailand und der Kampf ums Veltlin (1620–1641)* (Zürich, 1995), pp.367–8. Rhetia included the Domleschg, Oberhalbstein, Bergell and Engadin valleys, plus the town and cathedral chapter of Chur. The Ten Parish League comprised Belfort, Davos, Klosters, Castels, Schiers, Schanfigg, Langwies, Churwalden, Maienfeld and Malans-Jenins.

71. W. Schaufelberger, *Der alte Schweizer und sein Krieg* (3rd ed., Frauenfeld, 1987).

72. T. A. Brady Jr, *Turning Swiss: Cities and Empire, 1450–1550* (Cambridge, 1985), pp.57–69; Carl, *Der Schwäbische Bund*, pp.451–9.

73. W. A. B. Coolidge, 'The Republic of Gersau', *EHR*, 4 (1889), 481–515.

74. Population from K. von Greyerz, 'Switzerland during the Thirty Years War', in Bussmann and Schilling (eds.), *1648: War and Peace*, I, pp.133–9 at 133. Seven cantons were Catholic: Uri, Schwyz, Unterwalden, Luzern, Fribourg, Solothurn and Zug. Six were Protestant: Zürich, Bern, Glarus, Basel, Schaffhausen and Appenzell.

75. R. C. Head, *Jenatsch's Axe: Social Boundaries, Identity and Myth in the Era of the Thirty Years' War* (Rochester, NY, 2008); Wendland, *Der Nutzen der Pässe*, 47–78, 101–26. For tensions generally: R. C. Head, ' "Nit alss zwo Gmeinden, oder Partheyen, sonder ein Gmeind". Kommunalismus zwischen den Konfessionen in Graubünden 1530–1620', in B. Kümin (ed.), *Landgemeinde und Kirche im Zeitalter der Konfessionen* (Zürich, 2004), pp.21–57.

76. Brady, *Turning Swiss*, p.36.

77. L. Hugo, 'Verzeichnis der freien Reichsdörfer in Deutschland', *Zeitschrift für Archivkunde, Diplomatik und Geschichte*, 2 (1836), 446–76.

78. Köbler, *Historisches Lexikon*, pp.338, 567–8. The others were Sulzbach (near Frankfurt), Soden in the Taunus mountains, Gochsheim and Sennfeld, both near Schweinfurt in Franconia.

79. Overviews in P. Blickle, 'Peasant revolts in the German empire in the late Middle Ages', *Social History*, 4 (1979), 223–39; Whaley, *Germany*, I, pp.135–47.

80. P. Blickle, *The Revolution of 1525* (2nd ed., Baltimore, 1985); G. Vogler, 'Reichsvorstellungen im Umkreis des Bauernkrieges', in Press (ed.), *Alternativen*, pp.23–42. The Twelve Articles are printed in T. Scott and B. Scribner (eds.), *The German Peasants' War: A History in Documents* (Atlantic Highlands, NJ, 1991), pp.253–6.

81. M. Bensing and S. Hoyer, *Der deutsche Bauernkrieg, 1524–26* (3rd ed., Berlin, 1975).

82. G. Franz, *Der deutsche Bauernkrieg* (Darmstadt, 1976), p.299; P. Blickle, *Der Bauernjörg. Feldherr im Bauernkrieg* (Munich, 2015), esp. pp.294–5.

83. For example, P. Blickle, *Obedient Germans? A Rebuttal* (Charlottesville, VA, 1997).

84. R. Po-chia Hsia, *Social Discipline in the Reformation: Central Europe, 1550–1750* (London, 1989), pp.146–8; D. W. Sabean, *Power in the Blood* (Cambridge, 1984), pp.144–73. The judicial changes are discussed on pp.632–6.

85. For example, Luebke, *His Majesty's Rebels*, pp.170, 174.

86. These eventually comprised the abbey and town of St Gallen, the imperial cities of Rottweil and Mulhouse, the community of Biel (Bienne), the county of Wallis (Valais), the principality of Neufchâtel, the bishopric of

Basel, and Rhetia. The bishop of Sitten (Sion) was an associate between 1475 and 1628.

87. R. Hauswirth, *Landgraf Philipp von Hessen und Zwingli* (Tübingen, 1968); T. A. Brady Jr, *The Politics of the Reformation in Germany: Jacob Sturm (1489–1553) of Strasbourg* (Atlantic Highlands, NJ, 1997); Fabian, *Die Entstehung des Schmalkaldischen Bundes*, pp.30–31, 37–9, 211–16.

88. F. Gallati, 'Eidgenössische Politik zur Zeit des Dreißigjährigen Krieges', *Jahrbuch für schweizerische Geschichte*, 44 (1919), 1–257 at 3–4.

89. Useful works among the substantial literature on this topic include G. Parker, *The Dutch Revolt* (London, 1977); M. Prak, *The Dutch Republic in the Seventeenth Century* (Cambridge, 2005), and J. L. Price's similarly titled book (Basingstoke, 1998). The republic's relationship to the Empire is discussed on p.229.

90. The need for English aid obliged the Dutch to accept the incompetent Robert Dudley, earl of Leicester, as 'governor general' from 1585 to 1587. For Archduke Matthias's involvement see B. Rill, *Kaiser Matthias* (Graz, 1999), pp.9–12, 32–40; J. I. Israel, *The Dutch Republic* (Oxford, 1995), pp.190–205.

91. H. H. Rowen, *The Princes of Orange: The Stadholders in the Dutch Republic* (Cambridge, 1988).

92. See the contributions by I. Auerbach, G. Schramm and H. G. Koenigsberger to R. J. W. Evans and T. V. Thomas (eds.), *Crown, Church and Estates* (Basingstoke, 1991), and the two articles by J. Pánek, 'Das Ständewesen und die Gesellschaft in den Böhmischen Ländern in der Zeit vor der Schlacht auf dem Weissen Berg (1526–1620)', *Historica. Les sciences historiques en Tchécoslovaquie*, 25 (1985), 73–120, and 'Das politische System des böhmischen Staates im ersten Jahrhundert der habsburgischen Herrschaft (1526–1620)', *MIÖG*, 97 (1989), 53–82.

93. T. Brockmann, *Dynastie, Kaiseramt und Konfession* (Paderborn, 2011), pp.39–43, 56–63.

94. J. I. Israel, *Dutch Primacy in World Trade, 1585–1740* (Oxford, 1989); M. 't Hart, *The Dutch Wars of Independence: Warfare and Commerce in the Netherlands, 1570–1680* (London, 2014).

95. T. Winkelbauer, 'Nervus belli Bohemici. Die finanziellen Hintergründe des Scheiterns des Ständeaufstands der Jahre 1618 bis 1620', *Folia Historica Bohemica*, 18 (1997), 173–223; P. H. Wilson, *Europe's Tragedy: The Thirty Years War* (London, 2009), pp.269–313.

96. English translation of the Confederation's charter in P. H. Wilson, *The Thirty Years War: A Sourcebook* (Basingstoke, 2010), pp.41–6. Discussion in J. Bahlcke, 'Modernization and state-building in an east-central European Estates' system: The example of the *Confoederatio Bohemica* of 1619', *PER*, 17 (1997), 61–73, and his 'Die Böhmische Krone zwischen staatsrechtlicher Integrität, monarchischer Union und ständischem Föderalismus', in T. Fröschl

(ed.), *Föderationsmodelle und Unionsstrukturen* (Munich, 1994), pp.83–103. P. Mat'a voices greater scepticism towards claims for the Confederation's innovations: ' "Monarchia/monarchey/da einer allein herrschet": The making of state power and reflections on the state in Bohemia and Moravia between the Estates' rebellion and Enlightenment reforms', in H. Manikowska and J. Pánek (eds.), *Political Culture in Central Europe (10th–20th Century)*, I, *Middle Ages and Early Modern Era* (Prague, 2005), pp.349–67.

97. Z. V. David, *Finding the Middle Way: The Utraquists' Liberal Challenge to Rome and Luther* (Washington DC, 2003), esp. pp.302–48.

98. J. Burkhardt, *Der Dreißigjährige Krieg* (Frankfurt, 1992), pp.85–7; F. Müller, *Kursachsen und der Böhmische Aufstand, 1618–1622* (Münster, 1997); J. Polišenský, *Tragic Triangle: The Netherlands, Spain and Bohemia, 1617–1621* (Prague, 1991).

99. H. Smolinsky, 'Formen und Motive konfessioneller Koexistenz in den Niederlanden und am Niederrhein', in K. Garber et al (eds.), *Erfahrung und Deutung von Krieg und Frieden* (Munich, 2001), pp.287–300; A. D. Anderson, *On the Verge of War: International Relations and the Jülich-Kleve Succession Crises (1609–1614)* (Boston, MA, 1999); M. Groten et al. (eds.), *Der Jülich-Klevische Erbstreit 1609* (Düsseldorf, 2011).

100. M. Kaiser, 'Die vereinbarte Okkupation. Generalstaatische Besatzungen in brandenburgischen Festungen am Niederrhein', in M. Meumann and J. Rögge (eds.), *Die besetzte res publica* (Münster, 2006), pp.271–314.

101. M. Kaiser and M. Rohrschneider (eds.), *Membra unius capitis. Studien zu Herrschaftsauffassungen und Regierungspraxis in Kurbrandenburg (1640–1688)* (Berlin, 2005); F. L. Carsten, *Princes and Parliaments* (Oxford, 1959), pp.258–340; L. Hüttl, *Friedrich Wilhelm von Brandenburg* (Munich, 1981), pp.171–84, 197–200.

102. W. Frijhoff and M. Spies, *1650: Hard-Won Unity* (Basingstoke, 2004).

103. H. Dreitzel, *Absolutismus und ständische Verfassung in Deutschland* (Mainz, 1992), p.134. See generally idem, *Monarchiebegriffe in der Fürstengesellschaft* (2 vols., Cologne, 1991).

104. Dreitzel, *Absolutismus*, pp.92–100, 134–7.

105. H. Dippel, *Germany and the American Revolution, 1770–1800* (Chapel Hill, NC, 1977); B. Stollberg-Rilinger, *Vormünder des Volkes? Konzepte landständischer Repräsentation in der Spätphase des Alten Reiches* (Berlin, 1999), pp.140–88; H. E. Bödeker, 'The concept of the republic in eighteenth-century German thought', in J. Heideking and J. A. Henretta (eds.), *Republicanism and Liberalism in America and the German States, 1750–1850* (Cambridge, 2002), pp.35–52.

106. Dreitzel, *Absolutismus*, pp.104–20; Stollberg-Rilinger, *Vormünder des Volkes?*, pp.120–26.

107. A. Flügel, *Bürgerliche Rittergüter. Sozialer Wandel und politische Reform in Kursachsen (1680–1844)* (Göttingen, 2000), pp.178–209.

108. M. Wagner, 'Der sächsische Bauernaufstand und die Französische Revolution in der Perzeption der Zeitgenossen', in H. Berding (ed.), *Soziale Unruhen in Deutschland während der Französischen Revolution* (Göttingen, 1988), pp.149–65; H. Gabel and W. Schulze, 'Peasant resistance and politicization in Germany in the eighteenth century', in E. Hellmuth (ed.), *The Transformation of Political Culture* (Oxford, 1990), pp.119–46.

CHAPTER 12: JUSTICE

1. As noted by H. Keller, *Ottonische Königsherrschaft* (Darmstadt, 2002), p.38.

2. P. Blickle, *Das Alte Europa* (Munich, 2008), pp.44–6.

3. M. Walker, 'Rights and functions: The social categories of eighteenth-century German jurists and cameralists', *JMH*, 50 (1978), 234–51; W. Schmale, 'Das Heilige Römische Reich und die Herrschaft des Rechts', in R. G. Asch and H. Duchhardt (eds.), *Der Absolutismus – ein Mythos?* (Cologne, 1996), pp.229–48 esp. 240–41. See also Goethe's illuminating comments about the purpose of imperial justice in the light of his own experience as a legal intern: *Collected Works*, 12 vols., ed. T. P. Saine and J. L. Sammons (Princeton, 1987), IV: *From my Life: Poetry and Truth*, p.389.

4. R. McKitterick, *The Frankish Kingdoms under the Carolingians* (Harlow, 1983), pp.98–103; B. Arnold, *Medieval Germany, 500–1300* (Basingstoke, 1997), pp.148–51, and his *Princes and Territories in Medieval Germany* (Cambridge, 1991), pp.30–32.

5. G. Franz, *Geschichte des deutschen Bauernstandes vom frühen Mittelalter bis zum 19. Jahrhundert* (Stuttgart, 1970), pp.57–60; H. K. Schulze, *Grundstrukturen der Verfassung im Mittelalter* (3rd ed., 3 vols., Stuttgart, 1995–2000), I, pp.143–5.

6. W. Hartmann, 'Autoritäten im Kirchenrecht und Autorität des Kirchenrechts in der Salierzeit', in S. Weinfurter (ed.), *Die Salier und das Reich* (3 vols., Sigmaringen, 1991), III, pp.425–46.

7. Schulze, *Grundstrukturen*, I, pp.91–4. See also pp.359–60.

8. B. H. Hill Jr, *Medieval Monarchy in Action* (London, 1972), pp.213–14.

9. R. van Dülmen, *Theatre of Horror: Crime and Punishment in Early Modern Germany* (Cambridge, 1990), esp. p.132; E. Schubert, *Fürstliche Herrschaft und Territorium im späten Mittelalter* (2nd ed., Munich, 2006), p.89; Blickle, *Das Alte Europa*, pp.138–9, 225.

10. J. Q. Whitman, *The Legacy of Roman Law in the German Romantic Era* (Princeton, 1990), pp.4–28.

11. E. Ortlieb, *Im Auftrag des Kaisers. Die kaiserlichen Kommissionen des Reichshofrats und die Regelung von Konflikten im Alten Reich (1637–1657)* (Cologne, 2001), pp.366–8.

12. H. Weill, *Frederick the Great and Samuel von Cocceji* (Madison, WI, 1961); J. Whaley, *Germany and the Holy Roman Empire, 1493–1806* (2 vols., Oxford, 2012), II, pp.514–15.

13. H. E. Strakosch, *State Absolutism and the Rule of Law* (Sidney, 1967); F. A. J. Szabo, *Kaunitz and Enlightened Absolutism, 1753–1780* (Cambridge, 1994), pp.180–85.

14. K. Härter, 'The early modern Holy Roman Empire of the German Nation (1495–1806): A multi-layered legal system', in J. Duindam et al. (eds.), *Law and Empire* (Leiden, 2013), pp.111–31.

15. Hill, *Medieval Monarchy in Action*, pp.166–8. For the following see ibid, pp.180–83, and more generally G. Althoff, *Spielregeln der Politik im Mittelalter: Kommunikation in Frieden und Fehde* (Darmstadt, 1997), pp.21–98.

16. A. Krah, *Absetzungsverfahren als Spiegelbild von Königsmacht* (Aalen, 1987), pp.58–60.

17. Arnold, *Medieval Germany*, pp.47–8.

18. E. J. Goldberg, *Struggle for Empire: Kingship and Conflict under Louis the German, 817–876* (Ithaca, NY, 2006), p.229; H. Wolfram, *Conrad II, 990–1039* (University Park, PA, 2006), pp.185–6, 189–90, 333–405; Keller, *Ottonische Königsherrschaft*, p.46.

19. Ibid, pp.38–40; G. Althoff, *Die Ottonen* (2nd ed., Stuttgart, 2005), pp. 104–6, and his *Spielregeln*, pp.53, 294.

20. T. Reuter, *Germany in the Early Middle Ages, c.800–1056* (Harlow, 1991), pp.214–16.

21. M. Becher, *Otto der Große* (Munich, 2012), pp.163–85.

22. Goldberg, *Struggle for Empire*, pp.229–30.

23. Krah, *Absetzungsverfahren*, pp.379–401.

24. Althoff, *Spielregeln*, pp.116–20.

25. J. Barrow, 'Playing by the rules: Conflict management in tenth- and eleventh-century Germany', *EME*, 11 (2002), 389–96 at 392.

26. Keller, *Ottonische Königsherrschaft*, pp.49–50.

27. G. Althoff, *Die Macht der Rituale: Symbolik und Herrschaft im Mittelalter* (Darmstadt, 2003), p.136. Henry's own supplication before Gregory VII is discussed on p.58. For the following see also T. Reuter, 'Unruhestiftung, Fehde, Rebellion, Widerstand. Gewalt und Frieden in der Politik der Salierzeit', in Weinfurter (ed.), *Die Salier und das Reich*, III, pp.297–325.

28. G. Althoff, 'Kaiser Heinrich VI', in W. Hechberger and F. Schuller (eds.), *Staufer & Welfen* (Regensburg, 2009), pp.143–55; W. Stürner, *Friedrich II.* (2 vols., Darmstadt, 2009), II, pp.9–75, 189–210.

29. S. Weinfurter, *The Salian Century* (Philadelphia, 1999), pp.72, 81.

30. T. Head, 'The development of the Peace of God in Aquitaine (970–1005)', *Speculum*, 74 (1999), 656–86; H. E. J. Cowdrey, 'The Peace and Truce of God in the eleventh century', *P&P*, 46 (1970), 42–67.

31. E. Boshof, *Königtum und Königsherrschaft im 10. und 11. Jahrhundert* (3rd ed., Munich, 2010), pp.112–13; K. Schnith, 'Recht und Friede. Zum Königsgedanken im Umkreis Heinrichs III.', *HJb*, 81 (1961), 22–57; Weinfurter, *Salian Century*, pp.98–104.

32. The 1152 and 1235 measures are printed in K. Zeumer (ed.), *Quellensammlung zur Geschichte der deutschen Reichsverfassung in Mittelalter und Neuzeit* (Tübingen, 1913), pp.7–8, 68–77. Further discussion in Arnold, *Medieval Germany*, pp.151–7, 184–91; Stürner, *Friedrich II.*, II, pp.313–16.

33. H. Vollrath, 'Ideal and reality in twelfth-century Germany', in A. Haverkamp and H. Vollrath (eds.), *England and Germany in the High Middle Ages* (Oxford, 1996), pp.93–104; B. Weiler, 'Reasserting power: Frederick II in Germany (1235–1236)', in idem and S. MacLean (eds.), *Representations of Power in Medieval Germany, 800–1500* (Turnhout, 2006), pp.241–72 esp. 247–9, 258–61.

34. E. Boshof, *Die Salier* (5th ed., Stuttgart, 2008), p.260; Arnold, *Princes and Territories*, pp.44–5.

35. B. Diestelkamp, 'König und Städte in salischer und staufischer Zeit', in F. Vittinghoff (ed.), *Stadt und Herrschaft* (Munich, 1982), pp.247–97 at 278–81.

36. T. Reuter, 'The medieval German *Sonderweg*? The Empire and its rulers in the high Middle Ages', in A. J. Duggan (eds.), *Kings and Kingship in Medieval Europe* (London, 1993), pp.179–211 at 190–94.

37. J. J. Schmauss and H. C. von Senckenberg (eds.), *Neue und vollständige Sammlung der Reichsabschiede* (4 vols., Frankfurt am Main, 1747), I, pp. 30–31; B. Weiler, 'Image and reality in Richard of Cornwall's German career', *EHR*, 113 (1998), 1111–42 at 1120–21.

38. H. Carl, *Der Schwäbische Bund, 1488–1534* (Leinfelden-Echterdingen, 2000), pp.33–4, 365–6.

39. F. R. H. Du Boulay, *Germany in the Later Middle Ages* (London, 1983), pp.83–90.

40. W. Troßbach and C. Zimmermann, *Die Geschichte des Dorfs. Von den Anfängen im Frankenreich zur bundesdeutschen Gegenwart* (Stuttgart, 2006), pp.86–9.

41. Schubert, *Fürstliche Herrschaft*, pp.67–70; Arnold, *Princes and Territories*, pp.186–210; Blickle, *Das Alte Europa*, pp.226–7. For this process in the Habsburg lands see A. Niederstätter, *Österreichische Geschichte, 1278–1411* (Vienna, 2004), pp.326–33.

42. E. Lacour, 'Faces of violence revisited: A typology of violence in early modern rural Germany', *Journal of Social History*, 34 (2001), 649–67.

43. S. Reynolds, *Kingdoms and Communities in Western Europe, 900–1300* (2nd ed., Oxford, 1997), pp.56–7; Schulze, *Grundstrukturen*, II, pp.168–9; Whitman, *The Legacy of Roman Law*, pp.35–7.

44. M. Prietzel, *Das Heilige Römische Reich im Spätmittelalter* (2nd ed., Darmstadt, 2010), p.15.

45. F. R. H. Du Boulay, 'Law enforcement in medieval Germany', *History*, 63 (1978), 345–55.

46. E. Schubert, 'Die Harzgrafen im ausgehenden Mittelalter', in J. Rogge and U. Schirmer (eds.), *Hochadelige Herrschaft im mitteldeutschen Raum (1200 bis 1600)* (Leipzig, 2003), pp.13–115.

47. Carl, *Der Schwäbische Bund*, pp.403–4.

48. B. Diestelkamp, *Rechtsfälle aus dem Alten Reich* (Munich, 1995), pp.11–12; R. Seyboth, 'Kaiser, König, Stände und Städte im Ringen um das Kammergericht 1486–1495', in B. Diestelkamp (ed.), *Das Reichskammergericht in der deutschen Geschichte* (Cologne, 1990), pp.5–23.

49. K. S. Bader, 'Approaches to imperial reform at the end of the fifteenth century', in G. Strauss (ed.), *Pre-Reformation Germany* (London, 1972), pp.136–61 at 148–50. The extensive literature is reviewed in R.-P. Fuchs, 'The supreme court of the Holy Roman Empire', *The Sixteenth-Century Journal*, 34 (2003), 9–27; E. Ortlieb and S. Westphal, 'Die Höchstgerichtsbarkeit im Alten Reich', *ZSRG GA*, 123 (2006), 291–304.

50. G. Schmidt-von Rhein, 'Das Reichskammergericht in Wetzlar', *NA*, 100 (1989), 127–40.

51. S. Jahns, *Die Assessoren des Reichskammergerichts in Wetzlar* (Wetzlar, 1986); B. Ruthmann, 'Das richterliche Personal am Reichskammergericht und seine politischen Verbindungen um 1600', in W. Sellert (ed.), *Reichshofrat und Reichskammergericht* (Cologne, 1999), pp.1–26. The court also had its own secretariat and archive.

52. J. Weitzel, 'Zur Zuständigkeit des Reichskammergerichts als Appellationsgericht', *ZSRG GA*, 90 (1973), 213–45; K. Perels, 'Die Justizverweigerung im alten Reiche seit 1495', *ZSRG GA*, 25 (1904), 1–51; H. Gabel, 'Beobachtungen zur Territorialen Inanspruchnahme des Reichskammergerichts im Bereich des Niederrheinisch-Westfälischen Kreises', in Diestelkamp (ed.), *Das Reichskammergericht*, pp.143–72 esp. 154–62; S. Westphal, *Ehen vor Gericht – Scheidungen und ihre Folgen am Reichskammergericht* (Wetzlar, 2008).

53. A. Wiffels, 'Der Große Rat von Mechelen', in I. Scheurmann (ed.), *Frieden durch Recht. Das Reichskammergericht von 1495 bis 1806* (Mainz, 1994), pp.374–82; F. Hertz, 'Die Rechtsprechung der höchsten Reichsgerichte im römisch-deutschen Reich und ihre politische Bedeutung', *MIÖG*, 69 (1961), 331–58 at 348.

54. S. Ullmann, *Geschichte auf der langen Bank. Die Kommissionen des Reichshofrats unter Kaiser Maximilian II. (1564–1576)* (Mainz, 2006); S. Ehrenpreis, *Kaiserliche Gerichtsbarkeit und Konfessionskonflikt. Der Reichshofrat unter Rudolf II., 1576–1612* (Göttingen, 2006); L. Auer, 'The role of the Imperial Aulic Council in the constitutional structure of the Holy Roman Empire', in R. J. W. Evans et al. (eds.), *The Holy Roman Empire, 1495–1806* (Oxford, 2011), pp.63–76.

55. W. Behringer, *Witches and Witch-Hunts: A Global History* (Cambridge, MA, 2004); B. Gehm, *Die Hexenverfolgung im Hochstift Bamberg und das Eingreifen des Reichshofrates zu ihrer Beendigung* (Hildesheim, 2000); W. Sellert and P. Oestmann, 'Hexen- und Strafprozesse am Reichskammergericht', in Scheurmann (ed.), *Frieden durch Recht*, pp.328–35.

56. S. Westphal, 'Der Umgang mit kultureller Differenz am Beispiel von Haftbedingungen für Juden in der Frühen Neuzeit', in A. Gotzmann and S. Wendehorst (eds.), *Juden im Recht. Neue Zugänge zur Rechtsgeschichte der Juden im Alten Reich* (Berlin, 2007), 139–61 at 152–4.

57. W. Sellert, 'Das Verhältnis von Reichskammergerichts- und Reichshofratsordnungen am Beispiel der Regelungen über die Visitation', in Diestelkamp (ed.), *Das Reichskammergericht*, pp.111–28; K. O. Frhr. v. Aretin, 'Kaiser Joseph II. und die Reichskammergerichtsvisitation 1766–1776', *ZNRG*, 13 (1991), 129–44. The religious cases are discussed on p.123.

58. R. Smend, *Das Reichskammergericht* (Weimar, 1911), pp.230–31; E. Ortlieb and G. Polster, 'Die Prozessfrequenz am Reichshofrat (1519–1806)', *ZNRG*, 26 (2004), 189–216.

59. As reported by BBC News on 19 April 2012. Further statistics in Diestelkamp, *Rechtsfälle*, pp.31–6; Whaley, *Germany*, II, pp.414, 432.

60. Ortlieb, *Im Auftrag*, pp.99–114; M. Fimpel, *Reichsjustiz und Territorialstaat* (Tübingen, 1999), pp.35, 54, 57, 293.

61. S. Westphal, *Kaiserliche Rechtsprechung und herrschaftliche Stabilisierung* (Cologne, 2002), pp.32–52; G. Benecke, *Society and Politics in Germany, 1500–1750* (London, 1974), p.277; Ortlieb, *Im Auftrag*, pp.90–97; B. Stollberg-Rilinger, 'Rang vor Gericht. Zur Verrechtlichung sozialer Rangkonflikte in der frühen Neuzeit', *ZHF*, 28 (2001), 385–418.

62. C. Kampmann, *Reichsrebellion und kaiserliche Acht. Politische Strafjustiz im Dreißigjährigen Krieg und das Verfahren gegen Wallenstein 1634* (Münster, 1992), and his 'Zur Entstehung der Konkurrenz zwischen Kaiserhof und Reichstag beim Achtverfahren', in Sellert (ed.), *Reichshofrat*, pp.169–98.

63. K. O. Frhr. v. Aretin, *Das Alte Reich, 1648–1806* (4 vols., Stuttgart, 1993–2000), III, pp.92–3; A. G. W. Kohlhepp, *Die Militärverfassung des deutschen Reiches zur Zeit des Siebenjährigen Krieges* (Greifswald, 1914), pp.58, 62–4.

64. D. Landes, *Achtverfahren vor dem Reichshofrat* (Frankfurt am Main, 1964).

65. W. Troßbach, 'Power and good governance: The removal of ruling princes in the Holy Roman Empire, 1680–1794', in J. P. Coy et al. (eds.), *The Holy Roman Empire, Reconsidered* (New York, 2010), pp.191–209, and his 'Fürstenabsetzungen im 18. Jahrhundert', *ZHF*, 13 (1986), 425–54.

66. See especially the works of W. Schulze, *Bäuerlicher Widerstand und feudale Herrschaft in der frühen Neuzeit* (Stuttgart, 1980), pp.73–85, 'Die veränderte Bedeutung sozialer Konflikte im 16. und 17. Jahrhundert',

in H.-U. Wehler (ed.), *Der Deutsche Bauernkrieg, 1524–1526* (Göttingen, 1975), pp.277–302, 'Peasant resistance in sixteenth- and seventeenth-century Germany in a European context', in K. von Greyerz, *Religion, Politics and Social Protest* (London, 1984), pp.61–98.

67. P. H. Wilson, *War, State and Society in Württemberg, 1677–1793* (Cambridge, 1995), pp.229–31; P. Milton, 'Intervening against tyrannical rule in the Holy Roman Empire during the seventeenth and eighteenth centuries', *GH*, 33 (2015), 1–29; Fimpel, *Reichsjustiz*, pp.245–6, and the works in n.65 above.

68. R. Sailer, *Untertanenprozesse vor dem Reichskammergericht. Rechtsschutz gegen die Obrigkeit in der Zweiten Hälfte des 18. Jahrhunderts* (Cologne, 1999), pp.468–73.

69. W. Troßbach, 'Bauernbewegungen in deutschen Kleinterritorien zwischen 1648 und 1789', in W. Schulze (ed.), *Aufstände, Revolten, Prozesse* (Stuttgart, 1983), pp.233–60; C. R. Friedrichs, 'German town revolts and the seventeenth-century crisis', *Renaissance and Modern Studies*, 26 (1982), 27–51; *NTSR*, XVIII, 421–68.

70. A. Suter, *'Troublen' im Fürstbistum Basel (1726–1740)* (Göttingen, 1985).

71. As argued by H.-U. Wehler, *Deutsche Gesellschaftsgeschichte* (5 vols., Munich, 2008), I, *passim*, and II, p.297.

72. J. Barth, *Hohenzollernsche Chronik oder Geschichte und Sage der hohenzollernschen Lande* (Sigmaringen, 1863), pp.532–6; J. Cramer, *Die Grafschaft Hohenzollern* (Stuttgart, 1873), pp.257–412; V. Press, 'Von den Bauernrevolten des 16. zur konstitutionellen Verfassung des 19. Jahrhunderts. Die Untertanenkonflikte in Hohenzollern-Hechingen und ihre Lösungen', in H. Weber (ed.), *Politische Ordnungen und soziale Kräfte im Alten Reich* (Wiesbaden, 1980), pp.85–112.

73. Auer, 'Imperial Aulic Council', pp.73–4.

74. D. M. Luebke, *His Majesty's Rebels: Communities, Factions and Rural Revolt in the Black Forest, 1725–1745* (Ithaca, NY, 1997); H. Rebel, *Peasant Classes* (Princeton, 1983), pp.199–229; T. Robisheaux, *Rural Society and the Search for Order in Early Modern Germany* (Cambridge, 1989), pp.175–98.

75. H. Gabel, *Widerstand und Kooperation. Studien zur politischen Kultur rheinischer und maasländischer Kleinterritorien (1648–1794)* (Tübingen, 1995); Benecke, *Society and Politics*, pp.276–8.

76. N. Schindler, *Rebellion, Community and Custom in Early Modern Germany* (Cambridge, 2002), pp.35–7. For the following also U. Rublack, 'State-formation, gender and the experience of governance in early modern Württemberg', in idem (ed.), *Gender in Early Modern German History* (Cambridge, 2002), pp.200–217; W. Troßbach, 'Widerstand als Normalfall. Bauernunruhen in der Grafschaft Sayn-Wittgenstein-Wittgenstein 1696–1806', *WZ*, 135 (1985), 25–111 at 88–90.

77. Sailer, *Untertanenprozesse*, p.466.

78. K. Härter, 'Die Sicherheit des Rechts und die Produktion von Sicherheit im frühneuzeitlichen Strafrecht', in C. Kampmann and U. Niggemann (eds.), *Sicherheit in der Frühen Neuzeit* (Cologne, 2013), pp.661–72.

79. Haas's memorandum is in *HHStA*, Titel und Wappen, Kart.3, Mappe 1, and printed in G. Walter, *Der Zusammenbruch des Heiligen Römischen Reichs deutscher Nation und die Problematik seiner Restauration in den Jahren 1814/15* (Heidelberg, 1980), pp.132–44. For the widespread belief that ordinary folk would suffer if the Empire was reorganized as a unitary state, see K. O. Frhr. v. Aretin, *Heiliges Römisches Reich, 1776–1806* (2 vols., Wiesbaden, 1967), I, pp.362–71.

80. J. Viscount Bryce, *The Holy Roman Empire* (5th ed., London, 1919), p.402.

81. Quoted in B. Stollberg-Rilinger, *Des Kaisers alte Kleider* (Munich, 2008), p.252.

82. Ibid, p.257; K. Härter, *Reichstag und Revolution, 1789–1806* (Göttingen, 1992), pp.653–68.

83. Quotations from S. Jahns, 'Die Personalverfassung des Reichskammergerichts unter Anpassungsdruck', in Diestelkamp (ed.), *Das Reichskammergericht*, pp.59–109 at 59; D. Beales, *Joseph II* (2 vols., Cambridge, 1987–2009), I, p.126. Further comments in similar vein in C. Hattenhauer, *Wahl und Krönung Franz II*. AD 1792 (Frankfurt am Main, 1995), pp.401–19; Stollberg-Rilinger, *Kaisers alte Kleider*, pp.274–80.

84. M. Walker, *Johann Jakob Moser and the Holy Roman Empire of the German Nation* (Chapel Hill, NC, 1981), pp.290–95, 301. For a more upbeat assessment of Moser's views see R. Rürup, *Johann Jacob Moser. Pietismus und Reform* (Wiesbaden, 1965), pp.141–52.

85. J. H. Zedler, *Große vollständige Universal-Lexicon aller Wissenschaften und Künste*, vol.43 (Leipzig, 1745).

86. E.g. G. Kleinheyer, 'Die Abdankung des Kaisers', in G. Köbler (ed.), *Wege europäischer Rechtsgeschichte* (Frankfurt am Main, 1987), pp.124–44 at 144. Goethe's mother quoted in H. Neuhaus, 'Das Ende des Alten Reiches', in H. Altricher and H. Neuhaus (eds.), *Das Ende von Großreichen* (Erlangen, 1996), pp.185–209 at 191.

87. J. G. Gagliardo, *Reich and Nation: The Holy Roman Empire as Idea and Reality, 1763–1806* (Bloomington, IN, 1980), pp.99–102.

88. K. O. Frhr. v. Aretin, 'Die Reichsidee um 1800', in F. Bosbach and H. Hiery (eds.), *Imperium / Empire / Reich* (Munich, 1999), pp.109–11; W. Burgdorf, *Reichskonstitution und Nation. Verfassungsreformprojekte für das Heilige Römische Reich deutscher Nation im politischen Schrifttum von 1648 bis 1806* (Mainz, 1998), and his 'Imperial reform and visions of a European constitution in Germany around 1800', *History of European Ideas*, 19 (1994), 401–8. See also pp.277–80.

89. A. Gotthard, *Das Alte Reich, 1495–1806* (3rd ed., Darmstadt, 2006), pp. 149–50; G. W. F. Hegel's *German Constitution* (1802), in T. M. Knox (ed.), *Hegel's Political Writings* (Oxford, 1969), pp.143–242.

90. M. Umbach, *Federalism and Enlightenment in Germany, 1740–1806* (London, 2000), pp.167–84; P. Burg, *Die deutsche Trias in Idee und Wirklichkeit. Vom Alten Reich zum deutschen Zollverein* (Stuttgart, 1989), pp.9–12; A. Kohler, 'Das Reich im Spannungsfeld des preussisch-österreichischen Gegensatzes. Die Fürstenbundbestrebungen, 1783–1785', in F. Engel-Janosi et al. (eds.), *Fürst, Bürger, Mensch* (Munich, 1975), pp.71–96; D. Stievermann, 'Der Fürstenbund von 1785 und das Reich', in V. Press (ed.), *Alternativen zur Reichsverfassung in der Frühen Neuzeit?* (Munich, 1995), pp.209–26; A. Hanschmidt, *Franz von Fürstenberg als Staatsmann* (Münster, 1969), pp.186–249.

91. E. Hirsch, *Die Dessau-Wörlitzer Reformbewegung im Zeitalter der Aufklärung* (Tübingen, 2003); M. Umbach, 'The politics of sentimentality and the German *Fürstenbund*, 1779–1785', *HJ*, 41 (1998), 679–704, and her 'Visual culture, scientific images and German small-state politics in the late Enlightenment', *P&P*, 158 (1998), 110–45.

92. Landesarchiv Münster, A267 Nos.2557–61, insurance scheme registers; T. C. W. Blanning, *Reform and Revolution in Mainz, 1743–1803* (Cambridge, 1974), pp.188–90.

93. E.g. by Umbach, *Federalism*, pp.161–2.

94. K. Härter, 'Reichsrecht und Reichsverfassung in der Auflösungsphase des Heiligen Römischen Reichs deutscher Nation', *ZNRG*, 28 (2006), 316–37 at 326; K. O. Frhr. v. Aretin, *Das Reich* (Stuttgart, 1986), p.393.

95. D. Petschel, *Sächsische Außenpolitik unter Friedrich August I.* (Cologne, 2000), pp.56–91; J. B. Knudsen, *Justus Möser and the German Enlightenment* (Cambridge, 1986).

96. T. Hartwig, *Der Überfall der Grafschaft Schaumburg-Lippe durch Landgraf Wilhelm IX. von Hessen-Kassel* (Hanover, 1911).

97. Aretin, *Das Alte Reich*, III, pp.354–61; W. Lüdke, 'Der Kampf zwischen Oesterreich und Preussen um die Vorherrschaft im "Reiche" und die Auflösung des Fürstenbundes (1789/91)', *MIÖG*, 45 (1931), 70–153.

98. W. Burgdorf, *Ein Weltbild verliert seine Welt. Der Untergang des Alten Reiches und die Generation 1806* (2nd ed., Munich, 2009), p.33.

99. Aretin, *Das Alte Reich*, III, pp.417–36, and his *Heiliges Römisches Reich*, I, pp.303–7, 317–18, 368–70.

100. Quoted in Neuhaus, 'Das Ende', p.200. Statistics from Sailer, *Untertanenprozesse*, p.17.

101. Quote from G. Schmidt, *Geschichte des Alten Reiches* (Munich, 1999), p.333. On Prussian fears of revolution see G. Birtsch, 'Revolutionsfurcht in Preußen 1789 bis 1794', in O. Büsch and M. Neugebauer-Wölk (eds.), *Preußen und die revolutionäre Herausforderung seit 1789* (Berlin, 1991), pp.87–101;

L. Kittstein, *Politik im Zeitalter der Revolution. Untersuchungen zur preußischen Staatlichkeit, 1792–1807* (Stuttgart, 2003), pp.32–42. For the level and character of protest see H. Berding (ed.), *Soziale Unruhen in Deutschland während der Französischen Revolution* (Göttingen, 1988).

102. Wehler, *Deutsche Gesellschaftsgeschichte*, I, pp.356–7. The literature on the German Jacobins is summarized in Whaley, *Germany*, II, pp.583–91.

103. H. Schultz, 'Mythos und Aufklärung. Frühformen des Nationalismus in Deutschland', *HZ*, 263 (1996), 31–67; Schmidt, *Geschichte*, pp.333–40.

104. T. C. W. Blanning, *The French Revolution in Germany: Occupation and Resistance in the Rhineland, 1792–1802* (Oxford, 1983); M. Rowe, *From Reich to State: The Rhineland in the Revolutionary Age, 1780–1830* (Cambridge, 2003); Kittstein, *Politik*, pp.43–7, 57–64.

105. K. Härter, 'Der Reichstag im Revolutionsjahr 1789', in K. O. Frhr. v. Aretin and K. Härter (eds.), *Revolution und konservatives Beharren* (Mainz, 1990), pp.155–74.

106. R. Blaufarb, 'Napoleon and the abolition of feudalism', in A. Forrest and P. H. Wilson (eds.), *The Bee and the Eagle: Napoleonic France and the End of the Holy Roman Empire, 1806* (Basingstoke, 2009), pp.131–54.

107. S. S. Biro, *The German Policy of Revolutionary France: A Study in French Diplomacy during the War of the First Coalition, 1792–1797* (2 vols., Cambridge, MA, 1957); T. C. W. Blanning, *The Origins of the French Revolutionary Wars* (Harlow, 1986).

108. C. Jany, *Geschichte der Preußischen Armee* (4 vols., Osnabrück, 1967), III, pp.252–9.

109. H. M. Scott, *The Birth of a Great Power System, 1740–1815* (Harlow, 2006), pp.202–13, 244–60; P. H. Wilson, *German Armies: War and German Politics, 1648–1806* (London, 1998), pp.303–30.

110. B. Simms, *The Impact of Napoleon: Prussian High Politics, Foreign Policy and the Crisis of the Executive, 1797–1806* (Cambridge, 1997); Kittstein, *Politik*, pp.365–408.

111. H. Angermeier, 'Deutschland zwischen Reichstradition und National-staat. Verfassungspolitische Konzeptionen und nationales Denken zwischen 1801 und 1815', *ZSRG GA*, 107 (1990), 19–101 at 53–4; Aretin, *Das Alte Reich*, III, pp.515–16.

112. Aretin, *Heilige Römisches Reich*, I, p.365.

113. W. Real, 'Die preußischen Staatsfinanzen und die Anbahnung des Sonderfriedens von Basel 1795', *Forschungen zur Brandenburgischen und Preußischen Geschichte*, 1 (1991), 53–100; P. G. Dwyer, 'The politics of Prussian neutrality, 1795–1805', *GH*, 12 (1994), 351–73.

114. Aretin, *Heilige Römisches Reich*, I, pp.365–6; Kittstein, *Politik*, pp.95–8.

115. D. E. Showalter, 'Hubertusberg to Auerstädt: The Prussian army in decline?', *GH*, 12 (1994), 308–33 at 324.

116. Kittstein, *Politik*, pp.119–38, 294–309.

117. Central to this critique was the anachronistic charge that Austria failed to exploit France's weakness in 1789 to recover Alsace and Lorraine as 'German' territory. E.g. V. Bibl, *Der Zerfall Österreichs* (2 vols., Vienna, 1922–4).

118. K. A. Roider Jr, *Baron Thurgut and Austria's Response to the French Revolution* (Princeton, 1987); H. Rössler, *Graf Johann Philipp Stadion. Napoleons deutscher Gegenspieler* (2 vols., Vienna, 1966); U. Dorda, *Johann Aloys Joseph Reichsfreiherr von Hügel (1754–1825)* (Würzburg, 1969).

119. Quoted in Aretin, *Heiliges Römisches Reich*, II, pp.250–55.

120. P. H. Wilson, 'German military preparedness at the eve of the Revolutionary Wars', in F. C. Schneid (ed.), *The Consortium on Revolutionary Europe, 1750–1850: Selected Papers, 2004* (High Point, NC, 2008), pp. 16–30; Härter, *Reichstag*, p.399. Britain briefly subsidized another 62,400 Prussians in 1794.

121. M. Hochedlinger, *Austria's Wars of Emergence, 1683–1797* (Harlow, 2003), pp.285, 425.

122. Gagliardo, *Reich and Nation*, pp.144–8, 166–70; Kittstein, *Politik*, pp.65–87.

123. Hertz, 'Die Rechtsprechung', pp.347–8; K. O. Frhr. v. Aretin, 'Das Reich und Napoleon', in W. D. Gruner and J. Müller (eds.), *Über Frankreich nach Europa* (Hamburg, 1996), pp.183–200 at 189.

124. W. D. Gruner, 'Österreich zwischen Altem Reich und Deutschem Bund (1789–1816)', in W. Brauneder and L. Höbelt (eds.), *Sacrum Imperium* (Vienna, 1996), pp.319–60 at 333.

125. K. Härter, 'Der Hauptschluß der außerordentlichen Reichsdeputation vom 25. Februar 1803', *GWU*, 54 (2003), 484–500; Walter, *Der Zusammenbruch*, pp.7–8. Events summarized by Aretin, *Das Alte Reich*, III, pp.489–98. The Reichsdeputationshauptschluß, is printed in Zeumer (ed.), *Quellensammlung*, pp.509–28.

126. D. Schäfer, *Ferdinand von Österreich. Großherzog zu Würzburg, Kurfürst von Salzburg, Großherzog der Toskana* (Cologne, 1988).

127. C. W. Ingrao, *The Habsburg Monarchy, 1618–1815* (2nd ed., Cambridge, 2000), p.228. See also H. Gross, 'The Holy Roman Empire in modern times', J. A. Vann and S. W. Rowan (eds.), *The Old Reich* (Brussels, 1974), pp.1–29 at 4–5.

128. Aretin, *Das Alte Reich*, III, p.503; Angermeier, 'Deutschland', 35–7.

129. D. Hohrath et al. (eds.), *Das Ende reichsstädtischer Freiheit, 1802* (Ulm, 2002).

130. For examples of how these arrangements were implemented, see the contributions by E. Klueting and R. Haas in T. Schilp (ed.), *Reform – Reformation – Säkularisation* (Essen, 2004).

131. O. F. Winter, 'Österreichische Pläne zur Neuformierung des Reichstages 1801–1806', *MÖSA*, 15 (1962), 261–335.

132. Aretin, *Das Reich*, pp.48–9. For the unions see E. Kell, 'Die Frankfurter Union (1803–1806)', *ZHF*, 18 (1991), 71–97.

133. *HHStA*, Staatskanzlei Vorträge 167; Dorda, *Reichsfreiherr von Hügel*, pp.173–5.

134. F. C. Schneid, *Napoleon's Conquest of Europe: The War of the Third Coalition* (Westport, CT, 2005), p.141. In return, Prussia ceded Ansbach-Bayreuth to Bavaria and Cleves to Napoleon. Bavaria also surrendered Berg, which was combined with Cleves as a new German satellite state allied to France.

135. Bavaria was allowed to annex the imperial city of Augsburg, and it received the Tirol, Vorarlberg, Trent and Brixen from Austria, which in turn was permitted to incorporate Salzburg. Francis's younger brother was given Würzburg by Bavaria, but French pressure delayed this part of the treaty. Austria was allowed to annex Venice in return for recognizing the new Italian kingdom. All three newly minted German sovereigns were obliged to marry into the Bonaparte family.

136. H. Ritter v. Srbik, *Das Österreichische Kaisertum und das Ende des Heiligen Römischen Reiches, 1804–1806* (Berlin, 1927), pp.40–41. Attitudes to the imperial title at this point are discussed further on pp.159–63.

137. Fesch was the son of Napoleon's grandmother by her second marriage to a Swiss officer. See K. Rob, *Karl Theodor von Dalberg (1744–1817). Eine politische Biographie für die Jahre 1744–1806* (Frankfurt am Main, 1984), pp.408–9.

138. M. Kaiser, 'A matter of survival: Bavaria becomes a kingdom', in Forrest and Wilson (eds.), *The Bee and the Eagle*, pp.94–111; Walter, *Der Zusammenbruch*, pp.19, 23–4.

139. Napoleon to Tallyrand, 31 May 1806, *Correspondance de Napoléon Ier, publiée par ordre de l'Empereur Napoléon III* (32 vols., Paris, 1858–70), XII, p.509.

140. Johann Philipp Stadion deliberately did not pass on Francis's request during his brief negotiations with France. Further discussion in P. H. Wilson, 'Bolstering the prestige of the Habsburgs: The end of the Holy Roman Empire in 1806', *International History Review*, 28 (2006), 709–36; G. Mraz, *Österreich und das Reich, 1804–1806* (Vienna, 1993).

141. Printed in Zeumer (ed.), *Quellensammlung*, pp.532–6. The others were Nassau-Usingen, Nassau-Weilburg, Hohenzollern-Hechingen, Hohenzollern-Sigmaringen, Salm-Salm, Salm-Kyrburg, Arenberg, Liechtenstein and von der Leyen.

142. Details in *HHStA*, Titel und Wappen, Kart.3; Rössler, *Stadion*, I, pp.225–55.

CHAPTER 13: AFTERLIFE

1. For example, T. Nipperdey, *Deutsche Geschichte, 1800–1918* (3 vols., Munich, 1983–92), I, p.14; J. Viscount Bryce, *The Holy Roman Empire* (5th ed., London, 1919), p.410; K. Epstein, *The Genesis of German Conservatism* (Princeton, 1966), pp.665–9.

2. H. Angermeier, 'Deutschland zwischen Reichstradition und Nationalstaat. Verfassungspolitische Konzeptionen und nationales Denken zwischen 1801 und 1815', *ZSRG GA*, 107 (1990), 19–101 at 20–21; W. Burgdorf, *Ein Weltbild verliert seine Welt. Der Untergang des Alten Reiches und die Generation 1806* (2nd ed., Munich, 2009), pp.203–4. See generally idem, ' "Once we were Trojans!" Contemporary reactions to the dissolution of the Holy Roman Empire of the German Nation', in R. J. W. Evans and P. H. Wilson (eds.), *The Holy Roman Empire, 1495–1806* (Leiden, 2012), pp.51–76.

3. H. Ritte v. Srbik, *Das Österreichische Kaisertum und das Ende des Heiligen Römischen Reiches, 1804–1806* (Berlin, 1927), p.67. See also Haas's opinions discussed on pp.636–7.

4. *HHStA*, Titel und Wappen, Kart.3 (Haas's and Fahrenberg's reports Aug. 1806); Prinzipalkommission Berichte, Fasz.182d (Hügel's report).

5. *HHStA*, Titel und Wappen, Kart.3 (Baron von Wessenberg's report 18 Aug. 1806).

6. G. Menzel, 'Franz Joseph von Albini, 1748–1816', *Mainzer Zeitschrift*, 69 (1974), 1–126 at 108; H. Rössler, *Napoleons Griff nach der Karlskrone. Das Ende des Alten Reiches, 1806* (Munich, 1957), p.65.

7. Palm has been anachronistically claimed as the first martyr in 'the cause of German nationalism': H. A. Winkler, *Germany: The Long Road West* (2 vols., Oxford, 2006–7), I, p.48.

8. Rössler, *Napoleons Griff*, pp.55–6; Burgdorf, *Weltbild*, pp.155–65.

9. Nipperdey, *Deutsche Geschichte*, I, p.14. See also W. Reinhard, 'Frühmoderner Staat und deutsches Monstrum', *ZHF*, 29 (2002), 339–57.

10. G. Walter, *Der Zusammenbruch des Heiligen Römischen Reichs deutscher Nation und die Problematik seiner Restauration in den Jahren 1814/15* (Heidelberg, 1980), pp.75–6. Austrian arguments can be followed in *HHStA*, Titel und Wappen, Kart.3, Gutachten zur Abdankungsfrage, esp. memorandum of 31 July 1806. A self-styled Prince Karl Friedrich Philipp von Wettinberg, living in Teddington, paid £4,000 for a full-page advertisement in the *Independent* newspaper on 24 Sept. 1999 to proclaim himself Emperor Charles VIII on the basis that the Empire had not been legally dissolved.

11. Walter, *Zusammenbruch*, pp.26–42, 76–95, 129. Sweden's protest is in *HHStA*, Titel und Wappen, Kart.3.

12. L. Kittstein, *Politik im Zeitalter der Revolution* (Stuttgart, 2003), pp. 293–354. Prussia's defeat is summarized by C. Telp, 'The Prussian army in the Jena campaign', in A. Forrest and P. H. Wilson (eds.), *The Bee and the Eagle* (Basingstoke, 2009), pp.155–71.

13. Burgdorf, *Weltbild*, p.164.

14. G. Mraz, *Österreich und das Reich, 1804–1806* (Vienna, 1993), pp.83–4. For an example of the integration of the former territories within a surviving principality, see P. Exner, 'Die Eingliederung Frankens – oder: wie wird man württembergisch und badisch?', *ZWLG*, 71 (2012), 383–448.

15. Landesarchiv Münster, A230 Rietberg Geheimer Rat Akten, Nr.1377, 14 May 1808.

16. L. Auer, 'Die Verschleppung der Akten des Reichshofrats durch Napoleon', in T. Olechowski et al. (eds.), *Grundlagen der österreichischen Rechtskultur* (Vienna, 2010), pp.1–13.

17. E.-O. Mader, *Die letzten 'Priester der Gerechtigkeit'. Die Auseinandersetzung der letzten Generation von Richtern des Reichskammergerichts mit der Auflösung des Heiligen Römischen Reiches Deutscher Nation* (Berlin, 2005).

18. I. Scheurmann (ed.), *Frieden durch Recht. Das Reichskammergericht von 1495 bis 1806* (Mainz, 1994), esp. p.342.

19. K. and A. Weller, *Württembergische Geschichte im südwestdeutschen Raum* (7th ed., Stuttgart, 1972), p.212; *Baden und Württemberg im Zeitalter Napoleons* (2 vols., issued by the Württembergisches Landesmuseum, Stuttgart, 1987). For general discussions of the reforms, see M. Broers, *Europe under Napoleon, 1799–1815* (London, 1996), pp.103–41, 167–77, 202–8; M. Rowe, 'Napoleon and the "modernisation" of Germany', in P. G. Dwyer and A. Forrest (eds.), *Napoleon and his Empire: Europe, 1804–1814* (Basingstoke, 2007), pp.202–40; A. Fahrmeir, 'Centralisation versus particularism in the "Third Germany"', in M. Rowe (ed.), *Collaboration and Resistance in Napoleonic Europe: State-Formation in an Age of Upheaval, c.1800–1815* (Basingstoke, 2003), pp.107–20.

20. S. A. Eddie, *Freedom's Price: Serfdom, Subjection and Reform in Prussia, 1648–1848* (Oxford, 2013).

21. K. Görich, *Friedrich Barbarossa* (Munich, 2011), p.639.

22. B. Demel, 'Der Deutsche Orden und seine Besitzungen im südwestdeutschen Sprachraum vom 13. bis 19. Jahrhundert', *ZWLG*, 31 (1972), 16–73 at 68–72.

23. Menzel, 'Franz Joseph von Albini', pp.109–10; R. Wohlfeil, 'Untersuchungen zur Geschichte des Rheinbundes, 1806–1813. Das Verhältnis Dalbergs zu Napoleon', *ZGO*, 108 (1960), 85–108; G. Schmidt, 'Der napoleonische Rheinbund – ein erneuertes Altes Reich?', in V. Press (ed.), *Alternativen zur Reichsverfassung in der frühen Neuzeit?* (Munich, 1995), pp.227–46.

24. Walter, *Zusammenbruch*, pp.59–70. For the following see E. Weis, 'Napoleon und der Rheinbund', in A. v. Reden-Dohna (ed.), *Deutschland und Italien im Zeitalter Napoleons* (Wiesbaden, 1979), pp.57–80.

25. D. E. Barclay, *Frederick William IV and the Prussian Monarchy, 1840–1861* (Oxford, 1995), p.188. See generally A. Zamoyski, *Rites of Peace: The Fall of Napoleon and the Congress of Vienna* (London, 2007), pp. 239–50; Walter, *Zusammenbruch*, pp.104–8.

26. T. Riotte, *Hannover in der britischen Politik (1792–1815)* (Münster, 2005), pp.193–208; W. D. Gruner, 'Österreich zwischen Altem Reich und Deutschem Bund (1789–1816)', in W. Brauneder and L. Höbelt (eds.), *Sacrum Imperium* (Vienna, 1996), pp.319–60 at 326–40.

27. P. Burg, *Die deutsche Trias in Idee und Wirklichkeit. Vom Alten Reich zum deutschen Zollverein* (Stuttgart, 1989), pp.46–54.

28. F. Quarthal, 'Österreichs Verankerung im Heiligen Römischen Reich deutscher Nation', in R. G. Plaschka et al. (eds.), *Was heißt Österreich?* (Vienna, 1995), pp.109–34 at 126–7.

29. Angermeier, 'Deutschland', 42–60. For Austrian policy see V. Press, *Altes Reich und Deutscher Bund. Kontinuität in der Diskontinuität* (Munich, 1995).

30. M. Hughes, 'Fiat justitia, pereat Germania? The imperial supreme jurisdiction and imperial reform in the later Holy Roman Empire', in J. Breuilly (ed.), *The State of Germany* (Harlow, 1992), pp.29–46 at 44–5.

31. K. Härter, 'Reichsrecht und Reichsverfassung in der Auflösungsphase des Heiligen Römischen Reichs deutscher Nation', *ZNRG*, 28 (2006), 316–37.

32. H. Fuhrmann, '"Wer hat die Deutschen zu Richtern über die Völker bestellt?" Die Deutschen als Ärgernis im Mittelalter', *GWU*, 46 (1995), 625–41.

33. E. Vermeil, *Germany's Three Reichs: Their History and Culture* (London, 1944), p.49.

34. Ibid, pp.383–4. See also C. Duhamelle, 'Das Alte Reich im toten Winkel der französischen Historiographie', in M. Schnettger (ed.), *Imperium Romanum – irregulare corpus – Teutscher Reichs-Staat* (Mainz, 2002), pp.207–19. Although he shares the common misconception of disjunction between 843 and 962, J.-F. Noël is a rare exception in offering a more positive assessment: *Le Saint-Empire* (Paris, 1976).

35. J. Pánek, 'Bohemia and the Empire: Acceptance and rejection', in R. J. W. Evans and P. H. Wilson (eds.), *The Holy Roman Empire, 1495–1806* (Leiden, 2012), pp.121–41 esp.131–7; R. Krueger, *Czech, German and Noble: Status and National Identity in Habsburg Bohemia* (Oxford, 2009), pp.191–217.

36. T. C. W. Blanning, 'The French Revolution and the modernization of Germany', *CEH*, 22 (1989), 109–29 at 116–18.

37. Angermeier, 'Deutschland', 42, 51–2. See also J. Whaley, 'Thinking about Germany, 1750–1815', *Publications of the English Goethe Society*, 66 (1996), 53–72.

38. M. Umbach (ed.), *German Federalism* (Basingstoke, 2002); A. Green, *Fatherlands: State-Building and Nationhood in Nineteenth-Century Germany* (Cambridge, 2001); D. Langewiesche, 'Föderative Nation, kulturelle Identität und politische Ordnung', in G. Schmidt (ed.), *Die deutsche Nation im frühneuzeitlichen Europa* (Munich, 2010), pp.65–80.

39. A. Green, 'The federal alternative? A new view of modern German history', *HJ*, 46 (2003), 187–202.

40. W. Doyle (ed.), *The Oxford Handbook of the Ancien Régime* (Oxford, 2012).

41. K. H. Wegert, *German Radicals Confront the Common People: Revolutionary Politics and Popular Politics, 1789–1849* (Mainz, 1992), esp. p.319; A. Green, 'Political institutions and nationhood in Germany', in L. Scales and O. Zimmer (eds.), *Power and the Nation in European History* (Cambridge, 2005), pp.315–32.

42. K. B. Murr, *Ludwig der Bayer: Ein Kaiser für das Königreich? Zur öffentlichen Erinnerung an eine mittelalterliche Herrschergestalt im Bayern des 19. Jahrhunderts* (Munich, 2008).

43. W. Burgdorf, ' "Das Reich geht mich nichts an". Goethes *Götz von Berlichingen*, das Reich und die Reichspublizistik', in Schnettger (ed.), *Imperium Romanum*, pp.27–52. See also idem, *Weltbild*, pp.266–7, 283–318.

44. Barclay, *Frederick William IV*, pp.31–2. See generally K. Herbers and H. Neuhaus, *Das Heilige Römische Reich* (Cologne, 2010), pp.298–302. Cologne Cathedral was completed in 1880.

45. L. L. Ping, *Gustav Freitag and the Prussian Gospel: Novels, Liberalism and History* (Bern, 2006); R. Southard, *Droysen and the Prussian School of History* (Lexington, KY, 1995); K. Cramer, *The Thirty Years' War and German Memory in the Nineteenth Century* (Lincoln, NB, 2007).

46. Burgdorf, *Weltbild*, pp.262–8.

47. Ludwig's son Otto ruled from 1832 until he was deposed by a military coup in 1862. Thereafter, Greece was ruled by monarchs from the Schleswig-Holstein-Sonderburg-Glücksburg family until the 'colonel's coup' of 1973.

48. M. Todd, *The Early Germans* (2nd ed., Oxford, 2004), pp.247–52; G. L. Mosse, *The Nationalization of the Masses: Political Symbolism and Mass Movements in Germany from the Napoleonic Wars through the Third Reich* (New York, 1975), pp.24–63.

49. The Habsburgs used a black double eagle surmounted by Rudolf II's dynastic crown as their dynastic imperial symbol between 1804 and 1918.

50. Hanover, Holstein, Nassau, Frankfurt, Hessen-Kassel and Hessen-Homberg were annexed by Prussia, while Parma, Lucca, Naples-Sicily, Tuscany, Modena and the Papal States disappeared into Italy.

51. B. Jelavich, *Modern Austria* (Cambridge, 1987), pp.72–147; F. Fellner, 'Reichsgeschichte und Reichsidee als Problem der österreichischen Historiographie', in Brauneder and Höbelt (eds.), *Sacrum Imperium*, pp.361–74; M. Stickler, 'Reichsvorstellungen in Preußen-Deutschland und der Habsburgermonarchie in der Bismarckzeit', in F. Bosbach and H. Hiery (eds.), *Imperium – Empire – Reich* (Munich, 1999), pp.133–54. For the hereditary title see pp.162–3.

52. E. E. Stengel, *Abhandlungen und Untersuchungen zur Geschichte des Kaisergedankens im Mittelalter* (Cologne, 1965), pp.140–46; Stickler, 'Reichsvorstellungen', pp.144–54.

53. R. Staats, *Die Reichskrone* (2nd ed., Kiel, 2008), pp.36–40.

54. A converted Cunard paddle steamer, previously called *Britannia*: W. Hubatsch et al., *Die erste deutsche Flotte, 1848–1853* (Herford, 1981), esp. p.54.

55. K. Görich, *Die Staufer* (2nd ed., Munich, 2008), p.14; F. Shaw, 'Friedrich II as the "last emperor" ', *GH*, 19 (2001), 321–39.

56. The statue was damaged and removed in 1945, but renewed and put back in 1993, perhaps rather insensitively on 1 September, the date celebrated throughout the Second Empire as 'Sedan Day', commemorating the victory over France in 1870.

57. J. Rüger, *The Great Naval Game: Britain and Germany in the Age of Empire* (Cambridge, 2007), pp.154–9.

58. M. Derndarsky, 'Zwischen "Idee" und "Wirklichkeit". Das Alte Reich in der Sicht Heinrich von Srbiks', in Schnettger (ed.), *Imperium Romanum*, pp.189–205; P. R. Sweet, 'The historical writing of Heinrich von Srbik', *History and Theory*, 9 (1970), 37–58; F. Heer, *The Holy Roman Empire* (London, 1968).

59. M. Hughes, *Nationalism and Society: Germany 1800–1945* (London, 1988); R. Chickering, '*We Men who Feel most German*': A Cultural Study of the Pan-German League, 1886–1914 (London, 1984). For the persistence of multilayered attachments see A. Confino, *The Nation as a Local Metaphor: Württemberg, Imperial Germany, and National Memory, 1871–1918* (Chapel Hill, NC, 1997).

60. Görich, *Die Staufer*, p.15.

61. B. Schneidmüller, 'Konsens – Territorialisierung – Eigennutz. Vom Umgang mit spätmittelalterlicher Geschichte', *FMS*, 39 (2005), 225–46 esp. 242–3; H. K. Schulze, *Grundstrukturen der Verfassung im Mittelalter* (3rd ed., 3 vols., Stuttgart, 1995–2000), I, pp.30–33; F. Graus,

'Verfassungsgeschichte des Mittelalters', *HZ*, 243 (1986), 529–89 at 551–9; P. N. Miller, 'Nazis and Neo-Stoics: Otto Brunner and Gerhard Oestreich before and after the Second World War', *P&P*, 176 (2002), 144–86.

62. H. Picker (ed.), *Hitlers Tischgespräche im Führerhauptquartier* (3rd ed., Stuttgart, 1977), p.463.

63. Herbers and Neuhaus, *Das Heilige Römische Reich*, p.301.

64. F.-L. Kroll, 'Die Reichsidee im Nationalsozialismus', in Bosbach and Hiery (eds.), *Imperium*, pp.179–96 at 187–90; M. Pape, 'Der Karlskult an Wendepunkten der deutschen Geschichte', *HJb*, 120 (2000), 138–81 at 163–6.

65. Staats, *Reichskrone*, p.35.

66. K. R. Ganzer, *Das Reich als europäischen Ordnungsmacht* (Hamburg, 1941); F. W. Foerster, *Europe and the German Question* (New York, 1940).

67. G. Wolnik, *Mittelalter und NS-Propaganda* (Münster, 2004), p.85.

68. Kroll, 'Reichsidee', pp.181–2.

69. M. Steinmetz, *Deutschland, 1476–1648* (East Berlin, 1965), pp.184–211; A. Dorpalen, *German History in Marxist Perspective* (Detroit, MI, 1985), pp.76–89.

70. J. Burkhardt, 'Europäischer Nachzügler oder institutioneller Vorreiter?', in Schnettger (ed.), *Imperium Romanum*, pp.297–316 at 300–301; T. Nicklas, 'Müssen wir das Alte Reich lieben?', *Archiv für Kulturgeschichte*, 89 (2007), 447–74 at 453–4.

71. H. J. Berbig, 'Der Krönungsritus im Alten Reich (1648–1806)', *ZBLG*, 38 (1975), 639–700 at 688.

72. Recently, Lenz has denied that the clerical figure depicts Pope Martin: *Badische Zeitung*, 3 July 2010; *Reutlinger General-Anzeiger*, 6 July 2014.

73. Further discussions of this aspect in J. Whaley, 'The old Reich in modern memory: Recent controversies concerning the "relevance" of early modern German history', in C. Emden and D. Midgley (eds.), *German Literature, History and the Nation* (Oxford, 2004), pp.25–49; P. H. Wilson, 'Still a monstrosity? Some reflections on early modern German statehood', *HJ*, 49 (2006), 565–76; T. C. W. Blanning, 'The Holy Roman Empire of the German Nation past and present', *Historical Research*, 85 (2012), 57–70.

74. A. Wieczorek et al. (eds.), *Die Staufer und Italien. Drei Innovationsregionen im mittelalterlichen Europa* (2 vols., Stuttgart, 2010). Further discussion in Schneidmüller, 'Konsens', 225–7.

75. E.g. H. Soly (ed.), *Charles V, 1500–1558* (Antwerp, 1998).

76. Quoted in R. Morrissey, *Charlemagne and France* (Notre Dame, IN, 2003), p.300. For an example of this interpretation see F. Pesendorfer, *Lothringen und seine Herzöge* (Graz, 1994), p.31.

77. http://www.karlspreis.de (accessed 8 Oct. 2013). See B. Schneidmüller, 'Sehnsucht nach Karl dem Großen', *GWU*, 51 (2000), 284–301 at 284–8; Morrissey, *Charlemagne and France*, pp.272–4.

78. O. v. Habsburg, *Idee Europa. Angebot der Freiheit* (Munich, 1976), p.42. See also his *Karl IV. Ein Europäischer Friedensfürst* (Munich, 1978).

79. G. Schmidt, 'Das frühneuzeitliche Reich – Sonderweg und Modell für Europa oder Staat der Deutschen Nation?', in Schnettger (ed.), *Imperium*, pp.247–77; J. Whaley, 'Federal habits: The Holy Roman Empire and the continuity of German federalism', in Umbach (ed.), *German Federalism*, pp.15–41 esp. 28. Schmidt and Whaley are the foremost exponents of the view that the early modern Empire was the first German nation state.

80. Chiefly P. C. Hartmann, *Das Heilige Römische Reich deutscher Nation in der Neuzeit, 1486–1806* (Stuttgart, 2005), p.28, *Kulturgeschichte des Heiligen Römischen Reiches 1648 bis 1806* (Vienna, 2001), pp.5, 76, 448, 'Bereits erprobt: Ein Mitteleuropa der Regionen', *Das Parlament*, 49–50 (3 and 10 Dec. 1993), 21. Broadly similar arguments have been advanced for the medieval Empire by J. Schatz, *Imperium, Pax et Iustitia. Das Reich* (Berlin, 2000).

81. Hartmann, *Kulturgeschichte*, pp.21, 55. Habsburg, *Idee Europa*, p.37, also presents the Empire as superior to the nation state.

82. Post on http://www.german-foreign-policy.com (29 Aug. 2006).

83. *Die Zeit*, no.26 (2000); *Frankfurter Allgemeine Zeitung*, 31 May 2000, no.5.

84. W. Heun, 'Das Alte Reich im Lichte der neueren Forschung', in H. Schilling et al. (eds.), *Altes Reich und neue Staaten 1495 bis 1806*, II, *Essays* (Dresden, 2006), pp.13–15; Reinhard, 'Frühmoderner Staat', 342–3.

85. B. Simms, 'The ghosts of Europe past', *The New York Times*, 9 June 2013. Further discussion in P. H. Wilson, 'The *Immerwährende Reichstag* in English and American Historiography', in H. Rudolph (ed.), *Reichsstadt, Reich, Europa. Neue Perspektiven auf dem Immerwährenden Reichstag zu Regensburg (1663–1806)* (Regensburg, 2015), pp.107-24

86. The classic definition of the sovereign state was articulated around 1900 by Max Weber: H. H. Gerth and C. Wright Mills (eds.), *From Max Weber: Essays in Sociology* (London, 1948), pp.78–80. Useful insight in J. J. Sheehan, 'The problem of sovereignty in European history', *AHR*, 111 (2006), 1–15.

87. H. Behr, 'The European Union in the legacies of imperial rule? EU accession politics viewed from a historical comparative perspective', *European Journal of International Relations*, 13 (2007), 239–62. For the following see S. Weichlein, 'Europa und der Föderalismus', *HJb*, 125 (2005), 133–52.

88. J. Zielonka, *Europe as Empire: The Nature of the Enlarged European Union* (Oxford, 2006); O. Wæver, 'Imperial metaphors: Emerging

European analogies to pre-nation-state imperial systems', in O. Tunander et al. (eds.), *Geopolitics in Post-Wall Europe* (London, 1997), pp.59–93.

89. P. H. Wilson, 'Das Heilige Römische Reich, die machtpolitisch schwache Mitte Europas – mehr Sicherheit oder ein Gefahr für den Frieden?', in M. Lanzinner (ed.), *Sicherheit in der Vormoderne und Gegenwart* (Paderborn, 2013), pp.25–34.

90. E. O. Eriksen and J. E. Fossum (eds.), *Democracy in the European Union: Integration through Deliberation?* (London, 2000); Zielonka, *Europe as Empire*, pp.165–6, 185.

Index

Aachen, imperial city: cathedral 681;
  coronations at 268, 273, 301, 305,
  309–10, 378, 717; as imperial centre
  36, 156, 180, 340, 379, 383; and
  imperial insignia 45, 273, 286, 311,
  673, 679; palace at 35, 36, 256, 270,
  273–4, 318, 332; unrest 577
Aalen, imperial city 545
Aargau 248, 588
Aargau, treaty (1712) 590
Abbas I 'the Great' (1557–1628), shah
  of Persia from 1586 150
abbeys: foundation 86; governance
  371–2, 525; identity 252; and
  imperial courts 635; influence 122,
  337, 374; military obligations 345,
  347; and monarchs 86–8, 332, 610;
  patronage 86–7; plundered 587;
  possession 372; secularization 135,
  650, 651; supervision 53, 91, 376;
  wealth 87, 89, 129, 132, 544, 545
Abbt, Thomas (1738–66) 290
Abodrites 202–3, 212, 214, 346
Abruzzi 354
Absolutism: alleged 596; defined 501;
  and Empire 423, 747; enlightened
  501–2, 539–40; 'imperial' 158, 501;
  in practice 531, 538–40
Acre 147
Adalbero Eppensteiner (980–1039),
  duke of Carinthia from c.1011 249
Adelbert (932–71), co-king of Italy
  950–61 298
Adelbert (d.1072), archbishop of
  Hamburg-Bremen from 1043 92

Adelheid (c.931–99), empress 85, 313,
  314–15
Adelheid of Savoy (d.1079) 297
administration: corruption 534;
  development 434–5, 511–12; financial
  367, 370, 533–4, 541–4, 594; district
  370; local 511–12, 519–22, 535; and
  written culture 54, 259–60, 320–25,
  367, 404, 479, 525–6, 535–6, 541, 561,
  594, 608–9, 628–9; see also officials
Adolf of Nassau (c.1250–98), German
  king from 1292; ability 302, 387;
  burial 67; deposition 302, 386–7,
  394–5; election 308, 386, 722;
  governance 723
Adolf II of Nassau (1423–75),
  archbishop of Mainz from 1461 625
Adrianople (Edirne) 148
Adso (c.910–92), abbot of Montier-en-
  Der 39
Africa 21, 143, 144, 145, 165, 167, 169,
  518, 701
Ageltrude of Benevento (d.923), empress
  313, 705
Agnes of Poitou (1024–77), empress
  197
Agnes of Waiblingen (1072–1143) 246
agrarian depression 376, 494–5
Al-Andalus, caliphate 145
Al-Kamil Al-Malik (d.1238), sultan of
  Egypt 146
Al-Rashid, Harun (786–809), caliph of
  Baghdad 145
Albert I (1255–1308), king from 1298:
  burial 67; character 386; election

885

515, 534, 620, 646; conflicts with
Habsburgs 73–4, 157–63399, 445,
454, 456, 458–62, 470, 477–8, 588,
645–65, 665, 734–5, 739, 742, 750,
751; cooperation with Habsburgs
154, 160, 455, 647, 746; imperial
ambitions 41, 156–7, 298, 443, 746;
and imperial princes 115, 129, 137,
158, 161, 175, 227, 456, 470, 477–8,
481, 534, 560, 567, 652, 746, 750,
752; influence in Empire 1, 114, 125,
127, 197–9, 215, 389, 392, 441, 442,
479, 627, 649, 651, 744; law 265,
604, 606, 659; literacy 277; monarchy
32, 40, 121, 234, 257, 274, 278, 301,
313, 318, 397, 535, 645; origins 2, 6–
7, 77, 155; and papacy 60, 63, 65, 68–
70, 75, 76, 145, 156–7, 161, 214, 392,
723, 724, 728; and Prussia 160, 162,
168, 474, 646, 648, 657, 752; society
503; and Swiss 589; taxation 383; as
threat 415; universities 71, 236, 276
Franche-Comté 196, 197, 200, 229–30,
727
Francia 26, 41, 700, 702
Francia, East: and Empire 41, 47;
extent 256; origins 35, 155, 340, 704–
5; rulers 256, 341–2; subdivision 183;
see also German kingdom
Francia, West: and Empire 41, 47;
extent 195, 198, 256; monarchy 155–
6, 201, 269, 315, 341–2; origins 35,
155, 340; subdivision 183, 704; see
also France
Francis I Stephen (1708–65), emperor
from 1745; election 424, 477, 478,
750; imperial ideal 159, 290; wife
222, 230
Francis II (1768–1835), emperor from
1792; abdication 2, 15, 135, 163, 639,
654, 656–7, 665, 674, 753; coronation
287, 752; daughter 647; defends
Empire 649, 651, 653; imperial
title 162, 219; interpretations 647;
successor 665
Franciscan order 39, 69, 724
Franco-Prussian War (1870–71) 667,
672
Franco-Spanish War (1635–59) 157,
175, 442, 744

François I (1494–1547), king of France
from 1515 157, 298, 746
François d'Anjou (1555–84), duke 595
Franconia, duchy: ducal title 361, 373,
640; economy 490, 495; feuding
in 398–9; nobles 556, 557–9, 561;
origins 24, 250, 336; political
composition 133, 185, 247; and
monarch 341, 343, 346, 348, 384,
392, 711; towns 575
Franconian Kreis: assembly 415; counts
412, 562; defence 461; demise 653;
finances 452; influence 564, 567;
membership 415
Frankenhausen, battle (1525) 287
Frankfurt, grand duchy 135, 659
Frankfurt am Main, imperial city:
attacked 573; book trade 275;
economy 469; elections in 286, 290,
310; as imperial centre 180, 185, 272,
323, 379, 388, 394, 405, 408, 434,
616, 664, 665, 739; influence 572;
Jewish population 104, 105–7, 285;
law 507; palace at 332; trade fair
463–4
Frankfurt an der Oder 507, 523
Frankfurt Parliament (1848–9) 668,
671, 674
Frankfurt Union (1803) 652, 663
Franks: and Christianity 79–82, 87;
dress 34, 300; economy 240, 487–90,
509; empire 24–6, 179–80, 184–91,
195, 200, 203, 238, 246, 335, 374,
582, 681; identity 237–8, 253, 438,
704; kingship 26–7, 34, 40–42, 335–
42; law codes 238, 605; legacy 34,
157, 256, 257, 342, 485, 681; nobles
34, 238, 236, 449–42, 702; origins 20,
24, 78, 237–8, 699–700; partitions
2–3, 25, 34, 35, 40–41, 47, 155, 180,
195, 256, 339, 340, 702, 704–5;
warrior culture 33–5, 43, 79, 82, 161,
201, 340; see also Carolingians
Franz Joseph (1830–1916), Austrian
emperor from 1848 665
Frederick 'the Fair' (1289–1330), anti-
king from 1314 69, 301, 313, 387,
388, 401, 428, 587, 724
Frederick I 'Barbarossa' (1122–90),
emperor from 1155; and Burgundy